Handbook of
THE ECONOMICS OF
EDUCATION

Handbook of
THE ECONOMICS OF EDUCATION

Volume 5

Edited by

ERIC A. HANUSHEK
Stanford University

STEPHEN MACHIN
University College London

LUDGER WOESSMANN
University of Munich

Amsterdam • Boston • Heidelberg • London • New York • Oxford
Paris • San Diego • San Francisco • Singapore • Sydney • Tokyo
North-Holland is an imprint of Elsevier

North-Holland is an imprint of Elsevier

Radarweg 29, PO Box 211, 1000 AE Amsterdam, The Netherlands
The Boulevard, Langford Lane, Kidlington, Oxford OX5 1GB, UK

Library of Congress Cataloging-in-Publication Data
A catalog record for this book is available from the Library of Congress

British Library Cataloguing-in-Publication Data
A catalogue record for this book is available from the British Library

ISBN: 978-0-444-63459-7

For information on all North-Holland publications
visit our website at https://www.store.elsevier.com/

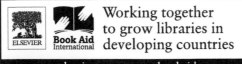

Working together
to grow libraries in
developing countries

www.elsevier.com • www.bookaid.org

Publisher: Zoe Kruze
Acquisition Editor: Kirsten Shankland
Editorial Project Manager: Hannah Colford
Production Project Manager: Jason Mitchell
Designer: Greg Harris

Typeset by SPi Global, India

INTRODUCTION TO THE SERIES

The aim of the *Handbooks in Economics* series is to produce Handbooks for various branches of economics, each of which is a definitive source, reference, and teaching supplement for use by professional researchers and advanced graduate students. Each Handbook provides self-contained surveys of the current state of a branch of economics in the form of chapters prepared by leading specialists on various aspects of this area of economics. These surveys summarize not only received results but also newer developments, from recent journal articles and discussion papers. Some original material is also included, but the main goal is to provide comprehensive and accessible surveys. The Handbooks are intended to provide not only useful reference volumes for professional collections, but also possible supplementary readings for advanced courses for graduate students in economics.

Kenneth J. Arrow and Michael D. Intriligator

Founding Editors

CONTENTS

CONTRIBUTORS

J.G. Altonji
Yale University, NBER, and IZA

P. Arcidiacono
Duke University, NBER, and IZA

G. Bulman
University of California, Santa Cruz

D. Epple
Carnegie Mellon University and NBER

R.W. Fairlie
University of California, Santa Cruz

D. Figlio
Northwestern University and NBER

P. Glewwe
University of Minnesota

E.A. Hanushek
Stanford University, NBER, CESifo, and IZA

K. Karbownik
Northwestern University

C. Koedel
University of Missouri — Columbia

A.M. Lavecchia
University of Toronto

H. Liu
Harvard University

L. Lochner
University of Western Ontario, CESifo, and NBER

S. Machin
University College London; Centre for Economic Performance, London School of Economics; and CESifo

A. Maurel
Duke University, NBER, and IZA

B. McCall
University of Michigan

A. Monge-Naranjo
Federal Reserve Bank of St. Louis and Washington University in St. Louis

K. Muralidharan
UC San Diego, NBER, BREAD, J-PAL

P. Oreopoulos
University of Toronto; National Bureau of Economic Research (NBER); Canadian Institute for Advanced Research (CIFAR)

M. Podgursky
University of Missouri — Columbia

R. Romano
University of Florida

K.G. Salvanes
Norwegian School of Economics

J. Smith
University of Michigan, NBER, IZA, and CESifo

M. Urquiola
Columbia University and NBER

L. Woessmann
University of Munich, Ifo Institute, CESifo, and IZA

C. Wunsch
IZA, CESifo, University of Basel, and CEPR

R. Zimmer
Vanderbilt University

Editors' Introduction

E.A. Hanushek*, S. Machin[†], L. Woessmann[‡]
*Stanford University, NBER, and CESifo
[†]University College London; Centre for Economic Performance, London School of Economics; and CESifo
[‡]University of Munich, Ifo Institute, and CESifo

That a fifth *Handbook of the Economics of Education* is now complete testifies to the substantive and influential body of research on education now being produced by economists. The ten original contributions to the volume cover a wide range of key, topical education research questions. In doing so, they draw upon research findings using a blend of economic theory and modern empirical methods.

As with prior volumes, each of the chapters has a forward looking perspective. While they review the current state of the art in each area, they use this as a building block in pointing to current puzzles and useful places for further development. Two things have changed, however, in the decade since the first volume was published. First, the research base — as we describe briefly below — has dramatically expanded in many of the overall areas covered. Second, with this expansion, the range of topics worthy of inclusion has itself expanded.

It is useful to place this work within the broader field of economics. The economics of education has become one of the most active areas of applied economic research. All top economics departments have individuals working in the area, and many economics of education researchers are now employed in positions in education and public policy schools. Papers on education now frequently appear in the profession's leading academic journals. The numbers in the following table make clear this publication trend. It shows decade by decade numbers, starting in the 1950s and going up to the first decade of the millennium, for a word-search based measure of the number of economics of education papers published in top economics journals. It rises from just 3 in the 1950s to 134 by the

Education publications in selected general-interest economics journals

	Decade					
	1950s	1960s	1970s	1980s	1990s	2000s
Number of papers	3	37	78	38	82	134
Number non-North American based	0	4	13	8	23	56
Percent non-North American based	0%	11%	17%	21%	28%	42%

Notes: Publications with the word Education, Schooling, School, or Human capital in the title in the following list of journals: *American Economic Review; Economic Journal; Econometrica; Economica; Journal of Political Economy; Quarterly Journal of Economics; RAND Journal of Economics; Review of Economic Studies*.
Source: Machin (2014).

2000s. The very clear internationalization of the area is also made clear, as the percentage of papers written by authors outside of North America rises from none of the three in the 1950s to 42% of those in the 2000s.

There are a number of reasons that lie behind this rise to prominence, and why it looks set to continue. One key factor has been the increased call from governments around the world to design evidence-based education policies. The nature of evidence provided via education research by economists is very well suited to meet this policy demand. Over and above this, the data available to study education have improved massively through time. The kinds of administrative data sources that are almost routinely used in much of today's research simply were not available two or three decades ago. Nor was the richness of survey data available for analysis of international differences in test scores now collected on pupils in a very large number of countries around the world (Hanushek and Woessmann, 2011). These are but two examples of the provision of more and better data available for education research. Moreover, it is clear that the influx of new data has dovetailed particularly well in economics of education research with the methodological advances that have been made in empirical economics. The study of experimental settings and a range of "quasi" or "natural" experiments that have been used to push the research frontier forwards have featured a lot in the new economics of education research.

These enablers of economics of education research have by now drawn in many new cohorts of researchers who have begun their academic research careers doing a Ph.D. on the economics of education, and subsequently become academics, policymakers, and education practitioners. This vibrant, and now sizable, young group of economists working on education augurs well for the economics of education field to continue to thrive in the future.

Volume 5 of the *Handbook of the Economics of Education* features ten chapters on contemporary issues in education. A couple of chapters, while ostensibly covering the same general areas as chapters in earlier volumes (ie, student loans and education in developing countries), underscore the dramatic advances in the fields over the past decade. However, the majority of the volume goes into new areas, for some of which (eg, technology, behavioral approaches, and teacher pensions) there was virtually no literature available a decade ago.

Handbook volumes appear at irregular intervals, but the explosion of research and articles in the economics of education suggest that this is not the last volume in the series.

REFERENCES

Hanushek, E., Woessmann, L., 2011. The economics of international differences in educational achievement. In: Hanushek, E., Machin, S., Woessmann, L. (Eds.), Handbook of the Economics of Education, vol. 3. Elsevier, Amsterdam.

Machin, S., 2014. Developments in economics of education research. Labour Econ. 30, 13–19. European Association of Labour Economists Special 25th Memorial Issue.

CHAPTER 1

Behavioral Economics of Education: Progress and Possibilities

A.M. Lavecchia*, H. Liu†, P. Oreopoulos*,‡
*University of Toronto, Toronto, Ontario, Canada
†Harvard University, Cambridge, Massachusetts, United States
‡National Bureau of Economic Research (NBER), Cambridge, Massachusetts, United States; Canadian Institute for Advanced Research (CIFAR), Toronto, Ontario, Canada

Contents

Abstract

Behavioral economics attempts to integrate insights from psychology, neuroscience, and sociology in order to better predict individual outcomes and develop more effective policy. While the field has been successfully applied to many areas, education has, so far, received less attention — a surprising oversight, given the field's key interest in long-run decision making and the propensity of youth to make poor long-run decisions. In this chapter, we review the emerging literature on the behavioral economics of education. We first develop a general framework for thinking about why youth and their parents

Handbook of the Economics of Education, Volume 5
ISSN 1574-0692, http://dx.doi.org/10.1016/B978-0-444-63459-7.00001-4

might not always take full advantage of education opportunities. We then discuss how these behavioral barriers may be preventing some students from improving their long-run welfare. We evaluate the recent but rapidly growing efforts to develop policies that mitigate these barriers, many of which have been examined in experimental settings. Finally, we discuss future prospects for research in this emerging field.

Keywords

Behavioral economics of education, Present bias, Education, Policymakers

The roots of education are bitter, but the fruit is sweet

Aristotle (384–322 BC)

1. INTRODUCTION

A 6-year-old does not go to school because she wants a better life. She must be persuaded that school is fun *now*, or given no better option. That's because her brain is not yet well developed.[1] While parts of her brain corresponding to motor and sensory processing mature early, higher cognitive areas like the prefrontal cortex, which underlie executive functions such as planning, working memory, and self-control, take longer to improve (Romine and Reynolds, 2005; Teffer and Semendeferi, 2012). Without them, the 6-year-old is simply not conditioned to think about long-run consequences from immediate actions.

Over time and with experience, a remarkable process of neural circuitry expansion and pruning occurs that makes it possible to hold information in mind before deciding what to do with it (Romine and Reynolds, 2005). The cortex (outer layers that primarily distinguish the primate brain) thickens as neural connections proliferate. Then, rarely used connections are selectively trimmed, improving efficiency, while others are grouped together, improving specialization (Fuster, 2002). Nerve cell conductivity also improves, allowing information to pass more quickly from one part of the brain to another so that the brain becomes more interconnected (Chick and Reyna, 2012; Giedd et al., 2012). Impulses, feelings, and distractions can then be held in check while imagining the future before reacting.

Until recently, many neuroscientists believed this maturation process occurred largely before puberty (Fuster, 2002). Neuroimaging studies have demonstrated otherwise: maturation takes more than 20 years, with the circuitry responsible for executive function

---

[1] Excellent overviews of brain development are provided by Fuster (2002), Romine and Reynolds (2005), Teffer and Semendeferi (2012), Johnson et al. (2009), and in the book, *The Adolescent Brain*, edited by Reyna et al. (2012).

being among the very last areas to fully develop (Fuster, 2002; Giedd et al., 2012; Romine and Reynolds, 2005; Teffer and Semendeferi, 2012). Patience, for example, increases as children grow (Bettinger and Slonim, 2007; Kosse and Pfeiffer, 2012; Thompson et al., 1997).[2] Preferences, therefore, change with age, and children spend most — if not all — of their school years with less interest in the future than their future adult selves (Read and Read, 2004). The timing is unfortunate, given the many important long-term investments that can occur during this period.

Teenagers are particularly more susceptible to overemphasizing the present due to their more fully developed limbic system, a midbrain area which registers desires for immediate rewards and pleasure (Chapman et al., 2012). The limbic system is highly sensitive to monetary, novel, and social rewards (Giedd et al., 2012). It also reacts more independently from other systems when in states of high emotional arousal or conflict — states that occur more frequently in teenage years (Galvan, 2012). While brain systems associated with higher order critical thinking skills also undergo a rapid expansion during childhood, they remain unrefined and less integrated until adulthood. Many neuroscientists suggest that the rapid development of the limbic system relative to executive function systems contributes to the observed increase in pleasure-seeking and risk-taking behavior (Atkins et al., 2012; Schneider et al., 2012).

Our tendency to overemphasize the present when making decisions involving immediate desires against long-term, incremental and uncertain benefits dissipates with age but does not go away. Even as adults, there is evidence that the tradeoff between immediate outcomes compared to distant ones is implemented in neural systems that yield hyperbolic discounting (Kable and Glimcher, 2007, 2010; McClure et al., 2004). A substantial research literature has firmly established that, in a variety of settings, adult responses deviate from those predicted by a time consistent intertemporal utility model that assumes a constant discount rate (Stanovich et al., 2012): future gains are discounted more than future losses, small changes to outcomes are discounted more than large changes (Frederick et al., 2002); small probability events, when emphasized, are discounted less than when not emphasized, and responses depend on context, emotional state (Rick and Loewenstein, 2008) and perceived social identity (Benjamin et al., 2010; Galvan, 2012). Sometimes we do not even try to think in the long-term, relying instead on rules of thumb or past habits (Stanovich et al., 2012).

The emerging field of behavioral economics attempts to integrate research from psychology, neuroscience, and sociology in order to better understand individual decision

---

[2] Late development in executive function also helps explain a declining time preference for immediate monetary gains against larger later gains (Giedd et al., 2012). Several researchers have found, starting as far back as childhood, a steady decline in people's willingness to forgo a fixed monetary future amount for a smaller immediate amount (Bettinger and Slonim, 2007; Green et al., 1994; Kosse and Pfeiffer, 2012; Stanovich et al., 2012; Steinberg et al., 2009; Thompson et al., 1997).

making and to develop policies that address the shortcomings in our decision-making processes. While classical economics often assumes that individuals always make correct short- and long-run trade-offs (ex-ante), behavioral economics instead suggests that deviations from time-consistent preferences due to cognitive and perceptual aspects of our brain's architecture, may lead to suboptimal outcomes (DellaVigna, 2009).

Behavioral economics seeks not to reject the standard intertemporal decision-making model but to enrich it by incorporating more realistic assumptions that sometimes lead to profound differences in predicted actions, including those that are of interest to practitioners and policy makers. To that end, the field has attracted wide and growing attention: compared to traditional programs with the same goals, interventions that draw from insights in behavioral economics may be more cost-effective, given that the research suggests that even small changes in the way choices are presented or in the way information is conveyed can lead to large changes in behavior.[3]

A prototypical example concerns saving for retirement. When deciding about whether to start saving for retirement, standard economic models assume that individuals are forward looking, are able to forecast how much they will need to save (or have access to services that help them do this), and face little difficulty following through with their plans. Several studies note, however, that the behavior of at least some people deviates from this model (eg, Benartzi and Thaler, 2007). Simply changing the default action, from having to opt-into pension plans to being automatically enrolled, or requiring individuals to make an active decision regarding their contributions, increases savings significantly (Beshears et al., 2013; Carroll et al., 2009; Chetty et al., 2014). Other areas in which behavioral economics has been actively applied include finance, health, and law (DellaVigna, 2009; Diamond and Vartiainen, 2007; Hough, 2013; Sunstein, 2000; Thaler, 2005; Thaler and Sunstein, 2008).

One discipline that has received less attention from behavioral economists is education. This is surprising to us, given the field's key interest in long-run decision making and the propensity of youth to make poor long-run decisions. Economic models usually describe education as a well-thought-out investment: if students exert little effort in school, it is because they feel it is *optimal* to do so (Becker, 1962). Clearly, this outcome need not be the case for a 6-year-old, and the slower development of the cortex suggests it need not be the case for a teenager either.

Education outcomes, ranging from performance on standardized tests to high school and postsecondary attainment, are determined by many factors including parental inputs, school inputs and environmental factors. But perhaps just as important are inputs from students themselves. Paying attention in class, doing homework, completing assignments on time, and attending lectures or tutorials are all important determinants of student

[3] Madrian (2014).

success. While parents and teachers may play a significant role in the extent to which these investments are undertaken, actions by students themselves ultimately determine the effectiveness of these inputs. These investments begin at early ages; the implication is that actions taken by as early as primary or middle school may have an important impact on later outcomes, especially if learning is cumulative. As a result, a serious consideration of the role of students in the production of education outcomes, even at an early age, is fundamental to both understanding differences in outcomes across students and for designing effective policies.

Overall, the area of education is a fruitful environment in which researchers and policy makers should consider possible deviations from the traditional human capital investment model and how behavioral economics might explain these deviations. This paper synthesizes the recent and growing literature on the behavioral economics of education and, in doing so, encourages others to recognize opportunities for further research. We discuss how policies that make learning opportunities easier, continually remind students of long-term goals, teach strategies to develop self-control, and encourage youth to take pride in their own skill development are promising approaches for helping foster academic achievement (Schneider and Caffrey, 2012).

With these ideas in mind, Section 2 describes a general framework for thinking about why youth may not take full advantage of education opportunities. We argue that brain development over time and environmental context play an important role in determining education outcomes, and that education itself may affect brain development and, therefore, individuals' preferences. This framework implies that the actions of students and parents may deviate from the predictions of the traditional human capital investment model because of tendencies to (1) focus too much on the present; (2) rely too much on routine and disregard information that is not salient; (3) focus too much on negative identities; and (4) make mistakes due to little information or too many options. In Section 3, we map the mechanisms discussed in Section 2 onto particular educational outcomes worth encouraging, such as attainment, attendance, and homework. While it is not possible to predict for any particular student whether such encouragement would make them better off, we discuss evidence why, for at least for some students, this is likely the case. Section 4 reviews the recent but rapidly growing efforts to develop policies that address behavioral barriers, many of which have been examined in experimental settings. We conclude in Section 5 by discussing prospects and possibilities for making further progress in this emerging field.

2. BARRIERS TO TREATING EDUCATION AS INVESTMENT

In considering why some individuals may not necessarily treat education as an investment, we find it helpful to conceptualize the process of long-term decision making as involving two broad systems — one that is forward looking and one that is not.[4] Economists often assume that individuals only use a rational, forward-looking system to maximize lifetime welfare given various resource constraints. While this simplifying assumption helps in many settings, research from neuroscience and psychology shows it can lead us astray in other settings, especially in cases where youth, still in cognitive development, are making the decisions.

Framing the discussion in terms of the dual system approach is a useful way to think about how the development of the brain interacts with current neurobiological evidence for how decision making is implemented. The current evidence suggests a model for intertemporal choice in which the brain produces subjective values for different outcomes, these values can be measured on a single common scale, and the largest-valued outcome chosen (Glimcher, 2014). However, evidence for signals can be found both in cortical areas (the medial prefrontal cortex) and in the limbic system (the striatum), and the interaction between these signals during a decision is still unclear. How these different signals are integrated across cortex and the striatum, possibly in the face of constraints and/or the state of development, can yield distant outcomes which are discounted and perhaps even ignored depending on a number of factors, including salience, stress, distractions, and age (Mani et al., 2013; Mullainathan and Shafir, 2013). The discounting or ignorance of long-term consequences is particularly useful for describing suboptimal education behavior. For the remainder of the chapter, it will be helpful to keep in mind four key implications from this model: (1) some students focus too much on the present; (2) some rely too much on routine; (3) some students focus too much on negative identities; and (4) mistakes are more likely to occur with many options or with little information. We discuss each implication in turn.

---

[4] Recent neuroscientific evidence rejects the overly dichotomous notion that there are separate, competing, neural systems for processing immediate versus delayed rewards (Glimcher and Fehr, 2014; Kable and Glimcher, 2007, 2010). Instead, it is increasingly recognized that multiple neurobiological systems interact with each other to yield hyperbolic discounting, and this might arise from neurobiological constraints (possibly in the interaction between multiple systems). The distinction is not important for our policy discussion. We have chosen a framework that highlights that the process of valuing immediate outcomes is different from the process of evaluating (much) later ones (Glimcher, 2014). We do not require that two separate neural values systems compete with one another, only that the systems which implement the intertemporal tradeoff are not yet fully developed prior to adulthood, and this leads to behavior or preferences which change with development. This work also distinguishes between overemphasizing the present versus overemphasizing outcomes that happen sooner rather than later. In an "As Soon As Possible" (ASAP) model, subjective values of outcomes are steeply discounted relative to the soonest currently available reward (Kable and Glimcher, 2010). Since the intertemporal decisions we focus on tradeoff immediate costs for longer-term, uncertain benefits, the implications of both models are very similar.

2.1 Some Students Focus Too Much on the Present

Assessing how you feel this instant is much easier than assessing how you expect to feel 10 years from now. Whereas System 1 quickly and intuitively gauges current feelings, System 2 is tasked with anticipating how one will feel in the future. This means that immediate costs associated with investments that yield future payoffs are salient and relatively easy to assess. On the other hand, future feelings seem vague and uncertain. The imbalance can lead to myopia, with System 1 downplaying the importance of the future and overemphasizing the present. System 1 also evaluates probabilities based on its assessment of what it finds to be salient and most important in the present.[5] In contrast, System 2 is more deliberate and weighs current and future benefits differently than System 1. The tendency to emphasize the present relative to the future varies both across people and within individuals, depending of factors such as stress, distractions or cognitive development (Kahneman, 2003; Kahneman and Frederick, 2002).

The differences between System 1 and System 2 in their weighting of current and future expected costs and benefits can potentially explain why individuals make a variety of poor economic choices. In the System 1 and System 2 framework, individuals may act myopically or in a manner that appears time-inconsistent: System 1 may react quickly and decide against a tradeoff with a cost today and a benefit tomorrow, especially if the current cost is particularly salient, but a tradeoff that requires the same cost tomorrow and a benefit the following period may require more abstract and deliberate thought for System 2 to peruse. The outcomes that result from this decision-making process are consistent with individuals having quasi-hyperbolic preferences, with System 1 and System 2 thinking underlying these preferences.[6] Recent empirical evidence of myopic behavior stemming from this System 1 and System 2 framework can be found in a variety of fields. The retirement savings literature, for example, finds that many people spend little time deciding how much to save for retirement, despite the complexity and importance of this decision (Benartzi and Thaler, 2007). When asked to reflect on their savings decisions, many believe that they should be saving more. A majority of them say they plan to start saving soon, yet fail to follow through with those plans (Choi et al., 2002).

Children and adolescents are especially prone to short-term thinking. For example, Bettinger and Slonim (2007) find that more than 43% of children (aged 5–16) in their sample made choices in line with hyperbolic discounting. When asked to choose between a $10 gift certificate to be distributed immediately after the experiment or a larger amount (up to $25) in 2 months, these children picked the immediate reward.

---

[5] See Kahneman (2003) and the citations therein, especially Kahneman and Tversky (1973) and Tversky and Kahneman (1983). Also see Fudenberg and Levine (2006) for a model treating System 2 as principal and System 1 as agent.

[6] Quasi-hyperbolic discounting is the most commonly used form of discounting to model the behavior of individuals with time-inconsistent preferences (ie, Laibson, 1997).

When asked to evaluate a similar tradeoff where the $10 gift certificate was distributed in 2 months or the same larger amount in 4 months, these children chose the latter. Bettinger and Slonim (2007) also find that more than 25% of children choose options inconsistent with *any* type of rational behavior, but that these irrational choices were less likely to occur among older children.

Present-biased behavior has important implications in education (Castillo et al., 2011; Golsteyn et al., 2014; Sutter et al., 2013; Wulfert et al., 2002). Doing homework, studying for exams, researching colleges or potential opportunities for financial aid and completing applications all involve salient upfront costs. At the same time, temptations to procrastinate abound; games, television, friends, and food are all much more attractive than an extra hour of studying. In many cases, the potential benefits from these actions may seem incremental, uncertain and distant. When deciding whether to stay home and complete homework or enjoy time with friends, more salient upfront costs may lead a student to overemphasize the costs of studying relative to the potential future benefits. Similarly, deciding against taking advanced (and difficult) math or science courses in high school may seem particularly appealing to a high school senior despite the fact that doing so would make it difficult to transition to higher-paying STEM fields in college (Harackiewicz et al., 2012).

These examples highlight how education decisions may be suboptimal when viewed through the System 1 and System 2 framework. Instead of reflecting forward-looking maximizing behavior, individuals can make decisions driven by System 1 that are very different than those they would make had they paused more to deliberate. Decisions may be high-stakes, such as which program of study to pursue or whether to attend college, or they may seemingly be low-stakes, such as whether to study for an extra hour. Over time, as the benefits of learning compound, marginal decisions on how much to study or practice also become consequential. That many of these decisions are made by students early in life makes myopic behavior more likely due to underdeveloped executive functioning skills. For instance, Castleman (2013) and Baum and Schwartz (2013) also note that the neurological systems in adolescents are particularly likely to favor immediate rewards, which may hinder the ability of students to be forward looking in their educational decisions.[7]

More education may itself improve executive function, thus helping minimize subsequent suboptimal decisions. Self-control, patience, and focus are skills that some studies suggest can be improved, though much work remains for understanding mechanisms and external validity.[8] Becker and Mulligan (1997) suggest that more schooling may reduce

---

[7] See footnote 9 for examples of empirical studies which suggest that discounting decreases with age, particularly from adolescence until about age 30.

[8] In a complementary review article on behavioral economics of education, Koch et al. (2015) focus on the development and importance of these kinds of noncognitive or soft skills. They discuss how soft skills fit in the education production function, both in terms of influencing education outcomes and being influenced by education. Some examples include differences in personality traits (Borghans et al., 2008), altruism (Benenson et al., 2007; Fehr et al., 2013), trust (Sutter and Kocher, 2007), and cooperation (Fan, 2000; Lergetporer et al., 2014).

the remoteness of students' future preferences. They argue that problem–solving tasks assigned to students in school teach them to imagine alternative scenarios, in particular those involving adult lives and their future selves. Another channel through which increased education may help students focus less on the present is by decreasing the current disutility from costly actions such as studying or completing assignments (Oreopoulos and Salvanes, 2011). If learning is cumulative, taking actions today which increase understanding of course material or improve essential skills such as reading, writing and numeracy, make it easier for students to understand future material.

Interestingly, the psychology literature identifies a mechanism through which additional schooling may make future educational investments less costly. With repetition and the acquisition of relevant skills, tasks that previously relied (almost) entirely on System 2 may migrate toward the automatic activity of System 1. Prototypical examples include driving a vehicle, mastering chess or performing at a high-level in sports (Kahneman, 2003; Kahneman and Frederick, 2002). A novice chess player will find that with practice and time, analyzing the board will become more automatic, intuitive, and effortless. As it relates to education, investments in schooling may initially appear costly and salient because they require significant cognitive effort in addition to time. With practice and better developed skills, however, these immediate costs may seem less daunting.

2.2 Some Students Rely Too Much on Routine

While the incorrect assessment of present versus future described above results in students optimizing poorly, relying too much on routine and automatic thinking can also lead to suboptimal outcomes. Our predisposition to automatically make decisions by relying on familiar knowledge leads to new information being discounted while familiar decisions and routines become the default.

We often rely and benefit from routine. It makes it easier to get through daily tasks without feeling mentally strained. It also frees up bandwidth to focus on new or more complicated tasks. Grade school is one example of a setting in which routines form to make daily life easier. For most children, showing up to class on weekdays becomes routine. Students do not have to decide each day whether to go.[9] When they complete a grade, they are automatically registered for the next. When they complete elementary school, a system is in place to help them to secondary school.

Problems arise, however, when routines must be disrupted in order to take advantage of opportunities for improving welfare. At the end of high school, for example, students that stick with their current routine will generally find themselves out of school (and out of work). Transitioning to college requires first deviating from one's daily routine to prepare to go, such as finding time to fill out forms, write entry essays, choose a program of

---

[9] Social norms, especially those of a student's family and friends may also be important. We expand on this point in the following section.

study, pick courses, and apply for financial aid. It also requires *changing* routine, such as a new commute, study schedule, work schedule, and social schedule. To deliberately address each of these tasks, students must resist relying on System 1's autopilot preferences. Failing to modify routine for any one of them may close or limit college options.

Another implication from following automatic thought patterns and routines is that new information (or awareness about the existence of new information) will only be relevant for decisions if it immediately comes to mind. Individuals may miss out on acquiring better information not only because they do not have enough money or time, but also because the cognitive processes underlying System 1 rely on immediate accessibility and the ease with which facts, attributes and thoughts come to mind (Kahneman, 2003). As a result of System 1's automatic thinking, individuals may not even realize that they should seek out new information. Students (or their parents) may make decisions using only readily available information or options, even if other information *seems* relatively easy to access.[10] This has significant implications for many situations in education, especially the transition to college.

To give one example, Hoxby and Avery (2013) find that bright students from disadvantaged backgrounds often fail to apply to selective colleges that have lower out-of-pocket costs than less selective schools they know about. This occurs despite the fact that information about various schools, programs and costs is available freely online. Sending information about school availability directly to students in the form of an information package appears to significantly increase application and enrollment rates at selective schools, a point we expand upon in Section 2.3 (Hoxby and Turner, 2013). Information about college options, tuition fees and even financial aid opportunities may be less accessible for students from low-income families (Avery and Kane, 2004; Dynarski and Scott-Clayton, 2006; Oreopoulos and Dunn, 2013; Scott-Clayton, 2012b) who are burdened by concurrent stressors associated with poverty and who are exposed to fewer resources from parents and high school counselors about the transition process (Castleman, 2013; Levine, 2013).

Even after entering college, issues of information inaccessibility persist. Scott-Clayton (2011) notes that information about available courses is located separately from information about degree or program requirements and college counselors often have insufficient time for individual students (Baum and Scott-Clayton, 2013). Due to this lack of convenient and timely access to relevant information, a student must disrupt her predisposition to rely on default choices and routine in order to choose the right courses.

---

[10] Students and their families may also ignore or discount new information because of biased beliefs about the information they already have (DellaVigna, 2009). For example, they may be overconfident that the information they already have is correct and subsequently decide not to see new information. While we know of no studies that explicitly test for biased beliefs in education due to overconfidence, Hoffman (2012) finds evidence that supports this hypothesis among business experts.

Moreover, the sudden lack of routine that accompanies college means that a student must not only expend more effort into planning his or her day, but also have enough self-control to follow up on these tasks.

With System 1's reliance on automatic thinking and routine, differences in exposure to information (even information freely and quickly available) may have important implications for student behavior. Without sufficient exposure, recent efforts by policymakers to improve the quantity and quality of information available to students and their families about college and financial aid are ultimately limited. Policies that expose information, compared to making it easily available, are more likely to be effective in a variety of fields, from consumer retail behavior to health.[11] For example, experimental evidence in Chetty et al. (2009) suggests that displaying the after-tax price of items at the grocery store can greatly affect consumers' purchasing decisions. While most consumers would normally have no trouble in computing the after-tax price of items, they would have to pause to do the relevant calculation. Our reliance on System 1 and its propensity to make quick decisions and focus only on salient factors implies that even simple optimizing decisions may not always be made. However, with a better understanding of our tendency to rely on routine, possibilities exist to leverage this knowledge to design more effective policies and improve individual outcomes.

2.3 Some Students Focus Too Much on Negative Identities

Concerns about identity predominate adolescent thinking and behavior (Akerlof and Kranton, 2000, 2002, 2010; Bishop, 2006; Coleman, 1961; Cusick, 1973; Everhart, 1983; Gordon, 1957; Hall, 1904; Haun et al., 2013; Hollingshead, 1975; Jackson, 1968; Roderick, 1993; Willis, 1977). The questions "what kind of person am I?" and "what are others like me doing?" serve as powerful reference points for deciding how to act. These extremely salient concerns about identity may have significant implications for how students tradeoff between immediate costs and long-term benefits from education. Akerlof and Kranton (2002) argue that students care about the extent to which their behavior deviates from that of their social group (eg, based on gender, race or being athletic or studious). For example, gendered norms surrounding socially appropriate levels of competition emerge and are sustained early on (Buser et al., 2014; Sutter and Glätzle-Rützler, 2015). In this context, investments in education, such as effort in school, depend

---

[11] In the field of health economics, Kling et al. (2012) show that the accessibility of information about Medicare prescription drug plans had a large effect on plan choice. Specifically, individuals in one experimental group were sent a one page letter with the web address to the Medicare website to view various drug plan options and prices. This group was also given information on how access and navigate the website. Individuals in the treatment group however were sent a different one page letter that detailed the cost of their current drug plan as well as the potential cost savings from switching to another plan. These relatively minor differences in the way information was presented led to large differences in plan choice and hundreds of dollars in cost savings for those in the treatment group.

not only on individual benefits, such as test scores and grades, but also on social benefits, such as whether a particular level of effort is consistent with the behavior of one's social group. If an individual's friends preoccupy themselves with trying to have fun while avoiding the subject of planning for the future, that individual will feel pressure to do the same in order to conform.[12] System 1's focus on the immediate present may lead students to overemphasize the current benefits associated with gratification from one's peer group relative to what their future selves or even their current, more reflective selves would prefer (Haun et al., 2013).[13] Since social interactions occur daily both in and outside of school from kindergarten and beyond, they are frequently a priority for many students. As a result, education decisions may overemphasize the value of immediate social gratification relative to a more deliberate consideration of long-term consequences.

Students may also fail to anticipate that their circumstances and friends may change. Imagining themselves with a career or family in the future may be difficult while still in school. Students may also forgo worthwhile education opportunities, such as going to a more selective out-of-state college, because they fear losing touch with their friends. In particular, they may not realize that their future interests, and ultimately their friends might change over time. This tendency is known as projection bias and may reinforce any predisposition toward being present-biased (Busse et al., 2012; DellaVigna, 2009; Loewenstein et al., 2003).

People hold multiple identities based on their gender, race, and other characteristics. Sociologists have long demonstrated that particular identities can be made more salient by prompting or "priming" individuals to focus on them (Benjamin et al., 2010). Identities may relate to social groups, but may also relate to attitudes, such as being "resilient," "capable," "incapable," or "unworthy." Attitudes can also be primed, for example by reading motivational passages or watching tragic movies (Dweck and Leggett, 1988; Dweck and Sorich, 1999). Priming students to focus on positive identities related to learning and intellectual curiosity may be one approach for trying to improve education outcomes.

2.4 Mistakes Are More Likely With Too Little Information or Too Many Options

A growing body of evidence suggests that many children and parents are not fully informed about education costs, benefits, and options. This especially applies to those from low-income backgrounds. Avery and Kane (2004) demonstrate that high school

---

[12] Bishop (2006) reviews the literature on how student effort is affected by social norms and by the threat of harassment of peers. We refer interested readers to Bishop's review in Volume 2 of this Handbook and the many citations therein.

[13] We expand on this point with evidence from a recent study by Bursztyn and Jensen in Section 4. Importantly, the benefits associated with gratification from one's peer group may either reinforce or mitigate the tendency to focus on the present.

students from low-income family backgrounds have very little understanding of actual college tuition levels, financial aid opportunities, and the admissions process. A report by the Advisory Committee on Student Financial Assistance (2001) notes that students and families, as well as adult learners, are often intimidated by news stories about college being unaffordable. These stories may contribute to the fact that individuals often greatly overestimate the cost of higher education (Horn et al., 2003). Usher (1998) finds that low-income individuals overestimate tuition costs by an average factor of two and under-estimate the average annual income differential between high school and university graduates. Misinformation or unawareness can lead to suboptimal outcomes, as high school students who view all postsecondary programs as unaffordable may miss out on significant returns. On the other hand, students only focused on university options may struggle to complete and miss out on more enjoyable careers from vocational schooling or other community college options.

While more information helps individuals make better decisions, more choice may not. Neoclassical economic models predict that giving individuals more choices makes them at least as well off as before. Expanding an individual's choice set increases the like-lihood that an option that best matches one's preferences is available. This argument, however, relies on two assumptions. First, individuals do not find it too difficult to survey the menu of choices and identify the option that is the best fit for them. Second, they are able to easily keep all choices in mind when making their decision (eg, when presented with a lengthy list of specials and entrées on a restaurant menu, you still remember promising options on page one by the time you get to page five). Yet, as discussed earlier, individuals have limited cognitive capacity and attention, and evaluating an abundance of choices requires cognitive effort, which may be especially costly if one's mental band-width is already burdened by other concerns.

Indeed, research in retail food purchases (Iyengar and Lepper, 2000), consumer credit (Bertrand et al., 2010), and finance (Benartzi and Thaler, 2007; Choi et al., 2004) suggests that people may respond unexpectedly to an abundance of choices. For example, Iyengar et al. (2005) find a strong negative correlation between the number of mutual funds offered in company pension plans and enrollment rates. Experimental evidence suggests that when presented with more choice, savers are more likely to choose the default option even if that option may not best suit their individual circumstances (Agnew and Szykman, 2005). Overwhelmed by the number of options, individuals may rely on heuristics characteristic of System 1 such as choosing the simplest or most familiar option or deferring their decisions indefinitely.

More recently, evidence that more choice doesn't necessarily lead to better decisions and outcomes has also been found in education. Scott-Clayton (2011) argues that the abundance of choices available to students in college for programs of study, courses and schedules may be contributing to high dropout rates, especially when combined with a lack of structure. Similarly, when students and parents are given the option of choosing primary and secondary schools, many choose the nearest school and sometimes fail to consider school quality (Hastings and Weinstein, 2008; Ross et al., 2013).

3. OPPORTUNITIES FOR IMPROVEMENT

In the human capital investment model all choices are ex-ante optimal. Observed actions like skipping class, ignoring homework, or dropping out of school stem from a well-thought-out decision in which alternative actions would likely leave one worse off. In contrast, behavioral theory does not assume that observed actions necessarily reveal what is ex-ante optimal; the roles of Systems 1 and 2 in decision-making imply that students make choices that do not always maximize lifetime well-being. In some cases, students may come to regret automatic or short-sighted decisions driven by System 1, wishing instead that they had considered future consequences more carefully. The fact that education attainment decisions may be suboptimal, relative to what students' future and more deliberate selves would prefer, suggests that policies designed to address barriers leading to these decisions have potential to improve outcomes and, ultimately, well-being.

How can policy makers know which behaviors are best to encourage? They cannot. As Bernheim and Rangel (2009) note, without additional assumptions or insights, researchers cannot distinguish at face value whether an observed behavior stems from a suboptimal choice or from the possibility that individuals are rationally weighing their own long-term costs and benefits. In the latter case, imposing constraints on individuals would make them worse off, but ultimately, the goal of interventions is to help individuals achieve their own goals, not to satisfy policymakers' preferences (Rabin, 2013). In this section, we draw attention to several domains in education where the ex-ante optimality of choices by parents and students is suspect, in turn suggesting that policies or tools to improve decisions and ultimately outcomes may be warranted.

One way in which we identify instances of suboptimal choices is through the success of "nudges." Nudges are interventions that encourage certain outcomes, but which do not meaningfully alter costs and restrict individual choice (Thaler and Sunstein, 2008). Seemingly trivial changes to upfront costs or to how choices are presented should not affect outcomes under models of rational decision making and yet, as we present evidence below, they do. Nudging opportunities likely exist because of our overreliance on System 1 thinking. Specifically, the salience of upfront costs together with seemingly vague and distant potential future benefits may lead students and parents to overemphasize the present. [14]

---

[14] Chetty (2015) advises against framing the debate on behavioral economics around whether individuals are rational or not. He argues for a more "pragmatic, policy-oriented" perspective by focussing instead on models that best predict behavior and improve policy. In our context, our framework is useful because it helps explain why students and parents react to nudges in the first place, and therefore may also serve as a useful framework for explaining overall low student grades, attainment, and skill development.

This section identifies potential opportunities for improvement across several domains in education. By discussing examples where nudges have meaningfully impacted behavior in educational contexts, we suggest that particular issues of interest to educators — such as encouraging more parental involvement, more time doing homework and becoming eligible for financial aid — may also serve as promising opportunities for nudges. Although a nudge that changes behavior does not necessarily prove that the underlying intervention improves welfare, it does require that researchers and policy makers seriously consider the possibility that preintervention decisions by students and parents may not have been ex-ante optimal (Bernheim and Rangel, 2009). On the other hand, an ineffective nudge is not evidence that economic agents optimize in the way that the human capital investment model predicts; it may simply be that the nudge targeted the incorrect behavioral barrier.

While students' ex-post regret and reflections about past behavior are not direct evidence that ex-ante decisions are suboptimal, it can also provide insights into why certain choices are made and identify possible opportunities for improvement. For example, that the majority of high school dropouts regret their decision to leave school while also attributing their decision to "too much freedom" and "not enough rules" suggests that the long-term consequences of their decisions may not always be at the top of mind (Bridgeland et al., 2006). In some cases, we argue that the large financial gains from encouraging a particular behavior, such as graduating from high school, parental involvement or increasing class attendance, is sufficient to be skeptical about the ex-ante optimality of preintervention behavior.

3.1 Parental Involvement

Parental inputs are critical in determining children's cognitive and noncognitive skills as well as education attainment (Cunha and Heckman, 2008; Todd and Wolpin, 2007). The decisions parents make early on for their children have consequences not only on their quality of schooling, but also on peers they interact with and their future dispositions toward learning. These inputs may also include personality traits such as risk attitudes, which may affect how students and parents both view long-term investments in education (Dohmen et al., 2011; Levin and Hart, 2003) and in turn, concrete decisions such as school choice (Wölfel and Heineck, 2012). Levels of parental involvement vary widely, with children from lower-income and minority families receiving less involvement, on average, than their higher-income classmates (Sirin, 2005).

Many traditional models attribute these differences to differences in returns to education for children from different socioeconomic backgrounds. Investing in education may be more costly for low-income parents, so choosing to invest less is optimal. Alternatively, parents may simply value education differently, although that valuation may be similarly impacted by the same behavioral barriers that affect students (eg, the low salience of long-term benefits). Another explanation is that low-income parents are less involved because they have less information about how to effectively invest. A policy that makes it easier to acquire information should therefore increase investment among affected parents relative to those who were not exposed to the policy. Recent experimental evidence suggests that small changes in the timing of information or in the way information is presented to parents can increase parental involvement and produce significant and often long-lasting results (Avvisati et al., 2014; Bergman, 2014). For example, Bergman (2014) finds virtually all parents who are offered text messages to inform them of their middle school child's incomplete homework agree to receive the messages, and that the children of these randomly selected parents perform significantly better than those whose parents do not receive the offer.

Given the strong association between academic achievement and long-run outcomes such as college attendance and earnings (Chetty et al., 2011), the magnitude of the effects from these small interventions suggests that either classroom information is difficult to obtain, or that the value from obtaining it is not salient enough for parents to want to access it. Stress exacerbates these barriers. Whether from money, time, or other circumstances, added stress reduces the brain's capacity to focus on other tasks, including parental involvement. As a result, simply making information more available may not be effective because stressed-out parents are distracted. Effective policies to increase parental involvement, therefore, may include those that reduce stress or make it easier to change routine.

3.2 Attendance

By the time high school students decide to drop out, there is typically a long history of truancy and absenteeism that extends as far back as early elementary school (Barrington and Hendricks, 1989). Efforts to target early disengagement and keep students in class may therefore help prevent at-risk students from falling into a downward spiral, in which missing school causes them to fall behind in their studies, which, in turn, makes them feel even less motivated to attend classes and puts them further behind (Lamdin, 1996; Peterson and Colangelo, 1996; Strickland, 1998). In college, absenteeism rises sharply when attendance is mostly voluntary. Past studies estimate about one-third of undergraduate college students regularly fail to show for class (Romer, 1993).

Both high school and college absenteeism are highly correlated with poor academic performance (Stanca, 2006). Past studies have struggled in determining whether these uniformly robust relationships represent direct causal influences. Dobkin et al. (2010) use a clever regression discontinuity design, in which college instructors insist on subsequent mandatory attendance for students with midterm grades below a specified cut-off. Students with grades just below the cut-off and facing mandatory attendance fare significantly better on the final exam than those with grades just above it.

A students' classroom environment clearly helps determine whether he desires to attend school. Students who feel engaged, motivated, and among friends are more likely to go (Brewster and Bowen, 2004; Catterall, 1998; Croninger and Lee, 2001; Lee and Burkham, 2003). Students may overemphasize these factors, however, and place less weight on the incremental and uncertain benefits from attendance. For example, the primary reason students gave for missing class in Dobkin et al.'s study was having slept in.

Students may also put off attending meetings outside the classroom, such as tutorials, after-school workshops, or advising. Unless attendance is mandatory, participation rates in these services are often very low. Some recent studies, discussed in detail below, suggest that mandatory tutoring or advising services are much more promising for boosting academic performance than voluntary ones. Our System 1 and 2 frameworks for decision-making point to the problems of leaving students to reorganize routines on their own. Bettinger et al. (2013) suggest that from this lack of structure, students manage time poorly and become disengaged.

3.3 Homework

Homework often involves trading off more enjoyable activities now for uncertain, incremental benefits later. Bridgeland et al. (2006) find that high school dropouts report that they were doing little, if any, homework prior to leaving school. More than 60% of these respondents indicated that they could have completed high school had they worked harder at it and done more. At the college level, experimental evidence suggests that completing homework assignments lowers the probability that students drop a course and significantly increases grades without lowering performance in other courses (Grodner and Rupp, 2013). Despite this, many students fail to complete assignments on time. For example, Bergman (2014) finds that more than 20% of students fail to complete assignments on time, with homework completion rates lower than in-class assignments.

Empirical evidence suggests a strong negative association between impatience and study habits, especially homework.[15] As one example, we consider the amount of self-reported study time at school or at home by students in the 1979 National Longitudinal Survey of Youth (NLSY79).[16] Fig. 1 shows the distributions of study times of those classified as patient or impatient using a measure of present bias introduced by DellaVigna and Daniele Paserman (2005) and also used in Cadena and Keys (2015). In Fig. 1, the average amount of time spent studying or working on class projects

[15] Oreopoulos and Salvanes (2011) also show a strong association between education attainment and individuals self-reporting they agree people should live for today and let tomorrow take care of itself.

[16] Specifically, we consider a sample of NLSY79 respondents who report being enrolled in school or college in 1981. The study time variable is defined as the sum of hours spent studying or working on class projects at school, on campus or away from school during the last 7 days.

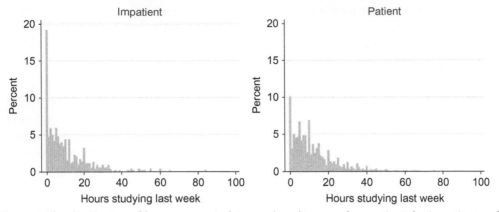

Figure 1 The distribution of hours spent studying and working on class projects by impatient and patient students.

is lower among impatient students. In particular, impatient students are more likely to report spending no time studying.[17] This example is consistent with the results from a large and growing literature in psychology which finds that children who are better able to exhibit self-control have better study habits, are more likely to regularly do homework, get better grades and have higher education attainment (Duckworth and Carlson, 2013; Duckworth and Steinberg, 2014; Duckworth et al., 2012). Importantly, this research suggests that the ability to self-regulate can be influenced and improved, leaving open the possibility that targeted interventions can lead to significant gains in education attainment.[18]

Notes: This sample includes all NLSY79 respondents reporting being enrolled in formal schooling in 1981. The graph shows the distribution of reported time spent studying or working on class projects between students classified as impatient (left panel) and those classified as patient (right panel). This measure of impatience was introduced by DellaVigna and Daniele Paserman (2005) and classifies a respondent as being impatient

---

[17] These relationships still hold in regressions that control flexibly for age, gender, race, mother's education (four categories), father's education (four categories), family income quartile as a child, poverty status as a child, magazines in the home as a child, newspapers in the home as a child, having a library card as a child, urban status and region indicators. In particular, NLSY79 respondents classified as "impatient" are 2.2% more likely to report spending no time studying (8.8% vs. 11%), and report studying 1.35 h fewer per week (7.09 vs. 8.44 h per week) than those classified as "patient."

[18] Duckworth et al. (2014) propose a model where agents choosing between an immediately rewarding activity and a valued distant goal can exercise self-control in several ways. When facing such a choice (such as checking Facebook instead of doing homework), agents can exercise self-control by anticipating the temptation and choosing to remove themselves from the situation (ie, study in an area without a computer, tablet or cell-phone) or by paying a cost to suppress directly the urge at the time the choice must be made.

surveyors report that the respondent was "impatient or restless" in any of the annual NLSY79 waves between 1980 and 1985. The study time variable is defined as the sum of hours spent studying or working on class projects at school, on campus or away from school during the last 7 days.

3.4 High School Completion

High school dropouts face daunting challenges over the rest of their lives. Among recent dropouts in the United States, 16% are unemployed and 32% live below the poverty line; those with jobs earn an average of only $12.75 per hour with the most common jobs found in the construction, food services, and landscaping services industries (Messacar and Oreopoulos, 2013). Labor-market outcomes remain bleak. Dropouts aged 50 earn an average of $16.50 an hour. In addition to difficulties in the labor market, social outcomes are worse for dropouts compared to any other education attainment group. More of them are separated or divorced, unhealthy, and unhappy.

There is, of course, no single explanation why students drop out of high school: conflicts at home, urgent financial difficulties, or unexpected pregnancies are only a few examples. Some dropouts say they are too poorly prepared to complete high school. Bridgeland et al. (2006) report a majority say they are unmotivated or uninspired to go to class, but most also say they regret their decision later in life and, with the benefit of hindsight, wish they had stayed. Present bias may be at play, as suggested by Cadena and Keys (2015), who find that adolescents classified by a surveyor as "impatient" are more likely to dropout, even if they stated an intention to finish. This behavior is difficult to reconcile with the human capital investment framework and suggests short-sightedness or the salience of an immediate distaste for school may be getting in the way of realizing larger lifetime gains.

Compulsory schooling laws have existed for decades (and sometimes more than a 100 years), primarily because of the belief that students wishing to leave school early are, in fact, better off by not doing so. For example, in the United Kingdom, Prime Minister David Cameron offers paternalistic reasons for wanting to raise the school leaving age from sixteen to eighteen, "Think about it: with your children, would you dream of just leaving them to their own devices, not getting a job, not training, nothing? No – you'd nag and push and guide and do anything to get them on their way ... and so must we" (Watt, 2013). Many studies have exploited historical differences in compulsory-schooling laws to examine whether high school students benefited from facing more restrictive dropout options. They often estimate substantial increases to adult annual earnings, in the range of 10% from an additional year of school due to facing more restrictive laws (Acemoglu and Angrist, 2001; Angrist and Krueger, 1992; Harmon and Walker, 1995, and Oreopoulos, 2005). Other studies find nonpecuniary benefits, such as less crime (Anderson, 2014; Lochner and Moretti, 2004), lower use of cigarettes and illicit drugs (Mensch and Kandel, 1988), improved health (Lleras–Muney, 2005; Meghir et al., 2013), reduced incidence of teen pregnancy (Black et al., 2005), and improved memory and other cognitive abilities (Banks and Mazzonna, 2011).[19]

To be clear, policies that force children to stay in school by threat of fine or jail are not nudges. Constraining all individuals toward one action relies on the strong assumption that everyone who would behave differently without the constraint would actually be worse off in that event.[20] As this is unlikely, compulsory-schooling legislation often does allow for exceptions. Students are often allowed to leave if they work full-time or are parents. Sometimes students are allowed to leave early after explicitly agreeing they understand the long-term risks from such actions. Enforcement is also not strict. To our knowledge, no parent has ever gone to jail under compulsory-schooling legislation and very few have been fined. However, the law serves to set expectations and efforts to encourage youth to stay in class. Truant students are given more attention. They or their parents are often first contacted by teachers, principals, or caseworkers in an effort to reengage the students and address reasons behind the truancy. More resources for addressing or enforcing truancy may also come from changes to compulsory-schooling laws. Ideally, while past evidence suggests that many high school dropouts (but not all) miss out on large lifetime benefits, effective approaches to keep students interested and engaged in learning are needed to help them make better choices to stay in school, even when dropping out is permissible.

[19] Two important caveats must be mentioned. First, estimated benefits to compulsory schooling vary widely outside North America (Brunello et al., 2009; Brunello et al., 2012; Devereux and Hart, 2010; Grenet, 2011; Meghir and Palme, 2005; Pischke and von Wachter, 2008). One possibility is that returns are individual-specific and even change over the life cycle. Studies that estimate returns by looking at different samples of workers in different age brackets might produce inconsistent results. Other explanations discussed by Grenet (2011) are that institutional factors, like minimum wage policies, affect returns, or that the implementation and enforcement of the laws vary across countries. Pischke and von Wachter (2008) suggest that the tracking of students into vocational or academic schools at early ages in some countries will result in different returns to basic labor market skills. The other caveat is that another recent study, Stephens and Yang (2014), calls into question the robustness of findings from some US studies that use changes in compulsory schooling laws over time. Estimated returns become small and statistically insignificant after trying to control for region-specific time trends. Their critique does not apply to findings from Angrist and Krueger (1992), who use static differences in school entry ages to estimate returns to compulsory schooling. Perhaps regional trend controls absorb a delayed effect. At the very least, the study suggests a need for additional research to determine whether these laws really did generate large returns. Even small average returns from compulsory schooling may still imply suboptimal behavior for some, since large and small effects are being averaged together. Under the human capital investment model, individuals affected by the laws should either be indifferent or expect to be negatively impacted. In this case, we should expect to find very low or even negative returns from constraining this entire group to stay on.

[20] Alternatively, the costs to those who would not have been worse off without the constraint are smaller than the perceived benefits for those who would have been worse off.

3.5 College Attainment

Past and recent evidence suggests that there are still large returns to a college degree that are also difficult to reconcile within a school investment model.[21] While benefits vary significantly across all college programs and occupations, college graduates enjoy an earnings premium in all major occupation sectors. The empirical evidence suggests that those at the margin of attending benefit at least as much as those from the more general college population at large (Zimmerman, 2014). Many researchers believe skill-biased technological change has caused a large growth in demand for college educated workers, especially those with skills that cannot easily be automated. Other empirical research argues that there are likely large nonmonetary returns to higher education, including higher job satisfaction and better health outcomes (Oreopoulos and Salvanes, 2011).

A possible behavioral explanation for no college experience is lack of encouragement and approval from friends and family. Qualitative research on the college decision-making process suggests that students develop predispositions toward higher education at an early age based in part on parents' experiences and level of encouragement, as well as friends' interests in going, the high school resources available to them, and access to college information (Cabrera and La Nasa, 2000). Salient information from these sources — as well as the social implications of a college-going identity — may therefore play an important role in actual attainment (Demming and Dynarski, 2009; Oreopoulos and Petronijevic, 2013).

Another behavioral barrier to college is having to change routine to get there. College transition costs are typically considered too small to matter in the education-investment model. However, there are many transition points from high school to college that require deliberate attention around short- and long-term trade-offs. Prospective students must decide where to go, how long to go, how to afford to go, and then actually apply. Upon gaining admission, they must choose courses, set up meetings, fill out forms, and finally show up for class. While many underprivileged students express intent to go on to college, they sometimes fail to complete application requirements (Avery and Kane, 2004). Some students plan to attend college, get accepted, and register for courses, yet fail to show up when their program begins. Others attend for years only to drop out before graduating despite often only requiring a few more credits (Cadena and Keys, 2015).

Benefits from college appear more associated with program completion, even for programs lasting 1 or 2 years. In the United States, earnings of workers who only complete some college are only marginally higher than the earnings of high school graduates (Oreopoulos and Petronijevic, 2013). Yet while college enrollment rates have risen over the past few decades, completion rates have not followed suit. As with high school

---

[21] See Oreopoulos and Petronijevic (2013) for one recent review of the estimates of the financial returns to postsecondary education. See also Baum et al. (2013).

dropout, reasons for college dropout may be from overreliance on System 1 thinking. Several promising behavioral policies designed for increasing college completion are discussed in Section 4.

3.6 Program Suitability

College-bound youth must choose where to go and what to study from a wide array of options. Without adequate deliberation, many of them may end up in places not best suited to their abilities or interests. Recent evidence suggests that high-achieving students from low- and middle-income families are less likely to apply to selective institutions to which they would likely be admitted (Baum and Scott-Clayton, 2013; Hoxby and Avery, 2013). Moreover, many students may not consider the breadth of program and school opportunities available to them (ie, vocational programs, relative to General Arts and Sciences programs at a local community college), especially if they are unfamiliar with them. Given that postsecondary completion rates, per-student instructional resources and career advising services vary widely across various institutions and programs, enrolling in schools that do not best match abilities and interests can be very costly for students. Mismatch between student interests and college services may also increase chances of dropout.

3.7 College Aid Savvy

Some students receiving college financial aid could be getting more. Others fail to qualify for aid entirely: each year, more than one million college students in the United States who are eligible for grant aid fail to complete the necessary forms to receive it (Council of Economic Advisors, 2009). Bird and Castleman (2014) estimate that nearly 20% of annual Pell Grant recipients in good academic standing fail to refile a FAFSA after their freshman year, and subsequently miss out on financial aid for the following academic year. Missing out on financial aid opportunities lowers the expected financial return to obtaining postsecondary credentials and, among those who do manage to apply for and receive financial aid, some could benefit from selecting a better financial aid package. The quality of a financial aid package is evaluated both by the quantity and the types of aid given: for instance, a financial aid package with a higher proportion of grants rather than loans or work-study funding is "better" because it may allow students to spend more time studying or enjoying leisure (Avery and Hoxby, 2003; Bettinger, 2004; Stinebrickner and Stinebrickner, 2003). However, Avery and Hoxby (2003) find that some students are just as attracted to financial aid in the form of work-study and loans as they are grants, despite the fact that grants are less costly. The authors also find that some students are attracted by superficial aspects of financial aid offers, such as calling grants "scholarships," and forgo better opportunities as a result.

An aversion to holding debt may also lead to students missing out on financial aid opportunities. In the human capital investment framework, the inability to borrow enough is the main reason why individuals who would benefit from attending college might not attend. This liquidity constraint can arise because the financial benefits of college occur in the future, while the costs of college must be paid in the present. Recent studies suggest that increasing numbers of students may face credit constraints, even when they have access to government aid (Lochner and Monge-Naranjo, 2012; Oreopoulos and Petronijevic, 2013). Yet, an inability to borrow is not the same as a preference not to borrow. Students are considered debt averse if they prefer more school, can borrow to go, but end up not going in order to avoid incurring debt. Such behavior occurs because immediate (psychological) discomfort from holding debt can lead to students underinvesting in education (Scott-Clayton, 2012a,b).[22] In one study of postsecondary financial aid applicants in Latin America, Caetano et al. (2011) find that survey respondents are about 10% less likely to choose arrangements labeled as "debt" or "loan" contracts, as opposed to other financially equivalent contracts without these labels. Baum and Schwartz (2013) argue that students with no alternative means of financing postsecondary education, particularly those from low-income or minority backgrounds, may be more likely to be reluctant to finance college with loans.

In addition to educational underinvestment, debt aversion may lead students to engage in suboptimal study strategies, such as working part-time when that time could be used for homework. It can also affect enrollment decisions and career choices. For example, law school applicants who were offered tuition *waivers* conditional on finding employment in the public sector, compared to tuition *loans* that are waived after finding employment in the public sector, were far more likely to both enroll in the program and have a public sector job (Field, 2009). Students, therefore, showed a strong preference to remain out of debt both while in school and after graduation.

3.8 College Cost Savvy

Low-income students and their parents are more likely to overestimate costs of attending college (Avery and Kane, 2004; Usher, 1998). Reports in the popular media that describe a crisis in student borrowing or that highlight extreme examples of students graduating with high debt levels may contribute to and further exacerbate the over-estimates of attending college among low-income families (Avery and Turner, 2012; Jabbar, 2011). But why don't families discount these extreme examples about the costs of obtaining postsecondary credentials? One reason may be that these reports are particularly easy to recall when beginning to think about the college application process and this accessibility may lead to suboptimal decisions.

---

[22] Aversion to holding debt may also be viewed in the standard rational economic framework if the variance to postcollege earnings is high and risk aversion is sufficiently high (Baum and Schwartz, 2013).

Lower-income families are also less likely to take advantage of government incentives to save for postsecondary education. The benefits of tax incentives for education saving, such as the 529 account in the United States, are highest for those with high incomes (Dynarski, 2004). Use of registered education savings plans (RESPs) in Canada is also concentrated among high-income and high-wealth families, despite the fact that the accounts were originally intended to lower the postsecondary among low-income families (Milligan, 2005). Students from low-income families who open an RESP account qualify for up to $2000 without any additional contribution, yet a large fraction of eligible students fail to do so. Making it easier to complete the application increases take-up rates substantially (Nayar, 2013).

4. POLICIES AND PROGRAMS TO ADDRESS BEHAVIORAL BARRIERS

This section reviews the growing literature of interventions designed to overcome behavioral barriers in education. Earlier we classified barriers into four general categories: (1) some students focus too much on the present, (2) some rely too much on routine, (3) some focus too much on negative identities, and (4) mistakes are more likely with many options or with little information. We selected interventions based on their likelihood of helping with at least one of these barriers. Some of them target a specific event, like helping complete an application. Some target a one-time change in school environment, like introducing more regular tests. Other interventions target recurring barriers and thus occur in multiple doses, like reminding students each week to attend tutorials. Whether a one-time or continuous intervention is preferred or warranted depends on a number of factors, especially cost and effectiveness. One-time interventions are not always cheaper. For example, a motivational presentation to think about the future is more expensive than a weekly email linking to motivational videos. With regard to the effectiveness of a behavioral intervention, a key determinant is the timing between it and when the actual decision being targeted needs to be made. In the case of applying to college, reminding students in Grade 11 will not be as effective as reminding them in Grade 12. Inviting students to an after-school presentation on college application completion will not be as effective as inviting them to complete the form now, in class. Follow-up interventions may also be necessary in order to sustain behavioral changes or to reinforce habits; as such, research on the duration of these behavioral changes will be valuable.

In most cases, the studies we discuss below use random assignment as the source of variation, allowing for convincing and straightforward causal inference. We also describe programs designed to address behavioral barriers that have been proposed but not yet rigorously tested or that are currently being evaluated and whose preliminary results seem promising. Our goal is both to review the evidence accumulated to date, and to encourage other researchers to develop and test new policies that leverage these ideas. We mention key examples in the text. Tables 1–5 provide a more comprehensive list. Whenever possible, we report the estimated effects of interventions for binary dependent variables in percentage points while results for outcomes such as test scores or grades are reported in standard deviations. In cases where grades are not standardized we report effects in terms of change in GPA points and note the baseline average. Unless otherwise indicated, all reported effects are statistically significant at conventional levels.

4.1 Interventions That Aim to Offset Immediate Costs With Immediate Benefits

One approach to address present bias is simply to remind students to think more about their future. For example, in an online study with at-risk undergraduate students from McGill University, a random sample was asked to take about 2 h to participate in a goal-setting exercise in which they wrote down specific long-term goals and proposed intermediate steps to achieve those (Morisano et al., 2010). The end-of-year Grade Point Average for students assigned to the exercise was half a point higher than control students assigned to a basic personality test, a 0.7 standard deviation difference. While a seemingly trivial exercise, "interrupting" individuals at the cusp of a decision involving short- and long-run trade-offs and encouraging them to think deliberately may effectively deter them from overemphasizing the present. Requiring students to regularly write or think about their future appears to be a promising avenue for additional research.

Another approach for addressing present bias is to offer immediate incentives that off-set immediate costs (Hershfield et al., 2011). Parents often adopt this strategy in offering small rewards (like television or dessert) for future-enhancing behavior (like doing home-work or eating vegetables). Yet, some social scientists advise caution on the use of exter-nal incentives to motivate behavior (Deci and Ryan, 2010). Students, they note, can be intrinsically motivated to learn based on their own desires for self-improvement, fun, and challenge, or they can be extrinsically motivated to do an unwanted task in order to attain a wanted outcome attached to it. Grades are themselves a type of extrinsic incentive to study and learn. A concern is that, by offering external incentives to make immediate tasks seem more worthwhile, students may become subsequently reliant on them or the incentive itself may become less attractive over time. Ideally, extrinsic incentives complement intrinsic motivation so that the extrinsic goal is self-endorsed and students recognize the importance of the behavior and appreciate the added incentive. Students may also come to internalize the incentivized behavior if their own self-confidence or self-identity from doing it improves. For example, conditions attached to a scholarship or nonmonetary award, such as a minimum GPA or required courses, may increase stu-dent effort if the student views the scholarship or award program as part of his or her identity.

Studies on the effectiveness of offering immediate incentives for improving grades or attendance yield mixed results (Gneezy et al., 2011). Table 1 summarizes these. One of the earliest experiments offered 3rd- to 6th-grade students in rural Ohio $15 for

Table 1 Interventions that aim to offset immediate costs with immediate benefits

Authors	Treatment	Data	Research Design	Findings
Panel A: primary, middle, or high schools				
Angrist and Lavy (2009)	Achievement Awards demonstration: $1500 for passing the Israeli high school matriculation exam	Administrative data for high school seniors from 40 low-performing Israeli schools	Field experiment (randomization at the school level)	Eligibility for the cash reward increase the probability of passing the matriculation exam by (i) 5.2% for boys and girls (29% vs. 24%) (not significant); (ii) 10.5% for girls (39% vs. 29%); (iii) −2.2% for boys (18% vs. 20%) (not significant)
Bettinger (2012)	$15 ($20) for each proficient (advanced) score in each state reading, math, writing, science, and social studies test	Administrative data for 3rd, 4th-, 5th-, and 6th-grade students in Coshocton, Ohio	Field experiment (randomization at the school-grade level)	Eligibility for the Coshocton Incentive Program (i) increased math test scores by 0.15 standard deviations; (ii) increased reading test scores by 0.01 standard deviations (not significant); (iii) increased social science test scores by 0.02 standard deviations (not significant); (iv) increased science test scores by −0.04 standard deviations
Dearden et al. (2009)	Education Maintenance Allowance (EMA): (i) ~$50 per week for each week of 12th- or 13th-grade attendance; (ii) ~$75 bonuses for term completions; (iii) $75–$200 for course completion	Survey data for low-income high school students in England	OLS and Propensity Score Matching	Eligibility for the EMA (i) increased full-time 12th-grade enrollment by 4.5% (74% vs. 69%); (ii) increase full-time 13th-grade enrollment by 6.7% (68% vs. 61%)

	Intervention	Data	Method	Findings
Fryer Jr. (2011)	(i) $2 payment for each book read in Dallas public schools (Earning by Learning); (ii) payment for performance on a series of tests in NYC public schools (NYC Spark); (iii) payment for grades in five core courses in Chicago (Paper Project)	Administrative data from 203 public schools in Chicago, Dallas, and New York City	Field experiment	(i) Earning by Learning: (a) 0.012 standard deviation increase in reading scores, (b) 0.079 standard deviation increase in math scores; (ii) NYC Spark: (a) −0.026 to 0.004 standard deviation increase in reading scores, (b) −0.031 to 0.062 standard deviation increase in math scores; (iii) Paper Project: (a) −0.006 standard deviation increase in reading scores, (b) −0.010 standard deviation increase in math scores. No main effect estimates above are significant
Guryan et al. (2015)	Financial incentives (prizes worth up to $5 per book read) combined with Project READS, a summer reading program	Administrative and survey data for 415 4th and 5th-grade students at a relatively wealthy, large urban school district in the northeastern U.S.	Field experiment and surveys to elicit reading level and preferences (randomization at the classroom level)	A one standard deviation increase in measured reading motivation at baseline lead treatment group students to read 1.3 more Project Reads books that were mailed to them, compared to the control group This estimated effect is highest (4.7 more books) for students whose mailed books were well-matched to their reading interests and level

Continued

Table 1 Interventions that aim to offset immediate costs with immediate benefits—cont'd

Authors	Treatment	Data	Research Design	Findings
Jackson (2010)	Texas Advanced Placement Incentive Program (APIP): pays students between $100 and $500 for taking and passing AP exams; substantial financial incentives for teachers	Administrative data from 57 Texas high schools for the 1994–2005 period	Difference in differences using schools that do not adopt the APIP as the control group	Eligibility for the APIP led to: (i) a 2.4% increase in the percentage of 11th- and 12th-graders taking AP exams; (ii) a 13.5% increase in the number of students scoring above 1100 (24) on the SAT (ACT); (iii) a 5% increase in the number of students attending college
Kremer et al. (2009)	The Girl's Scholarship Program (Kenya):Girls who place in the top 15% of all girls in the program (treatment) schools on standardized tests received a scholarship to cover school fees and supplies for 2 years	Administrative data for 6th-grade girls at Kenyan primary schools	Field experiment	Eligibility for the scholarship increased test scores by 0.13 standard deviations during the program year
Levitt et al. (2012)	(i) Incentives to improve test score performance framed as gains and losses; (ii) pecuniary versus nonpecuniary rewards; (iii) immediate versus nonimmediate rewards	Administrative data for more than 7000 elementary and high schools from three school districts near Chicago	Field experiment	(i) 0.08–0.17 standard deviation improvement in test scores for incentives framed as losses relative to those framed as gains; (ii) −0.1 to 0.25 standard deviation improvement in test scores for nonfinancial incentives relative to financial incentives for elementary school students; (iii) nonimmediate awards have no effect on test scores
Oswald and Backes-Gellner (2014)	Eligibility to year a bonus equal to the monthly salary for apprenticeship students. The bonus is tied to grade performance on courses related to the apprenticeship program	Administrative and survey data for 238 vocational students in Switzerland	OLS	Students whose apprenticeships offered bonuses experienced a 0.36 standard deviation GPA increase. This effect is higher (by approximately 0.8 standard deviations) for students identified as impatient using a survey

Study	Intervention	Data	Method	Results
Riccio et al. (2013)	Opportunity NYC: Various health, workforce, and education incentives directed at children including: (i) \$25 per month for 95% school attendance; (ii) \$300 to \$600 for passing or proficiency on standardized exams (amount varies for primary/middle/high school students); (iii) \$25 per parent–teacher conference attended (up to 2 per year)	Administrative and survey data for more than 11,000 children in New York	Field experiment	Students in 4th grade at random assignment: effects on math proficiency (i) 2.1% in Year 1 (not significant) (73% vs. 71%); (ii) 1.7% in Year 2 (not significant) (80% vs. 79%) Students in 7th grade at random assignment: effects on math proficiency: (i) 0.8% in Year 1 (not significant) (60% vs. 59%); (ii) −1.6% in Year 2 (not significant) (62% vs. 64%)
Rodréguez-Planas (2012)	Quantum Opportunity Program (QOP): \$1.25 per hour devoted to prescribed educational and developmental activities + a lump sum payment matching their earnings paid upon obtaining a high school diploma or GED and enrolled in postsecondary education or training	Administrative and survey data from low-achieving students from low-performing high schools entering 9th grade in 1995 in the United States	Field experiment	Eligibility for the QOP: (i) increased high school or GED completion by 4.3% (68% vs. 64%) (not significant); (ii) increased postsecondary education enrollment by 5% (32% vs. 27%)
Springer et al. (2015)	Students who attended 25% and 75% of their allotted supplemental education services (SES) tutoring hours received (i) a signed certificate of recognition from the district superintendent; OR (ii) \$25 plus an additional \$50 upon completing 100% of allotted hours	Administrative data for more than 300 primary and middle school students	Field experiment	Students randomly assigned to receive the nonmonetary award (certificate) attended 43% more tutoring hours than control group students (60% vs. 17%) Students randomly assigned to receive the monetary award attended 6% more tutoring hours than control group students (23% vs. 17%) (not significant)

Continued

Table 1 Interventions that aim to offset immediate costs with immediate benefits—cont'd

Authors	Treatment	Data	Research Design	Findings
Panel B: postsecondary education				
Angrist et al. (2009)	The Student Achievement and Retention Project (STAR) (i) GPA based scholarship (SFP); (ii) mentoring from upper-year undergraduates (SSP); (iii) SFP + SSP	Administrative data for first-year students at a large public Canadian university	Field experiment	Students randomly assigned to the SFP treatment arm (i) 0.01 standard deviation increase in first-year GPA (not significant); (ii) −0.02 standard deviation increase in second-year GPA (not significant). Students randomly assigned to the SFP + SSP treatment arm (i) 0.23 standard deviation increase in first-year GPA; (ii) 0.08 standard deviation increase in second-year GPA (not significant)
Angrist et al. (2014b)	$100 reward for course grades of 70% + $20 for each percentage point higher than this	Administrative data for first and second-year students at a large public Canadian university	Field experiment	Students randomly assigned to the treatment group (i) earned first-year GPAs −0.021 standard deviations higher than those for the control group (not significant); (ii) earned a second-year GPA 0.107 standard deviations higher than those for the control group (not significant)
Barrow et al. (2014)	For each of two semesters, (i) $250 for at least half-time enrollment; (ii) $250 for a "C−" average or better at the end of midterms; (iii) $500 for maintaining a "C−" average; (iv) optional counseling	Administrative data for low-income parents beginning community college in Louisiana	Field experiment	Students randomly assigned to the treatment group (i) earned 3.345 more credits (10.7 vs. 7.4 credits) during first year; (ii) earned first-year GPAs 0.068 points higher (2.23 vs. 2.17 GPA) (not significant)

Study	Program	Data	Method	Results
Castleman (2014)	(i) Florida Medallion Scholars (FMS) scholarship: 75% of public college tuition and fees paid for students with a 3.0 high school GPA and at least 20 on the ACT (or 970 on the SAT); (ii) Florida Academic Scholars (FAS) scholarship: 100% of public college tuition and fees paid for students with a 3.5 high school GPA and at least 28 on the ACT (or 1270 on the SAT)	Administrative data for Florida high school graduates and post-secondary attendees	Differences-in-differences design	Students eligible for FMS were 3% more likely to graduate with a BA 5 years after high school (not significant) (41% vs. 38%) Students eligible for FAS were 10% more likely to graduate with a BA 5 years after high school (54% vs. 44%)
Cohodes and Goodman (2014)	John and Abigail Adams Scholarship Program (MA): MA public school tuition waived for students who score in the top 25th percentile of their school district and attain minimum absolute benchmarks on the statewide 10th-grade test; must maintain 3.0 GPA in college	Administrative data for Massachusetts public high school students (Massachusetts Department of Elementary and Secondary Education, National Student Clearing House)	Regression discontinuity design on 10th-grade test scores	Eligibility for the MA scholarship (i) increased the likelihood of enrolling in a college immediately by 1.7% (80% vs. 78%); (ii) decreased the likelihood of graduating from a college within 6 years by 2.5% (64% vs. 66%)
Cha and Patel (2010)	$1800 for earning a grade of "C" or better in 12 or more credits or $900 for a "C" or better in 6–11 credits. All payments made at the end of each semester	Administrative data for low-income Ohio college students with children and eligible for TANF	Field experiment	Students randomly assigned to the treatment group earned 2.0 more credits (15.4 vs. 13.4 credits)
Cornwell et al. (2005)	Georgia Hope: Full tuition/fees at GA public colleges for students with a 3.0 high school GPA; must maintain a 3.0 GPA in college	Administrative data for all undergraduate students enrolled at the University of Georgia	Difference in differences using non-Georgia residents as the control group	Eligibility for the Georgia Hope scholarship (i) decreased the likelihood of freshman full course load enrollment by 4.2% (77% vs. 81%); (ii) decreased the likelihood of completing a freshman full course load by 6% (58% vs. 64%)

Continued

Table 1 Interventions that aim to offset immediate costs with immediate benefits—cont'd

Authors	Treatment	Data	Research Design	Findings
De Paola et al. (2012)	(i) €700 for students with the 30 highest cumulative scores on all exams; (ii) €250 for students with the 30 highest cumulative scores on all exams	Administrative data from first-year business students at the University of Calabria	Field experiment	Students randomly assigned to the €700 reward treatment (i) scored 0.19 standard deviations higher on exams; (ii) earned 2.335 more credits (20.8 vs. 18.5 credits) Students randomly assigned to the €250 reward treatment (i) scored 0.16 standard deviations higher on exams; (ii) earned 2.194 more credits (20.7 vs. 18.5 credits)
Dynarski (2008)	Arkansas (AR): $1000 to $2500 for tuition and fees at AR colleges for students with at least 19 on the ACT and a 2.5 core high school GPA; Georgia: full tuition/fees at GA public colleges for students with a 3.0 high school GPA; must maintain a 3.0 GPA in college	Survey (census, 1% PUMS) data for all 22- to 34-year-olds in 2000	Difference in differences design using other states (not GA or AR) as the control group	The fraction of the age 22–34 population with a college degree increased by 2.98% in states that enacted merit scholarship programs (GA and AR) (37% vs. 34%)
Ford et al. (2012)	Future to Discover (FTD): "Learning Accounts" up to $8000 in funds for college-related expenses	Administrative data from high schools in two Canadian provinces	Field experiment	Eligibility for Learning Accounts increased postsecondary enrollment by 8% (71% vs. 63%)
Leuven et al. (2010)	(i) €681 for completion of all first-year requirements; (ii) €227 for completion of all first-year requirements	Administrative data from first-year business and economics students at the University of Amsterdam	Field experiment	Students in the €681 treatment arm were 4.6% more likely to complete first-year requirements (24% vs. 19.5%) (not significant) Students in the €227 treatment arm were 0.7% more likely to complete first-year requirements (20% vs. 19.5%) (not significant)

Study	Incentive	Data	Method	Results
Leuven et al. (2011)	(i) €1000 for the student with the top microeconomics exam score; (ii) €3000 for the student with the top microeconomics exam score; (iii) €5000 for the student with the top microeconomics exam score	Administrative data from first-year business students at the University of Amsterdam	Field experiment (prerandomization students could select which treatment arm (€1000,3000,5000) they wanted to be eligible for)	Students randomly assigned to the treatment groups (i) were 6.8% more likely to attend the first tutorial meeting (81% vs. 74%); answered 0.895 (€1000 incentive), 1.246 (€3000 incentive), and −0.629 (€5000 incentive) more questions correctly on the 35-question final exam
MacDonald et al. (2009)	$750 each of three semesters for (i) obtaining a 2.0 GPA or higher; (ii) meet eligibility requirements for the following semester; (iii) completing at least 12 hours of tutorial, case management or career workshops	Administrative data for at-risk community college students in Ontario, Canada	Field experiment	Students randomly assigned to the treatment group earned GPAs (i) 0.07 points higher during the first semester of college (2.18 vs. 2.11) (not significant); (ii) 0.12 points higher during the second semester (2.06 vs. 1.88); (iii) 0.01 points higher during the third semester (2.10 vs. 2.09) (not significant). Larger effects were observed for women and older students
Miller et al. (2011)	$1000 each of four semesters for (i) obtaining a 2.0 GPA or higher; (ii) enrolling full time; (iii) completing two extra advisor meetings per semester	Administrative data for low-income students starting at the University of New Mexico	Field experiment	Students randomly assigned to the treatment group (i) earned 0.0 more first semester credits (baseline average of 12.8 credits) (not significant); (ii) earned 0.6 more second semester credits (8.7 vs. 8.1 credits) than students in the control group

Continued

Table 1 Interventions that aim to offset immediate costs with immediate benefits—cont'd

Authors	Treatment	Data	Research Design	Findings
Richburg-Hayes et al. (2011)	Up to $1300 each of two or three semesters, paid in installments for achieving (i) registration; (ii) continued mid-semester enrollment; (iii) a 2.0 GPA in at least six credits	Administrative data for New York City community college students between ages 22 and 35 who also required remediation	Field experiment	Students randomly assigned to the treatment group (i) earned 0.6 more first semester credits (8.7 vs. 8.1 credits); (ii) were 7.4% more likely to enroll full time (60% vs. 53%); (iii) experience no difference in GPA than students in the control group
Scott–Clayton (2011)	West Virginia's PROMISE scholarship: WV public college tuition waiver for students we earn a 3.0 high school GPA and an ACT score of 21 or higher + maintain a 3.0 college GPA (with credit requirements)	Administrative data from public colleges in West Virginia	Regression discontinuity design on ACT score	Eligibility for the PROMISE scholarship increases the likelihood that a student (i) maintains a 3.0 GPA in college by 6.3% (46% vs. 40%); (ii) graduates with a BA within 4 years by 6.7% (43% vs. 37%)
Sjoquist and Winters (2012a)	Arkansas (AR): $2500 for tuition and fees at AR colleges for students with at least 19 on the ACT and a 2.5 core high school GPA; Georgia: full tuition/fees at GA public colleges for students with a 3.0 high school GPA; must maintain a 3.0 GPA in college	Survey (census, 5% PUMS) data for all 22- to 34-year-olds in 2000	Difference in differences design using other states (not AR or GA) as the control group	The fraction of the age 22 to 34 population with a college degree increased by 0.9% (not significant) in states that enacted merit scholarship programs (GA and AR) (35% vs. 34%)
Sjoquist and Winters (2012b)	25 state-based merit aid programs with requirements on high school GPA, ACT/SAT scores, college credit enrollment, and college GPA	Survey data from the 2000 census (1% and 5% PUMS) and the 2000 to 2010 American Community Survey	Difference in differences design using nonmerit scholarship states as the control group	The fraction of the age 24–30 population with a college degree increased by −0.2% (not significant) in states that enacted merit scholarship programs (38.6% vs. 38.8%)

obtaining grades above a proficiency cut-off in four subjects (Bettinger, 2010). Math scores increased by 0.15 standard deviations in the year incentives were offered, but this effect dissipated the year after, with no effects found in Reading, Social Science, and Science. Using an array of award schemes for primary and middle school students in an impressive variety of settings, Fryer (2011) found very modest or no effects. One exception was an experiment in Dallas, in which 2nd-grade students were paid to read books rather than to do well on tests. Reading scores improved by 0.25 standard deviations, suggesting that incentivizing learning *inputs*, like reading or homework time, may be more promising than incentivizing learning outputs like grades.

The effects of financial incentives may be sensitive to context, such as the age of students or timing of payments. For instance, Levitt et al. (2012) find that an incentive offered immediately before a test and awarded minutes after improves performance, whereas offering the same incentive awarded a month later does not. Perhaps performance incentives are more effective when awarded soon after the exertion of effort required to achieve them (Levitt et al., 2012).In a recent paper, Oswald and Backes-Gellner (2014) find that apprenticeship students in Switzerland identified as impatient respond more to a financial incentive to improve grades.[23]

Participation incentives compared to grade incentives target lower performing students and generally show more promise. Dearden et al. (2009) evaluate a program in the United Kingdom offering low-income high school students money for staying in school beyond the minimum dropout age. The fraction in school for at least two additional years increased from 61% to 68%. Ford et al. (2012) examine The Future to Discover program in New Brunswick, which provided high school students, starting in Grade 9, "learning accounts" that accumulated to $8000 by time of graduation and could only be used for college-related expenses. College enrollment and graduation increased by 8% for students randomly offered these accounts compared to a control group. Annual information and reminders about the learning accounts, plus verification that students and parents understood the program, may have increased salience and interest.

Many colleges and universities offer financial incentives in the form of merit scholarships. One of the more rigorous studies of an existing program exploits a regression discontinuity design to look at West Virginia's PROMISE scholarship and finds substantial increases in four and 5-year graduation rates (Scott-Clayton, 2011). The PROMISE scholarship provides a tuition waiver to students who maintain a minimum GPA and course load. Students who receive the scholarship are more than 6% more likely to receive at least a 3.0 GPA through college (46% vs. 40%) and are 7% more

---

[23] Guryan et al. (2015) find that elementary school students who initially enjoyed reading, responded more to a financial incentive to read more books over the summer. Although Guryan et al. (2015) do not measure impatience, financial incentives that aim to address short-term impatience may have heterogeneous impacts depending on how well-matched the curriculum is to students abilities and interests.

likely to graduate within 4 years than students who just missed out on receiving the award (33% vs. 26%). Importantly, the effects on GPA disappear in the final year of college, when the scholarship cannot be renewed, suggesting that students are motivated to work harder as a result of the financial incentive.

Experimental evidence on the effectiveness of college merit scholarships is less impressive. Angrist et al. (2009), for example, test the effects of offering $1000 to $5000 awards for first-year undergraduates to attain grade averages above 70%, with and without additional mentorship support. Females offered both the scholarship incentive and mentor support receive grades 0.30 standard deviations higher by the end of the first and second year compared to a control group. The second-year results are important, as they suggest sustained effort or learning, even after incentives are removed, yet the program had no significant long-term impact on females offered only the scholarship and no impact on males. A follow-up experiment offering large course-based incentives for incrementally higher grades above 70%, plus mentorship support, failed to generate significant long-term effects (Angrist et al., 2014b).

An alternative type of merit aid targets course credit accumulation for students already enrolled in college in an effort to encourage on-time completion and retention. The lower (or nonexistent) grade thresholds make these programs more expensive since a larger fraction of students achieve the credit target, including those who would have achieved it without the incentive. Several recent experiments suggest these kinds of merit-awards can increase retention. Barrow et al. (2014) find significant effects on credit accumulation from an experiment paying college students in Louisiana for enrolling at least half-time and attaining C-averages or better. Similar experiments were initiated in other states, all targeting low-income college students using credit accumulation incentives and grade targets no greater than C-averages. Results show small but significant increases in cumulative earned credits by the first or second term (Miller et al., 2011; Richburg-Hayes et al., 2011). MacDonald et al. (2009) also find significant increases in GPA and retention from a Canadian experiment offering community college students $750 for each of three semesters for obtaining a GPA above 2.0, maintaining a full course load, and accessing a minimum amount of student services. Graduation rates were 3% higher for the treatment group (27% vs. 24%) and 9% higher among students from low-income backgrounds (34% vs. 25%).

Significant latitude exists in designing immediate incentives to offset immediate costs, including the type of incentive, the target population, and whether it encourages performance outputs or specific inputs. The current research does not generate obvious conclusions on the potential of these approaches (Table 1 summarizes this research). Impacts have generally been modest or nonexistent, although they have not been negative, as some would predict given that extrinsic rewards could potentially crowd out intrinsic motivation. Thus far, the research literature has mainly focused on offering money, with one exception being Springer et al. (2015), who find large effects on tutorial attendance from offering middle-school students certificates of completion signed by the district superintendent, compared to the monetary gift certificates given to control students. Nonmonetary incentives might appeal to students in ways that monetary ones do not.

Present bias arises not just from an immediate preference for leisure but also an immediate preference for spending money. College financial aid is typically distributed only at the beginning of the semester and deposited into a bank account. Once the challenges and distractions that accompany the start of a college semester begin, students may forget that these funds are intended to last for the whole year. The Aid Like A Paycheck program seeks to combat this short-sightedness by changing the way financial aid is delivered. After first paying off tuition and fees, students receive their remaining aid in equal biweekly installments tied to academic requirements. Researchers are looking at whether the program affects work hours, grades, and, ultimately, graduation (Ware et al., 2013).

4.2 Interventions That Help Reduce Inertia and Change Routine

Relying on routine usually makes our lives easier by reducing cognitive costs of decision making, but sometimes it can lead us astray as we ignore other available opportunities. In this section, we review policies and programs designed to change routines or encourage students and parents to reconsider their default plans. Tables 2–4 summarize this research, respectively categorized by whether interventions target students, parents, or environment.

4.2.1 Text Messages, Email Reminders, Mailings, and Videos

Many students who commit to attending a particular college in spring are nowhere to be found on campus the following fall. Whether due to forgetfulness regarding paperwork, a lack of true interest, or anxiety regarding a new environment, as many as 20% of recent high school graduates in the United States who accept offers of admission fail to actually enroll after their senior year. This phenomenon is commonly known as summer melt (Castleman and Page, 2014a; Castleman et al., 2012). In a study of approximately 5000 recent high school graduates who had indicated intent to go to college, Castleman and Page (2015) asked whether low-cost reminders could effectively reduce summer melt. Some students were randomly assigned to receive text messages in the summer between high school and college informing them of tasks required by their intended college and offering additional assistance if needed. These students were 3% more likely ultimately to enroll at a 2-year college (but not 4-year college) than students who received no intervention (23% vs. 20%). Treatment effects were concentrated among those with less definite college plans and less access to college-planning supports.[24]

---

[24] A similar strategy can be adopted in targeting potential high school dropouts. For example, in August of each year, retired teachers and guidance counselors attempt to telephone 11th- and 12th-grade students in Toronto not yet registered for the upcoming school year, but not yet graduated. They do not leave voice mail, but rather keep trying until they speak with the student. In 2011, of the 1667 students contacted, the callers reached all but 15 and convinced 864 to come back. Of those, 300 graduated that year (Hammer, 2012).

Another example of a low-cost intervention with minimal personal contact comes from Hoxby and Turner (2013), who focus on high-achieving students from low-income family backgrounds. The authors were interested in this group's tendency to disproportionately apply to less selective colleges, despite being able to get into better schools. Across the United States, 39,000 students were randomly selected into a treatment or control group. The treatment group received a package of information about more selective colleges, an application fee waiver, and encouragement to apply. The package listed differences in graduation rates across schools, instructional resources of various selective colleges, instructions on how to apply, and expected out-of-pocket costs of attending. Students from the treatment group applied to more colleges, and were 40% more likely to apply to a selective college[25] (92% vs. 52%) and 5% (9% vs. 4%) more likely to enroll in a selective school. Importantly, Hoxby and Turner (2013) find no evidence that students induced to attend more selective colleges are persisting at lower rates than their control group peers, suggesting that the high-achieving, low-income students who were induced to apply to and enroll in more selective colleges by the intervention were not underprepared.

Providing information about education's benefits can also increase motivation to attend. Jensen (2010) surveys students from the Dominican Republic and finds that while the measured returns to schooling are high, the returns perceived by students are extremely low. Students presented with information on the higher measured returns reported increased perceived returns several months later and an increase in schooling by 0.20 years, on average.

How information is presented or *who* is targeted matter as well. Dinkleman and Martinez (2014) examined effects from showing 8th-grade Chilean students DVDs of young disadvantaged adults describing their path toward college or vocational schools. While the presentation increased understanding about financial aid, there was little change in students' expectations of overall educational attainment. In Finland, Kerr et al. (2014) evaluate an experiment in which high school seniors across 97 randomly chosen schools were provided with information about average earnings and employment outcomes for graduates across a variety of postsecondary programs. While they find evidence of information updating, they find no impact on school choice or program of study.

4.2.2 Personal Assistance

Text messages, email reminders, mailings, and video presentations cost little, but are also easy to ignore. A more intensive approach to helping students with inertia is personal assistance, in the form of one-on-one help from someone trusted and someone with experience. These opportunities to speak directly to students offer an important social component to nudge attempts and can be tailored to individual circumstances.

---

[25] Here, we define "selective college" as an institution five percentiles above schools for which the student was prepared to attend. See Hoxby and Turner (2013).

Table 2 Interventions to help reduce inertia and change routine for students

Authors	Intervention	Data	Research design	Findings
Panel A: text messages, email reminders, mailings, and videos				
Castleman and Page (2014b)	12 text message reminders about refiling the FAFSA to renew financial aid after the freshman year	Administrative data from the National Student Clearinghouse and uAspire (a nonprofit organization) for 808 college students in Boston and Springfield, Massachusetts	Field experiment	Community college students randomly assigned to receive text message reminders were 12% (19%) more likely to persist into their sophomore year (baseline persistence rate of 64%). The intervention had no effect on 4-year college students (baseline persistence rate of 87%)
Castleman and Page (2014a)	Text message reminders and mentoring support to complete college enrollment process	Administrative data from Texas, Massachusetts and Pennsylvania	Field experiment	Students randomly assigned to receive text message reminders were 3% more likely to enroll in a 2 year college (23% vs. 20%). Treatment effects were largest for students with moderate high school GPAs and less defined college plans
Dinkleman and Martinez (2014)	15 minute informational video on the higher educational experience of 23 adults, including information on eligibility for financial aid	Survey and administrative data for more than 6000 8th-grade students in Chile	Field experiment (randomization at the school level)	Students randomly assigned to receive treatment were 6% more likely to be enrolled in college-preparation high school (66% vs. 60%). Effects were largest for students randomly assigned to take DVDs home to view with their families
Hoxby and Turner (2013)	Mailed semi-customized information on college options plus application fee waiver for high-achieving, low-income students	Administrative data from 12,000 high school seniors in the United States	Field experiment	Treated students (i) applied to 2.2 more colleges (6.9 vs. 4.7 schools); (ii) 40% more likely to apply to a selective college (92% vs. 52%); (iii) 5% more likely to enroll in a selective school (8.8% vs. 3.5%)

Continued

Table 2 Interventions to help reduce inertia and change routine for students—cont'd

Authors	Intervention	Data	Research design	Findings
Jensen (2010)	Information on the difference in earnings between university, secondary and primary school educated men between the ages of 30 and 40	Survey data from 8th-grade boys in the Dominican Republic	Field experiment (randomization at the school level)	Students randomly assigned to receive information on the returns to education (i) were 4.1% more likely to enroll in school for 9th-grade (59% vs. 55%); (ii) completed 0.2 more years of schooling (10 vs. 9.8 years of schooling). Treatment effects were largest for the least poor students
Kerr et al. (2014)	Information session on the earnings differences between various postsecondary degrees and program	Survey and administrative data for the 3500 Finnish graduating high school students	Field experiment (randomization at the school level)	The college application and enrollment behavior of students randomly assigned to the information treatment was no different than control group students
McGuigan et al. (2012)	Information on the potential earnings benefits and net costs of attending college, as well as information on financial aid options. Treated students also received a postcard and a five-minute video on the same topic	Survey data for more than 12,000 high school students at 56 schools in London	Field experiment (randomization at the school level)	Students randomly assigned to the treatment group were (i) 3.9% less likely to believe that the costs of higher education are a barrier to attending (7.8% vs. 11.7%); (ii) 3.3% more likely to believe that university graduates have better labor force outcomes (83.7% vs. 80.4%); (iii) 0.6% more likely to express university application intentions (59.6% vs. 59%) (not significant)
Nguyen (2008)	Information on the returns to education delivered through (i) presenting national statistics on the average returns to education; (ii) a role model; (iii) national statistics and a role model	Administrative and survey data for primary school students in Madagascar	Field experiment (randomization at the school level)	Students randomly assigned to receive information on the returns to education through national statistics scored 0.24 standard deviations higher on standardized tests Students randomly assigned to receive information on the returns to education through a mentor score 0.08 standard deviations higher on standardized tests (not significant)
Oreopoulos and Dunn (2013)	Short video on the potential earnings gains from postsecondary education (PSE), costs of PSE, eligibility for financial aid and a personalized financial aid calculator to estimate financial aid	Survey data from 1600 low-income high school students (five high schools) in Toronto, Canada	Field experiment	Among students unsure about their education attainment, random assignment to treatment led to a (i) 24.1% decrease in the belief that costs are a barrier to attending college (37.6% vs. 61.7%); (ii) 15% increase in community college aspirations (23% vs. 8%); (iii) 23% increase in university aspirations (65% vs. 42%)

Panel B: personal assistance

Avery (2013)	Tutoring and college application assistance	Administrative data from the College Possible Program	Field experiment	Students randomly assigned to the College Possible program were (i) 30% more likely to apply to a 4-year college; (ii) 44% more likely to apply to a selective institution; (iii) 15% more likely to enroll in a 4-year college
Berman and Bos (2010)	Counseling or college options, costs and application procedure	Administrative data from the Los Angeles Unified School District	Field experiment	Students randomly assigned to receive treatment were (i) 5% more likely to write the SAT (83% vs. 78%); (ii) 2% more likely to apply to a college (96% vs. 94%); (iii) 5% more likely to enroll at a state-college (55% vs. 50%); (iv) no more likely to be enrolled in college overall
Bettinger et al. (2012)	(i) Personalized advice in completing FAFSA (FAFSA Treatment Group); (ii) Personalized financial aid estimates and encouragement to complete the FAFSA on their own (Information Only Treatment Group)	Administrative data from H&R Block in Ohio and North Carolina, the Department of Education and the National Student Clearing House	Field experiment	Students randomly assigned to the FAFSA Treatment group were (i) 16% more likely to complete a FAFSA (56% vs. 40%); (ii) 11% more likely to be enrolled in college and receive financial aid (41% vs. 30%); (iii) 9.4% more likely to be enrolled full time (31% vs. 22%); (iv) 8% more likely to be enrolled in college for 2 years (36% vs. 28%). Students randomly assigned to the Information Only Treatment group had outcomes similar to those in the control group
Carrell and Sacerdote (2013)	Personalized mentoring and assistance in completing financial aid and college application forms	Administrative data from New Hampshire high schools	Field experiment	Students randomly assigned to receive coaching were (i) 5.4% more likely to enroll in college (57.2% vs. 51.8%); (ii) 5.6% more likely to enroll in a 4-year college (28.3% vs. 22.7%); (iii) no more likely to enroll in a 2-year college; (iv) 13% more likely to be enrolled in college 2 years after high school (47% vs. 34%)

Continued

Table 2 Interventions to help reduce inertia and change routine for students—cont'd

Authors	Intervention	Data	Research design	Findings
Castleman et al. (2012)	Counseling to relieve information and financial barriers to mitigate summer melt	Administrative data from seven high schools in Rhode Island	Field experiment	Students randomly assigned to receive counseling were (i) 15% more likely to be enrolled in college full time (47% vs. 32%); (ii) 15% more likely to be enrolled in a 4-year college (41% vs. 26%); (iii) no more likely to be enrolled in a 2-year college; (iv) 19% more likely to have followed through with intentions from senior year (56% vs. 37%)
Castleman et al. (2014)	Counseling to low-income high school graduates to mitigate summer melt	Administrative data from high schools in Massachusetts and Georgia	Field experiment	Students randomly assigned to receive counseling were (i) 3.3% more likely to enroll in college in the fall (86% vs. 82.7%); (ii) 5% more likely to be enrolled in college in their sophomore year (71% vs. 66%)
Panel C: coaching and advising				
Borghans et al. (2013)	Advice from counseling while in secondary school on college program choices	Survey data from more than 4000 high school graduates in the Netherlands	OLS and instrumental variables	Meeting with a high school counselor is associated with a reduction in the likelihood that a student wishes they had chosen a different program by 2% (20% vs. 22%). Male students and those with parents from low socioeconomic statues are affected the most by high school counseling
Bettinger and Baker (2014)	Coaching to improve college completion	Administrative data from eight public and private colleges from InsideTrack	Field experiment	Students randomly assigned to InsideTrack were 4% more likely to complete college (35% vs. 31%)
Cook et al. (2014)	Mandatory intensive math tutoring and weekly social-cognitive skill training	Administrative data for 106 at-risk ninth and 10th-grade high school students in Chicago	Field experiment	Students randomly assigned to receive treatment scored (i) 0.51 standard deviations higher on standardized math tests (TOT 0.65 standard deviations); (ii) earned 0.43 standard deviations higher math GPAs (TOT 0.58 standard deviations); (iii) −0.06 standard deviations higher on standardized reading tests (not significant)

By making the application process more convenient and appealing, personal assistance reduces procrastination. Offering help to "get it done now" in an existing interaction minimizes disruption and lowers opportunity costs of time. Personal assistance could also help reduce anxiety about making mistakes; it speeds up and simplifies the process, avoiding the need for detailed instructions and review. Offering assistance may increase perceptions about the value in the help being offered: personal encouragement may empower individuals to more fully consider the possibility of change.

Bettinger et al. (2012) offer an example of the power of personal assistance with an experiment that takes place in H&R Block offices, which provide income tax preparation services primarily for lower- and middle-income families across the United States. Families in Ohio and North Carolina were randomly assigned into one of three groups. The first group was given personalized assistance in completing the FAFSA; after preparing the family's tax return, H&R Block professionals offered families the opportunity to complete the application, a process which typically took an additional ten minutes. Using software which took advantage of information on the family's tax return to prepopulate most of the FAFSA questions, treatment recipients were not only guided through the application process, but also provided with a financial aid estimate and tuition estimates at nearby colleges. A second treatment group were provided with the same information and aid estimates as the first, but were left to complete the FAFSA on their own.

Relative to the control group, FAFSA application rates and college enrollment rates did not increase for students whose families received the Information Only Treatment. The full personal assistance treatment, however, was very effective: On average, graduating high school students whose families received the FAFSA Treatment were 16% (56% vs. 40%) more likely to have filed the FAFSA than those in the comparison group, and were 8% (35% vs. 27%) more likely to attend college for at least 2 years. This suggests that those induced to enroll were not underprepared for college.[26]

A number of studies explore the potential for personal assistance to help with other aspects of the college application process. We mention three key ones here. First, Avery (2013) evaluates the College Possible program, a comprehensive mentoring intervention that targets disadvantaged students in Minnesota. In addition to free tutoring services designed to help students improve their ACT scores, College Possible provides students with personalized assistance in choosing a college and completing paperwork. Students randomly assigned to receive treatment were 30% more likely to apply to 4-year colleges and submitted almost five more applications, on average, than students in the comparison

---

[26] Building on the positive effects of targeted personal assistance, the U.S. Department of Education's FAFSA Completion Project notifies high schools of students who have not completed a FAFSA. Such information allows guidance counselors to provide targeted assistance, ask students until they complete the form, or offer positive (eg, a discounted prom ticket) or negative incentives (eg, can't go to the prom without filling out a FAFSA).

group. The results also suggest that program participants were induced to apply to 4-year colleges relative to 2-year colleges. If these low-income students were prepared to attend 4-year colleges but would otherwise have applied to 2-year schools, then the College Possible program may be alleviating information constraints about programs at 4-year institutions, leading students to be matched with programs that better meet their abilities and interests. Indeed, students eligible for the program were 15% more likely to enroll in a 4-year college than those in the control group.

Second, Carrell and Sacerdote (2013) study the effects of a program designed to increase college enrollment rates among New Hampshire high school seniors who had demonstrated an interest in applying to a postsecondary program, but who failed to begin the application process by January of their senior year. Students randomly assigned to a treatment group received personalized assistance to help complete college applications, with all of their application fees paid for. Students offered this service had college enrollment rates 15% higher than the comparison group (65% vs. 50%), with the majority of the effect concentrated among female students. The percentage of students attending college for at least 2 years also increased.[27]

Finally, Castleman et al. (2012) evaluate an intervention in seven urban Rhode Island schools that randomly offered active college counseling to high school graduates during the summer before college in seven urban schools. Program recipients received assistance from counselors throughout the summer to secure additional financial aid, complete necessary paperwork and alleviate any other concerns about going to college. The authors found that eligibility for the program increased college enrollment rates by 15% (60% vs. 45%). Similarly strong effects were found for full-time enrollment at 4-year colleges.

4.2.3 Coaching and Advising

The examples above demonstrate how a program's application process can itself prevent individuals interested in the program from taking it up, and how personal assistance can be a very effective tool to help. The approach could also be useful in many other settings besides college applications, such as helping students choose courses to place them on an academic track or toward timely graduation, helping them open an education savings plan, helping them with good time management, or reminding them to utilize student services. As a specific example, Bettinger and Baker (2014) evaluate the InsideTrack program, where mostly nontraditional college students were randomly assigned a coach whose job was to contact and motivate students regularly (through email, text, and phone) to help set goals and develop a strategy toward achieving them. Coaches were

---

[27] A similar project is underway in Canada, in which a three class workshop is incorporated into the 12th-grade curriculum at low-college-transition schools: First, students are assisted in picking programs they are interested in and can get into; second, they apply in class, for free, and third, they are assisted in applying for financial aid.

proactive, providing outreach without waiting for students to ask. Students offered the program for one school year were about 5% more likely to persist the following year and 4% more likely to complete their degree after 2 years (35% vs. 31%). While the mechanisms behind these effects are not entirely clear, coaching could be helping to address several behavioral barriers discussed in Section 2.[28]

However, making similar coaching services available does not guarantee participation because students may procrastinate, ignore the opportunity, or not believe in its effectiveness; the proactive outreach of the coaches — and other forms of mandatory assistance — may be important for addressing these limitations. In Chicago, disadvantaged 9th- and 10th-grade students were randomly provided with mandatory intensive tutoring, during school-hours, along with weekly social-cognitive skill training.[29] Students participated in 1 h of tutoring, as part of their everyday class schedule. While the weekly skill training sessions were voluntary, because they took place during the school day, they were preferred over the alternative of going to class. Had the tutoring been voluntary or the training less convenient, it is not likely that participation would have remained above 70%. As a result of the program and its high participation rate, math test scores increased remarkably by 0.65 standard deviations.

4.2.4 Helping Parents

The assumption that parents make education-investment decisions on behalf of their children is common in economics. However, everyday concerns related to parents' own jobs and careers, household finances and other family responsibilities may distract them from paying more deliberate attention to their children's educational progress. In this context, parents may fail to incorporate low-stakes but important investments, such as asking about their children's day at school or encouraging daily homework completion in their children's daily routines. This can occur even if parents realize that greater involvement can improve their child's academic outcomes. If the path to more parental involvement were simpler or more salient, perhaps behavior would change. Below we present some examples of interventions that adopt this approach.

Avvisati et al. (2014) test whether an intervention that encourages parents to incorporate greater involvement in their child's middle school as part of their daily routine improves behavior and academic performance. Prior to randomization, middle school parents in a Parisian suburb were asked whether they wanted to volunteer to participate in a series of seminars in which parental interest in the daily activities at their child's

---

[28] Some schools are beginning to consider mobile nudges as a means to provide electronic coaching advice and motivation. The University of Washington Tacoma, for example, offers students a personalized mobile support system called "Persistence Plus," which "helps keep students on track by delivering a mobile 'nudge', a daily text message that reminds them about quizzes and tests, helps with time, stress, and performance management, and encourages appropriate behavioral responses" (Fuhrman, 2014).

[29] Cook et al. (2014).

Table 3 Interventions to help reduce inertia and change routine for parents

Authors	Intervention	Data	Research design	Findings
Avvisati et al. (2014)	Three meetings, focused on how parents can help their children do well in school (with an emphasis on homework completion), every 2–3 weeks from November to December	Administrative data from 6th-grade students from a school district outside of Paris, France	Field experiment (randomization done after consent; randomization at class level so can get peer effects)	Treated parents are 3.4% more likely to contact the school regularly (82% vs. 79%) and 6.7% more likely to monitor their child's homework (27% vs. 21%) Children of parents eligible for the intervention accumulate 25% fewer absences and achieve French grade 0.12 standard deviations higher than those of nontreated students
Banerji et al. (2013)	Three interventions in rural India (i) ML: mother literacy and numeracy intervention; (ii) CHAMPS: teaching mothers about education system and how to help their children; (iii) ML + CHAMPS	Survey data from 480 villages in two Indian states	Field experiment	ML treatment mothers were 3% more likely to review their child's school work (25% vs. 22%). CHAMPS treatment mothers were 6.5% more likely to review their child's school work (28.5% vs. 22%) Children of treated mothers scored 0.037–0.069 standard deviations higher on numeracy tests than children of untreated mothers
Benhassine et al. (2013)	Small "labeled cash transfer" (LCT) to fathers of children in poor rural communities	Survey data for more than 47,000 primary school students in five Moroccan regions	Field experiment	Students of families randomly assigned to receive LCTs were (i) 5.1% less likely to drop out of school after 2 years (2.5% vs. 7.6%); (ii) 7.9% more likely to complete primary school (72.3% vs. 64.4%)
Bergman (2014)	Biweekly calls/texts/emails to middle and high school parents about missed assignments and tests	Administrative data from 462 students in grades 6–11 at a school in Los Angeles	Field experiment	Students whose parents were eligible for treatment experienced (i) a 0.23 standard deviation increase in GPA, sensitive to past GPA as a control; (ii) marginal increase in test scores; (iii) improvement in classroom behavior (iv) 6% less likely to exhibit (teacher reported) unsatisfactory classroom behavior (20% vs. 26%); (v) 6.9% more likely to exhibit (teacher reported) excellent classroom behavior (41% vs. 34%) Treated parents were 7.9% more likely to attend parent–teacher conferences (23% vs. 15%)

Study	Intervention	Data	Method	Results
Bursztyn and Coffman (2012)	Solicited whether parents would be willing to choose a cash transfer (CT) program over their a CCT program that included a feature which monitored children's school attendance	Survey data from 210 families with adolescent children in Brazil	Framed field experiment	Treated parents willing to give up about 6% of monthly income to keep the CCT with monitoring. When offered an alternative technology that sent text messages to the parent when the child was absent from school, parents were willing to switch from the CCT to the CT
Harackiewicz et al. (2012)	Parents were mailed two mailed brochures and the link to a website that discussed the value of STEM courses	Administrative and survey data from Wisconsin 10th- and 11th-grade students and their families	Field experiment	Students of parents eligible for treatment enrolled in nearly one more semester of STEM courses than students of untreated parents (8.31 vs. 7.50 semesters) Treated parents were 17% more likely to value STEM courses and 17% more likely to have conversations about the importance of advanced STEM courses with their children
Kraft and Dougherty (2013)	Daily phone calls/text messages to parents of 6th- and 9th-grade students at MATCH charter school in Boston. Messages focused on what child did that day, what assignments and homework was assigned and ways for the child to improve	Administrative data from 6th- and 9th-grade charter school students in Boston	Field experiment (randomization at the class level)	Students of parents eligible for treatment (i) increased homework completion by 5.9% (85 %vs. 79%); (ii) increased in-class participation by 0.59 times per day (6.84 vs. 5.25 times per day)
Kraft and Rogers (2015)	Weekly calls/emails/text messages to parents of high school students highlighting (i) what the student was doing well behaviorally or academically; OR (ii) what the student needed to improve on	Administrative data for 576 summer program high school students	Field experiment	Students of parents who received messages highlighting positive behavior were 4.5% more likely to earn course credit (88.7% vs. 84.2%) (not significant) Students of parents who received improvement messages were 8.8% more likely to earn course credit (93% vs. 84.2%)

school, homework completion and supervision were stressed as factors of student success. The authors then randomly assigned some volunteer parents to participate in these seminars while other volunteer parents received no intervention.[30] Eligibility to attend the seminars led to substantial increases in parent involvement, as reported by parents and corroborated by teachers (who were not aware which parents were assigned to treatment), as well as on student behavior. Treated parents scored 0.27 standard deviations higher on an overall parenting score. Students of treated parents accumulated 25% fewer absences and were less likely to be disciplined for misbehaving than untreated students. Additionally, the increase in parental involvement led to significant improvements in academic outcomes. Students in the treatment classes overall had French (language) grades that were 0.12 standard deviations higher than that of the control group, although test scores did not significantly improve. Kraft and Rogers (2015) examine a related program in which teachers sent parents weekly one-way communication about advice on what students needed to improve in class (as opposed to messages that focused on what students were doing well in class). The probability a student earned course credit by 9% (96% vs. 87%).

In Los Angeles, parents with middle and high school children were randomly selected to participate in a pilot that informed them of missing homework and absences through email and text messages (Bergman, 2014). Parents selected for this treatment were more likely to report accurate beliefs about their children's missed assignments, as well as 7.9% (23% vs. 15%) more likely to attend parent–teacher conferences compared to those in a comparison group. Impressively, this inexpensive intervention improved student GPAs by 0.23 standard deviations, as well as attendance, assignment completion, in-class work habits, and cooperation.

Harackiewicz et al. (2012) tested an intervention that sent parents brochures promoting the career benefits from studying science, technology engineering and mathematics courses (often referred to as STEM courses). Parents were also directed to a web site and given advice on how to discuss these benefits with their children. On average, 10th- and 11th-grade students whose parents were randomly assigned this information increased their enrollment in STEM courses by nearly a semester. Additionally, parents reported increased positive perception of STEM courses and indicated that the materials provided helped them discuss the importance of course selection with their children. Students of

---

[30] As a result of the timing of the randomization, some students of parents who both volunteered and were assigned to receive treatment were placed in classrooms with students from nonvolunteer, nontreated parents. Other students of volunteer parents who were not assigned to participate in the seminars were also in classrooms with nonvolunteer, nontreated students. This allowed the authors to test whether peer effects led to change in the behavior of nontreated students who happened to be in the same classroom as volunteer, treated students. Interestingly, the authors find evidence of peer effects: classmates in the treatment classes were 2.4% less likely to be punished for disciplinary reasons and 4.6% more likely to earn higher behavior marks.

college educated parents were the most likely to respond to the treatment by taking additional advanced STEM courses; given that these students are more likely than their peers to have passed foundational STEM courses early in high school, it is possible that the most prepared students were also the students more encouraged to enroll.

Beyond the classroom, behavioral economists are now examining interventions that could be brought into the home. For example, Ariel Kalil and Susan Mayer are currently studying how disadvantaged parents might more frequently engage in educational play with their child. Parents with children in Chicago preschools are given electronic tablets with education games installed. Some are randomly provided information about the importance of educational play, then asked to select a preschool staff member to help "keep score" on playtime spent with the child. Parents also receive advice for scheduling playtime and awards of recognition for meeting goals. More explicitly, Banerji et al. (2013) examine the effects of training parents in rural India about concrete ways to engage with their child's learning. Treated mothers were 6.5% (24% to 52%) more likely to review their children's school work, though math test scores for children of these parents improved only marginally.

4.2.5 Changing Defaults and Adding Structure

The interventions discussed above address students' tendency to stick to routine by providing salient reminders, information, or personal assistance to help consider other options. Another approach is to change routine externally by changing default options or by imposing more structure (Scott-Clayton, 2012b). One clear example of this comes from the ACT college entrance exam. Before fall 1997, students who took the ACT were allowed to send their test scores to three schools for free, with each additional report costing $6. Nearly 80% of ACT takers sent exactly three reports. After fall 1997, students were allowed to send an additional (fourth) free report, while the cost of additional reports remained the same. Pallais (2013) finds that after allowing students to send four reports for free, less than 20% of ACT takers sent three test score reports and more than 70% sent exactly four reports, suggesting that the default number of free reports dominated student application behavior. Allowing an additional free report also changed types of schools some students applied to. Specifically, low-income students submitted more applications and were more likely to apply to a selective institution. With only three default submissions, some students for whom applying to a selective school would have been a realistic option may have decided not to apply in order to retain three safer options.

As another example of changing defaults, Oreopoulos and Ford (2014) propose helping all 12th-grade students from disadvantaged high schools to apply to at least one postsecondary program in class, for free. They develop an experiment in Canada in which a three class workshop is incorporated into the 12th-grade curriculum at low-college-transition schools: first, students receive assistance in picking programs they are interested in and can get into; second, they apply in class, for free; and third, they receive assistance in applying for financial aid. The slogan of the program is "Keep Your Options Open"; by exiting high school with both an offer of acceptance from a program that the student helped choose and a financial aid package, the idea of going to college becomes less abstract. The path becomes more salient and easier to take.

Encouraging students to follow better routines can also occur through imposing more structure. Elementary and secondary school students follow a clearly defined path to graduation, including taking mandatory courses and completing frequent tests. College programs, on the other hand, often expect students to independently determine what they need to learn through homework, readings, and attending lectures. Attending class and doing coursework is optional in many cases; the expectation is that students are already able to prioritize school work in spite of the many demands on their time and tempting alternatives to studying. In some cases, adding structure to coursework and academic programs may actually "free up" students' time to be more productive. The additional freedoms that accompany going to college, such as living independently for the first time, parties, or nonacademic extra-curricular activities may lead students to procrastinate. Although adding more structure to academic programs, either through mandatory attendance or homework, reduces flexibility in students' schedules, it may also make procrastination seem more costly and improve course performance. Structure may also help students get a clearer picture of what behaviors are necessary to be successful in college.

With these ideas in mind, the Guttman Community College was established in 2012 in New York with an all new academic curriculum and core structure to improve students' chances of graduation. Entering students commit to attending full time and are required to attend a 3-week Summer Bridge Program in August that sets academic expectations, encourages students to understand their strengths and challenges as a learner, builds social networks, introduces the school's electronic resources, and provides a refresher in reading, writing, and mathematics. All students take the same courses in the first year, including an interdisciplinary liberal arts and science course, ethnography, statistics, and composition. Each student is assigned a "student success advocate," whose job is to help with the college transition in first year. Students choose a major by the end of their first year, with a set curriculum. Scheduling of writing assignments and tests are coordinated among faculty throughout the year.

Another way to restructure the college environment is to create resources for student support, coupled with incentives so that students actually utilize them. Students participating in the Accelerated Study in Associate Program (ASAP) across several City University of New York (CUNY) campuses are required to (1) enroll full time, (2) take developmental courses, (3) graduate within 3 years, (4) take a noncredit seminar about goal setting and academic planning, (5) attend tutoring frequently, (6) meet with an assigned advisor at least twice a month, (7) meet with a career and employment specialist once a semester and (8) take block-scheduled classes so that students have similar

Table 4 Interventions to help reduce inertia and change routine by changing defaults and adding structure

Authors	Intervention	Data	Research design	Findings
Ariely and Wertenbroch (2002)	Students allowed to choose and commit to deadlines for assignments vs. traditional firm deadlines	Administrative data from an executive-education course at MIT	Field experiment (randomization done at course section level) and lab experiment	(i) Students allowed to choose assignment deadlines, on average, chose to precommit to less-flexible, evenly spaced deadlines; (ii) Students required to submit at evenly spaced deadlines performed better on a proof-reading task than those with flexible deadlines
Dobkin et al. (2010)	Mandatory attendance policy for students scoring below the median on the class midterm	Administrative data from three large undergraduate economics classes	Regression discontinuity design	(i) The mandatory attendance policy increased attendance rates by 28%; (ii) A 10% increase in attendance led to a 0.16 standard deviation increase in final exam scores
Duckworth et al. (2011)	Mental Contrasting with Implementation Intentions (MCII) intervention: students are asked to (i) articulate a goal, including why achieving it is positive; (ii) named a critical obstacle to achieving the goal; (iii) outline strategies for how they intended to deal with the obstacle	Administrative data from school and PSAT records for 66 10th-grade students at a selective high school	Field experiment	Students randomly assigned to the MCII intervention completed 56 more PSAT-prep questions than students in the control group (140 vs. 84)
Grodner and Rupp (2013)	Mandatory homework assignments worth 10% of the final course grade	Administrative data from an undergraduate economics class in North Carolina	Field experiment	3.5–5.7% increase in test scores for students assigned to the mandatory homework group
Oreopoulos et al. (2014)	Comprehensive intervention for at-risk high school students including: mandatory (free) tutoring sessions, one-on-one and group mentoring, free public transit tickets (conditional on school attendance), up to $1000 for college tuition and fees, college application assistance and fee waivers	Administrative data for more than 6000 disadvantaged high school students in Toronto, Ontario	Difference-in-differences	Eligibility for the Pathways to Education Program increases: (i) 5-year high school graduation rates by 15% (60% vs. 45%); (ii) college enrollment rates by 19% (57% vs. 38%); (iii) math and English test scores by 0.15 standard deviations

Continued

Table 4 Interventions to help reduce inertia and change routine by changing defaults and adding structure—cont'd

Authors	Intervention	Data	Research design	Findings
Pallais (2013)	Before 1997, college applicants were able to send three free ACT score reports to schools for free. After 1997, four free reports were allowed with additional reports costing $6	American Freshman Survey	OLS and difference-in-differences	Before 1997, more than 70% of ACT takers sent exactly three reports. After 1997, fewer than 20% sent exactly three reports and 70% sent exactly four reports After 1997, students applied to colleges with 0.35–0.50 points higher on the ACT
Pennebaker et al. (2013)	Daily online testing with personalized feedback	Administrative data from an undergraduate psychology course at the University of Texas at Austin	OLS (comparing "treated" students with those from prior cohorts)	Students in course sections with daily online testing (i) scored 6% higher on tests in the psychology course (77% vs. 71%); (ii) scored marginally higher on other courses taken the following semester. Results were strongest for low-income students
Scrivener and Weiss (2013)	Comprehensive community college program intervention: mandatory full-time enrollment, mandatory block classes, "quick" graduation, financial assistance, mentoring and career counseling	Administrative data from six CUNY colleges	Field experiment	Students randomly assigned to the treatment group (i) 9.5% more likely to be enrolled in college after 2 years (67.8% vs. 58.3%); (ii) accumulated 7.6 more credits by the end of the second year of college (37.9 vs. 30.4 credits); (iii) 5.7% more likely to complete their associate's degree after 2 years (14.5% vs. 8.7%)
Stanca (2006)	Mandatory attendance policy on college course performance	Survey data from an undergraduate economics course at the University of Milan	OLS and IV with panel data	A 1% increase in lecture attendance was associated with a 0.1% increase in test scores

classmates and faculty can coordinate across courses. In exchange for fulfillment of these requirements, the program waives tuition fees, provides free public transportation passes, pays for all textbooks, and offers social activities (Scrivener and Weiss, 2013).

ASAP students are 9.5% more likely than the comparison group to be enrolled in college by the end of their second year (58.3% vs. 67.8%). They earn 7.6 more total credits (37.6 vs. 30.0) and are 5.7% more likely to have completed an associate's degree after 2 years than students in the control group (14.5% vs. 8.7%). Results at the third year are expected to show even larger effects, given that program participants are required to graduate within 3 years. Though these results are encouraging, determining which aspects of ASAP contribute the most to student success will be important for allocating scarce resources in the most effective way. Oreopoulos et al. (2014) evaluate a similar program offered to disadvantaged high school students and estimate large impacts on high school graduation and college enrollment.

Changing the class environment to incorporate more structure can also improve student outcomes through both creating a regular routine and by limiting the potential for procrastination. For example, courses with assignments or exams due only at the end lead many students to wait until the end to study. Frequent, mandatory assignments can combat these tendencies to procrastinate. Moreover, these relatively low-stakes assignments provide the opportunity for students to be given regular feedback on their performance, allowing confidence to be built by successes and making the benefits of learning more salient. Grodner and Rupp (2013) test whether mandatory regular homework assignments improve academic performance for undergraduate students in North Carolina. Students randomly selected into a treatment group were required to submit regular homework assignments that were worth 10% of their final grade. The remaining 90% was comprised of marks on four exams, each worth 22.5% of their final grade. Students in the control group were evaluated only based on the four exams (each worth 25%); the homework assignments were voluntary and ungraded. The authors find that students who were required to complete homework assignments scored between 3.5% and 5.7% higher on tests than students in the control group.

Aside from the temptation to procrastinate on homework, college students are also tempted to avoid coming to class altogether. As we discussed earlier, absenteeism is common in many college programs and courses; those that take place early in the morning find it especially difficult to encourage regular attendance. Dobkin et al. (2010) find that a mandatory attendance policy in one class raises overall academic performance. In their quasi-experimental design, students were informed after their midterms that attendance would become mandatory for those who scored below the median. This policy increased attendance by 28% for students scoring just below the median on the midterm. Those at the margin of being required to attend class also increased final exam scores by more than 0.46 standard deviations compared to those who just missed the requirement. Notably, grades in other courses were not affected.

Aside from required assignments, the timing of due dates may also be important for improving academic performance. Many college courses cluster deadlines at the end of the term, but giving students 3–4 months to finish their assignments may exacerbate tendencies to procrastinate. Students who are aware of this tendency may want tools that help them commit to certain deadlines,[31] while students who are not short sighted and have no procrastination problems may prefer traditional end of term deadlines that provide the most scheduling flexibility. To test whether students have a preference for precommitment for assignment deadlines, Ariely and Wertenbroch (2002) randomly assigned multiple sections of a semester-long course to one of two conditions. In the choice condition, students in one section of the course were allowed to choose their own deadlines for three papers. Students were free to choose any deadline but were required to commit to these dates by the end of the first week of the term. As the control group, students in the other section were given fixed, evenly spaced deadlines for the same papers. Surprisingly, students in the choice group chose to commit to submitting their assignments in relatively evenly spaced intervals throughout the term. On average, students chose to submit the first paper 42 days before the end of the term, the second 26 days before the end of the term and the third 10 days early. The fact that students chose to constrain themselves through earlier deadlines suggests that at least some of them attempted to mitigate their expected procrastination.

To test whether allowing students more flexibility to choose deadlines improves performance, the authors hired proofreaders for a 3-week field experiment, in which they were randomly assigned to one of three groups. The first group was asked to submit one proofread document at the end of each week. The second group was allowed to submit their documents anytime, as long as they were all submitted by the end of 3 weeks. Finally, similar to the choice condition in the first study, a third group committed to self-imposed deadlines for the documents. As in the previous study, the authors found that participants assigned to the third group chose deadlines that were spread out. These proofreaders also performed better on the tasks than those randomly assigned to submit all three tasks by the end of the third week (group 2). However, those who were allowed to choose their own deadlines performed worse than those who were required to submit a task weekly (group 1), suggesting that some were unable to choose deadlines "optimally" to maximize their performance. Altogether, these results suggest that setting fixed deadlines can improve academic outcomes, especially for students who have a tendency to procrastinate. These results may also be particularly relevant for increasingly prevalent online courses, which encounter higher dropout rates than traditional courses (Price and Shireman, 2013).

---

[31] For example, this would be the case if students were sophisticated time-inconsistent discounters (ie, Laibson, 1997).

4.3 Interventions That Strengthen Positive Identities

The need for social interaction and the need to feel liked are powerful influences on behavior (eg, Akerlof and Kranton, 2002, 2010). These influences can have negative consequences, such as when hard-working students are harassed for making less future-oriented classmates feel bad,[32] or when peers collectively focus on enjoying the present, reinforcing each others' present bias. One approach to mitigate negative social influences is to help students focus on more positive identities. Social psychologists have repeatedly demonstrated that individuals behave differently when prompted or "primed" to think of themselves as associated with one group compared to another (Mangels et al., 2012; Steele, 1997; Steele and Aronson, 1995). For instance, in Cohen et al. (2006), 7th-graders from a school with a large proportion of low-income and minority students were randomly assigned to one of two groups. In the treatment group, students were asked at the start of the semester to consider and write about which value was most important to them. In the control group, students chose a "least important" value, but explained why those values might be important to other people. Treated African-American students had significantly higher fall semester grades than those in the control group, closing the racial achievement gap by 40% with an increase of more than 0.25 GPA points on a four-point scale.

In another experimental study, university freshmen in a treatment group read results from an upperclassman survey that emphasized that feeling out of place in college during one's first year was a common, temporary phenomenon. The treated freshmen were then asked to write an essay and record a video for future freshmen, in which they related the survey results to their present experience. In contrast, freshmen in the control group read a survey and wrote an essay and speech on how college could change their preexisting political attitudes. The African-American participants in the treatment group showed steady improvements in GPA across the 4 years of college, reducing the racial gap in GPA between African Americans and European Americans by 52% overall — without any intermediate interventions (Walton and Cohen, 2011).Ultimately, reducing students' immediate concerns about their social identity or feeling out of place can lead to significant long-term gains. Early evidence also suggests that an urban boarding school program may insulate like-minded students from other students with different priorities (Curto and Fryer, 2014).

Students may also identify themselves as failures, or less able than others. A substantial amount of research by Dweck (2007) and others suggests that the beliefs about themselves that people bring to new situations and opportunities can affect how much they learn and how well they do. Students who think that most of the factors contributing to success are innate also are more likely to become discouraged from initial setbacks, or avoid more

---

[32] A more specific example is the case of "Acting White," where black peers impose costs on their members trying to do well at school (Austen-Smith and Fryer, 2005).

Table 5 Interventions that strengthen positive identities

Authors	Intervention	Data	Research design	Findings
Abdulkadiroglu et al. (2015)	Enrollment in a school taken over by a charter school	Administrative data for 3173 charter school students in Boston and New Orleans	Matching and 2SLS	Enrollment in a New Orleans charter school due to a grandfathering eligibility rule increases math (English) test scores by 0.21 (0.14) standard deviations. Enrollment in a Boston Charter school increases math (English) test scores by 0.32 (0.39) standard deviations
Angrist et al. (2012)	Enrollment in a KIPP academy. The KIPP curriculum requires students to adhere to a behavioral code	Classroom and administrative data for 531 middle school students in Lynn Massachusetts	Field experiment	Reading and math scores of lottery winners increase by 0.12 and 0.34 standard deviations. Special needs students and students with limited English proficiency show larger gains
Angrist et al. (2014a)	Enrollment in Boston charter schools. The school adheres to a "No Excuses" pedagogy, focusing on discipline and academic success	Administrative data for 8851 applicants to six Boston-area charter high schools	Field experiment	Lottery winners have a 24% (44% vs. 20%) increase in the likelihood of qualifying for a state university scholarship, take one more AP exam on average (1.63 vs. 0.59 exams), are 18% more likely to enroll in a 4-year college (59% vs. 41%), and 11% less likely to enroll in a 2-year college (8% vs. 19%)
Aronson et al. (2002)	Participants were taught that intelligence is not a finite endowment and that it can grow with effort. They were also asked to write a pen-pal letter to a fictitious, struggling middle school student explaining that intelligence is malleable	Administrative data from 109 Stanford University undergraduate students	Field experiment	African-American students randomly assigned to the treatment group earned GPAs that were (i) 0.27 points higher than those assigned to an unrelated pen-pal treatment (3.32 vs. 3.05 GPA); (ii) 0.22 points higher than those assigned to the control group (3.32 vs. 3.10 GPA). Effects were smaller and insignificant for white students
Blackwell et al. (2007) (Study 2)	Eight sessions over 8 weeks teaching students that the brain is malleable and that intelligence grows with effort	Administrative data from 91 7th-grade students in New York City	Field experiment	0.55 standard deviation GPA increase from the spring of 7th grade to the spring of 6th grade for students randomly assigned to receive the treatment, relative to the control group

Study	Description	Data	Method	Findings
Bursztyn and Jensen (2015)	Students given the opportunity to sign up for a free SAT prep course were told that their decision to sign up for the course would be kept private from everyone except their classmates OR private from everyone, including their classmates	Administrative and survey data for more than 800 low-income high school students in Los Angeles	Field experiment	Students randomly assigned to have their sign up decision disclosed to their classmates were 11% less likely to sign up for the course (61% vs. 72%) Among students taking two honors classes, those randomly assigned to have their sign up decision disclosed were (i) 25% less likely to sign up if they happened to be in a nonhonors class during the experiment (54% vs. 79%); (ii) 25% more likely to sign up if happened to be in an honors class during the experiment (97% vs. 72%)
Bursztyn and Jensen (2015)	Students using an in-class, computer-based learning system to prepare for high school exit exams given access to information on the top three performers in their class (and school). The names of top performers for the course were revealed partway through the semester and without prior notice	Administrative data on prep question performance for 13,000 remedial math and English students in 200 high schools	OLS	Disclosing the names of top performers is associated with one fewer correct answer per day (7 vs. 8 per day) For students in the top quartile of performance before the disclosure change, making the names of top performers public is associated with three fewer correct answers per day (9.5 vs. 12.5 per day)
Cohen et al. (2006)	Targeted reaffirmations of personal adequacy and self-integrity	Administrative data from a 7th-grade school	Field experiment	Students randomly assigned to the treatment group earned a fall semester GPA 0.3 points higher than the control group (on a four-point scale). Treatment effects were largest for African-American students; those for white students were small and insignificant
Curto and Fryer (2014)	Enrollment at an urban boarding school 5 days per week	Classroom and administrative data for 221 low-income 6th- to 8th-grade students in Washington D.C. and Baltimore	Field experiment	Reading and math test scores for lottery winners increase by 0.21 and 0.23 standard deviations respectively. Effect sizes are larger for females (0.38 and 0.27 standard deviations)

Continued

Table 5 Interventions that strengthen positive identities—cont'd

Authors	Intervention	Data	Research design	Findings
Dee (2014)	To test whether stereotype threat due to being a student-athlete affects academic performance, participants were primed by asking whether their athletic commitments interfered with academic commitments prior to writing a test	Administrative data for 91 students and student-athletes at Swarthmore College	Framed field experiment	Student-athletes randomly assigned to the stereotype condition scored 0.84 standard deviations lower on a standardized (GRE) test
Dobbie and Fryer (2011)	Enrollment in the Harlem Children's Zone	School and administrative data for 842 lottery applicants for elementary and middle school students	Field experiment	Math and scores increased by 0.23 standard deviations for middle-school lottery winners. Elementary school lottery winners experienced 0.19 and 0.14 standard deviation higher math and reading scores
Fryer (2014)	Injecting charter schools best practices into low-performing public schools	Administrative data for 12,000 elementary and high school students in Huston, Texas	Field experiment and matching	Students at schools that adopted the best practices experienced standardized math test score increases of 0.14 standard deviations. Test score gains were higher for elementary schools (0.20 standard deviations) than for high schools (0.10 standard deviations)
Gollwitzer et al. (2011)	Participants are asked to write about potential barriers to completing a foreign language quiz successfully	Classroom data from 49 German elementary school students and 63 U.S. middle school students	Field experiment	Treated participants scored slightly more than one point higher (6.23 vs. 5.13 out of 10) on the vocabulary quiz

Study	Description	Sample	Method	Results
Good et al. (2003)	In three treatment conditions, middle school students were either taught that (i) intelligence is malleable; (ii) academic struggles are common at the beginning of middle school (attribution condition); (iii) a combination of the first two interventions	138 middle school students in rural Texas	Field experiment	Students randomly assigned to the malleable intelligence condition scored 8% higher on a standardized math test (82% vs. 74%). Students randomly assigned to the attribution condition scored 11% higher on a standardized math test (85% vs. 74%). Students randomly assigned to receive both interventions scored 10% higher on the standardized math test (84% vs. 74%)
Morisano et al. (2010)	Web-based program that asked participants to write about their ideal future, their goals toward this future, and the concrete steps for achieving these goals	Administrative data for 85 undergraduates at McGill University with GPAs below 3.0	Field experiment	Students randomly assigned to the treatment group (i) earned a GPA 0.48 standard deviations higher that the control group, one semester after the intervention (2.91 vs. 2.46 GPA); (ii) All students in the treatment group took a full course load, while only 80% of students in the control group did so
O'Rourke et al. (2014)	An educational game that emphasized that intelligence is malleable. Children are awarded points for effort, persistence and strategy	Administrative data on performance in the educational game Refraction for more than 15,000 children	Field experiment	Children randomly assigned to experimental condition (which emphasized that intelligence is malleable (i) persisted in the game for 29 more seconds (median 118 vs. 89 seconds); (ii) completed 1.2 more levels of the game, on average (6.7 vs. 5.5 levels)
Walton and Cohen (2011)	College freshmen were asked read reports from fictitious upperclassmen who described that feeling out of during one's first-year of college was a temporary phenomenon. Students were then asked to record a video detailing their experiences for future students	Administrative data for 92 freshmen students at a large university campus	Field experiment	African-American students randomly assigned to the control group experienced a 0.3 GPA point increase (3.65 vs. 3.35 GPA)

Continued

Table 5 Interventions that strengthen positive identities—cont'd

Authors	Intervention	Data	Research design	Findings
Walton et al. (2015)	A short intervention designed to help foster a sense of belonging among female engineering students in male dominated (more than 80%) fields	Administrative and survey data for 228 first-year engineering students from three successive cohorts at the University of Waterloo, Canada	Field experiment	Female students randomly assigned to the treatment group experienced a 4% increase in first-year GPA in Engineering courses (77.5% vs. 73.5%)
Wilson and Linville (1982)	Students were shown booklets and videos of upperclassmen who described that struggles during freshman year were temporary and that academic performance would likely improve in subsequent years	Administrative data for 40 freshmen students at Duke University	Field experiment	Students randomly assigned to the treatment group (i) were 20% (80%) less likely to drop out of college by the end of their sophomore year; (ii) experienced a 0.34 GPA increase (2.92 vs. 2.58 GPA). Students in the control group experienced no GPA increase (2.82 vs. 2.87 GPA)
Wilson and Linville (1985)	Students were given information that grades in freshman year are typically low but improve throughout one's college career	Administrative data for 80 freshmen students at the University of Virginia	Field experiment	Students randomly assigned to the treatment group experienced GPA increases of approximately 0.2 GPA points (2.8 vs. 2.6 GPA) from the first to second semester of their freshman year
Yeager et al. (2014) (Study 2)	30 min intervention designed to help students recognize a self-transcendent purpose for education	338 middle-income 9th-grade students in California	Field experiment	Students randomly assigned to receive the self-transcendent purpose intervention experienced a GPA increase of 0.11 GPA points (3.04 vs. 2.93 out of 4). The impact of treatment was even larger for students with a preintervention GPA below 3.0 (2.1 vs. 1.9)

challenging tasks after initial successes. In contrast, students who assume that effort matters most view failure more as an indication that they do not currently know enough, and should learn more, or that they have to increase the amount of time and effort spent on that activity. As an example of the consequences of these different mindsets, Wilson and Linville (1982) randomly assigned 40 Duke University freshmen to watch pretaped videos and read accounts of upperclassmen's initial academic struggles in adjusting to college life. Upperclassmen in the videos recalled having a low GPA during their own freshmen year, but that their grades began to improve later in their college careers as they grew accustomed to the increased workload and academic expectations at the university. In contrast, students in the control group watched videos of the same upperclassmen in which the older students described their academic and nonacademic interests. The authors found that students randomly assigned to the treatment group were 20% less likely to drop out of college by the end of their sophomore year (from a baseline dropout rate of 25%). Students in the treatment group also earned better grades; their GPAs increased by 0.34 points (on a four-point scale) from the first semester of their freshmen year to the end of their sophomore year, while the GPAs of those in the control group were unchanged. [33] Similar results have been replicated in other settings.[34]

Another approach to improving students' academic identities at younger ages is to reduce negative subjective experiences by teaching that the brain is malleable and that through hard work, intelligence can be improved. Blackwell et al. (2007) tested this intervention in an experimental setting on 7th-grade students in New York City. Specifically, once a week for 8 weeks, students randomly selected into a treatment group were taught that intelligence is not fixed and that through effort, intellectual ability can improve. Students in the control group were only taught study skills. As is common with middle school students, the GPAs of those in the control group fell from 2.7 to about 2.4 (on a four-point scale) between the spring of 6th grade and the spring of 7th grade. The grades of students assigned to the treatment group, however, remained unchanged, which corresponds to a 0.55 standard deviation increase relative to the control group. Yeager and Walton (2011) and Walton (2015) discuss how these seemingly small interventions can have such large and lasting effects. They argue that timely interventions which reinforce students' academic identities can improve outcomes by decreasing the likelihood that small failures cause students to believe that academic success is unachievable. This, in turn, mitigates the potential that a self-reinforcing cycle of disbelief in one's abilities leads to even worse academic performance. Identity interventions

---

[33] In particular, if the treatment led relatively weaker, less prepared students to drop out, the average preparedness of students in the control group would have been higher than the treatment group, biasing the effect on GPA downward.

[34] Wilson and Linville (1985) replicate the findings from their initial study for a larger sample of freshmen students at the University of Virginia. See Yeager and Walton (2011) and the citations therein for other replications and similar interventions.

may also occur at an institutional level: in addition to including a more structured curriculum, the KIPP charter school system's values include "High Expectations" and "Choice and Commitment," which together imply that students can achieve difficult goals through their own willpower. Evaluations of KIPP and similar "No Excuses" charter school programs suggest that these underlying values may be associated with higher test scores and academic achievement (Abdulkadiroglu et al., 2015; Angrist et al., 2012, 2014a; Dobbie and Fryer, 2011; Fryer, 2014). We describe other studies that examine the effect of reinforcing students' academic identities on various outcomes in Table 5.

4.4 Interventions That Simplify Options and Combat the Paradox of Choice

Helping students and parents navigate situations with an abundance of information or choices can also lead to improved outcomes. Often, simplifying how information is conveyed can help students and their families focus on the criteria that matters most. This can be especially helpful in the domain of school choice. Even at the primary and high school levels, evaluating and selecting a school requires comparing hundreds of options on several criteria (ie, test score performance and nonacademic features of the school). Faced with navigating complex information on numerous options, parents may simply choose the path of least resistance, such as enrolling their child in the closest school. Hastings and Weinstein (2008) examine whether simplifying how information on school quality is presented affects the choices parents make. Parents at Charlotte–Mecklenburg Public School District schools randomly selected into a control group received the district's standard information package on school quality — a 100-page book with descriptions of each school in the district. Parents at treated schools were given a simplified one-page information sheet ranking schools by their previous year's test score performance. The authors find that parents in the treatment group were 6–7.5% more likely than parents in the control group to choose a school other than their child's default school. Importantly, this simplified information led parents to choose higher quality schools; on average test scores of schools that parents in the treatment group selected score 0.1 standard deviations higher than those selected by the control group. Students in the treatment group also subsequently perform better than their control group peers, suggesting that simplifying the way information is presented can improve academic outcomes through better matching students with schools that best fit their abilities and interests.

5. CONCLUSION

By taking into account our frequent difficulty in making short and long-run trade-offs, behavioral economics has made significant inroads in many different domains. Education represents a relatively new avenue for behavioral economics, one that holds many opportunities. Since executive brain function, which helps focus on the future and control impulses, does not mature fully until an individual's mid-twenties, children and adolescents are even more susceptible than adults to "behavioral barriers" which may lead them to miss out on education opportunities. We categorize these barriers into four categories: (1) some students focus too much on the present, (2) some rely too much on routine, (3) some students focus too much on negative identities, and (4) mistakes are more likely with many options or with little information.

The immaturity of a child's brain also provides opportunities. Students may be more responsive to interventions that target behavioral barriers. This review presents some very promising examples: An online goal-setting exercise raised semester grades by 0.7 standard deviations; setting up a college fund of $8000 for disadvantaged 9th-grade students increased college graduation rates by 8%; text messaging college-bound students preparation advice in their summer after high school increased enrollment by 3%; help for 10 min completing the college financial aid application increased enrollment by 8%; informing parents through email of middle school children's absences and missed assignments raised GPA by 0.2 standard deviations; mandatory college class attendance increased final exam scores by 0.6 standard deviations; asking 7th-grade students to write about which value was most important to them and why increase end of semester GPA by 0.25 points; and teaching middle school students intelligence is not fixed and that through effort, intellectual ability can improve increased grades by 0.6 standard deviations.

Opportunities abound to simplify applications or schedules, make them more salient, remind students and parents of education opportunities, and motivate them to want to learn. The area is ripe for inquiry. The examples we've presented here suggest that interventions shaped by behavioral theory are likely cost-effective and easy to implement, while delivering significant results. At the same time, not all interventions are successful: increases in elementary students' tests scores disappear the next year, while associated financial incentives report very modest effects. Similarly, merit aid scholarships for college freshmen do not appear to generate long-term changes in behavior. Context, population, timing, and details are all crucial — if subtle changes make a big difference, then it is understandable that not all changes would do so. Future work should explore the conditions under which those changes are successful, especially for high touch interventions that may require more effort and more resources. But ultimately, these opportunities are exciting, testable and tenable. And for a 6-year-old who struggles to get to school, and then, to sit still, they may have the potential to make a real difference — even if she doesn't know it yet.

ACKNOWLEDGMENTS

We are extremely grateful to Chris Avery, Ben Castleman, Stefano DellaVigna, Angela Duckworth, Alex Haslam, Mitchell Hoffmann, Kory Kroft, David Laibson, Susan Mayer, Helena Skyt Nielsen, Uros Petronijevic, Todd Rogers, Aloysius Siow, Mel Stephens, Ryan Webb, and Ludger Woessmann for providing helpful and detailed comments.

REFERENCES

Abdulkadiroglu, A., Angrist, J.D., Hull, P.D., Pathak, P.A., 2015. Charters Without Lotteries: Testing Takeovers in New Orleans and Boston. IZA Discussion Paper No. 8985.

Acemoglu, D., Angrist, J.D., 2001. How large are human-capital externalities? Evidence from compulsory-schooling laws. In: Bernanke, B.S., Rogoff, K. (Eds.), NBER Macroeconomics Annual 2000. MIT Press, Cambridge, MA, pp. 9–74.

Advisory Committee on Student Financial Assistance, 2001. Access Denied: Restoring the Nation's Commitment to Equal Educational Opportunity. Department of Education, Washington, D.C.

Agnew, J.R., Szykman, L.R., 2005. Asset allocation and information overload: the influence of information display, asset choice and investor experience. J. Behav. Finance 6 (2), 57–70.

Akerlof, G.A., Kranton, R.E., 2000. Economics and identity. Q. J. Econ. 115 (3), 715–753.

Akerlof, G.A., Kranton, R.E., 2002. Identity and schooling: some lessons for the economics of education. J. Econ. Lit. 40 (4), 1167–1201.

Akerlof, G.A., Kranton, R.E., 2010. Identity Economics: How Identities Shape Our Work, Wages, and Well-Being. Princeton University Press, Princeton, New Jersey.

Anderson, D.M., 2014. In school and out of trouble? The minimum dropout age and juvenile crime. Rev. Econ. Stat. 96 (2), 318–331.

Angrist, J.D., Krueger, A.B., 1992. The effect of age at school entry on educational attainment: an application of instrumental variables with moments from two samples. J. Am. Stat. Assoc. 87 (418), 326–336.

Angrist, J.D., Lavy, V., 2009. The effects of high stakes high school achievement awards: evidence from a randomized trial. Am. Econ. Rev. 99 (4), 1384–1414.

Angrist, J.D., Lang, D., Oreopoulos, P., 2009. Incentives and services for college achievement: evidence from a randomized trial. Am. Econ. J. Appl. Econ. 1 (1), 1–29.

Angrist, J.D., Dynarski, S.M., Kane, T.J., Pathak, P.A., Walters, C.R., 2012. Who benefits from KIPP? J. Policy Anal. Manage. 31 (4), 837–860.

Angrist, J.D., Cohodes, S.R., Dynarski, S.M., Pathak, P.A., Walters, C.R., 2014a. Stand and deliver: effects of Boston's charter high schools on college preparation, entry and choice. J. Labor. Econ. 34 (2) Forthcoming.

Angrist, J., Philip Oreopoulos, D., Williams, T., 2014b. When opportunity knocks, who answers? New evidence on college achievement awards. J. Hum. Resour. 49 (3), 572–610.

Ariely, D., Wertenbroch, K., 2002. Procrastination, deadlines, and performance: self-control by precommitment. Psychol. Sci. 13 (3), 219–224.

Aronson, J., Fried, C.B., Good, C., 2002. Reducing the effects of stereotype threat on African American college students by shaping theories of intelligence. J. Exp. Soc. Psychol. 38 (2), 113–125.

Atkins, S.M., Bunting, M.F., Bolger, D.J., Dougherty, M.R., 2012. Training the adolescent brain: neural plasticity and the acquisition of cognitive abilities. In: Reyna, V.F., Chapman, S.B., Dougherty, M.R., Confrey, J. (Eds.), The Adolescent Brain: Learning, Reasoning, and Decision Making. American Psychological Association, Washington, D.C.

Austen-Smith, D., Fryer Jr., R.G., 2005. An economic analysis of 'acting white'. Q. J. Econ. 120 (2), 551–583.

Avery, C., 2013. Evaluation of the College Possible Program: Results from a Randomized Controlled Trial. NBER Working Paper 19562, National Bureau of Economic Research.

Avery, C., Hoxby, C.M., 2003. Do and Should Financial Aid Packages Affect Students' College Choices? NBER Working Paper 9482, National Bureau of Economic Research.

Avery, C., Kane, T.J., 2004. Student perceptions of college opportunities: the Boston coach program. In: Hoxby, C.M. (Ed.), College Choices: The Economics of Where to Go, When to Go, and How to Pay for It. University of Chicago Press, Chicago, pp. 355–394.

Avery, C., Turner, S., 2012. Student loans: do college students borrow too much – or not enough? J. Econ. Perspect. 26 (1), 165–192.

Avvisati, F., Gurgand, M., Guyon, N., Maurin, E., 2014. Getting parents involved in deprived schools. Rev. Econ. Stud. 81 (1), 57–83.

Banerji, R., Berry, J., Shotland, M., 2013. The Impact of Mother Literacy and Participation Programs on Child Learning: Evidence from a Randomized Evaluation in India. Abdul Latif Jameel Poverty Action Lab (J-PAL), Cambridge, MA.

Banks, J., Mazzonna, F., 2011. The effect of education on old age cognitive abilities: evidence from a regression discontinuity design. Econ. J. 122 (560), 418–448.

Barrington, B.L., Hendricks, B., 1989. Differentiating characteristics of high school graduates, dropouts and nongraduates. J. Educ. Res. 82 (6), 309–319.

Barrow, L., Richburg-Hayes, L., Rouse, C.E., Brock, T., 2014. Paying for performance: the education impacts of a community college scholarship program for low-income adults. J. Labor. Econ. 32 (3), 563–599.

Baum, S., Schwartz, S., 2013. Student Aid, Student Behavior, and Educational Attainment. The George Washington University Graduate School of Education and Human Development.

Baum, S., Scott-Clayton, J., 2013. Redesigning the Pell Grant Program for the Twenty-First Century. The Hamilton Project.

Baum, S., Kurose, C., Ma, J., 2013. How College Shapes Lives: Understanding the Issues. Trends in Higher Education Working Paper Series, October 2013.

Becker, G., 1962. Investment in human capital: a theoretical analysis. J. Polit. Econ. 70 (2), 9–49.

Becker, G.S., Mulligan, C.B., 1997. The endogenous determination of time preferences. Q. J. Econ. 112 (3), 729–758.

Benartzi, S., Thaler, R., 2007. Heuristics and biases in retirement savings behavior. J. Econ. Perspect. 21 (3), 81–104.

Benenson, J.F., Pascoe, J., Radmore, N., 2007. Children's altruistic behavior in the dictator game. Evol. Hum. Behav. 28 (3), 168–175.

Benhassine, N., Devoto, F., Duflo, E., Dupas, P., Pouliquen, V., 2013. Turning a Shove into a Nudge? A 'Labeled Cash Transfer' for Education. NBER Working Paper 19227, National Bureau of Economic Research.

Benjamin, D.J., Choi, J.J., Joshua Strickland, A., 2010. Social identity and preferences. Am. Econ. Rev. 100 (4), 1913–1928.

Bergman, P., 2014. Parent–Child Information Frictions and Human Capital Investment: Evidence from a Field Experiment. Working paper.

Berman, J., Bos, J., 2010. Evaluation of the SOURCE Program: An Intervention to Promote College Application and Enrollment among Urban Youth. BPA Report. Berkley Policy Associates, Oakland.

Bernheim, B.D., Rangel, A., 2009. Beyond revealed preference: choice theoretic foundations for behavioral welfare economics. Q. J. Econ. 124 (1), 51–104.

Bertrand, M., Karlan, D., Mullainathan, S., Shafir, E., Zinman, J., 2010. What's advertising content worth? Evidence from a consumer credit marketing field experiment. Q. J. Econ. 125 (1), 263–306.

Beshears, J., Choi, J.J., Laibson, D.I., Madrian, B.C., 2013. Simplification and savings. J. Econ. Behav. Org. 95, 130–145.

Bettinger, E., 2004. How financial aid affects persistence. In: Hoxby, C.M. (Ed.), College Choices: The Economics of Where to Go, When to Go, and How to Pay for It. University of Chicago Press, Chicago, pp. 207–237.

Bettinger, E., 2010. Need Based Aid and Student Outcomes: The Effects of the Ohio College Opportunity Grant. Working Paper.

Bettinger, E., 2012. Paying to learn: the effect of financial incentives on elementary school test scores. Rev. Econ. Stat. 94 (3), 686–698.

Bettinger, E., Baker, R., 2014. The effects of student coaching in college: an evaluation of a randomized experiment in student mentoring. Educ. Eval. Policy Anal. 36 (1), 3–19.

Bettinger, E., Slonim, R., 2007. Patience among children. J. Public Econ. 91 (1–2), 343–363.

Bettinger, E., Long, B.T., Oreopoulos, P., Sanbonmatsu, L., 2012. The role of application assistance and information in college decisions: results from the H&R block FAFSA experiment. Q. J. Econ. 127 (3), 1205–1242.

Bettinger, E., Boatman, A., Long, B.T., 2013. Student supports: developmental education and other academic programs. Future Child. 23 (1), 93–115.

Bird, K., Castleman, B.L., 2014. Here Today, Gone tomorrow? Investigating Rates and Patterns of Financial Aid Renewal Among College Freshman. EdPolicy Works Working Paper Series No. 25, May 2014.

Bishop, J.H., 2006. Drinking from the fountain of knowledge: student incentive to study and learn-externalities, information problems and peer pressure. In: Hanushek, E.A., Welch, F. (Eds.), In: Handbook of Economics of Education, vol. 2. Elsevier, Amsterdam, pp. 909–944.

Black, S.E., Devereux, P.J., Salvanes, K.G., 2005. The more the merrier? The effect of family size and birth order on children's education. Q. J. Econ. 120 (2), 669–700.

Blackwell, L.S., Trzesniewski, K.H., Dweck, C.S., 2007. Implicit theories of intelligence predict achievement across and adolescent transition: a longitudinal study and an intervention. Child Dev. 78 (1), 246–263.

Borghans, L., Duckworth, A., Heckman, J., ter Weel, B., 2008. The economics and psychology of personality traits. J. Hum. Resour. 31 (1), 27–56.

Borghans, L., Golsteyn, B.H.H., Stenberg, A., 2013. Does Expert Advice Improve Educational Choice? IZA Discussion Paper No. 7649.

Brewster, A.B., Bowen, G.L., 2004. Teacher support and the school engagement of Latino middle and high school students at risk of school failure. Child Adolesc. Soc. Work. J. 21 (1), 47–65.

Bridgeland, J.M., DiIulio Jr., J.J., Morison, K.B., 2006. The Silent Epidemic: Perspectives of High School Dropouts. Civic Enterprises, Chicago, IL.

Brunello, G., Fort, M., Weber, G., 2009. Changes in compulsory schooling, education, and the distribution of wages in Europe. Econ. J. 119 (536), 516–539.

Brunello, G., Weber, G., Weiss, C.T., 2012. Books Are Forever: Early Life Conditions, Education and Lifetime Income. IZA Discussion Paper No. 6386.

Bursztyn, L., Coffman, L.C., 2012. The schooling decision: family preferences, intergenerational conflict, and moral hazard in the Brazilian favelas. J. Polit. Econ. 120 (3), 359–397.

Bursztyn, L., Jensen, R., 2015. How does peer pressure affect educational investments. Q. J. Econ. 130 (3), 1329–1367.

Buser, T., Niederle, M., Oosterbeek, H., 2014. Gender, competitiveness and career choices. Q. J. Econ. 129 (3), 1409–1447.

Busse, M.R., Pope, D.G., Pope, J.C., Silva-Risso, J., 2012. Projection Bias in the Car and Housing Markets. NBER Working Paper 18212, National Bureau of Economic Research.

Cabrera, A.F., La Nasa, S.M., 2000. Understanding the college-choice process. New Dir. Inst. Res. 107, 5–22.

Cadena, B.C., Keys, B.J., 2015. Human capital and the lifetime costs of impatience. Am. Econ. J. Econ. Policy 7 (3), 126–153.

Caetano, G., Patrinos, H.A., Palacios, M., 2011. Measuring Aversion to Debt: An Experiment Among Student Loan Candidates. Working Bank Policy Research Working Paper No. 5737.

Carrell, S.E., Sacerdote, B., 2013. Late Interventions Matter Too: The Case of College Coaching New Hampshire. NBER Working Paper 19031, National Bureau of Economic Research.

Carroll, G.D., Choi, J.J., Laibson, D.I., Madrian, B.C., Metrick, A., 2009. Optimal defaults and active decisions. Q. J. Econ. 124 (4), 1639–1674.

Castillo, M., Ferraro, P.J., Jordan, J.L., Petrie, R., 2011. The today and tomorrow of kids: time preferences and educational outcomes of children. J. Public Econ. 95 (11–12), 1377–1385.

Castleman, B.L., 2013. Prompts, Personalization, and Pay-Offs: Strategies to Improve the Design and Delivery of College and Financial Aid Information. The George Washington University Graduate School of Education and Human Development.

Castleman, B.L., 2014. The Impact of Partial and Full Merit Scholarships on College Entry and Success: Evidence from the Florida Bright Futures Scholarship Program. EdPolicy Works Working Paper No. 17, February 2014.

Castleman, B.L., Page, L.C., 2014a. A trickle or a torrent? Understanding the extent of summer "melt" among college-intending high school graduates. Soc. Sci. Q. 95 (1), 202–220.

Castleman, B.L., Page, L.C., 2014b. Freshman Year Financial Aid Nudges: An Experiment to Increase FAFSA Renewal and College Persistence. EdPolicy Works Working Paper Series No. 29, June 2014.

Castleman, B.L., Page, L.C., 2015. Summer nudging: can personalized text messages and peer mentor outreach increase college going among low-income high school graduates? J. Econ. Behav. Org. 115, 144–160.

Castleman, B.L., Arnold, K., Wartman, K.L., 2012. Stemming the tide of summer melt: an experimental study of the effects of post-high school summer intervention on low-income students' college enrollment. J. Res. Educ. Eff. 5 (1), 1–17.

Castleman, B.L., Page, L.C., Schooley, K., 2014. The forgotten summer: does the offer of college counseling after high school mitigate summer melt among college-intending, low-income high school graduates? J. Policy Anal. Manage. 33 (2), 320–344.

Catterall, J.S., 1998. Risk and resilience in student transitions to high school. Am. J. Educ. 106 (2), 302–333.

Cha, P., Patel, R., 2010. Rewarding Progress, Reducing Debt: Early Results from Ohio's Performance-Based Scholarship Demonstration for Low-Income Parents. MDRC Report, October. MDRC, New York and Oakland.

Chapman, S.B., Gamino, J.F., Anand Mudar, R., 2012. Higher-order strategic gist reasoning in adolescence. In: Reyna, V.F., Chapman, S.B., Dougherty, M.R., Confrey, J. (Eds.), The Adolescent Brain: Learning, Reasoning, and Decision Making. American Psychological Association, Washington, D.C.

Chetty, R., 2015. Behavioral economics and public policy: a pragmatic perspective. Am. Econ Rev, 105 (5), 1–33.

Chetty, R., Looney, A., Kroft, K., 2009. Salience and taxation: theory and evidence. Am. Econ. Rev. 99 (4), 1145–1177.

Chetty, R., Friedman, J.N., Rockoff, J.E., 2011. The Long-Term Impacts of Teachers: Teacher Value-Added and Student Outcomes in Adulthood. NBER Working Paper 17699, National Bureau of Economic Research.

Chetty, R., Friedman, J.N., Leth-Petersen, S., Nielsen, T., Olsen, T., 2014. Active vs. passive decisions and crowd-out in retirement savings accounts: evidence from Denmark. Q. J. Econ. 129 (3), 1141–1219.

Chick, C.F., Reyna, V.F., 2012. A fuzzy trace theory of adolescent risk taking: beyond self-control and sensation seeking. In: Reyna, V.F., Chapman, S.B., Dougherty, M.R., Confrey, J. (Eds.), The Adolescent Brain: Learning, Reasoning and Decision Making. American Psychological Association, Washington, D.C.

Choi, J.J., Laibson, D.I., Madrian, B.C., Metrick, A., 2002. Defined contribution pensions: plan rules, participant choices, and the path of least resistance. In: Poterba, J. (Ed.), Tax Policy and the Economy. MIT Press, Cambridge, MA.

Choi, J.J., Laibson, D.I., Madrian, B.C., 2004. Plan design and 401(k) savings outcomes. Natl. Tax J. 57 (2), 275–298.

Cohen, G.L., Garcia, J., Apfel, N., Master, A., 2006. Reducing the racial achievement gap: a social-psychological intervention. Science 313 (5791), 1307–1310.

Cohodes, S., Goodman, J., 2014. Merit aid, college quality and college completion: Massachusetts' Adams scholarship as an in-kind subsidy. Am. Econ J Appl. Econ. 6 (4), 251–285.

Coleman, J.S., 1961. The Adolescent Society. The Free Press, New York.

Cook, P.J., Dodge, K., Farkas, G., Fryer Jr., R.G., Guryan, J., Ludwig, J., Mayer, S., Pollack, H., Steinberg, L., 2014. The (Surprising) Efficacy of Academic and Behavioral Intervention with Disadvantaged Youth: Results from a Randomized Experiment in Chicago. NBER Working Paper 19862, National Bureau of Economic Research.

Cornwell, C., Lee, K.H., Mustard, D.B., 2005. Student responses to merit scholarship retention rules. J. Hum. Resour. 40 (4), 895–917.

Council of Economic Advisors: National Economic Council, 2009. Simplifying Student Aid: The Case for an Easier, Faster and More Accurate FAFSA. Executive Office of the President, Washington, D.C.

Croninger, R.G., Lee, V.E., 2001. Social capital and dropping out of high school: benefits to at-risk students of teachers' support and guidance. Teach. Coll. Rec. 103 (4), 548–581.

Cunha, F., Heckman, J.J., 2008. Formulating, identifying and estimating the technology of cognitive and noncognitive skill formation. J. Hum. Resour. 43 (4), 738–782.

Curto, V.E., Fryer Jr., R.G., 2014. The potential of urban working schools for the poor: evidence from SEED. J. Labor. Econ. 32 (1), 65–93.

Cusick, P., 1973. Inside High School. Holt, Rinehart & Winston, New York.

Dearden, L., Emmerson, C., Frayne, C., Meghir, C., 2009. Conditional cash transfers and school dropout rates. J. Hum. Resour. 44 (4), 827–857.

Deci, E.L., Ryan, R.M., 2010. Self-determination. In: Weiner, I.B., Craighead, W.E. (Eds.), Corsini Encyclopedia of Psychology. In: vols. 1–2. Wiley, New York.

Dee, T., 2014. Stereotype threat and the student athlete. Econ. Inq. 52 (1), 173–182.

DellaVigna, S., 2009. Psychology and economics: evidence from the field. J. Econ. Lit. 47 (2), 315–372.

DellaVigna, S., Daniele Paserman, M., 2005. Job search and impatience. J. Labor Econ. 23 (3), 527–588.

Demming, D., Dynarski, S., 2009. Into College, OUT of poverty? Policies to Increase the Postsecondary Attainment of the Poor. NBER Working Paper 15387, National Bureau of Economic Research.

Devereux, P.J., Hart, R.A., 2010. Forced to be rich? Returns to compulsory schooling in Britain. Econ. J. 120 (549), 1345–1364.

Diamond, P., Vartiainen, H. (Eds.), 2007. Behavioral Economics and Its Applications. Princeton University Press, Princeton.

Dinkleman, T., Martinez, C., 2014. Investing in schooling in Chile: the role of information about financial aid for higher education. Rev. Econ. Stat. 96 (2), 244–257.

Dobbie, W., Fryer Jr., R.G., 2011. Are high-quality schools enough to increase achievement among the poor? Evidence from the Harlem Children's Zone. Am. Econ. J. Appl. Econ. 3 (3), 158–187.

Dobkin, C., Gil, R., Marion, J., 2010. Skipping class in college and exam performance: evidence from a regression discontinuity classroom experiment. Econ. Educ. Rev. 29 (4), 566–575.

Dohmen, T., Falk, A., Huffman, D., Sunde, U., 2011. The intergenerational transmission of risk and trust attitudes. Rev. Econ. Stud. 79 (2), 645–677.

Duckworth, A.L., Carlson, S.M., 2013. Self-regulation and school success. In: Sokol, B.W., Grouzet, F.M. E., Mueller, U. (Eds.), Self-Regulation and Autonomy: Social and Developmental Dimensions of Human Conduct. Cambridge University Press, New York, pp. 208–230.

Duckworth, A.L., Steinberg, L., 2014. Understanding and Cultivating Self-Control. Working Paper.

Duckworth, A.L., Grant, H., Lowe, B., Oettingen, G., Gollwitzer, P.M., 2011. Self-regulation strategies improve self-discipline in adolescents: benefits of mental contrasting and implementation intentions. Educ. Psychol. 31 (1), 17–26.

Duckworth, A.L., Quinn, P.D., Tsukayama, E., 2012. What no child left behind leaves behind: the roles of IQ and self-control in predicting standardized achievement test scores and report card grades. J. Educ. Psychol. 104 (2), 439–451.

Duckworth, A.L., Gendler, T.S., Gross, J.J., 2014. Self-control in school-age children. Educ. Psychol. 49 (3), 199–217.

Dweck, C.S., 2007. Mindset: The New Psychology of Success. Random House, New York.

Dweck, C.S., Leggett, E.L., 1988. A social-cognitive approach to motivation and personality. Psychol. Rev. 95 (2), 256–273.

Dweck, C.S., Sorich, L.A., 1999. Mastery-oriented thinking. In: Snyder, L.C.R. (Ed.), Coping: The Psychology of What Works. Oxford, University Press, New York, pp. 232–251.

Dynarski, S.M., 2004. Who benefits from the education saving incentives? Income, educational expectations and the value of the 529 and Coverdell. Natl. Tax J. 57 (2), 359–383.

Dynarski, S., 2008. Building the stock of college-educated labor. J. Hum. Resour. 43 (3), 924–937.

Dynarski, S., Scott-Clayton, J., 2006. The cost of complexity in federal student aid: lessons from optimal tax theory and behavioral economics. Natl. Tax J. 59 (2), 319–356.

Everhart, R.B., 1983. Reading, Writing, and Resistance: Adolescence and Labor in a Junior High School. Routledge and Kegan Paul, Boston, MA.

Fan, C.-P., 2000. Teaching children cooperation – an application of experimental game theory. J. Econ. Behav. Org. 41 (3), 191–209.

Fehr, E., Rützler, D., Sutter, M., 2013. The development of egalitarianism, altruism, spite and parochialism in childhood and adolescence. Eur. Econ. Rev. 64, 369–383.

Field, E., 2009. Educational debt burden and career choice: evidence from a financial aid experiment at NYU law school. Am. Econ. J. Appl. Econ. 1 (1), 1–21.

Ford, R., Frenette, M., Nicholson, C., Kwakye, I., Shek-wai Hui, T., Hutchison, J., Dorber, S., Smith Fowler, H., Hébert, S., 2012. Future to Discover: Post-secondary Impacts Report. Social Research and Demonstration Corporation (SDRC), Ottawa, Ontario.

Frederick, S., Loewenstein, G., O'Donoghue, T., 2002. Time discounting and time preference: a critical review. J. Econ. Lit. 40 (2), 351–401.

Fryer Jr., R.G., 2011. Financial incentives and student achievement: evidence from randomized trials. Q. J. Econ. 126 (5), 1755–1798.

Fryer Jr., R.G., 2014. Injecting charter school best practices into traditional public schools: evidence from field experiments. Q. J. Econ. 129 (3), 1355–1407.

Fudenberg, D., Levine, D.K., 2006. A dual-self model of impulse control. Am. Econ. Rev. 96 (5), 1449–1476.

Fuhrman, T., 2014. Keeping students on track with a mobile 'nudge'. Campus Technology. (July 17). http://campustechnology.com/Articles/2014/07/17/Keeping-Students-on-Track-With-a-Mobile-Nudge.aspx?Page=1. Accessed August 23, 2014.

Fuster, J.M., 2002. Frontal lobe and cognitive development. J. Neurocytol. 31 (3–5), 373–385.

Galvan, A., 2012. Risky behavior in adolescents: the role of the developing brain. In: Reyna, V.F., Chapman, S.B., Dougherty, M.R., Confrey, J. (Eds.), The Adolescent Brain: Learning, Reasoning, and Decision Making. American Psychological Association, Washington, D.C.

Giedd, J.N., Stockman, M., Weddle, C., Liverpool, M., Wallace, G.L., Reitano Lee, N., Lalonde, F., Lenroot, R.K., 2012. Anatomic magnetic resonance imaging of the developing child and adolescent brain. In: Reyna, V.F., Chapman, S.B., Dougherty, M.R., Confrey, J. (Eds.), The Adolescent Brain: Learning, Reasoning, and Decision Making. American Psychological Association, Washington, D.C.

Glimcher, P.W., 2014. Value-based decision making. In: Glimcher, P.W., Fehr, E. (Eds.), Neuroeconomics. second ed. Academic Press, New York (Chapter 10).

Glimcher, P.W., Fehr, E., 2014. Neuroeconomics, second ed. Academic Press, New York.

Gneezy, U., Meier, S., Rey-Biel, P., 2011. When and why incentives (don't) work to modify behavior. J. Econ. Perspect. 25 (4), 191–210.

Gollwitzer, A., Oettingen, G., Kirby, T.A., Duckworth, A.L., Mayer, D., 2011. Mental contrasting facilitates academic performance in school children. Motiv. Emot. 35 (4), 403–412.

Golsteyn, B.H.H., Grönqvist, H., Lindahl, L., 2014. Adolescent time preferences predict lifetime outcomes. Econ. J. 124 (580), F739–F761.

Good, C., Aronson, J., Inzlicht, M., 2003. Improving adolescents' standardized test performance: an intervention to reduce the effects of stereotype threat. Appl. Dev. Psychol. 24, 645–662.

Gordon, W.C., 1957. The Social System of the High School. The Free Press, Chicago.

Green, L., Fry, A.F., Myerson, J., 1994. Discounting of delayed rewards: a life-span comparison. Psychol. Sci. 5 (1), 33–36.

Grenet, J., 2011. Is extending compulsory schooling alone enough to raise earnings? Evidence from French and British compulsory schooling laws. Scand. J. Econ. 115 (1), 176–210.

Grodner, A., Rupp, N.G., 2013. The role of homework in student learning outcomes: evidence from a field experiment. J. Econ. Educ. 44 (2), 93–109.

Guryan, J., Kim, J.S., Park, K., 2015. Motivation and Incentives in Education: Evidence from a Summer Reading Program. NBER Working Paper 20918, National Bureau of Economic Research.

Hall, G.S., 1904. Adolescence. Appleton, New York.

Hammer, K., 2012. TDSB uses a personal touch to bring dropouts back to school. The Globe and Mail. http://www.theglobeandmail.com/news/national/tdsb-uses-a-personal-touch-to-bring-dropouts-back-to-school/article4219643/Accessed August 23, 2014.

Harackiewicz, J.M., Rozek, C.S., Hulleman, C.S., Hyde, J.S., 2012. Helping parents to motivate adolescents in mathematics and science: an experimental test of a utility-value intervention. Psychol. Sci. 23 (8), 899–906.

Harmon, C., Walker, I., 1995. Estimates of the economic return to schooling for the United Kingdom. Am. Econ. Rev. 85 (5), 1278–1286.

Hastings, J.S., Weinstein, J.M., 2008. Information, school choice, and academic achievement: evidence from two experiments. Q. J. Econ. 123 (4), 1373–1414.

Haun, D.B.M., van Leeuwen, J.C., Edelson, M.G., 2013. Majority influence in children and other animals. Dev. Cogn. Neurosci. 3, 61–71.

Hershfield, H.E., Goldstein, D.G., Sharpe, W.F., Fox, J., Yeykelis, L., Carstensen, L.L., Bailenson, J.N., 2011. Increasing saving behavior through age-progressed renderings of the future self. J. Mark. Res. 48, S23–S37.

Hoffman, M., 2012. How Is Information (Under-) Valued? Evidence from Framed Field Experiments. Working Paper.

Hollingshead, A.B., 1975. Four Factor Index of Social Status. Yale University, New Haven, CT. Unpublished manuscript.

Horn, L.J., Chen, X., Chapman, C., 2003. Getting Ready to Pay for College: What Students and Their Parents Know About the Cost of College Tuition and What They Are Doing to Find Out: NCES Report No. 2003-030. National Center for Education Statistics, Washington, D.C.

Hough, D.E., 2013. Irrationality in Health Care: What Behavioral Economics Reveals About What We Do and Why. Stanford Economics and Finance, Palo Alto.

Hoxby, C.M., Avery, C., 2013. The Missing "One-Offs": The Hidden Supply of High-Achieving, Low-Income Students. Brookings Papers on Economic Activity.

Hoxby, C.M., Turner, S., 2013. Expanding College Opportunities for High-Achieving, Low Income Students. SIEPR Discussion Paper 12-014, Stanford Institute for Economic Policy Research.

Iyengar, S.S., Lepper, M.R., 2000. When choice is demotivating: can one desire too much of a good thing? J. Pers. Soc. Psychol. 79 (6), 995–1006.

Iyengar, S.S., Huberman, G., Jiang, H., 2005. How much choice is too much? Contributions to 401 (k) retirement plans. In: Mitchell, O.S., Utkus, S.P. (Eds.), Pension Design and Structure: New Lessons from Behavioral Finance. Oxford Scholarship Online.

Jabbar, H., 2011. The behavioral economics of education: new directions for research. Educ. Res. 40 (9), 446–452.

Jackson, P.W., 1968. Life in Classrooms. Holt, Rinehart, and Winston, New York.

Jackson, C.K., 2010. A little now for a lot later: a look at a Texas advanced placement incentive program. J. Hum. Resour. 45 (3), 591–639.

Jensen, R., 2010. The (perceived) returns to education and the demand for schooling. Q. J. Econ. 125 (2), 515–548.

Johnson, S.B., Blum, R.W., Giedd, J.N., 2009. Adolescent maturity and the brain: the promise and pitfalls of neuroscience research in adolescent health policy. J. Adolesc. Health 45 (3), 216–221.

Kable, J.W., Glimcher, P.W., 2007. The neural correlates of subjective value during intertemporal choice. Nat. Neurosci. 10, 1625–1633.

Kable, J.W., Glimcher, P.W., 2010. An "as soon as possible" effect in human intertemporal decision making: behavioral evidence and neural mechanisms. J. Neurophysiol. 103 (5), 2513–2531.

Kahneman, D., 2003. Maps of bounded rationality: psychology for behavioral economics. Am. Econ. Rev. 93 (5), 1449–1475.

Kahneman, D., Frederick, S., 2002. Representativeness revisited: attribute substitution in intuitive judgment. In: Gilovich, T., Griffin, D., Kahneman, D. (Eds.), Heuristic and Biases: The Psychology of Intuitive Judgment. Cambridge University Press, New York, NY, pp. 49–81.

Kahneman, D., Tversky, A., 1973. On the psychology of prediction. Psychol. Rev. 80 (4), 237–251.

Kerr, S.P., Pekkarinen, T., Sarvimaki, M., Uusitalo, R., 2014. Educational Choice and Information on Labor Market Prospects: A Randomized Field Experiment. Working Paper.

Kling, J.R., Mullainathan, S., Shafir, E., Vermeulen, L.C., Wrobel, M.V., 2012. Comparison friction: experimental evidence from medicare drug plans. Q. J. Econ. 127 (1), 199–235.

Koch, A., Nafziger, J., Nielson, H.S., 2015. Behavioral economics of education. J. Econ. Behav. Org. 115, 3–17.

Kosse, F., Pfeiffer, F., 2012. Impatience among preschool children and their mothers. Econ. Lett. 115 (3), 493–495.

Kraft, M.A., Dougherty, S.M., 2013. The effect of teacher-family communication on student engagement: evidence from a randomized field experiment. J. Res. Educ. Eff. 6 (3), 199–222.

Kraft, M.A., Rogers, T., 2015. The underutilized potential of teacher-to-parent communication: evidence from a field experiment. Econ. Educ. Rev. 47, 49–63.

Kremer, M., Miguel, E., Thorton, R., 2009. Incentives to learn. Rev. Econ. Stat. 91 (3), 437–456.

Laibson, D.I., 1997. Golden eggs and hyperbolic discounting. Q. J. Econ. 112 (2), 443–477.

Lamdin, D.J., 1996. Evidence of student attendance as an independent variable in education production functions. J. Educ. Res. 89 (3), 155–162.

Lee, V.E., Burkham, D.T., 2003. Dropping out of high school: the role of school organization and structure. Am. Educ. Res. J. 40 (2), 353–393.

Lergetporer, P., Angerer, S., Glätzle-Rützler, D., Sutter, M., 2014. Third-party punishment increases cooperation in children through (misaligned) expectations and conditional cooperation. Proc. Natl. Acad. Sci. 111 (19), 6916–6921.

Leuven, E., Oosterbeek, H., van der Klaauw, B., 2010. The effect of financial rewards on students' achievement: evidence from a randomized experiment. J. Eur. Econ. Assoc. 8 (6), 1243–1265.

Leuven, E., Oosterbeek, H., Sonnemans, J., van der Klaauw, B., 2011. Incentives versus sorting in tournaments: evidence from a field experiment. J. Labor Econ. 29 (3), 637–658.

Levin, I.P., Hart, S.S., 2003. Risk preferences in young children: early evidence of individual differences in reaction to potential gains and losses. J. Behav. Decis. Mak. 16 (5), 397–413.

Levine, P.B., 2013. Simplifying Estimates of College Costs. The Hamilton Project, Washington, D.C. Policy Memo 2013-06.

Levitt, S.D., List, J.A., Neckermann, S., Sadoff, S., 2012. The Behavioralist Goes to School: Leveraging Behavioral Economics to Improve Educational Performance. NBER Working Paper 18165, National Bureau of Economic Research.

Lleras-Muney, A., 2005. The relationship between education and adult mortality in the United States. Rev. Econ. Stud. 72 (1), 189–221.

Lochner, L., Monge-Naranjo, A., 2012. Credit constraints in education. Annu. Rev. Econ. 4, 225–256.

Lochner, L., Moretti, E., 2004. The effect of education on crime: evidence from prison inmates, arrests, and self reports. Am. Econ. Rev. 94 (1), 155–189.

Loewenstein, G., O'Donoghue, T., Rabin, M., 2003. Projection bias in predicting future utility. Q. J. Econ. 118 (4), 1209–1248.

MacDonald, H., Bernstein, L., Price, C., 2009. Foundations for Success: Short-Term Impacts Report. Report to the Canada Millennium Scholarship Foundation.

Madrian, B.C., 2014. Applying insights from behavioral economics to policy design. Annu. Rev. Econ. 6, 663–688.

Mangels, J.A., Good, C., Whiteman, R.C., Maniscalo, B., Dweck, C.S., 2012. Emotion blocks the path to learning under stereotype threat. Soc. Cogn. Affect. Neurosci. 7 (2), 230–241.

Mani, A., Mullainathan, S., Shafir, E., Zhao, J., 2013. Poverty impedes cognitive function. Science 341 (6149), 976–980.

McClure, S.M., Laibson, D.I., Loewenstein, G., Cohen, J.D., 2004. Separate neural systems value immediate and delayed monetary rewards. Science 306 (5695), 503–507.

McGuigan, M., McNally, S., Wyness, G., 2012. Student Awareness of Costs and Benefits of Educational Decisions: Effects of an Information Campaign. CEE Discussion Paper 139, Centre for the Economics of Education.

Meghir, C., Palme, M., 2005. Educational reform, ability and family background. Am. Econ. Rev. 95 (1), 414–424.

Meghir, C., Palme, M., Simeonova, E., 2013. Education, Cognition and Health: Evidence from a Social Experiment. NBER Working Paper 19002, National Bureau of Economic Research.

Mensch, B.S., Kandel, D.B., 1988. Dropping out of high school and drug involvement. Sociol. Educ. 61 (2), 95–113.

Messacar, D., Oreopoulos, P., 2013. Staying in school: a proposal for raising high school graduation rates. Issues Sci. Technol. 29 (2), 55–61.

Miller, C., Binder, M., Harris, V., Krause, K., 2011. Saying on Track: Early Findings from a Performance-Based Scholarship Program at the University of Mexico: MDRC Report, August. .

Milligan, K., 2005. Who uses RESPs and why. In: Beach, C.M., Boadway, R.W., McInnis, R. (Eds.), Higher Education in Canada. John Deutsch Institute for the Study of Economic Policy, Queen's University, Kingston, Ontario, pp. 467–494.

Morisano, D., Hirsh, J.B., Peterson, J.B., Pihl, R.O., Shore, B.M., 2010. Setting, elaborating, and reflecting on personal goals improves academic performance. J. Appl. Psychol. 95 (2), 255–264.

Mullainathan, S., Shafir, E., 2013. Scarcity: Why Having Too Little Means So Much. Times Books: Henry Hold and Company, LLC, New York.

Nayar, 2013. SmartSaver: Final Evaluation Report: Online Report Accessed August 31, 2014. http://www.theomegafoundation.ca/documents/SmartSAVER%20Final%20Evaluation%20Report.pdf.

Nguyen, T., 2008. Information, Role Models and Perceived Returns to Education: Experimental Evidence from Madagascar. MIT Working Paper.

O'Rourke, E., Haimovitz, K., Ballwebber, C., Dweck, C.S., Popovic, Z., 2014. Brain Points: A Growth Mindset Incentive Structure Boosts Persistence in an Educational Game. In: Proceedings of the SIGCHI Conference on Human Factors in Computing Systems – CHI 2014.

Oreopoulos, P., 2005. Canadian Compulsory Schooling Laws and Their Impact on Educational Attainment and Future Earnings. Statistics Canada Analytical Studies Branch Research Paper No. 251.

Oreopoulos, P., Dunn, R., 2013. Information and college access: evidence from a randomized field experiment. Scand. J. Econ. 115 (1), 3–26.

Oreopoulos, P., Ford, R., 2014. Life after high school: an experiment to help all high school seniors during class through the college application process. In progress.

Oreopoulos, P., Petronijevic, U., 2013. Making college worth it: a review of research on the returns to higher education. Future Child. 23 (1), 41–65.

Oreopoulos, P., Salvanes, K.G., 2011. Priceless: the nonpecuniary benefits of schooling. J. Econ. Perspect. 25 (1), 159–184.

Oreopoulos, P., Brown, R.S., Lavecchia, A.M., 2014. Pathways to Education: An Integrated Approach to Helping At-Risk High School Students. NBER Working Paper 20430, National Bureau of Economic Research.

Oswald, Y., Backes-Gellner, U., 2014. Learning for a bonus: how financial incentives interact with preferences. J. Public Econ. 118, 52–61.

Pallais, A., 2013. Small differences that matter: mistakes in applying to college. J. Labor Econ. 33 (2), 493–520.

De Paola, M., Maria, V.S., Nistico, R., 2012. Monetary incentives and student achievement in a depressed labor market: results from a randomized experiment. J. Hum. Cap. 6 (1), 56–85.

Pennebaker, J.W., Gosling, S.D., Ferrell, J.D., 2013. Daily online testing in large classes: boosting college performance while reducing achievement gaps. PLoS One. 8 (11), e79774.

Peterson, J.S., Colangelo, N., 1996. Gifted achievers and underachievers: a comparison of patterns found in school files. J. Counsel. Dev. 74 (4), 399–407.

Pischke, J.-S., von Wachter, T., 2008. Zero returns to compulsory schooling in Germany: evidence and interpretation. Rev. Econ. Stat. 90 (3), 592–598.

Price, J.A., Shireman, R.M., 2013. Go to Class! Participate! Study! How Might Altered Incentives – Including Cash Rewards – Affect Student Success in College? The George Washington University, Graduate School of Education and Human Development.

Rabin, M., 2013. Healthy habits: some thoughts on the role of public policy in healthful eating and exercise under limited rationality. In: Oliver, A. (Ed.), Behavioural Public Policy. Cambridge University Press, New York, pp. 115–147.

Read, D., Read, N.L., 2004. Time discounting over the lifespan. Org. Behav. Hum. Decis. Process. 94 (1), 22–32.

Reyna, V.F., Chapman, S.B., Dougherty, M.R., Confrey, J. (Eds.), 2012. The Adolescent Brain: Learning, Reasoning, and Decision Making. American Psychological Association, Washington, D.C.

Riccio, J., Dechausay, N., Miller, C., Nunez, S., Verma, N., Yang, E., 2013. Conditional Cash Transfers New York City: The Continuing Story of the Opportunity NYC – Family Rewards Demonstration: MDRC Report, September.

Richburg-Hayes, L., Sommo, C., Welbeck, R., 2011. Promoting Full-Time Attendance Among Adults in Community College: Early Impacts from the Performance-Based Scholarship Demonstration in New York: MDRC Report, May.

Rick, S., Loewenstein, G., 2008. The role of emotion of economic behavior. In: Lewis, M., Haviland-Jones, J., Barrett, L.F. (Eds.), Handbook of Emotions. Guilford Publications, New York, pp. 138–156.

Roderick, M., 1993. The Path to Dropping Out. Auburn House, Westport, MA.

Rodríguez-Planas, N., 2012. Longer-term impacts of mentoring, educational services, and learning incentives: evidence from a randomized trial in the United States. Am. Econ. J. Appl. Econ. 4 (4), 121–139.

Romer, D., 1993. Do students go to class? Should they? J. Econ. Perspect. 7 (3), 167–174.

Romine, C.B., Reynolds, C.R., 2005. A model of the development of frontal lobe functioning: findings from a meta-analysis. Appl. Neuropsychol. 12 (4), 190–201.

Ross, R., White, S., Wright, J., Knapp, L., 2013. Using Behavioral Economics for Postsecondary Success. ideas42, New York.

Schneider, S.L., Caffrey, C.M., 2012. Affective motivators and experience in adolescents' development of health-related behavior patterns. In: Reyna, V.F., Chapman, S.B., Dougherty, M.R., Confrey, J. (Eds.), The Adolescent Brain: Learning, Reasoning, and Decision Making. American Psychological Association, Washington, D.C.

Schneider, S., Peters, J., Bromberg, U., Brassen, S., Miedl, S., Banaschweski, T., Barker, G.J., Conrod, P., Flor, H., Garavan, H., Heinz, A., Ittermann, B., Lathrop, M., Loth, E., Mann, K., Martinot, J.-L., Nees, F., Paus, T., Rietschel, M., Robbins, T.W., Smolka, M.N., Spangel, R., Ströhle, A., Struve, M., Schumann, G., Büchel, C., 2012. Risk taking and the adolescent reward system: a potential common link to substance abuse. Am. J. Psychiatry 169 (1), 39–46.

Scott-Clayton, J., 2011. On money and motivation: a quasi-experimental analysis of financial incentives for college achievement. J. Hum. Resour. 46 (3), 614–646.

Scott-Clayton, J., 2012a. What explains trends in labor supply among U.S. undergraduates. Natl. Tax J. 65 (1), 181–210.

Scott-Clayton, J., 2012b. The Shapeless River: Does a Lack of Structure Inhibit Students' Progress at Community Colleges. CCRC Working Paper No. 25, Community College Research Center.

Scrivener, S., Weiss, M.J., 2013. More Graduates: Two-Year Results from an Evaluation of Accelerated Study in Associate Programs (ASAP) for Developmental Education Students. MDRC Policy Brief, December.

Sirin, S.R., 2005. Socioeconomic status and academic achievement: a meta-analytic review of research. Rev. Educ. Res. 75 (3), 417–453.

Sjoquist, D.L., Winters, J.V., 2012a. Building the stock of college-educated labor revisited. J. Hum. Resour. 47 (1), 270–285.

Sjoquist, D.L., Winters, J.V., 2012b. State Merit-Based Financial Aid Programs and College Attainment. IZA Discussion Paper No. 6801, Institute for the Study of Labor.

Springer, M.G., Rosenquist, B., Swain, W.A., 2015. Monetary and non-monetary student incentives for tutoring services: a randomized controlled trial. J. Res. Edu. Eff. 8 (4), 453–474.

Stanca, L., 2006. The effects of attendance on academic performance: panel data evidence for introductory microeconomics. J. Econ. Educ. 37 (3), 251–266.

Stanovich, K.E., West, R.F., Toplak, M.F., 2012. Judgment and decision making in adolescence: separating intelligence from rationality. In: Reyna, V.F., Chapman, S.B., Dougherty, M.R., Confrey, J. (Eds.), The Adolescent Brain: Learning, Reasoning and Decision Making. American Psychological Association, Washington, D.C.

Steele, C.M., 1997. A threat in the air: how stereotypes shape intellectual identity and preference. Am. Psychol. 52 (6), 613–629.

Steele, C.M., Aronson, J., 1995. Stereotype threat and the intellectual test performance of African-Americans. J. Pers. Soc. Psychol. 69 (5), 797–811.

Steinberg, L., Graham, S., O'Brien, L., Woolard, J., Cauffman, E., Banich, M., 2009. Age differences in future orientation and delay discounting. Child Dev. 80 (1), 28–44.

Stephens Jr., M., Yang, D.-Y., 2014. Compulsory education and the benefits of schooling. Am. Econ. Rev. 104 (6), 1777–1792.

Stinebrickner, R., Stinebrickner, T.R., 2003. Working during school and academic performance. J. Labor Econ. 21 (2), 473–491.

Strickland, V., 1998. Attendance and Grade Point Average: A Study: Report No. SP038147. National Center for Research on Teacher Learning, Fast Lansing, MI (ERIC Document Reproduction Service No. ED423224).

Sunstein, C., 2000. Behavioral law and economics. In: Arkes, H., Lopes, L., Baron, J. (Eds.), Cambridge Series on Judgement and Decision Making. Cambridge University Press, Cambridge.

Sutter, M., Glätzle-Rützler, D., 2015. Gender differences in competition emerge early in life and persist. Manag. Sci. 61 (10), 2339–2354.

Sutter, M., Kocher, M.G., 2007. Trust and trustworthiness across different age groups. Games Econ. Behav. 59 (2), 364–382.

Sutter, M., Kocher, M.G., Glätzle-Rützler, D., Trautmann, S.T., 2013. Impatience and uncertainty: experimental decisions predict adolescents' field behavior. Am. Econ. Rev. 103 (1), 510–531.

Teffer, K., Semendeferi, K., 2012. Human prefrontal cortex: evolution, development and pathology. In: Hofman, M.A., Falk, D. (Eds.), Progress in Brain Research: Evolution of the Primate Brain from Neuron to Behavior. Elsevier B.V., Amsterdam, The Netherlands, pp. 191–218.

Thaler, R., 2005. Advances in behavioral finance. The Roundtable Series in Behavioral Economics, vol. 2 Princeton University Press, Princeton.

Thaler, R., Sunstein, C., 2008. Nudge: Improving Decisions About Health, Wealth and Happiness. Penguin Books, New York.

Thompson, C., Barresi, J., Moore, C., 1997. The development of future-oriented prudence and altruism in preschoolers. Cogn. Dev. 12 (2), 199–212.

Todd, P.E., Wolpin, K.I., 2007. The production of cognitive achievement in children: home, school and racial test score gaps. J. Hum. Cap. 1 (1), 91–136.

Tversky, A., Kahneman, D., 1983. Extensional versus intuitive reasoning: the conjunction fallacy in probability judgment. Psychol. Rev. 90 (4), 293–315.

Usher, A., 1998. Income-Related Barriers to Post-Secondary Education, Council of Ministers of Education. Canada Working Paper as Part of Postsecondary Education Project, Learner Pathways and Transitions.

Walton, G.M., 2015. The new science of wise psychological interventions. Curr. Dir. Psychol. Sci. 23 (1), 73–82.

Walton, G.M., Cohen, G.L., 2011. A brief social-belonging intervention improves academic and health outcomes of minority students. Science 331 (6023), 1447–1451.

Walton, G.M., Logel, C., Peach, J.M., Spencer, S.J., Zanna, M.P., 2015. Two brief interventions to mitigate a "chilly climate" transform women's experience, relationships, and achievement in engineering. J. Educ. Psychol. 107 (2), 468–485.

Ware, M., Weissman, E., McDermott, D., 2013. Aid Like a Paycheck: Incremental Aid to Promote Student Success. MDRC Policy Brief, September.

Watt, N., 2013. Cameron promises 'land of opportunity' where young people must earn or learn. The Guardian.

Willis, P., 1977. Learning to Labour. Saxon House, Westmead.

Wilson, T.D., Linville, P.W., 1982. Improving the academic performance of college freshman: attribution therapy revisited. J. Pers. Soc. Psychol. 42 (2), 367–376.

Wilson, T.D., Linville, P.W., 1985. Improving the performance of college freshmen with attributional techniques. J. Pers. Soc. Psychol. 49 (1), 287–293.

Wölfel, O., Heineck, G., 2012. Parental risk attitudes and children's secondary track choice. Econ. Educ. Rev. 31 (5), 727–743.

Wulfert, E., Block, J.A., Ana, E.S., Rodriguez, M.L., Colsman, M., 2002. Delay of gratification: impulsive choices and problem behaviors in early and late adolescence. J. Pers. 70 (4), 533–552.

Yeager, D.S., Walton, G.M., 2011. Social-psychological interventions in education: they're not magic. Rev. Educ. Res. 81 (2), 267–301.

Yeager, D.S., Henderson, M.D., Paunesku, D., Walton, G.M., D'Mello, S., Spitzer, B.J., Duckworth, A.L., 2014. Boring but important: a self-transcendent purpose for learning fosters academic self-regulation. J. Pers. Soc. Psychol. 107 (4), 559–580.

Zimmerman, S., 2014. The returns to college admission for academically marginal students. J. Labor Econ. 32 (4), 711–754.

CHAPTER 2

Education Research and Administrative Data

D. Figlio*, K. Karbownik[†], K.G. Salvanes[‡]
*Northwestern University and NBER, Evanston, IL, United States
[†]Northwestern University, Evanston, IL, United States
[‡]Norwegian School of Economics, Bergen, Norway

Contents

Abstract

Thanks to extraordinary and exponential improvements in data storage and computing capacities, it is now possible to collect, manage, and analyze data in magnitudes and in manners that would have been inconceivable just a short time ago. As the world has developed this remarkable capacity to store and analyze data, so have the world's governments developed large scale, comprehensive data files on tax programs, workforce information, benefit programs, health, and education. While these data are collected for purely administrative purposes, they represent remarkable new opportunities for expanding our knowledge. This chapter describes some of the benefits and challenges associated with the use of administrative data in education research. We also offer specific case studies of data that have been developed in both the Nordic countries and the United States, and offer an (incomplete) inventory of data sets used by social scientists to study education questions on every inhabited continent on earth.

Keywords

Education research, Administrative data, Linked data, Education registers, Empirical methods

Handbook of the Economics of Education, Volume 5
ISSN 1574-0692, http://dx.doi.org/10.1016/B978-0-444-63459-7.00002-6

1. INTRODUCTION

Thanks to extraordinary and exponential improvements in data storage and computing capacities, it is now possible to collect, manage, and analyze data in magnitudes and in manners that would have been inconceivable just a short time ago. From 1986 to 2007, the world's capacity to store data increased from 539 MB per capita to 44,716 MB per capita, with 81% of that growth occurring over the last 7 years of that time period (Hilbert and Lopez, 2011). Over the same time period, computing speed increased at an even faster pace — from 0.09 million instructions per second on general-purpose computers in 1986 to 239 million instructions per second in 2000 to 28,620 million instructions per second in 2007 (Hilbert and Lopez, 2011). And while we do not have comparable statistics for the past 7 years, computing speed and capacity growth has surely continued unabated.

As the world has developed this remarkable capacity to store and analyze data, so have the world's governments developed large-scale, comprehensive data files on tax programs, workforce information, benefit programs, health, and education. Today, in many countries around the world, governments collect, maintain, and store an archive of information regarding a vast range of behaviors and outcomes over an individual's entire lifetime (Card et al., 2010a). Governments have established statistical offices to maintain and use these data to produce official statistics about their populations. In the education sector, governments have invested large sums of funds to develop longitudinal data systems. For example, in the United States, the federal Department of Education has invested over $750 million to help states build, populate, and maintain these data systems. Much of this innovation in the United States came about as part of school accountability systems, and accountability systems still provide the backbone for the country's most frequently used databases.

At the same time, because administrative data sets are established for administrative purposes, they are not designed in a manner that makes them readily available for scholarly activity. In many locations, the data sets are administered by officials who also implement the policies for which these data were collected, and those who control access to the data may not be interested in evaluation of the policies they oversee. Moreover, the structure of administrative data — with a set of records for each administrative event, be it a point in time record about school attendance or workforce participation, a test score, a disciplinary infraction, a residential move, or a class taken — offers both complications and new opportunities of statistical analysis along a vast range of substantive areas.

While these data are collected for purely administrative purposes, they represent remarkable new opportunities for expanding our knowledge and, through the conduct of analyses with more comprehensive data and better sources of exogenous variation than could typically be used in times past, challenging conventional wisdom in many areas based on previous research utilizing other sources like surveys. Administrative data also facilitate study of research questions that have heretofore not been possible to study credibly at all. Researchers who are able to access these data, especially those able to link data across administrative domains, have the ability to make extraordinary scientific advances by exploiting the population-wide data sets combined with the increased opportunity for identification of causal effects through exogenous variation by, for instance, policy changes, natural disasters, and other shocks that affect some groups of people but not others. In addition to natural experiments, these data can facilitate the conduct of field experiments, where the subjects of short-term experiments can be followed administratively for a longer period of time in manners that would have been impossible or prohibitively expensive to do absent large-scale administratively collected data. The new insights from these studies have extraordinary potential to inform education policy and practice, and we document some cases where new policies have been based upon insights from these studies. Indeed, the massive growth in the quality and diversity of economic research on educational topics is certainly related to the increased availability of good administrative data.

This chapter describes some of the benefits and challenges associated with the use of administrative data in education research. We also offer specific case studies of data that have been developed in both the Nordic countries and the United States, and offer an (incomplete) inventory of data sets used by economists to study education questions on every inhabited continent on earth.

2. THE BENEFITS OF USING ADMINISTRATIVE DATA IN EDUCATION RESEARCH

Administrative data sets are not a panacea. They are limited to certain locations, which can decrease generalizability. It's hard to know whether a research study from Colombia or North Carolina or Norway or Romania will translate into different contexts. Administrative data sets often measure variables in a manner that is conducive to administration of programs, say, but are not necessarily ideal for research purposes. And administrative data sets are not necessarily structured in a manner that ensures data quality similar to the one in purpose built research data sets.

That said, while traditional purpose-built data sets have many strengths, administrative data sets offer a number of clear advantages for empirical research in education. One clear advantage involves the ability to study population-level data. This ability offers a number of remarkable new possibilities. Perhaps the most obvious involves statistical power — in contrast to data sets with hundreds or thousands of observations, administrative data sets with many times that number of observations mean that it is often (depending on research design) possible to detect modest but meaningful relationships with much greater precision than was previously possible. But there are at least two other distinct advantages of administrative data that are afforded by the large magnitudes of observations. One involves the ability to detect rare events that might be useful for identification: In administrative data sets, it is often possible to make twin comparisons or study children from three-child families; to investigate the effects of extremely rare climatic or seismic events; or to study specific economic events like plant closures (Card et al., 2010a; Roed and Raaum, 2003). In traditional purpose-built data sets, it is rare to have sufficient numbers of observations to be able to carry out analyses of these types. Another major advantage of having large-scale administrative data is the ability to study heterogeneous effects of educational policies and practice: With very large numbers of observations, it becomes possible to see whether the effects are similar across wildly different groups of individuals, and if they differ, how they differ, and for whom.

Allowing for new identification strategies and for the ability to see how generalizable results are across groups are two major advantages of the population-level nature of administrative data, but they are not the only benefits. Because data coverage is universal, it becomes feasible that one can link administrative data from one domain (eg, education) to data from another domain (eg, workforce or health). While it is certainly possible to compare across domains in nonadministrative settings, doing so is considerably more difficult because people would have to be purposefully longitudinally followed, and because a cross-section of educational data, say, and a cross-section of health data may only include some of the same individuals by happenstance. Administrative data, by virtue of their population-level nature and the frequency of data observation, allow the researcher to follow individuals or entities over time, so that there is a panel structure to the data.

Administrative data sets also provide novel types of variables typically not found in nonadministrative data (Einav and Levin, 2013). They can offer new opportunities, for instance, to look at measures of delinquency, of changing geographical location, of social networks, and of health instances that are nearly impossible to study in any other manner. The real-time nature of administrative data also provides new opportunities to study the effects of educational policies and practices that are very recent; and offers the chance for researchers to make their scholarship much more relevant to the specific policy decisions that policymakers must make right away than are studies that make use of retrospective information (Einav and Levin, 2013). And of course, natural experiments need not be rare events to be better-studied using administrative data sets: Because natural experiments are unannounced, and often occur via chance or quirks, it is very difficult to set up a prospective study that will permit the evaluation of a natural experiment; with administrative data that cover a population and that are recorded regularly, it is much more feasible to ex post identify and study these natural experiments (Roed and Raaum, 2003).

The preceding description of advantages of administrative data makes clear the benefits of these data for identifying causal effects. But these data are also highly beneficial for the identification of structural parameters of human behavior for multiple reasons. First of all, the population-level nature of administrative data means that these data are representative of a given population. In addition, the administrative data, through the variety of records across a set of domains, both simultaneously and over time, allows the structural analyst with the opportunity to simultaneously model a set of complex relationships that would almost surely not be possible to uncover using retrospectively collected data (Roed and Raaum, 2003). The lack of a specific structure of administrative data can also facilitate reduced-form analyses, because data that are recorded as a series of observations but without a distinct structure can be rearranged to build rectangular panel data sets that have precisely the properties that are more ideal for the specific empirical task at hand (Einav and Levin, 2013).

Another benefit of administrative data is that data quality is likely to be simply better than retrospective data collection. Rather than ask people whether they participated in a given program 20 years ago, scholars who make use of administrative data can observe directly whether the individuals participated — according to the authorities who paid for the participation and therefore had a strong interest in correctly recording the occurrence! Also because of the mandatory nature of participation in the activities that generate administrative data, these data are much less likely to suffer from attrition problems or nonresponse problems than are data collected through voluntary means (Card et al., 2010a). Likewise, administrative data are likely to be less subject to overreporting or underreporting of key variables.

Administrative data also facilitate the study of intergenerational issues. It is possible, at least in some contexts, to match children's administrative records to that of their parents, and even grandparents. While it is certainly possible to purposefully follow families longitudinally, the risk of attrition is surely greater when attempting to move from one generation to the next than if it is possible to directly match individuals using administrative means (Roed and Raaum, 2003). And, in the case of questions that require a long amount of time to study in real time (eg, intergenerational issues), the time horizon over which intergenerational questions may be studied can be shrunk considerably with administrative data.

Using administrative data has major practical value as well. Importantly, different countries have extremely different policy environments. While it is possible that in some circumstances, a study conducted in Denmark would be just as relevant to Chile as would be a study conducted in Chile, or vice versa, there are many cases — because of different institutions and different populations — where it makes the most sense to study a specific question in the location where the policy environment is what the researcher most wishes to study. And, of course, this demonstrates the real benefit of comparative work across jurisdictions: If a result is similar across very different populations or very different policy environments, this lends additional credence to the idea that the result is general. Likewise, we can learn a lot from studying how different are the outcomes in jurisdictions where the policy environment is very different from one another. In sum, some research is transferrable and we can learn a lot from work done in other countries, but other research is best conducted locally, suggesting a benefit to many countries developing, maintaining, and sharing with researchers their administrative data (Card et al., 2010a).

In summary, administrative data are more comprehensive than are purpose-built survey data, and can be collected with frequently far more accurate information. Furthermore, the costs of conducting research with administrative data are much lower as well, at least once the data systems are developed. Once data structures are established, linking and extracting more records from administrative data cost only the time of the programmer, and the marginal cost of adding additional individuals or periods of data to the analytical sample is extremely small, suggesting remarkably large economies of scale associated with administrative data (Roed and Raaum, 2003). While there are obviously many important roles for purpose-built survey data — not least the fact that only with purpose-built data it is possible to study precisely the questions that one wishes to study in exactly the manner in which one wishes to study them — it is also evident that administrative data offer numerous new opportunities to conduct research on questions that were previously impossible to study, or at least to study so well. Indeed, administrative data and survey data, while sometimes substitutes, can frequently be considered complements, as when administrative data can reduce the set of questions that need to be answered via surveys, or when administrative data can be used to serve as a check on the reliability of retrospective information collected via surveys (Roed and Raaum, 2003). Administrative data can also be thought of as complementary to the conduct of field experiments, as the costs of tracking and following up with field experiment participants are much lower, and the data frequently much better, when the field experiments can be linked with data collected by governments for administrative purposes (Card et al., 2010a). For all of these purposes, having a high degree of access to administrative data makes a wide range of empirical studies in education more feasible and more believable.

3. CASE STUDIES

The Nordic countries, notably Denmark, Sweden, Norway, Finland and to some extent Iceland, established administrative registers in the mid-1960s. When population-wide social security systems were established, there was a need for a unique personal identifier in order to follow people across jobs and other labor market states and collect information on earned pension points. These population-wide identifiers were then adopted for all administrative registers from birth registers to cause of death registers, and included in registers covering education and labor market participation, as well as for linking members of families together. The core of these registers is thus the universal system for identification numbers covering everybody from date of birth (or immigration) and identical across all administrative units. The identification number system was based on the 1960 census and for some of the countries also local (municipality level) registries of populations. This also implies then that people born several decades prior to 1960 are covered. And for instance, for Norway, a job has been done more recently to uncover time and place of birth, and for some registers and cohorts also parental background.

The Nordic countries have established mechanisms to share these data with members of the research community for specific research projects, and several research groups in each country have now access to portions of the register data linking some of these data sets depending on the focus of research.[1] In the case of each research project, both the administrative units who administer the data as well as the National Data Inspection Authority must consent to the use and matching of registers based on a detailed application procedure. Since the registers contain sensitive and very private information, the national statistical offices link the registers for research purposes and provide identification numbers for researchers that are different from the actual administrative identification numbers.

There are some common core data sets in all the Nordic countries such as family links, several education registers for test scores at different levels, completed education etc., and labor market outcomes and income. The countries do, however, differ to some degree when it comes to, for instance, availability and access to health data, vital statistics, etc. The Nordic countries also differ in terms of how far back in time data sets are linked and available for potential research use. Of course, being data collected for administrative purposes, when data are available to study the introduction of a given program or policy, it is generally by good fortune rather than prospective design, and it is also the case that many policy programs are unique to each country.

In this section we offer three case studies of some of the data potentially available to researchers in different jurisdictions, and how they have been used. Our case studies are two Nordic countries — Norway and Sweden — as well as the state of Florida. These are not intended to be complete overviews, but are rather examples of some representative uses of administrative registers. When appropriate, we also mention some complementary work conducted outside of the countries featured in the case studies.

3.1 Norway

Most of the research using register-based data sets in Norway has exploited the joint advantages of access to long panels of data combined with parental background and child outcomes along many dimensions, and the fact that population-wide data provides the opportunity of using policy reforms back in time for identifying causal effects. In education research, one example of this strategy is assessing the causal effect of parental education on children education exploiting a mandatory school reform for parents

---

[1] This overview focus on registers used for research with a focus on education in wide sense and a lot of register-based research using Norwegian data is not included. For instance, Roed and Raaum (2003) describe the collection of registers for one research group focusing mainly on labor market outcomes.

(Black et al., 2005a). In this paper, a parent cohort from the late 1940s to the late 1950s and their children are used to estimate the intergenerational transmission of education, using the panel structure of the data as well as the family links. In addition, a mandatory school reform rolled out across 700 municipalities in a period of 10 years for the parental generation, which is used to identify the causal effect of the educational transmission across generations. Due to the population-wide data set, the analysis could also be undertaken for different education subgroups, for instance, whether mothers or fathers or both were affected by the reform, and for different education levels.[2]

Family links for the whole population combined with the long-term panel structure following people from birth to adulthood have also been essential in the recent research using register data in Norway and the other Nordic countries. Examples of this line of research are Black et al. (2005b, 2007). Both these papers study family dynamics in the sense of the effect of family size and birth order, or child health on a set of long-term outcomes in education and the labor market. Both papers need to match long-term outcomes from a large set of registers measuring adult outcomes, such as several measures of education (years of education, completing high school, college attendance), as well as outcomes in the labor market including working and annual earnings. In Norway, a person register that links family members to one another by relationship facilitates the study of questions such as birth order effects by family size (Black et al., 2005b). Black et al. (2007) further use a register of twins, including monozygotic twins, to identify the effects child health on long-term outcomes. For child health birth weight was used which required merging in the Norwegian birth registry. Bharadwaj et al. (2013) use a very similar data set to assess the effect on test scores in school of medical treatment just after birth for just above or just below very low birth weights.

Early investment and long-term outcomes has been another important part of the agenda for Norwegian researchers using these data sets — especially using family policies for identification. One of the obvious advantages of using the Norwegian data register data is that since the data goes long back, many of the family policies and education policies which were part of the developing welfare state can be analyzed. A notable example of this approach is Havnes and Mogstad (2011) who study the long-run effects on children's education and labor market outcomes by exploiting the fact that a day care reform was rolled out across municipalities in the late 1970s and early 1980s. Similarly, Bettinger et al. (2014) investigate a program that increased parents' incentives to stay home with children under the age of 3. They assess the effect on older siblings' 10th grade GPA, and find support for a positive effect that seems to be driven by mother's reduced labor force participation. Another reform used for identifying the effect of even earlier investment in children on adult outcomes, is an extension of a maternity leave program that came into

---

[2] See Bjorklund and Salvanes (2011) for an overview of the international literature on the intergenerational mobility of education, also discussing other identification strategies.

force on July 1, 1977. This sharp cutoff in eligibility depending on the exact date of birth is well-suited for a regression discontinuity design approach (Carneiro et al., 2015), and here especially the value of large population-level data is on display, as one requires very large data sets in order to execute very data intensive nonparametric approaches. Interestingly, fairly strong effects on children's medium and long-term outcomes were found for staying longer home after birth with the mother. On the other hand, analyzing extensions of the maternity leave reform of up to 1 year fully covered leave, and using the same estimating strategy does not seem to give a positive effect on children's outcomes (Dahl et al., 2015). There clearly seem to be decreasing returns also to this input in the production function of children.

Several other strategies have been exploited to assess the effect of early investment, especially related to the effect of parental income, on in-school education outcomes, and a variety of long-run outcomes. Rege et al. (2011) evaluate the effect on children's test score in middle school using job loss from mass layoffs for identification. They find an asymmetry in the effect of father's and mother's job loss — a negative effect on grade point average in 9th grade for father's job loss and a positive effect of mothers. The authors interpret their results as not an effect of income but of distress form job loss which is strongly negative for men. Black et al. (2013) analyze the effect of child care subsidies on children's long-term education using a sharp discontinuity in the price of childcare in Norway. They find significant positive effect of the subsidies on children's middle school performance. This suggests a positive shock of disposable income on children's school performance. Carneiro et al. (2014) use very similar data to assess the effect of timing and possible dynamic complementarities of parents' income on children's short- and long-term outcomes both in completed years of education and performance in the labor market. The rich data provides an opportunity to use nonparametric methods, and supports findings that not only the discounted lifetime income but also timing matter, which supports the dynamic complementarities hypothesis.

Since the early 2000s grades in high school and middle school have been available as well as national tests for some years in primary school. The register of school grades combined with school resources and information on teachers have been exploited to answer a more traditional questions in the literature on the economics of education. Leuven and Roenning (2015) use grades in middle school to study the effect of class size on students' achievement exploiting a version of the Maimonides rule, while Haegeland et al. (2012) use the same pupil performance register, but a wider school resource measure and different identification strategy — a local hydro power plant tax. Both find small effects of resource use on children's school performance. Thanks to the population-wide register data comprising all pupils at a grade level, peer effects may be identified. Leuven and Roenning (2015) use the same performance register but add in detailed information on school grade mixing. They find positive effects on pupils mixed with older peers. Black et al. (2011) exploit this and assess the effect of the quality of peers using within school changes across years in the composition of pupils. Using data going longer back in time, they are able to assess the long-term peer effects. In another paper, Black et al. (2013) analyze the role of school starting age on cognitive outcomes such as IQ tests for boys at age 18, and for longer-run outcomes such as educational attainment, teenage pregnancy, and earnings. The important issue in this literature is to separate school starting age from test age. Exploiting variation in the mapping between year and month of birth and the year the military test is taken, allowed the analysis to distinguish the effects of school starting age from pure age effects. Findings provide evidence for a very small positive effect of starting school younger on IQ scores measured at age 18. In contrast, they find evidence of much larger positive effects of age at test, and these results are very robust.

Another well-studied area in the economics of education where long panels of register data may be helpful in making progress is in answering the seemingly simple question of what are the returns to education? Exploiting Norwegian population panel data with nearly career long earnings histories, a detailed picture of the causal relationship between schooling and earnings over the life cycle can be analyzed (Bhuller et al., 2015). These authors estimate internal rates of returns over lifetime earnings from age 17 to the mid-60s for many cohorts, and make use of a direct measure of lifetime earnings instead of approximating earnings using 1 year or an age groups, and thus, avoiding the problems of Mincer life-cycle bias. When doing so, they find evidence that the estimated returns to schooling are biased downward.

Administrative data have already been in use, in particular in the Scandinavian countries, for some years, and the enhanced knowledge from these studies have already informed policies and we are starting to see the fruits of these new insights in active policies. In Norway, the most striking example is a strong focus that politicians have recently put on preschool or early investment in children. As a part of a surge in the interest in early investment in children and children outcomes, the focus among researchers in Norway has been to exploit the possibility for assessing long-term outcomes in education and the labor market. Both the effect of maternity leave, a daycare roll out for preschool children as well as other programs increasing, for instance, parents' time use in preschool children, have painted quite a consistent picture of the importance of early investment for medium and long-term cognitive outcomes. These findings — together with the international evidence — have informed the public debate and later led to policy proving stronger incentives for more resource use in preschools in Norway, for instance. Different from the system in the United States, in the Scandinavian countries the way that this type of research may penetrate the public debate and also inform the ministries and politicians, is mainly through forming groups of academic "experts" in a particular area. The "experts" document the new insights from research in the area, and write a report to the Government. In this case a group of experts, including economists who do research on early investment using administrative data, drafted a review of the findings and also came up with concrete suggestions for how to improve both the coverage and quality of preschools in Norway (NOU 2010:8). Based on reports like this a white paper will be written to the Parliament with suggestion of a law change or suggestion for reallocation of money to preschools. There are also several other examples for Norway of how new research based on administrative data informs politicians and leads to law changes outside the area of education, for instance, from newly gained information on how the labor market functions.

3.2 Sweden

The Swedish data infrastructure is constructed in a very similar way to Norwegian data described in the section earlier. The data comes from local and national registers and is maintained by municipalities and Statistics Sweden. Each Swedish resident is assigned a unique and permanent identification number at the time of their birth and each immigrant is assigned a similar number if they immigrate to Sweden for more than 6 months.[3] These unique numbers are recorded in every administrative database, be it local or national, and allow merging different registers together. They are also used in surveys and experimental studies (Fredriksson et al., 2013; Golsteyn et al., 2014; Hinnerich et al., 2011; Jalava et al., 2015; Meghir and Palme, 2005).[4]

Historically Sweden conducted only population censuses at national level and maintained birth and death records at parish level. Similar to Norway, this changed in the 1960s when Statistics Sweden (SCB) started building their registry data. Today SCB maintains four core registers that together contain more than 50 different thematically focused subregisters. These four core data sets cover population (eg, employment or education registers), activity (eg, earnings or pupils registers), real estate (eg, prices or GIS registers), and business (eg, patent or schools registers). In addition to these SCB registers, the National Board of Health and Welfare maintains more than 70 registers with individual level medical diagnoses.[5] The registers are accessible to research community through SCB, various research institutes (eg, the Research Institute in Industrial Economics, IFN) or governmental agencies (eg, the Institute for Evaluation of Labour Market in Education Policy, IFAU). Access is granted on project-by-project basis and each application undergoes detailed investigation. Different registers are merged by SCB and researchers obtain data sets with a new unique, but randomly generated, individual identifiers.

---

[3] When the system was created in the 1960s all the living Swedes were also assigned unique identifiers retrospectively.

[4] Jalava et al. (2015) evaluate short-term effects of experimental intervention in Stockholm schools, and their subsequent research will merge in registry data to study longer-run outcomes.

[5] Similar data exist in a number of locations including Manitoba (Currie et al., 2010) and Denmark (Dalsgaard et al., 2014).

Due to security and data management reasons SCB maintains different educational databases under different "big registers," and hence for a given project these need to be merged with one another. For instance, Fredriksson et al. (2013) investigate the long-run effects of class size, and their baseline data set is actually a purpose-built longitudinal survey run by the Department of Education at Gothenburg University. However, since the subjects in this survey all have unique identification numbers it is possible to link them back to other administrative data sources. In particular, the authors add data on class size from class registers, parental information from multigenerational registers, medium-term achievement from compulsory school pupil registers and military draft registers, completed education from education registers, earnings from statement of earnings registers and wages from wages and staff for public and private sector registers. On the one hand, this decomposition illustrates the complexity of the data structure and emphasizes the crucial role of unique personal identifier. On the other hand, such a complex structure enhances the security of the very sensitive personal information and improves the management of the data.

The long panels and retrospective assignment of unique individual identifiers allow studying life-cycle and multigenerational effects also in the case of Sweden. Meghir and Palme (2005) study the effects of comprehensive schooling reform that among other elements increased the length of compulsory schooling, and was introduced in the late 1940s. They utilize survey data on two cohorts that are then linked to registry data which provide individual educational attainment and earnings. Meghir et al. (2012) utilize the same reform, richer data set and show that it not only reduces the criminal activity of the treated generation but also of their children. Even more data demanding endeavor is undertaken by Palme et al. (2015) where they combine Swedish registers and historical survey records to estimate the intergenerational persistence of human capital, measured by educational attainment, across four generations.

Both Norway and Sweden share two very unique and purpose-built data sets: military assessment and adoptions. The former one provides physical, cognitive, and noncognitive assessment of all males at the age of 18–19 (Lundborg et al., 2014).[6] The latter one contains all persons who were born in Sweden between 1962 and 1996 and adopted by both parents (Bjorklund et al., 2006; Holmlund et al., 2011).[7] Together with the ability to link these data to population registers they provide social scientists with extremely powerful analytical tool. There are also several other purpose-built survey data sets in Sweden. Fredriksson et al. (2013) use the Gothenburg University panel mentioned above containing cognitive test scores for 13-year-olds. Golsteyn et al. (2014) use the

---

[6] Since the mid-2000s, the draft is no longer mandatory in Sweden, so the data does not provide information on the whole population. The draft continues to be mandatory in Norway. Finland has also mandatory military draft (Kerr et al., 2013).

[7] The register is now expanded to cover more recent birth cohorts.

Stockholm Birth Cohort Study, which contains information on children's time preferences at age 13. In the paper, the authors link this survey to administrative data and conclude that adolescent time preferences predict outcomes up to five decades later in life.

Although Sweden, and likewise Norway and Denmark, seem like ideal places for empirical studies on the intersection of family, health, education, and labor markets, there are still many challenges in carrying out this research in reality. The two main obstacles in educational research are that authorities tend to be reluctant to allow the conduct of field experiments, as well as the lack of longitudinal assessment data. Scandinavia, including Sweden, lags far behind the United States in the implementation of the field experiments related to student incentives (Fryer, 2014), student support (Cook et al., 2014), teacher incentives (Imberman and Lovenheim, 2015), school choice (Deming et al., 2014), or school management (Fryer, 2014). Given the problems with tracking students over time in the United States, the Scandinavian administrative data infrastructure is ideal to study long-run consequences and potential positive and negative spillovers of policy interventions, and field experiments are current gold standard in policy evaluation.

That said, the Scandinavian countries do have a fair degree of assessment data of late. Sweden, similar to Denmark and Norway, introduced in recent years some form of longitudinal assessments in their compulsory schools. The longitudinal assessment data in Sweden began in 2009 and comprise of tests given in grades 3, 6 and 9. The assessment data in grades 3 and 6 have not been widely used in research thus far.[8] Before this reform Swedish students were only assessed at the age 16. These data on compulsory school exit exams are available since 1988, and have been often used, for example, by Almond et al. (2009) who study the effects of prenatal exposure to radioactive fallout on school outcomes. It is worth noting that unlike in the United States all tests in Scandinavian countries are low stakes and the Swedish Education Agency explicitly states that they " .. are not examination, but should be part of the teacher information about student's knowledge …." In fact, except for Stockholm and Malmo, these virtually do not matter for high school admissions as children are guaranteed a place in their closest high school (Karbownik, 2014).

Sweden and Denmark, unlike Norway, have also implemented a large-scale refugee placement policy in a nearly random way. The placement assignment could be seen as random conditional on observables because the individual could not choose their first place of residence and there was no direct interaction between a refugee and placement officers. This does not guarantee that immigrants were randomly assigned to neighborhoods, in fact they were not, but the placement selection was based on observable

---

[8] Raw scores are not kept by the authorities and for the early schooling test it is only the pass/fail indicator that is recorded in the registers. Although, from research perspective the more continuous score measure is very valuable this is a clear example where the research needs do not cross with the administrative needs, and indeed this data serves primarily administrative purposes for which a binary coding is sufficient.

attributes of immigrants and these are all available in administrative data. This policy has been extensively studied not only for its labor market consequences for immigrants themselves (Edin et al., 2003) but also for the educational consequences of their children (Aslund et al., 2011).[9]

Sweden is also the only one of the Scandinavian countries that introduced some form of charter schools. Unlike in the United States these have not been introduced with a random component and allow only for differences-in-differences type of identification. Sandstrom and Bergstrom (2005) study the effects of the reform, and the competition it induces, on quality of public schools. Bohlmark and Lindahl (2015) study its long-run consequences. Hensvik (2012) utilized the same reform to understand how competition affects teacher mobility and wages. Wikstrom and Wikstrom (2005) document that school competition leads to grade inflation, and that voucher schools inflate their students' grades more heavily. Sweden has also introduced two other market oriented educational reforms that have been evaluated by researchers. The first transferred the funding responsibilities from central government to local municipalities (Fredriksson and Ockert, 2008). The second allowed individual level wage bargaining between teachers and principals (Bohlmark et al., 2012). Yet another school choice reform was introduced in Stockholm in 2000, and changed the high school admission system from one largely based on place of residence to another entirely based on compulsory school performance, ie, change from zoning to open enrollment. Soderstrom and Uusitalo (2010) document that the reform lead to sharp changes in student composition in Stockholm schools, while Karbownik (2014) shows that these changes in student quality lead to changes in teacher labor supply.

3.3 Florida

Due to the decentralized nature of education in the United States, there exists no prospect of national educational data records, at least in the foreseeable future. However, a number of states and school districts have established systems in which students can be followed longitudinally and matched to schools and, in some cases, their teachers over time. The three states with the longest-standing state level student longitudinal data systems that have been widely available for researchers are Florida, North Carolina, and Texas.

Florida has maintained statewide records of student test scores that are longitudinally comparable (initially in grades 4, 5, 8, and 10, and soon thereafter expanded to grades 3

---

[9] The Danish study uses the placement policy to study the effects of early exposure to neighborhood crime on subsequent criminal behavior of the youth (Damm and Dustman, 2014). Nekby and Pettersson-Lidbom (2015) provide an in-depth discussion about the validity of the empirical strategy utilized in the Swedish context, and their results contradict findings in, for example, Dahlberg et al. (2012). The comparison of these studies highlights the need for broad access to registry data by the research community so that empirical findings could be replicated and reassessed by independent research teams.

through 10) since the 1997–98 school year within its Education Data Warehouse (EDW). The EDW also includes information on high school graduation, grade retention, student attendance, disciplinary infractions, school assignments, home language, immigrant status, disability, race/ethnicity, gender, school transcripts, and a measure of student poverty, along with other measures. Florida assigns a unique identification number that remains with the student no matter which school district he or she attends within the state. Since 2001–02, Florida has linked students with their teachers in each class — permitting the matching of staff databases that include teacher credentials to their students.

A large number of papers have made use of these student-level longitudinal data to study a wide range of research questions. For example, Chiang (2009), Figlio and Rouse (2006), Rouse et al. (2013), and West and Peterson (2006) identify the effects of changing school-level accountability pressure on student test performance in public schools, and Figlio and Lucas (2004b) investigate the degree to which school accountability policies affect student sorting across schools. Sass (2006) and Booker et al. (2011) study the effects of charter schools on test scores and later outcomes. Figlio and Hart (2014) measure the degree to which public schools respond to the competitive pressure associated with school voucher systems. Harris and Sass (2011) study the effects of a variety of teacher qualifications and in-service training on teachers' contributions to student achievement, while Chingos and West (2012) investigate the relationship between measured teacher value added and labor market returns when those teachers leave teaching. Winters and Greene (2012) study the effects of a test-based promotion policy. Schwerdt and West (2013) evaluate the role of grade configuration on student outcomes. Burke and Sass (2013) identify classroom peer effect relationships.

The Florida Department of Education, in conjunction with other state of Florida agencies, has successfully linked K-12 data with a variety of postsecondary data sources, including information on postsecondary education and training, employment and earnings records, military service and criminal justice records. These matched data sets, known as the Florida Education and Training Placement Information Program (FETPIP), have followed students in Florida beginning with the 1996–97 high school graduation cohort, so earnings data are now available for individuals as late as their early mid-careers. A number of important papers have been written that have linked FETPIP data to K-12 education records. For instance, Clark and Martorell (2014) compare labor market outcomes of students who barely passed high school graduation examinations to those who barely failed these examinations to identify the degree to which a high school diploma has signaling value in the labor market.[10] Other papers follow people from the education data sets into the labor market. In a particularly inventive use of these data, Chingos and West (2012) relate teachers to students' test scores to obtain measures of teacher "value added," and then observe whether teachers with higher measured value

[10] Clark and Martorell (2014) also make use of data from Texas to perform a parallel exercise in that state.

added command higher labor market earnings in the event in which they leave public school teaching. Both of these papers offer glimpses into the types of analyses that are possible when it is feasible to link education records — both those of students and those of teachers — to labor market records.

In recent years, it has become possible to track Florida students not just forward into the labor market but also backward to early childhood program participation and birth records. For a series of projects by Figlio, Roth and coauthors, the Florida Departments of Education and Health have matched the birth records of all children born in Florida between 1992 and 2002 to the school records observed by the Department of Education. To date, over 1.6 million children's administrative records have been matched between agencies for these research purposes.[11] These matched data have made it possible to study questions ranging from the educational consequences of poor neonatal health (Figlio et al., 2014) through the effects of early interventions for autism spectrum disorders on children's educational outcomes (Currie et al., 2014) to the spillover effects of having disabled siblings on children's cognitive development (Black et al., 2014c). The earliest of these birth cohorts are, at the time of writing, old enough to have graduated from high school, so soon it will be possible to follow children born in Florida through their K–12 schooling career and, thanks to the FETPIP data, into postsecondary education, the labor market, the military, and the criminal justice system.

These matched administrative data from Florida highlight some major benefits possible by virtue of the fact that they are drawn from population-level data. Consider, for instance, the three papers described in the preceding paragraph: None of these research projects could have been carried out without the benefit of population-level data because they each require large-scale data to study relatively rare events. Figlio et al. (2014) compare twin pairs with discordant birth weights; Currie et al. (2014) study children with autism spectrum disorders, accounting for fewer than 1% of the population; and Black et al. (2014c) identify the effects of disabled siblings by comparing the outcomes of first and second-born children in three-plus-sibling families. Traditional surveys that follow children and families longitudinally are not equipped to study rare occurrences such as these. With population-level data, many new research programs can be launched at a fraction of the cost of purpose-built survey-based databases, and still more research programs that were previously infeasible or impossible to undertake are now possible to carry out.

These Florida data provide some distinct advantages over data sets observed in other jurisdictions. The ability to follow students longitudinally, to observe frequent assessment

---

[11] These data sets are linked by name, date of birth, and social security number (a national identification number). This three-factor linkage allows for much more accurate matching of data across administrative data domains than would have occurred with fewer linking factors (eg, name and data of birth alone). See Figlio et al. (2014) for details.

data and other student outcomes, and to link students to teachers — attributes not found except for very recently in some European registry data — allows researchers to study certain questions in the United States that are difficult to study in many other jurisdictions. Now that it is possible to link school records to later labor market data, and backward to birth and early childhood records, Florida is developing some attributes of the registries found in northern European countries. On the other hand, linked data for Florida children are only available for relatively recently born children, and no information about parents, except that observed on a child's birth records, are currently linkable to children in Florida. In addition, given the fact that the United States is an open economy with high degrees of mobility across states, it is natural that there would be considerable attrition from even the most complete records. For instance, the birth records-school records linked data employed by Figlio et al. (2011) and others include only 81% of the children born in Florida between 1992 and 2002; the remaining children either left the state of Florida or enrolled in private schools and never were included in the public school records. While careful checks of other data sources make clear that virtually all of the children whom one would have expected to have been matched between these data sets were ultimately matched, this highlights the shortcomings of matched birth and school records in the United States context. Nonetheless, the data from Florida highlight some of the limitless possible population-level research programs that matched administrative data sets could facilitate in the United States and around the world.

As in the Scandinavian context, research using administrative data from Florida has led to substantial policy changes. Noteworthy examples include how school voucher policy in Florida (and in several other states in the United States) has been influenced by research documenting the effects of school vouchers on selection, participation, and competition; and how the state changed its compensation policies regarding the accumulation of teacher credentials (in particular, National Board Certification) once research identified the degree to which the attainment of this credential influenced — or failed to influence — teacher performance in the classroom. These examples, coupled with other cases both in Florida as well as around the country, such as how North Carolina maintained an early childhood enrichment program when presented with research evidence documenting its efficacy, or how Washington changed its teacher retention policies after research showed the relatively limited relationship between teacher experience and value added in the classroom, demonstrate the ways in which administrative data in education have not only led to scholarly advances but also are beginning to result in research-driven policy and practice changes.

4. CHALLENGES ASSOCIATED WITH THE USE OF ADMINISTRATIVE DATA

We have so far stressed the important advantages of administrative registers as compared to survey data — fewer issues with recall and other measurement problems; since its population-wide the data set is representative; less problems with attrition compared to surveys that follow the sampled populations over time; less problems with nonresponse; and the ability to study heterogeneous effects and rare and infrequent events. Combined with data for public policies in the past, many credible policy evaluations such as education policies and family policies as described above can be analyzed. Complete family links makes it possible to exploit other "experiments" for identification such as comparing siblings and twins as well as the use of adoptees. The long panel structure of administrative registers makes it possible to assess the effects of policy programs both for short- and long-terms outcomes across a large number of outcomes and across many administrative units.

However, there are certain limitations or restrictions related to the use of administrative register data, and we try to distinguish between three different aspects of restrictions as compared to surveys designed for particular research questions.

4.1 Limited Information/Less Flexibility Than With Purpose-Built Surveys

Administrative registers are collected for different reasons than research, and in particular in one area they have limitations as compared to purpose-built surveys. Very little information on cognitive skills other than achievement and attainment or social and behavioral skills are available in most register data. Variables that potentially are very important in understanding, for instance, school choices such as motivation and attitudes, and more general psychological traits, for instance, as measured by Big five components are not available. Some of these questions are available in some countries in military data for men, but usually only for a limited number of years.

This lack of important information on, for instance, reasons for education choices or effort is a challenge, but several new strategies are being used to mediate this limitation. Several research groups in the Nordic countries are now combining surveys with registers data, as well as lab experiments and randomized field experiments with register data.

One example connected to the economics of education undertaken is in Norway, where pupils just prior to the decision to attend high school, were surveyed on the "Big five" personality traits and on the information about the labor market (Almas et al., 2015). The idea in the project was to use incentivized lab experiments to tease out preferences for willingness to compete, risk taking, patience etc., together with an ability test, a survey regarding the "Big five," time use on homework etc., and a quite intensive survey on the students' knowledge of the labor market and the returns to education. Parents and students provided consent to follow these students through the education system and into the labor market, and to match to parental background from register data. Many research questions may be analyzed using this resource — for instance, to understand high drop-out rates better. This type of approach also facilitates field experiments in school, and then allows following pupils through the education system, into the labor market. Hence, the lack of information in the administrative data sets may be compensated in different ways.

4.2 Technical Issues With the Use of Administrative Registers

Depending on the country, issues of a more technical nature might be an obstacle in the use of administrative registers. One such obstacle is the ability to match administrative registers across administrative units. For instance, important research topics can be analyzed by connecting school outcomes to long-term outcomes such as income and completed education, or even outcomes such as fertility, crime, and marriage. In many countries, and notably the Nordic countries a common identification number is utilized across all administrative units and across all registers. Furthermore, even if the different administrative registers are collected and owned in principle by the different units, a law for statistical usage for research purposes enables researchers to use merged registers across administrative units. De-identified and merged data are made available through the national statistical offices. But in many countries a unique personal identification number either does not exist, or there are legal restrictions to merge across administrative units.[12] For example, in the United States only a few states have linked children's social security numbers, which are used for all labor market and benefits data, to their birth records, and in many states it is actually illegal to link social security numbers to education records. In cases like these, it becomes extremely difficult to link data across administrative data domains. While many states in the United States are making strong progress in linking education and workforce data, thanks to the leadership of the Data Quality Campaign, a national organization dedicated to promoting the development, implementation, and use of high-quality administrative education data sets, and other allied groups, this is a difficult and slow-going process.

Another issue is, of course, that it is hard to follow people moving to other countries since they may change citizenship, or even if people are studying and working abroad it is hard to follow them in terms of income or graduation. Hence, attrition of samples might be an issue. One will be able to identify which country they move to and the reason for moving, but not outcomes. This is of course a limitation, but the same limitation is shared by standard surveys. This issue is certainly compounded in countries like the United States where people move freely and often between states but individual states maintain their own birth records, health records, education records, and workforce data. In recent years, it has become possible in rare circumstances to match school records to tax data from the Internal Revenue Service in order to follow children living in one state to adult outcomes in another state (see, eg, Chetty et al., 2014a,b), and we are hopeful that more cases like that will occur in the future.

[12] Another legal restriction was in place, until recently, in Finland where the possibility of indirect identification of individuals in small groups prevented researchers from using registry data in full capacity.

Since the administrative data sets are not designed for research in the first place, they are not particularly well documented (with some exceptions). This also means that there is a big investment aspect of using these data sets as compared to more standard surveys — for instance, in the United States some of the surveys are publicly available and very well documented. The larger research groups in the Nordic countries using several matched registers have used the data sets over a long time and spent a considerable amount of resources in checking the data and understanding its structure, the content of the variables, and the changing definitions of these variables over time. Due to changes in tax laws for instance, also the definition of earnings provided in these data sets may change. These changes are not always easily available to outsiders of the administrative units collecting the data. And of course, it is always possible that the administrative data sets are incomplete or have other errors in them, because their purpose was never for research quality but rather for recording activities such as governmental program participation and compliance. As a consequence, these data may not have been subjected to the same type of quality assurance/quality control that is standard in the case of data sets collected specifically for research purposes.

4.3 Political Issues Related to Anonymity

An important issue with using administrative registers is that they cannot be made available publicly, due to security and confidentiality concerns. Given that unique personal identifiers exist, most countries with these data sets have developed secure systems for making them available to researchers or research groups. In the Nordic countries (with the exception of Finland where a slightly different system is in place), very similar system have been developed over time where the Statistical agencies play an important role in merging and de-identifying data for researchers, generally through research centers that have been through a quite extensive application procedure with data authorities, owners of data and the national statistical offices.

For all of the Nordic countries there are several research groups with access to the same or very overlapping collection of administrative data sets, and no research group has the "monopoly" to certain registers. The advantage is, of course, that research can be replicated by other researchers. This is true to an increasing degree in a number of other countries, such as the United Kingdom, Chile, the Netherlands, and numerous states in the United States, to name a few. Governments must balance the costs associated with potential security breaches against the very large benefits of making data available to a wide range of researchers, who have insights and expertise in a larger set of substantive research issues. It is imperative that researchers work diligently to ensure that they treat administrative data with care and maintain high degree of security so that justifiably worried stewards of administrative data can feel more confident that sharing data with scholars provides high benefits to citizens with extremely low risks of security breaches or other forms of negligent behavior.

5. THE USE OF ADMINISTRATIVE DATA AROUND THE WORLD

We begin this section by specifying different types of administrative data used in educational research. In Tables 1–4 we mostly focus on student or teacher registries; however, we also consider principals, preformal schooling children and other individuals for whom we observe administrative educational records. These tables are divided by whether the data sets are matched or unmatched to other records, and whether or not they are linked to surveys or experiments. Table 1 lists papers that use a single administrative data source; Table 2 lists papers that matches individuals across various administrative data sources; Table 3 lists papers that use a single administrative data source which is matched to either survey or experimental data; Table 4 lists papers that matches individuals both across various administrative data sources and to either survey or experiment. We group the papers by continent, country, region (state) and provide abbreviated bibliographic information.

Table 1 Survey of papers using administrative education data

(1)	(2)
Country/region	Authors, publication year, and title
Austria: Linz	Schneeweis and Zweimuller (2012) Girls, Girls, Girls: Gender Composition and Female School Choice
England	Machin et al. (2007) New Technology in Schools: Is There a Payoff?
England	Ray et al. (2009) Value Added in English Schools
England	Dustmann et al. (2010) Ethnicity and Educational Achievement in Compulsory Schooling
England	Holmlund et al. (2010) Does Money Matter for Schools?
England	Burgess and Briggs (2010) School Assignment, School Choice and Social Mobility
England	Gibbons and Silva (2011a) Faith Primary Schools: Better Schools or Better Pupils?
England	Gibbons and Telhaj (2011) Pupil Mobility and School Disruption
England	Keslair et al. (2012) Every Child Matters? An Evaluation of "Special Educational Needs" Programmes in England
England	Lavy et al. (2012) The Good, the Bad, and the Average: Evidence on Ability Peer Effects in Schools
England and Wales	Burgess et al. (2013) A Natural Experiment in School Accountability: The Impact of School Performance Information on Pupil Progress
England	Burgess and Greaves (2013) Test Scores, Subjective Assessment, and Stereotyping of Ethnic Minorities
England	Geay et al. (2013) Non-Native Speakers of English in the Classroom: What Are the Effects on Pupil Performance?
England	Gibbons et al. (2013) Everybody Needs Good Neighbours? Evidence from Students' Outcomes in England

Continued

Table 1 Survey of papers using administrative education data—cont'd

(1) Country/region	(2) Authors, publication year, and title
England	Allen and Burgess (2013) Evaluating the Provision of School Performance Information for School Choice
England	Almond et al. (2015) In Utero Ramadan Exposure and Children's Academic Performance
Finland	Hakkinen et al. (2003) School Resources and Student Achievement Revisited: New Evidence from Panel Data
Germany: Hesse	Muhlenweg and Puhani (2010) The Evolution of the School-Entry Age Effect in a School Tracking System
Italy	Barbieri et al. (2011) The Determinants of Teacher Mobility: Evidence Using Italian Teachers' Transfer Applications
Italy	Angrist et al. (2014) Is a Small Moment: Class Size and Moral Hazard in the Mezzogiorno
Israel: Jerusalem	Angrist and Lavy (2001) Does Teacher Training Affect Pupil Learning? Evidence from Matched Comparisons in Jerusalem Public Schools
Israel	Gould et al. (2004) Immigrating to Opportunity: Estimating the Effect of School Quality Using a Natural Experiment on Ethiopians in Israel
Israel	Lavy and Schlosser (2005) Targeted Remedial Education for Underperforming Teenagers: Costs and Benefits
Israel	Lavy (2008) Do Gender Stereotypes Reduce Girls' or Boys' Human Capital Outcomes? Evidence from a Natural Experiment
Israel	Gould et al. (2009) Does Immigration Affect the Long-Term Educational Outcomes of Natives? Quasi-Experimental Evidence
Israel	Lavy and Paserman (2012) Inside the Black Box of Ability Peer Effects: Evidence from Variation in the Proportion of Low Achievers in the Classroom
Israel	Cohen-Zada et al. (2013) Allocation of Students in Public Schools: Theory and New Evidence
Netherlands	Leuven et al. (2007) The Effect of Extra Funding for Disadvantaged Pupils on Achievement
Netherlands: Rotterdam	Heers et al. (2014) The Impact of Community Schools on Student Dropout in Pre-Vocational Education
Sweden	Waldo (2007) On the Use of Student Data in Efficiency Analysis—Technical Efficiency in Swedish Upper Secondary School
Canada: British Columbia	Bedard and Dhuey (2006) The Persistence of Early Childhood Maturity: International Evidence of Long-Run Age Effects
Canada: British Columbia	Smith (2010) How Valuable Is the Gift of Time? The Factors That Drive the Birth Date Effect in Education
Canada: British Columbia	Friesen et al. (2010) Disabled Peers and Academic Achievement
Canada: British Columbia	Coelli and Green (2012) Leadership Effects: School Principals and Student Outcomes

Table 1 Survey of papers using administrative education data—cont'd

(1)	(2)
Country/region	**Authors, publication year, and title**
Canada: British Columbia	DeCicca and Smith (2013) The Long-Run Impacts of Early Childhood Education: Evidence from a Failed Policy Experiment
Canada: Ontario	Card et al. (2010b) School Competition and Efficiency with Publicly Funded Catholic Schools
Canada: Ontario	Leach et al. (2010) The Effects of School Board Consolidation and Financing on Student Performance
Trinidad and Tobago	Jackson (2010) Do Students Benefit from Attending Better Schools? Evidence from Rule-Based Student Assignments in Trinidad and Tobago
Trinidad and Tobago	Jackson (2012a) Single-Sex Schools, Student Achievement, and Course Selection: Evidence from Rule-Based Student Assignments in Trinidad and Tobago
Trinidad and Tobago	Jackson (2013a) Can Higher-Achieving Peers Explain the Benefits to Attending Selective Schools? Evidence from Trinidad and Tobago
USA: Alaska	Tuck et al. (2009) Local Amenities, Unobserved Quality, and Market Clearing: Adjusting Teacher Compensation to Provide Equal Education Opportunities
USA: California	Clark et al. (2009) Selection Bias in College Admissions Test Scores
USA: California (San Diego)	Koedel (2009) An Empirical Analysis of Teacher Spillover Effects in Secondary School
USA: California	Jepsen (2010) Bilingual Education and English Proficiency
USA: California (San Diego)	Koedel and Betts (2010) Value Added to What? How a Ceiling in the Testing Instrument Influences Value-Added Estimation
USA: California (San Diego)	Koedel and Betts (2011) Does Student Sorting Invalidate Value-Added Models of Teacher Effectiveness? An Extended Analysis of the Rothstein Critique
USA: California (San Diego)	Zimmer et al. (2012) Examining Charter Student Achievement Effects across Seven States
USA: Colorado	Briggs and Weeks (2009) The Sensitivity of Value-Added Modeling to the Creation of a Vertical Score Scale
USA: Colorado (Denver)	Goldhaber and Walch (2012) Strategic Pay Reform: A Student Outcomes-Based Evaluation of Denver's Procomp Teacher Pay Initiative
USA: Colorado (Denver)	Zimmer et al. (2012) Examining Charter Student Achievement Effects across Seven States
USA: District Columbia	Curto and Fryer (2014) The Potential of Urban Boarding Schools for the Poor: Evidence from SEED
USA: Florida	Figlio and Lucas (2004b) What's in a Grade? School Report Cards and the Housing Market
USA: Florida	Tyler et al. (2004) The Devil's in the Details: Evidence from the GED on Large Effects of Small Differences in High Stakes Exams

Continued

Table 1 Survey of papers using administrative education data—cont'd

(1) Country/region	(2) Authors, publication year, and title
USA: Florida	West and Peterson (2006) The Efficacy of Choice Threats within School Accountability Systems: Results from Legislatively Induced Experiments
USA: Florida	Figlio and Rouse (2006) Do Accountability and Voucher Threats Improve Low-Performing Schools?
USA: Florida	Sass (2006) Charter Schools and Student Achievement in Florida
USA: Florida	Greene and Winters (2007) Revisiting Grade Retention: An Evaluation of Florida's Test-Based Promotion Policy
USA: Florida	McCaffrey et al. (2009) The Intertemporal Variability of Teacher Effect Estimates
USA: Florida	Greene and Winters (2009) The Effects of Exemptions to Florida's Test-Based Promotion Policy: Who Is Retained? Who Benefits Academically?
USA: Florida	Chiang (2009) How Accountability Pressure on Failing Schools Affects Student Achievement
USA: Florida	Winters et al. (2010) The Impact of High-Stakes Testing on Student Proficiency in Low-Stakes Subjects: Evidence from Florida's Elementary Science Exam
USA: Florida	Feng (2010) Hire Today, Gone Tomorrow: New Teacher Classroom Assignments and Teacher Mobility
USA: Florida	Harris and Sass (2011) Teacher Training, Teacher Quality and Student Achievement
USA: Florida	Booker et al. (2011) The Effects of Charter High Schools on Educational Attainment
USA: Florida	Chingos and Peterson (2011) It's Easier to Pick a Good Teacher Than to Train One: Familiar and New Results on the Correlates of Teacher Effectiveness
USA: Florida	Chingos (2012) The Impact of a Universal Class-Size Reduction Policy: Evidence from Florida's Statewide Mandate
USA: Florida	Winters et al. (2012) Observed Characteristics and Teacher Quality: Impacts of Sample Selection on a Value Added Model
USA: Florida	Winters and Greene (2012) The Medium-Run Effects of Florida's Test-Based Promotion Policy
USA: Florida	Weiss and May (2012) A Policy Analysis of the Federal Growth Model Pilot Program's Measures of School Performance: The Florida Case
USA: Florida	Schwerdt and West (2013) The Impact of Alternative Grade Configurations on Student Outcomes through Middle and High School
USA: Florida	Mihaly et al. (2013) Where You Come from or Where You Go? Distinguishing Between School Quality and the Effectiveness of Teacher Preparation Program Graduates
USA: Florida	Feng and Sass (2013) What Makes Special-Education Teachers Special? Teacher Training and Achievement of Students with Disabilities

Table 1 Survey of papers using administrative education data—cont'd

(1) Country/region	(2) Authors, publication year, and title
USA: Florida	Winters et al. (2013) The Effect of Same-Gender Teacher Assignment on Student Achievement in the Elementary and Secondary Grades: Evidence from Panel Data
USA: Florida	Burke and Sass (2013) Classroom Peer Effects and Student Achievement
USA: Florida	Cowen and Winter (2013) Do Charters Retain Teachers Differently? Evidence from Elementary Schools in Florida
USA: Florida	Figlio and Hart (2014) Competitive Effects of Means-Tested School Vouchers
USA: Florida	Sass et al. (2014) Value-Added Models and the Measurement of Teacher Productivity
USA: Florida (Miami-Dade)	Taylor (2014) Spending More of the School Day in Math Class: Evidence from a Regression Discontinuity in Middle School
USA: Florida (Miami-Dade)	Loeb et al. (2012) Effective Schools: Teacher Hiring, Assignment, Development, and Retention
USA: Florida (unnamed)	Figlio (2006) Testing, crime and punishment
USA: Illinois	Fitzpatrick and Lovenheim (2014) Early Retirement Incentives and Student Achievement
USA: Illinois	Gates et al. (2006) Mobility and Turnover Among School Principals
USA: Illinois (Chicago)	Cullen et al. (2006) The Effect of School Choice on Participants: Evidence from Randomized Lotteries
USA: Illinois (Chicago)	Jacob and Levitt (2003) Rotten Apples: An Investigation of the Prevalence and Predictors of Teacher Cheating
USA: Illinois (Chicago)	Neal and Schanzenbach (2010) Left Behind by Design: Proficiency Counts and Test-Based Accountability
USA: Illinois (Chicago)	Jacob and Lefgren (2004b) Remedial Education and Student Achievement: A Regression-Discontinuity Analysis
USA: Illinois (Chicago)	Jacob and Lefgren (2004a) The Impact of Teacher Training on Student Achievement: Quasi-Experimental Evidence from School Reform Efforts in Chicago
USA: Illinois (Chicago)	Booker et al. (2011) The Effects of Charter High Schools on Educational Attainment
USA: Illinois (Chicago)	Jacob (2013) The Effect of Employment Protection on Teacher Effort
USA: Illinois (Chicago)	Aaronson et al. (2007) Teachers and Student Achievement in the Chicago Public High Schools
USA: Illinois (Chicago)	Jacob and Lefgren (2009) The Effect of Grade Retention on High School Completion
USA: Illinois (Chicago)	Jacob (2005) Accountability, Incentives and Behavior: The Impact of High-Stakes Testing in the Chicago Public Schools
USA: Illinois (Chicago)	Cullen et al. (2005) The Impact of School Choice on Student Outcomes: An Analysis of the Chicago Public Schools

Continued

Table 1 Survey of papers using administrative education data—cont'd

(1) Country/region	(2) Authors, publication year, and title
USA: Illinois (Chicago)	Steinberg (2014) Does Greater Autonomy Improve School Performance? Evidence from a Regression Discontinuity Analysis in Chicago
USA: Illinois (Chicago)	Cortes et al. (2013) Educating Bright Students in Urban Schools
USA: Illinois (Chicago)	Jacob and Walsh (2011) What's in a Rating?
USA: Illinois (Chicago)	Robertson (2011) The Effects of Quarter of Birth on Academic Outcomes at the Elementary School Level
USA: Illinois (Chicago)	Cortes et al. (2014) Intensive Math Instruction and Educational Attainment: Long-Run Impacts of Double-Dose Algebra
USA: Kentucky	Streams et al. (2011) School Finance Reform: Do Equalized Expenditures Imply Equalized Teacher Salaries?
USA: Kentucky	Barrett and Toma (2013) Reward or Punishment? Class Size and Teacher Quality
USA: Kentucky	Cowen et al. (2012) Teacher Retention in Appalachian Schools: Evidence from Kentucky
USA: Kentucky	Kukla-Acevedo (2009) Do Teacher Characteristics Matter? New Results on the Effects of Teacher Preparation on Student Achievement
USA: Louisiana	Imberman et al. (2012) Katrina's Children: Evidence on the Structure of Peer Effects from Hurricane Evacuees
USA: Louisiana	Sacerdote (2012) When the Saints Go Marching Out: Long-Term Outcomes for Student Evacuees from Hurricanes Katrina and Rita
USA: Massachusetts	Goodman (2008) Who Merits Financial Aid? Massachusetts' Adams Scholarship
USA: Massachusetts	Goodman (2010) Skills, Schools, and Credit Constraints: Evidence from Massachusetts
USA: Massachusetts	Goodman (2014) Flaking Out: Student Absences and Snow Days as Disruptions of Instructional Time
USA: Massachusetts (Boston)	Abdulkadiroglu et al. (2009) Strategy-Proofness Versus Efficiency in Matching with Indifferences: Redesigning the NYC High School Match
USA: Massachusetts (Brookline)	Angrist and Lang (2004) Does School Integration Generate Peer Effects? Evidence from Boston's Metco Program
USA: Massachusetts (Boston)	Abdulkadiroglu et al. (2014) The Elite Illusion: Achievement Effects at Boston and New York Exam Schools
USA: Massachusetts (Boston)	Abdulkadiroglu et al. (2011) Accountability and Flexibility in Public Schools: Evidence from Boston's Charters and Pilots
USA: Massachusetts (Boston)	Pathak and Shi (2014) Demand Modeling, Forecasting, and Counterfactuals, Part I
USA: Michigan	Gershenson (2012) How Do Substitute Teachers Substitute? An Empirical Study of Substitute-Teacher Labor Supply

Table 1 Survey of papers using administrative education data—cont'd

(1) Country/region	(2) Authors, publication year, and title
USA: Michigan	Andrews et al. (2010) The Effects of the Kalamazoo Promise on College Choice
USA: Michigan	Brummet (2014) The Effects of School Closings on Student Achievement
USA: Minnesota (Twin Cities)	Hinrichs (2011) When the Bell Tolls: The Effects of School Starting Times on Academic Achievement
USA: Missouri	Ransom and Sims (2010) Estimating the Firm's Labor Supply Curve in a "New Monopsony" Framework: Schoolteachers in Missouri
USA: Missouri	Koedel et al. (2014) Who Benefits from Pension Enhancements?
USA: Missouri	Costrell and Podgursky (2010) Distribution of Benefits in Teacher Retirement Systems and Their Implications for Mobility
USA: North Carolina	Rothstein (2010) Teacher Quality in Educational Production: Tracking, Decay, and Student Achievement
USA: North Carolina	Jackson (2013b) Worker Productivity, and Worker Mobility: Direct Evidence from Teachers
USA: North Carolina	Fruehwirth (2014) Can Achievement Peer Effect Estimates Inform Policy? A View from Inside the Black Box
USA: North Carolina	Clotfelter et al. (2009a) The Academic Achievement Gap in Grades 3 to 8
USA: North Carolina	Kinsler (2012) Beyond Levels and Growth: Estimating Teacher Value-Added and its Persistence
USA: North Carolina	Goldhaber (2007) Everyone's Doing It, But What Does Teacher Testing Tell Us About Teacher Effectiveness?
USA: North Carolina	Clotfelter et al. (2009b) Teacher Credentials and Student Achievement in High School: A Cross-Subject Analysis with Student Fixed Effects
USA: North Carolina	Jacob et al. (2010) The Persistence of Teacher-Induced Learning
USA: North Carolina	Clotfelter et al. (2006) Teacher-Student Matching and the Assessment of Teacher Effectiveness
USA: North Carolina	Murnane and Olsen (1990) The Effects of Salaries and Opportunity Costs on Length of Stay in Teaching: Evidence from North Carolina
USA: North Carolina	Jackson (2009) Student Demographics, Teacher Sorting, and Teacher Quality: Evidence from the End of School Desegregation
USA: North Carolina	Jackson and Bruegmann (2009) Teaching Students and Teaching Each Other: The Importance of Peer Learning for Teachers
USA: North Carolina	Ost (2014) How Do Teachers Improve? The Relative Importance of Specific and General Human Capital
USA: North Carolina	Jackson (2012b) School Competition and Teacher Labor Markets: Evidence from Charter School Entry in North Carolina
USA: North Carolina	Wiswall (2013) The Dynamics of Teacher Quality

Continued

Table 1 Survey of papers using administrative education data—cont'd

(1) Country/region	(2) Authors, publication year, and title
USA: North Carolina	Clotfelter et al. (2008) Would Higher Salaries Keep Teachers in High-Poverty Schools? Evidence from a Policy Intervention in North Carolina
USA: North Carolina	Henry et al. (2014) Teacher Preparation Policies and Their Effects on Student Achievement
USA: North Carolina	Fuller and Ladd (2013) School-Based Accountability and the Distribution of Teacher Quality across Grades in Elementary School
USA: North Carolina	Carruthers (2012a) The Qualifications and Classroom Performance of Teachers Moving to Charter Schools
USA: North Carolina	Clotfelter et al. (2011) Teacher Mobility, School Segregation, and Pay-Based Policies to Level the Playing Field
USA: North Carolina	Player (2010) Nonmonetary Compensation in the Public Teacher Labor Market
USA: North Carolina	Bifulco and Ladd (2006) The Impacts of Charter Schools on Student Achievement: Evidence from North Carolina
USA: North Carolina	Rothstein (2009) Student Sorting and Bias in Value-Added Estimation: Selection on Observables and Unobservables
USA: North Carolina	Clotfelter et al. (2009c) Are Teacher Absences Worth Worrying About in the United States?
USA: North Carolina	Condie et al. (2014) Teacher Heterogeneity, Value-Added and Education Policy
USA: North Carolina	Ahn (2014) A Regression Discontinuity Analysis of Graduation Standards and Their Impact on Students' Academic Trajectories
USA: North Carolina	Miller (2013) Principal Turnover and Student Achievement
USA: North Carolina	Strain (2013) Single-Sex Classes & Student Outcomes: Evidence from North Carolina
USA: North Carolina	Goldhaber et al. (2013a) Is a Good Elementary Teacher Always Good? Assessing Teacher Performance Estimates across Subjects
USA: North Carolina	Cratty (2012) Potential for Significant Reductions in Dropout Rates: Analysis of an Entire 3rd Grade State Cohort
USA: North Carolina	Miller and Mittleman (2012) High Schools That Work and College Preparedness: Measuring the Model's Impact on Mathematics and Science Pipeline Progression
USA: North Carolina	Carruthers (2012b) New Schools, New Students, New Teachers: Evaluating the Effectiveness of Charter Schools
USA: North Carolina	Kinsler (2011) Understanding the Black–White School Discipline Gap
USA: North Carolina	Guardiano et al. (2011) Can Districts Keep Good Teachers in the Schools That Need Them Most?
USA: North Carolina	Clotfelter et al. (2007) Teacher Credentials and Student Achievement: Longitudinal Analysis with Student Fixed Effects
USA: North Carolina	Gates et al. (2006) Mobility and Turnover Among School Principals

Table 1 Survey of papers using administrative education data—cont'd

(1)	(2)
Country/region	**Authors, publication year, and title**
USA: North Carolina	Clotfelter et al. (2005) Who Teaches Whom? Race and the Distribution of Novice Teachers
USA: North Carolina	Ladd and Walsh (2002) Implementing Value-Added Measures of School Effectiveness: Getting the Incentives Right
USA: North Carolina	Jackson (2014) Teacher Quality at the High-School Level: The Importance of Accounting for Tracks
USA: North Carolina	Mansfield (2014) Teacher Quality and Student Inequality
USA: North Carolina	Ahn and Vigdor (2014) When Incentives Matter Too Much: Explaining Significant Responses to Irrelevant Information
USA: North Carolina	Macartney (2014) The Dynamic Effects of Educational Accountability
USA: North Carolina (Charlotte-Mecklenburg)	Deming (2014) Using School Choice Lotteries to Test Measures of School Effectiveness
USA: North Carolina (Wake)	Edwards (2012) Early to Rise? The Effect of Daily Start Times on Academic Performance
USA: North Carolina (Wake)	McMullen and Rouse (2012b) School Crowding, Year-Round Schooling, and Mobile Classroom Use: Evidence from North Carolina
USA: North Carolina (Wake)	McMullen and Rouse (2012a) The Impact of Year-Round Schooling on Academic Achievement: Evidence from Mandatory School Calendar Conversions
USA: North Carolina (Wayne)	Bastian et al. (2013) Incorporating Access to More Effective Teachers into Assessments of Educational Resource Equity
USA: New Jersey	Ou (2010) To Leave or Not to Leave? A Regression Discontinuity Analysis of the Impact of Failing the High School Exit Exam
USA: New York	Boyd et al. (2013) Analyzing the Determinants of the Matching of Public School Teachers to Jobs: Disentangling the Preferences of Teachers and Employers
USA: New York	Brewer (1996) Career Paths and Quit Decisions: Evidence from Teaching
USA: New York	Lankford and Wyckoff (1997) The Changing Structure of Teacher Compensation, 1970–94
USA: New York (New York City)	Abdulkadiroglu et al. (2009) Strategy-Proofness Versus Efficiency in Matching with Indifferences: Redesigning the NYC High School Match
USA: New York (New York City)	Abdulkadiroglu et al. (2009) The Elite Illusion: Achievement Effects at Boston and New York Exam Schools
USA: New York (New York City)	Schwartz et al. (2004) The Impact of School Reform on Student Performance: Evidence from the New York Network for School Renewal Project
USA: New York (New York City)	Hermann and Rockoff (2012) Worker Absence and Productivity: Evidence from Teaching

Continued

Table 1 Survey of papers using administrative education data—cont'd

(1) Country/region	(2) Authors, publication year, and title
USA: New York (New York City)	Rockoff and Lockwood (2010) Stuck in the Middle: Impacts of Grade Configuration in Public Schools
USA: New York (New York City)	Zabel (2008) The Impact of Peer Effects on Student Outcomes in New York City Public Schools
USA: New York (New York City)	Schwartz and Stiefel (2006) Is There a Nativity Gap? New Evidence on the Academic Performance of Immigrant Students
USA: New York (New York City)	Rubenstein et al. (2009) Spending, Size, and Grade Span in K-8 Schools
USA: New York (New York City)	Wiswall et al. (2014) Does Attending a STEM High School Improve Student Performance? Evidence from New York City
USA: New York (New York City)	Leos-Urbel et al. (2013) Not Just for Poor Kids: The Impact of Universal Free School Breakfast on Meal Participation and Student Outcomes
USA: New York (New York City)	Winters (2012) Measuring the Effect of Charter Schools on Public School Student Achievement in an Urban Environment: Evidence from New York City
USA: New York (New York City)	Kane et al. (2008) What Does Certification Tell Us About Teacher Effectiveness? Evidence from New York City
USA: Ohio	Zimmer et al. (2014) Charter School Authorizers and Student Achievement
USA: Ohio	Zimmer et al. (2012) Examining Charter Student Achievement Effects across Seven States
USA: Ohio (Cincinnati)	Taylor and Tyler (2012) The Effect of Evaluation on Teacher Performance
USA: Ohio (Cincinnati)	Kane et al. (2011) Identifying Effective Classroom Practices Using Student Achievement Data
USA: Pennsylvania	Ferguson et al. (2006) The Effects of Defined Benefit Pension Incentives and Working Conditions on Teacher Retirement Decisions
USA: Pennsylvania (Philadelphia)	Zimmer et al. (2012) Examining Charter Student Achievement Effects across Seven States
USA: Texas	Cullen et al. (2013) Jockeying for Position: Strategic High School Choice under Texas' Top Ten Percent Plan
USA: Texas	Reback (2008) Teaching to the Rating: School Accountability and the Distribution of Student Achievement
USA: Texas	Booker et al. (2007) The Impact of Charter School Attendance on Student Performance
USA: Texas	Hanushek et al. (2007) Charter School Quality and Parental Decision Making with School Choice
USA: Texas	Hanushek et al. (2004b) Disruption Versus Tiebout Improvement: The Costs and Benefits of Switching Schools
USA: Texas	Clark et al. (2009) Selection Bias in College Admissions Test Scores
USA: Texas	Hanushek et al. (2004a) Why Public Schools Lose Teachers

Table 1 Survey of papers using administrative education data—cont'd

(1) Country/region	(2) Authors, publication year, and title
USA: Texas	Hendricks (2014) Does It Pay to Pay Teachers More? Evidence from Texas
USA: Texas	Rivkin et al. (2005) Teachers, Schools, and Academic Achievement
USA: Texas	Currie et al. (2009) Does Pollution Increase School Absences?
USA: Texas	Hanushek et al. (2002) Inferring Program Effects for Special Populations: Does Special Education Raise Achievement for Students With Disabilities?
USA: Texas	Sanders (2012) What Doesn't Kill You Makes You Weaker. Prenatal Pollution Exposure and educational Outcomes
USA: Texas	Hanushek et al. (2009) New Evidence about Brown v. Board of Education: The Complex Effects of School Racial Composition on Achievement
USA: Texas	Zimmer et al. (2012) Examining Charter Student Achievement Effects across Seven States
USA: Texas	Tyler and Lofstrom (2010) Is the GED an Effective Route to Postsecondary Education for School Dropouts?
USA: Texas	Tyler et al. (2004) The Devil's in the Details: Evidence from the GED on Large Effects of Small Differences in High Stakes Exams
USA: Texas	Klopfenstein (2004) Advanced Placement: Do Minorities Have Equal Opportunity?
USA: Texas (Houston)	Imberman and Lovenheim (2015) Incentive Strength and Teacher Productivity: Evidence from a Group-Based Teacher Incentive Pay System
USA: Texas (Houston)	Imberman et al. (2012) Katrina's Children: Evidence on the Structure of Peer Effects from Hurricane Evacuees
USA: Utah	Ni and Rorrer (2012) Twice Considered: Charter Schools and Student Achievement in Utah
USA: Washington	Gritz and Theobald (1996) The Effects of School District Spending Priorities on Length of Stay in Teaching
USA: Washington	Goldhaber and Theobald (2013) Managing the Teacher Workforce in Austere Times: The Determinants and Implications of Teacher Layoffs
USA: Washington	Krieg (2008) Are Students Left Behind? The Distributional Effects of the No Child Left Behind Act
USA: Washington	Goldhaber et al. (2013b) The Gateway to the Profession: Assessing Teacher Preparation Programs Based on Student Achievement
USA: Washington	Krieg (2011) Which Students Are Left Behind? The Racial Impacts of the No Child Left Behind Act
USA: Washington	Krieg (2006) Teacher Quality and Attrition
USA: Washington	Theobald and Gritz (1996) The Effects of School District Spending Priorities on the Exit Paths of Beginning Teachers Leaving the District
USA: Washington	Theobald (1990) An Examination of the Influence of Personal, Professional, and School District Characteristics on Public School Teacher Retention

Continued

Table 1 Survey of papers using administrative education data—cont'd

(1) Country/region	(2) Authors, publication year, and title
USA: Wisconsin	Imazeki (2005) Teacher Salaries and Teacher Attrition
USA: Wisconsin (Milwaukee)	Zimmer et al. (2012) Examining Charter Student Achievement Effects across Seven States
USA: unnamed	Springer (2008) The Influence of an NCLB Accountability Plan on the Distribution of Student Test Score Gains
USA: unnamed	Matsudaira et al. (2012) An Integrated Assessment of the Effects of Title I on School Behavior, Resources, and Student Achievement
USA: unnamed	Imberman (2011b) The Effect of Charter Schools on Achievement and Behavior of Public School Students
USA: unnamed	Bui et al. (2014) Is Gifted Education a Bright Idea? Assessing the Impact of Gifted and Talented Programs on Students
USA: unnamed	Lockwood and McCaffrey (2009) Exploring Student-Teacher Interactions in Longitudinal Achievement Data
USA: unnamed	Engberg et al. (2014) Evaluating Education Programs That Have Lotteried Admission and Selective Attrition
USA: unnamed	Imberman (2011a) Achievement and Behavior in Charter Schools: Drawing a More Complete Picture
USA	Belfield and Levin (2004) Should High School Economics Courses Be Compulsory?
Chile	Urquiola and Verhoogen (2009) Class-Size Caps, Sorting, and the Regression-Discontinuity Design
Chile	Mizala and Roumaguera (2000) School Performance and Choice: The Chilean Experience
Chile	Thieme et al. (2013) A Multilevel Decomposition of School Performance Using Robust Nonparametric Frontier Techniques
Chile	Bellei (2009) Does Lengthening the School Day Increase Students' Academic Achievement? Results from a Natural Experiment in Chile
Peru	Dell (2010) The Persistent Effects of Peru's Mining Mita
China: Beijing	Lai (2010) Are Boys Left Behind? The Evolution of the Gender Achievement Gap in Beijing's Middle Schools
Kenya	Lucas and Mbiti (2014) Effects of School Quality on Student Achievement: Discontinuity Evidence from Kenya
Australia: Queensland	Leigh (2010) Estimating Teacher Effectiveness from Two-Year Changes in Students' Test Scores

Unmatched administrative source studies.

Note: This table lists studies which make use of unmatched administrative data, and that have been published or announced as forthcoming between January 1990 and July 2014 in the following outlets: *American Economic Journal: Applied Economics*, *American Economic Journal: Economic Policy*, *American Economic Review*, *Econometrica*, *Economic Journal*, *Economics of Education Review*, *Education Finance and Policy*, *Journal of Human Resources*, *Journal of Labor Economics*, *Journal of Political Economy*, *Journal of Public Economics*, *Quarterly Journal of Economics*, *Review of Economic Studies*, *Review of Economics and Statistics* and NBER Working Papers: Education Program. All the papers in the table used at least one administrative data set in the analysis and these data were not matched across registers or to other external data sources.

Table 2 Survey of papers using administrative education data

(1) Country/region	(2) Authors, publication year, and title
Denmark	Heinesen (2010) Estimating Class-Size Effects using Within-School Variation in Subject-Specific Classes
Denmark	Damm and Dustman (2014) Does Growing Up in a High Crime Neighborhood Affect Youth Criminal Behavior?
Finland	Kerr et al. (2013) School Tracking and Development of Cognitive Skills
Germany: Hesse, Bayern, Schleswig-Holstein	Dustmann and Schonberg (2012) Expansions in Maternity Leave Coverage and Children's Long-Term Outcomes
Norway	Falch and Strom (2005) Teacher Turnover and Non-Pecuniary Factors
Norway	Black et al. (2005b) The More the Merrier? The Effect of Family Size and Birth Order on Children's Education
Norway	Black et al. (2005a) Why the Apple Doesn't Fall Far: Understanding Intergenerational Transmission of Human Capital
Norway	Black et al. (2007) From the Cradle to the Labor Market? The Effect of Birth Weight on Adult Outcomes
Norway	Black et al. (2010) Small Family, Smart Family? Family Size and the IQ Scores of Young Men
Norway	Rege et al. (2011) Parental Job Loss and Children's School Performance
Norway	Black et al. (2011) Too Young to Leave the Nest? The Effects of School Starting
Norway	Havnes and Mogstad (2011) No Child Left Behind: Subsidized Child Care and Children's Long-Run Outcomes
Norway	Haegeland et al. (2012) Pennies from Heaven? Using Exogenous Tax Variation to Identify Effects of School Resources on Pupil Achievement
Norway	Loken et al. (2012) What Linear Estimators Miss: The Effects of Family Income on Child Outcomes
Norway	Falch and Naper (2013) Educational Evaluation Schemes and Gender Gaps in Student Achievement
Norway	Bharadwaj et al. (2013) Early Life Health Interventions and Academic Achievement
Norway	Black et al. (2013) Under Pressure? The Effect of Peers on Outcomes of Young Adults
Norway	Bettinger et al. (2014) Home with Mom: The Effects of Stay-at-Home Parents on Children's Long-Run Educational Outcomes
Norway	Black et al. (2014b) Does Grief Transfer Across Generations? In-Utero Deaths and Child Outcomes
Norway	Black et al. (2014a) Care or Cash? The Effect of Child Care Subsidies on Student Performance
Norway	Havens and Mogstad (2014) Is Universal Child Care Leveling the Playing Field
Sweden	Wikstrom and Wikstrom (2005) Grade Inflation and School Competition: An Empirical Analysis Based on the Swedish Upper Secondary Schools

Continued

Table 2 Survey of papers using administrative education data—cont'd

(1) Country/region	(2) Authors, publication year, and title
Sweden	Sandstrom and Bergstrom (2005) School Vouchers in Practice: Competition Will Not Hurt You
Sweden	Bjorklund et al. (2006) The Origins of Intergenerational Associations: Lessons from Swedish Adoption Data
Sweden	Almond et al. (2009) Chernobyl's Subclinical Legacy: Prenatal Exposure to Radioactive Fallout and School Outcomes in Sweden
Sweden: Stockholm	Sund (2009) Estimating Peer Effects in Swedish High School Using School, Teacher, and Student Fixed Effects
Sweden	Andersson et al. (2011) Do You Want Your Child to Have a Certified Teacher?
Sweden	Aslund et al. (2011) Peers, Neighborhoods, and Immigrant Student Achievement: Evidence from a Placement Policy
Sweden	Hall (2012) The Effects of Reducing Tracking in Upper Secondary School: Evidence from a Large-Scale Pilot Scheme
Sweden	Hensvik (2012) Competition, Wages and Teacher Sorting: Lessons Learned from a Voucher Reform
Sweden	Gronqvist and Hall (2013) Education Policy and Early Fertility: Lessons from an Expansion of Upper Secondary Schooling
Sweden	Fredriksson et al. (2013) Long-Term Effects of Class Size
Sweden	Lundborg et al. (2014) Parental Education and Offspring Outcomes: Evidence from the Swedish Compulsory School Reform
Canada: Manitoba	Oreopoulos et al. (2008) Short-, Medium-, and Long-Term Consequences of Poor Infant Health: An Analysis Using Siblings and Twins
Canada: Manitoba	Currie et al. (2010) Child Health and Young Adult Outcomes
USA: Arkansas	Costrell and McGee (2010) Teacher Pension Incentives, Retirement Behavior, and Potential for Reform in Arkansas
USA: Florida	Figlio (2007) Boys Named Sue: Disruptive Children and Their Peers
USA: Florida	Figlio et al. (2010) Who Uses a Means-Tested Scholarship, and What Do They Choose?
USA: Florida (Alachua)	Carrell and Hoekstra (2010) Externalities in the Classroom: How Children Exposed to Domestic Violence Affect Everyone's Kids
USA: Florida	Clark and See (2011) The Impact of Tougher Education Standards: Evidence from Florida
USA: Florida	Chingos and West (2011) Promotion and Reassignment in Public School Districts: How Do Schools Respond to Differences in Teacher Effectiveness?
USA: Florida	Chingos and West (2012) Do More Effective Teachers Earn More Outside the Classroom?
USA: Florida	Figlio et al. (2014) The Effects of Poor Neonatal Health on Children's Cognitive Development
USA: Georgia	Scafidi et al. (2007) Race, Poverty, and Teacher Mobility

Table 2 Survey of papers using administrative education data—cont'd

(1) Country/region	(2) Authors, publication year, and title
USA: Illinois	Doyle (2007) Child Protection and Child Outcomes: Measuring the Effects of Foster Care
USA: Illinois (Chicago)	Jacob (2004) Public Housing, Housing Vouchers, and Student Achievement: Evidence from Public Housing Demolitions in Chicago
USA: Illinois (Chicago)	Cho (2009) The Impact of Maternal Imprisonment on Children's Educational Achievement: Results from Children in Chicago Public Schools
USA: Massachusetts	Angrist et al. (2013) Explaining Charter School Effectiveness
USA: Missouri	Podgursky et al. (2004) The Academic Quality of Public School Teachers: An Analysis of Entry and Exit Behavior
USA: North Carolina	Goldhaber and Anthony (2007) Can Teacher Quality Be Effectively Assessed? National Board Certification as a Signal of Effective Teaching
USA: North Carolina	Goldhaber and Hansen (2009) National Board Certification and Teachers' Career Paths: Does NBPTS Certification Influence How Long Teachers Remain in the Profession and Where They Teach?
USA: North Carolina	Goldhaber et al. (2007) A Descriptive Analysis of the Distribution of NBPTS-Certified Teachers in North Carolina
USA: North Carolina (Charlotte-Mecklenburg)	Billings et al. (2014) School Segregation, Educational Attainment, and Crime: Evidence from the End of Busing in Charlotte-Mecklenburg
USA: North Carolina (Charlotte-Mecklenburg)	Deming (2011) Better Schools, Less Crime?
USA: North Carolina (Charlotte-Mecklenburg)	Hastings et al. (2007) The Effect of Randomized School Admissions on Voter Participation
USA: North Carolina (Charlotte-Mecklenburg)	Deming et al. (2014) School Choice, School Quality, and Postsecondary Attainment
USA: New York (New York City)	Dobbie and Fryer (2011) Are High-Quality Schools Enough to Increase Achievement Among the Poor? Evidence from the Harlem Children's Zone
USA: New York (New York City)	Dobbie and Fryer (2014) The Impact of Attending a School with High-Achieving Peers: Evidence from the New York City Exam Schools
USA: New York (New York City)	Boyd et al. (2006) How Changes in Entry Requirements Alter the Teacher Workforce and Affect Student Achievement
USA: Texas	Clark and Martorell (2014) The Signaling Value of a High School Diploma
USA: Texas	Lyle (2006) Using Military Deployments and Job Assignments to Estimate the Effect of Parental
USA: unnamed	Chetty et al. (2014a) Measuring the Impacts of Teachers I: Evaluating Bias in Teacher Value-Added Estimates

Continued

Table 2 Survey of papers using administrative education data—cont'd

(1) Country/region	(2) Authors, publication year, and title
USA: unnamed	Chetty et al. (2014b) Measuring the Impacts of Teachers II: Teacher Value-Added and Student Outcomes in Adulthood
USA: unnamed	Engel et al. (2010) Military Deployments and Children's Academic Achievement: Evidence from Department of Defense Education Activity Schools
USA	Tyler et al. (2000) Estimating the Labor Market Signaling Value of the GED
Taiwan	Gimenez et al. (2013) Parental Loss and Children's Well-Being

Multiple matched administrative sources studies.

Note: This table lists studies which make use of administrative data matched across multiple registers, and that have been published or announced as forthcoming between January 1990 and July 2014 in the following outlets: *American Economic Journal: Applied Economics, American Economic Journal: Economic Policy, American Economic Review, Econometrica, Economic Journal, Economics of Education Review, Education Finance and Policy, Journal of Human Resources, Journal of Labor Economics, Journal of Political Economy, Journal of Public Economics, Quarterly Journal of Economics, Review of Economic Studies, Review of Economics and Statistics* and NBER Working Papers: Education Program. All the papers in the table used at least two administrative data sets in the analysis and these data sets were matched together. We excluded from this table studies that matched a single administrative data source to non-administrative external data sources such as surveys.

It is not our purpose to provide an encyclopedic review of all papers making use of administrative data around the world, but we wanted to offer a very wide-ranging sampling of the current state of the use of administrative data throughout the world. We therefore sought to systematically survey a large number of leading economics outlets that publish papers in the economics of education. Specifically, we browsed all articles published or accepted for publication between January 1990 and July 2014 in the *American Economic Journal: Applied Economics, American Economic Journal: Economic Policy, American Economic Review, Econometrica, Economic Journal, Economics of Education Review, Education Finance and Policy, Journal of Human Resources, Journal of Labor Economics, Journal of Political Economy, Journal of Public Economics, Quarterly Journal of Economics, Review of Economic Studies*, and *Review of Economics and Statistics*, as well as all 2014 NBER Working Papers from the Education program published until the end of July 2014. Although we recognize that this list is far from being comprehensive, we covered 350 papers from 28 countries and all continents except for Antarctica.

In the tables, we organize countries by regions of the world — Europe, North America, South America, Asia, Africa, and Oceania — and then order all papers within country and state (region) by publication date.[13] It is clear that the majority of research (published in these outlets at least) makes use of data from North America (253 papers), and in particular the United States (240 papers). It is possible that this is a substantial overstatement of the North American share of education economics research using

[13] We treat Israel as part of Europe for our accounting purposes.

Table 3 Survey of papers using administrative education data

(1)	(2)
Country/region	Authors, publication year, and title
England	Clark (2009) The Performance and Competitive Effects of School Autonomy
England	Gibbons and Silva (2011b) School Quality, Child Wellbeing and Parents' Satisfaction
England	Apps et al. (2013) The Impact of Pre-School on Adolescents' Outcomes: Evidence from a Recent English Cohort
England	Ouazad and Page (2013) Students' Perceptions of Teacher Biases: Experimental Economics in Schools
England	Burgess et al. (2015) What Parents Want: School Preferences and School Choice
France: Paris	Avvisati et al. (2014) Getting Parents Involved: A Field Experiment in Deprived Schools
Israel	Angrist and Lavy (2009) The Effects of High Stakes High School Achievement Awards: Evidence from a Randomized Trial
Israel	Lavy (2009) Performance Pay and Teachers' Effort, Productivity, and Grading Ethics
Israel	Lavy and Schlosser (2011) Mechanisms and Impacts of Gender Peer Effects at School
Israel	Lavy (2013) Gender Differences in Market Competitiveness in a Real Workplace: Evidence from Performance-Based Pay Tournaments among Teachers
Netherlands: Amsterdam	Cabus and De Witte (2011) Does School Time Matter?—On the Impact of Compulsory Education Age on School Dropout
Netherlands: unnamed	Meyer and Van Klaveren (2013) The Effectiveness of Extended Day Programs: Evidence from a Randomized Field Experiment in the Netherlands
Netherland: Amsterdam	Buser et al. (2014) Gender, Competitiveness, and Career Choices
Romania	Pop-Eleches and Urquiola (2013) Going to a Better School: Effects and Behavioral Responses
Sweden	Hinnerich et al. (2011) Are Boys Discriminated in Swedish High Schools?
Mexico	Behrman et al. (2015) Aligning Learning Incentives of Students and Teachers: Results from a Social Experiment in Mexican High Schools
USA: California	Fairlie and Robinson (2013) Experimental Evidence on the Effects of Home Computers on Academic Achievement among Schoolchildren
USA: Colorado (Denver)	Fryer (2014) Injecting Charter School Best Practices into Traditional Public Schools: Evidence from Field Experiments
USA: Florida (Alachua)	Figlio and Lucas (2004a) Do High Grading Standards Affect Student Performance?
USA: Florida	Harris and Sass (2014) Skills, Productivity and the Evaluation of Teacher Performance
USA: Illinois (Chicago)	Fryer (2011) Financial Incentives and Student Achievement: Evidence from Randomized Trials

Continued

Table 3 Survey of papers using administrative education data—cont'd

(1) Country/region	(2) Authors, publication year, and title
USA: Illinois (Chicago)	Fryer (2014) Injecting Charter School Best Practices into Traditional Public Schools: Evidence from Field Experiments
USA: Illinois (Chicago)	Cook et al. (2014) The (Surprising) Efficacy of Academic and Behavioral Intervention with Disadvantaged Youth: Results from a Randomized Experiment in Chicago
USA: Indiana (Gary)	Hanushek (1992) The Trade-Off Between Child Quantity and Quality
USA: North Carolina (Charlotte-Mecklenburg)	Hastings and Weinstein (2008) Information, School Choice, and Academic Achievement: Evidence from Two Experiments
USA: New York (New York City)	Rockoff et al. (2012) Information and Employee Evaluation: Evidence from a Randomized Intervention in Public Schools
USA: New York (New York City)	Fryer (2011) Financial Incentives and Student Achievement: Evidence from Randomized Trials
USA: New York (New York City)	Fryer (2013) Teacher Incentives and Student Achievement: Evidence from New York City Public Schools
USA: New York (New York City)	Dobbie and Fryer (2013) Getting Beneath the Veil of Effective Schools: Evidence from New York City
USA: New York (New York City)	Rockoff et al. (2011) Can You Recognize an Effective Teacher When You Recruit One?
USA: New York (New York City)	Boyd et al. (2011) The Effectiveness and Retention of Teachers with Prior Career Experience
USA: Ohio (Coshocton)	Bettinger (2012) Paying to Learn: The Effect of Financial Incentives on Elementary School Test Scores
USA: Texas (Dallas)	Fryer (2011) Financial Incentives and Student Achievement: Evidence from Randomized Trials
USA: Texas (Houston)	Fryer (2014) Injecting Charter School Best Practices into Traditional Public Schools: Evidence from Field Experiments
USA: Washington	DeArmond and Goldhaber (2010) Scrambling the Nest Egg: How Well Do Teachers Understand Their Pensions, and What Do They Think About Alternative Pension Structures?
USA: Wisconsin (Milwaukee)	Kasman and Loeb (2013) Principals' Perceptions of Competition for Students in Milwaukee Schools
USA: unnamed	Barrow et al. (2009) Technology's Edge: The Educational Benefits of Computer-Aided Instruction
USA: unnamed	Jacob and Lefgren (2008) Can Principals Identify Effective Teachers? Evidence on Subjective Performance Evaluation in Education
USA: unnamed	Jacob and Lefgren (2007) What Do Parents Value in Education? An Empirical Investigation of Parents' Revealed Preferences for Teachers
Chile	Dinkelman and Martinez (2014) Investing in Schooling in Chile: The Role of Information about Financial Aid for Higher Education
Chile	McEvan and Shapiro (2008) The Benefits of Delayed Primary School Enrollment: Discontinuity Estimates Using Exact Birth Dates

Table 3 Survey of papers using administrative education data—cont'd

(1) Country/region	(2) Authors, publication year, and title
Chile	Paredes (2014) A Teacher Like Me or a Student Like Me? Role Model Versus Teacher Bias Effect
Chile	McEwan (2013) The Impact of Chile's School Feeding Program on Education Outcomes
Chile	Anand et al. (2009) Using School Scholarships to Estimate the Effect of Private Education on the Academic Achievement of Low-Income Students in Chile
Chile	McEwan (2003) Peer Effects on Student Achievement: Evidence from Chile
Colombia	Angrist et al. (2006) Long-Term Educational Consequences of Secondary School Vouchers: Evidence from Administrative Records in Colombia
Colombia	Bettinger et al. (2010) Are Educational Vouchers Only Redistributive?
Colombia: Bogota	Barrera-Osorio et al. (2011) Improving the Design of Conditional Transfer Programs: Evidence from a Randomized Education Experiment in Colombia
Peru	Beuermann et al. (2014) One Laptop per Child at Home: Short-Term Impacts from a Randomized Experiment in Peru
Uruguay	Manacorda (2012) The Cost of Grade Retention
Venezuela	Ortega (2010) The Effect of Wage Compression and Alternative Labor Market Opportunities on Teacher Quality in Venezuela
China: Beijing	Lai et al. (2011) The Contributions of School Quality and Teacher Qualifications to Student Performance Evidence from a Natural Experiment in Beijing Middle Schools
China: Beijing	Lai et al. (2009) The Adverse Effects of Parents' School Selection Errors on Academic Achievement: Evidence from the Beijing Open Enrollment Program
Benin	Blimpo (2014) Team Incentives for Education in Developing Counties: A Randomized Field Experiment in Benin
Kenya: Busia and Teso	Kremer et al. (2009) Incentives to Learn
Kenya: Busia and Teso	Glewwe et al. (2009) Many Children Left Behind? Textbooks and Test Scores in Kenya
Kenya	Lucas and Mbiti (2012) Access, Sorting, and Achievement: The Short-Run Effects of Free Primary Education in Kenya
Uganda	Reinikka and Svensson (2011) The Power of Information in Public Services: Evidence from Education in Uganda

Unmatched administrative source studies matched to surveys or experiments.

Note: This table lists studies which make use of administrative data matched with surveys or experiments, and that have been published or announced as forthcoming between January 1990 and July 2014 in the following outlets: *American Economic Journal: Applied Economics, American Economic Journal: Economic Policy, American Economic Review, Econometrica, Economic Journal, Economics of Education Review, Education Finance and Policy, Journal of Human Resources, Journal of Labor Economics, Journal of Political Economy, Journal of Public Economics, Quarterly Journal of Economics, Review of Economic Studies, Review of Economics and Statistics* and NBER Working Papers: Education Program. All the papers in the table used in the analysis single administrative data set that was matched to survey and/or experimental data.

Table 4 Survey of papers using administrative education data

(1) Country/region	(2) Authors, publication year, and title
Denmark	Joensen and Nielsen (2009) Is There a Causal Effect of High School Math on Labor Market Outcomes?
Denmark	Gupta and Simonsen (2010) Non-Cognitive Child Outcomes and Universal High Quality Child Care
Denmark	Jensen and Rasmussen (2011) The Effect of Immigrant Concentration in Schools on Native and Immigrant Children's Reading and Math Skills
Israel: Tel-Aviv	Lavy (2010) Effects of Free Choice Among Public Schools
Norway	Naper (2010) Teacher Hiring Practices and Educational Efficiency
Sweden	Meghir and Palme (2005) Educational Reform, Ability, and Family Background
Sweden	Golsteyn et al. (2014) Adolescent Time Preferences Predict Lifetime Outcomes
USA: Illinois (Chicago)	Arteaga et al. (2014) One Year of Preschool or Two: Is It Important for Adult Outcomes?
USA: Illinois (Chicago)	Jacob et al. (2014) Human Capital Effects of Anti-Poverty Programs: Evidence from a Randomized Housing Voucher Lottery
Chile	Bharadwaj et al. (2013) Early Life Health Interventions and Academic Achievement

Multiple matched administrative sources studies matched to surveys or experiments.
Note: This table lists studies which make use of administrative data matched across multiple registers and additionally to nonadministrative based data source, and that have been published or announced as forthcoming between January 1990 and July 2014 in the following outlets: *American Economic Journal: Applied Economics, American Economic Journal: Economic Policy, American Economic Review, Econometrica, Economic Journal, Economics of Education Review, Education Finance and Policy, Journal of Human Resources, Journal of Labor Economics, Journal of Political Economy, Journal of Public Economics, Quarterly Journal of Economics, Review of Economic Studies, Review of Economics and Statistics* and NBER Working Papers: Education Program. All the papers in the table used in the analysis at least two administrative data sets that were matched together, and then further matched to survey and/or experimental data.

administrative data because of possible publication biases of the journals that we selected for inclusion, but again, our charge is not to be comprehensive in our survey. A large fraction of papers in the list make use of data from Europe (85 papers), while smaller shares makes use of data from South America (18 papers), Africa (6 papers), Asia (4 papers), and Oceania (1 paper). Within Europe the majority of papers come from England, Israel, Norway, and Sweden. These four countries comprise 77% of European output. Within United States, the majority of research comes from North Carolina, Florida, Texas, Chicago, and New York City; however, nearly half of the States in the Union contributed at least one paper to the list, and given the large investments in data infrastructure throughout the United States we expect the geographic spread to continue in the future. That said, it is not an accident that so many papers make use of data from North Carolina, Florida, Texas, Chicago, and New York City, as these are major US jurisdictions that facilitate research more than most. Among other countries

Chile contributed 11 papers, while Canada 9. There is also growing output based on Kenyan data. It is also clear from Tables 1–4 that majority of the research output utilizes only a single administrative data source (eg, school records) which could be related to both limited data infrastructure and matching restrictions (eg, in the United States). At the same time it is relatively rare that researchers are able to match individuals across multiple administrative data sets, say birth and school records, and also to survey or experiment — only 10 out of 350 paper we identified and primarily from outside of the United States.

As stated in the introduction, the use of administrative data is a rather new phenomenon and it has been made possible due to the increase in computational power, decrease in storage prices and enhanced cooperation between governmental agencies and researchers all over the world. The first papers from our list were published in *Economics of Education Review* (Theobald, 1990) and in the *Journal of Human Resources* (Murnane and Olsen, 1990). The former one used data from Washington, while the latter one from North Carolina, and both papers investigated the role that different variables play in teacher retention. In fact through the 1990s the surveyed journals published only seven papers using administrative data and six of these were studying the teacher labor market. One reason for the focus on teachers in the early use of administrative data is the fact that due to bureaucracy and budgeting, the records of public school employees were compiled and stored centrally by state departments of education long before researchers expressed interest in them, while few countries around the world systematically collected student achievement information.

In the 2000s, there was a rapid increase in the amount of scientific output using administrative data with 114 papers published in our list. The diversity also increased and papers used not only data on teachers and students but also on individuals pre- and post- their schooling years. Finally, between 2010 and July 2014 the scientific journals we surveyed have already published nearly 230 papers. This massive increase was driven mostly by the United States, but in every year more and more countries contribute to the global "data village." The first papers in our list using European data were published in 2001 using data from Jerusalem, from South America in 2000 using Chilean data, from Asia in 2009 using data from Beijing, and from Africa in 2009 using Kenyan data.

Akin to the examples provided in our Norway, Sweden, and Florida case studies, we observe a substantial variation in the types of registry data used internationally. This depends both on data infrastructure itself but also on the institutional setting in a particular country, state or region under investigation. For example, even though Norway has very high-quality long-run data it is difficult to study the long-run effects of school competition in this country because there is no variation in the competitive pressure faced by different schools. Similarly, although Sweden has introduced school competition to its institutional setting and hence it is possible to study whether such policies have long lasting effects, it is actually impossible to look at these effects in a short-run, ie, in a manner comparable to the United States, because Sweden did not test its pupils using standardized assessments. Yet another problem is the possibility to link different data registers, and from this perspective in most states in the United States it is not possible to study the effects of, for example, neonatal health on schooling outcomes (Table 2). The data simply do not allow a clean match between birth records and school records due to lack of unique personal identifier. Notable exception here is Florida that assigns their newborns social security numbers. Useful but not perfect way around this last problem is widely used in historical research probabilistic matching of individuals (Ferrie and Long, 2013). This method has been applied to some modern data sets like birth and school records in North Carolina (Ladd et al., 2012) but the match rates based on these procedures are not ideal and they are sensitive to the type of populations under scrutiny.

The examples in the paragraph above illustrate the complexity behind research projects involving registry data but also point out to the need of both data infrastructure and credible variation in studying economic and educational phenomena. The agenda becomes even more complex when the research objectives involve long-run effects of particular interventions, their spillovers or understanding the mechanisms through which these interventions operate. In this case population-level administrative registries are particularly essential as these research projects often involve matching subjects in field experiments to themselves decades later (Aslund, et al., 2011) or to subjects' siblings (Black et al., 2014c). Furthermore, when the goal is to elicit mechanisms through which the policies operate then most often the survey instruments need to be applied to the studied populations and then matched back to the original registers (Burgess et al., 2015).

Due to the institutional issues brought up in the paragraphs above researchers in different countries seem to specialize in studying very specific questions based on the registers that are available to them, and the policy environments that they face. Scandinavian countries produce mostly studies that involve rather lower quality educational measures for which they compensate with the fact that individuals can be tracked from their birth to their death and often also across generations.[14] These countries do not have longitudinal student assessment data but are the only locations in the world where the whole population of males undergoes physical, intellectual, and emotional evaluations at the time of entering adulthood.[15] On the other side of this spectrum are countries like England or the majority of the US states that have regular student assessments but do not allow merging different databases. A few notable exceptions to that rule are, for instance, Florida, Texas, Chicago, Charlotte-Mecklenburg (North Carolina), and

[14] A notable exception here is Finland where research community has not have until recently such a wide access to national registers as in Denmark, Sweden, or Norway.

[15] The mandatory military draft has been revoked in Sweden in the mid-2000s but the data for the cohorts 1952–2002 can still be used. At the same time as discussed in our case studies Sweden is in the process of rolling out longitudinal student assessments in their compulsory schooling system in grades 3, 6, and 9.

New York City that allow linking student records to subsequent postsecondary education (Booker et al., 2011), criminal records (Deming, 2011), or labor market outcomes (Clark and Martorell, 2014). These are generally rare because they require agreements and cooperation of multiple governmental agencies.[16] A longitudinal data set that follows kids from birth through childhood, adolescence to adulthood is also available for the province of Manitoba, Canada. These data are somewhat in-between Scandinavian and United States registers because although they allow tracking individuals longitudinally, they do not allow for more complex familial linkages or longitudinal student assessment. There are also few data sets with longitudinal components outside of Scandinavia or North America. For instance, it is possible to link birth records to schooling records in Chile (Bharadwaj et al., 2013), link birth records to death records to schooling records in Taiwan (Gimenez et al., 2013), or link schooling interventions to long-run outcomes in Israel (Lavy, 2014).

The growth in access to administrative data across the world is crucial from the policy point of view because it allows direct testing of external validity of particular economic phenomena in different institutional setting. In fact we see more and more multistate or multicountry studies in recent years, eg, Fryer (2014) or Bharadwaj et al. (2013).[17] The concern with external validity and ability to study the same policies in multiple locations is the more important in experimental work that necessarily focuses on rather narrow populations, but is becoming a "gold standard" in policy evaluations. The single-country multisite studies are important from national policy point of view, especially in diverse countries like United States or France, because it is not obvious that intervention which works in Chicago Public Schools or East Paris will work in more affluent areas like Greenwich, Connecticut or Neuilly-sur-Seine. Another broader question is whether similar policies give the same effects in culturally, economically, or institutionally different environment. In this case researchers have to rely on rare interventions that are universal across many countries, like for example standardized treatment of low birth weight babies. These studies are extremely valuable because they often allow research community to understand a more fundamental background of human social behavior. They also allow studying externalities of particular policies interacting with different institutional environments.

---

[16] Note that in Scandinavia, unlike in the United States, the multiple registers are handled by a single agency and even though Department of Defense administers the military draft and Department of Education coordinates the 9th grade assessments the research proposal is submitted and processed through a single Data Inspection Authority.

[17] There is fewer published cross-country than cross-state studies, however, we should see more and more of the former ones coming in the next few years. Another notable example is study of Bedard and Dhuey (2006) which combines results from Canada based on administrative data and from other countries based on various survey data.

In the remaining part of this section, we focus on particular questions relevant to educational research agenda, and how these have been addressed in different countries or states. We start off with the fundamental question of how early childhood environment affects educational, and potentially long-run outcomes. Given the advantages and disadvantages of various administrative data sets described in the paragraphs above, it is not surprising that this research question has been dominated by studies based on Scandinavian data (Table 2). The excellent data infrastructure in Denmark, Sweden, and Norway allows tracking individuals not only from their birth to their death but also across multiple generations and familial connections as children are linked to their biological parents using unique identifiers, and the parents are in turn linked to their siblings using unique identifiers. Except for the three aforementioned Scandinavian countries early childhood has also been studied in two other European countries: England (Almond et al., 2015) and Germany (Dustmann and Schonberg, 2012). In North America we have a birth order study from Indiana (Hanushek, 1992) which is the only study from the 1990s on our list that was not focused specifically on teachers but used an experimental population from Gary Income Maintenance Experiment merged to children schooling records. The other papers include birth weight effects estimates from Canada (Oreopoulos et al., 2008) and Florida (Figlio et al., 2014), in-utero pollution exposure study from Texas (Sanders, 2012) and an influential foster care system evaluation from Illinois (Doyle, 2007). A paper from Taiwan investigates the effects of parental loss on children's well-being (Gimenez et al., 2013) while a paper based on Chilean and Norwegian data studies the role of health interventions at birth (Bharadwaj et al., 2013). Some of these papers, due to their use of administrative data, documented new and important empirical phenomena. Figlio et al. (2014) are among the first to document that neonatal health and parental socioeconomic status are likely complements rather than substitutes — a common perception was rather that wealthier parents can better compensate for lower health capital of their children than poorer parents. Bharadwaj et al. (2013) show that health interventions in countries as different as Chile and Norway can yield fairly similar effects which boosts the confidence that earl life interventions effectiveness is not necessarily tied to specific institutional environment or wealth of the society.

Across different countries and institutional settings the most often studied question seems to be the role of school technology or the education production function. These topics range from the questions of how gender composition of classrooms influences female school choice in Austria (Schneeweis and Zweimuller, 2012), or how ethnic and immigrant concentration in schools affects cognitive development of children in Denmark (Jensen and Rasmussen, 2011)[18] and England (Dustmann et al., 2010), through

---

[18] The Danish study is the more important because it merges PISA data with registry data which in a longer-run will allow benchmarking the PISA test scores against economically meaningful variables like university graduation or income. Since PISA is used globally to compare the efficiency of educational systems it seems imperative to understand how PISA scores translate into long-run outcomes. To our knowledge Denmark is the only country that successfully merged their PISA samples to administrative records.

mandatory school entry and exit ages in Germany (Muhlenweg and Puhani, 2010) and the Netherlands (Cabus and De Witte, 2011) to school resources in Norway (Haegeland et al., 2012), Canada (Leach et al., 2010) and New York City (Rubenstein et al., 2009). There is also a substantial variation in the kind of inputs that are investigated in different states within the Union. They span from the role of the quantity of math instruction hours in Florida (Taylor, 2014) through teacher cheating in Chicago (Jacob and Levitt, 2003) to the role of school crowding in North Carolina (McMullen and Rouse, 2012b) or paying students for grade completion in Ohio (Bettinger, 2012).

There are also multisite studies within the United States that explore the role of same school inputs in very different school environments, and thus, allow for assessment of generalizability of the interventions. An example of such study would be Fryer's (2014) investigation of the role of importing best charter school practices to traditional public schools in Chicago, Denver, and Houston. His results are remarkably similar across Denver and Houston, the two experimental samples, and are smaller for Chicago, where only quasiexperimental variation is available. Notably Denver and Houston differ both in terms of demographics and institutional setting so the similarity of the estimates is noteworthy. It is also the case that Chicago implemented a slightly less intensive program which could account for the difference in the effects. Another example of this kind of cross sites within-country research is Abdulkadiroglu et al. (2014) who investigate the role of school composition on student achievement in Boston and New York. In both cities they find little evidence that attending elite schools has a causal effect on test scores or college quality. Similar findings are confirmed in Kenyan setting (Lucas and Mbiti, 2014) but Jackson (2010) finds large gains from attending elite schools in Trinidad and Tobago. This set of papers unlike the health interventions at birth suggests that some educational policies might be generalizable with country but not across countries.

One particular school attribute that gained a lot of attention in the educational research agenda involves class size (Angrist and Lavy, 1999; Chetty et al., 2011). Neither of these two papers used administrative educational data sets, but there exists evidence on this topic from at least four countries and two states using educational administrative data. This question has been studied in Denmark (Heinesen, 2010), Italy (Angrist et al., 2014), Sweden (Fredriksson et al., 2013), and in the United States in Florida (Chingos, 2012). Using different identification strategies and data these papers generally find conflating results. Danish, Italian, and Swedish studies confirm the previous results based on survey data that smaller classes generate significant advantages in later life schooling and labor market outcomes. On the contrary the Florida case-study and also another paper using Norwegian registry data (Leuven et al., 2008) do not find much of an effect of a reduction in class size. It is particularly interesting that the Swedish and Norwegian studies use an identical identification strategy but find very different results. This point makes clear the value of cross-context replication and studies.

The two remaining studies of class size in our list are somewhat different. Complementary research from Kentucky (Barrett and Toma, 2013) documents that principals are more likely to assign more effective teachers to larger classes, potentially to compensate for the negative class-size effects. Finally, a Chilean (Urquiola and Verhoogen, 2009) paper makes a more methodological point by documenting an inverted-U cross-sectional relationship between class size and household income as well as stacking of schools' enrollments at multiples of the class-size cap. These two data facts could invalidate non-experimental or regression discontinuity estimates of the class size in liberalized market settings where schools are free to set prices and/or turn away students, and households are free to sort between schools. The manipulation of a class-size rule that can potentially invalidate the regression discontinuity estimates has also been documented in Israel (Cohen-Zada et al., 2013). Comprehensive administrative data facilitated these studies that otherwise would be harder to conduct.

Another hotly debated in the past decades educational policy topic has been the role of school choice and competition. Around the world, governments have recently implemented and researchers evaluated various forms of choice and competition. Outside the United States the countries that contributed to this broad research agenda are England, Israel, and Sweden in Europe, Canada and United States in North America, Colombia and Chile in South America, and China in Asia. However, not all of these countries study the same phenomena that we encapsulate in a single broad term of school choice. For example, outside the United States, the effects of voucher and charter schools on student outcomes are examined in England (Clark, 2009), Sweden (Sandstrom and Bergstrom, 2005), Chile (Mizala and Roumaguera, 2000), and Colombia (Angrist et al., 2006; Bettinger et al., 2010). These papers, with the exception of early Chilean descriptive work, point towards beneficial effects of vouchers on student achievement. An interesting modification of the voucher system type of competition is studied in Ontario, Canada (Card et al., 2010b) where non-Catholics are subject to monopoly of public schools while Catholics (40% of children in the province) can choose between sending their kids to secular public schools or to separate schools. The authors also find test score gains due to increased competition in Ontario.

These effects have also been investigated in the United States for Florida (Figlio and Hart, 2014), Chicago (Booker et al., 2011), Massachusetts (Angrist et al., 2013), New York City (Winters, 2012), Texas (Booker et al., 2007), and Utah (Ni and Rorrer, 2012). The results generally suggest heterogeneous effects of charters which might be either due to the fact that they apply different identification strategies or due to differential role of institutional settings. Research by Zimmer et al. (2012) examines the role of charter schools more comprehensively by looking simultaneously at seven states but it is important to note that their analysis is based on individual fixed effects and not on random or quasirandom variation. They find mixed results for charter school effects and point out that their results rely heavily on the assumptions they make along the way. This study with such an external validity would not be possible without administrative data available in multiple sites within the United States. There is also research that considers lotteries and open enrollment to schools that are not necessarily private schools. Cullen et al. (2006) find little evidence for improvements of achievement of lottery winners in Chicago, while Deming et al. (2014) find increases in college attainment among lottery winners in Charlotte-Mecklenburg. Free school choice seems to also benefit students in Israel (Lavy, 2010). Clearly, more work is needed in order to gauge the degree to which specific programs and identification strategies are responsible for differing research findings.

Another strand of this agenda considers the role of parents in school choice in England (Burgess et al., 2015), Beijing (Lai et al., 2009), and Charlotte-Mecklenburg (Hastings and Weinstein, 2008). There is also research that considers the importance of accurate information on school quality when school choice is available in England (Allen and Burgess, 2013); and that examines the potential negative spillovers from school choice, like grade inflation in Sweden (Wikstrom and Wikstrom, 2005). Finally, competition and school choice may affect not only students but also their teachers, and we discuss this research agenda below where we focus more broadly on the labor market for teachers.

Much of the early research using administrative data focused on the labor market for teachers but the interest in this topic did not decline over time. In fact other countries and states started contributing papers studying teachers. In the United States, we observe researchers in a large number of states investigating the labor market for teachers; specific examples include the use of administrative data in Alaska, Arkansas, Colorado, Florida, Illinois, Georgia, Kentucky, Michigan, Missouri, North Carolina, New York, Ohio, Pennsylvania, Texas, Washington, and Wisconsin. Outside of the United States teachers have been studied in Israel, Italy, Norway, Sweden, and Venezuela. The most widely studied question is likely the teacher labor supply and mobility that has been investigated within the United States in Florida (Feng, 2010), Georgia (Scafidi et al., 2007), Kentucky (Cowen et al., 2012), Michigan (Gershenson, 2012), Missouri (Podgursky et al., 2004), North Carolina (Jackson, 2013b), New York (Brewer, 1996), Texas (Hanushek et al., 2004a), Washington (Theobald, 1990), Wisconsin (Imazeki, 2005); and internationally in Italy (Barbieri et al., 2011), Norway (Falch and Strom, 2005), Sweden (Karbownik, 2014), and Venezuela (Ortega, 2010).[19] The broad conclusion from these papers is that school quality and working conditions matter for attracting and retaining teachers, particularly those of higher quality, but particular factors differ across sites in both whether they matter and how much they matter.

Another related topic that is present only in the United States research, to the best of our knowledge, is the role of teacher retirement and the retirement benefits. This particular question has been studied in Arkansas (Costrell and McGee, 2010), Illinois (Fitzpatrick and Lovenheim, 2014), Missouri (Koedel et al., 2014), Pennsylvania

---

[19] Many of these states and countries contributed multiple studies on the topic of teacher labor supply and mobility.

(Ferguson et al., 2006), and Washington (DeArmond and Goldhaber, 2010). Some other studies consider the role of incentives in improving teacher performance in Denver (Goldhaber and Walch, 2012), Chicago (Jacob, 2013), Kentucky (Barrett and Toma, 2013), New York City (Fryer, 2013), Houston (Imberman and Lovenheim, 2015), and outside of the United States in Israel (Lavy, 2009).

A lot of attention in the United States has also been given to the interaction between the schools, teachers and their students. School accountability was introduced voluntarily by many states in the 1990s but with the introduction of the federal No Child Left Behind law in 2002 the remaining states were required to start measuring the relative performance of their students, which by extension allowed calculations of value added measures, assessment of teacher effectiveness and as an unintended side-effect produced large quantities of administrative data on teacher and their students (Figlio and Loeb, 2011). Based on our selection of journals we found value added or accountability research from San Diego (Koedel and Betts, 2010), Colorado (Briggs and Weeks, 2009), Florida (Sass et al., 2014), Chicago (Aaronson et al., 2007), North Carolina (Rothstein, 2010), Texas (Rivkin et al., 2005), and Washington (Krieg, 2011). Outside of the United States, value added models have also been examined in two other English speaking countries, mainly England (Ray et al., 2009) and Australia (Leigh, 2010).

There are many other research themes that we did not cover in this brief review and which gained considerable attention in the research community. To name a few from our extensive but incomplete list, registry data have been used to study: the introduction of new technologies to schools in England (Machin et al., 2007), experimental evidence on schools influence on parents' involvement in education in France (Avvisati et al., 2014), experimental evidence on gender differences in competitiveness and its consequences for educational choices in the Netherlands (Buser et al., 2014), the role of school quality in Romania (Pop-Eleches and Urquiola, 2013), experimental evidence on learning incentives in Mexico (Behrman et al., 2015), perceived effects of school quality on housing market (Figlio and Lucas, 2004b), the role of peer effects utilizing student reshuffling due to extreme events (Imberman et al., 2012) or the ability of principals to recognize effective teachers (Jacob and Lefgren, 2008). We also have not mentioned some unique educational data sets used worldwide to address very specific research questions. These would be GED takers in Florida and Texas (Tyler et al., 2004), principals in Illinois and North Carolina (Gates et al., 2006), college entry exam takers in Michigan (Andrews et al., 2010), or anthropometric measurements of school children in Peru (Dell, 2010).

In summary, there is a growing prevalence in the use of administrative data in educational research and in this section we hoped to provide some brief overview of this phenomenon internationally. We did not and could not aim to be complete here, however, our goal was to provide useful examples of applications and data types utilized in different countries. It is clear that there are many opportunities to study new questions in new environments, and we expect that the explosion in the use of administrative data in education research will only continue to expand rapidly.

6. CONCLUSIONS

It is evident that administrative data present a world of opportunity, and while there are clearly challenges associated with the use of administrative data, the benefits of collecting these data and using them for research and policy purposes surely outweigh the costs involved. While administrative data are not a substitute for many purpose-built survey data, in the cases in which they are substitutes they have the potential to save taxpayers considerable amounts of money while delivering better-quality data, and of course there are many ways in which administrative data can make survey data better, more cost-effective, and more flexible. The availability of these data has led to new research questions that had previously not been addressable being studied; the overturning of conventional wisdom through higher-quality research designs made possible by better data; and more data-driven policymaking in education. All of these are victories for both research and policy. Given the remarkable progress of computing power and capacity, it is in the best interest of both science and policy to make good use of these administratively collected data while following best practices in data security and ethics. Furthering partnerships and trust relationships between the entities that collect and administer these administrative data and members of the scholarly community, and developing de-identified data sets that will protect privacy and confidentiality while furthering research will benefit taxpayers, policy makers and scholars alike.

REFERENCES

Aaronson, D., Barrow, L., Sander, W., 2007. Teachers and student achievement in the Chicago public high schools. J. Labor Econ. 25 (1), 96–135.

Abdulkadiroglu, A., Pathak, P.A., Roth, A.E., 2009. Strategy-proofness versus efficiency in matching with indifferences: redesigning the NYC high school match, Am. Econ. Rev. 99 (5), 1954–1978.

Abdulkadiroglu, A., Angrist, J.D., Dynarski, S.M., Kane, T.J., Pathak, P.A., 2011. Accountability and flexibility in public schools: evidence from Boston's charters and pilots. Q. J. Econ. 126 (2), 699–748.

Abdulkadiroglu, A., Angrist, J., Pathak, P., 2014. The elite illusion: achievement effects at Boston and New York exam schools. Econometrica 82 (1), 137–196.

Ahn, T., 2014. A regression discontinuity analysis of graduation standards and their impact on students' academic trajectories. Econ. Educ. Rev. 38, 64–75.

Ahn, T., Vigdor, J.L., 2014. When Incentives Matter Too Much: Explaining Significant Responses to Irrelevant Information. NBER Working Paper No. 20321.

Allen, R., Burgess, S., 2013. Evaluating the provision of school performance information for school choice. Econ. Educ. Rev. 34, 175–190.

Almas, I., Cappelen, A., Salvanes, K.G., Sorensen, E., Tungodden, B., 2015. Willingness to compete: family matters. Manage. Sci. http://pubsonline.informs.org/doi/pdf/10.1287/mnsc.2015.2244.

Almond, D., Edlund, L., Palme, M., 2009. Chernobyl's subclinical legacy: prenatal exposure to radioactive fallout and school outcomes in Sweden. Q. J. Econ. 124 (4), 1729–1772.

Almond, D., Mazumder, B., van Ewijk, R., 2014. In utero Ramadan exposure and children's academic performance. Econ. J. http://onlinelibrary.wiley.com/doi/10.1111/ecoj.12168/abstract.

Anand, P., Mizala, A., Repetto, A., 2009. Using school scholarships to estimate the effect of private education on the academic achievement of low-income students in Chile. Econ. Educ. Rev. 28 (3), 370–381.

Andersson, C., Johansson, P., Waldenstrom, N., 2011. Do you want your child to have a certified teacher? Econ. Educ. Rev. 30 (1), 65–78.

Andrews, R.J., DesJardins, S., Ranchhod, V., 2010. The effects of the Kalamazoo Promise on college choice. Econ. Educ. Rev. 29 (5), 722–737.

Angrist, J.D., Lang, K., 2004. Does school integration generate peer effects? Evidence from Boston's Metco program. Am. Econ. Rev. 94 (5), 1613–1634.

Angrist, J.D., Lavy, V., 1999. Using Maimonides' rule to estimate the effect of class size on student achievement. Q. J. Econ. 114 (2), 533–575.

Angrist, J.D., Lavy, V., 2001. Does teacher training affect pupil learning? Evidence from matched comparisons in Jerusalem public schools. J. Labor Econ. 19 (2), 343–369.

Angrist, J., Lavy, V., 2009. The effects of high stakes high school achievement awards: evidence from a randomized trial. Am. Econ. Rev. 99 (4), 1384–1414.

Angrist, J., Bettinger, E., Kremer, M., 2006. Long-term educational consequences of secondary school vouchers: evidence from administrative records in Colombia. Am. Econ. Rev. 96 (3), 847–862.

Angrist, J.D., Pathak, P.A., Walters, C.R., 2013. Explaining charter school effectiveness. Am. Econ. J. Appl. Econ. 5 (4), 1–27.

Angrist, J.D., Battistin, E., Vuri, D., 2014. Is a Small Moment: Class Size and Moral Hazard in the Mezzogiorno. NBER Working Paper No. 20173.

Apps, P., Mendolina, S., Walker, I., 2013. The impact of pre-school on adolescents' outcomes: evidence from a recent English cohort. Econ. Educ. Rev. 37, 183–199.

Arteaga, I., Humpage, S., Reynolds, A.J., Temple, J.A., 2014. One year of preschool or two: is it important for adult outcomes? Econ. Educ. Rev. 40, 221–237.

Aslund, O., Edin, P.-A., Fredriksson, P., Gronqvist, H., 2011. Peers, neighborhoods, and immigrant student achievement: evidence from a placement policy. Am. Econ. J. Appl. Econ. 3 (2), 67–95.

Avvisati, F., Guragand, M., Guyon, N., Maurin, E., 2014. Getting parents involved: a field experiment in deprived schools. Rev. Econ. Stud. 81 (1), 57–83.

Barbieri, G., Rossetti, C., Sestito, P., 2011. The determinants of teacher mobility: evidence using Italian teachers' transfer applications. Econ. Educ. Rev. 30 (6), 1430–1444.

Barrera-Osorio, F., Bertrand, M., Linden, L.L., 2011. Improving the design of conditional transfer programs: evidence from a randomized education experiment in Colombia. Am. Econ. J. Appl. Econ. 3 (2), 167–195.

Barrett, N., Toma, E.F., 2013. Reward or punishment? Class size and teacher quality. Econ. Educ. Rev. 35, 41–52.

Barrow, L., Markman, L., Rouse, C.E., 2009. Technology's edge: the educational benefits of computer-aided instruction. Am. Econ. J. Econ. Policy 1 (1), 52–74.

Bastian, K.C., Henry, G.T., Thompson, C.L., 2013. Incorporating access to more effective teachers into assessments of educational resource equity. Educ. Finance Policy 8 (4), 560–580.

Bedard, K., Dhuey, E., 2006. The persistence of early childhood maturity: international evidence of long-run age effects. Q. J. Econ. 121 (4), 1437–1472.

Behrman, J.R., Parker, S.W., Todd, P.E., Wolpin, K.I., 2015. Aligning learning incentives of students and teachers: results from a social experiment in Mexican high schools. J. Polit. Econ. 123 (2), 325–364.

Belfield, C.R., Levin, H.M., 2004. Should high school economics courses be compulsory? Econ. Educ. Rev. 23 (4), 351–360.

Bellei, C., 2009. Does lengthening the school day increase students' academic achievement? Results from a natural experiment in Chile. Econ. Educ. Rev. 28 (5), 629–640.

Bettinger, E., 2012. Paying to learn: the effect of financial incentives on elementary school test scores. Rev. Econ. Stat. 94 (3), 686–698.

Bettinger, E., Kremer, M., Saavedra, J.E., 2010. Are educational vouchers only redistributive? Econ. J. 120 (546), F204–F228.

Bettinger, E., Haegeland, T., Rege, M., 2014. Home with mom: the effects of stay-at-home parents on children's long run educational outcomes. J. Labor Econ. 32 (3), 443–467.

Beuermann, D.W., Cristia, J., Cueto, S., Malamud, O., Cruz-Aguayo, Y., 2014. One laptop per child at home: short-term impacts from a randomized experiment in Peru. Am. Econ. J. Appl. Econ. 7 (2), 53–80.

Bharadwaj, P., Loken, K.V., Neilson, C., 2013. Early life health interventions and academic achievement. Am. Econ. Rev. 103 (5), 1862–1891.

Bhuller, M., Mogstad, M., Salvanes, K., 2015. Life cycle earnings, education premiums and internal rates of return. J. Labor Econ.

Bifulco, R., Ladd, H.F., 2006. The impacts of charter schools on student achievement: evidence from North Carolina. Educ. Finance Policy 1 (1), 50–90.

Billings, S.B., Deming, D.J., Rockoff, J., 2014. School segregation, educational attainment, and crime: evidence from the end of busing in Charlotte-Mecklenburg. Q. J. Econ. 129 (1), 435–476.

Bjorklund, A., Salvanes, K.G., 2011. Education and family background: mechanisms and policies. In: Handbook of Economics of Education, vol. 3. North Holland, Amsterdam, pp. 201–247.

Bjorklund, A., Lindahl, M., Plug, E., 2006. The origins of intergenerational associations: lessons from Swedish adoption data. Q. J. Econ. 121 (3), 999–1028.

Black, S.E., Devereux, P.J., Salvanes, K.G., 2005a. Why the apple doesn't fall far: understanding intergenerational transmission of human capital. Am. Econ. Rev. 95 (1), 437–449.

Black, S.E., Devereux, P.J., Salvanes, K.G., 2005b. The more the merrier? The effect of family size and birth order on children's education. Q. J. Econ. 120 (2), 669–700.

Black, S.E., Devereux, P.J., Salvanes, K.G., 2007. From the cradle to the labor market? The effect of birth weight on adult outcomes. Q. J. Econ. 122 (1), 409–439.

Black, S.E., Devereux, P.J., Salvanes, K.G., 2010. Small family, smart family? Family size and the IQ scores of young men. J. Hum. Resour. 45 (1), 33–58.

Black, S.E., Devereux, P.J., Salvanes, K.G., 2011. Too young to leave the nest? The effects of school starting age. Rev. Econ. Stat. 93 (2), 455–467.

Black, S.E., Devereux, P.J., Salvanes, K.G., 2013. Under pressure? The effect of peers on outcomes of young adults. J. Labor Econ. 31 (1), 119–153.

Black, S.E., Devereux, P.J., Loken, K.V., Salvanes, K.G., 2014a. Care or cash? The effect of child care subsidies on student performance. Rev. Econ. Stat. 96 (5), 824–837.

Black, S.E., Devereux, P.J., Salvanes, K.G., 2014b. Does Grief Transfer Across Generations? In-Utero Deaths and Child Outcomes. NBER Working Paper No. 19979.

Black, S.E., Breining, S., Figlio, D.N., Guryan, J.G., Karbownik, K., Nielsen, H., Roth, J., Simonsen, M., 2014c. Spillovers in the Family: The Educational Consequences of Having a Disabled Sibling. Mimeo.

Blimpo, M.P., 2014. Team incentives for education in developing countries: a randomized field experiment in Benin. Am. Econ. J. Appl. Econ. 6 (4), 90–109.

Bohlmark, A., Lindahl, M., 2015. Independent schools and long-run educational outcomes – evidence from Sweden's large scale voucher reform. Economica 82 (327), 508–551.

Bohlmark, A., Gronqvist, E., Vlachos, J., 2012. The Headmaster Ritual: The Importance of Management for School Outcomes. IFAU Working Paper 2012:16.

Booker, K., Gilpatric, S.M., Gronberg, T., Jansen, D., 2007. The impact of charter school attendance on student performance. J. Public Econ. 91, 849–876.

Booker, K., Sass, T.R., Gill, B., Zimmer, R., 2011. The effects of charter high schools on educational attainment. J. Labor Econ. 29 (2), 377–415.

Boyd, D., Grossman, P., Lankford, H., Loeb, S., Wyckoff, J., 2006. How changes in entry requirements alter the teacher workforce and affect student achievement. Educ. Finance Policy 1 (2), 176–216.

Boyd, D., Grossman, P., Ing, M., Lankford, H., Loeb, S., O'Brien, R., Wyckoff, J., 2011. The effectiveness and retention of teachers with prior career experience. Econ. Educ. Rev. 30 (6), 1229–1241.

Boyd, D., Lankford, H., Loeb, S., Wyckoff, J., 2013. Analyzing the determinants of the matching of public school teachers to jobs: disentangling the preferences of teachers and employers. J. Labor Econ. 31 (1), 83–117.

Brewer, D.J., 1996. Career paths and quit decisions: evidence from teaching. J. Labor Econ. 14 (2), 313–339.

Briggs, D.C., Weeks, J.P., 2009. The sensitivity of value-added modeling to the creation of a vertical score scale. Educ. Finance Policy 4 (4), 384–414.

Brummet, Q., 2014. The effects of school closings on student achievement. J. Public Econ. 119, 108–124.

Bui, S.A., Craig, S.G., Imberman, S.A., 2014. Is gifted education a bright idea? Assessing the impact of gifted and talented programs on students. Am. Econ. J. Econ. Policy 6 (3), 30–62.

Burgess, S., Briggs, A., 2010. School assignment, school choice and social mobility. Econ. Educ. Rev. 29 (4), 639–649.

Burgess, S., Greaves, E., 2013. Test scores, subjective assessment, and stereotyping of ethnic minorities. J. Labor Econ. 31 (3), 535–576.

Burgess, S., Wilson, D., Worth, J., 2013. A natural experiment in school accountability: the impact of school performance information on pupil progress. J. Public Econ. 106, 57–67.

Burgess, S., Greaves, E., Vignoles, A., Wilson, D., 2015. What parents want: school preferences and school choice. Econ. J. http://onlinelibrary.wiley.com/doi/10.1111/ecoj.12153/abstract.

Burke, M.A., Sass, T.R., 2013. Classroom peer effects and student achievement. J. Labor Econ. 31 (1), 51–82.

Buser, T., Niederle, M., Oosterbeek, H., 2014. Gender, competitiveness, and career choices. Q. J. Econ. 129 (3), 1409–1447.

Cabus, S.J., De Witte, K., 2011. Does school time matter?—On the impact of compulsory education age on school dropout. Econ. Educ. Rev. 30 (6), 1384–1398.

Card, D., Chetty, R., Feldstein, M., Saez, E., 2010a. Expanding Access to Administrative Data for Research in the United States. White Paper, National Science Foundation, Washington, DC.

Card, D., Dooley, M.D., Payne, A., 2010b. School competition and efficiency with publicly funded catholic schools. Am. Econ. J. Appl. Econ. 2 (4), 150–176.

Carneiro, P., Lopez-Garcia, I., Salvanes, K.G., Tominey, E., 2014. Intergenerational Transmission, Human Capital Formation and the Timing of Parental Income. Working Paper, Norwegian School of Economics.

Carneiro, P., Loken, K., Salvanes, K.G., 2015. A flying start? Long term consequences of maternal time investments in children during the first year of life. J. Polit. Econ. 123 (2), 365–412.

Carrell, S.E., Hoekstra, M.L., 2010. Externalities in the classroom: how children exposed to domestic violence affect everyone's kids. Am. Econ. J. Appl. Econ. 2 (1), 211–228.

Carruthers, C.K., 2012a. The qualifications and classroom performance of teachers moving to charter schools. Educ. Finance Policy 7 (3), 233–268.

Carruthers, C.K., 2012b. New schools, new students, new teachers: evaluating the effectiveness of charter schools. Econ. Educ. Rev. 31 (2), 280–292.

Chetty, R., Friedman, J.N., Hilger, N., Saez, E., Schanzenbach, D., Yagan, D., 2011. How does your kindergarten classroom affect your earnings? Evidence from project STAR. Q. J. Econ. 126 (4), 1593–1660.

Chetty, R., Friedman, J.N., Rockoff, J.E., 2014a. Measuring the impacts of teachers I: evaluating bias in teacher value-added estimates. Am. Econ. Rev. 104 (9), 2593–2632.

Chetty, R., Friedman, J.N., Rockoff, J.E., 2014b. Measuring the impacts of teachers II: teacher value-added and student outcomes in adulthood. Am. Econ. Rev. 104 (9), 2633–2679.

Chiang, H., 2009. How accountability pressure on failing schools affects student achievement. J. Public Econ. 93, 1045–1057.

Chingos, M.M., 2012. The impact of a universal class-size reduction policy: evidence from Florida's statewide mandate. Econ. Educ. Rev. 31 (5), 543–562.

Chingos, M.M., Peterson, P.E., 2011. It's easier to pick a good teacher than to train one: familiar and new results on the correlates of teacher effectiveness. Econ. Educ. Rev. 30 (3), 449–465.

Chingos, M.M., West, M.R., 2011. Promotion and reassignment in public school districts: how do schools respond to differences in teacher effectiveness? Econ. Educ. Rev. 30 (3), 419–433.

Chingos, M.M., West, M.R., 2012. Do more effective teachers earn more outside the classroom? Educ. Finance Policy 7 (1), 8–43.

Cho, R.M., 2009. The impact of maternal imprisonment on children's educational achievement: results from children in Chicago public schools. J. Hum. Resour. 44 (3), 772–797.

Clark, D., 2009. The performance and competitive effects of school autonomy. J. Polit. Econ. 117 (4), 745–783.

Clark, D., Martorell, P., 2014. The signaling value of a high school diploma. J. Polit. Econ. 122 (2), 282–318.

Clark, D., See, E., 2011. The impact of tougher education standards: evidence from Florida. Econ. Educ. Rev. 30 (6), 1123–1135.

Clark, M., Rothstein, J., Schanzenbach, D.W., 2009. Selection bias in college admissions test scores. Econ. Educ. Rev. 28 (3), 295–307.

Clotfelter, C.T., Ladd, H.F., Vigdor, J., 2005. Who teaches whom? Race and the distribution of novice teachers. Econ. Educ. Rev. 24 (4), 377–392.

Clotfelter, C.T., Ladd, H.F., Vigdor, J.L., 2006. Teacher-student matching and the assessment of teacher effectiveness. J. Hum. Resour. 41 (4), 778–820.

Clotfelter, C.T., Ladd, H.F., Vigdor, J.L., 2007. Teacher credentials and student achievement: longitudinal analysis with student fixed effects. Econ. Educ. Rev. 26 (6), 673–682.

Clotfelter, C.T., Glennie, E., Hall, H., Vigdor, J., 2008. Would higher salaries keep teachers in high-poverty schools? Evidence from a policy intervention in North Carolina. J. Public Econ. 92, 1352–1370.

Clotfelter, C.T., Ladd, H.F., Vigdor, J.L., 2009a. The academic achievement gap in grades 3 to 8. Rev. Econ. Stat. 91 (2), 398–419.

Clotfelter, C.T., Ladd, H.F., Vigdor, J.L., 2009b. Teacher credentials and student achievement in high school: a cross-subject analysis with student fixed effects. J. Hum. Resour. 45 (3), 655–681.

Clotfelter, C.T., Ladd, H.F., Vigdor, J.L., 2009c. Are teacher absences worth worrying about in the United States? Educ. Finance Policy 4 (2), 115–149.

Clotfelter, C.T., Ladd, H.F., Vigdor, J.L., 2011. Teacher mobility, school segregation, and pay-based policies to level the playing field. Educ. Finance Policy 6 (3), 399–438.

Coelli, M., Green, D.A., 2012. Leadership effects: school principals and student outcomes. Econ. Educ. Rev. 31 (1), 92–109.

Cohen-Zada, D., Gradstein, M., Reuven, E., 2013. Allocation of students in public schools: theory and new evidence. Econ. Educ. Rev. 34, 96–106.

Condie, S., Lefgren, L., Sims, D., 2014. Teacher heterogeneity, value-added and education policy. Econ. Educ. Rev. 40, 76–92.

Cook, P.J., Dodge, K., Farkas, G., Fryer, R.G., Guryan, J., Ludwig, J., Mayer, S., Pollack, H., Steinberg, L., 2014. The (Surprising) Efficacy of Academic and Behavioral Intervention with Disadvantaged Youth: Results from a Randomized Experiment in Chicago. NBER Working Paper No. 19862.

Corten, K.E., Moussa, W.S., Weinstein, J.M., 2013. Educating bright students in urban schools. Econ. Educ. Rev. 37, 286–297.

Cortes, K., Goodman, J., Nomi, T., 2014. Intensive Math Instruction and Educational Attainment: Long-Run Impacts of Double-Dose Algebra. NBER Working Paper No. 20211.

Costrell, R.M., McGee, J.B., 2010. Teacher pension incentives, retirement behavior, and potential for reform in Arkansas. Educ. Finance Policy 5 (4), 492–518.

Costrell, R.M., Podgursky, M., 2010. Distribution of benefits in teacher retirement systems and their implications for mobility. Educ. Finance Policy 5 (4), 519–557.

Cowen, J.M., Winter, M.A., 2013. Do charters retain teachers differently? Evidence from elementary schools in Florida. Educ. Finance Policy 8 (1), 14–42.

Cowen, J.M., Butler, J.S., Fowles, J., Streams, M.E., Toma, E.F., 2012. Teacher retention in Appalachian schools: evidence from Kentucky. Econ. Educ. Rev. 31 (4), 431–441.

Cratty, D., 2012. Potential for significant reductions in dropout rates: analysis of an entire 3rd grade state cohort. Econ. Educ. Rev. 31 (5), 644–662.

Cullen, J.B., Jacob, B.A., Levitt, S.D., 2005. The impact of school choice on student outcomes: an analysis of the Chicago public schools. J. Public Econ. 89, 729–760.

Cullen, J.B., Jacog, B.A., Levitt, S., 2006. The effect of school choice on participants: evidence from randomized lotteries. Econometrica 74 (5), 1191–1230.

Cullen, J.B., Long, M.C., Reback, R., 2013. Jockeying for position: strategic high school choice under Texas' top ten percent plan. J. Public Econ. 97, 32–48.

Currie, J., Hanushek, E.A., Kahn, M.E., Neidell, M., Rivkin, S.G., 2009. Does pollution increase school absences? Rev. Econ. Stat. 91 (4), 682–694.

Currie, J., Stabile, M., Manivong, P., Roos, L.L., 2010. Child health and young adult outcomes. J. Hum. Resour. 45 (3), 517–548.

Currie, J., Figlio, D., Goodman, J., Persico, C., Roth, J., 2014. A Population Level Study of the Effects of Early Intervention for Autism. Mimeo.

Curto, V.E., Fryer, R.G., 2014. The potential of urban boarding schools for the poor: evidence from SEED. J. Labor Econ. 32 (1), 65–93.

Dahl, G., Loken, K., Mogstad, M., Salvanes, K., 2015. What is the case for paid maternity leave? Rev. Econ. Stat.

Dahlberg, M., Edmark, K., Lundqvist, H., 2012. Ethnic diversity and preferences for redistribution. J. Polit. Econ. 120 (1), 41–76.

Dalsgaard, S., Nielsen, H.S., Simonsen, M., 2014. Consequences of ADHD medication use for children's outcomes. J. Health Econ. 37, 137–151.

Damm, A.P., Dustman, C., 2014. Does growing up in a high crime neighborhood affect youth criminal behavior? Am. Econ. Rev. 104 (6), 1806–1832.

DeArmond, M., Goldhaber, D., 2010. Scrambling the nest egg: how well do teachers understand their pensions, and what do they think about alternative pension structures? Educ. Finance Policy 5 (4), 558–586.

DeCicca, P., Smith, J., 2013. The long-run impacts of early childhood education: evidence from a failed policy experiment. Econ. Educ. Rev. 36, 41–59.

Dell, M., 2010. The persistent effects of Peru's mining mita. Econometrica 78 (6), 1863–1903.

Deming, D.J., 2011. Better schools, less crime? Q. J. Econ. 126 (4), 2063–2115.

Deming, D.J., 2014. Using School Choice Lotteries to Test Measures of School Effectiveness. NBER Working Paper No. 19803.

Deming, D.J., Hastings, J.S., Kane, T.J., Staiger, D.O., 2014. School choice, school quality, and postsecondary attainment. Am. Econ. Rev. 104 (3), 991–1013.

Dinkelman, T., Martinez, C.A., 2014. Investing in schooling in Chile: the role of information about financial aid for higher education. Rev. Econ. Stat. 96 (2), 244–257.

Dobbie, W., Fryer, R.G., 2011. Are high-quality schools enough to increase achievement among the poor? Evidence from the Harlem Children's Zone. Am. Econ. J. Appl. Econ. 3 (3), 158–187.

Dobbie, W., Fryer, R.G., 2013. Getting beneath the veil of effective schools: evidence from New York City. Am. Econ. J. Appl. Econ. 5 (4), 28–60.

Dobbie, W., Fryer, R.G., 2014. The impact of attending a school with high-achieving peers: evidence from the New York City exam schools. Am. Econ. J. Appl. Econ. 6 (3), 58–75.

Doyle, J.J., 2007. Child protection and child outcomes: measuring the effects of foster care. Am. Econ. Rev. 97 (5), 1583–1610.

Dustmann, C., Schonberg, U., 2012. Expansions in maternity leave coverage and children's long-term outcomes. Am. Econ. J. Appl. Econ. 4 (3), 190–224.

Dustmann, C., Machin, S., Schonberg, U., 2010. Ethnicity and educational achievement in compulsory schooling. Econ. J. 120 (546), F272–F297.

Edin, P.-A., Fredriksson, P., Aslund, O., 2003. Ethnic enclaves and the economic success of immigrants – evidence from a natural experiment. Q. J. Econ. 11 (1), 329–357.

Edwards, F., 2012. Early to rise? The effect of daily start times on academic performance. Econ. Educ. Rev. 31 (6), 970–983.

Einav, L., Levin, J., 2013. The Data Revolution and Economic Analysis. NBER Working Paper No. 19035.

Engberg, J., Epple, D., Imbrogno, J., Sieg, H., Zimmer, R., 2014. Evaluating education programs that have lotteried admission and selective attrition. J. Labor Econ. 32 (1), 27–63.

Engel, R.C., Gallagher, L.B., Lyle, D.S., 2010. Military deployments and children's academic achievement: evidence from department of defense education activity schools. Econ. Educ. Rev. 29 (1), 73–82.

Fairlie, R.W., Robinson, J., 2013. Experimental evidence on the effects of home computers on academic achievement among schoolchildren. Am. Econ. J. Appl. Econ. 5 (3), 211–240.

Falch, T., Naper, L.R., 2013. Educational evaluation schemes and gender gaps in student achievement. Econ. Educ. Rev. 36, 12–25.

Falch, T., Strom, B., 2005. Teacher turnover and non-pecuniary factors. Econ. Educ. Rev. 24 (6), 611–631.

Feng, L., 2010. Hire today, gone tomorrow: new teacher classroom assignments and teacher mobility. Educ. Finance Policy 5 (3), 278–316.

Feng, L., Sass, T.R., 2013. What makes special-education teachers special? Teacher training and achievement of students with disabilities. Econ. Educ. Rev. 36, 122–134.

Ferguson, J., Strauss, R.P., Vogt, W.B., 2006. The effects of defined benefit pension incentives and working conditions on teacher retirement decisions. Educ. Finance Policy 1 (3), 316–348.

Ferrie, J., Long, J., 2013. Intergenerational occupational mobility in Britain and the U.S. since 1850. Am. Econ. Rev. 103 (4), 1109–1137.

Figlio, D.N., 2006. Testing, crime and punishment. J. Public Econ. 90, 837–851.

Figlio, D.N., 2007. Boys named sue: disruptive children and their peers. Educ. Finance Policy 2 (4), 376–394.

Figlio, D.N., Hart, C.M.D., 2014. Competitive effects of means-tested school vouchers. Am. Econ. J. Appl. Econ. 6 (1), 133–156.

Figlio, D.N., Loeb, S., 2011. School accountability. In: Handbook of Economics of Education, vol. 3, pp. 383–421.

Figlio, D.N., Lucas, M.E., 2004a. Do high grading standards affect student performance? J. Public Econ. 89, 1815–1834.

Figlio, D.N., Lucas, M.E., 2004b. What's in a grade? School report cards and the housing market. Am. Econ. Rev. 94 (3), 591–604.

Figlio, D.N., Rouse, C.E., 2006. Do accountability and voucher threats improve low-performing schools? J. Public Econ. 90, 239–255.

Figlio, D.N., Hart, C.M.D., Metzger, M., 2010. Who uses a means-tested scholarship, and what do they choose? Econ. Educ. Rev. 29 (2), 301–317.

Figlio, D.N., Guryan, J., Karbownik, K., Roth, J., 2014. The effects of poor neonatal health on children's cognitive development. Am. Econ. Rev. 104 (12), 3921–3955.

Fitzpatrick, M.D., Lovenheim, M.F., 2014. Early retirement incentives and student achievement. Am. Econ. J. Econ. Policy 6 (3), 120–154.

Fredriksson, P., Ockert, B., 2008. Resources and student achievement – evidence from a Swedish policy reform. Scand. J. Econ. 110 (2), 277–296.

Fredriksson, P., Ockert, B., Oosterbeek, H., 2013. Long term effects of class size. Q. J. Econ. 128 (1), 249–285.

Friesen, J., Hickey, R., Krauth, B., 2010. Disabled peers and academic achievement. Educ. Finance Policy 5 (3), 317–348.

Fruehwirth, J.C., 2014. Can achievement peer effect estimates inform policy? A view from inside the black box. Rev. Econ. Stat. 96 (3), 514–523.

Fryer, R.G., 2011. Financial incentives and student achievement: evidence from randomized trials. Q. J. Econ. 126 (4), 1755–1798.

Fryer, R.G., 2013. Teacher incentives and student achievement: evidence from New York City public schools. J. Labor Econ. 31 (2), 373–407.

Fryer, R.G., 2014. Injecting charter school best practices into traditional public schools: evidence from field experiments. Q. J. Econ. 129 (3), 1355–1407.

Fuller, S.C., Ladd, H.F., 2013. School-based accountability and the distribution of teacher quality across grades in elementary school. Educ. Finance Policy 8 (4), 528–559.

Gates, S.M., Ringel, J.S., Santibanez, L., Guarino, C., Ghosh-Dastidar, B., Brown, A., 2006. Mobility and turnover among school principals. Econ. Educ. Rev. 25 (3), 289–302.

Geay, C., McNally, S., Telhaj, S., 2013. Non-native speakers of English in the classroom: what are the effects on pupil performance? Econ. J. 123 (570), F281–F307.

Gershenson, S., 2012. How do substitute teachers substitute? An empirical study of substitute-teacher labor supply. Econ. Educ. Rev. 31 (4), 410–430.

Gibbons, S., Silva, O., 2011a. Faith primary schools: better schools or better pupils? J. Labor Econ. 29 (3), 589–635.

Gibbons, S., Silva, O., 2011b. School quality, child wellbeing and parents' satisfaction. Econ. Educ. Rev. 30 (2), 312–331.

Gibbons, S., Telhaj, S., 2011. Pupil mobility and school disruption. J. Public Econ. 95, 1156–1167.

Gibbons, S., Silva, O., Weinhardt, F., 2013. Everybody needs good neighbours? Evidence from students' outcomes in England. Econ. J. 123 (571), 831–874.

Gimenez, L., Chou, S.-Y., Liu, J.-T., Liu, J.-L., 2013. Parental loss and children's well-being. J. Hum. Resour. 48 (4), 1035–1071.

Glewwe, P., Kremer, M., Moulin, S., 2009. Many children left behind? Textbooks and test scores in Kenya. Am. Econ. J. Appl. Econ. 1 (1), 112–135.

Goldhaber, D., 2007. Everyone's doing it, but what does teacher testing tell us about teacher effectiveness? J. Hum. Resour. 42 (4), 765–794.

Goldhaber, D., Anthony, E., 2007. Can teacher quality be effectively assessed? National board certification as a signal of effective teaching. Rev. Econ. Stat. 89 (1), 134–150.

Goldhaber, D., Hansen, M., 2009. National board certification and teachers' career paths: does NBPTS certification influence how long teachers remain in the profession and where they teach? Educ. Finance Policy 4 (3), 229–262.

Goldhaber, D., Theobald, R., 2013. Managing the teacher workforce in austere times: the determinants and implications of teacher layoffs. Educ. Finance Policy 8 (4), 494–527.

Goldhaber, D., Walch, J., 2012. Strategic pay reform: a student outcomes-based evaluation of Denver's ProComp teacher pay initiative. Econ. Educ. Rev. 31 (6), 1067–1083.

Goldhaber, D., Choi, H.-J., Cramer, L., 2007. A descriptive analysis of the distribution of NBPTS-certified teachers in North Carolina. Econ. Educ. Rev. 26 (2), 160–172.

Goldhaber, D., Cowan, J., Walch, J., 2013a. Is a good elementary teacher always good? Assessing teacher performance estimates across subjects. Econ. Educ. Rev. 36, 216–228.

Goldhaber, D., Liddle, S., Theobald, R., 2013b. The gateway to the profession: assessing teacher preparation programs based on student achievement. Econ. Educ. Rev. 34, 29–44.

Golsteyn, B., Gronqvist, H., Lindahl, L., 2014. Adolescent time preferences predict lifetime outcomes. Econ. J. 124 (580), F739–F761.

Goodman, J., 2008. Who merits financial aid?: Massachusetts' Adams scholarship. J. Public Econ. 92, 2121–2131.

Goodman, J., 2010. Skills, schools, and credit constraints: evidence from Massachusetts. Educ. Finance Policy 5 (1), 36–53.

Goodman, J., 2014. Flaking Out: Student Absences and Snow Days as Disruptions of Instructional Time. NBER Working Paper No. 20221.

Gould, E.D., Lavy, V., Paserman, D.M., 2004. Immigrating to opportunity: estimating the effect of school quality using a natural experiment on Ethiopians in Israel. Q. J. Econ. 119 (2), 489–526.

Gould, E.D., Lavy, V., Paserman, M.D., 2009. Does immigration affect the long-term educational outcomes of natives? Quasi-experimental evidence. Econ. J. 119 (540), 1243–1269.

Greene, J.P., Winters, M.A., 2007. Revisiting grade retention: an evaluation of Florida's test-based promotion policy. Educ. Finance Policy 2 (4), 319–340.

Greene, J.P., Winters, M.A., 2009. The effects of exemptions to Florida's test-based promotion policy: who is retained? Who benefits academically? Econ. Educ. Rev. 28 (1), 135–142.

Gritz, M.R., Theobald, N.D., 1996. The effects of school district spending priorities on length of stay in teaching. J. Hum. Resour. 31 (3), 477–512.

Gronqvist, H., Hall, C., 2013. Education policy and early fertility: lessons from an expansion of upper secondary schooling. Econ. Educ. Rev. 37, 13–33.

Guardiano, C.M., Brown, A.B., Wyse, A.E., 2011. Can districts keep good teachers in the schools that need them most? Econ. Educ. Rev. 30 (5), 962–979.

Gupta, N.D., Simonsen, M., 2010. Non-cognitive child outcomes and universal high quality child care. J. Public Econ. 94, 30–43.

Haegeland, T., Raaum, O., Salvanes, K.G., 2012. Pennies from heaven? Using exogenous tax variation to identify effects of school resources on pupil achievement. Econ. Educ. Rev. 31 (5), 601–614.

Hakkinen, I., Kirjavainen, T., Uusitalo, R., 2003. School resources and student achievement revisited: new evidence from panel data. Econ. Educ. Rev. 22 (3), 329–335.

Hall, C., 2012. The effects of reducing tracking in upper secondary school: evidence from a large-scale pilot scheme. J. Hum. Resour. 47 (1), 237–269.

Hanushek, E.A., 1992. The trade-off between child quantity and quality. J. Polit. Econ. 100 (1), 84–117.

Hanushek, E.A., Kain, J.F., Rivkin, S.G., 2002. Inferring program effects for special populations: does special education raise achievement for students with disabilities? Rev. Econ. Stat. 84 (4), 584–599.

Hanushek, E.A., Kain, J.F., Rivkin, S.G., 2004a. Why public schools lose teachers. J. Hum. Resour. 39 (2), 326–354.

Hanushek, E.A., Kain, J.F., Rivkin, S.G., 2004b. Disruption versus Tiebout improvement: the costs and benefits of switching schools. J. Public Econ. 88, 1721–1746.

Hanushek, E.A., Kain, J.F., Rivkin, S.G., Branch, G.F., 2007. Charter school quality and parental decision making with school choice. J. Public Econ. 91, 823–848.

Hanushek, E.A., Kain, J.F., Rivkin, S.G., 2009. New evidence about brown v. board of education: the complex effects of school racial composition on achievement. J. Labor Econ. 27 (3), 349–383.

Harris, D.N., Sass, T.R., 2011. Teacher training, teacher quality and student achievement. J. Public Econ. 95, 798–812.

Harris, D.N., Sass, T.R., 2014. Skills, productivity and the evaluation of teacher performance. Econ. Educ. Rev. 40, 183–204.

Hastings, J.S., Weinstein, J.M., 2008. Information, school choice, and academic achievement: evidence from two experiments. Q. J. Econ. 123 (4), 1373–1414.

Hastings, J.S., Kane, T.J., Staiger, D.O., Weinstein, J.M., 2007. The effect of randomized school admissions on voter participation. J. Public Econ. 91, 915–937.

Havens, T., Mogstad, M., 2014. Is universal child care leveling the playing field. J. Public Econ. 127, 100–114.

Havnes, T., Mogstad, M., 2011. No child left behind: subsidized child care and children's long-run outcomes. Am. Econ. J. Econ. Policy 3 (2), 97–129.

Heers, M., Van Klaveren, C., Groot, W., Van den Brink, H.M., 2014. The impact of community schools on student dropout in pre-vocational education. Econ. Educ. Rev. 41, 105–119.

Heinesen, E., 2010. Estimating class-size effects using within-school variation in subject-specific classes. Econ. J. 120 (545), 737–760.

Hendricks, M.D., 2014. Does it pay to pay teachers more? Evidence from Texas. J. Public Econ. 109, 50–63.

Henry, G.T., Bastian, K.C., Fortner, C.K., Kershaw, D.C., Purtell, K.M., Thompson, C.L., Zulli, R.A., 2014. Teacher preparation policies and their effects on student achievement. Educ. Finance Policy 9 (3), 264–303.

Hensvik, L., 2012. Competition, wages and teacher sorting: lessons learned from a voucher reform. Econ. J. 122 (561), 799–824.

Hermann, M.A., Rockoff, J.E., 2012. Worker absence and productivity: evidence from teaching. J. Labor Econ. 30 (4), 749–782.

Hilbert, M., Lopez, P., 2011. The world's technological capacity to store, communicate, and compute information. Science 332, 60–65.

Hinnerich, B.T., Hoglin, E., Johannesson, M., 2011. Are boys discriminated in Swedish high schools? Econ. Educ. Rev. 30 (4), 682–690.

Hinrichs, P., 2011. When the bell tolls: the effects of school starting times on academic achievement. Educ. Finance Policy 6 (4), 486–507.

Holmlund, H., McNally, S., Viarengo, M., 2010. Does money matter for schools? Econ. Educ. Rev. 29 (6), 1154–1164.

Holmlund, H., Lindahl, M., Plug, E., 2011. The causal effect of parents' schooling on children's schooling: a comparison of estimation methods. J. Econ. Lit. 49 (3), 615–651.

Imazeki, J., 2005. Teacher salaries and teacher attrition. Econ. Educ. Rev. 24 (4), 431–449.

Imberman, S.A., 2011a. Achievement and behavior in charter schools: drawing a more complete picture. Rev. Econ. Stat. 93 (2), 416–435.

Imberman, S.A., 2011b. The effect of charter schools on achievement and behavior of public school students. J. Public Econ. 95, 850–863.

Imberman, S.A., Lovenheim, M., 2015. Incentive strength and teacher productivity: evidence from a group-based teacher incentive pay system. Rev. Econ. Stat. 97 (2), 364–386.

Imberman, S.A., Kugler, A.D., Sacerdote, B.I., 2012. Katrina's children: evidence on the structure of peer effects from hurricane evacuees. Am. Econ. Rev. 102 (5), 2048–2082.

Jackson, C.K., 2009. Student demographics, teacher sorting, and teacher quality: evidence from the end of school desegregation. J. Labor Econ. 27 (2), 213–256.

Jackson, C.K., 2010. Do students benefit from attending better schools? Evidence from rule-based student assignments in Trinidad and Tobago. Econ. J. 120 (549), 1399–1429.

Jackson, C.K., 2012a. Single-sex schools, student achievement, and course selection: evidence from rule-based student assignments in Trinidad and Tobago. J. Public Econ. 96, 173–187.

Jackson, C.K., 2012b. School competition and teacher labor markets: evidence from charter school entry in North Carolina. J. Public Econ. 96, 431–448.

Jackson, C.K., 2013a. Can higher-achieving peers explain the benefits to attending selective schools? Evidence from Trinidad and Tobago. J. Public Econ. 108, 63–77.

Jackson, K.C., 2013b. Match quality, worker productivity, and worker mobility: direct evidence from teachers. Rev. Econ. Stat. 95 (4), 1096–1116.

Jackson, C.K., 2014. Teacher quality at the high-school level: the importance of accounting for tracks. J. Labor Econ. 32 (4), 645–684.

Jackson, C.K., Bruegmann, E., 2009. Teaching students and teaching each other: the importance of peer learning for teachers. Am. Econ. J. Appl. Econ. 1 (4), 85–108.

Jacob, B.A., 2004. Public housing, housing vouchers, and student achievement: evidence from public housing demolitions in Chicago. Am. Econ. Rev. 94 (1), 233–258.

Jacob, B.A., 2005. Accountability, incentives and behavior: the impact of high-stakes testing in the Chicago public schools. J. Public Econ. 89, 761–796.

Jacob, B.A., 2013. The effect of employment protection on teacher effort. J. Labor Econ. 31 (4), 727–761.

Jacob, B.A., Lefgren, L., 2004a. The impact of teacher training on student achievement: quasi-experimental evidence from school reform efforts in Chicago. J. Hum. Resour. 39 (1), 50–79.

Jacob, B.A., Lefgren, L., 2004b. Remedial education and student achievement: a regression-discontinuity analysis. Rev. Econ. Stat. 86 (1), 226–244.

Jacob, B.A., Lefgren, L., 2007. What do parents value in education? An empirical investigation of parents' revealed preferences for teachers. Q. J. Econ. 122 (4), 1603–1637.

Jacob, B.A., Lefgren, L., 2008. Can principals identify effective teachers? Evidence on subjective performance evaluation in education. J. Labor Econ. 26 (1), 101–136.

Jacob, B.A., Lefgren, L., 2009. The effect of grade retention on high school completion. Am. Econ. J. Appl. Econ. 1 (3), 33–58.

Jacob, B.A., Levitt, S., 2003. Rotten apples: an investigation of the prevalence and predictors of teacher cheating. Q. J. Econ. 118 (3), 843–877.

Jacob, B.A., Walsh, E., 2011. What's in a rating? Econ. Educ. Rev. 30 (3), 434–448.

Jacob, B.A., Lefgren, L., Sims, D.P., 2010. The persistence of teacher-induced learning. J. Hum. Resour. 45 (4), 915–943.

Jacob, B., Kapustin, M., Ludwig, J., 2014. Human Capital Effects of Anti-Poverty Programs: Evidence from a Randomized Housing Voucher Lottery. NBER Working Paper No. 20164.

Jalava, N., Joensen, J., Pellas, E.M., 2015. Grades and rank: impacts of non-financial incentives on test performance. J. Econ. Behav. Organ. 115, 161–196.

Jensen, P., Rasmussen, A.W., 2011. The effect of immigrant concentration in schools on native and immigrant children's reading and math skills. Econ. Educ. Rev. 30 (6), 1503–1515.

Jepsen, C., 2010. Bilingual education and English proficiency. Educ. Finance Policy 5 (2), 200–227.

Joensen, J.S., Nielsen, H.S., 2009. Is there a causal effect of high school math on labor market outcomes? J. Hum. Resour. 44 (1), 171–198.

Kane, T.J., Rockoff, J.E., Staiger, D.O., 2008. What does certification tell us about teacher effectiveness? Evidence from New York City. Econ. Educ. Rev. 27 (6), 615–631.

Kane, T., Taylor, E.S., Tyler, J.H., Wooten, A.L., 2011. Identifying effective classroom practices using student achievement data. J. Hum. Resour. 46 (3), 587–613.

Karbownik, K., 2014. Do Changes in Student Quality Affect Teacher Mobility? Evidence from an Admission Reform. IFAU Working Paper 2014:15.

Kasman, M., Loeb, S., 2013. Principals' perceptions of competition for students in Milwaukee schools. Educ. Finance Policy 8 (1), 43–73.

Kerr, S.P., Pekkarinen, T., Uusitalo, R., 2013. School tracking and development of cognitive skills. J. Labor Econ. 31 (3), 577–602.

Keslair, F., Maurin, E., McNally, S., 2012. Every child matters? An evaluation of "special educational needs" programmes in England. Econ. Educ. Rev. 31 (6), 932–948.

Kinsler, J., 2011. Understanding the black–white school discipline gap. Econ. Educ. Rev. 30 (6), 1370–1383.

Kinsler, J., 2012. Beyond levels and growth: estimating teacher value-added and its persistence. J. Hum. Resour. 47 (3), 722–753.

Klopfenstein, K., 2004. Advanced placement: do minorities have equal opportunity? Econ. Educ. Rev. 23 (2), 115–131.

Koedel, C., 2009. An empirical analysis of teacher spillover effects in secondary school. Econ. Educ. Rev. 28 (6), 682–692.

Koedel, C., Betts, J., 2010. Value added to what? How a ceiling in the testing instrument influences value-added estimation. Educ. Finance Policy 5 (1), 54–81.

Koedel, C., Betts, J.R., 2011. Does student sorting invalidate value-added models of teacher effectiveness? An extended analysis of the Rothstein critique. Educ. Finance Policy 6 (1), 18–42.

Koedel, C., Ni, S., Podgursky, M., 2014. Who benefits from pension enhancements? Educ. Finance Policy 9 (2), 165–192.

Kremer, M., Miguel, E., Thornton, R., 2009. Incentives to learn. Rev. Econ. Stat. 91 (3), 437–456.

Krieg, J.M., 2006. Teacher quality and attrition. Econ. Educ. Rev. 25 (1), 13–27.

Krieg, J.M., 2008. Are students left behind? The distributional effects of the no child left behind act. Educ. Finance Policy 3 (2), 250–281.

Krieg, J.M., 2011. Which students are left behind? The racial impacts of the no child left behind act. Econ. Educ. Rev. 30 (4), 654–664.

Kukla-Acevedo, S., 2009. Do teacher characteristics matter? New results on the effects of teacher preparation on student achievement. Econ. Educ. Rev. 28 (1), 49–57.

Ladd, H.F., Walsh, R.P., 2002. Implementing value-added measures of school effectiveness: getting the incentives right. Econ. Educ. Rev. 21 (1), 1–17.

Ladd, H.F., Muschkin, C., Dodge, K., 2012. From Birth to School: Early Childhood Initiatives and Third Grade Outcomes in North Carolina. Mimeo.

Lai, F., 2010. Are boys left behind? The evolution of the gender achievement gap in Beijing's middle schools. Econ. Educ. Rev. 29 (3), 383–399.

Lai, F., Sadoulet, E., De Janvry, A., 2009. The adverse effects of parents' school selection errors on academic achievement: evidence from the Beijing open enrollment program. Econ. Educ. Rev. 28 (4), 485–496.

Lai, F., Sadoulet, E., de Janvry, A., 2011. The contributions of school quality and teacher qualifications to student performance: evidence from a natural experiment in Beijing middle schools. J. Hum. Resour. 46 (1), 123–153.

Lankford, H., Wyckoff, J., 1997. The changing structure of teacher compensation, 1970–94. Econ. Educ. Rev. 16 (4), 371–384.

Lavy, V., 2008. Do gender stereotypes reduce girls' or boys' human capital outcomes? Evidence from a natural experiment. J. Public Econ. 92, 2083–2105.

Lavy, V., 2009. Performance pay and teachers' effort, productivity, and grading ethics. Am. Econ. Rev. 99 (5), 1979–2011.

Lavy, V., 2010. Effects of free choice among public schools. Rev. Econ. Stud. 77 (3), 1164–1191.

Lavy, V., 2013. Gender differences in market competitiveness in a real workplace: evidence from performance-based pay tournaments among teachers. Econ. J. 123 (569), 540–573.

Lavy, V., 2014. Long Run Effects of Free School Choice: College Attainment, Employment, Earnings, and Social Outcomes at Adulthood. Mimeo.

Lavy, V., Paserman, M.D., 2012. Inside the black box of ability peer effects: evidence from variation in the proportion of low achievers in the classroom. Econ. J. 122 (559), 208–237.

Lavy, V., Schlosser, A., 2005. Targeted remedial education for underperforming teenagers: costs and benefits. J. Labor Econ. 23 (4), 839–874.

Lavy, V., Schlosser, A., 2011. Mechanisms and impacts of gender peer effects at school. Am. Econ. J. Appl. Econ. 3 (2), 1–33.

Lavy, V., Silva, O., Weinhardt, F., 2012. The good, the bad, and the average: evidence on ability peer effects in schools. J. Labor Econ. 30 (2), 367–414.

Leach, J., Payne, A.A., Chan, S., 2010. The effects of school board consolidation and financing on student performance. Econ. Educ. Rev. 29 (6), 1034–1046.

Leigh, A., 2010. Estimating teacher effectiveness from two-year changes in students' test scores. Econ. Educ. Rev. 29 (3), 480–488.

Leos-Urbel, J., Schwartz, A.E., Weinstein, M., Corcoran, S., 2013. Not just for poor kids: the impact of universal free school breakfast on meal participation and student outcomes. Econ. Educ. Rev. 36, 88–107.

Leuven, E., Roenning, M., 2015. Classroom grade composition and pupil achievement. Econ. J.

Leuven, E., Lindahl, M., Oosterbeek, H., Webbink, D., 2007. The effect of extra funding for disadvantaged pupils on achievement. Rev. Econ. Stat. 89 (4), 721–736.

Leuven, E., Oosterbeek, H., Roenning, M., 2008. Quasi-experimental estimates of the effects of class size on achievement in Norway. Scand. J. Econ. 110 (4), 663–693.

Lockwood, J.R., McCaffrey, D.F., 2009. Exploring student-teacher interactions in longitudinal achievement data. Educ. Finance Policy 4 (4), 439–467.

Loeb, S., Kalogrides, D., Beteille, T., 2012. Effective schools: teacher hiring, assignment, development, and retention. Educ. Finance Policy 7 (3), 269–304.

Loken, K.V., Mogstad, M., Wiswall, M., 2012. What linear estimators miss: the effects of family income on child outcomes. Am. Econ. J. Appl. Econ. 4 (2), 1–35.

Lucas, A.M., Mbiti, I.M., 2012. Access, sorting, and achievement: the short-run effects of free primary education in Kenya. Am. Econ. J. Appl. Econ. 4 (4), 226–253.

Lucas, A.M., Mbiti, I.M., 2014. Effects of school quality on student achievement: discontinuity evidence from Kenya. Am. Econ. J. Appl. Econ. 6 (3), 234–263.

Lundborg, P., Nilsson, A., Rooth, D.-O., 2014. Parental education and offspring outcomes: evidence from the Swedish compulsory school reform. Am. Econ. J. Appl. Econ. 6 (1), 253–278.

Lyle, D.S., 2006. Using military deployments and job assignments to estimate the effect of parental. J. Labor Econ. 24 (2), 319–350.

Macartney, H., 2014. The Dynamic Effects of Educational Accountability. NBER Working Paper No. 19915.

Machin, S., McNally, S., Silva, O., 2007. New technology in schools: is there a payoff? Econ. J. 117 (522), 1145–1167.

Manacorda, M., 2012. The cost of grade retention. Rev. Econ. Stat. 94 (2), 596–606.

Mansfield, R.K., 2014. Teacher quality and student inequality. J. Labor Econ. 33 (3), 751–788.

Matsudaira, J.D., Hosek, A., Walsh, E., 2012. An integrated assessment of the effects of title I on school behavior, resources, and student achievement. Econ. Educ. Rev. 31 (3), 1–14.

McCaffrey, D.F., Sass, T.R., Lockwood, J.R., Mihaly, K., 2009. The intertemporal variability of teacher effect estimates. Educ. Finance Policy 4 (4), 572–606.

McEvan, P.J., Shapiro, J.S., 2008. The benefits of delayed primary school enrollment: discontinuity estimates using exact birth dates. J. Hum. Resour. 43 (1), 1–29.

McEwan, P.J., 2003. Peer effects on student achievement: evidence from Chile. Econ. Educ. Rev. 22 (2), 131–141.

McEwan, P.J., 2013. The impact of Chile's school feeding program on education outcomes. Econ. Educ. Rev. 32, 122–139.

McMullen, S.C., Rouse, K.E., 2012a. The impact of year-round schooling on academic achievement: evidence from mandatory school calendar conversions. Am. Econ. J. Econ. Policy 4 (4), 230–252.

McMullen, S.C., Rouse, K.E., 2012b. School crowding, year-round schooling, and mobile classroom use: evidence from North Carolina. Econ. Educ. Rev. 31 (5), 812–823.

Meghir, C., Palme, M., 2005. Educational reform, ability, and family background. Am. Econ. Rev. 95 (1), 414–424.

Meghir, C., Palme, M., Schnabel, M., 2012. The Effect of Education Policy on Crime: An Intergenerational Perspective. NBER Working Paper No. 18145.

Meyer, E., Van Klaveren, C., 2013. The effectiveness of extended day programs: evidence from a randomized field experiment in the Netherlands. Econ. Educ. Rev. 36, 1–11.

Mihaly, K., McCaffrey, D., Sass, T.R., Lockwood, J.R., 2013. Where you come from or where you go? Distinguishing between school quality and the effectiveness of teacher preparation program graduates. Educ. Finance Policy 8 (4), 459–493.

Miller, A., 2013. Principal turnover and student achievement. Econ. Educ. Rev. 36, 60–72.

Miller, L.C., Mittleman, J., 2012. High schools that work and college preparedness: measuring the model's impact on mathematics and science pipeline progression. Econ. Educ. Rev. 31 (6), 1116–1135.

Mizala, A., Roumaguera, P., 2000. School performance and choice: the Chilean experience. J. Hum. Resour. 35 (2), 392–417.

Muhlenweg, A.M., Puhani, P.A., 2010. The evolution of the school-entry age effect in a school tracking system. J. Hum. Resour. 45 (2), 407–438.

Murnane, R.J., Olsen, R.J., 1990. The effects of salaries and opportunity costs on length of stay in teaching: evidence from North Carolina. J. Hum. Resour. 25 (1), 106–124.

Naper, L.N., 2010. Teacher hiring practices and educational efficiency. Econ. Educ. Rev. 29 (4), 658–668.

Neal, D., Schanzenbach, D.W., 2010. Left behind by design: proficiency counts and test-based accountability. Rev. Econ. Stat. 92 (2), 263–283.

Nekby, L., Pettersson-Lidbom, P., 2015. Revisiting the relationship between ethnic diversity and preferences for redistribution. Scand. J. Econ.

Ni, Y., Rorrer, A.K., 2012. Twice considered: charter schools and student achievement in Utah. Econ. Educ. Rev. 31 (5), 835–849.

Oreopoulos, P., Stabile, M., Walld, R., Roos, L.L., 2008. Short-, medium-, and long-term consequences of poor infant health: an analysis using siblings and twins. J. Hum. Resour. 43 (1), 88–138.

Ortega, D.E., 2010. The effect of wage compression and alternative labor market opportunities on teacher quality in Venezuela. Econ. Educ. Rev. 29 (5), 760–771.

Ost, B., 2014. How do teachers improve? The relative importance of specific and general human capital. Am. Econ. J. Appl. Econ. 6 (2), 127–151.

Ou, D., 2010. To leave or not to leave? A regression discontinuity analysis of the impact of failing the high school exit exam. Econ. Educ. Rev. 29 (2), 171–186.

Ouazad, A., Page, L., 2013. Students' perceptions of teacher biases: experimental economics in schools. J. Public Econ. 105, 116–130.

Palme, M., Lindahl, M., Massih, S.S., Sjogren, A., 2015. Long-term intergenerational persistence of human capital: an empirical analysis of four generations. J. Hum. Resour. 50 (1), 1–33.

Paredes, V., 2014. A teacher like me or a student like me? Role model versus teacher bias effect. Econ. Educ. Rev. 39, 38–49.

Pathak, P.A., Shi, P., 2014. Demand Modeling, Forecasting, and Counterfactuals, Part I. NBER Working Paper No. 19859.

Player, D., 2010. Nonmonetary compensation in the public teacher labor market. Educ. Finance Policy 5 (1), 82–103.

Podgursky, M., Monroe, R., Watson, D., 2004. The academic quality of public school teachers: an analysis of entry and exit behavior. Econ. Educ. Rev. 23 (5), 507–518.

Pop-Eleches, C., Urquiola, M., 2013. Going to a better school: effects and behavioral responses. Am. Econ. Rev. 103 (4), 1289–1324.

Ransom, M.R., Sims, D.P., 2010. Estimating the firm's labor supply curve in a "new monopsony" framework: schoolteachers in Missouri. J. Labor Econ. 28 (2), 331–355.

Ray, A., McCormack, T., Evans, H., 2009. Value added in English schools. Educ. Finance Policy 4 (4), 415–438.

Reback, R., 2008. Teaching to the rating: school accountability and the distribution of student achievement. J. Public Econ. 92, 1394–1415.

Rege, M., Telle, K., Votruba, M., 2011. Parental job loss and children's school performance. Rev. Econ. Stud. 78 (4), 1462–1489.

Reinikka, R., Svensson, J., 2011. The power of information in public services: evidence from education in Uganda. J. Public Econ. 95, 956–966.

Rivkin, S.G., Hanushek, E.A., Kain, J.F., 2005. Teachers, schools, and academic achievement. Econometrica 73 (2), 417–458.

Robertson, E., 2011. The effects of quarter of birth on academic outcomes at the elementary school level. Econ. Educ. Rev. 30 (2), 300–311.

Rockoff, J.E., Lockwood, B.B., 2010. Stuck in the middle: impacts of grade configuration in public schools. J. Public Econ. 94, 1051–1061.

Rockoff, J.E., Jacob, B.A., Kane, T.J., Staiger, D.O., 2011. Can you recognize an effective teacher when you recruit one? Educ. Finance Policy 6 (1), 43–74.

Rockoff, J.E., Staiger, D.O., Kane, T.J., Taylor, E.S., 2012. Information and employee evaluation: evidence from a randomized intervention in public schools. Am. Econ. Rev. 102 (7), 3184–3213.

Roed, K., Raaum, O., 2003. Administrative registers: unexplored reservoirs of scientific knowledge? Econ. J. 113 (488), F258–F281.

Rothstein, J., 2009. Student sorting and bias in value-added estimation: selection on observables and unobservables. Educ. Finance Policy 4 (4), 537–571.

Rothstein, J., 2010. Teacher quality in educational production: tracking, decay, and student achievement. Q. J. Econ. 125 (1), 175–214.

Rouse, C.E., Hannaway, J., Goldhaber, D., Figlio, D., 2013. Feeling the Florida heat? How low-performing schools respond to voucher and accountability pressure. Am. Econ. J. Econ. Policy 5 (2), 251–281.

Rubenstein, R., Schwartz, A.E., Stiefel, L., Zabel, J., 2009. Spending, size, and grade span in K-8 schools. Educ. Finance Policy 4 (1), 60–88.

Sacerdote, B., 2012. When the saints go marching out: long-term outcomes for student evacuees from hurricanes Katrina and Rita. Am. Econ. J. Appl. Econ. 4 (1), 109–135.

Sanders, N.J., 2012. What doesn't kill you makes you weaker: prenatal pollution exposure and educational outcomes. J. Hum. Resour. 47 (3), 826–850.

Sandstrom, M.F., Bergstrom, F., 2005. School vouchers in practice: competition will not hurt you. J. Public Econ. 89, 351–380.

Sass, T.R., 2006. Charter schools and student achievement in Florida. Educ. Finance Policy 1 (1), 91–122.

Sass, T.R., Semykina, A., Harris, D.N., 2014. Value-added models and the measurement of teacher productivity. Econ. Educ. Rev. 38, 9–23.

Scafidi, B., Sjoquist, D.L., Stinebrickner, T.R., 2007. Race, poverty, and teacher mobility. Econ. Educ. Rev. 26 (2), 145–159.

Schneeweis, N., Zweimuller, M., 2012. Girls, girls, girls: gender composition and female school choice. Econ. Educ. Rev. 31 (4), 482–500.

Schwartz, A.E., Stiefel, L., 2006. Is there a nativity gap? New evidence on the academic performance of immigrant students. Educ. Finance Policy 1 (1), 17–49.

Schwartz, A.E., Stiefel, L., Kim, D.Y., 2004. The impact of school reform on student performance: evidence from the New York network for school renewal project. J. Hum. Resour. 39 (2), 500–522.

Schwerdt, G., West, M.R., 2013. The impact of alternative grade configurations on student outcomes through middle and high school. J. Public Econ. 97, 308–326.

Smith, J., 2010. How valuable is the gift of time? The factors that drive the birth date effect in education. Educ. Finance Policy 5 (3), 247–277.

Soderstrom, M., Uusitalo, R., 2010. School choice and segregation: evidence from an admission reform. Scand. J. Econ. 112 (1), 55–76.

Springer, M.G., 2008. The influence of an NCLB accountability plan on the distribution of student test score gains. Econ. Educ. Rev. 27 (5), 556–563.

Steinberg, M.P., 2014. Does greater autonomy improve school performance? Evidence from a regression discontinuity analysis in Chicago. Educ. Finance Policy 9 (1), 1–35.

Strain, M.R., 2013. Single-sex classes & student outcomes: evidence from North Carolina. Econ. Educ. Rev. 36, 73–87.

Streams, M., Butler, J.S., Cowen, J., Fowles, J., Toma, E.F., 2011. School finance reform: do equalized expenditures imply equalized teacher salaries? Educ. Finance Policy 6 (4), 508–536.

Sund, K., 2009. Estimating peer effects in Swedish high school using school, teacher, and student fixed effects. Econ. Educ. Rev. 28 (3), 329–336.

Taylor, E., 2014. Spending more of the school day in math class: evidence from a regression discontinuity in middle school. J. Public Econ. 117, 162–181.

Taylor, E.S., Tyler, J.H., 2012. The effect of evaluation on teacher performance. Am. Econ. Rev. 102 (7), 3628–3651.

Theobald, N.D., 1990. An examination of the influence of personal, professional, and school district characteristics on public school teacher retention. Econ. Educ. Rev. 9 (3), 241–250.

Theobald, N.D., Gritz, M.R., 1996. The effects of school district spending priorities on the exit paths of beginning teachers leaving the district. Econ. Educ. Rev. 15 (1), 11–22.

Thieme, C., Prior, D., Tortosa-Ausina, E., 2013. A multilevel decomposition of school performance using robust nonparametric frontier techniques. Econ. Educ. Rev. 32, 104–121.

Tuck, B., Berman, M., Hill, A., 2009. Local amenities, unobserved quality, and market clearing: adjusting teacher compensation to provide equal education opportunities. Econ. Educ. Rev. 28 (1), 58–66.

Tyler, J.H., Lofstrom, M., 2010. Is the GED an effective route to postsecondary education for school dropouts? Econ. Educ. Rev. 29 (5), 813–825.

Tyler, J.H., Murnane, R.J., Willett, J.B., 2000. Estimating the labor market signaling value of the GED. Q. J. Econ. 115 (2), 431–468.

Tyler, J.H., Murnane, R.J., Willett, J.B., 2004. The devil's in the details: evidence from the GED on large effects of small differences in high stakes exams. Econ. Educ. Rev. 23 (4), 339–349.

Urquiola, M., Verhoogen, E., 2009. Class-size caps, sorting, and the regression-discontinuity design. Am. Econ. Rev. 99 (1), 179–215.

Waldo, S., 2007. On the use of student data in efficiency analysis—technical efficiency in Swedish upper secondary school. Econ. Educ. Rev. 26 (2), 173–185.

Weiss, M.J., May, H., 2012. A policy analysis of the federal growth model pilot program's measures of school performance: the Florida case. Educ. Finance Policy 7 (1), 44–73.

West, M.R., Peterson, P.E., 2006. The efficacy of choice threats within school accountability systems: results from legislatively induced experiments. Econ. J. 116 (510), C46–C62.

Wikstrom, C., Wikstrom, M., 2005. Grade inflation and school competition: an empirical analysis based on the Swedish upper secondary schools. Econ. Educ. Rev. 24 (3), 309–322.

Winters, M.A., 2012. Measuring the effect of charter schools on public school student achievement in an urban environment: evidence from New York City. Econ. Educ. Rev. 31 (2), 293–301.

Winters, M.A., Greene, J.P., 2012. The medium-run effects of Florida's test-based promotion policy. Educ. Finance Policy 7 (3), 305–330.

Winters, M.A., Trivitt, J.R., Greene, J.P., 2010. The impact of high-stakes testing on student proficiency in low-stakes subjects: evidence from Florida's elementary science exam. Econ. Educ. Rev. 29 (1), 138–146.

Winters, M.A., Dixon, B.L., Greene, J.P., 2012. Observed characteristics and teacher quality: impacts of sample selection on a value added model. Econ. Educ. Rev. 31 (1), 19–32.

Winters, M.A., Haight, R.C., Swaim, T.T., Pickering, K.A., 2013. The effect of same-gender teacher assignment on student achievement in the elementary and secondary grades: evidence from panel data. Econ. Educ. Rev. 34, 69–75.

Wiswall, M., 2013. The dynamics of teacher quality. J. Public Econ. 100, 61–78.

Wiswall, M., Stiefel, L., Schwartz, A.E., Boccardo, J., 2014. Does attending a STEM high school improve student performance? Evidence from New York City. Econ. Educ. Rev. 40, 93–105.

Zabel, J.E., 2008. The impact of peer effects on student outcomes in New York City public schools. Educ. Finance Policy 3 (2), 197–249.

Zimmer, R., Gill, B., Booker, K., Lavertu, S., Witte, J., 2012. Examining charter student achievement effects across seven states. Econ. Educ. Rev. 31 (2), 213–224.

Zimmer, R., Gill, B., Attridge, J., Obenauf, K., 2014. Charter school authorizers and student achievement. Educ. Finance Policy 9 (1), 59–85.

CHAPTER 3

Charter Schools: A Survey of Research on Their Characteristics and Effectiveness

D. Epple*, R. Romano[†], R. Zimmer[‡]
*Carnegie Mellon University and NBER, Pittsburgh, PA, United States
[†]University of Florida, Gainesville, FL, United States
[‡]Vanderbilt University, Nashville, TN, United States

Contents

Abstract

The charter school movement is nearing its 25th anniversary, making this an opportune time to take stock of the movement by addressing the following questions: Where do charter schools locate? Who do they serve? Who manages them? Who teaches in them? Most importantly, what are the effects of charter schools on the academic performance of students who enroll in charters and on students who remain in traditional public schools? We review research findings that shed light on these questions.

Handbook of the Economics of Education, Volume 5
ISSN 1574-0692, http://dx.doi.org/10.1016/B978-0-444-63459-7.00003-8
139

Keywords

Charter School Effectiveness, Charter School Operation

1. INTRODUCTION

The charter school movement is nearing its 25th anniversary, making this an opportune time to take stock of the movement by addressing questions such as: Where do charter schools locate? Who do they serve? Who manages them? Who teaches in them? Most importantly, what are the effects of charter schools on the academic performance of students who enroll in charters and on students who remain in traditional public schools (TPSs)?

Charter schools in the United States were first introduced in St. Paul, Minnesota in 1992. The sponsors envisioned a new form of public schools, operating outside the cultural and regulatory bounds of TPSs, as laboratories for educational innovation. At the outset of the charter movement, critics argued that charter schools would drain public resources away from charter schools and raised concerns as to whether charter schools would serve all populations, including minorities, lower-ability and special-needs populations (Cobb and Glass, 1999; Fiske and Ladd, 2000; Frankenberg and Lee, 2003). Supporters, in contrast, argued that given the greater freedom from regulations, charter schools would be innovative and create competitive pressure on all schools to improve, while at the same time improving racial integration by letting families choose schools outside of neighborhoods where housing is racially segregated and by promoting fuller and richer integration in classrooms *within* schools where all students have chosen to attend (Finn et al., 2000; Kolderie, 2004; Nathan, 1998).

These debates are not new, as most of these same arguments occur over the use of vouchers. In contrast to attitudes toward vouchers, however, the public view of charter schools is largely favorable, with opinion polls showing that public support of charter schools has grown over time. The 2014 PDK/Gallup Poll of public attitudes toward public schools (2014, p. 19) finds 70% of respondents favor the idea of charter schools,[1] double the proportion reporting a favorable view in 2002. At the same time, however, public understanding of charter schools is muddled, with 48% believing that charter schools are free to teach religion, 57% believing that charter schools can charge tuition, 68% believing that charter schools can choose students on the basis of ability, and only 50% knowing that charter schools are public schools.

Our review proceeds as follows. In Section 2 we summarize the defining characteristics of charter schools and provide an overview of the charter authorization process,

---

[1] Phrasing of the question matters somewhat; the proportion favoring charters falls from 70% to 63% when the question does not refer to charters as public schools.

charter funding, and types of charter organizations. Section 3 provides a largely descriptive summary of the geographic distribution of charter schools, comparisons of demographic characteristics of charter and TPS students including evidence on cream skimming, and comparison of characteristics of charter and TPS teachers. To set the stage for review of evidence on charter effectiveness, we detail in Section 3.4 the methodological challenges in evaluating charter effectiveness and discuss strengths and weaknesses of alternative approaches that have been utilized. Section 4 then summarizes the evidence on charter effectiveness. In Section 5 we discuss research that seeks to go inside the black box to investigate how effectiveness varies with charter school educational models, teacher characteristics, and other factors. Evidence on the response of TPSs to competition from charter schools is reviewed in Section 6. A brief conclusion is provided in Section 7.

2. WHAT IS A CHARTER SCHOOL?

A charter school is a public school chartered under the auspices of a state government. While charter laws vary across states, two defining characteristics are: (1) charter schools cannot charge tuition and (2) charter schools are not permitted to impose admission requirements and, if oversubscribed, must select from their applicants by lottery.

For charter schools to operate within a state, the state government must pass legislation determining how charter schools will be financed and delineating procedures for chartering of schools. At present (August 2015), 41 states plus the District of Columbia permit charter schools to operate.[2] States delegate power to grant charters to "authorizers." There is considerable variation across states in delegation of this power, with several states designating more than one authorizer. In 2010/11, charters could be authorized by local school districts in 31 states, the state education agency in 21, an independent charter board in 7, a higher education institution in 9, a municipal government office in 2, and a non-for-profit organization in 1. Sixteen states designated only one authorizer while the remainder designated two or more National Alliance for

---

[2] A total of 42 states plus the District of Columbia have passed Charter School Laws at some point in time. In Washington State, the state Supreme Court recently declared the law unconstitutional. In Mississippi, the charter law expired in 2009, but a new charter law was passed in 2013 and two schools were authorized in August 2015.

http://www.charterschoolboard.ms.gov/Pages/default.aspx Hence, we count Mississippi among the 41 states permitting charter schools in 2015. Due to lags in data availability, we sometimes rely on data from earlier years in this review. Depending on the year, the number of states with charter schools may be reported as 40, 41, or 42. We note the year for which data are reported in all instances.

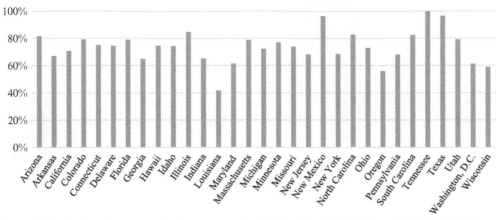

Figure 1 Charter funding per student as a percent of TPS funding, FY 2011. *From Batdorff, M., Maloney, L., May, J., Speakman, S., Wolf, P., Cheng, A., 2014. Charter School Funding: Inequity Expands (www. uaedreform.org/charter-funding-inequity-expands/).*

Public Charter Schools (NAPCS).[3] In some states, a request for authorization to create a charter school goes first to the local school district in which the charter would locate, with potential for appeal to the state education agency if the district declines to grant a charter.

Charter laws typically specify that a charter school receive a specified payment from the local district for each district student who attends the charter school. The payment per student averaged 80% of local district expenditure per student in 2009/10, with the percentage being lower, 72%, in urban areas (NAPCS). However, these differences do not necessarily take into account the fact that charter schools often rely on local school districts for certain services, including busing. In addition, the composition of student populations may differ between the two types of schools. For example, charter schools typically serve fewer special needs students, which are more costly to educate. Batdorff et al. (2014) investigate funding for each state with the objective of taking account of differences in student composition to compare funding charter schools receive to the amount district schools would have received to educate the same students. They found that the average charter school student in the United States is funded 28.4% below the average TPS student, a differential of $3814. Fig. 1, drawn from the Batdorff et al. data, shows charter funding as a percentage of district funding levels by state for FY2011. As is evident from the figure, the percentage varies widely across states, ranging from a low near 40% in Louisiana to virtual parity in Tennessee. Batdorff et al. (2014) also provide an analysis of sources of funding disparities in FY2011 aggregated to the national level. As detailed in their Figure M20, they find that, on average, charter schools obtain 25% less funding per student than TPS funding per student. Expressed in dollars

---

[3] We make frequent use of the extensive database on charter schools maintained by the NACPS: http://dashboard.publiccharters.org/dashboard/home.

inflation-adjusted to year 2007, this is $2998 per student.[4] Detailing the sources of the difference, they find that charters receive $506 less federal revenue per student than TPSs and $484 more state funding per student than TPSs. Hence, combining federal and state funding, the net difference between charters and TPSs is quite small. Strikingly, they find that funding from local governments sources is $3449 less for charters than for TPSs. Charters received $492 more per student than TPSs from indeterminate sources than TPSs — state records were inadequate to determine the exact funding source. Even if these indeterminate funds were entirely from local governments, the disparity in local funding between charters and TPSs would be sufficient to account for the overall 25% funding differential. They find lack of public funding for facilities to be an important source of the public funding disparity, but differences in policies with respect to local funding go well beyond differences in facilities funding. Previous research has found that charters appeal to philanthropic organizations for financial support, particularly for funding facilities (Farrell et al., 2012; Nelson et al., 2000). Batdorff et al. (2014) find that funding from "other" (including philanthropic) sources is relatively small and comparable in magnitude for charters and TPSs — on the order of 5% of per student revenue for both.

Charter operators may be part of an Education Management Organization (EMO), a Charter Management Organization (CMO), or freestanding. Both EMOs and CMOs operate multiple schools, the key distinction being that the former are for-profit and the latter nonprofit. CMOs have also been more successful in raising philanthropic support than TPSs, EMOs, or freestanding charter schools. This support has added to the controversy surrounding charter schools as many opponents see private organizations having too much influence in the future of public schools (Reckhow, 2013).

It is natural to expect that successful charter school models will be "franchised," and this is in fact the case.[5] From 2007/08 to 2010/11, the percentage of charter schools that were freestanding declined from 78% to 68%, while the percentage in CMOs grew from 12% to 20%, and the percentage in EMOs increased from 10% to 12% (NAPCS). EMO student share is greater than school share. In 2010/11 (NAPCS) 61% of charter students were in freestanding charters, 19% in CMOs, and 20% in EMOs (NAPCS).

Information about the extent of CMO operations is provided in recent studies by Farrell et al. (2012) and Furgeson et al. (2012a,b) using broadly similar definitions.[6]

---

[4] To adjust to current year 2015 dollar values, these figures should be multiplied by 11%.

[5] "Success" in this context means ability to attract students and secure adequate funding while also succeeding in obtaining renewal of charters from the relevant charter authorizers. We discuss in a subsequent section the evidence on academic performance of charter schools.

[6] They identified 40 such CMOs operating a total of 292 schools in 14 states, located primarily in Texas, California, Arizona, Ohio, Illinois, New York, and the District of Columbia. They note that, with a broader definition — any nonprofit operating two or more schools — there are roughly 130 CMOs serving on the order of 250,000 students. In contrast, with the exception of the for-profit organization of Edison schools (eg, Gill et al., 2005), EMOs appear to be less studied and accurate counts are not as readily available.

3. LOCATION AND CLIENTELE

Fig. 2 shows the nationwide growth in number of students served by charter schools and charter school share of total public school enrollment. While charter school share is still relatively small, 4.5%, charter enrollment has increased rapidly, roughly quadrupling from 2000 through 2012. In this section, we compare charter and TPSs and provide evidence about changes over time. We shall frequently reference Table 1, which provides a national comparison on a broad range of characteristics, including enrollment, location, and demographics.[7]

3.1 Where Do Charter Schools Locate?

3.1.1 Variation Across States

Fig. 3A shows the large variation across states in charter school share of public school enrollment. In this figure, states are ordered from highest to lowest based on charter share of enrollment within state. Eleven states have charter shares of 5% or higher; Arizona leads with a 12% share. In Fig. 3B, states are ordered by state share of national charter enrollment. We see that California alone has 20% of all US charter enrollment, followed by Florida and Texas with 9% each, Arizona with 7%, Michigan with 6%, and

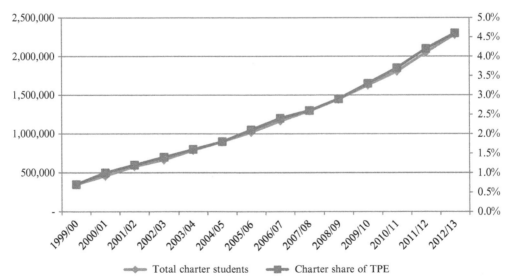

Figure 2 Charter enrollment growth. *Data from National Alliance for Public Charter Schools (http:// dashboard.publiccharters.org/dashboard/home).*

[7] Except where indicated, the data are for the 2010–11 academic year — the most recent year for which all variables in the table are available.

Table 1 Selected Charter School and Student Statistics, 2010/11*

	Charter	Traditional public
Number of states authorizing charter schools	41 states and DC (Year 2015)	
Enrollment (number)	1,805,002	47,419,367
Enrollment share of TPE[a]	3.7%	96.3%
Expenditure per student	$10,011	$14,014
Demographics (as % of enrollment)		
African American	29.2%	15.5%
Hispanic	27.2%	22.9%
White non-Hispanic	36.0%	53.0%
Other	7.6%	8.7%
FRL (as % of enrollment)[b]	50.6%	47.8%
Location[c]		
% Urban	55.8%	28.3%
% Suburban	28.9%	46.8%
% Rural	15.2%	24.9%
Charter grades		
K–8 as % of TPE	3.8%	96.2%
High school as % of TPE	3.5%	96.5%
Students per teacher[d]		
Primary selfcontained	22.5	21.6
Primary departmentalized	26.9	26.2
Middle selfcontained	21.9	16.7
Middle departmentalized	24.0	25.5
HS selfcontained	23.7	17.6
HS departmentalized	22.2	24.2
Combined selfcontained	22.6	15.3
Combined per school	22.7	18.2
Students per school		
K–8	366.0	460.6
High school	324.2	624.1
NAEP proficiency		
Fourth grade reading	29.0%	33.0%
Fourth grade math	34.0%	40.0%
Eighth grade reading	27.0%	32.0%
Eighth grade math	31.0%	34.0%
Eighth grade science	24.0%	31.0%
Limited English proficiency (2007/08)	16.5%	11.2%
Special education	11.9%	12.4%

[a]Total public enrollment = charter enrollment + traditional public enrollment.
[b]Eligible for free or reduced-price lunch.
[c]Percentage is by enrollment (not schools).
[d]In self-contained classes, a given group of students is instructed in multiple subjects by the same teacher while in departmentalized classes different subjects are taught by different teachers.
*Data from National Alliance for Public Charter Schools (http://dashboard.publiccharters.org/dashboard/home) and 2010/11 school year except where noted. **Data from University of Arkansas EdReform 2014 report, which uses "nationalized" data from 40 metropolitan areas in 30 states (and the District of Columbia). Figures in 2014 dollars.

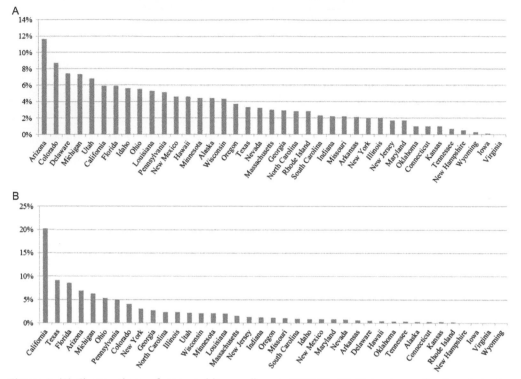

Figure 3 (A) Charter share of state public enrollment, 2010/11. (B) State share of national charter enrollment, 2010/11. *Figures calculated from the Common Core of Data: National Center for Education Statistics, Common Core of Data, "Public Elementary/Secondary School Universe Survey, 2010–11."*

Ohio and Pennsylvania each with 5%. These seven states account for 61% of all US charter school enrollment.

3.1.2 Variation Across City, Suburban, and Rural Districts

We see from Table 1 that charter school enrollments are more heavily concentrated in urban areas relative to TPS enrollment share, with much lower concentrations in suburban and rural areas. We next detail variation across the 30 metropolitan areas with the largest charter shares of metropolitan area charter enrollment in 2010/11. Fig. 4A shows the national charter share for each of these metropolitan areas, while Fig. 4B shows the share of the local market served by charters in each of these 30 metropolitan areas. From Fig. 4A, we see that, in seven of these metropolitan areas, charter schools serve 10% or more of the metropolitan area public student population. From Fig. 4B, we see that seven of these metro areas each have more than 3% of national charter enrollment with Los Angeles leading with 6.5% of US charter students. Strikingly, these 30 metro areas

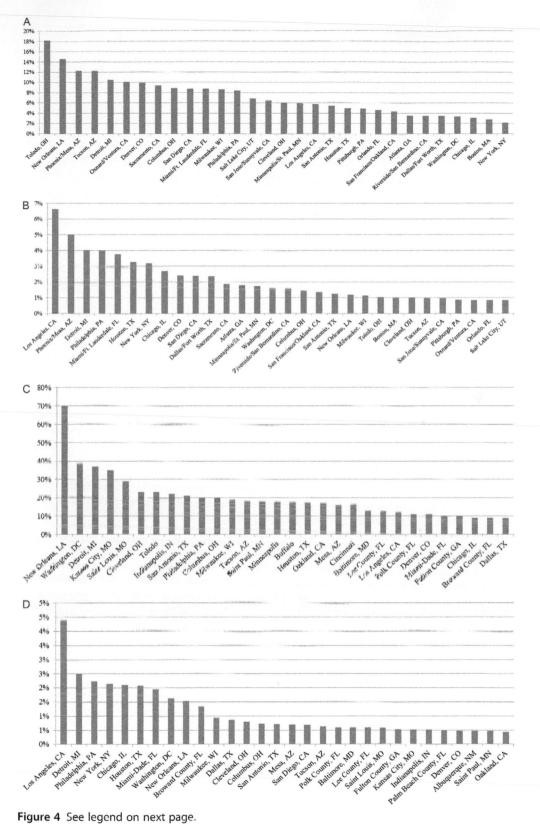

Figure 4 See legend on next page.

together comprise 63% of total US charter enrollment. Focusing on central city districts, we see in Fig. 4C that New Orleans charters have by far the largest charter share of any central city district,[8] followed in order by Washington, DC, Detroit, and Kansas City, all having a central city district charter share of 35% or more. From Fig. 4D, we see that six of these cities each have more than 2% of national charter enrollment; Los Angeles leads with 5% of US charter students, followed by Detroit, Philadelphia, New York City, Chicago, and Houston. These 30 cities together serve 34% of US charter students. Thus, while charter schools currently serve less than 5% of the US public school population, these figures show the variation across locations in charter enrollment and highlight the salient role that charter schools play in some US educational markets.

Econometric research has investigated charter school location. Glomm et al. (2005) study charter school location in Michigan, finding that charters are located in communities with diverse populations as measured by heterogeneity in race and adult education. Bifulco and Buerger (2012) investigate charter school location in New York. They find, as in Glomm et al. (2005), that charters tend to be located in districts where the population is diverse, while also finding that charters tend to locate where expenditure per student is high, teacher costs are low, and public school achievement is relatively low. In both of the preceding papers, the authors are careful to emphasize that the analysis is reduced-form and leaves open the issue of causality. While not focused on charter school location per se, Imberman (2011) instruments for charter location, using measures of building availability in order to estimate causal effects of charter schools on outcomes of students in public schools. His first-stage regression results demonstrate the important role of building availability on charter school location. (Imberman's results regarding impacts on student achievement are discussed later in our review of "indirect effects.") Recent research has sought to develop structural models of charter school entry and choice. Mehta (2012) models charter school entry in North Carolina, abstracting from heterogeneity in student demographic characteristics. Using panel data for Washington, D.C. schools for the period from 2002 through 2003, Ferreyra and Kosenok (2015)

Figure 4 (A) Charter share of public school enrollment in 30 US metro areas (metro areas consist of the MSAs surrounding the cities listed, with districts matched to MSA by zip code as defined by the U.S. Department of Labor), 2010/11. (B) Share of national charter enrollment in 30 US metro areas (metro areas consist of the MSAs surrounding the cities listed, with districts matched to MSA by zip code as defined by the U.S. Department of Labor), 2010/11. (C) Charter share of public school enrollment in 30 US cities, 2010–11 SY. (D) Share of national charter enrollment in 30 U.S. cities, 2010–11 SY. *Figures calculated from the Common Core of Data: National Center for Education Statistics, Common Core of Data, "Public Elementary/Secondary School Universe Survey, 2010–11."*

---

[8] The city of New Orleans abolished traditional public schools effective with the 2014/15 academic year with public education in the city now offered entirely by charter schools.

estimate an equilibrium model of charter entry decisions and household choice among schools. They find heterogeneity in household preferences, with African-American and Hispanic households having higher preference for charters than whites, and with poor households favoring charters more than those with higher incomes. They also find high fixed costs to be a deterrent to entry in areas where charters would attract enrollment.

3.2 Student Selection: Who Do Charter Schools Serve?

By law, charter schools are required to select students by lottery when they are oversubscribed. In this sense, charter schools cannot selectively admit students. This does not imply that student composition of charter schools will replicate the composition of public schools. Charter school student body composition will be affected by charter school location. Furthermore, charter schools may selectively market themselves to families. In addition, charter and TPSs may differ in appeal to differing clienteles, leading to differences in school composition. In this section, we review and assess differences in characteristics of charter and public school students.

Comparisons using national data for 2010/11 in Table 1 show that charter shares of students served by grade level (elementary and high school) are roughly the same as share of overall student population served. Charter schools, on average, are smaller than TPSs. Charter middle schools are about 80% the size of TPS middle schools, and charter high schools are about half the size of traditional public high schools. Class sizes by grade level for the most common modes of instruction are shown in Table 1.[9] For these school configurations, class sizes are relatively similar between charter and TPSs. There are other school configurations, not shown in the table, that serve smaller shares of the student population. In schools that combine across grade levels, for example, charter schools have substantially higher student/teacher ratios than TPSs, though it is not clear to what extent this reflects differences in grade levels served in combined schools. Overall, it is clear that the smaller average class sizes observed in the past for charters relative to TPSs no longer prevails.

We next turn to comparison of the demographic composition of charter and TPS students at varying levels of geographic disaggregation.

3.2.1 National, State, Metropolitan, and District Comparisons

Following Powell et al. (1997), Fitzgerald et al. (1998), RPP (2000), Miron and Nelson (2002), and Frankenberg et al. (2010), we begin by comparing average characteristics of students in charter and TPS schools at varying degrees of geographic disaggregation. We then turn to a review of findings with respect to student selection into and retention in

---

[9] In selfcontained classes, a given group of students is instructed in multiple subjects by the same teacher while in departmentalized classes different subjects are taught by different teachers. Selfcontained classes are relatively rare outside of primary grades.

charter schools that use strategies to take account of the demographic variation across charter school locations, competitors, and other factors.

The proportion of students reported as eligible for free or reduced-price lunch (FRL) in charter schools has grown markedly over time, as shown in Fig. 5A, from roughly 30% in 2001 to 50% in 2010. As shown in Table 1, the proportion of FRL students is now nearly the same in charters (51%) and TPSs (48%). This increase may reflect a growing proportion of poor students in charter schools, and/or an increase in charter school participation in the National School Lunch Program.

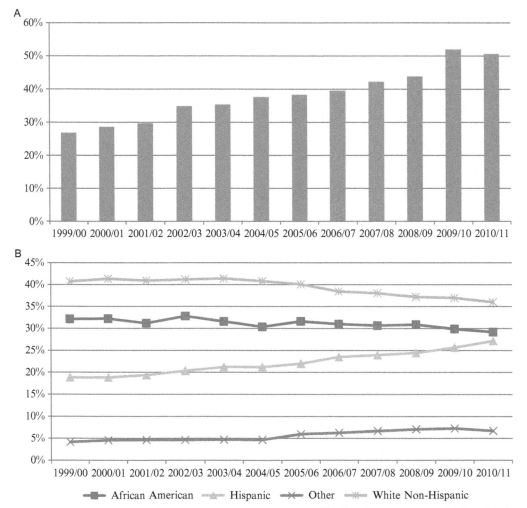

Figure 5 (A) Percentage of charter school students eligible for free or reduced-price lunch. (B) Percentages of charter school students by race and ethnicity. *Data from National Alliance for Public Charter Schools (http://dashboard.publiccharters.org/dashboard/home).*

Charter school composition by race and, ethnicity has changed over time, as shown in Fig. 5B. The most noteworthy change is the growth in percentage of Hispanic students in charter schools, which increased from 19% to 27% between 2001 and 2010. The proportion of charter students that are African-American declined by approximately 4% over this period, and the proportion white declined by approximately 5%. Overall, as seen in Table 1, charter enrollment share of minority students is higher than TPSs, and the share of white students is correspondingly lower. The charter share of African-American students stood at 29% in 2010–11, almost double the share of African-American students in TPSs. The share of Hispanic student was 27%, roughly 5% higher than in TPSs.

While sector-wide comparisons of the proportion of charter and TPS students in particular subgroups are useful to describe the population being served, they provide little information about the extent to which individual schools are integrated. In other words, the fact that the entire sector (charter or TPS) in a district serves a wide range of student populations does not tell us anything about integration. A district where the TPSs have equal shares of students from each race might have schools that are highly integrated (ie, each school has a mix of students that looks like the district-wide average), or it might have schools that are fully segregated (eg, one-third of the schools are 100% white, one-third are 100% black, and one-third are 100% Hispanic).

Table 2 provides a summary at the national level of segregation by race and FRL status. The first row shows that the proportion of schools with more than 80% one race is approximately 38% in charters and 41% in TPSs. Likewise, the second row shows that the proportion with more than 60% one race or ethnicity is also relatively similar in the two sectors, at 65% in charters and 67% in TPSs. By these measures, segregation is relatively high in both charters and TPSs. These figures are far from the full story. The third row shows that the proportion of charter schools with more than 80% white students is 14.5%, while the proportion of TPSs schools with more than 80% white is 31%. The proportion of charters with more than 80% nonwhite is 41%, roughly double that for

Table 2 Segregation and poverty in public charter schools

	Charter	Noncharter
More than 80% single race/ethnicity	38.3%	41.1%
More than 60% single race/ethnicity	64.6%	67.2%
More than 80% white	14.5%	30.7%
More than 80% nonwhite	40.6%	21.8%
More than 60% white	29.1%	48.2%
More than 60% nonwhite	50.7%	32.3%
More than 80% FRL	36.5%	23.6%
More than 60% FRL	42.5%	35.8%
Less than 20% FRL	8.4%	12.6%

Figures calculated from the Common Core of Data: National Center for Education Statistics, Common Core of Data, "Public Elementary/Secondary School Universe Survey, 2010–11."

TPSs. The final three rows of Table 2 show concentrations with respect to poverty. More than one-third of charter schools have at least 80% of students eligible for FRL as compare to slightly less than one-fourth for TPSs. Approximately 60% of charters have at least half of their student eligible for FRL as compared to 54% of TPSs. In summary, then, charters and public schools exhibit substantial and similar degrees of racial and, ethnic segregation, but schools with a high degree of segregation are more likely to be charters if predominantly nonwhite and are more likely to be TPSs if predominantly white. Charter schools also exhibit more segregation by poverty than TPSs.

We next investigate segregation across central city school districts. Fig. 6A shows the proportion of schools with more than 80% FRL students for the 30 cities with highest charter enrollment. The proportions are strikingly high in some cities. For example, in Chicago and New Orleans, 90% of charter schools have more than 80% students on FRL. In 19 of the 30 cities, the proportion of charters with greater than 80% FRL students is higher than the proportion of TPSs with greater than 80% FRL students. The reverse is true in the remaining 11 cities.

Using a similar approach, we investigate segregation by race or ethnicity. Fig. 6B shows the proportion of schools with more than 80% of students with one race for the 30 cities with highest charter enrollment. Again, this proportion is strikingly high in some cities, led by New Orleans with 92% and Detroit with 87%. The figure shows the proportions in charters and TPSs to be relatively similar for most of these cities. A similar conclusion emerges in Fig. 6C which uses a 60% rather than 80% concentration by one race or ethnicity. Continuing the investigation of segregation by race and ethnicity, we show in Fig. 6D the proportions of schools with more than 80% nonwhite students and in Fig. 6E the proportions of schools with more than 80% white students. From Fig. 6D, we see that, in most of the 30 cities, the proportion of charters schools with more than 80% nonwhite is greater than the proportion of TPSs with more than 80% nonwhite students. Fig. 6E shows, not surprisingly, that within these cities, few schools in either sector have more than 80% white students. Fig. 6F and G tell a similar story when segregation is measured with more than 60% nonwhite and 60% white respectively.

It is important to note that there are exceptions to the general pattern summarized above. St. Paul, Minnesota is one such exception. Fig. 6D shows that the proportion of schools greater than 80% nonwhite is approximately the same for charters and TPSs in St. Paul, MN, while Fig. 6E shows that the proportion of schools more than 80% white is markedly higher in charters than TPSs. Reports by the Institute on Metropolitan Opportunity (IMO), (2013) and by its predecessor, the Institute on Race and Poverty (2008, 2012), have highlighted the racial segregation of charter schools relative to TPSs in Minneapolis-St. Paul area. The IMO (2013) report points to charters locating in mixed-race suburbs and attracting predominantly white students as increasing white segregation in charters and, thereby, increasing nonwhite segregation in TPSs. Understanding why this phenomenon is occurring in Minneapolis-St. Paul area is an important research issue.

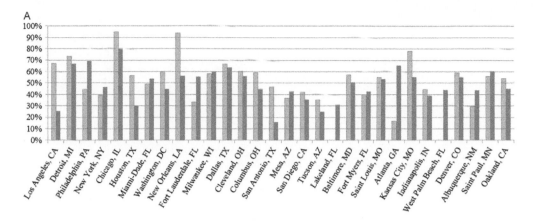

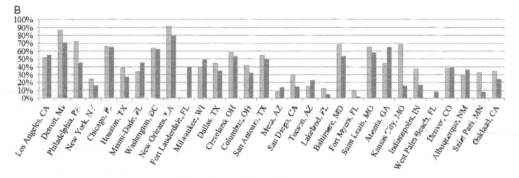

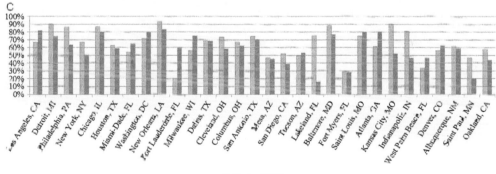

Figure 6 (A) Proportion of city schools with >80% FRL, 2010/11. (B) Proportion of city schools with >80% single race/ethnicity, 2010/11. (C) Proportion of city schools with >60% single race/ethnicity, 2010/11.

(Continued)

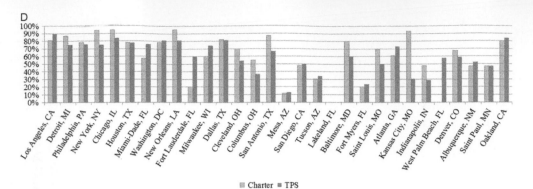

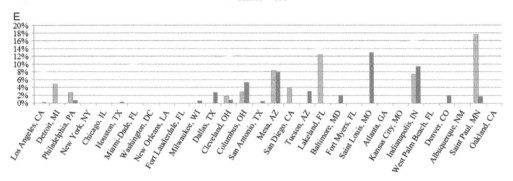

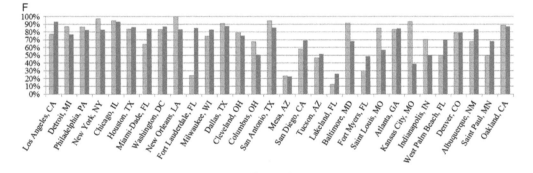

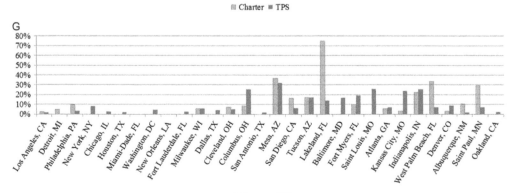

Figure 6—Cont'd (D) Proportion of city schools with >80% nonwhite, 2010/11. (E) Proportion of city schools with >80% white, 2010/11. (F) Proportion of city schools with >60% nonwhite, 2010/11. (G) Proportion of city schools with >60% white, 2010/11. *Figures calculated from the Common Core of Data: National Center for Education Statistics, Common Core of Data, "Public Elementary/Secondary School Universe Survey, 2010–11."*

Turning to the metropolitan level, we see in Fig. 7A, that the proportion of schools with greater than 80% FRL is generally higher in charters than in TPSs. However, in some low poverty metro areas (eg, Sacramento, Oxnard/Venture, Orlando, Salt Lake City), charter FRL share is lower than TPS FRL share. The proportion of charter schools with greater than 80% nonwhite is greater than in TPSs in almost all the metropolitan areas shown in Fig. 7B. By contrast, as shown in Fig. 7C, the proportion of charters with greater than 80% white is generally lower than in TPSs.

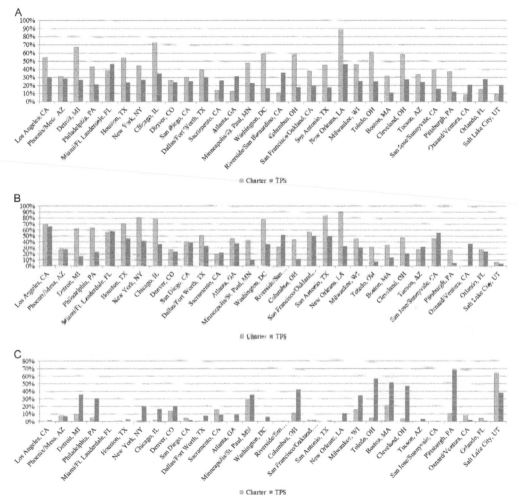

Figure 7 (A) Proportion of metro area schools with >80% FRL, 2010/11. (B) Proportion of metro area schools with >80% nonwhite, 2010/11. (C) Proportion of metro area schools with >80% white, 2010/11. *Figures calculated from the Common Core of Data: National Center for Education Statistics, Common Core of Data, "Public Elementary/Secondary School Universe Survey, 2010–11."*

Table 3 Demographic comparison of students in TPS, feeders, and charters, 2010/11

	Feeders	Charters
Number of schools	29,797	5068
Average enrollment (per school)	677	336
Total students enrolled	20,172,202	1,704,418
Students in poverty	54%	54%
English language learners	13%	9%
Special education students	11%	8%
White	40%	35%
Black	17%	29%
Hispanic	34%	28%
Asian/Pacific islander	5%	3%
Native American	1%	1%

Data from Center for Research on Education Outcomes (CREDO) study of 27 representative states: Cremata, E., Davis, D., Dickey, K., Lawyer, K., Negassi, Y., Raymond, M., Woodworth, J., 2013. National charter school study. CREDO. http://credo.stanford.edu/documents/NCSS%202013%20Final%20Draft.pdf.

We next discuss comparisons at a finer grained geography. Table 3 from the CREDO study compares the demographic composition of charters to that of traditional public feeder schools from which charter students are drawn. From the table, we see that proportion of FRL students is 54% for both feeders and charters, both being 5% higher than in the universe of TPSs.[10] We see in Table 1 that charter schools serve a much higher proportion of African-American students than do TPSs, 29% versus 17%. Charters also serve a higher proportion of Hispanic students (27%) than do TPSs (23%), but they serve a smaller proportion than their feeder-school counterparts (34%). The latter suggests that charter schools locate in areas that have a relatively high proportion of Hispanic students, but, in those locations, they draw a smaller fraction of Hispanics than their TPS counterparts.

Another measure of clientele served is academic performance. Charter school students nationwide have lower NAEP reading and math scores than TPS students in both 4th and 8th grades, and lower science scores in 8th grades. A central research question is whether the lower achievement of charter school students is a result of student selection, relative educational quality, or both. We discuss in the next section evidence on student selection into charter schools and, in Section 3.4, the extent and nature of achievement differentials that might be attributable to differences in quality of education in the two sectors.

Still another domain for comparing clienteles served is special needs students. As shown in Table 1, enrollment shares nationwide of limited English proficiency are

---

[10] Charter school participation in the National School Lunch Program in charters may be less extensive than TPS participation. If so, the actual proportion of poor students in charter schools may be higher than reflected in reported FRL eligibility.

substantially higher in charters than TPSs, while enrollment shares of special needs students are lower in charters than in TPSs. Relative to the neighborhoods in which they locate, Table 3 indicates that charters schools serve a smaller proportion of English language learners than their feeder-school counterparts, 9% versus 13%, and a smaller proportion of special education students, 8% versus 11%.[11] Given the higher proportion English language learners served nationwide in charters than in TPSs, this suggests, as with Hispanic students, that charters locate in areas with high proportions of LEP students but, in those neighborhoods, they attract a smaller proportion of LEP students than their public school counterparts.

3.2.2 Within-School Diversity of Charters Relative to Public Schools

The above analyses show differences in populations served by charter relative to TPSs. These differences arise both from charter school location and selection into charter schools conditional on location. It is clearly of interest to disentangle the two. To accomplish this, research has examined the movement of students from TPSs to charter schools using longitudinal student-level data. This method allows researchers to track students as they move from school to school and examine whether students who exit TPSs to charter schools move to schools with a greater or lower concentration of students of the same race or, ethnicity. In addition, using the same approach, researchers can examine whether below- or above-average achieving students are exiting TPSs. In both cases, the approach provides a more refined counterfactual than making sector-wide comparisons.

However, this method does not provide a comprehensive picture of the student sorting resulting from charter schools, because it includes only the charter students who enter charter schools after having previously been enrolled in TPSs; it does not identify a counterfactual for students who enroll in charter schools beginning in kindergarten.[12] Nonetheless, this addition to the picture of the changing peer environments of individual students who move to charter schools is valuable in capturing the effects of charters at

---

[11] Note that the results from CREDO in Table 3 show a lower overall proportion of English Language Learners than shown by the LEP data in Table 1. Two potential reasons are the following. The former are for 2010/11 whereas the latter are for 2007/08. The other is source of data. As explained in footnote 14 of the CREDO report: "Data on English language learners and special education students is available by state for all public schools from the National Center for Education Statistics, but it is not disaggregated to the school level to allow for computations by charter designation. For the 27 states, CREDO collected these data at the school level from each state education department and compiled the proportions for charter schools in those states."

[12] In fact, in evaluating the effect on racial segregation, a very appealing approach would be to use lottery data and examine the racial makeup of the school a lottery "loser" attends and compare that to the racial makeup of schools lottery "winners" attend. This analysis would include not only students switching schools midstream (eg, a student who switches from a TPS in 2nd grade and attend a charter school in 3rd grade), but also include students who start out in a charter school in the entry grade. At this point, no study has conducted this type of evaluation.

the neighborhood level whereas comparisons at higher levels of aggregation do not capture the enormous local variation in schools, and comparisons at the neighborhood level after charter entry do not fully capture the effects of charters on school composition relative to that prevailing prior to charter entry. Only a handful of studies have used this approach, partially because it requires longitudinal student-level data, which can be difficult to obtain. When this approach has been used, the results for the segregation analysis have been mixed across the racial groups, but less so for the cream skimming question.

In an early study, Booker et al. (2005) examined the effect of charter schools on the stratification of students in terms of both ability and race using data from California and Texas. In both states, African-American students transferred to charter schools with higher concentrations of black students than the schools they attended previously. In Texas, white students also moved to charter schools with higher concentrations of whites than at their TPSs, but the opposite was true in California. Hispanic charter students in both states had fewer Hispanic peers than they had in their prior TPSs. In terms of measured ability, transfer students had lower test scores than the average student at their TPSs. These findings support the inferences discussed earlier from the evidence in Tables 1 and 3. In both states, charters attracted a disproportionate share of students with low test scores relative to the TPSs the students exited.

In another early study using longitudinal student-level data, Bifulco and Ladd (2007) examined data from North Carolina focusing on racial distribution and found that charters have increased the racial isolation of black and white students. On average, black charter students left schools that were 53% black for charters that were 72% black. Similarly, white charter students left TPSs that were 72% white to charters that were 82% white.[13] Both black and white charter students had more peers from college educated parents than at their previous TPS, but the percentage increase in college educated parents was about 6 times larger for whites than for blacks. On net, black students transferred to charters with lower average test scores than their previous schools, while white students transferred to charters with higher average test scores than their previous public schools. In a more recent study in North Carolina, Ladd et al. (2014) noted that while charter schools once served disproportionally black students, that has changed in recent years and has been increasingly serving white students. This suggests that the dynamics of who charter schools serve may evolve over time.

In probably the most geographically comprehensive study to date, Zimmer et al. (2009) used longitudinal student-level data to examine how charters affected peer composition in five urban districts and two states. They found modest effects of charters on the racial mix of schools. In some locations, black and white students tended to attend

---

[13] As we note previously, this is the kind of impact that IMO (2013) sees in the Minneapolis-St. Paul area, though without the strong identification strategy of the student-level longitudinal approach employed by Bifulco and Ladd (2007).

charters with a higher concentration of students of their same race than at their previous TPS, but these differences were generally small. Overall, across the seven jurisdictions, the average increase in the Black concentration experienced by a Black transfer student was 3.8%, versus an average increase of 1.3% in the White concentration experienced by transferring white students, and an average decline of 5.9% in the Hispanic concentration experienced by transferring Hispanic students.[14]

The study also looked at the ability distribution of students transferring to charter schools. In most cases, the charter students were near or slightly below the test score average for the TPS that they previously attended. Compared to their immediate peers in the TPSs they exited, students transferring to charter schools had slightly higher test scores in two of seven locations, while in the other five locations the scores of the transferring students were identical to or lower than those of their TPS peers. Same-race comparisons indicate lower prior scores for charter students in five of seven sites among African-Americans and in four of seven sites among Hispanics. For White students the pattern was slightly different: In four of seven sites, white students entering charter schools had higher prior achievement than their white peers in both subjects, and in one other site they had higher scores in one of two subjects. These results for white students had little effect on the overall averages because white students constituted a minority of charter students in every location, and less than one-quarter of charter students in the four locations where their scores were consistently higher than those of their white peers.

Garcia et al. (2008) extended this research on cream skimming by adding a somewhat nuanced comparison while examining Arizona charter schools. They compared the achievement levels of students exiting TPSs to enroll in charter schools with those of students exiting TPSs to enroll in other types of schools, such as other TPSs. Overall, they find that students who transfer from TPSs to charter schools have lower prior achievement levels than students transferring to other TPSs.

Two other studies that examine the racial mix of students are worth noting. The first of these studies surveyed parents about the choice to attend a school and compared their answer to their actual revealed preferences by the choice they made (Weiher and Tedin, 2002). They found that the parents reported similar values on school attributes irrespective of race and SES. In practice, however, parents' choices were often at odds with their avowed preferences. While 60% of parents ranked high-school test scores as a primary factor in choosing a school, the majority of these parents picked a charter school with lower average test scores than the TPS that their student left. Similarly, few parents mentioned race as a factor in choosing a school, but parents tended to pick schools with higher concentrations of students in their racial group than at their previous school. These results may suggest that race plays a role in choices families make. However, in a more recent

---

[14] These averages give equal weight to each jurisdiction rather than weighting by the number of students or schools.

study, Butler et al. (2013) used the U.S. Department of Education's Early Childhood Longitudinal Program data (which includes a rich set of observable characteristics) and examined educational enrollment choices families make across a large array of schools, including charter schools, and found that once a rich set of variables are included, race was not driving decisions to attend charter schools, but socioeconomic characteristics did.

In addition to concerns around issues of race and possible cream skimming, critics have raised questions about whether all students have access to charter schools, including special education students. As we saw in Table 3, charter schools do serve fewer special education students than their TPS feeder-school counterparts. Investigation of this phenomenon has been undertaken for two school districts, New York (Winters, 2013) and Denver (Winters, 2014). In Denver, Winters finds that the gap begins in elementary school, with a 1.7% difference in Kindergarten. This gap arises because fewer IEP students apply to charter schools. The gap then grows to 7.2% by 5th grade. Two features underlie this growth. Charters are less likely that TPSs to classify a student as IEP and more likely to declassify a student from IEP status. This accounts for half the growth in the percentage gap. Accounting for the other half of the growth, non-IEP students switching schools are more likely to move to a charter than a TPS, increasing the proportion of non-IEP students. Winters finds that differences in application rates lead to a 4.4% gap in 5th grade. This gap subsequently declines to 3.4% as more IEP students enter than exit charter schools. Winters' (2013) findings for elementary schools in New York City point to differential application rates at the kindergarten level coupled with differences between charters and TPSs in classification of IEP students as the factors giving rise to the gap in New York City. Difference in exit rates of IEP students between charters and TPSs play little role in either Denver or New York City, suggesting that the gap is not due to charter schools "counseling out" IEP students. Winters finds no significant differences across students with different types of disabilities in propensity to apply to charters versus TPSs in Denver, but substantial differences in New York City. For example, almost all students with autism apply to TPSs in New York City.

As Winters emphasizes, these findings suggest the need for research to clarify the reasons for differential rates of application of special-needs student to charters relative to TPSs. It remains to be determined whether the gap arises because of actual or perceived differences between charters and TPSs in services for IEP students, because parents are concerned that a special needs child is more likely to be reclassified in a charter, or other factors influencing parental decisions. Study of reasons for differences in rates of IEP classification and declassification is also needed. The role of finance policies also warrants further study. As Bifulco and Buerger (2012) emphasize, there are substantial differences across states in the degree to which funding to charters varies with IEP or LEP status or with other student characteristics that affect costs of education. Also, further investigation is needed to determine whether the findings for Denver and New York apply more broadly.

These issues have been explored a bit further with a couple of studies, but with not the same focus on the implications for student achievement. Instead, these studies focus on student moves and why they are made. In the first of these studies, Hanushek et al. (2007) use Texas student-level longitudinal data to track student moves between schools of varying quality and make the case that students exiting charter schools are motivated by school quality. More specifically, the authors found that higher achieving charter schools have lower exit rates than lower achieving charter schools, and the authors argue that much of the student mobility in charter schools is motivated to improve their educational situation.

In a more recent study, Zimmer and Guarino (2013) explore this issue with a different angle to examine whether they can find any empirical evidence of charter schools pushing out low-performing students. Some critics argue that charter schools may have an incentive to push out these students to raise their academic profile and to reduce costs (Ravitch, undated). Using longitudinal student-level data from an anonymous district, the authors examine the achievement levels of students exiting charter schools relative to students exiting TPSs. First using an informal descriptive model, they did find that the academic performance of students exiting charter schools as measured by test scores is slightly less than students remaining in charter schools, but they also found this to be true in TPSs. In a formal linear probability model controlling for observable student characteristics, the authors find that low-performing students were no more likely to exit charter schools than TPSs. The authors note that this does not prove charter schools are not pushing out low-performing students as they cannot distinguish the reasons students leave a particular school, but the evidence they provide is not supportive of the claim. They acknowledge their analysis is of only one location and argue that researchers should explore the validity of the claims in a larger set of locations.

While the research reviewed above has made major headway on the issue of cream skimming, important open issues remain. Disruptive behavior has been found to be a significant channel by which students generate adverse impacts on the learning of classroom peers (Carrell and Hoekstra, 2010). To the extent the data permit, it would be of interest in future work to investigate whether there are differences in behavioral measures (infractions, suspensions, absenteeism, tardiness) between students who apply for charter schools and those who do not, and whether students who exit charters exhibit more or fewer behavioral problems than those who remain. It would also be of interest to investigate treatment effects of charter schools on behavioral measures, as, for example, in the Engberg et al. (2014) study of magnet schools.

Synthesizing the findings on charter school demographic composition, we read the evidence as follows. Charter schools tend to locate in urban areas with high concentrations of minority and low-income students. This, rather than selection conditional on location, is the primary factor giving rise to the high degree of segregation by race/ethnicity and by FRL status that characterizes the majority of charter schools. The evidence further indicates, however, that household school choice decisions following charter school entry tend to perpetuate and sometimes accentuate such segregation. This is not to suggest that charter school authorizers would grant a charter to an applicant seeking to exploit opportunities to increase segregation, but increased segregation could be seen as a side effect of entry for charter schools striving towards desirable educational objectives. We return to this issue later in our discussion of school specialization.

3.3 Teachers in Charter Schools

Charter school teachers differ in their characteristics and in facets of their employment. Here we present comparative descriptive statistics about charter school teachers, while discussing research that seeks to explain differences in Section 5. Table 4 summarizes a number of differences between teachers in charter schools and TPSs, also providing corresponding values for private schools when available. All values are drawn from the 2011/12 Schools and Staffing Survey, a nationally representative sample conducted by the National Center for Education Statistics. We highlight some comparisons of charter school teachers to those in TPSs. We leave to the reader examination of differences with respect to private schools.

Minority teachers make up a substantially larger proportion of teachers in charter schools than in TPSs, perhaps reflecting the frequent urbanicity and concentration of

Table 4 Teacher characteristics in traditional public, charter, and private schools, 2011/12

	Traditional public	Charter	Private
Percent white, non-Hispanic	82.3	69.9	88.3
Percent black, non-Hispanic	6.6	11.8[a]	3.6
Percent Hispanic	7.6	13.1	5.2
Percent male	23.6	25.1	25.9
Average age	42.6	37.4	43.8
Percent younger than 30	14.7	31	16.7
Average teaching experience (years)	14	8.7	14.2
Average years at current school	8.1	3.6	8.3
Percent less than 4 years' teaching experience	10.7	26.3	16.1
Percent highest degree = bachelor's	39.4	52.3	48.5
Percent regular full time	92.8	91	79.2
Required hours (typical week)	30.7	32	38.3
Total hours per week	52.2	53.5	52.1
Average school year earnings	$55,400	$46,300	$41,900
Percent teachers receiving supplemental comp for student performance/average amount	4.0/$1400	15.8/ $1300	0.5[a]/ $1100[a]
Percent any professional development	99.0	98.3	N/A

[a]CV of estimate between 30% and 50%.
All values from Goldring, R., Gray, L., Bitterman, A. Characteristics of Public and Private Elementary and Secondary School Teachers in the U.S.: Results From the 2011–12 Schools and Staffing Survey, First Look, National Center for Education Statistics 2013–314, Department of Education, August 2013.

minorities in many charter schools. Gender differences are minor. Research has emphasized the relative youthfulness of charter school teachers and their relative lack of teaching
experience. More than a quarter of charter school teachers have less than 4 years of teaching experience. Moreover, the average tenure of teachers in charter schools is just 3.6
years as compared to 8.1 years in TPSs. This relates to teacher turnover in charter schools,
a major issue to which we return. Charter school teachers have less training; 52.3% have a
bachelor's degree as their most advanced degree, while the corresponding percentage in
TPSs is 39.4, this because 56.8% of TPS teachers have a more advanced degree. Charter
school teachers earn substantially less and a higher percentage have part of their earnings
linked to student performance, though not a large proportion of earnings. Charter school
teachers are required to work modestly longer hours. As we saw in Table 1, average class
sizes are broadly comparable between charter and TPSs.

Other data on charter school teachers are not systematically collected, but various
studies clarify other differences between charter school teachers and TPS teachers. Charter school teachers are frequently not certified or not certified in the area in which they
teach, while states require TPS teachers to be certified. This is why many TPS teachers
have master's degrees, which is required for certification in many states. In 2011, of the
then 41 states that authorized charter schools, only 23 of them had the same certification
requirements for charter school teachers as for TPS teachers.[15] Fourteen states of the latter
do not require that 100% of charter teachers be certified, the minimum percentage ranging from 30 to 90. The remaining states do not require certification, though the charter
authorizer might impose requirements. It should be noted that No Child Left Behind
(NCLB) requires teachers of core subjects in all public schools, including charters, to
be "highly qualified," which has likely induced more certification in charter schools.
Podursky and Ballou (2001) provide early data for 1997–98 from a survey they conducted
of teachers in seven states that had charter schools.[16] The proportion of charter
schools that had more than 50% of teachers not certified was about 18.5%, with virtually
no such TPSs. Stuit and Smith (2009) and Cannata and Penaloza (2012) provide more
recent data. Stuit and Smith analyze data from the 2003–04 Schools and Staffing Survey
and Cannata and Penaloza develop data for 2007–08 for charters in eight states, matched
to TPSs by state, geographic area, student racial and socioeconomic composition, and
size. Stuit and Smith report that 14.5% of teachers in charters had no certification, the
corresponding percentage in TPSs equal to 1.5. Matching does not reduce this gap;
Cannata and Penaloza found 18.7% of charter teachers held less than full certification
as compared to 3.2% in the matched TPSs. In the "No Excuses" charter schools in Boston

---

[15] Here we are paraphrasing Exstrom's (2012) summary on certification requirements, which she derives
from NCES (2011).
[16] The survey is not necessarily representative as they examined states with charter laws supporting relatively
strong autonomy and due to possible selection in response.

studied in Abdulkadiroğlu et al. (2011), 56.7% of high-school teachers are licensed to teach in their assignment relative to 88.8% in Boston TPSs.

The data on whether teachers attended highly selective colleges are mixed. Baker and Dickerson (2006) use data from 18 states and the District of Columbia from the 1999 Schools and Staffing Survey (SASS). Using Barron's college selectivity rankings, they report that 12.1% of charter teachers graduated from the top two selectivity groups, the percentage in TPSs equal to 8.1. In a more recent study with broader geographic coverage, Stuit and Smith (2009) report virtually no difference, with about 25% graduating from a selective undergraduate institution. In their matched sample for eight states, Cannata and Penaloza (2012) find that charter school teachers attend somewhat less selective colleges. TPS teachers are also more likely to earn their degrees from education departments (Stuit and Smith, 2009).

Unionization of charter school teachers is drastically lower than in TPSs. In Podursky and Ballou's (2001) early sample only 8% of charter school teachers engaged in collective bargaining. Stuit and Smith (2009) report 39% of charter teachers are unionized, while 95.4% of TPS teachers are in unions. NAPCS reports that only 12.3% of charter school teachers were unionized in 2009–10. Among those that were unionized, 64% were unionized by state law.

Tenure is much rarer in charter schools than in TPSs. Podursky and Ballou (2001) report that only 15% of the charter schools they studied awarded tenure and 63% of teachers were on 1-year contracts. Turnover of charter school teachers is substantial and substantially higher than in TPSs. For example, 25% of teachers in charter schools left their school in 2003–04 in the Stuit and Smith (2009) data, while the comparable percentage in TPSs was 14.

Whether these differences can affect the performance of charter schools is an open question. In Section 4, we examine the evidence of the effectiveness of charter schools, including whether operational features affect school outcomes. But first, in the next section we examine the challenges of estimating these effects.

3.4 Evaluating Charter Schools: Methodological Issues

Among the various aspects of the charter debate, none is more contentious than whether charter schools are having a positive effect on student achievement. As previously noted, advocates argue that charter schools could not only have a direct effect on students attending charter schools, but could have systemic effects on students attending TPSs through competitive pressure — ie, because TPSs now have to compete for students, they will work harder and smarter in educating students. In this section, we lay the groundwork for discussion of charter school effectiveness by discussing alternative empirical approaches and their strengths and weaknesses.

In the case of direct effects, an analysis is complicated by the fact that students and their families choose to attend charter schools. This choice may imply these students are different as they may be more engaged students and families than a typical student attending a TPS. Alternatively, students attending charter schools could be students who have not had success in traditional settings and are trying charter school as a last resort. Therefore, any observed differences in performance between students in charter and TPSs may not result from weaker or superior educational services in charter schools, but result from different unobserved characteristics of students. If these unobserved characteristics are not accounted for in a research study, they can create a "selection bias" and could lead researchers and policymakers to invalid conclusions.

The most obvious and strongest approach for dealing with the selection bias is to assign students randomly to charter and TPSs from a pool of all students. However, such random assignment has not occurred. This is not surprising since randomly assigning students in such a way would run counter to the reform itself as part of the theory behind charter schools is to have students match their needs and interest to the offerings of the schools. Forcing a student to attend a randomly assigned school would break this link. In lieu of a pure randomized design, researchers have often used one of four approaches: (1) lottery-based design (which simulates randomized design), (2) fixed-effect approaches, (3) matching procedures, (4) Ordinary Least Squares (OLS) regression designs, and (5) instrumental variable (IV) approaches.

Among these approaches, many argue that the lottery-based design is the most rigorous as it relies upon lottery assignment of oversubscribed schools as a natural experiment proxying random assignment to schools. As such, however, these evaluations answer a narrower question: Do outcomes improve for students who enroll in oversubscribed schools? The efficacy of the lottery schools is found by comparing the subsequent outcomes of lottery "winners" who attend the oversubscribed school with those of "losers" who are denied admission and attend another school. However, the results would only have inferences to oversubscribed schools. In fact, one would expect schools with wait lists to be the best schools, so the results may offer little insights into the performance of undersubscribed schools Zimmer and Engberg (forthcoming).[17] In addition, many students who enter an oversubscribed school may enter the school outside of the lottery including a sibling exception and a lottery analysis may not have inferences about these students. Furthermore, Tuttle et al. (2012) raise challenges to employing the approach correctly as often schools do not keep careful records of students who entered a school through a lottery or outside of lottery as one example of a challenge.

[17] It should also be noted that researchers often employ a "lottery fixed effect" in these analyses as there is not one lottery for all charter schools, but often a lottery for each charter school and the lottery fixed effect is designed to control for differences across lotteries, including the number of students on the wait list. However, the lottery fixed effect approach weights charter schools with longer wait lists more than charter schools with shorter wait lists, which makes the results less generalizable as the results may be driven by a select number of charter schools with long wait lists (Reardon, 2009).

A further concern is attrition, which can come in two forms. First, a student assigned to a charter school via a lottery may attend less than the full set of grades offered at a charter school (eg, a student assigned to a charter high school may only attend 9th grade and then transfer out) or may not attend at all. Furthermore, a "lottery loser" could end up in undersubscribed charter school or could enter a charter school at a later date. Second, a student could exit the data set altogether as a student might end up attending a private school, move outside of the jurisdiction of the data set (eg, move out of a district), or drop out of school. To the degree that either form of attrition is nonrandom, it can create bias.

There are two ways to address the first form of attrition. First, a researcher could do an intention-to-treat (ITT) analysis, in which a student, for research purposes, maintains his or her original assignment to a charter school or TPS regardless of the type of school a student actually attends. This approach maintains the random assignment, which guards against bias, but answers the policy question of what impact does randomly assigning a student to a charter school (but not necessarily attendance) have on student outcomes. Obviously, this is a less important question than the impact actual attendance at a charter school has on outcomes. Therefore, researchers, in addition or as alternative to doing an ITT analysis, often conduct a treatment-on-treated (TOT) analysis, in which a researcher employs an IV approach using the random assignment as an instrument. This analysis focuses on the question of the impact actual attendance has on student outcomes, but has the drawback of reduced breadth of inferences that comes with an IV approach (which we shall describe later). So there is a tradeoff of the two approaches with the ITT approach having greater breadth of inferences, but answering a less policy relevant question, while the TOT approach answers a more policy relevant question, but has less breadth of inferences.

For the second form of attrition in which students disappear from the analysis, neither an ITT or TOT analysis will alleviate the possible bias. The concern is that students attriting out of a data set may be very different than students who remain. For instance, in analysis of magnet schools, Engberg et al. (2014) found that more affluent students exited the data set of the urban district they were examining as many students exited for a suburban district or private school if they did not get into a magnet school via the lottery. In that case, the authors use a bounding technique to regain an unbiased estimate, but the approach provides a less precise estimate. While some lottery studies do not provide explicit discussion of the attrition issue, Abdulkadiroğlu et al. (2011) provide evidence that differential attrition of lottery winners and losers is small, and Dobbie and Fryer (2011a) provide evidence that their results are robust to correction for potential differential attrition.

When lottery-based analyses are not possible, a fixed-effect approach with student-level longitudinal data is often used. A fixed-effect approach minimizes the problem of selection bias by comparing the academic gains of individual students over time switching between a TPS and a charter school (ie, "switchers"). An advantage of this method over the lottery approach is that it applies to schools with and without waiting lists for admission. However, some researchers have raised concerns with this approach (Ballou et al., 2007; Hoxby and Murarka, 2007). These critics note that the fixed-effect approach does not provide an estimate for students who attend charter schools for the duration of the analysis (ie, "nonswitchers") as the analysis requires a comparison of student outcomes in both contexts. Switchers may differ from nonswitchers in important ways, so the results may not be applicable for students who are continuously enrolled in a charter school. Researchers also wonder about the motivation of students switching into charter school midway through their educational careers. For instance, Hoxby and Murarka (2007) argue that a fixed-effect approach cannot account for the possibility that students who, for example, perform poorly on a test may be especially likely to transfer to a charter school the following year. The dip in the performance could be a real dip caused by poor educational instruction, a disruption in a student's life unrelated to a school, or it could be just noise in test scores.[18] Regardless of the reason for the dip, the fixed-effect approach could produce biased estimates. Even absent bias, studies that rely on student-level fixed effects answer a different — but also narrow question: Are student outcomes for students who switch between a TPS and a charter schools better while the student attends a charter school versus a TPS?

A recent set of studies by CREDO, a research center at Stanford headed by Margaret Raymond, used an alternative approach to the fixed-effect and lottery approaches (CREDO, 2009, 2013a). These studies, which have been cited often both by researchers and stakeholders in the charter debate, used what they term a virtual control records (VCR) approach, which is a matching procedure where a "virtual" match for each charter student is found in a TPS. These students are matched based on known demographic attributes, grade in school, eligibility or participation in special support programs (including free and reduced lunch programs, English language learner status and special education status), and a baseline test result. Much like the fixed-effect approach, the VCR approach has the advantage over lottery-based studies in that a broad set of charter schools can be included, not just oversubscribed schools. However, as with the fixed-effect approach, the internal validity of the analysis requires stronger assumptions than in lottery studies as the approach assumes that students that have similar observed characteristics and baseline test scores also have similar unobservable characteristics. Relative to the fixed-effect approach, the VCR approach has the advantage of including a broad set of students as the analysis is not restricted to only students switching between schools. It includes all students who have a baseline test score in a charter school. However, the need to have a

---

[18] All tests have some level of noise in their measurement, and some students will score lower or higher on a single administration of a test than the average score they would receive if they took multiple, similar tests. Thus, a student could score poorly on a particular test in 1 year and then the next year score higher as they bounce back to a score more reflective of their learning.

baseline test score implies a potential limitation in the question the analysis can answer, as it cannot examine the accumulated impact for many students who first attend a charter school prior to baseline tested grade. For instance, if a student enters a charter school in Kindergarten and the first year a student is tested is 3rd grade, which would be the baseline test score used for matching students between charter and TPSs, the analysis will estimate the differential gain or loss between charters and TPSs from this baseline test score to test scores in later grades (eg, 4th grade, 5th grade). If charter schools are the most or least beneficial to students during these early grades, the analysis would miss that part of the charter school contribution.

A fourth approach is the most basic approach — an OLS regression model with school type as the independent variable of interest and controlling for observed student characteristics. Like the matching approach, this approach could be more inclusive of schools and students in the analysis and could lead to valid estimates if the researcher has a large set of observable characteristics including characteristics associated with student and family motivation. But having a baseline test score would be an essential control variable for the analysis and therefore faces the same challenge as the matching approach of using a baseline test score. Together, this suggests, much like the matching approach, the OLS approach has strong assumptions. Later, when we aggregate the findings from previous research in summary tables, we shall combine the matching and OLS research design studies into one category and only highlight those studies that have received the most attention.

A fifth and final approach, which is less frequently used in examining effectiveness of charter schools (relative to the fixed-effect and lottery-based approaches), is an instrumental variable (IV) approach. An IV approach uses an "instrument" to control for the choices students and their families make, and reduces the selection bias in estimating the effects of charter schools on student outcomes. A valid instrument must impact the choice of a charter versus TPS but must not itself affect the educational outcome. While an IV approach could have advantages relative to the lottery-based design and fixed-effect approaches as it may be more inclusive of students and schools, it is often difficult to find an "instrument" that is correlated with the choice families make and uncorrelated with ultimate educational outcomes. Another limitation of the IV approach is that the effect only applies to individuals who are at the margin on the instrument used (Angrist et al., 1996). For example, in the context of charter schools, distance to a charter school has been used as an instrument. This may be a valid instrument, but the results only apply to individuals on the margin based on distance from a charter. From a policy perspective, we would like to know the charter effect for the broader population, but the IV estimates do not provide this. So again, this approach answers the question of effectiveness for a narrow population. This approach has often been used when the outcome measure is not a repeated outcome measured both during and after treatment, such as test score, but often a single measured outcome that only occurs after treatment, such as graduation rates or college attendance.

These methodological considerations suggest that differences in findings across studies could result from differences in research approaches in addition to alternative policy settings in which charter schools are examined. We shall discuss this point further as we synthesize findings across the existing literature.

4. EFFECTIVENESS OF CHARTER SCHOOLS

In the last decade or so, there has been a rapid expansion of the number of studies that have examined the direct effects of charter schools; and, at this point, it would be hard to provide an accurate account of all the studies. However, only a subset of these studies has tried to address the selection bias inherent in estimating a direct effect. Nevertheless, the number of studies with rigorous research designs is numerous and there are too many to summarize individually. Therefore, we synthesize the findings by research designs using tables highlighting the more prominent studies as well as studies that have looked at unique outcomes. We synthesize by research design because, as we noted above, each research design is answering somewhat narrowly defined and different questions with different inferences. It should be noted that these studies have typically estimated average effects across all schools. While these researchers have recognized that there can be wide variation of performance across schools, they have not generally provided estimates of the variance in performance.

4.1 Achievement Effects

We first synthesize across fixed-effect studies as this approach was used by the earliest and most often cited studies (Bifulco and Ladd, 2006; Booker et al., 2007; Hanushek et al., 2007; Imberman, 2011; Sass, 2006; Zimmer et al., 2003) and has been the most widely used approach for estimating charter effects. In Table 5, we synthesize the effects across the fixed-effect studies. Across the various geographic locations,[19] researchers have generally found no overall average effect, small positive, or even small negative average effects. Digging deeper into some of these studies, researchers have often found that student achievement for charter schools in their initial years are often negative, but student achievement improve as these schools mature (Bifulco and Ladd, 2006; Booker et al., 2007; Hanushek et al., 2007; Ni and Rorrer, 2012; Sass, 2006; Zimmer et al., 2012). This suggests that policymakers should not expect charter schools to have a positive impact overnight, and it may take time for these schools to have an impact, if ever.

As previously mentioned, some have argued that the assumptions of the fixed-effect model are too strong and studies relying upon lotteries to assign students randomly to a charter and TPSs are more conclusive (Hoxby and Murarka, 2007). Based on this

[19] By our count, the fixed effect approach has been used in studies evaluating charter schools in at least 12 states.

Table 5 Summary of student fixed effect estimates

Study	Location (years)	Research design	Average impact
Zimmer et al. (2003)	California	Fixed effects	No reading effect for elementary students; small negative effect in math No math effect for secondary students; small positive effects in reading
Solomon and Goldschmidt (2004)	Arizona	Fixed effects	Positive reading effect for elementary students attending charter schools for 3 years compared to students attending TPSs for 3 years Negative reading effects for secondary students attending charter schools for 3 years compared to students attending TPSs for 3 years
Zimmer and Buddin (2006)	Los Angeles and San Diego	Fixed effects	No math or reading effect for Los Angeles elementary students; small negative effects for San Diego elementary students in math and reading Mixed small effects across locations for secondary students
Sass (2006)	Florida	Fixed effects	Small negative math and reading effects in grades 3–10
Bifulco and Ladd (2006)	North Carolina	Fixed effects	Negative math and reading effects in grades 4–8
Booker et al. (2007)	Texas	Fixed effects	Negative math and reading effects in grades 4–8
Hanushek et al. (2007)	Texas	Various models including fixed effects[a]	Negative combined reading and math effects in grades 4–8
Zimmer et al. (2009; 2012)	Chicago	Fixed effects	Chicago: no effect in math; small negative effect in reading
	Denver		Denver: moderate positive effect in math; no effect in reading
	Milwaukee		Milwaukee: small positive effect in math; no effect in reading
	Philadelphia		Philadelphia: no effect in math or reading
	Ohio		Ohio: moderately large negative effect in math; small negative effect in reading
	San Diego		San Diego: no effect in math or reading
	Texas		Texas: moderately large negative effect in math; small negative effect in reading
Imberman (2011)	Anonymous District	Fixed effect and IV#	No math, reading, or language arts effects

Table 5 Summary of student fixed effect estimates—cont'd

Study	Location (years)	Research design	Average impact
Nicotera et al. (2011)	Indianapolis	Fixed effects	Results vary by whether the analysis uses spring to spring test score gains analysis or fall to spring test score gains Strong positive math effects and no effect in reading for the spring to spring analysis Strong positive math and reading effects for the fall to spring analysis
Ni and Rorrer (2012)	Utah	Two approaches: (1) HLM (2) GMM with fixed effects	Both approaches show small negative effects in math and language arts in grades 1–6; no effect in language arts grades 7–11

[a]While other approaches are used in these papers, we focused on fixed-effect results here.

argument, along with the Institute Educational Science' (IES) emphasis on randomized control trials when funding research, a number of lottery-based studies have recently emerged after the wave of fixed-effect studies. As Table 6 suggests, these studies have been much more supportive of charter schools with nearly all of these studies finding positive effects — in some cases, quite large effects (Abdulkadiroğlu et al., 2011; Curto and Fryer, 2011; Hoxby and Rockoff, 2004; Hoxby et al., 2009; Tuttle et al., 2013; Wong et al., 2014) — with only one finding no effect, a study by Mathematica of charter middle schools (Gleason et al., 2010). However, even this study, while finding no positive effects on average across all schools, found some positive effects for urban charter middle schools. Therefore, many advocates for charter schools fixate on the lottery-based studies arguing that these studies have stronger research design, but generally fail to note that these studies have weaker external validity than fixed effect studies or observational studies in general.

Because both fixed-effect and the lottery-based approaches received a fair amount of criticism, two recent studies by CREDO used the VCR matching procedure discussed in the previous section (CREDO, 2009, 2013a). In these studies, CREDO tried to address the external validity weaknesses of lottery-based and the fixed-effect studies by including all schools, not just oversubscribed schools of a lottery-based study, and a larger set of students, not just the switchers of a fixed-effect study. While we previously noted that the VCR approach examines the effect of charter schools relative to a baseline test, which limits the ability to study impacts in the early grades, these studies were unique in that they included longitudinal student-level data from multiple states. The two CREDO

Table 6 Summary of estimates from lottery based analyses

Study	Location	Research design	Average impact
Hoxby and Rockoff (2004)	Chicago	Random assignment based on lottery data	Positive effects in math of 6–7% and in reading of 5–6%
Hoxby et al. (2009)	New York City	Random assignment based on lottery data	Small positive effect in both math and reading
Abdulkadiroğlu et al. (2010)	Boston	Random assignment based on lottery data along with observational analyses	Moderately large positive effects in English and large effects in math
Dobbie and Fryer (2011a)	Harlem Children Zone	Random assignment based on lottery data	Very large math and ELA positive effects both in elementary and middle-school grades
Curto and Fryer (2011)	SEED schools in D.C.	Random assignment based on lottery data	Moderate to large effects in math and reading
Gleason et al. (2010)	National Sample of Middle Schools	Random assignment based on lottery data	Null average effects for student achievement and behavioral outcomes. Did find a positive effect for low-income, low-performing students, but negative effects for more advantaged students
Wong et al. (2014)	Los Angeles	Random assignment based on lottery data	Improved math English test scores, greater school retention, and lower rates of engaging in ≥ 1 very risky behaviors, but no difference in risky behaviors, such as any recent use of alcohol, tobacco, or drugs

studies included 16 and 27 states,[20] respectively. To our knowledge, the only other studies that can make a claim of using data from multiple states are studies using OLS regression approaches, a RAND study using a fixed-effect approach (Zimmer et al., 2009, 2012), and the Mathematica charter middle-school study (Gleason et al., 2010) using the lottery-based approach.[21]

CREDO presented results in a unique way, reporting the proportion of charter schools that outperformed their locally matched TPS, which made their findings easier

---

[20] The 2009 study includes 15 states plus the District of Columbia, while the 2013 study actually included 25 states plus the District of Columbia and New York City.

[21] Mathematica also had a national study of charter schools managed by charter management organizations (CMOs) (Tuttle et al., 2013) and a study of schools managed by the individual CMO of KIPP, but these studies were not meant to be representative of charter schools in general.

to interpret for a lay audience, including the media. CREDO found in the 2009 study that 17% of charter schools outperformed TPSs in math, but this number grew to 29% in the 2013 study. On a similar note, CREDO found that 31% performed worse than their TPSs counterpart in the 2009 study, but only 19% in the 2013 study. While this suggests some improvement between the timeframes of the studies, the 2013 study's overall national estimate of charter schools suggests little average impact with no statistically significant difference in math and a slight positive effect in reading of 0.01 of a standard deviation. In general, these results have been interpreted in two ways. The more optimistic view is that overall performance of charter schools is improving over time. The more negative view is that many students' performance in many charter schools are still lagging behind students in TPSs and, overall, the results across the two studies do not show a pattern of systematic improvement.

In Table 7, we summarize the matching studies as well as the national OLS regression studies. While these studies are often thought to impose stronger assumptions for controlling for selection bias, and therefore raise more internal validity concerns among researchers, they have disproportionally received national attention. For instance, the 2004 AFT study by Howard Nelson was highlighted in front page story in the *New York Times*.[22] Because this study used National Assessment of Educational Progress (NAEP) data which do not track individual students over time, many researchers criticized not only this study,[23] but criticized the *New York Times* for reporting what many believed to be a study with weak controls for selection bias (Carnoy et al., 2006). In fact, a full page advertisement appeared in the *New York Times* shortly after the story came out criticizing both the study and the *New York Times* reporting.[24] Within weeks, Hoxby (2004) used an OLS approach using school-level proficiency data across states comparing the performance of charter schools to nearby TPSs. While many viewed this design as an improvement, many argued that these results were also suspect and left many policymakers and observers confused.[25] In the end, many argued for stronger approaches when examining charter schools.

The most recent set of papers have examined charter schools in Texas (Baude et al., 2014) and North Carolina (Ladd et al., 2014) with a variant of the OLS approach using value-added models. Baude and colleagues argued that using the value-added approach as opposed to a fixed-effect or lottery-based approach represents an improvement because any competitive effects on the quality of TPSs (which will weaken these schools as counterfactuals) will be amplified as these methods base their comparisons solely on those TPSs from which the charter school students are drawn even though these public schools likely

---

[22] http://www.nytimes.com/2004/08/17/education/17charter.html.

[23] http://educationnext.org/grayladywheezing/.

[24] https://www.edreform.com/wp-content/uploads/2013/04/NY-Times-Ad-Ed-Week-Version.pdf.

[25] http://www.ecs.org/html/Document.asp?chouseid=5588.

Table 7 Summary of results from matching and OLS regression approaches

Study	Location	Research design	Average impact
AFT (2004)	National	OLS regression of cross sectional data	Average 4th-grade achievement was higher for TPSs than in charter schools, both for students overall and for low-income students
Hoxby (2004)	National	OLS regression of cross sectional data using TPSs located near charter schools as the comparison group	Charter students were 3% more likely than noncharter students in nearby schools to be proficient in reading and 2% more likely to reach proficient levels in mathematics
CREDO (2009)	16 states	Matching approach	Across all states, 17% of charter schools outperformed TPSs in math; 31% performed worse than their TPSs counterpart
Furgeson et al., 2012a,b	Twenty-two anonymous CMOs from several states	Matching approach	Evaluated as a group, the 22 CMOs had positive but not statistically significant test score impacts for all four academic subjects that were evaluated. Impacts varied greatly across CMOs. For example, in math 10 CMOs had significant positive impacts and 4 had significant negative impacts. Larger CMOs tended to have more favorable impacts
CREDO (2013a)	27 states	Matching approach	Across all states, 29% of charter schools outperformed TPSs in math; 19% performed worse than their TPSs counterpart. Overall average impact of no effect in math and slight positive effect in reading
Baude et al. (2014)	Texas	Value-added model	In recent years, charter schools have improved performance with moderate to large effect sizes in math and reading, respectively
Ladd et al. (2014)	North Carolina	Value-added model as well as fixed effect approach	In the value-added model, which is the approach the authors emphasize, the results suggest that, as a whole, charter schools have improved performance over time. The authors also suggest that charter schools are leading to higher parental satisfaction where the authors use a demographic adjusted proportion of parents who keep their children in the school the next year relative to similar parents whose children are in TPSs

face the strongest competitive pressures. Both papers focus on the evolution of charter schools over time, and both find that while charter schools generally lagged behind TPSs in the early years of the movement in each state, eventually, charter schools either tend to meet or surpass the performance of TPSs.[26] In addition, Ladd and colleagues found have higher parental satisfaction for parents in charter schools.

Comparing the results across the studies using lottery-based and observational approaches of OLS, matching and fixed effects, the studies using lottery-based approaches are much more positive. As previously noted, one could argue that the lottery-based findings should be the only ones trusted as lottery-based approach employs an approach that best mimics a randomized design providing a stronger guard against self-selection.[27] However, there are a number of reasons why the set of findings from the lottery-based approach and observational approaches could differ beyond the rigor of the approach. First, many of the locations studied in the two sets of approaches do not overlap. Because each state has its own charter laws and the local environments can affect the adoption of charter schools, the performance of charter schools could vary from location to location. Therefore, both sets of results could be right with results varying not because of the research approach, but because of the location. In one case in which the location overlapped across the different approaches, the results for the VCR approach were similar to the results from the lottery-based approach (CREDO, 2013b). Second, the two sets of studies could be evaluating two very different sets of charter schools and even different sets of students within the same charter schools (Zimmer and Engberg, 2013). As noted previously, while the fixed effect and matching approaches tend to include all charter schools with tested students, a lottery-based approach only uses oversubscribed schools and only students who enter these via a lottery. In addition to the CREDO (2013b) study, others have addressed these issues by using both lottery-based and observational approaches for the same set of schools and found substantively similar results (Abdulkadiroğlu et al., 2011; Furgeson et al., 2012a,b; Tuttle et al., 2013).[28] This suggests that differences in schools rather than differences in methodologies underlie the differences in findings. Evidence in this regard is provided by Abdulkadiroğlu et al. (2011) in their demonstration that the observational approach for their lottery sample gives

[26] Ladd et al. (2014) also employed a fixed effect model, which showed no effect for students switching between sectors.

[27] An alternative explanation is that charter schools are more likely to be oversubscribed if they locate in areas where the TPSs are low quality. Therefore, part of the explanation for the strong performance could be that the nearby TPS are really poor performing (Deming, 2014). This does not suggest that the results are wrong in these analyses, it just raises questions of whether the results would hold if charter schools were scaled up to different locations with higher performing nearby TPSs.

[28] At the very least, Zimmer and Engberg (2013) advocate that researchers using lottery-based analysis should examine whether students in undersubscribed schools or enter an oversubscribed schools outside of lottery have similar observable characteristics and value added gains in test scores as a check to see whether there are red flags of making inferences beyond the population examined.

comparable findings to their lottery estimates. They go on to note that the observational approach suggests that "… the charter schools in our lottery study are among the best in Boston. Observational estimates of the effect of time spent in charter schools that were not included in the lottery study are economically and statistically significant, but only about half as large as the corresponding estimates for lottery-sample schools." It is fair to say that researchers have not come to consensus on charter school effectiveness because these differences in findings. An interpretation that fits the evidence is that some charter schools, including especially the oversubscribed schools, are in fact much more effective with respect to student achievement than there counterpart TPSs, while the majority of charter schools are not superior, and some are inferior, to their counterpart TPSs.

Differences in findings may also arise from peer effects associated with student selection. While the requirement for oversubscribed schools to choose students by lottery precludes selective admission by charters, charters may induce self-selection by adopting a more challenging curriculum, more demanding standards for conduct, longer school days, more stringent graduation requirements, or other policies that attract more able and motivated students. It is natural to wonder, for example, whether charter schools with "No Excuses" policies may induce such favorable selection. As summarized in, Abdulkadiroğlu et al. (2011, p. 704): "No Excuses schools are characterized by small size, frequent testing, a long school day and year, selective teacher hiring, and a strong student work, ethic. Other features include an emphasis on discipline and comportment, teacher-led whole-class instruction, and the absence of computer-aided instruction." Charter schools in Boston studied by Abdulkadiroğlu et al. (2011) had 35% more hours of middle-school instruction per year than Boston Public Schools (BPS), and 26% more hours of high-school instruction. Evidence of more stringent graduation requirements is provided in Angrist et al. (2013a,b). Boston charter high schools students in their study have 7.6% higher 12 grade repetition than their lotteried-out counterparts.[29]

As noted previously, and as Angrist et al. (2013a,b) highlight in a thorough discussion and analysis, there are three broad channels by which selection could give rise to differential performance between charter and TPSs.[30] The most obvious channel is if charter schools attract more academically able students than TPSs. A second is if less able students exit charter schools at a higher rate than in TPSs. A third is if peers in charter schools generate greater positive spillovers than in TPS counterparts. Lottery studies effectively

---

[29] This grade repetition appears to be concentrated almost entirely among male students: The 4-year male graduation rate from charter high schools studied by Angrist et al. (2013a,b) is 22.5% lower ($p = 0.03$) than lotteried-out counterparts, with that differential falling to 2.2% ($p = 0.82$) after 5 years. The corresponding values for female students are 4.2 and 1.3, with neither being significant.

[30] These issues are also explored by Baude et al. (2014) and Ladd et al. (2014). Ladd and colleagues argue that the recent improvement of charter schools in North Carolina is the result of increased quality of students attracted and recruited to charter schools, which they argue leads to improved peer effects. In contrast, Baude and colleagues argue that peer effects have not played a major role in school improvement in Texas.

address the first channel by exploiting random selection of students. The random selection exploited in lottery studies also addresses the second channel effectively if students who ever attended a charter school are thereafter counted as charter school students, as in the Angrist et al. (2013a,b) analysis of Boston charter high schools.

The third channel may, however, remain, even in lottery studies. Students who are not selected in charter school lotteries may attend schools with less beneficial peer attributes than those who are selected. This channel does not invalidate the estimated impact of charter schools in lottery studies, but gains achieved via peer effects have different policy implications than gains achieved through superior delivery of education. Investigating the potential role of peer effects, Angrist et al. (2013a,b) find, after eliminating transition grades, a 15% higher switch rate out of charter schools ($p = 0.08$) as compared to switches made by lottery losers. The compositional effect of this differential switching gives rise to a 0.13σ differential in both baseline math ($p - 0.07$) and baseline reading ($p = 0.07$) scores in the first postlottery year. The differential declines in subsequent years. Angrist et al. (2013a,b) go on to investigate whether the peer-effect benefits of this differential in peer baseline achievement can account for the superior academic outcomes in the charter schools. They conclude it does not. The same conclusion is reached for charter middle schools in Boston by Abdulkadiroğlu et al. (2011).

A recent Mathematica study summarized by Nichols-Barrer et al. (2014) undertakes a detailed assessment of the potential role of peer characteristics and potential peer effects in 19 KIPP middle schools. They find that students admitted to KIPP schools are observationally similar to students in nearby public middle schools. Similar patterns of attrition are also found for both types of schools, with lower achieving students being more likely to leave both types of schools. However, KIPP schools have lower replacement rates and replace with higher achieving students. They conclude that, taking even the high end of peer-effect estimates from the literature, the resulting differential in peer achievement is not nearly large enough to account for the differential in academic outcomes between KIPP middle schools and their TPS middle-school counterparts.

As noted by Nichols-Barrer et al. (2014), peer spillovers might arise from bringing together highly motivated students that select into charter schools, and such peer benefits might not be captured by peer mean achievement. It is also plausible that concentrating such students together in schools, as occurs among lottery winners, would result in beneficial peer effects not realized by comparably motivated lottery losers. If peer motivation does convey spillover benefits, it is possible that No Excuses charter schools adversely affect noncharter TPSs by drawing the most motivated students out of TPSs. It should be noted, however, that the equivalence found by Abdulkadiroğlu et al. (2011) between the lottery approach and the observational approach provides evidence against this peer-effect argument. Assuming more motivated students select charter schools, the observational approach, which cannot match on unobserved motivation, will then have a less motivated control group than the lottery losers. Hence, the achievement difference between lottery winners and equally motivated lottery losers should be smaller than the difference between lottery winners and the less motivated observational control group. The fact that no such difference is found suggests that unobserved motivation may not be a major factor. Devising additional research strategies to investigate the potential for peer spillover effects that might arise from unobserved motivation remains an important research issue for the lottery approach.

An alternative approach is directly to evaluate the no-excuses model by implementing it in existing public schools. While, to our knowledge, this has not been done by those who operate no-excuses charter schools,[31] a remarkable set of experiments has been undertaken to investigate whether implementing changes deemed best practices from charter school into public schools can deliver the achievement gains found in no-excuses charter schools. In an experiment in Houston, five practices identified by Dobbie and Fryer (2013) were introduced into 20 low-performing Houston schools in a randomized trial. As summarized by Fryer (2014), the five practices were "… increased time, better human capital, more student-level differentiation, frequent use of data to alter the scope and sequence of classroom instruction, and a culture of high expectations." In particular, the following were among changes that were implemented: Time in school was increased by 21%, 19 of 20 principals were replaced and 46% of teachers left or were removed, tutoring software was provided along with extra tutoring support to students determined to be of high need, more frequent assessment examinations were employed to evaluate student progress and identify students needing extra help, and an effort was made to inculcate high expectations including having schools and parent signing contracts analogous to those used in no-excuses charter schools.

Analyzing the results, Fryer (2014) finds statistically significant annual gains in math of 0.15 of a standard deviation and small, statistically insignificant gains in reading.[32] Lower impacts on reading than math are not unusual in lottery studies of charters, though significant positive effects are often found, eg, Abdulkadiroğlu et al. (2011). Fryer goes on to describe and analyze interventions similar in spirit that were conducted in Denver and Chicago. In Denver, there were seven schools in the treatment group, and estimated impacts are comparable to those in Houston. In Chicago, there were 29 schools, but

[31] KIPP contracted with Denver Public Schools in 2004 to operate a school that had been closed by the state due to poor academic performance. KIPP withdrew in 2007 citing inability to find a qualified leader for the school. See Sherry (2007) and also an interview with KIPP spokesman Steve Mancini: http://www. cpr.org/news/story/denvers-cole-college-prep-close.

[32] Fryer notes two issues that potentially affect the results. He observes (p. 36) that publicity in advance of the experiment might have induced selective attrition in advance of the experimental treatment that is not captured in the analysis. He also notes (p. 37) that students in the treated elementary schools are 1.4% more likely than the control schools to be missing a test score, and he indicates that the bounding approach of Lee (2009) (trimming the 1.4% of the treatment group with the highest annual gains) systematically alters the results.

selection was not by randomization. Using a matching approach, Fryer estimates treatment effects in math about one-third the size found in Houston and small reading gains on the order of those found in Houston.

Fryer provides a cautionary summary of the daunting challenges to be overcome in broader implementation of these changes in TPSs. For example, in the 20 treatment schools in Houston, as noted 46% of teachers left or were removed and 19 of 20 principals were replaced, with then 300 candidates interviewed in the process of replacing those who were removed. Fryer also points to fidelity of implementation as an ongoing challenge, noting the difficulties often encountered in efforts to scale up interventions. Nonetheless, the Houston experiment is encouraging with respect to potential gains from injecting charter best practices into low-performing TPSs.

4.2 Effects on Other Outcomes

In some cases, researchers have moved beyond examining test scores alone and are examining other outcomes, for example alternative student measures while the students are attending charter schools including behavioral outcomes (like risky health choices) or attendance outcomes (Imberman, 2011; Wong et al., 2014). Other researchers have examined long-term outcomes including high school graduation rates as well as college preparation, attendance, persistence, and type (2-year vs. 4-year colleges) and, recently, earnings (Angrist et al., 2013a,b; Booker et al., 2009, 2011, 2014; Dobbie and Fryer, 2013; Furgeson et al., 2012a,b). These studies have used a variety of approaches including fixed effects (for outcomes measured multiple times like attendance and behavioral), matching procedures, IVs (using proximity to charter schools as an instrument), and lotteries, each having strengths and weakness as previously discussed. However, across these approaches, unlike the test score results, the findings, summarized in Table 8, have been more consistently positive.

Coupling the overall results of the achievement and alternative-outcomes literatures together, it could be argued that while charter schools are not having a consistent effect on test scores, there is emerging research suggesting that they are having more consistent positive effects on alternative outcomes, which is consistent with some research of vouchers. For example, Wolf et al. (2010) found no statistically significant effect on test scores for Washington, D.C. voucher recipients, but did find effects on high-school graduation. In some cases, researchers have found this within their charter studies. Imberman (2011), using a fixed-effect approach in an anonymous district, found little effect on test scores, but large effects on attendance and behavioral outcomes. Similarly, Zimmer et al. (2009) found little effect on test scores, but found positive and substantial effects on high-school graduation and attending college in Chicago. It is too soon to know whether this pattern will hold up as other researchers examine these outcomes in other places and over time. However, if it does, this may explain why charter schools continue to be popular,

Table 8 Summary of results of analyses of noncognitive outcomes

Study	Location	Research outcomes	Research design	Average impact
Booker et al. (2011)	Chicago and Florida	Examined high-school graduation and college attendance of students attending charter high schools	Probit model with the restriction that all students previous attended a charter school in 8th grade. Also controlled for observable characteristics and conducted a bivariate probit approach using proximity as an instrument	Increased probability of graduating high school and attending college of 7–15%, depending upon location and outcome
Imberman (2011)	Anonymous District	Examine the effect of behavioral and attendance outcome as measure of noncognitive skill formation	Fixed effect	Schools that begin as charters (startups) generate large improvements in discipline and attendance, while no such effect was observed for conversion charter schools
Furgeson et al. (2012a,b)	Anonymous CMOs	Examined high-school graduation and college attendance in Charter Management Organizations (CMOs)	Graduation data were obtained for six CMOs. College attendance data were obtained for four CMOs. Method entailed comparison of charter students to matched students in home district of each charter school	Combined data for six CMOs showed positive but insignificant effects on college attendance. Evaluated separately, three CMOs had large significant positive impacts on college attendance, two an insignificant positive effect, and one a large significant negative effect. Combined data for four CMOs showed positive but insignificant effects college attendance. Evaluated separately, two CMOs had large significant positive impacts on college attendance and two had insignificant effects
Angrist et al. (2013a,b)	Boston	Examined postsecondary outcomes	Random assignment based on lottery data	Positive impacts on measures of college preparation (such as SAT scores), no statistically significant impact on high-school graduation, and an effect of shifting students from 2-year colleges into 4-year colleges

Dobbie and Fryer (2013)	Promise Academy in the Harlem Children's Zone	The effects of high-performing charter schools on human capital, risky behaviors, and health outcomes	Random assignment based on lottery data	The study found a 14.1% increased likelihood to enroll in college and females are 12.1% less likely to be pregnant in their teens, and males are 4.3% less likely to be incarcerated. The study found no impact on selfreported health
Booker et al. (2014)	Chicago and Florida	Evaluate high-school graduation, college attendance, labor outcomes	Probit and OLS models (depending upon whether it was dichotomous our continuous outcome) with the restriction that all students previous attended a charter school in 8th grade. Also controlled for observable characteristics and conducted a bivariate probit and IV approach using proximity as an instrument	Increased probability of graduating high school, attending college, and persisting in college of 7–13%, depending upon location and outcome. In addition, the analysis was the first to examine labor outcomes and found an advantage of about 12% for students who attended a charter school
Wong et al. (2014)	Los Angeles	Examined risky behaviors	Random assignment based on lottery data for three high-performing charter schools. ITT analysis excluding applicants to the three focus schools who went to an alternative high-performing charter school in 9th grade	No significant difference in behaviors denoted risky (eg, alcohol, tobacco, drug use). Significantly lower incidence in charter sample of behaviors denoted very risky (eg, binge drinking, substance use at school, gang participation)

even with a lack of consistent evidence that charter schools outperform students in TPSs. It may be that families have goals for their child beyond improving test scores and families see charter schools as a means of achieving these goals, even if they do not achieve the goal of improving test scores.

5. INSIDE THE BLACK BOX

Controlling for differences in students, it is of obvious interest to explain differences in educational outcomes between charter school students and those attending other schools.

5.1 Charter School Teachers

We first examine research on charter schools and teachers. While identifying effective teachers and measuring their relative productivity is challenging and controversial, that teachers affect educational outcomes is unquestioned. The relative autonomy charter schools have in hiring, rewarding, utilizing, and firing teachers is touted by charter proponents as a key advantage relative to TPSs. As noted previously, charter schools are usually not bound by unions, nor must they follow state regulations like those governing awarding of tenure. Charter schools usually face reduced teacher certification constraints if any. On the other hand, charter schools frequently serve students that may be more difficult to teach, locate where it is less desirable to live, lack state-of-the-art facilities, and may face tighter budget constraints.

In Section 3 we provided some descriptive statistics about charter school teachers. Among other differences relative to TPS teachers, charter school teachers are younger, less experienced, less educated, less credentialed, and they earn less. We discuss research that seeks to explain differences in observable characteristics of charter school teachers. The linkage between observable teacher characteristics and effectiveness of teachers is, however, mixed. Of the 34 "high quality estimates" of the effect of a master's degree on student performance, Hanushek and Rivkin (2006) report that 91% of the estimates are insignificant and the remaining 9% find a negative effect. Of the 37 high quality estimates on teacher experience, 56% find no statistically significant effect, though 41% find a significantly positive effect. As summarized in Hanushek and Rivkin (2006), further investigation has found that teachers develop their skills very quickly, mainly in the first year, this nonlinearity in experience effects on teacher effectiveness likely explaining the mixed result. Of the 17 high quality estimates on teacher salary, 82% find no significant effect, though the remaining studies find a significantly positive effect. An alternative approach to using teacher characteristics in assessing their effectiveness is to estimate teacher effectiveness directly as a fixed-effect on student scores. This approach has been applied in some analyses of charter schools. Thus, we also discuss this research, including a summary of the technique and issues in applying it.

The stock of teachers in charter schools depends on who is hired and who continues, whether by choice or dismissal. As noted in Section 3, teacher turnover in charter schools is substantial if not extreme. We first discuss research that regards the stock of teacher characteristics in charter schools. Next we discuss research concerned with the characteristics of teachers that continue to teach. Last, we discuss research on teachers that move to charter schools from TPS schools.

Much of the research investigating differences in charters and TPS teachers relies on a version of a regression with a teacher characteristic as the dependent variable, a dummy variable if the teacher is in a charter school, and with a set of other explanatory variables like characteristics of the school including student characteristics. Some issues to keep in mind in evaluating this research are as follows. Giving a causal interpretation to the charter school effect is open to question since charter school entry is endogenous. If, for example, charter school entry is more probable in areas where the local teachers are relatively ineffective (eg, gaining approval is easier), then the charter school may need to hire from a weaker pool of teachers to staff its classes. Of course, researchers take steps to address this kind of issue.

A second issue is that the "charter effect" is likely to combine supply- and demand-side effects. If, for example, teachers that are less effective in increasing test scores are present in charter schools it could be because charter schools value this trait less and/or because highly effective teachers are averse to working in charter schools. Again, research has paid some attention to this confluence, but a lack of economic modeling that frames the empirical research makes it difficult to interpret the estimates.

A third issue is that an estimated charter effect on their teachers is arguably a residual effect, suggesting some element of charter schools that remains unexplained. With this view, the ideal would be to have a model that controls for practices and specific characteristics of schools that fully explains equilibrium teacher characteristics with then no residual effect of working in a charter school. This is the "black box issue" applied to teachers. The research generally seeks to identify charter effects independent of specific practices and school characteristics, but residual effects remain large. It is also possible that some teachers simply have an aversion (or preference) to work in a charter school, eg, as a result of their political views.

Baker and Dickerson (2006) examine whether teaching in a charter school predicts teachers that come from more highly ranked undergraduate institutions. The hypothesis is that the flexibility in hiring that charter schools have (eg, not having to satisfy certification requirements) and in retaining teachers (eg, through their salary policies) will lead them to employ teachers from better undergraduate institutions. Data on teachers is for 18 states and Washington D.C. from the 1999 SASS, including TPSs, charter schools, Catholic schools, and private non–Catholic schools, specifically, members of the National Association for Independent Schools (NAIS). Key factors that are investigated are whether the state requires 100% or less certification of charter school teachers, a ranking of the autonomy of charter schools in the state developed by the Center for Education Reform, and the relative supply of graduates from highly ranked schools by state. College rankings are based on Barron's, where the variable used in their analysis are dichotomous with "highly competitive" or "most competitive" considered as selective colleges.

Logit estimation predicts whether a teacher went to a selective college using dummy variables for the type of school and other controls. These equations are specified separately for states that require 100% versus less than 100% certification for charter teachers.[33] Results from SUR logit regressions for states that require 100% certification and those that do not are as follows. The estimates imply that the odds a charter-school teacher will have attended a selective college is twice that of a TPS teacher[34] and highly significant in states that do not require 100% certification, and 1.3 times as high and significant at the 10% level in states that do. The analogous estimates for NAIS schools are highly significant and, respectively, equal to 4.7 and 3.3. The "state high quality supply share," which measures the state supply of graduates from selective colleges has a large and significant coefficient. Catholic schools are not significantly different from TPSs in hiring teachers from selective colleges, with point estimates less than 1. Rural and percentage in poverty in the school are usually significant with point estimates less than 1. Evidence on the effect of salary is mixed, with average salary either not significant or increasing the probability of a teacher having a degree from a selective college.

The analysis provides evidence that barriers to hiring teachers in TPSs from selective colleges play a role in limiting their presence. While the analysis considers both supply- and demand-side factors to some degree, it cannot well identify the preference of graduates from selective colleges to work in certain types of schools relative to school demands to hire them. As we noted in Section 3, the more recent evidence on charter school teachers indicates the same or fewer graduates from relatively selective colleges. One can only speculate as to why these changes have occurred.

Cannata and Penaloza (2012) examine supply- and demand-side factors determining charter school teacher characteristics, and how these vary across charter schools that are managed differently. Part of the analysis concerns identifying which teachers actively chose their school rather than essentially taking the only available job. A related question investigated is whether charter school teachers have more of a choice as to where they work as compared to TPS teachers. Identifying teachers that have made a real choice about where to work arguably permits more credible investigation about what characteristics of the school determined their choice.

---

[33] Regressions are also conducted separating by the ranking of autonomy of charter schools, and by states for some states. Regressions that, alternatively, use interactions are also run. Similar results obtain to those we report.

[34] An odds ratio is a ratio of probabilities. For example, if a charter teacher attends a selective college with probability 0.2 and a TPS teacher with probability 0.1, the odds of a charter teacher attending a selective college are twice as high as for a TPS teacher.

The authors surveyed teachers during the 2007–08 school year in 59 charter schools and 59 matched TPSs in California, Colorado, Delaware, Indiana, Michigan, Minnesota, New Mexico, and Wisconsin. A total of 1015 charter school teachers and 1300 TPSs teachers were surveyed. Schools were matched on being in the same state, geographic proximity, grade-range served, racial-ethnic composition, socioeconomic status, and size. Despite the latter matching, charter schools were still substantially different, with fewer students per school and a significantly higher proportion of black students. Among the surveyed charter schools, 19% are operated by Best Academy (an EMO that operates in multiple states), 8% were operated by other for-profit and not-for-profit CMOs, and 73% were independent charters.

The survey had teachers report whether they "chose this school over positions at other schools because they wanted to teach here," or "this was the only opening for which I was qualified," or "I was assigned to this school." Those that answered "yes" to the first choice are considered to have made an "active choice." Teachers that made an "active choice" were asked further questions about what influenced their choice, assigning a number from a 5-point scale to 21 school characteristics (eg, "principal support" or "like-minded educators"), while also listing the top three characteristics that determined their choice. Part of the analysis regresses whether the teacher made an active choice on teacher and school characteristics, including a charter dummy variable, or using dummy variables for the three charter affiliation types. For teachers that made an active choice, their rankings of school characteristics are regressed on the same set of explanatory variables. Estimation is also done using propensity scores as another explanatory variable (using a regression of charter on school characteristics), as an additional control for school characteristics.

Mean analysis supports what has generally been found, that charter teachers are less experienced, less likely to be certified, are less likely to have graduate degrees, are more likely to be black, and are more likely to have become teachers while changing job type. Selectivity of the college attended is here lower in charter schools. However, there are important differences across the categories of charter affiliation. Only Best Academy teachers attended significantly less selective colleges. Best Academy teachers were also significantly less likely to be black.

Regarding having made an active choice, no statistical difference in the means between TPSs and all charter schools is found. However, in the estimation controlling for teacher and school characteristics, charter school teachers were more likely to have made an active choice. This is driven mainly by the nonaffiliated charter schools, with the coefficient estimate on active choice for Best Academy charter teachers insignificant. Prior experience, being black (or other minority, non-Hispanic), and teaching in a school with a higher percentage of FRL students significantly predict active choice.

School characteristics like "principal support" that an actively choosing teacher ranked as among the top three in choosing their job are assigned a 1 in logit regressions on school and teacher characteristics and a dummy variable for either charter school or a set of dummy variables for the three different charter school affiliations. Charter teachers significantly favored "agreeing with the school's mission" and "autonomy over teaching" relative to TPS teachers, and significantly cared less about "close to where I live," "positive reputation," and "job security." Again, though, these preference differences are explained by teachers in nonaffiliated and other-affiliation schools, with no significant differences expressed by teachers in the Best Academy schools (in the regressions without propensity scores).

The salient take-away from the paper is as the authors express: "... the data suggest that charter school teachers are a diverse group and the variation between different types of charter schools may be just as important as the difference between teachers in charter and TPSs (p. 16)." In particular, the evidence is that the "Best Academy" teachers are very different from other charter school teachers.

Cowen and Winters (2013) and Carruthers (2012) use value-added estimation of teacher effectiveness in their analyses of charter school teachers. The key application to teachers of the value-added approach estimates teacher effectiveness semiparametrically using teacher fixed effects. We briefly describe the approach, borrowing heavily from Hanushek and Rivkin (2006), and then go on to discuss its application to charter schools.[35]

With multiple years of data, the approach regresses student scores on past score or scores, student characteristics, time variant peer student characteristics in the classroom and school, other time variant school characteristics (eg, per student expenditure), and a teacher fixed effect. The teacher fixed-effect estimates the achievement (score) gain attributable to the teacher if certain conditions are met, providing an overall measure of teacher effectiveness. Thus, the approach is silent about observable characteristics of teachers that might determine or be correlated with effectiveness, but provides a summary measure.

To provide an unbiased estimate, the approach assumes that teacher effects are constant across students and settings, though the fixed effect could be interacted with say previous student score if value added to the test depends on the student's baseline. It also assumes that any unobservable classroom/school characteristics are random, obviously a strong assumption. If, for example, highly motivated students are able to get into relatively effective teachers' classes, then estimates of teacher effectiveness will be biased. Hanushek and Rivkin (2006) discuss some techniques to alleviate concerns about nonrandomness.

The multiyear specification controls for random measurement error and random classroom variation of unobservables. School fixed effects are sometimes used, thus controlling for time invariant unobserved school impacts, identification then within schools.

---

[35] See Hanushek and Rivkin (2006) for references and a more complete discussion.

With school-fixed effects, however, the distribution of teacher effectiveness in schools must remain constant since the effectiveness estimate is relative to peer teachers. The multiyear approach also assumes teacher effectiveness is time invariant, which is reasonable for relatively short periods especially with more experienced teachers.

Estimates using the approach indicate large differences in teacher effectiveness. Comparing, for example, teachers at the 5th to the 95th effectiveness percentile, Hanushek (1992) finds that a good teacher increases average student learning of low-income minority students by one grade level relative to a bad teacher. Kane and Staiger (2008) provide experimental support for the approach by showing that value-added estimates of teacher effectiveness prior to their random assignment of teachers to classrooms provided unbiased estimates of teacher effects and explained "just over half of the teacher-level variation in average student achievement during the experiment (p. 3)."

While their focus is on the relative pattern of teacher attrition in charters versus TPSs, Cowen and Winters' (2013) value-added estimates of teacher effectiveness are of interest in their own right. They use a rich data set containing scores in Florida on reading and math on the required standardized (FCAT) exam for all grade-school students for the years 2002–03 through 2008–09. They also have data on all teachers in charter schools and TPSs, and can well connect students to their teachers. Grade-school students take the exam in 3rd, 4th, and 5th grade, and they use the 4th and 5th grade scores to estimate teacher effectiveness, with a rich set of control variables including the student's 3rd grade score. Estimates with a school-fixed effect are highly correlated with estimates without the school-fixed effect. Using multiple-year lagged scores has minor effects on the effectiveness estimates, this suggesting nonrandom student classroom assignment may not be introducing bias. They estimate teacher effectiveness separately for teachers with less than 4 years of experience and for more experienced teachers.

Their estimated probability density of effectiveness of TPS teachers in Florida is rightward shifted relative to charter teachers in both reading and math, more so in math. The relatively higher effectiveness of TPS teachers is statistically significant, with mean difference about one-tenth of a standard deviation. They state: "we caution readers against an unrestrained interpretation of these results as evidence that TPS teachers vastly exceed charter teachers," noting that there is the "possibility that TPS teachers are simply more effective instructors for the standardized statewide exam (p. 27)." Their caveat notwithstanding, they provide interesting evidence that charter teachers are less effective, consistent with the research finding less experienced and less educated teachers in charter schools. We discuss Carruthers (2012) value-added evidence below as it pertains to the subset of teachers that move to charter schools from TPSs.

As reported above, teacher turnover in charter schools is significant and significantly higher than in TPSs. Stuit and Smith (2009) use data from 2003–04 Schools and Staffing Survey administered by NCES and the 2004–05 Teacher Follow-Up Survey to investigate differences in teacher turnover between charter schools and TPSs, and what explains these differences. Variation in school policies, teacher characteristics, school characteristics including management of charter schools, and labor-market conditions are considered. Turnover can be moving to a new school or leaving the profession. Sixteen states are in the sample, with 1,753,390 TPS teachers in 45,820 schools and 35,570 charter school teachers in 1900 schools.

Overall, 25% of charter teachers turned over after 2003–04, compared to 14% in TPSs. In charter schools, 14% left the profession, while 7% in TPSs left the profession. They perform multinomial logit regression, with "stayed in the school" as the reference choice and "moved to a new school" and "left the profession" the alternative choices. In addition to a dummy variable for being a charter school teacher, they include interactions for whether the charter school is new (has been operation for 3 years or less), whether it is managed by an EMO, and whether it has converted from a TPS or is a "start-up" charter schools. Controls for teacher and school characteristics, and for a variety of "organizational conditions" are also included, the latter consisting of 11 variables including, unionization, a dichotomous hours-per-week measure, and principal and teacher involvement and control measures obtained from surveying them.

We summarize some of the findings focusing on the logit estimated odds ratio of leaving the profession versus staying at one's school. The estimated odds of a teacher leaving a charter school that is not new, is not a conversion charter, and is not managed by an EMO are 3.3 times higher than for a TPS teacher and significant at the 1% level. The estimated odds for a conversion charter school is significantly lower, but remains well above that for a TPS. Whether the charter school is managed by an EMO or is new does not have a significant effect on predicted turnover. The estimated effects on moving to another school are in the same direction with the same charter characteristics significant (though of somewhat different magnitudes).

Variables that are significant in increasing the probability of leaving the profession are being under 30 or over 50, being uncertified, teaching in a secondary school, working more than 60-hours-per-week, and reporting being dissatisfied with one's school. Variables that significantly reduce the probability of leaving the profession are having an education degree, teaching in a large school, and having the principal have substantial power over hiring. Some variables not found to be significant are being a minority teacher, having attended a selective college, teaching in an urban school, and teacher reporting of having administrative support, being involved in instructional decision making, the cooperative atmosphere among teachers, and satisfaction with salary.

While there are a number of differences between charter TPS schools and observable characteristics of teachers that are significant in predicting leaving the profession, the "residual" associated with being a charter school teacher (in any kind of charter school) remains quite high. Of interest is explaining the remaining large difference in turnover, including identifying differences in forced changes versus differences in teacher choices. The follow-up survey provides some insight into this.

The follow-up survey was administered to a sample of teachers in 2004–05 with questions that varied depending on whether the teacher left the profession or continued to teach in some school. The authors classify reasons teachers reported for leaving the profession into three categories, "life changes," "voluntary attrition," or "involuntary attrition," the only choice in the latter category being "school staffing action." Examples of explanation for leaving the profession in the second category are "for better salary or benefits" and "dissatisfied with teaching as a career." Significantly more teachers reported leaving the profession in TPSs due to life changes than teachers in charter schools, and the reverse for both voluntary and involuntary reasons. For charter-school teachers, 14.9% reported leaving the profession due to a school staffing action, while only 5.9% of TPS teacher reported the same, the difference highly significant. As the authors point out, this might provide evidence of charter schools having more power to get rid of less effective teachers, but might also be due to more frequent closing of charter schools and efforts to comply with new restrictions imposed by NCLB. Charter school teachers also reported significantly more frequently "dissatisfaction with previous school" as a (voluntary) reason for leaving the profession. Overall, the evidence is that a mixture of voluntary and forced actions explains the higher frequency of charter school teachers leaving the profession. "Laid off or involuntarily transferred" was reported as a reason for moving schools significantly more often by TPS teachers, as was "opportunity for a better teaching assignment" and "did not have enough autonomy." The responses explaining moving suggest TPS teachers have more opportunity to continue to teach. Stuit and Smith's analysis is informative and provocative, but direct evidence about whether charter schools are relatively able to retain more effective and/or get rid of less effective teachers is not provided.

Cowen and Winters (2013) employ their estimates of teacher effectiveness to this end. They perform multinomial logit analysis predicting whether teachers stay in their school, transfer within their district, transfer between districts, or exit teaching in Florida. In addition to controls for numerous observable teacher and school characteristics (including salary), they include their estimate of teacher effectiveness (based on both math and reading scores in separate regressions), a charter-school dummy variable, and the latter interacted with the effectiveness estimate. They find that less effective teachers exit teaching in Florida with significantly higher probability and teachers exit charter schools with significantly higher probability, the former arguably consistent with findings on observables and the latter consistent with all the evidence. We should add that the regressions control for teacher experience and its square, so the exit of teachers estimated to be relatively ineffective is independent of experience effects. The most important finding, though, is that the interaction coefficient in regressions using both the reading- and math-based effectiveness measures is not significant and with point estimates very close to 0. Thus, they find no evidence that charter schools are better or worse than TPSs in improving the effectiveness of their teacher pool. Whether this reflects equal efficaciousness, attrition beyond control, or some combination of offsets is an open question.

The last research we discuss examines the flow of teachers into charter schools. Carruthers (2012) focuses on the effectiveness of teachers that leave TPSs for charter schools, while Jackson (2012) is most concerned with the effects of charter school competition on TPS teachers. We first discuss Carruthers (2012). She uses a rich panel data set on teachers, students, and schools for the years 1997–2009 in North Carolina. Her data on student scores allows only value-added estimation of teacher effectiveness for those initially in TPS schools.

Carruthers's initial analysis focuses on teacher observables. Mobile teachers (any that move out of TPS schools) are less experienced and have degrees from less selective colleges. Teachers that move to charter schools have yet weaker credentials, are more likely to be unlicensed, and are more likely to be black. Multinomial logit is conducted to predict when teachers move out of their TPS, with the alternatives to staying being move to a charter school, move to another TPS, move temporarily out of sample, or move permanently out of sample, controlling for teacher characteristics and characteristics of the sending schools. Relative to staying, teachers that have high licensing scores, have attended selective colleges, have less than 3 years of experience, and are nonwhite are more likely to move to charter schools. Movers to charter schools are more likely to come from schools that are more nonwhite and schools where students are performing below grade level, relative to those that stay. Females are less likely to make this move. This methodology cannot, however, investigate how charter schools draw teachers relative to similar TPS schools (because the default option is to remain in a school).

The next analysis then examines how moving from a TPS to a charter school, relative to moving to a noncharter school, predicts various teacher measures, controlling for characteristics of the sending and receiving school. Relative to moving to a similar TPS, charter schools draw from other TPS schools less experienced teachers, fewer teachers that attended selective colleges, fewer teachers holding graduate degrees, and teachers with lower scores on licensing exams. However, if we examine just licensed teachers, the latter findings are attenuated and reversed for licensing scores. Also, teachers that have been working for more than 25 years are more likely to move to charter schools than another TPS, and, especially, if they are licensed.

Motivated by the mixed evidence on observable teacher characteristics, Carruthers turns to effectiveness estimated by the value-added approach. Having scores for students of teachers in TPS schools, she estimates teacher effectiveness as a fixed-effect on student math and reading scores (in separate regressions), controlling for student characteristics and peer school characteristics; and, in part of the analysis, for school-fixed effects. The means of the fixed effects of teachers moving to charter schools are lower than for all TPS teachers and for teachers that move to other TPSs (which is also lower than the mean of all teachers). To control for characteristics of the sending and receiving school, she runs regressions like the previous ones but now predicting estimated teacher effectiveness, with moving anywhere compared to moving to a charter school. The regressions that use teacher effectiveness estimated without school-fixed effects show that teachers that move to charter schools are significantly less effective than those that move at all, and the latter are already less effective than all initial TPS teachers. This could, however, reflect a bias in teacher effectiveness since it could be that teachers are moving to charters from schools with less motivated students. But the analysis with school-fixed effects in estimating effectiveness find similar results, though charter schools drawing less effective teachers (than other TPS) is only significant for effectiveness measured using reading (not math) scores. Another finding in the analysis estimating teacher effectiveness is that first-year teachers are less effective, consistent with other research. This estimation also provides a baseline to interpret the quantitative estimates: "Thus the difference between a teacher moving to the charter sector and a teacher moving elsewhere is 38–47 percent of the effectiveness gap between new and more experienced teachers (p. 253)."

As the author points out, it is possible that charter schools hire relatively effective new teachers as the analysis regards only teachers that move from TPSs. However, 36.1% of charter school teachers in her data did teach initially in TPS schools, and other evidence (eg, Cowen and Winters, 2013) does not indicate offsetting hiring practices. Again, whether differences in teacher effectiveness in charter schools is explained by demand or supply factors remains an open question.

Jackson (2012) focuses on the labor-market effects of entry of charter schools, but he also provides evidence of the effectiveness of teachers that leave TPSs to teach in charter schools. His data is also from North Carolina for the years 1995 to 2005. He estimates teacher effectiveness of TPS teachers using fixed effects in the value-added model, but also does so using a vector of observable teacher characteristics in place of the fixed effect. The "predicted effectiveness" of teachers equals the coefficient-estimate weighted teacher characteristics used to explain student test scores. The predicted effectiveness approach has the advantage of allowing an estimate of teacher effectiveness for those not in the data used in estimation.[36] Jackson finds that switching from a TPS to a charter school predicts observable teacher characteristics as in Carruthers (eg, less experience), but also significantly predicts a lower "predicted effectiveness." This provides a nice complement to Carruthers's findings.

---

[36] Jackson uses only data from the period (1995–98) prior to charter school entry in his fixed effects estimation of teacher effectiveness to avoid potential biases from charter school entry. Entry of charter schools might lead to selection of new teachers into TPS schools. It also possible that entry of charter schools induces teachers facing competition to work harder, thus affecting their fixed effect estimate. This, then, limits substantially the data on teacher effectiveness that can be used in the subsequent analyses since there are no estimates for teachers that enter the data after the estimation period, which does not hold for the "predicted effect" alternative. On the other hand, the "predicted effect" measure of teacher effectiveness relies on observables that at least individually have not generally been good predictors of student scores as discussed above.

Jackson's main analysis uses difference-in-difference to examine the causal effect of local charter-school competition on TPS teachers. He presents evidence supporting the notion that teacher markets are localized. He regresses TPS school-level teacher variables (eg, log of average salary) on school and time fixed effects and a dummy variable for the presence of least one nearby charter school (eg, with 10 miles) that serves the same grade level. Thus, identification is within school. He finds significant positive effects on TPS teacher salaries, especially in hard-to-staff schools (in the top quarter of ethnic minority and percentage minority). Turnover at TPSs facing competition is not increased. The interpretation given to the findings is that supply and demand effects cancel as TPSs strive to retain teachers, but both forces imply higher salaries in TPSs. Teacher quality, measured by their predicted value, declines slightly at hard-to-staff TPSs, mainly explained by reduced teacher experience.[37] This paper provides appealing evidence on the equilibrium effects of charter competition in the teacher labor market.

The evidence from Florida and North Carolina is that charter schools as a group have somewhat less effective teachers and are no better in improving their teaching pool. This is consistent with the evidence on the overall effectiveness of charter schools in these states (Bifulco and Ladd, 2006; Sass, 2006). While this aggregate evidence suggests charter schools face challenges in outperforming TPSs, this may well reflect newness of the charter school movement. Moreover, the value-added evidence and the evidence on observable teacher characteristics indicate large variation in teachers in charter schools. No-excuses charter schools in Boston hire relatively more TFA teachers and alumni (Angrist et al., 2013a,b). In their study of effectiveness of New York City charter schools, Dobbie and Fryer (2013) find "… input measures associated with a traditional resource-based model of education — class size, per pupil expenditure, the fraction of teachers with no teaching certification, and the fraction of teachers with an advanced degree — are not correlated with school effectiveness in our sample." Thus, their evidence for charters accords with evidence regarding teachers summarized in Hanushek and Rivkin (2006). They find instead that the most important of nine human capital measures is frequent teacher feedback. They report "the typical teacher at a high-achieving elementary school receives feedback 15.89 times per semester, compared to 10.23 times at other charter schools. The typical teacher at a high-achieving middle school receives feedback 16.50 times per semester, over twice as much as teachers at other charter schools." More research is needed on teachers in charter schools that employ alternative educational models to add understanding of how differences in management of charter schools impacts teacher effectiveness. It is of interest to investigate this as well in the context of the value-added approach.

Regressions show that teacher characteristics in schools vary with the environment, independent of charter status. But the charter effect remains important. This suggests there is much more to explain about what makes charter school teachers different.

---

[37] This effect is short lived.

Some effort has been made to examine demand-side versus supply-side effects on charter school teachers, but regressions that are run are reduced forms. This clouds interpretation of the coefficients. Developing models that lead to structural estimation are likely to help understand differences in charter school teachers, which are likely to differ substantially across the variety of quasimarkets in which they operate. Thus, modeling charter schools to guide estimation is an important, though challenging, undertaking to advance understanding of charter school teachers.

5.2 Nonteacher Differences

While the average effects on educational outcomes across all charter schools within or across locations are important from a policy standpoint, they may not tell the full story as these effects could vary by policy environment, or by types of charter schools, or even school by school as operational features and practices vary. As we have already noted, findings across geographic locations vary, which may be a function of the policies in place across locations. For instance, some states have very liberal policies in terms of setting up charter schools, while others have much more conservative laws. Most studies have not examined charter schools across multiple locations. Therefore, individual studies have generally not tried to draw conclusions about the effect of variation of charter policies. Only the 2009 CREDO study has tried to bridge this gap and the results suggest that charter schools perform poorly in states in which charter schools operate under a cap limiting the number of charter schools or have multiple possible authorizers. In contrast, states where charter schools have an appeal process for adverse decision on an application have stronger charter school performance. These conclusions should be viewed as initial insights as the differences in effects were small and the policy variable could only vary across 16 states.[38]

A few studies have examined whether charter school type or the operational features affects outcomes. For instance, using student-level data from California, Buddin and Zimmer (2005) examined whether there were differential effects across conversion and startup charter schools and classroom-based versus nonclassroom-based charter schools, which often use online curriculum. The research showed some differences between conversion and startup charter schools, but the differences were generally small. However, the differences were much larger between classroom-based and nonclassroom-based charter schools with the nonclassroom-based charter schools having lower achievement. This result is consistent with a study of Ohio charter schools that found virtual schools performing poorly relative to TPSs and other charter schools

---

[38] Two studies have explored the charter authorizer issue further. The first study examined charter schools in Minnesota in which there are four possible types of authorizers and found no differential effects, but did find greater variation among charter schools authorized by nonprofits (Carlson et al., 2012). The second study examined charter schools in Ohio in which there are again four possible authorizers and found that charter schools authorized by nonprofit had lower achievement gains (Zimmer et al., 2014).

(Zimmer et al., 2009). It is consistent at well with findings for Pennsylvania, which has among the highest proportion of online charter students. The CREDO (2011) report on Pennsylvania charter schools found that all eight cyber schools then operating performed significantly and substantially worse on both mathematics and reading than TPSs.[39]

While some of the authors in these studies cautioned against drawing strong conclusions of these virtual/nonclassroom-based schools as they note that these schools typically serve unique students, it does raise some concerns about the rapid expansion of these types of schools in a number of states. In addition, as a major conclusion, the same authors emphasized that charter schools should not be thought of as a monolithic group.[40]

As the above discussion indicates, charter school performance can vary by type of school and possibly by policy environment. It is also possible that charter schools' performance may vary from school to school. By design, charter schools are given a great deal of autonomy, which may result in some schools doing quite well, while other schools may flounder. Studying educational practices poses challenges of classification, measurement, and causality. A small set of studies have collected information about the educational operation and practices of individual charter schools and tried to identify factors that led to improved performance. In some cases, researchers were not been able to identify many effective operational strategies or practices, which may be the result of small sample sizes and the challenges of identify nuanced differences in operations and practices (Tuttle et al., 2013; Zimmer and Buddin, 2007). However, other studies have found positive effects for factors such as teachers' focus on academic achievement (Berends et al., 2010), intensive coaching of teachers (Furgeson et al., 2012a,b), strong behavioral policies (Angrist et al., 2013a,b; Dobbie and Fryer, 2011b; Furgeson et al., 2012a,b; Tuttle et al., 2013), increased instructional time, high dosage tutoring, frequent teacher feedback, using data to guide instruction (Dobbie and Fryer, 2011b), and a general philosophy of "no excuse" policies, which includes strict discipline (Angrist et al., 2013a,b). Given that an original impetus for charter schools was for these schools to be incubators of effective educational operations and practices, more studies need to open the "black box" of these schools to identify key features that other schools could adopt.

---

[39] Perhaps in response to negative findings, Pennsylvania in 2013 rejected all eight applications for new cyber charters (Chute, 2013).

[40] There have also been evaluations of different types of CMOs and of CMOs as a whole. Mathematica evaluated the performance of CMOs using a matching strategy with student-level data and found no statistically significant effect overall for test scores or graduation, but did find a great deal of variation across CMOs (Furgeson et al., 2012a,b). In a second Mathematica study of KIPP schools, which is a well-known CMO operator, Tuttle et al. (2013) used a lottery-based approach in evaluating 13 middle schools and found strong positive effects in math, but no statistically significant effect in reading. The authors then employed observational approaches and found consistent results with these same 13 schools. Bolstered by the consistency of the results across the approaches, the authors then applied the same observational approaches to 41 KIPP schools and found strong positive effects for KIPP schools across multiple subjects. Again, these results suggest that charter schools should not be viewed as monolithic group.

The above discussion highlights the importance of school specialization, which is closely related to questions of validity of research approaches. If a single educational model were the best model for all students, then internal validity would imply external validity. But students differ, and there are likely to be gains from specializing educational models to fit the differing interests and capabilities of students. The greater the extent of such beneficial specialization, the more challenging is the issue of external validity as findings from a given subpopulation would tend to apply more narrowly.[41]

While specialization along some dimensions (eg, curriculum) is likely to be important, the potential for beneficial specialization does not imply that schools should differ on all dimensions. It is quite possible that some "best practices" should be part of all educational models, perhaps some or all of the elements highlighted by Dobbie and Fryer (2011b) and the related no-excuses approach.

It is also possible that educationally beneficial specialization can run counter to other social objectives. Two hypothetical examples illustrate. Suppose that a charter school provider develops an educational approach for minority students that offers superior educational outcomes to those given by the alternative TPSs. This might lead to increased racial or ethnic segregation. Suppose that TPSs provide superior services and opportunities for special needs students. This might give rise to disproportionate attendance of special needs students in TPSs. In these hypothetical scenarios, specialization enhances educational outcomes but increases segregation. In comparison of charters and TPSs, charter entry that increases segregation is often treated as negative evidence, per se, against charters. The extent to which beneficial specialization implies increased segregation has been little explored, but grappling with this difficult issue may well be unavoidable as expansion of the charter school sector continues.

6. COMPETITIVE EFFECTS

While competitive effects of charters on TPSs have received less attention than direct effects of charters on their students, competitive effects may be as important, if not more important. Despite recent growth, the charter school share remains comparatively small, with notable exceptions in some cities (Fig. 4C). Even if the recent pace of growth continues, it will be many years before the charter sector school grows sufficiently to have large widespread direct effects. Meanwhile, there is potential for charter schools to have substantial effects on the broader educational system via innovation and through competitive forces. We have discussed charter school innovations that might prove beneficial

---

[41] Recall that instances in which lottery-based and observational approaches have been applied to the same set of schools, similar impacts have been found. This favors external validity for those studies rather than gains associated with charter school specialization to unobserved characteristics of students in their self-selected applicant pools (Abdulkadiroğlu et al. (2011); Furgeson et al., 2012a,b; Tuttle et al., 2013).

in application in TPSs. We now turn to review of research assessing charter impacts on TPSs via competitive pressures.[42]

6.1 Financial Impacts

Financial impacts are among the most visible impacts of charters on TPSs. Charter schools draw students from TPSs, and, in doing so, they draw resources from TPSs. The channels of these financial impacts on TPSs may include payment from TPSs to charters as well as changes in state and federal funding from programs that link funding to enrollments. There has been relatively limited research providing systematic evidence of how TPSs adapt to the loss of finances associated with charter school growth. There are, however, studies that enumerate impacts and challenges of adjustment. A report of the Institute on Metropolitan Opportunity (2013) summarizes financial impacts on Minneapolis-St. Paul. Schafft et al. (2014) study funding and financial impacts in Pennsylvania. Bifulco and Reback (2014) provide instructive case studies of TPSs' financial adaptation to enrollment declines in Albany and in Buffalo New York.

From this research, the follow issues emerge. First, as charter schools draw enrollments from TPSs, the latter confront the painful task of closing schools to reduce the resulting excess school capacity while also confronting the challenges of attempting to reduce administrative and teaching staff levels. Teacher employment and tenure contracts often specify that any layoffs must be in reverse order of seniority. This and the higher pay received by senior relative to junior teachers imply that reduction in number of teachers is proportionately larger than the reduction in expenditures for teachers. Adjustment problems are often aggravated by the fact that a charter school does not draw students from a single TPS school. Rather, a given charter will draw some students from multiple TPS schools, resulting in declining class sizes in multiple TPS schools. Hence, closing one or more schools to address district excess capacity then entails reassignment of many students. Students forced by school closings to change schools may be more likely to contemplate nondistrict options than they would if they were not required to relocate (Epple et al., 2014). Second, charter schools create uncertainty. For example, if a charter school closes on short notice, the TPS district school must absorb those students.

District administrators find themselves grappling with these financial impacts while, at the same time, attempting to maintain or increase quality so as to avoid loss of more students. If fixed costs imply TPS cost per student rises as students leave for charters, per student payment to charters will rise as well if, as is typically the case, charter funding

---

[42] We should also note that if charter schools do indeed create competitive effects, these indirect effects could be the threat to the estimates of the direct effect we discussed in the previous section. More specifically, if charter schools are creating competitive effects for TPSs, then the TPSs would no longer serve as a good counterfactual. The performance of TPS students would be inflated by the fact that the achievement of students improved as a result of TPS competing with charter schools.

per student is tied to district per student funding. This may stimulate a vicious (from the district perspective) cycle in which rising payments per student induce charter school entry, further district enrollment losses occur, district cost per student and associated charter payment per student rise, and so on. An alternative perspective is that this dynamic increases the urgency with which TPSs reduce costs in response to enrollment losses. Moreover, fixed costs aside, the typical lower per student funding in charter schools (Fig. 1) implies district saving that could be used to increase TPS funding. Another dimension in which a TPSs district may be impacted is in market evaluation of the district's creditworthiness. Moody's (2013) highlighted potential adverse impacts of charters on credit ratings of struggling urban districts. There is no doubt that competitive pressures on TPS finances from charter schools are intense in urban districts experiencing rapid charter growth. These financial impacts and district responses are worthy of more study.

6.2 Challenges in Estimating Competitive Impacts on Effectiveness of TPSs

Estimating the impact of competition from charters on educational effectiveness of TPS is difficult for two reasons, one of which is conceptual and the other methodological. The conceptual challenge has two parts. First, it is difficult to establish good proxies for competitive pressure. The current literature generally assumes we know how a competitive threat is perceived by relevant actors. While the vast majority of research has used proximity to charter schools as proxy for whether a TPS feels competitive pressure, it may be more complicated. Competitive pressure may only occur when charter schools gain a significant portion of the "market share" of students. Or, pressure may only occur if there is a view that charter schools are outperforming a TPS, which hurts the reputation of a TPS. Or, the individual charter school may need to take a significant share of student from an individual TPS. Or, it could be a combination of all of the above.

The second conceptual challenge is associated with the complexity of providing education in general as education is provided through multiple layers, including teachers within classrooms who are managed by principals who are in turn provided resources and instructional and curriculum guidelines by the district. While actors in any single layer may feel competitive pressure, it might not ultimately affect the performance of students if the other layers are not equally motivated to improve. Alternatively, it might only matter that particular layers feel competitive pressures. For instance, a perceived competitive threat by teachers may be the only thing that matters because they are at the front lines of providing education. Or, it could be that the key to improving school-wide performance is to motivate the principal. Or, it might not matter whether principals or teachers feel competitive pressure if many of the curriculum, instructional, and staffing decisions are made at the district level. In addition, each of these actors within these layers may perceive competitive threats differently, and each may have a different ability to react to these threats.

Adding to the complexity of drawing conclusions across studies is the real possibility that charter schools have different competitive effects in different types of environments. For instance, a growing trend among districts nationwide is to offer intradistrict choice through open enrollment, whereby families can choose among all schools within the district, or through magnet schools. Other districts use a more traditional enrollment assignment based on geographic residency. Charter schools may have very different competitive effects in these environments. For districts with preexisting school choice, an already competitive market may diminish the competitive pressure created by charter schools. In contrast, the introduction of charter schools in a noncompetitive market with no choice program could have a much more dramatic effect. In addition, some districts may have growing enrollments and existing schools may be overcrowded. Here, charter schools could serve as a "release valve" for these districts. Other districts may have declining enrollments and the loss of additional students to charter schools could exert real fiscal pressure on existing schools. These observations suggest that developing theoretical models could help to guide empirical research on competitive effects.

The challenges we described so far do not include the methodological challenges, which are significant. If a researcher examines whether the performance of TPSs changes when charter schools are introduced nearby, they may not know whether any change in performance is a result of changing student population or changing performance. For instance, a charter school could be introduced into a neighborhood and begin attracting students away from a nearby TPS. If the students choosing a charter school are disproportionally low performing, than the average test scores for students within TPS may improve, not because the quality of education of the TPS is improving, but because the school has less low-performing students. In addition, there may be observable and unobservable characteristics of students and individual TPSs that should be accounted for when examining competitive effects. Furthermore, charter schools do not locate at random. Instead, they may locate in neighborhoods for a variety of reasons, including operators' perception of how well they can compete with TPSs based on both observable and unobservable characteristics of TPSs.

Researcher can address some of these methodological challenges by using student-level longitudinal data. Longitudinal data can help control for changing population of students within a TPS by actually tracking the students moving in and out of a TPS. Furthermore, longitudinal data can help control for both observable and unobservable differences of students and schools by using a combination of student- and school-fixed effects known as spell effects, which compares the performance of the same students in the same school over time. However, many researchers have not had access to these types of data and have used school-level data instead. In our review, we shall focus primarily on studies that have used longitudinal data. Nevertheless, there is some question of whether longitudinal data fully addresses all of the methodological challenges, especially the nonrandom location of charter schools. Therefore, it is our view that the analysis on the question of competitive effects is not as strong as research on some of the other questions.

6.3 Competitive Impacts of Charters on TPS Effectiveness

The earliest (and some of the most cited) works on competitive effects actually used school-level data. The first was a study by Hoxby (2003) in which she examined whether the share of charter students in a district affects tests scores in Michigan TPSs. She found positive effects. In a second study, also using Michigan data, but using distance to authorizers as instrument for charter location, Bettinger (2005) found no evidence that competition from a nearby charter improved test scores in TPSs. Several more recent studies have used longitudinal student-level data generally employing a combination of student- and school-fixed effects for the identification strategy. We summarize these studies, including their research design in Table 9.[43]

Among the studies listed in Table 9, Imberman's (2007) made the strongest attempt to address the nonrandom location of charter schools by his use of longitudinal student-level data and his analysis of a variety of outcomes (ie, behavior, attendance, test scores). He also used a variety of approaches including school-fixed effects, school-fixed-effects combined with school-specific time-trends, and instrumental variables. The results varied based on the approach, with the fixed-effect showing positive effects in some cases (depending on the measure of the outcome), while the IV approach showed negative effects. As part of his analysis, Imberman makes the case that the IV approach is the most trusted approach and suggests that charter schools could actually have a negative impact on TPSs because they change the peer environments within schools and reduce the resources within schools. At the very least, his analysis underscores the importance of the identification strategy for estimating competitive effects.

In a unique study, Cremata and Raymond (2014) examine competitive effects in Washington, D.C. However, they approach the question with a different conceptual framework. Much like some of the previous research, they include measures such as market share and attrition from TPS to charter schools as a proxy for competitive pressure, but they also factor in the quality of the charter school in their analysis. They argue that a

---

[43] Among these studies, Zimmer and Buddin (2009) is a bit more nuanced in approach as they examined competitive effects using both principal surveys and student-level test score data in California. The survey results showed that TPS principals felt little pressure from charters to improve performance or modify practices. The student achievement analysis employed both student and school fixed effects and used an array of alternative measures for school competition including distance to nearest charter school, a charter school within 2.5 miles, number of charter schools within 2.5 miles, and percentage of students lost to charter schools. No evidence that charter competition was improving the test score performance of students in nearby TPSs was found.

Table 9 Summary of competitive effects

Study	Location	Research design	Average impact
Hoxby (2003)	Michigan	Use a competition proxy of the share of charter students in a district affects tests scores. For the analysis, uses a difference-in-differences approach	Mostly positive effects across subjects and grades
Bettinger (2005)	Michigan	Use a competition proxy of number of charter schools within 5 miles and uses difference-in-differences approach as well an instrumental variable approach	No effects
Bifulco and Ladd (2006)	North Carolina	Use a competition proxy of charter schools within 2.5 miles radius using a student fixed-effect model	No effect in math or reading
Sass (2006)	Florida	Use a competition proxy of charter schools within 2.5 miles radius. The author uses a combination school and student fixed-effect model	Positive effect on math, no effect on reading
Booker et al. (2008)	Texas	Use a competition proxy of charter schools within 5 miles radius. The authors use a combination school and student fixed-effect model	Positive math and reading effect
Zimmer and Buddin (2009)	California	Use various competition proxies including number of charter schools within 2.5 miles as well as the number of students lost to charter schools. The authors use a combination school and student fixed-effect model. The authors also surveyed TPS to examine changes in practices as a response to charter schools	No effect on student achievement and very little changes in operation and practice of TPSs in reaction to charter schools
Zimmer et al. (2009)	Chicago Denver Milwaukee Philadelphia Ohio San Diego Texas	Use a competition proxy of charter schools within 5 miles radius. The authors use a combination school and student fixed-effect model	No effect except a small positive effect in both math and reading in Texas
Imberman (2011)	Large urban anonymous district	Used a variety of approaches including school-fixed effects, school-fixed-effects combined with school-specific time-trends, and instrumental variables	The results varied based on the approach, with the fixed-effect showing positive effects in some cases, while the IV approach showed negative effects
Winters (2012)	New York City	Use a competition proxy of percentage of students who left TPS for a charter school. The author uses a student fixed-effect approach	Mostly positive math and reading effects

Table 9 Summary of competitive effects—cont'd

Study	Location	Research design	Average impact
Nissar (2012)	Milwaukee	Use a competition proxy of charter schools within 2.5 miles radius using a student fixed-effect model	Positive math and reading effects
Cremata and Raymond (2014)	Washington, D.C.	As a proxy for competition, include measures such as market share and attrition from TPS to charter schools as a proxy for competitive pressure, but they also factor in the quality of the charter school in their analysis	Positive math and reading competitive effects when TPSs face competitive pressure from higher quality charter schools

TPS may be much more responsive if they are experiencing competition from a high quality charter school versus a low quality charter school. They find that charter school quality is important as TPSs improve (as measured by reading and math test scores) when they face competitive pressure from higher quality charter schools. Therefore, competitive pressure may not be entirely a function of losing students or market share to a charter school, but losing students and market share to high quality charter schools. The Washington D.C. setting is noteworthy in that DC is second only to New Orleans among central city districts in market penetration of charters (Fig. 3C). During the 4-year period of the Cremata and Raymond study, 2005/06 to 2008/09, the charter share in DC grew from 27% to 41%. This large and growing presence of charters is arguably the kind of setting in which charter competitive effects are likely to be manifest.

Finally, in a different twist on the debate surround competitive effects, three papers have recently emerged that not only look at the impact of charter schools on enrollment patterns in TPSs, but also in private schools. Toma et al. (2006) and Chakrabarti and Roy (2010) exclusively focused on Michigan, while Buddin (2012) conducted a national evaluation. In each case, the researchers examined how enrollment patterns of TPSs and private schools are affected as charter school enrollment changes either within the same district or same county. Across all studies (although to different degrees) the researchers found that private schools disproportionally lose students to charter schools relative to TPSs. This may imply that charter schools actually exert stronger competitive effects on private schools than TPSs as private schools are so financially sensitive to losing students and their tuition dollars.

In aggregate, the current body of evidence on the competitive effects of charter schools is mixed, which may be disappointing to the advocates of charter schools. However, while charter schools have large shares in some districts as seen in Fig. 4C, charters do not represent a large share of enrollment in most districts. Where charters have small shares, it may be unrealistic to expect charter schools to exert much of a competitive effect. In addition, many of these studies examine the effects of charter schools from nearly a decade ago. Much has changed since then, especially in some urban areas, and it could be charter schools are now exerting more pressure on TPSs. From this perspective, the Cremata and Raymond (2014) discussed above may be indicative of the kind of competitive effects charters have when charter presence is large and growing.

7. SUMMARY AND CONCLUSIONS

Since their inception in the early 1990s, charter schools have grown to serve roughly 5% of US public school students. Charters are located disproportionately in urban areas. Charter school penetration varies greatly across states and localities. Seven states account for 61% of total charter enrollments; 30 metropolitan areas account for 63% of total charter enrollments. The concern that charter schools would induce white flight from public schools has proven to be largely unfounded; the charter sector enrolls higher proportions of African-American and Hispanic students than TPSs. Charters enroll proportionately fewer special needs students than TPSs, which raises some concerns about the accessibility of these schools to all students. Class sizes in charter schools are comparable to those in TPSs. On the whole, teachers in charter schools are less experienced, are less credentialed, are less white, and have fewer advanced degrees. They are paid less, their jobs are less secure, and they turnover with higher frequency. Value added estimation of teacher effectiveness in Florida and North Carolina shows charter school teachers to be weaker in increasing test scores. Research explaining differences in teachers is in an early stage, and the relevance of differences in teachers to educational outcomes in charter schools is an open question.

The effectiveness of charter schools is far from uniform. Lottery studies of oversubscribed charter schools generally find favorable effects on achievement, often very large effects. The "No Excuses" model, in particular, has been found to deliver large gains. The invention of this educational model is arguably the most important innovation that can be credited to the charter movement. Whether this model can be implemented and can yield comparable gains in nonselective TPSs remains very much an open issue. A recent experiment in the Houston school district suggests that this may be possible, while also illustrating the tremendous challenges facing such implementation. At the opposite end of the quality spectrum, online "cyber" schools appear to be a failed innovation, delivering markedly poorer achievement outcomes than TPSs.

Taken as a whole, the evidence suggests that, accounting for differences in population served, charter schools are not, on average, producing student achievement gains any better than TPSs. However, policy prescriptions to withdraw support for charter schools, rationalized by this mediocre average performance, fail to recognize that a substantial number of charters significantly outperform the average TPS. The evidence also suggests that individual charter schools seem to improve as they mature and the charter school sector as a whole is improving over time, largely from closure of underperforming schools. This research points to the important role that charter authorizers can play in weeding out ineffective charter schools, a role that many charter authorizers have yet to embrace. Recent findings also suggest that charter school performance on behavioral and attainment (years of schooling) outcomes may be stronger than achievement outcomes. Finally, research on the impacts of charter schools on the academic performance of TPS through competitive pressures has generally found modest effects, though one recent study provides evidence that TPSs produce larger achievement gains when confronted with competition from high quality charter schools.

It is common to end a review such as this with the admonition that more research is needed, and this is surely true. As this review indicates, however, research has already contributed a great deal to our knowledge about charter schools. Given the variation in charter schools, research that focuses on specific educational practices and their environments may have the most potential to be informative. While the charter movement is now nearing its 25th year, roughly half of the current charter share of public school enrollments has been garnered in the past 7 years. In this respect, it is still far from mature. Polls indicate that the charter movement has gained widespread support among the public. If charter schools continue to grow, their direct and indirect effects may become more important. Increased stability of the charter sector itself may have significant impacts, eg, by providing more stable employment opportunities for principals and teachers. Continuing to collect and analyze data on charter schools is crucial. It remains to be seen whether, as it continues to mature, the charter movement will fulfill fully the as yet unrealized aspirations of its founders.

ACKNOWLEDGMENTS

We thank Melanie Zaber for outstanding research assistance.

REFERENCES

Abdulkadiroğlu, A., Angrist, J.D., Dynarski, S.M., Kane, T.J., Pathak, P.A., 2011. Accountability and flexibility in public schools: evidence from Boston's charters and pilots. Q. J. Econ. 126 (2), 699–748

AFT (American Federation of Teachers), 2004. Charter Schools Achievement on the 2003 National Assessment of Educational Progress. American Federation of Teachers, Washington, DC.

Angrist, J., Imbens, G., Rubin, D., 1996. Identification of causal effects using instrumental variables. J. Am. Stat. Assoc. 91 (23), 222–455.

Angrist, J.D., Cohodes, S.R., Dynarski, S.M., Pathak, P.A., Walters, C.D., 2013a. Charter Schools and the Road to College Readiness: The Effects on College Preparation, Attendance and Choice. Boston Foundation and New Schools Venture Fund, Boston.

Angrist, J.D., Pathak, P.A., Walters, C.R., 2013b. Explaining charter school effectiveness. Am. Econ. J. Appl. Econ. 5 (4), 1–27.

Baker, B., Dickerson, J., 2006. Charter schools, teacher labor market deregulation, and teacher quality: evidence from the schools and staffing survey. Educ. Policy 20 (5), 752–778.

Ballou, D., Teasley, B., Zeidner, T., 2007. Charter schools in Idaho. In: Berends, M., Springer, M.G., Walberg, H.J. (Eds.), Charter School Outcomes. L. Erlbaum Associates, New York, pp. 221–241.

Batdorff, M., Maloney, L., May, J., Speakman, S., Wolf, P., Cheng, A., 2014. Charter School Funding: Inequity Expands. University of Arkansas, Fayetteville, AR.

Baude, P.L., Casey, M., Hanushek, E.A., Rivkin, S.G., 2014. The Evolution of Charter School Quality. NBER Working Paper: 20645.

Berends, M., Goldring, E., Stien, M., Cravens, X., 2010. Instructional conditions in charter schools and students' mathematics achievement gains. Am. J. Educ. 116, 303–335.

Bettinger, E.P., 2005. The effect of charter schools on charter students and public schools. Econ. Educ. Rev. 24 (2), 133–147.

Bifulco, R., Buerger, C., 2012. The Influence of Finance and Accountability Policies on Charter School Locations. Working Paper, Syracuse University.

Bifulco, R., Ladd, H.F., 2006. The impact of charter schools on student achievement: evidence from North Carolina. J. Educ. Finance Policy 1 (1), 50–90.

Bifulco, R., Ladd, H.F., 2007. School choice, racial segregation, and test-score gaps: evidence from North Carolina's charter school program. J. Policy Anal. Manage. 26 (1), 31–56.

Bifulco, R., Reback, R., 2014. Fiscal impacts of charter schools: lessons for New York. Educ. Finance Policy 9 (1), 86–107. Winter.

Booker, K., Zimmer, R., Buddin, R., 2005. The Effect of Charter Schools on School Peer Composition. RAND Working Paper: WR-306-EDU. Retrieved January 3, 2013, from, http://www.ncspe.org/publications_files/RAND_WR306.pdf.

Booker, T.K., Gilpatric, S.M., Gronberg, T.J., Jansen, D.W., 2007. The impact of charter school student attendance on student performance. J. Public Econ. 91 (5–6), 849–876.

Booker, T.K., Gilpatric, S.M., Gronberg, T.J., Jansen, D.W., 2008. The effect of charter schools on traditional public school students in Texas: are children who stay behind left behind? J. Urban Econ. 64 (1), 123–145.

Booker, K., Sass, T., Gill, B., Zimmer, R., 2009. Achievement and Attainment in Chicago Charter Schools: RAND Technical Report. Retrieved July 16, 2014 from: http://lbr.rand.org/content/dam/rand/pubs/technical_reports/2009/RAND_TR585-1.pdf.

Booker, K., Sass, T., Gill, B., Zimmer, R., 2011. The effects of charter high schools on educational attainment. J. Labor Econ. 29 (2), 377–415.

Booker, K., Gill, B., Sass, T., Zimmer, R., 2014. Charter High School's Effect on Educational Attainment and Earnings. Available at: http://www.mathematica-mpr.com/~/media/publications/PDFs/education/charter_long-term_wp.pdf.

Buddin, R., 2012. The Impact of Charter Schools on Public and Private School Enrollments Cato Institute Policy Analysis No. 707. Available at SSRN: http://ssrn.com/abstract=2226597.

Buddin, R., Zimmer, R., 2005. Student achievement in charter schools: a complex picture. J. Policy Anal. Manage. 24 (2), 351–371.

Butler, J.S., Carr, D., Toma, E.F., Zimmer, R., 2013. School attributes and distance: tradeoffs in the school choice decision. J. Policy Anal. Manage. 32 (4), 785–806.

Cannata, M., Penaloza, R., 2012. Who are charter school teachers? Comparing teacher characteristics, job choices, and job preferences. Educ. Policy Anal. Arch. 20 (29), 1–25.

Carlson, D., Lavery, L., Witte, J.F., 2012. Charter school authorizers and student achievement. Econ. Educ. Rev. 31 (2), 254–267.

Carnoy, M., Jacobsen, R., Mishel, L., Rothstein, R., 2006. Worth the price? Weighing the evidence on charter schools? Educ. Finance Policy 1 (1), 151–161.

Carrell, S.E., Hoekstra, M.L., 2010. Externalities in the classroom: how children exposed to domestic violence affect everyone's kids. Am. Econ. J. Appl. Econ. 2 (1), 211–228.

Carruthers, C., 2012. The qualifications and classroom performance of teachers moving to charter schools. Educ. Finance Policy 7 (3), 233–268.

Chakrabarti, R., Roy, J., 2010. Do Charter Schools Crowd Out Private School Enrollment? Evidence from Michigan: Federal Reserve Bank of New York, Staff Report No. 472.

Chute, E., 2013. Pennsylvania withholds OK for 8 cyber charter schools. Pittsburgh Post-Gazette. (January 29).

Cobb, C.D., Glass, G.V., 1999. Ethnic segregation in Arizona charter schools. Educ. Policy Anal. Arch. 7(1).

Cowen, J., Winters, M., 2013. Do charters retain teachers differently? Evidence from elementary schools in Florida. Educ. Finance Policy 8 (1), 14–42.

CREDO, 2009. National Charter School Study. http://credo.stanford.edu/documents/NCSS%202013%20Final%20Draft.pdf.

CREDO, 2011. Charter School Performance Pennsylvania. http://credo.stanford.edu/reports/PA%20State%20Report_20110404_FINAL.pdf.

CREDO, 2013a. National Charter School Study. http://credo.stanford.edu/documents/NCSS%202013%20Final%20Draft.pdf.

CREDO, 2013b. Charter School Performance in New York City. http://www.nyccharterschools.org/sites/default/files/resources/CredoReport2013.pdf.

Cremata, E.J., Raymond, M., 2014. The competitive effects of charter schools: evidence from the district of Columbia. In: Paper Presented at Association of Education, Finance, and Policy Conference. Available at:http://www.aefpweb.org/annualconference/download-39th.

Curto, V.E., Fryer, R.G. Jr., 2011. Estimating the Returns to Urban Boarding Schools: Evidence from SEED. National Bureau of Economic Research (NBER) Working Paper 16746.

Deming, D., 2014. Using school choice lotteries to test measures of school effectiveness. Am. Econ. Rev. Pap. Proc. 104 (5), 406–411.

Epple, D., Jha, A., Sieg, H., 2014. The Superintendent's Dilemma: Managing School District Capacity as Parents Vote with Their Feet. Working Paper.

Dobbie, W., Fryer Jr., R.G., 2011a. Are high-quality schools enough to increase achievement among the poor? Evidence from the Harlem children's zone. Am. Econ. J. Appl. Econ. 3, 158–187.

Dobbie, W., Fryer Jr., R.G., 2013. The Medium-Term Impacts of High-Achieving Charter Schools on Non-Test Score Outcomes. Working Paper, Princeton University, Princeton, NJ.

Dobbie, W., Fryer Jr., R.G., 2011b. Getting beneath the veil of effective schools: evidence from New York City. Am. Econ. J. Appl. Econ. 5 (4), 28–60.

Engberg, J., Epple, D., Sieg, H., Zimmer, R., 2014. Evaluating education programs that have lotteried admission and selective attrition. J. Labor Econ. 32 (1), 27–63.

Exstrom, M., 2012. Teaching in charter schools. In. National Conference of State Legislatures, July.

Farrell, P., Wohlstetter, W., Smith, J., 2012. Charter management organizations: an emerging approach to scaling up what works. Educ. Policy 26 (4), 499–532.

Ferreyra, M.M., Kosenok, G., 2015. Charter School Entry and School Choice: The Case of Washington, D.C. Policy Research working paper; no. WPS 7383. World Bank Group, Washington, DC.

Finn, C.E., Manno, B.V., Vanourek, G., 2000. Charter Schools in Action: Renewing Public Education. Princeton University Press, Princeton, NJ.

Fiske, E., Ladd, H., 2000. When Schools Compete: A Cautionary Tale. Brookings Institution, Washington, D.C.

Fitzgerald, J., Harris, P., Huidekiper, P., Mani, M., 1998. 1997 Colorado Charter Schools Evaluation Study: The Characteristics, Status, and Student Achievement Data of Colorado Charter Schools. The Clayton Foundation, Denver, CO.

Frankenberg, E., Lee, C., 2003. Charter schools and race: a lost opportunity for integrated education. Educ. Policy Anal. Arch.. 11 (32). Retrieved from, http://epaa.asu.edu/epaa/v11n32/.

Frankenberg, E., Siegel-Hawley, G., Wang, J., 2010. Choice Without Equity: Charter School Segregation and the Need for Civil Rights Standards. Civil Rights Project, UCLA. Retrieved January 3, 2013, from, http://civilrightsproject.ucla.edu/research/k-12-education/integration-and-diversity/choice-without-equity-2009-report/frankenberg-choices-without-equity-2010.pdf.

Fryer, R.G., 2014. Injecting Charter School Best Practices into Traditional Public Schools: Evidence from Field Experiments. Harvard University, Boston. Retrieved January 25, 2016 at: http://scholar.harvard.edu/files/fryer/files/2014_injecting_charter_school_best_practices_into_traditional_public_schools.pdf.

Furgeson, J., Gill, B., Haimson, J., Killewald, A., McCullough, M., Nichols-Barrer, I., et al., 2012a. Charter-School Management Organizations: Diverse Strategies and Diverse Student Impacts. Mathematica Policy Research, Inc., Princeton, NJ. Updated Edition.

Furgeson, J., Brian, G., Haimson, J., Killewald, A., McCullough, M., Nichols-Barrer, I., Teh, B.-R., Verbitsky-Savitz, N., 2012b. The National Study of Charter Management: Organization (CMO)

Effectiveness Charter-School Management Organizations: Diverse Strategies and Diverse Student Impacts. Mathematical Policy Research, Princeton, NJ.

Garcia, D.R., McIlroy, L., Barber, R.T., 2008. Starting behind: a comparative analysis of the academic standing of students entering charter schools. Soc. Sci. Q. 89 (1), 199–216.

Gill, B.P., Hamilton, L., Lockwood, J.R., Marsh, J., Zimmer, R., Hill, D., Pribesh, S., 2005. Inspiration, Perspiration, and Time: Operations and Achievement in Edison Schools, Santa Monica, Calif.: RAND Corporation. MG-351-EDU. As of November 5, 2008: http://www.rand.org/pubs/monographs/MG351/.

Gleason, P., Clark, M., Tuttle, C.C., Dwoyer, E., 2010. The Evaluation of Charter School Impacts: Final Report (NCEE 2010-4029). U.S. Department of Education, Institute of Education Sciences, National Center for Education Evaluation and Regional Assistance, Washington, DC.

Glomm, G., Douglas, H., Te-Fen, L., 2005. Charter school location. Econ. Educ. Rev. 24, 451–457.

Hanushek, E., 1992. The trade-off between child quantity and quality. J. Political Econ. 100 (1), 84–117.

Hanushek, E., Rivkin, S., 2006. Teacher quality. In: Hanushek, E., Welch, F. (Eds.), In: Handbook of the Economics of Education, vol. 2. Elsevier B.V, North-Holland, Amsterdam, The Netherlands, pp. 1051–1078 (Chapter 18).

Hanushek, E.A., Kain, J.F., Rivkin, S.G., Branch, G.F., 2007. Charter school quality and parental decision making with school choice. J. Public Econ. 91 (5), 823–848.

Hoxby, C.M., 2003. School choice and school productivity: could school choice be a tide that lifts all boats? In: Hoxby, C.M. (Ed.), The Economics of School Choice. University of Chicago Press, Chicago, pp. 287–342.

Hoxby, C.M., 2004. A Straightforward Comparison of Charter Schools and Regular Public Schools in the United States. Retrieved January 25, 2016 at: http://www.wacharterschools.org/learn/studies/hoxbyallcharters.pdf.

Hoxby, C.M., Murarka, S., 2007. Charter Schools in New York City: Who Enrolls and How They Affect their Students' Achievement. National Bureau of Economic Research, Cambridge, MA. Retrieved November 5, 2008, from, http://www.nber.org/~schools/charterschooleval/nyc_charter_schools_technical_report_july2007.pdf.

Hoxby, C.M., Rockoff, J.E., 2004. The Impact of Charter Schools on Student Achievement. Unpublished Paper, Department of Economics, Harvard University.

Hoxby, C., Kang, J., Murarka, S., 2009. Technical Report: How New York City's Charter Schools Affect Achievement, New York City Charter Schools Evaluation Project. Retrieved July 5, 2013 at: http://users.nber.org/~schools/charterschooleval/how_nyc_charter_schools_affect_achievement_technical_report_2009.pdf.

Imberman, S.A., 2007. The Effect of Charter Schools on Non Charter Students: An Instrumental Variable Approach. NSCPE Working Paper. Accessed on August 1, 2014 from: http://www.ncspe.org/publications_files/OP149.pdf.

Imberman, S.A., 2011. Achievement and behavior in charter schools: drawing a more complete picture. Rev. Econ. Stat. 93 (2), 416–435.

Institute on Metropolitan Opportunity, 2013. Charter Schools in the Twin Cities: 2013 Update. University of Minnesota Law School, Minneapolis, MN.

Institute on Race and Poverty, 2008. Failed Promises: Assessing Charter Schools in the Twin Cities. University of Minnesota Law School, Minneapolis.

Institute on Race and Poverty, 2012. Update of 'Failed Promises: Assessing Charter Schools in the Twin Cities'. University of Minnesota Law School, Minneapolis, MN.

Jackson, C.K., 2012. School competition and teacher labor markets: evidence from charter school entry in North Carolina. J. Public Econ. 96, 431–448.

Kane, T., Staiger, D., 2008. Estimating Teacher Impacts on Student Achievement: An Experimental Evaluation. National Bureau of Economic Research Working Paper #14607.

Kolderie, T., 2004. Creating the Capacity for Change: How and Why Governors and Legislatures Are Opening a New-Schools Sector in Public Education. Education Week Press, Bethesda, MD.

Ladd, S., Clotfelter, C., Holbein, J.B., 2014. The Evolution of the Charter School Sector in North Carolina. In: Paper to be Presented at the Annual Meeting of the Association for Public Policy Analysis and Management, Albuquerque, New Mexico.

Lee, D.S., 2009. Training, wages, and sample selection: estimating sharp bounds on treatment effects. Rev. Econ. Stud. 76, 1071–1102.

Mehta, N., 2012. Competition in Public School Districts: Charter School Entry, Student Sorting, and School Input Determination. Working paper, University of Western Ontario, June 14, 2012.

Miron, G.N., Nelson, C., 2002. What's Public About Charter Schools? Corwin Press, Inc., Thousand Oaks, CA.

Moody's, 2013. Charter Schools Pose Greatest Credit Challenge to School Districts in Economically Weak Urban Areas. October 15.

Nathan, J., 1998. Controversy: charters and choice. In: The American Prospect. vol. 9. November–December, available at www.prospect.org.

National Center on Education Statistics, 2011. Digest of Education Statistics.

Nelson, F.H., Muir, E., Drown, R., 2000. Venturesome Capital: State Charter School Finance Systems. U.S. Department of Education, Washington, DC.

Ni, Y., Rorrer, A.K., 2012. Twice considered: charter schools and student achievement in Utah. Econ. Educ. Rev. 31 (5), 835–849.

Nichols-Barrer, I., Gill, B.P., Gleason, P., Tuttle, C.C., 2014. Does student attrition explain KIPP's success? Educ. Next. 14(4).

Nicotera, A., Mendiburo, M., Berends, M., 2011. Charter school effects in Indianapolis. In: Berends, M., Cannata, M., Goldring, E. (Eds.), School Choice and School Improvement: Research in State, District and Community Contexts. Harvard Education Press, Cambridge, MA.

Nissar, H., 2012. Heterogeneous Competitive Effects of Charter Schools in Milwaukee. NCSPE Working Paper.

PDK/Gallup Poll, 2014. The 46th Annual PDK/Gallup Poll of the Public's Attitudes Toward the Public Schools. http://pdkintl.org/programs-resources/poll/.

Podursky, M., Ballou, D., 2001. Personnel Policy in Charter Schools. Thomas B. Fordham Foundation, Washington, DC.

Powell, J., Blackorby, J., Marsh, J., Finnegan, K., Anderson, L., 1997. Evaluation of Charter School Effectiveness. SRI International, Menlo Park, CA.

Ravitch, D., undated. Florida Model Does Not Work, Letter to New Mexico State Legislators. Reprint Retrieved July 30, 2013, from, http://www.independentsourcepac.com/diane-ravitch-letter-to-new-mexico-legislature.html.

Reardon, S.F., 2009. Review of "How New York City's Charter Schools Affect Achievement" Boulder and Tempe: Education and the Public Interest Center & Education Policy Research Unit. Retrieved August 25, 2014 from, http://epicpolicy.org/thinktank/review-How-New-York-City-Charter.

Reckhow, S., 2013. Follow the Money: How Foundation Dollars Change Public School Politics. Oxford University Press, New York, NY.

RPP International, 2000. The state of charter schools: 2000. U.S. Department of Education, Office of Educational Research and Improvement, Washington, DC.

Sass, T.R., 2006. Charter schools and student achievement in Florida. Educ. Finance Policy 1 (1), 91–122.

Schafft, K.A., Erica, F., Ed, F., William, H., Stephen, K., Bryan, M., 2014. Assessing the Enrollment Trends and Financial Impacts of Charter Schools on Rural and Non-Rural School Districts in Pennsylvania. Department of Education Policy Studies, Penn State University, State College, PA. Retrieved January 25, 2016 at: http://www.rural.palegislature.us/documents/reports/Charter_School_2014.pdf.

Sherry, A., 2007. New start at Cole ends this spring: charter KIPP pulls plans to revamp all grades at middle school. Denver Post. 03/13/2007 http://www.denverpost.com/specialreports/ci_5421560.

Solomon, L., Goldschmidt, P., 2004. Comparison of traditional public schools and charter schools on retention, school switching, and achievement growth. The Goldwater Institute, Phoenix, AZ.

Stuit, D., Smith, T., 2009. Teacher Turnover in Charter Schools. www.vanderbilt.edu/schoolchoice/documents/stuit smith ncspe.pdf.

Toma, E., Zimmer, R., Jones, J., 2006. Beyond achievement: enrollment consequences of charter schools in Michigan. Adv. Appl. Microecon. 14, 241–255.

Tuttle, C.C., Gleason, P., Clark, M., 2012. Using lotteries to evaluate schools of choice: evidence from a national study of charter schools. Econ. Educ. Rev. 31, 237–253.

Tuttle, C.C., Gill, B., Gleason, P., Knechtel, V., Nichols-Barrer, I., Resch, A., 2013. KIPP Middle Schools: Impacts on Achievement and Other Outcomes. Mathematica Policy Research, Washington, DC.

Weiher, G.R., Tedin, K.L., 2002. Does choice lead to racially distinctive schools? Charter schools and household preferences. J. Policy Anal. Manage. 21 (1), 79–92.

Winters, M., 2012. Measuring the effect of charter schools on public school student achievement in an urban environment: evidence from New York City. Econ. Educ. Rev. 31 (2), 293–301.

Winters, M., 2013. Why the Gap? Special Education and New York City Charter Schools. Center for Reinventing Public Education, Seattle, WA.

Winters, M., 2014. Understanding the Charter School Special Education Gap: Evidence from Denver, Colorado. Center for Reinventing Public Education, Seattle, WA.

Wolf, P., Gutmann, B., Puma, M., Kisida, B., Rizzo, L., Eissa, N., Carr, M., 2010. Evaluation of the DC Opportunity Scholarship Program: Final Report, NCEE 2010-4018. U.S. Government Printing Office, Washington, DC. http://ies.ed.gov/ncee/pubs/20104018/pdf/20104018.pdf.

Wong, M.D., Coller, K.M., Dudovitz, R., Kennedy, D.P., Buddin, R., Chung, P.J., Shapiro, M.F., Kataoka, S.H., Brown, A.F., Tseng, C.H., Bergman, P., 2014. Successful schools and risky behaviors among low-income adolescents. J. Pediatr. Available at: http://pediatrics.aappublications.org/content/early/2014/07/16/peds.2013-3573.abstract.

Zimmer, R., Buddin, R., 2007. Getting inside the black box: examining how the operation of charter schools effects performance. Peabody J. Educ. 82 (2–3), 231–273.

Zimmer, R., Buddin, R., 2009. Is charter school competition in California improving the performance of traditional public schools? Public Adm. Rev. 69 (5), 831–845.

Zimmer, R., Engberg, J., 2013. Can Broad Inferences be Drawn from Lottery Analyses of School Choice Programs? An Exploration of Appropriate Sensitivity Analyses. NCSE Working Paper #220. Accessed July 16, 2014 at: http://www.ncspe.org/publications_files/OP220.pdf.

Zimmer, R., Engberg, J., forthcoming. Can broad inferences be drawn from lottery analyses of school choice programs? An exploration of appropriate sensitivity analyses. School Choice J.

Zimmer, R., Guarino, C.M., 2013. Is there empirical evidence that charter schools "push out" low-performing students? Educ. Eval. Pol. Anal. 35, 461–480.

Zimmer, R., Buddin, R., Chau, D., Gill, B., Guarino, C., Hamilton, L., et al., 2003. Charter School Operation and Performance: Evidence from California. MR-1700. RAND, Santa Monica, CA.

Zimmer, R., Gill, B., Booker, K., Lavertu, S., Sass, T., Witte, J., 2009. Charter Schools in Eight States: Effects on Achievement, Attainment, Integration, and Competition. MG-869. RAND, Pittsburgh.

Zimmer, R., Gill, B., Booker, K., Lavertu, S., Witte, J., 2012. Examining charter school achievement in seven states. Econ. Educ. Rev. 31 (2), 213–224.

Zimmer, R., Gill, B., Attridge, J., Obenauf, K., 2014. Charter school authorizers and student achievement. Educ. Finance Policy 9 (1), 59–85.

Zimmer, R.W., Buddin, R., 2006. Charter school performance in two large urban districts. J. Urban Econ. 60 (2), 307–326.

CHAPTER 4

Competition Among Schools: Traditional Public and Private Schools

M. Urquiola
Columbia University and NBER, New York, NY, United States

Contents

Abstract

This chapter considers research on the effects of competition between private and public schools. It focuses on three questions: (1) Do children experience higher achievement gains in private school? (2) If so, is this because private schools are more productive? (3) Does competition from private schools raise public school productivity and/or otherwise affect those "left behind"? The chapter shows that unless each of these questions is answered, one cannot form a full assessment on the desirability of private school entry. Voucher experiments suggest that question 1 can be answered in the affirmative for some subgroups and in some contexts. Such work cannot typically isolate channels, however, and hence does not address question 2. Question 3 has been primarily studied by papers on large-scale voucher programs. These suggest that private school entry results in nonrandom sorting of students, but are less clear on the effects. The bottom line is that despite demand for clear, simple conclusions on the effects of competition from private schools, research does not yet provide these.

Handbook of the Economics of Education, Volume 5
ISSN 1574-0692, http://dx.doi.org/10.1016/B978-0-444-63459-7.00004-X

Keywords

Competition, Private schools, Sorting, School productivity

1. INTRODUCTION

There is a long-standing perception among economists (eg, Smith, 1776; Friedman, 1955) that competition can improve school markets' performance. Traditionally, competition has been envisioned to take the form of entry by private schools into markets previously dominated by public schools. The conjecture is that such entry can enhance the accumulation of skill, or at least reduce the cost of its production.

It is not surprising that this seems plausible to many observers. After all, in some settings the counterfactual to a larger private sector is a public sector in which it at least casually appears difficult to terminate transparently underperforming teachers, reduce rampant absenteeism, or introduce meaningful curricular experimentation.

This chapter provides an overview of what economic research has revealed — and what knowledge gaps remain — on the effects of competition between "traditional" public and private schools. The exact meaning of this label will depend on the setting, but it leaves aside, for example, somewhat more recent institutional forms, such as charter schools in the USA.[1]

The chapter organizes the issues by focusing on three sets of questions:

1. Do children experience higher achievement gains in private than in public schools?
2. If private schools raise achievement more, is this because these schools are more productive? (We shall understand a given school to be more productive than another if it produces more skill given the same resources.)[2]
3. Does competition from private schools raise public school productivity? Does the existence of private schools otherwise affect those "left behind" in public schools?

The chapter first sets out a simple framework to show that unless *each* of these questions can be answered, one cannot form a full assessment on the desirability of greater competition from private schools. The discussion emphasizes three further points. First, economic theory suggests that none of these questions has an answer that is clear a priori; the effect of competition on school market performance is therefore an empirical question. Second, question 1 can be credibly answered if one has exogenous variation in private school attendance as provided, for example, by many voucher experiments. Third, such experiments do not typically provide answers to questions 2 and 3; analyses of large-scale voucher reforms are better suited to tackling these, but face significant methodological challenges related to identification and nonrandom sorting of students.

---

[1] The evidence on charter schools is covered elsewhere in this volume.

[2] Hoxby (2002b) provides a useful introduction to the importance of school productivity in the analysis of competition between schools. Our definition is different than the one she uses, but in the same spirit.

The chapter then considers the existing evidence. Rather than attempt to provide an exhaustive survey, it focuses on the research and settings that potentially provide the most credible answer to these questions, but which also help frame future avenues for research.[3] Specifically, on question 1 the discussion centers mainly on evidence from the USA, Colombia, and India. On questions 2 and 3, it focuses on evidence from Chile and Sweden.

To preview the findings, the literature has made significant strides in answering question 1. Randomized experiments show that in some settings students acquire greater skill if they attend private rather than public school, although a perhaps surprisingly large proportion of estimates suggest an impact that is statistically indistinguishable from zero.

This type of work has made less progress providing answers to question 2. It does provide some evidence consistent with private schools producing skills at lower financial cost (most instances of this result originate in low-income countries and at the primary level; there is little evidence on whether it generalizes beyond that). However, effectively tackling question 2 requires disentangling all the possible *channels* through which a private school effect operates. This is typically not feasible in the contexts of the randomized work. This has important implications, since the case for expanding the private sector is much stronger if one can make the case that higher achievement in private schools reflects higher productivity. Otherwise it could reflect potentially zero-sum mechanisms related to peer effects, for example.

Addressing question 3 ideally requires exogenous cross market variation in the extent of private enrollment. Not surprisingly experiments to date have not achieved this. As an alternative, some research has focused on large-scale voucher reforms that have induced substantial expansions in some countries' private sectors, with variation across markets. Such analyses have the advantage of potentially revealing the general equilibrium effects of competition from private schools; but they face challenges related to identification, and to the fact that private entry is frequently associated with nonrandom sorting of students across sectors. A mixed assessment of the effects of competition also emerges from this work. Specifically, while growth in the private sector seems to have resulted in sorting and stratification, its impact on learning appears more mixed. Finally, given the difficulty in isolating effects on the public sector (which answering question 3 requires) some of this work looks at aggregate effects. Here again mixed results emerge. To cite the most aggregate evidence, some countries with large voucher-induced private school growth have seen their relative performance in international tests improve significantly; others have seen it decline. In addition, here again it is difficult to isolate specific channels.

The bottom line is that despite demand for clear, simple conclusions on the effects of competition from private schools, research does not yet provide these. For now,

---

[3] For reviews of related literature, see Ladd (2002), Neal (2002), McEwan (2004), Gill et al. (2007), Levin (2008), Barrow and Rouse (2009), and Epple et al. (2015).

the evidence seems more mixed than observers have usually expected. Further, the existing research underlines that educational markets are complex (MacLeod and Urquiola, 2013).

The gaps in knowledge around questions 1–3 suggest pathways for future research. Aside from these, an important area for future work concerns how competition-related policies themselves may be better designed. Indeed, the heterogeneity in results itself suggests that the impact of competition from private schools may depend on how and in what context it is introduced, as has been found, for instance, in the case of school decentralization (Galiani and Schargrodsky, 2002; Hanushek et al., 2013).

The remainder of the chapter proceeds as follows. Section 2 presents a simple framework to organize ideas. Section 3 reviews the evidence, and Section 4 concludes.

2. A SIMPLE FRAMEWORK

Studying the effects of introducing private schools into a public school market raises many analytical issues. This section presents a basic framework to organize some of these. The objective is not to derive estimating equations, but rather to provide — by making simplifying assumptions and abstracting from multiple issues — a closed form illustration of the different mechanisms that questions 1–3 (Section 1) raise. One theme will be that in realistic settings in which relevant variables are unobserved and functional forms are more complicated, it is difficult to get a sense of the direction and/or the magnitude of each mechanism.

Consider a market in which students differ only according to their ability, A. Suppose that the skill of a student i who attends school s is given by

$$T_{is} = \alpha_s + f(A_i) + g(\bar{A}_s). \tag{1}$$

Note that there is a peer effect: a student's outcome is a function not just of her own ability, A_i, but also of the average ability of students at her school, $\bar{A}_s$. This peer effect should be thought of broadly. It could reflect a direct externality in the sense that students learn from more able classmates; alternately, it might reflect that the parents of more able children more effectively discipline school administrators. α_s is the school's productivity (ie, its contribution to skill that is independent of peer ability). As stated, we shall understand a given school to be more productive than another if it produces more skill given the same resources. Thus, by our definition productivity would also be independent of resources other than peer effects, such as spending per pupil, that are not in Eq. (1) — again the point will be that even assuming away such other issues clear answers to questions 1–3 are hard to obtain.

In using Eq. (1) to assess competition between private and public schools, an important step is to specify the functional form of peer effects and the distribution of students across the two sectors. This reflects that in reality, it is likely to be the case that the children who use private schools are not a random sample of the population.

Drawing on Hsieh and Urquiola (2003) and to simplify matters, suppose that initially all students attend a single public school. Further assume that both own ability and peer quality have a linear effect on learning outcomes. Thus skill is given by

$$T_i^0 = \alpha_{\text{pub}} + \beta A_i + \gamma \bar{A}, \tag{2}$$

where α_{pub} is the public school productivity, β indicates the impact of own ability, and γ that of peer ability. $\bar{A}$ is the average ability over all students. The superscript on T indicates this is the initial situation.

To simplify further, suppose that $A_i = i$ (ie, students are indexed by ability) and that i is uniformly distributed in the interval [0,1]. With this, the initial mean achievement is

$$\bar{T}_{i \in [0,1]}^0 = \alpha_{\text{pub}} + \frac{\beta}{2} + \frac{\gamma}{2}, \tag{3}$$

where $\bar{T}_{i \in [0,1]}^0$ denotes the mean skill in the public school when it contains all children, $i \in [0,1]$.

Now suppose that a private school with productivity α_{priv} enters the market. Assume that a simple form of "cream skimming" takes place: all students $i \in [\frac{1}{2}, 1]$ enroll in the private school, while those $i \in [0, \frac{1}{2})$ remain in the public sector. This is a stark assumption; while it simplifies matters, any form of nonrandom sorting will render relevant several issues discussed below.

The average achievement in the private school is

$$\bar{T}_{i \in [\frac{1}{2},1]}^{\text{priv}} = \alpha_{\text{priv}} + \frac{3\beta}{4} + \frac{3\gamma}{4}, \tag{4}$$

and the average in the public school is now

$$\bar{T}_{i \in [0,\frac{1}{2})}^{\text{pub}} = \alpha_{\text{pub}}^* + \frac{\beta}{4} + \frac{\gamma}{4}, \tag{5}$$

where the asterisk on α_{pub}^* indicates that the public sector productivity may change in the presence of the private school — that is the public school productivity may no longer be that which prevailed in the initial situation.

The remainder of this section uses the above expressions to discuss challenges in answering questions 1–3.

2.1 Question 1: Do Children Experience Higher Achievement Gains in Private Than in Public Schools?

In our example the children $i \in [\frac{1}{2}, 1]$ switch to private school. For these individuals the change in achievement — the effect of going to the private rather than the public school — is

$$\bar{T}_{i \in [\frac{1}{2},1]}^{\text{priv}} - \bar{T}_{i \in [\frac{1}{2},1]}^0 = (\alpha_{\text{priv}} - \alpha_{\text{pub}}) + \frac{\gamma}{4}, \tag{6}$$

where $\overline{T}^{0}_{i\in[\frac{1}{2},1]}$ denotes the mean score they would have had in the original public school. There are two sources of gains for these children: a productivity effect, if $\alpha_{priv} > \alpha_{pub}$, and a peer group effect given by the last right-hand side term. The latter arises because they are now isolated from the lowest ability children.

Suppose one were able to carry out an experiment in which two children of identical ability $i \in [0, \frac{1}{2})$ in the public school were eligible to transfer to the private school. If only one was randomly selected to do so, a comparison of their outcomes would approximate (Eq. 6).[4] In other words, such an experiment would provide a reduced form estimate of the causal impact of switching from a public to a private school.

If this impact is positive, then the first part of question 1 can be answered in the affirmative (ie, children experience greater achievement in private school). Below we shall discuss papers that essentially implement such an analysis.

2.2 Question 2: If Private Schools Raise Achievement More, Is This Because These Schools Are More Productive?

As stated, a randomized experiment can under some assumptions provide a credible approximation to Eq. (6). Note, however, that in general such an estimate does not identify the source of this difference. Specifically, with strong assumptions on aspects such as functional form, Eq. (6) decomposes the gain into a productivity effect ($\alpha_{priv} - \alpha_{pub}$), and a peer group effect, $\frac{\gamma}{4}$. Such a decomposition is hard to achieve empirically. For example, sorting may happen along unobservable characteristics that are therefore impossible to control for. Further, peer effects, to the extent they exist, are unlikely to follow a simple linear-in-means specification like Eq. (2). The literature on peer effects is complex and far from delivering a consensus on a functional form. In fact, the findings in Carrell et al. (2013) suggest that at least in some settings a stable functional form may not exist.[5]

In short, the existing research — even when it can credibly estimate the reduced form impact of attending a private school — does not isolate whether at least part of this effect is due to higher private school productivity.

As Hsieh and Urquiola (2003) point out this has two important consequences. First, to the extent that the gain measured in Eq. (6) is at least partially due to a peer effect, then this gain will not be independent of the size of the private sector or of the sorting its growth induces. For instance, the advantage conferred by transferring to a private school may dissipate as the private sector grows and incorporates weaker children. To illustrate, in our setup the measured private advantage would have been higher if only the children $i \in [\frac{4}{5}, 1]$ had transferred to private school, as the private peer quality would be higher in that case.

---

[4] This abstracts from impacts on the public sector productivity, to which we return in discussing question 3.
[5] See Epple and Romano (2011) and Sacerdote (2011) for further reviews on peer effects.

Second, a positive estimate of Eq. (6) does not necessarily imply that average achievement would grow if the private sector is expanded. Given the assumptions we have made here, if a positive difference $\overline{T}^{\text{priv}}_{i \in [\frac{1}{2}, 1]} - \overline{T}^{0}_{i \in [\frac{1}{2}, 1]}$ is only due to a peer effect, then private expansion will be zero sum. More generally, the aggregate effect of private expansion could be positive or negative.

The bottom line is that a credible positive reduced form estimate of Eq. (6) — such as some randomized studies deliver — is sufficient to answer question 1; it is not sufficient to answer question 2, and hence must be treated with caution in assessing the desirability of further private expansion. This does not even address the complications raised by question 3, to which we now turn.

2.3 Question 3: Does Competition From Private Schools Raise Public School Productivity? Does the Existence of Private Schools Otherwise Affect Those "Left Behind" in Public Schools?

As the previous section suggests, the case for expanding the private sector is much stronger if private schools have higher productivity. In addition, welfare effects could arise from private expansion if it induces the public sector to change its own productivity, or if it affects public school children through other channels.

This is difficult to analyze experimentally — it would be hard to implement a scheme that, for example, significantly manipulated private school entry across randomly selected markets. Instead, the literature has focused on large-scale, nationwide voucher reforms that have induced large changes in private enrollment in some markets.

The above setup can be used to think about how private school entry affects public performance in such settings. A first pass measure of this is provided by simply comparing the mean public sector achievement before and after private entry:

$$\overline{T}^{\text{pub}}_{i, [0, \frac{1}{2}]} - \overline{T}^{0}_{i, [0, 1]} = (\alpha^*_{\text{pub}} - \alpha_{\text{pub}}) - \frac{\beta}{4} - \frac{\gamma}{4}. \tag{7}$$

Expression (7) is a first pass partially because it compares different sets of students ($i \in [0, \frac{1}{2}]$ and $i \in [0,1]$), but it is useful because this difference is typically readily observed. This expression shows that to answer question 3 one would ideally want to decompose this change into three effects. First, there is the public sector's productivity change $\alpha^*_{\text{pub}} - \alpha_{\text{pub}}$. Second, there is a composition effect, $\frac{\beta}{4}$ — the public sector does worse simply because it has lost the most able children. Third, there is a peer effect given by $\frac{\gamma}{4}$. This is the consequence of public school children having lost the ability to interact with higher ability children, and is the mirror image of the peer-related gain for private school students in Eq. (6).

Empirically achieving a decomposition like that in Eq. (7) is difficult. Again, relevant variables might be unobserved, and functional forms may be more complicated than we have assumed here.

A clear prior on the direction of at least some of the components in Eq. (7) could provide analytical leverage to guess the direction of the others. However, theoretical work does not provide a clear prediction on the direction of any of these effects.

First, consider the productivity difference $\alpha^*_{\text{pub}} - \alpha_{\text{pub}}$. One might expect it to be positive, but McMillan (2005) shows that it could be negative, and it is useful to consider the main aspects of his argument. His model features two types of households, low and high income; the latter are willing to pay more for school quality than the former. Schools can influence their productivity by exerting effort. Competition ensures that the private schools provide an efficient level of effort. That is, some private schools serve high-income students and charge high tuition for high effort; others serve low-income households and charge low tuition for low effort. The public school sector can also choose between the two effort levels. If it exerts high effort it attracts both types of students — the high income prefer it in this case to tuition-charging private schools. In contrast, if it exerts low effort, it only gets the low-income students. Now suppose the public sector is initially exerting high effort, and a voucher is introduced. This lowers the cost of private schooling and may lead the private sector to grow as it enrolls more high-income households. If this happens, public schools choose to lower their effort to the level required to retain only low-income students. Hence competition may lower public school productivity.

Second, one might think that the sorting terms in Eq. (7) would be easy to sign, but note that here we have assumed straightforward cream skimming. As discussed below, many voucher programs that expand private schooling are targeted at lower-income children. In addition while in many countries some private schools serve the elite, in many other (particularly developing) countries the private sector also includes low-cost schools that serve low-income households.

The bottom line is that in general it will be hard to determine the sign on $\alpha^*_{\text{pub}} - \alpha_{\text{pub}}$, that is, to establish if competition from private schools forces public schools to become more productive. This matters because productivity gains are in a real sense the whole point of introducing competition.

Furthermore, it is possible for private entry to hurt those "left behind" in public schools even if one assumes that the effects on productivity are positive. The intuition is illustrated by the last term on the right-hand side of Eq. (7): *if* there are peer effects, and *if* private school entry leads to cream skimming, then the overall impact on the public sector could be negative even if there is a positive productivity effect.

It is again useful to discuss briefly some theoretical examples of this, and we cover three. First, Manski (1992) presents a theoretical and computational framework in which students are heterogeneous along their household income and motivation. Manski uses this to assess whether vouchers equalize educational outcomes. His setup features an externality in that students benefit from motivated peers at school. He shows that as the voucher level rises, motivated students tend to transfer to private schools, especially in poor communities. This renders the effects of vouchers ambiguous, much as in our simple framework. Manski's own conclusion is illustrative: "The immediate lesson is that qualitative analysis cannot determine the merits of alternative school finance policies. Qualitatively plausible arguments can be made both for public school finance and for voucher systems. Hence, informed assessment…requires quantitative analysis…The educational effects of systemic *choice* on low income young people appear to be neither uniformly positive nor negative."

Second, Epple and Romano (1998) consider a broadly similar setup in that students vary according to their income and ability. A key innovation is that schools charge tuition that can be tailored to students according to these two traits. This generates "diagonal" stratification on the income-ability plane. Intuitively, because school quality increases with peer ability, private schools set lower tuition for high-ability students; in addition, higher-income households with low-ability children pay a tuition premium to enable them to attend high-quality schools. The model still features the result that average peer quality in the public schools declines as private entrants "cream skim" higher-income/higher-ability students from the public schools. Epple and Romano (2008) extend this work by using estimates from Hoxby (2000) in a computational exercise. They assume private schools are more productive than public schools. In this case, as in Eq. (7), the overall effect is still ambiguous.

Third, the ambiguity need not arise from true human capital externalities as in Manski (1992) and Epple and Romano (1998). MacLeod and Urquiola (2009) show that private growth may hurt those left in public schools through informational channels. Specifically, they assume that an individual attends school and accumulates skill as a function of her innate ability, her effort, and her school's value added. The key assumption is that individual innate ability is more readily observed by schools than by employers. In this sense schools perform two services: they supply productivity, but they also provide information. For example, an employer might use the fact that a graduate is from a certain school to make inferences regarding her ability. This is a version of signaling (Spence, 1973) but one that originates in *which* school children attend, as opposed to *whether* they attend. This again produces a setting in which private school growth can hurt those left behind, since their low ability is revealed to employers by their failure to gain admission to a selective private school.[6]

In closing, note that one theme in the discussion surrounding questions 2 and 3 is that it is difficult to decompose the different mechanisms potentially unleashed by competition from private schools. One alternative — particularly when looking at the large-scale reforms used to analyze question 3 — is to simply analyze a single, market-level net effect.

[6] MacLeod and Urquiola (2009) refer to K-12 schools. MacLeod and Urquiola (2015) extend similar informational mechanisms to the college setting, and MacLeod et al. (2015) present empirical evidence that such mechanisms are operative.

If panel data for multiple local school markets are available then one can take differences over time removing market-specific fixed characteristics. In addition, looking at aggregate outcomes nets out composition effects like the second term in Eq. (7). We shall review such evidence below. Nevertheless, considering aggregate effects is still not ideal because it confounds the impact of productivity improvements and the net effect of peer group composition.

Below we review studies on large-scale voucher reforms that essentially implement such an analysis. It should be noted that two challenges remain. First, it may be difficult to account for factors that give rise to endogenous differential voucher growth across markets. Second, market-specific factors other than the voucher may impact a market over the time period under analysis.

3. THE EVIDENCE

This section reviews the evidence on the three questions considered above.[7] Dealing with these questions sequentially naturally imposes an ordering in terms of the types of evidence considered. Specifically, question 1 has been most credibly analyzed in the context of small-scale experiments involving the distribution of a limited number of targeted vouchers. In contrast, the papers that address questions 2 and 3 generally consider large-scale voucher reforms — namely, situations in which vouchers are distributed to anyone wishing to use them, without income or geographic restrictions.

3.1 Question 1: Do Children Experience Higher Achievement Gains in Private Than in Public Schools?

The most credible evidence on question 1 comes from small-scale voucher programs, as these often (eg, when they involve explicit or implicit randomization) provide a way to control for selection into private school. This makes it more likely that performance differences in public-private comparisons reflect the net effect of causal mechanisms. A large number of small-scale voucher programs potentially offer such evidence. For instance, Epple et al. (2015) count 66 voucher programs in the USA; 9 funded by tax revenues, 7 via tax credits, and 50 by private foundations.

This section begins by reviewing some of the evidence that has emerged from these programs; it then turns to studies set in Colombia and India.

3.1.1 United States

The largest voucher program in the USA is that in Milwaukee, Wisconsin. It began in 1990 with the distribution of about 800 vouchers giving students the opportunity to

---

[7] In some cases the review of the US evidence draws on Epple et al. (2015); that on Colombia on MacLeod and Urquiola (2013) and that on India on Urquiola (2015).

attend private school. Eligibility for the vouchers was restricted to students with household incomes below 175% of the federal poverty level. The beneficiaries were selected via lottery, such that the performance of the lottery losers provides a natural and credible counterfactual for that of the winners. Barrow and Rouse (2009) point out that the data collected as part of the program made available an additional comparison group: a random sample of low-income students from the Milwaukee Public Schools.

Using the latter comparison group Witte et al. (1995) find that the program had no statistically significant impact on test scores. Using the former comparison group, Greene et al. (1996) find statistically significant positive impacts in both math and reading. Using both comparison groups, Rouse (1998) finds significant impacts in math but not in reading. Recent research on Milwaukee faces greater difficulty exploiting randomization, as growth in the number of vouchers offered reduced the need for lotteries.[8]

Another relevant voucher program is that enacted by the US Congress for Washington, D.C. in 2003. The design is broadly similar to Milwaukee's in that it also features the use of lotteries. Using data on 2000 eligible applicants, Wolfe et al. (2010) and Wolfe et al. (2013) find that winning a voucher had no significant effects on test scores, but a relatively large impact on graduation: the intent to treat effect is about 12% points relative to a base graduation rate of 70%.

The Milwaukee and Washington, D.C. programs are publicly funded. Additional evidence comes from typically smaller, privately funded targeted programs. For example, Peterson et al. (2003) analyze programs with lottery-based voucher distribution in New York, Washington, D.C., and Dayton.[9] Averaging over all three programs they find a positive effect on math and reading scores for African Americans, although none for a group consisting of all other ethnic groups. When analyzed separately, the positive effect for African Americans persists only in New York (see also Howell et al., 2002; Mayer et al., 2002). However, Krueger and Zhu (2004) revisit the New York data and show that this last finding is sensitive to how ethnicity is coded, as well as to how one handles students with missing baseline scores.

Chingos and Peterson (2012) use more recent data to look at college enrollment as an outcome in the New York program. Although they find no effect on aggregate, they again find a statistically significant and substantial positive impact on African Americans.

To summarize, voucher experiments in the USA in principle allow one to identify the causal impact of switching a small number of children from public to private schools. The results often point to an absence of an achievement gain on average. There does appear to be a positive impact on black students, although this appears to be more robust when

---

[8] Witte et al. (2012) use a matched sample and report statistically significant effects in reading but none in math.

[9] These are the School Choice Foundation program in New York City, the Washington Scholarship Fund program in Washington, D.C., and the Parents Advancing Choice in Education program in Dayton, OH.

graduation rather than test scores are the outcome. In short, the US-based evidence on question 1 — which as emphasized above must be complemented with evidence on questions 2–3 to get a full sense of the effect of competition — does not provide robust evidence that an expansion of the private sector would significantly raise achievement. This overall conclusion is qualitatively similar to that in two recent reviews of the US evidence by Barrow and Rouse (2009) and Neal (2009).[10] To the extent that our conclusion is slightly more positive regarding the effects on subgroups, it reflects recent evidence that points in that direction.

3.1.2 Colombia

Additional evidence comes from Colombia, where from 1992 to 1997, a few larger municipalities operated a secondary school voucher program.[11] The stated goal of this program was to increase enrollment in grades 6–11, using private-sector participation to ease public-sector capacity constraints that mostly affected low-income households. As a result, the vouchers were targeted at entering sixth-grade students who were: (i) residing in low-income neighborhoods, (ii) attending public school, and (iii) accepted to begin the next academic year at a participating private school. When there was excess demand, the vouchers were generally allocated via lotteries.

Angrist et al. (2002) find that 3 years after the allocation, lottery winners were 10% points more likely to finish the eighth grade, and scored 0.2 standard deviations higher on achievement tests. In addition, they were less likely to work while in school, or marry/cohabit as teenagers. Using a similar design, Angrist et al. (2006) find that positive effects persist in longer term outcomes: voucher winners were 15–20% more likely to complete secondary school, and, correcting for differences in test taking between lottery winners and losers, the program increased college admissions test scores by two-tenths of a standard deviation.

In terms of identifying an effect like Eq. (6), the Colombian voucher experiment raises three important caveats. First, the vouchers were renewable contingent on grade completion, and thus the program included an incentive component — voucher winners faced a stronger reward for doing well at school. Therefore, the superior test performance of lottery winners might be due to external incentives rather than to the type of school attended per se.

---

[10] For example, Neal (2009) states that: "Measured solely by achievement and attainment effects, existing evidence does not support the view that private schools are generally superior to public schools in all settings." Barrow and Rouse (2009) conclude that "[t]he best research to date finds relatively small achievement gains for students offered education vouchers, most of which are not statistically different from zero."

[11] For further background on the Colombian voucher system, and for comparisons to others, see King et al. (1997), Angrist et al. (2002), and Epple et al. (2015).

Second, both lottery winners and losers tended to enroll in private schools, particularly in larger cities. Focusing on Bogota and Cali, Angrist et al. (2002) point out that while about 94% of lottery winners attended private school in the first year, so did 88% of lottery losers. This is not surprising to the extent that: (i) a high private enrollment rate in secondary was symptomatic of the very supply bottlenecks that the program was implemented to address, and (ii) applicants were required to be accepted at a private school. The latter likely increased the probability that households with preferences for private schooling applied, and that even lottery losers might have found private options they liked and were therefore willing to pay for independently. Since the reduced-form estimates in these papers are based upon a comparison of lottery winners and losers, they may in some cases measure a "private with incentives versus private without incentives" effect, rather than the effect of private versus public schooling per se.

Finally, the institutional setup implies that many voucher winners who, again, would have attended private school even if they did not win the lottery, used the vouchers to "upgrade" to more expensive private schools. Angrist et al. (2002) observe that the maximum tuition the voucher covered was roughly equivalent to the cost of a low-to-mid-price private school, and that it was common for voucher recipients to supplement this amount. Thus, part of the effect of winning a lottery could reflect access to greater resources, as opposed to a public/private differential.

To summarize, these studies support the hypothesis that the Colombian voucher program enhanced student performance, but they may not directly isolate the benefit of attending a private school as in Eq. (6).

3.1.3 India

India provides another interesting example of a privately funded voucher experiment. As Muralidharan and Sundararaman (2015) point out, in 2008 a foundation began distributing vouchers in 180 villages in Andra Pradesh. The vouchers were sufficient to cover about the 90th percentile of the private school fees in these markets. Baseline tests were conducted at all private and public schools in these villages. All the test takers were then allowed to apply for a limited number of vouchers.

Randomization took place in two steps. First, 90 villages were randomly selected to receive vouchers, and 90 remained in a control group. Second, within the 90 treatment villages, about 2000 of 3000 applicant households were randomly selected to receive vouchers (about 1200 of these actually made use of them). As we shall discuss below, this double randomization allows this paper to move beyond question 1.

Muralidharan and Sundararaman (2015) find that after 4 years of treatment, lottery winners did not have higher test scores than losers in Telugu (the local language), math, English, science, and social studies; in contrast, they did perform significantly better in Hindi. Using other survey evidence, Muralidharan and Sundararaman (2015) point out that these results are consistent with the allocation of instruction time at private schools. Namely, relative to public schools, private schools seem to devote time to Hindi at the expense of other subjects. This is in turn consistent with parents valuing learning on this subject (perhaps due to labor market returns) above others that are regularly tested.

In addition, Muralidharan and Sundararaman (2015) collected data on school costs. They find that private schools in the villages considered have expenditures that are only one-third of those in public schools. Thus, they emphasize that even if private schools produced no greater gains in Hindi — as in the other five tested subjects — they would still be providing substantial cost savings.

It is worth mentioning that there is evidence of lower private school costs in other settings; particularly in low-income countries. For example, Andrabi et al. (2008) describe that the private sector in Pakistan includes for-profit schools that charge very low fees — in their survey rural private schools charge about $18 a year. Andrabi et al. (2008) provide further information on where these savings originate. Consistent with the majority of educational expenditure in developing countries going to salaries, they find that they reflect that many private schools hire young, single, untrained local women as teachers. They pay them much less than the trained teachers (who are more likely to be men) more common in public schools.

There is nothing a priori wrong with this — these teachers are essentially producing comparable learning for much a lower cost and clearly find the employment opportunity worthwhile. At the same time, this may limit the relevance of such savings to other countries, or even to other educational levels within the same countries. Specifically, Andrabi et al. (2008) highlight that most private expansion in Pakistan has taken place at the primary level. Secondary education might require private schools to hire trained and more specialized teachers, which could drive up their costs up significantly.

To summarize, the literature on whether private schools provide learning gains in excess of those observed among public schools has produced mixed results. There is evidence of greater private gains for some subgroups and outcomes in some settings. But the estimated effects do not seem to be of a regularity or magnitude such that transferring students into private schools would by itself substantially and reliably raise achievement. This finding is consistent with a broader literature on the effects that attending a higher-achieving school or class has on academic performance, even when these transfers occur within a given (public or private) sector. Here again some papers find little or no effect (eg, Cullen et al., 2005, 2006; Clark, 2010; Duflo et al., 2011; Abdulkadiroglu et al., 2014) and some find positive effects (eg, Jackson, 2010; Pop-Eleches and Urquiola, 2013), but no uniform pattern emerges. Beyond this there is evidence of heterogeneous effects in that in some cases some groups (eg, low socioeconomic status individuals) seem to derive higher gains from private enrollment. This is also consistent with some papers in the literature on attending more selective schools or universities (eg, Dale and Krueger, 2002, 2014; Card and Giuliano, 2014).

3.2 Question 2: If Private Schools Raise Achievement More, Is This Because These Schools Are More Productive?

The previous section illustrates that some studies have used experiments to credibly answer question 1. Specifically, there is some evidence that in some cases and for some outcomes, private schools can raise achievement more than public schools, and at lower cost. Question 2 asks whether this reflects higher productivity on the part of private schools. As emphasized in Section 2, this is quite relevant to what these findings imply about the impact of competition more broadly. The more a private advantage is due to a productivity differential, the less likely it is to reflect potentially zero sum (or even negative) mechanisms related to sorting.

In general, the experiments that credibly answer question 1 do not provide a clear answer to question 2. This can be illustrated relative to several of the studies reviewed above. For example, in the study on India, Muralidharan and Sundararaman (2015) find that private schools produced higher learning in Hindi. The result is consistent with private schools being more focused on or better at teaching Hindi. But it is also consistent with a peer effect. For instance, suppose that parents who value Hindi are more likely to choose private schools in the absence of vouchers, and are also more likely to speak Hindi at home or expose their children to television programming in Hindi. This would be analogous to the setting in many countries where parents who value instruction in English (Hindi plays a similar "lingua franca" role in India) are more likely to use private schools. As a result lottery winners may be more exposed to and interact with children who know Hindi. In such a situation the greater achievement of lottery winners could be due to a peer effect, as in Eq. (6). A similar issue emerges in any setting in which some factor is in fixed supply (at least in the medium term); for example, parents who especially value Hindi or well-trained teachers.

One experimental paper that makes an interesting attempt to get around this issue is Bettinger et al. (2010), which also covers the Colombian case reviewed above. This paper attempts to find a setting in which voucher lottery winners did not enjoy a better peer group than losers. If one can thus sign the peer effect in Eq. (6) then one can argue that the effect of switching children to the private sector is mainly working through school productivity. Specifically, Bettinger et al. (2010) focus on applicants who requested vocational schools. As in many countries, these tend to be less selective. On average, therefore, the lottery winners that transferred to these school experience worse peer groups than those they would have encountered in public schools. Yet they still experienced higher achievement. A caveat is that this may not be the case along unobservables.

To summarize, although it is challenging to implement, research that illuminates the channels through which private enrollment affects skill would be of distinct value.

3.3 Question 3: Does Competition From Private Schools Raise Public School Productivity? Does the Existence of Private Schools Otherwise Affect Those "Left Behind" in Public Schools?

As the discussion surrounding Eq. (6) illustrated, question 1 can in principle be addressed in any setting in which private schools exist. All that is needed is exogenous variation in who enrolls in the private as opposed to the public sector. Of course identifying such variation is much easier said than done, but that is essentially what, by using lotteries, the papers reviewed in Section 3.1 achieve.

In contrast, answering question 3 requires settings in which there is variation in the size of the private sector across markets. Such variation can be found in the cross section in many countries. For instance, Epple et al. (2015) cite several countries that have implicitly or explicitly implemented large-scale voucher programs, where large-scale refers to programs in which vouchers are distributed nationwide to any child who wishes to use them. To the extent that households (and schools) react differentially to the introduction of vouchers across jurisdictions, cross-market variation in private enrollment emerges. Such variation can emerge even in the absence of voucher programs provided that private school entry is allowed. For instance, at any given point there is variation in the private enrollment rate across metropolitan areas in the USA or villages in India.

The expectation suggested by Friedman (1962) is that, all else equal, achievement will be higher where the private sector has a greater reach. The concern immediately arises that the "all else equal" clause is violated because such variation is endogenous: market characteristics correlated with higher private enrollment may be the real drivers of market performance. The resulting bias could go either way. For example, it may be that private enrollment is higher in areas that have a higher concentration of motivated or high-income parents. This might cause one to overestimate the beneficial impact of private participation. On the other hand, it could be that private enrollment is higher where public teacher unions most adversely affect performance, with the opposite effect.

As hard as it is to design and run an experiment awarding vouchers, it would be much harder to implement an experiment that induced cross-market variation in private enrollment (and prevented migration, for instance). In part because of this, another part of the literature has focused on large-scale voucher programs and their associated changes in the private share. This yields two analytical advantages. First, it allows analyses to include "market fixed effects," essentially comparing the performance of the same areas before and after significant expansion in private enrollment. This holds constant factors that are potentially fixed over time, such as the prevalence of motivated parents or persistent dysfunction in the public sector. Nevertheless, this is not equivalent to experimental variation and in this sense studies that tackle question 3 are often at a disadvantage relative to randomized experiments focused on question 1.

Second, and quite aside from identification concerns, large reforms may be better suited to revealing the general equilibrium effects of competition. For instance, it may be that the truly beneficial or deleterious effects of private school participation do not really reveal themselves until a market has a chance to experience substantial entry and exit of private schools. In this sense the studies that look at large-scale reforms may have an analytical advantage over small-scale voucher experiments.

A final note before proceeding to the evidence is that even if one were to assume that the fixed effects strategy delivers identification, Eq. (7) suggests that it will be difficult to separately identify effects on the productivity of the public sector from those affecting children through mechanisms like peer effects. As discussed in Section 2 one alternative is to look at the aggregate effect (including both private and public schools), and some of the papers reviewed below attempt that.

The remainder of this section focuses on two reforms that introduced "unrestricted" voucher schemes — those of Chile and Sweden. Although we shall not discuss them here because work on these cases has less directly addressed question 3, we note that Denmark, Holland, and New Zealand have also implemented large-scale school funding schemes that effectively function as voucher systems.[12] A final section makes brief reference to evidence from Canada, India, and the USA. These three countries have not implemented large-scale reforms and so they are not as suited to considering question 3, although there is nonetheless relevant research.

3.3.1 Chile

In 1981, Chile introduced a voucher system that led to perhaps the largest policy-induced expansion in private schooling in history.[13] Prior to this three types of schools were in operation: (i) public schools were managed by the National Ministry of Education and accounted for about 80% of enrollments, (ii) unsubsidized private schools catered to upper-income households and accounted for about 6% of enrollments, and (iii) subsidized private schools did not charge tuition, received limited lump sum subsidies, were often Catholic, and accounted for roughly 14% of enrollments. The reform transferred public schools to municipalities, simultaneously awarding them a per-student

---

[12] See Epple et al. (2015) for further description of these cases. For further reference on Denmark, see Justesen (2002); on Holland: Patrinos (2002) and Levin (2004); on New Zealand: Adams (2009), Ladd and Fiske (2001), and Lubienski et al. (2013).

[13] This section draws on Hsieh and Urquiola (2006), Urquiola and Verhoogen (2009), and McEwan et al. (2008). Here we use Chile as a setting to analyze question 3. It has also been used to analyze questions 1 (and to a lesser extent 2), but the literature has had more trouble arriving at identification as clear as that in the randomized studies reviewed above. For further background on the Chilean voucher system, its evolution, and its comparison to others, see Gauri (1998), McEwan and Carnoy (2000), Bellei (2007), Mizala and Urquiola (2013), and Neilson (2013).

subsidy sufficient to cover their costs. In addition, subsidized (or "voucher") private schools began to receive exactly the same per-student subsidy as municipal schools. Unsubsidized private schools continue to operate largely as before.

While all schools must participate in annual standardized exams, private schools generally operate under fewer restrictions. They can be religious and/or for-profit. They are allowed to implement admissions policies, albeit with increasing restrictions in recent years, at least in principle. After 1994 private voucher schools were allowed to charge tuition add-ons. Public schools are more constrained in many of these dimensions. They are not allowed to turn away students unless oversubscribed, and cannot charge tuition at the primary level; they essentially do not at the secondary level either.

These changes resulted in substantial private school entry. By 2009, about 57% of all students attended private schools, with voucher schools alone accounting for about 50%. Recent years have seen further reforms. In 1997, schools charging tuition add-ons were forced to provide exemptions on these for a percentage of low-income students. Recent legislation aims to eliminate the add-ons in the coming years. In 2008 the voucher was increased for low-income students, albeit only for schools agreeing to conditions including limitations on the selection of students. The recent reforms also include ending the ability of private voucher schools to operate for-profit, and further prohibitions on the selection of students. As often, the implementation details surrounding these reforms will be important.

Recall that several of the difficulties raised in answering question 3 arise due to sorting. Thus a crucial question is whether Chile's reform led to stratification, as would be predicted, for example, by theoretical models such as Epple and Romano (1998). Hsieh and Urquiola (2006) suggest that this indeed happened. In general terms, there was a "middle class" exodus from public schools consistent with cream skimming. There is also evidence that dynamics leading to stratification have continued both between and within sectors, and that at this point Chile displays one of the highest levels of school stratification by socioeconomic status in the OECD (see, for instance, Mizala and Urquiola, 2013; Valenzuela et al., 2013).[14]

Thus the analytical issues induced by sorting and highlighted in Section 2 are relevant in Chile. For example, Hsieh and Urquiola (2003) point out that addressing question 3 with a regression in the spirit of Eq. (7) suggests that private competition worsens public performance. Specifically, public schools have lower average test scores in areas with more private enrollment. While this could reflect an adverse effect of private schooling on public sector productivity, it could also be driven exclusively by sorting and peer effects.

---

[14] For other examples of school market liberalization leading to stratification, see Mbiti and Lucas (2009) on Kenya. For related evidence in the USA, see Urquiola (2005).

As stated, one way of netting out the effects of sorting is to focus on whether areas in which the private sector grew more displayed relative aggregate improvement. In this spirit, Hsieh and Urquiola (2006) apply a difference-in-differences approach to municipal-level data for 1982–96, suggesting that while areas with greater private growth display clear signs of greater stratification, they display no relative advantage in terms the evolution of achievement on standardized tests and years of schooling. As stated above the key caveat — despite the use of some candidate instrumental variables (eg, population density) — is that private entry into school markets is endogenous. For instance, if outcomes had been declining in areas where the private sector grew more, these effects would underestimate the salutary effects of competition.[15]

Bravo et al. (2010) consider the labor market rather than test score effects of the growth of private enrollment. The idea they exploit is that individuals who were more "exposed" to the 1981 reform — measured by the number of years they were still in school after the reform — should fare better. As in Hsieh and Urquiola (2006), this could reflect a host of mechanisms, and the idea is to capture an aggregate effect. They use a structural approach to analyze individuals' dynamic school and labor market choices. That said, the identification challenges cited above are still present, as are the need for several simplifying assumptions.[16] The authors use 2002 and 2004 survey data (with retrospective questions) to estimate the model. They then use simulations and compare the outcomes of individuals who were exposed to the post-1981 regime for their whole school career to those who were never exposed. A key finding is that individuals' average lifetime earnings are not affected by the reform, although this reflects different impacts at different educational levels: attending primary school after the reform raised earnings, but attending secondary school tended to reduce them. The latter result in turn reflects that while educational attainment rose with the reform, this postponed individuals' entry into the labor force and lowered the return to secondary education. Despite the lack of an overall effect on earnings, the authors find that the reform resulted in generalized and significant gains in average discounted lifetime utility. These arise from the utility of time spent attending school and not working.

---

[15] One alternative to considering the performance of certain markets over time is to use cross-sectional variation. In other work, Auguste and Valenzuela (2006) use a 2000 round of standardized tests to implement a cross sectional variant of this approach, using distance to a nearby city as an instrument for the private share. They also find evidence of cream skimming, but in contrast to Hsieh and Urquiola (2006) significant positive effects on achievement. Finally, Gallego (2006) implements a similar cross-section specification on 2002 testing data using the density of priests per diocese as an instrument for the prevalence of voucher schools, and also finds substantial effects of the competition proxy on average student achievement. Yet again questions surround the exogeneity of this variation.

[16] For example, Epple et al. (2015) note that for tractability the model assumes individuals are of "just" three types. This limits the extent to which sorting effects can be analyzed.

Another way of getting at whether greater private participation has improved aggregate performance is by looking at Chile's performance in international tests. If the effects of a growing private share were substantial, then one would expect Chile's performance in international (or national) tests to have improved over time, and/or for the country to be an outlier in performance relative to GDP per capita. Hsieh and Urquiola (2006) point out that over the first two decades after the reform, Chile's relative performance worsened. Hanushek et al. (2012) point out, however, that this trend then reversed. Specifically after dropping from 1999 to 2003, Chile's eighth-grade math and science scores increased substantially from 2003 to 2011. They estimate that Chile had the second-highest growth rate among 49 countries they studied. On the other hand, recent news reports indicate that this progress significantly decelerated or stagnated, depending on the subject, by the 2013 round.

In looking at such long-term trends, however, identification issues begin to loom even larger. For instance, while the decade that featured the most improvement saw further expansion in the private school share, it also featured: substantial increases in GDP per capita and educational expenditures, expansions in pre-school enrollments, reforms to rules governing university admissions, and reforms to the voucher system itself. Thus, it is very difficult to causally assign periods of improvement (or for analogous reasons, lack of improvement) to the growth in the private sector.

Chile is one setting where the literature has turned to considering whether the design of competition-related policies matters. For example, Hsieh and Urquiola (2006) briefly point out that private schools may not have been competing on productivity but rather on peer composition. In theoretical work, MacLeod and Urquiola (2009) and MacLeod and Urquiola (2015) formalize this notion. The essential idea again goes back to Friedman, who suggested that competition will improve outcomes as firms endeavor to develop reputations for quality. MacLeod and Urquiola thus ask: What is a school's reputation? Suppose it is given by the average skill of its graduates — good schools are those whose graduates have skills that are useful in the labor market or perhaps in higher education. This implies that schools' reputations depend not just on their value added, but also on the quality of students they admit. The implication they work out is that vouchers systems will work better if they restrict private schools' ability to select students. In essence, they suggest that voucher systems that borrow elements used for charter schools in the USA — which must select students via lotteries, for example — will be more likely to ensure that competition from private schools leads to greater value added.

In broadly related empirical work, Neilson (2013) asks how the design of voucher payments may affect the incentive that schools have to engage in supply side responses (eg, by raising their productivity). This paper considers a recent reform of the Chilean voucher system: the introduction of targeted vouchers in 2008. This reform in most cases eliminated tuition charges for poor students, and increased the payments to schools when they took on such children. Neilson's point is that this may have significant effects, as in some cases the Chilean market actually features — despite a universal voucher system — little competition between schools in poor neighborhoods. This reflects that low-income households can be very sensitive to distance and price. Using a structural model he calculates that the introduction of targeted vouchers allowed the effective prices of private schools for lower-income households to drop. This prompted schools to compete for these customers by raising productivity, since the targeted voucher made more expensive schools attractive to poor students. Although subject to several assumptions, the results suggest that in the case of Chile the introduction of targeted vouchers raised school value added and reduced the performance gap between poor and nonpoor children significantly.

3.3.2 Sweden

Prior to the early 1990s, almost all Swedish children attended municipal schools.[17] The national government funded these and hired teachers as well. A 1991 reform introduced three changes. First, the government awarded lump sum funding to municipalities. Second, "open enrollment" plans were instituted at the municipal level, such that in principle students could attend any school in their jurisdiction. Third, the government mandated that municipalities fund independent schools with a per-student payment equivalent to the resources they would have spent themselves.

As in Chile, independent schools may be religious and/or operated for-profit. They are not allowed to charge tuition add-ons, and must be open to all students regardless of their municipality of origin, ethnicity, or religion. At the compulsory level, admissions priority depends on proximity to the school, wait list (first-come, first-served), and sibling presence. Ability-based admissions are allowed at the secondary level.

Like Chile's, Sweden's voucher reform can be used to analyze question 3. Sandstrom and Bergstrom (2005) focus on whether individuals in public schools perform better if they live in municipalities that have a larger share of independent schools. As discussed this is difficult to ascertain as results could be driven by sorting. In addition the paper uses cross-sectional variation, but it nonetheless provides a useful introduction to the outcomes and issues. Specifically Sandstrom and Bergstrom (2005) report that independent and public schools indeed enroll different types of students. For example, independent school students are more likely to be immigrants and/or to have parents with higher income and education (see also Bjorklund et al. (2005) on this issue).

Sandstrom and Bergstrom (2005) implement a Heckman correction and, to address the endogeneity of private entry, use variables approximating whether local authorities are "hostile" to independent schools. Specifically, they proxy for this attitude using measures of the extent to which municipalities contract out responsibilities to the private

---

[17] For further reference on the setup of Sweden's voucher system, see Bohlmark and Lindahl (2007, 2008) in addition to several papers cited in this section.

sector. The assumption is that this attitude will only affect educational outcomes through the channel that municipalities with less hostility will be less likely to block private school entry. The key finding is that the presence of greater independent school competition results in better public performance in a GPA–type measure, as well as in standardized mathematics exams and in an indicator for whether students passed all three exams necessary for high school admission (see also Ahlin (2003) for related results).

Given the concerns generated by sorting another possibility is to look at aggregate effects. Bohlmark and Lindahl (2008) ask if outcomes improved by more in municipalities that experienced more extensive private entry. This analysis has advantages — and raises analogous caveats — to the work on Chile presented by Hsieh and Urquiola (2006). In implementing this approach Bohlmark and Lindahl (2008) focus on three types of outcomes measured at different points of students' careers: (i) GPA after the first year and at the end of high school, (ii) a dummy for having completed at least 1 year of higher education within 6 years of leaving compulsory schooling, and (iii) years of schooling 8 years after leaving compulsory school.

After showing that there are at most slight differences in preexisting trends in municipalities' performance along these dimensions, Bohlmark and Lindahl (2008) find: (i) a small positive effect of vouchers on average ninth-grade GPA, (ii) little evidence that the positive ninth-grade effect persists to the end of high school, and (iii) no evidence of effects on university attendance and years of schooling.

Bohlmark and Lindahl (2012) extend this analysis using data for a longer time span — all cohorts finishing ninth grade from 1988 to 2009. They look at average performance according to the growth of the independent sector in 284 municipalities. This leads to significantly more positive conclusions. Specifically, outcome measures include combined test scores in language and math at the end of ninth grade, combined grades in these subjects at the end of ninth grade, the fraction of students completing at least one semester of university education, and average years of schooling at age 24. All of these measures are found to increase with the share of independent-school students.

As noted above, mobility of students across districts argues for aggregation of districts to define the "market" as the set of districts among which students may choose. When Bohlmark and Lindahl conduct the same analyses after aggregating to the local labor market level, the findings with respect to test scores and grade gains prove to be robust in magnitude and significance, but the effects on college attendance and years of schooling do not.

Bohlmark and Lindahl (2012) make two additional points. First, they attribute the more positive results in the longer-term study to the fact that the independent school sector did not grow immediately, with growth picking up only around 2004. Second, they contrast their findings for Sweden to Hsieh and Urquiola's (2006) conclusions on Chile. They observe that their more favorable findings are consistent with the predictions of the reputational model of MacLeod and Urquiola (2009). Specifically, the idea is that competition will be most effective when it is not associated with significant sorting, as in this case parents' preferences for schools will be more likely to be driven by school productivity as opposed to school peer composition.

Some recent work suggests some caution with respect to the test score-related results in Bohlmark and Lindahl (2012) (the ones that are most robust to aggregation). Specifically, while the content of these tests is nationally standardized, they are graded locally at each school. A concern is that independent schools might be grading more leniently. This was recently analyzed in a regrading exercise described by Tyrefors Hinnerich and Vlachos (2013). Independent graders reexamined tests from different schools. The authors point out that independent schools were more likely to have their grades lowered after a second examination. It is possible that the independent schools — perhaps under greater pressure to please parents and to compete — engaged in more grade inflation.[18]

Finally, as in Chile, one can look at the evolution of Sweden's performance in international test scores (with analogous threats to identification). Sweden has seen significantly deteriorating performance in the years since vouchers were implemented. Perhaps this is not surprising; as in Chile, there is consensus in Sweden that the voucher program has not been a panacea and is in need of reform.

3.4 Evidence From Small-Scale Programs Related to Question 3: Canada, India, and the USA

Evidence on question 3 can also originate from smaller-scale programs. For instance, Chan and McMillan (2009) consider the effects on public school performance of a private school tax credit in Ontario. This is analogous to the tax-credit funded voucher programs in the USA analyzed by Epple et al. (2015). This credit was implemented on short notice in 2001, and became available to families in January 2002. The plan provided a credit that was scheduled to grow in increments over 5 years, although it was canceled before the end of this period. Using the 2002–03 private school enrollment share in a public school attendance zone as their measure of private school competition, Chan and McMillan find that a one standard deviation increase in competition is associated with a statistically significant 0.1 standard deviation increase in the percentage of public school students achieving the provincial performance standard for grade 3.

Turning to India, the experimental design in Andra Pradesh was unique in that randomization involved not only students but also towns/markets. This allows Muralidharan and Sundararaman (2015) to go beyond the usual comparison (lottery winners vs lottery losers) and address potential externalities on children who remain in public school, thus addressing question 3. For example, by comparing nonapplicants in towns that did not receive vouchers to nonapplicants in towns that did, they obtain an estimate of the effects

---

[18] This brief synopsis is based on correspondence with the authors, as the article cited is in Swedish. In addition, see the reporting in Fisman (2014).

on children "left behind" in the public sector. The authors find little if any evidence of such effects.

The USA has also not implemented a large-scale national voucher scheme like Chile or Sweden. This is in part due to its very decentralized school system. This decentralization introduces competition, however, because it provides choice between public school districts rather than between private and public schools. Such competition lies outside the scope of this chapter, but it bears mentioning that here again the literature has produced mixed results rather than a distinct sense that greater competition raises achievement (eg, Hoxby, 2000; Rothstein, 2007). Similarly, there are different claims as to whether Tiebout choice leads to stratification (eg, Clotfelter, 1998; Hoxby, 2000; Urquiola, 2005). Finally, there is also literature on the effects of private voucher-induced competition on public school performance in the USA (eg, Hoxby, 2002a; Chakrabarti, 2013;Figlio and Hart, 2006, 2014) with the caveats surrounding the discussion around Eq. (7) and also raised in presenting the evidence on Chile and Sweden.

To summarize, question 3 is most squarely addressed by the literature on large-scale voucher reforms. This work offers relevant analytical advantages, not least the fact that it allows one to observe situations in which the entry of private schools may display its full effect. This very characteristic, however, also introduces complications, such as the difficulty of isolating causal relationships. Keeping that in mind, the conclusions that emerge from this research also offer a mixed assessment of the impact of competition from private schools. First, there is relatively strong indication that private school entry can lead to stratification by socioeconomic status and other characteristics — although this would seem to depend on the institutional design in question. Second, the effects of competition on achievement appear more mixed.

4. CONCLUSION

This chapter has illustrated that assessing the impact of competition from private schools requires addressing a host of questions. If each of the three questions raised in this chapter cannot be clearly answered, then a full understanding of the consequences of competition is not attainable.

In terms of question 1, the evidence from randomized experiments suggests that transferring children from public to private schools may indeed increase their achievement. Yet the evidence is surprisingly mixed given the usual expectation. In particular, multiple experiments suggest little or no improvement for multiple outcomes. The most positive effects, at least in the USA, emerge for subgroups of generally lower socioeconomic status students. Work in Colombia finds systematically positive results, subject to some interpretation-related issues. All of these results are based on experimental designs, and so conform to a high standard in terms of identification.

In terms of question 2, the experimental evidence does not reveal if a private advantage originates in a particular channel (eg, higher private school productivity) although there is suggestive evidence that in low-income countries and at low-educational levels, the private sector can deliver cost savings. The difficulty in isolating channels has important implications. For instance, the case for transferring children to the private sector is significantly weakened if at least part of the private advantage is not due to productivity differences.

In addition, question 3 raises the need to assess the effects of private entry on the students that remain in the public sector. This is generally not possible in the context of randomized experiments, and so researchers have considered large-scale voucher programs that provide a chance to study how given educational markets change when there is substantial private entry. This research has produced mixed evidence. On the one hand, the findings suggest that greater private participation can cause more sorting/stratification. On the other hand, the evidence on achievement effects is mixed. A challenge in this area is credibly establishing causality. For instance, the effects of large-scale reforms take a long time to observe — making it hard to disentangle the effects of private entry, for example, from those of other reforms or events.

The gaps in knowledge around questions 1–3 suggest pathways for future research. In addition, the variety of impacts observed suggests that the effect of competition from private schools may be endogenous to how it is designed. For example, it may be that to successfully enhance the effects of competition from private schools it is not enough to introduce vouchers that are generally in the spirit of Friedman (1962), but that careful attention must be put on the design of these vouchers and/or the rules that govern private entry. Further the effects of competition-related policies may depend on context (Hanushek et al., 2013). Exploring this may be a productive area for future research.

ACKNOWLEDGMENTS

For useful conversations and/or comments, I am thankful to Dennis Epple, Eric Hanushek, Chang-Tai Hsieh, Stephen Machin, Bentley MacLeod, Evan Riehl, Richard Romano, and Ludger Woessmann. All remaining errors are my own.

REFERENCES

Abdulkadiroglu, A., Angrist, J., Pathak, P., 2014. The elite illusion: achievement effects at Boston and New York exam schools. Econometrica 82 (1), 137–196.

Adams, M., 2009. Tomorrow's schools today: New Zealand's experiment 20 years on. Mercatus Center, George Mason University. Mimeo.

Ahlin, A., 2003. Does school competition matter? Effects of a large-scale school choice reform on student performance. Department of Economics, Uppsala University, Working Paper 2003:2.

Andrabi, T., Das, J., Khwaja, A., 2008. A dime a day: the possibilities and limits of private schooling in Pakistan. Comp. Educ. Rev. 52 (3), 329–355.

Angrist, J., Bettinger, E., Bloom, E., Kremer, M., King, E., 2002. The effect of school vouchers on students: evidence from Colombia. Am. Econ. Rev. 92 (5), 1535–1558.

Angrist, J., Bettinger, E., Kremer, M., 2006. Long-term consequences of secondary school vouchers: evidence from administrative records in Colombia. Am. Econ. Rev. 96 (3), 847–862.

Auguste, S., Valenzuela, J.P., 2006. Is it just cream skimming? School vouchers in Chile. Fundacion de Investigaciones Economicas Latinoamericanas. Mimeo.

Barrow, L., Rouse, C., 2009. School vouchers and student achievement: recent evidence and remaining questions. Am. Rev. Econ. 1, 17–42.

Bellei, C., 2007. The private-public school controversy: the case of Chile. Harvard PEPG Working Paper 05-13. Working paper.

Bettinger, E., Kremer, M., Saavedra, J.E., 2010. Are educational vouchers only redistributive? Econ. J. 120 (546), F204–F228.

Bjorklund, A., Clark, M., Edin, P.A., Frederiksson, P., Krueger, A., 2005. The Market Comes to Education in Sweden. Russell Sage Foundation, New York.

Bohlmark, A., Lindahl, M., 2007. The impact of school choice on pupil achievement, segregation and costs: Swedish evidence. IZA Working Paper 2786. Mimeo.

Bohlmark, A., Lindahl, M., 2008. Does school privatization improve educational achievement? Evidence from Sweden's voucher reform. IZA Working Paper 3691. Mimeo.

Bohlmark, A., Lindahl, M., 2012. Independent schools and long-run educational outcomes: Evidence from Sweden's large scale voucher reform. IZA Working Paper 6683. Mimeo.

Bravo, D., Mukhopadhyay, S., Todd, P., 2010. Effects of school reform on education and labor market performance: evidence from Chile's universal voucher system. Quant. Econ. 1 (2), 47–95.

Card, D., Giuliano, L., 2014. Does gifted education work? For which students? National Bureau of Economic Research Working Paper No. 20453. Mimeo.

Carrell, S.E., Sacerdote, B.I., West, J.E., 2013. From natural variation to optimal policy? The importance of endogenous peer group formation. Econometrica 81 (3), 855–882.

Chakrabarti, R., 2013. Do vouchers lead to sorting under random private school selection? Evidence from the Milwaukee voucher program. Econ. Educ. Rev. 34, 191–218.

Chan, P., McMillan, R., 2009. School choice and public school performance: evidence from Ontario's tuition tax credit. University of Toronto. Mimeo.

Chingos, M., Peterson, P., 2012. The effects of school vouchers on college enrollment. Brookings Institution. Mimeo.

Clark, D., 2010. Selective schools and academic achievement. B.E. J. Econ. Anal. Policy Adv. 10, 1.

Clotfelter, C., 1998. Public school segregation in metropolitan areas. National Bureau of Economic Research Working Paper No. 6779. Mimeo.

Cullen, J., Jacob, B., Levitt, S., 2005. The effect of school choice on student outcomes: an analysis of the Chicago public schools. J. Public Econ. 89 (5–6), 729–760.

Cullen, J.B., Jacob, B.A., Levitt, S.D., 2006. The effect of school choice on student outcomes: evidence from randomized lotteries. Econometrica 74 (5), 1191–1230.

Dale, S.B., Krueger, A.B., 2002. Estimating the payoff to attending a more selective college: an application of selection on observables and unobservables. Q. J. Econ. 117 (4), 1491–1527.

Dale, S.B., Krueger, A.B., 2014. Estimating the effects of college characteristics over the career using administrative earnings data. J. Hum. Resour. 49 (2), 323–358.

Duflo, E., Dupas, P., Kremer, M., 2011. Peer effects, teacher incentives, and the impact of tracking: evidence from a randomized evaluation in Kenya. Am. Econ. Rev. 101 (5), 1739–1774.

Epple, D., Romano, R.E., 1998. Competition between private and public schools, vouchers, and peer-group effects. Am. Econ. Rev. 88 (1), 33–62.

Epple, D., Romano, R.E., 2008. Competition between private and public schools, vouchers, and peer-group effects. Int. Econ. Rev. 49, 1395–1435.

Epple, D., Romano, R.E., 2011. Peer effects in education: a survey of the theory and evidence. In: Benhabib, J., Bisin, A., Jackson, M. (Eds.), Handbook of Social Economics. Elsevier Science, North Holland.

Epple, D., Romano, R., Urquiola, M., 2015. School vouchers: a survey of the economics literature. J. Econ. Lit. NBER Working Paper No. 21523.

Figlio, D., Hart, C., 2006. Do accountability and voucher threats improve low-performing schools? J. Public Econ. 90, 239–255.

Figlio, D., Hart, C., 2014. Competitive effects of means-tested school vouchers. Am. Econ. J. Appl. Econ. 6 (1), 133–156.

Fisman, R., 2014. Sweden's school choice disaster. Slate, July 14, 2014.

Friedman, M., 1955. The role of government in education. In: Solo, R. (Ed.), Economics and the Public Interest. Trustees of Rutgers College, New Brunswick, NJ.

Friedman, M., 1962. Capitalism and Freedom. University of Chicago Press, Chicago.

Galiani, S., Schargrodsky, E., 2002. Evaluating the impact of school decentralization on education quality. Economia 20 (2), 275–314.

Gallego, F., 2006. Voucher school competition, incentives, and outcomes: evidence from Chile. MIT. Mimeo.

Gauri, V., 1998. School Choice in Chile. University of Pittsburgh Press, Pittsburgh.

Gill, P., Timpane, M., Ross, K., Brewer, J., Booker, K., 2007. Rhetoric versus reality: what we know and what we need to know about vouchers and charter schools. Rand Corporation. Mimeo.

Greene, J., Peterson, P., Du, J., 1996. The effectiveness of school choice: the Milwaukee experiment. Harvard University Education Policy and Governance Occasional Paper 97 1. Mimeo.

Hanushek, E., Peterson, P., Woessmann, L., 2012. Achievement growth: international and U.S. State trends in student performance. Program on Education Policy and Government Report No. 12-03, Taubman Center for State and Local Government, Harvard Kennedy School. Mimeo.

Hanushek, E.A., Link, S., Woessmann, L., 2013. Does school autonomy make sense everywhere? Panel estimates from PISA. J. Dev. Econ. 104, 212–232.

Howell, W.G., Wolf, P.J., Campbell, D.E., Peterson, P.E., 2002. School vouchers and academic performance: results from three randomized field trials. J. Policy Anal. Manage. 21 (2), 191–217.

Hoxby, C., 2000. Does competition among public schools benefit students and taxpayers? Am. Econ. Rev. 90 (5), 1209–1238.

Hoxby, C., 2002. How school choice affects the achievement of public school students. In: Hill, P. (Ed.), Choice With Equity. Hoover Press, Stanford.

Hoxby, C., 2002. School choice and school productivity (or could school choice be a tide that lifts all boats?). National Bureau of Economic Research. NBER Working paper.

Hsieh, C.T., Urquiola, M., 2003. When schools compete, how do they compete? An assessment of Chile's nationwide school voucher program. National Bureau of Economic Research Working Paper No. 10008. Mimeo.

Hsieh, C.T., Urquiola, M., 2006. The effects of generalized school choice on achievement and stratification: evidence from Chile's school voucher program. J. Public Econ. 90, 1477–1503.

Jackson, C.K., 2010. Do students benefit from attending better schools? Evidence from rule based student assignments in Trinidad and Tobago. Econ. J. 120 (549), 1399–1429.

Justesen, M., 2002. Learning from Europe: the Dutch and Danish school systems. Adam Smith Institute Mimeo. Mimeo.

King, E., Rawlings, L., Gutierrez, M., Pardo, C., Torres, C., 1997. Colombia's targeted education voucher program: features, coverage, and participation. The World Bank Series on Impact Evaluation of Education Reforms Working Paper No. 3. Mimeo.

Krueger, A., Zhu, P., 2004. Another look at the New York City voucher experiment. Am. Behav. Sci. 47 (5), 658–698.

Ladd, H., 2002. School vouchers: a critical view. J. Econ. Perspect. 16 (4), 3–24.

Ladd, H., Fiske, E., 2001. The uneven playing field of school choice: evidence from New Zealand. J. Policy Anal. Manage. 20 (1), 43–64.

Levin, J., 2004. Differences in educational production between Dutch public and religious schools. National Center for the Study of Privatization in Education Occasional Paper 93. Mimeo.

Levin, H., 2008. Issues in educational privatization. In: Fiske, E., Ladd, H. (Eds.), Handbook of Research in Education Finance and Policy. Routledge, New York, NY, pp. 391–401.

Lubienski, C., Lee, J., Gordon, L., 2013. School autonomy and equity in the New Zealand education market: a geographic analysis of organizational behavior and access. University of Illinois. Mimeo.

MacLeod, W.B., Urquiola, M., 2009. Anti-lemons: school reputation and educational quality. National Bureau of Economic Research Working Paper No. 15112.

MacLeod, W.B., Urquiola, M., 2013. Competition and educational productivity: incentives writ large. In: Glewwe, P. (Ed.), Education Policy in Developing Countries. University of Chicago Press, Chicago, pp. 127–145.

MacLeod, W.B., Urquiola, M., 2015. Reputation and school competition. Am. Econ. Rev. 105 (11), 3471–3488.

MacLeod, W.B., Riehl, E., Saavedra, J.E., Urquiola, M., 2015. The big sort: college reputation and labor market outcomes. National Bureau of Economic Research Working Paper No. 21230. Mimeo.

Manski, C., 1992. Educational choice (vouchers) and social mobility. Econ. Educ. Rev. 11 (4), 351–369.

Mayer, D., Peterson, P., Myers, D., Tuttle, C., Howell, W., 2002. School choice in New York City after three years: an evaluation of the school choice scholarships program: final report. Mathematica Policy Research, Inc.

Mbiti, I., Lucas, A., 2009. Access, sorting, and achievement: the short-run effects of free primary education in Kenya. Southern Methodist University.

McEwan, P., 2004. The potential impact of vouchers. Peabody J. Educ. 79 (3), 57–80.

McEwan, P., Carnoy, M., 2000. The effectiveness and efficiency of private schools in Chile's voucher system. Educ. Eval. Policy Anal. 22 (3), 213–239.

McEwan, P., Urquiola, M., Vegas, E., 2008. School choice, stratification, and information on school performance. Economia 8 (2), 1–42.

McMillan, P., 2005. Competition, incentives, and public school productivity. J. Public Econ. 89, 1131–1154.

Mizala, A., Urquiola, M., 2013. Parental choice and school markets: the impact of information on school effectiveness. J. Dev. Econ. 103, 313–335.

Muralidharan, K., Sundararaman, V., 2015. The aggregate effect of school choice: evidence from a two-stage experiment in India. Q. J. Econ. 130 (3), 1011–1066.

Neal, D., 2002. How vouchers could change the market for education. J. Econ. Perspect. 16 (4), 25–44.

Neal, D., 2009. Private schools in education markets. In: Berends, M., Springer, M., Balou, D., Walberg, H. (Eds.), Handbook of Research on School Choice. Routledge, New York, NY.

Neilson, C., 2013. Targeted vouchers, competition among schools, and the academic achievement of poor students. Yale University. Unpublished manuscript.

Patrinos, H., 2002. Private educational provision and public finance: The Netherlands as a possible model. National Center for the Study of Privatization in Education Occasional Paper No. 59. Working Paper.

Peterson, P., Howell, W., Wolf, P., Campbell, D., 2003. School vouchers: results from randomized experiments. In: Hoxby, C. (Ed.), The Economics of School Choice. The University of Chicago Press, Chicago, pp. 107–144.

Pop-Eleches, C., Urquiola, M., 2013. Going to a better school: effects and behavioral responses. Am. Econ. Rev. 103 (4), 1289–1324.

Rothstein, J., 2007. Does competition among public schools benefit students and taxpayers? Comment. Am. Econ. Rev. 95 (5), 2026–2037.

Rouse, C., 1998. Private school vouchers and student achievement: an evaluation of the Milwaukee parental choice program. Q. J. Econ. 113 (2), 553–602.

Sacerdote, B., 2011. Peer effects in education: how might they work, how big are they, and how much do we know thus far? In: Hanushek, E., Machin, S., Woessmann, L. (Eds.), Handbook of Education. Washington, D.C.

Sandstrom, M., Bergstrom, F., 2005. School vouchers in practice: competition won't hurt you. J. Public Econ. 89, 351–380.

Smith, A., 1776. The Wealth of Nations. W. Strahan and T. Cadell, London.

Spence, M., 1973. Job market signaling. Q. J. Econ. 3, 355–374.

Tyrefors Hinnerich, B., Vlachos, J., 2013. Systematiska skillnader mellan interna och externa bedömningar av nationella prov en uppföljningsrapport. Appendix 5 in "Olikheterna är för stora. Omrättning av nationella prov i grund och gymnasieskolan 2013", Skolinspektionen Dnr U2011/6544/GV. Mimeo.

Urquiola, M., 2005. Does school choice lead to sorting? Evidence from Tiebout variation. Am. Econ. Rev. 95 (4), 1310–1326.

Urquiola, M., 2015. Progress and challenges in achieving an evidence-based education policy. Latin Am. Econ. Rev. 24 (12).

Urquiola, M., Verhoogen, E., 2009. Class-size caps, sorting, and the regression discontinuity design. Am. Econ. Rev. 99 (1), 179–215.

Valenzuela, J., Bellei, C., De Los Rios, D., 2013. Socioeconomic school segregation in a market-oriented educational system. the case of Chile. J. Educ. Policy 29, 1–24.

Witte, J.F., Sterr, T., Thorn, C., 1995. Fifth year report: Milwaukee parental choice program. University of Wisconsin. Mimeo.

Witte, J.F., Carlson, D., Cowen, J.M., Fleming, D., Wolf, P., 2012. Voucher longitudinal educational growth study fifth year report. SCDP Evaluation Report. Mimeo.

Wolfe, P., Gutmann, B., Puma, M., Kisida, B., Rizzo, L., Eissa, N., Carr, M., 2010. Evaluation of the D.C. opportunity scholarship program final report. National Center for Education Evaluation. Mimeo.

Wolfe, P., Kisida, B., Gutmann, B., Puma, M., Eissa, N., Rizzo, L., 2013. School vouchers and student outcomes: experimental evidence from Washington, DC. J. Policy Anal. Manage. 32 (2), 246–270.

CHAPTER 5

Technology and Education: Computers, Software, and the Internet

G. Bulman, R.W. Fairlie
University of California, Santa Cruz, California, United States

Contents

Abstract

A substantial amount of money is spent on technology by schools, families, and policymakers with the hope of improving educational outcomes. This chapter explores the theoretical and empirical literature on the impacts of technology on educational outcomes. The literature focuses on two primary contexts in which technology may be used for educational purposes: (i) classroom use in schools and (ii) home use by students. Theoretically, information and communications technology (ICT) investment and computer-aided instruction (CAI) use by schools and the use of computers at home have ambiguous implications for educational achievement; expenditures devoted to technology necessarily offset inputs that may be more or less efficient, and time allocated to using technology may displace traditional classroom instruction and educational activities at home. However, much of the evidence in the schooling literature is based on interventions that provide supplemental funding for technology or additional class time, and thus favor finding positive effects. Nonetheless, studies of ICT and CAI in schools produce mixed evidence with a pattern of null results. Notable exceptions to this pattern occur in studies of developing countries and CAI interventions that target math rather than language. In the context of home use, early studies based on multivariate and instrumental variables approaches tend to find large positive (and in a few cases negative) effects while recent studies based on randomized control experiments tend to find small or null effects. Early research focused on developed countries while more recently several experiments have been conducted in developing countries.

Keywords

Computers, Software, Internet, Technology, Schoolchildren, Education, ICT

Handbook of the Economics of Education, Volume 5
ISSN 1574-0692, http://dx.doi.org/10.1016/B978-0-444-63459-7.00005-1

1. INTRODUCTION

Schools and families around the world spend a substantial amount of money on computers, software, Internet connections, and other technology for educational purposes. The use of technology is ubiquitous in the educational system in most developed countries. For example, essentially all instructional classrooms in US public schools have computers with Internet access (U.S. Department of Education, 2013). Most countries in Europe also have high rates of computer access in schools (European Commission, 2013). In addition to school level investment in technology, central governments frequently play an active role in providing or subsidizing investment in computer and Internet access. The US federal government spends more than $2 billion and recently increased the spending cap to $3.9 billion per year on the E-rate program, which provides discounts to schools and libraries for the costs of telecommunications services and equipment (Federal Communications Commission, 2014; Puma et al., 2000; Universal Services Administration Company, 2010). England provided free computers to nearly 300,000 low-income families at a total cost of £194 million through the Home Access Programme.[1] A growing number of schools are experimenting with one-to-one laptop or tablet programs that provide a computer to each student and often allow the student to take the computer home (Maine Education Policy Research Institute, 2007; Texas Center for Educational Research, 2009; Warschauer, 2006).[2] These programs are potentially expensive — for example, equipping each of the 50 million public school students in the United States with a laptop would cost tens of billions of dollars each year even if these laptops were replaced only every 3 years.

Families also spend a substantial amount of money on computers, software, and Internet connections each year. In the United States, for example, 86% of schoolchildren have access to a computer at home. Although current levels of access to home computers and Internet connections among schoolchildren are very high, access is not evenly distributed across countries or across the population within countries. Less than one-quarter of schoolchildren in Indonesia, for example, have access to a computer at home that they can use for schoolwork. In the United States, 98% of the 12 million schoolchildren living in households with $100,000 or more in income have access to a computer at home, but only 67% of the 12 million schoolchildren living in households with less than $25,000 in income have access. These disparities in access to home computers and the Internet are known as the Digital Divide.

---

[1] The Euro 200 Program in Romania and the Yo Elijo Mi PC Program in Chile are additional examples of government programs providing computers to low-income children.
[2] Extensive efforts to provide laptops to schoolchildren also exist in many developing countries. For example, the One Laptop per Child program has provided more than 2 million computers to schools in Uruguay, Peru, Argentina, Mexico, and Rwanda, and started new projects in Gaza, Afghanistan, Haiti, Ethiopia, and Mongolia. See http://one.laptop.org/about/countries.

A better understanding of how computer technology affects educational outcomes is critical because it sheds light on whether such technology is an important input in the educational production process and whether disparities in access will translate into educational inequality. This chapter explores the theory and literature on the impacts of technology on educational outcomes. Although technology is a broad term, the chapter focuses on the effects of computers, the Internet, and software such as computer-assisted instruction, which are currently the most relevant forms of new technology in education.[3] The discussion focuses primarily on the impacts of computers, the Internet and software on educational outcomes instead of impacts on other forms of human capital such as computer skills (although we discuss several such studies).[4] We consider studies that examine the impacts of technology on measurable educational outcomes, such as grades, test scores, retention, graduation, and attendance. Attention is also largely, but not entirely, restricted to studies from the economics literature.

The literature focuses on two primary contexts in which technology may be used for educational purposes: (i) classroom use in schools and (ii) home use by students. These contexts differ fundamentally in terms of who makes the investment decision and who controls how the technology is used. Districts and schools determine the level of technology investment and control how it is used in the classroom to aid instruction. Parents and students make decisions over investment in computers, the Internet, software, and other technologies at home. One unifying theme of the discussion is that the use of technology is placed in the context of educational production functions commonly discussed in the economics literature.

Investment in computer hardware, software, and connectivity may offset other inputs that affect student achievement in the context of the household and the school. Likewise, time spent using computers offsets other educational or recreational activities. We discuss the extent to which the estimates in the literature reflect these tradeoffs. Investment in computers for schools is divided into two broad areas: (i) investment in information and communications technologies (ICTs) generally, such as computer hardware and Internet connections and (ii) specific software used for computer-aided instruction (CAI). Computer use at home poses a unique challenge for estimation as the context is less conducive

---

[3] The Census Bureau and Bureau of Labor Statistics define personal computers as "desktop, laptop, netbook, notebook or tablet computers" in the latest Current Population Survey (2012).

[4] Computer skills training (CST) or computer science, which are vocational or academic subjects with benefits in the labor market, have generally been of less interest in the area of the economics of education. Angrist and Lavy (2002) note that "CST skills seems undeniably useful, just as typing was a useful skill taught in American high schools earlier in the twentieth century, but most of the recent interest in the educational use of computers focuses on CAI and not CST." We also do not focus on the analysis of the relationship between technology and the labor market for which there has been an extensive literature. See Autor (2001), Autor et al. (1998), DiMaggio and Bonikowski (2008), DiNardo and Pischke (1997), Freeman (2002), and Krueger (1993) for a few examples.

to policy interventions and randomized trials. We examine the literature based on cross-sectional evaluations relative to more recent studies based on experimental and quasi-experimental designs.

Section 2.1 discusses rates of computer use in schools. Section 2.2 highlights important theoretical considerations when interpreting estimates of the effects of technology in schools. Section 2.3 presents estimates from studies focusing on ICT and CAI investment in schools. Section 3.1 presents rates of access to computers at home, and Section 3.2 discusses theoretical considerations. Section 3.3 presents estimates of the effects of home computer use with an emphasis on differences in research design. Section 4 concludes and offers suggestions for future research.

2. TECHNOLOGY USE IN SCHOOLS

2.1 Estimates of Rates of Technology Use in Schools

Access to computers in public schools has increased manifold in the last 30 years. In the United States, there were only 0.008 computers per student in 1984, or 1 computer per 125 students (Coley et al., 1997). Fig. 1 displays recent trends in the number of computers per student based on data from the National Center for Educational Statistics (NCES). As recently as 1998, there were 0.15 computers per student and only half of these computers had Internet access. The most recent data available from the NCES, which is from 2008, indicates that there are 0.32 computers per student and essentially all computers have Internet access.

Germany, the United Kingdom, Japan, and other OECD countries also have high levels of computer access. Table 1 reports the average number of computers available per student for the 50 most populous countries in the world with data reported in the 2012 Programme for International Student Assessment (PISA) conducted by the OECD. These data indicate that there are 0.95 computers per 15-year-old student in the United States, 1.02 in the United Kingdom, 0.65 in Germany, and 0.56 in Japan. PISA data contain, to the best of our knowledge, the most uniform measure of computer access across all countries, but provide estimates of the number of computers per student that are much higher than most other sources. For example, the PISA estimates are nearly three times higher for the United States than those reported by the NCES, which is likely partly due to counting the number of "available" computers to students of a specific age, including those shared with students in other grades, but is also partly due to the most recent NCES data being from 2008.[5]

---

[5] To create their measure of computers per student, PISA uses responses to the following two questions: "At your school, what is the total number of students in the <national modal grade for 15-year-olds>?," and "Approximately, how many computers are available for these students for educational purposes?" This measure is different than those collected by other institutions such as the U.S. Department of Education, the European Commission, and UNESCO. These institutions consider the total number of school computers and the total number of school students.

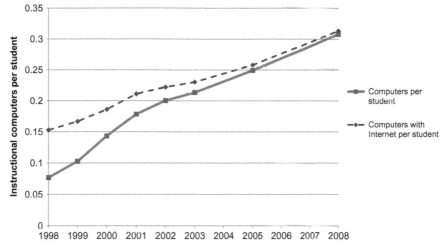

Figure 1 Number of instructional computers and instructional computers with Internet access per public school student. *Source: U.S. National Center for Educational Statistics, from various years of the Digest of Educational Statistics.*

Table 1 Number of available computers in school for each student, Programme for International Student Assessment (PISA), OECD 2012

Country	Available computers per student	Proportion of computers with Internet
Argentina	0.49	0.71
Australia	1.53	1.00
Austria	1.47	0.99
Belgium	0.72	0.97
Brazil	0.20	0.92
Bulgaria	0.56	0.97
Canada	0.84	1.00
Chile	0.49	0.95
Colombia	0.48	0.71
Costa Rica	0.53	0.83
Croatia	0.32	0.96
Czech Republic	0.92	0.99
Denmark	0.83	0.99
Finland	0.46	1.00
France	0.60	0.96
Germany	0.65	0.98
Greece	0.24	0.99
Hong Kong	0.73	1.00
Hungary	0.64	0.99
Indonesia	0.16	0.56

Continued

Table 1 Number of available computers in school for each student, Programme for International Student Assessment (PISA), OECD 2012—cont'd

Country	Available computers per student	Proportion of computers with Internet
Ireland	0.64	1.00
Israel	0.38	0.91
Italy	0.48	0.96
Japan	0.56	0.97
Jordan	0.35	0.84
Kazakhstan	0.80	0.57
Korea (South)	0.40	0.97
Malaysia	0.19	0.87
Mexico	0.28	0.73
Netherlands	0.68	1.00
New Zealand	1.10	0.99
Norway	0.79	0.99
Peru	0.40	0.65
Poland	0.36	0.98
Portugal	0.46	0.97
Romania	0.54	0.95
Russia	0.58	0.82
Serbia	0.24	0.83
Singapore	0.67	0.99
Slovak Republic	0.77	0.99
Spain	0.67	0.99
Sweden	0.63	0.99
Switzerland	0.68	0.99
Thailand	0.48	0.95
Tunisia	0.51	0.63
Turkey	0.14	0.96
United Arab Emirates	0.69	0.83
United Kingdom	1.02	0.99
United States	0.95	0.94
Vietnam	0.24	0.80

Note: To create the measure of computers per student, PISA uses responses to the following two questions: "At your school, what is the total number of students in the <national modal grade for 15-year-olds>?," and "Approximately, how many computers are available for these students for educational purposes?."

Table 2 presents the results of the European Commission's survey of school computer access and use. The survey reveals rates of computer access more similar to those in the United States for several countries, including Austria, Denmark, and Spain. Across all EU countries represented in the study, there are 0.20 computers per student in the 8th grade and 0.33 computers per student in the 11th grade. More than 50% of middle school students in the EU reported using a computer during lessons at least once each week.

Table 2 Number of computers in school per student, European Commission 2012

Country	4th Grade	8th Grade	11th Grade general	11th Grade vocational
Austria	0.13	0.23	0.55	0.18
Belgium	0.13	0.24	0.35	0.29
Cyprus	0.16	0.29	0.64	0.29
Czech Republic	0.18	0.21	0.29	0.20
Denmark	0.33	0.31	0.22	0.51
Estonia	0.24	0.28	0.26	0.21
European Union	0.16	0.20	0.33	0.24
Finland	0.17	0.21	0.52	0.25
France	0.13	0.19	0.38	0.29
Greece	0.06	0.05	0.06	0.08
Hungary	0.16	0.18	0.24	0.19
Ireland	0.14	0.21		0.21
Italy	0.06	0.09	0.18	0.09
Latvia	0.15	0.17	0.20	0.16
Lithuania	0.11	0.20	0.27	0.17
Luxembourg	0.23			
Malta	0.32	0.12		0.15
Poland	0.13	0.14	0.17	0.13
Portugal	0.12	0.18	0.29	0.18
Slovakia	0.16	0.17	0.27	0.19
Slovenia	0.13	0.13	0.73	0.22
Spain	0.31	0.31	0.45	0.23
Sweden	0.29	0.70		0.89

Note: Data from Digital Agenda for Europe: A Europe 2020 Initiative, European Commission.

It is clear that the computer has become a regular part of classroom instruction in developed countries.[6]

Interestingly, in the United States, schools serving students from the lowest income households have an almost identical number of computers per student as schools serving wealthier households (U.S. Department of Education, 2013), though the quality of these computers may differ. However, there is a notable digital divide across countries. Many developing countries still have relatively low rates of computer and Internet access. PISA reports computer access rates in Brazil, Romania, Turkey, and Vietnam that are approximately one-fourth those in developed countries. UNESCO (2014) reports that the

---

[6] Simple counts of computers and Internet connections provide only a general sense of each country's level of technology adoption. Potentially important differences in the quality of technology and the intensity of technology use (e.g. hours per day) are rarely documented in a systematic way.

Philippines has more than 400 students per computer.[7] Due to a lack of uniform data over time, it is difficult to determine the rate at which computer access is changing in many countries and how persistent the digital divide is likely to be (Table 4).

2.2 Theoretical Issues

Access to computers in schools may improve student outcomes in several ways. Computer software has the potential to provide self-paced instruction that is typically difficult to achieve in group instruction (Koedinger et al., 1997). Likewise, the content of instruction may be individualized to the strengths and weaknesses of the student. Because students can use instructional programs without the direct supervision of a teacher, ICTs and CAI hold the promise of increasing the overall amount of instruction that students receive (Barrow et al., 2009; Cuban, 1993), while still allowing parents and teachers to monitor student progress. The Internet represents a potentially valuable resource for finding out information about a wide range of educational topics and for reducing the coordination costs of group projects. Computers, the Internet, software, and other technologies, because of their interactive nature, may engage schoolchildren in ways that traditional methods cannot (Cuban, 2001). Further, enhanced computer skills may alter the economic returns to education, especially in fields in which computers are used extensively. These factors, in addition to the direct benefits of being computer literate in the workplace, society and higher education, are behind the decision to invest in ICT and CAI in schools.

The most relevant policy question of interest is whether schools are choosing the optimal levels of technology relative to traditional inputs. That is, with limited financial resources and instructional time, can schools, district, states, or countries increase academic achievement by investing more in technology. The answer to this question necessarily involves a trade-off between inputs. Financial investment in computers, Internet connections, software, and other ICTs is likely to offset investment in traditional resources such as teachers and textbooks. Likewise, time spent using computers in the classroom may offset traditional group instruction by the teacher or independent learning by the student. These tradeoffs imply that the theoretical predictions of the effect of ICT and CAI investment are ambiguous.

Computer resources can be added to a standard model of education production (for examples in the literature see Figlio, 1999; Hanushek, 1979, 1986; Rivkin et al., 2005; Todd and Wolpin, 2003). The binding constraints in such models are the budget for school resources and the amount of class time available for instruction. With these

---

[7] The United Nations Educational, Scientific and Cultural Organization (UNESCO) Institute for Statistics has recently been tasked with improving global data on ICT availability and use (UNESCO, 2009). While UNESCO has produced reports for several regions since 2012 (Latin America, the Caribbean, and the Arab States), the coverage is still quite limited.

constraints, the comparison of interest is the effectiveness of a dollar invested in ICT relative to a dollar invested in traditional school resources and, analogously, the effectiveness of an hour of classroom time allocated to CAI relative to an hour of traditional instruction. In practice, however, the literature frequently estimates the effect of supplemental investment in ICT and supplemental class time using CAI.[8] These estimates of the effect of ICT and CAI reflect whether technology can have a positive effect on education in the absence of constraints.

We consider a model of value-added education that provides a framework in which to discuss the empirical studies discussed in the following section.[9]

$$A_{it} = f\left(X_{it}, A_{it-1}, S_{it}, C_{it}, T_{it}^{S}, T_{it}^{C}\right) \text{ s.t. } P_t^S S_{it} + P_t^C C_{it} \le B_t \text{ and } T_{it}^S + T_{it}^C \le T \quad (1)$$

A measure of academic achievement, A_{it}, is assumed to depend on the characteristics of a student and his or her family, X_{it}, prior year achievement, A_{it-1}, investment in traditional and computer resources, S_{it} and C_{it}, and time allocated to traditional and computer instruction, T_{it}^S and T_{it}^C. The investments S_{it} and C_{it} can be thought of as a per-student average allocation if they are not chosen at the student level, subject to prices P_t^S and P_t^C and a per-student budget B_{it}. Likewise, the amount of time spent on traditional and computer instruction is constrained by total available instructional time T. Note that this model could also be considered at the level of a specific subject of interest. Conversely, if schools or districts cannot choose individual specific input levels, academic outcomes and inputs could be in the aggregate (e.g. the median score on a math exam).

If schools choose the optimal levels of investment and time allocation, then an exogenous reallocation toward technology will result in a negative or zero effect on the educational outcome. If schools do not make optimal choices, then the resulting change is likely to depend on several factors. Shifting investment to technology may have a direct effect on the quality of instruction. Greater investment in technology could improve the effectiveness of time dedicated to computer-based instruction and the corresponding reduction in traditional resources may reduce the effectiveness of time dedicated to traditional instruction. Of course, complementarities between certain technologies and teacher skills could offset some of the negative effect on traditional instruction. These effects, holding the respective time allocations fixed, will be positive if $\partial A / \partial C > \partial A / \partial S$. However, schools may change the allocation of instructional time in response to the change in resources. For example, a school with more computers may allocate more time to computer-based instruction and less to group instruction led by a teacher. Thus the total

---

[8] The distinction between estimates based on inputs that are supplements to, rather than substitutes for, traditional instruction is rarely made adequately in the literature. A notable exception is Linden (2008), which makes the distinction the focal point of parallel experiments — one that substitutes for traditional instruction with CAI and another that provides supplemental CAI outside of regular school hours.

[9] See Hanushek (1979) for an early discussion of value-added models in the economics of education literature.

effect of changing the allocation of financial resources may also reflect a reallocation of instructional time, $[\partial A/\partial C + \partial A/\partial T^C * \partial T^C/\partial C] - [\partial A/\partial S + \partial A/\partial T^S * \partial T^S/\partial S]$.

This model can be extended to account for different assumptions about the allocation of classroom time. First, computers may increase the total amount of instruction a student receives if teachers must divide their time between group and individual instruction. In this scenario, some traditional class time, T^S, is wasted for students and CAI can fill in these down periods. This should cause increased investment in ICT, and CAI in particular, to be more likely to have a positive effect on educational outcomes. Alternatively, students may use computers for noninstructional activities that offset instructional time. Furthermore, mechanical problems with technology could create instructional downtime. That is, some computer-based instructional time, T^C, may be wasted and thus crowd out more productive instruction. This should cause ICT investment to be more likely to have a negative effect. We discuss each of these adjustments to the model and the implications for interpreting estimates in the literature.

Barrow et al. (2009) propose a model to argue that CAI may increase total instructional time during a class period or school day. They assume that a teacher j divides class time between providing group instruction, T_j^G, and individualized instruction for each student i, T_{ij}. Each student receives group instruction and his or her share of individual instruction. Computer instruction, T_i^C, provides supplemental instruction during periods when the teacher is giving individual instruction to other students. This model differs from the baseline model presented above in that CAI replaces down time rather than traditional instruction. The revised constraints make these trade-offs clear.

$$T_{jt}^G + T_{ijt} + T_{it}^C \leq T \quad \text{and} \quad T_{jt}^G + \sum T_{ijt} \leq T_j \tag{2}$$

The return to computer-based instruction, $\partial A/\partial T^C$, is not offset by a reduction in traditional instruction, $\partial A/\partial T^S$. Modeled in this way, CAI will improve academic outcomes if it provides any academic benefit: $f\left(X_{it}, A_{it-1}, T_{it}, T_t^G, T_{it}^C\right) \geq f\left(X_{it}, A_{it-1}, T_{it}, T_t^G, 0\right)$.[10]

Belo et al. (2014) model a case in which time spent using computers is not necessarily productive. For example, students may use computers to watch videos or engage in social networking activities that do not improve traditional academic outcomes. In this case, computer time T^C is divided between learning time T^L and distraction time T^D. Thus the new time constraint is $T_{it}^S + T_{it} + T_{it}^L + T_{it}^D \leq T$. This implies that the difference in

---

[10] Note that time not allocated to active teacher or computer instruction is modeled to have no academic benefit for the student. In practice, time spent receiving individualized computer instruction is substituting for whatever the students would have been doing during this time, which may have been independent learning. Thus the estimated effect of CAI in this model may be the benefit of CAI relative to independent learning.

the marginal returns, $\partial A/\partial T^C - \partial A/\partial T^S$, depends on both the effectiveness of T^L relative to T^S and the share of T^C that is spent on noninstructional activities. These two models highlight that the effects of CAI estimated in the literature may stem from differences in the quality of the two types of instruction or changes in productive instructional time.

In practice, many empirical studies identify the effects of ICT investment using policies that increase investment in technology at "treated" schools but not at "control" schools without an offsetting reduction in traditional resources. For example, policies exploited by Angrist and Lavy (2002) and Leuven et al. (2007) create some schools that are "winners" and receive larger shares of national ICT investment.[11] These designs seem to favor finding a positive effect relative to a design in which investment must satisfy the budget constraint. Specifically, there does not need to be an offsetting reduction in traditional resources. That is, these designs may estimate $[\partial A/\partial C + \partial A/\partial T^C * \partial T^C/\partial C]$ $-[\partial A/\partial T^S * \partial T^S/\partial S]$ without the offsetting effect $\partial A/\partial S$. Further, there could be an income effect that increases investment in traditional resources (e.g. if funding normally used for computers is used to hire teachers' aides). Thus a positive effect could be found even if the marginal dollar of investment in technology is not more effective than the marginal dollar invested in traditional resources, and (perhaps) even if technology has no benefit for educational production. Despite the fact that these designs favor finding positive effects, they could nonetheless produce negative estimates if time is reallocated to computer-based instruction and this has smaller returns than traditional instruction (e.g. if a high fraction of computer time is noninstructional). It is also possible that schools may reallocate funds away from traditional instruction to maintain or support investments in technology.

An analogous discussion is relevant for interpreting the results in the CAI literature. If CAI substitutes for traditional instruction, then the estimated effect is a comparison of the marginal effects of traditional instruction and CAI (i.e. $\partial A/\partial T^C - \partial A/\partial T^S$). This is the economic and policy question of interest. However, many policies and experiments used to evaluate CAI increase a student's instructional time in a specific subject (e.g. Rouse and Krueger, 2004) or total instructional time (e.g. Banerjee et al., 2007). This occurs when nonacademic classes or classes dedicated to other subjects are reallocated to the subject being considered, or when instruction is offered outside of regular school hours. That is, the estimated effects in the literature frequently reflect an increase in T rather than just an increase in T^C and the corresponding reduction in T^S. Thus the results should be interpreted as some combination of the effect of substituting CAI for traditional instruction and increasing instructional time. It is worth noting that the benefits of CAI, like those of ICT more broadly, may be attenuated if students use computers for nonacademic purposes instead of the intended instruction.

---

[11] Goolsbee and Guryan (2006) exploit the E-Rate subsidy that results in varying prices of computing across schools and thus has both a price and an income effect.

Therefore, many empirical studies on ICT and CAI are structured in favor of finding positive effects on academic outcomes. Interpreting and comparing the estimates in the literature requires careful consideration of whether computer resources are supplementing or substituting for traditional investment. Estimates across studies are also likely to differ due to variation in treatment intensity (the amount of financial investment or the number of hours dedicated to computer use), the duration of the treatment, the quality of the investment, and the quality of the traditional investment or instruction that is offset.

2.3 Empirical Findings
2.3.1 Information and Communication Technologies Investment
Research on the effects of ICT investment in schools has closely mirrored the broader literature on the effects of school investment (see, e.g. Betts, 1996; Hanushek, 2006; Hanushek et al., 1996). Early studies of ICT in the education literature focused on case studies and cross-sectional comparisons (see Kirkpatrick and Cuban, 1998; Noll et al., 2000 for reviews). Studies in the economics literature have often exploited natural policy experiments to generate variation over time in ICT investment (e.g. Angrist and Lavy, 2002; Goolsbee and Guryan, 2006; Leuven et al., 2007; Machin et al., 2007). Recent studies of CAI have generally relied on randomized control trials (RCTs) (e.g. Banerjee et al., 2007; Carrillo et al., 2010; Mathematica, 2009; Mo et al., 2014; Rouse and Krueger, 2004). This section focuses on three important dimensions of variation in the literature: (1) the type of investment (ICT or CAI); (2) the research design (cross-sectional, natural experiment, or RCT); and (3) the interaction of the investment with traditional instruction (supplemental or substituting).

Fuchs and Woessmann (2004) examine international evidence on the correlation between computer access in schools (and homes) and performance on PISA, an internationally administered standardized exam. They show that simple cross-sectional estimates for 32 countries might be biased due to the strong correlation between school computers and other school resources. The authors note that evidence based on cross-sectional differences must be interpreted cautiously. Omitted variables are likely to generate positive bias in cross-country comparisons. However, cross-sectional estimates within countries may exhibit negative bias if governments target resources to schools that serve higher proportions of students from low-income households. Once they control for an extensive set of family background and school characteristics, they find an insignificant relationship between academic achievement and the availability of school computers.

Most recent research on ICT investment has exploited policies that promote investment in computer hardware or Internet access. The majority of studies find that such policies result in increased computer use in schools, but few studies find positive effects on educational outcomes. This is in spite of the fact that many of these studies exploit policies that provide ICT investment that supplements traditional investment. The results suggest that ICT does not generate gains in academic outcomes or that schools allow computer-based instruction to crowd out traditional instruction. Regardless, a null result in this context is a stronger result than if there was a binding constraint that required substitution away from investment and time allocated to other inputs.

Angrist and Lavy (2002) find higher rates of computer availability in more disadvantaged schools in Israel, which may be due to the Israeli school system directing resources to schools on a remedial basis. Thus cross-sectional estimates of the effect of computer access are likely to be biased downward. To address this, the authors exploit a national program that provided computers and computer training for teachers in elementary and middle schools. The allocation of computers was based on which towns and regional authorities applied for the program, with the highest priority given to towns with a high fraction of stand-alone middle schools. They present reduced-form estimates of the effect of the program on student test scores and they use the program as an instrumental variable to estimate the effect of CAI (defined broadly) on test scores.[12] Survey results indicate that the computers were used for instruction, but the authors find negative and insignificant effects of the program on test scores. While the identification strategy estimates the effects of supplemental financial investment in ICT, it did not necessarily result in supplemental class time, so the estimates may reflect the tradeoff between computer aided and traditional instruction. The authors argue that computer use may have displaced other more productive educational activities or consumed school resources that might have prevented a decline in achievement.

The finding that ICT investment generates limited educational gains is common in the literature. Leuven et al. (2007) exploit a policy in the Netherlands that provided additional funding for computers and software to schools with more than 70% disadvantaged students. Using a regression discontinuity design (RDD), they find that while additional funding is not spent on more or newer computers, students do spend more time on a computer in school (presumably due to new software). But the estimates suggest a negative and insignificant effect on most test score outcomes. The authors come to a similar to conclusion as Angrist and Lavy (2002) that computer instruction may be less effective than traditional instruction.

In the United States, Goolsbee and Guryan (2006) examine the federal E-Rate subsidy for Internet investment in California schools. The subsidy rate was tied to a school's fraction of students eligible for a free or reduced lunch, which generated variation in the rate of Internet investment, creating both an income and price effect.[13] Schools that

---

[12] An identifying assumption for the instrumental variables interpretation is that CAI is the sole channel by which computers would positively or negatively affect academic performance.

[13] The authors attempt to exploit discrete cutoffs in prices to implement a regression discontinuity design. Unfortunately, this does not result in a strong enough first stage to generate reliable estimates, so they exploit time variation in a difference-in-differences design.

received larger subsidies had an incentive to offset spending on traditional inputs with spending on Internet access. The authors find increased rates of Internet connectivity in schools, but do not find increases in test scores or other academic outcomes. The authors note that access to the Internet may not improve measurable student achievement and that promoting early adoption of technology may result in schools investing too soon in technologies and thus acquiring inferior or higher-cost products. In a more recent paper, Belo et al. (2014) examine if broadband use generates a distraction that reduces academic performance in Portugal. They find very large negative effects when using proximity to the internet provider as an instrument for the quality of the internet connection and time spent using broadband.

More recently, Cristia et al. (2014) examine the introduction of the Huascaran program in Peru between 2001 and 2006. The program provided hardware and noneducational software to a selected set of schools chosen on the basis of enrollment levels, physical access to the schools, and commitment to adopt computer use. Using various weighting and matching techniques, they find no effect of the program on whether students repeat a grade, drop out, or enroll in secondary school after primary school. These studies highlight the importance of considering the policy estimates in the context of an educational production function that considers classroom inputs and time allocation. Despite ICT funding being supplemental to traditional investment, computers may reduce the use of traditional inputs given time constraints.

There are, however, exceptions to the finding that ICT investment does not generate educational gains. Machin et al. (2007) exploit a change in how government ICT funds are allocated in England to generate variation in the timing of investment. This approach results in generally positive estimates for academic outcomes. The authors note that their results may be positive and significant in part because the schools that experienced the largest increases in ICT investment were already effective and thus may have used the investment efficiently. Barrera-Osorio and Linden (2009) find somewhat inconclusive results with statistically insignificant, but positive point estimates of effects, when they evaluate a randomized experiment at one hundred public schools as part of the "Computers for Education" program in Colombia. The program provided schools with computers and teacher training with an emphasis on language education, but they find that the increase in computer use was not primarily in the intended subject area, Spanish, but rather in computer science classes. Teacher and student surveys reveal that teachers did not incorporate the computers into their curriculum.

A recent trend in educational technology policy is to ensure that every student has his or her own laptop or tablet computer, which is likely to be a much more intensive treatment (in terms of per-student time spent using a computer) than those exploited in the policies discussed above. One of the first large scale one-to-one laptop programs was conducted in Maine in 2002, in which all 7th and 8th grade students and their teachers were provided with laptops to use in school. Comparing writing achievement before and after the introduction of laptops, it was found that writing performance improved by approximately one-third of a standard deviation (Maine Education Policy Research Institute, 2007). Grimes and Warschauer (2008) and Suhr et al. (2010) examine the performance of students at schools that implemented a one laptop program in Farrington School District in California relative to students at nonlaptop schools. They find evidence that junior high school test scores declined in the first year of the program. Likewise, scores in reading declined for 4th grade students during the first year. At both grade levels, however, the scores increased in the second year, offsetting the initial decline. This pattern may reflect the fixed costs of adopting computer technology effectively. The changes in these cases are relatively modest in magnitude, but are statistically significant.

A study of the Texas laptop program by the Texas Center for Educational Research (2009) exploited trends in 21 schools that adopted the program relative to a matched control group. Schools were matched on factors including district and campus size, region proportion of economically disadvantaged and minority students, and performance on the Texas Assessment of Knowledge and Skills (TAKS). The laptop program was found to have some positive effects on educational outcomes. Cristia et al. (2012) were able to exploit a government implemented RCT to estimate the effect of a laptop policy in Peru. After 15 months, they find no significant effect on math or language test scores and small positive effects on cognitive skills.

Taken as a whole, the literature examining the effect of ICT investment is characterized by findings of little or no positive effect on most academic outcomes. The exception to this is mixed positive effects of one-laptop initiatives. The modest returns to computer investment is especially informative in light of the fact that nearly all of the estimates are based on policies and experiments that provided supplemental ICT investment. The lack of positive effects is consistent across studies that exploit policy variation and RCTs. Because these initiatives do not necessarily increase class time, the findings may suggest that technology-aided instruction is not superior to traditional instruction. This finding may be highly dependent on specifically what technology is adopted and how it is integrated into a school's curriculum. The studies above generally do not specify the way in which ICT was used. In the next section, we examine studies that focus on the use of specific, well-defined software programs to promote mathematics and language learning.

2.3.2 Computer-Assisted Instruction

CAI is the use of specific software programs on computers in the classroom.[14] Frequently these programs are individualized or self-paced in order to accommodate differences in student ability or speed. CAI lends itself to evaluation using RCTs because access to software can be offered at the student or classroom level. CAI frequently targets a specific

---

[14] Computer-aided instruction (CAI), computer-aided learning (CAL), and E-learning are used synonymously in the economics and education literatures.

subject area that is tested before and after the software is introduced. Kulik and Kulik (1991) and Liao (1992) summarize the early education literature, which generally suggests positive effects. The evidence from economic studies is mixed and suggests that the characteristics of the intervention are important. Studies in this area differ significantly in the extent to which CAI is a substitute or a supplement to traditional instruction. Interestingly, evidence of positive effects appears to be the strongest in developing countries. This could be due to the fact that the instruction that is being substituted for is not as of high quality in these countries.[15]

Rouse and Krueger's (2004) evaluation of "Fast ForWord," a language and reading program, is one of the earliest examples of evaluating a specific CAI using an RCT. They conducted a randomized study that exploited within-school, within-grade variation at four schools that serve a high fraction of nonnative English speakers in the northeastern United States. The intervention pulled students out of their otherwise scheduled classes to receive 90–100 min of individualized CAI. The instruction these students missed was not necessarily in reading and language, so treated students received supplemental instruction in this subject area as a result. Despite the construction of the experiment, which favors gains in reading and language skills, they find little to no positive effects across a range of standardized tests that should be correlated with reading and language skills. The authors argue that computers may not be as effective as traditional classroom instruction.

In a large randomized study, the U.S. Department of Education and Mathematica Policy Research (2007; 2009) evaluated six reading and four math software products for students in elementary, middle, and high school. Randomization was across teachers within the same schools. Nine of the ten products were found to have no statistically significant effect, while the tenth product (used for 4th grade reading) had a positive effect. The study also examined how usage and effects changed between the first and the second years of implementation, allowing the researchers to test if teacher experience with the products was an important determinant of outcomes. They found that usage actually decreased on average in the second year and there were no positive effects.

Some studies, however, find positive effects of CAI initiatives. Barrow et al. (2009) exploit a within-school randomization at the classroom level in three large urban districts in the United States. They find statistically significant positive effects of CAI when treated classes are taught in the computer lab using prealgebra and algebra software. They also find some evidence that the effects are larger for classrooms with greater enrollment, which is consistent with the predictions of their model of time allocation (discussed in Section 2.2). The authors note that such effects may not translate to different software

---

[15] There are well-documented deficiencies in teacher quality and attendance and other education factors in developing countries. For example, Chaudhury et al. (2006) examine the rate of teacher absenteeism, which is 19%, and teacher effort in Bangladesh, Ecuador, India, Indonesia, Peru, and Uganda.

or different schools, but conclude that the positive findings suggest that CAI deserves additional evaluation and policy attention especially because it is relatively easy to implement compared with other interventions.

Banerjee et al. (2007) note that the generally insignificant effects of computer interventions in developed countries may not hold in developing countries where computers may replace teachers with less motivation and training. They test an intervention in India in which trained instructors guided students through two hours of computer instruction per week, one hour of which was outside of the regular school day. Thus the intervention was a combination of guided computer instruction by a supplemental instructor and additional class time. They find that the intervention has large and statistically significant effects on math scores, but also find significant fade-out in subsequent years. However, Linden (2008) finds very different results when attempting to separate the effects of in-class "substitution" for standard instruction from out-of-school "complements." Using two randomized experiments, test score effects for 2nd and 3rd graders in India were large and negative for the in-school intervention and insignificant and positive for the out-of-school intervention. The negative in-school results could stem from the fact that the program was implemented in "well-functioning network of NGO-run schools" or that the specific software being used was ineffective. That is, both the nature of the technology and what is being substituted for are important considerations when evaluating effect sizes.

Carrillo et al. (2010) find positive effects of the Personalized Complementary and Interconnected Learning software in Ecuador. The program was randomized at the school level and provided three hours of individualized math and language instruction to treated students each week. The initiative produced positive gains on math scores and no effect on language scores. Mo et al. (2014) conduct a randomized experiment at 72 rural schools in China. The intervention provided 80 minutes of supplemental math instruction (math-based computer games) per week during what would otherwise be a computer skills class. The intervention was estimated to generate an increase in math scores of 0.17 standard deviations for both 3rd and 5th grade students. It is important to note that the instruction was supplemental both in terms of providing additional mathematics instruction and not offsetting another academic subject.[16]

In an analysis of randomized interventions (both technological and nontechnological) in developing countries, Kremer et al. (2013) hypothesize that CAI tailored to each student may be the most effective. McEwan (2015) concludes that computer-based interventions in primary schools have higher average effects (0.15 standard deviations) than

[16] The authors note that their results may differ from Linden (2008) due to the fact "that by integrating the CAL program during a relatively unproductive period of time … the substitution effect may have been minimized."

teacher training, smaller classes, and performance incentives. However, he makes the important point that it is "misleading" to compare effect sizes without considering cost.

2.3.3 Computer Skills

Computer use in schools may benefit students in two ways: through the acquisition of computer skills that are useful in the labor market; and through the acquisition of basic skills such as math, reading, and writing. The economics literature has provided different justifications for focusing on the effectiveness of computers as a pedagogical tool for acquiring basic skills. Angrist and Lavy (2002) argue that computer skills training (CST) "seems undeniably useful" whereas the evidence for CAI "is both limited and mixed". Fuchs and Woessmann (2004) provide the antithetical justification for focusing on CAI, arguing that the literature finds little evidence that computer skills have "direct returns on the labor market" whereas the returns to basic academic skills are undeniable. There is clearly a need for more research on the effect of computer skills on labor market outcomes.

Most of the studies discussed in this paper do not estimate the effect of ICT on computer skills. A primary challenge is that academic exams do not provide a direct measure of computer skills, so these benefits may go unmeasured. For example, Goolsbee and Guryan (2006) note that ICT may "build skills that are unmeasured by standard tests." Several studies find evidence that enhance education in computer skills may be the primary result of many initiatives. For example, Barrera-Osorio and Linden (2009) find a significant increase in computer use in computer science and not in any other subject. Likewise, Bet et al. (2014) find that increased availability of technology affected time spent teaching digital skills, but computers were not used in math and language. Recent one-to-one laptop program policies have highlighted the need for "21st century skills," which go beyond basic computer skills and are likely even more difficult to measure.

2.3.4 Online College Courses

A new and rapidly growing area of research related to CAI is estimating the effectiveness of online instruction for college courses. In this context, online education is frequently a method for delivering traditional instruction (e.g. streaming videos of college lectures). The primary question of interest is how student performance in online courses compares to performance in the equivalent traditional course. Evidence from the first wave of studies appears to show that, at this time, Internet courses are less effective than in-person instruction. However, because online courses are lower cost per student, performance differences do not necessarily mean that online courses are not cost effective. Further, online courses may expand the number of students able to take courses due to financial, enrollment, or geographic constraints.

Several recent studies exploit randomized assignment of students to online and in-person education at the college level. Figlio et al. (2013) conduct a randomized experiment at a US university and find evidence that in-person instruction results in higher performance in introductory microeconomics, especially for males, Hispanics, and lower-achieving students. Alpert et al. (2015) use a random experiment to evaluate instruction in an introductory economics course by traditional face-to-face classroom instruction, blended face-to-face and online instruction, and exclusive online instruction. They find evidence of negative effects on learning outcomes from online instruction relative to traditional instruction, but no evidence of negative effects from blended instruction relative to traditional instruction. Bowen et al. (2014) conduct an experiment at six college campuses to compare traditional instruction to "hybrid" in-person and online instruction for a statistics course. They find no significant performance difference in performance between the two groups. Bettinger et al. (2014), using variation in access to in-person courses as an instrument, find lower performance and higher variation for students enrolled in online courses. Patterson (2014) proposes internet distractions as a possible reason for reduced performance in online courses. He conducts an experiment which finds that student performance improves when they use a commitment device to limit access to certain webpages. In related work, Joyce et al. (2014) find experimental evidence that the frequency of class meetings remains important even when course materials are available online.

Summary

Several patterns emerge when evaluating the effects of computer use in schools. Divisions in the literature emerge in terms of the nature of the intervention being studied, the research design, the parameter being estimated, and the school context. We provide an overview of each study and its key characteristics and findings in Table 3. The most prominent distinction is the division between ICT and CAI focused studies, which tend to coincide with methodological differences. The high cost of ICT hardware and connections, and the fact that it does not target specific students has meant that the majority of rigorous empirical research has exploited natural experiments generated by government policies. In contrast, several studies evaluating CAI software, which can target specific classrooms or students, have used RCT designs. It is important to note that despite the division between these two types of studies, ICT investment is likely to be a necessary condition for making CAI available.[17]

Both ICT and CAI produce somewhat mixed evidence of the effect of computers on student outcomes, though there appears to be more evidence of positive effects in studies of CAI. There are several reasons why CAI studies may be more likely to find positive effects. One explanation is methodological. Beyond differences in research design, it may

---

[17] This has a direct analogue in the economics of education literature more broadly. Many studies examine how funding affects student outcomes (with little regard for the specific inputs the funding makes possible) while other studies examine the effects of specific inputs.

Table 3 Overview: studies of technology use in schools

ICT study	Country	Investment	Grade	Design	Funding	Intensity	Results
Angrist and Lavy (2002)	ISR	Computers	4, 8	Policy d-in-d	Supplemental	Goal: 10:1 comp-stud ratio	Insign, neg
Fuchs and Woessmann (2004)	Many	Computers	10	Cross-section	N/A	N/A	Insign
Goolsbee and Guryan (2006)	USA	Internet	K-12	Policy d-in-d	Subsidy	20–90% Internet discount	Insign
Leuven et al. (2007)	NLD	Computers, software	8	Policy RD	Supplemental	$90 ICT per pupil	Insign, neg
Machin et al. (2007)	GBR	Computers	K-6	Policy d-in-d	Supplemental	Various (avg 5% ICT)	Lang pos, math insign
Maine Ed Policy Research (2007)	USA	Laptop	7, 8	Single diff		1-1 Laptop	Positive
Grimes and Warschauer (2008)	USA	Laptop	K-8	Policy d-in-d	Supplemental	1-1 Laptop	Mixed
Barrera-Osorio and Linden (2009)	COL	Computers	3–11	RCT	Supplemental	Avg 8.3 computers/school	Insign
Texas Center for Ed Research (2009)	USA	Laptop	6, 7, 8	Policy d-in-d	Supplemental	1-1 Laptop	Insign, pos
Suhr et al. (2010)	USA	Laptop	4, 5	Policy d-in-d	Supplemental	1-1 Laptop	Insign, pos
Cristia et al. (2012)	PER	Laptop	K-6	RCT	Supplemental	1-1 Laptop	Insign
Cristia et al. (2014)	PER	Computers, Internet	K-7	Policy d-in-d	Supplemental	~40% ICT increase	Insign
Belo et al. (2014)	POR	Internet	9	IV	Supplemental	Various	Neg

CAI study	Country	Investment	Grade	Design	Instr. time	Intensity	Results
Rouse and Krueger (2004)	USA	Language	K-6	RCT	Supplemental	6–8 weeks, 7–8 h per week	Insign
Banerjee et al. (2007)	IND	Math	4	RCT	Supplemental	2 years, 2 h per week	Positive
Mathematica Research (2007; 2009)	USA	Math, language	K-12	RCT	Substitute	1 year, various	Insign
Barrow et al. (2009)	USA	Math	7–12	RCT	Substitute	1 year, daily class	Positive
Carrillo et al. (2010)	ECU	Math, language	3–5	RCT	Substitute	2 years, 3 h per week	Math pos, lang insign
Mo et al. (2014)	CHN	Math	3, 5	RCT	Supplemental	1.5 years, 1.5 h per week	Positive

be the case that targeted CAI is more likely to generate positive effects than broader ICT initiatives. Specifically, CAI studies are more likely to result in supplemental instructional time. That is, while ICT studies may reflect a tradeoff between time allocated to computer-based instruction and traditional instruction, CAI estimates may reflect the net increase in instruction and therefore be biased in favor of positive findings. Further, ICT investment may not result in an increase in educational software and may increase computer use that detracts from traditional instruction (e.g. noneducational computer games, social networking, or internet use). By contrast, CAI studies focus narrowly on specific software and the educational outcomes that these are likely to affect.

Some of the notable exceptions to the pattern of null effects occur in studies set in the context of developing, rather than developed countries. This may indicate that the quality of the education or other activities being substituted for is lower. There also appears to be some evidence that interventions which target math are more likely to generate positive effects than interventions that target language. This could be due to the relative ease of making effective software for math relative to language or the relative ease of generating gains in math.

The finding that the results do not adhere to clear patterns should not be surprising. Policies and experiments differ in cost, the type of treatment (the specific hardware or software provided), the length of the intervention (number of years), the intensity of the treatment (hours per day), whether they supplement or substitute for other inputs, the grade levels treated, and the academic subject targeted. We highlight these differences in Table 3. Also, relatively little attention is given in the literature to heterogeneity in treatment effects by student characteristics, which is likely due in part to the finding of no effect overall in many studies. Nonetheless, some studies do differentiate the effects by gender and by baseline academic performance. While no patterns by gender emerge, some studies find evidence that computer resources benefit lower performing students more than the highest performing students (e.g. Banerjee et al., 2007; Barrow et al., 2009).

3. TECHNOLOGY USE AT HOME BY STUDENTS

3.1 Estimates of Rates of Technology Use at Home by Students

Computer and Internet use at home has grown rapidly over the past two decades. It is astonishing that only 20 years ago less than one-fourth of the US population had access to a computer at home (see Fig. 2). Only 17 years ago, less than one-fifth of the US population had an Internet connection at home. The most recent data available for the United States, which are for 2012, indicate that roughly 80% of the population has access to a home computer and 75% of the population has access to an Internet connection at home (U.S. Census Bureau, 2012).

Schoolchildren have even higher rates of access to computers and the Internet at home. Eighty-six percent have access to computers and 83% have access to the Internet.

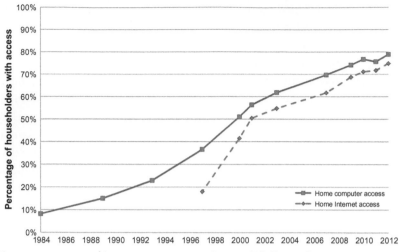

Figure 2 Home computer and Internet access rates. *Source: U.S. Census Bureau, computer and Internet use: Table 4. Households with a computer and Internet use: 1984 to 2012, from various years of the Current Population Survey.*

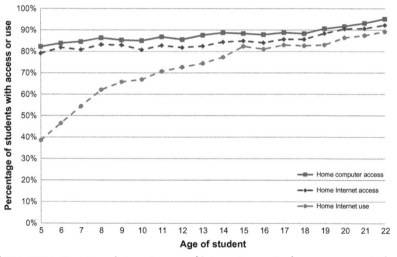

Figure 3 Home computer access, Internet use, and Internet use rates by age among students. *Source: Author's calculations from Current Population Survey microdata 2012.*

These rates are considerably higher than when the Current Population Survey (CPS) first collected information on home computer access. In 1984, roughly 15% of children had access to a computer at home (U.S. Census Bureau, 1988). Access to home computers and the Internet also rises with the age of the student (see Fig. 3). Home Internet use rises especially sharply with the age of the student.

Surveys from the 2012 PISA conducted by the OECD provide information on computer and Internet access at home among schoolchildren across a large number of countries. Table 4 reports estimates for the 50 largest countries in the world with available data. In most developed countries a very large percentage of schoolchildren have access to a computer at home that they can use for schoolwork. In contrast, schoolchildren in developing countries often have very low levels of access. For example, only 26% of schoolchildren in Indonesia and 40% of schoolchildren in Vietnam have access to a home computer. In most developed countries a very large percentage of schoolchildren also report having an Internet connection. Although data availability is more limited for Internet connection rates, the PISA data provide some evidence that children in developing countries have lower levels of access than developed countries. Only 52% of schoolchildren in Mexico, for example, report having an Internet connection at home. These patterns of access to home computers and Internet among schoolchildren generally follow those for broader household-based measures of access to home computers and the Internet published by the OECD (2014) and International Telecommunications Union (2014a).[18] ITU data indicate that 78% of households in developed countries have Internet access compared with 31% of households in developing countries (ITU, 2014b).

Over the past decade the percentage of students with home computers has increased. Fig. 4 displays trends in home computer access from 2003 to 2012 for selected large countries with available data. Home computer rates for schoolchildren have been very high in high-income countries such as the United States and Germany over the past decade. Other large countries have experienced rapid improvements in access to computers among schoolchildren over the past decade. Russia has caught up with high-income countries, and access to computers in Brazil grew from 36% as recently as 2006 to 72% in 2012. Schoolchildren in Mexico and Turkey have also seen rapid improvements in access to home computers over the past decade. Access to home computers has grown over the past decade for Indonesian schoolchildren, but remains relatively low.

Even with very high rates of access to home computers and the Internet in developed countries, large disparities remain within countries.[19] In the United States, for example, 9 million schoolchildren do not have access to the Internet at home with the lack of access being disproportionately concentrated among low-income and disadvantaged minority

[18] See Caselli and Coleman (2001), Wallsten (2005), Dewan et al. (2010), Andrés et al. (2010), and Chinn and Fairlie (2007, 2010) for a few examples of previous studies of disparities in computer and Internet penetration across countries.

[19] See Hoffman and Novak (1998), Mossberger et al. (2003), Warschauer (2003), Ono and Zavodny (2007), Fairlie (2004), Mossberger et al. (2006), and Goldfarb and Prince (2008) for examples of previous studies of disparities in computer and Internet use within countries.

Table 4 Percentage of students with computer at home for schoolwork and Internet connection at home, Programme for International Student Assessment (PISA), OECD 2012

Country	Computer at home for schoolwork	Internet connection at home
Argentina	84%	
Australia	98%	98%
Austria	98%	99%
Belgium	97%	99%
Brazil	72%	
Bulgaria	93%	
Canada	97%	
Chile	86%	78%
Colombia	63%	
Costa Rica	74%	71%
Croatia	94%	96%
Czech Republic	97%	98%
Denmark	99%	100%
Finland	99%	100%
France	97%	
Germany	98%	99%
Greece	92%	88%
Hong Kong	99%	99%
Hungary	94%	94%
Indonesia	26%	
Ireland	95%	98%
Israel	94%	96%
Italy	97%	97%
Japan	70%	89%
Jordan	83%	75%
Kazakhstan	66%	
Korea (South)	95%	95%
Malaysia	68%	
Mexico	57%	52%
Netherlands	98%	99%
New Zealand	94%	94%
Norway	99%	99%
Peru	52%	
Poland	97%	95%
Portugal	97%	96%
Romania	87%	
Russia	93%	93%
Serbia	95%	90%
Singapore	95%	98%
Slovak Republic	92%	94%
Spain	96%	96%
Sweden	99%	99%
Switzerland	98%	99%
Thailand	63%	
Tunisia	57%	
Turkey	68%	59%
United Arab Emirates	93%	
United Kingdom	97%	
United States	91%	
Vietnam	40%	

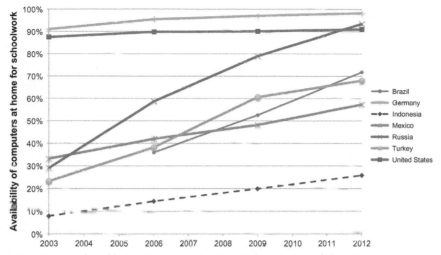

Figure 4 Percentage of students with computer at home for schoolwork for selected countries, OECD. *Source: OECD, Programme for International Student Assessment (PISA).*

schoolchildren.[20] Among schoolchildren living in households with $25,000 or less of income 67% have access to a home computer and 59% have access to the Internet at home, whereas 98% of schoolchildren living in households with $100,000 or more in income have access to a home computer and 97% have access to the Internet at home. Large disparities also exist across race and ethnicity. Among African-American schoolchildren 78% have home computers and 73% have home Internet access, and among Latino schoolchildren 78% have home computers and 71% have home Internet access. In contrast, 92% of white, non-Latino schoolchildren have home computers and 89% have home Internet access.

Disparities in access to home computers within countries and across countries may contribute to educational inequality. However, the rapidly expanding use of computers and the Internet at home in developing countries might have implications for relative trends in educational outcomes.

3.2 Theoretical Issues

In addition to teacher and school inputs, student and family inputs are important for the educational production function. The personal computer is an example of one of these inputs in the educational production process, and there are several reasons to suspect that it is important. First, personal computers make it easier to complete course assignments

---

[20] These estimates are calculated from October 2012 Current Population Survey, Internet Use Supplement microdata.

through the use of word processors, the Internet, spreadsheets, and other software (Lenhart et al., 2001, 2008). Although many students could use computers at school and libraries, home access represents the highest quality access in terms of availability, flexibility and autonomy, which may provide the most benefits to the user (DiMaggio and Hargittai, 2001). Children report spending an average of 16 min per day using computers for schoolwork (Kaiser Family Foundation, 2010). Access to a home computer may also improve familiarity with software increasing the effectiveness of computer use for completing school assignments and the returns to computer use at school (Mitchell Institute, 2004; Underwood et al., 1994; Warschauer and Matuchniak, 2010). As with computers used in school, owning a personal computer may improve computer specific skills that increase wages in some fields. Finally, the social distractions of using a computer in a crowded computer lab may be avoided by using a computer at home.

On the other hand, home computers are often used for games, social networking, downloading music and videos, communicating with friends, and other forms of entertainment potentially displacing time for schoolwork (Jones, 2002; Kaiser Family Foundation, 2010; U.S. Department of Commerce, 2004).[21] Children report spending an average of 17 min per day using computers for playing games and an average of 21 min per day using computers for watching videos and other entertainment (Kaiser Family Foundation, 2010). A large percentage of computer users report playing games at least a few times a week (Lenhart et al., 2008). Time spent using social networking sites such as Facebook and Myspace and other entertainment sites such as YouTube and iTunes has grown rapidly over time (Lenhart, 2009). Children report spending an average of 22 min per day using computers for social networking (Kaiser Family Foundation, 2010). Computers are often criticized for displacing more active and effective forms of learning and for emphasizing presentation (e.g. graphics) over content (Fuchs and Woessmann, 2004; Giacquinta et al., 1993; Stoll, 1995). Computers and the Internet also facilitate cheating and plagiarism and make it easier to find information from noncredible sources (Rainie and Hitlin, 2005). In the end, it is ambiguous as to whether the educational benefits of home computers outweigh their distraction and displacement costs.

Beltran et al. (2010) present a simple theoretical model that illustrates these points in the context of a utility maximization problem for a high school student. A linear random utility model of the decision to graduate from high school is used. Define U_{i0} and U_{i1} as the ith person's indirect utilities associated with not graduating and graduating from high school, respectively. These indirect utilities can be expressed as:

$$U_{i0} = \alpha_0 + \beta_0' X_i + \gamma_0 C_i + \lambda_0 t(W_i, C_i) + \theta Y_0(Z_i, C_i) + \varepsilon_{i0} \tag{3}$$

and

---

[21] Similar concerns were expressed earlier over television crowding out schoolwork time (see Zavodny, 2006, for example).

$$U_{i1} = \alpha_1 + \beta_1' X_i + \gamma_1 C_i + \lambda_1 t(W_i, C_i) + \theta Y_1(Z_i, C_i) + \varepsilon_{i1}, \tag{4}$$

where X_i, Z_i, and W_i may include individual, parental, family, geographical, and school characteristics; C_i is the presence of a home computer; Y_0 and Y_1 are expected future earnings; and t is the child's achievement (e.g. test score), and ε_i is an additive error term. X_i, Z_i, and W_i do not necessarily include the same characteristics because the individual, family and other characteristics affecting utility, test scores and expected future earnings may or may not differ. Achievement is determined by the characteristics, W_i, and the presence of computers is allowed to have different effects on the utility from the two educational choices. Expected earnings differ between graduating from high school and not graduating from high school, and are functions of the characteristics, Z_i, and home computers.

In the model, there are three major ways in which home computers affect educational outcomes. First, there is a direct effect of having a home computer on the utility of graduating from high school, γ_1. Personal computers make it easier to complete homework assignments through the use of word processors, spreadsheets, Internet browsers and other software, thus increasing the utility from completing schoolwork. Home access to computers offers more availability and autonomy than school access and may familiarize students with computers increasing the returns to computer use in the classroom. Second, access to home computers may have an additional effect on the utility of staying in school beyond making it easier to finish homework and complete assignments. In particular, the use of home computers may "open doors to learning" and doing well in school (Cuban, 2001; Peck et al., 2002), and thus encourage some teenagers to graduate from school. Third, personal computers also provide utility from games, email, chat rooms, downloading music, and other noneducation uses creating an opportunity cost from doing homework. The higher opportunity cost increases the utility of not graduating from high school. On the other hand, the use of computers at home, even for these noneducational uses, keeps children off the street, potentially reducing delinquency and criminal activities. These activities increase the utility from dropping out of school. The two opposing factors make it difficult to sign the effect of computers on the utility from not graduating from high school, γ_0.

Another way in which personal computers affect the high school graduation decision is through their effects on academic achievement. Computers could improve academic performance directly through the use of educational software and focusing time use on content. Computers and the Internet, however, may displace other more active forms of learning, emphasize presentation over content, and increase plagiarism. Therefore, the theoretical effects of computers on academic achievement, dt/dC, and thus on the utility from graduating from high school, $\lambda_1 dt/dC$, is ambiguous. Finally, computer skills may improve employment opportunities and wages, but mainly in combination with a minimal educational credential such as a high school diploma, implying that $dY_1/dC > dY_0/dC$.

Focusing on the high school graduation decision, we assume that the individual graduates from high school if $U_{i1} > U_{i0}$. The probability of graduating from high school, $y_i = 1$, is:

$$
\begin{aligned}
P(y_i = 1) &= P(U_{i1} > U_{i0}) \\
&= F\big[(\alpha_1 - \alpha_0) + (\beta_1 - \beta_0)' X_i + (\gamma_1 - \gamma_0) C_i + \theta(Y_1(Z_i, C_i) - Y_0(Z_i, C_i)) \\
&\quad + (\lambda_1 - \lambda_0) t(W_i, C_i)\big],
\end{aligned}
\tag{5}
$$

where F is the cumulative distribution function of $\varepsilon_{i1} - \varepsilon_{i0}$. In Eq. (5), the separate effects of computers on the probability of graduating from high school are expressed in relative terms. Home computers have a direct effect on the graduation probability through relative utility, and indirect effects through improving achievement and altering relative earnings. The net effect of home computers on high school graduation, however, is theoretically ambiguous.

Vigdor et al. (2014) model the adolescent's maximization problem as one of allocating time and money across competing uses. Adolescents devote time t_i and pay a monetary cost p_i to engage in different activities within the set of all potential activities. Each activity contributes directly to the adolescent's utility, and some activities also contribute indirectly to utility through building human capital and increasing future living standards. Utility can be written as $U = U(A, S(A))$, where A is the vector of activity choices and $S(A)$ is the future living standard given these activity choices. Not all activities increase future living standards, and adolescents place at least some weight on future living standards in the their computation of utility. Adolescents also face a time constraint and a budget constraint. The solution to the resulting utility maximization problem equates the ratio of prices of any two activities to the ratio of marginal utilities of the two activities.

Using this framework, the introduction of home computers and broadband Internet can be viewed as a shock to the prices and time costs of various activities. Vigdor et al. (2014) provide several examples in which computer technology reduces the prices and time costs of activities, and thus potentially increases their use. They note that access to word processing software reduces the cost of revising a term paper, and access to broadband reduces the cost of conducting research for an essay. Computer and broadband access also reduce the marginal cost of playing games or engaging in multiparty conversations with friends. The first two examples of activities presumably have a positive impact on expected future living standards, whereas the impact on expected future living standards of games and social networking is less clear. Even if these two activities have positive returns, they might have smaller returns to future living standards than the activities that they displace.

Vigdor et al. (2014) also note that the simple model could be expanded to incorporate the cost of technology. Although the adolescent is unlikely to purchase computers with his/her own money, the family's purchase of computers and Internet service could crowd out other "educational" expenditures. Another issue is that the maximization problem requires adolescents to make decisions with long-run consequences, and they may not be "neurologically" developed enough to make such decisions. This is less of a problem, however, if adolescents have at least weak preferences for building human capital and improving future living standards. Another point that Vigdor et al. raise is that in many cases the realized time allocations of adolescents will be determined not only by their own preferences, but by constraints placed on them by parents, teachers, and other adults. The model could be revised to incorporate these restrictions on activities, but one important implication is that the impact of computer technology on educational outcomes could vary with parental supervision.

These theoretical models provide some insights into how home computers might exert both positive and negative influences on educational outcomes, and demonstrate that the net total effect is difficult to determine. Families and students are likely to make decisions about computer purchases and Internet subscriptions in part based on these comparisons. If households are rational and face no other frictions, those households without computers have decided not to buy a computer because the returns are relatively low. However, it is also possible that various constraints prevent households from investing in home computers even if the returns are high. Parents may face credit constraints, be unaware of the returns to computer use, not be technically comfortable with computers, and have concerns about privacy. There is reason to suspect that these constraints might be important, given that households without computers tend to be substantially poorer and less educated than other households. Thus, the effect of computers for such families is an open and important question.

3.3 Empirical Findings

3.3.1 Effects of Home Computers and the Internet on Educational Outcomes

Although the theoretical models provide some insights into how home computers might exert positive and negative effects on the educational outcomes, they do not provide a prediction of the sign and magnitude of the net effect. A small, but growing empirical literature estimates the net effects of home computers on a wide range of educational outcomes. The literature on the topic has evolved over time primarily through methodological improvements. Earlier studies generally regress educational outcomes on the presence of a home computer while controlling for student, family, and parental characteristics. More recent studies focus on quasi-experimental approaches and randomized control experiments.

One of the first studies to explore whether home computers have positive educational effects on children was Attewell and Battle (1999). Using the 1988 National Educational Longitudinal Survey (NELS), they provide evidence that test scores and grades are positively related to access to home computers among 8th graders even after controlling for differences in several demographic and individual characteristics including typically unobservable characteristics of the educational environment in the household.[22]

Using data from the 2001 CPS, Fairlie (2005) estimates the relationship between school enrollment and having a home computer among teenagers. Controlling for family income, parental education, parental occupation, and other observable characteristics in probit regressions for the probability of school enrollment, he finds a difference of 1.4 percentage points (base rate of 85%). In a subsequent paper, Beltran et al. (2010) use panel data from the matched CPS (2000–04) and the National Longitudinal Survey of Youth (1997–2002) to estimate the relationship between home computers and subsequent high school graduation. They find that teenagers who have access to home computers are 6–8 percentage points more likely to graduate from high school than teenagers who do not after controlling for individual, parental, and family characteristics. Using detailed data available in the NLSY97, they also find that the estimates are not sensitive to the inclusion of difficult-to-find characteristics of the educational environment in the household and extracurricular activities of the student.[23] Estimates indicate a strong positive relationship between home computers and grades, a strong negative relationship with school suspension, and suggestive evidence of a negative relationship with criminal activities.

Schmitt and Wadsworth (2006), using the British Household Panel Survey (1991–2001), find a significant positive association between home computers and performance on the British school examinations. The results are robust to the inclusion of individual, household and geographical controls, including proxies for household wealth and prior educational attainment. Fiorini (2010) provides evidence on the impacts of home computers among young Australian children ages 4 to 7. She shifts the focus from access to home computers to computer use among children (although some results include computer access as an instrumental variable for computer use). Using data from the Longitudinal Study of Australian Children (2004–06), she finds evidence of a positive relationship between computer use and cognitive skills among young children.

In contrast to these findings of positive effects of home computers on educational outcomes, Fuchs and Woessmann (2004) find a negative relationship between home computers and student achievement using data from 31 developed and emerging countries among teenagers. Using the PISA database, they find that students with home computers have significantly lower math and reading test scores after controlling for student, family

---

[22] They include measures of the frequency of child-parent discussions of school-related matters, parents' familiarity with the parents of their child's friends, attendance in "cultural" classes outside of school, whether the child visits science or history museums with the parent, and an index of the educational atmosphere of the home (e.g. presence of books, encyclopedias, newspapers, and place to study).

[23] The controls include religion, private school attendance, whether a language other than English is spoken at home, whether there is a quiet place to study at home, and whether the child takes extra classes or lessons, such as music, dance, or foreign language lessons.

and school characteristics and country fixed effects. They find a large positive association between home computers and test scores in bivariate comparisons without controls.

Although regressions of educational outcomes on home computers frequently control for numerous individual, family and school characteristics, they may nonetheless produce biased estimates of causal effects due to omitted variables. In particular, if the most educationally motivated families (after controlling for child and family characteristics) are more likely to purchase computers, then a positive relationship between academic performance and home computers may capture the effect of immeasurable motivation on academic performance. Conversely, if the least educationally motivated families are more likely to purchase computers, perhaps motivated by their entertainment value, then estimates will be downward biased.

To address these concerns, a few recent studies (including some discussed above) estimate the impacts of home computers on educational outcomes using instrumental variable techniques, individual-student fixed effects, and falsification tests. Fairlie (2005) addresses the endogeneity issue by estimating instrumental variable models. Bivariate probit models of the joint probability of school enrollment and owning a home computer result in large positive coefficient estimates (7 7 percentage points). Use of computers and the Internet by the child's mother and father, and MSA-level home computer and Internet rates are used as exclusion restrictions. Some supporting evidence is provided that these variables should affect the probability of the family purchasing a home computer but should not affect academic performance after controlling for family income, parental education and occupation, and other factors. Beltran et al. (2010) also estimate bivariate probits for the joint probability of high school graduation and owning a home computer and find point estimates similar to those from a multivariate regression. Similar exclusion restrictions are used with the addition of the presence of another teenager in the household. Fiorini (2010) uses instrumental variables for computer use in her study of young Australian children and generally finds larger positive estimates of computer use on test scores than in OLS regressions. The number of older siblings and Internet use at work by men and women at the postcode level are used as exclusion restrictions.

Another approach, first taken by Schmitt and Wadsworth (2006), is to include future computer ownership in the educational outcome regression. A positive estimate of future computer ownership on educational attainment would raise concerns that current ownership proxies for an unobserved factor, such as educational motivation. Future computer ownership, however, is not found to have a positive relationship with educational outcomes similar to the positive relationship found for contemporaneous computer ownership (Beltran et al., 2010; Schmitt and Wadsworth, 2006). Along these lines of falsification tests or "pencil tests" (DiNardo and Pischke, 1997), Schmitt and Wadsworth (2006) do not find evidence that other household assets that proxy for wealth such as dishwashers, driers, and cars have similar effects on educational attainment. Similarly, Beltran et al. (2010) do not find evidence of a positive relationship between educational attainment and having a dictionary or cable television at home, which also might be correlated with unobserved educational motivation or wealth.

A couple of studies address selection concerns by estimating fixed effect models. The inclusion of student fixed effects controls for differences in unobservable characteristics that are time-invariant. Vigdor et al. (2014), using panel data from North Carolina public schools, find modestly sized negative effects of home computer access and local-area access to high-speed Internet connections on math and reading test scores when including fixed effects. In contrast, they find positive estimates when student fixed effects are excluded. Beltran et al. (2010) find that adding student fixed effects results in smaller positive point estimates that lose significance.

Malamud and Pop-Eleches (2011) address the endogeneity problem with a RDD based on the effects of a government program in Romania that allocated a fixed number of vouchers for computers to low-income children in public schools. The basic idea of the RDD is that schoolchildren just below the income threshold for eligibility for a computer voucher are compared to schoolchildren just above the income threshold. The two groups of schoolchildren close to the threshold have nearly identical characteristics and differ only in their eligibility for the computer voucher. Estimates from the discontinuity indicate that Romanian children winning vouchers have lower grades, but higher cognitive ability as measured by Raven's Progressive Matrices.

A few randomized control experiments have been conducted to evaluate the effects of home computers on educational outcomes. The first random experiment involving the provision of free computers to students for home use was Fairlie and London (2012). The random-assignment evaluation was conducted with 286 entering students receiving financial aid at a large community college in Northern California.[24] Half of the participating students were randomly selected to receive free computers. After 2 years, the treatment group of students who received free computers had modestly better educational outcomes than the control group along a few measures. Estimates for a summary index of educational outcomes indicate that the treatment group is 0.14 standard deviations higher than the control group mean. Students living farther from campus and students who have jobs appear to have benefitted more from the flexibility afforded by home computers. The results from the experiment also provide the only evidence in the literature on the effects of home computers for postsecondary students.

Fairlie and Robinson (2013) also conduct a random experiment, but shift the focus from college students to schoolchildren. The experiment includes 1123 students in grades 6–10 attending 15 schools across California. All of the schoolchildren participating in the study did not have computers prior to the experiment and half were randomly selected to receive free

---

[24] The focus on the impacts of computers on community college students is important, unlike 4-year colleges where many students live on campus and have access to large computer labs, community college students often have limited access to on-campus technology.

computers. The results indicate that even though there was a large effect on computer ownership and total hours of computer use, there is no evidence of an effect on a host of educational outcomes, including grades, standardized test scores, credits earned, attendance, and disciplinary actions. No test score effects are found at the mean, at important cutoffs in the distribution (e.g. passing and proficiency), or at quantiles in the distribution. The estimates are precise enough to rule out even moderately sized positive or negative effects. Consistent with these results, they find no evidence that treatment students spent more time on homework and that the computers had an effect on turning homework in on time, software use, computer knowledge, or other intermediate inputs in education. Treatment students report spending more time on computers for schoolwork, but they also report spending more time on computers playing games, social networking and for other entertainment.

Most of the evidence in the literature focuses on the effects of home computers on the educational outcomes of schoolchildren in developed or transition economies. A couple of previous studies use random experiments to examine the impacts of one laptop per child (OLPC) laptops on educational outcomes in developing countries.[25] Beuermann et al. (2012) examine the impacts of randomly providing approximately 1000 laptops for home use to schoolchildren in grades 1 through 6 in Peru.[26] They find that the laptops have a positive, but small and insignificant effect on cognitive skills as measured by the Raven's Progressive Matrices test (though the effect is significant among children who did not already have a home computer before the experiment). Teachers reported that the effort exerted in school was significantly lower for treatment students than control students and that treated children reported reading books, stories, or magazines less than control children. Mo et al. (2012) randomly distribute OLPC laptops to roughly half of a sample of 300 young schoolchildren (grade 3) in China.[27] They find some evidence that the laptops improved math test scores, but no evidence of effects on Chinese tests. They also find that the laptops increased learning activity use of computers and decreased time spent watching television.

[25] Although the One Laptop per Child program in Peru (Cristia et al., 2012) and the Texas laptop program (evaluated with a quasi-experiment in Texas Center for Educational Research, 2009) were initially intended to allow students to take computers home when needed in addition to using them in school, this did not happen in most cases. In Peru, some principals, and even parents, did not allow the computers to come home because of concerns that the laptops would not be replaced through the program if they were damaged or stolen. The result is that only 40% of students took the laptops home, and home use was substantially lower than in-school use. In Texas, there were similar concerns resulting in many schools not allowing computers to be taken home or restricting their home use. The main effect from these laptop programs is therefore to provide one computer for every student in the classroom, rather than to increase home access.

[26] Recipients of the laptops were also provided with an instruction manual and seven weekly training sessions.

[27] The laptops included some tutoring software and one training session was provided.

3.3.2 Heterogeneity in Home Computer Effects

The effects of home computers on educational outcomes might differ across subgroups of the student population. For example, minority students might benefit more or less from having a home computer because of more limited opportunities for alternative places of access, social interactions with other computer users, and learning about use from parents, siblings, and friends. Girls and boys may differ in how they use computers possibly resulting in differential effects. Several studies estimate separate home computer effects by demographic group and other student characteristics. For example, in Attewell and Battle's (1999) study of home computer effects on the test scores and grades of 8th graders they find evidence of stronger positive relationships between home computers and educational outcomes for higher SES children, boys, and whites. Fiorini's (2010) study of the impacts of home computer use on cognitive and noncognitive skills among Australian children ages 4 to 7 finds evidence of larger effects for girls and children with less educated parents. Fairlie (2012a) finds larger effects of home computers on educational outcomes for minority college students than nonminority college students (Table 5).

As with school-based interventions, the evidence is mixed with several studies not finding evidence of heterogeneity in the effects of home computers. For example, Beltran et al. (2010) estimate regressions that include interactions between home computers and race, income or gender and, in almost all cases, do not find statistically significant interaction effects. Fairlie and Robinson (2013) and Fairlie (2015) find no evidence of heterogeneous treatment effects by pretreatment academic achievement, parental supervision, propensity for nongame use, grade, race, or gender. Beuermann et al. (2012) find some evidence of a larger reduction in school effort for younger Peruvian children, but essentially no difference in effects on cognitive skills for younger children and no difference in effects on school effort and cognitive skills by gender. In their study of Romanian schoolchildren, Malamud and Pop-Eleches (2011) do not find evidence of differential effects by gender, but do find that younger children experience larger gains in cognitive skills. Given the lack of consistency in findings across studies for any subgroup, it is difficult to draw strong conclusions on this question.

3.3.3 Effects on Computer Skills and Other Outcomes

Several previous studies examine the impacts of home computers on computer skills. There is some evidence of positive impacts, but surprisingly the overall evidence is not universally strong. For example, Fairlie (2012b) finds evidence of positive effects of home computers on computer skills among college students, whereas Fairlie and Robinson (2013) find no evidence of home computers on computer knowledge or skills among schoolchildren. Among young children in Peru, Beuermann et al. (2012) find strong evidence that the OLPC laptops improved scores on a proficiency test in using the laptop, but find no effects on skills for using a Windows based computer or using the Internet. Mo et al. (2012) finds large positive effects on computer skills from OLPC

Table 5 Overview: studies of computer use at home

Study	Country	Investment	Grade/age	Design	Data	Outcome	Results
Attewell and Battle (1999)	USA	Computer	Grade 8	Cross-section	NELS	Test scores	Positive
Fuchs and Woessmann (2004)	Many	Computer	Teenagers	Cross-section	PISA	Test scores	Negative
Fairlie (2005)	USA	Computer	Teenagers	Cross-section	CPS	Enrolled	Positive
Schmitt and Wadsworth (2006)	GBR	Computer	Age 15–17	Cross-section, IV	BHPS	A-level exams	Positive
Beltran et al. (2010)	USA	Computer	Teenagers	Cross-sect, FE, IV	CPS — NLSY	Graduate, grades, suspension	Positive
Fiorini (2010)	AUS	Computer use	Age 4–7	Cross-sect, IV	LSAC	Cognitive skills	Positive
Malamud and Pop-Eleches (2011)	ROM	Computer	School aged	RD	Survey	Grades/cognitive skills	Negative/positive
Vigdor et al. (2014)	USA	Computer, Internet	Grades 5–8	Cross-sect, FE	NC records	Test scores	Negative
Beuermann et al. (2012)	Peru	Computer	Grades 1–6	RCT	Survey	Cognitive skills	Mixed
Fairlie and London (2012)	USA	Computer	College	RCT	CC records	Grades, transfer courses	Positive
Mo et al. (2012)	CHN	Computer	Grade 3	RCT	Survey	Test scores/ television	Positive/negative
Fairlie and Robinson (2013)	USA	Computer	Grades 6–10	RCT	CA records	Grades, test scores, attend	Insign
Bauernschuster et al. (2014)	DEU	Internet	Age 7–16	IV	GSOEP	Social activities	Insign, pos

laptops for young children in China. Finally, Malamud and Pop-Eleches (2011) find that winning a computer vouchers increased computer knowledge, fluency and applications, but not web and email fluency among Romanian children.

Research has also focused on the impacts of specific types of computer use or impacts on other educational or social outcomes. For example, a few studies have explored the effects of Facebook use among college students on academic outcomes and find mixed results (see Junco, 2012; Kirschner and Karpinski, 2010; Pasek and Hargittai, 2009, for example). Bauernschuster et al. (2014) use German data to examine the effects of broadband Internet access on children's extra-curricular school activities such as sports, music, arts, and drama and do not find evidence of crowd out. Finally, Beuermann et al. (2012), using data from Peru's randomization across and within schools, do not find evidence of spillovers to classmates and friends (though close friends appear to become more proficient at using a laptop).

Summary

A few patterns emerge from the review of the empirical literature on home effects. First, studies using multivariate regressions and instrumental variable models tend to show large positive (and in some cases negative) effects, but studies using randomized control experiments tend to show zero or small positive effects. As noted above, the contrast in findings may be due to selection bias. Fairlie and London (2012) find evidence that nonexperimental estimates for community college students are nearly an order of magnitude larger than the experimental estimates. Second, most studies estimate impacts on grades and test scores, but many studies examine additional outcomes such as homework time, enrollment and graduation. Although there are some differences in results across outcomes they are generally consistent within the same study. The lack of consistent variation in findings for different outcome measures is at least a little surprising because we might expect intermediate inputs such as homework time and grades that are related to effort to be affected more by potential crowd-out or efficiency gains than test scores which capture the amount of information children learned during the school year. Although not the focus of the chapter, we also review a few papers examining impacts on computer skills and find some evidence of positive effects. But perhaps these findings are not surprising as there is no reason to suspect a negative influence.

Most of the earlier research was on the United States and other developed countries, but several recent studies examine home computer impacts in developing countries. The research focusing on developing countries tends to find smaller impacts, but it is difficult to disentangle this from their methodological focus on random experiments. Theoretically, the effects might be very different in the United States and other countries with a greater reliance on technology throughout the educational system. Finally, several studies explore heterogeneity in the effects of home computers on educational outcomes. Most of the studies examining heterogeneity focus on main demographic groups such as race and gender, but studies also examine heterogeneity by pretreatment academic performance, parental supervision, and propensity for entertainment use of computers. The evidence on heterogeneity is decidedly mixed with no clear evidence even for the same group across studies.

Overall, these results suggest that increasing access to home computers among students who do not already have access is unlikely to greatly improve educational outcomes, but is also unlikely to negatively affect outcomes.

4. CONCLUSIONS

Theoretically, the net effects of ICT investments in schools, the use of CAI in schools, and the use of computers at home on educational outcomes are ambiguous. Expenditures and time devoted to using computers, software, the Internet, and other technologies may be more efficient than expenditures on other educational inputs or may be less efficient. New technologies may displace other more effective instructional and learning methods and distract schoolchildren, or they may represent an effective learning tool and engage schoolchildren in learning. Thus, it is perhaps not surprising that the findings from the rapidly growing empirical literature on the effects of computers, the Internet and computer-assisted instruction are mixed.

The implications from these findings suggest that we should not expect large positive (or negative) impacts from ICT investments in schools or computers at home. Schools should not expect major improvements in grades, test scores and other measures of academic outcomes from investments in ICT or adopting CAI in classrooms, though there might be exceptions such as some CAI interventions in developing countries. Existing and proposed interventions to bridge the digital divide in the United States and other countries, such as large-scale voucher programs, tax breaks for educational purchases of computers, and one-to-one laptop programs with check-out privileges are unlikely to substantially reduce the achievement gap on their own.

An important caveat to this tempered conclusion, however, is that there might be other educational effects of having a computer that are not captured in measurable academic outcomes. For example, computers may be useful for finding information about colleges and financial aid. They might be useful for communicating with teachers and schools and parental supervision of student performance, attendance and disciplinary actions through the spreading use of student information system software (e.g. School Loop, Zangle, ParentConnect, and Aspen). Similar to other aspects of society, schools, professors, and financial aid sources are rapidly expanding their use of technology to provide information and course content to students. A better understanding of these potential benefits is important for future research.

More research is clearly needed in additional areas. First, more research is needed on benefit-cost analyses of computers, Internet connections, software, and other technologies with attention devoted to whether expenditures on these interventions are substituting for other inputs or represent new expenditures. The cost of various interventions is rarely documented or considered. Though purchase costs are declining, maintenance costs may be high and devices may become obsolete or need to be replaced frequently. Second, more research is needed on the shape of the educational returns to technology. For example, are the marginal benefits from a few hours of computer use in the classroom high, but then decline rapidly when computers are used more extensively in the classroom? Third, more research is needed on the related question of online education. There is considerable momentum towards offering online courses by colleges, massive open online courses (MOOCs), creation of online colleges, and "flipped" classrooms, but we know relatively little about their effectiveness relative to costs. Fourth, more research is needed on the impacts of specific uses of computers. For example, computer use for researching topics might be beneficial, whereas computer use for practicing skills may displace other more productive forms of learning (Falck et al., 2015). Each new use of computer technology poses new possible benefits in terms of customization and flexibility, but also creates potential pitfalls that may interfere with education.[28] One of the fundamental challenges of studying the effects of computer technology on educational outcomes is that research consensus often lags the implementation of new initiatives. Computer technology is expanding rapidly from desktop computers to laptops, iPads, and phones, and from educational software to Internet learning applications and social media.

REFERENCES

Alpert, W.T., Couch, K.A., Harmon, O.R., 2015. Online, Blended, and Classroom Teaching of Economics Principles: A Randomized Experiment. University of Connecticut, Department of Economics Working Paper.

Andrés, L., Cuberes, D., Diouf, M., Serebrisky, T., 2010. The diffusion of the Internet: a cross-country analysis. Telecommun. Policy 34 (5), 323–340.

Angrist, J., Lavy, V., 2002. New evidence on classroom computers and pupil learning. Econ. J. 112 (482), 735–765.

Attewell, P., Battle, J., 1999. Home computers and school performance. Inf. Soc. 15, 1–10.

Autor, D.H., 2001. Wiring the labor market. J. Econ. Perspect. 15 (1), 25–40.

Autor, D., Katz, L., Krueger, A., 1998. Computing inequality: have computers changed the labor market? Q. J. Econ. 113 (4), 1169–1214.

Banerjee, A., Cole, S., Duflo, E., Linden, L., 2007. Remedying education: evidence from two randomized experiments in India. Q. J. Econ. 122 (3), 1235–1264.

Barrera-Osorio, F., Linden, L.L., 2009. The Use and Misuse of Computers in Education: Evidence from a Randomized Experiment in Colombia. Policy Research Working Paper 4836, Impact Evaluation Series No. 29, The World Bank.

Barrow, L., Markman, L., Rouse, C.E., 2009. Technology's edge: the educational benefits of computer-aided instruction. Am. Econ. J. Econ. Policy 1 (1), 52–74.

[28] See Los Angeles Unified School District's one-to-one iPad program for a high-profile example of the challenges of adopting new and relatively untested technology. Several schools attempted to abandon the program after students bypassed security filters in order to access the Internet, which was not intended. The program was suspended in light of possible flaws in the bidding process for technology provision.

Bauernschuster, S., Falck, O., Woessmann, L., 2014. Surfing alone? The internet and social capital: evidence from an unforeseeable technological mistake. J. Public Econ. 117, 73–89.

Belo, R., Ferreira, P., Telang, R., 2014. Broadband in school: impact on student performance. Manag. Sci. 60 (2), 265–282.

Beltran, D.O., Das, K.K., Fairlie, R.W., 2010. Home computers and educational outcomes: evidence from the NLSY97 and CPS. Econ. Inq. 48 (3), 771–792.

Bet, G., Ibarrarán, P., Cristia, J., 2014. The Effects of Shared School Technology Access on Students' Digital Skills in Peru. Inter-American Development Bank, Research Department, Washington, DC, United States. Mimeographed document.

Bettinger, E., Fox, L., Loeb, S., Taylor, E., 2014. Changing Distributions: How Online College Classes Alter Student and Professor Performance. Working Paper.

Betts, J., 1996. Is there a link between school inputs and earnings? Fresh scrutiny of an old literature. In: Burtless, G. (Ed.), Does Money Matter? The Effect of School Resources on Student Achievement and Adult Success. Brookings Institution, Washington, D.C, pp. 141–191.

Beuermann, D.W., Cristia, J.P., Cruz-Aguayo, Y., Cueto, S., Malamud, O., 2012. Home computers and child outcomes: short-term impacts from a randomized experiment in Peru. Inter-American Development Bank Working Paper No. IDB-WP-382.

Bowen, W.G., Chingos, M.M., Lack, K.A., Nygren, T.I., 2014. Interactive learning online at public universities: evidence from a six-campus randomized trial. J. Public Policy Anal. Manage. 33 (1), 94–111.

Carrillo, P., Onofa, M., Ponce, J., 2010. Information Technology and Student Achievement: Evidence from a Randomized Experiment in Ecuador. Inter-American Development Bank Working Paper.

Caselli, F., Coleman II, W.J., 2001. Cross-country technology diffusion: the case of computers. Am. Econ. Rev. 91, 328–335.

Chaudhury, N., Hammer, J., Kremer, M., Muralidharan, K., Rogers, F.H., 2006. Missing in action: teacher and health worker absence in developing countries. J. Econ. Perspect. 20 (1), 91–116.

Chinn, M.D., Fairlie, R.W., 2007. The determinants of the global digital divide: a cross-country analysis of computer and internet penetration. Oxf. Econ. Pap. 59, 16–44.

Chinn, M.D., Fairlie, R.W., 2010. ICT use in the developing world: an analysis of differences in computer and internet penetration. Rev. Int. Econ. 18 (1), 153–167.

Coley, R.J., Cradler, J., Engel, P.K., 1997. Computers and Classrooms: The Status of Technology in U.S. Schools: ETS policy information report: 1-69.

Cristia, J.P., Ibarrarán, P., Cueto, S., Santiago, A., Severin, E., 2012. Technology and Child Development: Evidence from the One Laptop per Child Program. Inter-American Development Bank Working Paper No. IDB-WP-304.

Cristia, J.P., Czerwonko, A., Garofalo, P., 2014. Does Technology in Schools Affect Repetition, Dropout and Enrollment? Inter-American Development Bank Working Paper No. IDB-WP-477.

Cuban, L., 1993. Computers meet classroom: classroom wins. Teach. Coll. Rec. 95 (2), 185–210.

Cuban, L., 2001. Oversold and Underused: Computers in the Classroom. Harvard University Press, Cambridge.

Dewan, S., Ganley, D., Kraemer, K.L., 2010. Complementarities in the diffusion of personal computers and the Internet: implications for the global digital divide. Inf. Syst. Res. 21 (4), 925–940.

DiMaggio, P., Bonikowski, B., 2008. Make money surfing the web? The impact of Internet use on the earnings of US workers. Am. Sociol. Rev. 73 (2), 227–250.

DiMaggio, P.J., Hargittai, E., 2001. From Digital Divide to Digital Inequality: Studying Internet Use as Penetration Increases. Working Paper No. 15, Princeton University.

DiNardo, J., Pischke, J.-S., 1997. The returns to computer use revisited: have pencils changed the wage structure too? Q. J. Econ. 112 (1), 291–304.

European Commission, 2013. Survey of Schools: ICT in Education – Benchmarking Access, Use and Attitudes to Technology in Europe's Schools: Digital Agenda for Europe. Final report: 1-159.

Fairlie, R.W., 2004. Race and the digital divide. Contributions to Economic Analysis & Policy, The Berkeley Electronic Journals 3 (1), 1–38. Article 15.

Fairlie, R.W., 2005. The effects of home computers on school enrollment. Econ. Educ. Rev. 24 (5), 533–547.

Fairlie, R.W., 2012a. Academic achievement, technology and race: experimental evidence. Econ. Educ. Rev. 31 (5), 663–679.

Fairlie, R.W., 2012b. The effects of home access to technology on computer skills: evidence from a field experiment. Inf. Econ. Policy 24 (3–4), 243–253.

Fairlie, R.W., London, R.A., 2012. The effects of home computers on educational outcomes: evidence from a field experiment with community college students. Econ. J. 122 (561), 727–753.

Fairlie, R.W., Robinson, J., 2013. Experimental evidence on the effects of home computers on academic achievement among schoolchildren. Am. Econ. J. Appl. Econ. 5 (3), 211–240.

Fairlie, 2015. Do boys and girls use computers differently, and does it contribute to why boys do worse in school than girls? B. E. J. Econom. Anal. Policy (Contributions) 94, 1–38.

Falck, O., Mang, C., Woessmann, L., 2015. Virtually No Effect? Different Types of Computer Use and the Effect of Classroom Computers on Student Achievement. CESifo Working Paper No. 5266.

Federal Communications Commission, 2014. The E-Rate Program. http://www.fcc.gov/e-rate-update.

Figlio, D.N., 1999. Functional form and the estimated effects of school resources. Econ. Educ. Rev. 18, 241–252.

Figlio, D., Rush, M., Lu, Y., 2013. Is it live or is it internet? Experimental estimates of the effects of online instruction on student learning. J. Labor Econ. 31 (4), 763–784.

Fiorini, M., 2010. The effect of home computer use on children's cognitive and non-cognitive skills. Econ. Educ. Rev. 29, 55–72.

Freeman, R.B., 2002. The labour market in the new information economy. Oxf. Rev. Econ. Policy 18, 288–305.

Fuchs, T., Woessmann, L., 2004. Computers and Student Learning: Bivariate and Multivariate Evidence on the Availability and Use of Computers at Home and at School. CESifo Working Paper No. 1321.

Giacquinta, J., Bauer, J.A., Levin, J., 1993. Beyond Technology's Promise: An Examination of Children's Educational Computing at Home. Cambridge University Press, New York.

Goldfarb, A., Prince, J., 2008. Internet adoption and usage patterns are different: implications for the digital divide. Inf. Econ. Policy 20 (1), 2–15.

Goolsbee, A., Guryan, J., 2006. The impact of internet subsidies in public schools. Rev. Econ. Stat. 88 (2), 336–347.

Grimes, D., Warschauer, M., 2008. Learning with laptops: a multi-method case study. J. Comput. Res. 38 (3), 305–332.

Hanushek, E.A., 1979. Conceptual and empirical issues in the estimation of educational production functions. J. Hum. Resour. 14 (3), 351–388.

Hanushek, E.A., 1986. The economics of schooling: production and efficiency in public schools. J. Econ. Lit. 24 (3), 1141–1177.

Hanushek, E.A., 2006. School resources. In: Hanushek, E.A., Welch, F. (Eds.), Handbook of the Economics of Education, vol. 2. North Holland, Amsterdam, pp. 865–908.

Hanushek, E.A., Rivkin, S.G., Taylor, L.L., 1996. Aggregation and the estimated effects of school resources. Rev. Econ. Statist. 78 (4), 611–627.

Hoffman, D.L., Novak, T.P., 1998. Bridging the racial divide on the internet. Science 280, 390–391.

International Telecommunications Union, 2014a. Core Indicators on Access to, and Use of, ICT by Households and Individuals, Latest Available Data. http://www.itu.int/en/ITU-D/Statistics/Pages/stat/default.aspx.

International Telecommunications Union, 2014b. Key ICT Indicators for Developed and Developing Countries and the World (Totals and Penetration Rates). http://www.itu.int/en/ITU-D/Statistics/Pages/stat/default.aspx.

Jones, S., 2002. The Internet Goes to College: How Students Are Living in the Future with Today's Technology. Pew Internet and American Life Project, Washington, D.C.

Joyce, T., Crockett, S., Jaeger, D.A., Altindag, O., O'Connell, S.D., 2014. Does Classroom Time Matter? A Randomized Field Experiment in Principles of Microeconomics. Working Paper.

Junco, R., 2012. Too much face and not enough books: the relationship between multiple indices of Facebook use and academic performance. Comput. Hum. Behav. 28 (1), 187–198.

Kaiser Family Foundation, 2010. Generation M^2: Media in the Lives of 8- to 18-Year Olds. Kaiser Family Foundation Study.

Kirkpatrick, H., Cuban, L., 1998. Computers make kids smarter—right? Technos Q. Educ. Technol. 7, 2.

Kirschner, P.A., Karpinski, A.C., 2010. Facebook® and academic performance. Comput. Hum. Behav. 26 (6), 1237–1245.

Koedinger, K.R., Anderson, J.R., Hadley, W H., Mark, M.A., 1997. Intelligent tutoring goes to school in the big city. Int. J. Artif. Intell. Educ. 8, 30–43.

Kremer, M., Brannen, C., Glennerster, R., 2013. The challenge of education and learning in the developing world. Science 340, 297–300.

Krueger, A.B., 1993. How computers have changed the wage structure: evidence from micro data. Q. J. Econ. 107 (1), 35–78.

Kulik, C.-L., Kulik, J., 1991. Effectiveness of computer-based instruction: an updated analysis. Comput. Hum. Behav. 7, 75–94.

Lenhart, A., Simon, M., Graziano, M., 2001. The Internet and Education: Findings from the Pew Internet & American Life Project. Pew Internet & American Life Project, Washington, DC.

Lenhart, A., Kahne, J., Middaugh, E., Macgill, A.R., Evans, C., Vitak, J., 2008. Teens, Video Games, and Civics: Teens' Gaming Experiences Are Diverse and Include Significant Social Interaction and Civic Engagement. Pew Internet and American Life Project, Washington, DC.

Lenhart, A., 2009. The democratization of online social networks: A look at the change in demographics of social network users over time. Pew Internet & American Life Project, Presentation at AoIR 10.0. (October 8, 2009).

Leuven, E., Lindahl, M., Oosterbeek, H., Webbink, D., 2007. The effect of extra funding for disadvantaged pupils on achievement. Rev. Econ. Statist. 89 (4), 721–736.

Liao, Y.-K., 1992. Effects of computer-assisted instruction on cognitive outcomes: a meta-analysis. J. Res. Comput. Educ. 24 (3), 367–380.

Linden, L.L., 2008. Complement or Substitute? The Effect of Technology on Student Achievement in India. Working Paper.

Machin, S., McNally, S., Silva, O., 2007. New technology in schools: is there a payoff? Econ. J. 117 (522), 1145–1167.

Maine Education Policy Research Institute, 2007. Maine's Middle School Laptop Program: Creating Better Writers. Maine Education Policy Research Institute, University of Southern Maine.

Malamud, O., Pop-Eleches, C., 2011. Home computer use and the development of human capital. Q. J. Econ. 126, 987–1027.

Mathematica, 2007. Effectiveness of Reading and Mathematics Software Products: Findings from the First Student Cohort: Report for U.S. Department of Education.

Mathematica, 2009. Effectiveness of Reading and Mathematics Software Products: Findings from Two Student Cohorts: Report for U.S. Department of Education.

McEwan, P.J., 2015. Improving learning in primary school of developing countries: A meta analysis of randomized experiments. Rev. Educ. Res. 85, 353–394.

Mitchell Institute, 2004. One-to-one Laptops in a High School Environment, Piscataquis Community High School Study Final. Report, Great Maine Schools Project.

Mo, D., Swinnen, J., Zhang, L., Yi, H., Qu, Q., Boswell, M., Rozelle, S., 2012. Can One Laptop per Child Reduce the Digital Divide and Educational Gap? Evidence from a Randomized Experiment in Migrant Schools in Beijing. Rural Education Action Project, Stanford University, Working Paper 233.

Mo, D., Zhang, L., Luo, R., Qu, Q., Huang, W., Wang, J., Qiao, Y., Boswell, M., Rozelle, S., 2014. Integrating Computer Assisted Learning into a Regular Curriculum: Evidence from a Randomized Experiment in Rural Schools in Shaanxi. Working Paper.

Mossberger, K., Tolbert, C., Stansbury, M., 2003. Virtual Inequality; Beyond the Digital Divide. Georgetown University Press, Washington, DC.

Mossberger, K., Tolbert, C., Gilbert, M., 2006. Race, place, and information technology. Urban Aff. Rev. 41 (5), 583–620.

Noll, R.G., Older-Aguilar, D., Rosston, G.L., Ross, R.R., 2000. The digital divide: definitions, measurement, and policy issues. In: Paper Presented at Bridging the Digital Divide: California Public Affairs Forum. Stanford University.

OECD, 2014. OECD Factbook 2014: Economic, Environmental and Social Statistics. http://www.oecd-ilibrary.org/economics/oecd-factbook-2014_factbook-2014-en.

Ono, H., Zavodny, M., 2007. Digital inequality: a five country comparison using microdata. Soc. Sci. Res. 36 (September 2007), 1135–1155.

Pasek, J., Hargittai, E., 2009. Facebook and academic performance: reconciling a media sensation with data. First Monday. 14. Number 5-4.

Patterson, R.W., 2014. Can Behavioral Tools Improve Online Student Outcomes? Experimental Evidence from a Massive Open Online Course. Working Paper.

Peck, C., Cuban, L., Kirkpatrick, H., 2002. Technopromoter dreams, student realities. Phi Delta Kappan 83 (6), 472–480.

Puma, M.J., Chaplin, D.D., Pape, A.D., 2000. E-rate and the digital divide: a preliminary analysis from the Integrated Studies of Educational Technology. Urban Institute, Washington, D.C.

Rainie, L., Hitlin, P., 2005. The Internet at School. Pew Internet and American Life Project, Washington, DC.

Rivkin, S.G., Hanushek, E.A., Kain, J.F., 2005. Teachers, schools, and academic achievement. Econometrica 73 (2), 417–458.

Rouse, C.E., Krueger, A.B., 2004. Putting computerized instruction to the test: a randomized evaluation of a "scientifically based" reading program. Econ. Educ. Rev. 23 (4), 323–338.

Schmitt, J., Wadsworth, J., 2006. Is there an impact of household computer ownership on children's educational attainment in Britain? Econ. Educ. Rev. 25, 659–673.

Stoll, C., 1995. Silicon Snake Oil: Second Thoughts on the Information Highway. Doubleday, New York.

Suhr, K., Hernandez, D., Grimes, D., Warschauer, M., 2010. Laptops and fourth-grade literacy: assisting the jump over the fourth-grade slump. J. Technol. Learn. Assess 9 (5), 1–45.

Texas Center for Educational Research, 2009. Evaluation of the Texas Technology Immersion Pilot: Final Outcomes for a Four-Year Study (2004–05 to 2007–08).

Todd, P.E., Wolpin, K.I., 2003. On the specification and estimation of the production function for cognitive achievement. Econ. J. 113 (2), 3–33.

Underwood, J., Billingham, M., Underwood, G., 1994. Predicting Computer Literacy: How Do the Technological Experiences of Schoolchildren Predict Their Computer Based Problem-Solving Skills? J. Inform. Tech. Teach. Educ. 3 (1), 115–125.

U.S. Census Bureau, 1988. Computer Use in the United States: 1984: Current population reports special studies, Series P-23, No. 155.

U.S. Census Bureau, 2012. Computer and Internet Access in the United States: 2012, Table 1. Reported Internet Usage for Individuals 3 Years and Older, by Selected Characteristics: 2012, http://www.census.gov/hhes/computer/publications/2012.html.

U.S. Department of Commerce, 2004. A nation online: entering the broadband age. U.S.G.P.O, Washington, D.C.

U.S. Department of Education, 2013. Digest of Education Statistics 2012 (NCES 2014–015). National Center for Education Statistics, Institute of Education Sciences, U.S. Department of Education, Washington, DC.

UNESCO Institute for Statistics, 2009. Guide to Measuring Information and Communication Technologies in Education: Technical paper no. 2: 1-140.

UNESCO Institute for Statistics, 2014. ICT in Education in Asia: A Comparative Analysis of ICT Integration and E-Readiness in Schools Across Asia. Information Paper No. 22: 1-64.

Universal Services Administration Company, 2010. Annual report.

Vigdor, J.L., Ladd, H.F., Martinez, E., 2014. Scaling the digital divide: home computer technology and student achievement. Econ. Inq. 52 (3), 1103–1119.

Wallsten, S., 2005. Regulation and internet use in developing countries. Econ. Dev. Cult. Chang. 53, 501–523.

Warschauer, M., 2003. Technology and Social Inclusion: Rethinking the Digital Divide. MIT Press, Cambridge.

Warschauer, M., 2006. Laptops and Literacy: Learning in the Wireless Classroom. Teachers College Press, New York.

Warschauer, M., Matuchniak, T., 2010. New technology and digital worlds: Analyzing evidence of equity in access, use, and outcomes. Rev. Res. Educ. 34 (1), 179–225.

Zavodny, M., 2006. Does watching television rot your mind? Estimates of the effect on test scores. Econ. Educ. Rev. 25, 565–573.

CHAPTER 6

Teacher Pensions

C. Koedel, M. Podgursky
University of Missouri — Columbia, Missouri (MO), United States

Contents

Abstract

Most educators in the United States receive retirement compensation via a subnational defined-benefit pension plan. These plans exert strong "pull" and "push" incentives over the course of the career and concentrate teacher retirements at relatively early ages compared to other professions. They also impose sharp penalties on geographically mobile teachers. Teacher pensions are a large and growing cost of public education. There are several reasons for the rising costs, but the biggest reason is that the unfunded liabilities of most plans are growing. The growth in unfunded liabilities is facilitated by the decoupling of contributions and benefits at the individual level, and represents a shift of wealth from young to older teachers in the United States. In response to fiscal pressures, some states are changing their plans, primarily for new teachers.

Keywords

Teacher pensions, Defined-benefit plans, Retirement, Cash-balance plans, Public educators

1. INTRODUCTION

Unlike most private-sector professionals, public educators in the United States are primarily enrolled in defined-benefit (DB) pension plans (Hansen, 2010, National Council on Teacher Quality, 2012). Upon retirement from a DB plan, educators receive a lifetime annuity that depends on their earnings and years of service. Although in principle DB plans can be designed so that annuity payments are directly tied to contributions over the course of the career, as a matter of practice payments and contributions are not linked in the plans that cover the majority of public educators. The decoupling of benefits and contributions at the individual level allows for peculiar labor supply incentives, and the cross–subsidization of retirement benefits across contemporaneous workers and generations of workers.

Substantial resources are devoted to fund educator retirement benefits. Based on data from 2012, on average across states teachers and their employers contributed approximately 20% of salaries to teachers' pension plans, and unfunded liabilities in state plans totaled over $300 billion (National Council on Teacher Quality, 2012).[1] Moreover, economists have argued that fund-reported cost and liability estimates are too low because the value of promised benefits has been understated by actuaries (Biggs, 2011; Biggs and Richwine, 2014; Novy-Marx and Rauh, 2009, 2011, 2014). Consistent with this concern, pension debts have been rising in most public pensions plans in the United States over the past decade, even in plans where educators and employers have ultimately made all actuarially required contributions (eg, Missouri).

In addition to being of interest due to their increasingly precarious financial situation, educator pension plans are also of interest because of the labor supply incentives that they create. The labor supply incentives are driven by compensation *backloading*, which is a term used to describe the feature of typical plans that wealth accrues very slowly early in the career and then very quickly toward the end of the career, as we illustrate below. The backloading has implications for initial recruitment and also creates powerful "pull" incentives that encourage educators who have already entered the profession to remain in teaching until they become eligible for pension collection. Once a teacher reaches collection eligibility the incentive structure shifts — usually sharply — and similarly strong "push" incentives encourage retirement. In many states, an educator who enters teaching in her mid–20s and works continuously will feel the "push" of the pension system by her mid-to-late 50s. The push effect is independent of promotions. Holding career duration and pension-plan mobility constant, a principal or superintendent will be pushed out by the pension system at the same point in the career cycle as a classroom teacher (Koedel et al., 2013a).

Concerns about the lack of workforce-quality benefits of teachers' pension incentives, along with the cost and fiscal volatility of many plans, have prompted the development of alternative retirement compensation options for public educators. As of 2012, 13 of the 50 states offered educators something other than a pure-DB pension plan.

---

[1] Based on combined employer-employee contribution rates to state pension plans for educators as reported by the National Council on Teacher Quality (2012). This figure excludes health insurance costs during retirement, which are important because most educators retire well before eligibility for Medicare (typically age 65) and many states and school districts provide access to free or heavily subsidized health insurance for retirees. Health insurance has become a large retirement benefit cost for many states and school districts but we do not examine retiree health benefits in this chapter. We refer interested readers to Clark (2010).

Alternative options across states include defined contribution (DC) plans, hybrid DB–DC plans, choice plans (where educators can choose from some combination of DB, DC, and hybrid plans) and cash-balance plans. While the overwhelming majority of public educators continue to be covered by a traditional DB plan, the retirement-benefit landscape in education is changing.

The purpose of this chapter is to provide an overview of pensions for public educators, with a primary focus on the United States. We begin by describing how educator pension plans work and reviewing the current policy landscape. Next we discuss the labor supply incentives created by backloading and review the literature on their implications for retirement behavior and workforce quality. Then we discuss the fiscal condition of educator pension plans and how their fiscal health has evolved over time, followed by an overview of recent efforts in some states to reform educator retirement systems and the tradeoffs that have come with the reforms. We conclude with a brief discussion of educator retirement plans in other developed countries, although we are not aware of any research studies on educator pensions outside of the United States.

2. BACKGROUND ON RETIREMENT BENEFIT PLANS FOR EDUCATORS

Compensation for educators in any year can be divided into current and deferred components (Lazear, 1986). Current compensation consists of direct salaries and other contemporaneous benefits like health coverage. Deferred compensation is delivered through pension payments and retiree health coverage. The latter is important for teachers because many retire before reaching the age of eligibility for Medicare (typically age 65), but we focus on the pension share of deferred compensation in this chapter.

As noted above, educators in 37 of the 50 states are covered by pure-DB pension plans. Of the remaining 13 states, 5 offer hybrid plans, which include DB and DC components, 6 others offer a choice between DB and alternative plans (eg, DC and hybrid plans), one state (Kansas) offers a cash-balance plan, and one state (Alaska) enrolls all educators in a DC plan.[2] Most of these plans are "contributory" in that both the educator and employer (either the district or the state) make a contribution toward funding the retirement benefit. Teacher contributions are exempt from federal and state income taxes.

---

[2] These summary statistics are as reported by the National Council on Teacher Quality (2012). They describe the situation for teachers newly hired in 2014 or later, with the exception of the cash-balance plan in Kansas which is effective in 2015. In some cases, incumbent teachers are in different "tiers" of plans, with the hybrid or DC plans only covering younger teachers. Thus, the vast majority of incumbent and experienced teachers are covered by traditional DB plans. In 28 states (eg, California, Texas, Ohio), teachers have their own plans, while in 23 others (eg, Florida, Maryland, Tennessee) teachers are in consolidated plans with other state and local workers. In addition, some teachers are in municipal teacher plans (eg, Chicago, New York, Saint Louis, Kansas City).

2.1 How Traditional, Final-Average-Salary DB Pension Plans Work

The DB plans that cover most public educators are typically administered at the state level and share a common structure (Costrell and Podgursky, 2009). The following general formula is used to determine the annual benefit at retirement:

$$B = F*YOS*FAS \qquad (1)$$

In Eq. (1), B represents the annual benefit or annuity, F is a formula factor, which is usually close to 2%, YOS indicates years of service in the system, and FAS is the teacher's final average salary, commonly calculated as the average of the final few years of earnings.[3] After retirement, the benefit (B) is also generally adjusted for inflation. In some states inflation adjustments are by statute and in others they are ad hoc. Often there are caps in place limiting cumulative adjustments.

The vesting period varies between 3 and 10 years across state plans. Vesting periods have been on the rise in recent years (National Council on Teacher Quality, 2012). Once vested, educators are eligible to collect a pension upon retirement. If an educator leaves the system prior to vesting she usually loses all employer contributions on her behalf but can recoup her own contributions, typically with interest.

The official "normal retirement age" in most plans is between ages 60 and 65. Normal retirement can also be entirely service-based — eg, at 30 years of system service. However, educators can often retire and collect benefits earlier. For example, the Missouri state pension plan has two provisions that facilitate retirement prior to the normal retirement age of 60. The first provision is referred to as "25-and-out." The 25-and-out provision allows an educator to retire and begin collecting benefits immediately, at any age, as long as she has 25 years of system experience. There is a modest penalty associated with retirements via 25-and-out, but it is less than what would be actuarially appropriate. The second provision that facilitates early retirement in Missouri is referred to as the "rule-of-80." The rule-of-80 states that at whatever point a teacher's combination of age and experience adds up to 80, she can retire and begin collecting benefits immediately and without penalty. This means, for instance, that a teacher who begins work at age 24 and works continuously would be eligible for full retirement benefits at age 52 with 28 years of experience. Most DB plans have similar provisions that facilitate retirements before the normal age.

In 27 of the 37 DB-only states, educators are also enrolled in Social Security. States covered by Social Security tend to have less-generous and less-costly pension plans given

---

[3] By contrast, the annuity payment in the national Social Security system is based on earnings averaged over an entire work career. These are called career-average DB plans. Other plans, common in private firms that have retained DB plans, are called cash balance plans. These allow pension wealth to accrue smoothly over an employee's work life. See Barr and Diamond (2010).

that educators and districts also contribute to Social Security.[4] Social Security is also a DB plan. However, unlike standard state plans, wealth accrual in Social Security is not heavily backloaded (as we illustrate below).

Two features of the benefit structure in state plans — both absent from Social Security — generate the backloading (Costrell and Podgursky, 2009; Friedberg and Turner, 2010). First are the generous early-retirement provisions similar to the ones we describe above for Missouri that are found in most plans. These provisions can substantially increase the number of years that career educators can collect pension payments, but are of little to no value to educators who leave the system early. Second is the way that final average salary is calculated. The *FAS* calculation is frozen at the time of exit and therefore does not account for inflation or life-cycle pay increases. This penalizes teachers who exit a plan mid-career. To illustrate, consider two individuals who end up with the same wage profile over the course of their respective 30-year careers. The first individual stays in the same system and her final payment is equal to $30*F*FAS$, where *FAS* is calculated using her last few years of earnings. The second individual switches systems after 15 years. Her final payment comes from the two systems and is equal to $\{15*F*FAS_1 + 15*F*FAS_2\}$, where FAS_1 is her final average salary at the time of her exit from the first system, unadjusted for inflation or career-cycle pay increases.

2.2 Pension-Wealth Accrual in Traditional DB Plans

For analytic tractability we define "pension wealth" as the present value of the future stream of pension payments earned at a given point in an educator's career. Pension wealth at time s, with collection starting at time j where $j \geq s$, can be calculated as:

$$\sum_{t=j}^{T} Y_t * P_{t|s} * d^{t-s} \tag{2}$$

In Eq (2), Y_t is the annual pension payment in period t, $P_{t|s}$ is the probability that the individual is alive in period t conditional on being alive in period s, d is a discount factor, and we set T to 101.[5]

Fig. 1 shows wealth-accrual profiles for a representative 24-year-old entrant into teaching based on the rules from three state plans: California, Missouri, and Tennessee. We discount to the point of entry using a discount rate of 4% for the calculations

---

[4] State and local employees (and thus public school teachers) were excluded from Social Security when the act was passed in 1935. However, amendments to the act in 1950, 1954, and 1956 allowed states to elect Social Security coverage for state and local workers if the workers voted to join (Munnell, 2000). Recent data from the Bureau of Labor Statistics shows that 27% of public school teachers are not covered by Social Security (U.S. Department of Labor, 2008, Table 5).

[5] At the point of initial collection Y_t is equal to the baseline benefit "B" from Eq. (1). Y_t can be cost-of-living adjusted during retirement.

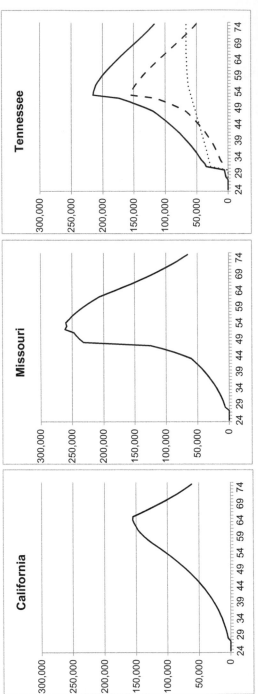
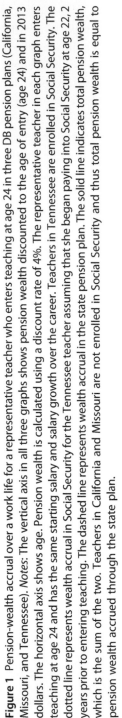

Figure 1 Pension-wealth accrual over a work life for a representative teacher who enters teaching at age 24 in three DB pension plans (California, Missouri, and Tennessee). *Notes:* The vertical axis in all three graphs shows pension wealth discounted to the age of entry (age 24) and in 2013 dollars. The horizontal axis shows age. Pension wealth is calculated using a discount rate of 4%. The representative teacher in each graph enters teaching at age 24 and has the same starting salary and salary growth over the career. Teachers in Tennessee are enrolled in Social Security. The dotted line represents wealth accrual in Social Security for the Tennessee teacher assuming that she began paying into Social Security at age 22, 2 years prior to entering teaching. The dashed line represents wealth accrual in the state pension plan. The solid line indicates total pension wealth, which is the sum of the two. Teachers in California and Missouri are not enrolled in Social Security and thus total pension wealth is equal to pension wealth accrued through the state plan.

in the figure.[6] Teachers in Tennessee are enrolled in Social Security and we show wealth accrual with and without Social Security benefits for the Tennessee teacher. Teachers in California and Missouri are not enrolled in Social Security.

The formula factors at full retirement (ie, at the maximum value) in California, Missouri, and Tennessee are 0.024, 0.025, and 0.015, respectively.[7] Full retirement eligibility for the representative teacher is reached at the aforementioned rule-of-80 in Missouri and at 30 years of service in Tennessee. In California full retirement eligibility is not reached until age 65, which is more than a decade later than in Missouri and Tennessee based on the work profile of our representative teacher. Thus, California teachers can collect full benefits for fewer years than their counterparts in the other states (this is not true just in the comparison with Missouri and Tennessee — most states allow teachers to retire and begin collecting full benefits earlier than in California).[8]

All three plans shown in Fig. 1 have a 5-year vesting rule — prior to vesting teachers accrue no pension wealth. Once vested, the marginal returns to work in terms of pension-wealth accrual are initially small and then rise quickly in all three plans. In Missouri, the pension wealth profile has a plateau. The spike at the front end of the plateau in Missouri coincides with the attainment of eligibility to collect benefits via 25-and out, which comes with a penalty that is less than what would be actuarially fair. To see why the 25-and-out provision generates such a large increase in pension wealth, consider the marginal value of that year of work for our representative entrant. If she exits after 24 years of service and prior to 25-and out eligibility, she will not be eligible to collect her first pension payment until age 56 under the rule-of-80, but by working the 25th year she can collect her first payment at age 49. The extra 7 years of payments facilitated by the 25-and-out provision, even after accounting for the collection penalty, drive the rapid pension-wealth increase at the front end of the plateau. The peak in Missouri occurs when the teacher has worked continuously up to the rule-of-80 amount, which is how she receives the most pension payments under full benefit eligibility (ie, without a collection penalty).

---

[6] We parameterize a starting wage and wage-growth profile to produce the graphs in Fig. 1. The starting wage and wage-growth profile are the same for the representative teacher in all three states for ease of comparison, and are determined by a wage function that we estimate as a cubic in teaching experience using administrative data from Missouri. The California teacher is from the newest tier of that system — currently retiring teachers in California are covered under a more generous and more backloaded set of rules. We assume that the Tennessee teacher began contributing to Social Security at age 22, prior to entering the pension system at age 24.

[7] The formula factor is increased from 0.0250 to 0.0255 for all service years for teachers in Missouri who put in at least 31 years of service. This benefit is reflected in the figure by the small bump in the pension-wealth profile at 31 years of work, which effectively extends the "plateau" in the graph.

[8] In all three states benefits can be collected prior to reaching full retirement eligibility but with a reduced formula factor.

The Tennessee plan is characterized by a pension-wealth spike at 30 years of service and a similar spike is present in the California plan.[9] In all three plans, pension-wealth begins to decline once educators become eligible for full retirement (ie, eligible for collection at the maximum formula factor). Wealth accrual declines because benefits cannot be collected while working. While the value of the monthly pension payment can be increased by posteligibility work (which can raise final average salary and years of service), the gains from the larger payments are more than offset by losses owing to forgone pension payments. We return to this point below when we discuss labor supply incentives.

The profiles in Fig. 1 are discounted to the point of entry into teaching at age 24. Changing the discounting horizon does not affect the shapes of the curves but does change the pension-wealth values on the vertical axis. Based on our parameterized real discount rate of 4%, the multiplicative factor required for discounting the profiles to age 55 rather than age 24 is approximately 3.4. Thus, the discounting horizon affects the strength of the incentives at different points in the work life. The graphs in the figure illustrate wealth accrual from the perspective of a new entrant. However, a teacher who is making a labor supply decision at a later stage in her career will face larger, and hence more potent, incentives.

The profile for the Tennessee teacher also provides the opportunity to compare the state plan to Social Security. Wealth accrual in Social Security is fairly flat owing to the Social Security system having a very different formula for determining benefits.[10] However, there is still a prominent spike in the Tennessee plan overall even after accounting for Social Security. This is because late in a teacher's career, the present discounted value of the stream of pension payments from the state plan far exceeds that of the Social Security payments. In essence, the Social Security benefit simply shifts up the peaked wealth-accrual profile in Tennessee.

Finally, Fig. 1 shows that total pension wealth for Missouri educators at the end of the career is much larger than in California and Tennessee, even when one accounts for Social Security in Tennessee. There are several factors that contribute to the gap in the profiles across states. In the comparison with Tennessee, the issue is that the Missouri formula factor is much higher. In the comparison with California, while the California

---

[9] Interestingly, Tennessee has a 25-and-out clause as well. However, unlike in Missouri the penalty for collecting under 25-and-out in Tennessee accounts for the age of collection — the younger the educator, the sharper the penalty. Accounting for age in an actuarially appropriate manner wipes out the pension-wealth gains from collection under 25-and-out in Tennessee. Thus, there is no deviation from the smooth accrual rate at 25 years of service in Tennessee.

[10] The flatness of the Social Security curve after age 65 also derives from the fact that since 1999 it has been possible to collect Social Security and continue working without penalty. As noted in the text, it is generally not possible to collect DB teacher pensions and continue working under the same plan. Teachers are free to "retire" in one state plan (eg, New York) and take a teaching position covered by another state plan (eg, New Jersey).

teacher can work up to a formula factor that approaches the Missouri formula factor (0.024 vs. 0.025), the Missouri teacher can retire with the high formula factor at a much younger age, which results in many more years of pension payments. Put differently, the California teacher must choose between more payments at a lower formula factor or fewer payments at a higher formula factor, whereas the Missouri teacher gets more payments and a high formula factor.[11]

2.3 Defined-Contribution, Hybrid, Cash-Balance, and Choice Plans

Alaska is the only state that exclusively offers a DC-only plan for educators, although educator retirement compensation in states with hybrid and choice options also have DC components. Retirement benefits in DC plans are entirely portable and directly tied to contributions. DC plans are best thought of as individual retirement savings accounts — there is no backloading. Educators are responsible for making their own investments in DC plans, although the investment choice set is typically constrained. DC plans come with investment risk for educators, which is a limitation relative to the DB alternative (where the investment risk is borne by the system). However, as noted by Koedel et al. (2014), DB plans are also risky, albeit in different ways (see discussion below).

As of 2012, educators in five states — Indiana, Michigan, Oregon, Rhode Island, and Virginia — were enrolled in hybrid retirement plans (National Council on Teacher Quality, 2012). Hybrid plans combine a less-remunerative and less-costly DB plan with a DC plan.[12] The DB component works like a traditional DB plan. Benefits are backloaded in hybrid plans owing to the DB component, but because the absolute level of pension-wealth in the DB component is lower, the impact of the backloading is reduced. Per above, the DC component is not backloaded.

In Kansas, all teachers hired after January 1, 2015 are enrolled in a cash-balance plan. Although rare in K–12 education, the Teachers Insurance and Annuity Association of America (TIAA) has similar plans that cover higher education employees. Cash-balance plans guarantee members a minimum rate of return, which is an implicit and generally desirable feature of traditional DB pension plans (at least from the pensioner's perspective). Cash-balance plans are like DC plans in sense that the value of the retirement benefit is directly tied to contributions, but unlike DC plans, employees do not make investment decisions (plan assets are managed by the pension fund) and do not bear investment risk. In addition, cash-balance plans offer automatic annuitization at retirement. Because of the

---

[11] Other aspects of the plans also contribute to differences in wealth accrual across states including the number of years used to calculate final-average-salary (the benefit becomes more valuable when fewer years are used) and differences in how cost-of-living adjustments are applied during benefit collection across plans. We do not go into detail about these other features of the plans in the text but they are incorporated into the graphs in Fig. 1.

[12] In hybrid plans teacher contributions are typically put in the DC plan and employer contributions in the DB plan.

direct link between contributions and benefits, wealth accrual in cash-balance plans is not backloaded and benefit cross-subsidization across teachers does not occur.

Finally, six states — Florida, Louisiana, Ohio, South Carolina, Utah, and Washington — offer educators a choice of retirement plans. The choices vary across states but include some combination of DB, DC, hybrid, and cash-balance plans.

3. INCENTIVES FOR EDUCATORS

Between pure-DB, hybrid, and choice states, the vast majority of public educators earn some or all of their retirement compensation via a DB pension plan. The prevalence of the DB pension structure in education stands in sharp contrast to the private sector, where fewer than one in five workers has DB pension coverage (Wiatrowski, 2012).

The wealth-accrual profiles in Fig. 1 illustrate the "pull" and "push" incentives that are built into these plans. The pull incentives on the front end encourage educators to remain in the system until reaching collection eligibility. Drawing on Lazear (1986), the conventional economic rationale for the backloaded compensation profile is to deter shirking. The idea is that if it is costly for employers to monitor effort, backloading can be used to raise the employee's cost of shirking under the assumption that if the employee is caught, she will be terminated prior to receiving the backloaded compensation. However, this rationale is a poor fit for public school teachers because most teachers earn tenure very early in their careers (as early as after 2 years of teaching — see Hanushek, 2009), which makes the threat of losing a pension not credible.[13]

Shortly after educators become eligible to collect a pension, the wealth-accrual profile begins to slope downward as educators enter the push region. Wealth accrual turns negative because benefits cannot be collected while working. Put differently, upon reaching collection eligibility there is an immediate spike in the opportunity cost of continued work.[14] Collection-eligible individuals who continue working could earn a fraction of their salary — typically a substantial fraction — without working at all or while working in an alternative career (even in a school covered by a different pension system). As noted above, although pensioners can increase the value of their monthly pension payments by increasing their years of service and final average salary even after they become

[13] Lazear (1986) analyzes the efficiency rationale for this type of incentive structure in the context of a competitive firm. A key factor in his model is the role of a pension as a performance bond to discourage shirking. See Jacob (2011) and Weisberg et al. (2009) for information about the infrequency with which tenured teachers in public schools receive unsatisfactory ratings and/or are removed from the classroom. An additional, general rationale for long-term government retirement plans is that they facilitate improved intergenerational risk sharing (eg, see Gollier, 2008; Schiller, 1999). The literature on the intergenerational risk-sharing benefits of public retirement plans is less concerned with the specifics of plan design and the political economy, which are the primary focus of this chapter.

[14] To offset the push incentive some states utilize deferred retirement option plans (DROPs). These plans allow educators to "retire" and continue working without losing pension benefits.

collection eligible, the increased value in pension payments caused by delaying retirement is more than offset by the fact that payments are forgone via continued work. Thus, there is a "push" from the pension system to retire. The mostly flat, then rapidly rising, and then declining profile of pension-wealth accrual exacerbates differences in career salary profiles for teachers relative to other professionals as documented by Vigdor (2008).

There is consensus in the literature that educators' retirement choices are responsive to the above-described pension incentives. Harris and Adams (2007) show that teachers exit into retirement at much younger ages relative to workers in other professions, which they note is consistent with teachers responding to their "push" incentives, but they find little evidence to suggest that the "pull" incentives affect mid-career attrition. Using data from Arkansas, Costrell and Podgursky (2009) show that retirements spike when teachers become eligible for full benefit collection, and that the distribution of retirements shifts in response to a change in retirement-eligibility rules. Costrell and McGee (2010) extend this work and find significant effects of pension-wealth accrual and peak values on retirement behavior for Arkansas teachers. Furgeson et al. (2006) study a temporary pension incentive program in Pennsylvania and find that an increase in teachers' retirement benefits generates a substantial behavioral response in terms of retirements. Fitzpatrick and Lovenheim (2014) also study a temporary incentive program, this time in Illinois, and similarly to Furgeson et al. find that teachers were highly responsive. Brown (2013) uses data from a permanent pension reform in California and finds significant changes in the clustering of retirements by age corresponding to pension rule changes. Finally, Ni and Podgursky (forthcoming) estimate a structural "option value" model of teacher retirements for Missouri teachers. They find that the Missouri DB plan concentrates retirements much more than would be the case under a plan with smoother wealth accrual.

The evidence on the responsiveness of teachers to their retirement incentives is consistent with the larger literature on workers in other occupations. For example, Coile and Gruber (2007) use nationally representative data from the Health and Retirement Study to show that Social Security and private pension benefits are significant determinants of retirement behavior. Chan and Stevens (2008) use the same data and also conclude that workers' labor supply decisions depend on their pension incentives. Their study additionally highlights the important role that information plays in influencing behavior. In particular, Chan and Stevens (2008) show that well-informed individuals appear to be much more responsive to their pension incentives than ill-informed individuals. However, while ill-informed individuals may act as if they are unresponsive to their pension incentives, they are actually responding to their perceived but incorrect understanding of how their pensions work.[15]

---

[15] Older studies showing that workers' retirement decisions are responsive to their accumulation of retirement wealth include Samwick (1998) and Stock and Wise (1990).

In addition to understanding responsiveness in general, economists are interested in determining whether responsiveness is related to teacher productivity. The nature of the relationship between the DB incentive structure and productivity is critical to understanding how pension plans influence workforce quality overall. At the point of initial recruitment, the effect of the pension structure on workforce quality depends on how teachers who differ by quality value deferred retirement compensation. We are not aware of any direct empirical evidence on how DB pensions influence selection into teaching, but economic theory suggests that heavily backloaded retirement plans will not be an effective recruiting tool for high-ability young teachers. One reason is that the backloading penalizes mobility and research shows that higher-ability individuals place higher ex ante probabilities on exiting teaching (Murnane and Olsen, 1990; Podgursky et al., 2004). Consistent with these earlier studies, Chingos and West (2015) and Goldhaber and Grout (2016) find that when given a choice, teachers who choose DC plans with mobile benefits are, on average, moderately more effective as measured by value-added to student test scores.[16] The evidence that higher-ability teachers prefer mobile retirement benefits is in line with the association between worker ability and mobility in the broader labor market. For example, Groes et al. (2015) show that across the top 80% of the ability distribution, job mobility is positively related to worker productivity. While direct evidence on selection is unavailable, taken together, the body of indirect evidence suggests that the backloaded structure of wealth accrual in DB pension plans will be unattractive to higher-ability individuals relative to the alternative of a more mobile retirement benefit plan, or simply higher salaries.

Conditional on entry into the workforce, the effects of the pull and push incentives on workforce quality depend on whether educator responsiveness is related to effectiveness. Starting with the pull incentives, quality will be improved if educators who would otherwise leave but are retained in teaching by these incentives are more effective than their replacements. One reason to expect a positive quality effect is that, on average, experienced teachers are more effective than novices (eg, see Clotfelter et al., 2006; Hanushek and Rivkin, 2006). Thus, all else equal, retention incentives that maintain a higher overall level of experience in the workforce should result in higher student achievement. However, the positive empirical relationship between educator effectiveness and experience is not a sufficient condition to ensure that the pull incentives will positively affect workforce quality. The quality effect depends on the effectiveness of educators whose behavior is altered by the DB structure and this is a selected group. For example, it may that an experienced educator who wants to leave teaching, but chooses to stay only because the pension-related costs of changing jobs are high, is not as effective as the average teacher of the same experience level.

---

[16] In Goldhaber and Grout (2016) the choice is between a DB and hybrid plan rather than a full DC plan.

Some empirical evidence is available on the effect of the pull incentives on workforce quality. Koedel et al. (2013b) divide teachers in Missouri into groups based on their observed retirement behaviors and compare teachers who are the most likely to have been retained by the pension system to other experienced teachers. In math they find that retained teachers are *less* effective than their similarly experienced peers and cannot be statistically distinguished from novices, while in reading retained teachers are no more effective than their similarly experienced peers but outperform new entrants. Fitzpatrick and Lovenheim (2014) use an early-retirement incentive program in Illinois in the late 1990s to provide evidence on the workforce-quality effects of the pull incentives. The Illinois program, which was temporary, offered teachers in the pull region of the pension structure the opportunity to exit the system prior to reaching collection eligibility without incurring the substantial cost that would normally come with doing so. Put differently, the program temporarily dulled the early-exit penalty in the Illinois pension system that generates the pull incentive. Fitzpatrick and Lovenheim show that a large number of experienced teachers elected to exit teaching via the program. However, they report that the program did not reduce test scores and likely increased them, despite the fact that it reduced the overall experience of the workforce. Thus, research evidence to date does not suggest that the pull incentives raise workforce quality and it is more consistent with these incentives resulting in the retention of less effective teachers on average.

Next we turn to the push incentives. If effectiveness declines after a certain age, it would support the use of the push incentives in DB pension plans to improve workforce quality (Lazear, 1986). However, two aspects of how the push incentives work call into question the likelihood that they are designed to improve quality. First, the push incentives in many plans begin to take effect immediately, or almost immediately, after the pull incentives cease. There is a logical inconsistency in connecting the pull and push incentives to workforce quality unless we believe that the experience-effectiveness profile turns very sharply from increasing to decreasing for most individuals. Compounding this issue is that in many states full retirement eligibility occurs at a "rule-of-X," where different educators hit "X" with different combinations of age and experience. This further implies that the pull and push incentives are not targeted around a central turning point in the relationship between age, experience and productivity.

A second reason to be skeptical that the push incentives are positively affecting workforce quality by incentivizing older workers with declining skills to leave is that in many states, educators feel the DB pension push at young ages — as early as their mid-to-late 50s. In fact, Podgursky and Ehlert (2007) report that the national median retirement age for teachers is 59 (based on data from the 2005 Schools and Staffing Survey).[17] Given that professionals in other sectors of the economy typically work much longer, it is not clear why productivity in education would begin to decline at such an early age.

---

[17] Harris and Adams (2007) also report steeply increasing exit rates for teachers starting in their mid-50s.

The only study of which we are aware that provides direct empirical evidence on the effect of the push incentives on workforce quality is Koedel et al. (2013b). They find that, on average, teachers who are observed working into the push region of the pension incentive structure are no more or less effective than other experienced teachers in terms of raising achievement and are more effective than novices.

4. PENSION PLAN FINANCING

As noted in the introduction, a substantial share of educational resources is devoted to funding educator retirement benefits. The National Council on Teacher Quality (2012) reports that as of 2012, combined employee-employer contribution rates to fund educator retirement benefits ranged from 15% to 29% of earnings across states. These contribution rates are determined by actuarial calculations, which economists have argued rely on assumptions that lead to a significant understatement of true pension costs (Biggs, 2011; Biggs and Richwine, 2014; Novy-Marx and Rauh, 2009, 2011, 2014).

Fig. 2 reports benefit costs for retirement, including Social Security, contributed by employers as a percentage of salary for public school teachers and private sector managers and professionals (these data are taken from the United States Department of Labor). Note that these costs do not include any employee contributions nor do they include employer payments for retiree health insurance. Two patterns are clear from the figure. First, benefit costs for public school teachers, which are currently 19.5% of salaries, are substantially above those for private-sector professionals and managers. Second, private-sector costs have been relatively flat over the previous decade whereas the costs for public school teachers exhibit a clear increasing trend.[18]

The primary driver of the pension cost increases for educators is amortization of previously accrued unfunded liabilities.[19] The National Council on Teacher Quality reports that unfunded liabilities increased between 2009 and 2012 in all but seven states. In 2013, the average percentage of earnings for a new entrant into teaching devoted to cover the "unfunded actuarially accrued liability" (UAAL) in state plans was roughly 10%.[20]

---

[18] Data from the U.S. Department of Labor on public school teacher pension costs (excluding Social Security) imply a 2014 pension cost of just over $1000 per student, up from an inflation-adjusted $500 per student in 2005. As a percentage of per student spending, pension costs grew from 4.9% to 8.9% over this period. See Costrell (2015).

[19] States generally follow standards of the Government Accounting Standards Board (GASB) with regard to reporting the liabilities of pension plans. Annual required contributions by GASB standards have two components. The first is "normal cost," which measures the cost of new pension obligations incurred in a given year. The second is payment sufficient to amortize the unfunded liabilities of the pension plans over 30 years.

[20] This figure is based on the authors' own calculations using data collected in actuarial valuation reports from state plans, supplemented with data from the Public Plans Database maintained by the Center for Retirement Research at Boston College.

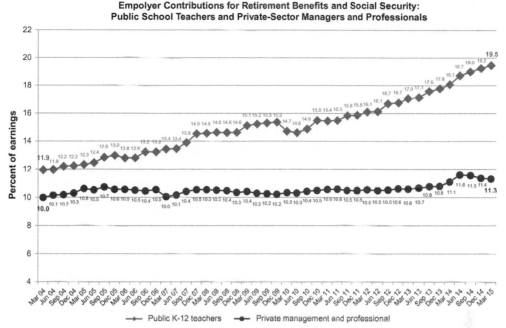

Figure 2 Employer pension costs as a percentage of salary: public school teachers and private sector managers and professionals. *Source: Costrell and Podgursky (2010), updated at: http://www.uaedreform.org/downloads/2013/12/quarterly-employer-contribution-chart-update.pdf. Bureau of Labor Statistics, National Compensation Survey, Employer Costs for Employee Compensation (Various Years).*

One factor driving the cost increases is that most pension plans have failed to meet their assumed rate of return — usually 8% — on their investment portfolio. In practice, the pension funds (and their actuaries) set contribution rates for teachers and employers by discounting liabilities at the assumed return on the portfolio (again 8%). However, because future liabilities must be paid, most economists believe that liabilities should be discounted or priced using a risk-free or low-risk rate (as is the federal requirement for private sector plans). Several studies have argued that actuarial cost calculations understate liabilities and that actual costs are much higher than what has been reported (Biggs, 2011; Biggs and Richwine, 2014; Novy-Marx and Rauh, 2009, 2011, 2014), which is consistent with the persistent accumulation of pension debt by state plans even in plans that ultimately make all actuarially required contributions.

States have responded in a number of ways to the weakening fiscal condition of educator pension plans. Some have increased required contribution rates. Others have created alternative plans as described above. Still others have created new, less-generous "retirement plan tiers" for incoming teachers that provide lower net benefits. These changes can be generally characterized as cross-cohort wealth transfers from young and not-yet-hired teachers to older, more senior teachers.[21]

A fundamental feature of DB pension plans that has contributed to their persistent underfunding is that for any individual benefits are not directly tied to contributions. Among other things, this facilitates benefit promises that do not require direct funding at the time when promises are made. Glaeser and Ponzetto (2014) develop a political economy model and show that this feature of pension financing promotes an inefficient allocation of resources where compensation via pensions is too high. In short, their model shows that politicians can appeal to pensioners without scaring off taxpayers by improving pension benefits. The key assumption in their model is that pension packages are "shrouded," meaning that public-sector workers better understand their value than ordinary taxpayers.

Shoag (2014) draws a parallel between modern public pension fund financing and a period of substantial debt-funded public investment in infrastructure in many states in the mid-19th century. Similarly to pension benefit promises today, the borrowing for the infrastructure projects increased long-term government liabilities. Projections of the proceeds from the infrastructure projects via presumed subsequent economic growth factored prominently into state budgets for repayment at the time. After a debt-fueled period of public investments in canals and state-chartered banks that ended in the 1840s, eight states and the territory of Florida had defaulted. Shoag (2014) reports that the combined debt of state governments by the early 1840s stood at over $200 million, up from $12.8 million in 1825.

As in the early 19th century with states' various canal and bank-charter projects, a rationale for not immediately funding pension promises is that the investment return on assets can be used to pay off liabilities when they come due. This rationale is appealing politically if politicians discount future deficits at high rates, as it allows them to promise benefits without making immediate payments to cover the costs. This type of situation is particularly dangerous if unrealistic investment returns are required in order for liabilities to be covered like with the infrastructure boom discussed by Shoag (2014), and as has been asserted by economists with regard to the assumed rate of return used by the actuaries for most public pension plans.

The fact that pension promises can be made without setting aside direct funding facilitates political gaming as in Glaeser and Ponzetto (2014). Koedel et al. (2014) provide

---

[21] Another disturbing shift has been toward increasing risk in the investment portfolio in an effort to meet or exceed the assumed rate of return and close funding gaps. Over the last 60 years, state and local pension funds (including teachers) have moved from investment portfolios which were overwhelmingly comprised of low-risk government securities, to portfolios in which equities and "alternative investments" such as real estate and hedge funds are more prevalent (Pew Charitable Trusts and the Laura and John Arnold Foundation, 2014).

direct evidence of such gaming in the educator pension plan in Missouri. They examine a series of enhancements to the Missouri plan in the late 1990s and early 2000s. The enhancements greatly improved the benefit formula for educators, and similar enhancements were made in most states during the same time period (National Conference of State Legislators, 1999, 2000, 2001). One reason for the widespread enhancements is that the stock market was producing abnormally high returns, which in the short run resulted in many pension funds showing an actuarial surplus. That is, the accounting books for many funds indicated that they had more assets than would be required to pay off future liabilities. A prudently operated fund would use excess returns generated during periods of above-average market performance to offset periods of below-average market performance. But because the system is easy to manipulate intertemporally, it facilitates rent capture when asset returns in the short run exceed long run expectations.

Koedel et al. (2014) show that the enhancements to the Missouri state pension plan were structured to transfer resources to experienced teachers and away from young teachers and teachers who had not yet entered the workforce. The key feature of the enhancements that facilitated the transfer is that they were implemented retroactively and required no additional contributions from educators. For example, one enhancement increased the formula factor in Missouri from 0.023 and 0.025. At the time when the legislation was enacted, all teachers were eligible for the improved formula factor despite the fact that experienced teachers had made all previous contributions to fund a less remunerative benefit.

This is an example of the intergenerational risk of DB pension plans, which is driven by the ability of current generations to extract resources from the system that they do not need to pay for and can leave for future generations to make up. Another form of wealth transfer that occurred in the late 1990s and early 2000s was from young teachers and future generations of teachers toward state governments. This type of transfer occurred when a number of state governments did not make necessary funding contributions on the behalf of employees when investment returns were high enough to mask the behavior (eg, California, Illinois).

An additional problem with the disconnect between benefit funding and benefit promises is that plans hold risky assets without pricing the risk (Biggs, 2011; Biggs and Richwine, 2014; Novy-Marx and Rauh, 2009, 2011, 2014). This practice is encouraged by voluntary accounting standards (promulgated by the Government Accounting Standards Board, GASB) that allow funds to discount future liabilities at the expected rate of return on the investment portfolio without considering risk. Thus, one way for funds to improve the asset-to-liability ratio is to shift to a riskier portfolio with a higher expected return. Because of compounding, even small changes in the expected rate of return over time can result in large changes in the apparent fiscal health of a pension plan. The cost of the risk borne by many state pension plans, which has thus far gone unaccounted for, will be left for future generations to address.

5. THE CHANGING US PENSION LANDSCAPE

The problems surrounding the financing of DB pension plans for educators, coupled with concerns that these plans offer little in the way of workforce quality improvement, have led some states to implement alternatively structured retirement plans as discussed in Section 2.[22] All of the available alternatives — hybrid, choice, DC, cash balance — share the common feature that they move a larger share of educators' retirement compensation into plans where benefits are tied directly to contributions. In DC and cash-balance plans, benefits are tied entirely to contributions. Choice and hybrid plans still maintain some disconnect between benefits and contributions for the share of retirement compensation delivered through the DB component, but the introduction of the non–DB component weakens the disconnect for total retirement compensation.[23]

Another response to pension funding problems has been to maintain the DB pension structure but with reduced benefits for new members. Benefits have been reduced in a number of ways. For example, since 2009 eleven states have increased the vesting period (National Council on Teacher Quality, 2012). Teachers who do not vest lose their employer contributions, which can then be used to support pension payments for the remaining workforce. States have also changed plan rules in ways that reduce the accrual of pension wealth for new teachers. Examples include raising the age or experience requirement for collection eligibility and changing the formula factor for new teachers.

Illinois is an example of a state that kept the DB structure but made sharp cuts in the benefit accrual rate for new teachers (those hired on or after January 1, 2011, who are referred to as "Tier II members"). The cuts in Illinois include a later retirement age, a cap on annual cost-of-living adjustments (COLAs) for retirees, and a cap on the allowable final average salary. The result is a much slower rate of pension-wealth accrual. Indeed, Costrell and Podgursky (2011) show that a typical Tier II teacher in Illinois entering at age 25 will accrue no net pension wealth until age 51. Note that the benefit cut comes with no relief in terms of contribution rates — Tier I (experienced) and Tier II (new) teachers both contribute 9.4% of their salaries toward their pensions.[24]

Finally, the increasing prevalence of public schools of choice in K–12 education merits brief mention on the issue of pensions. Charter schools in 16 states can currently

---

[22] It should also be noted that there is evidence that teachers value a marginal dollar of retirement benefits at much less than a marginal dollar of salary. In an analysis of an Illinois pension enhancement that permitted active teachers to purchase additional service years (and hence higher retirement annuities) at a very steep discount, Fitzpatrick (2015) finds that teachers implicitly valued a marginal dollar of retirement benefits at less than 20 cents.

[23] Chingos and West (2015) and Goldhaber and Grout (2016) show that in an environment with retirement-plan choice, a large fraction of teachers choose the more mobile option (either a pure DC plan as in Chingos and West or a hybrid plan with a DC component as in Goldhaber and Grout).

[24] A number of other states have also made reforms along these lines in recent years including Alabama, Louisiana, and New York (eg, see National Conference of State Legislators, 2012a,b).

opt out of state pension plans. When given the opportunity many charters schools do opt out, but the share varies from state to state. Charter schools that opt out are free to develop their own retirement plans and evidence suggests that they tend to implement DC plans similar to many private employers (Olberg and Podgursky, 2011). The effect of charter school innovation in this area has not been rigorously examined in research to date.

6. TEACHER PENSIONS IN OTHER OECD COUNTRIES

The World Bank describes a "three pillar" taxonomy for characterizing national retirement systems. The first pillar represents a mandatory public system, such as the United States Social Security system. The second pillar represents privately managed, mandatory savings plans, and the third pillar privately managed voluntary plans (Baily and Kirkegaard, 2009). Teachers in most OECD countries are members of "first pillar" national plans, similarly to public school teachers in the United States who are also enrolled in Social Security. They are also typically part of "second pillar" mandatory plans. The latter are generally DB plans and the final-average-salary structure found in the United States is common. However, some of the more problematic features of US final-average-salary DB plans have been eliminated or ameliorated in other countries.[25]

Consider two types of mobility for teachers: geographic and occupational. The pension-relevant aspect of geographic mobility in the United States involves crossing pension boundaries, which for all practical purposes coincide with state lines. Geographic mobility is less of an issue in many other countries because occupational plans cover an entire nation. But even in countries with multiple subnational plans, such as Canada, province-wide plans can accommodate a great deal of geographic teacher mobility because provinces are so large and because there is reciprocity between provinces, unlike among United States. For example, the Ontario teacher pension plan, a final-average-salary DB plan resembling many US state plans that covers roughly 300,000 active and retired teachers, has reciprocity arrangements with other Canadian provinces.[26]

In the case of occupational mobility, most occupational DB plans in other countries are not based on an annuity formula that freezes nominal salaries at the time of exit. Again using the Ontario plan as an example, the final average salary is increased annually by a cost of living index for teachers who exit covered employment. No such adjustment is

---

[25] We only briefly touch on the international pension landscape because we could not find any research on occupational plans for educators outside of the United States (although there have been many comparative studies of the retirement benefit systems of various countries, these tend to focus only on the large public plans and not on educator plans specifically — eg, see Baily and Kirkegaard, 2009, Dan and Diamond, 2010; Muir and Turner, 2011; Organization for Economic Cooperation and Development, 2013; Turner, 2010).

[26] http://www.otpp.com/documents/10179/712513/-/4fc371f9-5c3f-41c0-a625-a4512020113e/Annual+Report.pdf.

made in state plans in the United States, where any cost-of-living adjustments occur only after collection begins. For example, in the United States if a teacher exits the profession 20 years prior to reaching collection eligibility her final average salary is frozen at her nominal earnings at the time of exit. Only after she begins collecting does her annuity increase with any cost-of-living adjustments. Returning to the discussion in Section 2.1, incorporating cost-of-living adjustments prior to collection eligibility for early exiters in US plans would greatly reduce the degree of compensation backloading.

It is not clear why educator pension plans in the United States impose such harsh penalties on mobile teachers relative to plans in other countries. The explanation may be political, as US plans redistribute pension wealth from young and mobile teachers to senior teachers and administrators (Costrell and Podgursky, 2009; Koedel et al., 2014). Representatives of the latter groups dominate the governing boards of these plans and are likely to be more politically influential. The interests of young and mobile teachers are better represented in pension plan design abroad — how this influences workforce quality and the fiscal sustainability of subnational pension plans outside of the United States merits attention in future research.

7. CONCLUSION

In contrast to most private-sector professionals, the vast majority of public educators in the United States are enrolled in final average salary DB pension plans. There is nothing inherent to the structure of DB plans that requires compensation to be backloaded. The United States Social Security system, for example, uses career average earnings in calculating the pension annuity. However, the state DB plans that cover most public educators are characterized by significant compensation backloading, primarily as a consequence of using final average salary to compute retirement annuities and offering service-based options (sometimes in combination with age) to facilitate retirements before the normal age. The backloading creates a somewhat unique incentive structure in education (shared with other public sector occupations) that merits greater consideration in labor-based education research.

Combined with their peculiar labor incentives, the weak fiscal condition of most state pension plans covering educators ensures that pension reform will continue to be an important topic for education research and policy in the United States moving forward. Because such a large share of the total resources currently devoted to educator compensation is devoted to financing current DB pension plans, reforming these plans has the potential to meaningfully affect the educator labor market along a number of dimensions, including how teachers are recruited and retained, and when they retire. Pension reform also has the potential to free up additional resources for K-12 schools that can be used in a more transparent way — for example, to improve teacher salaries and/or to purchase additional educational inputs.

REFERENCES

Baily, M.N., Kirkegaard, J.F., 2009. U.S. Pension Reform: Lessons from Other Countries. Peterson Institute for International Economics, Washington, DC.

Barr, N., Diamond, P., 2010. Pension Reform: A Short Guide. Oxford University Press, Oxford.

Biggs, A., 2011. An options pricing method for calculating the market price of public sector pension liabilities. Pub. Budget. & Fin. 31 (3), 94–118.

Biggs, A.G., Richwine, J., 2014. Putting a price on teacher pensions. In: Peterson, P.E., Nadler, D. (Eds.), The Global Debt Crisis: Haunting U.S. and European Federalism. Brookings, Washington, DC.

Brown, K., 2013. The link between pensions and retirement timing: lessons from California teachers. J. Public Econ. 98 (1), 1–14.

Chan, S., Stevens, A.H., 2008. What you don't know can't help you: pension knowledge and retirement decision-making. Rev. Econ. Stat. 90 (2), 253–266.

Chingos, M.W., West, M.R., 2015. Which teachers choose a defined contribution pension plan? Evidence from the Florida retirement system. Educ. Finance Policy 10 (2), 193–222.

Clark, R.L., 2010. Retiree health plans for public school teachers after GASB 43 and 45. Educ. Finance Policy 5 (4), 438–462.

Clotfelter, C.T., Ladd, H.F., Vigdor, J.L., 2006. Teacher-student matching and the assessment of teacher effectiveness. J. Hum. Resour. 41 (4), 778–820.

Coile, C., Gruber, J., 2007. Future social security entitlements and the retirement decision. Rev. Econ. Stat. 89 (2), 234–246.

Costrell, R.M., 2015. School pension costs have doubled over the last decade, now top $1000 per student nationally. Teacher Pensions Blog (July 20). http://www.teacherpensions.org/blog/school-pension-costs-have-doubled-over-last-decade-now-top-1000-pupil-nationally.

Costrell, R.M., McGee, J.B., 2010. Teacher pension incentives, retirement behavior, and potential reform in Arkansas. Educ. Finance Policy 5 (4), 492–518.

Costrell, R.M., Podgursky, M.J., 2009. Peaks, cliffs and valleys: the peculiar incentives in teacher retirement systems and their consequences for school staffing. Educ. Finance Policy 4 (2), 175–211.

Costrell, R.M., Podgursky, M.J., 2010. Distribution of benefits in teacher retirement systems and their implications for mobility. Educ. Finance Policy 5 (4), 519–557.

Costrell, R.M., Podgursky, M.J., 2011. Teacher retirement benefits. Educ. Next (Fall), 61–69.

Fitzpatrick, M.D., 2015. How much are public school teachers willing to pay for their retirement benefits? Am. Econ. J. Econ. Policy. 7 (4), 165–188.

Fitzpatrick, M., Lovenheim, M., 2014. Early retirement incentives and student achievement. Am. Econ. J. Econ. Policy 6 (3), 120–154.

Friedberg, L., Turner, S., 2010. Labor market effects of pensions and implications for teachers. Educ. Finance Policy 5 (4), 463–491.

Furgeson, J., Strauss, R.P., Vogt, W.B., 2006. The effects of defined benefit pension incentives and working conditions on teacher retirement decisions. Educ. Finance Policy 1 (3), 316–348.

Glaeser, E.L., Ponzetto, G.A.M., 2014. Shrouded costs of government: the political economy of state and local public pensions. J. Public Econ. 116, 89–105.

Goldhaber, D., Grout, C., 2016. Which plan to choose? The determinants of pension system choice for public school teachers. J. Pension Econ. Finance 15 (1), 30–54.

Gollier, C., 2008. Intergenerational risk-sharing and risk-taking of a pension fund. J. Public Econ. 92 (5–6), 1463–1485.

Groes, F., Kircher, P., Manovskii, I., 2015. The U-shapes of occupational mobility. Rev. Econ. Stud. 82 (2), 659–692.

Hansen, J.S., 2010. An introduction to teacher retirement benefits. Educ. Finance Policy 5 (2), 402–437.

Hanushek, E.A., 2009. Teacher deselection. In: Goldhaber, D., Hannaway, J. (Eds.), Creating a New Teaching Profession. Urban Institute, Washington, DC, pp. 165–180.

Hanushek, E.A., Rivkin, S.G., 2006. Teacher quality. In: Hanushek, E.A., Welch, F. (Eds.), Handbook of the Economics of Education, vol. 2. North Holland, Amsterdam, pp. 1052–1078.

Harris, D.N., Adams, S.J., 2007. Understanding the level and causes of teacher turnover: a comparison with other professions. Econ. Educ. Rev. 26 (4), 325–337.

Jacob, B., 2011. Do principals fire the worst teachers? Educ. Eval. Policy Anal. 33 (4), 403–434.

Koedel, C., Ni, S., Podgursky, M., 2013a. The school administrator payoff from teacher pensions. Educ. Next 13 (4), 8–13.

Koedel, C., Podgursky, M., Shi, S., 2013b. Teacher pension systems, the composition of the teaching work-force, and teacher quality. J. Policy Anal. Manage. 32 (3), 574–596.

Koedel, C., Ni, S., Podgursky, M., 2014. Who benefits from pension enhancements? Educ. Finance Policy 9 (2), 165–192.

Lazear, E.P., 1986. Retirement from the labor force. In: Ashenfelter, O., Layard, R. (Eds.), Handbook of Labor Economics, vol. I. Elsevier Science, Amsterdam, pp. 305–355.

Muir, D.M., Turner, J.A., 2011. Imagining the Ideal Pension System: International Perspectives. W.E. Upjohn Institute for Employment Research, Kalamazoo, MI.

Munnell, A., 2000. The Impact of Mandatory Social Security Coverage of State and Local Workers: A Multi-State Review. AARP, Washington, DC.

Murnane, R., Olsen, R., 1990. The effects of salaries and opportunity costs on length of stay in teaching: evidence from North Carolina. J. Hum. Resour. 25 (1), 106–124.

National Conference of State Legislators, 1999. Pensions and Retirement Plan Issues in 1999 State Legislatures: Policy report.

National Conference of State Legislators, 2000. Pensions and Retirement Plan Issues in 2000 State Legislatures: Policy report.

National Conference of State Legislators, 2001. Pensions and Retirement Plan Enactments in 2012 State Legislatures: Policy report.

National Conference of State Legislators, 2012. Pensions and Retirement Plan Enactments in 2012 State Legislatures: Policy report. (updated April, 2013).

National Council on Teacher Quality, 2012. No One Benefits: How Teacher Pension Systems Are Failing Both Teachers and Taxpayers: Policy report.

Ni, S., Podgursky, M., forthcoming. How teachers respond to pension system incentives: new estimates and policy applications. J. Labor Econ.

Novy-Marx, R., Rauh, J., 2009. The liabilities and risks of state-sponsored pension plans. J. Econ. Perspect. 23 (4), 191–210.

Novy-Marx, R., Rauh, J., 2011. Public pension promises: how big are they and what are they worth? J. Finance 66 (4), 1207–1245.

Novy-Marx, R., Rauh, J., 2014. Revenue demands of public employee pension promises. Am. Econ. J. Econ. Policy 6 (1), 193–229.

Olberg, A., Podgursky, M.J., 2011. Charting a New Course to Retirement: How Charter Schools Handle Teacher Pensions. Fordham Institute, Washington, DC (June).

Organization for Economic Cooperation and Development, 2013. Pensions at a Glance. Paris (November).

Pew Charitable Trusts, The Laura and John Arnold Foundation, 2014. State Public Pension Shifts Over Past 30 Years. Washington, DC (June).

Podgursky, M., Ehlert, M., 2007. Teacher Pensions and Retirement Behavior. CALDER Working Paper No. 5.

Podgursky, M., Monroe, R., Watson, D., 2004. Academic quality of public school teachers: an analysis of entry and exit behavior. Econ. Educ. Rev. 23 (6), 507–518.

Samwick, A.A., 1998. New evidence on pensions, social security, and the timing of retirement. J. Public Econ. 70 (2), 207–236.

Schiller, R.J., 1999. Social Security and institutions for intergenerational, intragenerational and international risk sharing. Carnegie-Rochester Conf. Ser. Public Policy 50, 165–204.

Shoag, D., 2014. Past and present high-risk investments by states and localities. In: Peterson, P.E., Nadler, D. (Eds.), The Global Debt Crisis: Haunting U.S. and European Federalism. Brookings, Washington, DC.

Stock, J.H., Wise, D.A., 1990. Pensions, the option value of work, and retirement. Econometrica 58 (5), 1151–1180.

Turner, J.A., 2010. Pension Policy: The Search for Better Solutions. W.E. Upjohn Institute for Employment Research, Kalamazoo, MI.

U.S. Department of Labor, Bureau of Labor Statistics, 2008. National Compensation Survey: Retirement Benefits in State and Local Governments in the United States, 2007 (May). http://stats.bls.gov/ncs/ebs/sp/ebsm0008.

Vigdor, J., 2008. Scrap the sacrosanct salary schedule. Educ. Next 8 (4), 36–42.

Weisberg, D., Sexton, S., Mulhern, J., Keeling, D., 2009. The Widget Effect: Our National Failure to Acknowledge and Act on Differences in Teacher Effectiveness. The New Teacher Project, New York.

Wiatrowski, W.J. 2012. The last private industry pension plans: a visual essay. Mon. Labor Rev. (December).

CHAPTER 7

The Analysis of Field Choice in College and Graduate School: Determinants and Wage Effects

J.G. Altonji[*], P. Arcidiacono[†], A. Maurel[†]
[*]Yale University, CT, United States; NBER, and IZA
[†]Duke University, NC, United States; NBER, and IZA

Contents

Handbook of the Economics of Education, Volume 5
ISSN 1574-0692, http://dx.doi.org/10.1016/B978-0-444-63459-7.00007-5

Abstract

As the workforce has become more educated, educational decisions are about what type of education to pursue as well as how much to pursue. In college, individuals somewhat specialize through their choice of college major. Further specialization occurs in graduate school. This chapter investigates how majors and graduate school affect labor market outcomes, as well as how individuals make these potentially important decisions. To do so, we develop a dynamic model of educational decision-making. In light of the model, we examine the estimation issues associated with obtaining causal effects of educational choices on earnings. We then examine ways that authors have overcome the selection problem, as well as the approaches authors have taken to estimate the process by which these educational decisions are made.

Keywords

College majors, Advanced degrees, Returns to schooling, Uncertainty

1. INTRODUCTION

The literature on the returns to education often focuses on the returns to years of schooling (Card, 1999), treating education as unidimensional. This may be a reasonable approach when there is relatively little specialization in school, as for example in secondary education in the United States.[1] But as the workforce has become more educated, educational decisions are about the type of education to pursue as well as about the quantity. While a liberal arts education is supposed to provide a broad background in many areas, there is nonetheless some specialization as individuals choose college majors that have different emphases in their coursework. Graduate education leads to even more specialization. An additional year of schooling in a Master's in Education program is quite different from that in engineering.

Wage difference across college majors are large. Using data from the 2009 American Community Survey, Altonji et al. (2012) show that the log wage gap between male electrical engineers and male general education majors is within two percentage points of the gap between college and high school graduates. Altonji et al. (2014b) and Gemici and Wiswall (2014) show that these differentials have been significantly increasing over time. With increases in the returns to skill, the incentives to obtain a graduate degree have also increased, with the share of individuals getting a Master's degree more than doubling between 1985 and 2010.

From an aggregate viewpoint, the distribution of college majors is an important input to the skill composition of tomorrow's workforce. In 2010, there were 209 federal

---

[1] Even in secondary education in the USA, there is a great deal of heterogeneity in the mix of courses that students take — both within high schools and across high schools. See Altonji et al. (2012) for a survey of the literature on the choice of high school curriculum and the labor market effects of high school curriculum.

programs designed to increase knowledge of Science, Technology, Engineering, and Math (STEM) fields and attainment of STEM degrees with overall spending of more than 3 billion dollars (Scott, 2013). The Governor of Florida has proposed freezing tuition for STEM majors (Alvarez, 2012), and the State of New York is offering free tuition for high-performing students who enroll in public institutions and are STEM majors, conditional on working in the state for at least 5 years (Chapman, 2014).

The raw wage differences across majors may, however, reflect a number of factors besides differential accumulation of human capital across majors. One obvious issue is selection. Perhaps those who major in the more apparently lucrative fields would also have earned more in other majors. Perhaps those who choose less lucrative majors would have earned even less in the better paying majors because their skills are a poor match with the work required. These issues become even more complicated given the importance of occupations in the labor market, to the degree that individuals are heterogeneous in their preferences for occupations, and to the degree that majors have heterogeneous effects on both the pecuniary and nonpecuniary returns to different occupations.

But even if some majors have a larger causal effect on productivity than others, the high-paying majors may be less attractive for students on other dimensions. For example, they may involve heavier university workloads or lead to less pleasant or fulfilling jobs. Initial interest in STEM majors at the undergraduate level, for example, is quite high. However, 48% switch out of STEM majors, with half dropping out and half switching to another major.

Universities may place less weight on student labor market prospects when deciding how much priority to give to increasing the number of STEM majors. For example, they may prefer a distribution of students across majors that is in line with the distribution of faculty members in their various departments. Princeton explicitly pushes students to consider departments with fewer students per instructor. And institutions may understate tradeoffs between nonpecuniary considerations and labor market prospects when counseling students. For example, the introduction to *Major Choices vol. II*, available on Princeton's website, states that its

> purpose is to encourage undergraduates to follow their intellectual passions and study what they love, with confidence in the fulfilling lives that lie ahead and the knowledge that in no way will their choice of major limit the career choices they may wish to make in the future.[2]

As a result of this push, departments with the largest percentage increases were classics, Slavic languages and literature, comparative literature, and religion.[3] But while we do not

---

[2] http://www.princeton.edu/pr/pub/mc/v2/home/index.htm.
[3] http://www.princeton.edu/main/news/archive/S11/45/32K06/index.xml.

present evidence for samples drawn exclusively from elite universities, the evidence for a broad set of schools suggests strongly that choice of major does limit career choice.

In this chapter, we investigate how majors and graduate school impact labor market outcomes, as well as how individuals make these potentially important decisions. In particular, we

1. document the trends in the number and earnings of different undergraduate majors and graduate programs (Section 2);

2. develop a model for how to think about the various factors that influence major choice (Section 3);

3. in light of the model, examine the estimation issues associated with obtaining causal effects of educational choices on earnings and discuss the progress to date on addressing these issues (Section 4);

4. review research on how individuals make postsecondary decisions regarding choice of major and graduate school, paying attention both to choices by the student as well as how choices by universities make particular fields of study more attractive (Sections 5.1 and 5.2); and

5. discuss work using subjective expectations data to get at student beliefs regarding the benefits of choosing particular educational paths (Section 5.3).

We cover some of the same ground as the recent survey by Altonji et al. (2012). However, we give much more emphasis to graduate education. As we document, graduate school attendance has grown rapidly over the past two decades. Now is a good time to pull together the existing literature on the demand for and return to graduate school, although it is still relatively sparse. We also give more emphasis to how students make choices and to the role that universities play in influencing them. And we highlight papers that collect subjective expectations as a way of eliciting student beliefs about the monetary and nonmonetary value of various fields of study and the career paths that they will lead to. These beliefs play a central role in models of education choice.

2. DESCRIPTIVES

We begin this chapter by providing descriptive evidence on the allocation of students across undergraduate majors and graduate degrees, together with the wage premia associated with the various combinations of undergraduate and graduate degrees. In Section 2.1, we examine the distribution of undergraduate majors among all individuals with a Bachelor's degree, discuss its evolution over time, and report the mean wages associated with each major. In Section 2.2, we turn to graduate degrees and discuss the trends in the number of individuals graduating with different types of advanced degrees, in particular Master's, PhD, MD, JD, and dental degrees. Finally, Section 2.3 focuses on the joint distribution of undergraduate and graduate degrees, and further presents descriptive results about the wage returns to different pairs of undergraduate and graduate degrees.

2.1 Undergraduate Degrees

Table 1 reports the distribution of majors among individuals with a Bachelor's degree between the ages of 27 and 58, using data from the 2013 American Community Survey. The five most common fields of study are Business (22.5%, includes Business Management, Accounting and General Business), Education (10.1%), Engineering (8.2%), Social Sciences (7.3%, includes Economics, Sociology, Anthropology and Archeology, Political Science, and Government), and Medical and Health Services (7.2%). More than half of college graduates have a Bachelor's degree in one of those areas. We also report the average hourly wage for each major. There are very large differences across majors in this dimension. For instance, individuals with an Engineering degree earn on average close to 80% more than individuals who obtained a degree in Education. Interestingly though, and consistent with nonpecuniary factors playing an important role when choosing a college major, Education majors account for a larger share of Bachelor's degrees than Engineering majors. In addition to Engineering, other high-paying college majors (with mean wages above $40 per hour) include Biology, Computer and Information Systems, Physical Sciences, Mathematics, and Transportation Sciences. On average, individuals who earned a Bachelor's degree in any of those fields of study earn at least 50% more than college graduates who obtained their Bachelor's degree in fields of study such as Education, Fine Arts, Public Administration, Family and Consumer Sciences, Theology, Cosmetology, and Culinary Arts. From the outset, it is important to keep in mind that those stark differences across majors are driven in part by the fact that students with different productivity levels tend to choose different majors. Accounting for endogenous sorting of students across majors is crucial to estimating the causal effect of college majors on wages. We will discuss this issue thoroughly in Section 4.

While the dramatic increase in college graduation rates in the last four decades has been the object of much attention, relatively little is known about the change in the distribution of undergraduate majors over time. Fig. 1 reports the evolution from 1981 to 2013 of the proportions of students graduating with a Bachelor's degree in Business, Life Sciences, Social Sciences, Engineering, Mathematics and Physical Sciences, Health, Education, Humanities, Fine Arts, and other fields, among all students receiving a Bachelor's degree in any given year.[4] Those shares are computed using data from the Higher Education General Information Survey (HEGIS) through 1985–86, and the Integrated Postsecondary Education Data System (IPEDS) from 1986–87 to 2012–13. Majors in Business, Social Sciences, Humanities, and Fine Arts, along with the majors included

---

[4] Other fields include those such as Communication and Journalism, Homeland Security, Law Enforcement and Firefighting, Park, Recreation, Leisure and Fitness Studies, Agriculture and Natural Resources, Public Administration, and Social Services, as well as Family and Consumer Sciences.

Table 1 Fraction of Bachelor's graduates by major

Major	Proportion (%)	Mean wage ($)
Business	22.5	35.86
Education	10.1	25.23
Engineering	8.2	45.20
Social Sciences	7.3	37.57
Medical and Health Services	7.2	35.93
Biology	4.8	43.07
Psychology	4.7	29.04
Communications	4.3	30.18
Fine Arts	4.2	25.15
Computer and Information Systems	3.9	40.01
Physical Sciences	3.0	41.33
English Language and Literature	2.9	30.96
History	1.9	34.63
Criminal Justice	1.9	27.98
Liberal Arts and Humanities	1.4	28.69
Public Administration	1.4	25.15
Mathematics	1.3	41.08
Agriculture	1.0	28.77
Physical Fitness	0.9	26.97
Linguistics	0.9	30.29
Engineering Technologies	0.8	36.89
Architecture	0.7	31.93
Family and Consumer Sciences	0.7	24.79
Interdisciplinary Studies	0.7	29.41
Environmental Science	0.6	29.73
Philosophy and Religion	0.6	31.99
Theology	0.6	22.43
Ethnic Studies	0.3	33.78
Transportation Sciences	0.3	40.37
Construction Services	0.2	33.88
Court Reporting	0.2	29.44
Communication Technologies	0.1	26.73
Cosmetology and Culinary Arts	0.1	20.61

Notes: Proportions reported for all college graduates with a BA degree or higher, between the ages of 27 and 58. Mean wage is annual earnings, divided by average hours worked per week times weeks worked in the past year. Mean wages are censored to be larger than $5 per h. and less than $400 per h.
Source: Data from American Community Survey, 2013 1-year PUMS.

in the other fields category, have been accounting for the highest share of Bachelor's degrees since the late 1980s. As of 2013, these majors accounted for as much as 68% of college graduates, up from 63% in 1981. Health majors have become more popular in the last 10 years. Those majors account for 9.8% of the Bachelor's degrees awarded

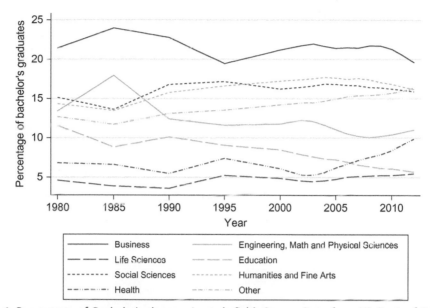

Figure 1 Percentage of Bachelor's degrees in each field. *Source: Data from US Dept. of Education (NCES), Higher Education General Information Survey (HEGIS), 1980–81 through 1985–86; Integrated Postsecondary Education Data System (IPEDS), 1990–91 to 2012–13.*

in 2013, which is about twice as much as in 2003. On the other hand, majors in Education, and, to a lesser extent, majors in Engineering, Math, and Physical Sciences have become less popular over time. In particular, the fraction of awarded Bachelor's in Education dropped from 12% in 1981 to only 6% in 2013. As of 2013, Life Sciences (the least popular field of study throughout this period) accounted for only 5% of the total number of Bachelor's degrees awarded during that year.

2.2 Graduate Degrees

The share of individuals receiving an advanced degree has increased substantially in the last 30 years. Fig. 2 reports the evolution of the number of individuals graduating with a Master's degree in the USA (restricted to permanent residents and US citizens) over the period 1985–2013, computed as a fraction of the total resident population of 24-year olds.[5] The share of individuals getting a Master's degree within each cohort has increased by 240% between 1985 and 2013, likely reflecting an increase in the demand as well as in the supply of those types of advanced degrees. It is worth noting that this trend is steeper than the growth in the number of Bachelor's degrees awarded each year (+86% over the period 1985–2013, see Fig. 3), reflecting a large increase in the rate at which college

---

[5] The number of degrees awarded each year, used in Figs. 2–7, is obtained from the HEGIS (1985–86) and IPEDS (1986–87 through 2012–13).

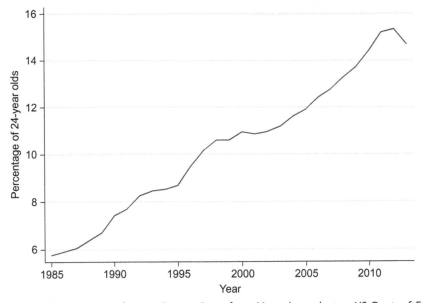

Figure 2 Share of Master's graduates. *Source: Data from Master's graduates: US Dept. of Education (NCES), Higher Education General Information Survey (HEGIS), 1985–86; Integrated Postsecondary Education Data System (IPEDS), 1990–91 to 2012–13. Population: US Census Bureau, Population Division; Quarterly US population estimates by age, sex, race, and Hispanic origin (1980–89); monthly intercensal estimates of the US population by age and sex (1990–2000); intercensal estimates of the resident population by single year of age, sex, race, and Hispanic origin for the USA (2000–10); annual estimates of the resident population by single year of age and sex for the USA (2011–13).*

graduates go on to a Master's program. While the share of individuals getting a Master's degree has increased significantly for all fields over that period, the growth has been particularly dramatic for Health and, to a lesser extent, Business (see Fig. 4).

Fig. 5 reports the proportions of students who graduated with a Master's degree in Business, Education, Health Professions, Other STEM, and Other non-STEM fields, among all students (again restricted to permanent residents and US citizens) receiving a Master's degree in any given year from 1985 to 2013.[6] Education and Business together account for around 50% of the Master's degrees awarded throughout this period. Education was, by a substantial margin, the most popular field until 2007, then followed in the most recent years by a steady decline in the proportion of Master's degrees awarded in this field. As of 2013, Education and Business accounted for pretty much the same

---

[6] Other STEM fields include Computer and Information Sciences, Engineering, Mathematics, Physical Sciences, and Social Sciences. Other non-STEM fields include fields such as Visual and Performing Arts, Theology, Public Administration and Social Services, English and Literature, Communication and Journalism, and Architecture, as well as Homeland Security, Law Enforcement, and Firefighting.

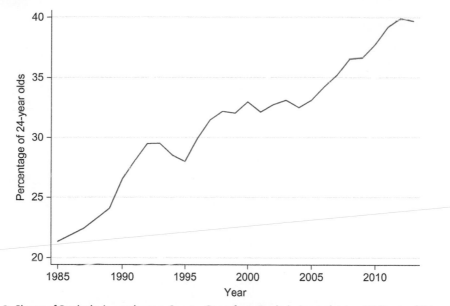

Figure 3 Share of Bachelor's graduates. *Source: Data from Bachelor's graduates: US Dept. of Education (NCES), Higher Education General Information Survey (HEGIS), 1985–86; Integrated Postsecondary Education Data System (IPEDS), 1990–91 to 2012–13. Population: US Census Bureau, Population Division; Quarterly US population estimates by age, sex, race, and Hispanic origin (1980–89); monthly intercensal estimates of the US population by age and sex (1990–2000); intercensal estimates of the resident population by single year of age, sex, race, and Hispanic origin for the USA (2000–10); annual estimates of the resident population by single year of age and sex for the USA (2011–2013).*

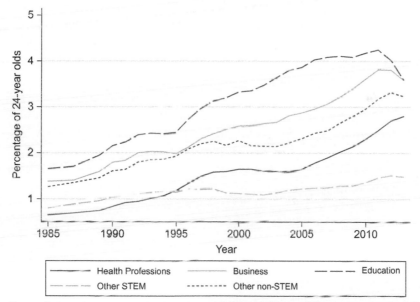

Figure 4 Share of Master's graduates broken down by field. *Source: Field of study: US Dept. of Education (NCES), Higher Education General Information Survey (HEGIS), 1985–86; Integrated Postsecondary Education Data System (IPEDS), 1990–91 to 2012–13. Population: US Census Bureau, Population Division; Quarterly US population estimates by age, sex, race, and Hispanic origin (1980–89); monthly intercensal estimates of the US population by age and sex (1990–2000); intercensal estimates of the resident population by single year of age, sex, race, and Hispanic origin for the USA (2000–10); annual estimates of the resident population by single year of age and sex for the USA (2011–13).*

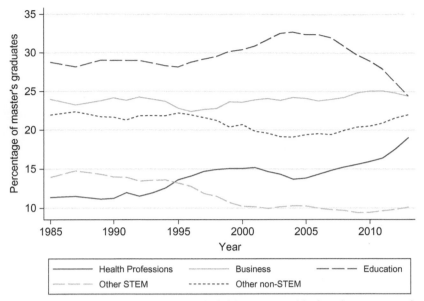

Figure 5 Percentage of Master's degrees in each field. *Source: Field of study: US Dept. of Education (NCES), Higher Education General Information Survey (HEGIS), 1985–86; Integrated Postsecondary Education Data System (IPEDS), 1990–91 to 2012–13.*

share of Master's degrees awarded in that year. It will be interesting to see whether the decline in the popularity of Education is confirmed in the next couple of years.

On the other side of the spectrum, Master's in Health and STEM are, throughout the period, the least popular fields. Notably, in 2013, about 10% of the Master's degrees were received in STEM fields, which represents less than half of the share of Master's degrees awarded in Business or Education.

PhD degrees have also become more prevalent over this period, while still accounting for only a small share of each cohort. Fig. 6 reports the evolution of the number of permanent residents and US citizens graduating with a PhD degree in the USA, as a fraction of the total resident population of 28-year olds. The share of individuals receiving a PhD degree has fluctuated between 0.6% and 1.1% over the period 1985–2013, with the number of PhD degrees awarded in 2013, as a share of 28-year-old US residents, being 70% higher in 2013 relative to 1985. Fig. 7 reports for each year the share of students who earned a PhD degree in STEM, Social Sciences, Humanities, Business, Education, and other fields, among all students receiving a PhD degree in that year.[7] Throughout

---

[7] STEM includes Biological and Medical Sciences, Mathematics and Statistics, Physical Sciences, Computer and Information Sciences, and Engineering. Social Sciences includes Economics, Sociology, Political Science, Psychology, Public Administration, and Social Services. Humanities includes Visual and Performing Arts, Foreign Languages, Literatures and Linguistics, English and Literature, and Theology. Finally, Other fields include Agriculture and Natural Resources, Architecture, Multi/Interdisciplinary Studies, Park, Recreation, Leisure and Fitness Studies, and Homeland Security, Law Enforcement, and Firefighting.

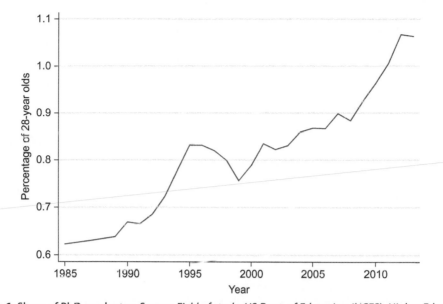

Figure 6 Share of PhD graduates. *Source: Field of study: US Dept. of Education (NCES), Higher Education General Information Survey (HEGIS), 1985–86; Integrated Postsecondary Education Data System (IPEDS), 1990–91 to 2012–13. Population: US Census Bureau, Population Division; Quarterly US population estimates by age, sex, race, and Hispanic origin (1980–89); monthly intercensal estimates of the US population by age and sex (1990–2000); intercensal estimates of the resident population by single year of age, sex, race, and Hispanic origin for the USA (2000–10); annual estimates of the resident population by single year of age and sex for the USA (2011–13).*

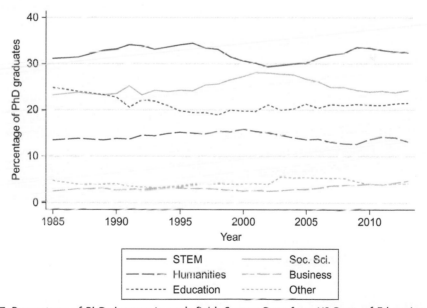

Figure 7 Percentage of PhD degrees in each field. *Source: Data from US Dept. of Education (NCES), Higher Education General Information Survey (HEGIS), 1985–86; Integrated Postsecondary Education Data System (IPEDS), 1990–91 to 2012–13.*

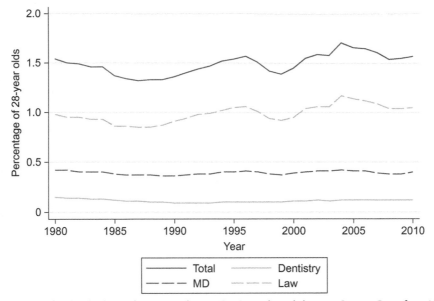

Figure 8 Share of individuals graduating with an MD, JD, or dental degree. *Source: Data from US Dept. of Education (NCES), Higher Education General Information Survey (HEGIS) degrees and Other Formal Awards Conferred Surveys (1980–85), Integrated Postsecondary Education Data System (IPEDS) Completions Survey (1987–99), IPEDS Completions Component (2000–10).*

this period, Business (and others) are the least popular fields, while STEM fields account for the highest fraction of PhD degrees. It is worth noting that, although the flow of new PhD degrees awarded each year has substantially increased over time, the distribution of fields within those types of degrees is similar in 2013 to what it was close to three decades ago. The most noticeable change occurs for Education, with a decrease in the share of PhD's in that field from 24.9% to 21.5%.

Turning to professional degrees, Fig. 8 plots the evolution of the number of individuals graduating with an MD, a JD, or a dental degree, as a fraction of the total resident population of 28-year olds. The share of individuals graduating with a dental degree or with an MD degree has been remarkably stable over the last 30 years, hovering around 0.1% and 0.4%, respectively. The share of JD degrees is somewhat more volatile, but remains of similar order of magnitude in the most recent years as 30 years ago (around 1%). Those patterns contrast sharply with the large increase in the share of individuals graduating with a Master's or a PhD degree over the same period.

Interestingly, Figs. 9 and 10 show that the number of applications to MD and JD programs fluctuate significantly more over the last 15 years than the number of matriculants and first-year enrollments, respectively.[8] These patterns are consistent with the demand

---

[8] The numbers reported for MD degrees in Fig. 9 also include the number of applicants, matriculants, and first-year enrollments to Doctor of Osteopathic Medicine (DO) programs.

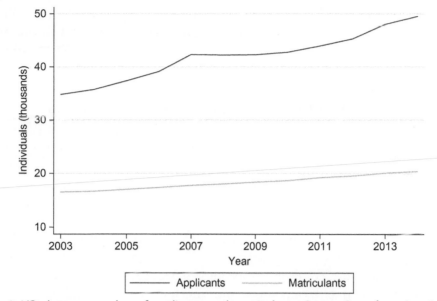

Figure 9 MD degrees: number of applicants and matriculants. *Source: Data from Association of American Medical Colleges.*

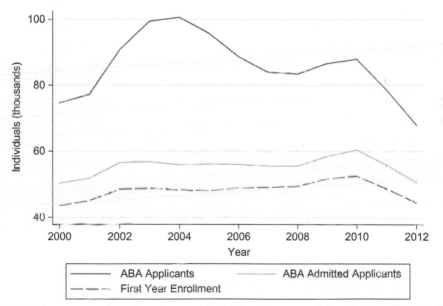

Figure 10 JD degrees: number of applicants, admitted applicants, and first-year enrollments. *Source: Data from Applicants: Law School Admission Council, National Decision Profiles (2015). Enrollment: American Bar Association, Section of Legal Education and Admission to the Bar.*

for those types of advanced degrees being constrained by the supply side. Fig. 9 further points to a significant increase over this period in the selectivity of MD programs, while Fig. 10 shows that rejection rates from JD programs are in fact slightly lower in 2012 than in 2000.

2.3 The Distribution of Undergraduate and Graduate Degrees

In this section, we provide basic facts about the joint distribution of undergraduate and graduate degrees. The source of the information is the 2010 sample of the National Survey of College Graduates (NSCG10). We report results for persons between the ages of 27 and 59, inclusive. The NSCG10 provides facts about the stock of college graduates at a point in time.[9] It complements the IPEDS and HEGIS, which we use to summarize trends in college and advanced degrees.[10]

Table 2 reports on the proportions of male and female college graduates with advanced degrees, by broad graduate degree type. The fractions of men and women with at least one advanced degree are almost identical: 0.353 and 0.344, respectively. However, the distribution is different, with women much more likely to have a Master's in Education or Psychology, and less likely to have a Master's in a business-related field, an MBA, a Master's in Computer and Mathematical Sciences, Engineering, or a medical degree. The gender differences in graduate degrees in part reflects gender differences in undergraduate fields. For example, the proportions of men and women with a Bachelor's in Education are 0.053 and 0.151, respectively, while the corresponding proportions in Engineering are 0.132 and 0.023, respectively.[11]

Table 3 reports on graduate degree attainment by field of undergraduate study. Column 1 provides the unweighted sample size for each major. Column 2 reports the fraction of college graduates with a Bachelor's degree in the specified field. Column 3 reports the fraction of college graduates in each field who obtain at least one advanced degree.[12] The remaining columns of each row report the fraction of persons in the specified

---

[9] The sample size does not permit a cohort analysis at the level of disaggregation by field that we use. One could use earlier waves of the NSCG to examine trends, but we have not done so.

[10] The IPEDS and HEGIS lack information on the interrelationship between undergraduate field and graduate degree type.

[11] See Table A.1, which is also based on NSCG10 but includes ages 24 through 59. All summary statistics and regression results based on the NSCG10 use sample weights.

[12] About 19.4% of the sample report a second undergraduate field, although this also includes minors. For persons with a second undergraduate field, we use the first major specified. Altonji and Zhong (2015) provide evidence that to a first approximation, the earnings and occupations of double majors are a weighted average of the earnings and occupation distribution associated with the separate fields, but with more of the weight on the first. Presumably, the presence of double majors in the sample will blur to some degree the connection between the specified undergraduate major and graduate degree type. Note also that some sample members report more than one graduate degree and are counted as having a graduate degree in more than one column of the table.

Table 2 Proportion of male and female college graduates with advanced degrees by degree type

	All (1)	Male (2)	Female (3)
Master's — Education field	0.077	0.042	0.108
Master's in Business-related field	0.020	0.027	0.013
Master's in Public Administration	0.005	0.006	0.004
Master's in Arts field	0.006	0.005	0.007
Master's in Humanities field	0.015	0.016	0.014
Master's — Other nonscience and engineering field	0.010	0.008	0.011
Master's in Psychology or Social Work	0.020	0.010	0.029
Master's — Other social and related sciences	0.011	0.011	0.010
Master's in Health Services Administration	0.003	0.002	0.003
Master's in Nursing	0.006	0.001	0.010
Master's — Biological/Agricultural/Environmental Life Sciences	0.008	0.008	0.008
Master's — Computer and Mathematical Sciences	0.014	0.021	0.008
Master's — Engineering	0.017	0.029	0.006
Master's — Physical and related sciences	0.004	0.005	0.002
Master's — Other science and engineering-related fields	0.018	0.011	0.023
MBA	0.046	0.060	0.034
Law	0.032	0.036	0.029
MD	0.023	0.031	0.015
PhD	0.029	0.038	0.020
Other professional degree	0.003	0.002	0.003
Has at least one advanced degree	0.348	0.353	0.344
N	56,133	30,367	25,766

Notes: The sample includes individuals ages 27–59. Estimates are weighted using sample weights.
Source: Data from National Survey of College Graduates 2010.

undergraduate field who obtained the graduate degree listed in the column heading. Consider engineering, in the NSCG sample, 7.4% of undergraduates obtained an engineering degree (column 2). Of these 39.5% obtained at least one graduate degree; 18.2% obtained a Master's in Engineering and 3.6% in Computer Science and Mathematical Sciences; and 7.7% obtained an MBA and 2.2% obtained a Master's in a business-related field.[13] The fractions are much lower for other nonscience-related graduate degrees.

The table supports the following generalizations. First, and not surprisingly, there is a strong link between the undergraduate major and graduate degree type.[14] The large

[13] The MBA category consists of Master's in Business Administration and Management, in Business and Managerial Economics, and in Business, General, and Other Business Management/Administrative Services. The category Master's in a business-related field consists of accounting, marketing, and financial management.

[14] Black et al. (2003) analyze the role of graduate degree attainment in earnings difference across undergraduate degrees using the 1993 National Survey of College Graduates. For a small set of majors, they present evidence on the distribution of graduate degrees by type of undergraduate degree.

Table 3 Fraction of undergraduate majors who obtain graduate degrees, by major and degree type

Major	Raw counts (1)	Fraction of college graduates (2)	Fraction with advanced degrees (3)	Master's — Education field (4)	Master's in Business-related field (5)	Master's in Public Administration (6)	Master's in Arts field (7)	Master's in Humanities field (8)	Master's — Other nonscience and engineering field (9)	Master's in Psychology or Social Work (10)	Master's — Other social and related sciences (11)	Master's in Health Services Administration (12)	Master's in Nursing (13)
Education	2138	0.108	0.425	0.360	0.002	0.000	0.004	0.007	0.007	0.014	0.003	0.001	0.001
English/ Languages/ Literature	891	0.039	0.447	0.121	0.007	0.010	0.005	0.102	0.029	0.009	0.020	0.000	0.000
Fine/ Performing Arts	681	0.043	0.209	0.046	0.006	0.001	0.085	0.007	0.005	0.007	0.002	0.000	0.004
Other Humanities	1035	0.054	0.415	0.112	0.007	0.005	0.009	0.095	0.016	0.016	0.014	0.001	0.000
Communications/ Journalism	648	0.043	0.182	0.058	0.006	0.001	0.005	0.007	0.039	0.004	0.009	0.000	0.001
Accounting	526	0.048	0.211	0.006	0.089	0.006	0.000	0.001	0.000	0.001	0.004	0.005	0.001
Business	2205	0.140	0.213	0.021	0.037	0.005	0.000	0.007	0.002	0.002	0.003	0.002	0.000
Marketing	446	0.031	0.216	0.018	0.082	0.000	0.000	0.000	0.015	0.001	0.002	0.000	0.000
Other non-S and E fields	326	0.021	0.228	0.060	0.001	0.020	0.006	0.000	0.042	0.006	0.004	0.001	0.000
Economics	1989	0.022	0.383	0.022	0.061	0.003	0.001	0.005	0.003	0.004	0.052	0.006	0.003
Political Science	2571	0.034	0.521	0.041	0.011	0.048	0.001	0.014	0.012	0.008	0.047	0.001	0.021
Psychology or Social Work	4467	0.063	0.431	0.081	0.007	0.005	0.002	0.008	0.009	0.193	0.009	0.003	0.003
Other social and related sciences	4303	0.057	0.377	0.084	0.008	0.009	0.005	0.018	0.021	0.049	0.055	0.001	0.032
Nursing	1596	0.030	0.232	0.004	0.002	0.001	0.000	0.001	0.002	0.003	0.001	0.014	0.157
Biological/ Agricultural/ Environmental Science	6824	0.067	0.505	0.034	0.010	0.002	0.001	0.005	0.003	0.006	0.006	0.004	0.004
Computer and Mathematical Sciences	5271	0.048	0.315	0.031	0.016	0.003	0.000	0.005	0.003	0.001	0.003	0.001	0.000
Engineering	11,907	0.074	0.395	0.004	0.022	0.001	0.003	0.002	0.004	0.000	0.003	0.000	0.000
Physical and related sciences	3874	0.023	0.574	0.029	0.009	0.001	0.000	0.006	0.006	0.001	0.007	0.003	0.001
Other S and E-related fields	4120	0.056	0.332	0.029	0.004	0.002	0.003	0.003	0.007	0.007	0.002	0.011	0.002
Total	55,818	1											

Major	Master's — Biological/ Agricultural/ Environmental Life Sciences (14)	Master's — Computer and Mathematical Sciences (15)	Master's — Engineering (16)	Master's — Physical and related sciences (17)	Master's — Other science and engineering related fields (18)	MBA (19)	Law (20)	MD (21)	PhD (22)	Other professional degree (23)
Education	0.002	0.004	0.001	0.000	0.007	0.009	0.003	0.001	0.018	0.001
English/ Languages/ Literature	0.002	0.006	0.001	0.000	0.007	0.028	0.068	0.012	0.040	0.001
Fine/ Performing Arts	0.000	0.003	0.001	0.000	0.014	0.002	0.010	0.001	0.013	0.000
Other Humanities	0.001	0.001	0.001	0.000	0.005	0.024	0.094	0.013	0.023	0.000
Communications/ Journalism	0.001	0.002	0.001	0.000	0.003	0.014	0.030	0.001	0.008	0.000
Accounting	0.000	0.009	0.001	0.000	0.001	0.079	0.008	0.000	0.004	0.000
Business	0.000	0.009	0.001	0.000	0.002	0.104	0.017	0.002	0.002	0.000
Marketing	0.000	0.001	0.000	0.000	0.003	0.088	0.002	0.000	0.001	0.002
Other non-S and E fields	0.002	0.002	0.000	0.000	0.021	0.031	0.027	0.001	0.004	0.000
Economics	0.001	0.011	0.005	0.000	0.003	0.094	0.090	0.011	0.027	0.000
Political Science	0.003	0.002	0.001	0.000	0.008	0.053	0.263	0.004	0.015	0.001
Psychology or Social Work	0.001	0.009	0.001	0.000	0.027	0.026	0.027	0.015	0.041	0.010
Other social and related sciences	0.003	0.002	0.002	0.000	0.018	0.031	0.054	0.007	0.021	0.003
Nursing	0.001	0.000	0.000	0.000	0.017	0.014	0.005	0.002	0.008	0.000
Biological/ Agricultural/ Environmental Science	0.005	0.005	0.004	0.003	0.036	0.030	0.014	0.185	0.077	0.009
Computer and Mathematical Sciences	0.004	0.129	0.018	0.001	0.009	0.050	0.010	0.009	0.033	0.001
Engineering	0.001	0.036	0.182	0.002	0.013	0.077	0.010	0.002	0.039	0.001
Physical and related sciences	0.013	0.020	0.045	0.125	0.012	0.032	0.017	0.088	0.181	0.007
Other S and E-related fields	0.006	0.008	0.006	0.000	0.128	0.030	0.006	0.060	0.020	0.010

Notes: Column 1 provides the unweighted sample size for each major. Column 2 reports the fraction of college graduates with a Bachelor's degree in the specified field. Column 3 reports the fraction of college graduates who obtain at least one advanced degree, by undergraduate field. Columns 4–23 report the share of the advanced degree specified in the column accounted for by the undergraduate major listed in the row. The sample includes individuals ages 27–59. Estimates are weighted using sample weights.
Source: Data from National Survey of College Graduates, 2010.

fraction of engineers who obtain a Master's in Engineering is echoed in the fact that 36.0% of education majors get an education-related Master's degree, 9.5% of Biology/Agricultural/Environmental Life Sciences majors get a Masters' in a life-sciences field, and 18.5% of these majors get a medical degree. Similarly, 14.1% of business majors get Master's degrees in a business-related field or an MBA; 15.7% of nurses obtain a Master's in Nursing, while only 0.6% of all undergraduates obtained a Master's in Nursing.

Second, aggregating across groups of majors within the same broad field obscures the links. Consider the social sciences, the percentage of economics majors who obtain an MBA or a business-related Master's degree is 15.5%. The percentage who obtain a law degree is 9.0%. In contrast, the corresponding values for political science are 6.4% for business and 26.3% for law. The differences with psychology are also very large.

Third, the degree of concentration in particular advanced degrees varies across under-graduate majors. One can see this by noting that the relative values of the row entries vary more for some majors than others. Table 4 makes this point more directly. Each row of Table 4 reports the share of the advanced degree specified in the column accounted for by the specified undergraduate major divided by the share of that major among all college graduates (column 2). If majors were equally represented in each graduate degree, all the cell values would be 1 (aside from sampling error). In the case of nursing, the value is 27.0 for a Master's degree in Nursing. That is, a person with a Master's degree in Nursing is *27.0 times* more likely to have majored in nursing than undergraduates as a whole. Undergraduate nursing majors are also substantially overrepresented in Health Services Administration, but are underrepresented in all other broad graduate programs. On the other hand, economics majors are overrepresented in several graduate degree types but are not massively overrepresented in any.

Finally, the extent to which particular advanced degrees draw from a broad set of majors varies considerably. This point is made most directly in Table 5. Each column of Table 5 reports the shares of the specified graduate degree that are contributed by the various undergraduate majors. MBA programs draw from a number of undergraduate majors, while graduate nursing draws almost entirely from undergraduate nursing majors. The columns of Table 4 also provide information on the same point. Again, the entries show the relative odds that a person in the major specified in the row has received a graduate degree of the type indicated in the column. These are the shares of a major in a graduate degree normalized by the size of the undergraduate major. One can see that the values are much more tightly concentrated around 1 for an MBA degree or a Master's degree in a business-related field than for fields such as nursing or engineering. In nursing and engineering, field-specific preparation at the undergraduate level may be critical.

Table 4 Ratio of the fraction of advanced degree recipients in college major to all college graduates in that major, by advanced degree type and college major (Prob(major m| grad degree f))/Prob(major m| college graduate)

Major	Raw counts (1)	Fraction of college graduates (2)	Fraction with advanced degrees (3)	Master's — Education Field (4)	Master's in Business-related field (5)	Master's in Public Administration (6)	Master's in Arts field (7)	Master's in Humanities field (8)	Master's — Other nonscience and engineering field (9)	Master's in Psychology or Social Work (10)	Master's — Other social and related sciences (11)	Master's in Health Services Administration (12)	Master's in Nursing (13)
Education	2138	0.081	0.425	4.65	0.10	0.01	0.73	0.49	0.75	0.69	0.27	0.54	0.25
English/ Languages/ Literature	891	0.059	0.447	1.56	0.38	1.95	0.74	6.91	2.97	0.46	1.95	0.06	0.05
Fine/ Performing Arts	681	0.063	0.209	0.59	0.28	0.15	13.88	0.45	0.49	0.33	0.15	0.00	0.73
Other Humanities	1035	0.054	0.415	1.45	0.36	0.96	1.55	6.46	1.65	0.79	1.33	0.23	0.05
Communications/ Journalism	648	0.043	0.182	0.74	0.31	0.19	0.77	0.46	4.02	0.19	0.81	0.00	0.21
Accounting	526	0.048	0.211	0.08	4.56	1.09	0.00	0.04	0.03	0.06	0.34	2.02	0.09
Business	2205	0.140	0.213	0.27	1.92	0.90	0.01	0.48	0.18	0.09	0.27	0.77	0.04
Marketing	446	0.031	0.216	0.24	4.21	0.03	0.02	0.03	1.54	0.05	0.15	0.16	0.00
Other non-S and E fields	326	0.021	0.228	0.77	0.06	3.90	0.97	0.00	4.33	0.28	0.38	0.42	0.00
Economics	1989	0.022	0.383	0.29	3.10	0.69	0.24	0.34	0.28	0.13	4.95	2.19	0.00
Political Science	2571	0.034	0.521	0.52	0.58	9.44	0.16	0.96	1.25	0.38	4.47	0.55	0.12
Psychology or Social Work	4467	0.063	0.431	1.05	0.38	0.89	0.27	0.57	0.92	9.65	0.91	1.35	0.45
Other social and related sciences	4303	0.057	0.377	1.08	0.40	1.79	0.87	1.20	2.10	2.48	5.24	0.46	0.32
Nursing	1596	0.030	0.252	0.05	0.11	0.23	0.04	0.10	0.21	0.13	0.13	5.30	26.96
Biological/ Agricultural/ Environmental Science	6824	0.067	0.505	0.44	0.49	0.40	0.18	0.36	0.31	0.29	0.58	1.44	0.68
Computer and Mathematical Sciences	527	0.048	0.315	0.40	0.84	0.59	0.06	0.33	0.34	0.05	0.28	0.38	0.00
Engineering	11,907	0.074	0.395	0.05	1.13	0.16	0.49	0.12	0.37	0.01	0.25	0.00	0.00
Physical and related sciences	3874	0.023	0.574	0.37	0.45	0.21	0.07	0.43	0.64	0.03	0.67	1.05	0.21
Other S and E-related fields	4120	0.056	0.332	0.37	0.18	0.38	0.54	0.19	0.76	0.37	0.15	4.9	0.36
Total	55,818	1											

Major	Master's — Biological/ Agricultural/ Environmental Life Sciences (14)	Master's — Computer and Mathematical Sciences (15)	Master's — Engineering (16)	Master's — Physical and related sciences (17)	Master's — Other science and engineering-related fields (18)	MBA (19)	Law (20)	MD (21)	PhD (22)	Other professional degree (23)
Education	0.19	0.25	0.07	0.10	0.39	0.19	0.09	0.06	0.68	0.23
English/ Languages/ Literature	0.21	0.41	0.06	0.02	0.40	0.61	2.14	0.52	1.51	0.36
Fine/ Performing Arts	0.02	0.62	0.08	0.11	0.77	0.04	0.31	0.06	0.51	0.10
Other Humanities	0.11	0.11	0.03	0.07	0.29	0.53	2.95	0.59	0.87	0.15
Communications/ Journalism	0.11	0.13	0.03	0.01	0.18	0.29	0.94	0.05	0.31	0.00
Accounting	0.01	0.65	0.05	0.03	0.04	1.72	0.26	0.02	0.16	0.00
Business	0.03	0.62	0.04	0.07	0.10	2.27	0.53	0.10	0.08	0.15
Marketing	0.02	0.06	0.02	0.02	0.19	1.92	0.05	0.00	0.04	0.87
Other non-S and E fields	0.23	0.17	0.01	0.00	1.19	0.68	0.85	0.06	0.15	0.00
Economics	0.07	0.80	0.32	0.03	0.18	2.04	2.83	0.49	1.03	0.05
Political Science	0.36	0.12	0.03	0.03	0.44	1.14	8.26	0.18	0.56	0.23
Psychology or Social Work	0.15	0.64	0.04	0.09	1.51	0.56	0.86	0.68	1.57	3.91
Other social and related sciences	0.38	0.17	0.10	0.13	1.04	0.67	1.69	0.33	0.80	1.25
Nursing	0.16	0.02	0.00	0.00	0.96	0.31	0.15	0.07	0.32	0.12
Biological/ Agricultural/ Environmental Science	11.86	0.35	0.22	0.79	2.04	0.66	0.45	8.33	2.92	3.69
Computer and Mathematical Sciences	0.47	9.19	1.06	0.32	0.50	1.09	0.31	0.39	1.25	0.32
Engineering	0.16	2.57	10.96	0.70	0.73	1.69	0.31	0.31	1.49	0.23
Physical and related sciences	1.64	1.46	2.69	36.08	0.68	0.70	0.53	3.97	6.89	3.01
Other S and E-related fields	0.69	0.56	0.34	0.07	7.22	0.66	0.18	2.69	0.76	3.96

Notes: Column 1 provides the unweighted sample size for each major. Column 2 reports the fraction of college graduates with a Bachelor's degree in the specified field. Column 3 reports the fraction of college graduates who obtain at least one advanced degree, by undergraduate field. Columns 4–23 report the ratio of the share of the advanced degree specified in the column accounted for by the undergraduate major listed in the row to the share of that major among all college graduates reported in column 2. The sample includes individuals ages 27–59. Estimates are weighted using sample weights.

Source: Data from National Survey of College Graduates, 2010.

Table 5 Fraction of advanced degree recipients in college major, by advanced degree type and college major

Major	Raw counts (1)	Fraction of college graduates (2)	Fraction with advanced degrees (3)	Master's — Education field (4)	Master's in Business-related field (5)	Master's in Public Administration (6)	Master's in Arts field (7)	Master's in Humanities field (8)	Master's — Other nonscience and engineering field (9)	Master's in Psychology or Social Work (10)	Master's — Other social and related sciences (11)	Master's in Health Services Administration (12)	Master's in Nursing (13)
Education	2138	0.081	0.425	0.50	0.01	0.00	0.08	0.05	0.08	0.07	0.03	0.06	0.03
English/ Languages/ Literature	891	0.039	0.497	0.05	0.01	0.08	0.05	0.27	0.12	0.02	0.08	0.00	0.00
Fine/ Performing Arts	681	0.043	0.207	0.03	0.01	0.01	0.59	0.02	0.02	0.01	0.01	0.00	0.03
Other Humanities	1055	0.054	0.415	0.08	0.02	0.05	0.08	0.35	0.09	0.04	0.07	0.01	0.00
Communications/ Journalism	648	0.045	0.182	0.03	0.01	0.01	0.03	0.02	0.17	0.01	0.03	0.00	0.01
Accounting	526	0.048	0.211	0.00	0.22	0.05	0.00	0.00	0.00	0.00	0.02	0.10	0.00
Business	2205	0.140	0.213	0.04	0.27	0.13	0.00	0.07	0.03	0.01	0.04	0.11	0.01
Marketing	446	0.031	0.216	0.01	0.13	0.00	0.00	0.00	0.05	0.00	0.00	0.00	0.00
Other non-S and E fields	326	0.021	0.228	0.02	0.00	0.08	0.02	0.00	0.09	0.01	0.01	0.01	0.00
Economics	1989	0.022	0.383	0.01	0.07	0.02	0.01	0.01	0.01	0.00	0.11	0.05	0.00
Political Science	2571	0.034	0.521	0.02	0.02	0.32	0.00	0.03	0.04	0.01	0.15	0.02	0.00
Psychology or Social Work	4467	0.063	0.431	0.07	0.02	0.06	0.02	0.04	0.06	0.61	0.06	0.09	0.03
Other social and related sciences	4203	0.057	0.377	0.06	0.02	0.10	0.05	0.07	0.12	0.14	0.30	0.03	0.02
Nursing	1596	0.030	0.232	0.00	0.00	0.01	0.00	0.00	0.01	0.00	0.00	0.16	0.80
Biological/ Agricultural/ Environmental Science	6824	0.067	0.505	0.03	0.03	0.03	0.01	0.02	0.02	0.02	0.04	0.10	0.05
Computer and Mathematical Sciences	5271	0.048	0.315	0.02	0.04	0.03	0.00	0.02	0.02	0.00	0.01	0.02	0.00
Engineering	11,907	0.074	0.395	0.00	0.08	0.01	0.04	0.01	0.03	0.00	0.02	0.06	0.00
Physical and related sciences	3874	0.023	0.574	0.01	0.01	0.00	0.00	0.01	0.01	0.00	0.02	0.02	0.00
Other S and E-related fields	4120	0.056	0.332	0.02	0.01	0.02	0.03	0.01	0.04	0.02	0.01	0.04	0.02
Total	55,818	1											

Major	Master's — Biological/ Agricultural/ Environmental Life Sciences (14)	Master's — Computer and Mathematical Sciences (15)	Master's — Engineering (16)	Master's — Physical and related sciences (17)	Master's — Other science and engineering-related fields (18)	MBA (19)	Law (20)	MD (21)	PhD (22)	Other professional degree (23)
Education	0.02	0.03	0.01	0.01	0.04	0.02	0.01	0.01	0.07	0.02
English/ Languages/ Literature	0.01	0.02	0.00	0.00	0.02	0.02	0.08	0.02	0.06	0.01
Fine/ Performing Arts	0.00	0.03	0.00	0.00	0.03	0.00	0.01	0.00	0.02	0.00
Other Humanities	0.01	0.01	0.00	0.00	0.02	0.03	0.16	0.03	0.05	0.01
Communications/ Journalism	0.00	0.01	0.00	0.00	0.01	0.01	0.04	0.00	0.01	0.00
Accounting	0.00	0.03	0.00	0.00	0.00	0.08	0.01	0.00	0.01	0.00
Business	0.00	0.09	0.01	0.01	0.01	0.32	0.07	0.01	0.01	0.02
Marketing	0.00	0.00	0.00	0.00	0.01	0.06	0.00	0.00	0.00	0.03
Other non-S and E fields	0.00	0.00	0.00	0.00	0.03	0.01	0.02	0.00	0.00	0.00
Economics	0.00	0.02	0.01	0.00	0.00	0.04	0.06	0.01	0.02	0.00
Political Science	0.01	0.00	0.00	0.00	0.02	0.04	0.28	0.01	0.02	0.01
Psychology or Social Work	0.01	0.04	0.00	0.01	0.10	0.04	0.05	0.04	0.10	0.25
Other social and related sciences	0.02	0.01	0.01	0.01	0.06	0.04	0.10	0.02	0.05	0.07
Nursing	0.00	0.00	0.00	0.00	0.03	0.01	0.00	0.00	0.01	0.00
Biological/ Agricultural/ Environmental Science	0.79	0.02	0.01	0.05	0.14	0.04	0.03	0.55	0.19	0.25
Computer and Mathematical Sciences	0.02	0.44	0.05	0.02	0.02	0.05	0.02	0.02	0.06	0.02
Engineering	0.01	0.19	0.81	0.05	0.05	0.12	0.02	0.02	0.11	0.02
Physical and related sciences	0.04	0.03	0.06	0.83	0.02	0.02	0.01	0.09	0.16	0.07
Other S and E-related fields	0.04	0.03	0.02	0.00	0.41	0.04	0.01	0.15	0.04	0.22

Notes: Column 1 provides the unweighted sample size for each major. Column 2 reports the fraction of college graduates with a Bachelor's degree in the specified field. Column 3 reports the fraction of college graduates who obtain at least one advanced degree, by undergraduate field. Columns 4–23 report the share of the advanced degree specified in the column accounted for by the undergraduate major listed in the row. The sample includes individuals ages 27–59. Estimates are weighted using sample weights.
Source: Data from National Survey of College Graduates, 2010.

2.3.1 Facts About Earnings

In Table 6, we provide descriptive evidence on the relative returns to various undergraduate and graduate degrees based on 1993 and 2010 NSCG surveys. The table reports coefficients from the regression of log earnings on 19 mutually exclusive indicators for undergraduate field of study and on 20 mutually exclusive indicators for advanced degree type. The model includes controls for gender, race/ethnicity interacted with gender, and a cubic in age interacted with gender. We control for mother's education category and father's education category but lack data on test scores and high school curriculum. The sample is restricted to full-time workers between the ages of 24 and 59, inclusive.[15] The sample only includes people with at least a Bachelor's degree. The returns are relative to a Bachelor's in Education. Column 1 reports coefficients on undergraduate major, with education as the excluded category. Column 2 reports coefficients on advanced degrees. Both columns come from the same regression.

The estimates show that the highest returns are in Engineering, the Physical Sciences, Computer and Mathematical Sciences, Accounting, and Nursing. The highest-paid major is Electrical and Communications Engineering, which pays 0.392 log points more than education. The next four highest-paid fields are Accounting (0.327), Computer and Mathematical Sciences (0.327), Economics (0.313), and Nursing (0.312). Political Science majors earn a 0.176 premium over teachers. English, Languages and Literature, other humanities (which includes History), other Social Sciences, and Psychology majors earn a small premium over education. The life sciences pay less than the physical sciences. The patterns are consistent with evidence from many other data sets for the USA, as we discuss in more detail in Section 4. Fine and Performing Arts is the lowest-paid major among the set broken out in the table, followed by education, being the second lowest, with other humanities a close third. Altonji et al. (2012) and other studies that report results for more disaggregated categories find a number of majors that pay less than education.

The results show a premium for a Master's in Education of 0.124 (0.01). The returns to Master's degrees in the sciences range from 0.053 (0.02) for Biology/Agricultural/Environmental Life Sciences to 0.229 (0.02) for Computer and Mathematical Sciences. The return is only 0.081 (0.01) for psychology/social work but 0.166 (0.02) for the other social sciences. It is 0.068 (0.01) for a miscellaneous category of fields outside of science and engineering, and is negative for the humanities (−0.106). The ranking of the returns for an MBA, Law, and MD match the ranking of the number of years of study these degrees typically require.

---

[15] Altonji et al. (2012) report the results of a similar regression using the log hourly wage rate as the dependent variable and a much larger set of degree categories. They lack information on parental education. Their data are from the 2009 ACS. The ACS is much larger, but it does not provide information on the field of study of graduate degrees.

Table 6 Return to undergraduate and graduate degrees

	Coef./SE		Coef./SE
Education	0.000	Master's — Education field	0.124
			(0.01)
English/Languages/	0.105	MBA	0.263
Literature	(0.02)		(0.02)
Fine/Performing Arts	−0.059	Law	0.503
	(0.02)		(0.02)
Other Humanities	0.013	MD	0.710
	(0.02)		(0.02)
Communications/	0.142	Other professional degree	0.328
Journalism	0.026		(0.03)
Accounting	0.328	PhD	0.208
	(0.02)		(0.01)
Business	0.184	Master's in Business-related field	0.336
	(0.02)		(0.03)
Marketing	0.237	Master's in Public Administration	0.208
	(0.03)		(0.03)
Other non-S and E fields	0.142	Master's in Arts field	0.060
	(0.02)		(0.03)
Economics	0.313	Master's in Humanities field	−0.106
	(0.02)		(0.03)
Political Science	0.176	Master's — Other nonscience and	0.068
	(0.02)	engineering field	(0.01)
Psychology or Social Work	0.079	Master's in Psychology or Social Work	0.081
	(0.01)		(0.01)
Other social and related	0.082	Master's — Other social and related	0.166
sciences	(0.01)	sciences	(0.02)
Nursing	0.312	Master's in Health Services	0.263
	(0.01)	Administration	(0.03)
Biological/Agricultural/	0.125	Master's in Nursing	0.192
Environmental Science	(0.01)		(0.02)
Computer and	0.327	Master's — Biological/Agricultural/	0.053
Mathematical Sciences	(0.01)	Environmental Life Sciences	(0.02)
Engineering	0.392	Master's — Computer and	0.229
	(0.01)	Mathematical Sciences	(0.02)
Physical and related sciences	0.230	Master's — Engineering	0.196
	(0.01)		(0.01)
Other S and E-related fields	0.271	Master's — Physical and related	(0.11)
	(0.02)	sciences	(0.02)
		Master's — Other science and	0.179
		engineering related fields	(0.02)

Notes: This table reports coefficients from a regression of ln(earnings) a set of indicator variables for undergraduate major and a set of indicator variables for graduate degree type. A BA in Education in the reference undergraduate major. The other control variables include a cubic in age interacted with gender, father's education (six categories) mother's education (six categories), gender interacted with race (six categories), and Hispanic. These data are from the National Survey of College Graduates 1993 and 2010. The sample consists of persons with at least a BA/BS degree and is restricted to full-time workers between the ages of 24 and 59. The regression is weighted using survey weights. $N = 144,635$. $R^2 = 0.282$.

The above model assumes that the return to undergraduate and graduate degrees are additively separable in a log specification. What about complementarity between undergraduate and graduate degrees in the labor market? Much of the complementarity presumably operates through preparation for graduate school. An individual's skill set upon completion of a Master's in Engineering depends upon having a base in science and engineering to build on. Application decisions and admission decisions will both reflect this dependence. The undergraduate English major who is studying for a Master's in Engineering is unusual. On the other hand, some graduate degrees, such as law and MBA programs, do not have strong prerequisites. The degree of complementarity is likely to differ across degree pairs.

Table 7 reports estimates of the return to various combinations of undergraduate and graduate degrees relative to an undergraduate degree in education with no graduate degree. The table was constructed from a regression that includes the main effects of the undergraduate degree categories with education omitted, and interactions between the undergraduate categories (including education) and the aggregated graduate degree categories shown in the table. The row label specifies the undergraduate field and the column label indicates highest degree. The table also reports the number of observations underlying the main effects of the majors and the interaction terms. We have suppressed entries with fewer than 15 observations.

Estimates of the return to undergraduate major relative to education are reported in the first column. They echo the results in Table 4, although the values differ to some extent. Some graduate degrees narrow differences across undergraduate fields, while others preserve or widen them. A Master's in Education narrows differentials substantially. For example, Engineering majors with a Master's in Education earn about the same amount as an Education major with a Master's degree, despite the fact that an engineer without a graduate degree earns 46% more than an education major without a graduate degree. If one regresses the returns to the undergraduate field/Master's in Education combinations that are reported in column 2 on the returns to undergraduate major in column 1, the intercept and slope are 0.196 (0.04) and 0.0172 (0.16).[16] Proceeding on to graduate school education has a leveling effect across undergraduate degree types, presumably because many of those who pursue Master's degrees in the education field work as teachers and school administrators within a relatively narrow pay band.

In the case of terminal Master's degrees outside education, the corresponding regression yields an intercept of 0.0526 and a slope of 1.19 (0.172). That is, Master's degrees raise the earnings of undergraduates by an amount that increases more than 1 for 1 with the relative return to the undergraduate major. For an MBA the intercept and slope are 0.421 (0.04) and 0.476 (0.13), respectively. This indicates that getting an MBA narrows

---

[16] This regression and those described in the next paragraph are limited to undergraduate majors with at least 20 cases for the specified graduate degree.

Table 7 Returns to combinations of undergraduate and graduate degrees coefficient (standard error) [unweighted cell count]

	Bachelors only	Master's — Education field	Non-MBA/ Educ/Law Master's	MBA	Law	MD
Education	0	0.242	0.196	0.331	0.588	0.588
	(0)	(0.01)	(0.03)	(0.05)	(0.08)	(0.15)
	[6877]	[4768]	[1007]	[127]	[68]	[34]
English/ Languages/ Literature	0.116	0.228	0.276	0.599	0.645	0.981
	(0.03)	(0.05)	(0.04)	(0.12)	(0.06)	(0.14)
	[2227]	[552]	[1293]	[123]	[231]	[65]
Fine/ Performing Arts	−0.026	0.205	0.108	0.35	0.699	0.789
	(0.03)	(0.05)	(0.03)	(0.1)	(0.09)	(0.15)
	[2139]	[174]	[777]	[38]	[34]	[29]
Other Humanities	0.042	0.19	0.024	0.55	0.711	0.678
	(0.03)	(0.05)	(0.04)	(0.08)	(0.06)	(0.12)
	[2581]	[449]	[1185]	[154]	[432]	[114]
Communications/ Journalism	0.201	0.009	0.341	0.694	0.577	
	(0.03)	(0.11)	(0.06)	(0.19)	(0.06)	
	[2079]	[89]	[330]	[66]	[54]	
Accounting	0.397	0.38	0.577	0.6	0.764	
	(0.02)	(0.15)	(0.07)	(0.06)	(0.06)	
	[3432]	[17]	[472]	[273]	[93]	
Business	0.24	0.274	0.477	0.451	0.718	0.836
	(0.02)	(0.08)	(0.05)	(0.04)	(0.06)	(0.21)
	[9370]	[195]	[1037]	[1073]	[252]	[21]
Marketing	0.291	0.442	0.476	0.596	0.799	
	(0.03)	(0.12)	(0.06)	(0.07)	(0.08)	
	[2020]	[27]	[219]	[142]	[21]	
Other non-S and E fields	0.196	0.203	0.35	0.435	0.453	0.874
	(0.02)	(0.03)	(0.02)	(0.07)	(0.05)	(0.03)
	[5654]	[180]	[1231]	[189]	[65]	[885]
Economics	0.375	0.089	0.631	0.647	0.818	0.629
	(0.03)	(0.06)	(0.04)	(0.04)	(0.04)	(0.15)
	[1711]	[38]	[682]	[311]	[272]	[28]
Political Science	0.244	0.068	0.446	0.516	0.697	1.112
	(0.02)	(0.07)	(0.03)	(0.05)	(0.03)	(0.13)
	[2211]	[164]	[801]	[204]	[1213]	[20]
Psychology or Social Work	0.116	0.218	0.251	0.537	0.672	0.95
	(0.02)	(0.02)	(0.02)	(0.05)	(0.06)	(0.07)
	[4007]	[719]	[2437]	[205]	[242]	[185]
Other social and related sciences	0.129	0.172	0.27	0.382	0.702	0.844
	(0.02)	(0.03)	(0.02)	(0.11)	(0.04)	(0.09)
	[4735]	[584]	[2089]	[249]	[392]	[75]

Table 7 Returns to combinations of undergraduate and graduate degrees coefficient (standard error) [unweighted cell count]—cont'd

	Bachelors only	Master's — Education field	Non-MBA/ Educ/Law Master's	MBA	Law	MD
Nursing	0.374	0.2	0.554	0.571	0.675	0.974
	(0.02)	(0.08)	(0.02)	(0.07)	(0.08)	(0.17)
	[1768]	[50]	[710]	[49]	[19]	[15]
Biological/ Agricultural/ Environmental Science	0.158	0.2	0.303	0.472	0.735	0.914
	(0.01)	(0.03)	(0.02)	(0.06)	(0.1)	(0.03)
	[6224]	[371]	[2954]	[270]	[116]	[2303]
Computer and Mathematical Sciences	0.411	0.246	0.53	0.544	0.788	1.006
	(0.01)	(0.03)	(0.02)	(0.05)	(0.1)	(0.09)
	[6733]	[282]	[2184]	[456]	[67]	[70]
Engineering	0.46	0.234	0.616	0.67	0.853	0.876
	(0.01)	(0.12)	(0.01)	(0.02)	(0.06)	(0.07)
	[16,663]	[67]	[7090]	[1592]	[155]	[132]
Physical and related sciences	0.291	0.208	0.423	0.503	0.753	0.967
	(0.02)	(0.06)	(0.02)	(0.05)	(0.09)	(0.03)
	[3854]	[146]	[2378]	[240]	[78]	[557]
Other S and E-related fields	0.348	0.18	0.413	0.621	0.507	1.038
	(0.03)	(0.06)	(0.03)	(0.07)	(0.12)	(0.1)
	[1791]	[75]	[723]	[129]	[24]	[177]

Notes: This table reports estimates of the return (in logs) to various combinations of undergraduate degrees and graduate degrees relative to an undergraduate degree in education with no graduate degree. The table was constructed from a regression that includes the main effects of the undergraduate degree categories with education omitted. It also includes interactions between the undergraduate categories and the aggregated graduate degree categories. The row label specifies the undergraduate field and the column label indicates highest degree. The table also reports the number of observations underlying the main effects of the majors and the interaction terms. We suppress results based on fewer than 20 cases. The other control variables include a cubic in age interacted with gender, father's education (six categories), mother's education (six categories), gender interacted with race (six categories), and Hispanic. These data are from the National Survey of College Graduates, 1993 and 2010. The sample consists of persons with at least a BA/BS degree and is restricted to full-time workers between the ages of 24 and 59. The regression is weighted using survey weights. $N = 144,635$. $R^2 = 0.284$.

the gap in earnings between low- and high-paying majors, although 0.48% of that gap is preserved. In the case of law, the intercept and the slope are 0.627 (0.04) and 0.305 (0.17), respectively. The point estimates suggest that in percentage terms, the payoff to law is higher on average for those coming from a lower-paying undergraduate degree. Medicine follows the same pattern, although the coefficient is very imprecise.

These estimates are undoubtedly affected in complicated ways by selection bias, and are imprecise.[17] Nevertheless, they suggest that the relative return to different fields of

[17] The slope coefficients are also biased toward zero by sampling error in the estimates coefficient on the undergraduate major in column 1 of Table 7. However, the variance of the coefficient estimates is large relative to sampling error variances, so this bias is small.

graduate study varies sharply across undergraduate majors. We return to this question when discussing the relatively limited evidence on return to graduate education in Section 4.6.

Math Test Scores, Course Content, and Earnings Differential Across Fields

A number of papers, including Paglin and Rufolo (1990), Weinberger (1999), Arcidiacono (2004), and Altonji et al. (2012), show that average scores on math and verbal tests differ substantially across undergraduate majors. Paglin and Rufolo (1990) show that the average Math GRE score for the major (toward the end or after college) explains 82% of the variance across fields of study in entry-level wages. Using the 2009 ACS, Altonji et al. (2012) find that average SAT math and SAT verbal test scores (taken before college) account for about 58% variance in the major-specific earnings coefficients. However, they point out that part of this reflects the association between the average scores and the major-specific averages of other unobserved student characteristics that matter for wage rates. These characteristics may influence wage rates regardless of major and occupation, and they may also influence wage rates by influencing occupational preferences. As we discuss in Section 4, controlling for an individual's test scores usually reduces the variance of major-specific earnings differences, but by less than controlling for the major-specific averages.[18] Some of the empirical studies that we discuss below examine the link between test scores and grades and major choice. Some examine the extent to which returns to a major depend on them.

Occupation Choice and Earnings Differentials Across Fields

Black et al. (2003), Ransom and Phipps (2010), and Altonji et al. (2012, 2014a) present evidence on the degree to which undergraduate majors are concentrated in particular occupations. Arcidiacono et al. (2014) also present evidence on this question using data from Duke students. Altonji et al. (2012, Figure 3) display the distribution of the major-specific proportions of graduates who work in the 10 most common three-digit occupations for the major. It is based on the 2009 ACS. The mode of the distribution is about 0.43 and the occupational concentration is larger for younger workers. They also report evidence on the proportion of workers in each occupation that is accounted for by the three most popular majors in that occupation. The fraction varies widely across occupations, in ways that generally coincide with conceptions about how specific the skill requirements of the occupations are. For example, Nursing, Psychology, and Multi-disciplinary or General Science majors account for 82.9% of all registered nurses between the age of 40 and 44. Accounting, Business Management and Administration, and Finance majors together account for 72.1% of all accountants and auditors in the same age range. On the other hand, the top three majors account for only 30.7% of first-line

---

[18] Noise in the student-level test scores may be part of the reason why the major-specific averages are more important.

supervisors/managers and sales workers and only 32.1% of marketing and sales managers. Majors differ in the strength of the link between preferences for fields of study and preferences for the mix of tasks associated with particular occupations. This is one reason why the strength of the links between particular occupations and fields of study varies. Differences in the degree to which occupational tasks require knowledge that is specific to particular fields of study are a second reason. Note that the connection between undergraduate field of study and occupation is also presumably affected by the connection between undergraduate field of study and graduate degree, and between graduate degree and occupation. We do not have quantitative evidence on this.

3. MODEL

In this section, we present a series of models that highlight a number of key factors in the decisions individuals make about what type of education to get, how much to get, and where to get it. The most important of these is the fact that individuals are uncertain about their ability and labor market returns as they relate to specific fields of study and occupations. What they learn about these variables over time depends on prior educational choices. The second is that past educational choices affect future education and labor market opportunities. We begin with a simple three-period model that highlights the role of uncertainty about ability, with only two field choices. In Section 3.2, we expand the number of majors, incorporate the choice of institution, add uncertainty about meeting graduation requirements, and add graduate school. In Section 3.3, we add occupation choice, giving special emphasis to the fact that treatment effects of a major on wage rates depend on effects of wages in a given occupation and effects on occupation choice through nonpecuniary benefits and search frictions. Section 3.4 discusses in more detail the role of learning about ability in the return to a specific field of study, the decision to change majors, and the decision to obtain additional education. Section 3.5 briefly discusses the role of the supply side of education — the implications of the fact that institutions set admissions requirements, and that they influence the pecuniary and nonpecuniary costs of particular fields of study, as well as the costs of changing majors.

3.1 A Simple Model of Dynamic Major Choice

We begin by specifying a three-period model in the spirit of Altonji (1993) to illustrate how uncertainty about one's abilities affects the dynamics of major choice. To save notation, we allow abilities to influence both pecuniary and nonpecuniary costs and benefits of schooling and labor market choices rather than separately introduce tastes.[19] In period 1, individuals choose between two majors, m or h, or choose not to attend college, n.

---

[19] This modeling assumption is also consistent with most of the empirical literature dealing with schooling choices in the presence of imperfect information on the part of the students.

Denote d_{ijt} as an indicator for whether individual i chose option j at time t. For the moment, we treat the decision not to attend college as terminal. In period 2, those individuals who chose one of the college options update their beliefs about their abilities and then choose again among the different schooling options and not attending college. In period 3, all agents work, reaping the benefits of their past educational decisions. Since no additional decisions are made in period 3, we collapse the period 3 payoffs into those for period 2.

In period 1, payoffs for each of the choices depend on the individual's abilities that, at least for the schooling choices, are uncertain. An individual's ability in major j, denoted by A_{ij}^{tot}, is given by the sum of two terms: A_{ij}, which is known in period 1, and ζ_{ij} which is initially unknown and only realized if the individual chooses j in either period 1 or 2. ζ_{ij} is i.i.d. $N(0, \sigma_j)$.[20] We normalize the utility payoff to not attending college at all to zero. For simplicity, we also make the stark assumption that the postschool utility flow if a person leaves school after one period is the same as the flow if the person never attends school, and thus is also zero. Relative to not attending college, the first period of school offers a one-period utility flow (which could be negative) but also the option value of completing school.

Denote A_{ij1} as the beliefs of the individual regarding his ability in option j in the first period, so that $A_{ij1} = A_{ij}$. Beliefs in period 2 depend on the choices made in period 1 and are given by

$$A_{ij2} = \begin{cases} A_{ij1} + \zeta_{ij} & \text{if } d_{ij1} = 1 \text{ for } j \neq n \\ A_{ij1} & \text{otherwise.} \end{cases}$$

Expected flow payoffs for each of the options depend on the individual's beliefs regarding their abilities. In addition, if the individual changes his schooling decision in period 2, the individual incurs a switching cost. We specify expected flow payoffs while in school in each period as the following linear functions ($j \in \{m, h\}$):

$$U_{ij1} = \alpha_{0j} + \alpha_{1j} A_{ij1}$$
$$U_{ij2} = \alpha_{0j} + \alpha_{1j} A_{ij2} - \alpha_{2j} I(d_{ij1} \neq 1).$$

In the third period, when everyone is working, the expected utility is

$$U_{3ij} = (\gamma_{0j} + \gamma_{1j} A_{ij2})(d_{ih2} + d_{im2}).$$

In the equation for U_{ij2}, $I(\cdot)$ is the indicator function, implying α_{2j} is the cost of switching to major j. The α_j terms represent expected utility while in school, while the γ_j terms give the expected utility in the final period as a function of A_{ij2} for those who complete college. Note that $U_{3ij} = 0$ if the person did not attend school or left school after one period.

---

[20] We relax this assumption by allowing for correlated learning across majors in Section 3.4.

Denoting the discount factor by β, individuals choose their educational decisions to sequentially maximize the discounted sum of their payoffs:

$$E\left\{\sum_{t=1}^{3}\sum_{j\in\{h,m,n\}}\beta^{t-1}d_{ijt}\left(U_{ijt}+\varepsilon_{ijt}\right)\right\},$$

where the ε_{ijt}, are idiosyncratic shocks. Note that the schooling options d_{ih2} and d_{im2} when $t=2$ are not available if i chose the labor market option d_{in1} when $t=1$. This simple model produces a number of implications for the dynamics of major choice:

1. *All else equal, individuals in the first period will choose the major with the higher variance on the unknown ability.*
   Analogous to the occupational choice model of Miller (1984), high variance majors should be sampled first. If the fit with the major is bad, then the individual can always choose a different major. Even if switching to another major is prohibitively costly, the option to drop out still works to insure against bad information draws.

2. *All else equal, individuals in the first period will choose the major that is most difficult to switch to.*
   Majors that have high switching costs due to, for example, the course material building on past material will also be more attractive in period 1, all else being equal (eg, Engineering vs History).

3. *The timing of information revelation matters.*
   Better prior information reduces the option value of high switching cost majors and of college in general. Better posterior information increases the option value associated with the high switching cost majors and for college in general. Dropping out in this model is rational, as individuals respond to the new information they receive.

4. *Ability sorting may be driven either by the payoffs in school or in the labor market.*
   Ability could matter only in the labor market ($\gamma_{1j}>0$, $\alpha_{1j}=0$) or only in school ($\gamma_{1j}=0$, $\alpha_{1j}>0$). In the former case, the school provides information about the individual's abilities which influence labor market productivity and the nonpecuniary value of work, but do not affect the utility received in school. In the latter case, it may be that everyone receives higher returns in one major over another, but low-ability individuals do not choose that major because of the difficulty of the subject matter in school.

5. *Changes in returns to particular majors elicit larger long-run supply responses than short-run responses, particularly for high switching cost majors.*
   Suppose the baseline returns to the different education options, the γ_{0j}'s, evolved stochastically. Because (i) switching majors is costly and (ii) schooling takes two periods, the response to changes in labor market returns is gradual. If switching costs in major j are high, fewer individuals will find it optimal to switch to major j in response to a positive shock to γ_{0j} after the first period. Asymmetries in response to shocks to major-specific labor market returns then arise due to differences in switching costs.

3.2 Heterogeneity in Schooling Options

3.2.1 Expanding the Choice Set

We now consider a model that expands the number of majors from 2 to J, allows for C institutions of higher education, incorporates uncertainty for graduation, and incorporates graduate school. We again treat the decision not to go to college as an absorbing state. Before obtaining a Bachelor's degree, individuals decide to begin schooling in one of the J majors at one of the C institutions. Not all the institutions grant Bachelor's degrees, incorporating the case of 2-year colleges. Individuals in college have a positive probability of graduating. If they do so, they then have the option of attending graduate school in one of J^g subjects.

Schools influence the choice of major — and in turn the choice of occupation — in part through the flow payoffs individuals receive. We generalize the within-school flow payoffs as follows:

$$U_{ijct} = \alpha_{0jc} + \alpha_{1jc}A_{ijt} + \alpha_{2jc}I(d_{ijt-1} \neq 1) + \alpha_{3jc}I(d_{ict-1} \neq 1) + \epsilon_{ijct}. \tag{1}$$

The specification above allows schools to differ along four dimensions: the intercept for major j (α_{0jc}), the return on ability for major j (α_{1jc}), the cost of switching to major j (α_{2jc}), and the cost of switching to school c (α_{3jc}).

6. *Consider two schools c and c' where $\alpha_{0jc} < \alpha_{0jc'}$ and $\alpha_{1jc} > \alpha_{1jc'}$. Then all else equal there is a cutoff A_{ijt} such that those above A_{ijt} would prefer school c and those below would prefer c'.*

   Schools with higher endowments may have higher payoffs, either through the effect of these resources on human capital or through the effect on the college experience. These effects, however, may differ by both major and academic preparation. For example, schools could tailor their curriculum to the preparation levels of their students. An introductory math course at one university may require more math background and proceed at a faster pace than the same course at another university. The effects can differ across majors because preparation may matter more for some majors than others.

7. *The cost of switching majors (α_{2jc}) may vary by school and the set of majors offered may vary as well, limiting responses to changes in the labor market.*

   When a major is not offered at a particular school, this is equivalent to $\alpha_{0jc} = -\infty$. Some schools in the United States specialize in particular majors such as engineering, while others do not offer engineering. In many countries, students are accepted into a particular major and switching majors entails starting the college application process over. When only a subset of majors are offered or when students must precommit to a major, the short-run response to an increase in the returns to another major will be limited, similar to implication 5.

   Up until now, we have treated the cost of switching as operating through the utility function. But there may be other costs associated with switching majors, such as an increase in graduation times. Denote C_{ijct} as an indicator for whether i has completed a degree in major j at school c by time t. Denote H_{it} as the history of educational choices and outcomes up until time t. Think of H_{it} as a vector of credits and grades in various courses. We treat graduation as a stochastic process that depends on A_{it} and H_{it} so that the individual's perceived probability of graduating is

$$Pr(C_{ijt} = 1) = f_{jt}(A_{it}, H_{it}),\tag{2}$$

where $f_{jt}(\cdot)$ maps $\{A_{it}, H_{it}\}$ into the unit interval.

8. *Switching may delay graduation more in some majors than in others. Later switches may delay graduation more than earlier switches.*

   Some courses of study may require that courses be taken in sequence or require more specific courses than other majors. The cost of delaying graduation may be particularly acute for those with limited finances for whom paying for an additional year of college could be especially burdensome.

   Should the individual graduate, the choice set changes. The person now must decide whether to enter the labor market or attend graduate school. Let n indicate as before the choice to enter the labor market. Denote g as an indicator for the highest level of educational attainment which, if the individual has graduated with a Bachelor's or a post-Bachelor's degree, includes their school and major for their last degree. Extending the baseline payoff for working to incorporate the expanded educational options, the payoff for working at time t is

$$U_{ingt} = \gamma_{0g} + \gamma_{1g}A_{ig} + \epsilon_{ingt}.$$

9. *All else equal, those who chose less lucrative schooling options will be more likely to attend graduate school. Further, graduate school serves as insurance against changes in demand for particular majors.*

   By attending graduate school, the individual can partly erase the earnings dependence from the previous schooling choice. If, for idiosyncratic reasons, similar individuals chose different majors, then persons choosing the lower-paying major should be more likely to pursue graduate work. However, this assumes that majors do not prepare students differently for graduate work, and ignores complementarities between undergraduate major and graduate degree type. In Section 2.3.1, we presented descriptive evidence that such complementarities differ substantially across graduate degree types. In this case, U_{ingt} would also depend on the undergraduate field j. Note also that if the earnings premium for a school–major combination falls, then individuals in those school–major combinations may find graduate school attractive, particularly if the change in the earnings premium is seen as persistent.

3.3 Heterogeneity in Occupations

We now extend the baseline model discussed in Section 3.1 by allowing for $K > 1$ occupations in the workforce. We distinguish the expected flow payoffs in school from the expected flow payoffs for working, and denote the expected flow payoff for i working in occupation k after graduating from major j as U_{ikj}. We specify this flow payoff as the sum of two parts: pecuniary and nonpecuniary. Both the pecuniary aspects (given by the expected wage) and the nonpecuniary aspects are functions of the individual's abilities (A_i) given by $w_{kj}(A_i)$ and $np_{kj}(A_i)$, respectively, so that

$$U_{ikj} = np_{kj}(A_i) + \gamma_1 w_{kj}(A_i) \tag{3}$$

with $\gamma_1 \geq 0$.

In this framework, individuals make their schooling and occupational choices to sequentially maximize the discounted sum of their payoffs:

$$E\left\{ \sum_{t=1}^{2} \sum_{j} \beta^{t-1} d_{ijt} \left(U_{ijt} + \varepsilon_{ijt} \right) + \sum_{j} \sum_{k} \beta^2 d_{ij2} d_{ik3} \left(U_{ikj} + e_{ikj} \right) \right\},$$

where $(\varepsilon_{ijt}, e_{ikj})_{k,j,t}$ is a vector of idiosyncratic shocks. Note that individuals now choose their occupation upon entering the labor market in period 3.

10. *The treatment effect of a major on wages operates through both the choice of occupation and the effects on wages in each occupation. These effects may be of opposite sign if majors affect the nonpecuniary benefits of occupations.*

Note that since individuals value more than just the wage on the job, they may prefer a major j over a major j' even though the treatment effect of major j relative to j' on future earnings is negative. Furthermore, the treatment effect of graduating from college with a given major j (relative to high school) on future earnings can also be negative even if the effects on earnings are positive within each occupation. Consider someone who chooses to complete a degree in education. Completing a degree in education may increase earnings in all occupations relative to not having a college degree. But if it also raises the nonpecuniary returns to working in an education occupation and working in education pays less than other occupations, then the unconditional effect of majoring in education (relative to no college degree) on earnings could be negative.

Even if some majors do not affect the nonpecuniary benefits of occupations, the unconditional effect on earnings may still be ambiguous. Namely, if the pecuniary returns for a particular major are larger in low-paying but high nonpecuniary benefits occupations, the probability of choosing a low-paying occupation may increase, leading to an overall negative effect on earnings.

In practice, individuals from different demographic subgroups may attach different values to the nonpecuniary aspects of the occupations. For instance, workplace flexibility is likely to be more important for women than men. Denoting by X_i a set of demographic characteristics for individual i, we can extend our framework by writing the nonpecuniary part of the flow payoff for occupation k as $np_{kj}(A_i, X_i)$.

11. *Treatment effects of major on wages may vary across individuals with identical wages in all occupations.*

    The treatment effect of graduating from college with any given major *j* may be lower for those individuals who place a greater emphasis on nonpecuniary job benefits, and are more likely to prefer relatively low-paying but high nonpecuniary benefit occupations.

3.3.1 Accounting for Search Frictions

We have implicitly assumed so far that, after graduating from college, individuals can always choose across all possible occupations. We now relax this assumption by allowing workers who graduated from major *j* to receive λ_{jk} job offers within each occupation *k*, where λ_{jk} may be zero for certain (major, occupation)-pairs.

12. *Individuals choose their college major by taking into account the occupation-specific effects of majors on wages, job offer arrival rates, and nonpecuniary benefits.*

    For instance, completing a college degree in Science (relative to Humanities) may lead to an increase in wages in science occupations, as well as in the job offer arrival rates and nonpecuniary returns to these occupations. Individuals take into account those three effects when deciding whether to major in Science.

3.3.2 The Effect of Labor Market Conditions

This framework can be extended to incorporate aggregate labor market conditions. Specifically, define U_{ikj}^S to be the expected flow payoff for individual *i* working in occupation *k* when the economy is in state $S \in \{R,E\}$ (recession or expansion, respectively) after graduating from major *j*. Wages within each occupation and major vary across the business cycle, resulting in the following expected flow payoff:

$$U_{ikj}^S = np_{kj}(A_i) + \gamma_1 w_{kj}^S(A_i).\tag{4}$$

13. *The effect of aggregate labor market conditions on wages may vary across majors, through both (i) the choice of occupation and (ii) the effect on wages within each occupation.*

    For instance, (i) jobs in education are likely to benefit less from good economic conditions than other occupations such as science, while (ii) workers with a science degree working in Science are likely to be less affected by a recession relative to those who work in science and graduated from another major.

    It follows that the allocation of students across majors may vary over the business cycle. Although this stylized framework abstracts from these considerations, it is worth noting that, in practice, the effect of labor market conditions on the decision to enroll in a given major will also depend on how persistent students anticipate the labor market conditions to be.

3.4 Evolution of Beliefs

Individuals have innate abilities in each of the J majors and K occupations with a population distribution that is multivariate normal. Let Σ denote the $(J + K) \times (J + K)$ population covariance matrix of the abilities. Abilities may be correlated across majors and occupations, resulting in a generally nondiagonal matrix Σ. Individual i's expectations of these abilities at time t are given by A_{it}, a $J + K$ vector, where A_{ijt} gives expected ability in major j and A_{ikt} gives expected ability in occupation k.[21]

These expectations evolve with the signals received across different choice paths. Specifically, consider the case in which individuals who attend college learn about their academic ability through their schooling performance, as measured by their GPA by the end of the year. Any discrepancy between the actual and expected GPA leads the individuals to update their belief in a Bayesian fashion. Since Σ is nondiagonal, GPA in a given college major j also provides some information about the abilities in other majors $j' \neq j$ as well as about the abilities in all occupations k. Similarly, those who enter the labor market and work in occupation k update their beliefs about their abilities in all occupations and all majors using their log-wage as a signal. Hereafter we relax the assumption that labor market is absorbing by allowing for college re-entry, which arises here as a natural consequence of learning about ability.[22]

Formally, denoting by $\Sigma_t(A_i)$ the posterior ability covariance matrix at the end of period t, ability beliefs are updated as follows:

$$A_{it} = \left[(\Sigma_{t-1}(A_i))^{-1} + \Omega_{it}\right]^{-1}\left[(\Sigma_{t-1}(A_i))^{-1}A_{it-1} + \Omega_{it}S_{it}\right] \tag{5}$$

$$\Sigma_t(A_i) = \left[(\Sigma_{t-1}(A_i))^{-1} + \Omega_{it}\right]^{-1}, \tag{6}$$

where Ω_{it} is a $(J + K) \times (J + K)$ matrix with zeros everywhere except for the diagonal element corresponding to the major or occupation of individual i in period t. The nonzero diagonal element is the inverse of the variance of the idiosyncratic shock affecting the GPA received in that major or the wage received in that occupation, respectively. S_{it} denotes a $J + K$ vector with zeros everywhere except for the element corresponding to the major or occupation of individual i in period t. That element is the ability signal received in t, that is, GPA if individual i is enrolled in college and the log-wage otherwise.

---

[21] The model discussed in this section shares the same features as the correlated learning model estimated in Arcidiacono et al. (2015). In that model, individuals are uncertain about their abilities in 2-year colleges, in 4-year colleges as STEM majors, and in 4-year colleges as non-STEM majors. They are also uncertain about their ability in the skilled and unskilled sectors of the labor market. We discuss other work that emphasizes learning about preferences and ability in Section 5.1.2.

[22] Of course, students receive other signals about their academic ability. They may also learn about their preferences for nonpecuniary aspects of a field of study and the occupations related to it through the experience of taking classes in the field.

This updating rule, which follows from the assumption that ability is normally distributed, boils down to the standard "signal-to-noise ratio times the signal plus noise-to-signal ratio times the prior belief" updating formula in the unidimensional case. As individuals accumulate signals, the prior ability variance shrinks toward zero, thus giving more weight to the prior about ability and less to the new signals when updating the ability beliefs.

14. *Treatment effects of majors on wages partly operate through learning about ability.*

    Suppose it is the case that individuals who enroll in a Science major acquire a better sense of their comparative advantage, both in terms of major-specific and occupation-specific abilities, than those who enroll in the Humanities. Then this informational edge would lead Science graduates to make better decisions in the labor market (from an ex-post optimality viewpoint). All else equal, this should result in higher wages.

15. *Individuals who do not perform as well as expected revise their major-specific ability downward and may, as a result, find it optimal to switch majors.*

16. *Individuals who leave college before graduating may subsequently decide to re-enroll in the same or a different major as they update their beliefs about the wage returns to graduation and the wage returns to the different majors.*

    Some of the individuals who leave college may find that their earnings are less than expected and may decide to re-enroll and get a Bachelor's degree. Depending on the correlation patterns across the different occupation and major-specific abilities, these individuals may either re-enroll in their initial major, or enroll in a new major.

3.5 Supply Side

Until now, we have focused on how individuals make their educational decisions taking the environment as given. Yet the production of degrees in various fields is also affected by the institutions of higher education. Consider the recent work by Hastings et al. (2013) and Kirkebøen et al. (2015), who analyze school and major choices in Chile and Norway, respectively. In these countries, individuals apply to school-major combinations and switching majors is very costly. Admissions into school-major combinations is determined by test scores, with programs taking those with the highest test scores into until all the spots are filled. This introduces discontinuities that can be used in the identification of the treatment effects of different majors on outcomes such as earnings. But the fact that these discontinuities exist suggest that, at least for some programs, the number of majors is not determined by demand but by supply. A clear next step in this research is to understand how schools are choosing the size of their programs.

Even when individuals are allowed to change their major, the school may make it more or less attractive to do so. Returning to the baseline model, schools influence the cost of effort and switching majors through the workload they require; α_{0j}, α_{1j}, and α_{2j} are in part choice variables of the universities. Universities affect these parameters through the allocation of resources across departments. To the extent that a department has low (high) demand relative to the funding provided by the university, the department may have incentives to make their major more (less) attractive through the assignment of workload or grading standards. As pointed out earlier, many individuals begin in STEM fields but switch out, with those switching out tending to have lower test scores. This might be indicative of STEM departments facing high demand given their teaching resources relative to non-STEM departments.

4. ESTIMATING THE RETURN TO COLLEGE MAJORS

In this section, we provide an overview of the literature on the returns to specific fields of study. We begin by highlighting the key sources of endogeneity that have to be addressed, focusing on the largely neglected problem posed by the fact that people choose occupations. We then discuss the methods and estimates.

4.1 Sources of Bias in Estimating the Return to College Majors

Estimating the return to specific college majors is a formidable task. Two main issues have been broadly recognized in the empirical literature. First, the absolute advantage of workers may differ across college majors for a number of reasons. For example, general labor market ability may be related to nonpecuniary preferences for particular majors. It also may affect the ability of students to complete more difficult ones, and the amount of study time they need to do so. Second, students may have occupation-specific talents that alter the relative payoffs of different majors. A student may be good at engineering and poor at teaching, and as a consequence have a relatively high return to engineering compared to teaching. As long as students choose their college major partly based on the labor market returns, this type of sorting on comparative advantage will typically result in biased OLS estimates of the returns to majors. Sorting based on comparative advantage is of course a pervasive issue in economics, and the subject of a vast econometrics literature on heterogenous treatment effects and essential heterogeneity.[23] The potential selection bias arising from absolute advantage is also common to many discrete choice problems.

A third source of bias is more subtle. As we discussed in Section 3.3, with heterogeneity in preferences across occupations, the treatment effect of a major on *observed* wages

---

[23] See, for example, Heckman et al. (2006). See also the seminal work of Roy (1951) on sorting based on comparative advantage, and subsequent empirical analyses by, among others, Heckman and Sedlacek (1985), Heckman and Honore (1990) in the context of the Roy's model, and more recent work by Eisenhauer et al. (2015) and D'Haultfoeuille and Maurel (2013) dealing with the empirical analysis of extensions of Roy's model.

operates through both the choice of occupation and through effects on wages in each occupation. The particular field that a college student chooses alters the distribution of wage rates and employment opportunities that the student will experience in each of the occupations in the economy. For example, a computer science degree presumably has a larger positive effect on the wage offer distribution for computer programming jobs than for social worker positions. If graduates simply maximize income, then they would choose the highest-paying occupation given their majors. In this case, the treatment effect on actual wage rates, abstracting from occupation, would be a natural summary of how field of study affects productivity. However, with occupation-specific preferences, the utility maximizing choice of occupation will depend on an individual's preferences for nonpecuniary characteristics of occupation. The observed wage rate of a computer science graduate will be affected both by the size of the treatment effects on potential wages in various occupations and by what occupation the graduate chooses to pursue given both pecuniary and nonpecuniary considerations. Consequently, preexisting differences across majors in occupation preferences, and the treatment effect of field of study on occupation preferences both influence the treatment effect of a major on wage rates.

To understand the implications better, consider what one could learn from an experiment in which individuals are forced to choose a major that is selected at random, and then forced to pursue a career in an occupation that is also chosen at random. This experiment would identify differences across fields in the vector of average treatment effects on potential wage rates in various occupations. Next consider an alternative experiment in which individuals are forced to choose a major that is selected at random but are then allowed to choose jobs freely. The alternative experiment would identify average treatment effects of majors on observed wages rates and on occupational choices. However, identifying the effect of majors on wages in an occupation is more complicated as the observed wage response depends on both the effects on occupation-specific potential wages and the distribution of occupational preferences. This poses a formidable estimation problem.

Consider an instrumental variables estimation strategy that relies on a vector of instruments that do not affect occupation-specific potential wages but influence choice of field of study by altering the nonpecuniary benefits of particular occupations. Such an IV strategy will not identify the Local Average Treatment Effects (LATE) for majors on realized wage rates, because variation in the instrument will be associated with variation in the types of jobs that individuals choose conditional on major. On the other hand, suppose that the instruments influence the monetary and/or nonpecuniary benefits during college of a particular field of study but do not influence the monetary returns or the nonpecuniary benefits of particular occupations. Then IV could identify the *LATE* of major choice on realized (not occupation-specific) wage rates.

To help frame the discussion, consider the following equation for the log wage rate of an individual i who majored in field j and is working in occupation k in period t.

$$\ln w_{ijkt} = \gamma_{00} + \gamma_{jk} + \gamma_A A_i + \gamma_{jA} A_i + \gamma_{kA} A_i + \gamma_{jkA} A_i + Q'_{c(i)} \gamma_{jQ} + X'_{it} \gamma_{jkX} + v_{ijkt}. \quad (7)$$

In Eq. (7), γ_{jk} is the average treatment effect of being assigned to field j and occupation k. We normalize γ_{jk} to be relative to an excluded field-occupation combination. All other variables are deviations from population averages. A_i is a vector-valued measure of the student's ability. The coefficient γ_A is the influence of A_i on wages in all occupation/field combinations. It captures the effect of ability on absolute advantage. The coefficient γ_{jA} is the effect of A_i on comparative advantage in j. It reflects the interaction between j and A_i in the production of general human capital that is valued in all jobs. It also reflects complementarity between A_i and the skills taught in j. Similarly, the coefficient γ_{kA} corresponds to the effect of A_i on comparative advantage in occupation k. The coefficient γ_{jkA} is the differential effect of A_i on the wages of those who study j and work in k. It arises from complementarity between the task requirements of k and field j, and captures the effect of A_i on comparative advantage in the field/occupation pair j,k. Since γ_A is defined to be the average effect of A_i over all field/occupation combinations, the γ_{jA} sum to 0 over j, γ_{kA} sum to 0 over k, and γ_{jkA} sum to 0 over j,k.

The vector $Q_{c(i)}$ is a vector of measures of the quality/selectivity of the college c that i attends. X_{it} includes demographic characteristics and labor market experience. The effects of these variables may depend on j and k. The error term captures random factors that influence wages in j, k at a particular point in time.

As noted in the theoretical discussion of choice of major in Section 3, students choose j in part based upon the labor market payoffs in the various occupations given their beliefs about A_i and X_{it}, and in part based upon nonpecuniary factors associated with alternative majors and associated occupations. Conditional on the major j, and absent search frictions, individuals would then choose to work in occupations k that yield the highest utility given the wage Eq. (7). In practice, though, search frictions imply that individuals may only get to choose among a subset of all possible occupations. The observed choice of k and the associated wage rate depends upon j, A_i, nonpecuniary factors, and labor market frictions. Fully modeling the selection rule that leads i to a field j, occupation k pair would be quite complicated. However, it will be difficult to estimate complementarities between fields of study and occupational wage rates without understanding the selection process.

Empirical evidence on interactions between occupation and major in earnings equations is very limited. Some studies include occupation fixed effects as an informal way to assess the extent to which the return to major operates within occupations rather than across occupations. Arcidiacono et al. (2014) obtain data from a sample of Duke University students on beliefs about potential earnings by occupation for both chosen major and for alternative majors. The data indicate that students believe that the monetary returns to particular majors vary substantially across occupations, consistent with the existence of complementarities between majors and occupations. Expected earnings for any given major-occupation pair are also found to be highly heterogenous across individuals. Lemieux (2014) is one of the few papers in the literature that uses multiple regression to estimate the system of potential wage equations for j, k pairs given by Eq. (7). Robst (2007), Nordin et al. (2010), Yuen (2010), Kinsler and Pavan (2015), Lemieux (2014), Lindley and McIntosh (2015), and Altonji et al. (2014a) show that college graduates receive a larger earnings premium when individuals report that the skill requirements of their occupation is a good match for their college major or when their occupation is typical for their major.

The wage equation used by most studies is

$$\ln w_{ijt} = \gamma_0 + \overline{\gamma}_j + \overline{\gamma}_A A_i + \overline{\gamma}_{jA} A_i + Q_{c(i)} \gamma_{jQ} + X_{it}' \overline{\gamma}_{jX} + v_{ijt}. \tag{8}$$

In the above equation, $\overline{\gamma}_j$ is the average treatment effect of major j relative to the reference major. It is a weighted average of the γ_{jk}. The parameter $\overline{\gamma}_A$ is the sum of γ_A and a weighted average of the γ_{kA}. The parameter $\overline{\gamma}_{jA}$ is the sum of γ_{jA}, a weighted average of the γ_{jkA}, and a term that reflects differences by j in the weighted average of the γ_{kA}. Thus all of the parameters reflect differences by major in occupation choice.

We now discuss the alternative approaches that have been taken to estimate variants of Eq. (8).

4.2 Multiple Regression with Controls for Ability

Most studies in the literature have used multiple regression to estimate variants of Eq. (8). Table 8 summarizes the results from a few studies. The studies differ primarily in the choice of control variables. Most include basic demographic variables such as race. Almost all either control for gender or estimate separate equations for men and women. Some include parental background measures such as parental income and education. Most include prior test scores and/or high school grades. Webber (2014) controls for personality traits that are associated with labor market success. A few papers, including James et al. (1989) and Altonji (1993), control for high school curriculum. A few studies, such as Rumberger and Thomas (1993) and Loury and Garman (1995), control for college quality or selectivity. Failure to control for college quality could lead to biased estimates if college quality directly affects wage rates and is correlated with major choice.

Much of what leads to different (true) returns to different majors is likely reflected in the different courses taken. Hamermesh and Donald (2008) is one of the few studies to explore the degree to which earnings effects depend on the course content of the major by adding counts of course credits in various subjects. They find that adding the course credits account for part of the difference across fields, with math and science courses entering positively. College grades also enter positively in a log specification. This implies that differences across fields in the level (as opposed to the log) of earnings are larger for those with high grades.

Table 8 Empirical studies of the earnings effects of college major

Study	Data and method	Types of controls used	Outcome variable	Majors	Results	
Regression or matching-based studies						
Berger (1988)	NLS; conditional logit and selection correction in the wage equation	Log of years of experience, graduation-1900, and their interaction; IQ score and Knowledge of the World of Work score; US male unemployment rate, race, health status, married, residence in a standard metropolitan statistical area, South, enrolled in school, log of annual weeks worked; selection correction	Log hourly wages for the 1974 male college graduates in 1986 USD, corrected for selection bias	Business Engineering Science Arts Ref. Cat.: Education	1 year experience 0.35 0.41 0.12 0.10	12 years experience 0.13 0.36 0.22 −0.07
James et al. (1989)	NLS 72 (men only); WLS	Family background, SAT, high school rank, academic track, math credits, Catholic high school various college-level variables, labor market variables	1985 log annual earnings	Business Engineering Math and Science Social Science Humanities	Without occupation or industry dummies 0.26 0.47 0.20 0.24 0.06	With occupation and industry dummies 0.15 0.45 0.12 0.18 −0.03
Altonji (1993)	NLS72; OLS	SAT, high school grades, self-assessment of college ability, various education interactions; experience and experience-squared, gender, race, family background; high school curriculum; postgraduate degree	Log of real hourly wage; coefficients on terminal majors presented (not all presented)	Business Engineering Physical Science Math and Computer Science Life Science Social Science Humanities Ref. Cat.: Education	Men 0.18 0.41 0.24 0.39 0.12 0.10 0.06	Women 0.24 0.28 0.07 0.23 0.21 0.01 0.00

Study	Data and method	Controls	Outcome	Field		
Rumberger and Thomas (1993)	Survey of recent college graduates (1987); hierarchical linear modeling, OLS	Family background, race, GPA, private college, college selectivity, labor market variables	1987 log annual earnings	Business Engineering Science and Math Health Social Science Ref. Cat.: Education	Men 0.18 0.39 0.26 0.30 0.08	Women 0.25 0.51 0.30 C.44 0.13
Loury and Garman (1995)	NLS72; OLS	College selectivity, years of education, parental income, GPA, SAT, weeks worked, rural dummy	Log weekly earnings, 1979 or 1986	Business Engineering and Science Social Science Humanities Ref. Cat.: Education	Whites 0.21 0.37 0.09 -0.16	Blacks 0.26 0.55 -0.10 0.03
Grogger and Eide (1995)	NLS72, HS&B; GLS	Standard tests, high school grade; family income; experience; race; educational attainment (not shown: with occupation controls), full-time workers only	Log hourly wage 1977-79, 1986	Business Engineering Science Social Science Ref. Cat.: Education	Men 0.16 0.28 0.06 0.02	Women 0.11 0.07 0.22 0.02
Hamermesh and Donald (2008)	Graduates of University of Texas, Austin, 1980–2000 (selected years); double selection correction (into employment and survey nonresponse)	High-school background, college achievement, demographic, postgrad degree, hours worked, quadratic in propensity scores for working and survey response	Log earnings (selected majors presented only)	Business (hard) Business (soft) Engineering Natural Science Social Science Humanities Ref. Cat.: Education	0.49 0.38 0.32 0.27 0.28 0.09	

Continued

Table 8 Empirical studies of the earnings effects of college major—cont'd

Study	Data and method	Types of controls used	Outcome variable	Majors	Results		
					Full sample	Men	Women
Chevalier (2011)	LDLHE (UK) — random sample of one cohort; OLS, quantile regression	Ethnicity, age, disability status, parental social class, fee status, type of school attended and A-level score	Log earnings 3 years after graduation	Physical Science	−0.10	−0.09	0.16
				Medicine	0.40	0.58	0.35
				Biology, Veterinary	−0.16	0.05	−0.23
				Mathematics	−0.04	0.16	−0.11
				Engineering and Tech	0.02	0.20	−0.09
				Business	−0.08	0.11	−0.14
				Finance and Accounting	−0.17	0.18	−0.05
				Economics	−0.04	0.20	−0.21
				Architecture and Planning	0.04	0.21	−0.04
				Social Studies	−0.10	0.07	−0.14
				Law	−0.06	0.20	−0.16
				Psychology	−0.17	0.03	−0.23
				Communication	−0.17	−0.05	−0.19
				Language and Literature	−0.16	0.08	−0.21
				History and Philosophy	−0.19	−0.06	−0.19
				Creative Arts	−0.18	−0.01	−0.24
				Ref. Cat.: Education			
						Regression	Correction for unobs. heterogeneity (0.5)
Webber (2014)	NLSY79, NLY97, and American Community Survey, National Survey of College Graduates 1993, 2003. (United States); OLS with controls. OLS with bias corrections for selection on unobservables based on Altonji et al. (2005)	See Section 4.1: age, black, Hispanic, AFQT, mother's education, Rotter Scale score, Rosenberg Self-Esteem test	Log (simulated) lifetime earnings.	STEM		0.69	0.38
				Business		0.65	0.40
				Social Science		0.52	0.35
				Arts/ Humanities		0.37	0.30
				Ref. Cat.: High School			

Study	Method	Controls	Outcome	Coefficients / Majors	Full sample	Highest Degree Bachelor's	Highest Degree Bachelor's — Men	Highest Degree Bachelor's — Women
Del Rossi and Hersch (2008)	NSCG 2003; OLS	Sex, race, whether Hispanic or Latino, whether married or living in a marriage-like relationship, married indicator, age, age squared; married * male	Log of total annual earnings in 2002.	Business	0.16	0.16	0.15	0.15
				Education	−0.09	−0.12	−0.13	−0.13
				Engineering	0.29	0.28	0.46	0.25
				Science/Math	0.14	0.15	0.16	0.13
				Ref. Cat.: Arts/Social Science [Single Major]				

Dynamic discrete choice model

Study	Method	Controls	Outcome	Coefficients / Majors	Struct. model, unobs. het — Males	Struct. model, unobs. het — Females
Arcidiacono (2004)	NLS72; dynamic discrete choice model	Demographics like gender and SAT scores	Log of earnings.	Science	0.20	0.20
				Business	0.13	0.24
				Social Science/Humanities	0.05	0.06
				Education	0.01	0.07
				Ref. Cat.: High School		

Study	Method	Controls	Outcome	Coefficients / Majors	Struct. model, unobs. het — 1992	Struct. model, unobs. het — 1998
Beffy et al. (2012)	French data; structural model of college major choice	Demographics, including gender, place of birth, parents' citizenship; year of labor market entry (1992 or 1998)	Log average monthly earnings, 1992-95 or 1998-01.	Returns to 4 years of college in:		
				Science	0.15	0.27
				Law, Economics, and Management	0.1	0.23
				Ref. Cat.: Humanities and Social Sciences		

Study	Method	Controls	Outcome	Coefficients / Majors	OLS	Struct. model (ATE)
Kinsler and Pavan (2015)	Baccalaureate and Beyond; OLS, structural model of human capital	SAT, GPA, demographics	Log wages (full time yearly equivalent).	Business	0.18	0.15
				Science	0.21	0.18
				Ref. Cat.: Other majors		

Continued

Table 8 Empirical studies of the earnings effects of college major—cont'd

Fuzzy regression discontinuity design using field-specific admissions thresholds

Study	Data and method	Types of controls used	Outcome variable	Majors	Results		
					Levels	Less selective	More selective
Hastings et al. (2013)	Chilean data; 2SLS–fuzzy RD design using instruments based on whether index of grades and test scores exceeds program-specific admission thresholds	Gender, socioeconomic status, relative proficiency in math and reading	Average earnings between 2005 and 2012, over mean sample earnings.	Business	0.06	−0.03	0.17
				Art/Architecture	−0.03	0.01	0.00
				Education	0.00	0.00	0.00
				Law	0.11	−0.04	0.19
				Health	0.21	0.10	0.27
				Sci/Tech	0.08	0.01	0.18
				Humanities	−0.05	−0.01	0.04
				Social Sciences	0.12	0.02	0.21

Study	Data and method	Types of controls used	Outcome variable	Majors	Return to completed field			
					Levels	Levels	Log spec.	Log spec.
Kirkebøen et al. (2015)	Norwegian data; 2SLS–fuzzy RD design using instruments based on whether index of grades and test scores exceeds program-specific admission thresholds	Application score (running variable), gender, cohort, and age at application	Earnings eight years after application.	Humanities	−0.05	−0.35	−0.19	−0.56
				Social Science	0.08	−0.20	−0.08	−0.3
				Health	0.07	−0.11	0.07	−0.19
				Education		−0.11		−0.12
				Science	0.26	−0.03	0.49	0.03
				Engineering	0.42	−0.08	1.28	0.11
				Technology	0.17	0.04	0.27	0.23
				Business	0.22		0.43	
				Law	0.25	−0.01	0.40	0.11
				Medicine	0.37	0.12	0.83	0.4
				Ref. Cat. Education, Educ is next-best field				

Source: A few entries in the table are taken from Altonji et al. (2012, Table 2). Webber (2014): Calculated from rows 2 and 5 of his Table 6. Percentage gains converted to log point. Arcidiacono (2004): Calculated from his Table 7. Beffy et al. (2012): Calculated from Table 3. Chevalier (2011): Estimates are based on his Table 2, column 6 and Table 3. Values renormed so that education is the reference category. We have excluded some majors that he reports results for. Kinsler and Pavan (2015): From Table 3, column 3. Del Rossi and Hersch (2008): From Table 3. Full sample, controlling for graduate/professional degrees. Hastings et al. (2013): From Table 5, column 3 and Table 6, columns 2 and 4. Values renormed so that education is the reference category. Kirkebøen et al. (2015): The first two columns are calculated from Table 4 using the average value across preferred fields of 46.15 (75.61) when teaching (business) is the next-best alternative. The second two columns (log spec.) are from Table A7, which reports log returns for preferred field/next-best alternative pairs based on a log specification.

The content of the coursework will also vary with how easy it is to switch majors. In much of Europe, individuals precommit to majors, allowing for more specialization at the cost of perhaps worse matches.

Some studies use hourly wage rates rather than earnings as the compensation measure, while some report results for both and comment on the degree to which earnings effects operate through hours rather than wage rates. Most studies find larger differences across fields in earnings effects than in wage effects, although the correlation between the two is high. Most studies condition on positive earnings.[24] Some studies condition on full-time work.

We now turn to the estimates, which are reported in the last columns of Table 8.[25] For each set of estimates, we identify the reference category. When possible, we have expressed the coefficients as relative to education. In some cases, the estimates are relative to high school.

Most studies find that the return to engineering is substantially larger than the return to education. In US studies, the differential is typically about 0.4 even when family background and prior test scores are included. There is also a substantial premium to business, although the estimate is typically below that of engineering. Social studies majors also earn more than education majors.

Controlling for occupation compresses the earnings differences across fields of study, as illustrated by the estimates from James et al. (1989) in the table, or the estimates in Altonji et al. (2012) mentioned earlier. One would expect this if complementarity between field of study and occupation-specific tasks that are highly valued in the labor market is key to differences in the payoffs to fields of study. But it may also be due in part to differences in compensating differentials for nonpecuniary characteristics of occupations, to unobserved heterogeneity in general labor market ability that is correlated with choice of field and occupation and to the fact that conditioning on occupation in an earnings regression is to some degree conditioning on the dependent variable.

Most studies find that controlling for prior test scores, family background, and/or high school curriculum reduces estimates of the differences, but the changes are not always large. For example, Hamermesh and Donald (2008) obtain very similar estimates when they add high school class rank and SAT scores to their basic model.[26] In Table 9,

---

[24] Hamermesh and Donald (2008) is the only paper we are aware of that corrects for selection into employment. They find that doing so reduces earnings differentials by between 10% and 20%.

[25] A few entries in the table are taken from a similar table in Altonji et al. (2012). We have included a number of more recent studies, including the handful that attempt to address bias from unobserved heterogeneity. We have converted estimates that are expressed as a percentage effect or in terms of actual earnings to log points.

[26] The fact that their sample is from only one university may affect class rank and SAT scores and other student characteristics, given the rank and SAT scores are used in determining admission at the University of Texas and also influence the decision to attend that school rather than somewhere else.

Table 9 Returns to undergraduate degrees using different sets of controls (NLSY79) coefficient (standard error)

	(1) Demographics	(2) Demographics and parental education	(3) Demographics, parental education, and ASVAB	(4) Demographics, parental education, ASVAB, and personality traits (Rotter and Rosenberg scales)
Engineering	0.284 (0.04)	0.282 (0.04)	0.285 (0.04)	0.316 (0.03)
Computer and Information Sciences	0.274 (0.04)	0.269 (0.04)	0.264 (0.04)	0.264 (0.04)
Military Sciences	0.256 (0.09)	0.253 (0.10)	0.232 (0.10)	0.185 (0.07)
Health Professions	0.232 (0.03)	0.230 (0.03)	0.225 (0.03)	0.221 (0.03)
Business and Management	0.200 (0.02)	0.197 (0.02)	0.193 (0.02)	0.183 (0.02)
Foreign Languages	0.191 (0.08)	0.176 (0.08)	0.173 (0.08)	0.182 (0.07)
Mathematics	0.180 (0.07)	0.178 (0.07)	0.166 (0.07)	0.163 (0.07)
Public Affairs and Services	0.162 (0.04)	0.158 (0.04)	0.157 (0.04)	0.149 (0.04)
Physical Sciences	0.149 (0.07)	0.134 (0.07)	0.134 (0.07)	0.133 (0.06)
Other fields	0.141 (0.05)	0.147 (0.05)	0.149 (0.05)	0.145 (0.05)
Architecture and Environmental Design	0.128 (0.06)	0.112 (0.06)	0.119 (0.06)	0.114 (0.05)
Social Sciences	0.096 (0.03)	0.083 (0.04)	0.086 (0.03)	0.079 (0.03)
Library Science	0.090 (0.10)	0.075 (0.10)	0.060 (0.11)	0.063 (0.09)
General Studies	0.083 (0.10)	0.067 (0.11)	0.056 (0.11)	0.039 (0.11)
Communications	0.073 (0.04)	0.066 (0.04)	0.072 (0.04)	0.093 (0.04)
Biological Sciences	0.049 (0.05)	0.045 (0.05)	0.036 (0.05)	0.032 (0.05)
Psychology	0.027 (0.05)	0.020 (0.05)	0.018 (0.05)	0.003 (0.05)

Table 9 Returns to undergraduate degrees using different sets of controls (NLSY79) coefficient (standard error)—cont'd

	(1) Demographics	(2) Demographics and parental education	(3) Demographics, parental education, and ASVAB	(4) Demographics, parental education, ASVAB, and personality traits (Rotter and Rosenberg scales)
Education	Ref.	Ref.	Ref.	Ref.
Letters	−0.017	−0.025	−0.029	−0.014
	(0.05)	(0.05)	(0.05)	(0.05)
Fine and Applied Arts	−0.017	−0.030	−0.019	−0.002
	(0.04)	(0.04)	(0.04)	(0.04)
Agricultue and Natural Resources	−0.063	−0.063	−0.063	−0.083
	(0.06)	(0.06)	(0.06)	(0.07)
Home Economics	−0.132	−0.145	−0.137	−0.095
	(0.07)	(0.07)	(0.07)	(0.07)
Area Studies	−0.145	−0.182	−0.191	−0.177
	(0.14)	(0.14)	(0.14)	(0.14)
Theology	−0.231	−0.244	−0.226	−0.199
	(0.08)	(0.08)	(0.08)	(0.08)

Notes: This table reports estimates of the return (in logs) to various undergraduate degrees relative to a high school degree with no college education. The table was constructed from a regression that includes the undergraduate degree categories and a dummy for some college education only. The other control variables include (1) a quadratic in age, gender, race, and Hispanic; (2) father's and mother's highest grade completed; (3) six components of the ASVAB test (Arithmetic Reasoning, Numerical Operation, Coding Speed, Mathematics Knowledge, Paragraph Comprehension, and Word Knowledge); and (4) Rosenberg Self-Esteem and Rotter Locus of Control Scales. These data are from the National Longitudinal Survey of Youth 1979. The sample is constructed by pooling across survey waves (1981–2012) the observations of persons with at least a high school degree, who are 24 years old or older and work 30 h or more per week. $N = 55,724$ observations (9117 individuals). Standard errors are clustered at the individual level.

we use the NLSY79 to explore how the returns change as we add additional controls to a model with fairly detailed field of study categories. The estimation sample is constructed by pooling across survey waves (1981–2012) the observations of individuals with at least a high school degree, who are 24 years old or older, and work 30 hours or more per week. In all four regressions we include dummy variables indicating whether individuals have a high school degree or some college education only. To make the results easier to assess, we have ordered the majors from the highest return to lowest return based on the specification with only controls for gender, race/ethnicity, and age, which we report in the first column. The returns to the various majors are computed relative to Education. Columns 2–4 report the estimated returns as we add the following controls to the baseline specification, namely father's and mother's highest grade completed, six components of the ASVAB test (Arithmetic Reasoning, Numerical Operation, Coding Speed,

Mathematics Knowledge, Paragraph Comprehension, and Word Knowledge), and measures of personality traits (Rosenberg Self-Esteem and Rotter Locus of Control Scales), respectively. Overall, the estimated returns do change somewhat as we add these different sets of controls, but for most majors these changes are pretty small. There are a few exceptions though, with the returns to a major in military sciences or general studies exhibiting sizable changes as we go from specification (1) to specification (4) (0.256–0.185 log-points and 0.083–0.039 log-points, respectively). In most cases the estimated returns (relative to Education) fall as we control for differences in parental education, cognitive ability, and personality traits. When interpreting these results, it is important to keep in mind that the ASVAB scores as well as the Rotter and Rosenberg scales are noisy and incomplete measures of cognitive and noncognitive ability. It follows that, even in the specification with the most comprehensive set of controls (Column 4), the estimated returns to the various majors are likely to be biased upward. The size of the bias from selection on unobservables is a key empirical question. We discuss papers that address selection on unobservables when estimating the returns to majors in Sections 4.3–4.5.

4.2.1 OLS Evidence on Heterogeneity in the Returns

For a few studies we present estimates separately for men and women. Grogger and Eide (1995) is a good example. The relative returns are positively correlated, and there is no clear pattern in the differences.

Brown and Corcoran (1997) report estimates using the 1984 SIPP panel for a sample of college graduates, but use field of highest degree (15 categories) rather than field of undergraduate degree with controls for graduate education. Gender differences in the returns to major are relatively small. Altonji (1993, Table A1) reports separate estimates for men and women in a regression that includes dummies for less than 2 years of college, more than 2 years but no degree, and 16 mutually exclusive indicators for highest degree consisting of 10 undergraduate and 6 graduate degree categories. Relative to no college, women receive a higher payoff to nontechnical fields than men do, and about the same return in technical fields. But relative to education and other nontechnical fields, men tend to receive a higher premium in business and STEM fields.[27] Using the ACS 2009 with minimal controls, Altonji et al. (2012, Supplemental Table 3) report estimates by gender of the effects of college major on log wages, with a degree in education as the reference category. They use 171 major categories. The effects relative to education are larger for men than women in most fields. However, the correlation in the estimates is large. The results suggest that the gender gap for those obtaining a degree in education is smaller than in most other fields. Chevalier (2011) finds that for women, education pays well relative to most other majors, while for men, most other fields pay better, with

---

[27] Brown and Corcoran include controls for high school curriculum. Altonji includes controls for high school curriculum, SAT Math and Verbal scores, high school grades, and the student's self-assessment of whether or not he is college material.

physical science being an odd exception. The correlation in the relative returns to the degrees is fairly strong at 0.597, especially given that this value is downward biased by sampling error in the regression coefficients.

Several studies examine the effects of ability measures on the relative returns to field of undergraduate degree. Altonji (1993, Table A3) finds that the gap between the return to a technical major and a nontechnical major is substantially larger for those with higher values of a set of ability measures. Webber's (2014) evidence based on NLSY79 is less clear. We discuss other evidence on this issue in the next section.

4.2.2 Estimation Using Selection on Observables as a Guide to Selection on Unobservables

Webber (2014) estimates the effects of some college and a college degree in STEM, Business, Social Sciences, and Arts and Humanities on log earnings using the NLSY79. In line with several prior studies, he measures the effects of bias from selection on observables by examining how the coefficients on the college degree parameters change when the AFQT test, mother's education, the Rotter score measure of self-control, and the Rosenberg Self-Esteem scale are added to the controls. In addition, he also examines the effects of selection on unobservables using the methodology proposed by Altonji et al. (2005). Altonji et al. provide a set of assumptions under which the strength of the relationship between selection into various education outcomes and the observed explanatory variables in the earnings model are informative about the degree of selection based upon unobserved characteristics. Webber reports the fraction of the premium (over high school) associated with the different degrees that is due to selection on unobservables under the assumption that the degree of selection on unobservables is the same as the degree of selection on the observables. The fractions are large, but the assumption that selection on unobservables is as strong as selection on the observables is extreme in a study of the effects of field choice on earnings.[28] Using a simulation methodology that involves the use of the American Community Survey as well as estimates of selection bias parameters that are based upon the NLSY79, Webber provides estimates of the effects of the majors on lifetime earnings under alternative assumptions about the degree of selection on unobservables relative to observables. When test scores and personality measures are excluded, the estimates indicate that STEM graduates earn 39.1% more than Arts/Humanities majors. The corresponding values for Business and Social Science Majors are 34.1% and 21.6%, respectively. Correcting for observable ability measures changes these percentages to 37.4%, 77.6%, and 16.4%. Under the assumption that the degree of selection on unobservables is half as large as selection on observables, the STEM, Business, and Social Science premiums over Arts/Humanities are reduced to a relatively

---

[28] This is because much of the variance in earnings at a point in time is due to measurement error or permanent and transitory shocks that occur after college decisions have been made. These components of measured earnings are not related to education choices and thus are not a source of selection bias.

modest 11%, 10.9%, and 4.9%, respectively.[29] As we note below, most of the other approaches to accounting for selection on unobservables show larger differences across fields in returns.

4.3 Control Function Approaches to Controlling for Selection on Unobservables

The OLS approaches assume that the control variables are sufficient to address the problem of unobserved variation in ability, family background, and high school preparation that may alter the estimated returns to specific fields of study. A few studies have attempted to address selection on unobservables based on absolute advantage and/or comparative advantage. Drawing on Heckman (1979) and Lee (1983), Berger (1988) deals with selection by constructing a control function based on a reduced form multinomial logit model of the choice among five fields — Education, Liberal Arts, Business, Science, and Engineering. The data are the NLS Young Men panel, which included men ages 14–24 in 1966. The sample is restricted to college graduates who do not get an advanced degree. The logit model includes variables that belong in A_i and X_{it} plus a set of additional variables that are assumed to alter major choice by shifting the nonpecuniary preferences for field of study but not to affect wage rates directly. These variables include father's occupation, an indicator for whether both parents were present in the household when the respondent was 14, mother's and father's education, college prep high school curriculum, and ethnic origin. Given the literature on intergenerational links, there is reason to believe that some of these variables have a direct effect on wages. Furthermore, to the extent that variables such as father's occupation affect occupation choice conditional on field of study, they would affect the weighting that defines the parameters in Eq. (8).

Berger finds substantial differences in the average payoff to major that are in line with many other studies in the literature (see Table 8). The pattern of the coefficients on the sample selection terms varies across fields of study. They are only statistically significant in the wage rate equations for Education majors and Liberal Arts majors. The coefficients indicate positive selection into these majors. The sign on the ability measures (IQ and Knowledge of the World of Work) are mixed across equations. The experience profiles of wages vary across majors but also depend on the birth cohort, so it is hard to draw strong conclusions about whether they differ by field.

Even though the use of a reduced form model of major choice is a straightforward way to address selection on unobservables when estimating Eq. (8), Berger is the only study

---

[29] Webber also reports that selection into college and into STEM and Business majors is less strongly related to ability measures in the NLSY97 cohort than in the NLS79 cohort. Part of the discrepancy may be due to differences in the test instruments used and to the fact that the test was administered to the NLSY97 cohort at younger ages.

we know of that has employed it. The lack of obvious choices for variables that influence choice of major but not wages may partially explain the lack of use.

4.4 Structural Modeling of Major Choice and Wages

Arcidiacono (2004) estimates the monetary return to fields of study as a piece of a full dynamic discrete choice model. The model considers the decisions of whether to remain in college (conditional on having applied), where to attend college, and field of study. A key purpose of the paper is to shed light on why students sort by ability across schools and majors, not simply to estimate wage equations. But modeling the education decision-making process is also the most natural way to get a handle on effects of heterogeneity in ability and on dynamic selection that is induced by the arrival of information about talent, tastes, and field-specific wages.

Students may transfer, and optimal choice depends on field of study and ability. The monetary payoff to college depends on college quality with a field-specific coefficient. The nonpecuniary costs of attending college and of effort depend on college quality as well as the match between the student and the college.[30]

The basic setup is as follows. The analysis is restricted to students who were admitted to at least one 4-year college. The college application decision and the set of colleges to which a student is admitted are treated as exogenous. These individuals presumably have at least some interest in college and the opportunity to attend. As in Altonji's (1993) stylized model, individuals are forward looking but uncertain about preferences, ability, and labor market opportunities. In the first period, an individual chooses a major and a college from the set she was admitted to, or she makes an irreversible decision to enter the labor market. After making these choices, college students get new information about ability from grades, and about preferences for particular programs of study.

In Period 2, those who were college students in the first period once again choose a major and choose a college from the set to which they were originally admitted.[31] Alternatively, they may leave school and enter the labor market. After Period 2, those who had remained in college get additional information about their ability and preferences, and enter the labor market.

For present purposes, the key equation of the model is the wage equation. Ability has three components. The first two are proxied by the SAT math and SAT verbal scores. These are assumed to be known at the start of college. The second is proxied by

---

[30] The effort level and associated utility cost to i of attending a college of a given quality $Q_{c(i)}$ depends on a major-specific term that depends on Q. It also depends on a term that is increasing in the mismatch between a student of ability A_i and $Q_{c(i)}$.

[31] Arcidiacono's results imply that ability sorting across majors is primarily due to heterogeneity in preferences for major and the workplace.

cumulative grades. In the model, as college progresses, agents learn about their general ability and subject-specific abilities only through grades. The flow of information affects choices about college major and whether to remain in school, but cumulative grades and test scores are assumed to fully summarize the agent's ability. Cumulative grades and test scores are included in the wage equation. Thus, in Arcidiacono's basic specification, all components of ability that influence wage rates are assumed to be observed by the econometrician. The wage equation of the model can be estimated consistently by ordinary least squares. However, Arcidiacono also estimates a second specification that includes fixed person-specific unobserved heterogeneity. The unobserved heterogeneity influences both the returns to each major as well as preferences. In the wage equation, this amounts to replacing the parameters $\overline{\gamma}_j$ with $\overline{\gamma}_{r(i)j}$ where $r(i)$ is i's type. He allows for two types. Thus the wages take the form:

$$\ln w_{ijt} = \overline{\gamma}_{r(i)j} + [SATM_i, SATV_i, Grades_i]' \overline{\gamma}_{Aj}$$
$$+ [SATM_{c(i)}, SATV_{c(i)}]' \gamma_{jQ} + X'_{it} \overline{\gamma}_{jX} + v_{ijt}. \tag{9}$$

The equation must be estimated jointly with the other equations of the model. Identification of the type parameters comes from the correlation between the various outcomes. For example, someone may have a high unobservable preference for engineering. This preference may be correlated with grades and wages in ways that are not accounted for by observables.

The results are as follows. In the two-type model, the premium relative to no college is highest in the natural sciences (which include engineering) followed by business. Social Sciences/Humanities have a 5% return, and education is slightly negative for males and has a return of 6% for women.[32]

The parameters on average test scores for the school and for the individual are constrained to be greater than or equal to zero. $SATM_i$ and $SATM_{c(i)}$ are typically positive and statistically significant for all majors except for Education. $SATM_i$ also substantially increases the return to the "no college" option, so the net positive effect on the return to college is small. A 100-point increase in SAT math has little effect on the premiums for the various majors relative to the return to no college. It increases the return to Natural Sciences and Business relative to Education by about 2.5%. The nonnegativity constraint binds in many cases for $SATV_i$ and $SATV_{c(i)}$. Indeed, a number of studies have noted that verbal test scores sometimes appear with a negative sign in regression models that include math test scores.[33] Since verbal skills will almost certainly raise productivity across a broad

---

[32] Similar findings with the same data are found in Arcidiacono (2005), who does not model the dynamics of major choice but does model the college application decision and the decisions by colleges as to whom to admit.

[33] See Kinsler and Pavan (2015) and Seki (2013), who use SAT math and verbal scores and study a sample of college graduates. Sanders (2015) finds a negative effect of verbal test scores using five different data sets.

array of jobs rather than lower it, a natural explanation for the negative coefficients is that conditional on grades and *SATM*, *SATV* is associated with preferences for occupations that pay less for nonpecuniary reasons. However, Sanders (2015) does not find much support for this interpretation. He finds that the negative return is concentrated in occupations for which interpersonal contact is important. He speculates that reading scores may proxy for introversion conditional on math scores. This is an interesting area for future research.

What about school quality? The results indicate that attending a school with a 100-point higher average math SAT score raises the return to Natural Sciences degree by 2.8% and a Social Sciences degree by 6%. These numbers are small compared to the differences in returns across majors.

A few other papers have taken a structural approach. Beffy et al. (2012) estimate a sequential model in which university entrants choose a field, and then decide on the (initially uncertain) level of education before entering the labor market. The model is estimated using data from two cohorts of students in France, where there is evidence that a large fraction of students complete a level of education that differs from the level they aspired to when starting college. The choice of field of study, which is the main focus of the paper, is based on both monetary and nonmonetary factors. The earnings equation allows the effects of field (Sciences, Humanities and Social Sciences, and Law, Economics and Management) to interact with the level (five levels, from dropout to graduate school) and to vary across cohorts. The equation includes controls for gender, foreign birth, and whether the parents are immigrants, but test scores and secondary school grades are not observed in the data. Unobserved heterogeneity is accounted for through the use of vectors of heterogeneity parameters that allow for correlation between earnings, field choice, and degree level (three heterogeneity types). Estimation results show that, for both cohorts (students entering the labor market in 1992 or 1998) and most of the levels of education, majoring in Science leads to the highest earnings, followed by Law, Economics and Management, and Humanities and Social Sciences. The returns to field of study are highly heterogeneous across cohorts and levels of education. Notably, for those graduating in 1992, receiving a *Maitrise* (4 years of college) in Science is associated with a 15.2% premium over a degree in Humanities and Social Sciences. The premium goes up to 27.3% for the individuals graduating in 1998. The returns to Science relative to Humanities and Social Sciences also tend to increase with the level of education.

Kinsler and Pavan (2015) also develop and estimate a structural model of field of study and labor market outcomes. Individuals first choose what to study and then choose a job type. They are endowed with two types of human capital, math and verbal, but are imperfectly informed about them when they are deciding what to study. Human capital accumulation depends upon choice of major. Individuals find out their true human capital when they finish school. They choose which sector to work in based upon wage rates, nonpecuniary factors, and random variation in the opportunities available to them.

Kinsler and Pavan estimate the model using the 1993 cohort of Baccalaureate and Beyond. They complement the structural analysis by providing descriptive information on test scores and grades, subject matter by field of study, and the occupation distribution. They also present regression evidence on the interplay between wage rates, field of study, and employment in a job that is related to their field of study.

Kinsler and Pavan report average treatment effects of the returns to business and science relative to an "Other" category. They obtain estimates of 0.145 for business and 0.184 for science. These are below the corresponding OLS estimates of 0.204 and 0.229 in the base specification and 0.185 and 0.214 when SAT math and verbal scores and major GPA are controlled for. Thus OLS overstates the difference in returns even with controls, in part because the controls are noisy measures of ability and human capital. Kinsler and Pavan also use the model to show that the monetary return to science does not vary much across the population. The return to business are actually a bit smaller for those who choose business. Finally, the paper presents both descriptive evidence and evidence from the model that the payoff to science and to the "Other" major category strongly depend on working in a job related to the major. In the case of Science, the difference is almost 30%. The payoff to business does not depend much on this, although the estimates are somewhat noisy.[34]

4.5 Using Variation in Access to Fields of Study to Identify Returns
4.5.1 Methods
The use of exogenous variation in access to fields of study is an alternative approach to identifying returns. In many universities, the access to some fields of study, such as Business or Computer Science, is restricted. When well-defined, measurable student characteristics are used to determine admission, and the admissions criteria are known or can be easily estimated, then the possibility of using variation in the probability of admission to particular programs of study arises. In the United States, one could in principle use grade point average cutoffs along with other criteria to identify the return to selective programs. This would require assembling information on the cutoffs at a few universities. One would also need detailed information on the college transcripts of students. Multiple states, including Florida, Texas, and North Carolina, have invested in student record systems that could in principle be used for this purpose. Variation over time in the field-specific admissions cutoffs would also be very helpful.

The research possibilities are greater in the many countries where public provision of higher education dominates, admission is to a specific college program, and the criterion is an index of test scores or secondary school grades. Bertrand et al. (2010b) and Hastings et al.'s (2013) (hereafter, HNZ) study for Chile and Kirkebøen et al.'s (2015) (hereafter

---

[34] Across a full set of 50 majors, Altonji et al. (2014a) find that earnings are 29% higher for those who work in a occupation that is among the top five most common one for the major.

KLM) study for Norway show the potential as well as the challenges.[35] As we mentioned previously, in both countries admission is to a school/field combination. Students provide a ranked list of their preferred programs. They are generally admitted to the most preferred program for which they exceed the admissions cutoff.[36] The cost of changing programs is very high, so crossing the admissions threshold has a very large, discontinuous effect on the odds that a student will matriculate in a particular program. This provides the potential for a fuzzy Regression Discontinuity (RD) design. At first glance, this seems straightforward. However, the appropriate use and interpretation of IV estimators, including those based on fuzzy RD designs, to estimate the effects of multiple unordered categorical choices raises very difficult issues that are still being sorted out. HNZ and KLM are an important start of what we expect to become a very active area of research.

To illustrate the regression discontinuity approach, consider a simple case where there are three fields and only one school. Let s_i denote i's test score. Denote s^j as the test score cutoff for field j. Order the fields according to their test score cutoffs: $s^2 > s^1 > s^0$ and, for ease of exposition, assume that the cutoff for field 0 never binds.

We can obtain the effect of crossing the threshold in field j on earnings by examining those who were near the threshold for field j. Let $\bar{t}_{i1}(\underline{t}_{i1})$ equal 1 if i (a) listed field 1 ahead of field 0 and (b) had a test score slightly above (below) s^1, and equal 0 otherwise. For now, assume that admission is perfectly determined by the student's score and field ranking (strict RD design). The average treatment effect for crossing the threshold for field 1 for those for whom $\bar{t}_{i1} = 1$ or $\underline{t}_{i1} = 1$ is given by

$$\Delta_1 = E(Y_i|\bar{t}_{i1} = 1) - E(Y_i|\underline{t}_{i1} = 1), \tag{10}$$

where Y_i is some measure of earnings. This treatment effect has a clear interpretation. It gives the expected earning from being assigned to field 1 ahead of field 0 for this subset of individuals.

The corresponding effect for crossing the threshold for field 2 is not as straightforward to interpret. Let $\bar{t}_{i2}(\underline{t}_{i2})$ equal 1 if i (a) listed field 2 first and (b) had a test score slightly above (below) s^2, and equal 0 otherwise. The average treatment effect for crossing the threshold for field 2 for those for whom $\bar{t}_{i2} = 1$ or $\underline{t}_{i2} = 1$ is given by

$$\Delta_2 = E(Y_i|\bar{t}_{i2} = 1) - E(Y_i|\underline{t}_{i2} = 1). \tag{11}$$

---

[35] Bertrand et al. (2010b) use an RD approach to study the returns to engineering colleges in India. They use variation across castes in admissions cutoff scores. We do not discuss their study in detail, because their estimates of earnings effects are too noisy to draw strong conclusions. Other countries that use indices based on grades and/or test scores heavily in the admissions process include Turkey and Columbia.

[36] Students are permitted to rank up to 8 school/field combinations in Chile and up to 15 in Norway. In the absence of these restrictions (which do not bind for most students), students have an incentive to rank schools in accordance with their preference and without regard to admissions chances.

The second term is now a mixture of earnings from those rejected by 2 who choose field 1 and others who choose field 0. Letting d_{ij} indicate being assigned to field j, the second term can be decomposed as:

$$E(Y_i|\underline{t}_{i2}=1)=E(d_{i0}|\underline{t}_{i2}=1)E(Y_i|\underline{t}_{i2}=1,d_{i0}=1)+E(d_{i1}|\underline{t}_{i2}=1)E(Y_i|\underline{t}_{i2}=1,d_{i1}=1).$$

In order to recover the treatment effect of assignment to field 2 relative to 1, either more data are needed or more structure need to be placed on the problem. HNZ take the latter approach, writing earnings as:

$$Y_i=\theta_i+(\gamma_0+\phi_{i0})d_{i0}+(\gamma_1+\phi_{i1})d_{i1}+(\gamma_2+\phi_{i2})d_{i2}. \tag{12}$$

The first term gives the absolute advantage across all fields. A major advantage of the RD design over OLS is that it eliminates the bias from the unobserved components of the absolute advantage term θ_i. The coefficients on the field of admission dummies d_{ij} include comparative advantage terms ϕ_{ij}. HNZ express the comparative advantage terms as depending on a function of observables, X_i, and unobservables, ν_{ij}:

$$\phi_{ij}=X_i\phi_j+\nu_{ij}. \tag{13}$$

Let ν_i be the vector of comparative advantage terms of which ν_{ij} is an element. HNZ assume no selection into fields based on unobservables that affect earnings for those near the cutoff:

$$E(d_{ij}|\underline{t}_{i2}+\bar{t}_{i2}=1,\theta_i,X_i,\nu_i)=E(d_{ij}|\underline{t}_{i2}+\bar{t}_{i2}=1,X_i). \tag{14}$$

Given enough data, we could then calculate the field-specific premia for those near the threshold and holding particular values of X_i. Namely, the premium for field 2 over field 1 is

$$\Delta_{21}(X_i)=E(Y_i|\bar{t}_{i2}=1,X_i)-E(Y_i|\underline{t}_{i2}=1,d_{i1}=1,X_i). \tag{15}$$

HNZ note that the assumption of no selection on ν_i might be a reasonable approximation if students are unaware of individual heterogeneity in returns and/or are not very responsive to earnings differentials when choosing majors. They provide some evidence supporting these assumptions in the Chilean context.[37] As HNZ point out, even under these conditions, the ν_{ij} could lead to bias if they are correlated with nonpecuniary preferences for fields that influence rankings and affect comparative advantage. For example, suppose that students who enjoy engineering and science courses are more likely to be

---

[37] For example, HNZ report that males, students from higher-socioeconomic status (SES) schools, and students who are strong at math are not more likely to apply to programs for which returns are estimated to be high for these subgroups. Hastings et al. (2015, 2016) provide evidence for Chile that applicants are poorly informed about the earnings and education costs of different college programs. This is particularly true for low-SES students. See Section 5.3 for a discussion of evidence on the role of expectations and learning in major choice.

good engineers. Or suppose that they are more likely to pursue occupations for which an engineering degree adds value. Then occupation- or major-specific abilities will be correlated with field rankings. Indeed, Arcidiacono's (2004) model assumes that the effects of ability on relative returns and on preferences are strongly related. The empirical significance of this issue is still an important research question.

KLM provide weaker conditions for identifying treatment effects when data on the next-best alternative, defined as the alternative that would have been chosen if the preferred alternative is not part of the choice set, is available. Identification is conditional on the standard IV/LATE assumptions, plus an assumption that they refer to as the "irrelevance and next-best alternative" condition. This condition states that if crossing the admissions threshold to field 1 does not induce i to choose 1, then crossing the threshold does not induce her to choose 2 either. Similarly, it states that if crossing the admissions threshold to field 2 does not induce her to choose 2, then it does not induce her to choose field 1 either. In this case, we compare differences in earnings for those who are either just above or below the threshold *and* who have the same next-best alternative. Let d_{i2k} denote whether i listed field k immediately after field 2. Under their assumption, in the strict RD case we can calculate the local average treatment effect of being admitted to 2 over the next-best alternative k using

$$\Delta_{2k}^* = E(Y_i|\bar{t}_{i2}=1, d_{i2k}=1) - E(Y_i|\underline{t}_{i2}=1, d_{i2k}=1). \qquad (16)$$

This is an important result that shows the value of information about next-best alternatives in this context.[38]

KLM, however, focus on degree completion rather than admission. They also report reduced form estimates for predicted admission based on crossing the admissions threshold. We would often rather obtain the effects of completing a field than being assigned to a field, so the degree completion results are of great interest. But, from a more general methodological viewpoint, it also raises the question of the conditions under which exogenous variation in *field assignment* can be used to identify the treatment effect of *field completion*. It is possible that the irrelevance condition may not hold for field completion even when it holds for admission.

Let g_{ij} indicate whether i completes a degree in field j. Assume for the moment that individuals only complete degrees in the fields for which they are initially assigned. KLM's estimate of the treatment effect for completing a degree in field 2 relative to field j would then be given by

---

[38] In practice, KLM use a fuzzy RD design as admission to the preferred field is not a deterministic function of the application score. They extend the previous result to a fuzzy RD setting by showing that these assumptions are sufficient to identify the LATE of being admitted to field 2 over the next-best alternative k.

$$\Delta_{2j}^c = E(Y_i | \bar{t}_{i2} = 1, d_{i2j} = 1, g_{i2} = 1) - E(Y_i | \underline{t}_{i2} = 1, d_{i2j} = 1, g_{ij} = 1), \qquad (17)$$

where the superscript c indicates completion.

In their baseline specification for effects of degree completion, KLM select their sample by restricting to individuals who have obtained a postsecondary degree. For the discontinuity in admissions to be used to recover the completion premium for field 2 relative to next-best alternative j, one needs to be in a scenario where this restriction does not lead to a sample selection bias. In particular, this empirical strategy leads to consistent estimates of the premium of interest if either of the following scenarios holds:

1. Degree completion is unrelated to factors that affect earnings, implying that expected earning in the degree completion state is the same for actual completers as well as noncompleters.
2. Crossing the admission threshold does not affect degree completion. Formally, for any individual i, $d_0^i(\bar{t}_{i2} = 1) = d_0^i(\underline{t}_{i2} = 0)$ where $d_0^i(\bar{t}_{i2} = 1)$ and $d_0^i(\underline{t}_{i2} = 0)$, respectively, denote the potential degree completion status for test scores above the admission cutoff for field 2 and below the admissions threshold for 2.

The first scenario is clear. The second scenario is more subtle. To see why this condition is needed if the first scenario does not hold, we turn back to HNZ's decomposition. Suppose completing a degree depends on θ_i but a higher θ_i is needed to complete a degree in field 2 than j. Then those who cross the admission threshold for field 2 and then graduate will be positively selected relative to those who do not cross the threshold, biasing upward the estimated treatment effect of completion. This condition is implied by what KLM refer to as the irrelevance condition.

KLM consider whether their results are sensitive to conditioning on degree completion. First, they show that, averaging across preferred and next-best alternative pairs, crossing the admissions cutoff for the preferred field has a negligible effect on the graduation rate. Second, they estimate models that include all individuals, not just college completers, and show that their estimates change very little. This is true even when they add a dummy for completing postsecondary education as an additional endogenous outcome. These findings provide reassurance that differential selection by field in who graduates conditional on admission to field j is a second-order issue for their analysis. While in the Norwegian context the second condition above appears to hold, it is possible that both conditions are violated in other contexts. These are important questions for future research.

4.5.2 Discontinuities in Practice

In practice, the data are not as clean as what we described above. Both HNZ and KLM see many individuals who either (i) cross the cutoff but do not attend their supposedly best available option or (ii) do not cross the cutoff but later are found to have attended that program. The first could result from students changing their minds and the second from individuals deciding to wait for another admissions cycle in the hopes of enrolling in their first-choice program. Furthermore, in KLM's analyses of effects of degree completion, some enroll in a program but may end up graduating in a different program or not graduating with a degree. There are also differences in college quality and many more majors than three. Some aggregation of majors is then necessary to obtain statistical precision, particularly if a small window around the test threshold is used.

HNZ consider combinations of schools and majors which they refer to as degree programs. Each of these programs is characterized by an admission cutoff that varies in an arguably unpredictable way from 1 year to another. HNZ first estimate the effects of crossing the various program-specific admission cutoffs on future earnings, for students whose test scores lie in the neighborhood of the admission cutoffs. They also examine how these effects vary across program selectivity, major, and socioeconomic background. As discussed above, though, these effects are complicated to interpret in a structural fashion as different "untreated" individuals who are just below the admission cutoff may end up enrolling in different degrees. HNZ address this issue by imposing the restriction that individuals do not choose their program based on their unobserved (to the econometrician) program-specific comparative advantage. Under this assumption, they are able to estimate the effects on future earnings of being admitted to the different programs relative to not being admitted to any selective program. Specifically, they rely on the following specification of the earnings equation, for the set of individuals applying to the program p:

$$Y_{ip} = f_p(s_{ip}) + \sum_{r=1}^{P}(\theta_r + X_i\psi_r)d_{ir} + \epsilon_{ip}, \tag{18}$$

where P denotes the total number of programs, d_{ir} is a dummy for admission into program r, and $f_p(s_{ip})$ is a smooth (program-specific) function of the difference between individual i's test score and the admission cutoff for program p. The authors then estimate Eq. (18) by instrumenting for the admission dummies d_{ir} and their interactions with the $X_i's$ using the threshold-crossing dummies $\bar{t}_{ir}$. Note that if individuals do in fact choose their program based on their unobserved comparative advantage, one would need to estimate instead a correlated random coefficient model in order to recover the payoffs to being admitted to each program.

KLM focuses on graduation rather than admission. Letting X_i now denote the set of observed characteristics such as gender, age, and the running variable, KLM use the following specifications for every next-best field k:

$$Y_i = \sum_{j \neq k}\beta_{jk}g_{ij} + X_i\gamma_k + \lambda_{jk} + \epsilon_i \tag{19}$$

$$g_{ij} = \sum_{j \neq k}\pi_{jk}\bar{t}_{ij} + X_i\psi_{jk} + \eta_{jk} + \zeta_i \quad \forall j \neq k, \tag{20}$$

where the first subscript refers to the preferred field and the second to the next-best alternative. Graduation in field j, g_{ij}, is then instrumented for with whether the individual crossed the test score threshold. To gain precision, they estimate the first stage for all next-best alternatives at once and then the second stage returns for all next-best alternatives at once, imposing the restrictions $\lambda_{jk} = \mu_k + \theta_j$ and $\eta_{jk} = \tau_k + \sigma_j$. They then show that their results are robust to including all interactions between preferred and next-best alternatives. They also show that their results are robust to including more flexible functions of the running variable.

In practice, the field-specific grade cutoffs vary across universities and over time within universities. That is, at a given point in time, s^2 might exceed s^1 at one school while s^1 exceeds s^2 at another. And at a given university, the ranking of the cutoffs change over time in some cases. Both KLM and HNZ take advantage of such variation. Cutoff reversals are particularly important in order to separately identify the returns to field j relative to field k, and the returns to field k relative to field j. KLM find little evidence of complementarities between school quality and fields of study in the Norwegian data. As a result, in their main analysis, KLM assume that the effect of school quality on earnings is the same for all fields. With this additive separable specification, one is justified in using variation across schools and the relative values of the admissions cutoffs to identify the β_{jk}. This increases the number of β_{jk} parameters that are identified.

4.5.3 Results Using the Fuzzy RD Approach

HNZ provide estimates of effects of admission to a program relative to the outside option of not being admitted to any selective program, which are not directly comparable to estimates of degree completion effects. One would expect them to lie below the effects of degree completion.[39] In any event, they find earnings effects of 25.6% (of the average sample earnings) of being admitted to a Health degree, 16.1% for a Social Sciences degree, 11.9% for a Science/Technology degree, 15.1% for a Law degree, and 10.1% for a Business degree. The effect of Education is 4.2%, while the effects of Art/Architecture and Humanities are essentially zero. The relative returns are broadly consistent with the literature that takes field choice as exogenous conditional on a rich control set. HNZ also estimate the effect of program selectivity on future earnings. They find that being admitted to a program in the bottom selectivity quartile, relative to not being admitted to any selective program, raises earnings by 4.7%. The effect is much larger for the highly selective programs (24.2% for the top quartile). The relative returns to fields of study depend upon the selectivity of the degree program j. For example, the return to admission to Law and Social Sciences programs are primarily associated with admission to highly selective degree programs. Here one should keep in mind that variation in

---

[39] They do not have information for their full sample about college completion rates that one might use to do a rough adjustment of these estimates.

selectivity arises from both variation in selectivity of the institution and variation in the selectivity of the specific program within the broad categories (eg, nursing vs. physician's degree in the health category). Interestingly, HNZ find that students from high SES backgrounds receive large gains (30.7%) from admission to highly selective business programs, while the return for low SES students is close to zero. On the other hand, the return to highly selective health programs is large and positive for both groups.

Table 4 of KLM reports the estimates of the returns to different fields (j) relative to next-best alternatives (k) parameters for almost all pairs of 10 fields. Here we emphasize two main findings.[40] First, there are large differences in the returns across fields.[41] For example, relative to the Teaching degree, returns are large and positive in all fields except the Humanities and Social Sciences. For engineers the *gain* over teaching is US$75,240, which is very large relative to the average of US$46,150 for teachers. Second, the pattern of the gains to j over k is broadly consistent with what we would expect given the difference in the average earnings of those who complete a degree in j and the average earnings of those who complete a degree in k. One can reject, however, the restriction that the estimates of the relative gains are equal to the corresponding differences among 10 return parameters, one for each field, as opposed to the series of pairs. HNZ's basic specification in the homogeneous returns case implies this restriction.[42]

Overall, recent work employing RD designs to establish the earnings effects of particular fields of study as well as the quality of an institution is a major step forward. There is scope for much more work. We would highlight two areas. The first is to build directly on the work of Bertrand et al. (2010b), HNZ, and KLM. Further work is required on how best to balance between the restrictiveness of the samples used to identify relative returns to particular pairs of fields, how best to handle unobserved heterogeneity in returns, and how best to address complementarity between the quality/selectivity of an institution in particular fields of study. It would also be valuable to make richer use of measures of socioeconomic background and high school preparation in studying heterogeneity in returns.

The second area is to combine the use of discontinuities in admissions with explicit modeling of how students rank schools and fields of study. One could start with a reduced form approach that relates student rankings of school/field programs to observed variables

---

[40] In addition to estimating relative returns, KLM also provide a rich analysis of how relative returns influence preferences, and provide evidence that students rank majors in part based upon them.

[41] Under the KLM's baseline specification, there are no college quality effects. KLM show that specifications that do add the effects of institutions indicate field of study are much more important than college quality, at least in Norway. Further, controlling for institution effects has little impact on the premiums associated with particular fields.

[42] KLM also provide OLS estimates of a reduced form model of the earnings effects of a predicted offer of admission to preferred field j for each preferred/next-best combination. The prediction is based on the threshold crossing instrument. See their Table A4.

and unobserved variables that are influenced by the pecuniary and nonpecuniary returns to particular fields of study and occupations. A more ambitious approach would be to work with a structural model of field and school choice.

4.6 Returns to Graduate Degrees

As noted in the previous section, one of the primary barriers to estimating the returns to college majors is the selection problem: those who are in high-paying majors may have also received high labor market returns in other majors. This issue is partly mitigated when estimating the returns to an MBA because MBA programs often require work experience before entry.[43] Seeing earnings absent the MBA degree makes it possible to control for individual fixed effects in the wage equation. Note that it is not obvious a priori that fixed effects will produce the correct estimate as selection may be occurring into the MBA program based on wage residuals. Those who have temporarily low wages may be more likely to enroll in MBA programs due to the lower opportunity cost. This is similar to estimating the effects of training programs where wages often dip immediately before enrollment, which is known as the "Ashenfelter dip" (Ashenfelter, 1978).

Arcidiacono et al. (2008) use panel data from those who registered to take the Graduate Management Admissions Test (GMAT) in 1990 to estimate the returns to different MBA programs. Four surveys were administered with the latest data coming in 1998. Note that this is already a selected sample in that the individual must have already been considering enrollment in an MBA program to take the test. Controlling for observed covariates such as GMAT scores, undergraduate grades, demographics, and other advanced degrees shows virtually no return for males unless they were attending a program in the top 25.[44] Top 10 (11–25) programs were associated with earnings that were 25% (20%) higher than those who did not obtain an MBA.

Controlling for individual fixed effects, however, substantially changes the results, reducing the importance of quality of the program. The returns to a top-10 MBA program fall to 19%, while the returns to attending a program outside the top 25 increase to 9%. The first finding is to be expected: those who attend the most selective MBA programs are likely those who have the highest unobserved abilities. That the return increases for those outside the top 25 is unexpected, particularly given that these students have significantly higher test scores and undergraduate grades than those who do not enter an MBA program. The authors show that the increase in returns is not being driven

---

[43] Arcidiacono et al. (2008) show that over 90% of MBA students entered their MBA programs with at least 2 years of work experience.

[44] The regression estimate based on the NCES in Table 6 is 0.284 for obtaining any MBA. The NCES covers a much broader population and does not have information on test scores and grades. The data in Arcidiacono et al. (2008) include only individuals who registered for the GMAT and so were at least considering obtaining an MBA. This suggests that those who are considering an MBA have stronger labor market skills than the general population conditional on the same degree attainment.

by the Ashenfelter dip. Rather, there is a component of skills that individuals who enter these programs are weaker on. Namely, individuals were asked about their perceptions of how the MBA program would help them. Individuals who enroll perceive that the MBA would improve their skills on in areas not measured by test scores, suggesting the possibility that these students are "book smart" but not "people smart."

Specialization within MBA tracks also affects future earnings. Using the same data set and identification strategy as Arcidiacono et al. (2008), Grove and Hussey (2011) examine the returns to specialties within MBA programs. Concentrating in finance or management information systems yields returns of 6% and 8%, respectively, above an MBA degree in another concentration. Returns to finance classes within an MBA program have also been shown in a study of University of Chicago MBAs by Bertrand et al. (2010a), who attribute part of the differences in the returns to an MBA between men and women to the share of courses in finance. This finding is consistent with Grove and Hussey (2011) who show that women are significantly less likely to choose a finance concentration.

Specialization is even more important in medical school. For example, the average surgeon earned $269,000 compared to $131,200 for family practice doctors (Bhattacharya, 2005). Bhattacharya (2005) considers a number of factors for the large income disparities across specialties. First, high-income specialties often require more hours, implying that the wage gap across specialties is not as large as the corresponding income gap. Second, although the time to graduation does not vary across specialties, physicians have a period where they serve as residents before they can become "board certified" and this period varies substantially across specialties. High-income specialties often have longer residency programs. For example, pediatrics residency programs typically take 3 years, while surgical residency programs take at least 5. Finally, the returns to skills may be higher for specialists and this induces high-skilled medical students to sort into these residency programs.

To assess the role that each of these explanations play in explaining the differences in labor market outcomes across specialties, Bhattacharya (2005) estimates a model of physician specialty choice and labor market earnings where unobserved factors (such as ability) influence both specialty choice and earnings via discrete factors. Using data from the 1991 Survey of Young Physicians, he shows that just moving from salaries to hourly wages reduces the surgery premium from 55% to 46% over family practitioners. Selection on observed and unobserved abilities reduces the premium to 41%, and accounting for differences in training program length reduces the premium to 31%. This is still a substantial "unexplained" gap, with two clear sources remaining. First, there may be a compensating differential for working as a specialist. Second, not all medical school graduates are able to work as surgeons due to limits on the number of residency slots. With the number of entering surgeons restricted, wages for surgeons (and other specialties where the residency caps bind) are high due to low supply.

Long residency programs and work hours may make the high-income specialties unattractive for those with family concerns, who are disproportionately female. Taking time away or reducing hours when one has a family limits the time medical school graduates have to recoup their investments. Chen and Chevalier (2012) suggest that female family practitioners would actually have higher lifetime earnings had they instead become physician assistants. Becoming a physician assistant requires 2-year of post-baccalaureate work (as opposed to 4 for medical school) with no residency programs. Using data from the Robert Wood John Community Tracking Physician Survey of 2004–05 and the American Academy of Physician Assistant's annual survey for 2005, they show that, not surprisingly, medical school graduates are stronger on such factors like undergraduate grade point average than those who graduate as physician assistants. Yet, given the (uncorrected for selection) wages for female physician assistants and the hours worked by female family practitioners, the net present value from working as a physician assistant would be on average higher than the net present value for female family practitioners. These results are driven by the extended time in medical school and low wages during residency programs coupled with female family practitioners working less hours than their male counterparts. Indeed, male family practitioners see higher lifetime earnings (again uncorrected for selection) as family practitioners than as physician assistants because they work more hours at the high postresidency wage.

Whether individuals are able to recoup their investments also depends on the returns to hours worked and the penalties associated with time away. Bronson (2015) provides evidence that the wage penalties associated with taking time off in occupations such as engineering are higher than in other majors and provides a partial explanation for why women may find the sciences unattractive. Goldin (2014) shows that in some occupations, the returns to hours worked is linear with low penalties for taking time off, but in other occupations, the last hour worked has a much higher return than the first hour and the penalties for taking time off are high. This latter group includes occupations associated with obtaining an MBA or a Law degree. Goldin (2014) finds no gender gap between male and female MBA and law school graduates 1 year after graduation but a substantial gap emerges later in life, in large part due to differences in labor supply decisions. In contrast, the returns to hours are linear in pharmacy; there is no penalty for part time. Bertrand et al.'s (2010a) regression analysis of MBAs from the University of Chicago indicates that the fact that men work more hours per week and have fewer spells of nonemployment leads to a substantial male advantage in earnings growth in the first 10 years after MBA completion. Using the GMAT registrant data employed by Arcidiacono et al. (2008), Gicheva (2013) estimates a regression model relating wage growth to a nonlinear function of weekly hours in the previous period. She finds a substantial effect of long work hours on hourly wage growth for MBAs. The point estimate is larger for MBAs than for persons who registered for the GMAT but did not receive an

MBA. Her estimates are quite consistent with Bertrand et al.'s (2010a) results on the link between weekly hours and wage growth.

Black et al. (2003) use the 1993 National Survey of College Graduates to see how the returns to graduate school may vary by undergraduate major. Recall from the theoretical model that those with low-paying undergraduate majors may have a greater incentive to go to graduate school if by doing so they erase some of the earnings disadvantage associated with their undergraduate major. However, it may be the case that graduate school builds on past human capital accumulation. Black et al. (2003) show results suggesting that the premium associated with being an Economics major over majors like History and English are just as high if one gets an MBA or a Law degree as it is without an advanced degree, suggesting the additional treatment effect of having an MBA or a law degree is the same across these undergraduate majors. An important caveat is that the estimates are calculated based on matching on demographics; there are no controls for things like test scores or for selection into graduate school. Furthermore, Black et al.'s (2003) findings are somewhat at odds with the evidence in Table 7, which we discussed earlier. This table shows for a broader set of majors using the 1993 and 2010 National Survey of College Graduates that in percentage terms, the gain from an MBA or a law degree is larger for individuals from low-paying majors than high-paying majors. Additional work on complementarity between undergraduate and graduate degrees is needed.

As is the case for undergraduates, excellent data are available on entry to graduate programs in other countries, expanding the possible identification strategies. A good example of this is Ketel et al. (2016), who examine the choice to enter medical school in the Netherlands.[45] Weighted lotteries determine whether an interested individual can enroll in medical school. Higher high school grades and exam scores are associated with higher probabilities of admittance, but even those with very low scores may be admitted at the expense of higher-achieving classmates.

Ketel et al. (2016) use winning the medical school lottery as an instrument for medical school completion in a log earnings regression.[46] They do this for many years, making it possible to trace out the effects over time. Ketel et al. (2016) show substantially higher earnings for medical school completers in all years after graduation, with earnings differences of almost 40% twenty-two years after high school.

Instrumenting for medical school completion — as opposed to assignment — raises two of the same issues that were discussed in Section 4.5.1. First, as pointed out by HNZ

---

[45] While entering medical school in the Netherlands, like many countries outside of the United States, takes place immediately after high school, the amount of training required places medical school under graduate education.

[46] Some students who won the lottery chose not to attend while others who lost chose to enter the lottery the following year. Ketel et al. (2016) use the outcome of the lottery the first time the individual enters as their instrument.

and KLM, what is the treatment effect relative to? Lottery losers are likely to pursue a degree in some other field and so the estimated effects are relative to some combination of earnings in different fields. Ketel et al. acknowledge this difficulty of interpretation. They shed some light on this question by documenting the distribution of fields of study chosen by the lottery losers. Second, winning the lottery may affect future earnings irrespective of whether individuals end up graduating from medical school, thus leading to a violation of the exclusion restriction required to identify the LATE. In the context of Ketel et al. (2016) where a large share (82%) of the lottery winners end up graduating from medical school, this potential threat is most likely of second-order importance.

In other contexts where noncompletion rates are higher, this could be a serious problem. Consider an extreme example where only half of those who win the lottery complete medical school with the other half dropping out and entering the labor market. Further assume that those who lose the lottery enter business school and graduate with probability one. In this case, the IV estimates will not give the return to completing medical school relative to completing business school, or relative to not completing any education. In fact, even if medical school completers earn more than business school completers, the IV estimate could still be negative if business school completers earn sufficiently more than medical school dropouts. The problem in this specific example is that the exclusion restriction does not hold because the instrument (indicator for winning the lottery) affects earnings not only via the treatment status (medical school completion), but also through the potential earnings in the untreated state (earnings of medical school dropouts for lottery winners, and earnings of business graduates for lottery losers). Using the terminology of KLM, this is a situation where the irrelevance condition does not hold because the instrument affects completion of postsecondary education. In this example the fact that the untreated state includes both dropping out from medical school and graduating from business leads to a violation of the exclusion restriction. In this setting, though, one can still produce a consistent estimate of the expected earnings gain from beginning medical school versus not, if one instruments for assignment to medical school in the earnings regression and as long as there is no effect of winning the lottery on the potential earnings in the untreated state (not assigned to medical school).

5. CHOICE OF MAJOR

As discussed in the previous section, the choice of college major has key implications in terms of future earnings and career prospects. In the last 10 years, the empirical literature has paid increasing attention to the determinants of college major choice, and in particular to the relative importance of expected earnings versus nonmonetary factors including abilities and preferences.

5.1 Demand Side

5.1.1 *The Role of Expected Earnings*

Although the results vary depending on the context and the methodology used, most of the recent evidence available points to a significant but quantitatively modest elasticity of college major choice to expected earnings. Beffy et al. (2012) use French data to estimate a sequential schooling decisions model where students choose their major by comparing the (rationally) expected earnings and nonmonetary characteristics associated with each major. In this framework, in the spirit of Altonji (1993), the potential level of education that would be completed within each major is uncertain to the individual at the time of the choice. Beffy et al. use variation across the business cycle in the relative returns to the different majors to identify the earnings elasticity of college major choice. They find significant but quantitatively small elasticities of major choice to expected earnings, ranging between 0.09 and 0.14 for majors in Sciences and in Humanities and Social Sciences, respectively.

Earlier work by Berger (1988) on this question uses a rational expectations framework where the utility for each major is also given by the sum of the present value of expected lifetime earnings in that major and a nonpecuniary major-specific component. Berger uses a sample drawn from the National Longitudinal Survey of Young Men (NLS), which is made up of individuals who entered the labor market from 1962 to 1977. Key to the identification of the earnings elasticity of college major choice is the assumption that college major choices vary over this period only through the monetary returns to majors. Consistent with the students being forward-looking when choosing their college major, Berger finds that expected lifetime earnings are a better predictor of the choice of college major than the earnings at the start of the career. In his model, students are only uncertain about the future earnings associated with each potential major. In particular, when forming their expectations over lifetime earnings, students implicitly assume that they would complete any of the potential majors.[47] This assumption comes in contrast with Altonji (1993) and subsequent work allowing for uncertainty regarding major completion. Montmarquette et al. (2002) estimate the effect of expected earnings on college major choice by allowing the completion probabilities to be smaller than one and to vary across individuals and majors. However, unlike Berger (1988) and Beffy et al. (2012), the major-specific expected earnings are estimated without controlling for selection into each major, thus implying that one needs to be cautious when interpreting the estimated choice elasticities.

Long et al. (2015) examines the effects of wages on major choice using US survey data (IPEDS and Current Population Survey [CPS]) combined with administrative data from Washington state over the period 1982–2012. Their estimate of the elasticity of major

---

[47] Berger also assumes independence from irrelevant alternatives, which is unlikely to hold in the context of college major choice.

choice to the lagged major-specific wage premia is 0.67. This value is substantially larger than the ones obtained by Beffy et al. (2012) and Wiswall and Zafar (2015) (discussed in Section 5.3). However, the analysis of Long et al. is descriptive in nature, and as a result this discrepancy is likely to partly reflect the fact that those elasticity parameters have different interpretations.

Blom (2012) uses ACS data on major choice for cohorts of college graduates who were 20 years old between 1976 and 2006. She uses the occupational composition of majors to construct region-specific time series of major-specific wage premia based on region/occupation/year-specific wage data from the CPS. For the combined period, she finds the elasticity of major share with respect to the major-specific wage is only 0.0166 for men and 0.0646 for women, estimates that are broadly consistent with Beffy et al. (2012) and Wiswall and Zafar (2015). Neither value is statistically significant. However, Blom also finds that the elasticities are positive and substantial for the early cohorts but negative and substantial for the later cohorts. The negative estimates are puzzling, and so caution is called for.[48] Long et al. (2015) find that the major choice elasticities display a large degree of heterogeneity across individuals and majors. In particular, their results suggest that enrollments are more sensitive to changes in earnings for those majors that are tightly associated with particular occupations, such as nursing.

5.1.2 Ability Sorting and Learning

The literature has also examined the effect of perceived ability on college major choice. As we discussed above, Arcidiacono (2004) estimates a dynamic model of college and major decisions where students are uncertain about their abilities. In this model, it may be optimal for students to dropout, switch majors, or switch colleges after observing their grades and updating their ability beliefs accordingly. Estimation results indicate that ability is an important factor in explaining the decision to enroll in a given major. Interestingly, Math ability is found to play a much more important role in major choice than verbal ability. Arcidiacono also finds that learning about ability is an important factor in the decision to switch majors or drop out of college. Finally, most of the ability sorting across majors appears to be driven by the heterogeneity across abilities in major-specific preferences.

Recent work by Arcidiacono et al. (2015) examines how students update their ability beliefs as they receive new information, and the extent to which this learning process

---

[48] Blom (2012) and Blom et al. (2015) use similar data to examine how general economic conditions influence major choice. They show that the aggregate unemployment rate at the age when college students are choosing their majors has a substantial positive effect on the probability that students choose a high-paying field. The shift toward higher-paying majors induced by a three-point in rise the unemployment rate leads to an increase in 1.5% increase in average wage rates for the cohort. Since these effects are permanent, they are large enough to offset a substantial part of the losses of students who graduate in a recession found by Kahn (2010), Oreopoulos et al. (2012), Altonji et al. (2014a), and others.

accounts for the observed transitions between college and work, as well as between STEM and non-STEM majors. To do so, Arcidiacono et al. use data from the NLSY97 to estimate a dynamic model where students decide at each period whether to attend college, either in a 2- or 4-year institution (in a STEM or non-STEM major), work part-time or full-time, or engage in home production. Unlike Arcidiacono (2004) and the other papers discussed below, their framework allows for correlated ability learning through college grades (in the different types of colleges and majors) and wages, as in the model discussed in Section 3.4. Arcidiacono et al. find that the ability components which are revealed over time account for a sizable share of the dispersion in grades and wages, with the abilities in STEM and non-STEM majors being highly, though not perfectly, correlated. However, grades earned in college, both in STEM and non-STEM majors, reveal little about future labor market performance. Inasmuch as college education should help prepare students for the labor market, the latter finding suggests that the screening mechanisms in place in college perform poorly. Overall, estimation results show that college exit and re-entry decisions as well as major switching are all affected by learning about ability.

Fricke et al. (2015) provides interesting evidence on the impact of exposure to a given field of study on college major choice. Specifically, Fricke et al. make use of a natural experiment at the University of St. Gallen (Switzerland) where first-year students, who have not chosen a major yet, have to write a research paper in business, economics, or law. Excess demand for business leads the university to assign the field of the paper randomly for the students who expressed a preference for business, thus making it possible to identify for those students the effect on major choice of exposure to economics and law. Having to write a paper in economics is found to increase by 2.7 percentage points the probability of majoring in economics, which is significant and large in comparison with the share of economics majors within this group (5.9%). Note that the mechanism at work here combines the exposure to additional information on the economics field along with the accumulation of skills in that field.

Using administrative data from the University of Toulouse, Pistolesi (2014) focuses on the effects of providing information to high-school students about their probability of graduating from college in a given field. Pistolesi uses a fuzzy RD design to identify the impact of receiving a negative or positive (as opposed to neutral) signal about future graduation prospects on enrollment in each field. While receiving a positive signal has virtually no effect on enrollment, receiving a negative signal has a strong negative effect (11 pp.) on the enrollment probability.

Should Higher Education Systems Require Students to Specialize Early?

The evidence that students are learning about field-specific wage rates and their preferences and talents while proceeding through school raises an important question about the optimal design of higher education systems: when should students specialize? Some jurisdictions, including England, France, Chile, and Norway, require students to choose a school and a field as part of the college admissions process. The cost of switching later are quite high. Others, such as Scotland, the USA, and Canada, either require or permit students to choose a field later. In such "late choice" systems, students typically take fewer field-specific courses. Malamud (2010, 2011) provides a simple model that highlights some of the tradeoffs. Students who specialize early can take more courses in their chosen field. This is a benefit if depth in that field area is valued in the labor market. It is a negative if more broad education is valued. The labor market value of depth versus breadth likely varies across fields of study and across individuals. Students who specialize earlier must do so with less information about the costs and benefits of pursuing particular fields of study. Consequently, early specializers may be more likely to pursue a field of study that they regret. Whether or not they will be more likely to switch away from the occupation that their chosen major prepared them for depends upon the degree of mismatch relative to the return to field-specific preparation in the occupation. Malamud shows that students in the English university system are more likely to switch to occupations that are different from those associated with their field of study than students in the Scottish system. However, Malamud (2011) shows that the consequences for wages are relatively small.

In an ambitious paper, Bordon and Fu (2015) estimate the equilibrium effects, in the presence of individual uncertainty about major-specific match quality, of switching from a college-major-specific admission system (as in Chile and many other countries) to a system where students choose their major after entering college (as in the USA and Canada). Bordon and Fu find that this would result in a 1% increase in average student welfare, which would disproportionally benefit females as well as low-income and low-ability students. However, the authors do not have data on college grades or other direct measures of the flow of information to the student about ability and preferences. They do observe dropout decisions, but because transfers across majors are very difficult and thus rare, the researchers do not have access to the information about transfer costs and learning about talent and preferences that observing them would provide. Consequently model specification appears to play an important role in identifying features that are key to assessing the gains from allowing students to delay specialization.

Bridet and Leighton (2015) address similar questions using panel data on college graduates from the USA from Baccalaureate and Beyond: 1993–2003. They specify a structural model of course selection and specialization with the following features. A particular program of study influences both the types of human capital acquired and what the student learns about her abilities and preferences. Changing fields while in college or after entering the labor market is costly. In the model, students enter college with prior beliefs about their type (say, engineering vs business). If they do not specialize initially, they acquire skills in both fields, and also obtain signals about their true type. Engineering courses raise productivity in engineering occupations more than in business occupations. The opposite is true of business courses. After specialization, students accumulate human capital in the chosen field. They do not acquire any more information about their type until they enter the labor market, at which point type is revealed. A student's choice of when to specialize is a key endogenous variable in the model. She does so when she is confident enough about her type given that the opportunity costs of additional time in school are rising and taking account of the size of the labor market gains from more depth in the field under consideration. Using information on test scores, course taking, grades, time to specialization, occupation, and wage rates, Bridet and Leighton estimate model parameters governing the rate at which students learn about type, the labor market return to field-specific knowledge when used in one's chosen field and when used in the alternatives, and the fixed cost of switching fields after graduation. The estimates suggest that a person working in her field of comparative advantage earns up to 20% more than a student in the same field who is poorly matched. This paper offers a number of original insights about the tradeoffs. Simulations indicate that changing the USA system to require that students specialize at college entry would increase the share who end up working outside their field of comparative advantage by 7%. Expected earnings would fall by 1.5%.

In summary, the work to date suggests that on net, allowing students to specialize later leads to modest gains in earnings and student welfare. However, much more work is needed to understand information flows and human capital production by fields. In addition, a full analysis must account for the effects of timing of specialization on higher education costs, and how early specialization influences student behavior in secondary school.[49]

5.1.3 Other Determinants
Gender-Specific Preferences

Rather than attempt to provide a comprehensive survey of the literature on gender differences in college major choice, we simply highlight a few recent studies.[50] Gemici and Wiswall (2014) examine the determinants of the gender gap in college major choice as well as its evolution over time. Their analysis is based on a dynamic model of human capital investments in terms of numbers of years of schooling and field of study, as well

---

[49] Timing of specialization may also matter in terms of peer effects on college major choice. The role played by students' peers on the decision to enroll in a given college major is an important question, which has not been the object of much attention in this literature. Notable exceptions include Sacerdote (2001) and De Giorgi et al. (2010). Using data from Dartmouth College and exploiting the random assignment of roommates among freshmen, Sacerdote (2001) finds no evidence of peer effects on college major choice. This finding contrasts with De Giorgi et al. (2010) who use data from Bocconi University and a different identification strategy based on the existence of partially overlapping peer groups. They conclude that peers have a significant influence on major choice.

[50] Older papers include Daymont and Andrisani (1984), who make use of measures of the importance the individual places on particular job characteristics, and Blakemore and Low (1984), who provide evidence that women choose majors with lower skill depreciation rates.

as labor supply, where agents are assumed to form rational expectations about future outcomes. The authors estimate this model by combining data from the National Survey of College Graduates (NSCG) with the Census and the CPS. Similar to Zafar (2013) (discussed in Section 5.3), their results provide evidence that differences in preferences for majors are the main driving force behind the gender gap in college major choice. Gender differences in the distribution of major-specific skills, while significant, are far less important in explaining the gender gap. Estimation results also show that males were more responsive than females to the increase of the relative prices of science and business skills during the 1980s and 1990s, leading to a widening of the college major gender gap during this period.

Earlier analysis on this question by Turner and Bowen (1999) also finds that differences in skills across males and females, as measured by SAT Math and Verbal scores, only account for less than half of the overall gender gap in major choice. Turner and Bowen conclude that other factors, in particular gender-specific preferences for majors, play a dominant role in explaining the significant gender differences in major choice.[51]

Parental Influence

A couple of papers have examined the role played by parents on the choice of college major. Notably, Zafar (2012, 2013) addresses this question using subjective expectations data collected from a sample of sophomores from Northwestern University. Zafar finds that getting approval of parents is one of the most important factors underlying the choice of majors. According to the students, the probability of the parents approving a given major increases with the social status as well as the wage returns associated with the major.

Risk Aversion

Several papers have also examined the influence of risk aversion on college major choice. Assuming that individuals have constant relative risk aversion preferences, Wiswall and Zafar (2015) find that students tend to exhibit a very high degree of relative risk aversion (around five). The authors further show that ignoring risk aversion in this context would

---

[51] Dickson (2010) uses administrative data from three public universities in Texas to show that women are less likely than men to begin college intending to major in Engineering and Computer Science relative to the social sciences conditional on SAT scores and high school class rank. Women are more likely to intend to major in the humanities relative to the social sciences. Dickson also shows that they are also less likely to graduate in Engineering and Computer Science and more likely to graduate in the humanities and other majors conditional on initial field choice. Morgan et al. (2013) analyze gender differences in initial interest in STEM-related occupations and early college major using the ELS 2002–06 panel data survey. The ELS panel follows students who were in 10th grade in 2002 for 4 years. They find that high school preparation and work-family orientation explain only a modest portion of the gender gap in college major choice. Gender differences in occupational plans play a strong role. See also Weinberger (2004), who surveyed women in a set of female-dominated majors and in economics and business about importance of course preferences, course difficulty, classroom atmosphere, taste for occupations, and labor market prospects in their decisions not to choose each of a set of alternative majors.

result in overestimating substantially the earnings elasticity of college major choice. Nielsen and Vissing-Jorgensen (2005) investigate the role played by risk aversion on the choice of postsecondary curriculum in Denmark and estimate a high degree of relative risk aversion of similar magnitude as in Wiswall and Zafar (2015). Saks and Shore (2005) also examine the impact of risk, as measured by the volatility of wages associated with different types of careers, on college major choice. Consistent with decreasing absolute risk aversion preferences, they find that students from wealthier backgrounds tend to choose riskier majors such as business.

5.2 Supply Side

That ability sorting occurs is partly a result of differences in expectations of the instructors across fields. Grading differences and workloads differ substantially across fields in ways that suggest competition for students. Dickson (1984) shows that fields that have low student to faculty ratios yield higher grades and Freeman (1999) shows that fields that pay less also give higher grades. The fields that are typically associated with low student to faculty ratios and low pay are courses in the humanities and social sciences, excluding economics. The differences in grading standards can be so dramatic as to swamp any comparative advantage students have in particular fields. For example, Johnson (2003) shows that students at Duke University who major in biology actually receive higher grades in the classes they take in all other departments, with the exception of chemistry and math classes. If grading standards were uniform across departments, we would expect students to have higher grades in courses in their own major due to sorting on comparative advantage.

When student demand for a course is low, perhaps due to poor labor market conditions in the field, faculty may have incentives to provide higher grades as a way of inducing more demand for their courses. Sabot and Wakeman-Linn (1991) and Johnson (2003) provide evidence that suggests students do respond to differences in grading standards. But perhaps the most compelling evidence is Butcher et al. (2014), who examine a policy at Wellesley College which required introductory (100 level) and intermediate (200 level) courses with at least 10 students to have average grades that did not exceed a B+. Average grades in STEM classes and economics were below this cutoff while on average courses in other disciplines were above it. Predictably, grades fell in the non-STEM or economics courses, by 0.17 points. But enrollments in these courses fell as well, falling by almost 19%, with majors in these fields falling a remarkable 30%. The drops in enrollment occurred despite grades also falling in courses in nontreated departments (STEM and economics) by 0.09 points. Grades might fall in a nontreated department because the cap was binding for some classes in that department even if the departmental average grade across all classes was below the cap. But it also could be an equilibrium response to increased demand for its courses.

Instructors have more tools to induce demand for their courses besides grades. Arcidiacono et al. (2012a) provide multiple pieces of evidence from Duke University suggesting that STEM and economics classes are on average more demanding than their humanities and social science counterparts. First, their results suggest that freshmen students study 50% more in STEM and economics classes than in humanities and social science classes. Second, students were 50% more likely to list a STEM or economics course as their most challenging class compared to random assignment. Finally, students were significantly more likely to report they were switching majors due to lack of pre-college academic preparation or academic difficulty of the subject matter if their initial major was in STEM or economics.

The differences in grading standards and workloads differentially affect persistence in the major. Giving lower grades affects those at the bottom of the distribution more than those at the top due to both censoring at the top grade as well as the risks of failing out. The effect of Wellesley's anti-grade-inflation policy on black students in non-STEM and economics courses was over twice as large as the overall effect, resulting in average grade drops for black students in these courses of 0.36 points (Butcher et al., 2014). That the effect was larger for black students is due to blacks being significantly more likely to be toward the bottom of the grade distribution as a result of facing a worse precollege educational environment. Data from Duke University showed 76.7% of African American males declaring an initial interest in a major in STEM or economics, yet only 35% obtain a degree in one of these majors. The corresponding numbers for white males are 68.7% and 63.6% (Arcidiacono et al., 2012a). So while African American males came in just as interested as white males in STEM or economics, white males finished at a much higher rate. Arcidiacono et al. (2012a) show that these cross-racial differences can be accounted for by controlling for differences in academic background, either as manifested in SAT scores and Duke's measures of application quality or in first year performance. Similarly, African Americans were much more likely to switch fields because of lack of academic preparation or course difficulty, yet accounting for differences in precollege preparation again eliminates the racial gap.

These findings suggest the possibility that a *relative* position in the academic preparation distribution of a school may have a positive effect on obtaining a STEM degree. A related possibility is that affirmative action policies, which result in under-represented minorities being more likely to be toward the bottom of the preparation distribution within a college, may work against minorities completing degrees in the sciences.[52] Arcidiacono et al. (2016) provides evidence from the University of California system that this is the case. Using data for the 3 years preceding the implementation of Proposition 209,[53] Arcidiacono et al. (2016) show that sorting out of STEM fields on the basis of low

---

[52] As noted by Arcidiacono and Lovenheim (2016), the literature suggests affirmative action affects where individuals attend college, not whether they attend at all.

[53] Proposition 209 went into effect in 1998 and banned the use of racial preferences in admissions for public institutions.

relative academic preparation happens at each school in the system. The effects are large enough that a student admitted under affirmative action at UC Berkeley would have a higher probability of graduating in the sciences at UC Riverside (but not necessarily a higher probability of graduating college overall). Smyth and McArdle (2004) do not directly address the effects of affirmative action, but do examine the effects of relative academic preparation on major choice. They use the selective and highly selective public and private institutions in the College and Beyond data set. They also find that a student's preparation relative to the school average positively affects the odds of attaining a STEM degree, controlling for the student's preparation. The findings of these two studies are at odds with Arcidiacono's (2004, 2005) results using NLS72 data and variants of the structural model discussed earlier. He finds that increases in college quality raise the probability of majoring in the sciences for all students. Arcidiacono and Lovenheim (2016) concludes that weight of the evidence is consistent with a positive relative preparation effect once the lowest quality institutions are excluded. More research is needed on this important topic.

While a number of papers have examined the role played by financial aid and tuition fees on college attendance, very little is known about their impact on college major choice. Two recent papers have addressed this question and reached different conclusions regarding the effect of differential pricing by major. Stange (2015) analyzes the effect of differential pricing by major on the allocation of students across majors. Exploiting the fact that universities throughout the USA have adopted a differential pricing policy at different times, Stange shows that college major shares, in particular in engineering, do respond to the adoption of the policy. The author also provides some evidence that women and minorities are disproportionally affected by the introduction of higher tuitions for engineering. Related work by Evans (2013) uses administrative data from public institutions in Ohio to examine the effect of being eligible for a Science and Mathematics Access to Retain Talent (SMART) grant on majoring in STEM. SMART grants, which are attributed based on merit and financial need (students need to have received a Pell Grant), provide students in their junior and senior years with up to $4000 per year, conditional on majoring in STEM. Evans estimates the impact of being eligible for a SMART grant using a regression discontinuity design, and concludes that it had a negligibly small effect on the probability to major in STEM.

5.3 Subjective Expectations

Key to the dynamic models discussed in the previous section are the assumptions made about individual beliefs. These include beliefs about the availability of different schooling options, the difficulty of the course material, and the labor market returns associated with different educational paths. These dynamic models often assume that individuals, while not possessing perfect information, have beliefs that are at least right on average and are aware of how their abilities translate into future labor market success.

Yet there is evidence that individuals — and in particular those from poorer households — may be lacking important information when making their college decisions. Hoxby and Avery (2013) show that students from poor households with very high SAT scores apply to schools of much lower quality than those from wealthier households. This occurs despite the fact that it would often be less expensive for these students to attend elite institutions, given the generous financial aid policies. The importance of knowledge about potential financial aid and how to receive it is also evidenced in Bettinger et al. (2012), who show that students who received help filling out their Free Application for Federal Student Aid (FAFSA) forms were significantly more likely to enroll in college.

Given the results in Hoxby and Avery (2013), Hoxby and Turner (2013) provided information to poor students with high SAT scores about their chances of getting into various types of schools as well as expected financial aid. Students who received this information were significantly more likely to apply and attend private institutions than the control group, though the overall rates of initial college attendance were unchanged. Informational issues are also studied in Pallais (2015), who examined how college application and enrollment decisions changed when the ACT increased the number of places scores are sent for free from three to four. This small change increased both the quality of colleges that low-income students applied to as well as the quality of the institution attended. This occurred even though the cost of submitting an extra score was only $6.

Lack of information may also be relevant once individuals enter college. Both Arcidiacono et al. (2011) and Stinebrickner and Stinebrickner (2014a) show that students substantially overestimate their first-year grades for two very different schools (Duke and Berea). Indeed, Arcidiacono et al. (2011) show that Duke students have virtually no information regarding their abilities to perform well in the classroom that is not already known by the university. Given that Duke is a very selective university with students who generally have highly educated parents, we would expect informational concerns to be even more prevalent at less-selective institutions.

Information concerns may be particularly important in light of the substantial differences in grading policies and study hours across majors as well as the predictability of who is going to leave the low-grading/high study time majors. Stinebrickner and Stinebrickner (2014b) provide direct evidence on this point. Stinebrickner and Stinebrickner (2014b) show that the student over-optimism regarding performance at Berea is primarily driven by over-optimism about science grades.

As students take more classes, they generally revise their expected performance in the sciences downward. This holds true even for students who persist in the sciences. Those students expect their science grades to be about 0.3 points lower in their junior year than in their freshman year. Those who begin in the sciences but then switch out have much larger downward revisions. Their expected science grades drop by about 0.7 points between freshmen and junior year.

The over-optimism about performance in the sciences is also reflected in perceived versus actual probabilities of persisting in or switching to different majors. Stinebrickner and Stinebrickner (2014b) show that those who begin in the sciences are much less likely to persist in the sciences than they perceive, while those who begin in the humanities are much more likely to persist. Similarly, those who do not begin in the sciences expect to finish in the sciences at much higher rates than actually occurs.

Subjective expectations data have also been used to examine beliefs about earnings in both actual and counterfactual majors. These beliefs can then be used to see how expected earnings affects choices, providing another way to obtain wage elasticities. Zafar (2013) was the first to pursue such a strategy using subjective expectations data from students at Northwestern. He found little evidence that expected future earnings are important to major choice. Rather, consistent with the literature using observational data, nonpecuniary components play a dominant role in major choice. Larger elasticities are found in Arcidiacono et al. (2012b) who surveyed students at Duke University. The two main differences between Arcidiacono et al. (2012b) and Zafar (2013) are that Arcidiacono et al. (2012b) focus on males and also elicit information on occupations.[54] For each major (both actual and counterfactual), students were asked expected earnings and the probabilities of pursuing different occupations.[55] Due to attenuation bias, one might expect to find larger earnings elasticity estimates when using subjective expectations data than rational forecasts of earnings based on a statistical model if students do not have fully rational expectations. On the other hand, measurement error in student reports of their subjective expectations will lead to attenuation bias in estimates based on student reports. Wiswall and Zafar (2015) find similar elasticities to Arcidiacono et al. (2012b) for a sample of NYU students despite not asking about occupations when they use an estimation strategy similar to Arcidiacono et al. (2012b).[56]

An important objective of Wiswall and Zafar (2015) is to address the possibility that major choice elasticities are upward-biased because (unobserved) preferences for majors are correlated with the expected earnings for majors. To circumvent this issue as well as to study how students update their beliefs, Wiswall and Zafar provided their sample with information about average salaries by field for the US population. Specifically, in the initial stage of the survey, for each of a set of majors, the NYU respondents were asked about

---

[54] There is some evidence in the literature (eg. Montmarquette et al., 2002) that expected earnings play a more important for males than females in the context of college major choice. This might explain part of the discrepancy between those two studies.

[55] Focus groups suggested that students had an easier time thinking about expected earnings for different majors when they were tied to occupations. Using data from the same survey as Arcidiacono et al. (2012b), Arcidiacono et al. (2014) examine the complementarities between majors and occupations in terms of expected earnings.

[56] Given the difference with the results from Zafar (2013), this suggests that the wording of the questions may be important for eliciting these beliefs.

the probability that they would graduate in that major and what they would earn if they did so. They were also asked about population averages of earnings for each major. In the intermediate stage, they were provided with the data on average earnings by major. In the final stage, the questions regarding probabilities of graduating with different majors and expected earnings by major were repeated. The authors essentially regress the change in major choice probabilities on the change in the vector of major-specific earnings (relative to earnings in the humanities). Since the unobserved tastes likely did not change between the two times the question was asked, the authors get an estimate of the income elasticity with the taste factor differenced out. The estimated income elasticities shrink substantially and are on the order of those found with observational data. However, this shrinking of the elasticities likely reflects more than the correlation of the unobserved preference with earnings. The change in information is a shock. To the extent that individuals have already committed, or at least partially committed, to majors through their coursework, then the elasticity measured here is to the shocks in the labor market while in school. The long-run responses for those who enter having not taken any coursework would likely be larger. More research is needed on this important question.

That students respond to information regarding average salaries suggests imperfect information regarding the market. Students in Wiswall and Zafar (2015) tend to overestimate, the average wages in certain fields, including economics and business and the humanities and arts, while they underestimate the average wages in some other fields, including engineering and computer science. For instance, students overestimate females' wages in engineering and computer science by as much as 31.1% on average. There is, however, a fair amount of heterogeneity across students. For example, the median student underestimates males' wages in the natural sciences by 10.5%, but 10% of the students overestimate wages in the natural sciences by more than 37.7%.

Arcidiacono et al. (2012b) examine how misinformation regarding labor market beliefs affects choices using a different approach than Wiswall and Zafar (2015). Arcidiacono et al. (2012b) asked students to report what the average Duke student would make in different occupation-major combinations. Then, under the assumption that Duke students are right on average about labor market returns, they forecast how choice of major would change if the expected returns were purged of errors regarding average labor market returns. Arcidiacono et al.'s (2012b) findings suggest that 7.8% of students would have chosen different majors had they had correct measurements of population returns. Note that this number is not the response to new information (in which case the response would be intermingled with switching costs), but how choices would have differed from the status quo if students already had the correct information. There are likely conflicting biases present. First, the response may be biased upward for the reasons suggested by Wiswall and Zafar (2015). But these responses may also be biased downward if students' forecasts of their future earnings have changed since they have committed to a major—the same issue faced by Wiswall and Zafar (2015). This will lead to an underestimate of the coefficient on future earnings in the utility function, which would then translate to smaller responses to correct information.

In the Chilean context, Hastings et al. (2015) survey college applicants about earnings as well as tuition costs associated with particular programs of study and conduct an information provision experiment.[57] An advantage of the study is that it includes individuals from a wide range of backgrounds who are considering institutions across the quality spectrum. The applicants were asked to list up to the top three institution-major degree programs to which they planned to apply. For each program they were then asked about expected earnings and the tuition costs they would experience if they enrolled in it. They were also asked about what the typical graduate in each program would earn. The results indicate that students overestimate earnings and have unbiased but highly variable beliefs about costs. Low-SES students are more poorly informed. They plan to choose degrees with lower net value (earnings net of costs) than other degrees that they would be likely to be admitted to.

A randomly chosen treatment group of the applicants were then provided with data on the earnings and cost outcomes of past students who was pursued the respondents' planned enrollment choices. The treatment group members were told whether they could obtain a higher net value by pursuing their first choice major at other institutions they were likely to get into (given admissions test data), and what the expected net gain would be. They were also told whether they were competitive for other degree programs that offer higher net value but featured an alternative major in the same broad field as their first degree choice, and the size of the expected net gain. Finally, the treatment group students were given access to a data base application that could be used to help them find institutions (given a specified test score) that they could get into and that offered a higher net value than their first choice major. They could also use it to find high net value majors in the same broad field as their chosen major. Hastings et al. study the effects of the infor mation treatment on enrollment in college and on degree program choice. They find that the effects are relatively small and are concentrated among low-SES students. The low-SES students become more likely to enroll in programs that lead to higher net returns. The results are qualitatively consistent with Hoxby and Avery (2013) and Hoxby and Turner's (2013) evidence of "undermatch." Ninety percent of the expected gain in expected earnings operates through major choice and ten percent through institution choice. The overall increase in returns is large relative to the cost of the treatment.

Many papers in this literature find that preferences for nonmonetary benefits of col-lege majors play a key role in the decision to enroll in a given major. This is the case of Wiswall and Zafar (2015), who find that tastes for each major are the most important determinant of college major choice. The authors also provide evidence of a substantial degree of individual heterogeneity in the preferences for each major. In particular, they find that males, Asians, and high-SAT Math students tend to exhibit stronger distastes for

[57] See also Hastings et al. (2016).

humanities. However, 80% of the variation in major-specific tastes remains unexplained by observable characteristics. Similarly, Zafar (2013) investigates the gender gap in college major choice using subjective expectations data collected from sophomore students at Northwestern University. He finds that gender differences in preferences for majors are, by far, the main determinants of the gender gap in college major choice. Gender differences in beliefs about ability and major-specific earnings, on the other hand, do not account for a significant share of the gender gap. Zafar also finds that differences in nonpecuniary outcomes across majors matter significantly more for females than for males. Note that the potential gains from providing students with better information about returns to field are limited to the degree that nonpecuniary factors dominate decisions about field.

5.4 Graduate School

We now turn to the choice to attend graduate school. Given the many different options both in level (Master's, PhD) and educational content, and given limited data, this literature is relatively underdeveloped and few broad conclusions can be drawn. We highlight three areas where work has been undertaken: (i) how the business cycle affects graduate school enrollment, (ii) the factors that influence the decision to obtain an MBA, and (iii) the determinants of specialty choice for medical students.

5.4.1 Demand for Graduate School and the Business Cycle

Bedard and Herman (2008) examine how the demand for postbaccalaureate degrees varies with the business cycle. Using five cohorts of the National Survey of Recent College Graduates (NSRCG),[58] Bedard and Herman estimate separate probit models for the decision to enter a PhD program, enter a professional program (JD, MD), or enter a Master's program. Consistent with the opportunity cost of schooling being low when the economy is poor, higher state unemployment rates[59] are associated with higher probabilities of entering a PhD program for men. Somewhat surprisingly, there is no effect of the state unemployment rate on enrollment in professional programs and the effect is actually negative and significant for enrolling in a Master's program for men.[60]

---

[58] The NSRCG data used comes from survey data taken every other year from 1993 to 2001. NSRCG focuses on those who have obtained a Bachelor of Science or a Master's degree in the past 2 years, with this paper focusing on those who obtained a Bachelor of Science.

[59] Controls include state and year effects.

[60] Results for women display a completely different pattern, with higher unemployment rates associated with increased professional school enrollment and no effect on PhD or Master's enrollment. To the extent that slots in professional programs are constrained, it may be the case that, when the unemployment rate is high, women crowd out some of the men who would otherwise be interested in entering a professional program. This might explain the lack of significant effects of the unemployment rate on professional program enrollment as a whole.

A possible explanation for Master's enrollment being pro-cyclical is that some Master's degrees in some fields (eg, business) require work experience. When the economy is poor, students will have had less work experience and may also be reluctant to give up their current positions. Some support for this is found. When Bedard and Herman interact the state unemployment rate with undergraduate major, they find that the pro-cyclical relationship is strongest among social science majors, arguably the group most likely to pursue an MBA.[61]

Johnson (2013) considers the same question as Bedard and Herman (2008) but uses data from the CPS. The advantage of doing so is twofold. First, the analysis is not limited to those who obtained a Bachelor of Science, implying humanities majors are included as well. Second, many individuals wait to go to graduate school, with about half of individuals starting graduate school more than 18 months after they finish their undergraduate degree. Weighed against this is the lack of information on undergraduate majors, no measures of ability, and small sample sizes. Overall, Johnson (2013) finds that the state unemployment rate positively affects graduate school enrollment for women with no effect for men. Johnson also provides evidence that higher unemployment rates shift individuals into part-time programs conditional on enrollment. When the type of program is modeled (Master's, PhD, or professional), the patterns become more similar to Bedard and Herman (2008) in that the reaction to changes in state unemployment rates for men and women with regard to Master's enrollment are opposite, with men being less likely to enroll in Master's programs when the unemployment rate is high. However, while the qualitative patterns are similar, the estimates are too noisy to say much at the program level.

5.4.2 Demand for MBAs

The only study we are aware of that examines the choice over which MBA program to attend is Montgomery (2002). Montgomery estimates a nested logit model where a set of MBA programs are in one nest, attending a part-time program is in another nest, with the final nest including the option to not attend at all. Montgomery estimates his model in two stages. First, he estimates the probability of choosing a particular full-time MBA program conditional on enrolling in a full-time MBA program. Second, he estimates the probability of enrolling in a part-time or full-time MBA program or not enrolling at all.

Like Arcidiacono (2004, 2005), Montgomery needs to make assumptions regarding what MBA programs are in the individual's choice set. Montgomery's data contain information about whether the individual was admitted to their first choice school. Montgomery estimates a probit on the probability of being admitted to the first-choice school conditional on characteristics of the school and the individual. The probit

---

[61] The other undergraduate majors were classified as Physical Science, Computer Science and Math, Life Science, and Engineering.

coefficients are then used to form admissions probabilities for every MBA program. Next, Montgomery draws from a uniform distribution to see whether or not each of the schools is available to the individual. This assumes that, conditional on observables, admissions outcomes are independent. Montgomery then reduces the choice set further to keep computation feasible by assuming the choice set consists of the chosen school (for those who attended an MBA program) plus 14 schools randomly drawn from the set that the first stage revealed that the individual would be admitted to.[62]

Conditional on attending graduate school, a number of measures of the quality of the program show up as important, including the ranking of the institution, and the average GMAT and undergraduate GPA of the student body. Conditional on these quality measures, higher tuition results in lower attendance. Average starting salaries of the graduates, however, show up negative, and are likely indicative of the noisy measures of quality.

Turning to the decision to enroll in an MBA program, it is important to note that substantial selection has already occurred, as Montgomery's sample comes from students who took the GMAT and therefore at least had a passing interest in enrolling in an MBA program. This makes the results difficult to interpret. We do see, however, some evidence of positive selection on the basis of the student's GMAT scores, with factors such as currently being employed and positive expectations on the employer providing tuition assistance making attending a part-time program more likely.

Gicheva (2012) delves deeper into the decision to enroll in a full- or part-time MBA program, though abstracting away from the choice of school. Her focus is on the specific incentives workers have to go either full- or part-time and how employers influence this decision. Gicheva develops a search model where workers have heterogeneous costs of changing employers and where workers and firms bargain over wages. Workers with high adjustment costs have lower incentives to invest in human capital because the high adjustments costs lowers their threat point with their firm. But since these workers are more likely to stay at their current position, the firm has an incentive to encourage their investment as the firm benefits from the worker being more productive. In the model, these mobility costs effectively translate into whether the skills acquired are general or firm-specific. If the worker has extremely high mobility costs, then the skills acquired through an MBA program will only be used at their current employer, implying that the worker has little bargaining power. The individual would be in a situation comparable to that of a worker who acquired firm-specific training.

Gicheva's model assumes that (i) full-time programs provide more networking opportunities than their part-time counterparts, so full-time graduates have higher offer arrival rates, and (ii) total cost of the program (tuition plus lost earnings) is lower

---

[62] While this procedure may seem arbitrary, Montgomery notes that using 30 schools instead gave similar results.

for part-time programs. Firms then have a incentive to subsidize part-time programs over full-time programs for two reasons. First, they are more likely to see a return on their investment due to the lower offer arrival rates associated with part-time programs. Second, individuals with high mobility costs will underinvest from the firm's perspective due the reasons above.[63] Using the same data as Montgomery (2002), Gicheva finds support for each of these predictions.

5.4.3 Demand for Medical School Specialties

The market for physicians is highly regulated. Individuals who graduate from medical school are generally required to enter a residency program that can last anywhere between 3 and 6 years, depending on the specialty. However, medical school graduates cannot enter any residency program they like. Rather, medical school graduates list their preferred residency programs, which is a combination of both a specialty (eg, surgery, pediatrics) and a teaching hospital. Residency programs also list their preferences over medical students. For some specialties, such as surgery, there is an excess supply of graduates: many more graduates list their top choice as surgery than there are surgical residency positions.

Nicholson (2002) is the only paper that explicitly takes into account the probability of matching in a residency program when estimating a model of physician specialty choice. Nicholson estimates a conditional logit of specialty choice where the key coefficient is on the expected present value of lifetime earnings.[64] This earnings measure is constructed by multiplying the probability of matching in a specialty (which depends on the student's abilities as measured by test scores) by the earnings stream associated with the particular specialty. Those who do not match in their preferred specialty receive the income associated with the lowest-paying specialty (family practice/pediatrics).

Two key assumptions are made. First, earnings in the different specialties only depend on gender and experience, not ability.[65] Second, ability does not affect preferences for particular specialties. This latter assumption is key to Nicholson's identification strategy. Namely, the lifetime earnings calculations depend on ability through the probability of

---

[63] See Acemoglu and Pischke (1998) for an analysis of why firms may pay for general training.

[64] Agarwal (2015) studies the National Residency Matching Program. He estimates preferences for residency programs in family medicine, and hospital preferences for residences, but does not examine choice of specialty.

[65] Support for this assumption is found in Nicholson and Souleles (2001), who show that subjective measures of expected income do not vary with MCAT scores once one conditions on specialty. However, their results are from one medical school. If sorting across medical schools is driven largely by ability, the variation in overall ability within a medical school may be small and test scores may be negatively correlated with other ability measures within schools even though if they are positively correlated across schools.

matching in different residency programs. Hence to the extent that ability is related to choice of medical specialties, this is indicative of individuals responding to financial incentives.

In contrast with the literature on the responsiveness of the undergraduate major choice to earnings, Nicholson (2002) finds a substantial earnings elasticity. Since the model is both nonlinear and depends on the wage level, the average earnings elasticity varies by specialty despite the common coefficient estimate on the lifetime earnings measure, ranging from 1.0 to 2.2 across the specialties.

As with the literature on major choice, assumptions must be made about what individuals would earn in counterfactual specialties if observational data are used to obtain the earnings elasticities. Sivey et al. (2012) avoid these issues by presenting Australian medical students with different scenarios regarding compensation and job characteristics about two specialties and asking which specialty they would choose. By varying the compensation schemes and job characteristics in the hypotheticals it is then possible to measure the importance of these factors in specialty choice. Sivey et al. (2012) find large earnings elasticities, on the order of 0.95 for general practitioners. Their estimates also reveal that medical students have a strong preference to avoid having little control of their hours of work and being on call, with the estimates suggesting a marginal willingness to pay of over $70,000 to go from being on call one in 4 nights to one being on call one in 10 nights.

Control of hours, average hours worked, and fraction of doctors who are female vary substantially across specialties. In 2014, residency applicants for surgery were 36% female while residency applicants for pediatrics were 71% female (AAMC, 2014). Goldin and Katz (2011) suggest that these differences are driven in part by workplace flexibility. They point to gastroenterology as a specialty that had very few women but, as the job became more routine due to recommendations for routine colonoscopies, many more women entered the specialty. To our knowledge, however, there is no work in economics that seeks to decompose the gender gap in specialty choice into, for example, workplace flexibility, monetary renumeration, and tastes.

6. CONCLUSION

Choice of major is an important determinant of future earnings and is strongly associated with the type of jobs that people hold. The evidence suggests that much of the effect of major on earnings is causal, with STEM and business-related majors leading the way. Indeed, even the choice of specialization within graduate programs has a large effect on earnings, be it choosing a more finance-related concentration in business school or choosing to be a surgeon in medical school. Further, although less clear, these positive effects appear to be present across the board: humanities majors would earn more had they majored in business. That they choose not to major in the more lucrative fields suggest compensating differentials in school or in the workplace, and an important role for heterogeneity in tastes for fields of study and the occupations they lead to.

One clear avenue for future research is to consider the ways universities affect major choice. For example, consider the regression discontinuity designs in Hastings et al. (2013) and Kirkebøen et al. (2015). Are the measures used to screen who gets access to particular slots the best measures for predicting performance in these fields, be it probabilities of persistence to graduation or future labor market earnings? Similarly, are the skills that translate into successful completion of STEM degrees in the USA the same skills that are rewarded in the labor market for these fields? If not, might there be more efficient ways to allocate university resources?

Another avenue is to consider the link between field of study and occupations. We summarized a small set of studies that indicate that particular majors may increase earnings in some occupations but not others. Much more research is needed. And differences in occupations in other dimensions, such as the penalty for time away from the workforce and the reward for long work hours, may be useful for understanding why students make the choices they do. As occupations change, so too may the composition of the majors that feed those occupations. On the labor market side, more research is also needed to understand the determinants of the distributions of occupations within each field of study.

We have summarized some of the research on how degree completion by field and future earnings varies across schools, but more work is needed in this area. Here are some of the questions that are key to evaluating policies concerning student advising, admissions, and which schools and degree programs to support through loans or grants. Do some schools have absolute advantage for most students? To what extent do outcomes depend on the match among the student, the field of study, and the school? What characteristics of students and schools matter? To what extent would providing students with more information about admissions chances, degree completion probabilities and the earnings of past graduates by field and school lead to better choices? What is the role for admissions preference policies and financial aid policies that increase access of students from disadvantaged backgrounds to elite programs? What about graduate degree programs?

Research into the determinants and consequences of field choice in higher education has taken off in recent years. Indeed, many of the papers we discuss are still in working paper form or were published in the last 2 or 3 years. There is much left to do, and we hope that the questions raised in this chapter will stimulate further research on this fascinating topic.

APPENDIX A: DISTRIBUTION OF MALE AND FEMALE COLLEGE GRADUATES BY FIELD

Table A.1 Distribution of male and female college graduates by field of degree

	All (1)	Male (2)	Female (3)
Education	0.106	0.053	0.151
English/Languages/Literature	0.039	0.025	0.051
Fine/Performing Arts	0.044	0.039	0.048
Other Humanities	0.054	0.055	0.053
Communications/Journalism	0.045	0.035	0.053
Accounting	0.047	0.051	0.043
Business	0.138	0.165	0.114
Marketing	0.030	0.032	0.029
Other non-S and E fields	0.021	0.025	0.019
Economics	0.022	0.032	0.013
Political Science	0.034	0.041	0.029
Psychology or Social Work	0.065	0.037	0.089
Other social and related sciences	0.057	0.042	0.070
Nursing	0.029	0.005	0.049
Biological/Agricultural/Environmental Science	0.068	0.073	0.064
Computer and Mathematical Sciences	0.048	0.071	0.029
Engineering	0.073	0.132	0.023
Physical and related sciences	0.023	0.034	0.014
Other S and E-related fields	0.056	0.054	0.058
Total	1	1	1
N	59,273	31,743	27,530

Notes: The sample includes individuals aged 24–59. Estimates are weighted using sample weights.
Source: Data from National Survey of College Graduates 2010.

ACKNOWLEDGMENTS

We thank Magne Mogstad, Matt Wiswall, and Seth Zimmerman for helpful comments. Luis Candelaria, Hye Yoon Chung, Brian Clark, Vivek Sumpathkumar, and Ling Zhong provided excellent research assistance.

REFERENCES

AAMC, 2014. Residency applicants of U.S. Medical School by specialty and sex, 2014. https://www.aamc.org/download/321560/data/factstable39.pdf.
Acemoglu, D., Pischke, J.S., 1998. Why do firms train? Theory and evidence. Q. J. Econ. 113 (1), 79–119.
Agarwal, N., 2015. An empirical model of the medical match. Am. Econ. Rev. 105, 1939–1978.
Altonji, J.G., 1993. The demand for and return to education when education outcomes are uncertain. J. Labor Econ. 11, 48–83.

Altonji, J., Zhong, L., 2015. The effects of double majors and advanced degrees on occupation choice and wages. Yale University.

Altonji, J., Elder, T., Taber, C., 2005. Selection on observed and unobserved variables: assessing the effectiveness of catholic schools. J. Polit. Econ. 113 (1), 151–184.

Altonji, J., Blom, E., Meghir, C., 2012. Heterogeneity in human capital investments: high school curriculum, college major, and careers. Ann. Rev. Econ. 4, 185–223.

Altonji, J., Kahn, L., Speer, J., 2014a. Cashier or consultant? Entry labor market conditions, field of study, and career success. NBER Working Paper No. 20531.

Altonji, J., Kahn, L., Speer, J., 2014b. Trends in earnings differentials across college majors and the changing task composition of jobs. Am. Econ. Rev. 104 (5), 387–393.

Alvarez, L., 2012. To steer students toward jobs, Florida my cut tuition for select majors. New York Times.

Arcidiacono, P., 2004. Ability sorting and the returns to college major. J. Econ. 121, 343–375.

Arcidiacono, P., 2005. Affirmative action in higher education: how do admission and financial aid rules affect future earnings? Econometrica 73, 1477–1524.

Arcidiacono, P., Lovenheim, M., 2016. Affirmative action and the quality-fit tradeoff. J. Econ. Lit. forthcoming.

Arcidiacono, P., Cooley, J., Hussey, A., 2008. The economic returns to an MBA. Int. Econ. Rev. 49 (3), 873–899.

Arcidiacono, P., Aucejo, E., Fang, H., Spenner, K., 2011. Does affirmative action lead to mismatch? A new test and evidence. Quant. Econ. 2, 303–333.

Arcidiacono, P., Aucejo, E.M., Spenner, K., 2012a. What happens after enrollment? An analysis of the time path of racial differences in GPA and major choice. IZA J. Labor Econ. 1, 1–24.

Arcidiacono, P., Hotz, V.J., Kang, S., 2012b. Modeling college major choices using elicited measures of expectations and counterfactuals. J. Econ. 166, 3–16.

Arcidiacono, P., Hotz, V., Maurel, A., Romano, T., 2014. Recovering ex ante returns and preferences for occupations using subjective expectations data. NBER Working Paper No. 20626.

Arcidiacono, P., Aucejo, E., Maurel, A., Ransom, T., 2015. College attrition and the dynamics of information revelation. Duke University.

Arcidiacono, P., Aucejo, E., Hotz, V., 2016. University differences in the graduation of minorities in stem fields: evidence from California. Am. Econ. Rev., forthcoming.

Ashenfelter, O., 1978. Estimating the effect of training programs on earnings. Rev. Econ. Stat. 60 (1), 47 57.

Bedard, K., Herman, D., 2008. Who goes to graduate/professional school? The importance of economic fluctuations, undergraduate field, and ability. Econ. Educ. Rev. 27, 197–210.

Beffy, M., Fougere, D., Maurel, A., 2012. Choosing the field of studies in postsecondary education: do expected earnings matter? Rev. Econ. Stat. 94, 334–347.

Berger, M., 1988. Predicted future earnings and choice of college major. Ind. Labor Relat. Rev. 41, 418–429.

Bertrand, M., Goldin, C., Katz, L., 2010a. Dynamics of the gender gap for young professionals in the financial and corporate sector. Am. Econ. J. Appl. Econ. 2 (3), 228–255.

Bertrand, M., Hanna, R., Mullainathan, S., 2010b. Affirmative action in education: evidence from engineering college admissions in India. J. Public Econ. 94 (1–2), 16–29.

Bettinger, E.P., Long, B., Oreopoulos, P., Sanbonmatsu, L., 2012. The role of application assistance and information in college decisions: results from the H&R Block FAFSA experiment. Q. J. Econ. 127, 1205 1242.

Bhattacharya, J., 2005. Specialty selection and lifetime returns to specialization. J. Hum. Resour. XL (1), 115–143.

Black, D., Sanders, S., Taylor, L., 2003. The economic reward for studying economics. Econ. Inq. 41 (3), 365–377.

Blakemore, A.E., Low, S.A., 1984. Sex differences in occupational selection: the case of college majors. Rev. Econ. Stat. 66, 157–163.

Blom, E., 2012. Labor market determinants of college major. Unpublished.

Blom, E., Cadena, B., Keys, B., 2015. Investment over the business cycle: insight from college major choice. IZA Discussion Paper No. 9167.

Bordon, P., Fu, C., 2015. College-major choice to college-then-major choice. Rev. Econ. Stud. 82, 1247–1288.

Bridet, L., Leighton, M., 2015. The major decision: labor market implications of the timing of specialization in college. Toulouse School of Economics.

Bronson, M., 2015. Degrees are forever: marriage, educational investment, and lifecycle labor decisions of men and women. Georgetown University.

Brown, C., Corcoran, M., 1997. Sex-based differences in school content and the male-female wage gap. J. Labor Econ. 15 (3), 431–465.

Butcher, K., McEwan, P., Weerapana, A., 2014. The effects of an anti-grade-inflation policy at Wellesley College. J. Econ. Perspect. 28 (3), 189–204.

Card, D., 1999. The causal effects of education on earnings. In: Ashenfelter, O., Card, D. (Eds.), Handbook of Labor Economics, Vol. 3A. Elsevier Science B.V., Amsterdam, pp. 1801–1863

Chapman, B., 2014. Top-performing high school seniors can get free ride to state colleges for science studies. New York Daily News.

Chen, M., Chevalier, J., 2012. Are women overinvesting in education? Evidence from the medical profession. J. Hum. Cap. 6 (2), 124–149.

Chevalier, A., 2011. Subject choice and earnings of UK graduates. Econ. Educ. Rev. 30, 1187–1201.

Daymont, T.N., Andrisani, P.J., 1984. Job preferences, college major, and the gender gap in earnings. J. Hum. Resour. 19, 408–428.

De Giorgi, G., Pellizzari, M., Redaelli, S., 2010. Identification of social interactions through partially overlapping peer groups. Am. Econ. J. Appl. Econ. 2, 241–275.

D'Haultfoeuille, X., Maurel, A., 2013. Inference on an extended Roy model, with an application to schooling decisions in France. J. Econ. 174, 95–106.

Dickson, V., 1984. An economic model of faculty grading practices. J. Econ. Educ. 15 (3), 197–203.

Dickson, L., 2010. Race and gender differences in college major choice. Ann. Am. Acad. Pol. Soc. Sci. 627, 108–124.

Eisenhauer, P., Heckman, J., Vytlacil, E., 2015. The generalized Roy model and the cost-benefit analysis of social programs. J. Polit. Econ. 123, 413–443.

Evans, B.J., 2013. Smart money: do financial incentives encourage college students to study science? Working paper.

Freeman, D., 1999. Grade divergence as a market outcome. J. Econ. Educ. 30 (4), 344–351.

Fricke, H., Grogger, J., Steinmayr, A., 2015. Does exposure to economics bring new majors to the field? Evidence from a natural experiment. NBER Working Paper No. 21130.

Gemici, A., Wiswall, M., 2014. Evolution of gender differences in post-secondary human capital investments: college majors. Int. Econ. Rev. 55, 23–56.

Gicheva, D., 2012. Worker mobility, employer-provided general training, and the choice of graduate education. Labour Econ. 19, 232–240.

Gicheva, D., 2013. Working long hours and early career outcomes in the high-end labor market. J. Labor Econ. 31 (4), 785–824.

Goldin, C., 2014. A grand gender convergence: its last chapter. Am. Econ. Rev. 104 (4), 1–30.

Goldin, C., Katz, L., 2011. The cost of workplace flexibility for high-powered professionals. Ann. Am. Acad. Pol. Soc. Sci. 638, 45–67.

Grogger, J., Eide, E., 1995. Changes in college skills and the rise in the college wage premium. J. Hum. Resour. 30, 280–310.

Grove, W., Hussey, A., 2011. Returns to field of study versus school quality: MBA selection on observed and unobserved heterogeneity. Econ. Inq. 49 (3), 730–749.

Hamermesh, D., Donald, S., 2008. The effect of college curriculum on earnings: an affinity identifier for non-ignorable non-response bias. J. Econ. 144 (2), 479–491.

Hastings, J., Neilson, C., Zimmerman, S., 2013. Are some degrees worth more than others? Evidence from college admissions cutoffs in Chile. NBER Working Paper No. 19241.

Hastings, J., Neilson, C., Zimmerman, S., 2015. The effects of earnings disclosure on college enrollment decisions. NBER Working Paper No. 21300.

Hastings, J., Neilson, C., Ramirez, A., Zimmerman, S., 2016. (Un)informed college and major choice: evidence from linked survey and administrative data. Econ. Educ. Rev., forthcoming.

Heckman, J., 1979. Sample selection bias as a specification error. Econometrica 47, 153–161.

Heckman, J.J., Honore, B., 1990. The empirical content of the Roy model. Econometrica 58, 1121–1149.

Heckman, J.J., Sedlacek, G., 1985. Heterogeneity, aggregation, and market wage functions: an empirical model of self-selection in the labor market. J. Polit. Econ. 93, 1077–1125.

Heckman, J.J., Urzua, S., Vytlacil, E., 2006. Understanding instrumental variables in models with essential heterogeneity. Rev. Econ. Stat. 88 (3), 389–432.

Hoxby, C., Avery, C., 2013. The missing "one-offs": the hidden supply of high-achieving, low-income students. Brook. Pap. Econ. Act. Spring, 1–50.

Hoxby, C., Turner, S., 2013. Expanding college opportunities for high-achieving, low income students. SIEPR Discussion Paper No. 12-014.

James, E., Alsalam, N., Conaty, J.C., To, D.L., 1989. College quality and future earnings: where should you send your child to college? Am. Econ. Rev. 79 (2), 247–252.

Johnson, V., 2003. Grade Inflation: A Crisis in College Education. Springer-Verlag, Inc., New York

Johnson, M., 2013. The impact of business cycle fluctuations on graduate school enrollment. Econ. Educ. Rev. 34, 122–134.

Kahn, L., 2010. The long-term labor market consequences of graduating from college in a bad economy. Labour Econ. 17 (2), 303–316.

Ketel, N., Leuven, E., Oosterbeek, H., van der Klaauw, B., 2016. The returns to medical school: evidence from admission lotteries. Am. Econ. J. Appl. Econ., forthcoming.

Kinsler, J., Pavan, R., 2015. The specificity of general human capital: evidence from college major choice. J. Labor Econ. 33, 933–972.

Kirkebøen, L., Leuven, E., Mogstad, M., 2015. Field of study, earnings, and self-selection. Q. J. Econ. forthcoming.

Lee, L.F., 1983. Generalized econometric models with selectivity. Econometrica 51 (2), 507–512.

Lemieux, T., 2014. Occupations, fields of study and returns to education. Can. J. Econ. 47 (4), 1–31.

Lindley, J., McIntosh, S., 2015. Growth in within graduate wage inequality: the role of subjects, cognitive skill dispersion and occupational concentration. Labour Econ. 37, 101–111.

Long, M., Goldhaber, D., Huntington-Klein, N., 2015. Do completed college majors respond to changes in wages? Econ. Educ. Rev. 49, 1–14.

Loury, L., Garman, D., 1995. College selectivity and earnings. J. Labor Econ. 13 (2), 289–308.

Malamud, O., 2010. Breadth versus depth: the timing of specialization in higher education. Labour 24 (4), 359–390.

Malamud, O., 2011. Discovering one's talent: learning from academic specialization. Ind. Labor Relat. Rev. 64 (2), 375–405.

Miller, R.A., 1984. Job matching and occupational choice. J. Polit. Econ. 92, 1086–1120.

Montgomery, M., 2002. A nested logit model of the choice of a graduate business school. Econ. Educ. Rev. 21, 471–480.

Montmarquette, C., Cannings, K., Mahseredjian, S., 2002. How do young people choose college majors? Econ. Educ. Rev. 21, 543–556.

Morgan, S., Gelbgiser, D., Weeden, K., 2013. Feeding the pipeline: gender, occupational plans, and college major selection. Soc. Sci. Res. 42, 989–1005.

Nicholson, S., 2002. Physician specialty choice under uncertainty. J. Labor Econ. 20, 816–847.

Nicholson, S., Souleles, N.S., 2001. Physician income expectations and specialty choice. NBER Working Paper. 8536.

Nielsen, H.S., Vissing-Jorgensen, A., 2005. The impact of labor income risk on educational choices: estimates and implied risk aversion. Working paper.

Nordin, M., Persson, I., Rooth, D.A., 2010. Education-occupation mismatch: is there an income penalty? Econ. Educ. Rev. 29, 1047–1059.

Oreopoulos, P., von Wachter, T., Heisz, A., 2012. The short- and long-term career effects of graduating in a recession. Am. Econ. J. Appl. Econ. 4, 1–29.

Paglin, M., Rufolo, A.M., 1990. Heterogeneous human capital, occupational choice, and male-female earnings differences. J. Labor Econ. 8 (1), 123–144.

Pallais, A., 2015. Small differences that matter: mistakes in applying to college. J. Labor Econ. 33, 493–520.

Pistolesi, N., 2014. The effect of advising students at college entrance: evidence from a French university reform. Toulouse School of Economics.

Ransom, M., Phipps, A., 2010. Career and occupational implications of undergraduate majors: evidence from the national survey of college graduates. Brigham Young University.

Robst, J., 2007. Education and job match: the relatedness of college major and work. Econ. Educ. Rev. 26, 397–407.

Roy, A.D., 1951. Some thoughts on the distribution of earnings. Oxf. Econ. Pap. 3, 135–146.

Rumberger, R., Thomas, S., 1993. The economic returns to college major, quality and performance: a multilevel analysis of recent graduates. Econ. Educ. Rev. 12 (1), 1–19.

Sabot, R., Wakeman-Linn, J., 1991. Grade inflation and course choice. J. Econ. Perspect. 5 (1), 159–170.

Sacerdote, B., 2001. Peer effects with random assignment: results for Dartmouth roommates. Q. J. Econ. 116, 681–704.

Saks, R.E., Shore, S.H., 2005. Risk and career choice. Adv. Econ. Anal. Policy 5, 1–43.

Sanders, C., 2015. Reading skills and earnings: why do doing words good hurt you're wages? Working paper.

Scott, G., 2013. Testimony before the subcommittee on early childhood, elementary, and secondary education, committee on education and the workforce, house of representatives.

Seki, M., 2013. Heterogeneous returns to U.S. college selectivity and the value of graduate degree attainment. Bank of Canada.

Sivey, P., Scott, A., Witt, J., Joyce, C., Humphreys, J., 2012. Junior doctors' preferences for specialty choice. J. Health Econ. 31, 813–823.

Smyth, F.L., McArdle, J.J., 2004. Ethnic and gender differences in science graduation at selective colleges with implications for admission policy and college choice. Res. High. Educ. 45, 353–381.

Stange, K., 2015. Differential pricing in undergraduate education: effects on degree production by field. J. Policy Anal. Manage. 34, 107–135.

Stinebrickner, T., Stinebrickner, R., 2014a. Academic performance and college dropout: using longitudinal expectations data to estimate a learning model. J. Labor Econ. 32, 601–644.

Stinebrickner, T., Stinebrickner, R., 2014b. A major in science? Initial beliefs and final outcomes for college major and dropout. Rev. Econ. Stud. 81, 426–472.

Turner, S.E., Bowen, W.G., 1999. Choice of major: the changing (unchanging) gender gap. Ind. Labor Relat. Rev. 55, 289–313.

Webber, D., 2014. The lifetime earnings premia of different majors: correcting for selection based on cognitive, noncognitive, and unobserved factors. Labour Econ. 28, 14–23.

Weinberger, C., 1999. Mathematical college majors and the gender gap in wages. Ind. Relat. 38 (3), 407–413.

Weinberger, C., 2004. Just ask! Why surveyed women did not pursue college majors or careers in information technology fields. IEEE Technol. Soc. 23 (2), 28–35.

Wiswall, M., Zafar, B., 2015. Determinants of college major choice: identification using an information experiment. Rev. Econ. Stud. 82, 791–824.

Yuen, J., 2010. Job-education match and mismatch: wage differentials. Persp. Labour Income 11, 1–26.

Zafar, B., 2012. Double majors: one for me, one for the parents? Econ. Inq. 50, 287–308.

Zafar, B., 2013. College major choice and the gender gap. J. Hum. Resour. 48, 545–595.

CHAPTER 8

Student Loans and Repayment: Theory, Evidence, and Policy

L. Lochner[*,†,‡], A. Monge-Naranjo[§,¶]

[*]University of Western Ontario, London, Ontario, Canada
[†]CESifo, Munich, Bavaria, Germany
[‡]NBER, Cambridge, MA, United States
[§]Federal Reserve Bank of St. Louis, St. Louis, Missouri, United States
[¶]Washington University in St. Louis, St. Louis, Missouri, United States

Contents

Handbook of the Economics of Education, Volume 5
ISSN 1574-0692, http://dx.doi.org/10.1016/B978-0-444-63459-7.00008-7

Abstract

Rising costs of and returns to college have led to sizeable increases in the demand for student loans in many countries. In the USA, student loan default rates have also risen for recent cohorts as labor market uncertainty and debt levels have increased. We discuss these trends as well as recent evidence on the extent to which students are able to obtain enough credit for college and the extent to which they are able to repay their student debts after. We then discuss optimal student credit arrangements that balance three important objectives: (i) providing credit for students to access college and finance consumption while in school, (ii) providing insurance against uncertain adverse schooling or post-school labor market outcomes in the form of income-contingent repayments, and (iii) providing incentives for student borrowers to honor their loan obligations (in expectation) when information and commitment frictions are present. Specifically, we develop a two-period educational investment model with uncertainty and show how student loan contracts can be designed to optimally address incentive problems related to moral hazard, costly income verification, and limited commitment by the borrower. We also survey other research related to the optimal design of student loan contracts in imperfect markets. Finally, we provide practical policy guidance for re-designing student loan programs to more efficiently provide insurance while addressing information and commitment frictions in the market.

Keywords

Human capital, Borrowing, Student loans, Default, Repayment, Income-contingent, Credit constraint

JEL Codes

D14, D82, H21, H52, I22, I24, J24

1. INTRODUCTION

Three recent economic trends have important implications for financing higher education: (i) rising costs of postsecondary education, (ii) rising average returns to schooling in the labor market, and (iii) increasing labor market risk. These trends have been underway in the USA for decades; however, similar trends are also apparent in many other developed countries. Governments around the world are struggling to adapt tuition and financial aid policies in response to these changes. In an era of tight budgets, postsecondary students are being asked to pay more for their education, often with the help of government-provided student loans.

While some countries have only recently introduced student loan programs, many American students have relied on student loans to finance college for decades.

Still, the rising returns and costs of education, coupled with increased labor market uncertainty, have generated new interest in the efficient design of government student loan programs. In this chapter, we consider both theoretical and empirical issues relevant to the design of student loan programs with a particular focus on the US context.

The rising returns to and costs of college have dramatically increased the demand for credit by American students. Since the mid-1990s, more and more students have exhausted resources available to them from government student loan programs, with many turning to private lenders for additional credit. Despite an increase in private student lending, there is concern that a growing fraction of youth from low- and even middle-income backgrounds are unable to access the resources they need to attend college (Lochner and Monge-Naranjo, 2011, 2012).

At the same time, new concerns have arisen that many recent students may be taking on too much debt while in school. Growing levels of debt, coupled with rising labor market uncertainty, make it increasingly likely that some students are unable to repay their debts. These problems became strikingly evident during the Great Recession, when many recent college graduates (and dropouts) had difficulties finding their first job (Elsby et al., 2010; Hoynes et al., 2012). For the first time in more than a decade, default rates on government student loans began to rise in the USA.

Altogether, these trends raise two seemingly contradictory concerns: Can today's college students borrow enough? Or, are they borrowing too much? Growing evidence suggests that both concerns are justified and that there is room to improve upon the current structure of student loan programs. This has led to recent interest in income-contingent student loans in the USA and many other countries.

We, therefore, devote considerable attention to the design of optimal student lending programs in an environment with uncertainty and various market imperfections that limit the extent of credit and insurance that can be provided. In a two-period environment, we derive optimal student credit contracts that are limited by borrower commitment (repayment enforcement) concerns, incomplete contracts, moral hazard (hidden effort), and costly income verification. We show how these incentive and contractual problems distort consumption allocations across postschool earnings realizations, intertemporal consumption smoothing via limits on borrowing, and educational investment decisions. We also summarize other related research on these issues and related concerns about adverse selection in higher education, as well as dynamic contracting issues in richer environments with multiple years of postschool repayment. Based on results from our theoretical analysis and the literature more generally, we discuss important policy lessons that can help guide the design of optimal government student loan programs.

The rest of this chapter proceeds as follows. Section 2 documents several recent trends in the labor market and education sector relevant to our analysis. We then describe current student loan markets (especially in the USA) in Section 3, before summarizing literatures on borrowing constraints in higher education (Section 4) and student loan repayment (Section 5). Our analysis of optimal student credit contracts under uncertainty and various information and contractual frictions appears in Section 6, followed by a discussion of important policy lessons in Section 7. Concluding remarks and suggestions for future research are reserved for Section 8.

2. TRENDS

2.1 Three Important Economic Trends

Three important economic trends have substantially altered the landscape of higher education in recent decades, affecting college attendance patterns, as well as borrowing and repayment behavior. These trends are all well-established in the USA, but some are also apparent to varying degrees in other developed countries. We focus primarily on the USA but also comment on a few other notable examples.

First, the costs of college have increased markedly in recent decades, even after accounting for inflation. Fig. 1 reports average tuition, fees, room, and board (TFRB)

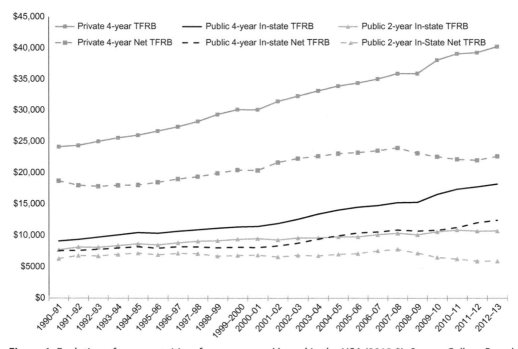

Figure 1 Evolution of average tuition, fees, room, and board in the USA (2013 $). *Source: College Board (2013) (online Tables 7 and 8), Trends in College Pricing.*

in the USA (in constant year 2013 dollars) from 1990–91 to 2012–13 for private non-profit 4-year institutions as well as public 4-year and 2-year institutions. Since 1990–91, average posted TFRB doubled at 4-year public schools, while it increased by 65% at private 4-year institutions. Average published costs rose less (39%) at 2-year public schools. The dashed lines in Fig. 1 report net TFRB each year after subtracting off tuition-waivers, grants, and tax benefits, which also increased over this period. Accounting for expansions in student aid, the average net cost of attendance at public and private 4-year colleges increased by "only" 64% and 21%, respectively, while net TFRB declined slightly (6%) at public 2-year schools. Driving some of these changes are increases in the underlying costs of higher education. Current fund expenditures per student at all public institutions in the USA rose by 28% between 1990–91 and 2000–01 reflecting an annual growth rate of 2.5% (Snyder et al., 2009, Table 360).[1] Expenditures per student have also risen in many other developed countries (OECD, 2013). In some of these countries, governments have shouldered much of the increase, while tuition fees have risen substantially in others like Australia, Canada, the Netherlands, New Zealand, and the UK.[2]

Second, average returns to college have increased sharply in many developed countries, including Australia, Canada, Germany, the UK, and the USA.[3] In the USA, Autor et al. (2008) document a nearly 25% increase in weekly earnings for college graduates between 1979 and 2005, compared with a 4% decline among workers with only a high school diploma. Even after accounting for rising tuition levels, Avery and Turner (2012) calculate that the difference in discounted lifetime earnings (net of tuition payments) between college and high school graduates rose by more than $300,000 for men and $200,000 for women between 1980 and 2008.[4] Heckman et al. (2008) estimate that internal rates of return to college versus high school rose by 45% for black men and 60% for white men between 1980 and 2000.

Third, labor market uncertainty has increased considerably in the USA. Numerous studies document increases in the variance of both transitory and persistent shocks to

---

[1] Jones and Yang (2014) argue that much of the increase in the costs of higher education can be traced to the rising costs of high skilled labor due to skill-biased technological change.

[2] Tuition and fees rose by a factor of 2.5 in Canada between 1990–91 and 2012–13. Australia, the Netherlands, and the UK all moved from fully government-financed higher education in the late 1980s to charging modest tuition fees by the end of the 1990s. Current statutory tuition fees in the Netherlands stand at roughly US$5000, while tuition in Australia now averages more than US$6500. Most dramatically, tuition and fees nearly tripled from just over £3000 to £9000 (nearly US$5000 to over US$14,500) at most UK schools in 2012. Tuition fees have also increased substantially in New Zealand since fee deregulation in 1991.

[3] See eg, Card and Lemieux (2001) for evidence on Canada, the UK, and USA; Boudarbat et al. (2010) on Canada; Dustmann et al. (2009) on Germany; and Wei (2010) on Australia. Pereira and Martins (2000) estimate increasing returns to education more generally in Denmark, Italy, and Spain, as well.

[4] These calculations are based on a 3% discount rate.

earnings beginning in the early 1970s.[5] Lochner and Shin (2014) estimate that the variance in permanent shocks to earnings increased by more than 15 percentage points for American men over the 1980s and 1990s, while the variance of transitory shocks rose by 5–10 percentage points over that period. A number of recent studies also document increases in the variances of permanent and transitory shocks to earnings in Europe since the 1980s.[6] The considerable uncertainty faced by recent school-leavers has been highlighted throughout the Great Recession with unemployment rates rising for young workers regardless of their educational background.[7] While very persistent shocks early in borrowers' careers clearly threaten their ability to repay their debts in full, even severe negative transitory shocks can make maintaining payments difficult for a few years without some form of assistance or income-contingency.

2.2 US Trends in Student Borrowing and Debt

Despite rising costs of college and labor market uncertainty, the steady rise in labor market returns to college has driven American college attendance rates steadily upward over the past few decades. The fraction of Americans that had enrolled in college by age 19 increased by 25 percentage points between cohorts born in 1961 and 1988, while college completion rates rose by about 7 percentage points over this time period (Bailey and Dynarski, 2011).

Along with the increase in college-going, the rising costs of and returns to college have led to a considerable increase in the demand for student loans in the USA.[8] Fig. 2 demonstrates the dramatic increase in annual student borrowing between 2000–01 and 2010–11 as reported by College Board (2011).[9] Not surprisingly, debt levels from student loans have also exploded, surpassing total credit card debt in the USA. Analyzing data drawn from a random sample of personal credit reports (FRBNY Consumer Credit Panel/Equifax, henceforth CCP), Bleemer et al. (2014) report that combined government and private student debt levels in the US quadrupled (in nominal terms) from $250 billion in 2003 to $1.1 trillion in 2013.

[5] See Gottschalk and Moffitt (2009) for a recent survey of this literature. More recent work includes Heathcote et al. (2010a,b), Moffitt and Gottschalk (2012), and Lochner and Shin (2014).

[6] Fuchs-Schundeln et al. (2010) document an increase in the variance of permanent shocks in Germany, while Jappelli and Pistaferri (2010) estimate increases in the variance of transitory shocks in Italy. Domeij and Floden (2010) document increases in the variance of both transitory and permanent shocks in Sweden over this period. In Britain, Blundell et al. (2013) find that increases in the variance of permanent and transitory shocks has been concentrated in recessions.

[7] See Elsby et al. (2010) and Hoynes et al. (2012) for evidence on unemployment rates during the Great Recession by age and education in the USA. Bell and Blanchflower (2011) document sizeable increases in unemployment throughout Europe for young workers with and without postsecondary education.

[8] Hershbein and Hollenbeck (2015) estimate that changes in the composition of college graduates (eg, parental education and income, race, institution of attendance, college major) explain very little of the increase in student borrowing between 1990 and 2008.

[9] Total Stafford loan disbursements also more than doubled in the previous decade (College Board, 2001).

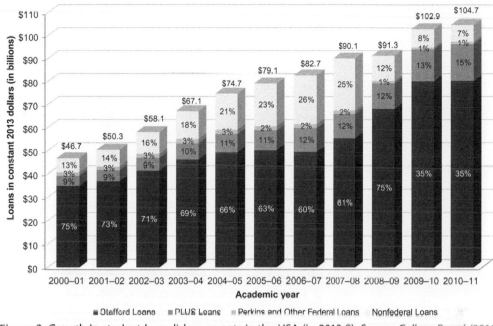

Figure 2 Growth in student loan disbursements in the USA (in 2013 $). *Source: College Board (2011).*

The dramatic increases in aggregate student borrowing and debt levels reflect not only the rise in college enrolment in the USA over the past few decades, but also an increase in the share of students taking out loans and greater borrowing among those choosing to borrow. Based on the CCP, Bleemer et al. (2014) show that the fraction of 25-year olds with government and/or private student debt rose from 25% in 2003 to 45% in 2013. Over that same decade, average student debt levels among 22- to 25-year olds with positive debt nearly doubled from $10,600 to $20,900 (in 2013 $). Akers and Chingos (2014) use the Survey of Consumer Finances (SCF) to study the evolution of household education debt (including both private and government student loans) over two decades for respondents ages 20–40. As shown in Fig. 3, the fraction of these households with education debt nearly doubled from 14% in 1989 to 36% in 2010, while the average amount of debt (among families with debt) more than tripled.[10] Altogether, these figures imply an eightfold increase in average debt levels (per person) among all 20- to 40-year-old households (borrowers and nonborrowers alike) between 1989 and 2010.[11]

---

[10] Brown et al. (2016) compare household debt levels in the CCP and SCF for the years 2004, 2007, and 2010. Their findings suggest that student loan debts appear to be under-reported by 24% (2004) to 34% (2010) in the SCF relative to credit report records in the CCP.

[11] In discussing the results of Akers and Chingos (2014), we refer to 20- to 40-year-old households as households in which the SCF respondent was between the ages of 20 and 40.

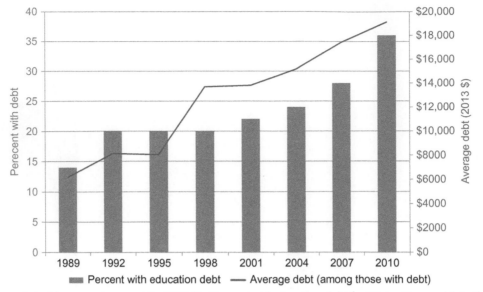

Figure 3 Incidence and amount (in 2013 $) of household education debt for 20- to 40-year olds in the USA. *Source: Akers and Chingos (2014, Table 1).*

Table 1 Education debt for baccalaureate degree recipients in NPSAS (2013 $)

Year graduating	Percent with education debt	Avg. cumulative student loan debt (per borrower)	Avg. cumulative student loan debt (per graduate)
1989–90	55	13,500	7300
1995–96	53	17,800	9300
1999–2000	64	22,900	14,600
2003–04	66	23,000	15,100
2007–08	68	25,800	17,600
2011–12	71	29,700	21,200

Source: Hershbein and Hollenbeck (2014, 2015).

With the CCP and SCF, it is difficult to determine debt levels at the time students leave school, so figures from these sources reflect both borrowing and early repayment behavior. By contrast, the National Postsecondary Student Aid Study (NPSAS) allows researchers to study the evolution of education-related debt accumulated during college. Using the NPSAS, Hershbein and Hollenbeck (2014, 2015) consider total student debt (government and private) accumulated by baccalaureate degree recipients who graduated in various years back to 1989–90 (see Table 1). They report that the fraction of baccalaureate recipients graduating with education debt increased by nearly one-third from 55% in 1992–93 to 71% in 2011–12, while average total student debt per graduating

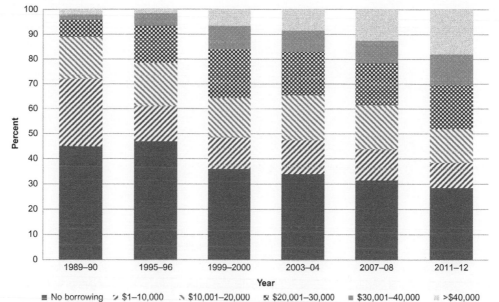

Figure 4 Distribution of cumulative undergraduate debt for baccalaureate recipients over time (NPSAS). *Source: Hershbein and Hollenbeck (2014, 2015).*

borrower more than doubled. Together, total student debt per graduate tripled between the 1989–90 and 2011–12 cohorts.

Fig. 4 documents the changing distribution of cumulative loan amounts among baccalaureate recipients over time in the NPSAS (Hershbein and Hollenbeck, 2014, 2015). The figure reveals different trends at the low and high ends of the debt distribution. The fraction of college graduates borrowing less than $10,000 (including nonborrowers) declined sharply in the 1990s but remained quite stable thereafter until the financial crisis in 2008. By contrast, undergraduate student debts of at least $30,000 increased more consistently over time, with the exception of the early 2000s when the entire distribution of debt was relatively stable. Since 1989–90, the fraction of college graduates that borrowed more than $30,000 increased from 4% to 30%. Though not shown in the figure, less than 1% of all graduates had accumulated more than $50,000 in student debt before 1999–2000, while 10% had by 2011–12 (Hershbein and Hollenbeck, 2014, 2015).

Fig. 5, from Steele and Baum (2009), reports the distribution of accumulated student loan debt separately for associate and baccalaureate degree recipients in the 2007–08 NPSAS. Students earning their associate degree borrowed considerably less, on average, than did those earning a baccalaureate degree. Roughly one-half of associate degree earners did not borrow anything, while only 5% borrowed $30,000 or more.

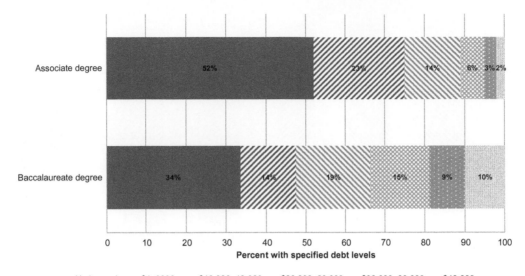

Figure 5 Distribution of cumulative student loan debt by undergraduate degree (NPSAS 2007–08). Data from 2007–08 NPSAS and includes US citizens and residents. Excludes PLUS loans, loans from family/friends, and credit cards. *Source: Steele and Baum (2009).*

It is important to note that students from all income backgrounds borrow from federal student loan programs and increasingly so. Fig. 6 documents the growth in average federal student loan amounts for dependent undergraduates by parental income quartile between 1989–90 and 2003–04 based on available NPSAS (Berkner, 2000; Wei and Berkner, 2008). This growth reflects increases at both the extensive margin (percent borrowing) as well as the intensive margin (amount per borrower) and is most pronounced for the highest income quartile. The sizeable increases in borrowing between 1992–93 and 1995–96 for all but the lowest income quartile coincide with the introduction of unsubsidized Stafford loans, which can be taken out irrespective of financial need.

The steady rise in total student borrowing over the late 1990s and 2000s belies the fact that government student loan limits remained unchanged (in nominal dollars) between 1993 and 2008. Adjusting for inflation, this reflects a nearly 50% decline in value. In 2008, aggregate Stafford loan limits for dependent undergraduate students jumped from $23,000 to $31,000, although this value was still more than 10% below the 1993 limit after accounting for inflation. Not surprisingly, a rising number of students have exhausted available government student loan sources over this period. For example, the share of full-time/full-year undergraduates that "maxed out" Stafford loans increased nearly sixfold from 5.5% in 1989–90 to 32.1% in 2003–04 (Berkner, 2000; Wei and Berkner, 2008).

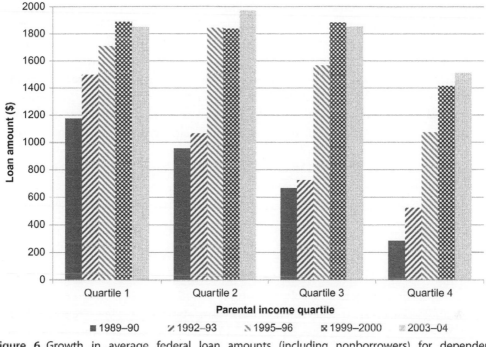

Figure 6 Growth in average federal loan amounts (including nonborrowers) for dependent undergraduates by parental income quartile. *Source: Berkner (2000) and Wei and Berkner (2000).*

Undergraduates turned more and more to private lenders to help finance their education prior to the 2008 increase in federal student loan limits and contemporaneous collapse in private credit markets. Between 1999–2000 and 2007–08, average debt from federal student loan programs declined by a few thousand dollars among baccalaureate degree recipients, but this was more than compensated for by a sizeable jump in private student loan debt (Woo, 2014). The top parts of each bar in Fig. 2 reveal the aggregate shift in undergraduate borrowing toward nonfederal sources (mostly private lenders), which peaked at 25% of all student loan dollars in 2007–08 before dropping below 10%.[12] Finally, data from the NPSAS shows that the fraction of undergraduates using private student loans rose from 5% in 2003–04 to 14% in 2007–08 before dropping back to 6% in 2011–12 (Arvidson et al., 2013).

Akers and Chingos (2014) discuss three important reasons that these increases in student borrowing do not necessarily imply greater monthly repayment burdens on today's borrowers: (i) earnings have increased significantly for college students, especially those

---

[12] These figures do not include student credit card borrowing, which has also risen over this period. In 2008, 85% of undergraduates had at least one credit card and carried an average balance of $3173 (Sallie Mae, 2008).

graduating with a baccalaureate degree or higher, (ii) nominal interest rates on federal student loans have fallen, and (iii) amortization periods for federal student loans have been extended.[13] Indeed, Akers and Chingos (2014) report that among 20- to 40-year-old households with positive education debt and monthly wage income of at least $1000, median student loan payment-to-income ratios remained relatively constant at 3–4% between 1992 and 2010, while average monthly payment-to-income ratios actually fell by half over the 1990s and have remained fairly stable thereafter. The incidence of high payment-to-income ratios (eg, at least 20%) also fell over this period. It is important to note, however, that these statistics (in all years) likely understate the financial burden of student loan payments on recent school-leavers, since they exclude very low-income households (wage income less than $1000 per month) from their analysis and since earnings levels are typically lowest in the first few years out of school.[14]

2.3 US Trends in Student Loan Delinquency and Default

Student loan delinquency and default rates provide another useful picture of borrowers' capacity and willingness to repay their student loan obligations. Fig. 7 reports official 2- and 3-year cohort default rates from 1987 to 2011. These default measures reflect the fraction of students entering repayment in a given year that default on their federal student loans within the next 2 or 3 years, respectively.[15] Despite increases in student debt levels over the 1990s, default rates declined considerably over this period. While largely unstudied, this decline likely reflects the increase in earnings associated with postsecondary schooling over that period as well as increased enforcement and collection efforts by the federal government.[16] After remaining relatively stable over the early 2000s, default rates on federal student loans began to increase sharply with the financial crisis of 2007–08 and the onset of the Great Recession. Two-year cohort default rates more than doubled from 4.6% in 2005 to 10% in 2011.

[13] Nominal interest rates on federal student loans fell from 8.3% in 1992 to 5.5% in 2010; average amortization periods on federal student loans increased from 7.5 to 13.4 years among 20- to 40-year-old households with debt (Akers and Chingos, 2014). Together, these imply a reduction in annual repayments of 42% for the same loan amount.

[14] The downward trend in payment-to-income ratios may also be driven, at least partially, by more severe under-reporting of student debt in the SCF as suggested by Brown et al. (2016). See footnote 10.

[15] Borrowers that are 270 days or more (180 days or more prior to 1998) late on their Stafford student loan payments are considered to be in default.

[16] Throughout the 1990s, the federal government expanded default collection efforts to garnish wages and seize income tax refunds from borrowers that default. The Department of Education began to exclude postsecondary institutions with high default rates (currently 30% or higher for 3 consecutive years) from participating in federal student aid (including Pell Grant) programs in the early 1990s. The 1998 change in the definition of default from 180 to 270 days late also contributed to some of the decline.

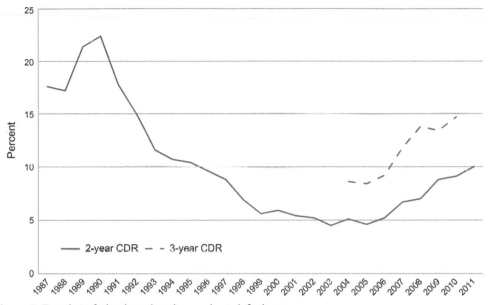

Figure 7 Trends in federal student loan cohort default rates.

Fig. 8 reveals that the decline in default rates over the 1990s was most pronounced among 2-year schools and 4-year for-profit institutions, which all had much higher initial default rates than 4-year public and private nonprofit schools.[17] Since 2005, default rates have increased most at for-profit institutions and public 2-year schools, which now stand at 13–15%. Default rates at these institutions are at least 5 percentage points higher than at other school types.

Default is only one very extreme form of nonpayment. Using CCP data, Brown et al. (2015) show high and increasing rates of delinquency (90 or more days late) on student loan payments (including government and private student loans) over the past decade. Among borrowers under age 30 still in repayment, the fraction delinquent on student loans increased sharply from 20% in 2004 to 35% in 2012. Using student loan records from five major loan guarantee agencies, Cunningham and Kienzl (2014) report that among students entering repayment in 2005, 26% had become delinquent and 15% had defaulted at some point over the next 5 years; another 16% had received a forbearance or deferment for economic hardship. Altogether, 57% had experienced a period where they did not make their expected payments.

[17] These figures are calculated from official default rates by institution as maintained by Department of Education.

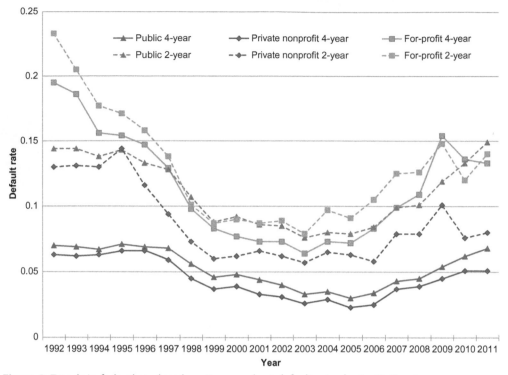

Figure 8 Trends in federal student loan 2-year cohort default rates by institution type.

2.4 Summary of Major Trends

Summarizing these trends for the USA, both the costs of and returns to college have risen dramatically in recent decades. On balance, the net returns to college have risen, which has led to important increases in college attendance rates. Student borrowing has also risen at both the extensive and intensive margins. While borrowing from government student loan programs has increased over this period, students have turned increasingly more to private lenders since the early 1990s to help fill the gap between sharply growing demand for credit and relatively stable or declining supply from government sources. Rising debt levels, coupled with an increase in labor market uncertainty, have given rise to higher delinquency and default rates on government and private student loans.

After discussing the current student loan environment in the USA and a few other countries, we return to some of these issues below in Sections 4 and 5, where we summarize evidence on borrowing constraints in higher education and the determinants of student loan repayment/default.

3. CURRENT STUDENT LOAN ENVIRONMENT

In this section, we describe the current student loan environment with an emphasis on the USA. However, we also provide a brief international context for student loan programs, devoting considerable attention to income-contingent loan repayment schemes.

3.1 Federal Student Loan Programs in the USA

Most federal loans are provided through the Stafford loan program, which awarded about $90 billion in the 2011–12 academic year, compared to $19 billion awarded through Federal Parent Loans (PLUS) and GradPLUS Loans combined, and just under $1 billion through the Perkins Loan program. For some perspective, total Pell Grant awards amounted to about $34 billion. See the College Board (2013) for these and related statistics. Important features of the main federal student loan programs are summarized in Table 2. We briefly discuss these programs in the following sections.

3.1.1 Stafford Loans

The federal government offers Stafford loans to undergraduate and graduate students through the William D. Ford Federal Direct Student Loan (FDSL) program.[18] Students are not charged interest on subsidized loans as long as they are enrolled in school, while interest accrues on unsubsidized loans. Only undergraduates are eligible for unsubsidized loans. In order to qualify for subsidized loans, undergraduate students must demonstrate financial need, which depends on family income, dependency status, and the cost of institution attended. Unsubsidized loans are available to both undergraduate and graduate students and can be obtained without demonstrating need. In general, students under age 24 are assumed to be "dependent," in which case their parents' income is an important determinant of their financial need.

Dependency status and year in college determine the total amount of Stafford loans a student is eligible for, as seen in Table 2. Dependent students can borrow as much as $31,000 over their undergraduate years, while independent students can borrow twice that amount.[19] Annual limits are lowest for the first year of college, increasing in the following 2 years.

---

[18] In the past, private lenders provided loans to students under the Federal Family Education Loan Program (FFEL), and the federal government guaranteed those loans with a promise to cover unpaid amounts. Regardless of the source of funds, the rules governing FDSL and FFEL programs were essentially the same. Prior to the introduction of unsubsidized Stafford loans in the early 1990s, Supplemental Loans to Students (SLS) were an alternative source of unsubsidized federal loans for independent students.

[19] Dependent students whose parents do not qualify for the PLUS program can borrow up to the independent student Stafford loan limits.

Table 2 Summary of current federal student loan programs

	Stafford		Perkins	PLUS and GradPLUS
	Dependent students	**Independent students**[a]		
Recipient	Students	Students	Students	PLUS: parents GradPLUS: grad. students
Eligibility	Subsidized: undergrad., financial need[b] Unsubsidized: all students		Financial need	No adverse credit history or cosigner required
Undergraduate limits				
Year 1	$5500	$9500	$5500	All need
Year 2	$6500	$10,500	$5500	All need
Years 3+	$7500	$12,500	$5500	All need
Cum. total	$31,000	$57,500	$27,500	All need
Graduate limits				
Annual	$20,500		$8000	All need
Cum. total[c]	$138,500		$60,000	All need
Interest rate	Undergrad.: variable, ≤8.25% Grad.: variable, ≤9.5%		5%	Variable, 10.5% limit
Fees	1.07%		None	4.3%
Grace period	6 months		9 months	Up to 6 months

[a]Students whose parents do not qualify for PLUS loans can borrow up to independent student limits from the Stafford program.
[b]Subsidized Stafford loan amounts cannot exceed $3500 in year 1, $4500 in year 2, $5500 in years 3+, and $23,000 cumulative.
[c]Cumulative graduate loan limits include loans from undergraduate loans.

Interest rates on Stafford loans are variable subject to upper limits of 8.25% for under-graduates and 9.5% for graduate students.[20] Fees are levied on borrowers of about 1%, which is proportionally subtracted from each disbursement. Students need not re-pay their loans while enrolled at least half-time, though interest does accrue on unsubsidized loans. After leaving school, borrowers are given a 6-month grace period before they are required to begin re-paying their Stafford loans.

[20] Interest rates for undergraduate and graduate students are equal to the 10-year treasury note plus 2.05% and 3.6%, respectively, subject to the upper limits. For the 2013–14 academic year, the rates equal 3.86% and 5.41% for undergraduates and graduates, respectively.

3.1.2 PLUS and GradPLUS Loans

The PLUS program allows parents who do not have an adverse credit rating to borrow for their dependent children's education. The GradPLUS program offers the same opportunities for graduate and professional students to borrow for their own education. Generally, parents and graduate students can borrow up to the total cost of schooling less any other financial aid given to the student. For this purpose, the cost of schooling is determined by the school of attendance and includes such expenses as tuition and fees, reasonable room and board allowances, expenses for books, supplies, and equipment. Interest rates are variable (10-year treasury note plus 4.6%) subject to a 10.5% limit, and fees of 4.3% of loan amounts are charged on origination. Graduate students enrolled at least half-time can defer all GradPLUS loan payments until 6 months after leaving school. Parents borrowing from the PLUS program can also request such a deferment.

3.1.3 Perkins Loans

The Perkins loan program targets students in need, distributing funds provided by the government and participating postsecondary institutions. Loan amounts depend on the student's level of need and funding by the school attended, but they are subject to an upper limit of $5500 per year for undergraduates and $8000 per year for graduate students. By far the most financially attractive loan alternative for students, Perkins loans entail no fees and a fixed low interest rate of 5% (see Table 2). Students are also given a 9-month grace period after finishing (leaving) school before they must begin re-payment of a Perkins loan.

3.1.4 Federal Student Loan Repayment and Default

Re-payment of student loans begins 6 (Stafford) or 9 (Perkins) months after finishing school with collection managed by the Department of Education. To simplify repayment, borrowers can consolidate most of their federal loans into a single Direct Consolidation Loan. Borrowers with Stafford or Direct Consolidation Loans have a number of repayment plans available to them.[21]

Under the *Standard Repayment Plan* and *Extended Repayment Plan*, borrowers make a standard fixed monthly payment based on their loan amount amortized over 10–30 years. For example, repayment periods are limited to 10 years for borrowers owing less than $7500, 20 years for borrowers owing less than $40,000, and 30 years for those owing $60,000 or more.[22] Borrowers may also choose the *Graduated Repayment Plan*, which starts payments at low monthly amounts, increasing payment amounts every 2 years over

---

[21] Payments for nonconsolidated Perkins Loans are fixed based on a 10-year amortization period.

[22] These repayment periods apply to borrowers who hold consolidated loans. For those with other nonconsolidated federal loans, the *Extended Repayment Plan* allows for repayment periods of up to 25 years for those with loans exceeding $30,000.

the 10- to 30-year repayment period. Final payments may be as much as three times initial payments under this plan. While the reduced starting payments of the *Graduated Repayment Plan* can be helpful for borrowers with modest initial earnings after leaving school, payments are not automatically adjusted based on income levels. Thus, payments under all of these debt-based repayment plans may be difficult for those who experience periods of unemployment or unusually low earnings. If these borrowers can demonstrate financial hardship, they may qualify for either a forbearance or deferment, which temporarily reduces or delays payments.[23]

Alternatively, borrowers may choose from a variety of income-based plans that directly link payment amounts to current income. The newest (and most attractive) of these plans is known as the *Pay As You Earn Plan* (PAYE). Under this plan, monthly payments are the lesser of the fixed payment under the 10-year *Standard Repayment Plan* and 10% of discretionary family income.[24] Borrowers on PAYE never pay more than the standard payment amount, and those with income less than 150% of the poverty level are not required to make any payment. Interest continues to accumulate even when payments are reduced or zero; however, any remaining balance after 20 years is forgiven.

It is important to point out that income-based repayment amounts and eligibility for forbearance/deferment do not depend on parental income or wealth, despite the important role these resources play in determining financial aid offerings at the time of enrolment. As documented in Section 5.3, parental support can be an important resource for former students that would otherwise have difficulties repaying their loans due to poor labor market outcomes; however, this form of support is not easily identified by lenders and is not currently considered by government student loan programs (except the PLUS program, which lends directly to parents themselves).

Loans covered by the federal system cannot generally be expunged through bankruptcy except in very special circumstances. Thus, the only way a borrower can "avoid" making required payments is to simply stop making them, or default. A borrower is considered to be in default once he becomes 270 days late in making a payment. If the loan is not fully re-paid immediately, or if a suitable re-payment plan is not agreed upon with the lender, the default status will be reported to credit bureaus, and collection costs may be added to the amount outstanding. Up to 15% of the

---

[23] Borrowers can request a deferment during periods of unemployment or when working full time but earning less than the federal minimum wage or 1.5 times the poverty level. Borrowers are entitled to deferments of up to 3 years due to unemployment or economic hardship. Borrowers can request a forbearance (usually up to 12 months at a time) due to economic hardship (eg, monthly payments exceed 20% of gross income).

[24] Discretionary income is the amount over 150% of the poverty guideline (based on family size and state of residence). In 2014, the federal poverty guideline for a single- (two-) person family was $11,670 ($15,730) in the 48 contiguous states, so the income-based payment amount for a single- (two-) person family is 10% of any income over $17,505 ($23,595).

borrower's disposable earnings can be garnished (without a court order), and federal tax refunds or Social Security payments can be seized and applied toward the balance.[25] In practice, these sanctions are sometimes limited by the inability of collectors to locate those who have defaulted. Wage garnishments are ineffective against defaulters that are self-employed. Furthermore, individuals can object to the wage garnishment if it would leave them with a weekly take-home pay of less than 30 (h/week) times the federal minimum hourly wage, or if the garnishment would otherwise result in an extreme financial hardship.

Just how costly are these punishments for those defaulting on their student loans? Of the $92 billion in delinquent student loans in 2011, the US Department of Education collected slightly over $1 billion through wage garnishments and $1.7 billion from income tax offsets (U.S. Department of the Treasury, 2012). Much more is eventually collected from defaulting borrowers as they rehabilitate their loans and continue their payments. The estimated lifetime recovery rate (net of collection costs) for Stafford loans disbursed in 2014 that will go into default at some point is roughly 85%.[26]

We do not know of any specific estimates of the impacts of student loan delinquency and default on future access to credit. Musto (2004) estimates a negative effect of personal bankruptcy on credit scores and access to new credit; however, these findings cannot be directly extrapolated to student loan delinquency and default since these actions do not lead to a discharge of debts as in the case of bankruptcy. Interestingly, the recent work of Albanesi and Nosal (2015) on the bankruptcy law reform of 2005 suggests that defaults on student loans may have even more detrimental consequences on credit scores and access to new credit than filing for bankruptcy, since the latter clears other forms of unsecured debt.

3.2 Private Student Loan Programs in the USA

As noted earlier, 14% of all undergraduates in 2007–08 turned to private student loan programs to help finance their education. Due to tightening private credit markets and expansions in the Stafford loan program, the fraction of undergraduates borrowing from private lenders dropped by more than half over the next few years (Arvidson et al., 2013). However, private student loans are still an important source of funding for some students, especially those attending more expensive private nonprofit and proprietary schools.

---

[25] Other sanctions against borrowers who default include a possible hold on college transcripts, ineligibility for further federal student loans, and ineligibility for a deferment or forbearance. Since the early 1990s, the government has also punished educational institutions with high student default rates by making their students ineligible to borrow from federal lending programs.

[26] See page S-31 of the Department of Education's *Student Loans Overview* for the Fiscal Year 2014 Budget Proposal available at http://www2.ed.gov/about/overview/budget/budget14/justifications/s-loansoverview.pdf.

Private loans are not need-based. Instead, students or their families must demonstrate their creditworthiness to lenders whose aim is to earn a competitive return. Private student loans are generally capped by the total costs of college less any other financial aid; however, lenders sometimes impose tighter constraints. Eligibility, loan limits, and terms generally depend on the borrower's credit score and sometimes depend on other factors that may affect repayment, such as the institution of attendance and degree pursued. In most cases, lenders require a cosigner (with an eligible credit score) to commit to repaying the loan if students themselves do not; a cosigner may also improve the terms of the loan. In this way, private student loan contracts, unlike those of government student loan programs, effectively incorporate the potential for postschool parental support. Among student loans distributed by some of the top private lenders in recent years, more than 90% (60%) of all undergraduate (graduate) borrowers had a cosigner (Arvidson et al., 2013). Interest rates charged on private loans are typically higher than those offered by federal student loan programs, especially for borrowers with poor credit records. Rates may be fixed or variable and are usually pegged to either the prime rate or the London Interbank Offer Rate (LIBOR).

Repayment terms typically range between 10 and 25 years, almost universally with fixed debt-based payments. Some programs require borrowers to begin repaying their loan shortly after taking it out, while others provide students with deferments during enrolment periods. Some even offer up to a 6-month grace period after students leave school. In some cases, lenders may offer opportunities for deferment/forbearance due to economic hardship. All of these attributes are at the discretion of the lender.

Since 2005, private student loans (like federal student loans) cannot be expunged through bankruptcy except in exceptional circumstances.[27] However, private lenders do not have the same powers as the federal government to enforce repayment. Most notably, lenders must receive a court judgment in order to garnish wages or seize a delinquent borrower's assets.

3.3 The International Experience

Many countries offer government student loans for higher education (OECD, 2013). In most cases, the general structure for these programs is similar to that of the USA in that students can borrow to help cover tuition/fees and living expenses, payments can be deferred until after leaving school, and repayment terms are debt-based.[28] Contingencies like deferment/forbearance for borrowers experiencing financial hardship are common; however, most countries do not offer explicit income-contingent repayment schemes.[29] Exceptions include Australia, Canada, Chile, New Zealand, the UK, and

---

[27] These limits on bankruptcy do not extend to other sources of financing like credit cards or home mortgages, which are also sometimes used to finance higher education.

[28] Even in Nordic countries like Denmark, Norway, and Sweden that charge zero or negligible tuition and fees, government loans are an important source of funding for student living expenses.

[29] None consider parental resources in determining repayment amounts.

Table 3 Summary of income-contingent repayment plans

	Australia	New Zealand	United Kingdom	Canada	United States
Program name	HECS-HELP		Maintenance and tuition fee loans	RAP[a]	PAYE[a]
Year adopted	1989	1992	1998	2009	2012
Collected with taxes?	Yes	Yes	Yes	No	No
Covers living expenses?	No	Yes	Yes	Yes	Yes
Interest rate[b]	CPI	0%	RPI + 0–3%	Prime + 2.5 or 5%	10-year T–Note + 2.05%
Fees	10%[c]	$60 initial, $40 annual	No	No	No
Minimum income threshold for payment?	Yes	Yes	Yes	Varies by family size	Varies by family size
Repayment begins	Income > threshold	Income > threshold	April after school ends	After school + 6 months	After school + 6 months
Repayment rate (% of income)	4–8%	12% (over threshold)	9% (over threshold)	0–20% (over threshold)	10% (over threshold)
Repayment rate increase with income?	Yes	No	No	Yes	No
Prepayment discount?	5%	No	No	No	No
Loan forgiveness?	No	No	After 30 years	After 15 years	After 20 years

[a]Eligibility for both RAP in Canada and PAYE in the USA requires financial hardship.
[b]In Australia, debt levels increase with inflation as determined by the consumer price index (CPI). In the UK, interest rates are linked to the Retail Price Index (RPI) and increase with borrower income levels. In New Zealand, an interest rate of 5.9% is charged for borrowers who move overseas. In Canada, the variable rate is prime + 2.5% and the fixed rate is prime + 5%.
[c]Australian borrowers who make up-front fee payments (rather than borrow) receive a 10% discount.

South Africa, which all have explicit income-contingent repayment programs. Because recent policy discussions often refer to these programs in Australia, New Zealand, and the UK, we discuss them in some detail along with similar plans in Canada and the USA.[30] Table 3 summarizes key aspects of these income-contingent loan programs.

[30] Chapman (2006) provides a comprehensive discussion of income-contingent programs around the world.

While the details of student loan programs in Australia, New Zealand, and the UK have changed over the years, repayment schemes have been fully income-contingent for many years. Students choose how much they wish to borrow each schooling period — Australian students can borrow up to tuition/fees, while New Zealand and UK students can also borrow to cover living expenses — and do not need to make any payments until after leaving school.[31] In all cases, repayment amounts depend on borrower income levels and are collected through the tax system. Borrowers with income below specified minimum thresholds need not make any payments, while payments increase with income above the thresholds. Annual income thresholds range from a low of 19,800 NZ dollars (roughly US$15,500) in New Zealand to £21,000 (roughly US$35,000) in the UK to a high of 51,300 Australian dollars (roughly US$45,000) in Australia. Borrowers in New Zealand and the UK pay 12% and 9%, respectively, of their income above this threshold toward their loan balance once they leave school. In Australia, those with incomes above the threshold must make payments of 4–8% of their total income with the repayment rate increasing in their income level.[32] Australian borrowers receive a 5% discount on any additional prepayments they make above the required amount.

In Australia and New Zealand, borrowers are expected to make payments until their student debt is paid off; although, student debts can be cancelled through bankruptcy in New Zealand (not Australia). Fees and interest rates charged on the loans will determine the number of years borrowers must make payments, even if they do not affect annual payment amounts. In Australia, students who attend Commonwealth-supported (ie, public) institutions do not face any explicit fees on HECS-HELP loans; however, a discount of 10% is granted for any amount over $500 paid up front for tuition. This effectively implies a 10% initiation fee on student loans.[33] Other than these fees, Australian students do not pay any real interest on their loans; although, the value of student debts is adjusted with the CPI to account for inflation. By contrast, New Zealand charges modest fees of $60 at the time a loan is established and $40 each year thereafter; however, it charges zero interest and does not adjust loan amounts for inflation.

The UK does not charge any initial fees on loans, but it charges interest based on the RPI. While in school, interest accrues at a rate equal to the RPI + 3%. After school, students with income below the income threshold of £21,000 face an interest rate equal to the RPI. Above the threshold, the rate linearly increases in income until £41,000 when it reaches a maximum of RPI + 3%. Any outstanding debt is cancelled 30 years after repayment begins; however, debts cannot be cancelled through bankruptcy.

---

[31] In most cases, New Zealand students can borrow for up to 7 full-time equivalent school years.

[32] Students in Australia and New Zealand must make payments while enrolled in school if they earn above the income thresholds when they are enrolled.

[33] Under the FEE-HELP program in Australia, which provides loans to students at institutions that are not subsidized by the government, an explicit 25% initiation fee is charged on all loans, but there is no discount on up-front payments.

Like the USA, Canada offers student loans under debt-based repayment contracts along with an option for income-contingent repayment for borrowers with low income levels.[34] Standard repayment terms (fixed payments based on 10- or 15-year amortization periods) are similar to those in the USA and include a 6-month grace period after school before repayment begins. Interest accrues at either a fixed (prime + 5%) or floating (prime + 2.5%) rate. Introduced in 2009, the Canada Student Loans Program's (CSLP) Repayment Assistance Plan (RAP) offers reduced income-based payments for borrowers with low postschool incomes. Like PAYE in the USA, RAP payments are given by the lesser of the standard debt-based payment and an income-based amount ranging from zero to 20% of income above a minimum threshold. Borrowers earning less than a minimum income threshold need not make any payments under RAP.[35] For low payment levels, interest payments are covered by the government. After 15 years, any debt still outstanding is forgiven. As in the USA, student loan debts cannot typically be expunged through bankruptcy. The official 3-year cohort default rate of 14.3% for loans with repayment periods beginning in 2008–09 was very similar to the corresponding rate of 13.4% for the USA.

3.4 Comparing Income-Contingent Repayment Amounts

Fig. 9 shows annual required payment amounts as a function of postschool income in Australia, New Zealand, and the UK, along with income-based payments on RAP in Canada and PAYE in the USA. All amounts have been translated into US dollars to ease comparison.[36] The figure clearly shows that repayments are lowest in the UK and, to a lesser extent, Australia. Canada appears to be the least generous (especially as incomes rise above $30,000); however, it is important to remember that actual RAP payment amounts never exceed standard debt-based payments. So, a student borrowing $20,000 at an interest rate of 5.5% (the current CSLP floating rate) would never be required to pay more than $2650 per year. Repayments in the USA are similarly capped; although, the current interest rate (3.96%) and corresponding annual payment ($2450) are slightly lower. Thus, for low student debt levels, Canadian and US repayments are similar to those in New Zealand at low- to middle-income levels and lower at higher incomes. Of course, debt-based payments in Canada and the USA are increasing with student debt levels. So, for example, debt-based payments for students borrowing $40,000 at current interest rates would be roughly $5300 in Canada and $4000 in the USA. In this case, payments are relatively high in Canada for borrowers with incomes between $30,000 and $60,000.

[34] In 2010–11, the Canada Student Loans Program provided $2.2 billion in loans to approximately 425,000 full-time students in all provinces/territories except Quebec, which maintains its own student financial aid system (Human Resources and Skills Development Canada, 2012).

[35] The minimum income threshold increases with family size beginning at CA$20,208 (in annual terms) for childless single borrowers.

[36] Based on September, 2014, exchange rates.

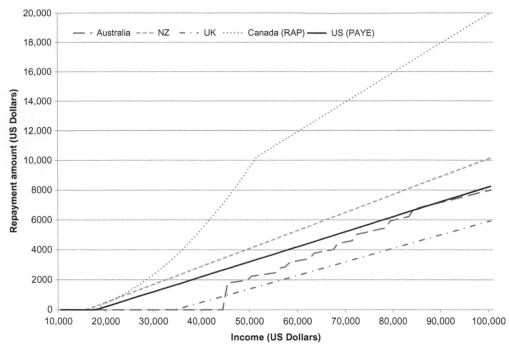

Figure 9 Income-contingent loan repayment functions for selected countries. *Notes:* All currencies translated to US dollars using Sept, 2014, exchange rates. Repayments for Canada and U.S. are for single childless persons and only reflect the income-contingent repayment amount which may exceed the debt-based payment.

4. CAN COLLEGE STUDENTS BORROW ENOUGH?

As noted in Section 2.2, an increasing number of American undergraduates exhaust their government student loan options, turning to private lenders for additional credit. The 2008 increase in Stafford loan limits effectively shifted the balance of student loan portfolios back toward government sources (see Fig. 2), but it is less clear whether this policy expanded total (government plus private) student credit. Regardless, without more regular increases in federal student loan limits, it is likely that continued increases in net tuition costs and returns to college will raise demands for credit beyond supply for many students.

While it is straightforward to measure the number of students who exhaust their government student loans — one-third of all full-time/full-year undergraduates in 2003–04 (Wei and Berkner, 2008) — the rise of private student lending over the past 20 years makes it much more difficult to determine how many potential students may be unable to borrow what they want and the extent to which constraints on borrowing distort behavior. Lochner and Monge-Naranjo (2011, 2012) argue that the increased supply of student credit offered by private lenders over the late 1990s and early 2000s likely did not meet the growing demands of many potential students.[37] However, there is little consensus regarding the extent and overall impact of credit constraints in the market for higher education.[38] We offer a brief review of evidence on borrowing constraints in the US education sector but refer the reader to Lochner and Monge-Naranjo (2012) for a more comprehensive recent review.[39]

A few studies directly or indirectly estimate the fraction of youth that are borrowing constrained. In their analysis of college dropout behavior, Stinebrickner and Stinebrickner (2008) directly ask students enrolled at Berea College in Kentucky whether they would like to borrow more than they are currently able to. Based on their answers to this question, about 20% of recent Berea students appear to be borrowing constrained. Given the unique schooling environment at Berea — the school enrolls a primarily low-income population but there is no tuition — it is difficult to draw strong conclusions about the extent of constraints in the broader US population, including those who never enroll in college. Based on an innovative model of intergenerational transfers and schooling, Brown et al. (2012) estimate the fraction of youth that are constrained based on whether they receive postschool transfers from their parents. Their estimates suggest that roughly half of all American youth making their college-going decisions in the 1970s, 1980s, and 1990s were borrowing constrained. Finally, Keane and Wolpin (2001) and Johnson (2013) use different cohorts of the National Longitudinal Survey of Youth (NLSY) to estimate similar dynamic behavioral models of schooling, work, and consumption that incorporate borrowing constraints and parental transfers. Using the 1979 Cohort of the NLSY (NLSY79), Keane and Wolpin (2001) estimate that most American youth were borrowing constrained in the early 1980s, whereas Johnson (2013) finds that few youth were constrained in the early 2000s based on the 1997 Cohort of the NLSY (NLSY97). In the latter analysis, students are reluctant to take on much debt due to future labor market uncertainty.[40] Unfortunately, the contrasting empirical approaches and sample populations used in these four studies make it difficult to reconcile their very different findings. There is little consensus regarding the share of American youth that face binding borrowing constraints at college-going ages.

---

[37] For example, private lenders almost always require a cosigner for undergraduate borrowers (Arvidson et al., 2013), so students whose parents have very low income or who have a poor credit record are unlikely to obtain private student loans.

[38] Caucutt and Lochner (2012) argue that credit constraints appear to distort human capital investments in young children more than at college-going ages.

[39] See Carneiro and Heckman (2002) for an earlier review of this literature.

[40] By contrast, Keane and Wolpin (2001) estimate very weak risk aversion among students. While the implied demands for credit are high, the costs associated with limited borrowing opportunities are low based on their estimates.

There is slightly more agreement about the extent to which binding constraints distort schooling choices. Most studies analyzing the NLSY79 find little evidence that borrowing constraints affected college attendance in the early 1980s. Cameron and Heckman (1998, 1999), Carneiro and Heckman (2002), and Belley and Lochner (2007) all estimate a weak relationship between family income and college-going after controlling for differences in cognitive achievement and family background. Cameron and Taber (2004) find no evidence to suggest that rates of return to schooling vary with direct and indirect costs of college in ways that are consistent with borrowing constraints. Even Keane and Wolpin (2001), who estimate that many NLSY79 youth are borrowing constrained, find that those constraints primarily affect consumption and labor supply behavior rather than schooling choices.

The rising costs of and returns to college, coupled with stable real government student loan limits, make it likely that constraints have become more salient in recent years (Belley and Lochner, 2007; Lochner and Monge-Naranjo, 2011). One in three full-time/full-year undergraduates in 2003–04 had exhausted their Stafford loan options, a sixfold increase over their 1989–90 counterparts (Berkner, 2000; Wei and Berkner, 2008). Despite an expansion of private student loan opportunities, family income has become an increasingly important determinant of who attends college. Youth from high-income families in the NLSY97 are 16 percentage points more likely to attend college than are youth from low-income families, conditional on adolescent cognitive achievement and family background; this is roughly twice the gap observed in the NLSY79 (Belley and Lochner, 2007). Bailey and Dynarski (2011) show that gaps in college completion rates by family income also increased across these two cohorts; although, they do not account for differences in family background or achievement levels. Altogether, these findings are consistent with an important increase in the extent to which credit constraints discourage postsecondary attendance in the USA.[41]

Although Johnson (2013) estimates that fewer youth are borrowing constrained in the NLSY97 compared to estimates in Keane and Wolpin (2001) based on the NLSY79, Johnson (2013) finds that raising borrowing limits would have a greater, though still modest, impact on college completion rates. His estimates suggest that allowing students to borrow up to the total costs of schooling would increase college completion rates by 8%.[42] Unfortunately, neither of these studies help explain the rising importance of family income as a determinant of college attendance observed over the past few decades.

---

[41] Belley and Lochner (2007) show that the rising importance of family income cannot be explained by a model with a time-invariant "consumption value" of schooling.

[42] Based on a calibrated dynamic equilibrium model of schooling and work with intergenerational transfers and borrowing constraints, Abbott et al. (2013) reach similar conclusions to those of Johnson (2013), further showing that long-term general equilibrium effects of increased student loan limits are likely to be smaller than the short-term effects due to skill price equilibrium responses and to changes in the distribution of family assets over time.

Credit constraints may also affect the quality of institutions youth choose to attend. Belley and Lochner (2007) estimate that family income has become a more important determinant of attendance at 4-year colleges (relative to 2-year schools) in recent years. However, this is not the case for income — attendance patterns at highly selective (mostly private) schools versus less-selective institutions. Kinsler and Pavan (2011) estimate that attendance at very selective institutions has become relatively more accessible for youth from low-income families due to sizeable increases in need-based aid that accompanied skyrocketing tuition levels. There is little evidence that youth significantly delay college due to borrowing constraints (Belley and Lochner, 2007).

Borrowing constraints affect more than schooling decisions. Evidence from Keane and Wolpin (2001), Stinebrickner and Stinebrickner (2008), and Johnson (2013) suggests that consumption can be quite low while in school for constrained youth. Constrained students also appear to work more than those that are not constrained (Keane and Wolpin, 2001; Belley and Lochner, 2007). Evidence from Belley and Lochner (2007) suggests that this distortion has become more important for high ability youth in recent years. Unfortunately, little attention has been paid to the welfare impacts of these distortions on youth.[43]

As we discuss further in Section 6, uninsured labor market risk can discourage college attendance in much the same way as credit constraints might. Youth from low-income families may be unwilling to take on large debts of their own to cover the costs of college when there is a possibility that they will not find a (good) job after leaving school. Indeed, standard assumptions about risk aversion coupled with estimated unemployment probabilities and a lack of insurance opportunities (ie, repayment assistance or income-contingent repayments) imply very little demand for credit in Johnson's (2013) analysis. Navarro (2010) also explores the importance of heterogeneity, uncertainty, and borrowing constraints as determinants of college attendance in a life-cycle model. His estimates suggest that eliminating uncertainty would substantially change who attends college; although, it would have little impact on the aggregate attendance rate. Most interestingly, he finds that simultaneously removing uncertainty and borrowing constraints would lead to sizeable increases in college attendance, highlighting an important interaction between borrowing limits and risk/uncertainty. The demand for credit can be much higher with explicit insurance mechanisms or implicit ones such as bankruptcy, default, or other options (eg, deferment and forgiveness in government student loans). Despite their importance, the empirical literature on schooling has generally paid little attention to the roles of risk and insurance. We examine these issues further in the remaining sections of this paper.

---

[43] The fact that schooling decisions are not affected in Keane and Wolpin (2001) suggests that the welfare impacts of the consumption and leisure distortions are probably quite small in their analysis.

5. DO SOME STUDENTS BORROW TOO MUCH?

Even if a growing number of American youth are finding it more difficult to finance the rising costs of higher education, increases in student borrowing and default rates raise concerns that some students may be borrowing too much. As we discuss further in the next section, an optimal student lending scheme should yield the same ex ante expected return from all borrowers; however, ex post returns will not generally be the same. In an uncertain labor market, unlucky borrowers will be asked to repay less, either through formal payment reductions (eg, deferment, forbearance, income-contingent repayments) or may even default. In this section, we discuss studies that empirically examine the determinants of student loan repayment and default.

In designing and evaluating student loan programs, it is important to quantify the expected payment amounts collected from different types of borrowers and to empirically identify the choices and labor market outcomes that influence actual ex post returns on student loans. Both government and private lenders are particularly interested in the ex ante expected returns on the loans they disburse. While default is a key factor affecting expected returns on student loans, other factors can also be important. For example, government student loans offer opportunities for deferment or forbearance, which temporarily suspend payments (without interest accrual in some cases). Income-contingent lending programs like "Pay As You Earn" can lead to full or partial loan forgiveness for borrowers experiencing low-income levels for extended periods, which clearly reduces expected returns on the loans. The timing of income-based payments can also influence expected returns if lenders have different discount rates from the nominal interest rates charged on the loans. Finally, the timing of default also impacts returns to lenders. It matters if a borrower defaults (without re-entering repayment) immediately after leaving school or after 5 years of payments, since the discounted value of payments is higher in the latter case. Ultimately, the creditworthiness of different borrowers (based on their background or their schooling choices) depends on their expected payment streams and not simply whether they ever enter default.

Despite the recent attention paid to rising student debt levels and default, surprisingly little is known about the determinants of student loan repayment behavior. Until very recently, the literature almost exclusively studied cohorts that attended college more than 30 years ago, measuring the determinants of default within the first couple years after leaving school.[44] Gross et al. (2009) provide a recent review of this literature. Among the demographic characteristics that have been examined, most studies find that default

---

[44] Dynarski (1994), Flint (1997), and Volkwein et al. (1998) study the determinants of student loan default using nationally representative data from the 1987 NPSAS that surveyed borrowers leaving school in the late 1970s and 1980s. Other early US-based studies analyze default behavior at specific institutions or in individual states. Schwartz and Finnie (2002) study repayment problems for 1990 baccalaureate recipients in Canada.

rates are highest for minorities and students from low-income families. The length and type of schooling also matter, with college dropouts and students attending 2-year and for-profit private institutions defaulting at higher rates. Finally, as one might expect, default rates are typically increasing in student debt levels and decreasing in postschool earnings.

A handful of very recent studies analyze student loan repayment/nonpayment among cohorts that attended college in the 1990s or later.[45] Given the important changes in the education sector and labor market over the past few decades, we focus attention on these studies; although, conclusions regarding the importance of demographic characteristics, educational attainment, debt levels, and postschool earnings for default are largely consistent with the earlier literature. In addition to studying more recent cohorts, these analyses extend previous work by exploring in detail three important dimensions of student loan repayment/nonpayment. First, using data on American students graduating from college in 1992–93, Lochner and Monge-Naranjo (2015) consider multiple measures of student loan repayment and nonpayment (including the standard measure, default) 10 years after graduation in order to better understand how different factors affect expected returns on student loans. Second, Deming et al. (2012) and Hillman (2014) use data for American students attending college in the mid-1990s and early 2000s to examine differences in default and nonpayment rates across institution types (especially for-profits vs public and nonprofits) as highlighted in Fig. 8. Third, Lochner et al. (2013) combine administrative and survey data to study the impacts of a broad array of available financial resources (income, savings, and family support) on student loan repayment in Canada over the past few years. We discuss key findings from these recent studies.

5.1 Student Loan Repayment/Nonpayment 10 Years After Graduation

Lochner and Monge-Naranjo (2015) use data from the 1993–2003 Baccalaureate and Beyond Longitudinal Study (B&B) to analyze different repayment and nonpayment measures to learn more about the expected returns on student loans to different borrowers. The B&B follows a random sample of 1992–93 American college graduates for 10 years and contains rich information about the individual and family background of respondents, as well as their schooling choices, borrowing, and repayment behavior.

Table 4 reports repayment status 5 and 10 years after graduation in B&B. In both years, 8% of all borrowers were not making any payments on their loans. In addition to default, deferment and forbearance are important forms of nonpayment, especially in the earlier period. Table 5 documents varying degrees of persistence for different repayment states. Among borrowers making loan payments (or fully repaid) 5 years after

---

[45] In addition to the studies discussed in detail, Cunningham and Kienzl (2014) examine default and delinquency rates by institution type and educational attainment for students entering repayment in 2005. Their findings are consistent with results surveyed in Gross et al. (2009).

Table 4 Repayment status for 1992–93 baccalaureate recipients 5 and 10 years after graduation (B&B)

Status	Years since graduation	
	5	10
Fully repaid	0.269	0.639
	(0.013)	(0.013)
Repaying or fully paid	0.920	0.917
	(0.008)	(0.007)
Deferment or forbearance	0.038	0.025
	(0.006)	(0.004)
Default	0.042	0.058
	(0.006)	(0.005)

Note: The table reports means (standard errors) for repayment status indicators based on the B&B sample of borrowers.
Source: Lochner and Monge-Naranjo (2015).

Table 5 Repayment status transition probabilities for 1992–93 baccalaureate recipients (B&B)

Repayment status 5 years after graduation	Repayment status 10 years after graduation		
	Repaying/ fully paid	Deferment/ forbearance	Default
Repaying or fully paid	0.939	0.020	0.040
	(0.006)	(0.004)	(0.005)
Deferment or forbearance	0.749	0.165	0.085
	(0.063)	(0.057)	(0.032)
Default	0.544	0.038	0.418
	(0.070)	(0.020)	(0.068)

Notes: The probability of each status in 2003 conditional on the status in 1998. Estimates based on the B&B sample of borrowers. Standard errors are listed in parentheses.
Source: Lochner and Monge-Naranjo (2015).

graduating, 94% remained in that state 5 years later while only 4% had entered default. Roughly half of all borrowers in default 5 years after school had returned to making payments (or fully repaid) after another 5 years, while 42% were still in default. Not surprisingly, deferment/forbearance is the least persistent state, since it is designed to provide temporary aid to borrowers in need. Among borrowers in deferment/forbearance 5 years after school, three-in-four were making payments (or had fully repaid), while 8.5% were in default 5 years later. The dynamic nature of student loan repayment status suggests that standard measures of default at any fixed date, especially in the first few years of repayment, provide a limited picture of lifetime payments and expected returns to lenders. One would expect greater persistence in nonpayment as time elapses; however, the literature is surprisingly silent on this issue.

Using student loan records, Lochner and Monge-Naranjo (2015) compute five different measures of repayment and nonpayment of student loans 10 years after graduation: the fraction of initial student debt still outstanding, an indicator for default status, an indicator for nonpayment status (includes default, deferment, and forbearance), the fraction of initial debt that is in default, and the fraction of initial debt that is in nonpayment. Analyzing the determinants of these repayment/nonpayment measures, they focus on the roles of individual and family background factors, college major, postsecondary institution characteristics, student debt levels, and postschool earnings. Table 6 reports estimates for all five repayment/nonpayment outcomes based on their most general specification that simultaneously controls for all of these potential determinants. Only variables that are statistically significant for at least one outcome are included.[46]

Among the individual and family background characteristics, only race is consistently important for all measures of repayment/nonpayment. Ten Years after graduation, black borrowers owe 22% more on their loans, are 6 percentage points more likely to be in default, 9 percentage points more likely to be in nonpayment, have defaulted on 11% more loans, and are in nonpayment on roughly 16% more of their undergraduate debt compared with white borrowers. These striking differences are largely unaffected by controls for choice of college major, institution, or even student debt levels and postschool earnings. By contrast, the repayment and nonpayment patterns of Hispanics are very similar to those of whites. Asians show high default/nonpayment rates (similar to blacks) but their shares of debt still owed or debt in default/nonpayment are not significantly different from those of whites. This suggests that many Asians who enter default/nonpayment do so after repaying much of their student loan debt. Looking across columns in Table 6, the estimated racial differences in default rates versus other (arguably better) measures of expected losses are sometimes sizeable (eg, modest black-white differences in default understate much larger differences in the fraction of initial debt that is in nonpayment) and highlight the value of looking beyond simple default rates if the goal is to better understand expected returns on student loans.

Among measures of family socioeconomic status, financial aid dependency status and parental income (when first applying for aid) are largely unimportant (and statistically insignificant so not reported in Table 6) for repayment/nonpayment after controlling for other factors. However, maternal college attendance is associated with a greater share of debt repaid after 10 years.

The B&B data reveal modest variation in repayment/nonpayment across college major choices; however, which majors are most successful in terms of repayment depends on the measure. Engineering majors owe a significantly smaller share of their debts (than "other" majors) after 10 years, while social science and humanities majors owe a larger share. Humanities majors are also in nonpayment on the greatest share of debt. Default

---

[46] The table notes detail all other variables included in the analysis.

Table 6 Effects of significant factors on student loan repayment/nonpayment outcomes 10 years after graduation

Variable	Share of UG debt still owed	Fraction in default	Fraction not paying	Default × share of debt still owed	Not paying × share of debt still owed
Black	0.216*	0.055*	0.085*	0.108*	0.158*
	(0.040)	(0.022)	(0.025)	(0.021)	(0.029)
Asian	0.107	0.072*	0.089*	0.003	0.008
	(0.062)	(0.033)	(0.038)	(0.033)	(0.045)
SAT/ACT Quartile 4	0.029	0.006	0.006	0.022	0.041*
	(0.028)	(0.018)	(0.020)	(0.015)	(0.020)
Mother some college	−0.047*	0.023	0.008	0.001	−0.014
	(0.021)	(0.014)	(0.016)	(0.011)	(0.015)
Mother BA+	−0.062*	0.003	−0.007	−0.019	−0.013
	(0.021)	(0.015)	(0.017)	(0.011)	(0.016)
Business	−0.020	−0.081*	−0.051	−0.024	−0.010
	(0.032)	(0.031)	(0.029)	(0.017)	(0.024)
Engineering	−0.090*	−0.018	−0.021	−0.016	−0.008
	(0.038)	(0.029)	(0.035)	(0.020)	(0.028)
Health	−0.007	−0.048	−0.020	−0.042*	−0.027
	(0.038)	(0.027)	(0.029)	(0.020)	(0.028)
Social Science	0.078*	−0.022	−0.014	−0.008	0.008
	(0.035)	(0.024)	(0.027)	(0.019)	(0.026)
Humanities	0.083*	0.001	0.023	0.031	0.081*
	(0.035)	(0.023)	(0.025)	(0.019)	(0.026)
HBCU	0.041	−0.005	−0.040	−0.060	−0.117*
	(0.069)	(0.038)	(0.044)	(0.037)	(0.050)
1997 earnings ($10,000)	−0.011*	−0.001	−0.003	−0.005	−0.004
	(0.005)	(0.004)	(0.005)	(0.003)	(0.004)
2003 earnings ($10,000)	−0.004	−0.008*	−0.012*	−0.001	−0.004*
	(0.003)	(0.003)	(0.003)	(0.001)	(0.002)
UG loan amount ($10,000)	0.133*	0.028*	0.039*	0.029*	0.034*
	(0.012)	(0.008)	(0.008)	(0.007)	(0.009)

Notes: The table reports estimated effects on reported repayment/nonpayment outcomes based on a sample of baccalaureate recipients in 1992–93. Outcomes are measured 10 years after graduation, and regressors are only included in this table if the estimated coefficient on that variable is statistically significant for at least one repayment/nonpayment outcome. In addition to regressors above, specifications also control for the following: gender; Hispanic; SAT/ACT quartiles 1–3; dependent status; parental income (for dependents); major indicators for public affairs, biology, math/science, history, and psychology; institutional control indicators for private for-profit and private nonprofit; Barron's Admissions Competitiveness Index indicators for most competitive, competitive, and noncompetitive; and state or region fixed effects. Standard errors in parentheses.
*$p < 0.05$.
Source: Lochner and Monge-Naranjo (2015).

rates are lowest for business majors, whereas health majors default on the lowest fraction of their debts (these are the only significantly different coefficients). In most cases, differences in these repayment measures across majors are modest compared with differences between blacks and whites. The increasing importance of college major as a determinant of earnings (Gemici and Wiswall, 2011) suggests that greater differences in repayment across majors for more recent students might be expected, but this is far from certain given the modest role of earnings differences in explaining variation in repayment/nonpayment by college major.

Not surprisingly, borrowers are less likely to experience repayment problems when they have low debt levels or high postschool earnings. As a ballpark figure for all repayment/nonpayment measures, an additional $1000 in debt can be roughly offset by an additional $10,000 in income. For example, an additional $1000 in student debt increases the share of debt in nonpayment by 0.3 percentage points, while an extra $10,000 in earnings 9 years after graduation reduces this share by 0.4 percentage points.

Given the importance of postschool earnings for repayment, one might expect that differences in average earnings levels across demographic groups or college majors would translate into corresponding differences in repayment/nonpayment rates — but this is not always the case. Despite substantial differences in postschool earnings by race, gender, and academic aptitude, differences in student loan repayment/nonpayment across these demographic characteristics are, at best, modest for all except race. And, while blacks have significantly higher nonpayment rates than whites, the gaps are not explained by differences in postschool earnings — nor are they explained by choice of major, type of institution, or student debt levels. Differences in postschool earnings (and debt) also explain less than half of the variation in repayment/nonpayment across college majors.

Despite large differences in national cohort rates between 4-year public and nonprofit schools on the one hand and for-profit schools on the other (see Fig. 8), the multivariate analysis of Lochner and Monge-Naranjo (2015) suggests little difference in repayment patterns across graduates from different types of institutions after controlling for borrower characteristics.[47] However, as noted by Deming et al. (2012), dropout rates are much higher at for-profit institutions. Since default rates are typically higher for dropouts than graduates (Gross et al., 2009), at least some of the default problem at 4-year for-profit schools may simply reflect an underlying dropout problem. We next discuss two recent studies that attempt to better understand the high observed default rates at for-profit institutions.

5.2 Default and Nonpayment at For-Profit Institutions

As Fig. 8 highlights, official cohort default rates have been highest at for-profit (and 2-year) institutions over most of the past two decades. Do the high default rates at for-profit schools indicate that these schools are doing something wrong — burdening

---

[47] Lochner and Monge-Naranjo (2015) include indicators for institutional control (public vs private non-profit vs for-profit) and college selectivity as measured by Barron's Admissions Competitiveness Index. Because coefficient estimates for all of these variables are insignificant in all specifications, they do not appear in Table 6.

their students with high debts while failing to provide a good education? Or, is it simply the case that these institutions enroll high-risk students that are more likely to experience repayment problems regardless of where they attend school? A few recent studies explore this issue.

Combining annual institution-level data on official 2-year cohort default rates with data from the Integrated Postsecondary Education Data System (IPEDS) in 2005–08, Deming et al. (2012) estimate that default rates at for-profit schools are 8.7 percentage points higher than at 4-year public schools and 5.7 percentage points higher than at 2-year community colleges, even when the sample is limited to open admission schools and differences in student composition, financial aid take-up, and various institutional offerings are accounted for.[48]

Deming et al. (2012) and Hillman (2014) use individual-level data from the Beginning Postsecondary Studies (BPS) to analyze the determinants of student loan default and nonpayment measured 5–6 years after students entered college. Both of these studies explore qualitatively similar specifications to those discussed earlier for Lochner and Monge-Naranjo (2015), so we do not discuss them in detail. We focus our discussion on the estimated differences in default or nonpayment between students attending for-profit schools versus public or nonprofit schools conditional on a broad range of other factors (eg, demographic and family characteristics, major/program type, degree received, debt levels, postschool income or unemployment).[49]

Deming et al. (2012) use the BPS cohort of first-time students entering 2-year and 4-year colleges in 2003–04 to study the impacts of attending for-profit institutions on a wide variety of educational outcomes. Accounting for a broad set of factors, they estimate that students attending for-profit schools experience higher levels of unemployment and lower earnings during the first few years after leaving school. Furthermore, for-profit students leave school with more debt and have student loan default rates that are 7–8 percentage points higher when compared with students that attended public and nonprofit schools. Hillman (2014) studies a similar sample (conditioning on similar factors) but estimates separate impacts of attending 2- and 4-year for-profit schools. His estimates suggest that students attending for-profit 2- and 4-year schools are 26% and 19%, respectively, more likely to default than students attending public 4-year colleges. One concern with both of these studies is the fact that students

---

[48] Specifically, they control for the fraction of students that are part-time, at least 25 years old, female, black, and Hispanic; the number of recipients and amounts disbursed for Pell grants and student loans; types of degree and highest degree offered; and indicators for institutional offerings of distance education, remedial course, job placement assistance, part-time employment services for students, and open admissions.

[49] Hershaff (2014) also uses individual-level data from the BPS and institution-level cohort default rate data combined with IPEDS to study differences in student loan repayment across students with Direct Loans relative to loans in the FFEL Guarantee program.

attending college for 4–5 years would have had little, if any, chance to default on their student loans by the time default is measured in the BPS.[50]

5.3 The Roles of Income, Savings, and Family Support

As we discuss further below, an efficient lending program should provide some form of insurance against uncertain labor market outcomes with payments depending on available resources. While lenders can expect some losses from impoverished borrowers, they should collect from those with adequate resources. Yet, measuring the full array of resources available to borrowers after they leave school can be challenging. Although labor market income is an important financial resource, access to other resources like personal savings, loans/gifts from families, or other in-kind assistance from families (eg, the opportunity to live at home) may be readily available.

Combining administrative data on student loan amounts and repayment with data from the Canada Student Loan Program's (CSLP) 2011–12 Client Satisfaction Surveys (CSS), Lochner et al. (2013) provide evidence on the link between a broad array of available resources (ie, income, savings, and family support) and student loan repayment in Canada. Because their data also contain questions soliciting borrowers' views on the importance of repaying student loans and the potential consequences of not doing so, they are able to account for heterogeneity in these factors when assessing the importance of income and other resources.

For perspective, the official 3-year cohort default rate of 14.3% for CSLP loans with repayment periods beginning in 2008–09 was very similar to the corresponding rate of 13.4% for the USA. More than one-in-four CSLP borrowers in their first 2 years of repayment were experiencing some form of repayment problem at the time of the CSS.

Lochner et al. (2013) estimate that postschool income has strong effects on student loan repayment for recent Canadian students. Borrowers earning more than $40,000 per year have nonpayment rates of 2–3%, while borrowers with annual income of less than $20,000 are more than 10 times as likely to experience some form of repayment problem. These sizeable gaps remain even after controlling for differences in other demographic characteristics, educational attainment, views on the consequences of nonpayment, and student debt. On the one hand, the very low nonpayment rates among borrowers with high earnings suggest that student loan repayment is well enforced in Canada. On the other hand, high delinquency and default rates among low-income borrowers signal important gaps in more formal insurance mechanisms like the CSLP's RAP.[51]

---

[50] Students have a 6-month grace period before they are expected to begin Stafford loan payments and another 9 months of missed payments before they would be considered to be in default.

[51] RAP is an income-contingent repayment scheme that reduces CSLP loan payments for eligible borrowers to "affordable" amounts no greater than 20% of gross family income. See Section 3.3 for further details on RAP.

Despite relatively high nonpayment rates for low-income borrowers, more than half of these borrowers continue to make their standard student loan payments. Other financial resources in the form of personal savings and family support are crucial to understanding this. Roughly half of all borrowers claim to have at least $1000 in savings, while 30% say they could expect to receive $2500 or more in financial support from their parents if they needed it. Low-income borrowers with negligible savings and little or no family support are more likely than not (59%) to experience some form of repayment problem, while fewer than 5% of low-income borrowers with both savings and family support do. Consistent with larger literatures in economics emphasizing the roles of savings and family transfers as important insurance mechanisms (Becker, 1991), Lochner et al. (2013) estimate that borrower income has small and statistically insignificant effects on the likelihood of repayment problems for those with modest savings and access to family assistance. By contrast, among borrowers with negligible savings and little or no family assistance, the effects of income on repayment are extremely strong. Measures of parental income when students first borrow are a relatively poor proxy for these other forms of self- and family-insurance, suggesting that efforts to accurately measure savings and potential family transfers offer tangible benefits.

Interestingly, these findings may offer an explanation for the poor repayment performance of American black students conditional on their postschool income, debt and other characteristics as discussed earlier. Given relatively low wealth levels among American blacks (Shapiro and Oliver, 1997; Barsky et al., 2002), it is likely that weaker financial support from parents at least partially explains their high nonpayment rates.

These findings also have important implications for the design of income-contingent repayment schemes. Lochner et al. (2013) estimate that expanding RAP to automatically cover all borrowers would reduce program revenues by roughly half for borrowers early in their repayment period.[52] This is because a more universal income-based repayment scheme would significantly reduce repayment levels for many low-income borrowers who currently make their standard payments. At the same time, little revenue would be raised from inducing borrowers currently in delinquency/default to make income-based payments, since the vast majority of these borrowers have very low-income levels.

Lochner et al. (2013) find that slightly more than half of all low-income borrowers have little self- or family-insurance. These borrowers currently have high delinquency/default rates and would surely benefit from greater government insurance as discussed in the next section. Yet, their results also suggest considerable caution is warranted before broadly expanding current income-contingent repayment schemes. Many low-income borrowers have access to savings and family support that enables them to make

---

[52] RAP currently requires borrowers to re-apply every 6 months with eligibility restricted to borrowers with low family income relative to their standard debt-based loan repayment amount. Any debt remaining after 15 years is forgiven. See Section 3.3 for further details on RAP.

standard payments. Lowering payments for these borrowers based on their incomes alone (without raising payment levels for others) could significantly reduce student loan program revenues. These results present important practical challenges regarding the appropriate measurement of borrower resources and the extent to which loan repayments should depend on broader family resources and transfers (to the extent possible).

6. DESIGNING THE OPTIMAL CREDIT PROGRAM

In this section, we use standard economic models to provide benchmarks on how credit and repayment for higher education should be designed in order to maximize efficiency and welfare. Using the same simple environment, we derive optimal credit contracts under a variety of incentive problems and contractual limitations. Starting from the "first best" — when investments maximize expected net income and all idiosyncratic risk is fully insured — we sequentially consider the impact on both investments and insurance of introducing limited commitment/enforcement, incomplete contracts, moral hazard (hidden action) and costly state verification (CSV). These incentive problems are standard in the theoretical literature of optimal contracts and are the staple in some applied fields (eg, corporate finance); however, only recently have they been systematically considered in studies of human capital investment as we discuss further below. We go beyond the usual approach of analyzing one incentive problem at a time, and consider models in which two or three co-exist.[53] While our analysis is largely normative, the implications of different models also provide useful insights about the observed patterns of repayment and default.

We first consider a two-period human capital investment framework with labor market risk in which we analytically characterize the nature of distortions introduced to investment and insurance by different incentive problems. At the end of the section, we discuss richer environments in which other forms of dynamic incentives and contractual issues may arise, reviewing the related literature on various incentive problems in financing human capital investment.

6.1 Basic Environment

Consider individuals that live for two periods, youth and maturity. Individuals are heterogenous in two broad characteristics: their ability, $a > 0$, and their initial wealth,

---

[53] We do not tackle the difficult problems associated with endogenous parental support discussed in the previous section. Doing so would require consideration of private information about family wealth for access to credit as in Mestieri (2012) and accounting for the hidden savings problem in the design of ex post loan repayments. This can have important implications for the optimal contract as discussed in Kocherlakota (2004) and Abraham et al. (2011); however, the contract in these environments can be quite difficult to characterize.

$W \geq 0$. Ability encompasses all personal traits relevant to a person's capacity to learn (when in school) and to produce (when working). Initial wealth, which can be used for consumption and/or investment includes not only resources available from family transfers but also potential earnings during youth. We take both a and W as given to focus on college education decisions. However, our analysis could be included in richer settings in which families invest in early schooling for children (shaping a) and deciding on bequest and inter vivos transfers (determining W).

A young person can invest in schooling, h, which augments his labor earnings in the next period. We assume that investment is in terms of consumption goods, but more general specifications in which the cost of investment is also in terms of time can be easily added without changing the substance of our results.[54] Postschool labor market earnings are given by

$$y = zaf(h),$$

where $f(\cdot)$ is a positive, increasing, continuous and strictly concave function that satisfies the Inada conditions. These assumptions ensure that investment in human capital is always positive. Ability a and the function $f(\cdot)$ are assumed to be known by everyone at the time of investing h.[55] Labor market earnings and, therefore, the returns to human capital investment are also shifted by labor market risk z, a continuous random variable with support $Z \subset \mathbb{R}_+$. The distribution of risk z is endogenous to the exertion of effort, e, by the individual. However, we assume that it is independent of (a, W) and human capital investment h. At this point, one can interpret e as either effort during school or during labor markets. What is essential is that a higher effort e leads to a higher (first order increase in the) distribution of risk z.[56]

Our baseline model assumes that z has continuous densities $\phi_e(\cdot)$ conditional effort e. For most of our analysis, we assume two levels of effort $e \in \{e_L, e_H\}$, where $e_L < e_H$; however, we briefly discuss settings with more effort options below.

Throughout this section, we assume that financial markets are competitive. Lenders, or more broadly, financial intermediaries, are assumed to be risk neutral. They evaluate streams of resources by their expected net present value, discounting future resources with a discount factor $q \in (0,1)$, the inverse of the risk-free rate $(1 + r)$. We also assume that the lender is free from incentive problems and can commit to undertake actions and deliver on contracts that ex post entail a negative net payoff. Finally, we assume

---

[54] In the context of college, it is useful to think of h as reflecting a combination of both years of schooling and quality of the institution. We clearly abstract from issues related to the tradeoff between quality and quantity of schooling to focus on the general nature of optimal loan contracts, especially the structure of postschool repayments.

[55] We, therefore, abstract from asymmetric information about ability that can lead to adverse selection. We discuss these issues below in Section 6.8.

[56] That is, for any function $p(\cdot)$ increasing in z, the conditional expectation $E[p(z)|e]$ is increasing in e.

equal discounting between the borrower and the lender (ie, $q = \beta$) to simplify the exposition.[57]

We assume that borrowers evaluate consumption/effort allocations (as of the time they decide their schooling) according to

$$u(c_0) - v(e) + \beta \int_Z u(c_1)\phi_e(z)\ dz, \tag{1}$$

where $u(\cdot)$ is the utility of consumption (an increasing and concave function) and $v(\cdot)$ is the disutility of effort (an increasing function).

We use this environment to study the optimal design of student loans. In this environment, a student loan contract is an amount of credit d given by the lender to the student in the youth period (while in school) in exchange for a repayment $D(z)$ after school from the student to the lender. The repayment $D(z)$ may depend on the realization of labor market risk z and may be negative for some z, indicating additional postschool transfers from the lender to the borrower. While we leave conditioning on all variables but z implicit, the repayment $D(z)$ may also depend on observed student characteristics as well as his investments in human capital. Along with the pair $\{d, D(z)\}$, an allocation of consumption, effort and human capital investment $\{c_0, c_1, e, h\}$ is chosen subject to the participation constraint of the lender,

$$d \leq q \int_Z D(z)\phi_e(z)\ dz. \tag{2}$$

Once discounted, the expected value (conditional on e) of repayments cover the cost of credit provided to the borrower. As for the borrower, initial consumption is given by

$$c_0 = W + d - h. \tag{3}$$

As students, individuals consume from their initial wealth W, plus resources borrowed from the lender (or deposited if $d < 0$) less resources invested in human capital. Second period consumption may be risky and is given by

$$c_1(z) = zaf(h) - D(z), \tag{4}$$

labor earnings less repayments (or plus insurance transfers from the lender if $D(z) < 0$).

In this environment, we consider a number of different incentive and contractual problems that restrict the design of $\{d, D(z); c_0, c_1, e, h\}$. We assume that initial wealth W, ability a, first period consumption c_0, and schooling investment h are always observable by creditors. However, we will consider environments in which there are limits on repayment enforcement (limited commitment), labor market outcomes $y = zaf(h)$

---

[57] Differences in discounting between the lender and the borrower lead to trends between c_0 and $c_1(z)$. Such trends could be easily added, but they would complicate the algebra without providing any additional insights.

are costly to observe (CSV), and effort e is not observable (moral hazard). In the first case, we also consider the possibility of incomplete contracts, in which repayments cannot be made contingent on labor market outcomes. We explore the optimal provision of credit and repayment design under each of these incentive problems.

6.2 Unrestricted Allocations (First Best)

The natural starting point is the case in which neither incentive problems nor contractual limitations distort investment and consumption allocations. In this case, the choice of $\{d, D(z); c_0, c_1, e, h\}$ maximizes the value of the borrower's lifetime utility (Eq. 1) subject to the break-even or participation condition for the lender (Eq. 2). The program reduces to choosing $\{d, D(z); e, h\}$, because expressions (3) and (4) pin down consumption levels in both periods.

We first derive the allocations conditional on effort and then discuss the determination of optimal effort. Consider the determination of $\{d, D(z); h\}$ conditional on $e = e_i$ for $i = L, H$ (leaving the conditioning implicit for now). From the conditions for d and $D(z)$, the optimal allocation of consumption over time satisfies

$$u'(c_0) = u'(c_1(z)). \tag{5}$$

Regardless of investment decisions, the optimal contract provides perfect insurance (ie, full smoothing of consumption over labor market risk). Since utility $u(\cdot)$ is strictly concave, the equality of marginal utilities also implies equality of consumption levels (ie, $c_1(z) = c_0$ for all z). This simple result highlights the fact that insurance is a crucial aspect of the ideal contract. When repayments can be arbitrarily contingent on the realization of risk, the optimal allocation pushes the lender to absorb all the risk. Full insurance could mean that the lender must make a positive transfer to the borrower ($D(z) < 0$) after school, even if the lender provided the financing for education and early consumption. Similarly, full insurance could mean that lucky borrowers end up paying the lender several times what they borrowed, which, as discussed below, may require an unreasonable level of commitment on behalf of borrowers.

With respect to optimal investment in human capital, combining the first-order conditions for d and h yields the condition

$$E[z|e_i]af'[h] = q^{-1}. \tag{6}$$

In the first best, the expected marginal return on human capital investment equals the risk-free rate (ie, the opportunity cost for the lender to provide credit). This result holds, because the borrower is fully insured by the lender and the lender is risk-neutral. Under these circumstances, it is natural for investment in human capital to maximize the expected return on available resources, regardless of the dispersion and other higher moments of labor market risk z.

Consider the stark predictions of this environment. Conditional on the level of effort, neither the implication of consumption smoothing in Eq. (5) nor the choice of investment in Eq. (6) depend on the individual's wealth W. First, the full insurance condition indicates that lifetime consumption profiles should be flat for all students: rich and poor, high and low ability alike. The values of W and a only determine the level of consumption, not its response to income shocks z or evolution over the lifecycle. Second, condition (6) indicates that all individuals invest at the efficient level, regardless of whether they need to borrow a lot or nothing at all. Conditional on effort, only ability a and the technology of human capital production determine investment levels. All other individual factors, including available resources W and preferences for the timing of consumption, should not influence educational investments given effort; these factors only affect the financing of investments. These sharp implications of the frictionless, complete markets model have provided the basis for various tests of the presence and importance of credit constraints.[58]

We now compare the utilities and allocations conditional on the two effort levels and determine which is optimal. Let $h^F(a, e_i)$ denote the first best level of human capital conditional on e_i (ie, the solution to Eq. (6) conditional on both levels of effort, $i = L, H$). Notice first that investments will be higher for high levels of effort, since $E[z|e_H] > E(z|e_L)$. For each effort level, the expected present value of resources for the borrower is given by $W - h^F(a, e_i) + qE[z|e_i]af[h^F(a, e_i)]$. Since the agent is fully insured, consumption in both periods would equal

$$c^F(W, a; e_i) = \frac{W - h^F(a, e_i) + qE[z|e_i]af[h^F(a, e_i)]}{1 + q}.$$

Consumption levels are strictly increasing in wealth W and ability a, as well as the expected realization $E[z|e_i]$. Since the latter is increasing in e, higher effort is also associated with higher consumption. Conditional on effort levels, the level of utilities, as of the time when investments are decided equal

$$U^F(W, a; e_i) = (1 + \beta)u[c^F(W, a; e_i)] - v(e_i).$$

Whether high effort is optimal in the first best (ie, whether $U^F(W, a; e_H) > U^F(W, a; e_L)$) depends on the counterbalance of wealth effects in the demand for consumption $c^F(W, a; e_i)$ versus the demand for leisure (ie, utility cost of higher effort). When utility is separable between consumption and effort as assumed here, leisure is a superior good. Given ability a, a sufficiently high wealth W implies that the marginal value of consumption is low, as is optimal effort (and investment). Given wealth W, individuals with higher ability would find it more desirable to exert higher effort. Thus, more able individuals would exhibit more investment due to both the direct impact of ability on earnings and the indirect impact of ability on effort.

---

[58] See Lochner and Monge-Naranjo (2012) for an overview of this literature.

We now study how different incentive problems distort investment in and insurance for human capital by reshaping the allocation of credit and the structure of repayments. To focus our discussion on these issues, we abstract from effort decisions until we introduce moral hazard in Section 6.5.

6.3 Limited Commitment

A crucial, yet often implicit, assumption in the solution of optimal credit arrangements is that both parties can fully commit to deliver their payments as contracted. In practice, borrowers sometimes default on their repayments, or at least face the temptation to do so. A rational lender should foresee these temptations and determine conditions under which default will take place. Formally, the lender can foresee the borrower's participation constraints necessary to preclude default. In this section, we consider the implications of borrower commitment problems. We first assume that repayment functions $D(z)$ can be made fully contingent on the actual realization of labor market risk z. Then, we examine the case in which these contingencies are ruled out.

6.3.1 Complete Contracts With Limited Enforcement

Limited commitment problems are often invoked for investments in education, because human capital is a notably poor collateral (Becker, 1975; Friedman and Kuznets, 1945). While human capital cannot be repossessed, the cost of defaulting on a loan might depend directly on the education of the individual as it determines his earnings. Then, the amount of credit a person could obtain would be endogenously linked to his investments in education, as these investments determine the amount of credit that the borrower can credibly commit to repay (Lochner and Monge-Naranjo, 2011, 2012).[59]

To formalize this argument, assume that once a borrower leaves school, he can always opt to default on a repayment $D(z)$ contracted earlier. But, default is not without its costs. For simplicity, assume that a defaulting borrower loses a fraction $\kappa \in (0,1)$ of his labor earnings, so his postschool consumption is $c_1^D(z) = (1 - \kappa)zaf(h)$. These losses could reflect punishments imposed by lenders themselves (eg, wage garnishments) or by others (eg, landlords refusing to rent or employers refusing to hire). Alternatively, the borrower could repay $D(z)$ yielding postschool consumption $c_1^R(z) = zaf(h) - D(z)$. For any realization z, borrowers compare the utility of these two consumption alternatives, repaying if and only if

$$u[zaf(h) - D(z)] \geq u[(1 - \kappa)zaf(h)]. \tag{7}$$

More simply, borrowers repay if and only if the cost of defaulting exceeds the repayment amount (ie, $\kappa zaf(h) \geq D(z)$).

---

[59] We only consider one-sided limited commitment problems where the lender can fully commit. This is natural when considering the optimal design of government credit arrangements.

Obviously, if reneging on the debt were costless ($\kappa = 0$), then no student loan market could be sustained, since no borrower would ever repay. Similarly, if κ is high enough, the temptation to default could be eliminated, and we would be back to the first best.

The restrictions (Eq. 7) can be seen as *participation constraints* on the borrower. As long as they are satisfied, the credit contract ensures that the borrower remains in the contractual arrangement. Any contract in which default occurs can be replicated by a contract without default by setting $D(z) = \kappa z a f(h)$. Since default is costly for the borrower and the lender does not necessarily recover all of those losses, optimal contracts in this setting would always prevent default. The optimal lending contract is similar to the first best problem only restricted so that condition (7) holds for all $z \in Z$.

Let $\lambda(z)$ be the Lagrange multipliers associated with the inequality (Eq. 7) for any realized z.[60] The optimal program maximizes the value of the borrower's lifetime utility (Eq. 1) subject to the break-even or participation condition for the lender (Eq. 2), the expressions (3) and (4) for consumption during and after school, and inequality (Eq. 7) for all $z \in Z$.

The first-order optimality conditions for this problem are straightforward. The optimal repayment value $D(z)$ conditional on the realization z implies the following relationship between $c_1(z)$ and c_0:

$$u'(c_0) = [1 + \lambda(z)]u'[c_1(z)].$$

For states of the world in which the participation constraint is not binding (ie, $D(z) < \kappa z a f(h)$), $\lambda(z) = 0$ and there is full consumption smoothing: $c_1(z) = c_0$. However, when the participation constraint is binding, $\lambda(z) > 0$ and $c_1(z) > c_0$. The participation constraint restricts the repayment that can be asked of the borrower for high labor market realizations. In turn, those restrictions limit the capacity of the student to borrow resources while in school, resulting in low school-age consumption relative to postschool consumption in high-earnings states.

From the first-order conditions for d and h, one can show that optimal human capital investment satisfies

$$af'[h]E\left[z\left(\frac{1+\kappa\lambda(z)}{1+\lambda(z)}\right)\right] = q^{-1}. \tag{8}$$

Notice that $E\left[z\left(\frac{1+\kappa\lambda(z)}{1+\lambda(z)}\right)\right] < E[z]$ as long as $\kappa < 1$ and some of the participation constraints bind (ie, $\lambda(z) > 0$) for some realizations of z. Comparing Eqs. (8) to (6), it is clear that, given concavity in $f(\cdot)$, the inability to fully commit to repayment reduces human capital investment below the first best level. The presence of limited commitment

---

[60] The multipliers are discounted and weighted by probabilities (ie, the term $q\phi(z)\lambda(z)$ multiplies the condition (7) for each z).

reduces the expected return on human capital due to the inability to effectively borrow against returns in the highest earnings states or to spread the resources from those states to other states with fewer resources.

In contrast to the unrestricted environment above, family resources W are a determinant of investment levels under limited commitment. Individuals with low wealth levels will want to borrow more while in school. This raises desired repayment amounts $D(z)$ in all future states, causing participation constraints to bind more often and more severely. Thus, poorer students face greater distortions in their consumption and investment allocations than wealthier students.

It is important to understand the nature of credit constraints that arise endogenously from the participation constraints associated with commitment problems. As with any other model of credit constraints, this environment predicts inefficiently low early consumption levels for those that are constrained (ie, a first-order gain could be attained by increasing early consumption and reducing postschool consumption for some labor market realizations). A more unusual aspect of constraints in this environment is that they arise due to an inability to extend insurance to fully cover high earnings realizations. The participation constraints do not restrict the ability to smooth consumption across adverse labor market outcomes, since the contract allows for negative repayments for low enough realizations of z. Rather, the limits arise due to the incentives of borrowers to default on high payments associated with strong positive earnings outcomes. The lender must reduce requested repayments in those states to drive the borrower to indifference between repaying and defaulting. This reduction in repayments must be met with less credit up front.[61] Finally, it is important to note that default never formally happens in equilibrium, because repayments $D(z)$ are designed to provide as much insurance as possible while avoiding default.

The ability to write fully contingent contracts is important for many of these results. As we show next, contracts and borrower behavior differ substantially if the repayment function $D(z)$ cannot be made contingent on labor market realizations.

6.3.2 Incomplete Contracts With Limited Enforcement

Now, consider the same contracting environment, only add the restriction that repayments cannot be made contingent on labor market realizations z. Instead, assume that any lending amount d is provided in exchange for a "promise" to repay a constant amount D. However, as in the previous section, the borrower retains the option to default, which will be exercised if it is in his best interest ex post. Of course, lenders are aware of this and

---

[61] An interesting illustration of limited commitment is the failure of Yale's Tuition Postponement Option, which was implemented in the 1970s and finally rolled back in 1999. The most successful participants "bought out" of their commitment to pay 4% of their income as specified by the plan. See http://yaledailynews.com/blog/2001/03/27/70s-debt-program-finally-ending/.

incorporate this possibility into the contracts they write. For simplicity, we assume that lenders do not recover any payments when borrowers default.[62]

With incomplete contracts, just two amounts (d, D) must balance multiple trade-offs. On the one hand, the fact that contracts cannot provide explicit insurance against downside risks leaves the option of default to take on that role, at least partially. On the other hand, borrowers no longer have an incentive to default when they experience high earnings realizations, since the repayment amount does not increase with earnings. As a result, limited commitment with incomplete contracts may generate default from borrowers with low earnings as an implicit — and imperfect — form of insurance against downside labor market risks. This insurance is implicitly priced by lenders as they incorporate the probability of default in the amount of credit d that they offer in exchange for a defaultable promise to repay a given amount D.

To develop the optimal contract, consider a person with ability a who enters the labor market with human capital investment h and student debt D. The decision of whether to honor the debt or default on it depends on the labor market realization z. If the borrower repays, his postschool consumption is $c_1(z) - zaf(h) - D$, while it is $c_1(z) = (1 - \kappa)zaf(h)$ if he defaults. The borrower is better off repaying when the realization z equals or exceeds the threshold

$$\tilde{z} \equiv \frac{D}{\kappa af(h)};$$

otherwise, he would be better off defaulting. Prior to learning z, the probability of default is given by $\Phi(\tilde{z}) = \int_0^{\tilde{z}} \psi(z)dz$. At the time schooling and borrowing/lending decisions are made, default is a stochastic event with the probability increasing in the amount of debt and decreasing in the borrower's ability and investment. Both ability and investment determine the borrower's earnings potential and are important factors for the credit contract.

Contemplating the probability of being defaulted upon, the participation constraint for the lender becomes

$$d \leq qD[1 - \Phi(\tilde{z})]. \tag{9}$$

The right-hand side is the discounted expected net repayment, where we have assumed that the lender receives zero in case of default. Borrowers pay an implicit interest rate of $D/d = q^{-1}[1 - \Phi(\tilde{z})]^{-1}$, which is increasing in the probability of default.[63]

---

[62] Assuming that the lender recovers a fraction of the defaulting costs simply adds an additional term in the break-even condition for the lender. See Lochner and Monge-Naranjo (2012) and the discussion in Section 6.6.2.

[63] Students with high enough wealth W may choose to save $(d < 0)$ receiving payment $- d/q$ after school.

The expected utility for a student with wealth W and ability a who invests h in his human capital, borrows d, and "promises" to repay D is

$$u[W + d - h] + \beta \left\{ \int_0^{\tilde{z}} u[(1-\kappa)zaf(h)]\phi(z)dz + \int_{\tilde{z}}^{\infty} u[zaf(h) - D]\phi(z)dz \right\}. \quad (10)$$

The first term reflects utility while in school, and the rest reflects expected postschool utility over both repayment and default states. Maximizing the borrowers utility (Eq. 10) subject to the lender's participation constraint (Eq. 9), the first-order conditions for d and D (after some basic simplifications and use of the expression for $\tilde{z}$) produce the following condition:

$$u'(c_0) = \frac{E\left[u'(c_1(z))|z > \tilde{z}\right]}{1 - \eta(\tilde{z})\frac{\tilde{z}}{D}},$$

where $\eta(\tilde{z}) \equiv \dfrac{\phi(\tilde{z})}{1 - \Phi(\tilde{z})} > 0$ is the hazard function for labor market risk z.[64] In this model, borrowing or lending does not lead to the standard Euler equation for the permanent income model (ie, $u'(c_0) = E[u'(c_1)]$), because here each additional unit of borrowing increases the probability of default and raises implicit interest rates. Even if early consumption is low relative to expected future consumption, borrowers may not want to take on more debt because of worsening interest rates on inframarginal dollars borrowed.

The first-order condition for investment h can be re-written as

$$E[z]af'(h)\left[\frac{E[zu'(c_1(z))] - \kappa\Phi(\tilde{z})E[zu'(c_1(z))|z < \tilde{z}]}{E[z]u'(c_0)\left[1 - qD\phi(\tilde{z})\,\tilde{z}\frac{f'(h)}{f(h)}\right]}\right] = q^{-1}.$$

Limited commitment with incomplete contracting produces a wedge (the term in brackets) between the expected marginal return to human capital and its marginal cost.

---

[64] The first-order conditions are as follows:

$$[d] : u'(c_0) = \lambda$$

$$[h] : u'(c_0) + \lambda q D\phi(\tilde{z}|e_H)\frac{\partial \tilde{z}}{\partial h} = \beta af'(h)\left\{(1-\tilde{\kappa})\int_0^{\tilde{z}} zu'\left[(1-\tilde{\kappa})zaf(h)\right]\phi(z|e_H)dz + \int_{\tilde{z}}^{\infty} zu'[zaf(h) - D]\phi(z|e_H)dz\right\}$$

$$[D]: \lambda\left[q(1 - \Phi(\tilde{z}|e_H)) - q\phi(\tilde{z}|e_H)\frac{\partial \tilde{z}}{\partial D}\right] = \beta\left\{\int_{\tilde{z}}^{\infty} u'[zaf(h) - D]\phi(z|e_H)dz\right\},$$

where λ is the Lagrange multiplier on the lender's participation constraint.

The human capital investment wedge consists of four distinct economic forces. The first two derive from the nature of constraints that arise when defaulters are disciplined via losses that depend on their earnings. First, human capital returns are reduced by a fraction κ in states that trigger default. This implicit tax on earnings unambiguously discourages investment. Second, human capital investments improve credit terms by reducing the likelihood of default. This force is captured by the expression $1 - qD\phi\big(\tilde{z}|e_H\big)\,\tilde{z}\dfrac{f'(h)}{f(h)} < 1$ in the denominator. This "credit expansion" effect encourages human capital investment. The third force derives directly from market incompleteness, which limits consumption smoothing. Imperfect insurance leads to a negative covariation between labor market realizations z and their valuation $u'(c_1)$, since c_1 is increasing in z. Hence, $E[z \cdot u'(c_1)] < E[z] \cdot E[u'(c_1)]$. This reduces the marginal value of investment relative to the case with full insurance, since individuals are unable to optimally allocate the uncertain returns on their investments across postschool labor market states. The fourth force comes from the fact that $u'(c_0) > E\big[u'(c_1(z))|z > \tilde{z}\big]$ (ie, that school-age consumption is too low relative to some postschool states when the returns of human capital arrive). Unless the credit expansion effect is particularly strong, it seems likely that this environment would yield under-investment in human capital and a positive relationship between family wealth W and human capital.

Combined with limited commitment, the absence of repayment contingencies has a number of important empirical and policy implications. First, as indicated already, default can occur in equilibrium. Second, if default occurs, it is for low realizations of z when both earnings and consumption are low. Third, the option of default serves a useful insurance role, since by defaulting, the borrower can maintain a higher level of consumption when his labor market outcomes are poor. Thus, eliminating default may be inefficient and could even reduce investment in human capital. Fourth, the probability of default is explicitly linked to the ability and educational investment decisions of borrowers. More able borrowers who invest more in their human capital, all else equal, should have lower default rates. Fifth, the model also shows how student loan terms and repayments need to be adjusted for the probability of default. The implicit interest rate is

$$q^{-1}\left[1 - \Phi\left(\frac{D}{\kappa a f(h)}\right)\right]^{-1}$$
, an equilibrium object that depends on ability a and human capital investment h, as well as the distribution of labor market shocks z, because of their impacts on the default rate.

Despite the simplicity and many attractive features of this framework, it is difficult to justify the lack of any explicit contingencies on either theoretical or empirical grounds. Theoretically, such an assumption requires prohibitively high costs of writing contracts or an inability of lenders to observe anything about the labor market success of borrowers. Empirically, we observe explicit (albeit limited) income contingencies in repayment in both government and private student loan markets as described in Section 3.

The model also abstracts from other important incentive problems that can distort human capital accumulation and its financing. We discuss several of these problems in the next few sections.

Finally, this framework is a weak normative guide, since it abstracts from a primal component on the design of student loan programs — the structure of loan repayments $D(z)$ — even when incorporating contingencies on repayment is costly.

6.4 Costly State Verification

Instead of arbitrarily ruling out contingent repayments, we now consider an environment in which lenders must pay a cost $\vartheta \geq 0$ to observe/verify the borrower's postschool earnings. Contingencies become costly, because the repayment $D(z)$ cannot be made contingent on z unless there is verification. If there is no verification, then the repayment is a fixed amount $\bar{D}$, which implicitly depends on the amount borrowed. To explore this friction in isolation, we abstract from other incentive problems until Section 6.6. The environment in this section is, therefore, a straight adaptation of Townsend's (1979) CSV model to the study of human capital and student loans.

As in Townsend (1979), we can solve for the optimal contract by considering truthful revelation mechanisms that specify a contingent repayment $D(z)$ in cases of verification, and a constant repayment $\bar{D}$ in all others.[65] It can be shown that, since contingencies in $D(z)$ are driven by insurance motives, verification will only occur for low realizations of $z < \bar{z}$, where the optimal value of threshold $\bar{z}$ must trade-off the provision of insurance against the cost of verification. Recognizing this, the participation condition for the lender can be written as

$$d \leq q\left[\int_0^{\bar{z}} D(z)\phi(z)dz - \vartheta\Phi(\bar{z}) + \bar{D}[1 - \Phi(\bar{z})]\right]. \qquad (11)$$

---

[65] More formally, as the borrower uncovers his realization z in the labor market, he makes an announcement $\hat{z}$ to the lender. Upon this announcement, the lender can either: (i) verify the announcement ($\chi(\hat{z}) = 1$) at cost ϑ to learn the true outcome and execute a payment $D^v(z, \hat{z})$ that depends on the realized and announced labor market outcomes; or (ii) not verify the borrower's announcement ($\chi(\hat{z}) = 0$), avoiding the cost ϑ, and request a repayment $D^a(\hat{z})$ based only on the announced $\hat{z}$. We assume that the lender can commit to carry out prespecified verification policies $\chi : Z \rightarrow \{0, 1\}$ that map announcements to verification decisions. The borrower knows this policy and therefore, knows the set of announcements that trigger verification and those that do not.

It is easy to see that the lender would not be able to tell apart different announcements for which $\chi = 0$. Borrowers that avoid being verified would announce the $\hat{z}$ associated with the lowest repayment. Therefore, for all states of the world in which there is no verification, the borrower repays $\bar{D} = \inf_{\{z : \chi(z) = 0\}}\{D^a(z)\}$. It is also the case that, upon verification, the lender can provide as much insurance as needed. The optimal contract would also rule out detectable deviations, for example, by setting zero consumption for borrowers they catch in a lie (ie, $z \neq \hat{z}$).

The first term in brackets reflects expected payments received (or paid if $D(z) < 0$) from the borrower if there is verification, while the second term reflects the expected costs of verification. The third term reflects expected repayments when there is no verification. Given any $\{d, D(z), \bar{D}, h\}$, a borrower's expected utility is

$$u[W + d - h] + \beta\left[\int_0^{\bar{z}} u[zaf(h) - D(z)]\phi(z)dz + \int_{\bar{z}}^{\infty} u[zaf(h) - \bar{D}]\phi(z)dz\right]. \quad (12)$$

The optimal student loan contract in this setting maximizes Eq. (12) subject to Eq. (11). Combining the first-order conditions for d and $D(z)$ yields

$$u'(c_0) = u'(c_1(z)) \text{ for } z < \bar{z}.$$

The optimal contract provides full consumption smoothing ($c_1(z) = c_0$) across school and postschool periods for "bad" states of the world in which verification occurs. Once z is truthfully learned by both parties, it is optimal for the risk neutral lender to absorb all residual risk. While left implicit above, borrower's characteristics such as ability a and wealth W, as well as aspects of the environment like verification costs ϑ and the distribution of labor market risk $\phi(z)$, determine the set $[0, \bar{z}]$ for which this takes place. These factors also affect the level of consumption c_0 for the early period and for the states of verification.

The previous result is useful to derive the optimal region for verification. Consumption $c_1(z)$ does not exhibit a jump at the threshold $\bar{z}$, because this would mean that the borrower could deviate and attain a first-order gain. The condition $c_1(\bar{z}) = c_0$ imposes a direct link between $\bar{z}$, $\bar{D}$, and c_0 in the form $\bar{z} = \dfrac{c_0 + \bar{D}}{af(h)}$. Since increases in the level of consumption under verification c_0 or in the required payment in the absence of verification $\bar{D}$ both increase the value of verification for the borrower, the region of verification must also increase to satisfy the lender's participation constraint. The verification region decreases with investment, because h improves the distribution of consumption under nonverification $c_1(z)$, which discourages verification.

With these conditions, the optimal loan program can be solved entirely in terms of $\{c_0, \bar{D}, h\}$. Let ψ denote the Lagrange multiplier on the lender's participation constraint (Eq. 11).[66] The first-order conditions for this problem imply that c_0 (consumption during school and after when there is verification) is set so that

---

[66] The concentrated Lagrangian in terms of $\{c_0, \bar{D}, h\}$ is

$$L = u(c_0) + \beta\left[u[c_0]\Phi(\bar{z}) + \int_{\bar{z}}^{\infty} u[zaf(h) - \bar{D}]\phi(z)dz\right]$$
$$+ \psi\left\{W + q\left[af(h)\int_0^{\bar{z}} z\phi(z)dz - (\vartheta + c_0)\Phi(\bar{z}) + \bar{D}[1 - \Phi(\bar{z})]\right] - h - c_0\right\},$$

where $\bar{z} = \frac{c_0 + \bar{D}}{af(h)}$.

$$u'(c_0) = \psi \left\{ 1 + \left[\frac{q \vartheta \phi(\bar{z})}{1 + q \Phi(\bar{z})} \right] \frac{1}{af(h)} \right\}. \tag{13}$$

The second term in braces represents the increased verification costs associated with a higher c_0. Aiming to save on costs of verification, the optimal contract reduces the level of c_0 and, therefore, student loan amounts. Similarly, after some simplification, the optimal level of $\bar{D}$ leads to the following condition

$$E[u'(c_1(z)) \mid z \geq \bar{z}] = \psi \left\{ 1 - \eta(\bar{z}) \frac{\vartheta}{af(h)} \right\}, \tag{14}$$

where $\eta(\cdot)$ is the hazard rate as defined above. As with c_0, the fixed level of debt repayment $\bar{D}$ is reduced also with the aim of reducing verification costs.

From expressions (13) and (14), it is clear that $u'(c_0) > E[u'[c_1(z)] \mid z \geq \bar{z}]$, and the implied behavior of consumption is consistent with the usual notion of credit constraints. This is also the case when we look at implications for optimal investment in human capital. From the first-order condition for h, we can show that investment in human capital satisfies

$$E[z] af'(h) \left\{ 1 + \left[\frac{1 - \Phi(\bar{z})}{E[z]} \right] \left(\left[1 - \frac{\vartheta \eta(\bar{z})}{af(h)} \right] \frac{\mathrm{Cov}[z, u'(c_1(z)) \mid z \geq \bar{z}]}{E[u'(c_1) \mid z \geq \bar{z}]} + \left[\frac{\vartheta \eta(\bar{z})}{af(h)} \right] E[\bar{z} - z \mid z \geq \bar{z}] \right) \right\}$$
$$= q^{-1}.$$

Notice that two distinct wedges reduce the marginal value of human capital and discourage investment. The first wedge arises from imperfect insurance and risky human capital investments, which generates a negative covariance between labor market outcomes and the marginal value of those returns for the borrower. The second wedge reflects the fact that higher investment levels lead to more verification, which is costly.

Costly verification of income yields an endogenous form of market incompleteness in which lenders require the same payment from all borrowers who receive "good" labor market shocks. In this respect, the model is similar to the limited commitment framework above, which exogenously rules out all explicit income contingencies (Section 6.3.2). However, the distinction between endogenous partial market incompleteness due to costly verification and exogenous full market incompleteness with limited commitment is quite important, since these two models yield very different implications for borrowers who receive adverse labor market outcomes. In the incomplete markets model with limited commitment, these unlucky borrowers enter default, which entails additional losses or penalties and reduces consumption levels below income levels. By contrast, under CSV, unlucky borrowers are audited and receive full insurance.

Empirically, we certainly observe default in countries without fully income-contingent loan programs like the USA and Canada. However, many borrowers with low postschool earnings also receive significant reductions in their payments through forbearance or deferment. Others also take advantage of more explicit income-contingent plans for low earners. Still, even low income borrowers do not appear to receive full insurance from student loan programs.[67] As we see next, introducing other forms of asymmetric information can help in understanding when this imperfect insurance might be desirable.

6.5 Moral Hazard

A college education not only requires readily observable investment expenditures like tuition, fees, and materials (h in our setting), but it also requires other student-specific inputs that may be more difficult to measure and control, like effort and the choice of school and courses appropriate for a student's talents and potential.[68] While these actions may be crucial for a successful college experience, they may also be "hidden" or difficult to control and monitor by lenders. We incorporate these hidden actions by explicitly modeling a costly effort e. When the lender does not observe this effort, a "moral hazard" problem can arise, as the costs of effort fall entirely on the borrower while the ensuing returns can be shared between the student and the creditor.

To examine the design of student loan contracts to deal with these incentives, we re-consider the determination of effort. Recall our assumption: High effort is costly, $v(e_H) > v(e_L)$, but also productive in that it improves the distribution of labor market shocks z. That is, the distribution of labor market risk under high effort dominates (in the first-order sense) the distribution under low effort. Even stronger, we assume a monotone likelihood ratio, that is, $l(z) \equiv \phi_{e_L}(z)/\phi_{e_H}(z)$ is strictly decreasing. We also assume that the support of z is the same under both levels of effort so there are no perfectly detectable deviations (realizations of z that can happen under one but not the other effort level). We restrict $l(z)$ to be bounded from below and from above.

The moral hazard problem arises, because the level of effort e cannot be directly controlled by the lender. Therefore, the level of investment h, the amount of credit d, and repayments $D(z)$ must be designed so that the borrower finds it in his own best interest to exert the effort expected by the creditor. For now, we consider a model in which moral hazard is the sole incentive problem. We defer to Section 6.6 cases in which moral hazard interacts with previously discussed contractual frictions.

Consider first a student with ability a and wealth W that faces a contract $\{d, h, D(\cdot)\}$ offered by a lender that expects he will exert the high level of effort, e_H. If the student conforms, he obtains an expected utility level equal to $U_H = u(c_0) - v(e_H) + \beta E[u[zaf(h) - D(z)]|e_H]$. If he instead deviates and shirks, his

---

[67] It is important to note that other forms of social insurance (eg, unemployment insurance, welfare) may effectively deliver a fixed minimal consumption level for a range of low postschool income levels.

[68] While we emphasize effort in school, our analysis applies equally to unobservable effort in the labor market (eg, job search effort) or to the tradeoff between higher-paying jobs and those that may be more appealing on other grounds (Rothstein and Rouse, 2011).

expected utility is $U_L = u(c_0) - v(e_L) + \beta E[u[zaf(h) - D(z)]|e_L]$. If the high effort e_H is to be implemented, the contract $\{d, D(z), h\}$ must satisfy the following *incentive compatibility constraint (ICC)* $U_H \geq U_L$:

$$[v(e_L) - v(e_H)] + \beta\left[\int_0^\infty u[zaf(h) - D(z)][\phi_{e_H}(z) - \phi_{e_L}(z)]dz\right] \geq 0. \qquad (15)$$

The optimal student loan contract is found by choosing $\{d, D(z); e, h\}$ to maximize the expected utility of the borrower (Eq. 1) subject the break-even or participation condition for the lender (Eq. 2) and the accounting expressions for consumption in both periods, Eqs. (3) and (4). If the optimal contract requires high effort from the student, then condition (15) must also be satisfied. Relative to the first best, the provision of insurance must give way, at least partially, to rewards for the student's success.

Let $\mu \geq 0$ denote the Lagrange multiplier associated with condition (15). Combining the first-order conditions for d and $D(z)$, it is straightforward to obtain the relationship

$$u'[c_1(z)][1 + \mu(1 - l(z))] = u'(c_0) \qquad (16)$$

between current and future consumption for any labor market outcome z. Since the likelihood ratio $l(z)$ is monotonically decreasing, when the ICC (Eq. 15) is binding, $\mu > 0$ and postschool consumption $c_1(z)$ is strictly increasing in z.[69] The economics underlying this result are clear: since effort is unobservable, the only way for the contract to induce high effort is to reward higher earnings with higher consumption. This is effective, because high realizations of z are more likely with high effort while low realizations of z are more likely with low effort. The lender must adhere to this rule in order to induce high effort even if he knows that the contract always induces high effort. The downside of these contracts is that unlucky students must bear low consumption even when they have exerted high effort. Finally, notice that if high effort is not optimal so the contract need not induce it, then $e = e_L$, $\mu = 0$, and full insurance can be provided: $c_1(z) = c_0$.

The first-order condition for human capital investment h can be written as

$$qaf'(h)\{(1 + \mu)E[zu'(c_1(z))|e_H] - \mu E[zu'(c_1(z))|e_L]\} = u'(c_0). \qquad (17)$$

On the left-hand side, the first term inside braces denotes the value of earnings from additional human capital. A term weighted by μ is added, because investments help relax the ICC. In the same vein, the negative term multiplied by μ reflects the negative impact on the ICC that arises from a higher value on the option to shirk. The right-hand side is simply the marginal cost of one unit of investment.

---

[69] If the likelihood ratio is declining enough in z, it is possible that optimal payments are decreasing over some z.

Interestingly, using the consumption optimality condition (16), we can replace the values for $u'[c_1(z)]$ in terms of $u'(c_0)$ and the ratio $l(z)$. After simplifying, the condition (17) reduces to the first best condition

$$af'(h)E[z|e_H] = q^{-1}.$$

As long as the contract induces the first best level of effort $e = e_H$, it also yields the first best level of investment h. More generally, it is optimal to design the contract so that the first best investment amount is chosen for whatever effort is exerted. Importantly, this implies that if the repayment schedule $D(z)$ is well-designed and can induce appropriate effort, the education prospects of students that need to borrow are the same as those coming from richer families that can self-finance their education. The "cost" of borrowing for economically disadvantaged students comes in the form of imperfect insurance.

The key with moral hazard is in the design of $D(z)$, which can be a difficult task. It is useful to illustrate this point using the well-known CRRA utility function $u(c) = \dfrac{c^{1-\sigma}}{1-\sigma}$ with $\sigma > 0$. The postschool consumption schedule (Eq. 16) becomes

$$c_1(z) = c_0[1 + \mu(1 - l(z))]^{1/\sigma},$$

which is delivered by setting the repayment to

$$D(z) = zaf(h) - c_0[1 + \mu(1 - l(z))]^{1/\sigma}.$$

Given the condition that $l(0) > 1$, the contract yields $c_1(z) < c_0$ for low values of z. That is, unsuccessful students experience a fall in their consumption after school. However, notice that some insurance is still being provided, as $D(z)$ may be negative. On the contrary, for high values of z, the likelihood ratio $l(z) < 1$, so successful students are rewarded with an increase in their consumption.

Even with this specific functional form, it is not possible to say much about the shape of $c_1(z)$ except that it is increasing. Likewise, except for the fact that $D(z)$ might be negative at low values of z, little more can be said regarding its shape unless more information is available on the distribution of labor market outcomes and the risk preferences of borrowers. In fact, not even the monotonicity of $D(z)$ can be established. A reliable empirical characterization of risks and preferences is necessary to characterize even the most general features of optimal student loan programs.

Thus far, we have emphasized the case in which high effort is optimal. This need not be the case if, for example, either a or W is so low that most of the resources generated by investment need to be repaid to the lender, leaving little for the borrower to consume. Low effort might also be efficient for very high wealth individuals, who place more value on leisure (ie, low effort) than the extra consumption that comes from exerting higher effort. If low effort is optimal, then investment for those exerting low effort is set to the first best under low effort: $af'(h)E[z|e_L] = q^{-1}$; since the ICC is not binding, $\mu = 0$ and full insurance is provided (ie, $c_1(z) = c_0$ for all z). The problem of moral hazard only distorts investment choices for those who are discouraged from putting forth high effort when it would otherwise be optimal. Since utility associated with high effort is distorted due to imperfect insurance while utility associated with low effort is not, there will be a set of (W,a) values for which effort and investment choices are distorted by moral hazard.

The sharp result that *conditional on effort* investment is not distorted (relative to the first best) generalizes to any number of potential effort choices. Additionally, if any two individuals with the same ability end up exerting the same effort, then they will also make the same educational investment yielding the same distribution for labor earnings, regardless of their family wealth.[70] However, the finding that either consumption or investment is distorted, but not both simultaneously, is special to the model with two effort levels. With a continuum of effort levels (and some regularity conditions), effort will generally be discouraged and the optimal contract will distort both investment and consumption relative to the first best.

Rather than exploring a richer structure for moral hazard, we now direct our discussion to the less explored environments in which moral hazard co-exists with other primal incentive problems, CSV and limited commitment.

6.6 Multiple Incentive Problems

In this section, we examine the optimal design of student loan programs in environments in which multiple incentive problems co-exist.

6.6.1 Costly State Verification and Moral Hazard

Consider now the case in which both the effort e of the student cannot be observed by the lender and the actual labor market outcome can only be verified by the lender at a cost $\vartheta > 0$. The loan contract must be designed to address both of these information frictions to provide as much insurance as possible to the borrower while making sure the creditor is repaid in expectation.

Because of the cost ϑ, the optimal verification policy will preserve the threshold property of Section 6.4: If the borrower realizes a labor market outcome z below a threshold $\bar{z}$, the lender will verify the outcome at cost ϑ and request repayment $D(z)$ (which can be negative) that is contingent on z. Otherwise, if $z \geq \bar{z}$, the lender will not bother to verify and the borrower repays a fixed amount $\bar{D}$. In both cases, the repayment can be set as a function of previously determined and known variables such as d, a, and h; however, we leave this conditioning implicit. Expressions for the lender's participation constraint (Eq. 11) and borrower's expected utility (Eq. 12) are the same as for the CSV model above.

---

[70] Similarly, suppose two individuals possess the same ability level but one lives in an environment with moral hazard and the other does not. If their wealth levels are such that they both end up exerting the same effort level, they will both make the same investment.

The contract must also induce the optimal level of effort. If low effort e_L is optimal, then there is no moral hazard problem and the optimal contracts are of the pure CSV case studied in Section 6.4. However, if high effort e_H is to be induced, then the contract must satisfy an ICC modified by the threshold property of the verification policy. That is, the expected discounted gains from better labor market outcomes should more than compensate the student for the cost of effort:

$$\beta\left[\int_0^{\bar{z}} u[zaf(h) - D(z)]\left[\phi_{e_H}(z) - \phi_{e_L}(z)\right]dz + \int_{\bar{z}}^{\infty} u[zaf(h) - \bar{D}]\left[\phi_{e_H}(z) - \phi_{e_L}(z)\right]dz\right]$$
$$\geq v(e_H) - v(e_L).$$

$$(18)$$

Given a student's ability a and wealth W, the optimal loan contract sets d, h, $\bar{z}$, $\bar{D}$, and $D(z)$ for $z < \bar{z}$ aiming to maximize Eq. (12) subject to the break-even constraint (Eq. 11) and the ICC (Eq. 18). As argued in the pure CSV case, consumption should not jump at the threshold of verification, so $c_1(\bar{z}) = \bar{z}af(h) - \bar{D}$. Therefore, we can write $\bar{D} = \bar{z}af(h) - c_1(\bar{z})$, and solve for it as a function of the threshold $\bar{z}$.

The first-order conditions for the amount of credit d and repayments $D(z)$ in a state of verification imply

$$u'[c_1(z)][1 + \mu(1 - l(z))] = u'(c_0) \quad \text{for all} \quad z < \bar{z},$$

$$(19)$$

where μ is the Lagrange multiplier on Eq. (18). When verification occurs, we recover exactly the same relationship between marginal utilities of consumption (and, therefore, consumption distortions) as in the pure moral hazard case (given μ).[71] Here, verification does not generally yield full consumption smoothing (as in the CSV model) due to the need to incentivize effort. However, if the conditional distributions of low-income realizations (ie, $z < \bar{z}$) are quite similar across effort levels, then $l(z)$ will be relatively flat in the relevant region and considerable consumption insurance can be provided at the low end of the income distribution. Moral hazard is less of a concern at high income realizations, since verification does not take place and payments are independent of income for $z \geq z$. For high z, consumption allocations are such that $u'[c_1(z)][1 + \mu(1 - l(z))] < u'(c_0)$.

The first-order condition for z implies that the threshold is set according to the condition

$$\frac{\partial \bar{D}}{\partial \bar{z}} = \vartheta\eta(\bar{z}|e_H)\left[\frac{u'(c_0)}{u'(c_0) - E[u'(c_1(z))(1 + \mu[1 - l(z)]) \mid z \geq \bar{z}; e_H]}\right],$$

$$(20)$$

where $\eta(\cdot|e_H)$ is again the hazard function as defined above (evaluated at $\bar{z}$ here) conditional on high effort. The left-hand side represents the increased fixed payment $\bar{D}$ needed when setting a higher verification threshold; the right-hand side compounds the increased

---

[71] However, note that the values of μ, c_0 and the range of z for which Eq. (19) holds now depend on the verification cost ϑ.

expected cost of verification with a measure of the consumption distortion outside the verification region. For $\vartheta > 0$, the latter (term in brackets) is greater than zero but less than one.

Finally, with respect to the optimal investment in human capital, the first-order condition for h can be written as

$$
E[z|e_H]af'(h)\left[\frac{E[\min\{z,\bar{z}\}|e_H]}{E[z|e_H]} + \frac{E\{[z-\bar{z}]u'[c_1(z)][1+\mu(1-l(z))]|z\geq\bar{z}; e_H\}}{E[z|e_H]u'(c_0)}\right]
$$
$$
= q^{-1},
$$

(21)

which is derived using condition (19) for $z < \bar{z}$. Verification costs leave upside risk uninsured, so the term inside brackets is strictly less than one, and investments in this environment are lower than the first best.

The combination of CSV and moral hazard produces a useful benchmark for the design of optimal student loan arrangements. On the one hand, this framework incorporates the desire to save on verification and other administrative costs. When income verification is costly, it should only occur when labor market outcomes are particularly low. In these cases, the commitment of lenders to verify some of the lower reports by the borrower provides them with the right incentives to truthfully report those states to reduce their payments. Doing so, the program can provide at least some insurance for the worst labor market realizations, precisely when borrower's are most in need of it. On the other hand, moral hazard implies that even for these unlucky borrowers the optimal arrangements must sacrifice some insurance and consumption smoothing in order to incentivize effort. Moral hazard also reduces the value of verification itself, since the ability to provide insurance is limited.

While the optimality conditions can be algebraically cumbersome, the general structure of the optimal contract is quite simple. To illustrate this point, consider the CRRA specification used earlier. For some positive values μ, c_0, and $\bar{z}$ (which should depend on a borrower's ability and wealth), the loan repayment is

$$
D(z) = \begin{cases} zaf(h) - c_0[1+\mu(1-l(z))]^{1/\sigma} - \vartheta & \text{if } z < \bar{z} \\ \bar{D} & \text{if } z \geq \bar{z} \end{cases}
$$

yielding postschool consumption

$$
c_1(z) = \begin{cases} c_0[1+\mu(1-l(z))]^{1/\sigma} & \text{if } z < \bar{z} \\ zaf(h) - \bar{D} & \text{if } z \geq \bar{z}. \end{cases}
$$

Above a certain threshold, the borrower absorbs all upside risk, paying a constant amount independent of z; however, downside risk is shared between the borrower and the lender. Absent moral hazard concerns, risk neutral lenders would absorb all downside risk; however, with moral hazard, it is optimal to make borrowers bear some of the downside risk to help incentivize effort. If low realizations are the smoking gun of low effort, then little insurance can be provided.

Finally, it is important to recognize that even if the contract is optimally designed, insurance may be quite limited and human capital will be lower than under full insurance in the first best. This naturally implies that human capital investments will be responsive to family wealth W among borrowers. Yet, such a relationship does not necessarily imply an inefficiency in existing credit arrangements, but instead it may signal that information or commitment frictions are important in the student loan market.

6.6.2 Limited Commitment: Default or Additional Constraints?

The previous arrangement was derived under the assumption that both the borrower and the lender could fully commit to any postschool payments. As we saw in the pure limited commitment model above, relaxing this assumption can have important implications for the optimal student loan arrangement. We now explore the interactions between limited commitment, moral hazard, and CSV — the three main credit market frictions we have considered. As above, assume that the borrower can always default on the repayment to the lender, but that doing so entails a cost that is proportional to his income. In addition to the lender's break-even or participation constraint and the incentive compatibility constraint, the contract must also respect the no-default restrictions $D(z) \leq \kappa z a f(h)$ for all z if default is to be avoided. As discussed below, however, default may sometimes be an optimal feature of contracts with costly verification.

Consider first the case with costless income verification ($\vartheta = 0$), but when both moral hazard and limited commitment constrain contracts. The optimal contract maximizes Eq. (1) subject to the participation condition for the lender (Eq. 2), the ICC condition (Eq. 15), and the no-default constraints (Eq. 7). As above, let μ be the Lagrange multiplier associated with the ICC and $\lambda(z)$ the multiplier associated with Eq. (7) for each z.

Following the same steps as in the previous models, the optimal allocation of consumption must satisfy

$$u'[c_1(z)][1 + \mu(1 - l(z)) + \lambda(z)] = u'(c_0).$$

For those states in which Eq. (7) does not bind, $\lambda(z) = 0$ and consumption smoothing is distorted only to induce high effort as in the pure moral hazard case. On the contrary, if the no-default constraint (Eq. 7) does bind, then $c_1(z) = (1 - \kappa)z a f(h)$ and the impact of $\lambda(z) > 0$ and $\mu > 0$ must be accommodated via lower borrowing d (and school-age consumption c_0) and lower human capital investment h, which must now satisfy the condition

$$E\left[z\left(\frac{1 + \mu(1 - l(z)) + \kappa\lambda(z)}{1 + \mu(1 - l(z)) + \lambda(z)}\right)\bigg|e_H\right] a f'(h) = q^{-1},$$

where the term in brackets is less than $E[z|e_H]$ if the no-default constraint binds for any z. Thus, incorporating limits on contract enforceability produces under-investment in human capital when there is moral hazard even if the efficient amount of ability is induced. As in the case without moral hazard (see Section 6.3.1), individuals under-invest, because they cannot spread the rewards from investment in very high-income states to other states nor can they fully borrow against these states. Moral hazard can further reduce investment relative to the pure limited commitment case, especially for individuals who are not induced to provide the efficient amount of effort.

Importantly, when $\vartheta = 0$, the ability to set $D(z)$ fully contingent on the realization z rules out default in equilibrium. Any contract that involves default in some states can always be replicated by a contract in which the borrower repays $\kappa zaf(h)$ in those states, which would make the lender strictly better off and the borrower no worse off. The fact that the lender can be made better off implies that he can also offer a better contract to the borrower that eliminates default.

This is not necessarily true when verification is costly (ie, $\vartheta > 0$). With costly verification, there will be some z for which the lender verifies the borrower's announced outcome (denoted by the indicator function $\chi(z) = 1$) and others for which he does not ($\chi(z) = 0$). In the latter case, the repayment is a constant amount $\bar{D}$ independent of z. For the set of all other realizations, the lender verifies and requests a payment of $D(z)$. Altogether, the borrower has three options once he observes z: (i) repay $\bar{D}$ without asking for verification; (ii) request verification and pay/receive an amount $D(z)$ that depends on z; or (iii) default and forfeit a fraction $\kappa zaf(h)$ of his income. In case (iii), the lender receives nothing.

Given repayment contract $\{D(z), \bar{D}\}$, the borrower will choose to default whenever $\kappa zaf(h) < D(z)$ in verification states and $\kappa zaf(h) < \bar{D}$ in nonverification states. Yet, lenders know this and will take it into account when designing contracts. On the one hand, it is possible that the optimal contract would set both $\bar{D}$ and $D(z)$ below $\kappa zaf(h)$ for all relevant values of z, thereby precluding default as when $\vartheta = 0$. On the other hand, with nonnegligible verification costs, it is possible that default is preferred by both borrower and lender alike for some realizations of z.

Under what conditions might default arise under optimal contacts? To answer this question, it is useful to think about default as just another repayment state or as part of a contract. For default to occur in equilibrium, it has to be that *both* borrowers and lenders would be better off if the borrower opts to default. For borrowers to prefer defaulting, repayment must be more costly than default, $D(z) > \kappa zaf(h)$. For lenders to prefer default, the cost of verification ϑ must exceed payments under verification. Taken together, default is only possible (though not assured) when $\vartheta > \kappa zaf(h)$.

Default becomes more attractive to lenders if they can capture some of the defaulting borrowers losses. To explore this possibility, suppose the borrower still loses a fraction κ of his income upon default, but assume that the lender can recover a fraction $\kappa^0 \leq \kappa$ of those losses.[72] That is, lenders recover $\kappa^0 zaf(h)$ from defaulted loans. If the lender chooses to verify, at most he would receive a payoff of $\kappa zaf(h) - \vartheta$ once verification costs are subtracted. Ex post, the lender would prefer to be defaulted upon if z falls below a threshold z^A defined by

---

[72] For example, it may be easier for lenders to collect penalties from defaulters with high income even if they do not actually verify their income.

$$z^A = \frac{\vartheta}{(\kappa - \kappa^0)af(h)}.$$

Among other things, this threshold reiterates the fact that default should not occur if verification is costless, since this implies $z^A = 0$. An alternative extreme arises when $\vartheta > 0$ and the lender captures all default losses, $\kappa^0 = \kappa$. If so, $z^A \to \infty$, and a lender would ex post always prefer to abandon the lending contract rather than verify it. However, this does not mean that verification never occurs. Ex ante, the lender may want to offer and *commit to deliver on* a contract in which $D(z)$ is low, or even negative for some z, in order to provide valuable insurance.

Default should be seen as an option for the lender in his design of the repayment function $D(z)$. The lender can always set the value of $D(z)$ below the cost of default and preclude that action by the borrower. The option of setting the repayment $D(z)$ above the default cost $\kappa z af(h)$ for some z, allows the lender to avoid having to pay the verification cost. This option can be used to save on verification costs and ultimately, allow lenders to offer better contracts to borrowers.

Altogether, the design of the optimal repayment function $\{\bar{D}, D(z)\}$ must meet a number of constraints and objectives: it must ensure that the expected repayment less any verification costs (plus any amounts received in the case of default) cover the lender's cost of funds; it must balance the provision of insurance with incentives to encourage effort by the student; and it must properly weigh the costs of verification with losses associated with default.[73] Like verification, default is one possible tool or option for the lender.

---

[73] Recall $\chi : Z \to \{0,1\}$ is an indicator function if there is verification ($\chi = 1$) or not ($\chi = 0$). Similarly, let $\xi : Z \to \{0,1\}$ be the indicator function of whether the participation condition of the borrower is binding ($\xi = 1$) or not ($\xi = 0$). Then, the break-even condition of the lender becomes

$$d \leq q \int_{z_i} \left\{ (1-\xi)[\chi(D(z) - \vartheta) + (1-\chi)\bar{D}] + \xi \kappa^0 z af(h) \right\} \phi_{e_H}(z) \, dz. \tag{22}$$

It can be shown that full repayment must occur for an upper interval $[\bar{z}, \infty)$. Hence, the expected discounted utility of the borrower is given by

$$u(c_0) + \beta \left[\int_0^{\bar{z}} \left\{ \xi u[c^D(z)] + \chi u[c^V(z)] \right\} \phi_{e_H}(z) \, dz + \int_{\bar{z}}^{\infty} u[z af(h) - \bar{D}] \phi_{e_H}(z) \, dz \right], \tag{23}$$

where $c^D(z) = (1-\kappa)z af(h)$ and $c^V(z) = z af(h) - D(z)$, are the consumption levels in the cases of default and verification, respectively. Finally, using Eq. (23), we can derive the relevant ICC for the optimal contracting problem.

The optimal contract maximizes initial utility (Eq. 23) subject to the break-even constraint (Eq. 22) of the financial intermediary, and subject to the relevant ICC (not derived here). Without loss of generality, we assume that contracted payments satisfy the participation constraints (Eq. 7) even in cases of default. However, in this case, default occurs whenever the constraints (Eq. 7) bind, because the borrower is indifferent between requesting verification or defaulting and the lender is strictly better off not having to verify. In those cases, $D(z) = \kappa z af(h)$. On the other hand, when Eq. (7) are slack and there is verification, then $D(z)$ is set according to the condition (19) as in the model when limited commitment is not a binding constraint. The threshold $\bar{z}$ for full repayment and the human capital investment level are set according to similar expressions as Eqs. (20) and (21) but with corrections for the regions of default.

In practice, optimal student loan contracts in this environment could be specified in different ways. Most simply, a student loan contract would specify a fixed payment $\bar{D}$; however, a borrower could always request a reduced repayment, have his income verified, and then pay the income-based amount $D(z)$. A borrower who fails to repay or ask for the income-based payment would be considered in default, triggering the specified punishments. This general structure characterizes the US and Canadian Government student loan programs as discussed in Section 3; however, these programs do not condition repayments explicitly on ability a and investment h as the optimal contract would.

We now discuss repayment patterns in terms of verification (V), default (D), and full repayment (R). We consider the most tractable case in which $\kappa^0 \rightarrow \kappa$, and $\vartheta > 0$, so $z^A = \infty$. The shape of the likelihood function $l(z)$ can give rise to a number of possibilities as shown in Fig. 10. In all four cases, the horizontal axis represents labor income realized after school, $zaf(h)$. The vertical axis reflects the level of consumption for

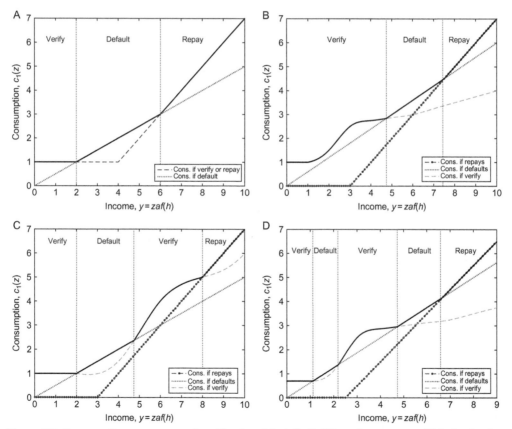

Figure 10 Consumption patterns and verification (V), default (D), and repayment (R) behavior in a model with costly state verification, moral hazard, and limited commitment. (A) No moral hazard: V, D, R. (B) Moral hazard: V, D, R. (C) Moral hazard: V, D, V, R. (D) moral hazard: V, D, V, D, R.

alternative responses of the borrower: fully repay (dashed line), default (dotted line) or partial payment $D(z) < \bar{D}$ based on verification (dash-dot line) as given by condition (19). The continuous line in each graph represents the upper envelope of these different responses (ie, the equilibrium postschool consumption level for the borrower).

Panel (A) reflects the case without moral hazard. In this case, the borrower asks for verification when earnings are low, triggering a repayment/transfer designed to yield him the same consumption as during school. For high earnings, he would rather just repay the constant amount $\bar{D}$. If default occurs, it is only for intermediate labor market outcomes. A similar pattern can arise when moral hazard is present, as shown in panel (B). Because higher effort is associated with better outcomes in the labor market, consumption under verification is strictly increasing in realized income, as required by the ICC on effort.

Panel (C) of Fig. 10, shows that a very different pattern can also emerge. If the function $l(z)$ is relatively flat at the low end of outcomes but particularly steep in the intermediate range (ie, effort has weak effects on the likelihood of low-income realizations but strong effects on the likelihood of intermediate realizations), then there can be two separate verification regions separated by a region of default. In this case, the region of default includes low to intermediate outcomes. Finally, as shown by panel (D), multiple regions of verification and default can alternate before reaching the full repayment region. This could happen when the function $l(z)$ switches multiple times from convex to concave and multiple steep regions of consumption under partial repayment lead to multiple crossings of this function with consumption under default.

Notice that for all possibilities, verification occurs at the low end of income realizations. This highlights two crucial aspects of the optimal contract. First, providing insurance for the worst income realizations is quite valuable. Second, default can be a useful but imperfect insurance tool that is always dominated by partial insurance at the very low end. Also, notice that full repayment is always the preferred option for high labor market outcomes. When labor market outcomes are very high, the marginal value of insurance is quite low. Given the desire to save on verification costs, a constant repayment amount is preferred to providing additional insurance and paying those costs. Furthermore, the losses associated with default grow with income, making a constant payment preferable to both borrower and lender.

6.7 Extensions With Multiple Labor Market Periods

Our two-period model abstracts from a number of interesting issues that would arise in a dynamic lifecycle setting in which loans are repaid over multiple periods after schooling. These issues arise when the incentive problems discussed in our two-period model remain active after borrowers finish school and enter labor markets. An extensive literature has studied variants of these dynamic incentive problems (eg, Chapters 20 and 22 in the textbook of Sargent and Lungqvist (2012)), although most of this literature has abstracted from the endogenous formation of human capital. We now briefly overview the main results from this literature and draw implications for the optimal design of student loan repayment. Throughout this discussion, we maintain the assumption that borrowers and lenders have the same rate of discount.

Begin by considering a multi-period extension of our model with no postschooling incentive problems. In particular, assume that after the exertion of effort e and investment h during school, both the borrower and lender observe the parameters and initial draw of the stochastic process $\{z_t\}_{t=1}^{T}$ that governs labor market and other risks during postschool years. With complete contracts, the structure of the contract will be essentially the same as in our two-period model. Since repayments in every period can be made fully contingent on the earnings realization, the borrower will be perfectly insured, consuming a constant amount every period. All risk is absorbed by the lender, who must receive a flow of repayments that fully covers the loan (in expected present value). Next, consider incomplete markets. In this case, the consumption allocation is given by a permanent income model in which the so-called natural borrowing limit — the maximum amount of debt that can always be repaid, even under the worst case realizations of $\{z_t\}_{t=1}^{T}$ — is determined by the amount invested in human capital.

Now, consider environments with limited commitment. As in the two-period model, the amount of repayments — and initial debt — may be limited by the outside option of the borrower, which might now be a concern in multiple periods. Generalizing our results on consumption allocations with complete markets, if the temptation to default is slack for some realization in any postschooling period, then consumption must equal that of the previous period. Yet, consumption smoothing is imperfect, since consumption must increase whenever the option to default is binding. Hence, consumption follows a nondecreasing path. In general, the set of states of the world for which consumption smoothing holds grows over time. Indeed, it is possible that at some point before retirement, consumption is fully smooth for all possible realizations of labor market risk. Repayments are designed so that the lender absorbs as much risk as possible — all of it when the participation constraint does not bind. In expectation, repayments must be declining over time, since they are permanently lowered every time the participation constraint binds.

Things can be quite different when moral hazard (hidden action) associated with labor market participation limits insurance. The optimal design of repayments will seek to use current and future consumption allocations to induce the borrower to exert optimal effort. In general, the ICCs bind when the borrower has the temptation to exert lower effort or to request a reduced repayment (or higher transfer from the lender). In these cases, the ICCs prescribe that the higher current consumption today must come at the cost of a reduction in all future consumption levels. On average, the borrower's consumption must be decreasing over time. Put another way, repayments to the lender must be increasing, on average, over time. This is commonly referred to as the "immiseration result."

There are cases in which the trend to higher repayments ends, such that consumption and repayments converge to a constant. In a paper that we discuss further below, Monge-Naranjo (2016) extend the model of unemployment insurance with moral hazard of Hopenhayn and Nicolini (1997) by allowing for a previous period of investment in human capital (with or without moral hazard during school). Thus, the model is designed to analyze how student loans should cope with a major risk for educational investments: unemployment following graduation from school. Monge-Naranjo (2016) demonstrate that the optimal credit arrangement should provide insurance to the borrower immediately after school, during the first period of unemployment, by providing transfers while the student finds a (suitable) job. However, those transfers should be declining as the unemployment spell continues. In this simple environment, all jobs are permanent, so as soon as the student finds employment, he should start repaying the lender a constant amount. The repayment amount should be set higher the longer the student had been unemployed. These two features of the optimal student loan contract provide some insurance to students while properly incentivizing them to look for jobs soon after graduation. In principle, the optimal contract could greatly enhance investments in human capital and improve the welfare of youth in need of financing to attend college.

6.8 Related Literature

Our model generates a number of lessons on how to design student loans that are self-financed, provide insurance, and optimally address a number of incentive problems, including limited commitment, moral hazard, and CSV. This framework not only generates endogenously restricted borrowing, but it also produces interesting patterns in terms of repayment and default. Some of these aspects deserve further exploration. Our analysis also omits a number of important incentive problems and the potential interactions of student loans with other public and private institutions. In particular, we have abstracted from issues of adverse selection (prior private information of borrowers about their potential returns on human capital or their willingness to repay), taxes, subsidies and other government interventions in credit markets, as well as social welfare programs like unemployment insurance. Rather than trying to tackle all of these issues within our framework above, we review recent and ongoing work in each of these areas.[74] For reasons of space, we only discuss the research most closely related to our objectives in this monograph.

---

[74] Friedman and Kuznets (1945) first raise the issue of income-contingent loans to deal with uncertainty and limited commitment problems, while Nerlove (1975) offers an early analysis of ex ante adverse selection and ex post moral hazard in reference to such loans.

A series of papers by Ionescu (2008, 2009, 2011), analyzes models with contractual frictions and incentive problems. The primary objective of these papers is to study college enrollment, borrowing, and default decisions when credit is subject to limited commitment and moral hazard. The analysis is directed specifically to existing government student loan programs and suggests that default rates are not generally higher among individuals that are most financially constrained. Instead, those that are constrained appear to be more restricted in terms of investment and borrowing. Most interestingly, she considers the impact of various forms of repayment flexibility (eg, lock-in low interest rates, switching to income-contingent repayments, or alternative bankruptcy discharges) in calibrated versions of her models. Consistent with our analysis above, she finds that the degree to which contingencies (repayment flexibilities) can be incorporated into student loan repayment schemes can have significant effects on schooling and welfare. More than hard borrowing constraints, the lack of insurance can be the limiting factor for schooling decisions.

Chatterjee and Ionescu (2012) consider student loans that offer insurance against the risk of failing college, a nontrivial risk for recent US college cohorts. Using a model that accounts for both adverse selection and moral hazard, their quantitative analysis suggests that offering loan forgiveness when a student fails college can lead to significant welfare gains without adverse impacts on enrollment or graduation rates. If forgiveness is also provided to students that choose to leave college without necessarily failing, the welfare gains are still positive but lower than under conditional forgiveness. Unconditional forgiveness raises enrollment and graduation but is less efficient because of the adverse incentives it produces.

Related and complementary work by Eckwert and Zilcha (2012) and Hanushek et al. (2014) studies the impacts of alternative repayment arrangements and government interventions in the market for student loans. Eckwert and Zilcha (2012) consider different repayment contracts in a model where individuals' abilities are heterogeneous and publicly known, but there is also exogenous labor market risk.[75] They abstract from borrowing for consumption purposes and from family transfers, further requiring that all investment expenditures must be borrowed. Using a three-period-lived overlapping generations (OLG) model, they contrast the resulting human capital, welfare and growth outcomes from three different student loan repayment schemes: (i) standard loan with fixed interest rate (ie, no insurance); (ii) insurance with pooling across abilities (ie, payments are a function of realized income but not initial ability), so there is cross-subsidization from high to low ability types; and (iii) insurance within ability groups, so there is no ex ante cross-subsidization. Their analysis produces two important conclusions. First, providing insurance conditional on ability (regime iii) is better for human capital investment, growth and welfare relative to a standard loan scheme (regime i).

---

[75] Alternatively, we can think of initial ability as a signal of true ability realized upon labor market entry.

Second, risk–pooling conditional on ability (regime iii), relative to unconditional pooling (regime ii), improves educational outcomes and also improves welfare as long as individuals are not too risk averse. Both of these conclusions highlight the importance of insurance and its counterbalance with proper incentives.

Hanushek et al. (2014) use a three-period-lived OLG environment with heterogeneity in ability, exogenous borrowing constraints, and intergenerational bequests to evaluate the implications of different stylized education policies for economic efficiency, inequality, and intergenerational mobility. In their framework, interventions can be welfare improving due to the borrowing constraint and the lack of insurance against uncertain labor market outcomes. They consider uniform education subsidies, merit-based subsidies, need-based subsidies, and loans with income-contingent repayment. Regarding the latter, students are restricted to borrow the full cost of college (or not at all) and must repay a constant fraction of their postschool income. While this structure, like that of government student loan programs in many countries, provides a limited form of insurance, it can also generate an adverse selection problem by encouraging lower ability students to attend (and borrow) for college even if their labor market returns are low. Their calibrated model produces a number of interesting results. First, merit aid performs poorly in terms of both equity and efficiency, because parental income and ability are highly correlated. Second, an income-contingent loan may end up subsidizing low ability children from well-off parents at the cost of high ability children from poor parents, because the latter repay more than the former. This highlights the problems with loan programs that effectively pool individuals of different abilities with ex ante cross-subsidization. Third, while income contingent loans can perform quite well in providing insurance and reducing inequality, a sizeable need-based aid program can perform better in terms of equity and efficiency. Finally, they demonstrate that general equilibrium responses to policy through changing skill prices are nontrivial.

Abbott et al. (2013) also study education subsidies and standard student loan programs (with debt-based repayments and no default) in a richer OLG general equilibrium environment with full lifecycles, incomplete markets, postschool labor market uncertainty, and inter vivos transfers. Based on their calibrated model, they conclude that current student loan programs in the USA improve welfare over the alternative of no government lending. However, further expansions of traditional student loans (without any income-contingencies) would have very minor effects on education choices and welfare.[76] Contrary to Hanushek et al. (2014), Abbott et al. (2013) do not consider different student loan repayment schemes; however, they do find that general equilibrium responses are important in evaluating policies.

---

[76] Keane and Wolpin (2001) and Johnson (2013) also find modest effects of expanding current loan limits (without income contingencies), while Navarro (2010) finds that expanding both loan limits and extending full insurance could have very large effects on enrollment decisions.

Adverse selection is the central focus of Del Rey and Verheyden (2013). They consider a number of policy interventions in an economy with competitive credit contracts under limited commitment, adverse selection (due to heterogeneous unobserved ability), and labor market risk. Different equilibria may arise depending on the degree of contract enforcement, for example, separating equilibria with some insurance if enforcement is high; pooling equilibria with no insurance (but with ex post default) with moderate punishments. The student loan market collapses if enforcement is too weak.

Del Rey and Verheyden (2013) highlight a number of policy insights. For example, a government subsidy to banks can lead to some credit in equilibrium even when enforcement is so weak that student credit markets would not survive in laissez faire. Also, by requiring universal participation and limiting private competition, the government might be able to enforce pooling across individuals of different ability/risk and provide partial insurance. However, as in Eckwert and Zilcha (2012), this would entail taxing high ability students to subsidize those of low ability. One concern is the extremely stylized nature of their model, binary choices and outcomes for nearly every dimension (eg, invest/not invest, successful/failure in school, high/low ability, borrow full schooling costs vs no investment/borrowing) and the extent to which their main results would hold in more realistic environments.

The papers mentioned thus far consider specific policy interventions without necessarily deriving optimal policies. Related to this, it is relevant to recall that the traditional problem of optimally designing taxes and other government transfer programs has been revisited over the last 15 years by the "New Dynamic Public Finance" literature, which has moved away from the Ramsey tradition (taking a set of taxes as given) toward the Mirrleesian tradition (deriving optimal taxes from an incentive-constrained contracting problem).[77] A few papers in this tradition (Bohacek and Kapicka, 2008; Bovenberg and Jacobs, 2011; Kapicka, 2014; Kapicka and Neira, 2014; Stantcheva, 2014) have included endogenous human capital formation in their analyses of optimal taxation, considering education subsidies as instruments to cope with tax distortions.

Most papers within the Mirrleesian paradigm derive optimal nonlinear taxes in environments in which labor income is observed but the underlying combination of ability, effort and human capital is not observed. Therefore, taxes must be set entirely as a function of observed earnings even if it would have been desirable to tax effort, ability, and human capital separately (the latter may or may not be observed). Taxes are set to maximize a welfare function, typically utilitarian, subject to an incentive compatibility constraint on each individual, to ensure that high ability (and/or human capital if unobserved) types do not exert low effort and impersonate a low ability (and/or human capital) type.

---

[77] See Golosov et al. (2007) for an overview of this literature.

Within the Mirless tradition, Stantcheva (2014) considers a model in which human capital is accumulated with both, real resources (eg, tuition) and training time (eg, on-the-job training). Labor market earnings are determined by not only human capital and labor effort, but also a stochastic yet persistent ability term. Her model allows for fairly general wage functions, which can change over time. Stantcheva (2014) assumes that the government does not observe ability (neither its initial realization nor its lifetime evolution).

In Stantcheva's framework, it is optimal for the government to subsidize human capital expenses, counterbalancing distortions on the taxation of wage and capital income, encouraging labor supply, and providing insurance against adverse draws of productivity in the labor market. Whether full deductibility of education expenses is optimal depends on whether the ability elasticity of wages is increasing in education. Similarly, whether training time must be deducted from taxes depends on whether labor effort raises (learning-by-doing) or lowers (on-the-job training) future earnings. While the optimal taxation program is quite complex, Stantcheva (2014) reports numerical results which suggest that simple linear age-dependent policies can come fairly close to the second best and that full deductibility of expenses might be close to optimal.

The public finance literature with optimal education subsidies and progressive taxes tackles the same basic economic problem as our optimal contracting formulation, namely, transferring resources across time (postschool to the schooling period) and across different postschool earnings realizations. Despite sharing similar objectives, the two formulations have notable differences in their emphases. First, the Mirrleesian problem assumes a utilitarian objective, such that redistribution across ex ante heterogeneous but unobserved abilities is an important aspect of the optimal policy. In our optimal contract formulation above, ability and wealth are observable and each loan must be paid in expectation. Therefore, the resulting allocations can be implemented by private markets or by the government. Moreover, it is straightforward to handle observed wealth heterogeneity in the optimal contracting formulation,[78] Some of the optimal allocations in the Mirrleesian framework may require the authority to tax or to regulate participation in markets, since as illustrated by the failure of the "Yale Plan" discussed above, students with the best earnings prospects may simply not join or find a way to drop out. Second, the public finance literature uses as instruments grants or deductions and progressive taxes, while the optimal contract formulation specifies loan amounts and their implied repayments. The bridge between the two formulations is illustrated by recent work by Findeisen and Sachs (2013, 2014) and Gary-Bobo and Trannoy (2014). They use a Mirrleesian problem to derive the optimal repayment for different loans from a menu available to borrowers. The menu of loans must be designed to deal with adverse

---

[78] In this respect, see the work of Mestieri (2012) that considers unobserved heterogeneity in both wealth and ability, giving rise to a role for entry exams.

selection and moral hazard (ex ante and ex post heterogeneity) including unobserved effort exertion while in the labor market.

The work by these two sets of authors is highly complementary. Gary-Bobo and Trannoy (2014) consider a more stylized environment (two ability types) and are able to prove that the optimal arrangement entails incomplete insurance (because of moral hazard as in our model) and typically involves cross-subsidization across students of ex ante different ability levels. More interestingly, loan repayments cannot be decomposed as the sum of an income tax (depending only on ex post earnings) and a loan repayment (depending only on student debt). Therefore, optimal loan repayments must be income-contingent, or equivalently, income tax must comprise a student loan tax.[79] Findeisen and Sachs (2013) consider a richer environment with a continuum of types.[80] Their numerical results also point to income-contingent repayment of loans. Most interestingly, they find that optimal repayment schemes for college loans can be well-approximated by a schedule that is linearly increasing in income up to a threshold and constant afterwards. This is somewhat similar to our model of moral hazard with CSV, but it is driven by the provision of ex ante incentives as opposed to saving on verification costs. The results of Findeisen and Sachs (2013) support our main conclusion that the welfare gains from optimally designed income-contingent repayment can be significant.

The work of Findeisen and Sachs (2013, 2014) and Gary-Bobo and Trannoy (2014) complements that of Hanushek et al. (2014) by characterizing the optimal repayment of loans given the specified economic environment. However, these papers abstract from risk and other life-cycle aspects that modern quantitative macro models consider essential. In this respect, Krueger and Ludwig (2013a,b) restrict attention to a class of parameterized taxes (constant marginal taxes with nonzero deductions) and uniform subsidies in order to find the best tax scheme within a richer life-cycle environment. Specifically, Krueger and Ludwig (2013a,b) use a model that allows for endogenous human capital formation, borrowing constraints and income risks with (exogenously) incomplete financial markets and no default.[81] Krueger and Ludwig find that the degree of tax progressivity and the education subsidy that would maximize a utilitarian welfare function are larger than in the current US status quo.

In addition to income taxes, there are a number of other government and private institutions that may also interact with student loan programs. In ongoing work (eg, Monge-Naranjo, 2016), we study the design of optimal student loan programs with and without the integration of unemployment insurance. This work considers a framework with an initial schooling investment choice and a multi-period postschool labor market with search frictions. After leaving school, individuals face labor market risk in

---

[79] Unfortunately, their analysis does not include differences in family wealth.

[80] Findeisen and Sachs (2014) enrich this setting further to deal with multiple dimensions of heterogeneity.

[81] They abstract from parents' inter vivos transfers and from wealth effects in labor supply.

terms of unemployment duration and moral hazard in job search as in Hopenhayn and Nicolini (1997). School success can also be distorted by hidden effort.

As in the models analyzed above, borrowing and investment are increasing in ability and optimal borrowing helps finance consumption during school. A number of interesting considerations and results arise from the optimal contract. First, borrowing and investments are set trying to minimize the possibility of "debt overhang," that is, situations in which debt is so high relative to potential income that it discourages the borrower from seeking (and maintaining) employment so much that it reduces expected payoffs for both the borrower and lender. Second, insurance is provided not only in the form of positive transfers to the unemployed but also in the form of time-varying repayment as a function of unemployment duration. The repayment must increase (in present value) with the duration of unemployment to encourage job seeking by the borrower. Third, the optimal contract delivers higher investments and (potentially greatly) higher welfare than other suboptimal arrangements, such as autarky, unemployment insurance alone, or the case in which unemployment insurance is not integrated with student loan repayment.[82] Finally, the optimal arrangement that arises from this environment highlights the importance of properly handling inter-temporal incentives. In particular, it suggests that as formulated, the debt-forgiveness component of current and newly proposed income-contingent repayments (eg, Dynarski and Kreisman, 2013), can unravel the incentives of young indebted workers early on. If so, arbitrary time-dependent debt forgiveness can reduce the capacity for optimally designed student loan contracts to provide incentives and insurance, and ultimately, credit.

7. KEY PRINCIPLES AND POLICY GUIDANCE

Our characterization and overview of optimal student loan arrangements under both information and commitment frictions produce a number of lessons that can help guide policy. We begin with three basic principles that should form the foundation of any efficient student loan program. We then discuss a number of specific lessons regarding the optimal structure of loan repayments, the costs of income verification, repayment enforcement and default, and borrowing limits.

7.1 Three Key Principles in the Design of Student Loan Programs

Three key principles are central to any well-designed student loan program, public or private.

---

[82] Earlier work by Moen (1998) shows that reducing interest payments during unemployment can help achieve efficient investment in human capital. His results derive from very different economic reasons related to a hold-up problem on the side of firms for the investment in human capital of the worker.

First, *insurance is a central aspect in the design of student loans*. School itself may be risky as many students fail to complete their desired course of study. Even successful graduates, as highlighted by the recent recession, can struggle to find a well-paying job, or any job at all, after leaving college. An efficient lending contract ought to provide as much insurance as feasible through income-contingent repayments. Even if the provision of contingencies involves nontrivial costs, it is always efficient to provide considerable insurance in terms of reduced payments or even transfers to borrowers experiencing the worst labor market outcomes. In the extreme, when contracts cannot be made contingent on income at all (ie, limited commitment with incomplete contracts), default serves as an implicit and imperfect form of insurance at the bottom of the income distribution. Inasmuch as lenders can pool loans across many borrowers or can engage in other forms of hedging, they should act as risk-fee entities, providing insurance to students against idiosyncratic risk in their educational investments but pricing the cost of that insurance in the terms of the loan.

Second, *incentive problems must be recognized and properly addressed*. Due to private information and repayment problems associated with limited enforcement mechanisms, the amount and nature of consumption insurance is limited. An optimal contract must address many often conflicting goals, such as providing the student with the appropriate incentives to study hard, search for a job, report their income, and repay their loans. Incentive problems are not only relevant for low earnings states, but they can also limit the income-contingency of repayments at the high end. Because of moral hazard and limited commitment, lenders rely on charging high repayments for lucky students. Moreover, incentive problems can vary over different stages of the loan, with adverse selection concerns prominent at the time of signing, hidden action problems and moral hazard concerns during school and in the labor market, and income verification and commitment problems during repayment. A central challenge in practice is to properly assess the nature and severity of these incentive problems in order to provide the right incentives to align the interests of the student and creditor.

A third practical principle is that *borrowers should fully repay the lender in expectation*. This does not mean that every borrower always repays in full. Borrowers will sometimes make only partial payments or may default entirely on the loan, while others end up paying more than the present value of the debt evaluated at the risk-free rate. Although there may be considerable uncertainty at the time borrowers take out their loans, contracts should be designed such that borrowers expect to repay loans in full when averaging across all possible outcomes and associated repayment amounts. This zero expected profit condition is natural in the case of competitive private loan contracts; however, governments could choose to subsidize student loans (paid for via tax revenue) as a way to subsidize higher education, motivated, possibly, by fiscal and human capital externalities.[83]

---

[83] See Lange and Topel (2006) and Lochner (2011) for recent surveys.

While this is feasible, we believe that any desired subsidies could be more efficiently offered directly in the form of grants, scholarships, or tuition reductions, all of which can be more easily targeted (across need and merit groups), are more transparent, and may entail lower administrative costs. Similarly, efforts to redistribute resources across different types of students are likely to be more efficiently achieved through direct transfers rather than via student loan programs, especially if the socially desirable investments are not entirely aligned with the borrowing and repayment incentives of individuals. Furthermore, efforts by government lenders to systematically extract profits from some borrowers to subsidize losses on others (based on ex ante known information) are likely to be undermined by competitive private creditors who would aim to poach the profitable ones.[84] For these reasons, as a practical guide, we advocate loan contracts, public or private, that lead to zero expected profits from all borrowers, assuming any government subsidies for education are provided directly rather than through government loan programs.

Altogether, an optimal student lending arrangement must strike the right balance between providing insurance and incentives to borrowers, while ensuring the lender is repaid in expectation.

7.2 The Optimal Structure of Loan Repayments

The optimal student loan arrangement must exhibit a flexible income-based repayment schedule to provide the maximal amount of insurance while ensuring proper incentives for borrowers to exert effort and honestly report their income. In practice, the income-contingent repayment schemes observed in the USA and other countries (see Section 3) offer some insurance to borrowers. Yet, optimal contracts are likely to look quite different. Students of different abilities, making different investments, and borrowing different amounts should generally face different repayment schedules. The optimal contract is unlikely to be characterized by a single income threshold below which payments are zero for all borrowers or by a single constant repayment rate as a fraction of income above the threshold. Indeed, the optimal contract may allow for additional transfers to borrowers experiencing the worst postschool outcomes.[85]

---

[84] Del Rey and Verheyden (2013) provide an interesting and provocative exception when adverse selection problems are so severe that a competitive separating equilibrium (with revenue neutral contracts) cannot be supported. As discussed, it may be optimal in this case for the government to support a student loan program with net expected losses if such a program can deter enough poaching by private lenders. While interesting, the empirical relevance of their case needs to be established.

[85] As we discuss further below, other forms of social insurance (eg, welfare, unemployment insurance, disability insurance) may provide for minimal consumption levels, eliminating the need for student loan repayment plans to provide additional transfers to borrowers earning very little after school. However, as we also discussed above, the optimal student loan should integrate in its design the presence of such programs.

An important lesson from our analysis is that the optimal contract aims to provide the greatest insurance at the bottom of the outcome distribution where it is most valuable. Absent moral hazard problems, consumption and not payments would be constant across all low income levels. At the same time, repayments may be considerably higher than the amount borrowed plus interest (with a modest risk premium) for the luckiest borrowers who experience very high earnings realizations; however, when income is costly to verify, repayments should be constant across all high income realizations, a feature that is typically observed in practice for student loans and other forms of debt. Relative to standard repayment schemes, the optimal design of repayments can lead to important gains in welfare and efficiency by providing additional consumption smoothing, by properly encouraging effort and income reporting, and by yielding efficient investments in education. We demonstrate that default can arise even under the optimal contract, an interesting feature not well-established in the literature. However, we argue that default should occur infrequently and not among those with the worst labor market outcomes, because insurance is better provided with verification and income-contingent repayment.

The optimal structure of repayments can be summarized as follows. In the absence of hidden effort, consumption would be smooth and repayments increasing one-for-one in income across states of the world for which income is observed (ie, verified) by the lender. The presence of moral hazard limits the amount of insurance that can be provided, because effort must be incentivized by linking payments and consumption to income levels. The more difficult it is to encourage proper effort, the less insurance can be provided and the less payments should increase with earnings.[86] When income is costly for the lender to observe, it is inefficient to write contracts fully contingent on high earnings levels. Instead, borrowers with sufficiently high earnings should be asked to pay a fixed amount and avoid going through the verification process. In this case, moral hazard is primarily a concern for low income realizations. Finally, imperfect enforcement mechanisms mean that lenders cannot always enforce high payments from lucky borrowers. This can be especially limiting when verification is quite costly and moral hazard problems are modest, because contracts would ideally specify high payments from those with high labor incomes. The combination of costly verification and limited commitment can also lead to default in equilibrium for low- to middle-income borrowers, though not the most unfortunate. It is important to note that these market frictions not only limit consumption smoothing across postschool earnings realizations, but they also limit the amount students can borrow for college and discourage educational investments. Credible evidence on the extent of these information and enforcement frictions is crucial if they are to be addressed appropriately.

---

[86] As a corollary, lenders should absorb all risk beyond the borrower's control (eg, aggregate unemployment risk due to business cycle fluctuations).

Because earnings tend to be low immediately after school and grow quickly at the beginning of workers' careers, average payments will also tend to start low and grow over time if loan programs are efficiently designed. However, this does not mean that efficiency can be obtained with a simple repayment schedule that exogenously increases payment amounts with time since leaving school (eg, the US *Graduated Repayment Plan*). While age-dependent repayment plans can help with intertemporal consumption smoothing, they cannot address labor market risks, including the possibility of extended periods of unemployment or unexpectedly low income later in workers' careers. Labor market risks can only be addressed with explicit income contingencies. Efficiency also requires that repayments be contingent (on current as well as past income) throughout worker careers, even if labor market risks eventually subside. As discussed in Section 6.7, it is optimal to link later repayments to earlier earnings reports to help encourage honest reporting and efficient effort by borrowers at those earlier ages. The efficiency gains from fully flexible, but potentially complex, repayment schedules relative to simpler but less flexible schemes can only be assessed with a greater empirical understanding of the extent of moral hazard and the dynamics of income risk.

7.3 Reducing the Costs of Income Verification

Income verification costs change the nature of the contract by limiting the contingency of repayments on income for high earnings states. With high enough costs, it may become too costly to link repayments to income over a broad range of income realizations. This can severely limit insurance and increase the likelihood of default. Together, these lead to reductions in credit and can discourage educational investments. Consequently, institutional reforms that lower the costs of verifying income and that facilitate the linking of payments to income can improve the flexibility of contracts to enhance consumption insurance, allow for greater borrowing, and increase investments. If verification costs can be reduced enough, default can be eliminated entirely.

These lessons favor integrating the monitoring of income and payment collection efforts with, for example, the collection of social security taxes, unemployment insurance contributions, or income taxes as suggested in the recent proposal by Dynarski and Kreisman (2013). Indeed, this is a key feature of income-contingent lending schemes in countries like Australia, New Zealand, and the United Kingdom (Chapman, 2006). By eliminating the duplication of costs, better terms can be offered to students. This also highlights one key advantage governments have over private lenders and educational institutions in the provision of student loans. As stressed above, the integration of student loan programs with other social insurance institutions such as unemployment insurance, can go well beyond the reduction of verification costs, and can include additional mechanisms to provide insurance and incentives.

7.4 Enforcing Repayment and the Potential for Default

When student loan contracts are designed optimally, default is just one of many "repayment" states. Although the potential for default can severely limit the amount of credit students receive, it can also provide a valuable source of insurance and collection when it is costly to incorporate contingencies into repayment contracts.

For extremely high verification costs, default may be the least expensive way to effectively provide insurance against some subpar labor market outcomes. At the other extreme, if income verification costs are low and contracts can efficiently be made contingent on all, or at least most, income levels, then flexible repayment schedules that link payments to income will always dominate default. As long as verification costs do not preclude any form of income-contingency, default should never occur in the very best or very worst states. Contracts should always be designed to ensure repayment from the highest earners, and they can better provide insurance than default at the low end with explicit contingencies.[87]

Default becomes a more attractive feature of loan contracts when lenders can capture some of the losses from defaulters (eg, wage garnishments). Indeed, better collection efforts that increase the amount creditors can seize in the event of default can theoretically lead to more not less default in equilibrium, as contracts would optimally adjust to take advantage of lower default losses.

Finally, it is important to recognize that the existence (or extent) of default need not imply any inefficiencies, especially if verification costs are high relative to the losses associated with default. Different labor market risks and their dependence on the exertion of effort by the student can lead to complex patterns in the incidence of default, verification and full repayment of loans in the optimal contract. In practice, of course, default is also more likely when contracts are not properly designed, especially in accounting for imperfect enforcement. If so, unusually high levels of default associated with poor ex post labor market outcomes would signal inefficiencies in the way that student credit is allocated and/or repayments are structured. More generally, the basic principle that lenders should be repaid in expectation demands that borrower types with high observed default rates make higher standard payments (when repaying) to offset the losses associated with default. The evidence discussed in Section 5 suggests that this is not the case with current government student loan programs.

7.5 Setting Borrowing Limits

The different credit contracts derived in Section 6 specify repayment functions, borrowing amounts, and investment levels as functions of all observable borrower characteristics (especially their family wealth and ability) and other factors that might affect the returns

---

[87] Default may be the efficient response for the lowest set of income realizations if other forms of social insurance provide a high enough consumption floor.

on their investments (eg, postsecondary institution, course of study). In those contracts, it was not necessary to impose a maximum credit amount, since the financial feasibility constraint was always imposed. Then, the amount of credit would also adjust to the initial characteristics of the individual and proposed investment and consumption decisions, and the lender was always repaid in expectation.

In practice, student loan programs specify repayment schedules as functions of the amount borrowed, the amount invested, and other relevant characteristics. In this case, we can think about the borrowing levels d specified by our contracts as limits lenders might place on different borrowers.

Given substantial heterogeneity in postsecondary institutions and college majors in terms of costs and postschool earnings distributions, the efficient loan scheme would link maximum loan amounts to college and major choices, as well as other relevant observed characteristics of the borrower (eg, student ability as measured by grades or aptitude tests). With asymmetric information, it might also be optimal to condition the amount of lending on the own contribution of the student and his family toward the cost of college. Section 5 documents the extent to which many of these factors affect default rates and expected repayment amounts under current government student loan programs. The considerable variation in default rates across many ex ante observable factors suggests that either loan limits or repayment rates need to be adjusted to better equalize expected returns across borrowers and to improve the efficiency of these programs.

7.6 Other Considerations

Our discussion has largely assumed that student loan programs themselves are the only source of insurance against adverse labor market outcomes. Yet, most countries have a broad social safety net, including welfare, unemployment insurance, and disability insurance in developed countries and informal family arrangements in both developed and developing countries. The optimal student loan contract should be designed with these in mind. For example, if other social programs provide a modest consumption floor for all workers, then it is unlikely that any postschool transfers from the lender to unlucky borrowers would be needed. Default may also be optimal for the most unlucky of borrowers when verification costs are nonnegligible, since there is no need for insurance through the loan contract. More generally, student loan contracts should take into consideration the provision of insurance and incentive effects of other social insurance mechanisms. Given dramatic differences across countries and even states within the USA, we might expect very different contracts to arise optimally in different locations.

The general environments and contracts we have discussed apply equally to public and private lenders. Yet, governments have some advantages over private creditors in terms of income verification, collection, and sometimes enforcement penalties; although, some of these advantages are not necessarily inherent. Private lenders can be given similar enforcement powers as in the 2005 changes to US bankruptcy regulations, and they may also be quite efficient at collection in some markets. Additionally, private credit markets may be more nimble and responsive to economic and technological changes. Adverse selection problems pose a particular concern with competitive lending markets, since they may prevent the market from forming for some types of students. Governments may be able to enforce participation in student loan markets to minimize adverse selection concerns or to form pooling equilibria where one would not arise in a competitive market. In these cases, it may be desirable to reduce competitive pressures, which might otherwise unravel markets. Of course, it can be very difficult to "enforce" full participation, unless governments are prepared to eliminate self-financing by requiring that all students borrow the same amount.

In the USA and Canada, both government and private student loan programs co-exist. In these cases, it is important for governments to account for the response of private lenders. For example, government programs that attempt to (or inadvertently) pool borrowers of different ex ante risk levels may be undercut by private creditors, leaving government loan programs with only the unprofitable ones.[88] A different form of adverse selection problem can also arise for specific schools or even states that try to provide flexible income-contingent loan programs for their students or residents: even if all students are forced to participate in the program, better students (or those enrolling in more financially lucrative programs) may choose to enroll elsewhere. For these reasons, federal student loan programs are likely to be more successful at overcoming adverse selection problems than state- or institution-based programs.

8. CONCLUSIONS

The rising costs of and returns to college have increased the demand for student loans in the USA, as well as many other countries. While borrowing and debt levels have risen for recent students, more and more appear to be constrained by government student loan limits that have not kept pace with rising credit needs. At the same time, rising labor market instability/uncertainty, even for highly educated workers, has made the repayment of higher student debt levels more precarious for a growing number of students. These trends have led to a peculiar situation where, ex ante, some students appear to receive too little credit, while ex post, others appear to have accumulated too much relative to their ability to repay. Together, these patterns suggest inefficiencies in the current student lending environment, making it more important than ever to carefully reconsider its design.

[88] As documented in Section 5, expected loan losses and default rates vary considerably based on ex ante observable factors. This suggests that government student loan programs do pool risk groups, which leaves them open to these concerns.

Optimal student credit arrangements must perform a difficult balancing act. They must provide students with access to credit while in school and help insure them against adverse labor market outcomes after school; however, they must also provide incentives for students to accurately report their income, exert efficient levels of effort during and after school, and generally honor their debts. They must also ensure that creditors are repaid in expectation.

We have shown how student loan programs can most efficiently address these objectives. When postschool incomes are costly to verify, optimal repayment plans will specify a fixed debt-based payment for high income realizations and income-based payments for all others. Absent moral hazard concerns, all but the luckiest borrowers should receive full insurance (ie, their payments should adjust one-for-one with income to maintain a fixed consumption level). More realistically, when moral hazard concerns are important such that borrowers must be provided with incentives to work hard in school and in the labor market, payments should typically increase (less than one-for-one) in income among those experiencing all but the best income realizations. The fact that loan contracts cannot always be fully enforced means that some borrowers may wish to default on their obligations, which further limits the contracts that can be written. When income verification costs are negligible, contracts should be written to avoid default, since the provision of explicit insurance would always be better. By contrast, high verification costs leave room for default as an efficient outcome for some income realizations, since it may be a relatively inexpensive way to provide partial insurance that does not require outlays to verify income. Importantly, we show that default is generally inefficient for borrowers experiencing the worst income realizations, since explicit insurance that can be provided with income verification always dominates in these cases. Yet, an important conclusion from our analysis is that the existence of default for some borrowers is not prima facie evidence of any inefficiency in student lending arrangements. We have also shown that optimal student loan programs will generally lead to lower educational investments for borrowers (relative to nonborrowers) when information and commitment concerns limit the loan contracts. The inability to fully insure all risk discourages investment, more so for students with fewer family resources to draw on.

We have also summarized a small but growing literature that examines the determinants of student loan default and other forms of nonpayment. While the existence of default itself does not necessarily imply inefficiencies in the system, the fact that expected losses associated with nonpayment appear to be quite high among some borrowers is inconsistent with the basic principle that lenders should be repaid in expectation. Fairly high default rates for some types of borrowers also suggest inefficiencies in terms of either inappropriately high loan limits (for them) or inadequate insurance for borrowers who experience very poor labor market outcomes. At the other extreme, it is possible that loan limits are too low for some student types that rarely default.

Finally, we have provided practical guidance for re-designing student loan programs to more efficiently provide insurance while addressing information and commitment frictions in the market. While some recommendations are relatively easy to make (eg, lowering verification costs by linking student loan collection/repayment to social security, tax, or unemployment collections), others require better empirical evidence on important features of the economic environment. In particular, the optimal design of income-based repayment amounts depends critically on the extent of moral hazard in the market, yet we know very little about how student effort responds to incentives. The literature on optimal unemployment insurance and labor supply can be helpful for determining the value of incentives in the labor market. Additional information on ex ante uncertainty, repayment enforcement technologies, and the costs of verification are also needed to design optimal student loan programs. Here, new data sources on education and borrowing behavior, labor market outcomes, and student loan repayment/default can be useful; however, these data will need to be analyzed with these objectives in mind.

ACKNOWLEDGMENTS

The views expressed are those of the individual authors and do not necessarily reflect official positions of the Federal Reserve Bank of St. Louis, the Federal Reserve System, or the Board of Governors. We thank Eda Bozkurt, Qian Liu, and Faisal Sohail for excellent research assistance and Elizabeth Caucutt, Martin Gervais, Steve Machin, and Youngmin Park for their comments.

REFERENCES

Abbott, B., Gallipoli, G., Meghir, C., Violante, G.L., 2013. Education policy and intergenerational transfers in equilibrium. NBER Working Paper No. 18782.

Abraham, A., Koehne, S., Pavoni, N., 2011. On the first-order approach in principal-agent models with hidden borrowing and lending. J. Econ. Theory 146 (4), 1331–1361.

Akers, B., Chingos, M.M., 2014. Is a student loan crisis on the horizon?. Brown Centre on Education Policy at Brookings Report.

Albanesi, S., Nosal, J., 2015. Insolvency after the 2005 Bankruptcy Reform. Federal Reserve Bank of New York Staff Report No. 725.

Arvidson, D., Feshbach, D., Parikh, R., Weinstein, J., 2013. The MeasureOne private student loan report 2013. http://www.measureone.com/reports.

Autor, D.H., Katz, L.F., Kearney, M.S., 2008. Trends in U.S. wage inequality: revising the revisionists. Rev. Econ. Stat. 90 (2), 300–323.

Avery, C., Turner, S., 2012. Student loans: do college students borrow too much-or not enough? J. Econ. Perspect. 26 (1), 165–192.

Bailey, M.J., Dynarski, S.M., 2011. Inequality in postsecondary education. In: Duncan, G.J., Murnane, R.J. (Eds.), Whither Opportunity? Rising Inequality, Schools, and Children's Life Chances. Russell Sage Foundation, New York, pp. 117–131.

Barsky, R., Bound, J., Charles, K., Lupton, J., 2002. Accounting for the black-white wealth gap: a nonparametric approach. J. Am. Stat. Assoc. 97 (459), 663–673.

Becker, G.S., 1975. Human Capital, second ed Columbia University Press, New York, NY.

Becker, G.S., 1991. A Treatise on the Family, Enlarged Edition. Harvard University Press, Cambridge, MA.

Bell, D.N., Blanchflower, D.G., 2011. Young people and the Great Recession. Oxf. Rev. Econ. Policy 27 (2), 241–267.

Belley, P., Lochner, L., 2007. The changing role of family income and ability in determining educational achievement. J. Hum. Cap. 1 (1), 37–89.

Berkner, L., 2000. Trends in Undergraduate Borrowing: Federal Student Loans in 1989-90, 1992-93, and 1995-96. U.S. Department of Education, National Center for Education Statistics, NCES 2000-151, Washington, D.C.

Bleemer, Z., Brown, M., Lee, D., van der Klaauw, W., 2014. Debt, jobs, or housing: what's keeping millennials at home?. Federal Reserve Bank of New York Staff Reports 700.

Blundell, R., Low, H., Preston, I., 2013. Decomposing changes in income risk using consumption data. Quant. Econ. 4 (1), 1–37.

Bohacek, R., Kapicka, M., 2008. Optimal human capital policies. J. Monet. Econ. 55 (1), 1–16.

Boudarbat, B., Lemieux, T., Riddell, W.C., 2010. The evolution of the returns to human capital in Canada, 1980-2005. Can. Public Policy 36 (1), 63–89.

Bovenberg, L., Jacobs, B., 2011. Optimal taxation of human capital and the earnings function. J. Public Econ. Theory 13 (6), 957–971.

Brown, M., Scholz, J.K., Seshadri, A., 2012. A new test of borrowing constraints for education. Rev. Econ. Stud. 79 (2), 511–538.

Brown, M., Lee, D., Haughwoutt, A., Scally, J., van der Klaauw, W., 2015. Measuring student debt and its performance. In: Hershbein, B.J., Hollenbeck, K. (Eds.), Student Loans and the Dynamics of Debt. W. E. Upjohn Institute for Employment Research, Kalamazoo, MI, pp. 37–52.

Brown, M., Haughwoutt, A., Lee, D., van der Klaauw, W., 2016. Do we know what we owe? A comparison of borrower- and lender-reported consumer debt. Federal Reserve Bank of New York Economic Policy Review. forthcoming.

Cameron, S., Heckman, J.J., 1998. Life cycle schooling and dynamic selection bias: models and evidence for five cohorts of American males. J. Polit. Econ. 106 (2), 262–333.

Cameron, S., Heckman, J.J., 1999. Can tuition policy combat rising wage inequality? In: Kosters, M.H. (Ed.), Financing College Tuition: Government Policies and Educational Priorities. American Enterprise Institute Press, Washington, D.C. pp. 76–124.

Cameron, S., Taber, C., 2004. Estimation of educational borrowing constraints using returns to schooling. J. Polit. Econ. 112 (1), 132–182.

Card, D., Lemieux, T., 2001. Can falling supply explain the rising return to college for younger men? A cohort-based analysis? Q. J. Econ. 116 (2), 705–746.

Carneiro, P., Heckman, J.J., 2002. The evidence on credit constraints in post-secondary schooling. Econ. J. 112 (482), 705–734.

Caucutt, E., Lochner, L., 2012. Early and late human capital investments, borrowing constraints, and the family. NBER Working Paper No. 18493.

Chapman, B., 2006. Income contingent loans for higher education: international reforms. In: Hanushek, E., Welch, F. (Eds.), Handbook of the Economics of Education. Vol. 2. Elsevier, Amsterdam, pp. 1435–1503.

Chatterjee, S., Ionescu, F., 2012. Insuring student loans against the risk of college failure. Quant. Econ. 3 (3), 393–420.

College Board, 2001. Trends in Student Aid. College Board Publications, New York, NY.

College Board, 2011. Trends in Student Aid. College Board Publications, New York, NY.

College Board, 2013. Trends in Student Aid. College Board Publications, New York, NY.

Cunningham, A.F., Kienzl, G.S., 2014. Delinquency: The Untold Story of Student Loan Borrowing. Institute for Higher Education Policy, Washington, D.C.

Del Rey, E., Verheyden, B., 2013. Loans, insurance and failures in the credit market for students. Working Paper.

Deming, D., Goldin, C., Katz, L., 2012. The for-profit postsecondary school sector: nimble critters or agile predators? J. Econ. Perspect. 26 (1), 139–164.

Domeij, D., Floden, M., 2010. Inequality trends in Sweden 1978-2004. Rev. Econ. Dyn. 13 (1), 179–208.

Dustmann, C., Ludsteck, J., Schoneberg, U., 2009. Revisiting the German wage structure. Q. J. Econ. 124 (2), 843–881.

Dynarski, M., 1994. Who defaults on student loans? Findings from the National Postsecondary Student Aid Study. Econ. Educ. Rev. 13 (1), 55–68.

Dynarski, S., Kreisman, D., 2013. Loans for educational opportunity: making borrowing work for today's students. The Hamilton Project Discussion Paper.

Eckwert, B., Zilcha, I., 2012. Private investment in higher education: comparing alternative funding schemes. Economica 79 (313), 76–96.

Elsby, M.W., Hobijn, B., Sahin, A., 2010. The labor market in the Great Recession. NBER Working Paper No. 15979.

Findeisen, S., Sachs, D., 2013. Education and optimal dynamic taxation: the role of income-contingent student loans. Working Paper.

Findeisen, S., Sachs, D., 2014. Designing efficient college and tax policies. Working Paper.

Flint, T., 1997. Predicting student loan defaults. J. High. Educ. 68 (3), 322–354.

Friedman, M., Kuznets, S., 1945. Income from Independent Professional Practice. NBER Books.

Fuchs-Schundeln, N., Krueger, D., Sommer, M., 2010. Inequality trends for Germany in the last two decades: a tale of two countries. Rev. Econ. Dyn. 13 (1), 103–132.

Gary-Bobo, R., Trannoy, A., 2014. Optimal student loans and graduate tax under moral hazard and adverse selection. CESIfo Discussion Paper No. 4279.

Gemici, A., Wiswall, M., 2011. Evolution of gender differences in post-secondary human capital investments: college majors. IESP Working Paper No. 03-11.

Golosov, M., Tsyvinski, A., Werning, I., 2007. New dynamic public finance: a user's guide. In: Acemoglu, D., Rogoff, K., Woodford, M. (Eds.), NBER Macroeconomics Annual 2006. Vol. 21. MIT Press, Cambridge, MA, pp. 317–388.

Gottschalk, P., Moffitt, R., 2009. The rising instability of U.S. earnings. J. Econ. Perspect. 23 (4), 3–24.

Gross, J., Cekic, O., Hossler, D., Hillman, N., 2009. What matters in student loan default: a review of the research literature. J. Stud. Financ. Aid 39 (1), 19–29.

Hanushek, E.A., Leung, C.K.Y., Yilmaz, K., 2014. Borrowing constraints, college aid, and intergenerational mobility. J. Hum. Cap. 8 (1), 1–41.

Heathcote, J., Perri, F., Violante, G.L., 2010. Unequal we stand: an empirical analysis of economic inequality in the United States: 1967-2006. Rev. Econ. Dyn. 13 (1), 15–51.

Heathcote, J., Storesletten, K., Violante, G.L., 2010. The macroeconomic implications of rising wage inequality in the United States. J. Polit. Econ. 118 (4), 681–722.

Heckman, J.J., Lochner, L.J., Todd, P.E., 2008. Earnings functions and rates of return. J. Hum. Cap. 2 (1), 1–31.

Hershaff, J., 2014. Moral hazard and lending: evidence from the federal student loan market. Working Paper.

Hershbein, B.J., Hollenbeck, K., 2014. The distribution of college graduate debt, 1990-2008: a decomposition approach - updated web tables and figures. W.E. Upjohn Institute Working Paper.

Hershbein, B.J., Hollenbeck, K., 2015. The distribution of college graduate debt, 1990-2008: a decomposition approach. In: Hershbein, B.J., Hollenbeck, K. (Eds.), Student Loans and the Dynamics of Debt. W.E. Upjohn Institute for Employment Research, Kalamazoo, MI, pp. 53–116.

Hillman, N., 2014. College on credit: a multilevel analysis of student loan default. Rev. High. Educ. 37 (2), 169–195.

Hopenhayn, H.A., Nicolini, J.P., 1997. Optimal unemployment insurance. J. Polit. Econ. 105 (2), 412–438.

Hoynes, H., Miller, D.L., Schaller, J., 2012. Who suffers during recessions? J. Econ. Perspect. 26 (3), 27–48.

Human Resources and Skills Development Canada, 2012. Canada Student Loans Program: Annual Report 2010-2011. Ottawa.

Ionescu, F., 2008. Consolidation of student loan repayments and default incentives. B.E. J. Macroecon. 8 (1), 1682.

Ionescu, F., 2009. The federal student loan program: quantitative implications for college enrollment and default rates. Rev. Econ. Dyn. 1094-202512 (1), 205–231.

Ionescu, F., 2011. Risky human capital and alternative bankruptcy regimes for student loans. J. Hum. Cap. 5 (2), 153–206.

Jappelli, T., Pistaferri, L., 2010. Does consumption inequality track income inequality in Italy? Rev. Econ. Dyn. 13 (1), 133–153.

Johnson, M., 2013. Borrowing constraints, college enrollment, and delayed entry. J. Labor Econ. 31 (4), 669–725.

Jones, J.B., Yang, F., 2014. Skill-biased technical change and the cost of higher education. State University of New York — Albany, Working Paper.

Kapicka, M., 2014. Optimal Mirrleesean taxation with unobservable human capital formation. Working Paper.

Kapicka, M., Neira, J., 2014. Optimal taxation in a life-cycle economy with endogenous human capital formation. Working Paper.

Keane, M., Wolpin, K.I., 2001. The effect of parental transfers and borrowing constraints on educational attainment. Int. Econ. Rev. 42 (4), 1051–1103.

Kinsler, J., Pavan, R., 2011. Family income and higher education choices: the importance of accounting for college quality. J. Hum. Cap. 5 (4), 453–477.

Kocherlakota, N., 2004. Figuring out the impact of hidden savings on optimal unemployment insurance. Rev. Econ. Dyn. 7 (3), 541–554.

Krueger, D., Ludwig, A., 2013. Optimal capital and progressive labor income taxation with endogenous schooling decisions and intergenerational transfers. Working Paper.

Krueger, D., Ludwig, A., 2013. Optimal progressive labor income taxation and education subsidies when education decisions and intergenerational transfers are endogenous. Am. Econ. Rev. Pap. Proc. 103 (3), 496–501.

Lange, F., Topel, R., 2006. The social value of education and human capital. In: Hanushek, E., Welch, F. (Eds.), Handbook of the Economics of Education. Vol. 1. Elsevier, Amsterdam, Netherlands, pp. 459–509.

Lochner, L., 2011. Nonproduction benefits of education: crime, health, and good citizenship. In: Hanushek, E., Machin, S., Woessmann, L. (Eds.), Handbook of the Economics of Education. Vol. 4. Elsevier, Amsterdam, Netherlands, pp. 183–282.

Lochner, L., Monge-Naranjo, A., 2011. The nature of credit constraints and human capital. Am. Econ. Rev. 101 (6), 2487–2529.

Lochner, L., Monge-Naranjo, A., 2012. Credit constraints in education. Ann. Rev. Econ. 4, 225–256.

Lochner, L., Monge-Naranjo, A., 2015. Default and repayment among baccalaureate degree earners. In: Hershbein, B.J., Hollenbeck, K. (Eds.), Student Loans and the Dynamics of Debt. W.E. Upjohn Institute for Employment Research, Kalamazoo, MI, pp. 235–284.

Lochner, L., Shin, Y., 2014. Understanding earnings dynamics: identifying and estimating the changing roles of unobserved ability, permanent and transitory shocks. NBER Working Paper No. 20068.

Lochner, L., Stinebrickner, T., Suleymanoglu, U., 2013. The importance of financial resources for student loan repayment. CIBC Working Paper No. 2013-7.

Mestieri, M., 2012. Wealth distribution and human capital: how borrowing constraints shape educational systems. Working Paper.

Moen, E.R., 1998. Efficient ways to finance human capital investments. Economica 65 (260), 491–505.

Moffitt, R.A., Gottschalk, P., 2012. Trends in the transitory variance of male earnings: methods and evidence. J. Hum. Resour. 47 (1), 204–236.

Monge-Naranjo, A., 2016. Student Loans and the Risk of Youth Unemployment. Federal Reserve Bank of St Louis Review, First Quarter 2016. Volume 98. (No. 1).

Musto, D.K., 2004. What happens when information leaves a market? Evidence from postbankruptcy consumers. J. Bus. 77 (4), 725–748.

Navarro, S., 2010. Using observed choices to infer agent's information: reconsidering the importance of borrowing constraints, uncertainty and preferences in college attendance. University of Wisconsin. Working Paper.

Nerlove, M., 1975. Some problems in the use of income-contingent loans for the finance of higher education. J. Polit. Econ. 83 (1), 157–183.

OECD, 2013. Education at a Glance 2013: OECD Indicators. OECD Publishing. http://dx.doi.org/10.1787/eag-2013-en.

Pereira, P., Martins, P., 2000. Does education reduce wage inequality? Quantile regressions evidence from fifteen European countries. IZA Discussion Paper No. 120.

Rothstein, J., Rouse, C.E., 2011. Constrained after college: student loans and early-career occupational choices. J. Public Econ. 95 (1-2), 149–163.

Sallie, Mae, 2008. How Undergraduate Students Use Credit Cards. Sallie Mae, Inc., Newark, DE

Sargent, T., Lungqvist, L., 2012. Recursive Macroeconomic Theory, third MIT Press, Cambridge, MA.

Schwartz, S., Finnie, R., 2002. Student loans in Canada: an analysis of borrowing and repayment. Econ. Educ. Rev. 21 (5), 497–512.

Shapiro, T., Oliver, M., 1997. Black Wealth/White Wealth: A New Perspective on Racial Inequality. Routeledge, New York, NY.

Snyder, T., Dillow, S., Hoffman, C., 2009. Digest of Education Statistics 2008. National Center for Education Statistics, Institute of Education Sciences, U.S. Department of Education, Washington, D.C.

Stantcheva, S., 2014. Optimal taxation and human capital policies over the life cycle. Working Paper.

Steele, P., Baum, S., 2009. How Much Are College Students Borrowing? College Board Publications, New York, NY.

Stinebrickner, T., Stinebrickner, R., 2008. The effect of credit constraints on the college drop-out decision: a direct approach using a new panel study. Am. Econ. Rev. 98 (5), 2163–2184.

Townsend, R.M., 1979. Optimal contracts and competitive markets with costly state verification. J. Econ. Theory 21 (2), 265–293.

U.S. Department of the Treasury, 2012. Fiscal year 2011 report to the congress: U.S. Government receivables and debt collection activities of federal agencies.

Volkwein, F., Szelest, B., Cabrera, A., Napierski-Prancl, M., 1998. Factors associated with student loan default among different racial and ethnic groups. J. High. Educ. 69 (2), 206–237.

Wei, H., 2010. Measuring economic returns to post-school education in Australia. Australian Bureau of Statistics Research Paper.

Wei, C.C., Berkner, L., 2008. Trends in Undergraduate Borrowing II: Federal Student Loans in 1995-96, 1999-2000, and 2003-04. National Center for Education Statistics, U.S. Department of Education, Washington, D.C.

Woo, J.H., 2014. Degrees of Debt — Student Borrowing and Loan Repayment of Bachelor's Degree Recipients 1 Year After Graduating: 1994, 2001, and 2009. National Center for Education Statistics, Institute of Education Sciences, U.S. Department of Education, Washington, D.C.

CHAPTER 9

Government-Sponsored Vocational Education for Adults

B. McCall*, J. Smith*,†,‡,§, C. Wunsch‡,§,¶,**
*University of Michigan, Ann Arbor, MI, United States
†NBER, Cambridge, MA, United States
‡IZA, Bonn, Germany
§CESifo, Munich, Germany
¶University of Basel, Basel, Switzerland
**CEPR, London, United Kingdom

Contents

Handbook of the Economics of Education, Volume 5
ISSN 1574-0692, http://dx.doi.org/10.1016/B978-0-444-63459-7.00009-9

Abstract

This chapter considers the literature on government-sponsored vocational training for adults, with a particular substantive focus on training provided via active labor market programs and a particular geographic focus on Western Europe and North America. We begin with a discussion of the underlying economic theory of investment in human capital over the life cycle and of government intervention in that process, along with models of participation in government programs and in particular services within those program. Building on the theory as well as on institutional knowledge and well-known empirical regularities related to participation in training, we then lay out the common applied econometric approaches to estimating the impacts of government-sponsored training for adults and consider important design and measurement issues common to studies in the empirical literature. Six case studies that consider the institutions and evaluation literatures in the United States, the United Kingdom, Germany, France, Sweden, and Denmark come next. These countries all provide a rich base of compelling empirical evidence and also serve to illustrate a wide variety of institutional choices and applied econometric methodologies. The penultimate section considers what we know about matching potential trainees to training and to particular training types, an important topic in light of the strong evidence of heterogeneity in treatment effects provided by the case studies. The final section summarizes the literature and its limitations and offers suggestions for future research.

Keywords

Education, Vocational Training, Active Labor Market Programs, Activation, Treatment Assignment, Incentives, Knowledge

1. INTRODUCTION

Countries today invest heavily in primary, secondary, and (at least in developed countries) postsecondary education.[1] Almost all of primary and secondary education is publicly provided as well as a substantial fraction of postsecondary education. Much of postsecondary education consists of traditional aged (18–24), full-time students seeking a baccalaureate degree.[2]

After leaving formal schooling, many adults continue to enhance their skills through employer-provided job training. However, government-sponsored vocational training plays a leading role in public policies used to combat the adverse employment effects of business cycle down turns and structural unemployment. It is these government-sponsored training programs that are the focus of this chapter. Most of the adults in these government-sponsored vocational training programs are currently unemployed, at an elevated risk of becoming unemployed, reentering the labor force after a long absence, or perhaps entering a new labor force through immigration.[3]

Government-sponsored vocational training programs form an integral part of the active labor market programs (ALMPs) of many developed countries. ALMPs are programs that help those receiving unemployment benefits find jobs. They are based on a mutual obligation between the benefit recipient and the government where the benefit recipient actively engages in job search and other undertakings to improve their employability and the government provides effective employment services and benefits. Governments may also subsidize apprenticeship programs that provide vocational training, although these programs are mainly for younger adults who have just left formal schooling.[4]

Government-provided vocational training can take place on-the-job or in the classroom. The training might provide basic-level, general work skills such as numeracy or literacy training or it could involve higher level, occupation-specific skills such as accountant or laboratory technician training. Vocational training might also entail the learning of entrepreneurial skills that enables an individual to become self-employed. Vocational training courses can last anywhere from a few weeks to several months. While vocational training might be provided through the public employment service (PES),

---

[1] In the United States in 2012, education expenditures amounted to 7.2% of GDP (see http://nces.ed.gov/programs/digest/current_tables.asp).

[2] In the fall of 2011 in the United States, of the 13.3 million individuals attending postsecondary education 6.6 million were enrolled at 4-year institutions, 7.9 million were enrolled full time, and 9.4 million were 24 or younger (see http://nces.ed.gov/programs/digest/current_tables.asp).

[3] For reasons of space, we do not cover vocational training programs specifically aimed at prisoners or former prisoners. See Cook et al. (2015) for a brief survey along with useful references.

[4] See Wolter and Ryan (2011) for a comprehensive review of the literature on apprenticeships.

which could require the approval of a caseworker, it may simply involve an individual enrolling in a course at a government-subsidized local community college.

While this chapter is broader than only government-sponsored vocational training provided through ALMPs, as the case studies below highlight, in many countries ALMPs are the main vehicle for the provision of government-sponsored vocational training. Also, internationally comparable data are only provided for ALMPs. So our cross-country comparisons, which are discussed next, focus on ALMPs.

Among Organisation for Economic Co-operation and Development (OECD) countries, there is substantial variation in the amount governments spend on ALMPs as well as the importance that vocational training plays within the set of ALMPs. ALMPs can be classified according to five objectives: incentives for retaining employment, incentives for creating employment, incentives for seeking and keeping a job, incentives for human capital enhancement, and improved labor market matching (Brown and Koettl, 2012).

The first two types of incentives are demand-side. Incentives to maintain employment include devices such as wage subsidies and job rotation while incentives for creating employment would include instruments such as job start-up support and hiring subsidies. The next two types of incentives are supply side. Incentives to seek and keep a job include both benefit sanctions and tax credits while incentives for human capital enhancement consist of subsidized on-the-job or classroom training. Finally, improved labor market matching would involve such things as job search assistance, employer intermediation services, and counseling and monitoring.

After enduring persistently high unemployment rates for many years, ALMPs underwent major reforms in Europe when employment policy became a main priority of the European Union (EU) in the late 1990s (see Kluve et al., 2007). The amount spent on ALMPs per person in the labor force for four EU countries (Austria, Denmark, Italy, and the Netherlands) is shown in Fig. 1. As can be seen in the figure, there is considerable cross-country variation in spending with Denmark almost always spending more than €800 per labor force person on ALMPs during the 1998–2012 period while the Netherlands was spending between €400 and €600, and Austria and Italy usually spending between €200 and €400.

During the Great Recession that began at the end of 2007 ALMP expenditures per labor force person increased dramatically for Denmark, rose slightly for Austria, remained fairly constant in the Netherlands, and decreased slightly in Italy. Unemployment rates, while rising substantially between 2007 and 2012 for both Denmark (3.2% to 6.3%) and Italy (4.9% to 8.9%), rose only moderately for the Netherlands (2.9% to 4.5%) and stayed constant for Austria (3.7% to 3.6%). We can see in Fig. 2 that the rapid increase in ALMP expenditures per labor force person in Denmark was insufficient to keep ALMP expenditures per unemployed person constant as they dropped from €25 thousand to €15 thousand before leveling off and then increasing somewhat. The Netherlands also saw

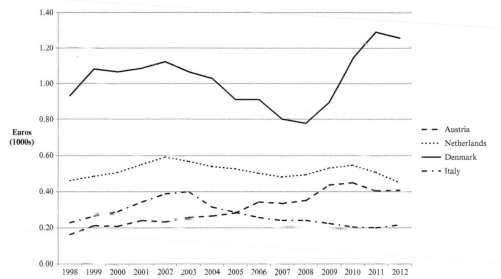

Figure 1 ALMP expenditures per labor force person. *Source: http://ec.europa.eu/eurostat/data/ database.*

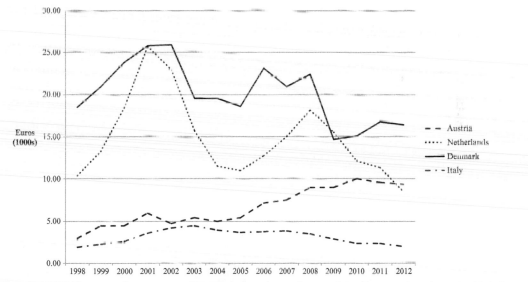

Figure 2 ALMP expenditures per unemployed person. *Source: http://ec.europa.eu/eurostat/data/ database.*

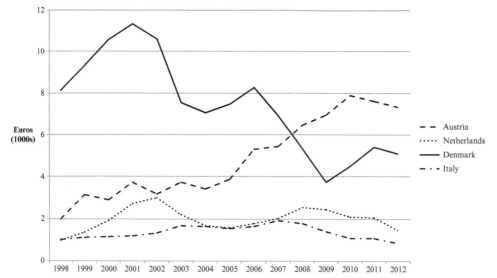

Figure 3 Training expenditures per unemployed person. *Source: http://ec.europa.eu/eurostat/data/database.*

a substantial drop in ALMP expenditures per unemployed person since 2008 while in Italy there has been a gradual decline since 2007. ALMP expenditures per unemployed person in Austria, on the other hand, increased from 2004 to 2010 and then decreased slightly thereafter.[5]

Training expenditures per unemployed person are presented in Fig. 3. Over most of the period Denmark's training expenditures per unemployed person exceeded the three other countries. However, since 2009 Austria has had higher training expenditures per unemployed person than Denmark. The Netherland's drop in training expenditures per unemployed person over the 2008–12 period was less pronounced than its drop in total ALMP expenditures while Austria's increase in training expenditures per unemployed person over this period was more rapid than its increase in total ALMP expenditures per unemployed person.

Looking across all OECD countries, in 2011 they spent about 0.56% of their GDP on ALMPs.[6] As shown in Fig. 4, Denmark, Finland, the Netherlands, and Sweden all spent more than 1% of their GDP on ALMPs. On the other hand, Chile, Israel, and the United

---

[5] Data for the European Union 15 countries (Austria, Belgium, Denmark, Finland, France, Germany, Greece, Ireland, Italy, Luxembourg, Netherlands, Portugal, Spain, Sweden, United Kingdom) are available from 2004 to 2011. It shows a decline in ALMP expenditures per unemployed person from €4.1 thousand to €3.2 thousand from 2007 to 2011.

[6] This includes government-sponsored classroom and workplace training as well as instruments such as training vouchers.

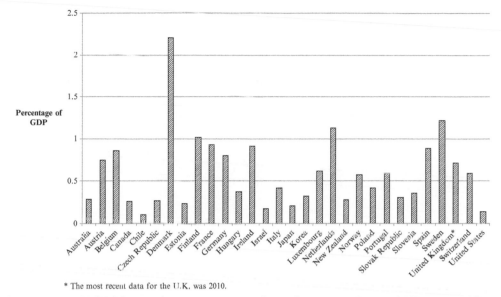

* The most recent data for the U.K. was 2010.

Figure 4 2011 Active labor market program expenditures by country. *Source: OECD.StatsExtract.*

States spent less than 0.2% of GNP on ALMPs. Across the OECD in 2011 job training comprised about 29% of ALMP expenditures. However, as Fig. 5 shows there is considerable variation across country. For example, for Austria, Finland, and Portugal the percentage of ALMP expenditures devoted to training exceeds 50% while for the Czech Republic, Poland, and the Slovak Republic less than 5% is spent on training.

In this chapter we focus our attention on countries in Western Europe and North America. These countries have a long history of experience with ALMPs and government-sponsored vocational training programs. They also tend to have more developed longitudinal data systems for tracking individuals' participation in such programs and their subsequent outcomes. Indeed, many of these countries willingly support evaluations of their government-sponsored training programs either through secondary data analysis or, in some cases, randomized controlled trials (RCT). So, unsurprisingly, much of the empirical research on the effectiveness of government vocational training programs comes from Western Europe and North America.

Even this set of countries, however, is too big for us to adequately cover in the space of a chapter. So, we have further narrowed our view and will provide detailed case studies of a handful of countries: Denmark, France, Germany, Sweden, the United Kingdom, and the United States. These countries differ in the extent of their investment (as measured by the percentage of GDP) in ALMPs, with Denmark and Sweden making large investments, France, Germany, and the United Kingdom making moderate investments, and the United States making a relatively small investment. However, even among the

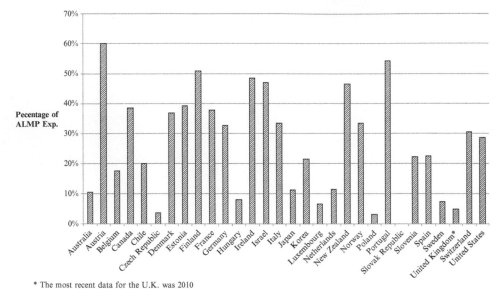

Figure 5 2011 Training expenditures as percentage of ALMP expenditures by country. *Source: OECD. StatExtracts.*

larger and moderate investors in ALMPs there are wide differences in the relative importance of government-sponsored vocational training. While Denmark devotes over 35% of its ALMP expenditures to training, Sweden only devotes about 7%. Germany and France devoted 33% and 38%, respectively, of ALMP expenditures to toward training but the United Kingdom only devotes about 5%.

The United States and Canada differ from most European countries in that they have only modest amounts of government-sponsored vocational training within their ALMPs. Instead, much of the government-sponsored vocational training in the United States and Canada occurs through government-subsidized 2-year colleges and technical schools that individuals seeking training can access directly.

Most of our review of the empirical literature then deals with studies concerning these six countries. Moreover, we concentrate on the more recent empirical research since reviews of earlier research are available elsewhere.[7] Our discussion of theoretical models and empirical methods, however, are more broadly applicable.

The next section of this chapter covers theoretical models of the provision of training. First we discuss the classic theory of human capital investment, including different types of human capital and their implications for who bears the cost of the investment. We then discuss the potential for market failures that could justify government intervention. Next we develop a formal model of human capital accumulation over the life cycle. A model

---

[7] See eg, Heckman et al. (1999) and Kluve et al. (2007).

with perfect certainty is considered first and then we incorporate uncertainty with individuals maximizing expected utility. It is this latter case that can explain why individuals in midcareer may need retraining.

Next, we analyze the possibility of training within the context of searching for a job while unemployed. We consider, for example, whether individuals optimally reduce their search effort when a training option becomes available only after being unemployed for a certain amount of time. We then explore the case with multiple training options and how to optimally determine what training option to pursue over time. Finally, a model that allows for equilibrium effects of training is developed. In situations where government intervention leads to a substantial increase in the supply of trained workers, equilibrium wages, and the return to training, will change. As we shall see, much of the empirical work that estimates the economic return to government-sponsored training programs ignores equilibrium considerations.

Section 3 of this chapter considers participation in training programs in a strictly voluntary situation, like that in the United States. Individuals will choose to participate in a training program if it increases their expected utility. On the other hand, individuals in some countries may be required to participate in training if they want to continue receiving benefits. In this case the decision an individual faces is whether to participate in training and continue receiving benefits, or not participate and lose benefits. We also consider the case of the optimal timing of training. An event such as a layoff may not cause an individual to immediately seek training. However, if the individual is unsuccessful at becoming reemployed given her current skill set she may decide at some point to enroll in a training program. Of course, at some point during an unemployment spell she may be assigned a caseworker that decides she needs training. If she refuses, she may face benefit sanctions.

The empirical methods used to evaluate training programs are discussed in Section 4. The goal of any evaluation is to estimate the causal effect of the program on a particular outcome (eg, wages or employment). While RCT are considered the "gold standard" for program evaluation (although they too have limitations that we shall discuss), it is rare that empirical researchers are able to conduct a RCT to evaluate a particular training program.

With only observational data, the main threat that researchers face in attempting to estimate the average effect of the treatment on the treated (ATT) is that they may lack some relevant information (variables) that is both related to whether or not an individual receives training and the outcome. Thus, it is necessary to use knowledge of the data, institutions, and selection and outcomes processes to identify the effect of training on outcomes. Researchers may also use the identifying restrictions imposed by economic theory to estimate training effects.

Sections 5 through 10 of the chapter describe the institutional framework of public-supported vocational training for each of the countries mentioned above. For each country, we also discuss the empirical research that estimates the effects of these training programs on various outcomes. Given the evidence that some training programs may be more effective for some individuals than for others, Section 11 discusses the matching of training programs to individuals. Should particular individuals be trained or not and, if so, what kind of training should they receive? What role does the caseworker play in determining the choice of the training program and do they have the appropriate incentives to make the best match? Also, we consider what type of caseworker behavior (eg, are they accommodating or not) leads to the best outcomes.

The last section of the chapter provides a summary, then discusses limitations of the literature, and offers what we see as useful directions for future research.

2. THEORY: PROVISION

In this section we cover theoretical aspects of the provision of publicly provided or subsidized job training programs. What are the benefits and costs to an individual and society of receiving job training? In the first section we introduce the classical human capital framework of Becker, Schultz, and others. Next, we expand this model to consider dynamic investment in human capital over the life cycle. One rationale for public provision of job training is that imperfect capital markets prevent individuals from investing in the optimal amount of human capital. In Section 2.4, we discuss this as well as other rationales for government intervention. Search models of the labor market with training, including situations with multiple training options, are considered next. In a partial equilibrium framework we shall see how the provision of training can change an individual's job seeking incentives. Finally, we examine job training from a general equilibrium perspective.

2.1 General Framework

In economics the training decision is usually viewed through the lens of human capital theory (Becker, 1993). In its simplest form human capital theory states that an individual will undertake training when the present discounted value of the benefits of training exceeds the cost of training. We first consider the situation with a single training opportunity available to an individual and where all values are known with certainty; that is, the individual has perfect foresight.

For simplicity assume that the direct cost of training is borne at time zero and equals c. Consider two income paths. Let y_t^0, $t = 0, 1, \ldots$ be the income path if the individual is not trained and y_t^1, $t = 0, 1, \ldots$ the income path when the individual is trained. Assume that capital markets are perfect and denote the market interest rate by r. Human capital theory states that an individual will undertake training when

$$\sum_{j=0}^{\infty}\frac{Y_j^1}{(1+r)^j}-\sum_{j=0}^{\infty}\frac{Y_j^0}{(1+r)^j}\geq c. \tag{1}$$

In the simple case where the per period return to investment is constant, $y_t^1 - y_t^0 = \alpha$ for $t = 1, 2, \ldots$, and assuming that in period zero an individual earns zero if trained (ie, $y_0^1 = 0$) and y_0^0 if not trained, an individual will invest in training if:

$$c + y_0^0 < \frac{\alpha}{r}. \tag{2}$$

This simple model yields several predictions: An individual will be more likely to invest in training the lower the direct cost (c), the lower the opportunity cost (y_0^0), the greater the return (α) and the lower the cost of borrowing (r).

More generally, let I_t represent the information that a person has accumulated by time t and let β denote the discount factor, $\beta = 1/(1 + r) < 1$. Suppose that there exists a training opportunity at time t_0. Assume that all the direct costs of training, c, are borne at time t_0. Now, however, we assume that future income streams if trained or not trained are not known with certainty but are instead stochastic processes. Denoted the stochastic income process by Y_t^1 if training takes place at t_0 and equals Y_t^0 if training does not take place. An individual who maximizes the expected present value of income will then undertake training at time t_0 if

$$E\left\{\sum_{j=0}^{\infty}\left(\frac{Y_{t_0+j}^1 - Y_{t_0+j}^0}{(1-r)^j}\right)\Big| I_{t_0}\right\} > c \tag{3}$$

or

$$E\left\{\sum_{j=0}^{\infty}\beta^j\left(Y_{t_0+j}^1 - Y_{t_0+j}^0\right)\Big| I_{t_0}\right\} > c \tag{4}$$

Again if we assume that the costs of training are borne in period zero and that period zero income equals zero if trained and that the returns to training are constant but potentially unknown at time t_0. Then a risk neutral individual will choose to invest in training if

$$E\left\{\tilde{\alpha}/r - Y_{t_0}^0 - c \Big| I_{t_0}\right\} \geq 0, \tag{5}$$

where $\tilde{\alpha}$ is the random variable of unknown but constant returns. Assuming that all values are known at time 0 except the return to training, we can rewrite Eq. (5) as

$$E[\tilde{\alpha}|I_{t_0}]/r - y_0^0 - c > 0. \tag{6}$$

An individual is more likely to invest in training the larger the expected returns to training in terms of increased earnings.

2.2 A Dynamic Model of Human Capital Investment

In this section we present a dynamic, discrete time, model of human capital accumulation that allows an individual to increase their human capital or skill level (S) over time by devoting some of their time to training (I).[8] We shall assume that skills depreciate over time at a constant rate (δ) so that an individual must spend some time training each period just to keep their skills constant. In particular, we assume that an individual's skill level at time $t+1$, S_{t+1}, satisfies the following: $S_{t+1} = (1-\delta)S_t + f(I_t)$ where f is an increasing and concave function of I_t.

As an individual's skill level increases so does the wage (W) they are paid by the market. Let g be an increasing function that relates the market wage an individual receives at time t to their skill level at time t so that $W_t = g(S_t)$.

We assume that capital markets are perfect so that an individual can borrow and save over time at the market interest rate, r. If there are no bequest motives and the time of death (T) is known with certainty, individuals will spend down all their assets (A) by the end of their lifetime ($A_{T+1} = 0$).

The utility an individual derives at time t depends on the amount they consume of a good (C_t) and the amount of leisure (L_t) they consume where the price of the consumption good is fixed at one. Utility is assumed to be additively separable over time where future utility is discounted by the discount factor β. Thus an individual's lifetime utility equals

$$\mathcal{U} = \sum_{t=0}^{T} \beta^t U(C_t, L_t) \tag{7}$$

and the goal of the individual is to maximize this lifetime utility subject to the constraints that there is a fixed amount of time each period that can be spent training, working, and consuming leisure, $1 = L_t + I_t + H_t$, where H_t is the fraction of time spent working, that the discounted lifetime amount spent on consumption equals discounted lifetime income:

$$\sum_{t=0}^{T} \left(\frac{1}{1+r}\right)^t C_t = A_0 + \sum_{t=0}^{T} \left(\frac{1}{1+r}\right)^t W_t H_t, \tag{8}$$

where A_0 is initial assets, that wages at time t satisfy $W_t = g(S_t)$, and that skills at time t satisfy $S_{t+1} = (1-\delta)S_t + f(I_t)$.

To solve this optimization problem it helps to rewrite it in a recursive dynamic programming format:

$$V_t(A_t, S_t) = \max_{C_t, L_t, I_t} [U(C_t, L_t) + \beta V_{t+1}(A_{t+1}, S_{t+1})], \tag{9}$$

where A_t and S_t are state variables representing the level of assets and skills at time t, respectively. The optimal value function V_t represents the optimal discounted utility

---

[8] In this model I can represent formal or informal training, both on and off the job.

achievable from time t forward given that the level of assets at time t equals A_t and the amount of skills at time t equal S_t. The relationship between assets at time $t + 1$ and t is governed by the equation:

$$A_{t+1} = (1+r)[A_t + W_t H_t - C_t],\tag{10}$$

while the relationship between skills at time t and $t + 1$ is:

$$S_{t+1} = (1-\delta)S_t + f(I_t).\tag{11}$$

Finally, the proportion of time devoted to leisure at time t must satisfy

$$L_t = 1 - I_t - H_t.\tag{12}$$

Rewriting the optimization problem in terms of C_t, H_t, and I_t, and substituting in the above constraints gives:

$$
\begin{aligned}
V_t(A_t, S_t) = \max{}_{C_t, H_t, I_t} \{ &U(C_t, 1 - I_t - H_t) \\
&+ \beta V_{t+1}(1+r)[A_t + g(S_t)H_t - C_t], (1-\delta)S_t + f(I_t)\}.
\end{aligned}
\tag{13}
$$

Differentiating the term in brackets in Eq. (13) with respect to the three arguments, and assuming interior solutions for C_t, H_t, and I_t, gives the first order conditions:

$$\partial U/\partial C - \beta(1+r)\partial V_{t+1}/\partial A = 0\tag{14}$$

$$\partial U/\partial L + \beta(1+r)\partial V_{t+1}/\partial A \, g(S_t) = 0\tag{15}$$

and

$$\partial U/\partial L + \beta \partial V_{t+1}/\partial S \, df/dI = 0\tag{16}$$

First order conditions (14) and (15) imply that

$$\frac{\partial U/\partial L}{\partial U/\partial C} = g(S_t) = W_t$$

or that the marginal rate of substitution between leisure and consumption equals the wage while the last two conditions (15) and (16) imply that

$$(1+r)W_t \partial V_{t+1}/\partial A = \partial V_{t+1}/\partial S \, df/dS\tag{17}$$

or that the marginal present value of devoting more time to work equals the marginal present value of job training.

Let C_t^*, L_t^*, H_t^*, and I_t^* represent the optimal values of C_t, I_t, H_t, and I_t.

$$\partial V_t/\partial A = \beta(1+r)\partial V_{t+1}/\partial A\tag{18}$$

and

$$\partial V_t \big/_{\partial S} = \beta \left[\partial V_{t+1} \big/_{\partial A} \, ^{dg} \big/_{dS} H_t^* + \partial V_{t+1} \big/_{\partial S} (1 - \delta) \right] \tag{19}$$

If we assume that the individual's discount factor satisfies, $\beta = 1 \big/_{1+r}$, then

$$\partial V_t \big/_{\partial A} = \partial V_{t+1} \big/_{\partial A} \equiv \lambda. \tag{20}$$

If we further assume that $dg/dS = w$ (ie, the return to skills is linear) then

$$\partial V_t \big/_{\partial S} = \beta \left[\lambda w H_t^* + \partial V_{t+1} \big/_{\partial S} (1 - \delta) \right]. \tag{21}$$

Now at time T we have

$$\partial V_T \big/_{\partial S} = \beta \lambda w H_T^* \tag{22}$$

substituting Eq. (22) into (21) yields

$$\partial V_{T-1} \big/_{\partial S} = \beta \left[\lambda w H_{T-1}^* + \beta \lambda w H_T^* (1 - \delta) \right]. \tag{23}$$

Substituting Eq. (23) into (21) then gives

$$\begin{aligned}
\partial V_{T-2} \big/_{\partial S} &= \beta \left[\lambda w H_{T-2}^* + \beta \left[\lambda w H_{T-1}^* + \beta \lambda w H_T^* (1 - \delta) \right] (1 - \delta) \right] \\
&= \lambda w \beta \left[H_{T-2}^* + \beta (1 - \delta) H_{T-1}^* + \beta^2 (1 - \delta)^2 H_T^* \right].
\end{aligned} \tag{24}$$

Continuing in this fashion we have

$$\partial V_{T-k} \big/_{\partial S} = \beta \lambda w \left[\sum_{j=0}^{k} H_{T-k+j}^* \beta^j (1 - \delta)^j \right] \tag{25}$$

or rewriting in terms of t:

$$\partial V_t \big/_{\partial S} = \beta \lambda w \left[\sum_{j=t}^{T} H_j^* \beta^j (1 - \delta)^j \right]. \tag{26}$$

Equating the last two first order conditions and substituting Eq. (26) gives

$$df \big/_{dI} (I_t^*) = \frac{\lambda W_t}{\beta \lambda w \left[\displaystyle\sum_{j=t}^{T} H_j^* \beta^j (1 - \delta)^j \right]} \tag{27}$$

The denominator on the right hand side of Eq. (27) is a decreasing function of t. The wage, assuming that the optimal investment in training/skills exceeds the amount of depreciation, is an increasing function of t. The function f is concave in I. So, the first derivative of f is a decreasing function of I. This implies that the optimal amount of training at time t, I_t^*, decreases with t. Intuitively, as a person ages, the amount of time that remains to realize the benefits from additional training decreases, which lowers the marginal benefits of additional training. In addition, the marginal costs of additional training in terms of forgone wages increases with age. These effects reinforce each other so that the optimal amount of training declines with age.

The solution just described assumed an interior solution for all t. However, for some t we might have $I_t^* > 0$ and $H_t^* = 0$. It is clear, though, that such a situation, wherein an individual focuses entirely on training would occur at the beginning of a career. There also may be some t where $H_t^* > 0$ and $I_t^* = 0$. These periods would always occur toward the end of a career. So this model does a good job of explaining the empirical phenomenon that people concentrate on schooling early in the life cycle. However, it cannot explain why in some situations individuals may invest heavily in training in midcareer. To explain this fact we need to introduce uncertainty.

If there is some source of uncertainty and assuming that individuals maximize expected utility equation (9) becomes

$$V_t(A_t, S_t) = \max{}_{C_t, L_t, I_t}[U(C_t, L_t) + \beta E\{V_{t+1}(A_{t+1}, S_{t+1})|I_t\}].$$

Uncertainty may enter in several different manners. For example, the amount of skills an individual has next period may be function of their skill level today S_t, the amount they invest in training today I_t, plus a random depreciation term $\tilde{\delta}_t$. In this scenario, $S_{t+1} = \left(1 - \tilde{\delta}_t\right)S_t + f(I_t)$.[9] For $\tilde{\delta}_{t-1}$ sufficiently small (eg, because a technological innovation made an individual's skills obsolete) an individual may substantially increase their investment in skills ($I_t \gg I_{t-1}$). So models with uncertainty can explain situations where in midcareer an individual (perhaps after a job displacement) decides to invest heavily in new skills.

2.3 Human Capital Specificity

Human capital may be general or specific. If human capital is general it raises an individual's productivity equally in all jobs. An example of this may be an individual's communication skills. Firm-specific human capital raises an individual's productivity only in the firm that provides the training. An example of this might be the particular organizational structure of the firm. Who does a person go to if they need some question answered?

Completely general or specific forms of human capital are the polar extremes. Intermediate cases would include, for example, occupation- or industry-specific human capital. In the former case, training of this type would raise an individual's productivity in jobs in the same occupation while the latter would only raise an individual's productivity in jobs in the same industry.

Theory predicts that employees bear the training cost for general human capital and that employers and employees share the costs of firm-specific human capital.[10] If a firm

---

[9] For example, $\tilde{\delta}$ could have a beta distribution.

[10] See, for example, Ehrenberg and Smith (2011) for more details.

invests in a worker's general human capital they cannot recoup their costs. A firm that tried to pay a trained worker less than the value of her posttraining marginal product in order to recoup the cost of the such training would lose the worker to another firm precisely because general human capital pays off at all firms.[11] For firm-specific human capital neither the employer nor employee would want to bear all the costs because then they risk being exploited by the other party. For example, if the employee bore all the costs the firm could threaten to fire the employee unless they gave the employer some of the increased productivity in terms of a wage reduction. The threat is credible since the employer is indifferent about whether the employee stays or goes.

Assuming that there are many employers who employ workers in a particular occupation and many employers in any particular industry, individuals would then also bear the costs of occupation-specific and industry-specific training. To the extent that capital markets are more imperfect for individual workers than for firms we might expect to see public subsidies of (or perhaps public provision of) general, occupation-specific, and/or industry-specific types of training rather than of (firm-) specific training. We turn to a discussion of market failures next.

2.4 Market Imperfections and Job Training

With a perfect capital market, as assumed above in our discussion of human capital investment over the life cycle, the only constraint on assets is that $A_T \geq 0$. Since there is no bequest motive, an individual would leave nothing behind so that optimally $A_T = 0$. An alternative model, which imposes an extreme form of credit market constraints, would be one that does not allow an individual to borrow at all. In this case, the individual would face asset constraints of the form $A_t \geq 0$, for all t. These additional constraints can only make an individual worse off. They are likely to be binding when A_0 is sufficiently low. For example, suppose $A_0 = 0$, which may be approximately true for individuals who are from low-income families. If utility functions are such that optimal consumption in every period is positive (eg, $U = C^\alpha L^\beta$ with $\alpha < 1, \beta < 1$) then in period 1 we cannot have a situation where $I_1^* > 0$ and $H_1^* = 0$. The individual must work at least a little in order to consume. Individuals faced with such borrowing constraints will underinvest in human capital relative to a situation with perfect capital markets. This sort of market failure provides one rationale for government intervention in education/training markets. Another reason for government intervention in terms of public provision of job training is that there may be positive externalities to society from job training (eg, reduced crime) that the individual does not incorporate into his/her individual decision-making when determining the optimal level of training to undertake.

---

[11] This story assumes that mobility costs are zero.

2.5 Job Search and Publicly Provided Training

This section develops a simple model of training with job search. We assume for simplicity that there is no wage uncertainty but that the probability of getting a job offer in a given period at a given wage, w, depends on search effort, which we denote by e. In particular, denote the probability of receiving a job offer in period t by $p(e)$ where we assume that p is a continuously differentiable function that is an increasing concave function of e, $p'(e) > 0$ and $p''(e) < 0$. To guarantee an interior solution we shall further assume that $\lim_{e \downarrow 0} p'(e) = \infty$ and $\lim_{e \to \infty} p'(e) = 0$. To simplify matters even further, it is assumed that the return per period while searching equals $b - e$ where b is the benefits received while not working. Once a job is found the individual will receive a wage of w_0 if no training is received and a wage of w_1 if training is received where $w_1 > w_0$. In all jobs it is assumed that there is an exogenous probability of job destruction that equals δ. Training is assumed to cost c units and delay job search by s periods. We assume an infinite time horizon and denote the discount factor by $0 < \beta < 1$. We shall initially assume that an individual can choose to enter a training program at any time during their job search process.

Let V denote the optimal value function associated with search, assuming that the individual has not yet received any job training. We shall denote by V^{U_0} the optimal value of continued search if the individual chooses not to receive job training that period and we let V^T denote the optimal value function if the individual chooses to receive training. So,

$$V = \max \left\{ V^{U_0}, V^T \right\}. \tag{28}$$

Now,

$$V^{U_0} = \max_e \left\{ b - e + \beta \left[p(e) V^{W_0} + (1 - p(e)) V \right] \right\}, \tag{29}$$

where V^{W_0} represents the optimal value associated with work at wage w_0. If an individual decides not to receive job training and searches with job search intensity e, then they receive a net benefit of $b - e$. With probability $p(e)$ they receive a job offer at wage w_0 and are employed next period which has the value V^{W_0}. With probability $1 - p(e)$ they do not get a job offer and are back in the same situation that they are in today, which has value V.

The value of training equals

$$V^T = b \left(\frac{1 - \beta^s}{1 - \beta} \right) - c + \beta^s V^{U_1} \tag{30}$$

where training is assumed to take s periods and cost c and V^{U_1} represents the value of unemployed search when the individual faces the wage w_1:

$$V^{U_1} = \max_e \left\{ b - e + \left[p(e) V^{W_1} + (1 - p(e)) V^{U_1} \right] \right\}. \tag{31}$$

The value function for an untrained individual while employed satisfies:

$$V^{W_0} = w_0 + \beta\left[\delta V + (1-\delta)V^{W_0}\right] \tag{32}$$

for $j=0, 1$. The individual earns w_0 this period and with probability δ her job is terminated. If terminated she enters unemployment where she still has the option to receive job training. Solving Eq. (32) for V^{W_0} yields:

$$V^{W_0} = \frac{w_0 + \delta\beta V}{1-(1-\delta)\beta}. \tag{33}$$

For an employed individual with training who can earn w_1 we have similar expressions for the value function

$$V^{W_1} = w_1 + \beta\left[\delta V^{U_1} + (1-\delta)V^{W_1}\right] \tag{34}$$

and

$$V^{W_1} = \frac{w_1 + \delta\beta V^{U_1}}{1-(1-\delta)\beta}, \tag{35}$$

where, other than receiving a higher wage than someone without job training, if a trained individual loses their job they no longer have the training option available to them and so their value of unemployed search equals V^{U_1}.[12]

It is clear, since none of the underlying variables change over time and the time horizon is infinite, that if $V^{U_0} = \max\left\{V^{U_0}, V^T\right\}$, then the individual will never choose to be trained and that if $V^T = \max\left\{V^{U_0}, V^T\right\}$, then training occurs at the outset of the (first) unemployment spell. If training doesn't occur then

$$V^{U_0} = \max_e\left\{b - e + \beta\left[p(e)V^{W_0} + (1-p(e))V^{U_0}\right]\right\} \tag{36}$$

and the optimal level of search effort, e_0^*, satisfies the first order condition:

$$\beta p'\left(e_0^*\right)\left[V^{W_0} - V^{U_0}\right] - 1 = 0. \tag{37}$$

Next we solve for the optimal value function V^{U_0}. Substituting Eq. (33) into (36) yields

$$V^{U_0} = b - e_0^* + p\left(e_0^*\right)\beta\left\{\frac{w_0 + \delta\beta V^{U_0}}{1-(1-\delta)\beta}\right\} + \left[1 - p\left(e_0^*\right)\right]\beta V^{U_0}.$$

Solving for V^{U_0} then gives

$$V^{U_0} = \frac{\left[b - e_0^*\right]\left[1-(1-\delta)\beta\right] + p\left(e_0^*\right)\beta w_0}{(1-\beta)\left[1-\beta(1-p(e_0^*)-\delta)\right]}. \tag{38}$$

---

[12] We are assuming that the training is (at least) industry-specific and that the job loss is due to a firm-specific idiosyncratic shock that does not affect the individual's productivity in other jobs in the industry.

Analogously we have

$$V^{U_1} = \frac{[b - e_1^*][1 - (1 - \delta)\beta] + p(e_1^*)\beta w_1}{(1 - \beta)[1 - \beta(1 - p(e_1^*) - \delta)]}.$$ (39)

Also after training is completed the optimal intensity of search satisfies

$$p'(e_1^*) = 1/\beta[V^{W_1} - V^{U_1}].$$ (40)

It is easy to show that since $w_1 > w_0$, $V^{U_1} > V^{U_0}$:

$$V^{U_1} = \frac{[b - e_1^*][1 - (1 - \delta)\beta] + p(e_1^*)\beta w_1}{(1 - \beta)[1 - \beta(1 - p(e_1^*) - \delta)]}$$

$$\geq \frac{[b - e_0^*][1 - (1 - \delta)\beta] + p(e_0^*)\beta w_1}{(1 - \beta)[1 - \beta(1 - p(e_0^*) - \delta)]}$$

$$> \frac{[b - e_0^*][1 - (1 - \delta)\beta] + p(e_0^*)\beta w_0}{(1 - \beta)[1 - \beta(1 - p(e_0^*) - \delta)]}.$$

$$= V^{U_0}$$

It is also clear that $V^{W_1} > V^{W_0}$ It is less obvious, however, that $e_1^* > e_0^*$ so that $p(e_1^*) > p(e_0^*)$. From Eq. (40) and the fact that $p'(e)$ is a decreasing function of e since p is a concave function, in order to establish this result we must prove that $V^W - V^U$ is an increasing function of w.

But,

$$V^W - V^U = \frac{w + \delta\beta V^U}{1 - (1 - \delta)\beta} - V^U$$

$$= \frac{w_1 + \delta\beta V^U - (1 - (1 - \delta)\beta)V^U}{1 - (1 - \delta)\beta}$$

$$= \frac{w - (1 - \beta)V^U}{1 - (1 - \delta)\beta}$$

So,

$$\frac{\partial(V^W - V^U)}{\partial w} = \frac{1}{1 - (1 - \delta)\beta}[1 - (1 - \beta)(\partial V^U/\partial e^* \times de^*/dw + \partial V^U/\partial w)]$$

$$= \frac{1}{1 - (1 - \delta)\beta}[1 - (1 - \beta)\partial V^U/\partial w]$$

$$= \frac{1}{1 - (1 - \delta)\beta}\left[1 - \frac{\beta p(e^*)}{1 - \beta(1 - p(e^*) - \delta)}\right]$$

$$= \frac{1}{1 - (1 - \delta)\beta}\left[\frac{1 - (1 - \delta)\beta}{1 - \beta(1 - p(e^*) - \delta)}\right]$$

$$= \frac{1}{1 - \beta(1 - p(e^*) - \delta)} > 0.$$

To summarize, in this model of training and job search if an individual chooses training they will do so immediately. Training, by assumption, will lead to s periods of no job search (a "locking in" period) while training occurs. After training ends, however, an individual with training will increase their search intensity relative to an individual with no training and is reemployed at a faster rate. Whether the expected duration of joblessness with training is longer than that without training depends on the length of training as compared to the posttraining increase in the per period probability of receiving a job offer.

The model above assumed that the individual was free to choose training each and every period. We now look at two models that limit training opportunities in two different ways. In the first case, we shall assume that an individual is offered a training opportunity with probability λ each period while unemployed. We shall assume that if the training offer is made to an unemployed individual, they will accept it if no job offer is made in the same period but that a job offer at the lower "no training" wage is preferable to training. Finally, we assume that training is only potentially offered for the current unemployment spell. Thus the value function for an unemployed individual who hasn't received training satisfies

$$V^{U_0} = \max_e \{ b - e + p(e)\beta V^{W_0} + [1 - p(e)][1 - \lambda]\beta V^{U_0} + [1 - p(e)]\lambda V^T \} \qquad (41)$$

and the first order condition for optimal search effort is

$$\beta p'(e_0^*) \left[V^{W_0} - (1 - \lambda) V^{U_0} - \lambda V^T \right] - 1 = 0$$

or

$$p'(e_0^*) = 1/\beta \left[V^{W_0} - (1 - \lambda) V^{U_0} - \lambda V^T \right]. \qquad (42)$$

Relative to the no training situation ($\lambda = 0$), the individual devotes less effort to job search before the training offer is received. This occurs since $V^T > V^{U_0}(\lambda = 0)$ by assumption. Also V^{U_0} is an increasing function of λ, so $(1 - \lambda) V^{U_0} + \lambda V^T > V^{U_0}(\lambda = 0)$. The value of being unemployed has increased when there is potentially a training opportunity, so search effort decreases. If a training offer is made, then an individual stops searching for s periods. Once search commences, as before, the search intensity and probability of a job offer increases relative to the no training situation.

A second type of training program would be one that is only offered (or potentially offered) to those whose unemployment spell exceeds some specific duration (eg, the New Deal program in the United Kingdom). This type of program would lead to a nonstationary model of job search. In our situation individuals who continue to be unemployed would reduce their search intensity as they approached the time where job training is offered. Suppose for simplicity that the training program is offered to every person when the unemployment spell equals t_0. Also assume that the individual benefits from the training program $V_{t_0}^T = V^T > V_{t_0}^{U_0} = V^{U_0}$ where V_t^j is the value function after t

periods of unemployment, $j = T$, U_0. It can be shown by backward induction that $V_t < V_{t+1}$ for $t = 1, \ldots, t_0 - 1$. The first order condition for optimal search effort at time t, e_t^*, for $t < t_0$ satisfies

$$\beta p'\left(e_t^*\right)\left[V^{W_0} - V_{t+1}\right] - 1 = 0. \tag{43}$$

Since $V_t < V_{t+1}$ Eq. (43) implies that $e_{t-1}^* > e_t^*$ and, hence, the conditional probability of reemployment decreases as the individual approaches the date at which training is offered.

2.6 Multiple Training Options

In this section we build a model of training similar to Heckman et al. (1999) where there are M training options plus a no training option. One difference between this model and that of Heckman et al. (1999) is that in this model there is uncertainty about how well an individual will do in any one of the training options. Assume that an individual is unemployed. If she (or her case worker) decides that she should not be trained she will receive job offers at a rate of η_0 per period and, once employed, will receive an (unskilled) wage rate of w_0 and bear the risk of job loss (destruction) of δ_0 per period.

Each of the M training options is characterized by a per period cost c_i, and a per period probability of completion of λ_i, $i = 1, \ldots, M$. There is also is a random variable $\widetilde{\alpha}_i$ that measures how successful the training program was at improving an individual's skills. The realization of the random variable occurs at the time of program completion. However before the training program is undertaken each individual (caseworker) has some beliefs about their potential success characterized by the c.d.f. F_i, $i = 1, \ldots, M$. The important point to notice is that these beliefs may differ across the different training programs. We assume, however, that the realizations of $\widetilde{\alpha}_i$ are independent.

Upon completion of training program i we assume that the individual's wage is an increasing function of their success. For simplicity we assume that $w_i = w_0 + a_i$ where α_i is the realization of $\widetilde{\alpha}_i$. It is also assumed that the job offer rate is an increasing concave function of α_i, $\eta_i(\alpha_i)$, while the job destruction rate is a decreasing convex function of α_i, $\delta_i(\alpha_i)$. Finally, we assume that while unemployed the individual receives some benefits denote by b. We shall denote the discount factor by β.

This problem satisfies the conditions of the multiarmed bandit (MAB) problem and has an index solution. Namely, the optimal strategy is to assign an index to each training option as well as the no training option and choose the option each period with the highest index (which is sometimes referred to as the Gittins index in honor of John Gittins who first solved the MAB problem).[13] The index for each option is computed as the reservation (or retirement) value Z that would make an individual indifferent between continuing the option or stopping and receiving Z, assuming that the option to stop is available each period in the future. Let x_i be the current state, assume that

---

[13] See Gittins (1979). For an application to job search models see McCall (1994).

the individual receives a reward in the current period that depends on the current state. Denote the reward function by $R(x_i)$. Finally, if an option is chosen it moves to a new state according to the transition probability function P_i that may depend upon the state x_i. Then the Gittins index for option i in state x_i satisfies:

$$Z_i(x_i) = R_i(x_i) + \beta \int_{\Omega_i} V_i(y, Z_i(x_i)) dP_i(y|x_i),$$

where V_i is the value function from the simple problem of continuing with project i or stopping and receiving Z.

For our particular application denote the case where training has yet to be completed by $x_i = (0, 0)$. When training has been completed at a level of success α_i, the state is denoted by $x_i = (\alpha_i, 0)$ if the individual is unemployed and $x_i = (\alpha_i, 1)$ if the individual is employed.

The Gittins index once training is completed and the individual is employed equals:

$$Z_i(\alpha_i, 1) = (w_0 + \alpha_i) + \beta(1 - \delta_i(\alpha_i)) \max\{V(\alpha_i, 1), Z_i(\alpha_i, 1)\} \\ + \beta\delta_i(\alpha_i) \max\{V(\alpha_i, 0), Z_i(\alpha_i, 1)\} \tag{44}$$

where the first term in parentheses is the current reward, the second term is when the individual remains employed next period that occurs with probability $1-\delta_i(\alpha_i)$ and the third term is when the individual loses their job that occurs with probability $\delta_i(\alpha_i)$. Assuming that individuals prefer to be employed at wage $w_0 + \alpha_0$, Eq. (44) can be simplified to

$$Z_i(\alpha_i, 1) = (w_0 + \alpha_i) + \beta(1 - \delta_i(\alpha_i))Z_i(\alpha_i, 1) + \beta\delta_i(\alpha_i)Z_i(\alpha_i, 1) \\ = \frac{w_0 + \alpha_i}{1 - \beta}.$$

The Gittins index while unemployed equals

$$Z_i(\alpha_i, 0) = b + \beta\eta_i(\alpha_i) \max\{V(\alpha_i, 1), Z_i(\alpha_i, 0)\} + \beta(1 - \eta_i(\alpha_i))Z_i(\alpha_i, 0).$$

But, the value of becoming employed when the "retirement" option $Z(\alpha_i, 0)$ is available satisfies

$$V(\alpha_i, 1, Z_i(\alpha_i, 0)) = w_0 + \alpha_i + \beta(1 - \delta_i(\alpha_i))V(\alpha_i, 1, Z_i(\alpha_i, 0)) + \beta\delta_i(\alpha_i)Z_i(\alpha_i, 0),$$

where have now made explicit the fact that V depends on Z, or

$$V(\alpha_i, 1, Z_i(\alpha_i, 0)) = \frac{w_0 + \alpha_i + \beta\delta_i(\alpha_i)Z_i(\alpha_i, 0)}{1 - \beta(1 - \delta_i(\alpha_i))}.$$

So,

$$Z_i(\alpha_i, 0) = b + \beta\eta_i(\alpha_i)\frac{w_0 + \alpha_i + \beta\delta_i(\alpha_i)Z_i(\alpha_i, 0)}{1 - \beta(1 - \delta_i(\alpha_i))} + \beta(1 - \eta_i(\alpha_i))Z_i(\alpha_i, 0)$$

or

$$Z_i(\alpha_i, 0) = \frac{b[1 - \beta(1 - \delta_i(\alpha_i))] + \beta\eta_i(\alpha_i)[w_0 + \alpha_i]}{[1 - \beta(1 - \delta_i(\alpha_i))][1 - \beta(1 - \eta_i(\alpha_i))] - \beta^2\delta_i(\alpha_i)\eta_i(\alpha_i)}$$

$$= \frac{b[1 - \beta(1 - \delta_i(\alpha_i))] + \beta\eta_i(\alpha_i)[w_0 + \alpha_i]}{(1 - \beta)[1 - \beta(1 - \delta_i(\alpha_i)) + \beta\eta_i(\alpha_i)]}.$$

It can be shown that $Z_i(\alpha_i, 0)$ is an increasing function of α_i.

Finally, the Gittins index before training has been completed satisfies

$$Z_i(0, 0) = b - c_i + \beta\lambda_i E\max\{V(\alpha_i, 0), Z_i(\alpha_i, 0)\}dF_i(\alpha) + \beta(1 - \lambda_i)Z_i(\alpha, 0).$$

This can be rewritten as

$$Z_i(0, 0) = b - c_i + \beta\lambda_i[1 - F_i(\alpha_i^*)]Z_i(0, 0) + \beta(1 - \lambda_i)Z_i(0, 0) + \beta\lambda_i\int_{\alpha_i^*}^{\infty}V_i(\alpha, 0)dF_i(\alpha),$$

where α_i^* is the "reservation value" of α_i such that for $\alpha_i < \alpha_i^*$ the retirement (stopping) option for $Z_i(0, 0)$ is preferred to continuing. Solving for $Z_i(0, 0)$ gives

$$Z_i(0, 0) = \frac{b - c_i + \beta\lambda_i\int_{\alpha_i^*}^{\infty}V_i(\alpha_i, 0)dF_i(\alpha)}{1 - \beta[1 - \lambda_i F_i(\alpha_i^*)]}.$$

Now,

$$V_i(\alpha_i, 0) = b + \beta\eta_i(\alpha_i)V_i(\alpha_i, 1) + \beta(1 - \eta_i(\alpha_i))V_i(\alpha_i, 0),$$

where

$$V_i(\alpha_i, 1) = w_i + \alpha_i + \beta(1 - \delta_i(\alpha_i))V_i(\alpha_i, 1) + \beta\delta_i(\alpha_i)V_i(\alpha_i, 0)$$

or

$$V_i(\alpha_i, 1) = \frac{w_i + \alpha_i + \beta\delta(\alpha_i)V_i(\alpha_i, 0)}{1 - \beta(1 - \delta(\alpha_i))}.$$

So,

$$V_i(\alpha_i, 0) = b + \beta\eta(\alpha_i)\left\{\frac{w_i + \alpha_i + \beta\delta(\alpha_i)V_i(\alpha_i, 0)}{1 - \beta(1 - \delta(\alpha_i))}\right\} + \beta(1 - \eta(\alpha_i))V_i(\alpha_i, 0).$$

Solving for $V_i(\alpha_i, 0)$ yields:

$$V_i(\alpha_i, 0) = \frac{b[1 - \beta(1 - \delta(\alpha_i))] + \beta\eta(\alpha_i)(w_i + \alpha_i)}{(1 - \beta)[1 - \beta(1 - \delta(\alpha_i)) + \beta\eta(\alpha_i)]}.$$

Thus, the M training programs are ranked by their Gittins indices. If none of them exceed the Gittins index of the no training option then the individual doesn't receive any training and there are no further considerations. If training option i is chosen, and the outcome is sufficiently successful (ie, $Z_i(\alpha_i, 0) \geq \max_{j \neq i} Z_j(0, 0)$), then the individual (caseworker) will consider no additional training program. However, if training is not successful $\left(Z_i(\alpha_i, 0) < \max_{j \neq i} Z_j(0, 0)\right)$ then the individual will try another training program (assuming at least one other training option dominates the no training option). As long as training costs are not too large relative to the amount of uncertainty in F_i training will have an option value. That is, all else equal, the Gittins index, $Z_i(0, 0)$, will be an increasing function of the riskiness (in terms of a mean preserving spread) of F_i.

To summarize, in this model there are several training options, one of which could be a no training option. The options differ not only in their expected costs and benefits but also in the uncertainty regarding costs and benefits. The optimal decision policy involves ranking the training options using indices and initially choosing the training option with the highest index. As information is revealed about this particular training option its index will be revised. If at some point the index for this training option falls below the "second-best" option then the optimal strategy is for the individual to discontinue the current training option and switch to the alternative training option that now has the highest index.

2.7 General Equilibrium Effects

Up to this point we have looked only at the individual's decision of whether or not to receive training. Public job training programs, however, typically involve a significant amount of the labor force so there may be general equilibrium effects as well (eg, Heckman et al., 1998a,b,c; Johnson, 1980).[14] In our situation, when many unemployed individuals receive training this would lead to downward pressure on the wage received by trained workers, w_1.

To consider this more formally, we shall develop an equilibrium search model using the Mortensen-Pissarides framework.[15] Let there be two types of employers, one type of employer uses untrained workers (type 0) and the other type employs trained workers (type 1). In the former case an employed worker produces y_0 per period while in the latter case an employed worker produces y_1, per period. The profit per period of an employer of type ℓ who has employed a worker is $y_\ell - w_\ell$, $\ell = 0, 1$. At the end of each period there is an exogenous probability δ that the worker-employer match will end. The value function for employer ℓ with a filled position is

---

[14] In the context of unemployment insurance see for instance, Davidson and Woodbury (1993) and for welfare, see Lise et al. (2004) and for social security see İmrohoroğlu and Kitao (2012).

[15] See Mortensen and Pissarides (1994) or McCall and McCall (2008).

$$J_\ell^e = \gamma_\ell - w_\ell + \beta \big[(1-\delta)J_\ell^e + \delta J_\ell^v \big]$$

where J_ℓ^v is the value of a job vacancy for employer $\ell, \ell = 0, 1$.

The value of a job vacancy to employer ℓ on the other hand satisfies

$$J_\ell^v = -k + \beta \big[q_\ell J_\ell^e + (1-q_\ell)J_\ell^v \big]$$

where k is the per period cost of maintaining the vacancy and q_ℓ is the probability of filling the vacancy at the end of the period, $\ell = 0, 1$ The probability q_ℓ however will depend on the number of unemployed individuals of type ℓ and the intensity with which each type of worker looks for a job, e_ℓ^*. In equilibrium, employers will enter the market until the value of a job vacancy J_ℓ^v equals 0.

Training will be simplified in order to make the model more tractable. We shall assume that training occurs instantaneously and that the per period probability of receiving training during an unemployment spell is λ. We also assume that when an employee-employer match is destroyed a previously trained worker loses the additional productivity $\gamma_1 - \gamma_0$ provided by that training. However, they may receive additional training in the current unemployment spell, again at rate λ. Our goal is to examine how equilibrium wages change when the government changes the rate at which workers are trained.

The value function for an unemployed worker who has yet to receive training is then

$$V^{U_0} = \max_e \big\{ b - e + p(e)\beta V^{W_0} + [1 - p(e)](1-\lambda)\beta V^{U_0}$$
$$+ [1 - p(e)]\lambda \beta V^{U_1}$$

while the value function for an unemployed trained worker satisfies Eq. (31). The value function for an employed untrained worker, V^{W_0}, satisfies

$$V^{W_0} = w_0 + \beta \big[\delta V^{U_0} + (1-\delta)V^{W_0} \big]$$

and the value function for an employed trained worker, V^{W_1}, satisfies

$$V^{W_1} = w_1 + \beta \big[\delta V^{U_0} + (1-\delta)V^{W_1} \big]. \tag{15}$$

There are two more features of the model that need to be specified. First, we need to specify how wages are determined. Here we assume a Nash bargaining solution where the surplus from a job match is split between the two parties with the employer receiving the fraction α of the surplus and the employee the fraction $(1-\alpha)$. The second feature is the way in which employers and employees become matched. Here we assume that there are two matching functions, $m_\ell, \ell = 0, 1$, one for trained individuals and the other for untrained individuals that depend on the optimal (equilibrium) search effort level of an unemployed worker, e_ℓ^*, the fraction of vacancies v_ℓ, and the fraction of unemployed workers, $u_\ell, \ell = 0, 1.$[16] That is, $m_\ell(e_\ell^*, v_\ell, u_\ell), \ell = 0, 1.$ We assume that m_ℓ is a decreasing function of u_ℓ, and an increasing function of e_ℓ^* and v_ℓ. For simplicity (and with some abuse of notation), we assume that

$$m_\ell(e_\ell^*, v_\ell, u_\ell) = p_\ell(e_\ell^*) m_\ell(v_\ell, u_\ell), \ell = 0, 1. \tag{46}$$

For an untrained job seeker the first order condition for the optimal search effort is then

$$p_0'(e_0^*) = 1 \div \beta m_0 [V^{W_0} - V^{U_0} - \lambda(V^{U_1} - V^{U_0})] \tag{47}$$

and for a trained job seeker equals

$$p_1'(e_1^*) = 1 \div m_1 \beta [V^{W_1} - V^{U_1}]. \tag{48}$$

From Eq. (47) and since $V^{U_1} > V^{U_0}$, when λ increases e_0^* decreases. Thus the direct effect of an increase in λ is to increase the fraction of trained workers in the economy. However, untrained workers respond to this increase in λ by reducing their search effort, which tends to offset this effect. In a long-run stationary equilibrium, the inflow rate into employment must equal the outflow rate into unemployment. The fraction employed for type ℓ jobs equals $f_\ell - u_\ell, \ell = 0, 1$ where f_ℓ is the fraction of type ℓ workers and $f_0 + f_1 = 1$. So, in a stationary equilibrium we have

$$0 = \delta(f_\ell - u_\ell) - p_\ell(e_\ell^*) m_\ell(v_\ell, u_\ell) u_\ell, \ell = 0, 1.$$

or

$$u_\ell = \left. \delta f_\ell \middle/ \delta - p_\ell(e_\ell^*) m_\ell(v_\ell, u_\ell) \right., \ell = 0, 1. \tag{49}$$

Also the fraction of trained workers must remain constant, so

$$0 = \delta(f_1 - u_1) - u_0 (1 - p_0(e_0^*) m_0(u_0, v_0)) \lambda$$

or

$$f_1 = \frac{\delta u_1 + u_0 (1 - p_0(e_0^*) m_0(u_0, v_0)) \lambda}{\delta}. \tag{50}$$

To simplify matters even further we assume that the matching functions are the same whether the unemployed worker is trained or untrained and that m is homogenous of degree zero. So,

$$u_\ell = \frac{\delta f_\ell}{\delta - p(e_\ell^*) m\left(1, \left. v_\ell \middle/ u_\ell \right.\right)}, \ell = 0, 1$$

---

[16] For an overview of matching functions see Petrongolo and Pissarides (2001). Also see Stevens (2007) for a microeconomics model that leads to a CES matching function, and Borowczyk-Martins et al. (2013) on accounting for bias when estimating matching functions.

or

$$u_\ell = \frac{\delta f_\ell}{\delta - p(e_\ell^*) m(1, \theta_\ell)}, \ell = 0, 1 \tag{51}$$

where $\theta_\ell \equiv {}^{v_\ell}/_{u_\ell}$ is a measure of labor market "tightness." From Eqs. (47) and (48) above we can see that as θ_ℓ increases optimal search effort decreases.

Equilibrium wages are determined by a Nash bargaining solution where the worker and firm split the joint surplus from the match with the employer getting the fraction α, where α is determined by the relative bargaining power of employers relative to employees. The joint surplus, S_ℓ, of the match equals

$$S_\ell = y_\ell + \beta\delta V^{U_\ell} + \beta(1-\delta)S_\ell, \ell = 0, 1 \tag{52}$$

where y^ℓ is the output in the current period and next period the job match is (exogenously) dissolved with probability δ where the worker receives V^{U_ℓ} and the firm receives 0 and with probability $1 - \delta$ the job match is not dissolved and the surplus equals $S_\ell, \ell = 0, 1$. Solving Eq. (52) for S_ℓ yields

$$S_\ell = \frac{y_\ell - \beta\delta V^{U_\ell}}{1 - \beta(1-\delta)}, \ell = 0, 1. \tag{53}$$

So the wage of a trained worker in equilibrium equals $(1-\alpha)S_1$ and the wage of an untrained worker equals $(1-\alpha)S_0$. As the training rate increases, we see from Eq. (50) that the direct effect is to increase the fraction of trained workers. By Eq. (51) this tends to increase the stationary unemployment rate of trained workers and decrease the stationary unemployment rate of untrained workers. Hence V^{U_0} increases and V^{U_1} decreases. From Eq. (49) and Nash bargaining this leads to a decrease in the equilibrium wage rate of trained workers and an increase in the equilibrium wage rate of untrained workers. The value of a trained vacancy then increases, leading to an increase in trained job vacancies and the value of an untrained vacancy declines leading to a drop in untrained job vacancies. So, $m(1, \theta_1)$ increases and $m(1, \theta_0)$ decreases, causing further indirect changes in u_1 and u_0.

To summarize, when the government increases the rate at which it trains unemployed workers this tends to increase the equilibrium fraction of workers in the economy who are trained. This increases the stock of trained workers which in turn pulls down the equilibrium wage of trained workers and raises the equilibrium wage of untrained workers. However, employers respond to these wage changes by increasing trained and decreasing untrained vacancies.

It is useful at this point to consider the implications of this for policy evaluation. Many econometric evaluations of policy changes measure the partial equilibrium benefit of training on the trained (a.k.a. the effect of the "treatment on the treated"). In our situation this corresponds to the effect of training a worker holding constant the equilibrium wages and job offer probabilities, where the latter is a function of equilibrium optimal search effort and equilibrium stationary unemployment and vacancy rates. They typically invoke the Stable Unit Treatment Value Assumption (SUTVA), which implies that the potential outcome of one unit does not depend on the assignments of other units. However, if a nonnegligible fraction of the economy is treated (as would be the case if the training rate, λ, changed from zero to, say, 0.3), equilibrium adjustments likely cause the SUTVA assumption to be violated. Thus, partial equilibrium estimators may result in misleading estimates of the effect of a policy change when the change affects a sizeable fraction of individuals in the economy. We discuss the estimation of general equilibrium treatment effects in Section 4.14.

3. THEORY: PARTICIPATION IN TRAINING PROGRAMS

There is a large literature that studies the determinants of participation in (or "take-up" of) various government-sponsored programs such as welfare (eg, Blank and Ruggles, 1996 and Daponte et al., 1999), Medicaid (eg, Card and Shore-Sheppard, 2004; Currie and Gruber, 1996), workers' compensation (eg, Card and McCall, 1996; Krueger, 1990), unemployment insurance (eg, Anderson and Meyer, 2003; McCall, 1995), disability insurance (eg, Benítez-Silva et al., 2004; Bound, 1989), and job training (eg, Ashenfelter, 1983; Heckman and Robb, 1985; Heckman and Smith, 2004; Heckman et al., 1999) The human capital model and, more generally, economic decision-making models of job training lead to predictions about when an individual will participate in a job training program.[17] Let D_t be a dichotomous random variable that equals one if an individual participates in training at time t, and zero, otherwise. In the simple model with a constant, known, return to training, $D_t = 1$ if and only if Eq. (2) is satisfied. However, the econometrician may not be able to fully observe the underlying parameters that guide an individual's decision. In this case, an empirical model can be derived from the perfect foresight model (2) by assuming that one or more of the underlying parameters are functions of both measured and unmeasured characteristics. This leads to an empirical specification of $\Pr(D_t = 1)$. For example, the discounted return to training may be modeled as

$$\alpha/r = g_1(\mathbf{X}_t) + v_{t1} \tag{54}$$

the direct cost of training as

$$c = g_2(\mathbf{X}_t) + v_{t2} \tag{55}$$

and the opportunity costs in terms of foregone earnings as

$$\gamma_t^0 = g_3(\mathbf{X}_t) + v_{t3} \tag{56}$$

---

[17] Currie (2006) surveys the literature on participation in social programs.

where $\mathbf{X}_t$ is a vector of observed characteristics, the g_k are functions of $\mathbf{X}_t$ and the ν_k are unobserved random error terms. Substituting Eqs. (54), (55), and (56) into Eq. (2) gives

$$g(\mathbf{X}_t) + g_2(\mathbf{X}_t) + g_3(\mathbf{X}_t) + \nu_{t1} + \nu_{t2} + \nu_{t3} \geq 0$$

or

$$g(\mathbf{X}_t) + \varepsilon_t \geq 0 \tag{57}$$

where $g = g_1 + g_2 + g_3$ and $\varepsilon_t = \nu_{t1} + \nu_{t2} + \nu_{t3}$. One can think of the left side of Eq. (57) as the net utility of participating in training; in this simple model, participation occurs when the net utility is nonnegative. Denote the cumulative density function of ε_t by F. Then the probability that an individual participates in training, $\Pr(D_t = 1 | \mathbf{X}_t)$, satisfies:

$$\Pr(D_t = 1 | \mathbf{X}_t) = F(g(\mathbf{X}_t)). \tag{58}$$

Typically, g is specified as a linear index function, $g(\mathbf{X}_t) = \mathbf{X}_t'\boldsymbol{\beta}$. With sufficient variation in $\mathbf{X}_t$, F is nonparametrically identified up to a scale factor (Matzkin, 1992). More realistically, the individual will not have perfect foresight. In this case they will participate in training at time t if Eq. (5) is satisfied. Of course, they may still possess more information than the econometrician. For example, they may observe $\mathbf{X}_t$ and some random variable γ_t. Thus, the individual would participate in training if

$$k(\mathbf{X}_t, \gamma_t) \equiv E\left\{ \tilde{\alpha} /_r - Y_t^0 - c | \mathbf{X}_t, \gamma_t \right\} \geq 0.$$

Denote the c.d.f. of γ_t by H. Assume that the econometrician does not observe γ_t. Then the probability of receiving training equals

$$\Pr(D_t = 1 | \mathbf{X}_t) = \int I[k(\mathbf{X}_t, \gamma_t) \geq 0] dH(\gamma_t | \mathbf{X}_t)$$

or, if it is assumed that γ_t and $\mathbf{X}_t$ are independent then

$$\Pr(D_t = 1 | \mathbf{X}_t) = \int I[k(\mathbf{X}_t, \gamma_t) \geq 0] dH(\gamma_t).$$

Nonparametric identification of both k and H is not feasible without more restrictions.

Some of the models discussed above imply that individuals participate in training programs at different times in an unemployment spell. One way to model this sort of dynamic participation is using a hazard model or more generally an event history framework (see Lancaster, 1992). Let T be the time spent unemployed until an individual participates in a public training program. Recall that the hazard function at time t is defined as

$$h(t|I_{t-}) = \lim_{\Delta t \to 0} \frac{\Pr(t < T \le t + \Delta t | T > t, I_{t-})}{\Delta t},$$

where I_{t-} is the information accumulated up to "just before" time t. If we assume that the information consists of a set of possibly time-varying variables $\mathbf{X}_t$ then we have

$$h(t|\mathbf{X}_s, s = (0, t]) = \lambda(t, \mathbf{X}_t),$$

where we have imposed the assumption that the hazard at time t only depends on the value current value of $\mathbf{X}$.

The proportional hazards model imposes the condition that the log hazard function is linearly separable in $\mathbf{X}$ and t:

$$h(t|\mathbf{X}_s, s = (0, t]) = \lambda_0(t)\phi(\mathbf{X}_t) \tag{59}$$

In many empirical studies ϕ takes the form

$$\phi(\mathbf{X}_t) = \exp(\boldsymbol{\beta}'\mathbf{X}_t) \tag{60}$$

so that the hazard at time t only depends on the value of $\mathbf{X}$ at time t. The survivor function, denoted by $S(t)$, equals the probability that T exceeds t. Assuming a proportional hazard function (59), it can be shown that

$$S(t|\mathbf{X}_s, s = (0, t]) = \exp\left(-\int_0^t \lambda_0(s)\phi(\mathbf{X}_s)ds\right) \tag{61}$$

If there is an unmeasured, time-constant variable, γ, that impacts the hazard function in a multiplicative fashion then we have

$$h(t|\mathbf{X}_s, s = (0, t], \gamma) = \lambda_0(t)\phi(\mathbf{X}_t)\gamma$$

and

$$S(t|\mathbf{X}_s, s = (0, t], \gamma) = \exp\left(-\gamma\int_0^t \lambda_0(s)\phi(\mathbf{X}_s)ds\right).$$

Denote the c.d.f. of γ by H. For identification purposes it is usually assumed that γ is independent of $\mathbf{X}_t$. Imposing this assumption and integrating out γ from the survivor function gives:

$$S(t|\mathbf{X}_s, s = (0, t]) = \int \exp\left(-\gamma\int_0^t \lambda_0(s)\phi(\mathbf{X}_s)ds\right)dH(\gamma)$$

Elbers and Ridder (1982) shows that λ_0, ϕ, and H are nonparametrically identified when $\mathbf{X}_t$ is time-constant and takes on at least two distinct values.[18]

---

[18] See also Heckman and Singer (1984).

In general, participating in a public job-training course may be only one of many reasons why an unemployment spell ends. For example, an individual may find a job before starting a training program. In this situation we typically observe both the duration of the unemployment spell and the reason why the unemployment spell ended. This sort of data is often analyzed using a competing risks model. Assume for simplicity that there are just two reasons ("risks") for a spell ending and denote them by 1 and 2. There are two underlying (latent) durations T_1 and T_2, but all that is observed is the "identified minimum," $T = \min(T_1, T_2)$, and an indicator variable of which outcome occurred $I(T = T_1)$. One question that arises is under what conditions we can identify the latent survivor function $S(T_1, T_2|\mathbf{X})$ from the identified minimum. This was addressed in the paper of Heckman and Honoré (1989), who showed that the latent survivor function S is nonparametrically identified when there are two continuous x-variables.

4. METHODS FOR EVALUATING VOCATIONAL TRAINING PROGRAMS

4.1 Introduction

This section reviews the standard econometric methods for evaluating vocational training programs. Three main features differentiate it from other surveys of econometric methods for program evaluation, such as (arranged in rough order of technical enthusiasm) Smith (2004), Blundell et al. (2005), Blundell and Costa-Dias (2009), Heckman et al. (1999), Imbens and Wooldridge (2009), Heckman and Vytlacil (2007a,b), and Abbring and Heckman (2007). First, we allocate our attention in rough proportion to the frequency with which particular econometric methods get used in this particular literature. Thus, for example, we spend relatively little time on regression discontinuity methods and relatively more time on methods that assume "selection on observed variables." Second, we have aimed the technical level at applied researchers rather than applied or theoretical econometricians, though we provide citations to the literature relevant to those audiences. Third, we include separate discussions of study design issues that commonly arise in the evaluation of vocational training programs, such as whether to define the "treatment" as being offered a course, starting a course or finishing a course.

The standard potential outcomes notation defined in the treatment effects literature allows us to increase the clarity and precision of the discussion at several points.[19] In the case of a binary treatment (eg, training versus no training) it defines two potential outcomes:

Y_{1i} denotes the outcome with treatment for individual "i,"

Y_{0i} denotes the outcome without treatment for individual "i,"

---

[19] Different disciplines, and different social networks within disciplines, have disparate citation practices regarding the potential outcomes framework, in part due to thinking about it at different levels of abstraction. Standard (in one place or another) citations include Frost (1920), Neyman (1923), Fisher (1935), Roy (1951), Quandt (1972), and Rubin (1974).

where Y can represent any outcome of interest. We follow the literature in using the terminology of treatments as a generic term for training and/or other services, such as job search assistance, that might substitute for (or be combined with) training in practice. Generalizing the potential outcomes framework to the case of multiple treatments is straightforward; see eg, Imbens (2000) or Lechner (2001).

Partial equilibrium evaluations conceive of these potential outcomes as fixed characteristics of individuals that do not depend on features of their environment such as who else gets training or how many others get training. The statistics literature calls this the "Stable Unit Treatment Value Assumption" (SUTVA). Economists would call this an assumption of no spillovers or, more generally, no equilibrium effects. We discuss relaxing the SUTVA assumption in the context of equilibrium evaluations later in this section.

The potential outcomes framework takes its name from the fact that any given individual at a particular time experiences only one of Y_{1i} and Y_{0i}. The outcome that the individual experiences can be measured but the outcome they do not experience cannot. This means that there is no simple, direct way to construct individual-specific impacts $\Delta_i = Y_{1i} - Y_{0i}$. It also motivates the interpretation of the problem of estimating the impact of training (or of treatments more generally) as a missing data problem. The researcher is missing the data on the potential outcome associated with the counterfactual treatment choice: what would have happened without treatment for the treated individuals and what would have happened with treatment for the untreated individuals.

The difficulty of constructing treatment effects for individuals leads to a focus in empirical work on average treatment effects of various sorts. The two most common are the average treatment effect on some population (ATE) and the average effect of treatment on the treated (ATET) individuals in some population. In terms of the potential outcomes notation, these become:

$$\Delta_{ATE} = E(Y_{1i} - Y_{0i})$$
$$\Delta_{ATET} = E(Y_{1i} - Y_{0i} | D_i = 1)$$

where the $E(\cdot)$ denotes the expectations operator, and where D_i is an indicator (ie, binary or dummy) variable for receipt of treatment. In words, then, $E(Y_{1i} - Y_{0i} | D_i = 1)$ denotes the mean impact of treatment on those who received it in the population. Both these parameters can be defined for subgroups based on characteristics not affected by treatment, eg, for men and women; we have more to say about such subgroups below.

Much of the literature, sometimes explicitly and much more often implicitly, assumes that training has the same effect on everyone who takes it. This "common effect" assumption appears in our notation as

$$\Delta_i = \Delta \quad \text{for all "}i."$$

In our view, this assumption has little relevance to the study of government-sponsored vocational training (nor, indeed, to the study of most other things), even when weakened to hold within subgroups groups defined by observed characteristics, so that

$$\Delta_i = \Delta(X_i).$$

We have several reasons for this view: First, as discussed in more detail below, the binary training indicator in many studies represents training by many different providers for many different occupations. Heterogeneous treatments suggest heterogeneous treatment effects. Second, we observe in many evaluation data sets, including those from experimental evaluations, that some individuals have zero earnings and no employment after training and others have positive earnings and employment. Except in the special (and unlikely) case of a common treatment effect of zero, this feature of the data necessarily implies heterogeneous treatment effects. Finally, when formally tested, as in Appendix E of Heckman et al. (1997b), the data typically reject the null of homogeneous treatment effects and provide substantively nontrivial lower bounds on the treatment effect variance. In light of all this, it rarely makes sense to talk about "the effect" of a training program.

Heterogeneous treatment effects matter in several ways: first, even if individuals do not know anything about their own treatment effect, if they know something about the variance of the treatment effects this may deter relatively risk-averse individuals from taking training. If individuals and/or gatekeepers such as caseworkers have some knowledge of the treatment effect at the individual level, this should lead to selection into training based on beliefs about that effect. In the presence of such selection we would expect, for example, that all else (eg, costs of participation) equal, the average treatment effect on the treated would exceed the treatment effect on the marginal trainee who is just indifferent (in expectation) between training and not training which in turn would exceed the average treatment effect in the population. In such a world, Δ_{ATET} may provide a misleading guide to the gains that would be realized by the additional trainees served due to an expansion of the program.

In a heterogeneous treatment effect world in which individuals select into training in part based on their beliefs about their treatment effect, different econometric estimators provide estimates of different parameters of interest. For example, instrumental variables estimators do not, in general, provide estimates of either Δ_{ATE} or Δ_{ATET} but rather something called the Local Average Treatment Effect (LATE), as we discuss in more detail below.

In addition, in a heterogeneous treatment effect world we can also define many other treatment effects parameters besides just Δ_{ATE} and Δ_{ATET}. For example, quantile treatment effects (QTEs) have attracted some limited interest in the more academic side of the government-sponsored training literature. QTEs reveal the effect of treatment on the full distribution of outcomes but require careful interpretation. A larger class of parameters of interest requires assumptions about the link between the treated and untreated outcomes, ie, about the joint distribution of Y_1 and Y_0. Examples of such parameters include the variance of the impacts of training and the fraction of trainees with a positive impact of training. Because the literature on training has not devoted much attention to these parameters (though it should devote more in our view) we refer the interested reader to the discussions in Heckman et al. (1997b) and Djebbari and Smith (2008).

4.2 Selection Into Participation

Before launching into our discussions of general applied econometric issues and specific estimators, we set the stage by introducing one (very) common version of the selection problem in evaluating training programs.

Fig. 6 displays data from the U.S. National Job Training Partnership Act (JTPA) Study (NJS), an experimental evaluation of the JTPA program that we describe in greater detail in the section on U.S. institutions and impact estimates. The JTPA study was unique in combining a random assignment evaluation of the JTPA program with collection (at a subset of the evaluation sites) of "ideal" comparison group data on eligible nonparticipants (ENPs). We present figures here for adult men ages 22 and above at the four sites with both experimental and comparison group data.[20]

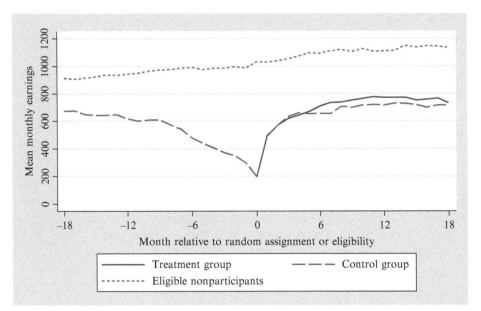

Figure 6 Mean earnings relative to RA/EL. *Source: Authors' calculation using US National JTPA Study Data.*

---

[20] Similar patterns emerge for adult women ages 22 and older, though the adult women exhibit less selection on time-invariant differences in levels. Similar patterns also emerge if we restrict the experimental samples to individuals recommended by their caseworker for classroom training in occupational skills (and possibly other services) prior to random assignment.

The figure contains three lines each of which presents mean earnings in a particular month of relative time for one of the three groups: the ENPs (the line of short dashes), the experimental treatment group (the solid line) and the experimental control group (the line of long dashes). Following Heckman and Smith (1999), time is measured relative to month zero, which is the month of random assignment for the experimental groups and the month of measured eligibility for the ENPs.[21]

Four features of the figure concern us here. First, comparing the experimental groups in the before period with the ENPs reveals the ubiquitous phenomenon known as Ashenfelter's (1978) dip. The dip consists of a reduction in the mean earnings of trainees in the period prior to training or, more precisely, of would-be JTPA participants in the period leading up to attempted participation. Though not apparent from the graph, the microfoundations differ from the aggregate pattern: most of the underlying variation consists of individuals experiencing sharp drops in earnings (usually to zero) upon job loss. Variation in the timing of job loss relative to the timing of (attempted) participation then generates the aggregate pattern of a falling mean. For more on the dip, see the discussions in Heckman and Smith (1999) and Heckman et al. (1999).

In terms of the simple model of program participation presented in Sections 2.1 and 3, the dip corresponds to selection into training based on serially correlated transitory negative shocks to earnings without training. For most, job loss implies a reduction in the opportunity cost of training. For those who lose a job in a declining industry and/or occupation, it may also imply a change in the relative value of changing industries or occupations. Dealing with this selection on the transitory component of the outcome poses an important obstacle to the production of compelling estimates of the causal effect of training in the absence of random assignment.

Second, looking at the period prior to the dip reveals what appears as a relatively constant mean difference between the ENPs and the experimental groups. This suggests additional selection into JTPA based on the "permanent" component of earnings without training. This combination of selection on both the permanent and transitory components of the outcome means that standard, simple solutions to the problem of nonrandom selection into training, such difference-in-differences, typically lack empirical plausibility.

Third, looking at the period just after random assignment for the two experimental groups does not reveal the familiar picture associated with investments in human capital wherein those investing start out behind due to reduced employment while they invest, called the "lock-in" effect in the training literature, and then overtake those not investing as the investment pays off. The reason for this is that some treatment group members receive job search assistance or subsidized on the job training rather than classroom training; these services act to speed rather than delay employment. Restricting the

---

[21] The treatment group line starts at month zero due to data limitations.

experimental sample to individuals recommended to receive classroom training (not shown) yields the traditional pattern.

Fourth, and finally, the behavior of earnings in the control group in the "post" period provide a guide to the extent of selection on longer-term trends in earnings without training. It could be, for example, that individuals with less cheery future earnings prospects differentially sort into training. In that case, designs that address only selection on transitory shocks and longer-term levels will yield upwardly biased estimates of the impact of training as a result of failing to take account of the selection on trends. Jacobson et al. (2005) pursue this line of analysis and find that it matters in their evaluation of community college training for displaced workers; see also Heckman and Hotz (1989).

Not all institutional settings and evaluation designs yield the patterns shown in Fig. 6. For example, in some countries few individuals will receive training early in an unemployment spell, as in the original implementation of the New Deal for Young People studied in Dorsett (2006) and Blundell et al. (2004). In other cases, an evaluation will compare trainees to other participants receiving lower intensity services. In such cases, both the trainee group and the comparison group will experience a dip, though the shapes of the dips may differ somewhat, as in Figures 1a–1d in the WIA evaluation of Andersson et al. (2013). We would also expect somewhat different patterns for voluntary versus "mandatory" training (where the latter could refer to training encouraged by the threat of benefit reductions) and for training chosen by the trainees rather than by a caseworker. The general point, which the example from the JTPA experiment highlights, is the importance of thinking about the underlying processes, in this case the earnings and participation processes, as in the models in Sections 2 and 3, and using these to motivate the choice of identification strategy when evaluating training programs. More narrowly, selection into training may take place on transitory shocks, on longer-term differences in levels, or even on longer-term differences in trends or some combination of these. All should get worried about in the process of designing a study.

4.3 Defining the Treatment

Most studies do not explicitly consider the question of how best to define what constitutes training, but that decision has important implications for both study design and interpretation. This section considers three aspects of that decision in detail. First, should the treatment of training consist of the offer of training, of starting a training program, or of finishing a training program? The offer of training has the virtue that it corresponds to what policy can, in most contexts, actually do. That is, in a regime of voluntary participation like those in the United States and Canada, caseworkers can offer training but some potential participants will choose not to take it, perhaps because they do not like the specific training options that turn out to be available or that the caseworker encourages them to undertake. In regimes where the trainee must take and complete the training offered (or find a job) in order to avoid losing their benefits, the distinction will matter less because most of those offered will take and complete the training, though different issues may arise, including stronger anticipation effects.[22]

Using the offer of training as the treatment also helps in sorting out the treatment timing issues discussed in more detail later on; an offer of training in June for a training course that starts in September will likely affect job search behavior in July and August and so in a meaningful sense the treatment starts with the offer. The downside to measuring treatment as the offer of training is that many of those who receive an offer will not start training at all or will start but not finish. In the case of the course starting in September but offered in June, for example, the potential trainee might find a job (or go to jail) in the interim, and so on. These and other factors also might arise during a training program and lead a participant not to complete his course; in addition, a training course is to some extent an experience good, so that some trainees may try out a course for a while and find that it does not provide the skills they expected, that they do not get along with the instructor, and so on, and so decide not to complete it. In both cases, defining the treatment as something other than completion results in attenuation of the treatment effect as those who never take up presumably have a zero treatment effect (or close to it) and those who drop out presumably have a lower average treatment effect than those who complete, though this depends on the relative proportions of those who drop out to take a job versus other reasons.

Defining treatment as completing training represents the third alternative. It has the great virtue of simplicity of interpretation. The estimated impact represents the impact of completing the training and, hopefully, now possessing the set of skills the training aims to provide. Completers will likely represent a more homogeneous group than either starters or offer recipients, and we would expect them to have more homogeneous treatment effects (as a censored distribution has a lower variance than the corresponding uncensored one). At the same time, two major drawbacks lead to relatively little adoption of this approach in the more scholarly evaluation literature. First, and less important, while clarifying the meaning of the treatment state, equating completion with treatment clouds the interpretation of the counterfactual, which now includes dropouts who receive partial treatment. Thus, the comparison becomes completing training versus not taking it or taking it and not completing it. If many trainees drop out for employment, such a comparison may make the training look less efficacious than it should absent very careful interpretation. Note that simply omitting the dropouts does not solve this problem, at least for the purposes of cost-benefit analysis, as dropouts consume real resources. Second, and more importantly in our view, coding training as completion tends, in practice, to go along with ignoring the in-program period in the evaluation. This in turn leads

---

[22] The US case study in Section 5 provides some evidence on the take-up rates of training offers for specific programs.

to excessively optimistic cost-benefit analyses that leave out the opportunity cost of training in terms of job search and foregone earnings. Put differently, both starting training and completing training after receiving an offer of training represent intermediate outcomes. Conditioning on them raises important conceptual and operational issues.

A second issue of treatment definition concerns receipt of multiple services as part of a spell of service receipt, only one of which consists of vocational training. For example, for individuals who do not link up with an employer during the course of their training, provision of formal job search assistance may follow the completion of training. The literature addresses this issue in three ways. The simplest strategy ignores the issue; to the extent this approach has a justification, it is that training should have an impact that dominates those of the lower intensity services typically combined with it. The second approach incorporates the additional services into the interpretation of the estimated training effects, so that the estimate becomes an impact of training plus possibly also subsequent services rather than just of training. Finally, some recent literature, most of it theoretical, formalizes the evaluation of sequences of treatments in the context of a "selection on observed variables" identification strategy (discussed in depth later on). This literature includes, eg, Lechner and Miquel (2010). In our view, this approach merits greater application in the literature, though data limitations often represent the barrier rather than researcher interest.[23]

Up to this point in our discussion of coding the treatment we have implicitly assumed the goal of coding up a binary treatment indicator. For many training programs, a binary treatment indicator represents a gross simplification, due to variation in the type and intensity of training provided. For example, a given program might provide 6-week courses in basic office skills as well as year-long courses in automotive repair among many other types of training. By collapsing this heterogeneity into a binary indicator the researcher, in an important sense, deliberately induces nonclassical measurement error in the training variable. On the other side, of course, lies the issue of statistical power. In a study with, say, 1000 trainees, an analysis based on a binary indicator for training will have substantially more power than an analysis that estimates separate effects for five different types of training, each received by 200 trainees.

At a broad level, the literature would benefit from a formal theory of optimal coarseness in the coding of treatment variables. Such a theory would formalize the relationship between features of the evaluation environment such as the extent and nature of heterogeneity in the training, the outcome residual variance, the treatment effect heterogeneity

---

[23] A related issue concerns individuals with multiple spells of training (or training and related services) with only a short break between them. The researcher faces the problem of how much time has to pass before the later training transforms from part of the treatment to part of the outcome. Typically, some relatively ad hoc determination is made in light of the data and institutions in a given context. For example, in evaluations of Canadian ALMPs, the break is typically 6 months; see eg, Human Resources and Skills Development Canada (2004).

(or prior beliefs about it based on other similar programs already evaluated), the sample size and so on and how finely to differentiate among training types in the analysis. The policy question of interest also matters: for example, for a program that cannot be killed for political reasons regardless of its cost-benefit performance it makes more sense to focus on using program resources effectively by emphasizing the most effective services. This implies an evaluation that estimates separate impacts for different training types.

In the absence of a formal theory of optimal coarseness in coding up training, researchers make choices less formally, and with more or less in the way of explicit justification. Most studies of training examine a binary treatment variable. In cases where low intensity services serve as the counterfactual when examining the impact of high intensity services, as in Heinrich et al. (2013) and Andersson et al. (2013) this still only divides the available treatments in two. Other studies, such as Plesca and Smith (2007) and Dorsett (2006) explicitly focus on the differential impacts of major treatment types in programs that offer several. In studies that compare training to other services or different types of training to one another the nature of the selection problem changes substantially. In choosing and justifying an identification strategy, the focus now becomes how individuals who select into the program get allocated to particular services, whether by their own choice or by a caseworker's choice or some combination of these and other factors. This selection problem may require a very different approach than the problem of nonrandom selection into the program at all, which is the selection problem that must be solved in an evaluation of training versus no services. A third strategy focuses on a single treatment type and ignores the remainder. A fourth strategy, applicable in contexts where the main differentiation among treatments occurs along a single dimension, such as duration, operationalizes treatment as continuous and estimates a "dose-response" function. Hirano and Imbens (2004) describe the econometric approach while Kluve et al. (2012) apply it in a training context.

4.4 Outcomes

The choice of outcome variables represents an important component of the design of studies of government-sponsored vocational training. Typically, researchers face important tradeoffs between cost and scope. This section highlights those tradeoffs as well as some important issues of measurement that often arise in this context, starting with labor market outcomes and then moving on to less traditional outcomes.

Labor market outcomes include employment, employment stability (eg, duration of first job spell or probability of returning to unemployment within a window), earnings, hours, wages, and job characteristics. Nearly every study looks at employment, and many go no farther. Particularly in European contexts where entitlements to public benefits last forever at some level, getting trainees off benefit and back to work often represents the top (or even only) priority for training programs, a priority naturally reflected in evaluations of those programs. The key downside to looking exclusively at employment lies in the difficulty of incorporating it directly into a cost–benefit analysis.

Earnings effects of training provide a more useful input to cost–benefit calculations. At the simplest level, assuming no effects on other outcomes (more on this below) or on nontrainees (more on that below as well), a simple comparison of the appropriately discounted stream of treatment-on-the-treated earnings effects (including the "lock-in" effect of reduced earnings during the in-program period) to the average costs of the program (appropriately adjusted for the marginal social cost of public funds) provides the answer to the evaluation question of whether to keep a program in its present form or to eliminate it.[24] More broadly, earnings impacts may represent one important input into a richer cost–benefit calculation that includes multiple perspectives, such as the trainee, the taxpayer, and the government.[25]

The literature on schooling typically focuses on log earnings. For example, the large literature on the oft-estimated Mincer equation regresses the natural log of earnings (or sometimes wages) on years of schooling, demographic characteristics, experience, and sometimes more. The Mincer equation format has an elegant theoretical justification, though one whose assumptions likely fail in practice.[26] The coefficient on schooling with log earnings as the dependent variable has an approximate interpretation as the percentage change in expected earnings for a 1 year increase in schooling.[27] A similar estimation setup with a binary training variable yields the analogous interpretation.

The pesky fact that the natural log of zero is undefined is the key difficulty with the natural log of earnings as dependent variable. In study populations with strong labor force attachment (eg, prime age male university graduates) simply dropping the small number of observations with zero earnings ("listwise deletion") may do little violence to the data. Working against this solution is the fact that populations enrolling in government-sponsored training often have exactly the opposite feature: many individuals with long spells of nonemployment and thus zero earnings. This then leads to unattractive choices regarding how best to deal with the zeros, such as recoding them to some small positive number and taking the log of that number, estimating selection models (typically with some implausible exclusion restriction like number of children or, in the good old days, with no exclusion restriction at all), or simply doing listwise deletion and hoping for the best.[28]

---

[24] See eg, Dahlby (2008) on the marginal social cost of public funds.

[25] A modest literature considers measurement error in earnings (and, not unrelated, differences between various survey and administrative earnings measures) and, in some cases, its relationship to impact estimates. See eg, Bound et al. (2001), Kornfeld and Bloom (1999), Smith (1997), and Wallace and Haveman (2007).

[26] See eg, Mincer (1974) and Heckman et al. (2007) for more on the Mincer model.

[27] See eg, Wooldridge (2013) Section 7.2 for the exact relationship.

[28] See Bushway et al. (2007) on the multifarious dimensions of folly associated with the empirical application of the selection model.

In contrast, the program evaluation literature typically looks at earnings levels rather than the natural log of earnings. We speculate that this difference in applied econometric norms has two sources. First, many programs target populations likely to have zero earnings, which accentuates the problems with the natural log just discussed. Second, many program evaluations incorporate a cost-benefit analysis, and impacts of training measured in levels allow, as noted above, very simple comparisons with costs measured in levels. Converting impacts in log points to levels is not that difficult, nor is conducting the cost-benefit analysis within the framework of internal rates of return, but small costs may suffice to change behavior. The choice of logs versus levels for the dependent variable affects not only the form of the analysis but can affect the substance: in addition to any effects of whatever is done about the zeros, the fact that least squares weights the observations differently in the two cases can lead to differences in both estimates of the substantive effect of training and in the statistical significance of those estimates.

Hours or, more generally, measures of the amount of time worked over some period of time and wages, defined as the rate of pay per unit of time worked, also feature in some studies. The interest here generally lies in decomposing the earnings impact of training, if any, into components due to increased employment, increased time spent working conditional on employment, and increased earnings per unit of time worked. Such decompositions illuminate the mechanisms via which training programs create their impacts. A program that affects employment chances but not wages or hours conditional on employment is different than a program that increases wages but not employment chances or hours. The latter arguably has increased the worker's human capital while the former may simply have connected trainees with employers faster than they would have on their own. Understanding how programs achieve their effects has important implications for policy choices around program content and design and for expectations about the persistence of short-run and medium-run impacts. At the same time, even with experimental data, obtaining program effects on wages poses a challenge due to nonrandom selection into employment (and thus an observed wage) that may differ between trainees and nontrainees. And, in Europe as well as the United States, many administrative datasets used for evaluating training programs lack data on hours worked.

Some studies consider job characteristics as outcomes. In a developing country context, examining whether the trainee gets a formal sector job provides a convenient summary measure of job quality. In the developed country contexts that constitute our main focus, such characteristics could include flexible hours, subsidized and/or on-site childcare, employer-paid health insurance of various sorts, and so on. Andersson et al. (2013), described in more detail in the US case study section, consider firm characteristics thought to relate to job quality, such as worker turnover at the firm. These characteristics play two important roles: they provide an additional dimension of outcomes that may affect a cost-benefit calculation, as when, in a US context, an evaluation that focuses solely on earnings impacts misses impacts on the probability of having employer-provided health insurance and they provide, in some cases, information on how the earnings impacts came about. For example, a finding that most trainees take jobs unrelated to the substantive context of their training might explain a null earnings impact, while a finding that workers end up at larger firms, which tend to pay more (see eg, the extensive literature surveyed in Brown, et al., 1990), could help account for a positive earnings impact.

Receipt of transfer payments or amount of transfer payments received represent additional labor market outcomes commonly studied in evaluations of training programs. Depending on the population, transfer payment receipt might correspond only approximately to one minus employment. Training may draw some individuals into the labor force and drive some others out. In some countries, the threat of mandatory training may push individuals into alternative transfer programs, such as disability benefits, where the requirement no longer binds. The extent of impacts on transfer payment receipt also plays a key role in the cost-benefit analysis from the perspective of either the government or the taxpayer.

For all labor market outcomes, the temporal length of the available data, both before and after training, matters for the quality of the analysis. Having sufficient data in the pretraining period plays a critical role in the credibility of studies that rely on selection on observed variables identification strategies, and on strategies that assume selection into training on fixed differences or time trends.

In the posttraining period, the literature demonstrates quite clearly that impacts not calculated over a sufficient period may (or may not) provide a misleading guide to the impacts of training. In some cases, such as the U.S. National Supported Work Demonstration, impacts remain rock solid for many years after the program, as shown in Couch (1992). In other cases, initially positive impacts fade out over time, as in the U.S. National Job Corps Study in Schochet et al. (2008). In yet other cases, impacts appear at some remove after training, as in Lechner et al. (2011) for German long-term training and Jacobson et al. (2005) for community college training in the United States. Researchers typically attribute impacts that appear only slowly to the time it takes workers to find employment that makes use of their training, and to accumulate some tenure at their new firm. What remains unexplained in the literature is the variation across programs in terms of the delay in impacts (and their failure to arrive at all in some cases, as with the men in Couch, 1992), though Lechner et al. (2011) are surely correct in their general suggestion that evaluations of programs with longer lock-in periods should have longer follow-up periods. A longer follow-up period also reduces the extent to which the analyst has to make assumptions about the time path of impacts in the period following the data when undertaking a cost-benefit analysis.

Some evaluations of training programs look for impacts on outcomes we find potentially problematic. First, consider the outcome "time to first employment." Finding a job sooner rather than later represents a good outcome in general, but not if it indicates a lower quality job match. One might imagine, for example, that a program that gets its participants enthused about job search and the importance of finding a job might lead them to take jobs that they otherwise might not take, and that then do not last as long. In such scenarios, impacts on time to first employment (or, put differently, duration of the initial unemployment spell) may provide a misleading guide to overall time employed and so require careful interpretation. See Dolton and Smith (2011) for a recent empirical example, and Ham and LaLonde (1996) and Eberwein et al. (1997) for thoughtful discussions of the challenging economic and econometric issues associated with attempting to estimate the effects of training on the lengths of spells of employment and of nonemployment in the context of nonrandom selection into employment and nonemployment that differs between trainees and nontrainees.

Second, we think that Smith et al. (2015) do an effective job of demolishing participant evaluation measures as presently implemented in evaluations of training programs; these measures ask trainees (in various ways, none of them supported by any actual research) whether or not the training program helped them. We conjecture that current participant evaluation measures have the sometimes helpful (for the evaluator and program operators, not for the taxpayer) feature of looking relatively positive even when more compelling econometric estimates of program impact tell a more negative story.

In addition to labor market outcomes, some studies of government-sponsored training also consider outcomes drawn from other domains, such as education, criminal behavior, fertility, health, and so on. Many evaluations of training programs measure impacts on the receipt of occupational or educational credentials. Impacts on arrests comprise a nontrivial component of the benefits of the Job Corps program, as discussed in McConnell and Glazerman (2001). Lechner and Wiehler (2011) find that training reduces fertility for women in Austria. Examining additional outcomes along these lines allows for a more comprehensive cost-benefit analysis and also sheds light on the mechanisms that lead to earnings impacts. For example, if training decreases women's fertility, that in turn may lead to greater labor force participation and thus to an earnings impact. Of course, looking at additional outcomes also adds to the cost of an evaluation, as additional data must be collected (or linked to, in the case of administrative records) and additional analyses performed. Finally, training may affect individuals who do not receive it, via eg, displacement and/or changes in skill prices. We discuss such equilibrium effects in Sections 2.7 and 4.14.

4.5 Comparison Group Selection

Most studies of government-sponsored training compare the trainees to some comparison group of individuals not trained, or at least not trained around the same time as the trainees being studied. Only the before-after estimator (or the "interrupted time series design" among those charging an especially high hourly rate) does not require a comparison group, and it is not widely used in this literature due to the "dip" discussed above. In the case of experiments and regression discontinuity designs (more on these below) the choice of untreated units is implicit in the identification strategy. For instance, an experiment creates its comparison group by randomly assigning some wannabe trainees not to receive training. In contrast, designs that assume selection on observed variables or bias stability, as with difference-in-differences, require explicit choice of a comparison group by the researcher.

To confuse matters somewhat, the literature uses the term "comparison group" in two distinct but related senses: the population from which the nontrainees are drawn and the set of nontrainees drawn from that population. To make these issues concrete, consider the evaluation of the U.S. Workforce Investment Act (WIA) by Heinrich et al. (2013) described in more detail in the section on the United States. This evaluation assumes selection on observed variables.

Unlike the situation in many European countries, where everyone looking for work registers as unemployed, and the population of registered unemployed non-trainees forms a natural comparison group in the first sense, in the United States and some other countries individuals may flow into a program like WIA from many directions: they may be unemployed and collecting unemployment insurance, they may be unemployed but not eligible for unemployment insurance due to an insufficient work history or benefit exhaustion, they may be reentering the labor market following a spell out of the labor force and so on. No single administrative data set in the US covers all of these source populations. In the Heinrich et al. (2013) paper, which relies exclusively on administrative data, the issue of data availability drives the comparison group selection process in the first sense of the term. In their analysis, they draw comparison observations from two distinct populations: individuals who claimed Unemployment Insurance (UI) benefits and individuals who registered with the Employment Service (ES). The virtue in each case lies in the availability of detailed administrative data. Two vices potentially counteract this virtue. First, using a comparison population that captures only one path into training means that some trainees may have no analogue (in terms of observed characteristics) within the comparison population. Second, even conditional on observed characteristics, individuals who select into claiming UI, or into participating in ES services, may differ in unobserved ways from the trainees, implying selection bias in the estimates. The authors, of course, address just these issues in justifying their choice of comparison populations.

Some Canadian evaluations of ALMPs that include training as an option, such as the evaluation of British Columbia Labour Market Development Agreement reported in Human Resources and Skills Development Canada (2004), use administrative data to define a comparison population but then select out particular observations within that population nonrandomly in order to collect additional information via surveys. In the case of the BC evaluation, unemployment insurance claimants comprised the comparison population but the evaluators drew untreated observations from within this population using matching (more on this below) based on the observed characteristics available in the administrative data. The actual impact evaluation compared program participants to comparison individuals in the survey sample. This setup illustrates the second notion of comparison group that appears in the literature, namely the subset of the comparison population that receives nonzero weight in the ultimate impact estimation.

The choice of comparison population interacts with the interpretation of the impact estimate. In the Heinrich et al. (2013) study, for example, ES participants received some job search services. Using them as a comparison group implies that the causal comparison is then WIA participation versus ES participation rather than WIA versus no WIA or WIA versus not WIA but maybe ES participation. Similarly, designs that compare training to lower intensity services within the same program as in the WIA training evaluation of Andersson et al. (2013) have a similar issue of interpretation. Comparisons like theirs have the advantage that everyone in the estimation participated in WIA. Thus, the selection problem at hand concerns selection into different services within WIA rather than selection into WIA. Depending on the nature of the institutions and the available data, this may represent a more easily solvable selection problem. In addition, in some contexts the training versus less intensive services comparison may have greater policy relevance than a comparison of training to no training. Using program applicants who end up not participating as a comparison group, as discussed in Bell et al. (1995), raises essentially the same issues: it saves the researcher from having to deal with selection into application, replacing that problem with the problem of dealing with selection into the program conditional on application. It also changes the nature of the causal estimand in ways that may or may not be helpful.

4.6 Timing and Dynamic Treatment Effect Issues

Consider the following setup: individuals become unemployed at some point in time. In each subsequent period, some of the unemployed find a job and some of the unemployed get training. For this example, we assume away labor force exits as well as other types of reemployment services. How best, in this context, to estimate the impact of training versus no training? Until recently, a common approach would compare individuals who received training in the first, say, 6 months of their unemployment spell to individuals who did not receive training in that interval (or maybe ever in that particular spell of unemployment). Sianesi (2004) and Fredriksson and Johansson (2008)[29] show that this approach can yield downward biased estimates of program impacts. The intuition is that conditioning on no treatment within some window implicitly conditions the comparison group on (part of) the outcome. For example, one possible reason an unemployed

---

[29] The working paper version, Fredriksson and Johansson (2004) addresses the issues we highlight here in greater detail than does the shorter published version.

individual does not receive training in the first 6 months after becoming employed is that she finds a job in the fourth month. This bias increases with the duration of the temporal window used to define the untreated comparison group.

Sianesi (2004) instead suggests an alternative setup in which individuals at risk of training at each possible duration who receive training in that period are compared with individuals with (at least) the same realized duration who do not receive training in that period. Thus, for example, one would (conditionally) compare individuals unemployed for at least 4 months who do and do not receive training in the fourth month of their unemployment spell. This strategy eliminates the bias from conditioning on future outcomes but at a cost, because the interpretation of the estimand changes. In particular, the estimand now equals the average effect of training in period k of the spell of unemployment versus not training in period k but possibly training in future periods for individuals with unemployment spells lasting at least k periods. This is a coherent and useful estimand but it does not fit as easily into a cost-benefit framework as a "training versus no training" estimand does. Note that estimates obtained using this estimation strategy cannot be used to determine optimal timing without additional assumptions beyond invoking the conditional independence assumption separately at each realized unemployment duration. The literature calls this the dynamic treatment effects framework. It has become the standard approach in countries with institutions and administrative data that provide a clear spell start date for everyone under study; see eg, Biewen, et al. (2014).

The so-called timing of events approach provides the most common alternative to the dynamic treatment effects approach in the recent applied literature. This general approach draws on the rich intellectual tradition of duration models in economics. The key to identification lies in the assumption of no (conditional) anticipation effects, which means in the training context that, conditional on observed characteristics, potential trainees do not know when in their spell of unemployment (or nonemployment) they will receive training. Thus, the plausibility of causal effects estimated using the timing-of-events strategy hinges critically on documenting institutional details that determine the information set of the potential trainee at each point in time. Abbring and van den Berg (2003) clearly exposit the identification approach underlying timing-of-events and contrast it to the traditional selection model approach as well as to dynamic panel data models. See also Fitzenberger et al. (2014) as well as Ba et al. (2015), who provide a critical take on this line of work.

4.7 Subgroups and Multiple Comparisons

Studies of government-sponsored vocational training frequently consider how their effects vary among groups of individuals defined by observed characteristics. Estimates of treatment effects for subgroups provide value in a number of ways. First, they provide the inputs to statistical treatment rules that aim to direct training (or other services) at those most likely to benefit from them; see eg, Berger et al. (2001), Manski (2001), Manski (2004), and Smith and Staghøcj (2010). Second, they may provide information about mechanisms. In the JTPA experiment, for example, one possible reason for the (statistically) zero impacts on youth is a requirement that sites faced to serve a larger fraction of the eligible population for youth than for adults. Third, theory may sometimes predict subgroup differences in treatment effects, as in Pitt et al. (2010); estimating subgroup impacts confronts the theory with evidence.

Consideration of subgroups raises the nettlesome statistical issue that goes by the name of the multiple comparisons problem, though this issue can also arise in evaluations of programs with no subgroups but a large number of outcome variables; see eg, Anderson (2008), Heckman et al. (2010), and Kling et al. (2007). To see the issue, imagine an evaluation with ten nonoverlapping subgroups. The researcher proudly notes that one of the ten subgroup estimates achieves statistical significance (in a test against the null of a zero impact) at the 10% level and perhaps substantive significance as well. The trouble with putting too much weight on such a finding is that under the null that all the subgroup impacts equal zero one would expect an average of one statistically significant subgroup effect across such evaluations.

The literature offers a variety of approaches to the multiple comparisons problem. A common one simply ignores it, as with the large tables of subgroup impacts in the 18- and 30-month impact reports from the JTPA experiment.[30] A second approach reduces the number of subgroups by requiring some sort of plausible ex ante theoretical or empirical motivation. A third approach adjusts the p-values required for statistical significance, so that more subgroups implies a higher statistical bar (ie, a lower p-value) before stars appear. A fourth approach requires researchers to announce in advance some limited set of subgroups they plan to examine; this approach prevents ex post fishing around to find some subgroup, somewhere in the data with a positive and statistically significant impact. Of course, the second, third, and fourth approaches can be combined in various ways. Schochet (2008a) provides a fine overview of the literature aimed at an applied audience. In our view, any sensible approach dominates doing nothing.

4.8 Methods: Field Experiments

Random assignment solves the problem of nonrandom selection into training by assigning would-be trainees at random to either receive training or not. Because of random assignment, in samples of reasonable size the randomized trainees have (statistically) equivalent distributions of both observed and unobserved characteristics. As a result, a simple comparison of the mean outcomes of the randomized-in trainees and the randomized-out nontrainees provides a compelling causal estimate of the impact of training, subject to some caveats we discuss in what follows. In notation

[30] See Bloom et al. (1993), Exhibits 4.15 and 5.14 and Orr et al. (1995), Exhibits 5.8, 5.9, 5.19, and 5.20.

$$E(Y_0|D=1, R=1) = E(Y_0|D=1, R=0)$$

where $R=1$ denotes randomization into the treatment (ie, training) group and $R=0$ denotes randomization into the control (ie, no training) group. Essentially, randomization produces a compelling causal estimate by forcing randomly chosen individuals who want to be trained (ie, have $D=1$) to experience the no-training outcome. Randomization also implicitly solves the problem of comparison group selection: trainees and nontrainees get drawn from the same population of wannabe trainees.

Governments in developed countries do not do randomization very often. A good approximation, in fact, is that only the US government uses random assignment to evaluate social and educational programs, though there are a few exceptions in the United Kingdom, Denmark, and elsewhere. When it randomizes, the US government (and the states, though usually only when lured by federal incentives) mainly randomize three groups of people: criminals, poor people, and students in public primary and secondary schools. Sometimes, it randomizes them to job training programs, as with the National Job Training Partnership Act (JTPA) Study of the late 1980s and early 1990s, the National Job Corp Study (NJCS) of the early 2000s, and the current Workforce Investment Act Gold Standard Experiment (WIAGSE). We talk about each of these evaluations in detail in the US case study in Section 5; here they serve mainly as sources of examples of various methodological problems and choices.

Randomization deliberately creates useful exogenous variation; for this reason, researchers tend to like experiments. At the same time, the literature has identified some conceptual and empirical issues that arise only in experiments or with special force in experiments. We consider those issues next, while referring the interested reader to Heckman and Smith (1995) and Heckman et al. (1999) for more extensive discussions.

The first set of issues relates to the interpretation of the experimental estimand. Obviously, where in the program participation process randomization occurs and what gets randomized critically affect the interpretation of the resulting experimental impact estimate. In the JTPA study, placement of random assignment relatively early in the participation process for cost reasons resulted in a substantial number of treatment group members who never enrolled in the program, thus complicating interpretation. Randomly assigning only access to JTPA in an institutional context rich with alternative programs providing similar services for free or at a modest price resulted in a substantial amount of control group substitution into these services. As Heckman et al. (2000) discuss in detail, dropout and substitution complicate the interpretation of the experimental results.[31]

The second set of issues relates to external validity. Experimental evaluations disrupt programs in ways that nonexperimental evaluations typically do not and also entail

---

[31] Of course, dropout from training also complicates the implementation and interpretation of nonexperimental evaluations. See eg, Paul (2015) for discussion and evidence from Germany.

nontrivial fixed costs at the site level to set up the random assignment process, train staff about how to use it and so on. Because of the disruption, local sites may decline to participate, as many did in the JTPA experiment. After initial attempts to obtain external validity by randomly selecting sites failed, the evaluation ended up approaching around 200 of the 600 JTPA program sites in order to obtain its decidedly nonrandom sample of 16 sites; see Doolittle and Traeger (1990) for more detail.

At the individual level, potential program participants may make different choices regarding application and/or preparation in the presence of random assignment, and the bureaucracy required in some countries for random assignment, such as having participants formally consent to be randomized, may yield nonrandom selection into the experiment from among all participants. The literature refers to the effects of these phenomena on the resulting estimates as randomization bias; Heckman et al. (1996) and Sianesi (2014) attempt to measure the extent of randomization bias empirically in the JTPA experiment and the U.K. Employment Retention and Advancement demonstration.

Experimental evaluations face a conflict between two other dimensions that affect external validity: the number of individuals trained and the number of individuals recruited into the program. Both cannot equal what they would in the world without the experiment. In the JTPA experiment, the evaluators chose to keep the number receiving services roughly the same, so as not lose external validity by changing the scale of the program. In order to fill the control group with a random assignment ratio of two treatment to one control then meant recruiting substantially deeper into the pool of eligibles than usual at the experimental sites. The sites believed (perhaps correctly, perhaps not) that these marginal recruits had lower impacts. The Job Corps experiment took a different approach: it adopted a random assignment ratio of (roughly) 19 treatments to one control, which minimized both additional recruiting and changes to program scale but required a very large number of sites to obtain a control group that provided sufficient statistical power to detect impacts of reasonable size.

As noted in Heckman and Smith (2000), it is important to keep in mind that relying on random assignment to solve the problem of selection bias does not make experimental studies immune from all the other issues that arise in empirical evaluations more generally. Experiments that rely on survey data may still have issues with attrition overall, and with differential attrition between the experimental treatment and control groups. Experiments may still face issues with outliers, and with measurement, of the dependent and independent variables. Experiments may still face issues of implementation fidelity (ie, does the program run the way it was intended) and with undermining by program operators as in Torp et al. (1993).

Stepping back to look at a wider view, experiments have occasioned a spirited methodological debate captured well in the contributions by Deaton (2010), Heckman (2010), and Imbens (2010). One dimension of this debate centers on the relative costs and benefits of design-based (or treatment effects) studies and "structural" analyses that seek to estimate externally valid policy-invariant parameters characterizing preferences and production functions. Our own view sees these approaches as complements rather than substitutes. Experiments provide valuable exogenous variation that can help to either identify structural parameters or to test structural models, as in eg, Todd and Wolpin (2006) and Lise et al. (2005). Indeed, one set of experiments, the U.S. Negative Income Tax (NIT) experiments, were purposefully designed to provide compelling estimates of structural wage and income elasticities (Ferber and Hirsch, 1981). In the other direction, structural models can suggest useful contexts for randomization.

A second dimension of this discussion centers on external validity or (more grandly) the ease with which knowledge cumulates across studies. A quite reasonable concern worries that a collection of experimental estimates, generated individually without any overall plan to systematically vary relevant features of the treatment or the population or the context across studies, will prove difficult or impossible to combine into knowledge that generalizes at least somewhat across time, space, and participant populations. We share this worry, but find it sometimes overstated, as existing variation has yielded useful broad conclusions via meta-analysis, as in Card et al. (2010) or Vivalt (2015). At the same time, while we sympathize with and support the idea of estimating policy-invariant structural parameters, and quite like many papers in this literature, we cringe a bit when we read papers that imagine that their estimate of "the elasticity" characterizes the heterogeneous responses of agents everywhere and always. Put differently, one researcher's valuable structure may be another researcher's misguided homogeneity.

A third component of this discussion addresses notions of a "hierarchy of evidence." Existing versions of such hierarchies typically put experimental studies at the top, as in Guyatt et al. (2008). The countervailing view argues that excessive focus on the methodological ordering of the supposed hierarchy distracts from careful evaluation of the quality of particular studies. We think of this as an empirical question regarding the relative magnitudes of within (methods) and between (methods) variation in the quality of individual studies. We are unaware of any systematic evidence regarding these relative magnitudes; our casual view of the evidence sees within variation as relatively more important but between variation as substantively important as well.

4.9 Methods: Selection on Observed Variables

The most commonly applied strategy for estimating the impacts of training programs assumes that the researcher can condition her way out of the problem of nonrandom selection into training. Various literatures calls this assumption "selection on observed variables" or "exogeneity" or "strict ignorability" or, most awkward of all, "unconfoundedness." Intuitively, the underlying economic substance consists of the belief that conditional on some particular set of observed characteristics potential participants choose whether or not to participate in a way unrelated to the untreated outcome.

In the potential outcomes notation, this corresponds to exogeneity in the context of the parametric linear regression model, ie, $E(U_0|D,X) = 0$, where X denotes a vector of conditioning variables not affected by treatment and U_0 denotes the unobserved component of the untreated outcome. In the context of semiparametric matching and weighting estimators, the marginally weaker assumption $E(Y_0|D=1,X) = E(Y_0|D=0,X)$ suffices.[32]

Thus, while no one who knew the literature would believe that individuals select at random into a training program absent formal random assignment, in a particular institutional context a researcher might make a compelling case that married men in their early 30s with exactly a high school degree and very similar employment, hours, and program participation histories over the past 5 years might select into training based on factors, such as distance to the local training center, unrelated to the untreated outcome of interest.

The literature offers the researcher a wide variety of alternative econometric estimators that implement a selection on observed variables identification assumption. These range from the standard parametric linear regression models taught in undergraduate econometrics courses through the matching methods imported to economics from the statistics literature to weighting methods originally developed to deal with survey nonresponse. The parametric linear model offers the advantages of statistical efficiency (in the world where the researcher manages to correctly specify the model).[33] Semiparametric and nonparametric estimators offer greater flexibility and, asymptotically, the correct form of the conditional mean function but at the cost of larger standard errors.

The applied literature has relied especially heavily on semiparametric estimators based on the propensity score, defined as the conditional probability of participation, $\Pr(D=1|X)$. These estimators combine a parametric (but flexible, at least in aspiration, if not in practice) propensity score model with nonparametric matching on the estimated propensity score or with weighting. We conjecture that semiparametric and nonparametric estimators have seen wider application in the training literature than almost anywhere else because of the availability of relative large sample sizes and the availability of experimental data to use in methodological studies.[34]

---

[32] In the context of the parametric linear regression model, this assumption suffices to identify a common effect of treatment. For matching estimators, this assumption suffices for the ATET; identification of the ATE requires a similar assumption for the treated outcome.

[33] Of course, a variety of parametric estimators exist for outcomes of various types, including logit and probit models for binary outcomes such as employment, duration models for outcomes such as the length of nonemployment spells, and so on.

[34] For additional detail, see the discussions of estimators in Heckman et al. (1997a, 1998b), Heckman et al. (1998a), Heckman et al. (1999), Dehejia and Wahba (1999, 2002), Imbens (2004), Smith and Todd (2005a,b), and Imbens and Wooldridge (2009). Frölich (2004), Huber et al. (2013), and Busso et al. (2014) provide Monte Carlo analyses. Heckman and Navarro (2004) contrast the differing roles of the propensity score in studies that assume selection on observed variables and in studies that assume selection on unobserved variables.

We now return to the question of how to justify an identification assumption of selection on observed variables. The conditional independence assumption (or its analogue for the parametric linear model) represents an implicit rather than an explicit model of participation and outcomes. Nonetheless, thinking about explicit models, such as those considered in Section 3, provides some guidance regarding what variables to include in the conditioning set. For example, even the simplest model will highlight the importance of variables that correlate with the opportunity cost of training.

The existing applied literature provides a treasure trove of evidence on variables that affect both training participation and labor market outcomes. This literature emphasizes the importance of conditioning on labor market outcomes prior to training (or the choice not to train, for the comparison group). As discussed in more detail in the section on longitudinal estimators, prior outcomes proxy both for the person-specific time-invariant unobserved component of outcomes as well as for serially correlated transitory unobserved variables. Another way to think about unconfoundedness recognizes that it requires variables that affect participation but that are not correlated with the outcome in the absence of training. These variables generate variation in training conditional on the variables thought to satisfy the conditional independence assumption. They are instruments, but instruments that the researcher does not, and need not, observe. Still, though, it pays to think about what these variables might be in the context of the institutions and economics of the context under study. Are they caseworker tastes? Random variation in information sets due to advertising or networks? Distance to the training program? Available training slots at a given point in time?

In addition to their direct value in providing compelling estimates of causal effects, when combined with data on a comparison group experiments provide indirect value by allowing methodological studies of the value of particular conditioning variables (or groups or types of variables) in nonexperimental evaluations based on a selection on observed variables identification strategy.[35] This literature began with the LaLonde (1986) and Fraker and Maynard (1987) papers that combined the data from the experimental evaluation of the National Supported Work Demonstration with comparison group data to study the performance of various identification strategies using the experimental impacts as a benchmark. Dehejia and Wahba (1999, 2002) and Smith and Todd (2005a,b) extended this line of work to matching and difference-in-differences matching (discussed below) estimators. Calónico and Smith (2015) replicate Smith and Todd (2005a), update it to account for developments in the related applied econometric literature, and attempt to clarify long-standing confusions in the literature regarding the meaning of the estimates obtained from these studies.

---

[35] The literature outside economics views these as members of the broader class of "within-study designs." See eg, Cook et al. (2009).

The nonexperimental component of the U.S. National JTPA Study took this idea very seriously indeed by collecting "ideal" comparison group data at four of the sixteen experimental sites for use in just such an exercise. The "ideal" data included individuals in (some of) the same local labor markets as those randomized, who met program eligibility rules at a defined point in time, and whose data came from the same survey instruments and administrative data sources as the individuals in the experimental component of the study. Heckman et al. (1998a) and Heckman et al. (1997a) use these data to (among many other things) study the value of particular conditioning variables; they find that "pre" period labor market outcomes (both earnings and labor force status), measured at relatively fine levels of temporal detail, have great value in reducing selection bias.

A closely related, but not quite as compelling, literature examines how much, if at all, the obtained impact estimates move when adding additional covariates to existing evaluation data sets. Under certain assumptions — see Heckman and Navarro (2004) and also Oster (2013) — coefficient stability in response to additional conditioning variables indicates that the original conditioning set solves the problem of nonrandom selection into training.[36] For example, Andersson et al. (2013) examine the value of conditioning on the characteristics of the most recent employer and, separately, of conditioning on 3 years of quarterly earnings information rather than two as done in earlier evaluations such as Heinrich et al. (2013) and find that neither set of variables matters much. Perhaps more surprisingly, Caliendo et al. (2014) add various psychometric measures to the standard (and very rich by North American standards) administrative data used for evaluating training programs in Germany and find that they do not move the estimates. Lechner and Wunsch (2013) offer the most thorough study along these lines. They examine the effects of combinations of groups of variables (eg, health, characteristics of most recent firm, earnings histories) in the context of the German data; their findings provide valuable guidance for future studies. In our view, more work along these lines with both experimental and nonexperimental data has great value, as does thinking more systematically about the generalizability of results of this sort across time, space, and institutions.

4.10 Methods: Difference-in-Differences and Related Longitudinal Methods

Longitudinal methods build on the availability of multiple periods of data to take account of types of selection bias less easily dealt with via selection on observed variables identification strategies. To see this more formally, we need to add an explicit time subscript to

---

[36] To see the intuition, suppose that there are two orthogonal unobserved factors A and B that both correlate with treatment and with the untreated outcome. If all of the conditioning variables represent proxies only for factor A, then adding them in sequence will lead eventually lead to stable estimates, but the problem of nonrandom selection into treatment will remain unsolved due to factor B.

our notation, so let "t" denote an "after" period and let "t'" denote a "before" period. The cross-sectional estimators we have considered up to this point compare trainees in "t" to nontrainees in "t," where the nontrainees result from random assignment of wannabe trainees in the case of experiments and from observational variation in the case of a selection on observed variables identification strategy. The worry that motivates the difference-in-difference estimator centers on a component of outcomes that does not vary over time (at least in an approximate, medium-run sense) and is not fully captured by the available conditioning variables. For example, suppose that

$$Y_{it} = \beta_0 + \beta_X X_{it} + \delta D_{it} + \mu_i + v_{it} \tag{62}$$

where μ_i denotes the time-invariant unobserved component of outcomes and v_{it} denotes the transitory unobserved component of outcomes and the remaining notation remains as before. With this data generating process, an identification strategy that only conditions on X fails in the case that participation in training depends in part on the unobserved component of the outcomes; this case is very likely in practice because the unobserved time-invariant component of the outcome affects the opportunity cost of training.

In contrast, the data generating process in Eq. (62) implicitly satisfies the "bias stability assumption" (BSA) that motivates the difference-in-differences estimator. In a general sense, the BSA has the form

$$E(Y_{0it}|X_{it}, D_{it}=1, D_{it'}=0) - E(Y_{0it}|X_{it'}, D_{it}=0, D_{it'}=0)$$
$$= E(Y_{0it'}|X_{it}, D_{it}=1, D_{it'}=0) - E(Y_{0it'}|X_{it'}, D_{it}=0, D_{it'}=0).$$

More specifically, in terms of the earnings process in Eq. (62), the bias equals the difference in person-specific fixed effects, and so is necessarily fixed over time:

$$E(\mu_i|X_i, D_{it}=1, D_{it'}=0) = E(\mu_i|X_i, D_{it}=0, D_{it'}=0).$$

The BSA states that the difference in the expected no-training outcomes of the trained and of the not trained is the same in period "t" and in period "t'." As a result, it can be differenced out, as in the parametric linear difference-in-differences estimator, which applies OLS to the following estimating equation:

$$Y_{it} - Y_{it'} = \beta_0 + \beta_X(X_{it} - X_{it'}) + \delta D_{it} + (v_{it} - v_{it'})$$

A different motivational path to the same applied econometric destination focuses on period-specific shocks that affect the trainees and the nontrainees equally. This motivation underlies the "common trends assumption" name often applied to the BSA, as in Blundell et al. (2004).

While we have focused on the particular case of parametric linear models and two periods of data in order to highlight the conceptual issues, the literature provides extensions along many dimensions, including additional time periods, more flexible conditioning on observed characteristics, and nonlinear outcome models.[37]

Two main issues bedevil the application of differences-in-differences evaluation methods in the context of training programs. The first concerns selection into training based on the transitory unobserved component of outcomes. Fig. 6 exhibits selection both on a serially correlated unobserved transitory component of the outcome and on a time-stable unobserved component. The differences-in-differences estimation framework, by design, deals only with the latter. Heckman and Smith (1999) show using the same JTPA data as in Fig. 6 that the difference-in-differences estimator has trouble dealing with the transitory shock; not surprisingly, the resulting estimates depend heavily on the particular "before" period used in their construction. Using periods well before training produces smaller estimates than using periods during the dip, as the latter conflate program impacts with recovery from the transitory shock that would occur even without training. The applied literature typically deals with this concern by combining differencing with conditioning, as in the "difference-in-differences matching" of Heckman et al. (1998a) or by symmetric differencing, as in Heckman and Robb (1985) or by simply choosing a "before" period prior to the dip based on inspection of the mean earnings behavior of trainees.[38]

The second issue that troubles the application of differences-in-differences to the training context concerns selection into training based on person-specific trends in outcomes. To see this, expand the earnings process in Eq. (62) above to include person-specific trends:

$$Y_{it} = \beta_0 + \beta_X X_{it} + \beta_D D_{it} + \mu_i + \beta_{ti} t + v_{it}$$

where β_{ti} denotes the time trend for individual "i." In the case where participation depends on the person-specific trends, difference-in-differences will provide inconsistent estimates, with the sign and magnitude of the inconsistency depending on (among other things) whether individuals with differentially steep trends select into or out of training. This issue has received relatively less attention in the literature than the issue of selection on the transitory unobserved component, despite an important early contribution by Heckman and Hotz (1989) that lays out the "random growth" estimator. That estimator takes account of person-specific trends in a manner analogous to the way the difference-in-differences estimator takes account of the person-specific intercepts. Moffitt (1991) provides an intuitive discussion that emphasizes the data requirements associated with particular longitudinal estimators.

---

[37] For additional time periods, see any textbook treatment of standard panel models, eg, Chapter 21 of Cameron and Trivedi (2005) or Chapter 10 of Wooldridge (2010). On more flexible conditioning, see eg, Heckman et al. (1998a). On nonlinear outcome models, see eg, Athey and Imbens (2006).

[38] See Heckman et al. (1999), Blundell et al. (2004), Jacobson et al. (2005), and Chabé-Ferret (2014) for further discussion.

An issue that receives too little attention in difference-in-differences style studies in general concerns the choice of dependent variable and its relation to the substantive content of the BSA. To make things concrete, consider again the earnings process defined in Eq. (62). In that model, if the dependent variable equals the level of earnings, then individuals with different values of the fixed effect μ_i have a persistent difference in average earnings levels, conditional on X. In contrast, if the dependent variable equals the natural log of earnings, then the BSA indicates a persistent proportional difference in average earnings. Moreover, the BSA for levels and the BSA for natural logs cannot simultaneously hold; at most one is correct. Yet papers that explicitly justify the choice of logs versus levels for their dependent variable when invoking the BSA remain scarcer than unicorns. See Heckman (1996) for further discussion. A closely related point concerns the application of difference-in-differences in nonlinear models. For example, assuming BSA in the context of a linear probability model with employment in some period as the dependent variable differs substantively from assuming BSA in the index of a probit model of employment. See the discussions in Blundell et al. (2004) and Lechner (2010) and, more generally, the literature on nonlinear difference-in-differences starting with Athey and Imbens (2006). Garlick (2014) provides a particularly clear discussion and some extensions.

Finally, we consider the extent to which conditioning on pretraining values of the outcome can substitute for, or even improve upon, the estimates obtained using the difference-in-differences estimator. The intuition underlying this approach notes that, assuming the variance of the transitory unobserved component does not dominate the overall variance of the outcome, a sufficient number of "before" period observations on the outcome provide a reasonable implicit estimate of the time-invariant unobserved component μ_i in Eq. (62). Moreover, we would expect conditioning on "before" period outcomes to go at least some ways toward accounting for selection on serially correlated transitory shocks, the v_{it} in Eq. (62) though of course such conditioning cannot, as emphasized by Chabé-Ferret (2014), deal with the transitory shock to the outcome without training, which does not appear in the data and yet may still affect both the training decision and outcomes in the "after" period assuming serially correlated shocks. And, more broadly, "pre" period outcomes should capture at least some, and maybe all or almost all, of the selection bias resulting from otherwise unobserved factors that affect both training choices and outcomes, such as physical appearance, health, attitudes, and so on.

The empirical literature provides a wealth of encouragement as well as evidence on the importance of conditioning on multiple "pre" periods of outcomes, as well as comparisons between doing so and doing difference-in-differences instead. Examples include Ashenfelter (1978), Ashenfelter and Card (1985), Card and Sullivan (1988), Heckman et al. (1998a), Dehejia and Wahba (1999, 2002), Imbens and Wooldridge (2009, Section 6.5.4), Dolton and Smith (2011), and Andersson et al. (2013). Of particular interest, particularly in light of the arguments in Chabé-Ferret (2014) is that several of these papers find that conditioning on "pre" outcomes (and other variables) sufficiently richly (meaning both number of "pre" periods and the flexibility of the conditioning) yields roughly the same estimates as obtained from a (conditional) difference-in-differences approach; Andersson et al. (2013) provide the most recent evidence along these lines in their evaluation of WIA training versus other services.

4.11 Methods: Instrumental Variables

An instrument in our context is a variable that affects outcomes only by affecting participation in training.[39] In more formal terms, it needs to satisfy two conditions: first, it needs to have a "first stage," which means it needs to have a substantively meaningful effect on the probability of training. Second, it needs to be exogenous, which means that it must be uncorrelated with the error term in the outcome equation. Estimation typically relies on two-stage least squares, with the first stage a linear probability model of the training indicator on the instrument and other exogenous covariates, and the second stage a linear regression of the outcome (eg, earnings) on the predicted value of the training indicator and the other exogenous covariates. In a loose sense, the first stage isolates some of the "good" (ie, not correlated with the error term) variation in training and the second stage uses that variation to estimate a treatment effect.

One of the most important developments in applied econometrics over the last two decades has been the realization that, in a heterogeneous effects world, the instrumental variables estimand requires careful interpretation. In the simplest case of a binary instrument, the IV estimator provides what the literature calls a "Local Average Treatment Effect" or LATE.[40] The LATE represents the average effect of treatment on the individuals whose training choices change when the instrument changes. To see how this works, consider an experimental evaluation of a training program with both treatment group dropout and control group substitution. In this context, we can use the randomly assigned treatment status as an instrument for training and obtain an estimate of the mean impact of training on individuals who would receive training if assigned to the treatment group but would not receive training if assigned to the control group. This is not an uninteresting estimand, but it is also not the ATET, as it omits the impacts on individuals who would receive training regardless of their assignment (the so-called "always takers").[41] See Heckman and Vytlacil (1998) and Angrist and Pischke (2009) for more on the interaction of instruments and heterogeneity.

---

[39] Strictly speaking, we could also frame experiments, regression discontinuity and difference-in-differences as instrumental variables estimators. Instead, we employ the narrower informal definition common in the literature.

[40] The applied statistics literature prefers "Complier Average Causal Effect" (CACE).

[41] Our discussion implicitly adopts the "monotonicity" assumption which holds that the instrument only shifts training participation in one direction.

While the literature provides a small library of instrumental variables studies of other related outcomes, such as years of schooling as reviewed in Card (2001), we know of only a single published paper in the training literature that relies on an instrumental variables strategy: Frölich and Lechner (2010).[42] They use variation in treatment intensity within local labor markets that straddle two (or more) Swiss cantons that have different probabilities of training to identify the effect of training on marginal trainees (ie, those who, arguably, would receive training in one canton but not another within the same local labor market).[43]

4.12 Methods: Regression Discontinuity

Regression discontinuity (RD) designs have enjoyed a renaissance within economics in recent years, with wide application particularly in studies of primary and secondary education.[44] The RD design relies on institutions that assign treatment based on some continuous (in the loose sense that most economists use that term) observed variable, such as a test score or a proposal rating score. The RD literature calls this observed variable the running variable. In the simplest case of a sharp design the probability of treatment changes from zero to one at the cutoff value. More general cases, called fuzzy designs, still have a discontinuity in the treatment probability at the discontinuity, but the probability of treatment on one or both sides of the discontinuity does not equal zero or one. For example, the treatment probability might jump from 0.3 to 0.8.

The RD estimand consists of the ratio of the limits of the outcomes and the treatment probabilities on the two sides of the discontinuity. In formal notation, it equals:

$$\Delta_{RD} = \frac{Y^+ - Y^-}{D^+ - D^-}$$

where S denotes the running variable, $S = S_0$ is the discontinuity, Y is the outcome of interest, D indicates treatment, $Y^+ = \lim_{S \downarrow S_0} E(Y|S)$, $Y^- = \lim_{S \uparrow S_0} E(Y|S)$, $D^+ = \lim_{S \downarrow S_0} E(D|S)$, and $D^- = \lim_{S \uparrow S_0} E(D|S)$. In words, Y^+ is the limit of the conditional mean of the outcome at the discontinuity when approaching from above, while Y^- is the corresponding limit when approaching from below. D^+ and D^- are the corresponding limits of the treatment probability so that in a sharp design the denominator equals 1.0 or -1.0.

---

[42] We exclude here the large number of papers that use randomly assigned treatment status as an instrument for training in the presence of dropout and/or substitution. The primary identification strategy in those studies is random assignment.

[43] The British Columbia Labor Market Development Agreement evaluation documented in Human Resources and Skills Development Canada (2004) attempted an instrumental variables strategy using distance from the training center as an instrument but no plausible results emerged from the exercise. See their footnote 38.

[44] Cook (2008) offers a fine intellectual history of regression discontinuity designs.

In a world where everyone with $S = S_0$ has a common effect of treatment, the RD estimand equals that common effect. In a heterogeneous treatment effect world, the RD estimand in a sharp design corresponds to the ATET for individuals with $S = S_0$ while the fuzzy design, under a monotonicity assumption, corresponds to the LATE for the compliers at $S = S_0$. In all cases, the estimand, strictly speaking, represents some treatment effect only for units with $S = S_0$. Generalization to units with other values of the running variable requires explicit justification; in our experience, the plausibility of such generalizations varies substantially across substantive contexts; see Wing and Cook (2013) for further discussion.

A wide variety of estimators exist for the RD design. All of them compare the outcomes of units (ie, individuals or classrooms or schools or whatever) with values of the running variable on the treated side of the cutoff value with the outcomes of units on the untreated side of the cutoff. They differ in terms of how much they impose in the way of parametric functional form and in the extent to which they restrict the analysis to observations close to the discontinuity. See van der Klaauw (2008), Imbens and Lemieux (2008), and Lee and Lemieux (2010) for methodological overviews.[45]

We have located only two studies that use regression discontinuity designs to look at the impact of training.[46] The first study, De Giorgi (2011), examines the New Deal for Young People (NDYP) in the United Kingdom. The NDYP is mandatory for individuals ages 24 and below whose unemployment spell reaches 6 months in duration. Individuals ages 25 and above receive a weaker treatment or no treatment. De Giorgi (2011) exploits this discontinuity in age by comparing the labor market and transfer receipt outcomes of individuals just under and just over 25 years of age when they reach 6 months unemployed. Two issues threaten the design in the NDYP context: anticipation (a.k.a. "threat") effects among the younger unemployed and spillover effects on the older workers. Threat effects, like those found in Black et al. (2003), would lead to differential selection out of the younger group but not the older group, prior to reaching 6 months unemployed. Spillovers could result from the fact that workers who differ in age by only a few days presumably represent close substitutes in production; treatment effects of NDYP on younger workers could lead to changes in the behavior of older workers as described in Sections 2.7 and 4.14 on general equilibrium issues. De Giorgi (2011) does a nice job of providing empirical evidence that neither issue leads to substantial bias in his estimated impacts.

The second study, Eyster et al. (2010), evaluates the High Growth Job Training Initiative (HGJTI). In particular, it utilizes an RD design to evaluate an aircraft assembly

---

[45] Recent methodological attention has focused on dealing with multiple discontinuities, as in Black et al. (2007a,b) and Bertanha (2014), multiple running variables, as in Wong et al. (2012), and estimator choice, as in Gelman and Imbens (2014).

[46] One could frame the Frölich and Lechner (2010) paper as an RD, but the authors do not.

training program operated by an HGJTI grantee called the Community Learning Center (CLC) in Texas. The CLC process included a usually-but-not-always applied cutoff on the Test of Adult Basic Education (TABE), yielding a fuzzy discontinuity with a reasonable first stage. Empirically, the results illustrate what happens with a high variance outcome such as earnings, combined with a relatively small sample size further reduced by focusing only on observations near the discontinuity for estimation: you get big standard errors. This argues for starting off with a power analysis, as in Schochet (2008b).

In our view, based on the success of RD methods at generating useful knowledge in the primary and secondary education world, and the rough similarity in institutional possibilities in the two areas, the as-yet-unrealized possibilities for valuable research using such designs to evaluate training programs seem endless. We encourage researchers to work with government agencies providing training to put in place the institutions required to generate RD estimates of the impacts of training.

4.13 Methods: Partial Equilibrium Structural Models

Partial equilibrium structural analyses of training write down explicit economic models of individual utility functions, budget sets and production functions in order to study how choices lead to outcomes within an interpretable economic framework. They seek to estimate policy-invariant structural parameters that allow convincing predictions of the effects of programs and policies not actually observed in the data.[47]

Structure does not represent an identification strategy in the same sense as the design-based strategies considered in the preceding sections. While, at the margin, structure in the form of (hopefully) theoretically- and/or empirically-motivated functional form assumptions may replace more compelling design-based identification, researchers typically prefer to combine the structure with compelling design-based identification when possible. In this sense, structural models and design-based identification strategies like those considered in the preceding sections represent complements in the production of knowledge.

We know of three partial equilibrium structural analyses of government-sponsored training programs: Cohen-Goldner and Eckstein (2008, 2010) and Adda et al. (2007). The two Cohen-Goldner papers study male and female immigrants from the former Soviet Union to Israel. In each case, they write down a dynamic discrete choice model on a quarterly time scale and use data on first 20 quarters after arrival in Israel to estimate the model. Identification comes from the modeling assumptions and the observational variation in the data as the institutional context provides no compelling exogenous variation in prices or policy. The model setup allows the authors to, for example, decompose the effect of training into effects on job offer arrival rates and wage offers.

---

[47] For broad general discussions on the place of structural approaches in empirical economics see eg, Keane (2010) and Wolpin (2013).

The Adda et al. (2007) paper uses the same general style of model to study training and subsidized employment in Sweden. Their paper builds on the rich Swedish register data but again relies on observational variation and structure for identification. In our view, the training literature would benefit from additional work within this class of models, but ideally integrating more compelling sources of variation, as in the Todd and Wolpin (2006) paper that combines a structural model with experimental data, and greater attention to the sensitivity of the obtained estimates to key modeling assumptions. Even without such variation, which necessarily limits the weight assigned to the existing empirical exercises, the models provide valuable interpretative frameworks for the design-based empirical work in other studies.

4.14 General Equilibrium

General equilibrium concerns lurk in the background of the many partial equilibrium evaluations of training described in this chapter, both design-based and structural. Most partial equilibrium evaluations implicitly assume away equilibrium effects; the occasional study will explicitly do so by invoking the SUTVA described above.

In the training context, the economics of equilibrium effects play out in one of three ways. The first mechanism is displacement: a training program trains someone for a particular occupation, they then take a job in that occupation that would have, in the world without the program, gone to someone else. As the person who would have gotten the job likely does not reside in the experimental control group or the nonexperimental comparison group, empirically important displacement effects imply that partial equilibrium evaluations overstate the impacts of the training program. In a model with endogenous search effort choice, the prospect of displacement may lead to changes in the optimal search effort of nontrainees as well, potentially reinforcing the initial effect.

The second mechanism is relative prices. If a training program trains a large number of participants in a particular skill, say cosmetology, they may flood the local labor market in this occupation and thereby reduce wages for both the trainees who find jobs and the preexisting stock of workers with the skill set. Once again, because the control or comparison group in a partial equilibrium evaluation will not include most (or all) of the nontrainees affected by the change in skill prices, the partial equilibrium will overstate the impact of the training. The search and matching model presented in Section 2.7 implicitly includes both of these mechanisms.

The first two mechanisms treat the amount of training as fixed, and just consider effects on individuals not (or not all) included in a partial equilibrium evaluation. The third mechanism concerns the amount of training undertaken. A policy that, for example, provides stipends to trainees who did not receive them before should, absent capacity constraints of some sort, increase the number of trainees. Those additional trainees imply stronger general equilibrium effects.

Two main empirical approaches characterize most attempts to estimate general equilibrium effects. In the first approach, the researcher examines local labor markets that feature different relative program scales. Forslund and Krueger (1997) describe and critique nonexperimental versions of this approach in the context of public relief work. Crépon et al. (2013a,b,c) randomly assign both program participants and local program scale in an equilibrium evaluation of an employment focused ALMP in France. In the second approach, the researcher writes down a structural equilibrium model and then calibrates or estimates it in order to obtain estimates for the equilibrium effects. Lise et al. (2004) calibrate an equilibrium search model to estimate the equilibrium effects of the Canadian Self-Sufficiency Project, a demonstration program which provided generous earnings subsidies to lone parents. They focus on the displacement effects induced by the subsidy via changes in the optimal search effort of those who are and are not eligible for the earnings subsidy. Similarly, Albrecht et al. (2009) calibrate an equilibrium search and matching model to obtain an estimate of the equilibrium effects of the large-scale Swedish "Knowledge Lift" program that emphasized general skills at the secondary school level (but also included some vocational training). They find substantively important equilibrium effects that work through changes in employer skill demand. In contrast, Heckman et al. (1998c) focus on wage and human capital investment effects and use a dynamic stochastic general equilibrium model to investigate the (quite large, in their view) effects on relative prices of "high school" and "university" human capital of a $500 per year university tuition subsidy (financed by a proportional tax so as to be revenue-neutral).[48]

We rely on examples from related literatures because we have not found a single study of government-sponsored vocational training that takes equilibrium considerations seriously. The absence of evidence on the equilibrium effects of government-sponsored vocational training for adults represents a real opportunity for policy-relevant and methodologically challenging research. And, of course, as the old saying goes, the absence of evidence is not evidence of the absence, in this case of substantively important general equilibrium effects in the training context.

4.15 Policy Evaluation and Evaluation Policy

To close the methods section, we want to step back from our narrow focus on policy evaluation and think about the big picture of evaluation policy. By evaluation policy we have in mind the set of decisions that governments make that determine how credibly they can evaluate the vocational training they provide to adult workers. These decisions determine the nature and extent of the data and variation in treatment status that individual evaluations have to work with. Evaluation policy includes decisions about what administrative data to collect (and at what quality level), how available to make it to

---

[48] Plesca's (2010) equilibrium evaluation of the US employment service and Cahuc and Le Barbanchon's (2010) equilibrium evaluation of job search counseling also merit mention in this context.

evaluation researchers, whether or not to undertake random assignment, whether or not to build credible sources of nonexperimental variation into training programs via eg, meaningful, measurable, and well-enforced discontinuities in eligibility for training or geographically staged rollout of new programs, whether to do evaluations "in-house" or to contract them out, and so on.

Our sense is that most countries have only an implicit evaluation policy, which is to say that they make local decisions on individual issues at different points in time without ever taking into account how the pieces fit together. In our view, lack of systematic evaluation policy results in too much money spent on training based on too little evidence and, in many cases, substantial amounts of time, effort, and money spent of evaluative research that does little to inform policy either because it addresses the wrong questions or, more often, because of its low quality.[49]

5. UNITED STATES

5.1 Types of Programs

The United States has three main types of programs providing government-sponsored job training: omnibus programs with (relatively) large budgets and participant numbers, large specialized programs offering homogeneous services to more narrowly defined populations, and various small programs serving particular populations. The omnibus programs comprise a sequence starting with the Manpower Demonstration and Training Act (MDTA) programs in the 1960s, through the Workforce Investment Act (WIA) program and onto, as of 2015, the new Workforce Innovation and Opportunity Act (WIOA) program. We describe the earlier programs very briefly and the WIA program in some detail, and also provide a brief discussion of the major innovations, such as they are, in WIOA, while urging the reader to consult LaLonde (2003) for more on the earlier programs.[50] In addition to the omnibus programs, we pay some attention to two of the larger specialized programs: the Job Corps and the programs operated under the Trade Adjustment Assistance (TAA) Act. We do not cover the minor programs. Our discussion draws with enthusiasm on the fine work of Barnow and Smith (2015).

5.1.1 Omnibus Programs

The first of the omnibus (or flagship) federal employment and training programs began in 1962 under the Manpower Development and Training Act (MDTA). It aimed to solve the problem of workers displaced by automation, though it gradually morphed over time into a program for relatively disadvantaged workers. The Comprehensive Employment

---

[49] See eg, Riddell (1991) and Smith (2011) for more on evaluation policy.

[50] We also neglect formalized performance management, which has played an important role in many US programs. See eg, Heckman et al. (2011).

and Training Act (CETA) program replaced MDTA in 1973. It broadened the service mix relative to MDTA and decentralized control over program operation, in part, to states and cities. Subsidized jobs in the public sector, called PSE for "public service employment" played an important role in CETA. They proved controversial due to concerns about fiscal substitution (ie, using federal dollars to support jobs that states and localities would have funded anyway, rather than "new" jobs).

The Job Training Partnership Act (JTPA) replaced CETA in 1982.[51] JTPA continued the tradition of state and local flexibility in implementation within a framework defined at the federal level, but put a greater focus on counties than cities relative to CETA. JTPA provided a mix of services including classroom training in occupational skills, adult basic education, subsidized on-the-job training at private firms and various forms of job search assistance. It did not provide PSE. It had separate funding streams and eligibility rules for adults and out-of-school youth and for dislocated workers (ie, individuals who recently became unemployed). The eligibility rules for adults and out-of-school youth focused that component of the program on the disadvantaged.

The Workforce Investment Act (WIA) of 1998 led to the replacement of JTPA by WIA in 2000. Like JTPA, WIA provided all services at no cost to the participant but did not provide any stipends and had separate funding streams with differing eligibility rules for adults, youths, and dislocated workers. WIA included three important organizational developments relative to JTPA: First, it mandated the creation of "one-stop centers" at which staff from a variety of programs would co-locate so that individuals in need of multiple services could obtain them by visiting a single physical location. Second, WIA defined a normative service sequence starting with core services (eg, job search assistance, placement assistance, and labor market information), and followed by intensive services (eg, assessment, counseling, and career planning) and then, if necessary, training. This structure sought to focus scarce training resources on those not moved into employment via less expensive core and intensive services. Core services are available to all workers, regardless of employment status or disadvantage. The law requires local programs to focus their training resources on the disadvantaged, though with less formal eligibility rules than under JTPA. Fidelity to the sequence varies across space, over time, and even among clients within a given office at a given time. It proves particularly problematic for clients who show up to WIA via referrals from providers of classroom training services. Third, WIA organizes the provision of classroom training via "individual training accounts," which function a bit like vouchers, though their use by WIA participants requires negotiation and approval of training plans by WIA caseworkers, and is limited to a set of approved training providers.[52]

---

[51] The JTPA was cosponsored by Dan Quayle and Ted Kennedy. The reader may decide for herself whether this makes JTPA a triumph of bipartisan cooperation or the programmatic analogue of broccoli ice cream.

[52] We have more to say about ITAs in Section 11.3 on demand-driven systems for allocating training.

The latitude granted to participants in the use of their ITAs also varies substantially across sites and over time.[53]

WIA is not, by international standards, a very large program in terms of either its budget or the number of workers it serves. Appendix B of Bradley (2013) provides some budget information: The adult, youth, and dislocated worker programs consumed about $2.5 billion in the fiscal year 2013, which is down a bit from funding levels during the Great Recession, even apart from the additional $3 billion dropped on the program under the American Recovery and Reinvestment Act (ARRA, the "stimulus"). Social Policy Research Associates (2013) presents statistics on WIA participants and the services they received. In program year 2012, the WIA adult program had just over 1.1 million exiters and the dislocated worker program had about 700,000. Among the adult exiters, 10.4% received some sort of classroom training, compared to about 14.0% of the dislocated worker exiters. In contrast, 100% of both groups received core services, and 26.4% of adults and 32.9% of dislocated workers received intensive services.[54] At a broad level, WIA provides some training, but mostly provides other employment-related services.

The Workforce Innovation and Opportunities Act (WIOA) of 2014 replaced WIA with WIOA as of 2015. WIOA preserves the basic structure of WIA, while making a number of changes related to the performance management system and allocations of funds at the margin between different activities and subgroups of participants. For our purposes, the most notable change is the formal elimination of WIA's normative service sequence.[55]

5.1.2 Large Specialized Programs: Job Corps and Trade Adjustment Assistance

The Job Corps, which dates back to the Great Society era of the early 1960s, provides a unique and expensive combination of services to disadvantaged youth in a (usually) residential setting. Participants receive room and board as well as a modest allowance.[56] Job Corps also differs from the omnibus programs just considered in being run directly by the federal government (with contractor assistance), rather than indirectly though the states. The program serves youth ages 16 to 24 who meet various eligibility criteria, including economic disadvantage and abstention from recreational drugs.[57] It provides a mix of academic training (aimed at GED attainment), vocational training, life skills training, and various health services. The vast majority of participants live in residence at one of the 100 or so Job Corps centers for several months. The program is not a large one in terms of numbers served: U.S. Department of Labor (2013a,b) reports only 40,792

---

[53] Blank et al. (2011) provide more detail on WIA's structure and implementation.

[54] See Table III-15 for the adults and Table II-14 for the dislocated workers.

[55] For more on WIOA, see U.S. Department of Labor (2015a) and National Skills Coalition (2014).

[56] See U.S. Department of Labor (2015b) for additional detail.

[57] According to U.S. Department of Labor (2013a) almost 9% of program terminations result from the failure of participants to maintain a sufficient level of purity in their precious bodily fluids.

enrollments in Program Year (PY) 2012. It does, however, spend a lot on each participant: Job Corps' budgetary authority for PY 2014 equals $1578 million. Assuming roughly the same number of participants as in PY 2012 implies expenditures of over $38,000 per participant in current dollars.

The TAA program (for workers; there are also TAA programs for firms and farmers, so that no one feels left out) aims to provide financial compensation and employment and training services to workers harmed by foreign trade.[58] As currently organized, it covers both manufacturing and service workers. Loosely speaking, workers petition in groups when they lose their jobs due to import competition or off-shoring. DOL has to certify their petition; once it does so, they become eligible for various benefits and services administered (mainly) at the state level via the same one-stop centers that deliver WIOA services.

The benefits available to certified workers include payment for approved training lasting up to 104 weeks, case management and employment services such as job search assistance, and job search and reallocation assistance for workers looking to move in pursuit of employment. Trade Readjustment Allowances (TRAs), which extend UI benefits for certified workers in approved training, complement the training and help support and encourage workers to undertake more serious retraining efforts. Certified workers also receive a generous refundable tax credit toward the purchase of health insurance for themselves and their families. Workers over 50 who obtain new jobs paying less than $50,000 per year can obtain "wage insurance" called "Reemployment Trade Adjustment Assistance" (RTAA) for up to 2 years. The benefit equals half the difference between their old wage and their new wage, up to a total of $10,000.[59] The current version of TAA dates back to the Trade Act of 2002; the program started under the Trade Expansion Act of 1962. Aspects of TAA were made more generous during the Great Recession as part of the ARRA. According to U.S. Department of Labor (2013a,b), in 2012 TAA certified 81,510 workers and, spent $575 million. Among the 131,011 TAA participants in 2012, about 41% received some sort of training. Classroom training in occupational skills formed the vast majority of all training paid for by TAA, with the remainder largely consisting of remedial and prerequisite training presumably designed to prepare the participants for later occupational training. Nationally, a bit over 9% of participants received a TRA.[60]

---

[58] Our TAA discussion builds in part on Collins (2012), who provides substantially more detail than we do here.

[59] The basic idea is to take tax dollars from workers who never had a job that paid them more than their marginal product due to labor and/or product market restrictions and to give those tax dollars to workers who lost such jobs and are sad about it.

[60] Schochet et al. (2012) show that, for the somewhat earlier cohorts and subset of states in the recent TAA evaluation (about which we say more later on) TAA training has a much longer average duration than training provided by WIA, as intended by the TAA program design. Their Table VI-3 reveals that "office and administrative support," "healthcare support," "installation, maintenance and repair," "healthcare practitioners and technical," and "transportation and material moving" comprise the five most popular occupational categories for training.

The fact that the United States largely decouples, in an institutional sense, its system of government-sponsored and/or subsidized vocational training (and, indeed, its ALMPs more generally) from its unemployment insurance and means-tested transfer systems make it quite different from the more centralized and integrated systems in eg, Denmark, France, Germany, and Sweden. This institutional difference manifests itself in a variety of ways. First, many programs outside the U.S. Department of Labor provide training (and other employment-related services). These include programs operated as part of the cash welfare system, which is overseen by the Department of Health and Human Services, and programs operated as part of the Food Stamp (now cleverly renamed Supplemental Nutrition Assistance Plan, or SNAP) program overseen by the Department of Agriculture.[61] Second, many individuals will obtain government-subsidized training without going through the UI system, the welfare system, or the ALMP system. They might go directly to a government-subsidized community college and enroll in a vocational course, with those eligible based on their income also possibly covering the already-subsidized tuition with a Pell Grant and/or government-subsidized student loans. Those same grant and loan programs also get used to pay for vocational training offered by private providers.[62] One result of all this is that a given community college vocational training classroom might include individuals having their way paid by the Workforce Investment Act, by a welfare-to-work program, by a Pell Grant, and out of their own pocket.

We focus in this case study on the training organized via ALMPs operated by the U.S. Department of Labor, recognizing that this may well represent only a solid minority of all of the vocational training provided to adults via government programs and/or with a government subsidy. We keep this narrow focus for two reasons: first, it maximizes the comparability of the US case study with the others included in the chapter. Second, as discussed in Barnow and Smith (2015), because of the institutional (and academic) separation of ALMPs and community colleges, it turns out to be remarkably difficult to obtain information about just the vocational training provided by community colleges.

5.2 Evidence of Impacts

The empirical literature on the effects of government-sponsored vocational training in the United States has a number of features that distinguish it from the corresponding literatures in the other countries we consider in our case studies (and, indeed, pretty much all other developed countries). First, it goes back much farther in time — clear back to the

---

[61] See Table 8.6 and related text in Barnow and Smith (2015) for more on the astounding variety of government-sponsored training programs in the United States.

[62] Kane's (2006) chapter in an earlier volume of this handbook reviews the extensive literature on the design and estimated effects of postsecondary student aid programs. For specific institutional details in the US context see U.S. Department of Education (2015a,b).

early evaluations of MDTA, Supported Work, and the Job Corps in the 1970s. Most other developed countries did not seriously engage with this topic until a decade or two later. Second, large-scale experimental evaluations, such as those of Supported Work, JTPA, the Job Corps, and WIA, play a key role in the US literature. Third, it has contributed in important ways to the development of applied econometric methods via the series of "within-study design" papers that begins with LaLonde (1986) and Fraker and Maynard (1987) and which makes use of experimental impacts as benchmarks for the study of nonexperimental identification strategies and estimators (we say more about this literature in the methods section). Fourth, it pays relatively more attention to cost-benefit concerns. Taken together, the US literature represents a surprisingly rich source of knowledge, particularly in light of the fact, noted in Section 1, that the United States consistently spends far less in relative terms on government-sponsored vocational training than many other developed countries.

In the remainder of the case study, we first briefly summarize the findings of the earliest evaluations, including those of Supported Work, MDTA, and CETA. We then consider in some detail the experimental evaluation of JTPA, the nonexperimental evaluations of WIA, the experimental evaluation of the Job Corps, and the nonexperimental evaluation of TAA. We conclude with a summary and some remarks on the avenues that we see as most profitable for future institutional innovation and research.

5.2.1 Early Evaluations

A number of evaluations of early employment and training programs merit brief mention because of their influence on the later literature both substantively and methodologically. The National Supported Work (NSW) Demonstration tested an intense, expensive intervention designed to ease individuals with severe barriers to labor market participation into work via experience in a supportive work environment with gradually increasing expectations; see Hollister et al. (1984) for an overview of the design and findings. It was one of the very first (along with the Negative Income Tax experiments) major social experiments. Among the four target groups, the long-term welfare recipients (all women) had substantial and lasting impacts, the young high school dropouts (both male and female) had no impacts, and the ex-addicts and ex-convicts had small positive impacts.[63] In addition to setting the stage, conceptually and institutionally, for future experimental evaluations, NSW helped develop the idea that, in the United States at least, disadvantaged women tend to benefit more from labor market programs than men do, and that typical interventions for youth add little value.

---

[63] Couch (1992) provides long-term impact estimates based on administrative data for the two groups, the welfare women and the men from the youth dropout, ex-addict, and ex-convict groups, created by LaLonde (1986).

The evaluation of the MDTA program in Ashenfelter (1978) first identified the empirically ubiquitous preprogram dip in mean earnings discussed in the methods section and the importance of effectively conditioning on pretraining labor market outcomes.

Finally, the suite of evaluations of the CETA program ably reviewed in Barnow (1987) and Dickinson et al. (1987) strongly influenced what followed both in terms of how researchers conceived of the methodological problems associated with evaluating training programs and in terms of the federal government's practical response to those problems, as did the related methodological paper by Ashenfelter and Card (1985). The CETA evaluations had the unique feature that they all relied on the same data on program participants from the CETA Longitudinal Manpower Survey (CLMS) combined with the same comparison group data from the Current Population Survey (CPS), both matched to longitudinal administrative data on earnings from the social security system.[64] Conducted by various groups of researchers, these evaluations provided widely varying impact estimates for CETA as a whole and for various service types within CETA, though they largely agreed on the ordering of impacts among subgroups, with adult women having the largest impacts, followed by youth (with quite modest absolute impacts in many cases), followed by adult men. Table 1 of Barnow (1987) and Table 2 in Dickinson et al. (1987) summarize this heterogeneity in findings; the latter paper dryly notes the obvious: "The wide diversity of estimated impacts reported in Table 2 greatly limits the usefulness of these studies in guiding policy decisions on the design and operation of employment and training programs."

The attempts to account for the variation in impact estimates consider a number of factors, which we divide into implementation, estimation, and identification, though the literature at the time does not frame them that way. Implementation choices include things like what age groups to include and what to do with participants who leave the program after only a few days. Particularly important in this context was the temporal alignment of the calendar year administrative data on earnings; for example, should someone who starts the program in July 1975 have 1975 as a preprogram year or a postprogram year or something in between? Estimation choices include things like estimating a parametric linear model, or doing various forms of matching (including bias-corrected matching), or estimating a linear model with propensity score weights and so on. Identification strategies used in the various studies include selection on observed variables, selection on time-invariant fixed effects, and selection on linear trends. Barnow (1987) and Dickinson et al. (1987) find that all three types of choices made a difference to the results, particularly the choice of identification strategy and the handling of the temporal alignment. But, in our view, the subsequent literature over-emphasized the sensitivity of the impacts to the identification strategy and under-emphasized the

---

[64] The CLMS part of the data can be obtained at the Upjohn Institute website: http://www.upjohn.org/Research/SpecialTopics/EmploymentResearchDataCenter

importance of implementation choices, many of which matter in the CETA context because of limitations in the underlying data. Right, wrong, or just overstated, the lesson the literature took away from the CETA studies played into the decision to undertake an experimental evaluation of JTPA.

5.2.2 JTPA

Formally called The National Job Training Partnership Act Study, or NJS, the major evaluation of the JTPA program consisted of a large-scale social experiment. The experiment randomly assigned applicants to JTPA at 16 sites around the United States and represented the first experimental evaluation of an on-going program (rather than a demonstration program set up for evaluation purposes like Supported Work). The experiment covered only the adult and out-of-school youth components of the program (Title II-A) and not the dislocated worker component (Title II-C). Site selection proved a controversial aspect of the evaluation. The federal structure of JTPA implies that sites must volunteer to participate; the NJS evaluators had to contact around 200 of the 600 JTPA sites, and offer substantial financial compensation, in order to obtain the final set of 16. As a result, external validity concerns have long surrounded the study. Doolittle and Traeger (1990) and Hotz (1992) provide additional detail on the travails of the site selection process.

Everyone randomly assigned in the NJS had been determined eligible for the program and recommended for specific service types by JTPA caseworkers. Based on the caseworker recommendations of service types, each member of the experimental sample belongs to one of three "treatment streams": (1) CT-OS, which means recommended for classroom training in occupational skills (and possibly other services not including subsidized on-the-job training); (2) OJT, which means recommended for subsidized on-the-job training (and possibly other services but not classroom training in occupational skills; and (3) Other, which means recommended only for services other than CT-OS or OJT, such as job search assistance, work experience and/or adult basic education, or, in a very small number of cases, recommended for both CT-OS and OJT. The prerandom-assignment service assignments did not bind the treatment group member's (or the caseworker's) later actions, but do predict reasonably strongly the service types treatment group enrollees actually received, particularly in the CT-OS stream, which will serve as our primary focus; see Table 4.4 in Kemple et al. (1993). In thinking about the experimental estimates by treatment type, it is important to keep in mind that treatment type is not randomly assigned, rather, individuals are randomly assigned conditional on the treatment type they work out with the caseworker. In total, 20,601 eligible applicants were randomly assigned. Of these, 7113 were in the CT-OS treatment stream, 7422 in the OJT treatment stream and 6066 in the "other" treatment stream. Broken down into the four demographic groups used for all of the analyses, they included 5626 adult men (ages 22 and older), 6607 adult women, 2348 male out-of-school youth (ages 16–21) and 2445 female out-of-school youth.[65]

For cost reasons, random assignment in the NJS took place relatively early in the participation process. In particular, it took place at the JTPA office rather than at the service provider office. This choice led to substantial amounts of treatment group dropout, defined as nonenrollment in JTPA. For instance, Table 4.2 of Kemple et al. (1993) reveals dropout rates of around 28% for both adult men and adult women. At the same time, the US institutional environment described above implied substantial amounts of control group substitution into alternative training (or sometimes the same training paid for by a different program or out of their own pockets). Unlike the WIA studies considered below, the NJS had survey measures of substitution, which allow estimation of the scope of the issue and so aid in interpretation of the experimental estimates. For example, Table II of Heckman et al. (2000) reveals that, within the CT-OS treatment stream, and based on survey responses regarding training, 48.8% of adult male and 56.1% of adult female treatment group members report receiving classroom training, compared to 27.4% of adult males and 33.3% of adult females in the control group.[66]

The experiment produced two major reports, Bloom et al. (1993) on outcomes over the first 18 months after random assignment and Orr et al. (1994) on outcomes over the 30 months after random assignment. The latter corresponds to the Orr et al. (1995) book and the Bloom et al. (1997) journal article.[67] Congress also requested that (what was then called) the US General Accounting Office investigate earnings impacts over a longer horizon; their findings appear in U.S. General Accounting Office (1996) but unfortunately do not differentiate impacts by treatment stream. We focus here mainly on the 30-month results and mainly, given our topic, on the results for the classroom training treatment stream.[68]

---

[65] These numbers come from the authors' calculations using the NJS data. Due to various types of nonresponse, plus difficulties obtaining UI administrative data for some sites, the samples used in the 18- and 30-month analyses are smaller. See eg, Exhibits 3.11 and 3.12 of Orr et al. (1995).

[66] In addition to survey measures of training the NJS also provides administrative data on services received from JTPA. Smith and Whalley (2015) compare the two measures of training in the experimental treatment group and find that they differ more than one might expect.

[67] The data from the NJS, including in particular the "ideal" comparison group of eligible nonparticipants collected alongside the experimental samples at four of the sites, had a large payoff in terms of methodological research as well. See eg, Heckman et al. (1997a), Heckman et al. (1998a), Heckman and Smith (1999). Put differently, the money spent on the evaluation created substantial value above and beyond that inherent in the process evaluation, impact estimates, and cost-benefit analysis

[68] The earnings measure in the 30-month study combines UI administrative data with survey data on earnings in an awkward way, though with the worthy intention of reducing potential bias due to survey nonresponse. The 18-month report relies solely on (hand-cleaned!) survey earnings. For more on the earnings measures in the JTPA data, see Kornfeld and Bloom (1999) and Smith (1997).

Exhibit 5.7 of Orr et al. (1995) provides "intent to treat" estimates of impacts on earnings in the 30 months after random assignment (RA) by treatment stream and demographic group. For both adult men and adult women, the data reveal modest lock-in effects over the first 6 months after RA: −$169 for women and −$255 for men. Over 7–18 months after RA, the adult women experience a positive mean impact of $434 and the men a positive impact of $632. Over the final 12 months of follow-up, the adult women gain $365 while the adult men gain $910. Due in part to both to large standard errors (earnings are a relatively high variance outcome in this population) and the relatively muted treatment comparison, none of these estimates differ from zero (or many other numbers) at conventional levels of statistical significance.[69]

Orr et al. (1995) present "impacts per enrollee" that account for treatment group dropout but not control group substitution. A better choice would be IV estimates of local average treatment effects of classroom training that use random assignment to the treatment group as an instrument for receipt of classroom training. That strategy, in turn, runs afoul of the fact that treatment group members also receive more other services that might affect earnings and the fact that the intensity of the classroom training received as measured by either hours or months is lower in the control group. Heckman et al. (2000) discuss these issues in great detail, and provide a variety of alternative nonexperimental estimates of the impact of receipt of training. They argue that, in general, the evidence suggests that the ITT experimental estimate substantially understates the true earnings effect of classroom training provided by JTPA for adults.

Some years after the NJS, JTPA also received one notable nonexperimental evaluation based solely on administrative data and relying on a "selection on observed variables" identification strategy. This study, summarized in Mueser et al. (2007) provides the intellectual foundation for the nonexperimental WIA studies we consider next.

5.2.3 WIA

Several studies provide nonexperimental evaluations of the WIA program using similar data and identification strategies. Some of these studies focus primarily on estimating the impact of WIA versus no-WIA (but possibly similar services provided by other programs). Other studies estimate this treatment comparison as well as estimating the impact of WIA training (and possibly core and intensive services) versus WIA core and/or intensive services but no training. One study estimates only this second parameter. Given our interest in government-sponsored training, we focus our attention

---

[69] Orr et al. (1995) note that ex post pooling of men and women yields statistical significance for impacts in the CT-OS stream. For both men and women, the OJT stream yields higher earnings impacts than the CT-OS stream. For women, the "other" stream mysteriously does as well. Nothing much works for youth; see their Exhibit 5.17.

here on Heinrich et al. (2013) and Andersson et al. (2013), both of which provide estimates of the impact of WIA training versus WIA without training (hereinafter just WIA training).[70]

Heinrich et al. (2013) combine WIA administrative data in a nonrandom, but arguably representative, sample of 12 states with data from the corresponding state UI systems. Their states fear having taxpayers learn about the effectiveness of the programs they pay for, and so choose to remain anonymous, so the set is known but state-level impact estimates do not have state names attached to them. They use the combined data to produce estimated impacts of WIA training conditional on enrollment. They produce separate estimates by state and quarter for 16 quarters (with enrollment in the first quarter) and then weight them by each state's contribution to the overall trainee sample.

The total sample size in the adult funding stream equals 95,590 of whom 27,325 receive training, in the dislocated worker stream, 20,002 out of 63,515 receive training. Basic descriptive statistics show that WIA serves more women than men (with men differentially in the dislocated group), relatively many African-Americans, relatively many adults in their 20s and 30s (though a bit older among the dislocated workers) and workers with around a high school diploma.

The analysis assumes selection on observed variables, where those variables include age, education, race / ethnicity, geographic indicators, and eight quarters of flexible employment and earnings histories. The literature suggests that these variables should do a reasonable job of addressing the selection problem, though of course one would like to have more direct measures of factors such as ability, motivation, and attractiveness rather than having to rely on labor market histories to proxy for them. The authors verify that their conditioning variables balance earnings more than eight quarters prior to enrollment, which provides a compelling specification test. Estimation uses many-to-one radius matching based on the estimated propensity score.

Heinrich et al. (2013) produce separate estimates for the two funding streams: "adults" and "dislocated workers." Within these groups they produce separate estimates for men and women. In the adult stream, the women have a modest three-quarter lock-in effect, followed by impacts that increase to around $800 per quarter. The men have no lock-in effect at all, something that the authors attribute to a higher rate of subsidized on-the-job training relative to women. Their impacts average about $500 per quarter in the later quarters. In sharp contrast, among the dislocated workers both men and women have large and long-lasting lock-in effects. These die out toward the end of the follow-up period, but meaningful positive impacts never appear for either group.

---

[70] Hollenbeck (2009) studies WIA versus no-WIA in Indiana, while Hollenbeck (2012) considers other states. Heinrich and Mueser (2014) consider how the effects of WIA vary with the aggregate unemployment rate; because this paper is as yet unpublished, even as a formal working paper, we do not consider it here. Heinrich et al. (2013) also produce estimates of the impact of WIA versus no WIA using comparison groups based on UI claimants and Employment Service (ES) registrants.

Two issues complicate the interpretation of these estimates. First, in some relatively small states that train a large fraction of their WIA enrollees, the authors run into common support issues, and so must drop a large fraction of the trainees from the estimation. This limits internal validity. Second, some comparison group members may substitute into non-WIA training. Because the sample consists of WIA enrollees, substitution is likely less important here than in the JTPA study already discussed. Still, because the data only include WIA training, the extent of such substitution in this set of studies remains unknown. In a common effect world, the substitution implies that the estimates understate the impact of training, while in a heterogeneous effects world (but one where WIA training does not differ much from non-WIA training) the estimates, once rescaled, represent effects on marginal trainees. Third, the dynamic treatment assignment issues (see the Section 4.6) that preoccupy much of the European literature do not matter in this context because nearly all WIA enrollees who will ever receive training do so in the calendar quarter of WIA registration or the next one. Fourth, the relatively modest scale of WIA compared to the relevant labor market implies that comparison group outcomes should not suffer much from general equilibrium effects, with the implication that such effects do not threaten internal validity. They might still matter for a cost-benefit analysis.

Andersson et al. (2013) provide both methodological and substantive insights. We discuss some of the former in the methods section and focus on their substantive results here. They provide estimates of the impact of WIA training in two anonymous states, one mid-Atlantic state (State A) and one Midwestern state (State B); their states do not overlap with those in Heinrich et al. (2013). Like them, Andersson et al. combine WIA program administrative records with administrative records from state UI systems. They obtain 25 calendar quarters of UI data for each observation, including the quarter of WIA enrollment and 12 quarters before and after. Unlike them, they additionally match in data from the US Census Bureau's Longitudinal Employer-Household Dynamics (LEHD) system, which provides information on employer characteristics for jobs held both before and after WIA enrollment. They utilize the information on preenrollment jobs as conditioning variables. The postenrollment job characteristics serve as outcome variables that help to sort out the mechanisms through which WIA impacts earnings and employment.

Andersson et al. (2013) consider adult WIA enrollees from 1999 to 2005, a period which includes the "dot com" recession and the start of the subsequent recovery. Sample (really population) sizes are large: for State A they have more than 15,000 adults and 10,000 dislocated workers, while in State B they have over 23,000 adults and 28,000 dislocated workers. State A has a bit less enthusiasm for training than State B, with training probabilities of 0.30 and 0.40 for adults and dislocated workers, respectively. The corresponding probabilities in State B equal 0.49 and 0.57. These moderate training probabilities mean that this analysis does not have support issues. The basic demographics of the enrollees (and of the trainees conditional on enrollment) look broadly similar to those in Heinrich et al. (2013). The authors note the similarity in the preprogram dips in mean earnings between enrollees who do and do not receive training and argue that this implies an easier selection problem for their "selection on observed variables" identification strategy to solve than researchers seeking to estimate the impact of WIA versus no WIA.

Andersson et al. (2013) estimate the probability of participation in training conditional on WIA enrollment and demographics, local labor market indicators, and a flexible set of variables capturing recent employment, earnings, and UI participation histories. They then obtain impact estimates using inverse probability weighting (IPW). They find strongly different impacts on earnings and employment for participants in the two WIA funding streams, and somewhat different impacts across states. In State A adults experience earnings reductions due to the lock-in effect for about three-quarters, followed by increasing impacts which stabilize at around $300 per quarter. In contrast, dislocated workers experience negative impacts that decline in magnitude from over $900 per quarter initially to around $125 per quarter toward the end of the 12 quarter follow-up period. The results for the adult stream participants in State B look similar to those in State A but with impacts that stabilize around $400 per quarter. Dislocated workers in State B experience a large and long-lasting negative lock-in effect like those in State A, but their impacts turn positive in the last three quarters of the follow-up period, leaving off at around $300.

The difference in earnings impacts, in both states, between enrollees in the adult and dislocated worker funding streams represents a real puzzle for the literature because nearly all dislocated enrollees could have been served under the adult stream, and many adult enrollees would qualify as dislocated workers. The impacts on job characteristics largely track the earnings impacts, with adults getting marginally better jobs and dislocated workers getting marginally worse jobs. Finally, a rough cost-benefit analysis finds that, in general, whether or not the training in the "adult" funding stream passes a cost-benefit test depends on assumptions about the duration of impacts outside the data, about training costs, and about the marginal social cost of public funds. In contrast, training provided under the dislocated worker stream essentially never passes a social cost-benefit test.

Results from the experimental evaluation of WIA, called the WIA Adult and Dislocated Worker Programs Gold Standard Experiment, lurk in the not-to-distant future of this literature. That experiment randomly assigned WIA enrollees at an almost-random sample of 28 WIA sites around the United States to one of three treatment arms: eligibility for WIA core services only, eligibility for WIA core and intensive services, and eligibility for WIA core, intensive, and training services. Comparisons of the second and third treatment arms will provide, after some massaging to deal with individuals in the third arm who do not take training, an analogue to the estimates from Heinrich et al. (2013) and Andersson et al. (2013).[71]

---

[71] See http://www.mathematica-mpr.com/our-capabilities/case-studies/evaluating-the-effectiveness-of-employment-and-training-services for additional details.

5.2.4 Job Corps

The Job Corps has endured two major evaluation efforts, a thorough and thoughtfully done nonexperimental evaluation during the late 1970s and, more recently, a large-scale experimental evaluation called the National Job Corps Study (NJCS). As noted in our methods discussion, the NJCS avoided issues with external validity resulting from non-random site selection, as in the NJS just described, by (at some cost) conducting random assignment at every Job Corps site in the continental US. In addition, it avoided external validity concerns associated with dipping much deeper into the pool of eligibles to fill in the control group by randomly assigning only (about) 7% of eligible applicants at each training center to the control group. For cost reasons, the evaluation did not include all of those randomly assigned to treatment in its research sample. The relatively small scale of the Job Corps in terms of number of trainees suggests little concern about equilibrium effects contaminating the control group (though they may remain relevant for a cost-benefit analysis).

Probably because it represents an expensive set of services, take-up in the treatment group proved quite high: 73% of those assigned to the treatment group actually enrolled in the Job Corps, and those who did so remained an average of 8 months. Moreover, the researchers did a good job of enforcing the assignment on the control group, as only 1.4% of control group members managed to enroll in Job Corps during their 3 year embargo period. Thus, the NJCS provides a clean experimental comparison between the offer of Job Corps plus all other programs available in the environment, and no offer of Job Corps, but still all of the other programs available in the environment. Unlike the case with the JTPA experiment, control group members cannot readily substitute into intense, expensive residential programs like the Job Corps. They can, and do, enthusiastically substitute into low- and medium-intensity education and training services, with 71.7% of the control group enrolling in an education or training program in the 48 months after random assignment, compared to 92.5% of the treatment group. However, not surprisingly, the amount of education and training received by the treatment group well exceeds that of the control group, with a difference in the means of about 710 h (including all the zeros in both cases).

Keeping in mind the complex treatment contrast induced by the experiment, we now consider the estimated impacts. We focus here on the impacts obtained using the matched social security administrative earnings records; see Schochet et al. (2008) and the references therein for more on the comparison of these impacts to the (somewhat different) impacts obtained using survey data and matched quarterly earnings from UI administrative records. The experiment randomized individuals who applied to the Job Corps between November 1994 and December 1995. The earnings data reveal substantial (and statistically significant) negative lock-in effects of −$270 in 1995 and −$179 in 1996, the period of treatment group participation in the Job Corps and shortly thereafter, followed by substantial (and statistically significant) positive impacts of $173 in 1997 and $218 in 1998. After that, the magnitudes fall and the stars (denoting statistical significance) disappear. Subgroup analysis reveals lower impacts for younger participants, for Hispanics, and, unusually in the US literature, for females.[72] The Job Corps also had important impacts on criminal behavior (as proxied by arrest and conviction rates) particularly in the short run, and on job quality, as proxied by various benefits, as of the 16th quarter after random assignment.

The NJCS includes a thorough cost-benefit analysis, detailed in McConnell and Glazerman (2001). The bottom line: due to the fade-out of the earnings impacts, and taking account of the benefits due to reduced criminal activity, the benefits to society do not exceed the substantial cost of around $16,500 per participant (in 1995 dollars). The program does pass a cost-benefit test from the point of view of the participant which, given the sad performance of many employment and training programs for youth in the United States, represents a minor feat in and of itself.

The broad brush findings from NJCS look surprisingly similar to those from the earlier, nonexperimental evaluation as presented in Mallar et al. (1982) and Long et al. (1981), though the earlier evaluation lacks longer-term follow-up data. In addition to increasing the credibility of the earlier evaluation (and providing another instance where thoughtfully applied nonexperimental methods combined with good data managed to mimic the results of an experiment) this also suggests that the mechanisms that bring about Job Corp's success have remained stable over time. The late 1980s evaluation of the Jobstart program summarized in Cave et al. (1993) also sheds light on mechanisms. Jobstart aimed, in broad terms, to provide a nonresidential (and thus much less expensive) version of the Job Corps. The quite disappointing impact estimates from the experimental Jobstart evaluation suggest that the residential aspect of Job Corps really matters for its effectiveness.

5.2.5 TAA

TAA recently experienced a large-scale nonexperimental evaluation, described in detail in Schochet et al. (2012). It primarily estimates the impact of receiving "significant TAA services" (ie, more than just case management) among a sample of workers certified under TAA between November 1, 2005 and October 31, 2006 from 26 states and with UI claims starting in a wider window around that year as allowed in the law. The comparison group consists of new UI claimants from the same time periods and the same local labor markets not certified under TAA. The evaluation identifies its effects via a "selection on observed variables" assumption with the conditioning variables drawn, in the primary analysis, from both survey data and UI and TAA administrative records; this yields a

---

[72] See Schochet et al. (2001) for more on the age differences in impacts and Flores-Lagunes et al. (2008) for more on the lack of strong impacts on Hispanic participants.

conditioning set somewhat richer than that used in the dislocated worker analyses in the Heinrich et al. (2013) WIA study.

Table 1 of Schochet et al. (2012) gives the main findings in terms of earnings and employment. TAA participants experience, as expected given the incentives for them to take relatively long training courses, a large and long-lasting negative lock-in effect: in the first four quarters the matched comparison group has 19.4 more weeks of employment and earn $12,674 more than the participants. Less expected is the persistence of the negative mean impacts through the fourth year of follow-up; in that year the comparison group still works 2.0 weeks more and earns $3273 more than the participants. The long-term effects turn out less negative for younger TAA participants; they generally do not differ between male and female participants. A quite extensive battery of sensitivity analyses does not dislodge the basic pattern of the findings.

5.2.6 Evaluations of Other Training Programs

The studies we consider in detail above barely scratch the surface of the total number of evaluations of government-sponsored and/or subsidized training programs in the United States, as a visit to the U.S. Department of Labor's Employment and Training Administration publication website will quickly demonstrate.[73] In choosing the studies to focus on, we have emphasized (1) training rather than other services, (2) major programs over minor ones, (3) high-quality studies with compelling identification, reasonable sample sizes, and high-quality data, and (4) programs operated by the U.S. Department of Labor.

Our choices about what to focus on imply that we omit evaluations of programs operated by other parts of the federal government, such as the welfare-to-work programs considered in eg, Greenberg and Robins (2011) and the Food Stamp / SNAP employment and training programs evaluated in Puma and Burstein (1994). We also omit evaluations of programs serving particular small groups, which often have sample size issues, and evaluations such as that of the High Growth Job Training Initiative by Eyster et al. (2010), which have methodological and/or data challenges. And we leave out the currently fashionable "sectoral training" programs under which taxpayers provide training for particular firms or small groups of firms, as in Maguire et al. (2010). Finally, and perhaps most importantly, we miss evaluations of vocational training provided via the community college system, as in the fine study by Jacobson et al. (2005). Consideration of this broader literature does not undermine any of our conclusions.

5.3 Overview and Conclusions

The United States spends much less on government-sponsored vocational training for adults than many European countries and organizes (disorganizes?) that training in a far more decentralized way. The literature does not provide much in the way of theory

---

[73] http://wdr.doleta.gov/research/keyword.cfm

or evidence for labeling that decentralization a feature or a bug. Certainly it makes life more interesting for researchers.

The United States has led the world in the use of experimental evaluations of its training programs. It has also excelled, at least in a relative sense, in the serious application of cost-benefit analysis to its programs, despite having pretty miserable data on program costs. On the negative side, the United States now lags behind many European countries in the quality and coverage of the administrative data available for evaluating training programs, and in the ease with which serious researchers can gain access to the data (with appropriate privacy protections). In common with the broader literature, the US literature is weak on estimating impacts relevant to program expansion or contraction at the margin, rather than program elimination. It also lacks compelling (or even not so compelling) estimates of the general equilibrium effects of government-sponsored vocational training.

Finally, the US literature suggests important general patterns in the impacts of training programs by demographic group, with the programs typically most effective for adult women, somewhat effective for adult men, and not very effective (or, in some cases, actually harmful) for youth. Though it dates back to the Supported Work demonstration in the 1970s, the literature still lacks either theoretical or empirical explanations for this pattern. More broadly, the US literature suggests that zero is sometimes, but not always, a good summary of the impact of training programs.

6. UNITED KINGDOM

6.1 Types of Programs

6.1.1 Education System

England, Northern Ireland, and Wales have a skill system based on qualification levels. Recently they switched from the National Qualifications Framework to the Qualifications and Credit Framework (QCF) [74] Both frameworks have nine qualification levels: entry level and levels 1–8. Much of the publicly supported training in the United Kingdom is designed to raise low-skilled individuals' qualification level.

Until recently, schooling was compulsory in England and Wales until the age of 16 [75] At the end of compulsory schooling (year 11) youth take the General Certificate of Secondary Education exams (GCSEs). GCSEs are compulsory in the core areas of math, science, and English. [76] Scores on the GCSE exams range from a high of A* (A "star") to a

---

[74] Scotland has its own system with 12 levels called the Scottish Credit and Qualifications System. See http://www.scqf.org.uk/framework-diagram/Framework.htm.

[75] Individuals are actually required to attend school until the end of the academic year in which they turn 16. The Education and Skills Act of 2008 will require individuals in 2015 to attend school or training, at least part time until age 18.

[76] Welsh is also compulsory in Wales and Irish in Northern Ireland.

low of G. Those scoring in the D–G range receive a level 1 qualification and those scoring in the A*–C range receive a level 2 qualification.[77] Usually students need to have received five or more A*–C scores in order to begin studying for the General Certificate of Education Advanced Level (A-level) exams. Typically individuals study three or four A-level subjects for 2 years (age 17–18) before taking the A-level exams. Passing the A-level exams is considered the equivalent of a level 3 qualification and is usually a requirement for university admission.

6.1.2 Apprenticeships and Traineeships

In England, Northern Ireland, and Wales anyone can apply for an apprenticeship if they are (i) 16 years of age or older, (ii) not in full-time education, and (iii) eligible to work in England. There are three levels of apprenticeship; intermediate level which is equivalent to passing five GCSEs, advanced level which is equivalent to passing two A-levels, and higher level which leads to National Vocational Qualification (NVQ) Levels 4 and above or a foundation degree.

Apprenticeships provide practical training in a job plus study toward related qualifications (usually 1 day a week). Apprenticeships are 1–4 years in length. An apprenticeship can lead to NVQs at levels 2, 3, 4, or 5, functional skills qualifications, in math, English, or ICT, a technical certificate such as a City & Guilds Progression Award, or knowledge based qualifications such as a Higher National Certificate. In England and Wales there are "one-stop" websites where individuals can search across the different apprenticeship vacancies and apply for apprenticeships.[78]

Apprentices are paid the national minimum wage the first day of their apprenticeship for hours of work or training that is part of the apprenticeship. Employers are reimbursed 100% of costs for apprentices who are 16–18 years of age and 50% of costs for apprentices who are 19–24 years of age. Starting in February 2012, small and medium-sized employers can also receive a £1500 apprenticeship grant in addition to any cost reimbursement.

During the 2012/13 academic year (August 2012–July 2013), around 869 thousand individuals participated in government-funded apprenticeships, with the majority (502 thousand) at the intermediate level. Almost 21% of apprenticeship participants were under 19 years old, 34% were between 19 and 24 years old, and 45% were 25 and older. Just over 52% of apprenticeship participants were female and about 89% were white. Apprenticeship success rates during the last few years have varied between 70% and 76% with the success rate for the 2011/12 academic year, equaling 73.8%.[79]

---

[77] Those with a U score receive no qualification.

[78] See https://apprenticeshipvacancymatchingservice.lsc.gov.uk /navms/forms/candidate/Apprenticeships. aspx for England and http://www.careerswales.com/en/ for Wales.

[79] Success rates are defined as the number of apprenticeship frameworks achieved divided the number of apprenticeship starts. An apprentice framework is the set of requirements listed for a particular apprenticeship that must be completed.

The most popular sectors for apprenticeships in 2012/13 were business, administration and law (29.0%), heath, public services, and care (23.5%), and retail and commercial enterprise (19.1%). The highest success rates for the 2011/12 academic year were in the leisure, travel and tourism (79.9%), education and training (79.4%), and information and communication technology (78.0%) sectors. The lowest success rate was for the arts, media, and publishing sector (60.3%).

In 2013, traineeships began being offered in England. Traineeships can last up to 6 months and are designed for young people who do not have the necessary skills for an apprenticeship. They provide the essential work preparation, math and English training along with work experience to make the youth "apprenticeship ready." Traineeships are delivered by training providers and employers provide the work experience placement. The training costs, including the trainee's pay, of traineeships are borne by the government. Between August 2013 and January 2014, there were 3300 traineeship starts in England. Individuals can apply to traineeships at the same one-stop website used for apprenticeships.

6.1.3 Further Education: Math and English

Originally called "Skills for Life" and rolled out in 2001, this program provides full funding for individuals aged 19 and older, excluding apprentices, to take GCSE level English and math if they do not currently have these qualifications at grades A*–C regardless of what other qualifications they hold. If on the other hand an individual needs to "retake" these examinations because they failed to achieve an A*–C grade, they are required to carry out the necessary learning and cannot simply retake the examination. Total participation in these programs was 1.05 million in 2012/13 of whom 597,000 individuals achieved at least one qualification. Among the participants in English and math, 146,000 or about 14% were in the English for Speakers of Other Languages (ESOL) program. About 118,000 (80%) in the ESOL program achieved at least one qualification in 2012/13.

6.1.4 Community Learning Programs

Community learning programs in England have several purposes some of which relate to increasing individual skill levels by, for example, improving a person's confidence and willingness to engage in learning, improving those skills that prepare people for training, employment, or self-employment, and improving digital, and financial literacy and/or communication skills. These programs and their funding are structured to encourage participation by disadvantaged individuals, including those living in rural areas, with low incomes, and/or with low skill levels. In the academic year 2012/13 funding was about £2.10 million with a total participation of 685,000 individuals of whom 514,000 participated in Personal and Community Development Learning programs, 66,000 in

Neighborhood Learning in Deprived Communities programs, 53,000 in Family English, Math, and Language, and 74,000 in Wider Family Learning programs.[80]

6.1.5 Training Programs for Individuals Receiving Assistance

First introduced in 1998, the New Deal was set of programs for individuals receiving assistance, either job seeker allowance (JSA) or employment and support allowance (ESA), that were designed to help them get back to work.[81] There were several programs for different groups of individuals receiving assistance: New Deal for Young People (NDYP), New Deal for those 25+ (ND25+), New Deal for Lone Parents (NDLP), and New Deal for those 50+ (ND50+).[82] The New Deal programs continued in the United Kingdom until Labour lost control of the government in 2010.

NDYP

For young people, the (mandatory) NDYP starts after receiving JSA for 6 months and involves intensive job search activities for 4 months, which is referred to as the Gateway period. If the individual is still unsuccessful at obtaining a job during the Gateway period they enter the next phase of the program that involves placement in one of several options, which lasts 6–12 months. Placement is determined by agreement between caseworker and individual. The Full-time Employment (EMP) option is a subsidized job where the employer agrees to provide training 1 day per week while the Full-time Education or Training (FTET) option is targeted toward individuals who lack skills and places the individual in either an education or training program. The Voluntary Sector (VS) option involves a work placement, typically in retail or service jobs, that allows an individual to gain experience. Placement in the Environmental Task Force (ETF) is typically a government job that has an environmental focus. The VS and ETF options gave individuals £400 spread over 6 months in addition to JSA benefits (De Giorgi, 2008; Dorsett, 2006).

ND25+

The ND25+ is similar to the NDYP except that the program began after 18 months of receiving JSA. There is a 16-week gateway period (2 weeks of which is a core gateway period of intensive training in job search and interview techniques). Followed by a selection of one of several options: (i) Employer Subsidy, (ii) Essential Skills Training, (iii) Education and Training Opportunities, and (iv) Preparation for Employment Program. If the individual has not found work after completing one of these options they

---

[80] See https://www.gov.uk/government/statistical-data-sets/fe-data-library-community-learning.

[81] JSA is what the British call unemployment insurance.

[82] Other programs where the New Deal for Disabled People, New Deal for Partners, and the New Deal for Musicians. These latter two programs were small compared to the others.

enter the Follow–Through stage that consists of weekly interviews with their personal advisor for 6 weeks (Department for Employment and Learning, 2014).

ND50+

The ND50+ is a voluntary program for individuals 50 and older who have been on JSA for at least 6 months. Individuals can meet with a personal advisor who gives them advice on how they can improve their job prospects.

NDLP

The NDLP is a voluntary program for single parents with children under 16 years of age. Individuals can qualify if they are out of work or working less than 16 h per week. Individuals receive support from a personal adviser (PA) at a Jobcentre Plus (more about these below) where they receive advice on job search and training opportunities and finding childcare.

NDC

In addition to these programs the government initiated a pilot program called the New Deal for Communities (NDC) that was started in 1999 with 39 of the most deprived neighborhoods in the United Kingdom. These communities were asked to submit proposals to the government concerning community improvement. By 2004 there were 2857 projects operating in these NDC areas. Nearly 500 of these projects were directed toward reducing unemployment including projects that supported NDC residents in developing their business (in terms of business advice or credit), helped residents start new businesses or self-employed activities, offered advice and information via job centers, opened or improved childcare facilities to enable residents to cope with work and parenthood, gave leadership/management courses, and gave vocational and skills training support.

Jobcentre Plus was first introduced in the United Kingdom in a set of Pathfinder Areas in October 2001. It was subsequently rolled out nationally over a 6-year period at a cost of nearly £2 billion. Similar in spirit to the one-stop centers in the United States, Jobcentre Plus brought the Employment Service and Benefits Agency under one roof providing an integrated (one-stop) service for working age individuals seeking social security benefits. There was a major upgrading of service delivery including modernized IT systems, performance targets for employment specialists working in Jobcentre Plus offices, and enhanced job brokering. The change for those receiving incapacity benefits (IB) was substantial. Before Jobcentre Plus there was no explicit work-focus associated with benefit delivery for IB recipients in the United Kingdom. After IB recipients were required to attend mandatory work focused interviews (WFIs) at a Jobcentre Plus, both at the start of a claim and again after receiving benefits for 36 months.

Other demonstration projects or pilots, for example, the Employment Retention and Advancement (ERA) demonstration that was launched in 2003, have been evaluated since 2000. We discuss these below.

After a pilot phase starting in April 2009, the Flexible New Deal (FND) was rolled out to half the country in October 2009. The program consisted of four stages (Adams et al., 2012; Vegeris et al., 2010). Stage one that begins at the start of a JSA claim lasts for 13 weeks. At the outset individuals are required to attend a New Jobseeker Interview where a Jobcentre Plus adviser provides an overview of the regime, assesses basic skills needs and enters into a Jobseeker's Agreement (JSAg) with the individual. In this stage claimants perform self-directed job search that is monitored via mandatory job search reviews every other week. If an individual is still claiming JSA after 3 months they enter Stage 2, which lasts 3 months. The job seeker attends a second meeting with a Jobcentre Plus adviser in which the JSAg is reviewed and additional training needs assessed. There is more intensive monitoring of job search activity during this period through the requirement to attend weekly review meetings for a 6-week period. Stage 3 begins after 6 months of claiming JSA and lasts for 6 months. Job seekers are obliged to engage more regularly with a Jobcentre Plus adviser and take part in job related activities. At the Initial Stage 3 Review, the job seeker agrees on an action plan, which outlines the activities they should undertake in order to find or move closer to work. Activities may include attending job preparation or preemployment training, work trials, or volunteering. Up to three of these activities may be mandatory, with failure to comply resulting in a benefit sanction.

Job seekers enter the FND if they are still claiming benefits after Phase 3 ends. The FND consists of a flexible package of work preparation and job search support. The design is that customers agree on an action plan of mandatory activities, which includes a minimum of four continuous weeks of full-time paid employment or work-related activity. All activity in the action plan is enforceable and can result in benefit sanctions by Jobcentre Plus for noncompliance. Throughout the FND, customers are required to attend Jobcentre Plus every 2 weeks to sign a declaration detailing that they are available for employment and are actively seeking work.

The plan was to rollout the FND to the remainder of the country a year later. However, when the new minority government took over in Great Britain in May 2010 the FND program was subsequently canceled and replaced by the Work Programme.

Current Programs
The Work Programme (WP) started in June 2011 and operates in Great Britain. It is the United Kingdom's main welfare to work program. Once individuals have received JSA or ESA payments for a certain length of time they are referred to the WP by their local Jobcentre. Participation in the WP may be mandatory or voluntary depending on various factors. The program can last for up to 2 years and is run by

service providers who have the freedom to implement their own approaches to help unemployed individuals find work.

JSA recipients 18–24-years-old are required to participate in WP after 9 months of receiving assistance payments while JSA recipients 25 and older are required to participate in WP if they have been receiving JSA payments for 12 months. JSA claimants facing significant disadvantages may be referred to WP after 3 months and participation at this point may be mandatory or voluntary depending on circumstances.

Mandatory Work Activity (MWA) is a work-related placement of short duration that is designed to help individuals on JSA gain skills that are useful for work. It usually involves a short 4-week placement that benefits the local community.

The Youth Contract was instituted specifically to help combat the high youth unemployment rates in Great Britain. It began in April 2012 and consisted of the Work Experience (WE) and Wage Incentive (WI) programs, Sector-Based Work Academies (SBWA), and additional support for Apprenticeships.

The WE program was designed to help young people on JSA gain insight into the world of work and give them practical experience to help them get a job before they become eligible for WP. It is a voluntary program and participants continue to receive JSA. Host employers are expected to allow time for job search and to let participants attend interviews with employers or at the Jobcentre Plus office. There were 147, 670 WE starts between April 2012 and May 2014.[83]

The WI program that began in April 2012 subsidized employers for hiring an 18–24-year-old attached to the Work Programme for 6 months and paying them at least the National Minimum Wage. If hired part time (16–29 h) they receive £1137.50 while if hired full time (30 + hours) they receive £2275. As of May 2014, there has been a total of 99,110 WI job starts.[84] The WI part of the Youth Contract was discontinued in August 2014 by the DWP because it believed it was no longer needed because of falling youth unemployment rates.

A SBWA can last up to 6 weeks and has three key components: (i) preemployment training paid for by DWP, (ii) a work-experience placement, (iii) a guaranteed job interview.[85] There were 60,790 SBWA starts in Great Britain from April 2012 through May 2014.[86]

The Skills Conditionality (SC) program began in August 2011 for individuals receiving JSA or ESA. If a Jobcentre Plus adviser considers skills to be the main barrier preventing an individual from finding employment they may require them to attend training as a condition of receiving benefits. Individuals first receive an initial skills assessment by

---

[83] See Department for Work and Pensions (2014a).
[84] See Department for Work and Pensions (2014a).
[85] See Department for Work and Pensions (2012a).
[86] See Department for Work and Pensions (2014a).

Jobcentre Plus and then are mandated to the appropriate training program at a college or training organization. Individuals who fail to comply with the terms of their mandate face benefit sanctions. When an individual is mandated to attend training courses the individual's childcare and travel costs are covered by Jobcentre Plus.

Between August 2011 and February 2014, there were 719 thousand referrals to training in Great Britain. About 56% of the referrals were for occupational training, 17% were for basic training, 12% were for ESOL, and 15% in other types of training.[87] Most of those referred to training were male (65%), white (72%), and between the ages of 25 and 44 (56%). Among referrals only about half actually start training (53%). Among training starts 55% were male, 73% were white and 56% were between the ages of 25 and 44.

As of August 2013, individuals 24 and older can apply for 24+ Advanced Learner Loans to help them fund college or QCF level 3 or 4 job training.[88] Loan repayments don't begin until April 2016 and a borrower doesn't pay anything back until they earn more than £21,000 a year. For the period August 2013 through July 2014, the number of learners with Advanced Learning Loans was 55,900 with an amount totaling £116 million or about £2070 per borrower.

6.2 Evidence of Impacts

Much of the empirical research investigating the impacts of ALMPs in the United Kingdom focuses on the New Deal program. So far there is little research investigating the impacts of the new set of programs that were initiated in 2011 after the Labor government was replace by a coalition government in May 2010. While some estimates of program effects are based on RCT or regression discontinuity design (RDD), much of the empirical research assumes selection on observed variables and uses propensity score matching (PSM) or assumes conditional bias stability and combines PSM with difference-in-differences (DID) estimation.

Some of the earlier research prior to the New Deal Program dealt with the Restart program that was begun in 1987 (Dolton and O'Neill, 1996, 2002). It was used to review the position of the long-term unemployed. Under the program unemployed individuals are interviewed after being on the unemployment register for 6 months. The unemployed individual meets with an official of the Employment Office and the interview is designed to help unemployed people find a job and reduce their dependency on unemployment benefits. This is achieved by placing workers in contact with employers or training agencies. In the program an unemployed individual faces sanctions if they fail to attend the interview or if it is deemed that they are not

---

[87] See Department for Work and Pensions (2014b).
[88] See https://www.gov.uk/advanced-learning-loans/overview for more information.

making genuine attempts to find work. Individuals continue to be interviewed every 6 months if they remain unemployed.

Dolton and O'Neill (1996) use an RCT to study the short-term effects of Restart. For a sample of individuals unemployed for 6 months some were randomly selected and asked not to attend the Restart interview. They would, however, be interviewed at 12, 18, etc. months of unemployment if they remained unemployed. This is the control group. The treatment group follows the normal Restart protocol and is required to attend the Restart interview at month 6. Dolton and O'Neill (1996) find that the median length of the unemployment spell is about 1 month shorter for the treatment group. They then use a competing risks model with three risks (job exit, training exit, signing off exit) to distinguish between alternative reasons for leaving unemployment. They find that the treatment group job exit hazard is statistically significantly higher than that of the control group. The estimated effect, however, is conditional on whether or not there was a job offer or a training offer (the former whose coefficient estimate is positive and statistically significant and the latter whose coefficient estimate is negative and statistically significant). Thus, the full magnitude of the effect on the job exit risk is unclear since Restart may increase the probability of a job offer and/or job-training offer. Dolton and O'Neill (1996) find no statistically significant effects of being assigned to the treatment group on the job training or signing-off risks, conditional on whether or not there was a job offer or a training offer.

Dolton and O'Neill (2002) examine the long-term effects of the Restart program on unemployment. While they find no statistically significant effect on the unemployment rate of women 5 years after the initial experiment, the unemployment rate of men who were in the treatment group was 6% lower than men in the control group.

Several studies have explored the effects of the New Deal for Young People on labor market outcomes (Beale et al., 2008; Blundell et al., 2004; De Giorgi, 2008; Dorsett, 2006). To identify the effect of NDYP on employment, Blundell et al. (2004) exploit age-based eligibility rules and the fact that before the NDYP was rolled out nationwide it was piloted in several areas. Using DID and PSM techniques they find that NDYP increased outflows to employment by about 5% in the first 4 months of the Gateway period. They also find some evidence that the effect may be lower in the long run as the estimates were higher when based only on the pilot period and find little evidence of substitution effects since the estimates when using 25–30-year-olds as the comparison group is similar to that based on an area based comparison group (nonpilot area).

The study by Dorsett (2006) used PSM techniques to compare the relative effect of the different options (EMP, FTET, VS, ETF) individuals may be placed in if they do not find a job during the Gateway period of NDYP on the probability of exit from registered unemployment and entry into employment. Contrary to the design of the program a sizeable fraction of individuals remain in the Gateway period well beyond 4 months. So, Dorsett creates a fifth option called the Extended Gateway (EGW). The estimated propensity score model includes a host of regressors including age, time and type of NDYP entry, marital status, disability, minority status, preferred occupation, region, local unemployment rate, previous JSA claim history, and the characteristics of claimants at the unit of delivery where an individual receives their services. This lends some credence to the conditional independence assumption underlying PSM.

In terms of the probability of remaining on the unemployment register, the EMP option is more effective at lowering this probability than the FTET, VS, or ETF options. For example, the estimated difference in the probability of unemployment between EMP and FTET is a statistically significant −12.2%. The estimated difference between the EMP and EGW options is not statistically significant. The EMP option, however, dominates all options in raising the probability of becoming employed.

De Giorgi (2008) uses a RDD to estimate the impact of NDYP exploiting the fact that those who have just turned 25 are no longer eligible for NDYP. He finds that the NDYP increases the chances of employment by a statistically significant 6–7%.

Beale et al. (2008) use a PSM-DID approach to estimate the effect of NDYP on the amount of time over a 4-year period a person spends receiving "Active Labor Market Benefits" (ALMB) which includes receipt of JSA or other benefits as well as participation in New Deal options, or the Worked-Based Learning for Adults and Basic Skills programs. The comparison group consists of individuals who are ineligible for NDYP because they are "slightly" too old (25–30 years old). Here the counterfactual is not JSA receipt but rather the ND25+ program that requires mandatory participation after 18 (21) months on JSA after (before) April 2001. The results in Beale et al. suggest that NDYP lowered the amount of time spent receiving of ALMB by 64 days over a 4-year period or a reduction of about 13%. While the propensity score distributions have substantial overlap, it is difficult to assess the appropriateness of the propensity score model since the model estimates are not reported.[89] Moreover, the authors do not report the standard errors associated with the point estimates.

Riley and Young (2001a) use quarterly data on outflows from unemployment by age group, unemployment duration group and destination (unsubsidized work, subsidized work, other destinations) and inflows to unemployment by age group to investigate NDYP. For some estimates, the authors use geographic variation across units of delivery both in terms of differences in when the NDYP was started and the "intensity of delivery" (which was measured by the average number of days that individuals receive personal advisor interviews) which differed across regions. Estimating a system of time-series equations they forecast what unemployment flows would have been in the absence of the NDYP (counterfactual) and compare these forecasts to the actual unemployment flows. They find that NYPD statistically significantly raised the outflow rate from

---

[89] The authors report the final propensity score model was determined by stepwise regression with variables included only when statistically significant at the 5% level.

unemployment of 18–24-year-olds without clear adverse effects on other age groups. They also find evidence that suggests that NDYP raised the outflow rate to work some of which is unsubsidized. However, in other research (Riley and Young, 2001b) using aggregate data on wages by age group or region and time-series regression analysis they found some evidence that the NDYP led to increased wages of 18–24-year-olds. The identification of causal effects in this paper hinges on the forecasting model being accurate. The assumptions underlying the forecasting model are similar to those in DID models, ie, that the relative difference between outflow and inflow rates would have remained the same between age-groups affected and unaffected by NDYP.

Evaluations of the New Deal for Lone Parents (NDLP) have focused on its effects on unemployment and employment (Dolton and Smith, 2011; Gregg et al., 2009; Knight et al., 2006), but also in some cases on its effects on the wellbeing of lone mothers and their children (Gregg et al., 2009). The study by Knight et al. (2006) used PSM techniques to explore the combined effects of NDLP and the Lone Parent Work Focused interview (LPWFI). The propensity score model included not only controls for when the eligible claim started, how long a person was on benefits before receiving eligible income support, whether a person received a disability premium, the person's age, gender, and region of residence, but also controls for the preprogram benefit history. The benefit receipt rate before the program began was nearly identical for the control and treated groups for samples of repeat/new recipients, suggesting a satisfactory match. The primary goal of LPWFI, which was mandatory, was to help movement into paid employment. Another goal was to encourage participation in NLDP, which was voluntary.

The main analysis of Knight and coauthors focuses on the combined effects of LPWFI and NDLP. Repeat/new claimants as well as existing claimants were followed for up to 18 months after eligibility began. For repeat/new claimants, Knight and coauthors find statistically insignificant combined effects of LPWFI and NDLP for the first year but then statistically significant, positive, and increasing effects thereafter implying that, of those who left income support, 11% would not have done so if these two programs had not been implemented. For existing claimants the combination of LPWFI and NDLP had an impact on benefit exit rates that varies and is not always positive. However, at 18 months the LPWFI/NDLP impact was positive and statistically significant at the 10% level. This implies that at 18 months after participation, of those existing claimants that left benefit, 19% would not have done so if they had not participated in LPWFI/NDLP.

The study by Gregg et al. (2009) investigates the combined effect of several programs including the NDLP on employment outcomes of lone mothers. Other major programs that began at approximately the same time were Working Families Tax Credit, the National Minimum Wage, and the National Childcare Strategy. Using a DID approach they find that these combined programs had a statistically significant positive effect on employment with point estimates ranging from 3.8% to 5.2% depending on the comparison sample used. Using a DID approach, Gregg et al. also find that these combined programs had statistically significant positive effects on lone mother's general health and life satisfaction. Identification in this paper hinges on the appropriateness of the common trends assumption in the DID model of which little evidence is presented.

Dolton and Smith (2011) use PSM to estimate the effect of NDLP on the probability of benefit receipt over time. Relative to earlier studies, they emphasize the inclusion of detailed benefit histories in the propensity score. They find that NDLP lowered the probability of future benefit receipt by a substantively important (and statistically significant) amount, with a larger effect on those with prior benefit histories consisting of continuous receipt of benefits (the "stock") than those with new or intermittent spells of benefit receipt (the "flow").

Romero (2009) investigates the effects of the New Deal Community program on employment outcomes. She uses data from a household survey that was conducted in NDC and comparison areas both before the introduction of NDC in 2002 and after its introduction in 2004. Using a DID-PSM approach Romero finds that NDC had a positive and statistically significant effect on employment but only among those who were low wage earners in 2002 (less than £299 per week).

On the other hand, the paper by Romero and Noble (2008) assesses whether the NDC had an effect on the likelihood that recipients of joblessness benefits, such as JSA or Incapacity Benefits/Severe Disability Allowances (IB/SDA), leave the benefit system. Using the Work and Pensions Longitudinal Study database and a DID estimation approach based on a fixed effect logit model they find that after the NDC program began, JSA and IB/SDA recipients living in NDC areas were statistically significantly more likely to leave the benefit system than JSA and IBS/SDA recipients living in comparison areas characterized by having the same levels of deprivation as the NDC areas but not included in the NDC program, although the effect size measured in terms of odds ratios is larger for IBS/SDA than JSA recipients.

The Employment Retention and Advancement (ERA) demonstration project operated in six Jobcentre Plus districts across the United Kingdom from 2003 to 2007. This demonstration tested the effectiveness of services oriented to helping participants keep jobs they have already found and advance within their firms using an experimental design. The treatment group received two types of support: personalized advisory support and financial incentives for completing training and working full time. ERA targeted three groups: (1) The "NDLP" group: Unemployed lone parents receiving income support (IS) and volunteering for NDLP; (2) The "WTC" group: Lone parents working part time and receiving Working Tax Credit (WTC), which supplements the wages of low-paid workers; (3) "The ND25+ group": Long-term unemployed people aged 25 or older receiving JSA who were required to participate in ND25+. Miller et al. (2008) analyzes the impact of ERA over a 2-year period for the ND25+ group, while Hendra et al. (2011) analyzes ERA's impact over a 5-year period for all groups.

Miller et al. (2008) reports that there were implementation difficulties in the first year of ERA, but that matters improved over time, as staff became more skilled and confident in delivering a postemployment intervention. They find that working ND25+ participants in ERA were much more likely than those in the control group to receive retention-related and advancement related help or advice from Jobcentre Plus staff. During the first 2 years, 44.2% of ND25+ customers in ERA were employed, compared with 42.2% of the control group with the effects concentrated in year 2.[90]

Hendra et al. (2011) find that ERA produced short-term earnings gains for the two lone parent target groups: the NDLP and WTC groups, which were made up mostly of women. These early gains were a result of increases in the proportion of participants who worked full time (at least 30 h per week). These gains, however, faded toward the end of the 5-year observation period. For the ND25+ target group ERA produced modest but persistent and statistically significant increases in employment (1.9–3.6% by year) and substantial, sustained, and statistically significant increases in average yearly earnings of between £312 and £464. These positive effects emerged after the first year and were still present at the end of the follow-up period. A statistically significant reduction in the probability of benefit receipt of 1.5% over the 5-year follow-up period was also observed for this group.

Another demonstration project that was conducted by the Department for Work and Pensions (DWP) and ran from November 2011 to July 2012 was the Support for the Very Long-term Unemployed (SVLTU) trailblazer scheme. The trailblazer was designed as a RCT wherein long-term JSA claimants who had completed the Flexible New Deal were assigned to one of three programs: Community Action Programme (CAP), On-going Case Management (OCM), and a "business as usual" control group.

The CAP treatment consisted of a 6-month work placement along with provider-led supported job search where the providers were contracted by DWP to source placements for claimants which delivered a community benefit. The OCM treatment consisted of a more intensive offer of flexible and personalized adviser-based support, as well as a set of mandatory activities, delivered by Jobcentre Plus through increased adviser interventions for 6 months. The control group received the standard Jobcentre Plus services that were job search reviews every other week plus additional appointments with advisers based on advisers' discretion and access to a menu of back to work support.

Rahim et al. (2012), who conducted a survey of the program participants, analyze several outcomes of the SVLTU demonstration project. They find no statistically significant differences between programs in relation to participants who entered paid employment, became self-employed or had accepted a job offer. They do find statistically

---

[90] The combined effect over the 2-year period was statistically significant at the 10% level while the effect in year 2, a 2.6% difference, was statistically significant at the 5% level.

significant differences in the fraction on JSA at the time of the survey (OCM 73%, CAP 80%, JCPO 76%). Rahim et al. (2012) also find no statistically significant difference in the average well-being scores of participants across the three groups. However, they do find that CAP participants on placements reported statistically significantly lower levels of anxiety, on average, when compared with other participants. Analysis of administrative data (Department for Work and Pensions, 2012a,b) finds that over the first 41 weeks those in the CAP group had nine fewer days of benefit receipt and those in OCM had 12 fewer days of benefit receipt than those in the control group, both of which are statistically significant.

The StepUP pilot provided a guaranteed job and support for up to 50 weeks. It was available for those in the 20 pilot areas who remained unemployed 6 months after completing their New Deal Option or Intensive Activity Period on ND25+. The subsidized jobs were 33 h a week to allow for job search during a normal working week. A StepUP job constituted a job offer under the Jobseeker's Agreement (JSAg), and sanctions could have been applied if a job was refused without good reason. There were two phases of support to individuals during the job: the "Retention Phase" during the first 26 weeks where the goal was to maximize retention in the StepUP job. The goal of the Progression Phase' during the final 26 weeks was to facilitate job search so that StepUP employees would move to an unsubsidized job in the labor market after the program ended.

Bivand et al. (2006) use survey data and a two-stage matching process to analyze the effects of StepUP on labor market outcomes. In the first stage, pilot areas were matched to comparison areas on the basis of labor market indicators. In the second stage individuals were matched according to the age, gender, detailed ethnicity code, disability status, the number of times the individual had been on the NDYP, the number of times the individual had been on the ND25+, and the last New Deal option/opportunity type. Bivand et al. find that individuals aged 18 to 24 who participated in StepUP had, on average, annualized earnings that were a statistically significant £3350 higher than their matched counterparts. The estimated difference in average earnings for the last 90 days between StepUP participants and their matched counterparts for the 25 to 29 or 30 to 49 age groups, although positive were not statistically significant. The estimated effect of StepUP on the average number of days worked in the last 90 days was not statistically significant for any age group.

As mentioned above, Jobcentre Plus was first introduced in 56 Pathfinder sites in 17 clusters across the United Kingdom. The second stage of implementation began in October 2002 and was mostly completed in March 2003, covering 24 districts. The remainder of the national rollout was scheduled in three successive waves between 2003/04 and 2005/06. Riley et al (2011) exploit this variation using different econometric approaches including DID, the random growth model (which allows time-trends to differ across treatment and comparison group) and PSM–DID to estimate the effect of the introduction of a Jobcentre Plus.[91] Based on the random growth model estimates, the authors find that for those receiving JSA benefit, the introduction of Jobcentre Plus statistically significantly increases the average quarterly claim exit rate by about 0.8%. For those receiving incapacity benefits, the introduction of Jobcentre Plus statistically significantly increased claim exit rates by about 2% in months 14 and 15 after its introduction.

From 2006 until 2011, the United Kingdom's Train to Gain (TTG) program was designed to encourage low-skilled workers to upgrade to NVQ level 2 or 3 by offering free training. Before the TTG program was implemented a pilot program called the Employer Training Pilots (ETP) was run in selected areas of England from 2002 and 2006. This pilot gave employers a financial incentive to offer qualification-based training to their low-skilled employees. The pilot started in 2002 in six areas, was expanded to six more areas in 2003, and finally added another eight areas in 2004 so that about one-third of the English workforce was covered. Using employee and employer survey data that was commissioned explicitly for evaluating ETP and a DID estimation approach, Abramovsky et al. (2011) find no statistically significant 1-year impact of ETP on employer provision of training or employees receipt of training. They also find no statistically significant effect on training receipt when using data from the Labor Force Survey, in the first year of the program or in years 2 and 3.

There are only a limited number of studies of the training programs put in place by the current government in 2011. Hillmore et al. (2012) analyze the early impacts of the Work Programme by comparing outcomes of individuals receiving JSA who were referred to WP to a matched set of individuals who were not referred to WP. Individuals were matched on age, sex, marital status, qualification, lone parent status, choice of preferred occupation, geographic district and the labor market characteristics of their local authority. Hillmore et al. (2012) combine DWP administrative data and administrative tax system data that contain spells of employment. Using data on referrals to WP between May 2011 through July 2011 and PSM techniques, Hillmore et al. (2012) find that in the first 3 months MWA decreased the likelihood of claiming benefit by up to 5%. After that the impact decreased, and equals zero at 21 weeks following the referral.

Using PSM methods and administrative DWP and tax data, Ainsworth et al. (2012) examine the early impacts of the Work Experience program. They find that WE decreased the likelihood of claiming benefits for 18–24-year olds by a statistically significant 6% 21 weeks after starting on placements and increased the likelihood of being in employment by nearly 8% 21 weeks after starting on placements.

In summary, most of the empirical studies of the effectiveness of various ALMPs employ PSM, DID or a combination of PSM and DID methods to estimate treatment effects. A few studies employ RCT but these are mostly done with pilot or demonstration

---

[91] Conducting a preprogram (placebo) test the authors find evidence that the common trends assumption of DID estimation is violated.

projects. The most analyzed policy program has been the New Deal, especially NDYP. Most estimates of the effect of NDYP find that it reduced the amount of time 18–24-year-olds spent unemployed (receiving benefits) and increased employment. However, there is some evidence that among the placement options the full-time training and education options were less effective at lowering unemployment than the employment option but more effective than the environmental task force option. There is also some empirical evidence that the NDLP was effective in lowering benefit receipt at least when combined with the lone parent work force interview.

Since the change of government in 2010, a set of new ALMPs have been introduced. While some features of the New Deal program have been retained (eg, the one-stop shopping aspect of the Jobcentre Plus) there have also been changes. To date little empirical research has been done on the short-run effectiveness of these new programs and not enough time has yet passed to judge their long-term effectiveness.

7. GERMANY

7.1 Types of Programs

In Germany, most publicly subsidized programs that provide basic education or further vocational training to adults are administered by the PES. The PES either pays for training directly, or it issues training vouchers which cover 50–100% of the direct cost of training. Moreover, the PES can pay income support to unemployed workers and wage subsidies for employed workers who participate in training. In addition to the programs administered by the PES, the Federal Ministry for Education and Research supports further vocational training of adults by covering parts of the direct cost of training and by providing income support during full-time education. Immigrants additionally have access to special programs funded by the Federal Office for Migration and Refugees.

In 2012, the German government spent about 2.5 billion EUR or 0.1% of GDP on publicly subsidized adult education (OECD, 2014). About 70% of expenditures are related to programs administered by the PES, about one forth is spent on programs supported by the Federal Ministry for Education and Research, and less than 5% go into programs for immigrants funded by the Federal Office for Migration and Refugees. Overall, there exist a variety of programs with different target populations and objectives. The programs can be grouped into four broad categories that are described in more detail in the following sections: basic education for adults, further vocational training, retraining, and training for career advancement.

7.1.1 Basic Education for Adults

There are four different types of programs that provide basic education to adults. The first one comprises literacy programs. Participants in literacy programs can receive financial support through all three channels: via a training voucher from the PES or the Federal

Ministry for Education and Research or, in case of immigrants, from the Federal Office for Migration and Refugees. Statistics only exist for the latter group. In 2012, about 10,000 immigrants participated in literacy programs, 60% of whom were women.[92]

The second group of programs provides financial support to obtain a certificate of secondary education. Unemployed workers with a vocational degree[93] or at least 3 years of work experience but no such certificate can receive a training voucher from the PES, which enables them to participate in preparatory classes for obtaining a certificate on the lowest secondary level.[94] A voucher will only be issued if the certificate is considered necessary for labor market integration and if there is a high probability of completing the necessary exams successfully. In addition, the Federal Ministry for Education and Research provides grants for adults seeking to obtain qualifications on any of the three secondary levels offered in Germany.[95] The grant is subject to a means test and is provided as a monthly payment (so-called training assistance). Part of it may be granted as an interest-free loan, which has to be re-paid after completion of the training.

The third group of programs provides financial support for low-skilled workers to obtain a first vocational degree. Both employed and unemployed workers qualify. They can receive a training voucher from the PES if they have at least 3 years of work experience. Additionally, unemployment insurance (UI) and welfare claimants continue to receive these payments during participation. For employed workers who attend training during their work hours, employers may receive a wage subsidy of up to 100% as compensation for the time their employees are absent from their work place. Since 2013, the German government has provided additional funding to support low-skilled workers in obtaining a first vocational degree. Workers qualify even with less than 3 years of work experience if they are older than 25 and receive UI or welfare payments.

The last group of programs consists of occupation specific combined German language and vocational training courses for immigrants.[96] They are financed by the European Social Fund (ESF) in cooperation with the Federal Office for Migration and Refugees. They are offered for all skill levels and a large variety of occupations. Both first and second generation immigrants can participate. The courses have four elements: occupation-specific German language lessons and vocational training in the classroom, firm visits, and internships in firms. Full-time courses have durations of up to 6 months,

---

[92] Bundesamt für Migration und Flüchtlinge (2013a).

[93] Germany has a formalized vocational education system with regulated apprenticeship and advanced vocational training that provides recognized formal degrees. For a detailed description of the German education system see Secretariat of the Standing Conference of the Ministers of Education and Cultural Affairs of the Länder in the Federal Republic of Germany (2013).

[94] So-called *Hauptschulabschluss*, which is the lowest attainable certified level of schooling in Germany.

[95] Besides the *Hauptschulabschluss*, there is the *Realschulabschluss*, which is equivalent to the British GCSE, and the *Abitur*, which is equivalent to the British A-levels or a high school diploma in the United States.

[96] *Programm zur berufsbezogenen Sprachförderung für Personen mit Migrationshintergrund* (ESF-BAMF).

part-time courses last up to 12 months. Since its introduction in 2009, about 130,000 immigrants have participated in the program. In 2012, about 24,000 immigrants participated in the program and total expenditures amounted to 53.5 million EUR. A total of 17% of participants had no school leaving certificate or vocational degree, 36% had a lower secondary degree, 33% had an upper secondary degree and 15% had a tertiary degree.[97]

7.1.2 Further Vocational Training and Related Programs for Jobseekers

The main target groups of programs administered by the PES are jobseekers who are unemployed or at risk of becoming unemployed after being notified of their dismissal.[98] The PES fully covers the direct cost of training for this group and continues to pay UI or welfare payments during participation. The objective of training for this group is to provide skills that improve the employment prospects of participants. Courses supported by training vouchers include occupation-specific classroom training, general vocational training such as computer courses, job-related training such as courses to obtain a driver's license for special vehicles like trucks or pallet transporters, as well as occupation-specific on-the-job training in a simulated work environment (so-called practice firms). The courses can last up to 12 months. The average duration is 4 months.

The PES also supports much shorter training programs belonging to the group of so-called measures for activation and vocational integration to which unemployed workers get assigned directly.[99] They have durations of 4–12 weeks and aim at removing smaller skill deficits. They comprise, for example, basic computer or language courses in the classroom. They also include short on-the-job training for a specific vacancy in a firm. This program lasts no more than 6 weeks and participants have the prospect of being hired for that specific vacancy at the end of the program. In addition to short vocational training, measures for activation and vocational integration of jobseekers comprise different forms of job search assistance. This includes training in job search skills, monitoring components such as availability checks, programs that comprise an assessment of the jobseekers' skills and employability, as well as suitability tests for specific occupations, vacancies or training programs. Since part of their objectives is to reveal qualification needs, these programs often precede more intensive training.

Since 2002, the German PES has also issued so-called activation and placement vouchers, which entitle the recipient to make use of activation and placement services

---

[97] Bundesamt für Migration und Flüchtlinge (2013a,b, 2014).

[98] In Germany, workers are notified of their dismissal well in advance. Notification periods of 3 months or longer are typical. Workers are obliged to register with the PES as jobseeker within a short period after they have been informed about their dismissal. From that point in time they are eligible for job search assistance provided by the PES.

[99] *Maßnahmen zur Aktivierung und beruflichen Eingliederung.* Before 2009, these measures had different names and the legal foundations were a bit different but the main characteristics are largely unchanged.

offered by external providers. UI recipients have a legal claim to receive such a voucher after 6 weeks of unemployment[100] but they are only issued on demand. The value of the voucher is typically 2000 EUR. The provider receives the first 1000 EUR shortly after the jobseeker has been successfully placed into a job. The rest is paid out after 6 months of employment. In 2012, about 540,000 vouchers have been issued but only 48,500 or 9% have been redeemed. Among those who make use of the voucher, women (36%), recipients aged above 50 (20%) as well as low-skilled recipients (29%) are under-represented.[101] Bernhard and Kruppe (2010) list the following potential reasons for the persistently low take-up rate: lack of initiative of jobseekers, lack of transparency in the provider market which overwhelms jobseekers, doubts about the quality of offered services, and cream-skimming by providers. The latter occurs because payment is success-based and there is no or only a small difference in the value of the voucher between easy and hart-to-place workers.[102]

7.1.3 Further Vocational Training for Employed Workers

The PES also supports employed workers who participate in further vocational training if they work in firms with less than 250 employees.[103] Vouchers are granted for training that takes place during work hours and employers are required to continue to pay the full salary. Moreover, training must go substantially beyond short job-specific further training but it is not required to provide a formal degree. The objective of this program is to encourage small and medium-sized firms, which typically engage less in further training, to invest more in the education of their workforce. Moreover, in order to direct investments toward groups which are usually underrepresented in further education, the reimbursement rates for training costs vary by target group. The PES covers up to 50% of the cost of training for workers aged below 45 and 75% of the cost if they are older than 45. For low-skilled workers without a formal vocational degree up to 100% of the training cost can be reimbursed and employers may additionally receive a wage subsidy.

In addition to the training vouchers issued by the PES, the Federal Ministry for Education and Research supports the participation of employed low-income workers in further vocational training. It pays a so-called education premium,[104] which is a

---

[100] This requirement changed over time. It was 3 months in the period 2002–04 and 2 months in the period 2008–10.

[101] Statistik der Bundesagentur für Arbeit (2013a).

[102] Only the second payment after 6 months of employment may vary. From 2002 to 2004, it was 500, 1000 or 1500 EUR for UI recipients with unemployment durations of no more than 6, 7–9, and more than 9 months (at the point in time where the voucher is issued), respectively. From 2005 to 2007 it was completely flat at 1000 EUR. Since 2008 caseworkers can decide to deviate from the usual 1000 EUR and grant up to 1500 EUR for workers who have been unemployed for more than a year.

[103] *Weiterbildungsförderung Geringqualifizierter und beschäftigter Arbeitnehmer im Unternehmen.*

[104] *Bildungsprämie.*

voucher that covers 50% of the tuition for courses that cost no more than 1000 EUR. Most of these courses are offered by publicly subsidized institutions, which explains their relatively low cost. Eligibility for the voucher is restricted to workers older than 25 years of age with annual income of no more than 20,000 EUR (40,000 EUR with a spouse). Since its introduction in 2008, more than 250,000 vouchers have been issued. Two-thirds of recipients are female and 40% work part time. Recently, the program has been prolonged until the end of 2017 with a planned distribution of 280,000 new vouchers.[105]

7.1.4 Retraining

The third group of programs is retraining which is administered by the PES. It is targeted at workers with some vocational training who have no prospect of working in their original occupation again in the future. Both employed and unemployed workers qualify and they are eligible if they have worked in an unskilled occupation for at least 4 years. The objective of the program is to qualify workers for a new occupation with better employment prospects. With typical durations of 18–24 months, this type of training comprises a substantial human capital investment. After successful completion, participants receive a formal vocational degree which is equivalent to an apprenticeship degree. Retraining is supported by the PES via training vouchers which usually cover 100% of the direct training costs. Additionally, recipients of income support continue to receive these payments during participation. For employed workers who participate retraining during their work hours, employers can receive a wage subsidy of up to 100% as compensation for the time their employees are absent from their work place.

7.1.5 Training for Career Advancement

The final group of programs consists of training for career advancement, which is funded by Federal Ministry for Education and Research. It is available to individuals who have already completed a formal vocational degree. The most common form of support is a so-called master grant.[106] Workers who want to obtain an advanced vocational degree in certain occupations have a legal claim to receive this grant. This includes advanced degrees as master craftsman (which has given the program its name), foreman, technician, or merchant, as well as advanced nonacademic degrees in health care, business administration, information technology or related occupations. An advanced vocational degree is a legal prerequisite for opening one's own business in these occupations. Hence, one additional objective of the program is to encourage workers in these occupations to start their own business. The government subsidizes 30.5% of the training costs and provides low-interest loans for the remaining part up to a total amount of 10,226 EUR. Moreover, the government covers the cost of living during full-time education subject to a means

[105] Bundesministerium für Bildung und Forschung (2013, 2014).
[106] *Meister-BAföG*.

test. In 2012, 168,000 individuals received this grant, 41% of whom took part in full-time education. Women made up 32% of all beneficiaries. Their relatively low share can be explained by a large share of beneficiaries being trained in manual and technical occupations. Total expenditures amounted to 546 million EUR.[107]

There are also two much smaller programs which are targeted at particularly talented adults. They are administered by the Foundation for the Support of Vocational Training for Gifted Adults which is funded by the Federal Ministry for Education and Research. Adults qualify if they already have a recognized vocational degree and performed particularly well during their apprenticeship or in a supra-regional occupational competition. Conditional on eligibility, admission is a discretionary choice made by selection committees in the institutions that govern vocational education in the respective occupation, eg, the chamber of commerce. Under the first program, employed young adults under age 25 can receive a so-called further training grant.[108] It is a 3-year grant of no more than 2000 EUR per year to finance advanced vocational training courses that beneficiaries attend while working. This includes, for example, obtaining a specific certificate, language courses, personnel management courses, and preparatory courses for exams to obtain an advanced vocational degree. In 2012, there were 6500 new beneficiaries, about 50% of whom were female.[109]

The second program is called career advancement grant.[110] It provides financial support for obtaining a university degree to workers with at least 2 years of work experience in their profession. Beneficiaries receive 750 EUR per month in full-time education and 2000 EUR per year when they remain employed during education. In 2012, 1400 new beneficiaries were admitted to the program, 62% of whom were women. The large share of females is due to an over-proportionally large share of training for occupations in the health and education sector. Only 13% of recipients were younger than 25. The majority of new beneficiaries (52%) were aged 26–30 and 5% were older than 45. A total of 59% of grant recipients participated in full-time education. In total, a bit more than 5000 adults have received this type of grant since its introduction in 2008.[111]

7.2 Assignment to and Use of Training Administered by the PES

The PES assigns workers to training either directly or by issuing a training voucher. The voucher specifies the training objective, an expiry date as well as possible restrictions in terms of the maximum duration of training or regional validity. Moreover, financial support is restricted to certified providers. Assignment to programs is a discretionary decision made by caseworkers. They assess whether a candidate has any skill deficits that are

---

[107] Bundesamt für Statistik (2013).
[108] *Weiterbildungsstipendium.*
[109] Stiftung Begabtenförderung berufliche Bildung (2013).
[110] *Aufstiegsstipendium.*
[111] Stiftung Begabtenförderung berufliche Bildung (2013, 2014).

sufficiently severe to justify financial support and that could be removed with any of the available programs. After establishing eligibility and consulting the candidate, the final decision is based on the candidate's personal characteristics, including education, work experience, past employment record and career prospects. Additionally, caseworkers take into account labor market conditions, in particular demand for specific skills, the supply of courses offered by providers, and available funding.

In 2012, a total of 308,000 individuals started a training program that was supported by a voucher from the PES, which corresponds to a take-up rate of about 85%. Kruppe (2009) investigates selectivity in voucher take-up. He reports that low-skilled workers, jobseekers with health problems, and persons with limited regional mobility are less likely to make use of the vouchers. Moreover, usage is particularly unlikely for jobseekers with multiple barriers to employment, mainly because of cream-skimming by providers. On the other hand, take-up is more likely the more specific the training objective stated on the voucher is because recipients find it easier to locate providers that offer specific types of courses.

Direct expenditures on training supported by vouchers (excluding income support) amounted to 353 million EUR. Additionally, about 1.1 million individuals entered short measures for activation and vocational integration, of which 32% took place in firms. Total direct expenditures for these measures amounted to 119 million EUR.[112] Unfortunately, public statistics do not report which share of participants and expenditures relates to vocational training as opposed to job search assistance and related measures within this group. There is also only limited information on the relative importance of different types of training that are supported by vouchers from the PES. In 2012, 14% of training participants started a course that awards a formal vocational degree after successful completion. Somewhat less than 10% of participants failed the final exams. The average duration of these courses was 19 months. The remaining training courses were much shorter with average durations of 4 months. Of all entrants into PES-supported training 46% were women, 14% foreigners, 10% were aged below 25, and 15% were aged above 50. About 6% of supported workers were employed and for approximately 40% of them employers received a wage subsidy. At least 13% of participants dropped out of the program prematurely, 36% of them because they found a job. For about 7% of participants it is not known whether they completed the program due to missing information in the administrative data.[113]

---

[112] Bundesagentur für Arbeit (2013a,b). This excludes income support payments during participation.

[113] Bundesagentur für Arbeit (2013a,b). Based on a comparison of planned and actual program durations as well as transitions to other labor market states Paul (2015) estimates that actual dropout rates were around 20% in earlier periods. This suggests that at least some of the nonclassified cases might be dropouts.

7.3 Evidence on Impacts

For Germany, there exists an extensive empirical literature about the impacts of publicly subsidized training on participants' labor market outcomes. The early literature from the 1980s and 1990s, which is surveyed in Wunsch (2005) and Jacobi and Kluve (2006), suffered from small sample sizes and methodological problems that were mainly due to the unavailability of good data. At the beginning of the new millennium, the German Institute for Employment Research (IAB) started to make high-quality administrative data available to the scientific community. As a result, a first wave of evaluation studies emerged that provides reliable and detailed results on the effectiveness of various types of programs for unemployed workers who participated in the programs in the early 1990s (Lechner and Wunsch, 2009; Lechner et al., 2007, 2011; Fitzenberger and Speckesser, 2007; Fitzenberger and Völter, 2007; Fitzenberger et al., 2008, 2013). Exploiting the richness and the long panel dimension of the data, all of these studies use selection-on-observables strategies to identify the program effects and implement them using propensity-score matching estimators.

A unique feature of these studies is that they are able to estimate the dynamics of the program effects — from the very short run to the long run — for up to 8 years after program start (Lechner et al., 2007, 2011; Fitzenberger and Völter, 2007; Fitzenberger et al., 2008). They show that all programs exhibit negative employment effects in the beginning, so-called locking-in effects, the magnitude and duration of which is closely tied to the average duration of the programs. They occur because of reduced search and placement efforts by, respectively, the jobseekers and caseworkers during participation. Soon after most participants completed the programs, the studies consistently find positive and long-lasting employment effects of the programs (for West Germany). Further vocational training increases the probability to be employed by about 10% and retraining by about 20%. Lechner et al. (2011) additionally provide a first step toward a cost-benefit analysis. By estimating the effects on cumulated time employed they assess the relative importance of the negative locking-in effects and the positive long-run effects. They show that short training programs with relatively small locking-in effects exhibit positive net effects on employment as early as 15 months after program start. In contrast, for retraining, which exhibits substantial locking-in effects, it takes 4.5 years for positive net effects to appear despite considerably higher long-run effects. Moreover, Lechner and Wunsch (2009) show that both the locking-in effects and the positive long-run effects are related to the business cycle. The locking-in effects are smaller in recessions because nonparticipants have more difficulties finding a job while participants attend the programs. This has a lasting effect on the long-run effects, which are larger when the program started during a recession.

In the early 2000s, after almost 10 years of persistently high unemployment, the German government started a series of substantial labor market reforms. A variety of new programs were launched, which now comprise the set of instruments described in the last section. The introduction of the new instruments was accompanied by systematic efforts to evaluate the effectiveness of these measures in improving labor market outcomes. The IAB has created a research data center (FDZ) that offers a large variety of high-quality survey and administrative data. Researchers have access to scientific use files or may use the data on-site in one of the FDZ's locations in Germany or the United States. As a result, a large number of evaluation studies have emerged and an increasing share of these studies is conducted by staff of the IAB as part of the systematic evaluation of German labor market policy.

An interesting feature of the German evaluation literature is that it almost entirely focuses on unemployed workers who participate in programs supported by the PES. The main reason for this is that most participants in publicly supported training actually fall into this group. This, in turn, can be explained by most measures having been introduced to solve Germany's unemployment problem following unification in 1990, which dominated the political agenda well in to the 2000s. It is only since the beginning of the German success story in the recent global recession that focus has shifted away from unemployed workers. With falling unemployment rates, attention has shifted toward to low-income workers, especially those who receive welfare payments because they earn less than the legally granted minimum. Often, these workers have no or little vocational training, or they work in low-skill occupations despite their original training. This is the reason why a number of new programs have been launched to support vocational training of low-skilled workers in recent years.

Another interesting feature of the German evaluation studies is that they are almost exclusively based on selection-on-observables strategies which are implemented using propensity-score matching estimators. There are several reasons for this. Firstly, the first wave of evaluation studies, which all used this approach, were perceived as some kind of "gold standard." Secondly, the quality of the data provided by the IAB actually makes this data-hungry strategy credible for the evaluation of many of the German programs, especially for publicly subsidized training (see the systematic investigation of the credibility of selection-on-observables strategies for the evaluation of training programs with the German data by Fitzenberger et al., 2013 and Lechner and Wunsch, 2013). Thirdly, the regular assignment process of participants to programs generates no other sources of exogenous variation that could be exploited for identification. As described in the last section, assignment to programs is a discretionary decision made by caseworkers of the PES, which is based on relatively well-defined criteria. Finally, there is strong resistance in the German government against randomization of participation. Assignment to training programs is to a large extent based on qualification needs. Resistance is based on the view that randomization would deny access to training to some needy individuals who would be able to participate under normal circumstances. In fact, German law only allows randomization in exceptional cases (Büttner, 2008). So far, to the best of our knowledge, there exist only two studies that use experimental designs and none of them studies publicly subsidized training for adults.[114]

The following sections summarize the evidence on the impacts of publicly subsidized training for adults that was conducted in West Germany in 2000 or later.[115] For some programs, there are no evaluation studies available, mainly because they are of minor importance due to a relatively small share in total expenditures. This includes literacy programs and all programs supported by the Federal Ministry for Education and Research. The discussion is organized by target group rather than by program type. The reason for this is twofold. Firstly, this is the way the literature emerged in Germany. Secondly, the data available in Germany do not allow separating out all of the different types of programs described above. For example, it is not possible to distinguish retraining from other programs that provide a vocational degree. Moreover, many studies that analyze short measures for activation and vocational integration do not distinguish between vocational training measures and job search assistance or related programs.

Before discussing the evidence in detail it is worth noting that there are three studies which go beyond a standard comparison of participation in various programs and nonparticipation. Kluve et al. (2012) employ the framework of Hirano and Imbens (2004) and estimate a continuous dose–response function that relates the duration of training to the probability of employment after training. To adjust for covariate imbalance they use the generalized propensity score for continuous treatments. Wunsch (2013) also estimates the effects of program duration. She uses a modified version of the sequential matching estimator proposed by Lechner (2009) which allows estimating effects for an arbitrary population of interest and takes dynamic selection into another period of training into account. Osikominu (2013) models the full path of transitions between different labor market states and training programs over time in an adapted hazard rate model with unobserved heterogeneity. Her approach accounts for dynamic selection into and out of training, and allows for the unbiased estimation of effects on postunemployment outcomes.

7.3.1 Programs for Unemployed Workers

The majority of studies investigate program effects for recipients of UI payments. Workers qualify for UI benefits if they have worked at least 12 out of the 24 months

---

[114] Büttner (2008) analyses the effects of programs that have the objective of testing jobseekers' availability for and willingness to work. Krug and Stephan (2013) use an experimental design to compare contracting-out of placement services to intensified counseling and placement efforts by caseworkers for hard-to-place unemployed workers.

[115] Results for East Germany are excluded because they are still affected by the transition process following unification.

preceding unemployment.[116] Following the biggest reform of postwar German labor market policy in 2005, unemployed recipients of means-tested welfare payments have become the new focus of attention. For the first time, all welfare recipients who are capable of working have access to the programs administered by the PES. This raised considerable interest in the effects of the programs for this particular group among both policy makers and researchers. Compared to recipients of UI, welfare recipients have on average less favorable labor market outcomes. They have either exhausted UI, which implies that they have been unemployed for at least 6–12 months, or they do not qualify for UI because of insufficient work experience. Moreover, they live in households with incomes below the legally granted minimum.

Besides focusing on different target groups, the studies differ quite a bit in terms of time period studied, grouping of the programs, and some methodological aspects. However, in terms of overall conclusions, the differences are relatively small. This is particularly true for short activation measures, which comprise vocational training, monitoring, and job search assistance elements. Job search assistance and jobseeker assessment programs outside of firms are usually found to be ineffective in raising employment rates of participants (Wunsch, 2013; Wunsch and Lechner, 2008), especially for welfare recipients (Bernhard and Kopf, 2014; Kopf, 2013; Thomsen et al., 2013). But participants in these measures are more likely to enter other types of programs afterwards (Kopf, 2013; Wunsch and Lechner, 2008). Moreover, there is some evidence that assignment to availability checks encourages workers to exit to employment or deregister as unemployed before program start (Büttner, 2008). Programs with a vocational training component fare better than programs focusing on aspects which are not of direct use for potential employers (Fitzenberger et al., 2013; Thomsen et al., 2013; Wunsch and Lechner, 2008). Overall, short activation measures outside of firms never increase employment rates by more than 5%, and there are no sizeable effects on postunemployment outcomes such as job stability (Osikominu, 2013). The two only studies that use mixed proportional hazard models with unobserved heterogeneity rather than matching methods to estimate program effects also find that the positive effects on the exit rate to employment disappear 6–12 months after program start (Hujer et al., 2006; Osikominu, 2013).

In contrast, all studies that separately analyze short activation measures taking place in firms consistently find large positive and long-lasting employment effects of around 15% based on matching methods (Achatz et al., 2012; Hartig et al., 2008; Kopf, 2013; Romeu Gordo and Wolff, 2011; Stephan, 2008; Stephan and Pahnke, 2011). These large effects have to be interpreted with caution, though. Short activation measures that take place in firms are suitability tests, often combined with on-the-job training, for a specific vacancy and with the prospect of being hired for that vacancy. When contrasting employment rates of participants with those of comparable unemployed nonparticipants, selection bias

---

[116] 12 out of 36 months before February 2006.

due to the availability of a specific job offer for participants but not for nonparticipants is not properly taken care of in these studies.[117] Studies that do not distinguish between different types of short activation measures mostly find positive effects on employment, at least for some groups of participants (Biewen et al., 2014; Huber et al., 2010; Zabel, 2013), which are possibly driven by the effects of in-firm measures.

The estimates of the effects of further vocational training programs are somewhat more diverse. All studies find negative locking-in effects for these programs which vary with the average duration of the programs. Whether the studies find positive employment effects later on depends somewhat on the sample, time period and methodology used. In general, the programs seem to be more effective for workers with less favorable employment prospects such as long-term unemployed workers (Biewen et al., 2014; Osikominu, 2013; Paul et al., 2013; Wunsch and Lechner, 2008). In line with this, studies that use stock samples of unemployed workers or unrestricted program inflows with higher shares of long-term unemployed jobseekers (Bernhard and Kruppe, 2012; Kluve et al., 2012; Stephan and Pahnke, 2011) report more positive results than studies that use inflow samples into unemployment (Wunsch and Lechner, 2008) or analyze training programs after the introduction of training vouchers that led to cream-skimming by providers (Paul et al., 2013). Moreover, studies that do not restrict future program participation of the comparison group tend to find more positive results than studies that require the control group not to have participated in any program for some time (Stephan, 2008; Wunsch and Lechner, 2008). Interestingly, this was not the case for programs conducted in the 1990s (Fitzenberger et al., 2008; Lechner et al., 2011). A possible reason for this is that further vocational training was the main program used in 1990s while later on the introduction of a range of other programs made a control group of unemployed workers who have not participated in further vocational training or any other program for some time more selective in terms of labor market outcomes.

Overall, in the studies that do find positive effects on employment, the estimated effects are in the order of magnitude of 5–10%. Moreover, Osikominu (2013) shows that participants benefit from improved outcomes post unemployment such as more stable employment spells and higher earnings. Concerning the relative performance of long versus short further vocational training the evidence suggests that programs with durations of more than 6 months are not cost effective. Long programs have substantial locking-in effects without producing significantly higher employment effects than shorter programs (Bernhard and Kruppe, 2012; Lechner et al., 2011; Paul et al., 2013; Wunsch and Lechner, 2008). In fact, Kluve et al. (2012) show that participating beyond 5–6 months does not lead to a further increase in the effectiveness of training. The only exception might be programs that award a formal vocational degree such as retraining.

---

[117] A similar problem exists for studies that estimate the effect of wage subsidies using matching methods, see the discussion in Schünemann et al. (2013).

With durations around 20 months they exhibit particularly large and long-lasting locking-in effects (Bernhard and Kruppe, 2012; Lechner et al., 2011; Paul et al., 2013; Wunsch and Lechner, 2008). However, evidence for both earlier and more recent programs suggests that employment effects of about 20% can be expected 3–4 years after program start (Lechner et al., 2011; Stephan and Pahnke, 2011). Here the question is whether the government is willing is to wait that long to recoup their investment.

7.3.2 Programs for Employed Workers

While there is plenty of evidence on the effects of programs for unemployed workers, there is only very little research on program for employed workers. So far, there exist only two studies for Germany. Görlitz (2010) analyzes a regional program that was implemented in 2006 in the German state of North-Rhine-Westphalia. The program had a lot of similarities with the national program that was also implemented in 2006. Both firms and employees of firms with less than 250 employees could receive a training voucher that reduced training costs by 50% per course up to a maximum of 750 EUR. The objective of the program was to increase training incentives for small and medium-sized firms. Görlitz (2010) exploits the introduction of the program in 2006 using variation across time, regions, and firm size. In line with the objective of the program, she studies the effects of the program on the firm level. Using data from the IAB Establishment Panel for 2001–07, she finds that the share of establishments that invest in training increased by 4–6%, while the training intensity of firms that invest in training remained unchanged.

Singer and Toomet (2013) provide first evidence on the effects of the national program that targets low-skilled employees and workers employed in firms with less than 250 employees independent of their skill level. For identification purposes the analysis is restricted to workers aged 45 or older in the latter group. The national program supports obtaining a first vocational degree, further vocational training, and retraining. Participants receive a training voucher that covers up to 100% of the training cost and for low-skilled workers a wage subsidy of up to 100% may be paid to employers. Singer and Toomet (2013) apply a dynamic matching approach similar to Crépon et al. (2009) and use individual administrative data from the IAB combined with administrative data on firms' employees that has been aggregated on the firm level (so-called IAB Establishment History Panel). They find that participation in the program increases the probability of remaining in paid employment by 1–2.5% within 2 years after training, mainly due to increased tenure in the firm where they were employed during participation. Moreover, they find that the effects are more pronounced for part-time workers and participants in longer programs. Looking at the effects separately by age suggests that postponed labor market withdrawal of elderly workers is the main driver behind the positive effects.

Together the two German studies suggest that training incentives for employed workers increase firms' likelihood to engage in further vocational training, stabilize employees' work careers, and improve the labor market attachment of elderly workers.

7.3.3 Combined German Language and Vocational Training Courses for Immigrants

Combined German language and vocational training courses for immigrants have only been introduced in 2009. Recently, the first evaluation of this program has been completed. Walter et al. (2014) analyze the short-run effects of participation in the program for up to 18 months after program start.[118] They use individual administrative data from the IAB and employ a propensity-score matching approach. For some outcome variables they additionally use data from a survey that was conducted about 6 months after the program ended. Only 8% of program participants were regularly employed before program entry, 50% were unemployed, 11% were in subsidized employment or some other program, 4% were in education, and 22% were engaged in some other nonmarket activity such as child care (mainly women). Moreover, the average unemployment duration of unemployed workers was over 40 months. Thus, program participants had very low labor market attachment.

Walter et al. (2014) find substantial locking-in effects of the programs. Participants exhibit 50–70% lower employment rates than comparable nonparticipants. Employment rates only recover very slowly. One year after program start the average employment effects are still negative but they become insignificant toward the end of the observation window after 18 months. However, there are large difference between men and women. For women, employment effects remain negative and statistically significant at around minus 20% 12 months after program start. In contrast, for men there are positive and sometimes significant employment effects of about 10% after 15 months. Hence, in terms of labor market integration, the program only seems to be successful for men. Walter et al. (2014) also report that the positive employment effects can reach up to 20% for participants age 45–54 and certain nationalities (Turkish, Asian, Arabian), although these effects are often not significant due to small sample sizes.

Walter et al. (2014) also find that directly after the end of the program, the probability of participating in another program, which can be interpreted as preparation for labor market integration, increases substantially. Twelve months after program start, men are 100% and women 80% more likely to participate in some other program. This also explains the slow recovery rate of employment effects. However, the positive effects on future program participation suggest that the program was at least successful in preparing participants with very low labor market attachments and insufficient German language

---

[118] Part-time courses last up to 12 months, full-time courses up to 6 months. The average duration of all courses was about 7 months (Walter et al., 2014).

skills for participation in other programs that are typically targeted at workers with fewer or less severe barriers to employment.

7.3.4 Summary

The evidence for Germany can be summarized as follows. All programs exhibit negative locking-in effects on employment in the short run, the magnitude and duration of which depends on average program duration. Depending on economic conditions and institutional features, training programs for unemployed workers may or may not have positive employment and earnings effects in the longer run. The effectiveness of training is positively related to the unemployment rate at program start and negatively related to incentive to use training to renew UI eligibility. Programs seem to be more effective for workers with less favorable employment prospects, and when they provide sizeable amounts of job-related or on-the-job training. Training incentives for employed workers seem to increase firms' likelihood to engage in further vocational training, to stabilize employees' work careers, and to improve the labor market attachment of elderly workers.

8. FRANCE

8.1 Types of Programs

Education for adults in France is organized by institutions called GRETA (Groupement d'établissement), which operate on the regional level and represent local training providers. They offer courses or entire programs to both private and public clients. For example, the PES purchases entire courses directly from providers or assigns unemployed workers on an individual basis. There exist a large number of programs but only some of them are subsidized.[119] In 2011, the French government spent about 5.8 billion EUR or 0.3% of GDP on publicly subsidized education for adults.[120] About 65% of expenditures relate to programs offered via the PES to unemployed workers, while 35% refer to programs that are open to other target groups as well. In contrast to many other European countries, there is no special income support during participation in education for adults. Nonemployed workers receive their regular compensation (unemployment insurance, disability benefits or social assistance) or an equivalent compensation that runs under a different name during participation but follows the same rules as the regular benefits. Training for employed workers is financed by employers or education insurance funds which, in turn, are also funded by firms. In some cases there are financial benefits for firms in order to promote firm-provided training.

---

[119] For a description of the French education system see European Commission (2011). For more information on GRETA visit http://www.education.gouv.fr/cid50753/la-formation-continue-des-adultes-a-l-education-nationale.html.

[120] References for expenditures on the various programs are provided below.

8.1.1 Basic Education for Adults

There exist only two types of publicly subsidized basic education programs for adults, both of which are organized outside the PES. The first one is called the key competencies program, which was introduced in 2009. Similar programs existed before but under different names. The objective of the program is to combat illiteracy and to develop the following key competencies: written comprehension and expression in French (mother tongue), introduction to a foreign language (mostly English), mathematics, basic competences in sciences and technology as well as the ability to develop one's own knowledge and competencies. Participants need a sufficiently good command of French and at least 9 years of schooling. The need for training has to be approved by the PES for unemployed workers, employers, and the PES for workers in subsidized employment and the training center for other employed workers. All courses are paid by the state and they last no longer than 400 h. In 2012, 55,000 individuals participated in the program with approval of the PES (Cavan, 2014). Total expenditures were about 40 million EUR (Garoche and Roguet, 2014).

The second type of programs comprises integration courses for foreigners. The French Bureau of Immigration and Integration assigns immigrants to French language courses, of which up to 400 h are supported by the state through tuition waivers. The courses also provide some knowledge about living in France. In 2011, 45,000 individuals participated with expenditures of 42 million EUR (Office Français de l' Immigration et de l'Intégration, 2012). Additionally, there exist so-called socio-linguistic workshops for immigrants who have lived in France already for some time but still lack appropriate language skills that facilitate integration. They also promote social integration, especially for women. The workshops are organized and financed by the Ministry of Immigration, Integration, National Identity and Solidarity Development. Finally, there are courses which provide migrant parents with information on the French school system, about the French society in general as well as children's and parents' duties related to schooling. Moreover, parents attend French language courses at the children's educational facilities. Participation is free and there are no special requirements. In 2010, only about 5000 parents participated in the program (Ministère de l'Intérieur, 2014).

8.1.2 Formal Vocational Qualification for Adults

In France, formal vocational qualifications within the French dual education system (vocational classroom training combined with practical training) can usually only be obtained in the age range 16–25. However, under certain conditions adults have access as well. Under the so-called apprenticeship contract program, adults older than 25 can participate in a regular apprenticeship if they have a recognized handicap or if they plan to found an enterprise which requires a particular qualification or certificate. Under the so-called professionalization contract program, adults older than 25 who are jobless, participating in an employment program or welfare recipients can obtain a formal vocational qualification or certificate in order to support re-entry into working life. They do not have to be registered with the PES. Public support is provided by the state or municipalities in the form of financial benefits for firms. These include exemptions from social security contributions, tax credits, financial benefits for handicapped apprentices, and lump-sum payments to cover some of the costs of training. Unfortunately, numbers on participants do not distinguish between regular apprentices and adults. However, there is some information on participation by age. About 45,000 individuals aged 22 or older were trained under an apprenticeship contract (Sanchez et al., 2014) and about 33,000 individuals aged 26 or older were trained under a professionalization contract (Sanchez, 2013).

8.1.3 Vocational Training Administered by the PES

The PES offers vocational training in three ways. Firstly, it purchases entire courses directly from providers. Secondly, the PES assigns workers to programs that are financed by the state or municipalities. Thirdly, it provides financial support to individuals who participate in selected training courses not directly offered by the PES on an individual basis. There are five types of programs. Firstly, there are short qualifying programs of no more than 400 h that prepare the participant for a specific vacancy by providing the qualifications or skills missing to fulfill the requirements of a specific vacancy. The employer reports the vacancy to the PES, the PES preselects candidates and the employer offers an employment contract to one of them. Employer and PES together develop a training plan and sign a contract with the candidate. Training takes place before employment starts. It can be classroom and/or on-the-job training. Employers receive financial aid for training the newly employed worker (up to 2000 EUR if inside the firm and up to 3200 EUR if outside the firm). In 2011, 43,000 individuals participated in such courses (Ministère du Travail de l'Emploi, de la Formation professionnelle et du Dialogue social, 2014) and public expenditures amounted to 80 million EUR (Garoche and Roguet, 2014).

The second type of programs consists of qualifying training programs with the objective of adapting the skills of the unemployed to the needs of the labor market and to support sectors with labor shortages. There are two groups of programs. The first one is directly financed by the PES and mainly comprises classroom training. The PES evaluates shortages on the labor market and decides which training programs are able to fill the gaps. It buys those training courses from suitable organizations and prescribes them to suitable candidates. In 2011, 67,000 individuals participated (Ministère du Travail de l'Emploi, de la Formation professionnelle et du Dialogue social, 2014) and expenditures amounted to 182 million EUR (Garoche and Roguet, 2014). Similar programs are also offered by the state and regional councils. The PES can approve participation in these courses, in which case it finances the course fees for participants. About 2000 additional participants were supported in this way in 2011 (Ministère du Travail de l'Emploi, de la Formation professionnelle et du Dialogue social, 2014). The second group is financed by the state or the municipality but assignment takes place via the PES. On the one hand, there are shorter programs of no more than 400 h with, at maximum, 9 weeks of practical training. The caseworker at the PES identifies the training needs of the jobseeker and develops a training plan together with the jobseeker. The objective is to facilitate a quick return to the labor market. On the other hand, there exists more formal vocational class-room training that awards a certificate or formal vocational qualification. The training lasts between 600 and 1500 h and focuses on qualifications required in the manufactur-ing, construction or service sectors. The PES assigns unemployed workers as part of a training plan if the caseworker has identified a need for this type of training. In 2012, 54,000 individuals participated in this type of training with expenditures of 65 million EUR (Ministère du Travail de l'Emploi, de la Formation professionnelle et du Dialogue social, 2014).

The third type of programs comprises short preparatory or vocational training courses that take place within subsidized employment in the nonmarket sector. Financial support is provided to employers in the form of recruitment subsidies, exemptions from social insurance contributions and training assistance. These programs are targeted at young unskilled workers as well as workers with difficulties in the labor market, such as long-term unemployed workers, workers with disabilities, or workers aged 50 or older who have not found employment within 3 months. The subsidized employment con-tracts last between 6 and 24 months, for certain target groups up to 5 years. They should include at least one training action and one supporting action such as assessment of skills and qualifications. There were about 392,000 signed contracts in 2011 (Bahu, 2014) and expenditures amounted to 2 billion EUR (Garoche and Roguet, 2014).

The fourth program type comprises support measures for workers who are subject to an enforced redundancy. The employer is obliged to offer this measure. If the firm refuses to do so, the PES steps in and imposes a sanction on the employer. Employer and employee sign a so-called career security agreement which contains one or more of the following measures: evaluation of skills, job search training, preparatory training for a specific job, occupational training or short employment measures. These measures last between 2 and 6 months. The agreement is for at most 12 months. Employees do not have to be registered at the PES, only if they are still unemployed after 12 months. They receive a special type of unemployment compensation which depends on tenure with the firm and is financed by the government. Moreover, the PES provides financial aid for the parts of the cost of training that are not covered by firms. Expenditures amounted to 80 million EUR in 2011 (Garoche and Roguet, 2014).

Finally, the PES provides individualized financial aid under various circumstances. Firstly, the PES supports training in the health, care or social sector which awards a state-approved certificate. Secondly, it finances preparatory courses for future craftsmen if no regional program exists. Thirdly, it finances courses that do not fall in any of the categories described in this section which are considered necessary for successful labor market integration. Fourthly, there is some income support in case unemployment benefits are exhausted before the end of training. It can be granted if the training is approved by the PES, leads to an accredited qualification and results in employment in a sector with an approved labor shortage. Lastly, there is also additional support for employers who want to retrain workers in order to facilitate reorganization. Firms with less than 250 employees are eligible if they plan to organize an internal reassignment of employees toward nonendangered jobs, fight problems resulting from inadequate skills, recruit job applicants and train them for particular jobs and/or organize a shift to part-time employment. The financial aid can be used to cover wages while the worker participates in external training courses. Training consists of occupational retraining or adaptation to new skills and competences, eg, new technology or production processes.

8.2 Evidence on Impacts

France is included in the case studies because the existing evidence on impacts includes papers that are particularly interesting either from a methodological point of view, or because they study aspects that are rarely considered elsewhere. The first evidence on the effects of training for unemployed adults for France was provided by Crépon et al. (2012). At the same time it is one of the first studies that analyzes effects on postunemployment outcomes, namely on the duration of the subsequent employment spell. To address the issue of selection into employment following unemployment or participation in training, Crépon et al. (2012) extend the timing-of-events framework introduced by Abbring and Van den Berg (2003) to account for training spell duration and unemployment recurrence. Moreover, they allow for selection into training based on both observed and unobserved characteristics. Crépon et al. (2012) analyze training programs for unemployed workers that took place in unemployment spells that started in the period 2001–05 based on rich administrative data. Two types of training are included: short qualifying programs that prepare for a specific vacancy and qualifying training programs with the objective of adapting the skills of the unemployed to the needs of the labor market and to support sectors with labor shortages. The authors find that training did not increase the exit rate from unemployment but statistically significantly reduced unemployment recurrence. On average, the transition rate from employment to unemployment decreased by 21%, which corresponds to an increase in employment duration of almost 340 days. Training with a duration of more than 1 year had even larger effects: it reduced unemployment recurrence by 38%. This is in line with the idea that training tailored to the needs of the labor market improves the quality of job matches between firms and jobseekers. Unfortunately, there are no cost-benefit calculations in this study.

Crépon et al. (2009) add to the literature on program evaluation in the presence of dynamic assignment to treatment. They combine the dynamic matching approach suggested by Fredriksson and Johansson (2008) with the ideas from the timing-of-events approach originating from Abbring and Van den Berg (2003). Their approach uses matching with duration outcomes and builds on a no-anticipation assumption combined with the assumption of conditional independence between the duration until treatment and the counterfactual durations until exit. They show that, in contrast to their approach, standard matching approaches use contaminated control groups because individuals in the control group participate in training during the period when outcomes are measured. Crépon et al. (2009) use similar data and consider the same types of training as Crépon et al. (2012). But they focus on unemployment spells starting in the period 2002–04. They show that the contamination rate was small and declining with unemployment duration in that particular case, resulting in small biases in the estimated effects of training versus no training.[121] However, if participation rates are much larger, contamination rates are higher and substantial biases may result when standard matching approaches are used. In terms of results regarding the effects of training the authors confirm the evidence from Crépon et al. (2012) that training in that period had little impact on unemployment duration.

Crépon et al. (2013a,b,c) study the role of information shocks in the evaluation of training programs for unemployed workers within the timing-of-events framework. The key identifying assumption underlying this approach is that unemployed workers either have no information about future treatment or do not react to the possibility of future treatment in any systematic way before actual assignment (no-anticipation assumption). Crépon et al. (2013a,b,c) scrutinize the validity of this assumption and analyze whether notification of future training directly affects unemployment duration. This is informative as to whether ignoring information shocks leads to biased estimates of the effects of training. The authors use administrative data similar to those of the earlier studies. Their sample comprises the universe of unemployment spells in the city of Paris in the period 2003–04. They find that notification has a negative effect on the exit rate from unemployment, which can be interpreted as an "attraction" effect as opposed to threat effects where workers try to avoid participation after notification (see eg, Rosholm and Svarer, 2008). Together with negative locking-in effects this decreases the exit probability around the treatment date. The authors also show that ignoring the effect of notification leads to an overestimation of the locking-in effects of the program because they absorb the notification effect. However, after 4 months, the negative initial effects are compensated by positive effects of training participation on the exit rate from employment, independent of whether notification effects are accounted for or not. Crépon et al. (2013a,b,c) conclude that the timing of information dissemination needs to be taken into account both in the evaluation of training and when deciding on their design.

---

[121] In fact, the approach that does not account for future program participation estimates a different parameter, the effect of training now versus no training now but potentially later.

Another innovation to the program evaluation literature has been brought forward by Ferracci et al. (2014). They propose an evaluation design that allows for certain spillover effects of training on nonparticipants via effects on local labor markets. Hence, they provide one way to scrutinize the validity of the stable unit treatment value assumption (SUTVA) implicit in almost all program evaluation studies. The authors propose an evaluation design that has similarities with sequential matching approaches for the evaluation of dynamically assigned sequences of programs (eg, Lechner, 2009). They combine a conditional independence assumption for training participation on the individual level within a given labor market with a second conditional independence assumption for training intensity across labor markets. Identification requires that there are no spillover effects of training across markets, only within markets. Estimation is based on a two-step matching procedure, first within markets and then across markets. Ferracci et al. (2014) use administrative data on unemployed workers merged with a survey of the predicted job vacancies at the local level collected yearly by the PES. They use quarterly 2.5% random samples of unemployment spells starting in 2002 or 2004. The training programs considered are the same as in the studies discussed above. The authors find that labor market outcomes of both participants in training and nonparticipants depend statistically significantly on the proportion of individuals treated in the relevant local labor market. The exit rate of participants from unemployment decreases steadily when regional treatment intensity increases. The exit rate of nonparticipants first decreases and then increases. Hence, there is evidence for spillover effects of training that violates SUTVA. The overall effect of training on the exit rate from unemployment is negative.

There are two additional studies that focus on specific programs that are of general interest. Cavaco et al. (2013) analyze support measures for displaced workers. They study a special program implemented in the mid-1990s, which was intended to improve reemployment prospects of displaced workers by a combination of job search assistance and retraining for a period of 6 months beginning just after the dismissal. The retraining component comprised intensive general and vocational education. The authors use rich survey data for a random sample of workers in certain regions who entered unemployment between April and June 1995. They employ propensity score matching to estimate the effects of the program where they control for firm size, type of mass layoff, gender, age, number of children, past employment history, local labor market conditions, skills, and type of job. Given selection into the program this seems a plausible set of control variables. Cavaco et al. (2013) find that participation in the program statistically significantly increased employment rates by about 6% 2–3 years after the start of training, mainly through an increase in permanent rather than temporary employment. The latter is particularly important as earlier research has shown that displaced workers are more likely to enter temporary employment in the absence of interventions (eg, Farber, 1999). Moreover, the effects are most pronounced for prime age workers. Again, no cost-benefit analysis is provided.

Blasco et al. (2012) use a multi-state multi-spell transition model with unobserved heterogeneity to investigate how participation in training affects labor market transitions. This paper is interesting for at least two reasons. Firstly, it is one of the rare papers that distinguish between training during nonemployment and training during employment. Secondly, it considers not only different labor market states during which training takes place but also different sequences of labor market states after training. The authors use nationally representative survey data collected in 2003 that contains retrospective information on monthly labor market status of individuals from May 1998 to May 2003. Blasco et al. (2012) find that training during nonemployment increases the exit rate to employment as well as posttraining employment stability. Training during employment increases the job retention rate for about 6 months but then increases the probability of leaving work for nonemployment. This suggests that training was mostly general rather than specific. However, training during employment also increases the exit rate from subsequent nonemployment to employment suggesting that future employers value training during previous employment. The disadvantage of this study is that it relies on strongly parametric methods, which raises doubts about the robustness of the results to less restrictive methods.

In summary, the evidence for France confirms that PES-provided training mostly has negligibly effects on participants' employment rates and only sometimes positive effects. However, even in the absence of positive effects on the exit rate from unemployment, the studies provide robust evidence that training increases postunemployment employment stability. The French studies also highlight some interesting methodological aspects regarding the validity of the no-anticipation assumption in the timing-of-events approach and the validity of the stable unit treatment value assumption; see the related discussion in Section 4.6.

9. SWEDEN

9.1 Types of Programs

Sweden is one of the most generous countries in terms of public support of adult education. Participation is heavily subsidized in terms of both coverage of direct cost and income support. In 2012, the Swedish government spent about 3.3 billion EUR or 1.4% of GDP on publicly subsidized adult education (OECD, 2014). The largest share of expenditures, namely 60%, is related to programs administered by the PES. These programs are targeted at unemployed workers or those who are at risk of becoming unemployed. About 25% of expenditures concern programs administered by communities. The majority of these programs provide basic education at the compulsory schooling or upper secondary level. About 12% of expenditures relate to further vocational training outside the PES that is supported by a national grant program which provides income support during training. Less than 5% of total expenses go into Swedish language courses for immigrants. Overall, the programs can be grouped into two broad categories that are described in more detail in the following sections: basic education for adults and further vocational training. Regarding the latter we distinguish between programs administered by the PES and programs administered by other institutions because they have different objectives and target groups.[122]

9.1.1 Basic Education for Adults

Under the so-called KOMVUX program,[123] communities offer basic education to adults aged 20 or older at the compulsory schooling or upper secondary level. In contrast to many other countries, participation is free of charge at the individual level. Financial support directly goes to the communities, who distribute the funds to training providers. Municipalities are required to admit adults who lack some skills usually acquired in compulsory school. Eligible adults have access to a guaranteed place in a course that helps them to gain the knowledge necessary to take part in society and working life. The skills provided are equivalent to those obtained when completing compulsory schooling. In addition, the KOMVUX program supports the completion of upper secondary education equivalent to either a high school degree, which provides access to college or university, or vocational training, which allows participants to work in a skilled occupation.[124] Additionally, there are independent, freely organized courses which provide some specific skills.[125] There are caseworkers who handle the applications on behalf of the municipalities. They evaluate the need for training based on past educational attainment, employment record and prospects, labor market needs and available training places. Precedence is given to highly motivated adults with the highest need for training, eg, those with short formal education and unemployed workers. Usually, the courses offered under the KOMVUX program are shorter than the programs at regular schools and they are tailored to the specific needs of the participants in terms of both content and organization (full time/part time, at day time/in the evening). Participants can attend KOMVUX courses for free and they receive a grade, certificate or diploma upon successful completion.

In 2012, the Swedish government spent 428 million EUR on the KOMVUX program. The largest share of 77% relates to education on the upper secondary level. There were 750,000 participants, 64% of whom were women and 11% of whom participated in basic courses on the compulsory schooling level; 38% of participants were younger than 25 and 11% were 45 or older. Dropout rates are quite high. A share of 18% dropped out of education on the upper secondary level and an even higher share of 24% did not

---

[122] For information on the Swedish education system and adult education see Ministry of Education and Research (2007, 2013).

[123] *Kommunal Vuxentutbildning.*

[124] *Yrkesvuxutbildning* or *Lärlingsvuxutbildning.*

[125] *Fristående kurser.*

complete courses on the compulsory schooling level. The dropout rate is somewhat higher for men (20%) than for women (17%) and a particularly large share of dropouts occurs in Swedish, English, and mathematics courses (around 30%). In contrast, dropout rates are much lower at around 10% for orientation courses and courses that provide either more general or specifically work-related knowledge. Dropouts mainly state the following reasons for leaving the program: family situation, health problems, course does not meet expectations, and lack of time.[126] The average duration of completed courses at the compulsory level is about 2 months while for courses at the upper secondary level it is 5–10 months. Younger adults spend about 2 months more in education than older ones and women about 4 months more than men (Stenberg, 2012).

There is a national grant program that provides income support during participation in KOMVUX.[127] The program also supports basic education at the compulsory schooling or upper secondary level outside of KOMVUX. In this case, adults attend regular schools rather than specific courses offered by municipalities. Adults aged 20 to 55 are eligible for so-called student aid during participation. Eligibility also requires that participants study at least half-time and for at least 3 weeks. The amount of aid depends on whether a person is studying full time or part time. For full-time education, the regular aid is about 245 EUR per week. For part-time education the amount is reduced accordingly. There is a basic grant which students do not have to repay and a supplementary loan which students do have to repay. The relative share varies with age, employment status and type of education.[128] Students with children receive an additional nonrepayable child allowance which varies with the number of children. The loan is higher by about 95 EUR per week for students aged 25 or older who have some work experience with some minimum income. The loan is also higher when the student has to cover additional expenses, eg, for housing. The student aid is not means-tested. Applicants have a legal right to receive the aid if they fulfill the personal eligibility requirements (age, repayment of past loans, grades from previously supported education) and the course requirements (eligible type of course, minimum intensity and duration). In 2012, the Swedish government spent 812 million EUR on student aid for basic education. A total of 25% of expenditures related to education at the compulsory schooling level. There were 93,000 participants, 62% of whom were women and 20% participated in courses at the compulsory schooling level.[129]

---

[126] Skolverket (2013a,b).

[127] *Studiemedel.*

[128] In the standard case, the grant part is about 75 EUR and the loan 170 EUR. The nonrepayable part is much higher at about 180 EUR and the loan is correspondingly much smaller at about 65 EUR for students aged 25 or older when they are unemployed and participate in vocational secondary education (*yrkesvux*) or when they study at the compulsory or upper secondary school level and do not already have an upper secondary qualification.

[129] Centrala Studiestödsnämnden (2013).

Basic education also includes Swedish language courses for immigrants. They provide basic language skills in Swedish and knowledge about Swedish society. Moreover, participants learn how to use computers as an aid in learning the language. They receive a grade or certificate after successful completion. Immigrants must be at least 16 years old and they must have a residence permit. The courses are free and offered full time or part time, during the day or in the evening. Participation may be combined with work, training or courses in other subjects. There are specialized courses which provide language training for specific occupations as well as for academics with a university degree from their native country. In 2012, the Swedish government spent 158 million EUR on such courses. A total of 108,000 immigrants participated in the courses, 57% of whom were women. The majority of participants (60%) were aged 25–39 years. Moreover, 27% of participants had upper secondary education and 34% tertiary education. The dropout rates are similar to those of the KOMVUX program. Only 77% of participants completed the courses in 2012. Again the dropout rate of men (27%) is higher than that of women (21%). Moreover, dropout rates seem to increase somewhat with the level of the course. The reasons for noncompletion are similar to the ones for KOMVUX.[130]

9.1.2 Further Vocational Training and Related Programs Administered by the PES

The Swedish PES offers a range of programs specifically targeted at workers who are unemployed or at risk of becoming unemployed. Jobseekers must register with the PES in order to have access to these programs. However, all unemployed workers who want to claim unemployment compensation must register anyway. The PES directly pays for off-the-job training with training providers. Additionally, all participants receive income support during participation. Workers aged 25 or older receive so-called activity support (*Aktivitetsstöd*). For those who qualify for UI payments this is equivalent to their unemployment benefits until exhaustion of UI, and 65% of the last daily wage thereafter. However, as with UI, a maximum of about 75 EUR per day and a minimum of about 35 EUR per day apply (5 daily benefits per week).[131] Workers who do not qualify for UI receive a flat payment of about 25 EUR per day for full-time participation or an appropriately adjusted amount for part-time courses. Participants who are younger than 25 receive a so-called development allowance (*Utvecklingsersättning*), which is a flat payment of about 15 EUR per day for participation in full-time education.

Programs offered by the PES can be grouped into four categories: preparatory measures, labor market training, job practice, and combined measures for long-term

---

[130] Skolverket (2013a,b).

[131] Workers qualify for UI if they have been insured for at least 12 months and have worked for at least 6 out of the last 12-month period without unemployment for at least 80 h per month. The replacement rate is reduced from 80% of the last daily wage during the first 200 days (100 days when under age 25 without children), to 70% for the next 100 days (350 days when 25 or older with children under age 18). The maximum benefit duration is 300 days (450 days with children under age 18).

integration of hard-to-place workers (the so-called job and development program). Assignment to the programs is a discretionary decision made by caseworkers of the PES conditional on eligibility. They assess the jobseekers' labor market situation, taking into consideration the vocational area and experience of the jobseeker, the current state of the labor market and available funds. On the basis of this, they decide whether any of the programs would be a good way to improve the jobseeker's chances of finding work. In 2012, the Swedish government spent almost 2 billion EUR on these measures.[132]

Preparatory measures (*förberedande insatser*) comprise a variety of short courses that last no more than 12 weeks and often precede other types of programs. They include job search assistance, training in job search skills, an assessment of the jobseekers' skills, work capacity and potential training needs, as well as labor market orientation. In 2012, about 140,000 jobseekers participated in the programs with expenditures of 247 million EUR or 13% of total expenses. More than half of participants (54%) were women, 17% were younger than 25, 11% were 55 or older, 39% were foreign born, 36% had no upper secondary education and a large share of 48% had a disability. The latter group mainly participated in courses that assess their work capacity. The dropout rate is 19% with similar values for men and women. However, this also includes exits to employment. Unfortunately, no information is available as to the share of exits to employment.[133]

Labor market training (*arbetsmarknadsutbildningen*) comprises vocational classroom-training which takes place at private or a municipality commissioned providers. The aim of the program is to improve participants' opportunities for finding work and to make it easier for employers to find labor with the right expertise. The types of courses offered depend on the state of the labor market. During recent years, most of supported courses have been within manufacturing, health and social care, and transport. Usually, the courses have durations of up to 6 months but jobseekers may also participate in a longer program if this is needed to fulfill the training objective. In 2012, about 58,000 jobseekers participated in labor market training leading to expenditures of 133 million EUR or 7% of total expenses. About 40% of participants were women, 38% were younger than 25, 7% were 55 or older, 37% were foreign born, 30% had no upper secondary education and 17% had a disability. At 17% the dropout rate is only slightly lower than for preparatory measures.[134]

Job practice (*praktik*) comprises different forms of work experience, on-the-job training and skill assessment. It takes place in firms but workers are not employed by the firm. Instead they receive income support from the PES. Firstly, jobseekers can be assigned to a work place for up to 6 months in order to receive vocational experience, vocational orientation or experience in working life. Secondly, there are two

---

[132] Arbetsförmedlingen (2013).
[133] Arbetsförmedlingen (2013).
[134] Arbetsförmedlingen (2013).

programs for jobseekers who lack or have little experience with Swedish working life and have registered with the PES only recently. On the one hand, they can participate in an assessment of professional skills which lasts up to 3 weeks. The assessment is intended to give participants the opportunity to demonstrate their skills to potential employers and to assess them. On the other hand, they can participate in a so-called trial opportunity which lasts up to 3 months. In this measure, participants come into contact with working life and potential employers in Sweden in an area that matches their education and experience. Thirdly and lastly, there is a program is called practical skills development that also targets jobseekers who have recently registered with the PES but it focuses on workers with previous vocational experience. The objective of the program is for the worker to remain in contact with working life and to further develop skills in the areas that match previous work experience and training. This program lasts no more than 3 months and should preferably be on a full-time basis. In 2012, about 76,000 jobseekers participated in job practice programs with expenditures of 51 million EUR or 3% of total expenses. Except for a larger share of females and foreign-born jobseekers, the composition of participants was similar to the one for labor market training: 47% were women, 38% were younger than 25, 7% were 55 or older, 42% were foreign born, 31% had no upper secondary education and 18% had a disability. At 15% the dropout rate (including exits to employment) is again somewhat lower than for both labor market training and preparatory measures.[135]

The last program offered by the PES is a combination of individually adapted measures for hard-to-place workers with the long-term objective of integrating them into the labor market (the so-called job and development program, *Jobb- och Utvecklingsgarantin*). The target group consists of long-term unemployed workers who still have not found employment after 1 year of search or program participation as well as jobseekers with special barriers to employment such as lone parents, jobseekers with disabilities, and immigrants. Workers can stay in the program until they have found a full-time job or (temporarily) leave the labor market for education, parental leave or health reasons. During the first phase of 150 days, workers receive intensive job search assistance, counseling, and individualized preparatory measures. During the second phase of 300 days, participants receive specifically targeted work experience, labor market training or occupational rehabilitation. If participants still have not found work after 90 weeks in the program, the PES provides a suitable subsidized work placement with an employer or service provider. The objective is to gain experience, credentials and references. In terms of expenditures, this intensive program is by far the most expensive one. In 2012, expenditures amounted to 1.4 billion EUR or 77% of total expenses on the programs discussed in this section. There were 177,000 participants, 47% of whom were women. Moreover, 17% of participants were younger than 25, 21% were 55 or older, 31% were foreign born, 29% had

---

[135] Arbetsförmedlingen (2013).

no upper secondary education and 28% had a disability.[136] Compared to the regular vocational training programs, the share of older workers and of jobseekers with a disability is considerably larger. Since the program does not comprise individual courses but a series of individually adopted measures with the sole purpose of integrating participants into the labor market, actual dropout rates without exits to employment or education are available. In 2012, 8% of participants dropped out.

9.1.3 Further Vocational Training Administered by Other Institutions

Further vocational training administered by other institutions than the PES is supported by the national grant program described earlier. Student aid is granted for participation in advanced vocational training or specialized further training courses mainly at community colleges[137] but also some other vocational training institutions.[138] The same eligibility criteria apply as for basic education: Adults must be at least 20 and no older than 55. Moreover, participants need to study at least half-time and for at least 3 weeks. Also the amount of student aid is the same. Participation is generally for free in Sweden but students must pay for textbooks and other study materials. In 2012, the Swedish government spent about 200 million EUR on student aid for further vocational training outside the PES. This corresponds to 42% of expenditures on student aid for adult education.[139]

9.2 Evidence on Impacts

Despite its relatively small size, Sweden is an important contributor to the literature on the effects of publicly subsidized vocational education for adults. Sweden has a long tradition in supporting adult education, which is among the most important components of Swedish labor market policy. Expenditures and participant numbers are large, which attracted interest in the effectiveness of these programs from both policymakers and researchers from early on. Sweden is one of the pioneers in making high-quality administrative data available to researchers. Moreover, the Swedish Ministry of Employment founded the Institute for Labour Market Policy Evaluation (IFAU, recently renamed as the Institute for Evaluation of Labour Market and Education Policy) which systematically evaluates Swedish labor market policies and supports evaluations by international researchers. Interest in the effectiveness of labor market policies peaked in the late 1990s and early 2000s after an unprecedented expansion of labor market programs in response to a severe recession in the early 1990s. This explains why the majority of Swedish evaluation studies analyze programs from the 1990s.

[136] Arbetsförmedlingen (2013).
[137] Folkhögskola.
[138] Kompletterande utbildning, kvalificerad yrkesutbildning, yrkeshögskola.
[139] Centrala Studiestödsnämnden (2013).

The following sections summarize the evidence on the impacts of publicly subsidized education for adults by program group. In contrast to Germany, there is not only extensive research on programs administered by the PES but also on basic education supported by communities. Moreover, because of the relatively large size of the programs, Sweden is also one of the few countries for which there exist quite a few studies that investigate the macroeconomic effects of the programs on wages and labor force participation as well as other spill-over effects such as displacement effects. However, similar to Germany the majority of studies focus on unemployed workers. The reason is that most studies investigate programs from the 1990s when unemployment was the most pressing problem in Sweden and most programs specifically targeted unemployed workers. In terms of methodology, the studies are more diverse than in Germany. In the mid-2000s, the Swedish PES even conducted a number of randomized experiments to evaluate some types of programs.

9.2.1 Basic Education for Adults

There are several studies that investigate the effects of the KOMVUX program. Within the program, most studies focus on education at the upper secondary level, or they group all courses together. Hence, there is no separate analysis for education at the compulsory schooling level. The main reason is probably sample size issues because only 10–15% of participants fall into this group. Most studies focus on the effects on earnings. One of the most important results from this literature is that long-run data is required to fully capture the effects of the program. It takes 7–8 years for positive earnings effects to appear. Based on data from the mid-1990s and conditional difference-in-differences methods, Stenberg (2010, 2011) finds that after about 10 years, the returns to 1 year in adult education are around 4%. Participant with low earnings before the program have higher returns resulting from both higher wages and more hours worked. However, cost-benefit calculations by Stenberg (2011) suggest that the returns are barely sufficient to cover societal costs. Stenberg et al. (2012, 2014) analyze the effects of programs in the late 1980s and mid-1990s on older participants aged 42–55 when entering KOMVUX. The earlier study used propensity-score matching which accounts for dynamic assignment to treatment (Fredriksson and Johansson, 2008); see the related discussion in Section 4.6. Hence, it estimates the effects of participating now rather than later. The second study combined matching with difference-in-differences to remove differences in pretreatment earnings. For older participants, Stenberg et al. (2012, 2014) only find positive effects on earnings for women that again only emerge after 7–8 years but no statistically significant effects for men. Moreover, they find no effects on the timing of retirement. Thus, investments in upper secondary education later in life only had small returns and did not delay exit from the labor market.

About half of the existing studies analyze a temporary expansion of adult education during the years 1997–2002 which is known as the adult education initiative or knowledge lift (*kunskapslyftet*). It was run through the KOMVUX system and aimed at providing low-skilled workers with upper secondary education to strengthen their position in the labor market. The program was introduced at the peak of unemployment in Sweden that followed the recession in the early 1990s. It mainly targeted unemployed workers but employed workers could also participate. The program focused on providing general skills such as English, Swedish or mathematics rather than vocational training for a specific occupation. The knowledge lift was by far the largest adult education program ever in Sweden. In the fall of 1997, about 220,000 adults or 2.5% of the Swedish population participated in the program compared to 300,000 pupils in regular upper secondary education (Albrecht et al., 2009).

Shortly after the introduction of the program Albrecht et al. (2005) find no effects on earnings but positive effects on employment for younger men aged 25–40 based on difference-in-differences and conditional probit analyses. Based on a longer observation period and a bivariate probit model, Stenberg (2005) finds that the program reduced the probability to be unemployed 5 years after program participation for previously unemployed workers. Moreover, Stenberg and Westerlund (2008) report positive earnings effects for long-term unemployed workers who spend at least two semesters in the program. The findings are based on difference-in-differences propensity score matching. Their cost-benefit calculations also suggest that the program becomes cost-effective after 5–7 years. In a follow-up study that is based on the same data and method but uses all unemployed rather than just long-term unemployed workers, Stenberg and Westerlund (2014) show that it takes about 4 years for women and 7 years for men for positive earnings effects to appear. Although especially the earlier studies use parametric methods, the results match quite well with the evidence on the effectiveness of KOMVUX in the 1980s and early to mid-1990 that is based on more advanced, semiparametric methods.

Given the large size of the knowledge lift program, spill-over effects on wages and employment of other workers in the economy are likely. The studies discussed so far are based on the assumption that such effects do not exist. If they do, these studies provide biased estimates of the program effects. Albrecht et al. (2009) calibrate an equilibrium search model with preprogram data and simulate both the partial effects which correspond to the estimates of the studies discussed above, and the general equilibrium effects. They find that program participants benefit most in terms of both earnings and employment. However, there are negative spill-over effects on employment of other low-skilled workers that did not upgrade their skills because more vacancies are being created for medium-skilled workers. This also creates positive spillover effects on the wages of non-participating medium-skilled workers. Moreover, the partial effects for participants are 1.5 to 2 times lower than the general equilibrium effects because of the additional effects on employment and wages. This suggests that the effects for participants reported in the microeconometric studies might be under-estimated and that the overall performance of the program might be more favorable than these studies suggest.

9.2.2 Further Vocational Training and Related Programs Administered by the PES

Most of the literature on PES-provided training focuses on labor market training and job experience programs. There is only one study that provides estimates for preparatory measures. Exploiting rich administrative data Nilsson (2008) applies propensity-score matching which accounts for dynamic assignment to treatment as proposed by Fredriksson and Johansson (2008). She estimates monthly program effects on employment 1 year after program start for several programs over the period 1992–2006. For preparatory measures there are mostly small negative effects over the entire 15-year period. In 2006 there is a small positive effect. It results from a positive effect of preparatory training in job search skills of 4% while all other programs, most of which only assess the skills and work capacity of participants, have small negative effects of 2%. This suggest that the average effects of preparatory measures may hide positive effects of more promising programs such as job search assistance and training in job search skills, which have been found to have small positive effects in many other contexts. In this respect, two studies by Hägglund (2009, 2011) are informative. They summarize the evidence from several regionally implemented randomized experiments that were designed to study the effects of intensified job search assistance via coaching and monitoring by caseworkers. Hägglund (2009) reports that the combined intervention reduced unemployment durations and increased employment and gross earnings for all participants but youth. Intensified monitoring alone, in contrast, was ineffective. Moreover, Hägglund (2011) reports considerable preprogram effects. Assignment to the treatment group increased exit rates from unemployment by about 50% before the assigned program started. When looking at destinations, the exit rate to employment increased by about 40%, while the exit rate to other states increased by about 55%. The latter mainly comprised exits to the sickness insurance system indicating important spillovers between this system and UI. Such interactions have also been documented for Sweden by Larsson (2006).

For labor market training there exist quite a large number of evaluation studies. Calmfors et al. (2002) survey the earlier literature which studies programs from the 1980s and early 1990s. Evaluations of training conducted during the 1980s, especially during the first half, quite consistently find positive effects on employment and/or earnings. Toward the end of the 1980s and at the beginning of the 1990s, when a severe recession started to hit the Swedish economy and a large expansion of training programs took place in response to rising unemployment rates, the findings start to become less favorable. Although the evidence is somewhat mixed and seems to depend somewhat on the methodology used, the majority of studies report statistically insignificant or negative effects of program participation on employment and earnings for programs in the early 1990s. Parametric models that allow for selection on unobserved variables (Andrén and Andrén, 2006; Andrén and Gustafsson, 2004) seem to yield more positive results than matching methods (Fredriksson and Johansson, 2003). Moreover, among studies that use similar methods and study the same training period, those that focus on short-run effects (Regnér, 2002) report more negative findings than studies with longer observation periods (Andrén and Andrén, 2006). This can be explained by initial locking-in effects of the programs which are well documented in later studies. Andrén and Gustafsson (2004) report interesting findings on the business-cycle dependence of effect heterogeneity. They find that the effects of labor market training on their participants' earnings become smaller during recession, especially for foreigners. This is somewhat contradicting later evidence for Sweden (Forslund et al., 2011) and for Germany (Lechner and Wunsch, 2009) but it might be explained by effect heterogeneity. Older and high-skilled workers seem to benefit more during good times, while younger and low-skilled workers benefit more during bad times.

Studies that analyze programs from the mid to late 1990s consistently find negative locking-in effects in the short run and at most statistically insignificant positive effects in the longer run despite using different methodologies (Adda et al., 2007; Richardson and Van den Berg, 2001; Sianesi, 2008). Sianesi (2008) provides the most comprehensive analysis of programs in the period 1994–99 based on propensity-score matching that accounts for dynamic assignment to treatment as proposed by Fredriksson and Johansson (2008). She finds substantial negative locking-in effects of 25% that disappear only slowly. The employment effects remain negative and statistically significant for more than 3 years and become insignificant thereafter.[140] Moreover, she finds that program participation has large positive effects on benefit collection. Directly after completion of the program about 6 months after program start the probability of benefit collection increased by 20%, mainly because participation leads to renewal of eligibility for unemployment insurance payments. The effect slowly decreases to about 5% in the longer run.

Stenberg (2005) and Stenberg and Westerlund (2014) compare the performance of labor market training via the PES to the knowledge lift for participants in 1997. The main difference between the two programs is that the latter mainly provides general training while the former focuses on specific vocational training. The earlier study is based on a parametric selection model that accounts for censoring. Stenberg (2005) finds that despite a reduction in unemployment incidence after 5 years, participants in the knowledge lift experience longer unemployment durations than participants in labor market training. Based on more convincing difference-in-differences propensity score matching, Stenberg and Westerlund (2014) analyze the effects on earnings. They show that participation in both programs leads to negative effects in the short run. However, for the

---

[140] Richardson and van den Berg (2001) employ a timing-of-events approach and estimate a duration model with unobserved heterogeneity. They study programs from 1993 to 2000 and find no significant effects on average unemployment duration. Adda et al. (2007) estimate a structural model and find negative effects of training on employment and no effects on earnings for younger unskilled males in programs conducted in the period 1996–98. In their study, training includes both classroom training and on-the-job training within the job experience program.

knowledge lift, they are much larger and last much longer. For labor market training they find positive earnings effects after only 1 year, while it takes 4 (women) to 7 years (men) for the knowledge lift. After 5–7 years, the two programs show similar returns for their participants (without adjusting for differences between participants). A direct comparison of the programs that adjusts for differences between participants as well as subgroup analyses reveal that females with only basic education seem to benefit more from general training than from specific training. However, these effects are not sufficient to offset the large negative effects of participating in the knowledge lift during the first years. Therefore, the results suggest that labor market training outperforms general training. An important drawback of the comparison is, however, that there is no distinction between earnings from employment and benefit payments, and that the effects on employment and unemployment rates are not considered. Sianesi (2008) finds that participation in labor market training has strong positive effects on benefit collection because it led to renewal of eligibility for unemployment insurance payments. The pattern of the effect she finds over time matches the pattern of the earnings effects reported by Stenberg and Westerlund (2014) remarkably well. Moreover, the largely negative employment effects of labor market training reported by Sianesi (2008) compared to positive employment effects of the knowledge lift reported by Albrecht et al. (2005, 2009) and the negative effects on unemployment reported by Stenberg (2005) point to a more favorable evaluation of the knowledge lift. Hence, in terms of relative cost-benefit considerations it is at least questionable whether labor market training outperforms general education for adults, at least for the late 1990s.

The two evaluation studies that analyze more recent training programs from the early and mid-2000s, which are based on the matching methods used by Sianesi (2004, 2008), report more positive results. For the period 2002–04, DeLuna et al. (2008) find negative locking-in effects on the exit rate to employment of 8% that vanish after about 9 months. After about 2.5 years the effect peaks at 13%, after which it declines slowly to about 9% 5.5 years after program start. After 3 years, participation reduced unemployment duration by about 25% compared to nonparticipation. The increase of the effects of training over time is confirmed by Nilsson (2008) who estimates effects for the period 1992–2006. The effects on employment 1 year after program start are smallest in the period 1995–96 after which they start to increase quite steadily. In 2000, they reached 8% and about 15% toward the end of the observation period.

Only a few studies investigate the performance of job practice programs. Sianesi (2008) investigates two types of programs covering the period 1994–99. She finds negative locking-in effects of around 10–15% that last about 6 months for placements with regular private and public employers, and more than 2 years for placements at nonprofit organizations and public employers. Thereafter, employment effects are statistically insignificant. However, there are again strong positive effects on benefit collection, which are even larger than those for labor market training: After 6 months the probability of benefit receipt increases by 40%. The effect then declines quickly to about 10% after which it declines slowly until it becomes insignificant 4–5 years after program start. Comparing job practice to labor market training, both Sianesi (2008) and Carling and Richardson (2004) conclude that programs that involve on-the-job training, and are thus more similar to regular jobs, perform better than vocational classroom training in the mid to late 1990s because participants spend less time out of employment.

Forslund et al. (2013) study job practice programs in a later period using the matching approach proposed by Fredriksson and Johansson (2008). For the period 1999–2002, they find locking-in effects in the form of positive effects on expected time to unsubsidized work which last about 1 year. However, after about 2 years, the expected time to work of participants is reduced by about 4%. In contrast, for the later period 2003–06, they find essentially no locking-in effects and the expected time to unsubsidized work is reduced by about 12% after almost 2 years. The authors also find positive effects on earnings and negative effects on the take-up of social assistance. Moreover, subgroup analyses suggest that women and high-skilled workers benefitted significantly more from job experience while workers aged 50 or older benefitted significantly less. Comparing job practice to labor market training they find that after almost 2 years, participants in job practice would have benefitted more from training while participants in training would have done equally well in training. However, in the short run both groups of participants have and would have been better off in job practice because the locking-in effects of training are larger and last much longer. In fact, Forslund et al. (2013) conclude from a simple cost-benefit calculation that the effects of training would have to persist for several years for training to outperform job practice.

Nilsson (2008) also finds a positive time trend in the effectiveness of job practice programs. From 2000, where the effects were close to zero, employment effects 1 year after program start increased to 7% in 2006. Without explicitly accounting for differences in the characteristics of participants, her results suggest that labor market training consistently performed better than job practice by around 10% since 2000. However, since she only reports effects 1 year after program start, there is no information regarding potential differences in locking-in effects, which are much larger for training according to Forslund et al. (2013).

Forslund et al. (2011) compare the relative performance of job practice and labor market training over the business cycle. They use data for the period 1999–2005 and apply a combination of nearest neighbor propensity score matching and Cox regressions in a design that exploits time and regional variation in the business cycle. They confirm the finding of Forslund et al. (2013) that job practice outperforms labor market training in the short run due to much larger locking-in effects of the latter. After about 6 months during a recession and about 9 months during a boom, labor market training starts to outperform job practice. After 2 years, labor market training increases the exit rate from unemployment to employment by almost 5% during a recession and 3% during a boom compared to job practice. In line with Lechner and Wunsch (2009), who investigate the business cycle dependence of the effects of training for Germany, Forslund et al. (2011) conclude that training should be used counter-cyclically, because the indirect costs of training in the form of locking-in effects are considerably smaller. They also confirm the result of the earlier study for Germany that lower locking-in effects during recessions coincide with larger positive long-run effects. However, in contrast to Lechner and Wunsch (2009) Forslund et al. (2011) only consider the relative effectiveness compared to job practice but not compared to nonparticipation. Yet the evidence presented by Nilsson (2008) suggests that both training and job practice were also effective compared to nonparticipation during the period under consideration.

Evidence on the so-called job and development program, which consists of a series of individually adapted measures for hard-to-place workers with the long-term objective of integrating them into the labor market, is limited. There are two studies based on matching methods which investigate similar programs that were predecessors of the program currently in place. Hägglund (2002) studies the short-run effects of the so-called activity guarantee for participants in 2000. He finds that the program increased the probability of being employed 12 months after program start by 35%. However, as Forslund et al. (2004) rightly note, this effect is entirely driven by placements into subsidized employment while the probability of holding a regular job remained unchanged. Moreover, participants who found unsubsidized employment were more likely to return to unemployment than nonparticipants. Liljeberg and Lundin (2010) investigate a more recent program (*jobbnättet*) that was implemented in Stockholm before introduction of the current program. They study participants in the period 2006–07 and have a somewhat longer observation period of 450 days. After a short locking-in period of no more than 2 months, Liljeberg and Lundin (2010) find positive effects on the exit rate from unemployment that steadily increase to 8% 7 months after program start. Thereafter, the effects decline to about 4% after 450 days. Time to unsubsidized employment is reduced by almost 7%, while time to any kind of job, including subsidized employment, is reduced by more than 15% after 450 days. The reduction in the time to a job that lasts at least 120 days is only 1–3% smaller which indicates, within the limits of a relatively short follow-up period, at least some stability of found employment. Liljeberg and Lundin (2010) also perform a simple cost-benefit comparison and conclude that the program was cost-effective.

As noted earlier, Sweden is one of the few countries for which there exist a number studies that investigate the macroeconomic effects of labor market programs administered by the PES. The relatively large size of the programs in terms of number of participants, especially during and following the recession in the early 1990s, raised a lot of interest in the effects on the labor market as a whole. Most of the evidence is summarized in Calmfors et al. (2002) and all studies focus on programs in the 1980s and 1990s. The authors also discuss the methodological issues related to reversed causality or simultaneity and how this has been addressed in the various studies they survey. All studies use different parametric methods to address the identification problem In the following, we only summarize the findings that Calmfors et al. (2002) classify as robust to different parametric approaches. Calmfors et al. (2002) conclude that there is little evidence for improved matching efficiency. There is quite strong evidence for large displacement effects of subsidized employment and, to a lesser extent, of job practice programs but not for labor market training. This has also been confirmed in a more recent study by Dahlberg and Forslund (2005). There is some weaker evidence that subsidized employment may have reduced regular employment despite reducing open unemployment. One particularly robust result is that large labor market programs have increased labor force participation although Johansson (2001) shows that this effect is only temporary. It mainly stems from participants renewing eligibility for UI which significantly reduces deregistration after benefit exhaustion. Calmfors et al. (2002) also report that there is some evidence for upward pressure of labor market programs on real wages. However, Forslund and Kolm (2004) reassess the earlier evidence and find no such evidence. They perform a number of checks in order to explain the differences in their findings to the earlier literature. They conclude that revisions in the National Accounts Statistics which affect the data used in both the earlier studies and theirs are the most likely explanation. Nakosteen et al. (2012) finally show that participation in labor market programs in the mid-1990s increased interregional mobility within Sweden for men while the evidence for women is mixed.

9.2.3 Special Programs for Immigrants

With a share of foreign-born residents in Sweden of about 15% and a net migration rate of about 0.7%, immigrants are an important target group of Swedish policy. Besides Swedish language courses for immigrants, for which there exist no evaluation studies, there are a number of introduction programs for immigrants. They are mainly administered by the PES and have various objectives that are mostly unrelated to training. However, there are two studies that report results for programs that are more closely related to the programs discussed in this chapter.

Åslund and Johansson (2011) study a program that was tried out in 20 Swedish municipalities from 2003 to 2006. Borrowing from programs previously used for disabled workers, the so-called special introduction program (SIN) targeted immigrants and refugees who are considered capable of starting to work immediately, but who are also long-term unemployed or at risk of becoming so. The program involves several steps, the most important one being assignment to a workplace for trial and training purposes (workplace introduction) with the prospect of being hired after the end of program. Based on a difference-in-differences approach applied within a competing risks duration framework, Åslund and Johansson (2011) find that participation in SIN increased the transition rate from unemployment to work experience schemes and that those who participated in the schemes had higher exit rates to employment.

Andersson Joona and Nekby (2009) study a trial introduction program (TIP) that was implemented in a randomized experiment in three Swedish municipalities in the period 2006–08. The purpose of TIP was to considerably shorten the time from being granted permanent residency to regular employment by enforcing earlier registration with the PES, flexible language instruction parallel with other labor market programs, and intensive counseling and coaching by PES caseworkers with considerably reduced caseloads. Andersson Joona and Nekby (2009) find that 3–24 months (depending on program entry) after program start, participating men are 6% more likely to have a regular job and 12% more likely to be enrolled in training offered by the PES. In contrast, there are no such employment effects for women and the effects on participation in PES training are only half of those for men. These gender differences are in line with results obtained for combined German language and vocational training programs for immigrants in Germany (Walter et al., 2014). Additional results from duration models suggest a significant reduction in the time to subsidized employment as well as a reduction in time to regular employment once the number of meetings with the caseworker or the type of intermediate PES program is taken into account. But again the effects are only statistically significant for men. Andersson Joona and Nekby (2009) conclude that TIP seems to improve the matching between individual needs and training programs as well as assignment to potentially more beneficial programs that speed up transitions to regular employment.

9.2.4 Summary

Given the large number of studies available for Sweden it is worthwhile to briefly summarize the main findings. There four main conclusions that can be drawn. Firstly, general training on the compulsory and upper secondary level succeeds is raising participants' earnings, but it takes a relatively long time for these positive effects to materialize. Secondly, the effectiveness of labor market training for unemployed workers depends on economic conditions and institutional features. For most years during the 1990s labor market training was ineffective. Since the early 2000s when the Swedish government abolished incentives to participate in training to renew UI eligibility, these programs show more positive employment effects. Thirdly, programs that involve on-the-job training and are thus more similar to regular jobs, on average perform better than vocational classroom training. Finally, extensive education programs for adults can have economically important spillover effects on employment and wages of nonparticipants, which raises concerns about the results from microeconometric studies that are based on the validity of the stable unit treatment value assumption that does not allow for such effects (see the discussions of equilibrium effects in Sections 2.7 and 4.14).

10. DENMARK

10.1 Types of Programs

In 2012, the Danish government spent about 1.8 billion EUR or 0.75% of GDP on publicly subsidized education for adults. Similar to other European counties, the largest part of programs is offered via the PES and targeted at unemployed workers. The PES assigns unemployed workers to both regular programs which are open to other groups as well, and special programs that are only offered by the PES. Regular programs include general education for adults and vocational training for adults. A share of 14% of total expenditures relates to the former and 11% to the latter. Special programs administered by the PES account for 75% of total expenditures (Finansministeriet, 2014a). The different types of programs are described in the following.

10.1.1 General Education for Adults

General education for adults is supported by a state educational support scheme (Statens Voksenuddannelsesstøtte, SVU) that provides employed or self-employed participants with income support during participation in education to compensate for their loss of labor income. Eligible workers apply for support on their own initiative. To be eligible for SVU, applicants must be a Danish citizen or resident, at least 25 years of age, they have to participate in education for at least 37 working hours, and they need approval for their absence from their employer. SVU is equivalent to 80% of the maximum unemployment benefit (423.60 EUR per week in 2012) and can be paid for up to 40 weeks of 37 h. In case there are course fees (see below), SVU beneficiaries can apply for additional support. In 2012, expenditures on SVU amounted to 6.5 million EUR or 2% of total expenditures on general education for adults. Unemployed participants continue to receive their regular unemployment compensation (unemployment insurance or welfare payments) and they are assigned to general education by the PES.

There are two types of general education, basic and higher education, with slightly different eligibility criteria regarding SVU income support. Basis education refers to programs on the primary or secondary level, higher education to the postsecondary level.[141] Applicants can receive SVU for basic education if they have at most 10 years of schooling and no more than 2 years of vocational training, or if they have not used their education for at least 5 years. The latter means that the applicant has not worked for at least 5 years or that he/she has worked in a job that only requires a lower level of education. Support for higher education is only granted if the level of education the person already has does not exceed the lowest postsecondary level, if a higher education has not been used for at least 5 years, or if the education has been received in a foreign country and is not accredited in

---

[141] For an overview of the Danish education system see Ministry of Children and Education (2012). For an overview of adult education in Denmark see The Danish Agency for International Education (2011).

Denmark. Moreover, there is a minimum work requirement of 3 out of the past 5 years for full-time workers and 2 out of 5 years for part-time workers. Additionally, only full-time courses are supported.

Basic education comprises four types of programs on different levels and with different target groups. Firstly, there exist preparatory courses that focus on improving basic literacy and numeracy skills (so-called preparatory adult education[142]). They are targeted at adults who do not have basic skills to follow education and training or to cope with working life. All adults who fall into this group have access to this program and participation is free. In the school year 2011/12, 39,500 individuals participated in this program, of whom three-quarters were foreigners, ie, without Danish citizenship. A share of 61% of participants were women, 25% under 25 years old, 8% over 55, 14% unemployed and 44% inactive, ie, out of the labor force. The dropout rate in 2012 was 21% (Undervisningsministeriet, 2014). According to a survey from 2005, the main reasons for dropout are a job, family reasons or dissatisfaction with the course (Danmarks Evalueringsinstitut, 2005). A share of 7% of total expenditures on general education for adults related to such preparatory courses in 2012 (Finansministeriet, 2014a).

The second type of basic programs targets adults with sufficient literacy and numeracy skills but who have never completed lower secondary education or who have a need to improve or supplement their basic education (so-called general adult education[143]). It provides a combination of single subject courses that complement existing education such that a compulsory or lower secondary school degree can be obtained through an exam at the end of the program. The courses have durations of 6–12 months with a flexible schedule that accommodates employment. Applicants who are not assigned by the PES have to see a guidance counselor who assesses their qualifications and training needs before admission. Employed and self-employed participants pay a small fee but otherwise the courses are free. In the school year 2011/12, 105,000 individuals participated in this program, of whom more than one-third were foreigners. A share of 59% of participants were women, 58% under 25 years old, 6% over 55, 7% unemployed and 68% inactive. The dropout rate in 2012 was 25% (Undervisningsministeriet, 2014). This program accounts for 21% of total expenditures on general education for adults in 2012 (Finansministeriet, 2014a).

The third type of basic programs offers similarly designed single subject courses on the upper secondary level to applicants with a lower secondary degree (so-called higher preparatory single subject courses[144]). In the school year 2011/12, 105,000 individuals participated in this program, of whom 18% were foreigners, 59% women, 64% under 25 years old, 2% over 55, 4% unemployed, and 55% inactive. The dropout rate in 2012 was 2% (Undervisningsministeriet, 2014). Expenditures in 2012 amounted 40% of total expenditures on general education for adults (Finansministeriet, 2014a).

---

[142] Forberedende Voksenundervisning (FVU).
[143] Almen Voksenuddannelse (AVU).
[144] Hf-enkeltfag.

The last group of basic education programs comprises Danish language courses which are offered for free to all newly arrived foreign nationals. Foreigners, who come to Denmark to work or study, have to attend a 250-hour "Danish for the labor market" course. Besides basic knowledge of Danish, it provides the necessary vocabulary needed for a specific job or type of education. These courses are specifically tailored to the labor market needs of each participant. All other foreigners as well as those who have completed the labor market course within 18 months can attend a Danish language training program on three different levels that follows a standardized schedule. In the school year 2011/12, 72,000 individuals participated in this program, of whom 58% were women, 24% under 25 years old, 1% over 55, 6% unemployed and 43% inactive (Undervisningsministeriet, 2014). At 3.5 million EUR, expenditures in 2012 were negligible compared to total expenditures on general education for adults (Finansministeriet, 2014a).

Higher education is supported on three postsecondary levels: occupation-oriented further education[145] that awards a so-called academy profession degree, diploma programs that correspond to the bachelor level at a university or equivalent institution, and master programs. Participants have to pay for their education but may apply for additional support under SVU. About 86,000 individuals participated in publicly supported higher education for adults in the school year 2011/12, 29% of whom participated in academy profession programs, 58% in diploma programs, and the remaining 13% in master programs (Undervisningsministeriet, 2014). Statistics on the composition of participants only exist for the two latter programs. A share of 66% of participants were women, 1% under 25 years old, 7% over 55, 2% unemployed and 5% inactive. The dropout rate was 2%. Higher education accounts for 27% of total expenditures on general education for adults in 2012 (Finansministeriet, 2014a).

10.1.2 Vocational Training for Adults

Vocational training for adults is supported through a state grant system (VEU-Godtgørelse) that is available to employed workers. For employed workers who are members of an unemployment insurance fund,[146] the fund administers everything in

---

[145] Videregående voksenuddannelse (VVU).

[146] Danish unemployment insurance funds (in Danish: A-kasse) are private nonprofit institutions that are supported by the state. In Denmark, employees are not obliged to insure themselves against unemployment. Some professions and trades have their own specialized A-kasse, but since September 2002 the A-kasser have the opportunity to choose to be multidisciplinary, ie, open for anyone. If members with unemployment insurance become unemployed, they are paid unemployment benefits based on their income of the last 3 months, subject to a maximum. Based on their status as private institutions, unemployment insurance organizations have a strong interest in seeing their unemployed members find a new job quickly. Therefore, unemployed members are *closely* mentored and have to provide evidence of their job applications. Although jobseekers have the right to look for jobs in their own profession or jobs that match their qualifications, this right lapses quite quickly if they don't find suitable work. In the end, they have to accept any job, even one for a lower qualification. Members pay a monthly contribution set by the fund which is independent of their salary. For more information see http://www.a-kasser.dk/unemployment-insurance.html.

connection with the VEU support. For all other employed workers the training institutions are responsible. As most beneficiaries are employed and receive their full salary during participation, the VEU allowance is primarily paid to employers as a partial wage reimbursement, which is unique compared to other countries. VEU is equivalent to 80% of the maximum unemployment benefit (423.60 EUR per week in 2012) and can be paid for up to 10 weeks of 37 h. In order to be eligible, workers must fulfill at least the entry level of education required for the desired vocational training and they must not already have the desired vocational training unless they have not used this education for at least 5 years. In 2012 expenditures on VEU grants accounted for 45% of total expenditures on vocational training for adults (Finansministeriet, 2014a). Unemployed participants continue to receive their regular unemployment compensation (unemployment insurance or welfare payments) and they are assigned to vocational training by the PES.

There are two types of vocational training for adults. Adult vocational training courses[147] are short programs with the objective of maintaining or upgrading existing vocational skills or acquiring new vocational skills in accordance with the short and long-run needs of the labor market. Courses last no more than 6 weeks, on average 3 days. Several such short courses can be and frequently are combined. Participants receive a certificate upon completion. There are user fees of about 15% of actual costs which are usually paid by employers. In 2012, 660,000 individuals participated in such courses, of whom 45% were women, 9% foreigners, 8% under 25, 17% over 55, 12% unemployed, and 7% inactive. The dropout rate was low at only 1% (Undervisningsministeriet, 2014). A share of 50% of total expenditures on vocational training for adults relates to this program (Finansministeriet, 2014a).

A small number of workers (857 in full-time equivalents in 2012) are supported in obtaining the necessary qualifications required for a vocational degree equivalent to an apprenticeship or similar formal vocational qualification (Finansministeriet, 2014a).[148] After an initial assessment of potentially missing skills and qualifications, beneficiaries attend a combination of various short adult vocational training courses and/or single-subject general training courses, possible combined with a short period of practical experience. The program targets low-skilled workers or workers with outdated skills as well as foreign workers whose education is not accredited in Denmark. Expenditures make up 5% of total expenditures on vocational training for adults (Finansministeriet, 2014a).

10.1.3 Special Programs Administered by the PES

Unemployed workers have free access to all types of general education and vocational training for adults described above via the PES. Additionally, the PES offers a range

---

[147] Arbejdsmarkedsuddannelse (AMU).
[148] Grundlæggende Voksenuddannelse (GVU).

of other programs with explicit training components. All of these programs should facilitate quick return to employment. Assignment to a program is the result of a discretionary decision made by caseworkers at the PES. Participation is compulsory and unemployment benefit sanctions are imposed in case of noncompliance. After 9 months of unemployment (12 months in the 1990s and early 2000s), jobseekers have a legal right to participate in an activation program. In 2012, 780,000 unemployed workers participated in an activation measure, 10% of whom were under 25 and 11% over 55 (Styrelsen for Arbejdsmarked og Rekruttering, 2014).

There are three relevant groups of activation measures. The first one is called counseling and upskilling. It includes all of the above regular general education and vocational training programs assigned by the PES as well as a variety of complementary courses specifically designed for unemployed workers. These courses include job search training, help with finding practical training, subsidized on-the-job training or education programs, Danish lessons as well as courses in mathematics and general skills. Program durations should not exceed 6 weeks during the first 9 months of unemployment. In 2012, 435,000 unemployed workers participated in such supplementary counseling and upskilling courses, of whom 19% were under 25 and 12% over 55 (Styrelsen for Arbejdsmarked og Rekruttering, 2014). Expenditures amounted to 532 million EUR in 2012 or 38% of total expenditure on special programs administered by the PES (Ekspertgruppen Beskæftigelsesindsats, 2014).

The second group of programs includes different job practice and on-the-job training programs. Practical training and workplace introduction programs are shorter programs that last no more than 6 months, take place within a firm and prepare participants for a specific job in that firm. Employers report offers to the PES which then places suitable job applicants. Employers have to ensure that the training plan is in line with the future occupational assignments. Direct costs are covered by employers but the government covers cost of living via the usual unemployment compensation. In 2012, 204,000 job applicants participated in this program (Styrelsen for Arbejdsmarked og Rekruttering, 2014). Upskilling jobs are regular jobs where employers receive subsidies for training job applicants for up to 6 weeks. The training must be complementary to the firm's own training activities. That is, the training must be general and not restricted to particular requirements of the firm, and it must be in a field where the firm does not offer training itself. This program is only used rarely. In order to overcome skill shortages and unemployment of unskilled workers, the PES also offers adult apprenticeship arrangements. They are equivalent to regular apprenticeships with practical training in a firm and classroom training in a training center and are subsidized for up to 2 years. Workers qualify if they have no corresponding vocational training, if they have not used earlier apprenticeship training for more than 5 years or if they have been unemployed for longer periods. About 500 adults participated in such arrangements in 2012 (Styrelsen for Arbejdsmarked og Rekruttering, 2014). Subsidies also exist for unemployed workers who participate in on-the-job training for professional, linguistic or social competencies in a firm. Subsidies are paid for no more than 1 year and have the purpose of training job applicants such that they can return to a job without any further aid. In total there were 73,000 subsidized employment contracts in 2012 (Styrelsen for Arbejdsmarked og Rekruttering, 2014). However, this includes contracts subsidized to maintain the jobs for workers with permanently reduced ability without an explicit training component. The share of these subsidies is relatively small, though.

Finally, there is a group of other programs with each of these programs having rather specific purposes. Firstly, job rotation aims to promote training offers by employers. Firms that send their employees to training can receive subsidies for hiring unemployed job applicants as temporary replacement for workers who attend training. There were 4200 cases in 2012 (Styrelsen for Arbejdsmarked og Rekruttering, 2014) with expenditures of 47 million EUR (Finansministeriet, 2014b). Secondly, workers who have received unemployment insurance benefits for at least 4 months can attend individually chosen regular training courses for up to 6 weeks during the first year of unemployment in order to update their professional skills or retrain. The PES must be involved in the process and the unemployment insurance fund has to approve the chosen training. In 2012, 34,000 UI recipients participated in such training courses, resulting in expenditures of 67 million EUR (Ekspertgruppen Beskæftigelsesindsats, 2014). Finally, the Danish government provides financial aid for firms facing large personnel cutbacks. This aid can be used for job search courses (up to 2 weeks), vocational training (up to 8 weeks) or as financial aid to compensate for hours reductions. Firms can apply for this aid if at least ten workers face redundancy in firms with 20–100 employees or at least 10% of the workforce in firms with more than 100 employees. Expenditures in 2012 amounted to 4 million EUR (Ekspertgruppen Beskæftigelsesindsats, 2014).

10.2 Evidence on Impacts

Denmark is an interesting case to look at for at least two reasons. Firstly, exceptionally informative administrative data are available to study the effects of training for adults. Secondly, Denmark is one of the few countries where the government has implemented a number of social experiments to evaluate different activation strategies for unemployment workers.[149] In fact, most of the empirical research for Denmark is based on these experiments. Moreover, as almost 80% of training for adults is prescribed by the PES, almost all empirical research focuses on training for unemployed workers that takes place via the PES.

[149] Recently, also France has run a number of social experiments. However, these experiments focus entirely on job search assistance and counseling without any general or vocational training component. See Behaghel et al. (2012), Crépon et al. (2013a,b). Similar efforts have been made in the United Kingdom; see http://www.mdrc.org.

Jespersen et al. (2008) provide the most comprehensive evaluation of training programs in Denmark with respect to both the scope of programs and time period considered. They focus on unemployment insurance recipients and analyze four types of programs: private job training where the employer receives wage subsidies during the training of an unemployed worker; public job training during subsidized nonmarket employment in a public institution; classroom training; and a residual category that includes heterogeneous programs both with and without a training component. The authors study short, medium, and long-run effects of the programs for up to 10 years after program start based on a stock sample of unemployed workers in 1995 whom they follow until the end of 2005. They use propensity score matching methods exploiting the richness of the Danish administrative data and evaluate both the benefits and costs of the program. Directly after program start, Jespersen et al. (2008) find the typical negative locking-in effects on employment during program participation. Training during subsidized private or public employment additionally has positive earnings effects during participation due to paid wages. After participation, only private job training exhibits lasting positive employment effects around 5% as well as earnings gains of about 9% in 2005, which seem to be driven by both training and the fact that participants hold a regular subsidized job for some time even after completion of the training part. The net benefit of the programs that trades off gains in income (earnings and transfers) against direct costs and paid subsidies is positive for private and public job training but negative for classroom training and all remaining programs. Thus, Jespersen et al. (2008) provide further evidence that training that is most closely related to a regular job seems to be most effective for unemployed workers.

Rosholm and Svarer (2008) study the same programs as Jespersen et al. (2008) but focus on UI eligible workers who became unemployed between January 1998 and June 2002. Moreover, their main objective is to test for possible preprogram effects, ie, they test whether the perceived risk of being assigned to a program affects the exit rate from unemployment. They use a timing-of-events approach to identify and estimate program effects. They allow actual participation in one of the four programs to have a differential effect during the program (locking-in period) and afterwards. Moreover, to measure threat effects they include the average hazard rate into programs over the next 13 weeks as a control variable and allow for different coefficients at different unemployment durations. Similar to Jespersen et al. (2008) the authors find the typical locking-in effects for private and public job training as well as classroom training. Furthermore, they find that private job training but not public job training has positive effects on the exit rate to employment after program participation. In contrast to Jespersen et al. (2008) they also find positive postprogram effects for classroom training, which could be explained by the different population studied (inflow sample rather than stock sample which oversamples long-term unemployed workers). As regards possible threat effects, Rosholm and Svarer (2008) find that a higher perceived risk of being assigned to a program increases the exit rate to employment and that this effect becomes larger the closer to the point where participation becomes compulsory after 12 months of unemployment. Thereafter, the threat effect declines and becomes statistically insignificant after 60 weeks of unemployment. The authors conclude that active labor market policy regimes shorten unemployment duration, even if actual program participation does not. However, since they do not allow for differential threat effects by program type it is unclear whether threat effects work that generally or whether they depend on the mix of offered programs or are even program-specific.

Munch and Skipper (2008) also study the same programs as Jespersen et al. (2008) but use a timing-of-events approach rather than matching. Moreover, they investigate effect heterogeneity for different subgroups of workers and focus on postunemployment outcomes. They find that general classroom training produces locking-in effects but subsequent positive effects on expected employment duration for young (below 25) and older (above 50) workers but negative impacts on accepted wage rates for all subgroups of participants.

Rosholm and Skipper (2009) use a social experiment conducted in 1994. This experiment randomized unemployed applicants for classroom training into treatment and control groups. In line with Jespersen et al. (2008) they find negative initial locking-in effects but no significant effects on time spent employed in the longer run. There are also no significant effects on subsequent wage rates. These findings support the credibility of the matching approach implemented by Jespersen et al. (2008) as opposed to the timing-of-events approach employed by Munch and Skipper (2008) which imposes more functional form restrictions.

Several studies exploit a more recent social experiment conducted in two Danish counties between November 2005 and February 2006. Half of the inflow into UI in this period was randomized into a treatment group that received the following intensified services (Graversen and Van Ours, 2008): (1) information letter in the second week of unemployment, (ii) a 2-week job search assistance program after 5–6 weeks, (iii) frequent meetings with caseworkers during weeks 7–18, (iv) mandatory participation in a training program after at most 18 weeks for at least 13 weeks (early activation). The studies investigate different aspects of the potential effects of the experimental treatment. Graversen and Van Ours (2008) and Rosholm (2008) find that intensified activation reduced average unemployment duration by about 20%. However, these effects materialize during the first 4 weeks after assignment to the treatment group before participation in job search assistance or training takes place, from which Graversen and Van Ours (2008) conclude that the effects do not result from participation in training. Rosholm (2008) investigates this issue further and shows that there are no effects of actual participation in job search assistance or training. However, there are sizeable threat effects of future program participation since jobseekers respond statistically significantly to higher perceived risk of participation. Graversen and Van Ours (2011) find further evidence for threat effects. They show that the activation effect increases with subjective costs of participation measured as the distance between the place of residence of the unemployed worker and the place where the activation took place. However, the quality of postunemployment jobs is unaffected by this distance. Blasco and Rosholm (2011) further investigate the effects of the activation program on postunemployment outcomes. They find that on top of reducing unemployment duration, the program reduced unemployment recurrence for men but not for women. For men, the duration of the subsequent employment spell increased by about 10%. Thus, the threat effect of the activation program does not seem to come at the expense of reduced match quality. One reason for this might be due to the design of the experiment. If participants left unemployment but returned within the period of the experiment they re-entered the experiment at the stage where they had left it. Vikström et al. (2014) address the issue that the above results on the mechanisms through which the program works are based on mixed proportional hazard models that require a number of quite restrictive assumptions. They apply nonparametric bounding methods to investigate the robustness of the earlier results from Rosholm (2008) and Graversen and Van Ours (2008, 2011). Largely in line with these studies they conclude that the activation package reduced unemployment duration through a combination of job search assistance, frequent meetings with caseworkers and possibly threat effects associated with perceived future program participation but not through participation in training. Gautier et al. (2012) finally show based on a difference-in-differences approach that the experiment had important spillover effects. They find that the nonparticipants in the experiment counties find jobs slower after the introduction of the activation program relative to workers in other comparable counties. This raises doubts about the large magnitude of the effects of the above microeconometric studies because they assume that no such spillover effects exist.

Maibom Pedersen et al. (2012) analyze a second experiment that was implemented in four Danish counties in 2008 in order to investigate which of the instruments used in the earlier experiment caused the large positive effects on the exit rate to employment. In particular, the intention was to separate the effects of more frequent meetings with caseworkers from the effects of early activation. Four different treatments were tested: (i) more frequent group meetings, (ii) more frequent individual meetings, (iii) early activation, (iv) early activation and more frequent group meetings. The authors find that more frequent meetings reduce average unemployment duration by about 5 weeks over 2 years leading to net cost savings of about 4750 EUR per new unemployment spell. Moreover, they confirm that early activation has no direct effect on the exit rate to employment but find that it increases exit rates to employment and reduces unemployment recurrence for men in response to the threat of future program participation. Hence, this study confirms the results from the earlier experiments but does not account for potential spillover effects in the experimental regions.

There are two studies which analyze program effects for immigrants. Heinesen et al. (2013) study the standard set of activation measures for unemployed workers but focus on immigrants from nonwestern countries who receive social assistance. They distinguish between subsidized employment which in Denmark includes training components, employment programs which offer nonmarket jobs in the public sector, and other programs including all other types of training. The authors use data for the period 1984–2004 and employ the timing-of-events approach of Abbring and van den Berg (2003). They find that all groups of programs statistically significantly increase the exit rate to employment with the effects being largest for regular subsidized employment. Moreover, there are no locking-in effects of the programs, which might be explained by the fact that the study focuses on particularly hard-to-place workers with low employment rates in the absence of any intervention. Clausen et al. (2009) analyze the effectiveness of different activation measures as well as Danish language courses for immigrants who received their residence permit in the period 2000–02. They also distinguish between subsidized regular employment and employment programs but additionally distinguish general education and training, mixed special courses designed to improve personal and vocational skills through combinations of different measures, counseling and upskilling measures, and subsidized private sector employment for vulnerable groups of immigrants. Based on a timing-of-events approach they find that subsidized private sector employment, which comprises on-the-job training, is by far the most effective program: it reduces mean unemployment duration by 14–24 weeks, while the other activation measures are largely ineffective. This is in line with the evidence for unemployed workers in general. Danish language courses also statistically significantly increase the exit to employment. One drawback of both studies is that they do not account for possible threat effects which would violate the no-anticipation assumptions underlying the timing-of-events approach, especially since sizeable threat effects have been found, for example, by Rosholm and Svarer (2008).

In summary, the evidence for Denmark confirms that PES-provided classroom training is largely ineffective in raising their participants' employment rates. Moreover, also in line with the evidence for other countries, programs that involve on-the-job training and are thus more similar to regular jobs, on average perform considerably better than vocational classroom training. The Danish studies also show that the possibility of future assignment to programs raises exit rates from unemployment due to a threat effect. Furthermore, the evidence suggests that — at least in the context of the Danish labor market — more frequent interactions with caseworkers are more effective in reducing unemployment duration than participation in various activation measures. Finally, there is another piece of evidence that large programs can have important spillover effects that violate the stable unit treatment value assumption at the center of microeconometric evaluation studies.

11. MATCHING PARTICIPANTS TO TRAINING

11.1 Does Match Matter?

One lesson from the empirical evidence summarized in the case studies is that the effectiveness of training varies considerably by type and duration of program, characteristics of participants, economic environment and institutional setup. Hence, in order to maximize the returns to public investments in training, matching the right types of participants to the right types of programs is crucial. Many studies make the point that the effectiveness of the programs could likely be improved by better targeting the programs to those who benefit most. There are a few studies that quantify the potential improvement in the average effectiveness of the programs. Plesca and Smith (2005) for the United States, Lechner and Smith (2007) for Switzerland, Wunsch and Lechner (2008) and Lechner et al. (2011) for Germany, and Staghøj et al. (2010) for Denmark show that a reallocation of workers to programs can result in sizeable improvements in the cost-effectiveness of the programs, even when subject to capacity constraints. Moreover, better educated workers or, more generally, workers with more favorable characteristics are often over-represented in training, independent of whether workers choose their own courses and providers or whether they have been assigned by caseworkers. Many studies provide evidence for this so-called creaming or cream skimming, eg, Bell and Orr (2002) for the United States, Hui and Smith (2002) for Canada, Coulter et al. (2012) for the United Kingdom and Hipp and Warner (2008) for Germany. Thus, the programs often do not seem to reach those who may be most in need of training or who might benefit most. The following sections summarize the literature on how different features of the matching process of participants to training affect outcomes.

11.2 Assignment by Caseworkers

In many countries, assignment to training programs is a discretionary decision made by caseworkers, especially when it comes to programs administered by the PES. Caseworkers assess whether a candidate has any skill deficits that are sufficiently severe to justify financial support and that could be removed with any of the available programs. After establishing eligibility and consulting the candidate, the final decision is usually based on the candidate's personal characteristics, including education, work experience, past employment record and career prospects. Additionally, caseworkers take into account local labor market conditions, in particular demand for specific skills, the supply of courses offered by providers, and available funding. Governments that rely on caseworker assignment typically argue that caseworkers have better knowledge about the labor market, required skills and the suitability of different training courses and that they can better judge the training needs of workers than the workers themselves. Indeed, many studies show that more frequent or more intensive interactions with caseworkers improve labor outcomes of jobseekers (eg, Hägglund, 2009; Maibom Pedersen et al., 2012; Van den Berg et al., 2012). However, only relatively little is known about the mechanisms through which caseworkers affect their clients. Caseworkers have many roles when they interact with jobseekers besides providing counseling services on job search and assignment to programs. On the one hand, they monitor jobseekers' search effort and possibly impose sanctions. On the other hand, they also motivate jobseekers, discuss their personal situation, provide support in coping with this situation, and offer new perspectives on their situation. The following sections summarize the existing evidence on the role of the assignment process of clients to different programs, a lot of which stems from qualitative research. Rigorous quantitative research remains quite limited.

11.2.1 Direct Evidence on the Role of Caseworkers

Some papers assess whether creaming leads to efficiency gains or losses. Heckman et al. (2002) use experimental data for the JTPA program, while Bell and Orr (2002) use experimental data for training provided to AFDC (Aid to Families with Dependent Children) recipients. Both studies find negligible effects of creaming on program impacts. The reasons for this finding differ, though. Heckman et al. (2002) find only little heterogeneity in the effects of participation in the JTPA program which explains why the allocation of participant matters little. Bell and Orr (2002), in contrast, draw their conclusion from the observation that based on the information caseworkers had at intake little could have been done to improve the average effectiveness of training for AFDC recipients. However, caseworkers' choices might have improved outcomes had they had knowledge about training impacts. Interestingly though, Bloom et al. (2003) also find that creaming had no systematic impact on the effectiveness of mandatory welfare-to-work programs in the United States. They pool data from three large-scale randomized experiments that together span a period of 15 years and cover 59 locations in seven states.

Lechner and Smith (2007) and Staghøj et al. (2010) compare allocations based on estimated program impacts with the actual allocation by caseworkers and random assignment. Exploiting rich administrative data for Switzerland, Lechner and Smith (2007) use propensity score matching to estimate training impacts on average employment rates. Staghøj et al. (2010) employ a timing-of-events approach with unobserved heterogeneity and estimate training impacts on average unemployment duration based on administrative data for Denmark. Both papers show that compared to random assignment caseworkers added little to the average effectiveness of training for unemployed workers. Although the actual allocation by caseworkers differed from random assignment and the effects of training were quite heterogeneous, average training outcomes were very similar. Moreover, alternative allocations of jobseekers to programs based on largest estimated effects could have increased average employment rates or reduced unemployment duration considerably even when taking capacity constraints into account. However, caseworkers could also have done much worse since allocations based on smallest impact would have resulted in considerably worse outcomes than the actual allocation. Plesca and Smith (2005) assess the benefits from reallocation based on estimated impacts for the JTPA program in the United States. They find potential for improvement for women but not for men.

On behalf of the Swiss State Secretariat for Economic Affairs (SECO), Frölich et al. (2007) conducted both qualitative and quantitative research on the question of how Swiss caseworkers and the organization of regional employment offices (REOs) affect the employment rates of their clients. They use administrative data for jobseekers and caseworkers combined with survey data on REOs and caseworkers. The microeconometric analyses control for differences in regional labor market conditions, the organization of regional employment offices, the characteristics of their clientele and characteristics of the caseworkers. As the outcome variable Frölich et al. (2007) consider average employment rates and they report results from both parametric models and propensity score matching. As a first key result the report by Frölich et al. (2007) and the accompanying paper by Behncke et al. (2010a) show that caseworkers who place less emphasis on a cooperative and consent-seeking relationship with their clients obtain higher average employment rates than those caseworkers with strong focus on these aspects. In a follow-up paper, Huber et al. (2014) investigate differences in program assignment as a potential mechanism underlying this result. Based on semiparametric mediation analysis, however, they find that less accommodating caseworkers do not use more effective combinations of labor market programs such as training. Hence, it must be other factors such as stricter monitoring, pressure to accept jobs, or other reasons that explain the positive employment effects of less cooperative caseworkers. This is indirectly supported by Frölich et al. (2007), who find that, in particular, stricter monitoring and sanctioning or more generally a focus on quick reemployment and employment-related measures yields better average employment rates than focusing on qualification. Based on Swiss administrative data Arni et al. (2015) also provide supporting evidence for this. They find that supporting qualification measures ("carrots") and more demanding, pressure-oriented measures such as monitoring, sanctions and workfare programs ("sticks") are compliments implying that a certain amount of both yields the most favorable results. However, they also find that a focus on "sticks" dominates focusing on "carrots."

Other evidence also supports the finding that a focus on job placement dominates a focus on training. Lagerström (2011) uses data on Swedish PES locations that randomize jobseekers to caseworkers and estimates whether caseworker fixed effects explain jobseekers' outcomes in terms of employment, earnings, and wages. He finds that caseworkers have a statistically significant impact on their clients' outcomes. However, the total variation explained by the caseworker fixed effects is small. He then investigates whether assignment to different programs or certain placement activities explain this finding. His results suggest that stronger emphasis on training has negative effects on jobseekers' outcomes compared to caseworkers who focus solely on supporting workers' search for a job or rely on employment-related measures. Bloom et al. (2003) report that more intensive use of basic education for welfare recipients reduced the average earnings effects of mandatory welfare-to-work programs in three large-scale experiments in the United States while emphasizing quick reemployment and personalized client attention increased earnings effects.

Weatherall and Markwardt (2010) investigate how caseworker behavior affects the employment status of unemployed workers in Denmark. They combine Danish register data for the period 2002–06 with survey data on caseworker behavior and estimate a multinomial logit model that controls for various worker characteristics. Caseworker behavior is measured by indices that have been formed from a battery of survey questions. They study the following types of behavior: tendency for creaming, professional distance, formalism, coercion, and other coping strategies. They confirm the result of Behncke et al. (2010a) that less cooperative behavior (more coercion) is positively related to employment rates. Moreover, they find that a tendency for creaming is positively correlated with higher transition rates out of unemployment, which might just be evidence for actual creaming, though. The also find that putting more emphasis on keeping a professional distance is negatively correlated with employment rates. However, Weatherall and Markwardt (2010) do not investigate the role of differential assignment to training or other labor market programs in explaining these findings.

Using Swiss data, Behncke et al. (2010b) investigate whether similarity of caseworkers and their clients in terms of gender, age, education and nationality affects clients' average employment rate. They apply statistical matching methods that control for regional labor market conditions, the organization of regional employment offices, characteristics of their clientele and other characteristics of the caseworkers. They find that belonging to the same social group as measured by the four characteristics increases employment rates by about three 3%. Based on the same data and methods, Frölich et al. (2007) additionally find that experience as caseworker and certified training that provides the necessary knowledge about the labor market, available programs and services as well as the social skills to cope with this particular clientele improve employment outcomes. Age, on the other hand, and having a college or university degree correlates negatively with employment rates. However, both studies again do not investigate the role of differential assignment to training or other labor market programs in explaining these findings.

Arni (2014) is currently working on a project that may provide interesting insights regarding this question. He investigates how caseworkers' beliefs and perceptions about the employment prospects of their clients affect their counseling strategies and program assignment decision. He is conducting a randomized experiment in selected Swiss REOs where a subgroup of caseworkers receive regular updates of their clients' estimated unemployment duration. Arni (2014) investigates how this profiling-like intervention affects caseworkers' beliefs, how this translates into potentially different counseling strategies and use of activation measures, and ultimately how this affects their clients' employment chances.

Based on the existing literature, it seems appropriate to conclude that caseworkers' assignment decisions are important because better targeting based on heterogeneous impacts of training has potential for large improvements in average program impacts. However, whether caseworkers can realize this potential depends on at least two things. Firstly, they need to know how they can improve assignment. This requires providing information on program impacts for different types of workers on a regular basis and in an accessibly way. Secondly, caseworkers must be willing to change their style of interaction with their clients, which might be the bigger challenge (see the discussion of Behncke et al., 2009, below). Moreover, the literature also suggests that other actions of the caseworkers, in particular their counseling and direct placement activities seem to be more important than program assignment. Rosholm (2014) rightly notes that caseworker meetings are less costly than training or other programs, in part because they have no locking-in effects. Moreover, they can be scaled up and down easily to accommodate business cycle fluctuations.

11.2.2 The Role of Organizational Features

A number of studies investigate how organizational features of the PES affect their clients' outcomes. A relatively well-studied feature is caseload. Almost all studies find that a lower caseload improves employment and/or earnings outcomes of clients, independent of applied methodology and the time period, country, and specific clientele studied. Jerger et al. (2001) study a locally implemented reduction in caseload for social assistance recipients in Germany in the period 1998–99 based on matching methods. Schiel et al. (2008) conduct a similar study for German long-term unemployed workers in the period 2002–05. Bloom et al. (2003) analyze earnings effects of mandatory welfare-to-work programs in the United States which have been obtained from three large-scale randomized experiments. Sheldon (2003a) studies the impact of caseload and other organizational features within an estimated matching function for Swiss PES locations in the period 1997–98. Koning (2009) uses Dutch data on PES locations in 2004 and estimates GLS models that control for client composition in terms of gender, age, education, and ethnicity as well as the local vacancy-to-jobseeker ratio. Hainmüller et al. (2011) use German PES data for the period 2007–08 and combine a difference-in-differences approach with matching techniques that control for a rich set of variables capturing local labor market conditions. Koning (2009) and Hainmüller et al. (2011) find that reducing caseload is cost-effective while Jerger et al. (2001) and Schiel et al. (2008), who study more disadvantaged clienteles, doubt the cost-effectiveness for this population.

Heinrich (2000) provides interesting evidence on how the organization of local, publicly funded providers of JTPA services in the United States affects JTPA participants' labor market performance. In particular, she compares for-profit providers with nonprofit providers. She finds that, in contrast to theoretical arguments, nonprofit providers were not more likely to serve more disadvantaged clients. Moreover, there were no systematic differences in the effectiveness in increasing participants' earnings and employment rates. However, including performance incentives in service providers' contracts (statistically and substantively) improved JTPA participants' average labor market performance independent of the type of provider.

There exists quite extensive qualitative research on the impact of organizational features of the PES in Switzerland due to several large evaluation projects initiated by the Swiss State Secretariat for Economic Affairs. For the period 2003–04, Frölich et al. (2007) analyze the correlation between organizational features of the PES and their clients' reemployment probability. They report that employer contacts are particularly important, especially direct interactions between caseworkers and employers, a good understanding of employers' needs, quick response to vacancies, and a good preselection of jobseekers for referrals to vacancies. The importance of employer contacts is also confirmed by Bellis et al. (2011) for Jobcentre Plus performance in the United Kingdom. Frölich et al. (2007) furthermore emphasize a cooperative attitude toward other institutions such as providers of training programs or external placement services. A similar finding is reported by Newton et al. (2012) for the United Kingdom. Additional factors that are positively related to PES performance listed by Frölich et al. (2007) include separation of monitoring activities from sanctioning decisions to reduce conflicts of roles, a relatively low administrative burden on caseworkers and caseworker changes after some time to induce new impulses in the activation process. They find negative correlations for a very cooperative, less stringent management style and disagreement between staff and supervisors. The latter has also been found by Bloom et al. (2003) for welfare recipients in the United States.

Based on a survey of Swiss PES locations in 2004, Egger and Partner (2006) study the determinants of PES performance, which is measured in terms of average job search duration, number of clients being unemployed for more than a year and number of clients who exhaust UI without finding employment. They list the following factors as correlates with high PES performance: early activation, employer contacts and knowledge about employers' needs, commitment and motivation of caseworkers, not too high a caseload, preventing long-term unemployment as an explicit target, and a simple organizational structure. In a follow-up study, Egger and Partner (2013) surveyed the eight most successful and five least successful Swiss REOs and study potential explanations for the differences in performance. They find that the most successful REOs place a high importance on performance targets, regularly assess the performance of individual caseworkers, put a relatively low administrative burden on caseworkers, have a good working atmosphere, have a good recruiting process and direct leadership of teams rather than multiple hierarchy levels, and their caseworkers regularly exchange their experiences.

The studies for Switzerland that have been summarized in the previous paragraphs control for differences in local labor market conditions and the composition of clients between PES locations. However, a rigorous analysis of underlying causal mechanisms is still missing. In this respect, the Swiss studies provide a number of interesting starting points for future research on the role of organizational features, caseworker characteristics, placement strategies and assignment to training or alternative programs for the labor market outcomes of jobseekers and other target populations.[150]

11.2.3 Statistical Tools to Assist Caseworkers in Their Decision

Many evaluation studies have emphasized that better targeting of training programs may improve the cost–effectiveness of training. In principle, targeting can serve two potentially conflicting goals: equity, ie, serving those most in need for services, or efficiency, ie, serving those for whom the cost–effectiveness of the programs is maximized. In order to improve targeting, two types of statistical tools to assist caseworkers in their assignment decision have been proposed.[151] Profiling systems take the perspective of equity, serving those more intensely with higher need for services. Need is measured in different ways. The most frequent profiling variable used is the expected probability of becoming long-term unemployed. The most prominent examples are the Job Seeker Classification Instrument (JSCI) in Australia (DEETYA, 1998) and the Worker Profiling and Reemployment System (WPRS) in the United States (Dickinson, et al., 1997). An example for a European system is Denmark (Rosholm et al., 2004). A model for the risk of becoming long-term unemployed is estimated based on past data and the coefficients are used to predict risk for new clients. Based on estimated risk, clients are then assigned to different types of activation measures or activation plans. Black et al. (2003) provide guidance for developing and implementing statistical profiling models. Berger et al. (2001) assess the performance of profiling systems in the United States. They show that many of the models did a bad job in predicting the profiling variable of interest. Moreover, even when the profiling variable had good predictive power, they found no systematic relationship between the profiling variable and program impacts, raising considerable doubts regarding the value of need-based systems.

Impact-based targeting systems address this concern by seeking to maximize program impacts directly. Based on estimates of program impacts for past participants, targeting systems predict the program type with the highest expected returns for each client taking into account effect heterogeneity with respect to type and duration of program, characteristics of participants, and potentially also economic environment. Famous examples include the Frontline Decision Support System (FDSS) in the United States (Eberts and O'Leary, 2002), and the Service and Outcome Measurement System (SOMS) in Canada (Colpitts, 2002). Frölich et al. (2003) summarize the arguments in favor of statistical targeting and challenges for implementation. Moreover, Plesca and Smith (2005), Lechner and Smith (2007), Wunsch and Lechner (2008), Staghøj et al. (2010), and

---

[150] The literature on the Restart program discussed in UK case study is also relevant in this context.

[151] For a nice summary of the earlier literature see Eberts et al. (2002).

Lechner et al. (2011) all quantify the potential gains from allocations based on estimated program impacts. Manski (2004) and Frölich (2008) propose alternative ways to implement statistical treatment rules. Frölich (2008) also proposes a way to analyze statistical inference on recommended treatment choice and how recommendations can be conveyed to caseworkers in a comprehensible way. Using Frölich's (2008) approach, Behncke et al. (2009) ran a pilot study that tested a statistical targeting system in selected regional employment offices (REOs) in Switzerland in 2005 (the so-called statistically assisted program selection, SAPS). Caseworkers in 21 REOs were randomized into treatment and control groups. The treatment group received a prediction of the program or set of programs with the largest expected impact on the reemployment probability for each client. The program impacts that served as inputs for SAPS were estimated from a large and very informative database for all types of programs and a variety of subgroups based on matching methods. SAPS was designed to serve as a supplementary input to the caseworkers' decision process. Caseworkers retained full discretion in their ultimate decision. The aim of the experiment was to investigate how SAPS affects caseworkers' assignment decisions, average program impacts and overall reemployment probabilities of jobseekers. The somewhat sobering result of the experiment was that caseworkers largely ignored the SAPS tool. Assignment decisions did not differ between the treatment and control groups. Anecdotal evidence points to relatively strong resistance to the tool among caseworkers. Some considered statistical estimates as inferior to their own experience. Others feared being proven wrong by the tool or that their decision power might be reduced or caseworkers might even be replaced in the future if the tool proved to be successful (Behncke et al., 2007). Similar concerns were raised during the development of the Canadian SOMS system and were one of the reasons why the Canadian government stopped its implementation in 2002. The SAPS experiment illustrates the challenges of moving from a system that gives caseworkers full discretion to a statistical targeting system. Achieving acceptance by caseworkers through communication of the merits of the tool and addressing potential fears as well as positive incentives to use the tool seem to be crucial in the process.

11.2.4 Optimal Assignment to Training
To conclude this section it should be noted that there is a small literature that approaches the question of optimal assignment of unemployed workers to training from a normative theoretical perspective. Pavoni and Violante (2005, 2007) developed a theoretical framework for studying optimal welfare-to-work programs. It allows for joint optimization of unemployment insurance and welfare payments on the one hand, and of the use of activation measures such as training on the other hand. Moreover, workers are heterogeneous with respect to their human capital which depreciates during unemployment. Based on a quantified version of this model it is possible to predict, given a desired level of generosity of the welfare system, the

optimal amount of benefits as well as the optimal timing and duration of training or other activation measures as a function of unemployment duration and the skill level of the worker. Based on a version of the model that is calibrated to the United States in the 1990s, Pavoni and Violante (2005) find that basic training is rarely optimal for high-skilled workers. Unskilled workers should optimally spend on average about 3 months in training and they should be assigned to training only if they are still unemployed after 12–48 months. The parsimonious use of training can be explained by the fact that this costly policy is compared to the situation where search incentives are optimized by appropriately chosen amounts of unemployment benefits and optimal use of less costly monitoring.

Wunsch (2007, 2013) adapted the model of Pavoni and Violante (2005, 2007) by including a second skill dimension (job search skills) and another policy instrument (job search assistance). Based on a version of the model that is calibrated to Germany in the early 2000s Wunsch (2007) finds that the minimum effectiveness required for training to be part of the optimal policy is relatively high. In fact it is higher than many of the empirical estimates of the impact of training. If, however, training is sufficiently effective, it should be used for low to intermediate skill levels and only if the worker has not found employment after some time. Moreover, the optimal duration of training is usually quite short.

Spinnewijn (2013) studies the optimal use of training in a similar framework. He shows that training should be used such that human capital converges to a stationary level for long unemployment durations. If the worker is below this level already at the start of unemployment he should be trained intensively immediately. If he is above, he should be trained with higher intensity only later to offset human capital depreciation. However, in contrast to the other studies Spinnewijn (2013) finds that training is always optimal and absorbing. Only the relative intensity of training versus search varies. All three studies find that implementing the optimal policy would result in sizeable welfare gains or cost savings compared to the actual systems implying that actual systems are suboptimal with respect to both the level of unemployment benefits and the use of training and other activation measures.

Pavoni et al. (2014) are currently working on a project where they study the optimal use of training based on an adapted version of the model developed by Pavoni and Violante (2007) that distinguishes between different types of training. They structurally estimate the parameters of the training technology and simulate the optimal use of formal education, classroom training and on-the-job training as a function of unemployment duration and the skill level of the worker. They consider the extreme case where search incentives and alternative policies are jointly optimized, the one where only the use of training is optimized and various intermediate cases. This provides much richer insights into the (potentially constrained by the benefit system) optimal design of training policies than the earlier studies.

11.3 Demand-Based Systems

During the past two decades an increasing number of countries have introduced demand-based systems in which individuals can select a training course and provider of their own choice. In the past, this mainly concerned training that was not administered by the PES. In recent years, some countries that traditionally used full-caseworker discretion for assignment of PES-administered programs have switched to more demand-based systems. The most prominent example is Germany, which introduced training vouchers for most PES-administered training programs in 2003. The main rationale for demand-based systems is that they maximize consumer choice, which in turn should maximize consumer utility and social welfare. If recipients can decide for themselves this may also reduce potential resistance to participation in mandatory training which may improve its effectiveness. Supporters of demand-based systems further argue that the need of providers to compete for participants will improve the quality of training. Opponents argue that recipients have too little information on available courses, providers, and labor market conditions to make the right decision from a societal and potentially even the individual perspective. They might also misjudge their own skills or pick courses that maximize consumption value rather than labor market or earnings prospects.

There are several types of demand-based systems which run under different names. The most common ones are training vouchers, bonuses or checks, and individual training or learning accounts (ITAs or ILAs). All of them involve a direct transfer from the government, either as the certified value of the voucher or as payments into ILAs. Sometimes, copayments by participants and/or employers are required. Dohmen et al. (2007), CEDEFOP (2000, 2009), and Groot and Van den Brink (2010) provide an overview of existing systems. Voucher systems exist or have been tested in Australia, Belgium, Germany, France, the Netherlands and the United States; ILAs in Austria, Canada, the Netherlands, Sweden, Switzerland, the United Kingdom and the United States. The following discussion mainly focuses on ITAs in the United States and training vouchers in Germany as the two most prominent examples but empirical evidence for other countries will be considered as well.

Barnow (2000, 2009) summarizes both the early and more recent evidence on voucher and ITA systems for targeted training programs in the United States. He concludes that the early evidence for vouchers for the economically disadvantaged is mainly negative, while the effects for dislocated workers are quite mixed. All programs that have positive impacts involve some assessment and counseling to determine what is most suitable for participants as well as screening of providers for training quality and placement rates. As part of the initiative to strengthen the reliance on market mechanisms, the first federal labor market training voucher system was introduced in the United States with the Workforce Investment Act (WIA) in 1998. WIA introduced individual training accounts (ITAs) for adults which enable individuals to choose a training course that best meets their skills from a list of eligible providers. They receive a voucher together with information on provider performance which allows recipients to make informed choices. Implementation of ITAs differed by local areas. Many states restrict training to certain occupations in high demand, or put cost and time limits on the vouchers. Moreover, some states have voluntary or compulsory counseling to guide customer choice. Thus, the ITAs introduced under WIA incorporate many of the features that describe more successful systems.[152]

The relative effectiveness of ITAs with different levels of control was evaluated by a randomized experiment which was funded by the U.S. Department of Labor. The experiment tested three approaches. The first approach required clients to receive intensive counseling. Counselors were supposed to direct clients to courses with high returns and they could reject clients' choices that did not meet this criterion. They also decided on the amounts of the ITA, which could exceed the amount of the other approaches, up to a maximum of 8000 USD in most sites. The second approach was similar to the one most frequently implemented in the transition to WIA. Counseling was also mandatory but less intensive. Counselors could not reject any choices from the list of approved providers. The ITA amount was fixed at 3000–5000 USD. The third approach differed from the second one only in that counseling was now voluntary and available upon request by the client. The experiment was implemented in eight sites between December 2001 and February 2004 and it involved about 8000 eligible customers. McConnell et al. (2006) and Perez-Johnson et al. (2011) summarize the results of the experiments as follows. Counselors were reluctant to direct choices and to limit training funds. Few clients requested voluntary counseling. Mandatory counseling delayed the start of training and discouraged participation in ITA-funded training but broadened the set of training options considered. The overall training rate was largely unaffected but the different approaches affected how training was funded. The different approaches led to very modest differences in mean earnings in the long term (15 to 22 quarters after random assignment) using both administrative data and survey data. These differences favor the structured choice model. Perez-Johnson et al. (2011) suggest that these differences likely result from the more generous ITAs available under the structured choice model rather than to the greater caseworker involvement and control.

Germany introduced training vouchers for most training programs administered by the PES in 2003. The new system is a mixture between caseworker discretion and free choice. The voucher specifies the training objective, an expiry date as well as possible restrictions in terms of the maximum duration of training or regional service providers, all of which are decided by the caseworker in the PES. Initially, caseworkers were instructed to issue vouchers only to workers for whom they predicted an exit rate from unemployment of at least 70% 6 months after completing training (so-called 70%-rule).

---

[152] See Ellis (2001) for a more detailed description.

This rule was abolished in 2005 in favor of individualized decisions regards need for training, employment prospects and success probabilities. Voucher recipients can choose courses within the restrictions stated in the voucher from a list of certified providers. Information about approved providers is accessible via an online database.

The take-up rate of training by voucher recipients is relatively stable at about 85% (Kruppe, 2009; Paul et al., 2013). Kruppe (2009) investigates selectivity in voucher take-up. For the period 2003–06, during most of which the 70%-rule was still in place, Kruppe (2009) reports that low-skilled workers, jobseekers with health problems, and persons with limited regional mobility are less likely to make use of the vouchers. Moreover, usage is particularly unlikely for jobseekers with multiple barriers to employment, mainly because of creaming by providers that were indirectly affected by the 70%-rule because they were evaluated by the share of participants in their programs who met the 70%-rule. On the other hand, take-up is more likely the more specific the training objective stated on the voucher is because recipients find it easier to locate providers that offer specific types of courses.

Bruttel (2005) summarizes the first experiences with the voucher system. He concludes that the advantages of the voucher system proclaimed by its supporters could not be realized to a large extent for three reasons: information asymmetries, in particular lack of information among low-skilled workers; lack of providers in certain regions which limits competition; and restricted potential for policy coordination due to the breakdown of links between the PES and private providers. Hipp and Warner (2008) reanalyze qualitative research on the effects of introducing vouchers both in Germany and the United States and compare the two systems. They also provide a theoretical discussion of the potential effects. They confirm the conclusions by Bruttel (2005) for Germany and show that similar problems occurred in the United States despite relatively large differences between the countries.

Rinne et al. (2013) combine matching with a difference-in-difference approach to estimate the effects of the introduction of the voucher system in 2003. They find that the effects of participating in training in terms of employment and earnings increased somewhat after the reform for skilled but not for unskilled workers. Paul et al. (2013) study the effects of awarding a voucher for the first 2 years of the new regime based on matching methods. In contrast to Rinne et al. (2013) they have data on both awarded and redeemed vouchers. They also document the strong positive selection in terms of employment outcomes (creaming). They find that awarding a voucher produced, on average, large and long-lasting negative locking-in effects on employment and no effects in the longer run. However, recipients without a vocational degree, in particular those who participated in courses that award such a degree benefited considerably in the long run. This result suggests that the strong creaming induced by the 70%-rule was actually harmful to the average effectiveness. Better targeting toward low-skilled workers could increase the average effectiveness considerably. Dörr and Strittmatter (2014) compare assignment to training and its effects on the effectiveness of training under the full-caseworker-discretion regime and the voucher regime. Based on conditional difference-in-differences approaches and decomposition methods they document how assignment changed in terms of different sets of participant characteristics as well as different program durations, and how this affected program impacts on employment and earnings. Overall they find that the prereform direct assignment regime produced more favorable program impacts in the short and medium-run. In the long run there were no statistically significant differences on average but positive effects of the voucher system for some shorter programs.

Schwerdt et al. (2012) report interesting results from a voucher experiment in Switzerland that was conducted in 2006. About 2500 participants in the Swiss Labour force survey were randomized into a treatment group that received vouchers for adult education with randomized values of roughly 200, 750, or 1500 USD which they could redeem within 6 months. The take-up rate was 18.4%. The voucher treatment increased participation rates in training by almost 13% in the treatment year. However, there were no statistically significant effects on average earnings, employment or participation in training in the subsequent year. Subsample analyses reveal, though, that low-skilled workers benefit from training, but they are least likely to participate due to positive self-selection into training. Schwerdt et al. (2012) also provide evidence for crowding-out of employer-financed training in response to the voucher program. They conclude that untargeted voucher programs are probably not an effective way to improve labor market outcomes by adult education.

Groot and Van den Brink (2010) report results from a randomized experiment conducted by Doets and Huisman (2009) in the Netherlands. It provided a group of low-skilled employed workers with ITAs of 1000 EUR. Within 3 years, training participation increased by 26%. However, Groot and Van den Brink (2010) calculate that there was a deadweight loss of about 40% due to the financing of training that would have taken place even in the absence of the ITA offer. An even higher number of about 50% is reported by Messer and Wolter (2009) for the Swiss voucher experiment. Van Wichelen (2005, 2008) even reports deadweight losses of up to 80% for a voucher program in Belgium that generously supported training of employed workers initiated by their employers.[153]

In summary, the existing literature provides no evidence for the superiority of demand-based systems over systems based on caseworker discretion. Quite the contrary, a lot of evidence suggests that self-selection into training leads to even stronger positive selection as take-up rates are considerably higher among higher-skilled workers than among low-skilled workers. One reason for this is that low-skilled workers find it particularly hard to choose among the many providers and available courses. Better targeting of vouchers to specific groups may not solve the problem entirely because take-up would

---

[153] See De Grier (2008) for a description of the Belgian program.

still be an issue. There is also no evidence for increased training quality measured by participants' labor market outcomes after participation speaking against one of the main arguments of supporters of training vouchers and ITAs. Moreover, demand-based systems weaken the link between those who issue vouchers and training providers thereby reducing the potential of policy coordination and giving providers the opportunity to cream participants in order to maximize placement rates. Reduced control over the choice of training that is supported by public funds also bears the potential for higher deadweight loss due to the crowding-out of training that would otherwise be funded by other sources. However, all of this does not mean that appropriately designed demand-based systems do not lead to superior outcomes. The existing evidence to date rather suggests that the design issue is harder than initially thought.

12. CONCLUSION

As we have seen in this chapter, government-sponsored training for adults is an important policy instrument to alleviate poverty, combat unemployment and manage structural change. Governments' financial investments in these programs are substantial, especially those of Scandinavian countries. So it is crucial to determine whether or not these programs are effective.

The empirical evidence of program effectiveness for the six countries this chapter focuses on mainly comes from studies of unemployed workers, who are the main target group for these programs. It finds that the effectiveness of labor market training programs for the unemployed depends on economic conditions and the institutional features of the program. Program effectiveness is positively related to the unemployment rate at the start of the program and negatively related to the incentive to use training as a means to renew benefit eligibility. Most programs exhibit negative locking-in effects in the short run, the magnitude and duration of which depends on average program duration. Also studies find that the possibility of labor market training for the unemployed increases exit rates from unemployment before the actual start of the program due to a threat effect. Empirical evidence furthermore finds that general training at the compulsory and upper secondary levels, which is usually not limited to unemployed workers, mostly succeeds in raising participants' earnings, but it can take a relatively long time for these effects to materialize. Extensive education programs for adults, however, can have economically important spillover effects on the employment and wages of nonparticipants, which raises concerns about the results from microeconometric studies that are based on the validity of the stable unit treatment value assumption that does not allow for such effects.

As regards effect heterogeneity, programs that involve on-the-job training and are thus more similar to regular jobs, on average perform better than vocational classroom training. Studies also find that programs are more effective for the unemployed with less favorable employment outcomes, especially with long elapsed unemployment duration.

There are also differences in program effects by gender and age. Many studies, especially for the United States and central Europe, find that training is most effective for adult women, somewhat effective for adult men, and not very effective (or, in some cases, actually harmful) for youth. Since heterogeneity matters it is important for empirical researchers to use methods that allow for arbitrary heterogeneity in effects and test for effect heterogeneity. If the aim is to maximize average program impacts then effect heterogeneity gives rise to a potential scope for improvement in matching participants to training.

The findings from the studies summarized in this chapter are largely in line with the results from a recent meta-study by Card et al. (2010). They analyze 199 impact estimates from 97 studies of active labor market policies between 1995 and 2007 that span 26 countries. Their findings can be summarized as follows: The distribution of medium and long-term outcomes is more favorable than the distribution of short-term outcomes. Often, meaningful positive effects only occur after 2–3 years. The latter are relatively unfavorable in the German-speaking countries but relatively favorable in the Anglo countries, which can be explained by heterogeneity in program types. Moreover, studies that use registered unemployment as their outcome tend to find more positive results than studies that directly use employment due to effects on labor force participation. Card et al. (2010) do not find systematic differences between experimental and nonexperimental studies, suggesting that the research designs used in recent nonexperimental studies are not systematically biased compared to an experimental benchmark.

One important conclusion from the existing evidence is that if empirical analyses find no or negative overall net benefits, governments should not necessarily eliminate training programs. This is because effect heterogeneity with respect to both participant characteristics and different types of programs means that some programs may lead to positive net benefits for some groups of unemployed. Moreover, many existing empirical analyses ignore possible threat effects that positively affect cost-effectiveness. Furthermore, there are cases where positive long-term effects on employment offset initial negative employment effects, but they require a sufficiently long observation period to be detected. Additionally, there is more and more evidence for longer-term positive effects on postunemployment outcomes such as employment stability even if there are no significantly positive effects on exit from unemployment or unemployment duration. However, many studies also find that more frequent interactions with caseworkers, monitoring and benefit sanctions are more effective in reducing unemployment duration than participation in other activation measures.

Turning to the empirical evidence on matching participants to training programs, there is no evidence for the superiority of demand-based systems over systems based on caseworker discretion. Demand-based systems also weaken the link between those who issue vouchers and training providers thereby reducing the potential of policy coordination and giving providers the opportunity to cream participants in order to maximize placement rates. The preponderance of evidence suggests that self-selection into training leads to even stronger positive selection as take-up rates are considerably higher among higher-skilled workers than among low-skilled workers. Reducing control over the choice of training that is government supported also runs the risk of higher deadweight loss due to the crowding-out of training that would otherwise be funded by other sources. Based on extant empirical studies, the issue of training program design has proven a much more difficult problem than was originally thought.

On the methodological front, as mentioned above it is important to use methods that allow for arbitrary effect heterogeneity and to check for effect heterogeneity by participant characteristics and different types of programs. Also, researchers need to pay more attention to the validity of the stable unit treatment value assumption and, if possible, check possible violations. The possibility of threat effects raises concerns about the validity of the no-anticipation assumption that underlies the timing-of-events approach and is inherent in most other approaches. These should be addressed explicitly. Furthermore, the dynamics inherent in the assignment process are often ignored or not appropriately accounted for by researchers. The existing evidence suggests that studies that account for these dynamics tend to yield somewhat more favorable results. Finally, regression discontinuity designs, which typically provide highly credible estimates, are strongly under-used in the evaluation of causal effect of government-sponsored training for adults. However, it would be easy enough to embed them in existing institutions, for example, by using scores for training needs, expected program impact, or the risk of becoming long-term unemployed in combination with some threshold value for program assignment.

Future research should center on the following issues: First, more evidence on causal impacts is needed for participants in training who are not unemployed or not at immediate risk of becoming unemployed, especially if programs have the objective of alleviating poverty or managing structural change. Second, more knowledge is needed about the effects of firm-provided training or more generally subsidized training for employed workers. Third, we agree with Card et al. (2010) that researchers should more thoroughly investigate welfare-relevant outcomes such as earnings and hours of work. Fourth, the literature should spend less time on generating impact estimates for programs that will never be abolished for political reasons and more time on generating knowledge about how to run these programs better. Fifth, more work is needed on the optimal design of the assignment process of programs to participants. The effects of institutional features, caseworker characteristics and strategies as well as different features of demand-based systems are not sufficiently well-understood. More rigorous evaluations of causal effects are needed. Sixth, researchers need to invest more in developing methods to appropriately account for the dynamics inherent in the assignment process. Seventh, we need more research that has as its primary goal estimating the general equilibrium effects of training, which also requires more work on methods to appropriately identify such effects. Eighth, more work would be desirable on the optimal duration and sequence of training as well as on better understanding the role of economic conditions at the time program participation takes place and thereafter. Finally, rigorous cost-benefit analyses are mainly limited to the United States, often due to the reluctance of governments to provide cost data, especially in many European countries. However, it is only possible to assess the cost-effectiveness of the billions of dollars spent on government-sponsored training for adults if researchers can and will take into account all potential benefits and costs of these programs.

ACKNOWLEDGMENTS

We thank Lars Skipper, the editors and participants in the 2014 CESifo education group meetings for helpful comments.

REFERENCES

Abbring, J.H., Heckman, J.J., 2007. Econometric evaluation of social programs, part III: distributional treatment effects, dynamic treatment effects, dynamic discrete choice, and general equilibrium policy evaluation. In: Heckman, J., Leamer, E. (Eds.), In: Handbook of Econometrics, vol. 6B. Elsevier, Amsterdam, pp. 5145–5303.

Abbring, J.H., van den Berg, G.J., 2003. The nonparametric identification of treatment effects in duration models. Econometrica 71 (5), 1491–1517.

Abramovsky, L., Battistin, E., Fitzsimons, E., Goodman, A., Simpson, H., 2011. Providing employers with incentives to train low-skilled workers: evidence from the UK employer training pilots. J. Labor Econ. 29 (1), 153–193.

Achatz, J., Fehr, S., Schels, B., Wolff, J., 2012. Ein-Euro-Jobs, betriebliche und schulische Trainingsmaßnahmen: Wovon junge Arbeitslose im SGB II am meisten profitieren. IAB-Kurzbericht Nr. 6/2012.

Adams, L., Oldfield, K., Riley, C., Skone James, A., 2012. Destinations of Jobseeker's Allowance, Income Support and Employment and Support Allowance Leavers 2011: Department for Work and Pensions, Research Report No. 791.

Adda, J., Costa Dias, M., Meghir, C., Sianesi, B., 2007. Labour Market Programmes and Labour Market Outcomes: A Study of the Swedish Active Labour Market Interventions. Institute for Labour Market Policy Evaluation, IFAU Working Paper No. 27.

Ainsworth, P., Hillmore, A., Marlow, S., Prince, S., 2012. Early Impacts of Work Experience. Department for Work and Pensions, London.

Albrecht, J., van den Berg, G.J., Vroman, S., 2005. The Knowledge Lift: The Swedish Adult Education Program That Aimed to Eliminate Low Worker Skill Levels: IZA Discussion Paper No. 1503.

Albrecht, J., van den Berg, G.J., Vroman, S., 2009. The aggregate labor market effects of the Swedish knowledge lift program. Rev. Econ. Dyn. 12 (1), 129–146.

Anderson, M., 2008. Multiple inference and gender differences in the effects of early intervention: a reevaluation of the Abecedarian, Perry Preschool, and early training projects. J. Am. Stat. Assoc. 103 (484), 1481–1495.

Anderson, P.M., Meyer, B.D., 2003. Unemployment insurance takeup rates and the after-tax value of benefits. Q. J. Econ. 112 (3), 913–937.

Andersson Joona, P., Nekby, L., 2009. TIPping the Scales Towards Greater Employment Chances? Evaluation of a Trial Introduction Program (TIP) for Newly-Arrived Immigrants Based on Random Program Assignment. IZA Discussion Paper No. 4072.

Andersson, F., Holzer, H., Lane, J., Rosenblum, D., Smith, J., 2013. Does Federally-Funded Job Training Work? Nonexperimental Estimates of WIA Training Impacts Using Longitudinal Data on Workers and Firms. NBER Working Paper No. 19446.

Andrén, T., Andrén, D., 2006. Assessing the employment effects of vocational training using a one-factor model. Appl. Econ. 38 (21), 2469–2486.

Andrén, T., Gustafsson, B., 2004. Income effects from labor market training programs in Sweden during the 1980s and 1990s. Int. J. Manpow. 25 (8), 688–713.

Angrist, J.D., Pischke, J.S., 2009. Mostly Harmless Econometrics: An Empiricist's Companion. Princeton University Press, Princeton, NJ.

Arbetsförmedlingen, 2013. Arbetsmaknadspolitiska Program – Årsrapport 2012.

Arni, P., 2014. Fitting Expectations? The Impact of Caseworker's Beliefs on Treatment Allocation and Outcomes in Unemployment Insurance – A Field Experiment. Mimeo, IZA, Bonn, Germany.

Arni, P., Lalive, R., van den Berg, G.J., 2015. Treatment versus Regime Effects of Carrots and Sticks. IZA Discussion Paper No. 9457.

Ashenfelter, O., 1978. Estimating the effect of training programs on earnings. Rev. Econ. Stat. 60 (1), 47–57.

Ashenfelter, O., 1983. Determining participation in income-tested social programmes. J. Am. Stat. Assoc. 78 (383), 517–525.

Ashenfelter, O., Card, D., 1985. Using the longitudinal structure of earnings to estimate the effect of training programs. Rev. Econ. Stat. 67 (4), 648–660.

Åslund, O., Johansson, P., 2011. Virtues of SIN can intensified public efforts help disadvantaged immigrants? Eval. Rev. 35 (4), 399–427.

Athey, S., Imbens, G.W., 2006. Nonlinear difference-in-differences. Econometrica 74 (2), 431–497.

Ba, B., Ham, J., LaLonde, R., Xianghong, L., 2015. Allowing for Forward Looking Behavior when Estimating Dynamic Treatment Effects. National University of Singapore, Singapore. Unpublished manuscript.

Bahu, M., 2014. Les contrats d'aide à l'emploi en 2012: Des entrées en hausse et des contrats toujours ciblés sur les publics en difficulté. Dares Analyses No. 021.

Barnow, B., 1987. The impact of CETA programs on earnings: a review of the literature. J. Hum. Resour. 22 (2), 157–193.

Barnow, B., 2000. Vouchers for federal training programs. In: Steuerle, C., Doorn Ooms, V., Peterson, G., Reischauer, R. (Eds.), Vouchers and the Provision of Public Services. Brookings Institution Press, Washington, DC, pp. 224–250.

Barnow, B., 2009. Vouchers in US vocational training programs: an overview of what we have learned. J. Labour Market Res. 42 (1), 71–84.

Barnow, B., Smith, J., 2015. Means-Tested Training Programs. University of Michigan, Ann Arbor. Unpublished manuscript.

Beale, I., Bloss, C., Thomas, A., 2008. The longer-term impact of the New Deal for Young People. Department for Work and Pensions, Working Paper No. 23.

Becker, G., 1993. Human Capital: A Theoretical and Empirical Analysis with Special Reference to Education. University of Chicago Press, Chicago.

Behaghel, L., Crépon, B., Gurgand, M., 2012. Private and Public Provision of Counseling to Job-Seekers: Evidence from a Large Controlled Experiment. IZA Discussion Paper No. 6518.

Behncke, S., Frölich, M., Lechner, M., 2007. Abschlussbericht zum Pilotprojekt; Statistisch Assistierte Programmselektion (SAPS). Abschlussbericht im Auftrag des SECO.

Behncke, S., Frölich, M., Lechner, M., 2009. Targeting labour market programmes – results from a randomized experiment. Swiss J. Econ. Statist. 145 (3), 221–268.

Behncke, S., Frölich, M., Lechner, M., 2010a. Unemployed and their caseworkers: should they be friends or foes? J. R. Stat. Soc. A. Stat. Soc. 173 (1), 67–92.

Behncke, S., Frölich, M., Lechner, M., 2010b. A caseworker like me – does the similarity between the unemployed and their caseworkers increase job placements? Econ. J. 120 (549), 1430–1459.

Bell, S., Orr, L., 2002. Screening (and creaming?) applicants to job training programs: the AFDC homemaker home health aide demonstration. Labour Econ. 9 (2), 279–301.

Bell, S., Orr, L., Blomquist, J., Cain, G., 1995. Program applicants as a comparison group in evaluating training programs: theory and a test. W.E. Upjohn Institute for Employment Research, Kalamazoo, MI.

Bellis, A., Sigala, M., Dewson, S., 2011. Employer Engagement and Jobcentre Plus. Department for Work and Pensions: Research Report No. 742.

Benítez-Silva, H., Buchinsky, M., Chan, H.M., Cheidvasser, S., Rust, J., 2004. How large is the bias in self-reported disability? J. Appl. Econ. 19 (6), 649–670.

Berger, M.C., Black, D.A., Smith, J., 2001. Evaluating profiling as a means of allocating government services. In: Lechner, M., Pfeiffer, F. (Eds.), Econometric Evaluation of Active Labour Market Policies. Physica, Heidelberg, pp. 59–84.

Bernhard, S., Kopf, E., 2014. Courses or individual counselling: does job search assistance work? Appl. Econ. 46 (27), 3261–3273.

Bernhard, S., Kruppe, T., 2010. Vermittlungsgutscheine für Arbeitslose – Oft ausgegeben und selten eingelöst. IAB-Kurzbericht 21/2010.

Bernhard, S., Kruppe, T., 2012. Effectiveness of further vocational training in Germany: empirical findings for persons receiving means-tested unemployment benefit. Schmollers Jahr. 132 (4), 501–526.

Bertanha, M., 2014. Regression Discontinuity Design with Many Thresholds. Stanford University, Stanford. Unpublished manuscript.

Biewen, M., Fitzenberger, B., Osikominu, A., Paul, M., 2014. The effectiveness of public sponsored training revisited: the importance of data and methodological choices. J. Labor Econ. 32 (4), 837–897.

Bivand, P., Brooke, B., Jenkins, S., Simmonds, D., 2006. Evaluation of StepUP Pilot: Final Report: Department for Work and Pensions, Research Report No. 337.

Black, D.A., Plesca, M., Smith, J.A., Shannon, S., 2003. Profiling UI Claimants to Allocate Reemployment Services: Evidence and Recommendations for States: Final Report to United States Department of Labor.

Black, D., Galdo, J., Smith, J., 2007a. Evaluating the Bias of the Regression Discontinuity Design Using Experimental Data. University of Chicago. Unpublished manuscript.

Black, D., Galdo, J., Smith, J., 2007b. Evaluating the worker profiling and reemployment services system using a regression discontinuity design. Am. Econ. Rev. Pap. Proc. 97 (2), 104–107.

Blank, R., Ruggles, P., 1996. When do women use AFDC & Food Stamps? The dynamics of eligibility vs participation. J. Hum. Resour. 31 (1), 57–89.

Blank, D., Heald, L., Fagnoni, C., 2011. An overview of WIA. In: Besharov, D., Cottingham, P. (Eds.), The Workforce Investment Act. Implementation Experiences and Evaluation Findings. W.E. Upjohn Institute for Employment Research, Kalamazoo, MI, pp. 49–78.

Blasco, S., Rosholm, M., 2011. The Impact of Active Labour Market Policy on Post-Unemployment Outcomes: Evidence from a Social Experiment in Denmark. IZA Discussion Paper No. 5631.

Blasco, S., Crépon, B., Kamionka, T., 2012. The Effects of On-the-job and Out-of-Employment Training Programmes on Labor Market Histories. CEPREMAP No. 1210.

Bloom, H., Orr, L., Cave, G., Bell, S., Doolittle, F., 1993. The National JTPA Study: Title II-A Impacts on Earnings and Employment at 18 Months. Abt Associates, Bethesda, MD.

Bloom, H., Orr, L., Bell, S., Cave, G., Doolittle, F., Lin, W., Bos, J., 1997. The benefits and costs of JTPA title II-A programs: findings from the national job training partnership act study. J. Hum. Resour. 32 (3), 549–576.

Bloom, H., Hill, C., Riccio, J., 2003. Linking program implementation and effectiveness: lessons from a pooled sample of welfare-to-work experiments. J. Policy Anal. Manage. 22 (4), 551–575.

Blundell, R., Costa-Dias, M., 2009. Alternative approaches to evaluation in empirical microeconomics. J. Hum. Resour. 44 (3), 565–640.

Blundell, R., Costa-Dias, M., Meghir, C., van Reenen, J., 2004. Evaluating the employment impact of a mandatory job search program. J. Eur. Econ. Assoc. 2 (4), 569–606.

Blundell, R., Dearden, L., Sianesi, B., 2005. Evaluating the effect of education on earnings: models, methods and results from the national child development survey. J. R. Stat. Soc. A. Stat. Soc. 168 (3), 473–512.

Borowczyk-Martins, D., Jolivet, G., Postel-Vinay, F., 2013. Accounting for endogeneity in matching function estimation. Rev. Econ. Dyn. 16 (3), 440–451.

Bound, J., 1989. The health and earnings of rejected disability applicants. Am. Econ. Rev. 79 (3), 482–503.

Bound, J., Brown, C., Mathiowetz, N., 2001. Measurement error in survey data. In: Heckman, J., Leamer, E. (Eds.), In: Handbook of Econometrics, vol. 5. North-Holland, Amsterdam, pp. 3705–3843.

Bradley, D., 2013. The Workforce Investment Act and the One-Stop Delivery System. Congressional Research Service, Washington, DC.

Brown, A., Koettl, J., 2012. Active Labor Market Programs: Employment Gain or Fiscal Drain?. IZA Discussion Paper No. 6880.

Brown, C., Hamilton, J., Medoff, J., 1990. Employers Large and Small. Harvard University Press, Cambridge, MA.

Bruttel, O., 2005. Delivering active labour market policy through vouchers: experiences with training vouchers in Germany. Int. Rev. Adm. Sci. 71 (3), 391–404.

Bundesagentur für Arbeit, 2013a. Arbeitsstatistik 2012 – Jahreszahlen. Amtliche Nachrichten der Bundesagentur für Arbeit, 60. Jahrgang, Sondernummer 1.

Bundesagentur für Arbeit, 2013b. Tabellenanhang Aktivierung in den Rechtskreisen SGB II und SGB III (2. Aktualisierung). http://statistik.arbeitsagentur.de/nn_4236 /Statischer-Content/Grundlagen/ Methodenberichte/Foerderstatistik/Methodenberichte-Foerderstatistik.html. retrieved August 7, 2014, 3:45 pm.

Bundesamt für Migration und Flüchtlinge, 2013a. Das Bundesamt in Zahlen 2012 – Asyl. Migration und Integration, Nürnberg.

Bundesamt für Migration und Flüchtlinge, 2013b. Berufsbezogene Deutschförderung: Das ESF-BAMF-Programm. Köln.

Bundesamt für Migration und Flüchtlinge, 2014. Das Bundesamt in Zahlen 2013 – Asyl. Migration und Integration, Nürnberg.

Bundesamt für Statistik, 2013. Meister-BAföG 2012: Zahl der Geförderten steigt weiter. https://www.destatis.de/ DE/PresseService/Presse/Pressemitteilungen/2013/07/PD13 _227_214 pdf. pdf?__blob=publicationFile. retrieved August 7, 2014, 3:25 pm.

Bundesministerium für Bildung und Forschung, 2013. Große Nachfrage nach der Bildungsprämie. http:// www.bmbf.de/_media/press/Pm1002-113.pdf. retrieved August 7, 2014, 3:56 pm.

Bundesministerium für Bildung und Forschung, 2014. 280.000 neue Bildungsgutscheine. http://www. bmbf.de/_media/press/PM0522-046.pdf. retrieved August 6, 2014, 5:04 pm.

Bushway, S., Johnson, B., Slocum, L.A., 2007. Is the magic still there? The use of the Heckman two-step correction for selection bias in criminology. J. Quant. Criminol. 23 (2), 151–178.

Busso, M., DiNardo, J., McCrary, J., 2014. New evidence on the finite sample properties of propensity score reweighting and matching estimators. Rev. Econ. Stat. 96 (5), 885–897.

Büttner, T., 2008. Ankündigungseffekt oder Maßnahmewirkung? Eine Evaluation von Trainingsmaßnahmen zur Überprüfung der Verfügbarkeit. J. Labour Market Res. 1/2008, 25–40.

Cahuc, P., Le Barbanchon, T., 2010. Labor market policy evaluation in equilibrium: some lessons of the job search and matching model. Labour Econ. 17 (1), 196–205.

Caliendo, M., Mahlstedt, R., Mitnik, O., 2014. Unobservable, but Unimportant? The Influence of Personality Traits (and Other Usually Unobserved Variables) for the Evaluation of Labor Market Policies. IZA Discussion Paper No. 8337.

Calmfors, L., Forslund, A., Hemström, M., 2002. Does Active Labour Market Policy Work? Lessons from the Swedish Experiences. Institute for Labour Market Policy Evaluation, IFAU Working Paper No. 2002:4.

Calónico, S., Smith, J., 2015. The Women of the National Supported Work Demonstration. University of Michigan, Ann Arbor, MI. Unpublished manuscript.

Cameron, C., Trivedi, P., 2005. Microeconometrics: Methods and Applications. Cambridge University Press, Cambridge.

Card, D., 2001. Estimating the return to schooling: progress on some persistent econometric problems. Econometrica 69 (5), 1127–1160.

Card, D., McCall, B.P., 1996. Is Workers' Compensation covering uninsured medical costs? Evidence from the "Monday Effect" Ind. Labor Relat. Rev. 49 (4), 690–706.

Card, D., Shore-Sheppard, L.D., 2004. Using discontinuous eligibility rules to identify the effects of the federal medicaid expansions on low-income children. Rev. Econ. Stat. 86 (3), 752–766.

Card, D., Sullivan, D., 1988. Measuring the effects of CETA participation on movements in and out of employment. Econometrica 56 (3), 497–530.

Card, D., Kluve, J., Weber, A., 2010. Active labour market policy evaluations: a meta-analysis. Econ. J. 120 (548), F452–F477.

Carling, K., Richardson, K., 2004. The relative efficiency of labor market programs: Swedish experience from the 1990s. Labour Econ. 11 (3), 335–354.

Cavaco, S., Fougère, D., Pouget, J., 2013. Estimating the effect of a retraining program on the re-employment rate of displaced workers. Empir. Econ. 44 (1), 261–287.

Cavan, N., 2014. La formation professionnelle des personnes en recherche d'emploi en 2012: hausse de 6% des entrées en formation. Dares Analyses No. 055.

Cave, G., Bos, H., Doolittle, F., Toussaint, C., 1993. JOBSTART: Final Report on a Program for School Dropouts. MDRC, New York, NY.

CEDEFOP, 2000. Demand-Side Financing – A Focus on Vouchers in Post-Compulsory Education and Training: Discussion Paper and Case Studies. CEDEFOP European Centre for the Development of Vocational Training, Thessaloniki.

CEDEFOP, 2009. Individual Learning Accounts. CEDEFOP European Centre for the Development of Vocational Training Panorama Series No. 163.

Chabé-Ferret, S., 2014. Symmetric Difference in Differences Dominates Matching in a Realistic Selection Model. Toulouse School of Economics. Unpublished manuscript.

Clausen, J., Heinesen, E., Hummelgaard, H., Husted, L., Rosholm, M., 2009. The effect of integration policies on the time until regular employment of newly arrived immigrants: evidence from Denmark. Labour Econ. 16 (4), 409–417.

Coalition, National Skills, 2014. Side-by-Side Comparison of Occupational Training and Adult Education & Family Literacy Provisions in the Workforce Investment Act (WIA) and the Workforce Innovation and Opportunity Act (WIOA), http://www.nationalskillscoalition.org/resources/publications/file/2014-10_WIOA-Side-by-Side.pdf.

Cohen-Goldner, S., Eckstein, Z., 2008. Labor mobility of immigrants: training experience, language, and opportunities. Int. Econ. Rev. 49 (3), 837–872.

Cohen-Goldner, S., Eckstein, Z., 2010. Estimating the return to training and occupational experience: the case of female immigrants. J. Econ. 156 (1), 86–105.

Collins, B., 2012. Trade Adjustment Assistance for Workers. Congressional Research Service, Washington, DC.

Colpitts, T., 2002. Targeting reemployment services in Canada: the service and outcome measurement system (SOMS) experience. In: Eberts, R.W., O'Leary, C.J., Wandner, S.A. (Eds.), Targeting Employment Services. W.E. Upjohn Institute for Employment Research, Kalamazoo, MI, pp. 283–301.

Cook, T., 2008. Waiting for life to arrive': a history of the regression-discontinuity design in psychology, statistics and economics. J. Econ. 142 (2), 636–654.

Cook, T., Steiner, P., Pohl, S., 2009. Assessing how bias reduction is influenced by covariate choice, unreliability and data analytic mode: an analysis of different kinds of within-study comparisons in different substantive domains. Multivar. Behav. Res. 44 (6), 828–847.

Cook, P., Kang, S., Braga, A., Ludwig, J., O'Brien, M., 2015. An experimental evaluation of a comprehensive employment oriented prisoner re-entry program. J. Quant. Criminol. 31, 355–382.

Couch, K., 1992. New evidence on the long-term effects of employment training programs. J. Labor Econ. 10 (4), 380–388.

Coulter, A., Day, N., Howat, N., Romanou, E., Coleman, N., 2012. The Jobcentre Plus Offer: Findings from the First Year of the Evaluation: Department for Work and Pensions, Research Report No. 814.

Crépon, B., Ferracci, M., Jolivet, G., van den Berg, G.J., 2009. Active labor market policy effects in a dynamic setting. J. Eur. Econ. Assoc. 7 (2–3), 595–605.

Crépon, B., Ferracci, M., Fougère, D., 2012. Training the unemployed in France: How does it affect unemployment duration and recurrence? Ann. Econ. Stat. 107 (108), 175–199.

Crépon, B., Duflo, E., Gurgand, M., Rathelot, R., Zamora, P., 2013a. Do labor market policies have displacement effects? Evidence from a clustered randomized experiment. Q. J. Econ. 128 (2), 531–580.

Crépon, B., Ferracci, M., Jolivet, G., van den Berg, G.J., 2013b. Information Shocks and the Empirical Evaluation of Training Programs During Unemployment Spells, Earlier Version: Analyzing the Anticipation of Treatments Using Data on Notification Dates. IZA Discussion Paper No. 5265.

Crépon, B., Gurgand, M., Kamionka, T., Lequien, L., 2013c. Is Counselling Welfare Recipients Cost-Effective? Lessons from a Random Experiment. CREST Série des Documents de Travail No. 2013-01.

Currie, J., 2006. The take-up of social benefits. In: Auerbach, A., Card, D., Quigley, J. (Eds.), Poverty, The Distribution of Income, and Public Policy. Russell Sage, New York, pp. 80–148.

Currie, J., Gruber, J., 1996. Health insurance eligibility, utilization of medical care, and child health. Q. J. Econ. 111 (2), 431–466.

Dahlberg, M., Forslund, A., 2005. Direct displacement effects of labour market programmes. Scand. J. Econ. 107 (3), 475–494.

Dahlby, B., 2008. The Marginal Social Cost of Public Funds. MIT Press, Cambridge, MA.

Danmarks Evalueringsinstitut, 2005. Forberedende voksenundervisning. Kvantitativ undersøgelse blandt deltagere. Availabke at: www.eva.dk/projekter/2004/evaluering-af-forberedende-voksenundervisning-fvu/evaluering-af-forberedende-voksenundervisning-fvu/evaluering-af-forberedende-voksenundervisning-fvu/download.

Daponte, B., Sanders, S., Taylor, L., 1999. Why do low-income households not use food stamps? Evidence from an experiment. J. Hum. Resour. 34 (3), 612–628.

Davidson, C., Woodbury, S., 1993. The Displacement effect of re-employment bonus programs. J. Labor Econ. 11 (4), 575–605.

De Giorgi, G., 2008. Long-term Effects of a Mandatory Multistage Program: The New Deal for Young People in the UK. Institute for Fiscal Studies, IFS Working Paper No. WP05/08.

De Giorgi, G., 2011. What Works for the Unemployed: Evidence from the New Deal in the UK. Stanford University, Stanford Unpublished manuscript.

De Grier, H.G., 2008. Training vouchers and active labour market policies: an easy or uneasy marriage? In: Pennings, F., Konijn, Y., Veldman, A. (Eds.), Social Responsibility in Labor Relations: European and Comparative Perspectives. Wolters Kluwer (Law & Business), Alphen aan den Rijn, pp. 379–390.

Deaton, A., 2010. Instruments, randomization and learning about development. J. Econ. Lit. 48 (2), 424–455.

DEETYA Department of Employment, Education, Training and Youth Affairs, 1998. The early identification of jobseekers who are at greatest risk of long-term unemployment in Australia. In: OECD, (Ed.), Early Identification of Jobseekers at Risk of Long-Term Unemployment: The Role of Profiling. OECD, Paris, pp. 31–61.

Dehejia, R., Wahba, S., 1999. Causal effects in nonexperimental studies: reevaluating the evaluation of training programs. J. Am. Stat. Assoc. 94 (448), 1053–1062.

Dehejia, R., Wahba, S., 2002. Propensity score matching methods for non-experimental causal studies. Rev. Econ. Stat. 84 (1), 151–161.

DeLuna, X., Forslund, A., Liljeberg, L., 2008. Effekter av yrkesinriktad arbetsmarknadsutbildning för deltagare under perioden 2002–04: Institute for Labour Market Policy Evaluation, IFAU Report No. 2008:1.

Department for Employment and Learning, 2014. New Deal 25+. Department for Employment and Learning, London.

Department for Work and Pensions, 2012a. Sector-Based Work Academies. Department for Work and Pensions, London.

Department for Work and Pensions, 2012b. Support for the Very Long Unemployed Trailblazer: Preliminary Analysis of Benefit Impacts. Department for Work and Pensions, London.

Department for Work and Pensions, 2014a. Youth Contract Official Statistics. Department for Work and Pensions, London.

Department for Work and Pensions, 2014b. Mandatory Programmes Official Statistics. Department for Work and Pensions, London.

Dickinson, K., Johnson, T., West, R., 1987. An analysis of the sensitivity of quasi-experimental net impact estimates of CETA programs. Eval. Rev. 11 (4), 452–472.

Dickinson, K., Kreutzer, S., Decker, P., 1997. Evaluation of Worker Profiling and Reemployment Services System. USA Department of Labor, Washington, DC.

Djebbari, H., Smith, J., 2008. Heterogeneous impacts in PROGRESA. J. Econ. 145 (1), 64–80.

Doets, C., Huisman, T., 2009. De effectiviteit van een individuele leerrekening. ECBO Expertisecentrum Beroepsonderwijs, Den Bosch.

Dohmen, D., Cleuvers, B.A., Fuchs, K., Günzel, J., Knauf, A., Kunzler, A., Reiss, M., Russo, S., Tirschmann, B., 2007. Current trends in the demand-led financing of further training in Europe – A synopsis. FiBS-Forum No. 40.

Dolton, P., O'Neill, D., 1996. Unemployment duration and the restart effect: some experimental evidence. Econ. J. 106 (435), 387–400.

Dolton, P., O'Neill, D., 2002. The long run effects of unemployment monitoring and work search programs: experimental evidence from the United Kingdom. J. Labor Econ. 20 (2), 381–403.

Dolton, P., Smith, J., 2011. The Impact of the UK New Deal for Lone Parents on Benefit Receipt. IZA Discussion Paper No. 5491.

Doolittle, F., Traeger, L., 1990. Implementing the National JTPA Study. MDRC, New York, NY.

Dörr, A., Strittmatter, A., 2014. Assignment Mechanisms, Selection Criteria, and the Effectiveness of Training Program. Univeristy of St. Gallen, Department of Economics Discussion Paper No. 2014-21.

Dorsett, R., 2006. The new deal for young people: effect on the labour market status of young men. Labour Econ. 13 (3), 405–422.

Eberts, R., O'Leary, C., 2002. A Frontline Decision Support System for Georgia Career Centers. W.E. Upjohn Institute for Employment Research, Working Paper No. 02-84.

Eberts, R., O'Leary, C., Wandner, S., 2002. Targeting Employment Services. W.E. Upjohn Institute for Employment Research, Kalamazoo, MI.

Eberwein, C., Ham, J., LaLonde, R., 1997. The impact of classroom training on the employment histories of disadvantaged women: evidence from experimental data. Rev. Econ. Stud. 64 (4), 655–682.

Egger, D., Partner, A.G., 2006. Wirkungsevalution der öffentlichen Arbeitsverwaltung – Evaluationsbericht. SECO Publikation Arbeitsmarktpolitik No. 18.

Egger, D., Partner, A.G., 2013. Detailanalyse der Unternehmensprozesse, Zuständigkeiten, Anreiz- und Führungssysteme der Regionalen Arbeitsvermittlungszentren. SECO Publikation Arbeitsmarktpolitik No. 33.

Ehrenberg, R.G., Smith, R.S., 2011. Modern Labor Economics: Theory and Public Policy, 11th ed. Pearson Addison Wesley, New York.

Ekspertgruppen om udredning af den aktive beskæftigelsesindsats, 2014. Veje til job – en arbejdsmarkedsind sats med mening. Available at: bm.dk/~/media/BEM/Files/Dokumenter/Pressemeddelelser/2014/Carsten%20Koch/Carsten%20Koch%20udvalget%20WEB%20pdf.ashx.

Elbers, C., Ridder, G., 1982. True and spurious duration dependence: the identifiability of the proportional hazard model. Rev. Econ. Stud. 49 (3), 403–409.

Ellis, N., 2001. Individual training accounts under the Workforce Investment Act of 1998: is choice a good thing? Geo. J. Pov. Law Pol. 8 (1), 235–256.

European Commission, 2011. Organisation of the education system in France 2009/2010. http://estudandoeducacao.files.wordpress.com/2011/05/franc3a7a.pdf.

Eyster, L., Smith Nightengale, D., Barnow, B., O'Brien, C., Trutko, J., Kuehn, D., 2010. Implementation and Early Training Outcomes of the High Growth Job Training Initiative. Final Report. Urban Institute, Washington, DC.

Farber, H.S., 1999. Alternative and part-time employment arrangements as a response to job loss. J. Labor Econ. 17 (4), 142–169.

Ferber, R., Hirsch, W., 1981. Social Experimentation and Economic Policy (Cambridge Surveys of Economic Literature). Cambridge University Press, New York, NY.

Ferracci, M., Jolivet, G., van den Berg, G.J., 2014. Evidence of Treatment Spillovers Within Markets. Rev. Econ. Stat. December 2014, 96 (5), 812–823.

Finansministeriet, 2014a. Finanslov for finansåret 2014. Tekst og anmærkninger (ajourført). § 20 Undervisningsministeriet. Available at: www.fm.dk/publikationer/2014/finanslov-for-finansaaret-2014/~/media/Publikationer/Imported/2014/AFL14/Finanslov%2020_WEB.pdf.

Finansministeriet, 2014b. Finanslov for finansåret 2014. Tekst og anmærkninger (ajourført). § 17 Beskæftigelsesministeriet. Available at: http://www.fm.dk/publikationer/2014/finanslov-for-finansaaret-2014/~/media/Publikationer/Imported/2014/AFL14/Finanslov%2017_WEB.pdf.

Fisher, R., 1935. The Design of Experiments. Oliver and Boyd, Edinburgh.

Fitzenberger, B., Speckesser, S., 2007. Employment effects of the provision of specific professional skills and techniques in Germany. Empir. Econ. 32 (2), 529–573.

Fitzenberger, B., Osikominu, A., Völter, R., 2008. Get training or wait? Long-run employment effects of training programs for the unemployed in West Germany. Ann. Econ. Stat. 91 (92), 321–355.

Fitzenberger, B., Orlanski, O., Osikominu, A., Paul, M., 2013. Déjà Vu? Short-term training in Germany 1980–1992 and 2000–2003. Empir. Econ. 44 (1), 289–328.

Fitzenberger, B., Osikominu, A., Paul, M., 2014. The Effects of Training Incidence and Duration on Labor Market Transitions. Universität Freiburg Unpublished manuscript.

Fitzenberger, B., Völter, R., 2007. Long-run effects of training programs for the unemployed in East Germany. Labour Econ. 14 (4), 730–755.

Flores-Lagunes, A., Gonzalez, A., Neumann, T., 2008. Learning but not earning? The impact of job corps training on Hispanic youth. Econ. Inq. 48 (3), 651–667.

Forslund, A., Kolm, A., 2004. Active labour market policies and real-wage determination: Swedish evidence. In: Polachek, S.W. (Ed.), In: Accounting for Worker Well-Being (Research in Labor Economics), vol. 23. Emerald Group Publishing, Bingley, pp. 381–441.

Forslund, A., Krueger, A., 1997. An evaluation of Swedish active labor market policy: new and received wisdom. In: Freeman, R., Topel, R., Swedenburg, D. (Eds.), The Welfare State in Transition: Reforming the Swedish Model. University of Chicago Press, Chicago, IL, pp. 267–298.

Forslund, A., Froberg, D., Lindqvist, L., 2004. The Swedish Activity Guarantee. OECD Social, Employment and Migration Working Papers No. 16.

Forslund, A., Fredriksson, P., Vikström, J., 2011. What active labor market policy works in a recession? Nordic Econ. Policy Rev. 1 (2011), 171–201.

Forslund, A., Liljeberg, L., von Trott zu Solz, L., 2013. Job practice: an evaluation and a comparison with vocational labour market training programmes. Institute for Evaluation of Labour Market and Education Policy, IFAU Working Paper No. 2013:6.

Fraker, T., Maynard, R., 1987. The adequacy of comparison group designs for evaluation of employment-related programs. J. Hum. Resour. 22 (2), 194–227.

Fredriksson, P., Johansson, P., 2003. Employment, Mobility, and Active Labor Market Programs. Institute for Labour Market Policy Evaluation, IFAU Working Paper No. 2003:3.

Fredriksson, P., Johansson, P., 2004. Dynamic Treatment Assignment: The Consequences for Evaluations Using Observational Data. IZA Discussion Paper No. 1062.

Fredriksson, P., Johansson, P., 2008. Dynamic treatment assignment—the consequences for evaluations using observational data. J. Bus. Econ. Stat. 26 (4), 435–445.

Frölich, M., 2004. Finite-sample properties of propensity-score matching and weighting estimators. Rev. Econ. Stat. 86 (1), 77–90.

Frölich, M., 2008. Statistical treatment choice. J. Am. Stat. Assoc. 103 (482), 547–558.

Frölich, M., Lechner, M., 2010. Exploiting regional treatment intensity for the evaluation of labor market policies. J. Am. Stat. Assoc. 105 (491), 1014–1029.

Frölich, M., Lechner, M., Steiger, H., 2003. Statistically assisted programme selection — international experiences and potential benefits for Switzerland. Swiss J. Econ. Statist. 139 (3), 311–331.

Frölich, M., Lechner, M., Behncke, S., Hammer, S., Schmidt, N., Menegale, S., Lehmann, Iten, R., 2007. Einfluss der RAV auf die Wiedereingliederung von Stellensuchenden. SECO Publikation Arbeitsmarktpolitik No. 20.

Frost, R., 1920. The Road Not Taken. In: Frost, R. (Ed.), Mountain Interval. Henry Holt, New York.

Garlick, R., 2014. Academic Peer Effects with Different Group Assignment Policies: Residential Tracking versus Random Assignment. Duke University, Durham, NC Unpublished manuscript.

Garoche, B., Roguet, B., 2014. Les dépenses en faveur de l'emploi et du marché du travail en 2011. Dares Analyses No. 018.

Gautier, P., Muller, P., Van der Klaauw, B., Rosholm, M., Svarer, M., 2012. Estimating Equilibrium Effects of Job Search Assistance. IZA Discussion Paper No. 6748.

Gelman, A., Imbens, G., 2014. Why High-order Polynomials Should Not Be Used in Regression Discontinuity Designs. NBER Working Paper No. 20405.

Gittins, J.C., 1979. Bandit processes and dynamic allocation indices. J. R. Stat. Soc. A. Stat. Soc. 41 ((2) Series B), 148–177.

Görlitz, K., 2010. The effect of subsidizing continuous training investments – evidence from German establishment data. Labour Econ. 17 (5), 789–798.

Graversen, B.K., van Ours, J.C., 2008. How to help unemployed find jobs quickly: experimental evidence from a mandatory activation program. J. Public Econ. 92 (10), 2020–2035.

Graversen, B.K., van Ours, J.C., 2011. An activation program as a stick to job finding. Labour 25 (2), 167–181.

Greenberg, D., Robins, P., 2011. Have welfare-to-work programs improved over time in putting welfare recipients to work? Ind. Labor Relat. Rev. 64 (5), 920–930.

Gregg, P., Harkness, S., Smith, S., 2009. Welfare reform and lone parents in the UK. Econ. J. 119 (535), F38–F65.

Groot, W., van den Brink, H.M., 2010. How Effective Are Training Accounts?. TIER Working Paper Series No. 10/25.

Guyatt, G., Oxman, A., Vist, G., Kunz, R., Falck-Ytter, Y., Alonso-Coello, P., Schünemann, H., 2008. GRADE: an emerging consensus on rating quality of evidence and strength of recommendations. Br. Med. J. 336 (7650), 924–926.

Hägglund, P., 2002. Första året med Aktivitetsgarantin – succé eller fiasko? Arbetsmarknad & Arbetsliv 8 (2), 95–109.

Hägglund, P., 2009. Experimental Evidence from Intensified Placement Efforts Among Unemployed in Sweden. Institute for Labour Market Policy Evaluation, IFAU Working Paper No. 2009:16.

Hägglund, P., 2011. Are there pre-programme effects of Swedish active labour market policies? Evidence from three randomised experiments. Econ. Lett. 112 (1), 91–93.

Haimmüller, J., Hofmann, B., Krug, G., Wolf, K., 2011. Do Lower Caseloads Improve the Effectiveness of Active Labor Market Policies? New Evidence from German Employment Offices. LASER Discussion Paper No. 52.

Ham, J., LaLonde, R., 1996. The effect of sample selection and initial conditions in duration models: evidence from experimental data. Econometrica 64 (1), 175–205.

Hartig, M., Jozwiak, E., Wolff, J., 2008 Trainingsmaßnahmen: Für welche unter 25-jährigen Arbeitslosengeld-II-Empfänger erhöhen sie die Beschäftigungschancen?. IAB-Forschungsbericht No. 2008/6.

Heckman, J., 1996. Comment. In: Feldstein, M., Poterba, J. (Eds.), Empirical Foundations of Household Taxation. University of Chicago Press, Chicago, pp. 32–38.

Heckman, J., 2010. Building bridges between structural and program evaluation approaches to evaluating policy. J. Econ. Lit. 48 (2), 356–398.

Heckman, J.J., Heinrich, C., Smith, J., 2002. The Performance of Performance Standards. J. Hum. Resour. 37 (4), (Autumn, 2002), 778–811.

Heckman, J., Honoré, D., 1989. The identifiability of the competing risks model. Biometrika 76 (2), 325–330.

Heckman, J., Hotz, V.J., 1989. Choosing among alternative methods of evaluating the impact of social programs: the case of manpower training. J. Am. Stat. Assoc. 84 (408), 862–874.

Heckman, J., Navarro, S., 2004. Using matching, instrumental variables, and control functions to estimate economic choice models. Rev. Econ. Stat. 86 (1), 30–57.

Heckman, J., Robb, R., 1985. Alternative methods for evaluating the impact of interventions. In: Heckman, J., Singer, B. (Eds.), Longitudinal Analysis of Labor Market Data. University of Cambridge Press for Econometric Society Monograph Series, New York, pp. 156–246.

Heckman, J., Singer, B., 1984. The identifiability of the proportional hazard model. Rev. Econ. Stud. 51 (2), 231–241.

Heckman, J., Smith, J., 1995. Assessing the case for social experiments. J. Econ. Perspect. 9 (2), 85–110.

Heckman, J., Smith, J., 1999. The pre-program earnings dip and the determinants of participation in a social program: implications for simple program evaluation strategies. Econ. J. 109 (457), 313–348.

Heckman, J., Smith, J., 2000. The sensitivity of experimental impact estimates: evidence from the national JTPA study. In: Blanchflower, D., Freeman, R. (Eds.), Youth Employment and Joblessness in Advanced Countries. University of Chicago Press, Chicago, pp. 331–356.

Heckman, J., Smith, J., 2004. The determinants of participation in a social program: Evidence from the Job Training Partnership Act. J. Labor Econ. 22 (2), 243–298.

Heckman, J., Vytlacil, E., 1998. Instrumental variables methods for the correlated random coefficient model. J. Hum. Resour. 33 (4), 974–987.

Heckman, J., Vytlacil, E., 2007a. Econometric evaluation of social programs, part I: causal models, structural models and econometric policy evaluation. In: Heckman, J., Leamer, E. (Eds.), In: Handbook of Econometrics, vol. 6. North-Holland, Amsterdam, pp. 4779–4874.

Heckman, J., Vytlacil, E., 2007b. Econometric evaluation of social programs, part II: using the marginal treatment effect to organize alternative econometric estimators to evaluate social programs and to forecast their effects in new environments. In: Heckman, J., Leamer, E. (Eds.), In: Handbook of Econometrics, vol. 6. North-Holland, Amsterdam, pp. 4875–5143.

Heckman, J., Khoo, M., Roselius, R., Smith, J., 1996. The Empirical Importance of Randomization Bias in Social Experiments: Evidence from the National JTPA Study. University of Western Ontario. Unpublished manuscript.

Heckman, J., Ichimura, H., Todd, P., 1997a. Matching as an econometric evaluation estimator: evidence from evaluating a job training programme. Rev. Econ. Stud. 64 (4), 605–654.

Heckman, J., Smith, J., Clements, N., 1997b. Making the most out of programme evaluations and social experiments: accounting for heterogeneity in programme impacts. Rev. Econ. Stud. 64 (4), 487–535.

Heckman, J., Ichimura, H., Smith, J., Todd, P., 1998a. Characterizing selection bias using experimental data. Econometrica 66 (5), 1017–1098.

Heckman, J., Ichimura, H., Todd, P., 1998b. Matching as an econometric evaluation estimator. Rev. Econ. Stud. 65 (2), 261–294.

Heckman, J., Lochner, L., Taber, C., 1998c. General-equilibrium treatment effects: a study of tuition policy. Am. Econ. Rev. 88 (2), 381–386.

Heckman, J., LaLonde, R., Smith, J., 1999. The economics and econometrics of active labor market programs. In: Ashenfelter, A., Card, D. (Eds.), In: Handbook of Labor Economics, vol. 3. North-Holland, Amsterdam, pp. 1865–2097.

Heckman, J., Hohmann, N., Smith, J., Khoo, M., 2000. Substitution and dropout bias in social experiments: a study of an influential social experiment. Q. J. Econ. 115 (2), 651–694.

Heckman, J., Lochner, L., Todd, P., 2007. Earnings functions, rates of return and treatment effects: the Mincer equation and beyond. In: Hanushek, E., Welch, F. (Eds.), In: Handbook of the Economics of Education, vol. 1. Elsevier, Amsterdam, pp. 307–458.

Heckman, J., Moon, S.H., Pinto, R., Savelyev, P., Yavitz, A., 2010. Analyzing social experiments as implemented: a reexamination of the evidence from the highscope perry preschool program. Quant. Econ. 1 (1), 1–46.

Heckman, J., Heinrich, C., Courty, P., Marschke, G., Smith, J., 2011. The Performance of Performance Standards. W.E. Upjohn Institute for Employment Research, Kalamazoo, MI.

Heinesen, E., Husted, L., Rosholm, M., 2013. The effects of active labour market policies for immigrants receiving social assistance in Denmark. IZA J. Migr. 2 (1), 1–22.

Heinrich, C., 2000. Organizational form and performance: an empirical investigation of nonprofit and for-profit job training service providers. J. Policy Anal. Manage. 19 (2), 233–261.

Heinrich, C., Mueser, P., 2014. Training Program Impacts and the Onset of the Great Recession. University of Missouri. Unpublished manuscript.

Heinrich, C., Mueser, P., Troske, K., Jeon, K., Kahvecioglu, D.C., 2013. Do public employment and training programs work? IZA J. Labor Econ. 2 (1), 1–23.

Hendra, R., Ray, K., Vegeris, S., Hevenstone, D., Hudson, M., 2011. Employment Retention and Advancement (ERA) Demonstration: Delivery, Take-Up, and Outcomes of In-Work Training Support for Lone Parents. Department for Work and Pensions, London.

Hillmore, A., Lally, J., Marlow, S., Prince, S., Pritchard, D., 2012. Early Impacts of Mandatory Work Activity. Department for Work and Pensions, London.

Hipp, L., Warner, M.E., 2008. Market forces for the unemployed? Training vouchers in Germany and the USA. Soc. Policy Adm. 42 (1), 77–101.

Hirano, K., Imbens, G., 2004. The propensity score with continuous treatments. In: Gelman, A., Meng, X. L. (Eds.), Applied Bayesian Modeling and Causal Inference from Incomplete-Data Perspectives. Wiley, New York, pp. 73–84.

Hollenbeck, K., 2009. Return on Investment Analysis of a Selected Set of Workforce System Programs in Indiana: Report submitted to the Indiana Chamber of Commerce Foundation, Indianapolis, Indiana.

Hollenbeck, K., 2012. Return on Investment in Workforce Development Programs. Upjohn Institute Working Paper No. 12-188.

Hollister, R., Kemper, P., Maynard, R., 1984. The National Supported Work Demonstration. University of Wisconsin Press, Madison, WI.

Hotz, V.J., 1992. Designing an evaluation of the job training partnership act. In: Manski, C., Garfinkel, I. (Eds.), Evaluating Welfare and Training Programs. Harvard University Press, Cambridge, MA, pp. 76–114.

Huber, M., Lechner, M., Wunsch, C., Walter, T., 2010. Do German welfare-to-work programmes reduce welfare dependency and increase employment? Ger. Econ. Rev. 12 (2), 182–204.

Huber, M., Lechner, M., Wunsch, C., 2013. The performance of estimators based on the propensity score. J. Econ. 175 (1), 1–21.

Huber, M., Lechner, M., Mellace, G., 2014. Why Do Tougher Caseworkers Increase Employment? The Role of Programme Assignment as a Causal Mechanism. Univeristy of St. Gallen, Department of Economics Discussion Paper No. 2014-14.

Hui, T.S., Smith, J.A., 2002. The Determinants of Participation in Adult Education and Training in Canada. MPRA Paper No. 17998.

Hujer, R., Thomsen, S.L., Zeiss, C., 2006. The Effects of Short-Term Training Measures on the Individual Unemployment Duration in West Germany. ZEW Discussion Paper No. 06-65.

Human Resources and Skills Development Canada, 2004. Summative Evaluation of Employment Benefits and Support Measures under the Terms of the Canada/British Columbia Labour Market Development Agreement: Final Report. HRSDC, Ottawa, ON.

Imbens, G., 2000. The role of the propensity score in estimating dose-response functions. Biometrika 87 (3), 706–710.

Imbens, G., 2004. Nonparametric estimation of average treatment effects under exogeneity: a review. Rev. Econ. Stat. 86 (1), 4–29.

Imbens, G., 2010. Better LATE than nothing: some comments on Deaton (2009) and Heckman and Urzua (2009). J. Econ. Lit. 48 (2), 399–423.

Imbens, G., Lemieux, T., 2008. Regression discontinuity designs: a guide to practice. J. Econ. 142 (2), 615–635.

Imbens, G., Wooldridge, J., 2009. Recent developments in the econometrics of program evaluation. J. Econ. Lit. 47 (1), 5–86.

İmrohoroğlu, S., Kitao, S., 2012. Social security reforms: benefit claiming, labor force participation, and long-run sustainability. Am. Econ. J. 4 (3), 96–127.

Jacobi, L., Kluve, J., 2006. Before and After the Hartz Reforms: The performance of Active Labour Market Policy in Germany. IZA Discussion Paper No. 2100.

Jacobson, L., LaLonde, R., Sullivan, D., 2005. Estimating the returns to community college schooling for displaced workers. J. Econ. 125 (1), 271–304.

Jerger, J., Pohnke, C., Spermann, A., 2001. Gut betreut in den Arbeitsmarkt? Eine Mikroökonometrische Evaluation der Mannheimer Arbeitsvermittlungsagentur. Mitt. Arbeitsmarkt Berufsforsch. 34 (4), 567–576.

Jespersen, S.T., Munch, J.R., Skipper, L., 2008. Costs and benefits of Danish active labour market programmes. Labour Econ. 15 (5), 859–884.

Johansson, K., 2001. Do labor market programs affect labor force participation? Swedish Econ. Policy Rev. 8 (2), 215–234.

Johnson, G.E., 1980. The theory of labor market intervention. Economica 47 (187), 309–329.

Kane, T., 2006. Public Intervention in Post-Secondary Education. In: Hanushek, E., Welch, F. (Eds.), In: Handbook of the Economics of Education, vol. 2. Elsevier, Amsterdam, pp. 1369–1401.

Keane, M., 2010. Structural vs. atheoretic approaches to econometrics. J. Econ. 156 (1), 3–20.

Kemple, J., Doolittle, F., Wallace, J., 1993. The National JTPA Study: Site Characteristics and Participation Patterns. MDRC, New York, NY.

Kling, J., Liebman, J., Katz, L., 2007. Experimental Analysis of Neighborhood Effects. Econometrica 75 (1), 83–119.

Kluve, J., Card, D., Fertig, M., Góra, M., Jacobi, L., Jensen, P., Leetmaa, R., Nima, L., Patacchini, E., Schaffner, S., Schmidt, C.M., van der Klaauw, B., Weber, A., 2007. Active Labor Market Policies in Europe: Performance and Perspectives. Springer, Berlin.

Kluve, J., Schneider, H., Uhlendorff, A., Zhao, Z., 2012. Evaluating continuous training programmes by using the generalized propensity score. J. R. Stat. Soc. A. Stat. Soc. 175 (2), 587–617.

Knight, G., Speckesser, S., Smith, J.A., Dolton, P.J., Azevedo, J.P., 2006. Lone Parents Work Focused Interviews/New Deal for Lone Parents: Combined Evaluation and Further Net Impacts. Department for Work and Pensions, London.

Koning, P., 2009. The effectiveness of public employment service workers in the Netherlands. Empir. Econ. 37 (2), 393–409.

Kopf, E., 2013. Short training for welfare recipients in Germany: which types work? Int. J. Manpow. 34 (5), 486–516.

Kornfeld, R., Bloom, H., 1999. Measuring program impacts on earnings and employment: do unemployment insurance wage reports of employers agree with surveys of individuals? J. Labor Econ. 17 (1), 168–197.

Krueger, A., 1990. Incentive effects of workers' compensation insurance. J. Public Econ. 41 (1), 73–99.

Krug, G., Stephan, G., 2013. Is the Contracting-Out of Intensive Placement Services More Effective than Provision by the PES? Evidence from a Randomized Field Experiment. IZA Discussion Paper No. 7403.

Kruppe, T., 2009. Bildungsgutscheine in der aktiven Arbeitsmarktpolitik. Sozialer Fortschritt 58 (1), 9–19.

Lagerström, J., 2011. How important are caseworkers – and why? New evidence from Swedish employment offices. Institute for Labour Market Policy Evaluation, IFAU Working Paper Series No. 2011:10.

LaLonde, R., 1986. Evaluating the econometric evaluations of training programs with experimental data. Am. Econ. Rev. 76 (4), 604–620.

LaLonde, R., 2003. Employment and training programs. In: Moffitt, R. (Ed.), Means-Tested Transfer Programs in the United States. University of Chicago Press, Chicago, IL, pp. 517–585.

Lancaster, T., 1992. The Econometric Analysis of Transition Data. Cambridge University Press, Cambridge.

Larsson, L., 2006. Sick of being unemployed? Interactions between unemployment and sickness insurance. Scand. J. Econ. 108 (1), 97–113.

Lechner, M., 2001. Identification and estimation of causal effects of multiple treatments under the conditional independence assumption. In: Lechner, M., Pfeiffer, F. (Eds.), Econometric Evaluation of Labor Market Policies. Physica, Heidelberg, pp. 43–58.

Lechner, M., 2009. Sequential causal models for the evaluation of labor market programs. J. Bus. Econ. Stat. 27 (1), 71–83.

Lechner, M., 2010. The estimation of causal effects by difference-in-differences methods. Found. Trends Econometrics. 4 (3), 165–224.

Lechner, M., Miquel, R., 2010. Identification of the effects of dynamic treatments by sequential conditional independence assumptions. Empir. Econ. 39 (1), 111–137.

Lechner, M., Smith, J., 2007. What is the value added by caseworkers? Labour Econ. 14 (2), 135–151.

Lechner, M., Wiehler, S., 2011. Kids or courses? Gender differences in the effects of active labor market policies. J. Popul. Econ. 24 (3), 783–812.

Lechner, M., Wunsch, C., 2009. Are training programs more effective when unemployment is high? J. Labor Econ. 27 (4), 653–692.

Lechner, M., Wunsch, C., 2013. Sensitivity of matching-based program evaluations to the availability of control variables. Labour Econ. 21 (1), 111–121.

Lechner, M., Miquel, R., Wunsch, C., 2007. The curse and blessing of training the unemployed in a changing economy: the case of East Germany after unification. Ger. Econ. Rev. 8 (4), 468–507.

Lechner, M., Miquel, R., Wunsch, C., 2011. Long-run effects of public sector sponsored training in West Germany. J. Eur. Econ. Assoc. 9 (4), 742–784.

Lee, D., Lemieux, T., 2010. Regression discontinuity designs in economics. J. Econ. Lit. 48 (2), 281–355.

Liljeberg, L., Lundin, M., 2010. Jobbnäret ger jobb: effecter av intensifierade arbetsförmedlingsinsatser föt att bryta långtidsarbetlöshet: Institute for Labour Market Policy Evaluation, IFAU Report No. 2010:2.

Lise, J., Seitz, S., Smith, J., 2004. Equilibrium Policy Experiments and the Evaluation of Social Programs. NBER Working Paper No. 10283.

Lise, J., Seitz, S., Smith, J., 2005. Evaluating Search and Matching Models Using Experimental Data. IZA Discussion Paper No. 1717.

Long, D., Maller, C., Thornton, C., 1981. Evaluating the benefits and costs of the job corps. J. Policy Anal. Manage. 1 (1), 55–76.

Maguire, S., Freely, J., Clymer, C., Conway, M., Schwartz, D., 2010. Tuning in to Local Labor Markets: Findings From the Sectoral Employment Impact Study. P/PV, Philadelphia, PA.

Maibom Pedersen, J., Rosholm, M., Svarer, M., 2012. Experimental Evidence on the Effects of Early Meetings and Activation. IZA Discussion Paper No. 6970.

Mallar, C., Kerachsky, S., Thornton, C., Long, D., 1982. Evaluation of the Economic Impact of the Job Corps Program: Third Follow-up Report. Mathematica Policy Research, Princeton, NJ.

Manski, C., 2001. Designing programs for heterogeneous populations: the value of covariate information. Am. Econ. Rev. 91 (2), 103–106.

Manski, C., 2004. Statistical treatment rules for heterogeneous populations. Econometrica 72 (4), 1221–1246.

Matzkin, R.L., 1992. Nonparametric and distribution-free estimation of the binary choice and the threshold-crossing models. Econometrica 60 (2), 239–270.

McCall, B.P., 1994. The effect of job heterogeneity on reservation wages. Int. Econ. Rev. 35 (3), 773–791.

McCall, B.P., 1995. The impact of unemployment insurance benefit levels on recipiency. J. Bus. Econ. Stat. 13 (2), 189–198.

McCall, B.P., McCall, J.J., 2008. The Economics of Search. Routledge, London.

McConnell, S., Glazerman, S., 2001. National Job Corps Study: The Benefits and Costs of Job Corps. Mathematica Policy Research, Washington, DC.

McConnell, S., Stuart, E., Fortson, K., Decker, P., Perez-Johnson, I., Harris, B., Salzman, J., 2006. Managing Consumer's Training Choices: Findings from the Individual Training Account Experiment. Mathematica Policy Research, Washington, DC.

Messer, D., Wolter, S., 2009. Money Matters: Evidence from a Large-Scale Randomized Field Experiment with Vouchers for Adult Training. IZA Discussion Paper No. 4017.

Miller, C., Bewley, H., Campbell-Barr, V., Dorsett, R., Hamilton, G., Hoggart, L., Homonoff, T., Marsh, A., Ray, K., Riccio, J.A., Vegeris, S., 2008. Implementation and Second Year Impacts for New Deal 25 Plus Customers in the UK Employment Retention and Advancement (ERA) Demonstration. Department for Work and Pensions, London.

Mincer, J., 1974. Schooling, Experience and Earnings. Columbia University Press, New York, NY.

Ministère de l'Intérieur, 2014. L'operation "Ouvrir l'école aux parents pour réussir l'intégration". Available at: http://www.immigration.interieur.gouv.fr/Accueil-et-accompagnement/Education-et-parentalite/L-operation-Ouvrir-l-ecole-aux-parents-pour-reussir-l-integration.

Ministère du Travail de l'Emploi, de la Formation professionnelle et du Dialogue social, 2014. Les données annuelles (2012) sur les personnes en recherche d'emploi entrées en formation (xls – 61 ko). Available at: http://travail-emploi.gouv.fr/etudes-recherches-statistiques-de,76/statistiques,78/politique-de-l-emploi-et-formation,84/formation-professionnelle,262/la-formation-professionnelle-des,2092.html.

Ministry for Education and Research, 2007. The Swedish Educational System. http://www.government.se/content/1/c6/07/92/85/f899a8ee.pdf.

Ministry for Education and Research, 2013. Adult Education and Training in Sweden. http://www.government.se/content/1/c6/22/31/75/087de557.pdf.

Ministry of Children and Education, 2012. Education and Training in Denmark. Facts and Key Figures. Available at: https://www.uvm.dk/~/media/UVM/Filer/English/PDF/120312%20Education%20and%20training%20in%20DK.pdf.

Moffitt, R., 1991. Program evaluation with nonexperimental data. Eval. Rev. 15 (3), 291–314.

Mortensen, D.T., Pissarides, C.A., 1994. Job creation and job destruction in the theory of unemployment. Rev. Econ. Stud. 61 (3), 397–415.

Mueser, P., Troske, K., Gorislavsky, A., 2007. Using state administrative data to measure program performance. Rev. Econ. Stat. 89 (4), 761–783.

Munch, J.R., Skipper, L., 2008. Program participation, labor force dynamics, and accepted wage rates. In: Fomby, T., Hill, R.C., Millimet, D.L., Smith, J.A., Vytlacil, E.J. (Eds.), In: Modelling and Evaluating Treatment Effects in Econometrics (Advances in Econometrics), vol. 21. Emerald Group Publishing Limited, Bingley, pp. 197–262.

Nakosteen, R., Westerlund, O., Zimmer, M., 2012. Active labor market programs and regional mobility: evidence from the Swedish recession 1994–1995. Contemp. Econ. Policy 30 (2), 178–194.

Newton, B., Meager, N., Bertram, C., Corden, A., George, A., Lalani, M., Metcalf, H., Rolfe, H., Sainsbury, R., Weston, K., 2012. Work Programme Evaluation: Findings from the First Phase of Qualitative Research on Programme Delivery: Department for Work and Pensions, Research Report No. 821.

Neyman, J., 1923. Statistical problems in agricultural experiments. J. R. Stat. Soc. A. Stat. Soc. 2 (2), 107–180.

Nilsson, P., 2008. Programeffekter 1992 till 2006. Arbetförmedlingen Working Paper No. 2008:1.

OECD, 2014. OECD Employment Outlook 2014. OECD, Paris.

Office Français de l' Immigration et de l'Intégration, 2012. Rapport d'Activité 2012. Available at: www.ladocumentationfrancaise.fr/var/storage/rapports-publics/134000761/0000.pdf.

Orr, L., Bloom, H., Bell, S., Lin, W., Cave, G., Doolittle, F., 1994. The National JTPA Study: Impacts, Benefits and Costs of Title II-A. Abt Associates, Bethesda, MD.

Orr, L., Bloom, H., Bell, S., Doolittle, F., Lin, W., Cave, G., 1995. Does Training for the Disadvantaged Work? Evidence from the National JTPA Study. Urban Institute Press, Washington, DC.

Osikominu, A., 2013. Quick job entry or long-term human capital development? The dynamic effects of alternative training schemes. Rev. Econ. Stud. 80 (1), 313–342.

Oster, E., 2013. Unobservable Selection and Coefficient Stability: Theory and Validation. NBER Working Paper No. 19054.

Paul, M., 2015. Many dropouts? Never mind! – employment prospects of Dropouts from Training Programs. Ann. Econ. Stat. 119–120, 235–267.

Paul, M., Dörr, A., Fitzenberger, B., Kruppe, T., Strittmatter, A., 2013. The Award of a Training Voucher and Labor Market Outcomes. Beiträge zur Jahrestagung des Vereins für Sozialpolitik 2013: Wettbewerbspolitik und Regulierung in einer globalen Wirtschaftsordnung - Session: Training and Apprenticeship, No. D07-V3.

Pavoni, N., Violante, G., 2005. Optimal Welfare-to-Work Programs. Federal Reserve Bank of Minneapolis, Discussion Paper No. 143.

Pavoni, N., Violante, G., 2007. Optimal welfare-to-work programs. Rev. Econ. Stud. 74 (1), 283–318.

Pavoni, N., Violante, G., Wunsch, C., 2014. Structural evaluation and optimal use of training in Germany. Mimeo, University of Basel, Switzerland, Unpublished Manuscript.

Perez-Johnson, I., Moore, Q., Santillano, R., 2011. Improving the Effectiveness of Individual Training Accounts: Long-Term Findings from an Experimental Evaluation of Three Service Delivery Models. Mathematica Policy Research, Princeton, NJ.

Petrongolo, B., Pissarides, C.A., 2001. Looking into the black box: a survey of the matching function. J. Econ. Lit. 39 (2), 390–431.

Pitt, M., Rosenzweig, M., Hassan, N., 2010. Human Capital Investment and the Gender Division of Labor in a Brawn-Based Economy. Yale Growth Center Discussion Paper No. 989.

Plesca, M., 2010. A general equilibrium analysis of the employment service. J. Hum. Cap. 4 (3), 274–329.

Plesca, M., Smith, J., 2005. Rules Versus Discretion in Social Programs: Empirical Evidence on Profiling in Employment and Training Programs. University of Maryland. Unpublished manuscript.

Plesca, M., Smith, J., 2007. Evaluating multi-treatment programs: theory and evidence from the U.S. Job Training Partnership Act. Empir. Econ. 32 (2–3), 491–528.

Puma, M., Burstein, N., 1994. The national evaluation of the food stamp employment and training program. J. Policy Anal. Manage. 13 (2), 311–330.

Quandt, R., 1972. Methods of estimating switching regressions. J. Am. Stat. Assoc. 67 (338), 306–310.

Rahim, N., Kotecha, M., Chanfreau, J., Arthur, S., Mitchell, M., Payne, C., Haywood, S., 2012. Evaluation of Support for the Very Long-Term Unemployed Trailblazer. Department for Work and Pensions, London.

Regnér, H., 2002. A nonexperimental evaluation of training programs for the unemployed in Sweden. Labour Econ. 9 (2), 187–206.

Richardson, K., van den Berg, G.J., 2001. The effect of vocational employment training on the individual transition rate from unemployment to work. Swedish Econ. Policy Rev. 8 (2), 175–213.

Riddell, C., 1991. Evaluation of manpower and training programs: the North American experience. In: OECD, (Ed.), The Evaluation of Manpower, Training and Social Programs: The State of a Complex Art. OECD, Paris, pp. 43–72.

Riley, R., Young, G., 2001a. Does Welfare-to-Work Policy Increase Employment? Evidence from the UK New Deal for Young People. National Institute of Economic and Social Research, London.

Riley, R., Young, G., 2001b. The Macroeconomic Impact of the New Deal for Young People. National Institute of Economic and Social Research, London.

Riley, R., Bewley, H., Kirby, S., Rincon-Aznar, A., George, A., 2011. The Introduction of Jobcentre Plus: An Evaluation of Labour Market Impacts. Department for Work and Pensions, London.

Rinne, U., Uhlendorff, A., Zhao, Z., 2013. Vouchers and caseworkers in training programs for the unemployed. Empir. Econ. 45 (3), 1089–1127.

Romero, R.G., 2009. Estimating the impact of England's area-based intervention 'New Deal for Communities' on employment. Reg. Sci. Urban Econ. 39 (3), 323–331.

Romero, R.G., Noble, M., 2008. Evaluating England's 'New Deal for Communities' programme using the difference-in-difference method. J. Econ. Geogr. 8 (6), 759–778.

Romeu Gordo, L., Wolff, J., 2011. Creating employment or keeping them busy? An evaluation of training programs for older workers in Germany. J. Aging Soc. Policy 23 (2), 198–218.

Rosholm, M., 2008. Experimental Evidence on the Nature of the Danish Employment Miracle. IZA Discussion Paper No. 3620.

Rosholm, M., 2014. Do Case Workers Help the Unemployed? Evidence for Making a Cheap and Effective Twist to Labor Market Policies for Unemployed Workers. IZA World of Labor No. 2014:72.

Rosholm, M., Skipper, L., 2009. Is labour market training a curse for the unemployed? Evidence from a social experiment. J. Appl. Econ. 24 (2), 338–365.

Rosholm, M., Svarer, M., 2008. The threat effect of active labour market programmes. Scand. J. Econ. 110 (2), 385–401.

Rosholm, M., Svarer, M., Hammer, B., 2004. A Danish Profiling System. University of Aarhus, Department of Economics, Working Paper No. 2004-13.

Roy, A.D., 1951. Some Thoughts on the Distribution of Earnings. Oxford Economic Papers No. 3.

Rubin, D., 1974. Estimating causal effects of treatments in randomized and non-randomized studies. J. Educ. Psychol. 66 (5), 688–701.

Sanchez, R., 2013. Le contrat de professionnalisation en 2012. Des embauches en baisse et des contrats plus courts, Dares Analyses No. 075.

Sanchez, R., Delort, A., Pesonel, É., 2014. L'apprentissage en 2012. Quasi-stabilité des entrées, hausse de la part des contrats courts. Dares Analyses No. 042.

Sheldon, G.M., 2003a. The Efficiency of Public Employment Services: A Nonparametric Matching Function Analysis for Switzerland. J. Prod. Anal. 20, 49–70.

Schiel, S., Schröder, H., Gilberg, R., 2008. Das arbeitsmarktpolitische Programm FAIR: Endbericht der Evaluation. In: Kruppe, T. (Ed.), Mehr Vermittlungen durch mehr Vermittler? Ergebnisse des Modellversuchs "Förderung der Arbeitsaufnahme" (FAIR). In: Bertelsmann, Bielefeld, IAB-Bibliothek, 312, pp. 1–263.

Schochet, P., 2008a. Technical Methods Report: Guidelines for Multiple Testing in Impact Evaluations (NCEE 2008-4018). National Center for Education Evaluation and Regional Assistance, Institute of Education Sciences, U.S. Department of Education, Washington, DC.

Schochet, P., 2008b. Technical Methods Report: Statistical Power for Regression Discontinuity Designs in Education Evaluations (NCEE 2008-4026). National Center for Education Evaluation and Regional Assistance, Institute of Education Sciences, U.S. Department of Education, Washington, DC.

Schochet, P., Burghardt, J., Glazerman, S., 2001. National Job Corps Study: The Impacts of Job Corps on Participants' Employment and Related Outcomes. Mathematica Policy Research, Princeton, NJ.

Schochet, P., Burghardt, J., McConnell, S., 2008. Does job corps work? Impact findings from the national job corps study. Am. Econ. Rev. 98 (5), 1864–1886.

Schochet, P., D'Amico, R., Berk, J., Dolfin, D., Wozny, N., 2012. Estimated Impacts for Participants in the Trade Adjustment Assistance (TAA) Program Under the 2002 Amendments. Mathematica Policy Research, Princeton, NJ.

Schünemann, B., Lechner, M., Wunsch, C., 2013. Do long-term unemployed workers benefit from targeted wage subsidies? Ger. Econ. Rev. 16 (1), 43–64.

Schwerdt, G., Messer, D., Woessmann, L., Wolter, S.C., 2012. The impact of an adult education voucher program: evidence from a randomized field experiment. J. Public Econ. 96 (7–8), 569–583.

Sianesi, B., 2004. An evaluation of the Swedish system of active labor market programs in the 1990s. Rev. Econ. Stat. 86 (1), 133–155.

Sianesi, B., 2008. Differential effects of active labour market programs for the unemployed. Labour Econ. 15 (3), 370–399.

Sianesi, B., 2014. Dealing with Randomisation Bias in a Social Experiment: the Case of ERA. Institute for Fiscal Studies, IFS Working Papers No. W14/10.

Singer, C., Toomet, O., 2013. On government-subsidized training programs for older workers. IAB-Discussion Paper No. 21/2013.

Skolverket, 2013a. Utbildningsresultat - Riksnivå - Kalenderår 2012: Skolverkets rapport Nr. 369.

Skolverket, 2013b. Kostnader – Riksnivå – Kalenderår 2012: Skolverkets rapport Nr. 377.

Smith, J., 1997. Measuring Earnings Levels Among the Poor: Evidence from Two Samples of JTPA Eligibles. University of Western Ontario, Canada. Unpublished manuscript.

Smith, J., 2004. Evaluating local economic development policies: theory and practice. In: Nolan, A., Wong, G. (Eds.), Evaluating Local Economic and Employment Development: How to Assess What Works Among Programmes and Policies. OECD, Paris, pp. 287–332.

Smith, J., 2011. Improving impact evaluation in Europe. In: Besharov, D., Cottingham, P. (Eds.), The Workforce Investment Act: Implementation Experiences and Evaluation Findings. W.E. Upjohn Institute for Employment Research, Kalamazoo, pp. 473–494.

Smith, J., Staghøej, J., 2010. Using Statistical Treatment Rules for Assign of Participants in Labour Market Programs. University of Michigan, Ann Arbor, MI. Unpublished manuscript.

Smith, J., Todd, P., 2005a. Does matching overcome LaLonde's critique of nonexperimental methods? J. Econ. 125 (1–2), 305–353.

Smith, J., Todd, P., 2005b. Rejoinder. J. Econ. 125 (1–2), 365–375.

Smith, J., Whalley, A., 2015. How Well Do We Measure Public Job Training? University of Michigan, Ann Arbor, MI. Unpublished manuscript.

Smith, J., Whalley, A., Wilcox, N., 2015. Are Program Participants Good Evaluators? University of Michigan, Ann Arbor, MI. Unpublished manuscript.

Social Policy Research Associates, 2013. PY 2012 WIASRD Data Book. SPRA, Oakland, CA. http://www.doleta.gov/performance/results/pdf/PY2012WIASRDDataBook.pdf.

Spinnewijn, J., 2013. Training and search during unemployment. J. Public Econ. 99 (1), 49–65.

Staghøj, J., Svarer, M., Rosholm, M., 2010. Choosing the best training programme: is there a case for statistical treatment rules? Oxf. Bull. Econ. Stat. 72 (2), 172–201.

Statistik der Bundesagentur für Arbeit, 2013a. Teilnehmer in Maßnahmen zur Förderung der beruflichen Weiterbildung (FbW). Nürnberg, April 2013.

Stenberg, A., 2005. Comprehensive education for the unemployed – evaluating the effects on unemployment of the adult education initiative in Sweden. Labour 19 (1), 123–146.

Stenberg, A., 2010. The impact on annual earnings of adult upper secondary education in Sweden. Int. J. Life. Educ. 29 (3), 303–321.

Stenberg, A., 2011. Using longitudinal data to evaluate publicly provided formal education for low skilled. Econ. Educ. Rev. 30 (6), 1262–1280.

Stenberg, A., 2012. Access to Education over the Working Life in Sweden: Priorities, Institutions and Efficiency. OECD Education Working Papers No. 62.

Stenberg, A., Westerlund, O., 2008. Does comprehensive education work for the long-term unemployed? Labour Econ. 15 (1), 54–67.

Stenberg, A., Westerlund, O., 2014. The Long-Term Earnings Consequences of General vs. Specific Training of the Unemployed. Institute for Evaluation of Labour Market and Education Policy, IFAU Working Paper No. 2014:3.

Stenberg, A., DeLuna, X., Westerlund, O., 2012. Can adult education delay retirement from the labour market? J. Popul. Econ. 25 (2), 677–696.

Stenberg, A., DeLuna, X., Westerlund, O., 2014. Does formal education for older workers increase earnings? — Evidence based on rich data and long-term follow-up. Labour 28 (2), 163–189.

Stephan, G., 2008. The effects of active labor market programs in Germany: an investigation using different definitions of non-treatment. Jahrb. NatlOkon. Stat. 228 (5/6), 586–611.

Stephan, G., Pahnke, A., 2011. The relative effectiveness of selected active labor market programs: an empirical investigation for Germany. Manch. Sch. 79 (6), 1262–1293.

Stevens, M., 2007. New microfoundations for the aggregate matching function. Int. Econ. Rev. 48 (3), 847–868.

Stiftung Begabtenförderung berufliche Bildung, 2013. Jahresbericht 2012. Bonn.

Stiftung Begabtenförderung berufliche Bildung, 2014. Jahresbericht 2013. Bonn.

Studiestödsnämnden, Centrala, 2013. Studiestödsstatistik, Återrapportering enligt regleringsbrevet för 2012.

Styrelsen for Arbejdsmarked og Rekruttering, 2014. Jobindsats Databank. http://www.jobindsats.dk/sw159.asp. Please follow the path: alle ydelser under ét – antal aktiverede og forløb – næste – område: hele landet – frekvens: år, 2012 – ydelsesgrupper i alt – cross at "tilbud" to find the data.

The Danish Agency for International Education, 2011. The Danish Education System. Available at: ufm.dk/en/publications/2011/files-2011/the-danish-education-system.pdf.

Thomsen, S.L., Walter, T., Aldashev, A., 2013. Short-term training programs for immigrants in the German welfare system: do effects differ from natives and why? IZA J. Migr. 2 (1), 1–20.

Todd, P., Wolpin, K., 2006. Assessing the impact of a school subsidy program in Mexico using a social experiment to validate a dynamic behavioral model of child schooling and fertility. Am. Econ. Rev. 96 (5), 1384–1417.

Torp, H., Raaum, O., Hernæs, E., Goldstein, H., 1993. The first Norwegian experiment. In: Jensen, K., Madsen, P.K. (Eds.), Measuring Labour Market Measures: Evaluating the Effects of Active Labour Market Policy Initiatives. Danish Ministry of Labour, Copenhagen, pp. 97–140.

U.S. Department of Education, 2015a. https://studentaid.ed.gov/sa/types/grants-scholarships/pell.

U.S. Department of Education, 2015b. https://studentaid.ed.gov/sa/types/loans.

U.S. Department of Labor, 2013a. Office of Job Corps, Quarterly Highlights Report, Program Year 2012, Through June 30, 2013. Department of Labor, Washington, DC.http://www.jobcorps.gov/Libraries/pdf/12_4th_qtr.sflb,

U.S. Department of Labor, 2013b. 2012 National TAA Program Statistics. http://www.doleta.gov/tradeact/TAPR_2012,cfm?state=US.

U.S. Department of Labor, 2015a. WIOA Fact Sheet. http://www.doleta.gov/wioa/pdf/WIOA-Factsheet.pdf.

U.S. Department of Labor, 2015b. Job Corps Policy and Requirements Handbook. U.S. Department of Labor, Office of Job Corps, Washington, DC. http://www.jobcorps.gov/pdf/prh.pdf.

U.S. General Accounting Office, 1996. Job Training Partnership Act: Long Term Earnings and Employment Outcomes: US General Accounting Office, GAO Report No. HEHS-96-40.

Undervisningsministeriet, 2014. Undervisningsministeriets databanken. http://statweb.uni-c.dk/databanken/uvmDataWeb/MainCategories.aspx?.

van den Berg, G., Kjeersgaard, L., Rosholm, M., 2012. To Meet or Not to Meet (Your Case Worker) – That Is the Question. IZA Discussion Paper No. 6476.

van der Klaauw, W., 2008. Regression-discontinuity analysis: a survey of recent developments in economics. Labour 22 (2), 219–245.

van Wichelen, L., 2005. Training Vouchers for Employers and Employees. Flemish Employment Administration, Brussels.

van Wichelen, L., 2008. Training Vouchers: A Simple Recipe for Success or Major Deadweight Loss Effects? Department of Work and Social Economy, Flemish Government, Belgium.

Vegeris, S., Vowden, K., Bertram, C., Davidson, R., Durante, L., Hudson, M., Husain, F., Mackinnon, K., Smeaton, D., 2010. Jobseekers regime and Flexible New Deal evaluation: A report on qualitative research findings. Department of Work and Pensions Research Report no 706.

Vikström, J., Rosholm, M., Svarer, M., 2014. The relative efficiency of active labour market policies: evidence from a social experiment and non-parametric bounds. Labour Econ. 24, 58–67.

Vivalt, E., 2015. How Much Can We Generalize from Impact Evaluations? New York University, New York Unpublished manuscript.

Wallace, G., Haveman, R., 2007. The implications of differences between employer and worker employment/earnings reports for policy evaluation. J. Policy Anal. Manage. 26 (4), 737–754.

Walter, T., Bonin, H., Butschek, S., Schütz, H., Schröder, H., Knerr, P., Steinwede, J., Thomsen, S.L., 2014. Evaluation "Programm zur berufsbezogenen Sprachförderung für Personen mit Migrationshintergrund (ESF-BAMF-Programm)" – Abschlussbericht. Im Auftrag des Bundesministeriums für Arbeit und Soziales, Bonn.

Weatherall, C.D., Markwardt, K.S., 2010. Caseworker Behavior and Clients' Employability. Social Policy and Welfare Services, Working Paper No. 04:2010.

Wing, C., Cook, T.D., 2013. Strengthening the regression discontinuity design using additional design elements: a within-study comparison. J. Policy Anal. Manage. 32 (4), 853–877.

Wolpin, K., 2013. The Limits of Inference Without Theory. MIT University Press, Cambridge, MA.

Wolter, S., Ryan, P., 2011. Chapter 11: Apprenticeship. In: Hanushek, R., Machin, S. (Eds.), In: Handbook of the Economics of Education, vol. IV. North-Holland, Amsterdam, pp. 521–576.

Wong, V., Steiner, P., Cook, T., 2012. Analyzing regression-discontinuity designs with multiple assignment variables: a comparative study of four estimation methods. J. Educ. Behav. Stat. 38 (2), 107–141.

Wooldridge, J., 2010. Econometric Analysis of Cross Section and Panel Data, second ed. MIT Press, Cambridge, MA.

Wooldridge, J., 2013. Introductory Econometrics: A Modern Approach, fifth ed. South-Western, Mason, OH.

Wunsch, C., 2005. Labour Market Policy in Germany: Institutions, Instruments and Reforms Since Unification. University of St. Gallen, Department of Economics, Discussion Paper No. 2005-06.

Wunsch, C., 2007. Optimal Use of Labor Market Policies. University of St. Gallen, Department of Economics, Discussion Paper No. 2007-26.

Wunsch, C., 2013. Optimal use of labor market policies: the role of job search assistance. Rev. Econ. Stat. 95 (3), 1030–1045.

Wunsch, C., Lechner, M., 2008. What did all the money do? On the general ineffectiveness of recent West German labour market programmes. Kyklos 61 (1), 134–174.

Zabel, C., 2013. Does activation increase lone mothers' employment chances? Effects of training and workfare for lone mothers receiving means-tested benefits in Germany. Int. J. Sociol Soc. Policy. 33 (7/8), 453–473.

CHAPTER 10

Improving Education Outcomes in Developing Countries: Evidence, Knowledge Gaps, and Policy Implications

P. Glewwe*, K. Muralidharan[†]
*University of Minnesota, St. Paul, Minnesota, United States
†University of California San Diego, La Jolla, California, United States; NBER, JPAL

Contents

Abstract

Improvements in empirical research standards for credible identification of the causal impact of education policies on education outcomes have led to a significant increase in the body of evidence available on improving education outcomes in developing countries. This chapter aims to synthesize this evidence, interpret their results, and discuss the reasons why some interventions appear to be effective and others do not, with the ultimate goal of drawing implications for both research and policy. Interpreting the evidence for generalizable lessons is challenging because of variation across contexts, duration and quality of studies, and the details of specific interventions studied. Nevertheless, some broad patterns do emerge. Demand-side interventions that increase the immediate returns to (or reduce household costs of) school enrollment, or that increase students' returns to effort, are broadly effective

Handbook of the Economics of Education, Volume 5
ISSN 1574-0692, http://dx.doi.org/10.1016/B978-0-444-63459-7.00010-5

at increasing time in school and learning outcomes, but vary considerably in cost-effectiveness. Many expensive "standard" school inputs are often not very effective at improving outcomes, though some specific inputs (which are often less expensive) are. Interventions that focus on improved pedagogy (especially supplemental instruction to children lagging behind grade level competencies) are particularly effective, and so are interventions that improve school governance and teacher accountability. Our broad policy message is that the evidence points to several promising ways in which the efficiency of education spending in developing countries can be improved by pivoting public expenditure from less cost-effective to more cost-effective ways of achieving the same objectives. We conclude by documenting areas where more research is needed, and offer suggestions on the public goods and standards needed to make it easier for decentralized and uncoordinated research studies to be compared across contexts.

Keywords

Education in developing countries, School enrollment and attendance, Learning outcomes, Demand for education, School inputs, Pedagogy, School governance, Policy evaluation, Cost effectiveness

1. INTRODUCTION

Governments in developing countries, international aid agencies, and almost all economists agree that an educated populace is necessary — though not necessarily sufficient — for long-run economic growth and, more generally, a high standard of living. The governments in these countries spend approximately one trillion dollars each year on education, and households spend hundreds of billions more (a precise amount is difficult to calculate) on their children's education. This spending, along with several other factors, has led to large increases in school enrollment at all levels in the past 25 years. Indeed, most children in developing countries now complete primary school and obtain at least some schooling at the secondary level.

Yet enrolling in school does not guarantee that children acquire the human capital that their schooling should provide. Indeed, there is ample evidence that in many developing countries children learn much less than the goals set out in the official curriculum. Also, in some of these countries a large fraction of children still are not finishing primary school, and there are still millions of children who never attend school at all. Moreover, high rates of enrollment often mask low rates of actual school attendance in many low-income settings.

Given this state of affairs, economists and other researchers who study education in developing countries have focused on two main questions. The first is: What education policies increase student enrollment, attendance, and completed years of schooling? The second is: What education policies increase student learning? Further, given the tight fiscal constraints under which developing country governments operate, a key question for researchers has been to identify the most cost-effective ways of achieving positive education impacts, and to identify the policies that are less cost effective.

Much research has been conducted in the last 25 years that attempts to answer these two questions, and this research has accelerated in the past 5–10 years. In particular, during the decade that has passed since the publication of the previous Handbook chapter on the economics of education in developing countries (Glewwe and Kremer, 2006) there has been a sharp increase in the quantity and quality of empirical research in developing countries. This growth in evidence has been facilitated by the increasing use of randomized experiments to evaluate the impacts of education interventions, as well as by the increasing availability of administrative and survey data sets on education in developing countries.

The growing body of this literature is reflected in the fact that there have been several other reviews of this literature in just the last 3 years, including Glewwe et al. (2013), Kremer et al. (2013), Krishnaratne et al. (2013), McEwan (2015), and Murnane and Ganimian (2014).[1] Further, the variation across these reviews in their interpretation of the research literature and of the corresponding policy implications has also prompted a recent survey of surveys by Evans and Popova (2015) to understand the source of this variation. The main conclusion of Evans and Popova (2015) is that the differences across these syntheses can partly be explained by the variation in the studies included in the reviews (due in part to differences in evidence-quality thresholds used for including studies), and partly by variation in how interventions are classified. They also recommend that future reviews combine a formal meta-analysis with a more narrative explanation of the specific interventions and contexts in order to better interpret the results and the variation across studies.

Given this proliferation of recent reviews of research on education in developing countries, this chapter aims to provide a framework that can be used to synthesize what can be learned from the evidence about the nature of education and human capital production in developing countries, and the ways in which governments can deploy their limited resources more effectively to achieve their goal of increasing the human capital of their citizens. While mechanical meta-analyses focus on classifying interventions and summarizing the estimates, we emphasize that many challenges arise when synthesizing the evidence to reach a definitive view of what works, and what does not. These challenges include variations in context, variations in duration of the evaluations and the outcomes studied, and perhaps most importantly variations in the details of the interventions themselves.

We therefore aim not only to summarize what has been found, but also to discuss and interpret these results and to discuss the reasons why some interventions appear to be effective and others do not, with the ultimate goal of drawing implications for both research and policy. Thus, in addition to summarizing and synthesizing the high-quality studies on education in developing countries, an important goal of this chapter is to provide a framework for understanding what the results *mean* in addition to summarizing what they *are*. In doing so, we also hope to provide guidance and suggestions for future

---

[1] This list does not even include other reviews that have reviewed education research in specific geographical settings, such as Muralidharan (2013), which focuses on India, and Conn (2014), which focuses on Africa.

research. Some of the key themes we seek to emphasize (especially relative to the chapter written a decade ago by Glewwe and Kremer, 2006) include the following, which are discussed in detail in Section 5 of the chapter.

First, the design of the details of any intervention matter enormously and should be more theoretically informed. Second, while the standard education production function approach seeks to estimate population average parameters, heterogeneity across students is likely to be a first order issue. Thus, the optimal policy is likely to be different at different points in the student learning distribution. Third, it is particularly important to try to understand *why* well-intentioned interventions may not have much of an impact on learning outcomes, and to aim such inquiry toward identifying binding constraints in the education system of interest. Fourth, interactions across components of an education system are likely to be of first order importance, which poses a challenge for most traditional research methods, which typically are not well suited to studying interactions. Finally, while several individual high-quality studies have been produced in the past decade, more public goods and standards for measurement and reporting need to be created to make it easier for highly decentralized (and often opportunistically conducted) research studies to be compared across contexts. This will contribute to a more systematic understanding of the most cost-effective ways to improve education outcomes in developing countries.

The plan of this review chapter is as follows. The next section presents recent trends in education outcomes in developing countries and places the performance of developing countries in perspective by accounting for the extent to which they over- or under-perform relative to their per capita income. Section 3 provides a theoretical framework for interpreting the evidence that will be reviewed later in the paper, discusses the empirical challenges in generating credible evidence on the impacts of policies to improve education, and outlines the methodology for determining how studies were selected to be included in this review. Section 4 presents our own review of the evidence to date, organized in a way that is consistent with the theoretical framework. Section 5 aims to interpret the body of evidence reviewed in Section 4, and discusses key themes that emerge for both research and policy. Section 6 concludes with a brief set of recommendations for education researchers, as well as for funders and users of such research.

2. TRENDS IN EDUCATION OUTCOMES, 1990 TO 2014

Primary and secondary school enrollment rates have increased in all regions of the developing world in the 50 years from 1960 to 2010, as seen in Table 1.[2] In 1960, primary

---

[2] Data are from the World Bank Edstats data based. Data are missing for some countries, especially in 1960. These are usually very small countries, but there are a few cases of missing data for very large countries. In particular, data are missing for China and the United States in 1960 and for Brazil in 2010. Limiting the data to countries with data in both 1960 and 2010 does not have a large effect on the figures in Table 1.

Table 1 Primary and enrollment rates, 1960 and 2010, by region

	Primary enrollment and completion				Secondary enrollment		
	Enrollment rate		Completion rate	Income adjusted residual (2010)	Enrollment rate		Income adjusted residual (2010)
Region	1960	2010	2010		1960	2010	
OECD countries	110	102	99	−8.0	52	102	−2.6
East Asia and Pacific	73	122	99	10.9	12	82	4.8
Eastern Europe and Central Asia	98	100	98	7.4	53	93	13.7
Latin America and Caribbean	88	108	98	4.2	14	85	3.1
Middle East and North Africa	54	108	98	1.7	10	85	−0.3
South Asia	56	111	92	8.0	18	61	2.0
Sub-Saharan Africa	41	101	68	−10.4	3	44	−12.1

school gross enrollment rates (GER) in the OECD countries[3] and in the countries of Eastern Europe and Central Asia (these are the countries and allies of the former Soviet Union) were above or very close to 100%, and were again close to 100% in 2010. Among developing country regions, the primary school GER in Latin America and East Asia were somewhat lower in 1960 (88% and 73%, respectively), but were over 100% in 2010. Farther behind in 1960 were South Asia (56%), the Middle East and North Africa (54%) and Sub-Saharan Africa (41%). Yet all three of these regions had achieved a 100% rate or higher by 2010.

While the primary GER data for 2010 suggest that all children in all regions are now completing primary school, this is not the case. GER can be misleading because they are calculated as the number of children enrolled in a particular level of school divided by the number of children in the population in the age range associated with that level. If some students repeat grades, or start school at a late age, they may still be in that level of schooling even though they are older than the associated age range. Repetition will, in general, increase GER and so a rate of 100% or even higher is consistent with a sizeable proportion of the population never finishing, and even never enrolling, in that level of schooling.

To assess more fully current progress in primary education it is most useful to examine what proportion of children *complete* primary school. This is shown in the third column of Table 1, for the year 2010 only since very few countries have completion data for 1960. By 2010 close to 100% primary school completion had been achieved in all other regions except South Asia and Sub-Saharan Africa. Yet South Asia is on course to reach full primary completion within a few years, having attained a 92% completion rate by 2010.

---

[3] The OECD countries are Australia, Austria, Belgium, Canada, Denmark, Finland, France, Germany, Greece, Iceland, Ireland, Italy, Japan, Luxembourg, the Netherlands, New Zealand, Norway, Portugal, Spain, Sweden, Switzerland, the United Kingdom, and the United States.

Even though Sub-Saharan Africa's primary school completion rate was only 68% in 2010, this is a large increase from 46% in 2000 (not shown in Table 1), and suggests that a rate close to 90% would be possible by 2020.

Secondary school GER data, by region, are shown for 1960 and 2010 in the fifth and sixth columns of Table 1. The rates in 1960 were only around 52–53% for the OECD countries and the Eastern European and Central Asian countries, but they had reached 100% by 2010. The rates in all five developing country regions were much lower, all below 20%, in 1960, with a very low rate of 3% for Sub-Saharan Africa. Yet by 2010 all regions of the developing world except for South Asia and Sub-Saharan Africa had rates of 80% or higher. In South Asia, the rate increased from 18% in 1960 to 61% in 2010, which is higher than OECD rate in 1960. In Sub-Saharan Africa, the rate increased from a very low rate of only 3% in 1960, reaching 44% in 2010, which is close to the OECD average in 1960.

These patterns raise the question of whether the variation in education attainment between OECD and developing countries are primarily driven by differences in per capita income. In other words, are developing countries lagging behind developed countries in terms of their enrollment rates given their income levels? This question is of little interest for primary school enrollment rates since all regions have attained average GER of 100% or higher. Indeed, Fig. 1 shows that the relationship between the primary GER and (log) per capita income in 2010 is essentially flat. Turning to the primary school completion rate, we find a strong positive correlation with the log of per capita income

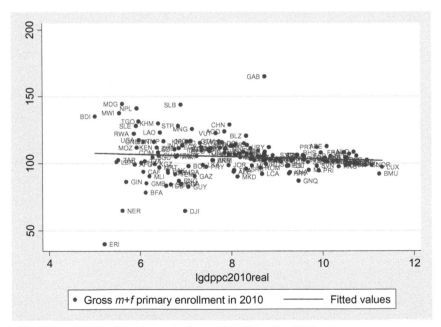

Figure 1 Primary gross enrollment rate by log real GDP/capita, 2010.

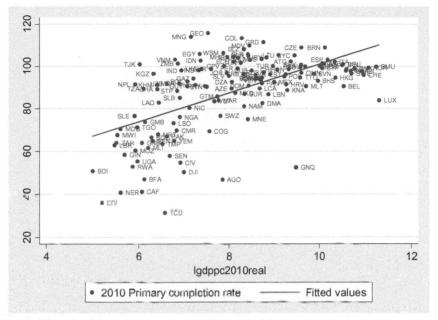

Figure 2 Primary completion rate by log real GDP/capita, 2010.

(Fig. 2). If developing countries are lagging behind the OECD countries even after conditioning on income, they would tend to lie below the line while the OECD countries would tend to be above the line. But this is not the case, as seen in the fourth column of Table 1. Indeed, the average residual for OECD countries is −8.0, which means that those countries tend to lie below the line, and so developing countries lie above it, on average. In other words, developing countries on average outperform on primary school completion rates conditional on per capita income. However, there is variation among developing countries, with East Asian, Eastern European and Central Asian, and South Asian countries generally well above the line while Sub-Saharan African countries are, on average, well below it (−10.4), even after accounting for their income levels.

Fig. 3 and the last column of Table 1 examine secondary school GER conditional on income. That relationship, from an analogous regression, is clearly positive. The last column in Table 1 investigates the performance of different groups of countries conditional on their income levels. On average, OECD countries have a slightly negative residual (−2.6), which implies that they perform slightly worse than average given their income level, so again developing countries, on average, perform somewhat better than average conditional on their income. Yet again there is variation among these countries, with Eastern Europe and Central Asian countries performing well above average, and Sub-Saharan African countries again performing well below average even after conditioning on their income levels.

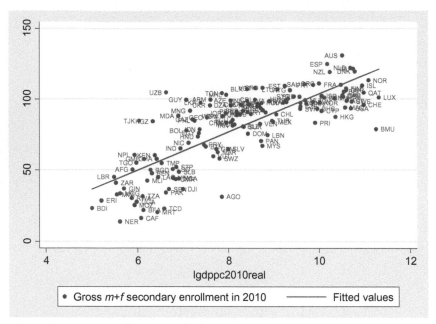

Figure 3 Secondary gross enrollment rate by log real GDP/capita, 2010.

Another way to assess the performance of developing countries in a way that controls for income levels is to examine school enrollment rates of developed countries when their income levels were similar to those of developing countries today. This is done in Table 2, examining three prominent developed countries: the United States, the United Kingdom, and France. Today's low-income developing countries (as defined by the World Bank), have a (purchasing power adjusted) per capita income in 2010 of $1307. France had a somewhat higher (unadjusted) per capita income ($1987) almost 200 years ago, in 1830. At that time, France's primary enrollment rate was only 39%, and its secondary enrollment rate was only 1%, well below the respective rates for low-income countries in 2010 (104% and 39%).

In Table 1, Sub-Saharan African countries seemed to perform poorly even after conditioning on their income levels, but Table 2 demonstrates that their performance is much better than those of today's developed countries when they had income levels similar to the average income level today in Sub-Saharan Africa. More specifically, in 2010 Sub-Saharan African countries had a (purchasing power adjusted) per capita income of $2148. The United States had a slightly higher (unadjusted) per capita income ($2582) almost 200 years ago, in 1830. At that time, its primary enrollment rate was only 55%, and its secondary enrollment rate was less than 1%, well below the respective average rates in Sub-Saharan Africa in 2010 (100% and 36%).

Table 2 Primary and secondary school gross enrollment rates: a historical perspective

Country or country group	Year	GDP/capita (2010 US$)	Enrollment rate Primary	Enrollment rate Secondary
Low-income developing countries	2010	1307	104	39
Middle income developing countries	2010	6747	109	69
South Asian countries	2010	3124	110	55
Sub-Saharan African countries	2010	2148	100	36
United States	1830	2582	55	<1
	1850	3085	68	<1
	1900	6827	88	37
United Kingdom	1890	6691	72	1
France	1830	1987	39	1
	1870	3130	74	1
	1930	7563	80	3

Sources: All 2010 figures are from World Development Indicators 2012. Note that the GDP/capita numbers are adjusted for purchasing power parity. Historical income data for the United States, United Kingdom, and France are from the Maddison-Project, http://www.ggdc.net/maddison/maddison-project/home.htm. Historical enrollment data from those countries were compiled by Peter Lindert, http://lindert.econ.uedavis.edu/data-and-estimates/lindert-data-for-cup-book.

South Asian countries also have relatively low levels of primary and secondary school enrollment, but their enrollment rates are much higher than those of the United States and France when they were at the average income level of South Asian countries in 2010 ($3124). In particular, the United States in 1850 and France in 1870 had very similar income levels, but their primary school enrollment rates were much lower (68% in the United States and 74% in France) than the average for South Asia in 2010 (110) and their secondary school enrollment rates were only about 1%, compared to 55% in South Asian countries today.

A final interesting historical comparison is with the United Kingdom, which had a much higher income in the 1800s relative to France and the United States. In 1890, the per capita income in the United Kingdom (in 2010 dollars) was $6691, which is similar to that of middle income countries in 2010 ($6747). However, in 1890, the primary and secondary school enrollment rates in the United Kingdom were only 72% and 1%, respectively. These are much lower than the 2010 rates for middle income countries, which were 109% and 69%, respectively.

These findings are similar to those of Deaton (2013) for health outcomes; he showed that populations in today's developing countries are much healthier than those in the developed countries a century earlier. These findings for health are almost certainly due to major advances in medicine over that period of time (such as the introduction of vaccinations and antibiotics), but it is not clear that analogous advances in education "technology" explain, even in part, the higher levels of education in today's developing countries compared to developed countries at the same income level in previous decades and centuries. Some possible explanations for these results include: (1) international campaigns for universal primary education,[4] which may have influenced global social norms in a way that persuaded governments in developing countries to prioritize primary education and also led to increased international donor funds to support this goal; (2) greater rates of democratization in developing countries now than in developed countries at a comparable level of per capita income, which may have created domestic political pressure for prioritizing education; and (3) greater returns to education in a world with more advanced technologies, many of which are complements to human capital.

We now examine international comparisons of learning outcomes, and the corresponding correlation with GDP per capita. There are two international learning assessment initiatives that administer comparable mathematics, reading and science tests to school-age children across a large number of developed and developing countries, the PISA and the TIMSS assessments. Both normalize the distributions of test scores so that the mean equals 500 and the standard deviation equals 100.

As others have shown (eg, Hanushek and Woessmann, 2015), students in many, and perhaps most, developing countries learn much less than students of the same age, or in the same grade, learn in OECD countries. However, OECD countries have much higher incomes than developing countries, and parents in OECD countries have much levels of education than do parents in developing countries. Thus, it should not be surprising that students in developed countries learn more each year, since their parents are likely to be both more educated and more able to afford additional school inputs, and the school system can afford more and higher quality inputs. So we conduct a similar exercise as in the case of school completion and plot cross-country test scores as a function of per capita income (Figs. 4–7).

To start, Fig. 4 examines the math scores of 15-year-old students in the 2012 PISA assessment. As expected, there is a general trend that countries with higher (log) incomes have higher test scores. The line in this figure is the least squares line for the all the points in the figure from a regression of test scores on a constant term and the log of per capita income. The OECD countries are "hollow" circles, while all other countries are solid ("filled") circles. However, there is no tendency for OECD countries to be "better than average" given their incomes — they are just as likely to be below the line as they are to be above it. This implies that developing countries as a whole are also found above the line as often as they are below it. Fig. 5 repeats this analysis for the 2012 PISA reading scores, and the results are similar. Similar patterns are seen in the TIMSS data, which are for younger children (in grade 4, so about 10 years old), as seen in Figs. 6 and 7.

The figures presented above provide useful perspective for understanding the challenges of improving human capital accumulation in developing countries. On one hand,

---

[4] Examples include the "Education for All" campaign and the Millennium Development Goals, the latter of which prioritized both universal primary education and the elimination of gender gaps in education.

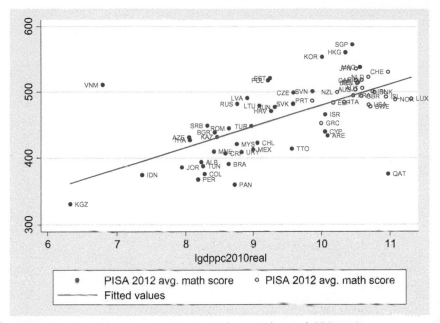

Figure 4 Mean age 15 math scores in 2012 (PISA), by 2010 log real GDP/capita.

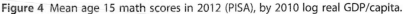

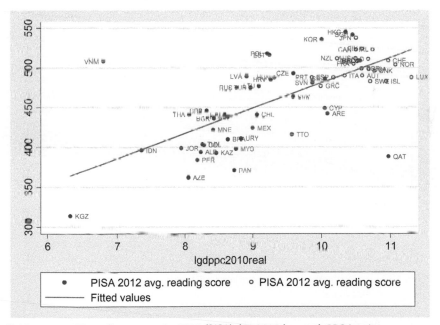

Figure 5 Mean age 15 reading scores in 2012 (PISA), by 2010 log real GDP/capita.

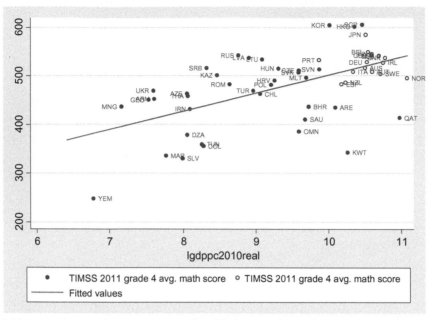

Figure 6 Mean grade 4 math scores in 2011 (TIMSS), by 2010 log real GDP/capita.

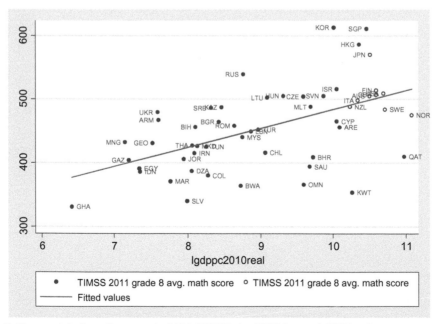

Figure 7 Mean grade 8 math scores in 2011 (TIMSS), by 2010 log real GDP/capita.

the data suggest that developing countries are doing a poor job of translating enrollment into learning outcomes. On the other hand, it is also possible to interpret the results as suggesting that developing countries "overperform" on enrollment conditional on per capita income, and perform "as expected" on learning outcomes conditional on per capita income.[5] Figs. 4–7 suggest that human capital accumulation will likely automatically improve as countries get richer both because parents of future cohorts will be more educated and because countries will have more resources to spend on education.

However, the key policy question of interest should be whether it is possible for developing countries to outperform the levels that would be predicted based on their income levels. One way of doing this is to identify education systems that are strong positive outliers on performance (conditional on per capita income) and to study the features of such education systems in a detailed case study to identify policies that could be translated to other settings for improved performance. For instance, Figs. 4 and 5 suggest that Vietnam is a strong positive outlier in this regard, and may be a role model for other developing country education systems. A second approach is to conduct micro-level (as opposed to system-level) research on the returns to different forms of education spending and reallocate resources from less to more efficient ways of spending limited resources. The advantage of this approach is that it allows for much better causal identification of the impacts (or nonimpacts) of specific categories of education policies, and policy recommendations based on such research is likely to be better grounded in credible evidence.[6] This is the approach that we will focus on for the rest of this chapter.

3. CONCEPTUAL ISSUES

In this section, we discuss two key conceptual issues. First, we present a simple theoretical framework to help organize our thinking to better understand how various policy and

---

[5] Note however, that the sample of students from developing countries who are tested in the TIMSS and PISA is much more nonrepresentative than the corresponding sample in OECD countries. Since these tests are conducted in school, they are only representative of students who are in school (and likely to be attending school regularly). Thus, it is likely that the true levels of learning in developing countries are considerably lower than those measured by TIMSS and PISA, and that these measured scores represent an upper bound on true levels of learning. If we had representative data on learning outcomes in all countries, it is possible that developing countries would be found to be "underperforming" relative to per capita income.

[6] For instance, it is possible that countries like Vietnam and Cuba (see Carnoy et al., 2007) outperform on education relative to per capita income because they were communist societies that (a) prioritized equality in education over outstanding individual achievements, (b) placed greater value on the "indoctrination" of citizens in party ideology and hence prioritized state-run education. A country case study would yield useful insights into such factors, but would not be able to credibly isolate the specific components of communist education systems that were responsible for the "positive deviance." Further, it is not clear whether replicating elements of the policies of these countries would work in the absence of a larger communist society. Nevertheless, we do not argue against the value of such system-level case studies, and consider them to be useful complements to the approach taken in this chapter.

household decisions may affect the production of skills and human capital by education systems. Second, we discuss the key empirical challenges to identifying the impacts of policies to improve education outcomes and discuss the process by which we identify the "high-quality" studies for which the evidence is summarized in Section 4.

3.1 Theoretical Framework

Education policy and research in developing countries have been motivated by finding answers to two key questions. The first one is "how to increase school enrollment and daily attendance among students," and the second one is "how to translate increases in student enrollment and attendance into improvements in skills and human capital." On school enrollment and attendance, a simple model of optimizing households in the tradition of Becker (1962) and Ben-Porath (1967) yields the result that households will invest in an additional year of education for their child only if the present discounted value of the expected increase in benefits exceeds the costs of doing so. Thus, policies that seek to improve school enrollment and attendance typically aim to increase the immediate benefits to households of sending their children to school or to reduce the costs of doing so. The magnitude of the impact of these policies will in turn depend on the distribution of the household and child specific factors, and the extent to which the policy increases the benefits of enrolling a child in school.

As summarized in the previous section, most developing countries have made substantial progress with regard to enrolling children in school; indeed, primary and secondary school enrollment rates are considerably higher than the rates in OECD countries when they were at comparable levels of per capita income. Nevertheless, while enrollment rates are high, in practice school attendance rates are quite varied and may not be as high.[7] This may be particularly true in cases where there is pressure on schools and parents to show high enrollment rates (in response to budget allocation rules and/or compulsory schooling laws). Thus, the challenge of "enrollment" is now better thought of as the challenge of "attendance" in most developing countries. However, the same theoretical framework of comparing costs and benefits of school enrollment can be applied to analyzing the household (and children's) decision of whether to attend school on a given day, and policies that seek to improve attendance similarly focus on increasing the returns to attending school on a given day (for instance through the provision of school meals) or on reducing the costs of doing so (for instance through improved school access).

---

[7] For instance, nationally representative survey data in India collected by the NGO Pratham as part of their annual ASER report finds that on average only 71.4% of students enrolled in primary schools were present during visits to schools, even though the enrollment rate was above 96%. Further, there is substantial variation across Indian states, with several large and economically and educationally backward states such as Bihar, Jharkhand, Uttar Pradesh, West Bengal, and Madhya Pradesh, with a cumulative population of over 500 million people having attendance rates as low as 50–60% (ASER, 2014).

The standard theoretical framework for understanding how various inputs at the household, school, and classroom level translate into learning outcomes is to specify and estimate an education production function. The production function for learning is a structural relationship that can be depicted as:

$$A = a(S, \mathbf{Q}, \mathbf{C}, \mathbf{H}, \mathbf{I}) \tag{1}$$

where A is skills learned (*achievement*), S is years of schooling, $\mathbf{Q}$ is a vector of school and teacher characteristics (*quality*), $\mathbf{C}$ is a vector of child characteristics (including "innate ability"), $\mathbf{H}$ is a vector of household characteristics, and $\mathbf{I}$ is a vector of school inputs under the control of households, such as children's daily attendance, effort in school and in doing homework, and purchases of school supplies.

The household decision making process on both school attendance (S) and the extent of household investments in education ($\mathbf{I}$) is based on optimizing household utility subject to the production function above and a set of constraints. Economists typically assume that each child is a member of a household in which the parents of that child maximize, subject to constraints, a (life-cycle) utility function. The constraints faced are the production function for learning, the impacts of years of schooling and of skills obtained on the future labor incomes of children, a life-cycle budget constraint, and perhaps some credit constraints or an agricultural production function (for which child labor is one possible input).

Assume that all elements in the vectors $\mathbf{C}$ and $\mathbf{H}$ are exogenous. Examples of such variables are credit constraints, parental tastes for schooling, parental education, and children's "ability." Some child characteristics that affect education outcomes (such as child health) could be endogenous; they can be treated as elements of $\mathbf{I}$, all of which are endogenous. Parental decisions regarding the endogenous variables, S and $\mathbf{I}$, depend on another important set of variables, the prices related to schooling, $\mathbf{P}$. These include school fees, prices for school supplies, and even wages paid for child labor. $\mathbf{P}$ does not appear in Eq. (1) because it has no direct effect on learning; its effect works through decisions made for the endogenous variables S and $\mathbf{I}$.

In the simplest scenario, assume that only one school is available and that parents cannot change the characteristics of that school. Thus all variables in $\mathbf{Q}$ and $\mathbf{P}$ are exogenous.[8] Parents choose S and $\mathbf{I}$ (subject to the above-mentioned constraints) to maximize household utility, which implies that both S and $\mathbf{I}$ can be expressed as functions of the four vectors of exogenous variables:

---

[8] In settings where households can choose from more than one school, it is possible that that $\mathbf{Q}$ and $\mathbf{P}$ may be endogenous even if they are fixed for any given school. Here, households maximize utility for each school in their schooling choice set, and then choose the school that leads to the highest utility. Conditional on choosing that school, they choose S and $\mathbf{I}$, as in the case where there is only one school from which to choose. In practice, rural settings are more likely to have limited choice across schools, while higher-density urban settings may feature more choice.

$$S = f(\mathbf{Q}, \mathbf{C}, \mathbf{H}, \mathbf{P}) \tag{2}$$

$$\mathbf{I} = g(\mathbf{Q}, \mathbf{C}, \mathbf{H}, \mathbf{P}) \tag{3}$$

Inserting Eqs. (2) and (3) into Eq. (1) gives the reduced form equation for (A):

$$A = h(\mathbf{Q}, \mathbf{C}, \mathbf{H}, \mathbf{P}) \tag{4}$$

This reduced form equation expresses a causal relationship, but it is not a production function because it reflects household preferences and includes prices among its arguments.

Policymakers are primarily concerned with the impact of education policies on eventual academic achievement, A. For example, reducing class size is a change in one element of $\mathbf{Q}$, and changing tuition fees is a change in one component of $\mathbf{P}$. Eqs. (2) and (4) show how such changes would affect S and A. Assuming that the costs of such changes are not difficult to calculate, the benefits in terms of increases in S and A can be compared to those costs. Of course, the costs should include costs borne by households from the policy change, so changes in $\mathbf{I}$, as expressed in Eq. (3), and in household leisure must be included in the overall cost figure (though in practice this is not easy to do).

Consider a change in one element of $\mathbf{Q}$, denoted by Q_i. Eq. (1) shows how changes in Q_i affect A holding all other explanatory variable constant, and thus provides the *partial* derivative of A with respect to Q_i. This represents a *production function parameter*. In contrast, Eq. (4) provides the *total* derivative of A with respect to Q_i as it allows for changes in S and $\mathbf{I}$ in response to the change in Q_i. This represents a *policy parameter*. Parents may respond to better teaching by increasing their provision of educational inputs; alternatively, if they consider better teaching a substitute for those inputs, they may reduce those inputs. In general, the partial and total derivatives could be quite different, and researchers should be clear which relationship they are estimating.

When examining the impact of policies on academic skills, A, should policymakers look at Eq. (1), or Eq. (4)? Eq. (4) is of interest because it shows what will actually happen to A after a change in one or more element in $\mathbf{Q}$ or $\mathbf{P}$; Eq. (1) will not show this because it does not account for changes in S and $\mathbf{I}$ in response to changes in $\mathbf{Q}$ and $\mathbf{P}$. Yet the partial derivative from Eq. (1) is also of interest because understanding the actual production function helps to identify the most cost-effective policies for improving education outcomes. Knowing the pure production function impact of a policy change may also better capture overall welfare effects. Intuitively, if parents respond to an increase in Q_i by reducing purchases of inputs $\mathbf{I}$, they will be able to raise household welfare by purchasing more of other goods and services. The reduced form impact (total derivative) reflects the drop in A due to the reduction in $\mathbf{I}$, but it does not account for the increase in household welfare from the increased purchase of other goods and services. In contrast, the production function impact, by holding $\mathbf{I}$ constant, captures the full impact before the benefit is shifted away from A to something not meaured by the reduced form impact. Thus, knowledge of the relationships in both Eqs. (1) and (4) is useful for policymakers; Eq. (4) shows what will happen to education outcomes, while Eq. (1) best captures the overall welfare effect.

In practice, there are two main challenges when attempting to estimate the relationship in either Eq. (1) or Eq. (4). The first is that these equations represent the relationship between inputs and the *total stock* of human capital. Thus, estimating the production function in Eq. (1) would require the econometrician to have data on *all prior inputs* into human capital — including early childhood experiences and even in-utero conditions. This is an extremely challenging requirement and is unlikely to be feasible in almost all settings. Thus, the standard approach to estimating education production functions is to treat the lagged test score as a sufficient statistic for representing prior inputs into learning, and to use a value-added model to study the impact of changing contemporaneous inputs into education on test scores (see Todd and Wolpin, 2003, for further details, including the assumptions needed for this approach to yield consistent estimates of production function parameters of interest).

Specifically, the estimating equation that is typically used has the following form:

$$A_{i,t} = \gamma A_{i,t-1} + \beta' X_{i,t} + \varepsilon_{i,t} \tag{5}$$

where $A_{i,t}$ represents test scores of child i at time t, $A_{i,t-1}$ represents the (lagged) test score at time $t-1$, and $X_{i,t}$ represents a full vector of contemporaneous home and school inputs. While the production function above is linear in $X_{i,t}$ and is typically estimated this way, the specification does not have to be very restrictive, because $X_{i,t}$ can include nonlinear (eg, quadratic) terms in individual inputs, and can also include interaction terms between specific sets of inputs.

However, even with the value-added specification of Eq. (5), the second challenge to consistently estimating β is that variation in the right-hand side variables is likely to be correlated with the error term $\varepsilon_{i,t}$. In other words, the observed school, teacher, and household characteristics are all likely to be correlated with unobserved (omitted) school, teacher, and household variables that directly determine learning outcomes — which will lead to biased estimates of β. In practice, this problem is quite likely to occur. For instance, communities and parents that care more about education are likely to be able to successfully lobby for more school inputs, and are also likely to provide unmeasured inputs into their children's education, which would lead to an upward bias on β when Eq. (5) is estimated using cross-sectional data.[9] In other cases, governments may target inputs to disadvantaged areas to improve equity, in which case areas with higher values of due to the program may have lower values of $\varepsilon_{i,t}$, leading to negative correlation between and $\varepsilon_{i,t}$ and thus downwardly biased estimates of β.

Relative to the evidence available when Glewwe and Kremer (2006) reviewed the literature, the largest advances in the empirical literature in the past decade have come from the increased prevalence of studies that pay careful attention to credibly identifying

---

[9] This problem is mitigated but not eliminated by including lagged test scores. While including the lagged test scores can help control for time invariant omitted variables, doing so does not eliminate concerns of contemporaneous omitted variables.

the causal impact of various education policies on learning outcomes. In particular, the sharp increase in the number of randomized experiments to study the impacts of education policies has greatly increased the volume of credible evidence on education in developing countries.[10]

The importance of accounting for omitted variable bias in the evaluation of education interventions is starkly illustrated by Glewwe et al. (2004), who compare retrospective and prospective studies of the impact of classroom flipcharts on learning outcomes. They find, using observational data, that flipcharts in classrooms appear to raise student test scores by 0.2 standard deviations of the distribution of students' test scores. However, when they conduct a randomized controlled trial (RCT) of flipcharts in classrooms, they find no impact on test scores at all, suggesting that the nonexperimental estimates were significantly biased upwards (even after controlling for other observable factors). These results underscore the value of field experiments for program evaluation in developing countries, and Glewwe et al. (2004) can be considered analogous to LaLonde (1986) in the US program evaluation literature, which showed that nonexperimental methods were not able to replicate the estimates from experimental evaluations of the impact of job training programs.

Note that the framework in Eq. (5) is quite general and can be used to examine policies that do not directly change $X_{i,t}$ but instead change the way schools are organized such as decentralization, promoting competition by removing restrictions on private schools, or developing incentive schemes that link teacher pay to student performance. In principle, these types of policies affect schooling outcomes by changing what happens in the classroom. For example, increased competition may change the behavior of teachers, and these behaviors can be included as components of the vector $\mathbf{Q}$. Further, Eq. (5) is also general enough to allow for both heterogeneity and complementarity in the impact of specific household and school inputs on learning outcomes. However, in practice, most studies focus mainly on credibly estimating the average value of $\boldsymbol{\beta}$ for specific changes in $X_{i,t}$ since the data requirements for credibly estimating heterogeneity and complementarities are more demanding.

3.2 Empirics

One of the main contributions of this chapter is its review of the evidence on the impacts of different types of education policies and programs on student learning and time in

---

[10] See the complementary chapter by Muralidharan (2016a) for further details on field experiments in education in developing countries, including a practical guide on how to conduct such experiments successfully. While there is some overlap between that chapter and this one, the focus of that chapter is methodological and aims to provide a user guide for running and interpreting field experiments in education in developing countries, whereas the focus of this chapter is more substantive and aims to synthesize the literature and what we have learned from it.

Table 3 Steps used to select papers used in conducting synthesis

Review step	Procedures used	Number of papers
1	Search EconLit and ERIC databases	13,437
	Review abstracts to eliminate duplicate papers and papers that did not estimate the impacts of school or teacher characteristics for a developing country	1017
2	Review full papers, eliminate papers based on lack of relevance or lack of quantitative analysis	320
3	Exclude papers that are not "high quality" (RCT, RDD, DD)	118
4	Number of high-quality studies that are RCT studies	80

school. However, as we highlight above, an important challenge for empirical research in this area is that of credible causal identification. We therefore limit our synthesis of the evidence to 118 high-quality studies conducted from 1990 to 2014.[11] In this section, we discuss the criteria for selecting these studies from the hundreds of relevant studies in the literature. To identify evaluations that have produced credible impacts of education programs or policies, the following four-step selection process was implemented. The number of studies corresponding to each step is shown in Table 3.

3.2.1 Step 1: Search for Possibly Relevant Papers/Reports and Read Their Abstracts

To begin, a search was conducted on a wide variety of sources, after which evaluations were systematically eliminated that did not meet a series of criteria for relevance and quality. To be included in the search, studies had to have been published in the (peer-reviewed) academic literature from 1990 to 2014, inclusive. Unpublished academic working papers written from 2010 to 2014 were also included. Academic working papers written before 2010 that had not yet been published by the end of 2014 were judged as likely to have some methodological flaws that have resulted in their not being published in peer-reviewed journals, so only academic working papers that were written from 2010 to 2014 were included.

The very first task was to conduct a search for journal articles published between 1990 and 2014 using two search engines for the economics and education literatures, respectively: EconLit and the Education Resources Information Center (ERIC). All papers that list both "education" as a keyword and any one of a list of 124 educational programs or policies as keywords (see the online Appendix for this list) were included in this initial sweep of the literature. The search was also limited to papers that include the name of at least one developing country or the term "developing country" or "developing

---

[11] Note that almost all papers that are cited with a 2015 publication date are either a revised or final versions of prior working papers that were available in 2014 or earlier, which (as explained below) are included in our review.

countries" in the abstract. Developing countries are defined using the International Monetary Fund's list of emerging and developing countries.

This initial search yielded 13,437 publications. For these papers, information found in the abstract (and, in some cases, by looking at the introduction or conclusion of the paper) was used to limit the studies to those that appear to be potentially relevant. In particular, this eliminated evaluations that did not focus on developing countries, or that did not estimate the impact of a program or policy on students' education outcomes.

In addition to published papers, a search was conducted of several prominent working papers series: National Bureau of Economic Research (NBER) working papers; World Bank Policy Research working papers; the Institute for the Study of Labor (IZA); the Center for Economic and Policy Research (CEPR); the CESIfo Research Network; the Rural Education Action Project (REAP) at Stanford University; and Oxford University's Young Lives Study. Papers listed as education papers on the Abdul Latif Jameel Poverty Action Lab's website were also searched. As mentioned above, working papers that appeared before 2010 were not included due to the assumption that high-quality working papers written before 2010 should have been published by 2014. As with the selection criteria for published papers, evaluations that do not focus on developing countries (for instance, several good studies from Israel were not included because Israel was not considered to be a developing country), or that do not estimate the impact of a program or policy on students' educational outcomes, were not included. The number of published papers and working papers that remained after reading their abstracts was 1017.

3.2.2 Step 2: Read Entire Paper/Report to Verify Relevance

In the second step, all of the evaluations that were not eliminated in the first step were read in full to obtain further information about each study. During this step, additional papers were eliminated for lack of relevance that was not evident from reading the abstracts. Possible reasons for lack of relevance were: (1) The evaluation did not focus on a developing country (which was not always clear in the abstracts); (2) The paper did not evaluate any type of education policy or program; and (3) The paper did not include quantitative analysis of the impact of an education policy or program on students' educational outcomes. After this step was completed, 320 papers remained that were relevant for this review of the literature.

3.2.3 Step 3: Retaining Only High-Quality Evaluations

In a third step, the evaluations that were not eliminated in the first two steps were reviewed for their quality. While regression analysis is commonly used to estimate the impact of a policy or program on an educational outcome, a very serious problem with regression analysis is that some factors that have a causal impact on the education outcome variables of interest are unlikely to be available in the data, which can lead to bias in regression estimates of the impacts of education policies and programs, and thus misleading results. This is the problem of *omitted variable bias*. Another problem with regression analysis is that regressions often included many school and teacher characteristics, but only to serve as control variables, and in many cases authors are not particularly interested in the coefficients associated with those variables, and so they should not be interpreted as estimates of the causal impacts of those variables.

Given these problems with regression estimation methods, all studies based on those methods alone are deemed not to be high-quality studies. Since matching estimators invoke similar assumptions, in particular the assumption that conditioning on (other) observed variables implies that (observed and counterfactual) education outcomes are independent of the program participation variable, studies based on matching methods were also excluded. This leaves three types of studies that are considered to be high-quality studies in this review. First, all evaluations based on a well-implemented RCT are included in the set of high-quality studies, as these studies avoid, or at least minimize, many types of estimation problems. Second, estimates based on a difference-in-differences (DD) regression (which requires longitudinal data) are deemed to be high-quality studies. Finally, evaluations based on regression discontinuity design (RDD) are also considered to be high-quality studies. The set of papers that were retained after this third step contained 118 "high-quality" studies.

3.2.4 Step 4: Identify RCT Evaluations

The fourth and final step of the review set an even higher bar for the quality of an evaluation. Well-implemented RCT studies arguably have the highest credibility, when implemented correctly. In particular, DD studies must rely on the parallel trends assumption, which can be difficult to verify, and RDD evaluations identify impacts only at the "cutoff point," strictly speaking. Of the 118 high-quality studies, about two-thirds (80) were RCTs. Note that we include high-quality non-RCT studies, but we typically give priority to the RCT evidence.

4. REVIEW OF THE EVIDENCE

This section reviews the evidence on the impacts of different types of education policies and programs on student learning and time in school. This is based on 118 high-quality studies conducted from 1990 to 2014. Following the theoretical framework above, we have organized this review as follows: First, we review interventions that are intended to increase the demand for schooling by students and their parents; second, we examine standard educational inputs that are typically provided through schools; third, we review the evidence on policies that are related to pedagogy; finally, we look at policies and programs related to the governance of schools, and to education systems more broadly.

The results of the high-quality studies discussed in this section are summarized in Tables 4–11. These tables list the number of estimates of positive and negative impacts for specific interventions, and they also break these down by whether the results are sta-tistically significant (at the 10% level). The number of studies from which these estimates come are shown in parentheses for each type of estimate (positive or negative, and sig-nificant or insignificant) for each intervention. While our discussion does not distinguish between positive and negative point estimates that are statistically insignificant, the tables present this breakdown to help the interested reader see the general direction of impacts even in cases where they are not significant.[12] Note that, unless otherwise indicated, we refer to impacts as "positive" or "negative" only if they are statistically significant at the 10% (or lower) significance level.

4.1 Demand-Side Interventions (Interventions That Focus on Households)

As discussed in Section 3.1, household decisions on whether to send their child to school are based on comparing the (perceived) costs and benefits of doing so. However, there are several reasons why household decisions may not be socially optimal. Possible reasons include: (1) Parents may not accurately perceive the returns to education, and therefore under- or overinvest in education; (2) Households may be credit constrained, which makes them unable to afford the upfront costs (both direct and indirect) of sending their children to school even though the investment in education has, on average, a positive expected value; (3) Households may be risk-averse, which may make them not invest in an extra year of education even if the average expected return is positive due to the var-iance of the actual return that their child will obtain; (4) Parents may have higher discount rates than the social planner, which may lead to suboptimal investments in education rel-ative to what is socially optimal; and (5) Parents may not account for the social spillovers from their child being educated (as is standard in any model with complementarities across the productivity of workers, such as Kremer, 1993), and so they may underinvest in their child's education.

Thus, the first class of interventions we review are those that aim to alleviate demand-side constraints to school enrollment and daily attendance. Table 4 summarizes the results for the impacts of these types of interventions on measures of time in school, such as daily attendance, current enrollment, and years of completed schooling, and Table 5 does the same for learning outcomes as measured by test scores. Below, we discuss these studies in more detail, grouping them into four general categories: information-based interventions, cash transfer programs, scholarship programs and other household interventions.

---

[12] This may be especially useful in cases where individual studies lack power to estimate statistically signif-icant impacts, but where multiple studies obtain insignificant estimates that are primarily either positive or negative.

Table 4 Summary of impacts on time in school of demand-side interventions

	Negative, significant	Negative, insignificant	Positive, insignificant	Positive, significant	Total studies
Information-based interventions					
Information on returns to education (all RCTs)	0 (0)	1 (1)	1 (1)	2 (1)	2
Career counseling (RCT)	1 (1)	0 (0)	0 (0)	0 (0)	1
School counseling (RCT)	0 (0)	0 (0)	1 (1)	1 (1)	1
Cash transfer programs					
Conditional cash transfer					
RCTs	0 (0)	0 (0)	3 (2)	24 (13)	13
Other high-quality studies	0 (0)	0 (0)	0 (0)	16 (7)	7
Unconditional cash transfers (RCT)	0 (0)	0 (0)	1 (1)	1 (1)	1
Labeled cash transfer (RCT)	0 (0)	0 (0)	0 (0)	2 (1)	1
Eliminating school fees (non-RCT)	0 (0)	2 (2)	1 (1)	1 (1)	2
Scholarship programs					
Merit-based scholarship (all RCTs)	0 (0)	0 (0)	1 (1)	3 (2)	2
Other household interventions					
Mother class on child learning (RCT)	0 (0)	0 (0)	1 (1)	0 (0)	1
Mother literacy class (RCT)	0 (0)	0 (0)	1 (1)	0 (0)	1
Combined mother literacy class and mother class on child learning (RCT)	0 (0)	0 (0)	1 (1)	0 (0)	1
Adult literacy program (non-RCT)	0 (0)	0 (0)	1 (1)	0 (0)	1
Female sanitary products (RCT)	0 (0)	1 (1)	0 (0)	0 (0)	1
Bicycle program (non-RCT)	0 (0)	0 (0)	0 (0)	1 (1)	1
Matching remittances funds for education (RCT)	0 (0)	0 (0)	1 (1)	1 (1)	1

Figures are number of estimates; figures in parentheses are number of papers/studies; statistical significance is at 10% level.

4.1.1 Information-Based Interventions

Several demand-side interventions are designed to provide information to students and their parents about the benefits of education and on how to take advantage of educational opportunities. Examples of such policies include providing information on the returns to education in the labor market and more general types of student counseling. The findings

Table 5 Summary of impacts on test scores of demand-side interventions

	Negative, significant	Negative, insignificant	Positive, insignificant	Positive, significant	Total studies
Information-based interventions					
Inform. on returns to schooling (RCT)	0 (0)	1 (1)	0 (0)	0 (0)	1
Career counseling (RCT)	0 (0)	1 (1)	0 (0)	0 (0)	1
Cash transfer programs					
Conditional cash transfer RCTs	0 (0)	1 (1)	1 (1)	3 (3)	5
Other high-quality studies	0 (0)	1 (1)	1 (1)	0 (0)	2
Unconditional cash transfers (RCT)	0 (0)	1 (1)	1 (1)	0 (0)	1
Labeled cash transfer (RCT)	0 (0)	0 (0)	1 (1)	0 (0)	1
Promise of high school financial aid (RCT)	0 (0)	1 (1)	0 (0)	0 (0)	1
Scholarship programs					
Merit-based scholarship (all RCTs)	0 (0)	1 (1)	0 (0)	6 (4)	4
Other household interventions					
Mother literacy classes (RCT)	0 (0)	0 (0)	1 (1)	0 (0)	1
Mother class on child learning (RCT)	0 (0)	0 (0)	0 (0)	1 (1)	1
Combined mother literacy class and mother class on child learning (RCT)	0 (0)	0 (0)	0 (0)	1 (1)	1

Figures are number of estimates; figures in parentheses are number of papers/studies; statistical significance is at 10% level.

from these studies are summarized in the first three lines of Table 4, which focuses on measures of time in school, and the first two lines of Table 5, which focuses on student learning as measured by test scores.

One potential reason why parents invest relatively little in their children's education is that they, or their children, may not be aware of sizeable returns to education in the labor market. Two high-quality studies have examined the impact on students' time in school of providing this type of information to parents and/or their children. As seen in the first line of Table 4, of the four estimates from these two studies, two (one from each study) are statistically insignificant while two (both from the other study) are significantly positive.

The first study of this type was by Jensen (2010), who implemented an RCT that provided information on (estimated) returns to schooling to boys in grade 8 from poor households in the Dominican Republic. This information was provided to these students in the form of a brief statement read to the students at the end of a survey. The motivation for this intervention was the finding that these students generally assumed that the returns to additional years of schooling were very low, which may explain their low rates of secondary school completion. Jensen found that the boys who received the information were 4.1% more likely to be in school 1 year after receiving the information (significant at the 10% level). He also found, using data collected 4 years later, that the boys who received the information were 2.3% more likely to finish secondary school (not significant) and had completed, on average, 0.2 more years of schooling (significant at the 5% level). The effects were strongest for the least poor of those in poor households, and weakest for the poorest of the poor households, which suggests that the latter may face other barriers, such as credit constraints.

In contrast, a similar but more intensive intervention in China by Loyalka et al. (2013) found little effect of providing information. They focused on boys and girls in grade 7 in poor rural areas of two Chinese provinces (Hebei and Shaanxi). As in the Dominican Republic, an initial survey suggested that these students had inaccurate information about the costs and benefits (in terms of future earnings) of education (in particular, they overestimated the cost of vocational education), and that they also lacked career planning skills. The intervention consisted of providing a 45 min information session on earnings associated with different levels of schooling. The evaluation was implemented as an RCT, and the main result is that the program had no significant effect on the dropout rate. The authors speculate that students felt that the quality of their schools was low, and thus they assumed that for their schools the additional time in school would not produce high returns, but they present no evidence to support this conjecture. Loyalka et al. (2013) also examined whether this intervention increased students' test scores, and found no significant effect, as seen in the first row of Table 5.

The Loyalka et al. study also examined another information-based initiative, that of providing four, 45-min sessions on career counseling. As seen in the second row of Table 4, this program had a significantly negative impact on time in school; the authors speculate that this may reflect that students learned that upper secondary and postsecondary entrance requirements were more difficult than they had previously thought. It had no statistically significant impact on student learning as measured by test scores, as seen in the second line of Table 5.

A somewhat similar information-based initiative, also in China, was a school counseling intervention that was evaluated by Huan et al. (2014). This program involved students in grades 7 and 8 who were preparing to take upper secondary school entrance exams. The main goal of the counseling was to reduce students' anxiety. Using an RCT to estimate the impact of this program, the authors found that it reduced the dropout rate by about 2% in the first half of the school year, an estimate that is significant at the 10% level, but there was no effect at the end of the school year (see the third line of

Table 4). The paper did not examine the impact of this intervention on student learning as measured by test scores.

4.1.2 Cash Transfer Programs

One of the most widely implemented demand-side programs during the last two decades, for which there is also a large amount of evidence, is conditional cash transfer (CCT) programs, which provide monetary payments to parents if their children are enrolled in school and have a high rate of attendance (usually 80% or 85%). Note that these programs address two different market imperfections that lead to suboptimal household investments in education. First, by providing resources to the household that can be used for the education of children, CCT programs alleviate credit and resource constraints that may make it difficult for households to bear the upfront direct and indirect costs of schooling. Second, by conditioning the provision of the cash transfer on enrollment, CCT programs aim to increase the *immediate* returns to households of investing in education and thereby reduce potential differences between the individually and socially optimal decisions regarding education of children, which were mentioned above.

While these programs focus on (and indeed condition on) enrollment and attendance, as opposed to test scores directly, to the extent that they increase enrollment and attendance they should also (hopefully) increase student learning. For a more detailed description, and an earlier assessment, of these programs, see Fiszbein et al. (2009). Beyond the question of whether CCTs are effective at improving time in school and learning outcomes, key related questions of interest include: (1) Is the "conditionality" actually necessary, or can it be dropped or replaced by "framing" the transfer as being for children's education (which would reduce the monitoring cost)? (2) Can the design of the CCT be modified to improve education outcomes, for example by adjusting the timing of payments and conditioning them on learning outcomes? (3) How does the impact of the program vary by the amounts of the transfers?

Since CCT programs provide payments to parents if their children are enrolled in school and maintain a high rate of attendance, one would expect that they increase the time that children spend in school. The results are summarized in the fourth and fifth rows of Table 4. Of the 43 estimates from 20 studies, almost all (40) are significantly positive (the other three are statistically insignificant). Thus the evidence is clear that this policy is effective at increasing time school. We now discuss these studies in some detail.

The most studied CCT program is Mexico's *PROGRESA* (later renamed as *Oportunidades*) program, which was both one of the first CCT programs in the world and, crucially, the first to be randomized to allow for credible estimation of its impact. It provided monthly cash payments to the mothers of children in grades 3–9 whose daily attendance rate in the previous month was 85% or higher. The amounts varied by grade, with grade 3 students receiving only about $7 per month and grade 9 students receiving either $22 (boys) or $25 (girls) per month.

Several studies have looked at the impact of *PROGRESA* on outcomes for students at different ages and after different durations of exposure. The first published study of its impact on time in school is that of Schultz (2004). He presents estimates, separately by grade for grades 3–9, of the impact of the program on enrollment in those grades, conditional on completing the previous grade. The largest effect is in the transition from primary to secondary school; conditional on completing grade 6 (completing primary school), students in the communities randomly assigned to the program had a grade 7 enrollment rate 8.7 percentage points higher than students in the control communities.

Behrman et al. (2009) provide estimates on grades of schooling completed that include both urban and rural areas, while Schultz included only rural areas. Another difference is that Behrman et al. (2009) examine children who were 6–14 years old in 2003, while Schultz examines a slightly older cohort: children who were 6–16 in 1999. The estimated impacts on boys' and girls' grades of school completed in Behrman et al. (2009) are small and statistically insignificant after 1.5 years of exposure to the program. In contrast, they obtain much larger and statistically significant estimated impacts after 5.5 years of exposure, impacts of 0.25 grades for boys and 0.32 for girls. A subsequent paper by the same authors, Behrman et al. (2011), also examined impacts after 5.5 years but it focused on an older cohort, children 9–15 years old in 1997, and is limited to rural areas. The children in this cohort, unlike those in the younger cohort considered in the earlier paper, are old enough to have completed their schooling and so the impact on grades of schooling completed is likely to be both larger and to be the full, final impact of the program. For girls aged 15–18 years old in 2003, and thus 9–12 years old when the program started in 1997, the program increased grades completed by about 0.7, and for boys of that age the impact was 0.9 to 1.0 additional grades completed. The impacts for older boys and girls (19–21 in 2003) were lower, especially for girls, likely because these children had fewer years of exposure to the program.[13]

More recent papers have examined CCT programs in other countries. Baird et al. (2011) estimated the impact of a CCT program for girls in Malawi on time in school. For girls already in school when the program started, the number of terms enrolled over the next 2 years increased by 0.535; since each year consists of three terms, this equivalent to one sixth of a year of schooling. Also, the daily attendance rate over the 2 years rose by 8.0 percentage points. They also find that variation in the size of the cash transfers had little effect on these outcomes. In a companion study, Baird et al. (2013) examined impacts of the same program for girls not in school when the program began, many of whom returned to school due to the program. They find a much larger impact on

---

[13] A third paper by these authors (and two others), Behrman et al. (2012), examined the short-term effects of the *PROGRESA* program on children in urban areas. After 1 year of program exposure both boys and girls who were aged 6–20 in 2002 had 0.11 higher grades completed; these effects are highly statistically significant.

terms enrolled over the 2-year period, an increase of 2.35 that is highly significant. This is equivalent to almost 1 year of schooling over a 2-year period.

Even more recently, Mo et al. (2013) estimated the impact of a CCT program on students in grade 7 in rural China. Households were offered about US$70 if their children had maintained an 80% or higher rate of attendance over one semester (4–5 months) of school. The authors find that the program reduced the dropout rate by 8%.

An interesting study by Barrera-Osorio et al. (2011) examined the impacts of three different versions of a CCT program in Colombia on daily attendance and enrollment among secondary school students. The first version was a standard CCT program that provided about $15 per month to students' families conditional on a daily attendance rate of 80% or higher in the previous month. The second version imposed the same conditionality but reduced the monthly payments to $10 per month and put $5 per month into a bank account that was made available around the time when students are preparing to enroll in the next year of schooling, which coincides with the time of year that educational related expenses are needed. Finally, the third version also provided payments of $10 per month for regular attendance but then put about $5 per month into a fund that was made available 6 years later, at the time of graduation from secondary school, but only if the student had enrolled in tertiary education. If the student did not enroll in tertiary education he or she had to wait another year before the money was made available. The objective was to provide an incentive to enroll in tertiary education.

All three versions of this intervention led to statistically significant increase in the daily rate of attendance. The first two interventions increased daily attendance by about 3 percentage points, while the third increased it by 5.6 percentage points. The first version, with no "forced savings," had no statistically significant effect on the enrollment rate. The second and third interventions both increased the enrollment rate by about 4 percentage points, increases that were statistically significant. These results suggest that adding a "forced savings" component to a CCT program could increase enrollment at the secondary and tertiary levels by a much larger amount than a CCT without that feature, and more generally that CCT programs can be made more effective by changing the design of those programs. These results also indicate that households may have difficulties committing to long-term investments in education, and that making "commitment devices" available leads to greater educational investments.

Colombia also has a national CCT program; it provides monthly cash grants to parents of children in primary school ($7 per month) and secondary school ($14 per month), conditional on a monthly attendance rate of 80%. The program, which started in 2002, was examined by Attanasio et al. (2010). Using difference-in-differences estimation, these authors found small (1.4 in urban areas and 2.8 in rural areas) but statistically significant percentage point increases in enrollment rates for children aged 8–13 years old, as well as larger (and also statistically significant) impacts for children aged 14–17 (4.7 percentage points for urban areas, and 6.6 for rural areas). Baez and Camacho (2011) also studied the impact of this program on time on school in Colombia, though they focused on more long-term impacts. They found that the program increased the probability of finishing secondary school by 3.9 percentage points.

Two papers have examined the impact of Nicaragua's CCT program, which focused on children in primary school, on time in school. Gitter and Barham (2008) examined the short-run impact, before the control group was allowed to participate in the program in 2003. They found that the program increased the current enrollment of 7–13-year-old children by 16.6 percentage points. Barham et al. (2013) examined the longer run effect of the program on boys; girls were not included in the study since their enrollment rates at ages 9–12 were quite high. Note also that this study had no pure control group; instead one set of randomly selected communities had the program for 5 years (2000 to 2005) while the other set had the program for only 2 years (2003 to 2005). They found that the program increased the number of grades attained by one-half (0.50).

There is only one high-quality study of a CCT program in a South Asian country, that of Chaudhury and Parajuli (2010) on Pakistan. The program targeted girls in grades 6–8. Their families received about $3 per month if their daughters' monthly attendance rate was 80% or higher. The evaluation was not based on an RCT, but instead uses difference-in-differences and regression discontinuity methods. The authors find that the program increased girls' enrollment by 8.7% (a 4 percentage point increase on a base of 43%).

Brazil's CCT program, originally called *Bolsa Escola* but now known as *Bolsa Familia*, is likely the largest such program in the world. At the time of the evaluations discussed below, it was targeted at 6–15-year-old children in poor households (it was later expanded to include older teenage children). Conditional on their child having an 85% attendance rate, parents received about $8 per month per child for up to three children. Unlike Mexico's *PROGRESA* program, Brazil's *Bolsa* program was not implemented as an RCT.

Two recent studies have examined Brazil's CCT program. De Janvry et al. (2012) applied difference-in-differences methods to household survey data; they found that the program reduced the dropout rate by 9.6 percentage points. Glewwe and Kassouf (2012) also used difference-in-differences estimation, but on school level data. They find that the Brazil program increased enrollment by about 3 percentage points and reduced the dropout rate by 3 percentage points. The likely cause of the difference in these two papers' estimated reductions in the dropout rates is that de Janvry et al. examined only four states in the poor Northeast region of Brazil, while Glewwe and Kassouf used nationwide data; the impact of the program is likely to be much larger among populations with higher poverty rates.

Honduras implemented a CCT program in the early 2000s for children aged 6–12 who were in grades 1–4. Conditional on daily attendance of 85% or higher, the mothers of these children received monthly payments of about $6. The program was implemented as an RCT. Galiani and McEwan (2013) found that it increased the enrollment rate by 8.3 percentage points, an estimate that is highly statistically significant.

Two recent studies have examined CCT programs in Cambodia. Barrera-Osorio and Filmer (2013) used an RCT to examine the impact of a standard CCT program that provided poor households (as measured by self-reported household characteristics) $10, twice per year, conditional on enrollment and maintaining passing grades. They found that the program increased the probability that students reach grade 6 increased by 17 percentage points, and more generally that their grades completed increased by 0.33 grades. They also examined a variant of the CCT program which targeted students in grades 4–6 if they scored well on a test at the end of grade 3.[14] This variant also provided $10, twice per year, to scholarship recipients who stayed enrolled, attended regularly, and maintained passing grades, all up to the end of grade 6. They find that this program increased students' probability of reaching grade 6 by 12 percentage points and increased the probability of an additional grade by 18 percentage points.

Filmer and Schady (2014) examined the medium-term impacts of a different Cambodian CCT program that provided scholarships to low-income students who graduated from primary school (finished grade 6). The scholarships paid for costs of schooling for grades 7, 8, and 9, conditional on staying in school and not repeating a grade. They were provided to approximately 20% of students, those who were deemed most at risk of dropping out based on information provided by those students. This estimation was done using regression discontinuity methods, taking advantage of the fact that eligibility for the program was determined by the dropout risk score; those whose risk score was just high enough to make them eligible for the program were compared to those whose score was slightly too low to make them eligible. Five years after the scholarships were offered, they find that the program increased the average number of grades completed by a statistically significant 0.6 years.

Two recent studies have examined the impact of cash transfer programs that did *not* condition the transfers on students' educational outcomes. The first is an *unconditional* cash transfer program in Malawi that was examined by Baird et al. (2011), the results of which are summarized in the sixth line of Table 4. Among girls who were already in school when the program started, the number of terms that they were enrolled over the next 2 years increased from 4.79 to 5.02, a small but statistically significant increase. The second is a "labeled" cash transfer program in Morocco that was examined by Benhassine et al. (2015). It provided monthly cash payments of $8 to $13 to primary

---

[14] The authors describe this as a merit-based scholarship program, but it differed from the merit-based scholarship programs discussed below because receipt of the scholarships was based on academic performance before the program started, so the program itself provided no incentive for students to increase their academic performance. Thus we view this program as a CCT program targeted at students whose past performance was relatively high.

school students' parents, with higher amounts for higher grades. The payments were "labeled" as assistance for costs of education, but there was no formal requirement that students enroll or attend school regularly for their parents to receive the payments. The results are summarized in the seventh line of Table 4. The authors find that the program increased the enrollment rate by 7.4 percentage points (average over boys and girls); this estimated impact is statistically significant. It did not matter whether the mother or father received the payment.

A final way to, in effect, transfer cash to parents whose children attend school is simply to reduce school fees. Indeed, in the past 10–20 years many developing countries, especially in Sub-Saharan African, have eliminated school fees at the primary level. There are two high-quality studies that examined the effect of such a program on students' time in school. The first is that of Borkum (2012). He used a regression-discontinuity approach to examine the impact of eliminating school fees in South African primary and secondary schools that served poor populations. Unlike the results for CCT programs, he found no effect of the elimination of school fees on enrollment at either the primary or the secondary level.

The second is a "scholarship" program that was not merit-based in China, which was evaluated by Yi et al. (2014). The program promised financial scholarships to pay for upper secondary school (either the vocational track or the academic track) to poor students in Shaanxi and Hebei provinces who were currently in lower secondary school (grades 7 and 9). There is no condition on this financial assistance other than being admitted to upper secondary school. Thus, this is essentially a fee reduction program. For students in grade 9, the intervention increased the rate of entry into upper secondary by 7.9 percentage points, which was statistically significant, but for those in grade 7 the increase was only 3.0 percentage points and not statistically significant.

Almost all of the assessments of cash transfer programs, both conditional and unconditional, have examined the impacts of those programs on students' time in school. Yet a few of the more recent studies have also examined their impact on student learning as measured by test scores. As shown in rows 3–6 of Table 5, some — but not all — cash transfer programs have also increased student learning. Seven high-quality studies have produced seven estimates of the impact of CCT programs on student learning. Three of these studies have found positive and statistically significant impacts on learning outcomes, while the results for the other four are statistically insignificant.

The first published study of the impact of a CCT program on test scores is that of Baird et al. (2011). As explained above, this CCT program focused on 13–22-year-old girls who were in school when the program started. The authors find that, for these girls, 2 years of exposure to the program increased English test scores and math scores by 0.14 and 0.12 standard deviations of the distribution of students' test scores (hereafter denoted as σ), respectively, both of which are statistically significant. The size of the transfers had little effect on these impacts. The follow up study by Baird et al. (2013), which (as explained above) focused on girls not in school when the program started (some of whom returned to school while others did not), found that 2 years of exposure to the program increased English test scores by 0.13σ and math scores by 0.16σ, both of which are statistically significant. They did not examine whether these impacts varied by the size of the transfer.

The Baez and Camacho (2011) study also examined the impact of the Colombia CCT program on student learning. The estimates are from 2009, and since the program began in 2002 they are long-run estimates of the impact, although the years of exposure varied from 2 to 7 years, depending on the age of the child. The overall impact on math scores was statistically insignificant while that for Spanish was negative and significant at the 10% level (-0.05σ). The average impact over these two subjects (see Table 4 of that paper) was statistically insignificant.[15] The lack of a positive impact, and perhaps even a negative impact on Spanish scores, could reflect some selection bias in that weaker students who did not receive CCT payments may have dropped out of school and so were not tested (which would increase the average test scores of those who remained in school); indeed, as discussed above this program greatly increased the probability of completing high school.

Mo et al. (2013) also examined the impact of the CCT program in rural China on the test scores of students in grade 7: the point estimate was very small and statistically insignificant. This may also reflect the fact that only students who stayed in school were tested; those who dropped out, who were more often from the control schools (as explained above), very likely had relatively low test scores, so if they had been tested it is possible that the results would have shown a positive impact of the program on learning.

The CCT program in Cambodia evaluated by Barrera-Osorio and Filmer (2013) also estimated the impact of that program on test scores. After 3 years of operation the impact on test scores was not significantly different from zero. Note that the test score data used in this study were obtained by testing children in their homes, which avoids the downward bias that could occur if only children who are still in school are tested.

The long-term impact of exposure to the Nicaraguan CCT program on (former) primary school students' test scores was examined by Barham et al. (2013). The children were exposed to the program when they were 9–12 years old, but the test score data were collected (for boys only) in 2010, 10 years after the start of the program. The results show that, 10 years after the start of the program, average test scores were 0.20σ (0.23σ for home language and 0.17σ for math) higher for the boys who were exposed longer (5 years instead of 2 years) to the CCT program, and these impacts are statistically significant.

---

[15] This average result is the one shown in Table 5; to minimize giving larger "weight" to studies that report many estimates for different population subgroups, Tables 4–11 use aggregate estimates across tests and grades whenever possible.

Finally, the study by Filmer and Schady (2014) that examined the long-term effects of a Cambodia program that provided (conditional) scholarships to low-income students who had graduated from primary school (finished grade 6) also examined student learning. The estimated impact on test scores 5 years after the program began (by which time many of the students were in grade 11) was small and not statistically significant. As in the Barrera-Osorio and Filmer (2013) study of Cambodia, test score data were obtained by testing children in their homes, avoiding downward bias that could occur if only children still in school are tested.

Recall that two studies have examined the impacts of other types of cash transfer programs. Baird et al. (2011) examined the impact of unconditional cash transfers in Malawi, While those transfers did increase enrollment, as explained above, they had no significant impact on students' test scores among the girls who were already in school when the program began. Lastly, the Moroccan "labeled" cash transfer program examined by Benhassine et al. (2015) had no effect on student test scores even though it did increase students' time in school.

The "scholarship" program in China evaluated by Yi et al. (2014), which was essentially a fee reduction program, also examined the impact of that program on student learning. As seen in seventh line of Table 5, this program had no significant impact on students' test scores.

To summarize the results for CCT programs, for which there is now a large amount of evidence, they almost always increase time in school, and in some cases they also increase student learning as measured by test scores. The significantly positive effects on time in school were found in all nine countries studied: Brazil, Cambodia, China, Colombia, Honduras, Malawi, Mexico, Nicaragua, and Pakistan. Regarding student learning, in two of five countries (Malawi and Nicaragua) estimates done several years after the end of the program show that CCT beneficiaries had higher cognitive skills, as measured by test scores. In contrast, in three other countries (Cambodia, China, and Colombia), there was no evidence of impacts on learning. However, data shortcomings, in particular lack of data on students who dropped out of school from the control groups, may downwardly bias the estimated impact on learning in the China and Colombia studies, but this potential bias does not apply to the two Cambodia studies.

Finally, one important limitation of the experimental evidence on CCT programs is that they typically do not allow us to evaluate alternative monetary values of the transfers, which is an important input into policy decisions. One approach that addresses this limitation is to use household and school level data to estimate a structural model of households' educational decisions, and to validate the model using the experimental CCT evaluations. While doing so is rather complicated and requires assumptions that may not hold, it has the advantage of enabling prediction of the impact of variation in programs, including variants that have not yet been implemented, on students' educational outcomes. Examples of such an approach are Todd and Wolpin (2006) and Attanasio et al. (2012).

4.1.3 Scholarship Programs

A further source of inefficiency on the demand side may come in translating school enrollment and attendance into learning outcomes. Since the returns to student effort typically take many years to realize, students who are present-biased may not exert adequate effort in school.[16] Thus, policies that help make the rewards from exerting effort to acquire human capital more immediate may be a promising option for improving student learning outcomes. A common way to do this (that may also alleviate resource constraints, as discussed above) is to provide merit-based scholarships to students, which provide tangible intermediate rewards on the basis of levels or improvements in student performance.

Two high-quality studies, both from Kenya, have examined the impact of merit-based scholarships on students' time in school. As seen in the ninth line of Table 4, three of the four estimates from these two studies find significantly positive effects (the fourth estimate is statistically insignificant). The first such study was that of Kremer et al. (2009), who conducted an experimental evaluation of a scholarship program in rural Kenya that targeted girls who were in grade 6 (Kenya's primary schools teach students from grade 1 to grade 8). At the beginning of the school year, girls in grade 6 were told that those who scored in the top 15% on end-of-year exams would be given, for each of the next 2 years (grades 7 and 8), an amount of money equal to $6.40, which was enough to cover school fees, and in addition their parents would be given an amount of money equal to $12.80. The second study in Kenya, by Friedman et al. (2011), was a follow-up of this 2009 study; it examined the educational outcomes of the same girls 4–5 years after the original program started (about 2 years after the program had ended). The earlier study found that the program significantly increased participation (daily attendance, where girls who leave school have a zero attendance rate) by 3.2 percentage points. The more recent study found that the program had significant positive impacts on enrollment in secondary school (8.6 percentage point increase) and current enrollment in any school (7.9 percentage point increase), but not on grades completed.

Consider next the impact of scholarship programs on student learning. Four studies, all RCTs, have examined the impact of providing scholarships based on student learning as measured by test scores. Their results are shown in the seventh line of Table 5. The findings are almost unanimous: five of the six estimates are significantly positive, while the sixth was statistically insignificant.

---

[16] An extensive literature in psychology documents that "fronto-cortal" brain development (that is associated with the ability to make long-term trade-offs) is completed only by the age of 18, and that youth and children below this age are less able to evaluate the long-term trade-offs that the neoclassical economic framework assumes will be made to reach optimal decisions regarding human capital investments. As a practical application of this point, this is partly why the juvenile justice system (for offenders under 18) is separate from the adult justice system.

The two Kenya studies, which were described above, found significantly positive effects. More specifically, Kremer et al. (2009) found a 0.27σ increase in scores on a grade 6 year-end exam, and Friedman et al. (2011) found that test scores were 0.20σ higher 4–5 years after the program started (2 years after it ended).

A more recent study is that of Blimpo (2014), who examined a program in Benin that randomly assigned 100 secondary schools to a control group or to one of three different types of scholarships: scholarships based on individual-level performance with respect to a set goal, with no limit on the number of scholarships offered; scholarships based on average performance for (randomly assigned) teams of four students, again with respect to a set goal and no limit on the number of scholarships; and a "tournament" in which 84 teams of four students each (randomly assigned) from 28 schools competed for a large prize that was given only to the three top performing teams. For the first two types, the payments were $10 per person ($40 for a team of four) for a relatively low level of performance, and $40 per person ($160 for a team of four) for a high level of performance. For the third type, the prizes were much larger, at $640 for each of the top three teams. All three types of incentives had similar (and statistically significant) impacts, increasing grade 10 test scores by 0.24σ to 0.28σ.

Finally, a scholarship program in China, evaluated by Li et al. (2014), was also based on a tournament. In one version (individual incentive), groups of 10 low-performing students would compete with each other in terms of improvement over time on their test scores. The top student received about $13, the second and third about $6, and the rest each received about $3. In the other version (peer incentive), each of ten low-performing students was paired with a high-performing student; prizes for the low performing students were the same as in the first version, but in this case the high-performing student also received a similar reward in order to encourage that student to assist the low-performing student with whom he or she had been paired.[17] The individual incentive intervention in China had no statistically significant impact. However, the authors find that combining student incentives with peer tutoring (where academically higher-achieving students were paired with lower achieving ones and both students were rewarded for improvements) increased the test scores of the weaker students by 0.27σ. Thus, in some cases it is possible that student incentives on their own may not be effective unless also accompanied by pedagogical support.

4.1.4 Other Household Interventions That Increase the Demand for Schooling

This section presents evidence on the remaining interventions shown in Tables 4 and 5. This set of interventions is diverse, but they have two common characteristics. First, they generally are intended to increase the demand for schooling, although in some cases

---

[17] This version could be interpreted as a hybrid intervention that involves peer tutoring as well as merit-based scholarships.

rather indirectly. Second, they are implemented directly with households rather than in schools.

One way to make schooling more effective, which should in turn increase the demand for schooling, is to provide information to mothers on how to develop their child's learning. Such an initiative was examined by Banerji et al. (2013), who also examined the impact of a mother literacy program and the combination of both programs. As seen in lines 10–12 of Table 4, neither of these two interventions, nor their combination, had an impact on children's time in school (as measured by enrollment and daily attendance). Turning to the effects on student learning, which are summarized in lines 9–11 of Table 5, the lessons on child learning led to small but statistically significant increases in the test scores (average over literacy and mathematics) of students in grades 1–4 (0.04σ), but there was no significant impact of the literacy class alone. Interestingly, a somewhat higher impact (0.06σ) on student test scores was found for women who took both classes. These impacts after 1 year of the program are relatively small, and there were no significant impacts on children's enrollment rates.

In a similar vein, Handa (2002) used a difference-in-differences approach to examine the impact of an adult literacy program in Mozambique on their children's enrollment rate. As seen in line 13 of Table 4, he found that the program had no effect. Yet a longer term program of the kind evaluated by Banerji et al. (2013) may have larger effects, and adult literacy is an outcome with positive value in itself beyond the impact on child outcomes.

The nonavailability of female sanitary products is often posited as a factor inhibiting female school participation after puberty. Oster and Thornton (2011) conduct an RCT to evaluate the impact of an intervention that provided female sanitary products to girls of secondary school age in Nepal, but found that the program had no effect on the daily attendance of secondary school girls (as seen line 14 of Table 4). This may have been because only 1% of girls actually stated that the lack of sanitary products was a binding constraint to school participation, suggesting that other constraints may have been more first order.

A more successful intervention for girls of secondary school age was a program in India that offered their families funds to purchase bicycles which their daughters could ride to attend secondary school. Muralidharan and Prakash (2013) used a difference-in-differences strategy (using triple and quadruple differences) to estimate the impact of this program on enrollment. They find that this program increased secondary school enrollment by 5.2 percentage points. For girls who lived more than three kilometers from the nearest secondary school, the impact was about 9 percentage points. These are very large impacts given that the initial enrollment rate for these girls was only 17.2%.

A final household-based intervention to increase the demand for schooling in Table 4 is a program that matched remittances sent by Salvadoran migrants in the United States to students of their choosing in El Salvador if those remittances are committed to educational purposes. Using an RCT, Ambler et al. (2014) found that when the match amount is three times the amount of remittance, the program increased enrollment in a private school by a statistically significant 10.9 percentage points. Note, however, that the overall increase in enrollment of 3.1 percentage points was not statistically significant.

To summarize this section, there is broad and consistent evidence that CCT programs successfully increase students' time in school. There is also evidence that scholarship programs may increase time in school and suggestive evidence that information-based interventions could serve this purpose. Turning to the impact of demand-side interventions on students' test scores, merit-based scholarships appear particularly effective, and in some cases CCT programs have also had positive impacts on test scores. Overall, the results suggest that interventions that increase the benefits of attending school (such as CCTs) increase time in school, while those that increase the benefits of higher effort and better academic performance (such as merit scholarships) improve learning outcomes. These results are consistent with theory and suggest that the outcomes that are explicitly rewarded by policies are more likely to be changed by those policies, and highlight the importance of theoretically informed program design.

4.2 Inputs

The majority of the costs of running a school system are typically input costs — including the costs of building schools, and the costs of operating schools (with teachers being a key input and teacher salaries typically being the largest component of education expenditure). Thus, it is no surprise that many studies have examined the impact of inputs, broadly defined, on students' educational outcomes. However, credibly studying the impact of school inputs is quite challenging given the limited number of studies with exogenous variation for these inputs. Thus, many studies that have examined inputs were deemed to not be credible enough to include in this review. As a result, many important categories of input interventions, such as school infrastructure, teachers' education levels, and teacher training, are not included in this review, and there are important evidence gaps in this area.

The impacts of inputs on students' time in school are shown in Table 6, while Table 7 provides results for the impacts of inputs on student learning, as measured by test scores. We organize our discussion of school inputs by classifying them into six broad categories: access to schools, pedagogical materials and facilities, teacher quality and quantity, provision of food, provision of medical services, and composite provision of better resources.

4.2.1 Access to Schools

Perhaps the most obvious school "input" is an actual school. More generally, access to schools affects both students' time in school and how much they learn. Access can be increased by: (1) Building new schools, which reduces the distance to the nearest school; (2) Increasing the hours per day, or the days per year, that schools are open; and

Table 6 Summary of impacts on time in school of school inputs

	Negative, significant	Negative, insignificant	Positive, insignificant	Positive, significant	Total studies
Interventions that increase access to schools					
Building new schools					
RCTs	0 (0)	0 (0)	0 (0)	3 (2)	2
Other high-quality studies	0 (0)	0 (0)	0 (0)	3 (3)	3
Providing school uniforms (RCT)	1 (1)	0 (0)	0 (0)	0 (0)	1
Pedagogical materials and facilities					
Textbooks (all RCTs)	0 (0)	0 (0)	2 (2)	0 (0)	2
Provision of libraries (RCT)	0 (0)	0 (0)	1 (1)	0 (0)	1
Multilevel teaching materials (RCT)	1 (1)	0 (0)	0 (0)	0 (0)	1
Multilevel teaching materials and parent-teacher partnership (RCT)	0 (0)	1 (1)	0 (0)	0 (0)	1
Teacher quantity and quality					
Extra teacher/materials (high quality)	0 (0)	0 (0)	0 (0)	2 (1)	1
Provision of food					
School meals					
RCTs	0 (0)	0 (0)	2 (2)	1 (1)	3
Other high-quality studies	0 (0)	3 (2)	1 (1)	0 (0)	2
Take-home rations					
RCTs	0 (0)	0 (0)	0 (0)	1 (1)	1
Other high-quality studies	0 (0)	0 (0)	1 (1)	0 (0)	1
School feeding/parent-teacher partnerships (RCT)	0 (0)	1 (1)	0 (0)	0 (0)	1
Medical services					
Deworming medicine (RCT)	0 (0)	0 (0)	0 (0)	1 (1)	1
Health insurance (high quality)	0 (0)	0 (0)	1 (1)	0 (0)	1
Large-scale provision of resources					
School infrastructure investment (RCT)	0 (0)	0 (0)	1 (1)	0 (0)	1
Support circles (RCT)	0 (0)	0 (0)	0 (0)	1 (1)	1

Figures are number of estimates; figures in parentheses are number of papers/studies; statistical significance is at 10% level.

Table 7 Summary of impacts on test scores of school inputs

	Negative, significant	Negative, Insignificant	Positive, insignificant	Positive, significant	Total studies
Interventions that increase access to schools					
Building new schools					
RCTs	0 (0)	0 (0)	0 (0)	2 (1)	1
Other high-quality studies	0 (0)	0 (0)	0 (0)	1 (1)	1
Hours per school day (high quality)	0 (0)	1 (1)	0 (0)	3 (2)	2
Pedagogical materials and facilities					
Textbooks (all RCTs)	0 (0)	2 (1)	1 (1)	0 (0)	2
Flipcharts (RCT)	0 (0)	0 (0)	1 (1)	0 (0)	1
Provision of libraries (RCT)	1 (1)	1 (1)	0 (0)	0 (0)	1
Multilevel learning materials (RCT)	0 (0)	1 (1)	0 (0)	2 (1)	1
Multilevel teaching materials and parent-teacher partnerships (RCT)	0 (0)	0 (0)	0 (0)	3 (1)	1
Teacher quantity and quality					
Pupil-teacher ratio					
RCTs	0 (0)	1 (1)	0 (0)	0 (0)	1
Other high-quality studies	3 (2)	1 (1)	0 (0)	0 (0)	2
Provision of food					
School meals					
RCTs	0 (0)	0 (0)	0 (0)	3 (2)	2
Other high-quality studies	0 (0)	2 (1)	1 (2)	1 (1)	2
Take-home rations (RCT)	0 (0)	0 (0)	0 (0)	1 (1)	1
School feeding /parent-teacher partnerships (RCT)	0 (0)	0 (0)	1 (1)	2 (1)	1
Medical services					
Deworming medicine (RCT)	0 (0)	1 (1)	1 (1)	0 (0)	1
Iron supplements (all RCTs)	0 (0)	1 (1)	2 (2)	1 (1)	2
Provision of eyeglasses (RCT)	0 (0)	0 (0)	0 (0)	1 (1)	1
Large-scale provision of resources					
Support circles (RCT)	0 (0)	0 (0)	1 (1)	0 (0)	1
Attending an elite public school (both are other high-quality studies)	0 (0)	0 (0)	1 (1)	1 (1)	2
Infrastructure/materials/teacher training (high quality)	0 (0)	0 (0)	2 (1)	2 (1)	1

Continued

Table 7 Summary of impacts on test scores of school inputs—cont'd

	Negative, significant	Negative, insignificant	Positive, insignificant	Positive, significant	Total studies
Unexpected school block grant (RCT)	0 (0)	0 (0)	0 (0)	1 (1)	1
Expected school block grant (RCT)	0 (0)	0 (0)	1 (1)	0 (0)	1
Incentivized community block grant (RCT)	0 (0)	1 (1)	1 (1)	0 (0)	1
Nonincentivized community block grant (RCT)	0 (0)	0 (0)	1 (1)	0 (0)	1

Figures are number of estimates; figures in parentheses are number of papers/studies; statistical significance is at 10% level.

(3) Removing barriers to enrollment, such as the lack of a school uniform (which are required in many developing countries).[18] This section examines all three types of interventions, starting with the building of new schools.

Five high-quality studies have examined the impact of building new schools on time in school. Each of these five studies examined a different country, so evidence is available from Afghanistan, Burkina Faso, Indonesia, Mozambique, and Pakistan. Building new schools reduces a very important *indirect* cost of attending school, the distance to the nearest school. More time spent traveling to school is time lost for other activities, including work, and greater distances may also lead to direct transportation costs and worries about safety. The first two rows of Table 6 show that there are two studies based on RCTs and three studies that use other high-quality estimation methods. All six estimates from these five studies show significantly positive impacts from building new schools on students' time in school.

The earliest of these five studies is that of Duflo (2001), who used difference-in-differences estimation to examine the impact of a massive school construction program in Indonesia in the 1970s on years of schooling in that country (the paper also examined the impact of years of schooling on wages, but that is not the topic of this chapter). She focused on boys born between 1950 and 1972, and found that an additional school built per 1000 school-age children increased years of education by 0.19 years.

The second study is that of Handa (2002), who used difference-in-differences estimation to estimate the impact of the construction of new primary schools in Mozambique on children's probability of being enrolled. He finds that the marginal probability of enrollment of boys and girls increased by 0.3 percentage points for each new primary school built within an "administrative post" area (administrative posts are relatively large

---

[18] Of course, tuition and other required school fees can effectively limit access as well, while cash transfer programs and scholarships can expand access. These interventions were discussed above in Section 4.1.

areas, with on average 21 primary schools). While this estimated impact is small, it is highly statistically significant (p-value < 0.01).

Alderman et al. (2003) conducted an RCT in Pakistan that provided funding to construct new (or support existing) private girls' primary schools; the support of existing schools made them affordable to poor families. In urban areas, the program increased the enrollment rate for girls by 25 percentage points, while in rural areas the enrollment rate increased by 15 percentage points.

A more recent study, based on an RCT conducted in Afghanistan, is that of Burde and Linden (2013). They examined the impact of the opening of primary schools on children of primary school age in rural villages of Afghanistan that did not have a school. In Ghor province, where this intervention took place, only 29% of families lived within 5 km of a primary school in 2007. The authors find very large impacts of that program on enrollment rates of children of primary school age in those villages. The program increased the enrollment rate by 51.5 percentage points for girls and by 34.6 percentage points for boys. The higher impact on girls likely reflects that they are often not allowed to travel to neighboring villages, some of which may have schools.

Finally, Kazianga et al. (2013) evaluated the impact of providing "girl friendly" schools in rural villages in Burkina Faso. These schools have amenities that are particularly attractive to girls, such as sources of clean water and separate latrines for boys and girls. Overall, opening these schools increased the enrollment rate of all children (average over boys and girls) by 18.5 percentage points, a very large effect that is highly statistically significant. This is the estimate included in Table 6; separate estimates indicate that the impact is 16.3 percentage points for boys and 21.9 percentage points for girls.

Together, these five studies from five different countries show that building schools in communities that do not have them can lead to very large increases in school enrollment. While the vast majority of primary school-age children in developing countries live very close to a primary school, for the small percentage who live much farther away building a school in their local community will likely have a very large effect on their probability of being enrolled.

Two of these five high-quality studies that examined the impact of building new schools on time in school also examined the impact of that intervention on student learning. As seen in the first two rows of Table 7, these two studies have produced three estimates of this impact. While the number of studies, and the number of estimates, is very small, the findings are unanimous: all three estimates are statistically significant and show that constructing new schools increases learning among children of school age.

Burde and Linden (2013) find that constructing new schools in rural Afghanistan had a large impact on test scores over a period of about 6 months, generating increases of 0.66σ for girls and 0.41σ for boys, both of which are highly statistically significant. These estimates include all children in those villages, not just those who are enrolled in school.

Similarly, Kazianga et al. (2013) find that building new "girl friendly" primary schools in rural Burkina Faso in villages that previous had no primary school increased test scores by 0.41σ. This result is an average over French and mathematics exams, and over girls and boys.

Perhaps the second most obvious "input" that affects students' educational outcomes (the first being providing an actual school) is the amount of time that children spend in school. For any given year, this time could be lengthened by increasing the number of hours per day that the school is open or by increasing the number of days per year that the school is in session. We found no high-quality studies that examined the impact of a longer school day on time in school, perhaps because it is rather obvious that longer school days by definition increase time in school, assuming that the rate of student absenteeism does not dramatically increase.

However, two high-quality studies have produced four estimates of the impact of an increase in the length of the school day on student learning, as seen in the third line of Table 7. Of these estimates, three are positive and significant and one is insignificant. The positive and significant estimates come from studies of Chile (Bellei, 2009) and Ethiopia (Orkin, 2013), both of which are based on difference-in-differences estimation. The one insignificant, estimate is also from the Orkin study. Overall, the evidence, while based on only two studies, is generally supportive of the common sense notion that longer school days increase student learning.

One high-quality study examined a third and final way to increase access to schools: provision of free school uniforms. Hidalgo et al. (2013) present results from an RCT in Ecuador that provided free school uniforms to poor primary school students in urban Ecuador. Surprisingly, they find that provision of free uniforms decreased daily attendance by 2 percentage points. Unfortunately, their data do not allow them to determine why provision of uniforms had this unexpected effect.

4.2.2 Pedagogical Materials and Facilities
Two RCT studies from Sub-Saharan Africa have examined the impact of textbooks on students' educational outcomes: Glewwe et al. (2009) and Sabarwal et al. (2014). These studies examined textbook distribution programs in Kenya and Sierra Leone, respectively. The results were surprising, and thus they merit further discussion.

The impact of these two programs on the time that students spend in school is examined in the fourth row of Table 6. Both of the two estimates (one from each of these two studies) are statistically insignificant; providing textbooks did not decrease dropping out or grade repetition in Kenya and did not increase daily attendance in Sierra Leone. However, in Kenya if one focuses on students in grade 8, who are relatively strong students (about half of students who start in grade 1 drop out before reaching grade 8), the program increased the probability that these students finished primary and enrolled in secondary school (not shown in Table 6, which shows only averages over all grades).

While textbooks may not increase students' time in school, one would expect that they would increase student learning. This is examined in the fourth row of Table 7, which summarizes the results of three estimates from the Kenya and Sierra Leone studies. Surprisingly, none of these three estimates is statistically significant. These findings are quite unexpected given that one would think that textbooks would have a strong impact, or conversely that lack of textbooks would have a strong negative effect, on student learning.

The study of Kenya by Glewwe, Kremer, and Moulin investigated the reasons behind the unexpected insignificant findings. The authors found that the textbooks provided, which were the official government textbooks, were too difficult for the average child to read in the region of Kenya (Busia and Teso districts) where the study took place. Indeed, when the sample is restricted to the top 20% of students (and, in some regressions, to the top 40% of students), as measured by their preintervention test scores, the textbooks did improve students' learning outcomes (not shown in Table 7).

For the study of Sierra Leone, by Sabarwal et al. (2014), the reason for the unexpected finding of no impact is rather obvious: few of the textbooks reached the students. In this RCT, the program was implemented by the Ministry of Education, and there was little follow up action to encourage the teachers and school administrators to distribute the textbooks to students; instead, most of the textbooks were kept in storage. The authors present evidence suggesting that school administrators stored most of the textbooks because they were unsure whether textbooks would be provided in future years. Overall, this small amount of evidence suggests that textbooks can have a positive impact when they are actually provided to students, and when the textbooks are at the appropriate level for those students, which was the case for the top students in Kenya. But if textbooks are too difficult, which was the case for most students in Kenya, or are never provided to the students, which was the case in Sierra Leone, they will have little or no effect on both time in school and student learning.

Another study from the same area of Kenya by the same authors (plus another author), Glewwe et al. (2004), used an RCT to examine the impact of the provision of "flip charts" (sets of large posters to place on an easel or hang on a wall) on students' test scores in Kenya. As seen in the fifth line of Table 7, the authors find that the provision of flip charts had no significant impact on student learning, and they note that nonexperimental estimates of the impact of this intervention find significant positive effects.

We found only one high-quality study of the impact of libraries on students' educational outcomes, a study of the provision of school libraries in India by Borkum et al. (2012). The authors used an RCT to examine the provision of both "in school" libraries and traveling libraries. As seen in the fifth line of Table 6, there was no effect of either library on students' daily attendance (which was already quite high, at around 90%). Turning to learning outcomes (sixth line of Table 7), "in school" libraries had no effect on students' language scores and the traveling libraries had an unexpected negative effect

(-0.22σ) on students' language scores. Thus in this setting school libraries did not lead to improved educational outcomes.

The last two pedagogical material interventions are from the same study, which examined primary schools in the Philippines. Tan et al. (1999) experimentally investigated the impact of the provision of "multilevel learning materials," as well as an intervention that combined those materials with "parent-teacher partnerships." The multilevel learning materials intervention by itself significantly reduced the probability of dropping out, but had no significant impact on dropping out when combined with parent-teacher partnerships (lines 6 and 7 of Table 6). The impact on test scores (in Filipino, math and English) was significantly positive for two of the three tests when only multilevel materials were provided, and for all three tests when those materials are combined with parent-teacher partnerships (lines 7 and 8 of Table 7). Of course, it is unclear what the relative contributions of two components are. Even the multilevel learning materials intervention by itself had many components (several different types of learning materials), so it is not clear which components led to increased student learning.

4.2.3 Teacher Quantity and Quality

Teachers vary in many ways, but we found no high-quality studies that have examined the impact of teacher characteristics on student learning or time in school.[19] However, one high-quality study has examined the impact of providing an extra teacher to very small primary schools in India, and three studies have examined the impact of variation in the pupil-teacher ratio. All four of these studies can be thought of as attempts to change the "quantity," as opposed to the "quality," of teachers. Indeed, a very important evidence gap is the lack of well-identified studies on the impact of teacher education and training on learning outcomes in developing countries.

Only one of these studies focused on the impact of the quantity of teachers on students' time in school. Chin (2005) used a DD approach to evaluate a program that provided extra teachers *and* additional educational materials (including blackboards) to very small primary schools in India. As seen in the eighth row of Table 6, she found that the program significantly increased students' primary school completion rates (by 1–2 percentage points), but it is not possible to determine how much of this effect is due to the extra teacher and how much is due to the additional educational materials.

Turning to the pupil-teacher ratio, three high-quality studies have produced five estimates of the impact of the pupil-teacher ratio on student learning. These results are summarized in the ninth and tenth rows of Table 7. Intuitively, one would expect that increased pupil-teacher ratios reduce learning because larger classes reduce opportunities for teachers to give individual attention to students. Indeed, three of the five estimates,

---

[19] We examine the impact of hiring contract teachers in Section 4.4.5 below. This is not a teacher characteristic per se, but rather pertains to the type of contract that a teacher has.

from two different studies, find a significantly negative effect. On the other hand, two of the five estimates, also from two studies, including the only RCT study, are statistically insignificant.

The two papers that produce the expected negative finding are those by Urquiola (2006) and Urquiola and Verhoogen (2009). Urquiola (2006) used regression discontinuity methods to estimate the impact of the pupil-teacher ratio on student learning in Bolivia. In particular, he used the fact that schools with pupil-teacher ratios above 30 can apply to the education authorities for another teacher, and he presents evidence that these schools often do obtain another teacher. He finds that schools that obtain another teacher, which greatly reduces the pupil-teacher ratio, have significantly higher language scores, but the effect on math scores is not statistically significant.

Urquiola and Verhoogen (2009) also use regression discontinuity methods to estimate the impact of class size on student test scores in Chile. The focus of the study is on children in grades K-8 in private schools (about half of students in Chile are enrolled in private schools). The authors found that increased class size has significantly negative impacts on both math and language test scores.

Duflo et al. (2012a, 2015) conducted an RCT in Kenya that randomly assigned some schools an extra contract teacher, and within those schools students were randomly divided into classes which were taught by the current teacher (who were civil-service teachers) and those taught by the contract teacher.[20] For the purpose of identifying the impact of the pupil-teacher ratio on student learning, the classes taught by the current (civil service) teacher can be compared to those taught by same type of teacher in the control schools, which have much larger pupil-teacher ratios. They find that although this reduction in class size led to higher test scores (about 0.09σ), this increase was not statistically significant.

In summary, while the amount of evidence is small, three of the four studies find evidence that reducing the pupil-teacher ratio improves students' time in school and their test scores. Yet the study on India could not distinguish the impact of an additional teacher from the impact of additional learning materials, and the one RCT study did not find a statistically significant impact of class size reductions on student learning. Clearly, more evidence on the size of these effects is needed. It is also important to bear in mind that reductions in class size can be very expensive, which implies that even if they do lead to better students outcomes there may be other interventions that achieve the same results at a lower cost. See Section 5 below for a brief discussion of the costs of some of the interventions discussed in this chapter.

4.2.4 Provision of Food

Child malnutrition is a common problem in many developing countries, and there is a large amount of evidence that well-nourished children have better educational outcomes

---

[20] The findings of this study on the impact of contract teachers are discussed below in Section 4.4.5.

(Glewwe and Miguel, 2008). The strongest evidence pertains to early childhood malnutrition, but it may also be the case that adequate nutrition during a child's time in school can improve his or her academic performance. Thus many developing countries have implemented programs that provide meals to students, and in some cases to their families as well. This section reviews the evidence on the effectiveness of such interventions based on eight high-quality studies.

The most common type of program that attempts to improve students' nutritional status is the provision of school meals. Lines 9 and 10 of Table 6 show the results from five studies in five different countries (Burkina Faso, Chile, India, the Philippines, and Uganda) that have estimated the impact of school meals on time in school. Of the seven estimates, six are statistically insignificant and one, for the program in Burkina Faso that was evaluated by Kazianga et al. (2012), finds (using an RCT) a significantly positive impact on enrollment of children aged 6–15 years old. This evidence indicates that in most cases school meals do not increase students' time in school. Even if school meals do not increase years of enrollment, one would think that it would increase daily attendance. Yet only one of the five studies, that of Alderman et al. (2012), measured the impact of school meals on daily attendance; the authors found no statistically significant, effect.

Of these five high-quality studies, four have examined the impact of school meals on student learning. As seen in lines 11 and 12 of Table 7, three of the seven estimates from these four studies are statistically insignificant and four are significantly positive. More specifically, McEwan (2013) found statistically insignificant impacts of a school feeding program on math and language test scores among grade 4 students in Chile. In neighboring Argentina, Adrogue and Orlicki (2013) found a small and statistically insignificant impact of school feeding on the mathematics test scores of students in grade 3, but a larger (0.17σ) and statistically significant impact on their language scores. Tan et al. (1999) found significantly positive impacts of a school feeding program in the Philippines on the math (0.25σ) and Filipino (0.16σ) of grade 1 students. Finally, Kazianga et al. (2012) found that school meals increase math scores by 0.10σ in Burkina Faso. These results suggest that school meal programs can — at least in some settings — increase student learning.

Two studies have examined the impact of take-home rations on students' education outcomes. The results on students' time in school are summarized in lines 11 and 12 of Table 6. Adrogue and Orlicki (2013) found no impact of such a program on student attendance in Argentina, but Kazianga et al. (2012) found a significantly positive 4.8 percentage point impact on the enrollment of children aged 6–15 in Burkina Faso. Only the latter program examined the impact of take-home rations on student learning; as seen in line 13 of Table 7, the Burkina Faso program increased students' math scores by 0.08σ, an impact that is statistically significant (p-value < 0.05).

Finally, the Tan et al. (1999) study also examined a program that combined school feeding with "parent-teacher partnerships." This combination had no effect on students' time in school, as seen in line 13 of Table 6, but it did lead to two (out of three) statistically positive impacts on student learning (line 14 in Table 7). However, it is not possible to determine the extent to which this is due to the school meals or to the parent-teacher partnerships.

4.2.5 Provision of Medical Services

A natural extension of the provision of food to improve students' educational outcome is the provision of basic medical services. This section examine four types of interventions for which there are high-quality studies: deworming programs; iron supplementation; health insurance; and the provision of eyeglasses.

Many individuals in developing countries have worm infections of various types (roundworm, hookworm, whipworm, and schistosomiasis). School-age children are particularly vulnerable to these types of infections, and those infections lead to anemia and other problems that may reduce children's attentiveness in school. Miguel and Kremer (2004) implemented an RCT to estimate the impact of providing deworming medicine to primary school students in rural Kenya. As seen in Table 6, this intervention increased students' time in school. More specifically, it reduced their absence rate by about 7–8 percentage points. However, as seen in Table 7, the authors did not find an impact of the program on students' test scores.

However, it is worth noting that a later study (not in the table) examines spillover effects of the Kenyan deworming program on younger siblings of children in treated communities and finds positive effects on the test scores of children who were less than 1 year old when the deworming program was implemented. Ten years after the program, Ozier (2014) finds that these children have large test score gains — equivalent to between 0.5 and 0.8 years of schooling. Further, a long-term follow up study of treated cohorts finds that 10 years after the program, women who were eligible for the program as school girls were 25% more likely to have attended secondary school, and men who were eligible were more likely to have completed primary school (Baird et al., 2015). The study also finds large positive labor market effects and estimates an annual financial return on investment of over 32%. Thus, it appears that the deworming program clearly improved long term human capital even though there were no short-term effects on test scores.

The other medical services initiative for which there is a high-quality study that examined impacts on students' time in school is a health insurance program in China that was evaluated by Chen and Jin (2012). They used a DD (combined with propensity score matching) estimation procedure. As seen in Table 6, they found no impact of the program on enrollment of children aged 6–16.

Turning to student learning outcomes, there are high-quality studies for two other types of interventions. One of them has some similarities to deworming, namely the provision of iron supplementation tablets. There are two high-quality studies, Luo et al. (2012) and Sylvia et al. (2013), both of which were conducted in China. As seen in

Table 7, there are four estimates from these two studies. Three are statistically insignificant, while the fourth is significantly positive. Together they provide some initial evidence that iron supplements can increase student learning, at least under some circumstances, but there are only two studies and both were conducted in the same country.

The last medical services intervention is the provision of eyeglasses. Glewwe et al. (2014) conducted an RCT to investigate the impact of this intervention on the learning of primary school students in rural China (they did not look at enrollment since it is already very close to 100%). The authors found that the eyeglasses significantly increased average test scores by at least 0.16σ.

4.2.6 Large-Scale Provision of Resources

The last set of input studies is a set of interventions that provided either entire packages of school inputs (broadly defined) or large amounts of money that schools could use to buy the inputs of their choice (or spend in other ways). As will be seen, these interventions are often quite different from each other.

One of the earliest published RCT studies in education is that of Newman et al. (2002), who examined a program in Bolivia that provided funds to schools to make infrastructure improvements. They estimated the impact of this program on the dropout rates of boys and girls in grade 7. As seen in Table 6, the program had no statistically significant impact on those dropout rates.

The other large-scale program for which there is a high-quality study that examined impacts on students' time in school is a program in Malawi that combines a remedial program for students who have dropped out of primary school, interactive radio instruction, a new type of curriculum and pedagogy ("Escuela Nueva") and mobilization of networks of families, friends and neighbors (which are referred to as "circles of support"). This intervention was evaluated using an RCT by Pridmore and Jere (2011). They find that this program significantly reduced the dropout rates (Table 6) but had no effect on the learning outcomes (Table 7) of primary school students in that country.

There are two studies that have examined the admittedly rather general policy of being admitted to an elite public school, which could be interpreted as devoting the resources required to transform a typical high school into an elite high school. Many developing (and developed) countries have elite public schools that restrict admission to the best students in the country, and that have much more qualified teachers and many other types of resources that are not found in a typical secondary school. Places in these schools are highly valued by many parents, and the students of these schools often have very successful careers, but it is not clear that those students' successes were due to their attending those elite schools. Two studies have examined this, one for Romania and the other for Kenya.

Pop-Eleches and Urquiola (2013) examined the effect of "going to a better school" in Romania. They find that students who are able to get into a better, more academically challenging school perform better on graduation tests. This indicates that "better" schools do lead to greater student learning, but it provides no information on which of the many characteristics that make a school "better" are the ones that bring about this improved performance.

In contrast, Lucas and Mbiti (2014) find, using regression discontinuity methods, essentially no evidence that going to an elite high school in Kenya leads to increased learning. The only possible exception is that students who attend such schools appear to do better on Swahili exams, which may reflect use of that language as the common language for communication among students outside of the classroom. Thus they attribute the success of graduates of those schools to characteristics that they already possessed that would have helped them be successful even if they had not attended an elite high school.

In a similar vein, in a paper for which the main contribution is methodological, Chay et al. (2005) examine Chile's P-900 program, which provided infrastructure, materials and teacher training to schools in Chile. They use a regression discontinuity approach to estimate the impact of this program. While two of the four estimates are significantly positive, it is virtually impossible to determine which component of the program led to increased student learning.

Finally, two recent studies have examined the impact of providing block grants, but in different ways. Das et al. (2013) examine a school block grant program in India. The authors show that when schools received large unexpected grants (about \$3 per student) students test scores increased by about 0.09σ. However, expected grants had little or no effect, because households decreased spending on education when they knew that the schools that their children were attending would receive the grants.

The second such study is by Olken et al. (2014). It examines a sort of cash transfer program that is targeted at entire villages, rather than households. The "incentivized" transfer provides villages with about \$10,000 and the promise of addition funds if the village scores well on 12 different health and education indicators. They also examined a similar but "unconditional" program where villages received the \$10,000 without any promise to provide additional funds based on health and/or education indicators. Neither program had any effect on students' test scores.

To summarize the evidence on the impact of standard "inputs" on students' educational outcomes, there is broad evidence that improving school access through building schools increases time in school and also typically improves learning outcomes (especially when the counterfactual is that children would not be going to school). However, there is more limited evidence to suggest that other categories of inputs have meaningful impacts on either time in school or test scores. It is important to caveat however that there are several categories of inputs for which we do not have much credible evidence on impacts — including teacher training and education. On a more positive note, however, there is evidence to suggest that some kinds of inputs, such as school health interventions, may be both effective as well as highly cost effective.

4.3 Pedagogy

As outlined in our theoretical framework (Section 3.1), a critical determinant of the extent to which increases in schooling inputs translate into improvements in learning outcomes is the way in which these inputs are used in practice and the way in which teaching and learning is organized. In other words, the "technology of instruction" is a key determinant of how inputs are translated into outcomes, and this section aims to review the evidence from high-quality studies in this area and to synthesize the implications of these findings for our understanding of education in developing countries.

In most developing countries, this "technology of instruction" has remained unchanged for decades, and consists of teachers using a "chalk and talk" method to teach a classroom of students. Classroom time is typically spent in a "lecturing" style starting from third grade, with students expected to follow the textbooks. This pedagogical method offers relatively little scope for differentiating instruction to account for the large heterogeneity in student ability and preparation levels within a typical classroom in a developing country. Instead, the focus is on completing the materials in the syllabus — typically specified in government-approved text books, with the goal of being able to answer questions and problems provided at the end of the chapter — which in turn will be tested in low- and high-stakes examinations. While some innovations in pedagogy are transmitted through teacher training programs, the evidence base for these innovations is typically not very strong.

An important point to note is that researchers have only recently started to use well-identified empirical strategies for identifying the impacts of pedagogical innovations on learning outcomes. Since most of the empirical innovations in improved causal identification have come from economists and statisticians, the focus of research in the economics of education has been more on questions of interest to economists, such as the impact on test scores of: programs designed to increase households' demand for education; inputs into the education production function; school resources; teacher pay levels and structure; information, choice and competition; and governance and accountability. Thus, there is a relative paucity of well-identified quantitative evidence on the critical question of how best to structure classroom instruction and pedagogy to most effectively improve learning outcomes in developing countries. Nevertheless, progress has been made on better understanding these issues in the past decade, which in turn has provided important insights into the nature of the education production function, and the binding constraints that confound attempts to improve education outcomes in developing countries. The rest of this section examines high-quality studies that have looked at the impact of pedagogy on student outcomes in developing countries; the results are summarized in Tables 8 and 9.

4.3.1 Supplemental Remedial Instruction and Teaching at the Right Level

Teaching effectively may be particularly challenging in many developing country contexts because of the higher variation, relative to developed countries, in the initial preparation of children when they enter school. This challenge has probably been magnified in the past two decades, since the focus on increasing school enrollment has brought several million first-generation learners into primary school systems in developing countries, which likely has led to a substantial increase in the entry-level variation in student abilities and preparation. Also, as Muralidharan and Zieleniak (2014) show, the variance in student learning levels within a cohort increases over time as they pass through the school system. How does a teacher effectively teach a classroom where students are so varied in their skill levels?

Remedial schooling interventions are one method that may be able to reduce the variance of achievement in the classroom and thus ensure that all students are progressing. Remedial programs offer the possibility of focusing on those students who are lagging behind and teaching at a level that is appropriate for their current level of skills. Ideally, such an intervention would increase their progress, and decrease the heterogeneity of student learning levels in a given grade. The evidence suggests that this may be the case, with several high-quality studies finding strong impacts of remedial instruction programs on learning outcomes, even when implemented by volunteers or informal teachers with little formal training and paid only a modest stipend that is several times lower than the salary of regular civil-service teachers.

The first rows of Tables 8 and 9 summarize the results from three studies that examined the impact on students' educational outcomes of interventions that focus on "teaching at the right level," which typically involves remedial/supplemental instruction and/or tutors or volunteers to provide that instruction. Only one of these studies examined the impact of teaching at the right level on students' time in school; as seen in Table 8, that study found no significant impact. All three studies considered impacts on student learning, and together they have produced six estimated impacts. As summarized in Table 9, two of these estimates are statistically insignificant while four are significantly positive. The following paragraphs discuss these studies in detail.

First, Banerjee et al. (2007) report results from an experimental evaluation of a program run by the education nonprofit organization Pratham that was specifically targeted at the lowest performing children in public schools in the Indian cities of Mumbai and Vadodara. The program provided an informal teacher hired from the community (known as a *Balsakhi* or "friend of the child") to schools, with an explicit mandate to focus on children in 3rd and 4th grade who had not achieved even basic competencies in reading and arithmetic. These children were taken out of the regular classroom for 2 hours

Table 8 Summary of impacts on time in school of pedagogy interventions

	Negative, significant	Negative, insignificant	Positive, insignificant	Positive, significant	Total studies
Teaching at the right level (RCT)	0 (0)	1 (1)	0 (0)	0 (0)	1
Computers, electronic games, and access to technology (high quality)	0 (0)	0 (0)	2 (1)	0 (0)	1

Figures are number of estimates; figures in parentheses are number of papers/studies; statistical significance is at 10% level.

Table 9 Summary of impacts on test scores of pedagogy interventions

	Negative, significant	Negative, insignificant	Positive, insignificant	Positive, significant	Total studies
Teaching at right level/ supplemental instruction (all RCTs)	0 (0)	1 (1)	1 (1)	4 (3)	3
Tracking/streaming (RCT)	0 (0)	0 (0)	0 (0)	2 (1)	1
Computers/electronic games					
RCTs	1 (1)	0 (0)	3 (3)	10 (6)	8
Other high-quality studies	3 (1)	0 (0)	0 (0)	0 (0)	1
Reading intensive pedagogy and reading materials (RCT)	0 (0)	0 (0)	2 (1)	2 (1)	1

Figures are number of estimates; figures in parentheses are number of papers/studies; statistical significance is at 10% level.

per day, and were provided with remedial instruction targeted at their current level of learning. This is the only study that examined the impact of teaching at the right level on a time in school variable. There is only one estimate and, as seen in Table 8, the impact of this program on daily attendance was statistically insignificant. In contrast, this program improved students' test scores (average of math and English scores) by 0.14σ after 1 year of the program, and by 0.28σ after 2 years. Most of the gains were observed for students who were "pulled out" of their regular classroom (who were at the lower end of the learning distribution) and not for those who continued in the regular class (though the latter students did experience a reduction in class size for 2 hours per day). The authors therefore interpret the results as being driven by the fact that the students who were pulled out were being taught at a level corresponding to their current proficiency, as opposed to the proficiency presumed by of the textbook.

Second, Banerjee et al. (2010) report results from several interventions designed to improve community participation in education in India. Of all the interventions tried, the only one that was found to be effective at improving learning outcomes was a remedial instruction program implemented by youth volunteers hired from the village, who were provided a week of training and then conducted after school reading camps for 2 to 3 months. These increases in learning were substantial (albeit starting from a low base), even though only 13.2% of students actually attended the camps. For the average child who could not read anything at the baseline, exposure to the remedial instruction program increased the fraction who were able to read letters by 7.9 percentage points. The instrumental variable estimates suggest that for children who were not able to read, the average impact of attending a camp raised the probability of being able to read letters by 60 percentage points, which is a very large effect.

A third piece of experimental evidence is provided by Lakshminarayana et al. (2013), who study the impact of a program run by the Naandi Foundation. The program recruited community volunteers to provide remedial education to children in a randomly selected set of villages in Andhra Pradesh. After an initial outreach to households to communicate program details, the volunteers provided 2 hours of remedial instruction per day after normal school hours in the students' school. The subject matter covered in these sessions was tailored to students' class-specific needs and learning levels, and aimed to reinforce the curriculum covered in school. After 2 years of this intervention, student test scores in program villages were 0.74σ higher than those in the comparison group, suggesting a large impact of the after-school remedial instruction program. Note, however, that the large magnitudes reported in this study (it is noteworthy that the large effects reported here are "intention to treat" estimates and not scaled up "treatment on the treated" effects) also reflect high program implementation quality and monitoring over a period of 2 years.

Finally, Banerjee et al. (2015) present results from multiple RCT's conducted across several Indian states in partnership with the education nonprofit organization Pratham to evaluate the impact of different models of implementing remedial instruction in public schools in a scaled up way.[21] Overall, they find support for the hypothesis that Pratham's instructional approach, which focuses on teaching children at a level that matches their level of learning, can significantly improve learning outcomes. They find that implementing the pedagogy in dedicated learning camps that are held outside of normal school hours, where teachers use learning-appropriate remedial materials, was effective in raising test scores. However, they found no impact of other models, which attempted to incorporate this pedagogy into the regular school day. The authors interpret their findings as suggesting that the remedial pedagogy was successful, but that it was difficult to get teachers to implement new curriculums during school hours, and that successfully scaling up remedial pedagogy within an existing schooling system can be challenging because teachers are focused on completing the syllabus prescribed in the textbook.

---

[21] Note that this study is not included in Tables 8 and 9 because the results are still preliminary. But we include it in the discussion because the underlying RCT's have been underway for several years and we are quite familiar with the studies.

One challenge in interpreting this body of evidence is that most interventions studied include both extra instructional time as well as teaching that is targeted at the level of the student. Nevertheless, the combination of evidence on tracking (see below) and on the success of programs that provide supplemental instruction targeted at the level of the student (and the descriptive evidence on learning trajectories over time) suggests that a likely binding constraint for why substantial increases in school inputs have not translated into much improvement in learning outcomes may be ineffective pedagogy.

The explanation that is most consistent with these findings is one articulated in Chapter 4 of Banerjee and Duflo (2011) and also by Pritchett and Beatty (2012), and in the conclusion of Glewwe et al. (2009), which is that the curriculum has been designed by highly educated elites and reflects a period of time when there was no expectation of universal primary education. Indeed, as they note, the historical purpose of education systems in many developing countries may not have been to provide "human capital" to all students as much as to screen gifted students for positions of responsibility in the state and the clergy. Note that such a design of an education system may also have been efficient in times when the structure of the economy was predominantly agrarian since the returns to education also depend on occupational choice, with lower returns in occupations that mainly involve physical labor (Munshi and Rosenzweig, 2006; Pitt et al., 2014). However, the design of curricula and textbooks in developing countries have typically not been adapted to the entry into the school system of millions of first-generation learners. Since teachers continue to follow the textbook as the default mode of instruction, and define their goals in terms of completing the curriculum over the course of year, it is not surprising that they are effectively "teaching to the top" of the distribution and that a large number of children are in the class but not learning because the lessons are too advanced for them.

Thus, improvements in pedagogy that make it possible to: (a) more effectively account for the variation in initial level of student preparation; (b) break the tight link between pedagogy and the textbook; and (c) move from a "selection" paradigm to a "human capital" paradigm, are likely to lead to significant improvements in the performance of developing country education systems.

4.3.2 Tracking of Classrooms

The findings above suggest that policies that reduce variation in student learning within a classroom could improve pedagogy. Indeed, an old question in the economics of education is whether students in a given grade benefit from being "tracked" into classrooms based on their initial learning levels or ability.[22] The main argument for tracking is that the reduction in variance in the ability levels of students in the classroom may make it

---

[22] See Betts (2011) for an excellent theoretical discussion on the tracking debate as well as a review of the empirical evidence from developed countries.

easier for teachers to more effectively match the difficulty level of the content and material they teach to the level of their students. The main argument against tracking is the concern that students who are tracked to "lower" level classrooms may suffer further from negative peer effects and from stereotyping and loss of self-esteem, which may place them on a permanently lower trajectory of learning. A further concern is that some education systems may track students very early using data that may be noisy and not sufficiently reliable for tracking.

Unfortunately, the problem of endogenous tracking and the lack of credible identification limits the extent to which we have good causal estimates of the impact of tracking. Fortunately, however, there is one high-quality study of tracking that was conducted in the context of a developing country, that of Duflo et al. (2011). They did not examine the impact of tracking on time in school but, as seen in the second row of Table 9, they examined the impact of tracking on student learning. More specifically, they conducted an experimental evaluation of tracking in Kenya and found that tracking and streaming of pupils appears to have a positive and highly significant effect on test scores in both the short term and the long term. Students in tracking schools scored on average 0.18σ higher than students in nontracking schools, and continued to score 0.18σ higher even 1 year after the tracking program ended, suggesting longer-lasting impacts than those found in many other education interventions.

Most importantly, Duflo, Dupas, and Kremer found positive impacts for students at all quartiles of the initial test score distribution and cannot reject that students who started out above the median score gained the same as those below the median; those in higher achieving classes scored 0.19σ higher than the higher achieving control school students, while those in lower achieving classes scored 0.16σ higher than the lower achieving control school students. Additionally, lower-achieving students gained knowledge in basic skills, while higher-achieving students gained knowledge in more advanced skills, suggesting that teachers tailored their classes to the achievement level of their students. Finally, since students just below and just above the median baseline score were otherwise similar, but experienced a sharp change in the mean test score of their peers, the authors are able to use this regression discontinuity method to show that tracking did not cause adverse peer effects.

4.3.3 Technology-Enhanced Instruction

Perhaps the most promising class of interventions for improving the effectiveness of pedagogy involves the greater use of technology in the classroom. Improvements in technology have played a central role in increasing productivity in almost every sector of the economy, and it is therefore widely believed that greater use of technology in classrooms should be a promising way to rapidly improve education outcomes in developing, and developed, countries. In particular, given that the basic nature of instruction has not changed in many decades, many "technology optimists" believe that technology-enhanced instruction has the potential to create "disruptive innovation," and thereby sharply improve education outcomes.

Some of possible channels of impact include: (1) cost-effective replication and scaling up of high-quality instruction using broadcast technology (such as radio and television-based instruction); (2) overcoming limitations in teacher knowledge and training, for example to teach more advanced concepts in science and mathematics or to teach a new language (such as English) for which there is growing demand but a limited supply of teachers with the requisite competence; (3) providing supplemental instruction at home; (4) better engaging children in the learning process through the use of interactive modules (such as educational games and puzzles); (5) customizing individual student learning plans; and (6) shortening the gap between the time when students' attempt to answer questions and demonstrate understanding of concepts and the time when the teacher provides feedback to students via corrected homework or exams. These interventions also range from being quite inexpensive, such as radio-based instruction, to very expensive, such as individual laptops for students under the "One Laptop per Child" (OLPC) initiative.

While promising, the high-quality evidence to date on the impact of technology-enhanced instruction on learning outcomes in developing countries suggests a need for caution. First, there is only one study that examines the impact of computers and information technology on students' time in school. Cristia et al. (2014) used a difference-in-differences approach to examine the impact of an intervention in Peru that increased access to computers and the internet to students in public secondary schools in Peru. Their results, summarized in the second row of Table 8, show no significant effect of the program on either repetition or dropout rates.

There is much more evidence on the impact of technology-enhanced instruction on student learning; the third and fourth rows of Table 9 indicate that there are 17 estimates from nine different studies. Yet these results point to widely varying magnitudes of impact, perhaps varying more than almost any other intervention considered in this chapter, including estimates that are significantly negative and others that are significantly positive. Further caution is in order because *all* but one of the studies discussed below are based on RCTs, with high contextual internal validity of the estimated impacts but uncertain external validity. Thus, the differences in estimated impacts are quite striking and point to the importance of context, and perhaps more importantly to the importance of program design in creating effective programs of technology-aided instruction.

Studies that find significant positive impacts of computer-aided learning (CAL) include Banerjee et al. (2007) and Linden (2008), both of which examined interventions in India, and Lai et al. (2011), Yang et al. (2013), Lai et al. (2013), and Mo et al. (2014), all four of which are studies of programs in China. Banerjee et al. (2007) found that a CAL program that provided 2 hours per week of computer-based math instruction in two cities in Western India was particularly effective at improving math scores, with very large positive effects of 0.48σ at the end of 2 years of the program, but that the gains were not long-lasting (the effects fell to 0.10σ 1 year after the program). They also report that the CAL intervention was not as cost effective as a remedial tutoring program in the same setting (the latter was discussed in Section 4.3.1).

Linden (2008) found positive effects of 0.29σ from an out-of-school CAL program after 1 year of the program. Lai et al. (2011) estimated the impact of a CAL program in schools for migrant children in Beijing, China, that provided two 40-minute sessions of remedial math instruction per week to children in grade 3; after 1 year their math scores were 0.14σ higher than those of children in the control group, a statistically significant effect. Yang et al. (2013) also studied a CAL program in three different provinces in China and find modest (0.12σ) but significant positive effects on test scores. Lai et al. (2013) estimated the impact of a CAL program similar to that implemented in Beijing, but it focused on Chinese language and was implemented in a remote Western province (Qinghai); they found significant increases in both Chinese (0.20σ) and math (0.22σ) after 1 year. Mo et al. (2014) examined a similar CAL program that provided remedial math instruction to boarding school students in another area of rural China and found that it led to significant improvements in math test scores for both 3rd-grade (0.25σ) and 5th-grade (0.26σ) students.

Studies that found no impact include Barrera-Osorio and Linden (2009) in Colombia, and Beuermann et al. (2013) in Peru. Barrera-Osorio and Linden studied a school-level program that provided computers and teacher training to randomly selected schools in Colombia and found no impact of the program on test scores in either Spanish or math. The authors argue that the lack of impact was because of poor implementation, with the teachers failing to incorporate the new technology effectively in their teaching.

Even more striking are the results in Beuermann et al. (2013), who studied the impact of the OLPC program in Peru using a large-scale randomized evaluation. They found that while the program increased the ratio of computers to students in schools from 0.12 to 1.18 in treatment schools, there was no impact on either school enrollment or test scores in math and language. The results are striking both because of the intensity of the program, with each child getting an individual laptop, and because children were permitted to take the laptop home, which allowed for a much more intense immersion in technology and greater access than any other study.

Finally, two studies found a negative impact: Linden (2008) and Malamud and Pop-Eleches (2011). Linden found that, in contrast with the positive impacts found from an after-school supplemental CAL program, a CAL program that was implemented in-class and thus substituted for regular instruction had a strong negative impact (−0.55σ) on test scores. The authors interpret these results as being driven by the difficulty of effectively modifying pedagogy within the classroom to incorporate technology, which could lead to a worsening of outcomes if effective preexisting instructional patterns are disrupted.

Malamud and Pop-Eleches (2011) used an RDD to study the impact of providing vouchers for purchasing computers to the families of middle-school students in Romania. They found that students who received the voucher had significantly lower GPA's (the results are not reported in standard deviations). They also found a possible explanation for this finding: students who received vouchers to buy a computer reported spending more time playing games and less time reading or doing homework.

These cautionary results are especially relevant for education policy, where it is tempting for politicians to want to scale up interventions like "computers for all" as a potential short-cut for addressing the challenges of education quality. Our summary of the evidence, as well as the brief discussion of the theoretical mechanisms, suggest that there are many good reasons to be excited about the *potential* for technology-enabled instruction to produce substantial improvements in students' learning outcomes. However, the evidence on the impact of greater use of technology in the classroom is mixed, and program impacts seem to depend crucially on the details of both the intervention and its implementation. In particular, it appears that the key success factor is the extent to which careful thought goes into integrating effective pedagogical techniques with technology. Much more, and much more careful, research is needed (on both process and impacts) before committing resources to scaling up these programs — especially those involving expensive investments in hardware — with scarce public funds.

4.3.4 Reading Intensive Pedagogy and Reading Materials

A final pedagogy intervention for which there is a high-quality study is a reading program in the Philippines. More specifically, Abeberese et al. (2014) conducted a randomized evaluation program of a reading program for grade 4 students in the Philippines. This program provided age-appropriate reading materials and trained teachers to incorporate reading into their teaching. Four months after the start of the program the reading scores of the students in the program schools were 0.13σ higher, although this fell to 0.06σ seven months after the start of the program. Both estimates are statistically significant. In contrast, there was no impact of the program on mathematics scores.

Overall, the evidence on pedagogy suggests that the quality of classroom pedagogy may be a key determinant of the extent to which increases in school inputs are translated into improvements in learning. In particular, there may be very large returns from focusing on foundational learning for *all* children in developing country school systems with a large number of first-generation learners. It is interesting to note that countries that strongly outperform their predicted test scores conditioning on levels of income (such as Vietnam and Cuba) feature egalitarian education systems that try to ensure basic skills for all students as opposed to identifying and focusing on very high achievers. This may be an example where a macro-level "systems" approach and a micro-level "interventions" approach may be yield similar insights.

4.4 Governance

The fourth critical determinant of education outcomes — in addition to policies to stimulate household demand for education, provision of school inputs, and pedagogical practices — is the quality of governance of the education system. We use the term governance to refer to a broad set of characteristics of education systems that relate to how efficiently they are managed. These include goal setting, personnel policy (hiring, training, retention, and promotions), accountability and monitoring, and performance management. More broadly, governance also includes decentralization, the extent of choice and competition in school markets, and the regulatory structure for private schools. In this section, we first discuss a body of evidence which suggests that poor governance in developing country education systems may be a first order constraint in translating inputs into outcomes, and then discuss evidence on policy options to improve school governance.

4.4.1 Measuring Governance

Perhaps the clearest indicator of weak governance in education is outright corruption whereby fiscal appropriations for education do not reach the targeted schools and communities. A striking instance of such corruption is provided by Reinikka and Svensson (2004), who showed that 87% of central government funds allocated to a school capitation grant (for nonwage expenditures) in Uganda never reached the schools, and that the median school in their representative sample had not received *any* of the funds. They show that most of the funds were captured by local officials and politicians. In a different context, Ferraz et al. (2012) document the impact of education corruption on students' educational outcomes in Brazil. Using data from an independent federal audit of local municipal finances they show that, conditional on a wide variety of student and municipality characteristics, municipalities where these audits detected corruption in education had test scores that were 0.35σ lower and also had higher dropout rates.

Another striking measure of weakness of school and teacher governance in developing countries is the high rate of teacher absence from schools. Chaudhury et al. (2006) present results from a multicountry study where enumerators made unannounced visits to public schools to measure teacher attendance and activity, and report an average teacher absence rate of 19%, with teacher absence rates of 25% in India and 27% in Uganda. In India, Kremer et al. (2005) report that not only were 25% of teachers absent from work, but another 25% were in school but not teaching and thus only about half of the teachers were found to be actually engaged in teaching activities. Muralidharan et al. (2014) present results from a nationally representative panel survey that revisited the rural villages surveyed by Kremer et al. (2005),[23] and find only a modest reduction in teacher

---

[23] The panel study did not include the urban areas surveyed by Kremer et al. (2005).

absence rates, from 26.3% to 23.7%.[24] They also calculate that the fiscal cost of teacher absence in India is $1.5 billion *each year*, highlighting the large costs of poor governance in education.

In addition to these two nationally representative studies, several other studies have also noted the high rates of teacher absence in India. Duflo et al. (2012b) find teacher absence rates in excess of 40% in informal schools run by an NGO in Rajasthan. Muralidharan and Sundararaman (2011, 2013a,b) and Muralidharan (2012) regularly document teacher absence with multiple unobserved visits to a representative sample of rural government-run primary schools in Andhra Pradesh, finding teacher absence rates ranging from 24% to 28% over the 5-year period from 2005–06 to 2009–10.

A recent literature has tried to measure management quality in schools using standardized surveys to codify management practices, following the method developed by Bloom and Van Reenen (2007). Bloom et al. (2015) measure variation in management practices across schools in several countries and find that: (a) average school management quality was poorest in the developing countries in their sample; (b) the variation in country-level management practices in education was higher than in other sectors such as healthcare and manufacturing; (c) management scores are positively correlated with students' test scores (though the test scores are in levels, rather than value-added); (d) there are large disparities in management practice scores even within countries — especially between government-run public schools and those with more managerial autonomy; and (e) having better management scores is not correlated with the demographic characteristics of students, but is correlated with the quality of governance (measured as greater accountability for student performance to an outside body), and with the degree of school leadership. The descriptive evidence summarized above all points to the likely importance of improving the governance of education systems in developing countries for improving outcomes. We now turn to evidence on specific ways of improving governance.

4.4.2 Monitoring

The most basic policy tool to reduce teacher absence is to increase the extent of monitoring and oversight of schools. This can include administrative (top-down) monitoring as well as community-based (bottom-up) monitoring. While there are no experimental studies of just improving monitoring (without also linking the improved monitoring to the introduction of teacher incentives), Muralidharan et al. (2014) use a nationally representative village-level panel dataset from India (collected in 2003 and then again in 2010) on teacher absence to study the correlations between changes in various school

---

[24] The absence rate of 25% given above includes both the rural and the urban sample, whereas the absence rate in the rural sample in 2003 was 26.3% (for the villages in the panel data set).

and management characteristics in this period and changes in teacher absence.[25] They find that increasing the probability of a school having been inspected in the past 3 months from 0 to 1 is correlated with a 7 percentage point reduction in teacher absence (or 30% of the observed absence rates). This estimate is similar in both cross-section and panel estimates, bivariate as well as multiple regressions, and with and without state or district fixed effects. Using the most conservative of these estimates, Muralidharan et al. (2014) calculate that increasing inspections and monitoring could be over 10 times more cost effective at increasing teacher-student contact time (through reduced teacher absence) than hiring additional regular teachers.

The remainder of this section summarizes the literature on the impact of school governance policies on students' educational outcomes. Results for studies that examine the impact of such policies on students' time in school are summarized in Table 10, and Table 11 does the same for students' test scores.

Evidence on the impact of monitoring on time in school is scarce and not encouraging, as seen in the first row of Table 10. Only two studies have considered this impact, those by Duflo et al. (2012b) and Banerjee et al. (2010). Both studies found insignificant effects of monitoring on student attendance.

The evidence of the impact of monitoring on student learning is only somewhat more encouraging. The first row of Table 11 presents the results for four experimental (RCT) studies. In only one of the four studies was there a significantly positive impact of monitoring on students' test scores. This is the study of Duflo et al. (2012b), who conducted a randomized evaluation of an intervention that monitored teacher attendance in informal

Table 10 Summary of impacts on time in school of governance interventions

	Negative, significant	Negative, insignificant	Positive, insignificant	Positive, significant	Total studies
Monitoring (all RCTs)	0 (0)	1 (1)	1 (1)	0 (0)	2
School-based management					
RCTs	0 (0)	7 (3)	5 (3)	1 (1)	3
Other high-quality studies	0 (0)	2 (1)	1 (1)	0 (0)	2
Teacher performance pay (RCT)	0 (0)	1 (1)	2 (1)	0 (0)	1
Private school (vouchers)					
RCTs	0 (0)	1 (1)	1 (1)	1 (1)	2
Other high-quality studies	0 (0)	1 (1)	0 (0)	0 (0)	1
Single-sex school (high quality)	0 (0)	0 (0)	0 (0)	1 (1)	1

Figures are number of estimates; figures in parentheses are number of papers/studies; statistical significance is at 10% level.

[25] This paper is not included in the studies summarized in Tables 10 and 11 in the following paragraphs because the outcome variable is teacher absence, not students' educational outcomes.

Table 11 Summary of impacts on test scores of governance interventions

	Negative, significant	Negative, insignificant	Positive, insignificant	Positive, significant	Total studies
Monitoring (all RCTs)	0 (0)	1 (1)	4 (3)	1 (1)	4
School-based management					
RCTs	0 (0)	9 (3)	7 (3)	2 (2)	5
Other high-quality studies	0 (0)	1 (1)	1 (1)	1 (1)	2
Teacher performance pay					
RCTs	0 (0)	1 (1)	2 (1)	5 (2)	3
Other high-quality studies	0 (0)	0 (0)	1 (1)	1 (1)	1
Contract teachers (all RCTs)	0 (0)	0 (0)	0 (0)	3 (2)	2
Private school (vouchers)					
RCTs	0 (0)	0 (0)	3 (2)	2 (2)	3
Other high-quality studies	0 (0)	2 (1)	2 (1)	0 (0)	2
Diagnostic feedback to teachers (RCT)	0 (0)	1 (1)	1 (1)	0 (0)	1

Figures are number of estimates; figures in parentheses are number of papers/studies; statistical significance is at 10% level.

schools in Rajasthan (India) using cameras with time-date stamps to record teacher and student attendance. The program not only monitored teachers, but also paid teacher salaries as a function of the number of valid days of attendance. They found that this program reduced teacher absence by half, but structural estimates of a model of labor supply suggest that the mechanism for this result was not the "monitoring" per se, but rather the incentives tied to the attendance. In contrast, no significant impact was found by Muralidharan and Sundararaman (2010), who experimentally studied the impact of a program that provided schools and teachers with low-stakes monitoring and feedback; they found that this program had no impact on either teacher attendance or test scores. These results suggest that while "monitoring" is an important tool in reducing teacher absence, "low-stakes" monitoring is unlikely to be very effective, and that it is "high-stakes" monitoring, that is monitoring with positive (negative) consequences for teacher presence (absence), which is more likely to be effective.

A different way to improve monitoring of schools is to increase the amount of "bottom-up" monitoring through the community. The evidence here is less encouraging. Banerjee et al. (2010) conducted an experimental evaluation of the impact of a community mobilization program to improve school quality in rural areas of the Indian state of Uttar Pradesh; they found no impact of various programs to build community involvement in schools in that state on community participation, teacher effort, or learning outcomes. This is consistent with the study of Muralidharan et al. (2014) which, using village-level panel data, found that the correlations between "bottom-up" measures of governance and monitoring, such as the frequency of PTA meetings, and teacher absence are negative but typically not significant, and that the magnitude of the correlations is always lower than that of the correlations between "top-down" inspections and teacher absence.

There is some positive evidence on the impact of community-based information campaigns (aimed at improving bottom-up monitoring) but the interventions have typically been quite intensive. Pandey et al. (2009) conducted an experimental evaluation of an information campaign to improve parental participation in village education committees (VEC's) in three states in India and found positive impacts on both process measures as well as learning outcomes, but the estimated impacts on learning outcomes were generally statistically insignificant. Moreover, the intervention was an intensive one that involved 8–9 village-level meetings in just 2 months. Meetings were advertised in advance with audio tapes, and the meetings included high-quality videos that were used to explain the rights of VECs as well as facilitators to answer questions.[26] While it may be possible to scale up such information interventions in a less intensive and thus more cost-effective way using mass media such as television and radio, there is limited evidence on the effectiveness of such "light-touch" information campaigns on improving school governance.

4.4.3 School-Based Management

Another approach to improve monitoring and accountability of schools and teachers is to decentralize more management authority to schools and communities — an approach that is broadly referred to as "school-based management" (SBM). The theory of change associated with this approach is to empower communities to take charge of their schools and in particular to make teachers more accountable to them. Several reforms based on this approach have been attempted around the developing world, but the empirical evidence on its success is both limited and mixed. Five high-quality studies, three RCTs and two non-RCT studies, have examined the impact of SBM on children's time in school. These five studies have produced 16 estimates, of which all but one are statistically insignificant, as seen in Table 10. Turning to student learning, seven high-quality studies have estimated the impact of SBM on students' test scores, as seen Table 11, of which five are RCTs and two are non-RCT studies. Most of the 21 estimates from these seven studies are statistically insignificant, but three estimates from three different studies are significantly positive. We discuss these studies further below.

Pradhan et al. (2014) conducted an experimental evaluation of a series of interventions that aimed to enhance community participation in school management in Indonesia. The specific interventions included implementing elections for school-committee

---

[26] This is similar to evidence from Uganda where researchers found large positive impacts of an information-based intervention to improve the functioning of community health centers (Bjorkman and Svensson, 2009). Note, however, that this intervention included specific measures to solve the collective action problem such as a joint meeting between communities and providers to identify changes that would be made by providers and communities, and to have similar follow up meetings as well.

memberships, providing grants and training to existing school committees, and facilitating "linkage" meetings between school committees and village councils. They found no significant impact on time in school measures and test scores for most of the interventions, except for a significantly positive impact on test scores of the "linkage" intervention, which facilitated the collaboration between the school committee and the village council. The authors suggest that this may be because the "linkage" intervention incorporated stakeholders from a more powerful community institution (the village council).

Beasley and Huillery (2014) also use a randomized experiment to evaluate a parent-empowerment program in Niger. The program provided grants to school committees to encourage parent participation in school management. However, the program had no impact on either time in school measures or test scores. The authors suggest that a possible explanation for the lack of impact is that parents do not have enough knowledge and information to make effective decisions to improve educational quality.

Lassibille et al. (2010) and Glewwe and Maïga (2011) both present experimental evaluations of the AGEMAD program in Madagascar, which aimed to strengthen school management at the district, subdistrict, school and teacher levels; both studies found no impact on student test scores of these interventions. The final experimental evidence on SBM is provided by a study in Kenya by Duflo et al. (2015), who found that training school management committees to evaluate the performance of contract teachers and to have influence on the renewals of contract teachers' contracts had a significantly positive impact on the performance of contract teachers and on students' test scores.

There are also difference-in-differences studies of two SBM programs in Mexico. Gertler et al. (2012) conducted a difference-in-differences analysis of the impact of the AGE program that empowered parents to improve school quality; they found that it reduced failure and grade repetition rates, but had no impact on dropout rates (they did not have data on test scores). They also found no impact in poor communities, suggesting that the AGE program may increase inequality across schools. Santibanez et al. (2014) also used a difference-in-differences strategy to evaluate the PEC-FIDE, another SBM program in Mexico, and found that the program had no general impact on students' test scores or time in school measures. The authors suggest that schools are more likely to allocate grants based on immediate benefits rather than improving structural governance. A final study by Yamauchi (2014), which combined difference-in-differences with propensity score matching, found a significantly positive impact of an SBM program on students' test scores in the Philippines. Note, however, that this intervention included not only SBM but also additional resources to implement the program, so the significantly positive effect reflects both the switch to SBM and the additional resources to the schools.

Overall, the results on monitoring suggest that there may be significant problems of both collective action and asymmetry in power between teachers and communities, especially in historically disadvantaged areas with low levels of education, that may make community-based monitoring less effective than top-down administrative monitoring.

This is a result that is consistent with the experimental findings of Olken (2007) in the context of monitoring corruption in Indonesia, and is also seen in comparisons of top-down and bottom-up school monitoring in the same context (Muralidharan et al., 2014). To the extent that community-based monitoring programs are effective, they seem to involve either intensive interventions, or specific components to mitigate the collective action problem such as coordination meetings with village councils or authority over specific aspects of school functioning (such as renewal of contract teachers).

4.4.4 Teacher Performance Pay

A common feature of the pay structure for teachers (and other civil-service employees) is the use of fixed salary schedules with little or no component of pay that is linked to performance. Since the effort exerted by teachers is a key determinant of education quality, a natural set of policy options to enhance governance in education would be to consider linking the compensation of teachers, as well as education administrators, to measures of performance. Reasons for the status quo of little or no link to performance include difficulties in measuring productivity of individual teachers, as well as concerns that linking pay to performance on measurable attributes of a job will lead to diversion of effort away from socially valuable tasks that may not be as well measured (Baker, 1992; Holmstrom and Milgrom, 1991). Nevertheless, the demonstrated low levels of teacher effort in developing countries (manifested by high rates of absence) have led both policymakers and researchers to consider the possibility that introducing performance-linked pay for teachers may improve outcomes. Four high-quality studies have been conducted on this topic in recent years in developing countries. As seen in Table 10, one of these studies examined the impact of this type of education policy on students' time in school. All four studies examined the impact of this type of intervention on test scores (see lines 4–5 in Table 11), most of which have found significantly positive impacts. These studies are discussed in detail in the following paragraphs.

Muralidharan and Sundararaman (2011) present experimental evidence on the impact of a program in the Indian state of Andhra Pradesh that provided bonus payments to teachers based on the average improvement of their students' test scores in independently administered learning assessments (with a mean bonus of 3% of annual pay). They found that at the end of 2 years of the program, students in incentive schools performed significantly better than those in control schools by 0.27σ and 0.17σ in math and language tests, respectively. Students in incentive schools also performed better on subjects for which there were no incentives, suggesting positive spillovers between improved performance on math and language and the untested subjects (science and social studies).

This study featured two different bonus payment interventions, and teachers were randomly assigned to each; the first intervention based bonuses on the average performance of groups of teachers, while the second based bonuses on each teacher's individual performance. In the first year, the treatment schools with group and individual-level teacher bonuses did equally well (with both having a significantly positive impact), but at the end of 2 years, students in individual-incentive schools scored better than those in group-incentive schools (0.33σ vs. 0.22σ for math, and 0.24σ vs. 0.09σ for language), though these differences were not statistically significant. Finally, the performance pay programs were implemented as a part of a larger set of experimental evaluations costing the same amount, which allowed the authors to compare the relative effectiveness of input- and incentive-based approaches to improve learning outcomes in the same setting. They find that the teacher incentive schools performed significantly better than other randomly chosen schools that received additional schooling inputs of a value similar to the cost of the teacher incentive program.

Second, Muralidharan (2012) presents evidence from a long-term follow up in the same setting, where teacher performance pay program was extended for 5 years to a sub-sample of the original schools, and finds that students who completed all of their 5 years in primary school under the individual teacher incentive program performed significantly better than those in control schools by 0.54σ and 0.35σ on math and language tests, respectively. The group teacher incentive program also had positive (and mostly significant) effects on student test scores, but the effect sizes were always smaller than those of the individual incentive program, and were not significant at the end of primary school for the cohort exposed to the program for 5 years. The paper estimates that the individual teacher performance pay program would be around 15 to 20 times more cost effective (including administrative costs) at improving learning outcomes than the default policy of reducing pupil-teacher ratios by hiring more teachers (even assuming the most generous estimates of the impact of pupil-teacher ratio reductions on test scores obtained in the same setting).

The third and final experimental study is Glewwe et al. (2010), who conducted an experimental evaluation of a teacher incentive program in Kenya that provided school-level group incentives using prizes for high-achieving schools. The prizes were awarded, using a tournament design, to the schools that had the best average student test scores and also to those that had the highest average improvements (to reward both the best schools as well as the most-improved ones). The authors report that the incentive program led to teachers increasing efforts in test-preparation but not in activities that would increase long-term learning (such as reduced absence rates). They found that students in treatment schools performed better on high-stakes tests but not on low-stakes tests, and also that these gains dissipated after the incentive program ended. They interpret their results as suggesting that teacher incentives may not be an effective strategy to promote long-term learning. Nevertheless, there are two important caveats. The first is that we now know that all interventions appear to have significantly high rates of test-score decay (see Andrabi et al., 2011) and that there may be important long-term gains in human capital even when test score gains decay (Chetty et al., 2011). Second, the group-nature of the incentive program (across 12 teachers) may have induced free riding and weakened the incentives faced by individual teachers (as seen in Muralidharan, 2012).

Further evidence in favor of the impact of performance pay for teachers on learning outcomes is from a nonexperimental study by Contreras and Rau (2012). They used a difference-in-difference procedure to evaluate the SNED program in Chile, which provided teacher bonus payments based on students' test scores and was rolled out in a scaled up way across all public schools. Their estimates indicate that this program led to a large (0.29σ) and significant increase in students' mathematics test scores.

Two other findings are relevant to this discussion of teacher performance pay. First, incentives can be based on teacher attendance rather than students' test scores. In particular, as discussed earlier, Duflo et al. (2012b) found that paying teachers on the basis of the number of days they are present in the school (as opposed to a flat salary that does not depend on performance) led to a halving of teacher absence rates (from 42% to 21%) and significant increases in student test scores (by 0.17σ). Thus, even if performance incentives on the basis of test scores is difficult to implement, it may be possible to increase student learning by using incentives on intermediate measures of effort, such as attendance, that are easier to measure and also less subject to concerns of multi-tasking. Second, it is worth noting that positive impacts of teacher performance pay on student learning outcomes have also been found in a developed country, Israel, for both group and individual teacher incentives (Lavy, 2002, 2009).

Taken together, these results suggest that even modest changes to compensation structures to reward teachers on the basis of objective measures of performance (such as attendance or increases in student test scores) can generate substantial improvements in learning outcomes at a fraction of the cost of a "business as usual" expansion in education spending. However, not all performance pay programs are likely to be effective, so it is quite important to design the bonus formulae well and to make sure that these designs reflect insights from economic theory. For instance, in the Andhra Pradesh experiment studies by Muralidharan and Sundararaman (2011), there was no reduction in teacher absence in the incentive schools, but teachers report higher levels of teaching activity (including extra classes) in incentive schools, suggesting that the incentives did not have any impact on the extensive margin of effort (attendance) for which there was no direct reward, but that they did have an impact on the intensive margin of teacher effort conditional on attending school. In contrast, Duflo et al. (2012b) found sharp increases in teacher attendance (which was monitored and rewarded), but no increase on teaching activity among those who were present, which is consistent with teacher activity being an unrewarded activity.

4.4.5 Teacher Contractual Structure

A different way to motivate teachers to exert effort would be to make employment contracts subject to periodic renewal, with contracts not being renewed for underperforming teachers. Widely used in the private sector, the performance-contingency of the employment contract can be a powerful motivator for effort. However, the majority of teachers tend to be employed in the public sector in both developing and developed countries, and public sector employment contracts typically feature lifetime tenure after a very short probationary period (if any).

Nevertheless, in recent years many developing countries have started to employ new teachers on short-term renewable contracts. The use of such "contract teachers" has been driven by a combination of lack of enough qualified teachers to match the needs of rapidly expanding school systems, the high cost of hiring them, and the reluctance of qualified teachers to serve in rural areas where the needs of the expanding education system are the greatest. Governments in several developing countries have responded to this challenge by staffing teaching positions with locally hired teachers on fixed-term renewable contracts; these teachers are not professionally trained and are paid much lower salaries than those of regular teachers.[27] The growing use of contract teachers in public schools has been one of the most significant trends in providing primary education in developing countries in the last two decades. Contract teachers comprise a third of public-school teachers across twelve countries in Africa (Bourdon et al., 2010) and their share among all public-school teachers in India grew from 6% in 2003 to 30% in 2010 (Muralidharan et al., 2014).

The use of contract teachers has been controversial. Supporters consider the use of contract teachers to be an efficient way to expand education access and quality to a large number of first-generation learners, and argue that contract teachers face superior incentives compared to tenured civil-service teachers. Opponents argue that using underqualified and untrained teachers may staff classrooms but will not produce learning outcomes, and that the use of contract teachers deprofessionalizes teaching, reduces the prestige of the entire profession, and reduces the motivation of all teachers (Kumar et al., 2005).

While there is very little evidence on the impact of changing the employment contract structure of teachers while holding all else constant, as seen in Table 11 there is evidence from two high-quality studies on the impact of "contract teachers" on students' test scores, although the specific ways in which such teachers differ from regular civil-service teachers vary across contexts. In the first study, Duflo et al. (2015) present results from an experimental evaluation of a program in Kenya that provided a randomly selected set of schools with an extra contract teacher. The extra contract teacher was provided to the first grade, and was used to reduce class size from around 80 to around 40. Half the students were randomly assigned to the contract teacher and the other half to the

---

[27] Contract teacher schemes have been used in several developing countries including Benin, Burkina Faso, Cambodia, Cameroon, Chad, Congo, India, Indonesia, Kenya, Madagascar, Mali, Nicaragua, Niger, Senegal, and Togo. See Duthilleul (2005) and Bourdon et al. (2010) for reviews of contract teacher programs. Contract teachers have also been widely employed in several states of India, and are also referred to as "para-teachers" (see Govinda and Josephine, 2004).

regular civil-service teacher. This design helps the authors distinguish between the effects of a class size reduction when taught by a regular teacher (measured by comparing student performance in classes with regular teachers across treatment and control schools — since the former schools would have half the class size), and the effects of being taught by a contract teacher (measured by comparing classrooms in treatment schools that were taught by contract teachers with those that were taught by regular teachers).

As explained above (Section 4.2.3), Duflo et al. (2015) found that simply reducing class sizes had no significant impact on test scores. More relevant for teacher contract structure is that they found that students who had the reduced class sizes *and* were also taught by a contract teacher scored significantly higher (0.29σ, averaged across subjects) than those in control schools. Even more relevant is that they found that holding class size constant, students taught by contract teachers scored significantly higher than those taught by civil-service teachers even though the contract teachers are paid much lower salaries.

The second high-quality study is that of Muralidharan and Sundararaman (2013a), who present experimental evidence from a program that provided an extra contract teacher to 100 randomly chosen government-run rural primary schools in the Indian state of Andhra Pradesh. At the end of 2 years, students in schools with an extra contract teacher performed significantly better than those in comparison schools by 0.16σ and 0.15σ in math and language tests, respectively. They also found that contract teachers were significantly less likely to be absent from school than civil-service teachers (16% vs. 27%). Finally, they implemented four different nonexperimental estimation procedures (using both within- and between-school variation as well as variation over time in pupil-teacher ratios in the same school) and found that they can never reject the null hypothesis that contract teachers are at least as effective in improving student learning as regular civil-service teachers. In fact, their point estimates typically suggest that the contract teachers are more effective than regular teachers, who are more qualified, better trained, and paid salaries five times higher than those of contract teachers.

It is also relevant to this discussion to highlight that all three of the studies on teaching at the right level, which were discussed in the previous section on pedagogy and found large positive effects on student learning outcomes of that intervention, used volunteer/informal/contract teachers with minimal formal training who were paid stipends that were at most one fifth of the salary of regular teachers. These results suggest that the superior work incentives of contract teachers may more than make up for their lack of formal teacher training. They also suggest that the binding constraint in translating increased education spending into improved learning outcomes may not be teacher training and qualifications (as is commonly believed) but teacher effort, which is (relatively) weak for civil-service teachers with lifetime employment security because there is no reward under the status quo for either effort or performance (and, conversely, few consequences for poor performance). Most relevant for policy perhaps is the fact that the results suggest that similar education outcomes can be had at much lower cost (since contract teacher salaries are much lower than those of civil-service teachers), and that it may be possible to significantly expand education quality for a given level of spending by making more use of contract teachers.

Nevertheless, scaling up the insights from this body of evidence into policy is nontrivial because of political challenges. This is best highlighted by Bold et al. (2013) who conduct a similar study in Kenya to the one conducted by Duflo et al. (2015) and find that the contract teacher program that they studied had a positive impact on student learning when implemented by a nonprofit partner, but that it had no impact when implemented by the government (partly because the program itself was not implemented). In practice, the scaling up of contract teacher programs has been politically challenging because of pressure from contract-teacher unions (especially when a large number of contract teachers are hired) to get "regularized." Muralidharan (2016b) discusses these practical challenges in more detail and presents an approach to potentially address them by making contract teachers the first stage of a performance-based career ladder.

4.4.6 Private Schools, Vouchers, and Public-Private Partnerships

Another important trend in primary education in developing countries over the past two decades has been the rapid growth of private schools, with recent estimates showing that private schools now account for over 20% of total primary school enrolment in low-income countries (Baum et al., 2014). The growing market share of fee-charging private schools is especially striking as it is taking place within a context of increased spending on public education and near universal access to free public primary schools. This raises important questions regarding the effectiveness of private schools in these settings and the optimal policy response to their growth.

Opponents of the growth of private schooling argue that it has led to economic stratification of education systems and has weakened the public education system by causing the middle class to leave the public-school system. They also worry that private schools compete by cream-skimming students, and attract parents and students on the basis of superior average *levels* of test scores, but that they may not be adding more value to the marginal applicant.[28] Others contend that private schools in developing countries have grown in response to failures of the public-schooling system, that they are more accountable and responsive to parents, that they have better management practices that ensure better teacher selection and accountability, and that the revealed preference of parents suggests that they are likely to be better than public schools. Supporters of private

---

[28] This concern is supported by several studies across different contexts, which find that highly demanded elite schools do not seem to add more value to student learning (see Zhang (2014) in China, Lucas and Mbiti (2014) in Kenya, Cullen et al. (2006) in Chicago, and Abdulkadiroglu et al. (2014) in Boston and New York).

schools recognize that their main weakness is that they are not accessible that to the poor who cannot afford to pay fees, and argue therefore that policymakers should be more open to voucher-like models that combine public funding with private provision of education.[29]

Thus, understanding the relative impact of public and private schools on learning outcomes is a first-order question for both research and policy. There are five high-quality studies of school voucher programs in developing countries that defrayed the cost of attending private schools. As seen in Table 10, three of these studies examined the impact of vouchers on time in school. Of the four estimated impacts, one is significantly positive and the other three are statistically insignificant. All five high-quality studies examined the impact of voucher programs on student learning. The summary information in Table 11 shows that two of the three RCT studies found a significant impact, but neither of the other high-quality studies found a significant impact. The following paragraphs discuss these studies in more detail.

Angrist et al. (2002) and Angrist et al. (2006) study the short and medium-term effects the PACES program in Colombia that provided vouchers (allocated by lottery) to students to attend private secondary schools.[30] They found that voucher winners performed significantly better both 3 and 7 years after receiving the voucher. More specifically, Angrist et al. (2002) find that the voucher winners scored 0.16σ higher on math and reading tests after 3 years, and that they completed more years of school and had lower rates of grade repetition. Angrist et al. (2006) find that the voucher winners have significantly higher high-school graduation rates (5.6 percentage points higher on a base of 25–30%), and that they scored 0.2σ higher on college-entrance exams (after controlling for differential attrition in the long-term follow-up study).

However, while both of these studies suggest that the PACES voucher program was highly effective, it may not be possible to interpret these results as reflecting only the differential "productivity" of private schools because the PACES program not only allowed students to use the vouchers to attend private schools, but it also allowed vouchers to be topped up by parents (to attend a better school than they could have afforded without a voucher), and required students to maintain minimum academic standards to continue receiving the voucher. Thus while the results point to the effectiveness of the PACES program, the estimates reflect a combination of private school productivity, additional education spending, and student incentives.

Muralidharan and Sundararaman (2015) present experimental evidence on the impact of a school-choice program in the Indian state of Andhra Pradesh that featured a unique

---

[29] See Tooley and Dixon (2007), Muralidharan and Kremer (2008), Goyal and Pandey (2009), and Tooley (2009).

[30] In Tables 10 and 11 we classify these two studies as RCTs because they are based on an actual lottery to determine eligibility for the vouchers. One could also classify them as "natural experiments."

two-stage randomization of the offer of a voucher (across villages as well as students). The design created a set of control *villages* that allows the authors to experimentally evaluate both the individual impacts of school choice (using the student-level lottery) as well as its aggregate effects including the spillovers onto nonapplicants and students who start out in private schools (using the village-level lottery).

At the end of 2 and 4 years of the school choice program, Muralidharan and Sundararaman (2015) find no difference between the test scores of lottery winners and losers on the two main subjects of Telugu (the native language of Andhra Pradesh) and math, suggesting that the large cross-sectional test-score differences in these subjects across public and private schools (of 0.65σ) mostly reflect omitted variables. However, they also find that private schools spend significantly less instructional time on Telugu (40% less) and math (32% less) than public schools, and instead spend more time on English, and on science and social studies. They also taught a third language, Hindi, which was not taught in public primary schools. When they conduct tests in these additional subjects after 4 years of the voucher program they find small positive effects of winning the voucher on English (0.12σ; p-value $= 0.098$), and science and social studies (0.08σ; p-value $= 0.16$), and large, positive effects on Hindi (0.55σ; p-value < 0.001).

Assuming equal weights across all subjects, they find that students who won a voucher had average test scores that were 0.13σ higher, a statistically significant effect, and that the average student who used a voucher to attend a private school scored 0.26σ higher ($p < 0.01$). However, this positive impact was driven mainly by Hindi (which was taught in private schools but not in public primary schools), and they find no impact of winning a voucher on average test scores excluding Hindi. However, even without assuming equal weights across subjects, Muralidharan and Sundararaman (2015) are able to infer that private schools were more productive than public schools because they were able to achieve similar Telugu and math test scores for the lottery winners with substantially less instructional time, and use the additional time to generate large gains in Hindi test scores. Further, the annual cost per student in the public-school system is over three times the mean cost per student in the private schools in the sample. Thus, students who win a lottery to attend private schools have slightly better test scores (better on Hindi and same on other subjects) even though the private schools spend substantially lower amounts per student.

Finally, two studies of Chile that were not RCTs found insignificant effects of attending a private school on Spanish and math test scores in that country. Lara et al. (2011) used a difference-in-differences approach to estimate the impact of vouchers to attend private schools on the test scores of students in grade 10 (all of whom were in public primary schools but some of whom used vouchers to move into private secondary schools). They find a very small positive impact (0.02σ) that is not statistically significant. Hsieh and Urquiola (2006) also use a difference-in-differences approach to examine the impact of using vouchers to enroll in a private school on the test scores of students in grades

4 and 8. They find negative but statistically insignificant effects on mathematics and language (Spanish) test scores.

Overall, the results from the three RCTs suggest that private schools were more productive (by being able to deliver similar learning outcomes in math and language at lower financial and time cost), but not necessarily more effective at raising test scores. Thus, from a policy perspective an important open question is to understand how public and privately managed schools would perform in a setting where the value of the voucher was set equal to the per-student spending in public schools. The two studies from Chile, where vouchers ensured similar levels of spending at private and public schools, suggests little effect, but Chile is very different from India, so it is difficult to generalize from one of these countries to the other. Further evidence from both countries, as well as others, would allow us to measure the extent to which the apparent greater productivity of private schools in India can translate into better absolute learning outcomes, and whether this finding extends to other countries.

4.4.7 Single-Sex Schools

A final governance intervention is single-sex schools, for which there is only one study. Jackson (2012) used regression discontinuity and difference-in-differences estimates to estimate the impact of single-sex schools on enrollment (as measured by taking a national examination) of grade 10 students in Trinidad and Tobago. He found, as seen in Table 10, that students who attend such schools are 7.3 percentage points more likely to take the national exam.

Overall, the summary of the evidence reviewed suggests that developing country education systems often feature weak governance, as seen by high rates of teacher absence and low levels of effort. Changing education system governance at scale is not easy given the political constraints involved. Nevertheless, the evidence suggests that interventions that improve governance of school systems — especially with regard to teacher effort and accountability — may have a large positive impact on learning outcomes in developing countries.

5. INTERPRETING THE EVIDENCE, AND IMPLICATIONS FOR FUTURE RESEARCH

As discussed in Section 3, an important goal for the empirical research on education in developing countries has been to estimate a series of partial derivatives of an education production function. Combining estimates of marginal returns to various possible education interventions with data on marginal costs would then allow researchers and policymakers to rank various interventions by the highest marginal return on investment. This is an implicit goal for many individual studies and typically an explicit goal for papers that aim to review the evidence. Given limited budgets and several competing uses for these funds, such a ranking could be used to help policymakers prioritize across competing potential investments. Further, reallocating public education expenditure away from ineffective forms of spending to more effective ones could potentially improve education outcomes even within a given budget.

In this section, we discuss the extent to which the evidence summarized in the previous section yields clear conclusions that would allow policymakers to use this evidence to improve the effectiveness of public spending on education. In attempting to draw such broad conclusions, we highlight the many challenges in interpreting the evidence, and discuss the implications for policy as well as for future research.

5.1 Challenges in Interpreting the Evidence

5.1.1 Production Function Parameters Versus Policy Parameters

The discussion in Section 3 highlighted the value of exogenously varying $Q_{i,t}$ to estimate the causal impact of $Q_{i,t}$ on education outcomes. Note however, that even random assignment of $Q_{i,t}$ may not yield the corresponding production function parameter β in Eq. (5).[31] This is because the production function parameter β is a partial derivative $\left(\partial A_{i,t} / \partial Q_{i,t} \right)$ holding *other inputs constant*. In practice, other inputs at the school or household level may endogenously respond to exogenous changes in $Q_{i,t}$, and the estimated parameter should therefore be more accurately interpreted as a policy parameter, which is a total derivative $\left(dA_{i,t} / dQ_{i,t} \right)$ that accounts for reoptimization by agents (students, parents, teachers, and school administrators) in response to an exogenous change in $Q_{i,t}$.

The extent to which the estimate from a well-identified evaluation of a change in $Q_{i,t}$ reflects reoptimization will depend critically on the duration of the study. A clear illustration is provided by Das et al. (2013), who studied a randomly assigned school grant program in India over a 2-year period and found significant positive effects on test scores at the end of the first year, but found no effect in the second year even though the grant was provided again in the second year, and was spent on very similar items in both years (books, school supplies, and classroom learning materials). They show that the most likely explanation for this result is that household spending on books and school supplies did not change across treatment and schools in the first year (when the school grant was unanticipated), but that households in treatment schools sharply cut back their spending on these categories in the second year (when the school grant was anticipated and could be accounted for in household decision making), and that this reduction offset around 80% of the per-student value of the grant. The authors therefore argue that the "first year" effect of the program is more likely to represent the "production function" effect of providing the school grant (since other factors did not have time to adjust), whereas the "second year" effect is closer to the "policy parameter" (which reflects household reoptimization).

---

[31] $Q_{i,t}$ is one of the $X_{i,t}$ variables in Eq. (5) that are school inputs.

This example highlights the importance of measuring as many intermediate inputs as possible to have a better idea about the mechanisms of program impact. However, in practice, it will be difficult to measure *all* possible intermediate inputs, and the extent to which they may have changed in response to the exogenously varied treatment. Thus, it is perhaps most accurate to interpret the "causal estimate" of β from experimental studies as the "policy effect" of $Q_{i,t}$ at the point when the outcomes are measured. While one could argue that experimental studies estimate production function parameters over short time periods, before agents have had an opportunity to reoptimize their behavior, it is: (a) difficult to confirm that this is true on every dimension of potential behavior modification and (b) much less likely to be true over longer time horizons.[32]

Note that this limitation is also present for nonexperimental methods, and is therefore not a criticism of experimental estimates per se. But it an important limitation to highlight because experimental estimates are often implicitly interpreted as representing the production function parameters of estimated equations such as Eq. (5).

One advantage of well-identified evaluations using large administrative data sets (based on, for example, RDDs) is that it may be possible to observe the policy effects over longer time horizons at a much lower marginal cost than in experimental studies (since the cost of conducting follow up surveys on experimental samples can be quite large, and the challenge of differential attrition grows over time). A good example of this is provided by Bharadwaj et al. (2013), who measured the impact of early childhood interventions several years later using administrative data in both Chile and Norway. Another good example is that of Pop-Eleches and Urquiola (2013), who present regression–discontinuity based estimates of the impact of going to a better school and also collect extensive data on household reoptimization in response to access to a better school. The main point, however, is that it is important to recognize that over time the estimates of program impact are more likely to represent policy effects as opposed to estimates of production function parameters.

5.1.2 External Validity

The challenges of external validity of even well-identified studies are well known (see Deaton, 2010, and the references cited therein, for further discussion). Even well-identified experimental estimates of program impacts are an estimate of the program interacted with a set of unobserved covariates — which are likely to be quite different across different contexts. These challenges are magnified in the context of writing a chapter such as this, which seeks to summarize evidence across a range of developing countries

---

[32] While the discussion may suggest that experimental estimates may be lower bounds of production function parameters and upper bounds of policy parameters, this need not be true if the unmeasured inputs are complements to the experimental intervention as opposed to substitutes (as was the case in Das et al., 2013).

that are located on different continents. This problem is well known among academic researchers, but can be understated in "systemic reviews" that compare interventions and estimates across contexts (see Pritchett and Sandefur, 2013, for a discussion). There is no good solution to this problem beyond conducting more studies and gathering more evidence by replicating evaluations of interventions in many settings. Unfortunately, the academic incentives to conduct such replication studies are limited.

5.1.3 Comparability of Interventions

Further, even when there are multiple studies of a similar intervention, there are almost always variations in the specific details of the intervention that make comparisons difficult. Take the case of teacher performance pay. While there are multiple high-quality studies on the subject, no two studies have the same formula for how teachers will be paid bonuses! Some of the design details that vary include individual versus group incentives, tournaments versus piece rates, linear versus nonlinear bonus formulae, formulae based on students reaching thresholds (such as the fraction who pass a test) versus those that reward improvements for all students.[33] Similarly, interventions of technology-enabled learning vary from simply providing hardware to different forms of integration of technology into pedagogy, practice, assessment, and customizing of learning pathways.

It is no surprise then that there is considerable variation in the estimated impact of even the same program in different contexts. The ranges of effect sizes from experimental evaluations of the same intervention documented by McEwan (2015) show that the variations within intervention type are often larger than those between intervention types. How then should we make policy-relevant inferences from the body of evidence summarized in Section 4 and in the other review papers written in the past 3 years? The following section considers this question.

5.2 Mapping the Evidence to a Deeper Understanding of Developing Country Education

We suggest here that one way of proceeding from well-identified individual studies to a deeper understanding of how best to improve education in developing countries is to think about whether the interventions or programs studied were alleviating a binding constraint to improving education quality.[34] In particular, we may learn as much from understanding why well-intentioned interventions do not work as expected as we may from interventions that are "successful."

---

[33] Indeed the question of optimal design of a teacher bonus system is by itself an important theoretical question that is not easy to answer (see Barlevy and Neal, 2012, for a discussion).

[34] The approach here is similar to that proposed by Dani Rodrik in the context of country-level growth diagnostics. See Rodrik (2008) for a discussion.

5.2.1 Understanding Nonimpact

In theory (as laid out in Section 3), finding that an intervention had a zero effect (or did not have a significant impact) should simply mean that the estimate of the associated β in Eq. (5), and thus the marginal impact of increasing $Q_{i,t}$, is insignificantly different from zero. In practice, however, it is important to distinguish between four different interpretations of a zero result.[35] These include: (a) poor implementation of the intervention, including corruption or administrative failures, which are often the binding constraint in many developing countries; (b) substitution away from other inputs provided by agents (including governments, schools, teachers, and households) in response to the treatment; (c) the intervention may help some students, but may not alleviate a binding constraint to education outcomes in the context being studied; and (d) absence of complementary inputs/reforms that may be needed for the intervention to be effective. Note that reasons (c) and (d) are consistent with the interpretation that the marginal impact of increasing $Q_{i,t}$ on outcomes is zero in a production function sense, but reasons (a) and (b) are not. Further, the distinction between (c) and (d) also matters for policy because the policy implication of (c) may be not to prioritize increasing $Q_{i,t}$ until the binding constraint is reduced or removed, whereas the policy implication of (d) would be to increase $Q_{i,t}$ as long as the complementary input is also increased.

These possibilities are illustrated across four different randomized evaluations of the impact of providing books and materials to students. (In some cases, these were directly provided as books, while in other cases the input was a grant to schools that was spent primarily on books and related materials.) Each of the four studies finds zero average impacts of providing books and materials, but each points to different possible reasons for the zero effects. Sabarwal et al. (2014) find no impact on test scores from the provision of textbooks to schools in Sierra Leone and attribute this to the fact that schools stored the textbooks instead of distributing them to students (which is a form of poor implementation). Das et al. (2013), described above, also find no net impact on test scores from the provision of a school grant (that was spent mostly on books and related materials) in India, but attribute it to households offsetting the intervention by reducing their own spending on these inputs.

Glewwe et al. (2009) also find no impact on test scores from providing textbooks to students in Kenya. But they do find positive impacts on students with the highest baseline test scores, and they suggest that their results are consistent with the fact that the majority of children could not read the English language textbooks to begin with, and thus could not benefit from the textbooks (whereas those who could read *did* benefit). Thus, in this case, the nonimpact is interpreted as suggesting that textbooks did not alleviate the binding constraint to learning in this context (which was the lack of sufficient reading skills).

---

[35] A fifth possibility, that the impact has no effect under almost any circumstances, is discussed below.

Finally, in ongoing work by one of us (Muralidharan), we again also find no impact on test scores from the provision of a large capitation grant to schools in Tanzania (the largest item that the grant was spent on was textbooks). However, this study was explicitly designed to test for complementarities with teacher effort (which was boosted by a separate intervention that paid teachers bonuses based on student performance) using a cross-cutting design with a sample size large enough to test for complementarities, and we find that the interaction effect of the school grant and teacher performance pay was significantly positive. In other words, the school grant on its own had no impact, but had a significant impact when provided in conjunction with a teacher performance pay intervention. Thus, it is likely that the performance pay treatment contributed to teachers making more effective use of the additional materials, but it is also true that having the materials allowed teachers to significantly improve student outcomes relative to teachers who increased effort due to performance-linked pay but had few or no textbooks to work with.

The broader point here is that these experiments, all of which found zero results, provide useful results in and of themselves, and yield an important policy conclusion that the marginal impact of providing only books and learning materials to students may be very low. On the other hand, the fact that four papers with the same result point to four different reasons for this nonimpact suggest that a "black box" experiment on its own may yield limited insights into the nature of the education production function and the true binding constraints to learning. Many more insights can be gained by collecting data on intermediate processes and inputs to better understand the factors that explain the observed "reduced form" zero estimates of program impact.

Of course, it is also possible that the true impact of a particular input is zero, with none of the above qualifications being applicable. A good example is provided by de Ree et al. (2015), who conducted an experimental evaluation of the impact of an Indonesian policy that unconditionally doubled teacher pay, and find that there was zero intensive margin impact of the salary doubling on student test scores. (They do not study the potential extensive margin benefits of improved teacher quality over time.) In this case, the program was well implemented, there was no measured crowding out of any other inputs, and there was no heterogeneity in the impacts across either teacher or student characteristics. While it is conceivable that some complementary intervention may have caused the salary doubling to have had a positive impact, the policy was implemented without any such intervention, and represents what was actually done. Thus, finding that the impact of a program that had a very large fiscal cost was zero is of value in itself, and is directly policy relevant given the number of settings where such policies are contemplated.

5.2.2 Drawing the Right Lessons From "Effective" Interventions

As discussed in Section 5.1.3, even when there are multiple high-quality studies of the same intervention, the details of the interventions often differ in important ways. Thus, even in cases where there is evidence to suggest that an intervention is "effective," we argue that it is more useful to focus on the principle illustrated by the successful intervention rather than a more mechanical conception of identifying interventions that "work." Overall, our assessment of the evidence to date is that interventions that expand schooling inputs may be less effective at improving learning outcomes than those that improve the effectiveness of pedagogy within classrooms and/or improve governance and the accountability of schools and teachers.

For instance, the fact that multiple studies find positive impacts of supplemental instruction targeted at the current learning level of the student (as opposed to the level of the textbook for the grade that the child is in) combined with evidence on flat learning trajectories from longitudinal data on learning outcomes (Muralidharan and Zieleniak, 2014) suggest that a key binding constraint to improving education quality in low-income countries is that students who are not functionally literate or numerate at the end of the second year of primary school may be learning very little in school in the subsequent years even if they stay enrolled. This may be an important reason for why expensive expansions in inputs and resources may be having little impact on learning outcomes, while inexpensive supplemental instruction programs are so effective at doing so (Banerjee and Duflo, 2011; Pritchett and Beatty, 2012).

Thus, the evidence to date suggests that the lack of foundational learning may be a critical binding constraint for education systems in low-income countries, and that policymakers would do well to prioritize giving attention to this constraint. The next step should be to identify specific models by which such foundational learning may be most effectively provided, and to iteratively pilot and evaluate such models to inform decisions on scaling up. The series of studies conducted on evaluating different models of "Teaching at the Right Level," which are summarized in Banerjee et al. (2015), is a good illustration of such an effort.

Similarly, the evidence strongly suggests that poor governance and accountability in education systems in low-income countries may be a critical constraint to improving learning outcomes. In particular, there is compelling evidence to suggest that pivoting public education spending from a business as usual input-augmentation strategy to an "inefficiency reduction" strategy may substantially improve education outcomes without increasing total spending. Two stark comparisons are provided by considering alternative ways of increasing teacher compensation, and of reducing class size.

De Ree et al. (2015) show that an unconditional doubling of teacher salaries in Indonesia had no impact on student learning outcomes, whereas Muralidharan and Sundararaman (2011) and Muralidharan (2012) show that a teacher performance pay program was highly effective, even though it spent only 3% of annual salary on the bonuses.[36] Similarly, Duflo et al. (2012b) show how changing the *structure* of teacher

---

[36] They show that the administrative cost of implementing the program was equal to at most another 3% of pay.

pay (from a flat salary to one that depends on the number of days attended) can substantially improve teacher attendance, even while not increasing the *level* of pay very much. These results provide a striking example of how pivoting public expenditure on teacher salaries (the largest component of education spending) from unconditional raises to performance-linked payments could sharply increase the efficiency of education spending.

Another example is provided by Muralidharan et al. (2014) who show that reducing teacher absence by investing in better school monitoring could be over ten times more cost effective at reducing the effective student-teacher ratio in schools (net of teacher absence) than the default policy of hiring more teachers. Thus, reallocating existing education expenditure away from less effective to more effective policies may substantially increase the total factor productivity (TFP) of publicly provided education in low-income countries.

Again, the specific details of how best to improve governance will depend on contextual factors, and the evidence presented in Section 4 should not be interpreted as calling for a universal scale up of any specific policy for improving governance. Rather, as the discussion above suggests, the evidence should best be interpreted as pointing to the likely large returns to investing in improving governance relative to a business as usual input-augmentation strategy.

5.3 Cost-Effectiveness and Making Individual Studies More Comparable

As discussed earlier, a key motivation for the empirical research on education in developing countries in the past decade has been to identify the relative cost-effectiveness of alternative ways to spend scarce public resources on education. Indeed, our discussion above has been motivated by cost-effectiveness and the possibility of improving education outcomes in a fiscally neutral way by reallocating spending from less cost-effective policies to more cost-effective ones. Nevertheless, analyzing the cost-effectiveness of every study reviewed in this chapter requires both the estimation of marginal benefits of different programs (the focus in the discussion so far) *and* data on the costs of these programs. Unfortunately, individual studies do not typically report cost data in a comparable way, which makes it challenging for us (and others) to present the evidence in this format.

Organizations such as the Abdul Latif Jameel Poverty Action Lab (J-PAL) are working to conduct such analyses, at least for experimental studies, but this is still challenging because studies do not typically report cost data in a systematic way, and often use customized measures of learning outcomes that are difficult to compare.[37] While the current default approach is to report per student cost per standard deviation of test scores improved of an intervention, this approach still has several shortcomings. First, the

---

[37] The authors of this chapter have served as former and current education program co-chairs of J-PAL, and the discussion reflects our experiences from attempting this exercise.

standard deviation of a test score can be sensitive to the range of question difficulty on the test, and the representativeness of the student sample in which the test was carried out. Second, the framework is not easy to apply to report on interventions that do not improve test scores, but reduce costs (technically, these would be infinitely cost-effective interventions on the margin). Third, the studies are typically carried out across several different contexts, which makes such cost-effectiveness comparisons difficult to interpret. Fourth, program costs are typically higher in smaller scale experiments than in scaled up settings where the fixed cost of program design can be amortized over a larger number of schools. The following paragraphs provide some results on cost-effectiveness, but the wide variation in results and the problems just mentioned imply that they should be regarded as exploratory rather than conclusive.

The three studies that found significant impacts of merit-based scholarships also report the amounts of the scholarships, although they do not report administrative and other costs of those programs. The Kenya girls' scholarship program studied by both Kremer et al. (2009) and Friedman et al. (2011) paid a total of $38 per scholarship recipient ($19 per year, including payments to parents, for 2 years) which implies a cost of about $6 per student since only about 15% of students received scholarships. The former study found impacts of 0.27σ at the end of the 2 year program, which implies a cost of $2 per 0.1σ increase, and the latter study found an impact of 0.20σ four to five years after the program, which implies a cost of $3 per 0.1σ increase. The more recent study by Blimpo found impacts of about 0.26σ after 1 year for all three variants of the incentive program, but the (average) payments to students varied by the intervention: the individual incentive cost about $9 per student, which implies a cost of $3 per 0.1σ increase; the team incentive cost $3 per student, which implies a cost of $1 per 0.1σ increase; and the team tournament incentive cost about $6 per year, which implies a cost of $2 per 0.1σ increase.

Three studies of CCT programs found significantly positive impacts on test scores: the studies by Baird et al. (2011) and Baird et al. (2013) of the same program in Malawi, and the study of Barham et al. (2013) on a CCT program in Nicaragua. The lowest cost intervention in the Baird et al. (2011) study provided payments of $5 per month for 10 months per year, and thus cost $50 per year. The payments were provided over a period of 2 years so the total cost was $100 per student. The impacts of the program on English and math scores, respectively, were 0.14σ and 0.12σ. Averaging over these impacts implies a cost of $77 per 0.1σ increase in student test scores. This is for girls who were already in school when the program began; Baird et al. (2013) examine the impact of the program on girls who were not in school when the program began. The impacts for these girls were slightly higher, 0.13σ and 0.16σ for English and math, respectively, but that paper did not investigate the size of the impact by the size of the grant, and so the estimates are for an average grant of $10 per month; averaging over these impacts implies a cost of $138 per 0.1σ increase in student test scores. Finally, Barham et al. (2013) evaluated a CCT program in Nicaragua that made educated-related payments of $133 per household per year. A typical household had one or two children in the program, so the cost per child could be $133 or $67 per year. The impact measured is of 3 years in the program, so total costs are $399 (one eligible child in household) or $200 (two eligible children in household) for the duration of the program. The estimated impact, averaged over language and math, was 0.20σ. Even assuming the lower cost of $200 this implies a cost of $100 per 0.1σ increase in student test scores.

Two studies of the introduction of computers found significantly positive effects and also had information about the cost of the intervention. Banerjee et al. (2007) found that providing four computers per school for children to share in primary schools in India increased math test scores by 0.48σ after 2 years, but 1 year after the program ended the impact was only 0.09σ. The program cost $15 per student per year, so $30 for 2 years. Using the estimated effect of 0.48σ the cost was $6 per 0.1σ increase in student test scores, but using the "long-run" estimate of 0.09σ the cost increases to $33 per 0.1σ increase in student test scores. Linden (2008) also provides cost estimates for the two computer interventions that he considered. The one that was successful, which took place out of school and so did not reduce instructional time during the school day, increased students' test scores by 0.29σ after 1 year and cost only $5 per student per year. This implies that the cost of increasing test scores was only about $2 per 0.1σ increase in student test scores. Overall, the cost-effectiveness of interventions that provide computers to students varies widely, depending on the specifics of the intervention (recall that many had no effect, and some even had negative effects) and, for at least one study, on how long the effects persists after the child is no longer in the program.

A final study to consider is the teacher incentive program evaluated by Muralidharan and Sundararaman (2011), which after 2 years increased students' test scores by 0.28σ when the teacher incentives were at the individual teacher level and by 0.15σ when the incentives were at the group (of teachers) level. The cost of the former was $222 per school, or about $3 per student, while the cost of the latter was $133 per school, or about $2 per student (the average school had about 80 students). These costs imply that both types of teacher incentive programs cost only about $1 per 0.1σ increase in student test scores.

These cost figures must be interpreted with caution, because most of them do not include administrative costs. Moreover, for the CCT interventions and the merit-based scholarship interventions much of the cost was not a cost to society as a whole but rather a redistribution of funds from taxpayers to program beneficiaries, and this redistribution may well have had poverty reduction benefits that should be included as benefits when making comparisons. Thus much more work needs to be done to compare the cost-effectiveness of these interventions. Yet it is clear that even among successful programs there is very wide variation in cost-effectiveness, which implies that more evidence is needed in order to improve students' educational outcomes in a way that maximizes those improvements given limited resources for achieving that goal. Indeed, having more comparable measures of costs and benefits would be very useful for education research and policy, and it would also be useful for funders of education research to create standardized templates for reporting costs and benefits that authors of individual studies should be encouraged to fill out to enable such comparisons (even though they should be interpreted with caution).

6. CONCLUSION

Improving education in developing countries is likely to promote both aggregate economic growth and the "inclusiveness" of this growth. As a result, national governments as well as international development organizations have prioritized and invested considerable resources in improving education attainment and outcomes in developing countries, and they continue to do so each year. This focus has resulted in sharp increases in school enrollment and completion rates in developing countries, and it is a reflection of this priority that these rates are substantially higher than what today's high-income countries had achieved at a comparable level of income per capita. At the same time, there is growing evidence that the extent to which extra years in school translates into additional human capital is much less than policymakers had hoped.

The past decade has seen a sharp increase in the number of high-quality empirical studies on the impacts of various education policies on improving enrollment, attendance, and learning outcomes. This chapter has summarized this evidence, and it has also attempted to interpret the body of evidence to date to guide both policymakers as well as researchers and funders of future research.

For policymakers, the main message from the summary of the evidence is that a "business as usual" approach of expanding spending on education (most of which is spent on increasing fairly standard inputs into education) is unlikely to have much impact on improving learning outcomes beyond that predicted by the cross-country relationship between per capita income and learning outcomes. On the other hand, interventions that focus on improved and more effective pedagogy (especially providing foundational literacy and numeracy skills to the millions of first-generation learners who are falling behind the pace of curriculum), and on improved governance of the education system (especially teacher performance and accountability) are likely to yield considerably greater returns on increased spending.

For researchers, we hope that this chapter provides a useful framework for organizing future research efforts, and helps direct attention to the areas where the knowledge gaps are particularly large. In particular, one point worth highlighting is that much of the high-quality empirical research in education in developing countries has been done by economists, and as a result the topics on which there is more evidence tend to be topics of interest to economists (such as household demand, information, inputs, and incentives). However, some of the most promising avenues for improving education in low-income settings may involve improving the design and delivery of classroom instruction. Thus, we believe that a fruitful area of future research is for researchers trained in rigorous empirical methods (especially in running field experiments) to collaborate with experts in curriculum and pedagogy to improve the empirical evidence base on effective pedagogy in low-income settings. Much more work is needed on the more "standard" topics as well, but it is likely to be more fruitful to focus attention on the optimal design of interventions (including many incentive-based ones) and testing alternative designs rather than simply testing whether some interventions work. In addition, we hope to have highlighted the importance of collecting intermediate data on mechanisms and context in order to shed more light not just on *whether* an intervention works, but also on *why* it may or may not have worked in the setting where it was studied.

Finally, for funders and international organizations, we urge that more attention be paid to the creating of "research public goods" including IRT-linked question item banks (that allow the results of different interventions in many parts of the world to be compared on a common scale), the creating of standardized templates for reporting cost information, and to encourage recipients of research funding to use these common platforms to enable greater comparability and improve the ability of individual studies to contribute to enhanced understanding of education in developing countries.

ACKNOWLEDGMENTS

We thank Amy Damon, Suzanne Wisniewski, and Bixuan Sun for collaboration in putting together the studies reviewed in this chapter. We also thank James Sayres and Eric Stephens for research assistance. Finally, we thank Eric Hanushek, Lant Pritchett, and the UK Department for International Development (DFID) for comments on preliminary versions of this chapter.

REFERENCES

Abdulkadiroglu, A., Angrist, J., Pathak, P.A., 2014. The elite illusion: achievement effects at Boston and New York exam schools. Econometrica 82, 137–196.

Abeberese, A.B., Kumler, T.J., Linden, L.L., 2014. Improving reading skills by encouraging children to read in school: a randomized evaluation of the Sa Aklat Sisikat reading program in the Philippines. J. Hum. Resour. 49 (3), 611–633.

Adrogue, C., Orlicki, M.E., 2013. Do in-school feeding programs have an impact on academic performance? The case of public schools in Argentina. Educ. Policy Anal. Arch. 21 (50), 1–23.

Alderman, H., Kim, J., Orazem, P.F., 2003. Design, evaluation, and sustainability of private schools for the poor: the Pakistan urban and rural fellowship school experiment. Econ. Educ. Rev. 22, 265–274.

Alderman, H., Gilligan, D.O., Lehrer, K., 2012. The impact of food for education programs on school participation in northern Uganda. Econ. Dev. Cult. Chang. 61 (1), 187–218.

Ambler, K., Aycinena, D., Yang, D., 2014. Channeling Remittances to Education: A Field Experiment Among Migrants from El Salvador. NBER Working Paper # 20262 [published as Ambler, Aycinena and Yang (2015)].

Ambler, K., Aycinena, D., Yang, D., 2015. Channeling remittances to education: a field experiment among migrants from El Salvador. Am. Econ. J. Appl. Econ. 7 (2), 1–27.

Andrabi, T., Das, J., Khwaja, A., Zajonc, T., 2011. Do value-added estimates add value? Accounting for learning dynamics. Am. Econ. J. Appl. Econ. 3 (3), 29–54.

Angrist, J., Bettinger, E., Bloom, E., King, E., Kremer, M., 2002. Vouchers for private schooling in Colombia: evidence from a randomized natural experiment. Am. Econ. Rev. 92 (5), 1535–1558.

Angrist, J., Bettinger, E., Kremer, M., 2006. Long-term educational consequences of secondary school vouchers: evidence from administrative records in Colombia. Am. Econ. Rev. 96 (3), 847–862.

ASER, 2014. Tenth Annual Status of Education Report. ASER Centre, New Delhi.

Attanasio, O., Fitzsimons, E., Gomez, A., Gutierrez, M.I., Meghir, C., Mesnard, A., 2010. Children's schooling and work in the presence of a conditional cash transfer program in rural Colombia. Econ. Dev. Cult. Chang. 58 (2), 181–210.

Attanasio, O.P., Meghir, C., Santiago, A., 2012. Education choices in mexico: using a structural model and a randomized experiment to evaluate progresa. Rev. Econ. Stud. 79, 37–66.

Baez, J.E., Camacho, A., 2011. Assessing the Long-Term Effects of Conditional Cash Transfers on Human Capital: Evidence from Colombia. World Bank Policy Research Paper No. 5681, World Bank, Washington, DC.

Baird, S., McIntosh, C., Ozler, B., 2011. Cash or condition? Evidence from a cash transfer experiment. Q. J. Econ. 26 (4), 1709–1753.

Baird, S.J., Chirwa, E., de Hoop, J., Özler, B., 2013. Girl Power: Cash Transfers and Adolescent Welfare. Evidence from a Cluster-Randomized Experiment in Malawi. NBER Working Papers 19479, National Bureau of Economic Research.

Baird, S., Hicks, J.H., Kremer, M., Miguel, E., 2015. Worms at Work: Long-Run Impacts of a Child Health Investment. UC Berkeley.

Baker, G., 1992. Incentive contracts and performance measurement. J. Polit. Econ. 100 (3), 598–614.

Banerjee, A., Duflo, E., 2011. Poor Economics. MIT Press, Cambridge, MA.

Banerjee, A., Cole, S., Duflo, E., Linden, L., 2007. Remedying education: evidence from two randomized experiments in India. Q. J. Econ. 122 (3), 1235–1264.

Banerjee, A., Banerji, R., Duflo, E., Gelnnerster, R., Khemani, S., 2010. Pitfalls of participatory programs: evidence from a randomized evaluation in education in India. Am. Econ. J. Econ. Policy 2 (1), 1–30.

Banerjee, A., Banerji, R., Berry, J., Duflo, E., Kannan, H., Mukherji, S., et al., 2015. Teaching at the Right Level: Evidence from Randomized Evaluations in India. MIT, Cambridge, MA.

Banerji, R., Berry, J., Shotland, M., 2013. The Impact of Mother Literacy and Participation Programs on Child Learning: Evidence from a Randomized Evaluation in India. Abdul Latif Jameel Poverty Action Lab (J-PAL), Cambridge, MA.

Barham, Tania, Macours, Karen, Maluccio, John A., 2013. More Schooling and More Learning?: Effects of a Three-Year Conditional Cash Transfer Program in Nicaragua After 10 Years. Inter-American Development Bank.

Barlevy, G., Neal, D., 2012. Pay for percentile. Am. Econ. Rev. 102 (5), 1805–1831.

Barrera-Osorio, F., Filmer, D., 2013. Incentivizing Schooling for Learning: Evidence on the Impact of Alternative Targeting Approaches. World Bank Policy Research Working Paper 6541.

Barrera-Osorio, F., Linden, L., 2009. The Use and Misuse of Computers in Education: Evidence from a Randomized Experiment in Colombia. World Bank Policy Research Working Paper #4836, Impact Evaluation Series No. 29.

Barrera-Osorio, M.B., Linden, L., Perez-Calle, F., 2011. Improving the design of conditional transfer programs: evidence from a randomized education experiment in Colombia. Am. Econ. J. Appl. Econ. 3, 167–195.

Baum, D., Lewis, L., Lusk-Stover, O., Patrinos, H., 2014. What Matters Most for Engaging the Private Sector in Education: A Framework Paper. The World Bank, Washington, DC.

Beasley, E., Huillery, E., 2014. Willing But Unable: Short-Term Experimental Evidence on Parent Empowerment and School Quality. J-PAL Working Paper.

Becker, G.S., 1962. Investment in human capital: a theoretical analysis. J. Polit. Econ. 70, 9–49.

Behrman, J.R., Parker, S.W., Todd, P.E., 2009. Schooling impacts of conditional cash transfers on young children: evidence from Mexico. Econ. Dev. Cult. Chang. 57 (3), 439–477.

Behrman, J.R., Parker, S.W., Todd, P.E., 2011. Do conditional cash transfers for schooling generate lasting benefits? A five-year followup of PROGRESA/Oportunidades. J. Hum. Resour. 46 (1), 93–122.

Behrman, J.R., Gallardo-Garcia, J., Parker, S.W., Todd, P.E., Velez-Grajales, V., 2012. Are conditional cash transfers effective in urban areas? Evidence from Mexico. Educ. Econ. 20 (3), 233–259.

Bellei, C., 2009. Does lengthening the school day increase students' academic achievement? Results from a natural experiment in Chile. Econ. Educ. Rev. 28, 629–640.

Benhassine, N., Devoto, F., Duflo, E., Dupas, P., Pouliquen, V., 2015. Turning a shove into a nudge? A "labeled cash transfer" for education. Am. Econ. J. Econ. Policy 7 (3), 86–125.

Ben-Porath, Y., 1967. The production of human capital and the life cycle of earnings. J. Polit. Econ. 75, 352–365.

Betts, J., 2011. The economics of tracking in education. In: Hanushek, E., Machin, S., Woessmann, L. (Eds.), Handbook of the Economics of Education, vol. 3. North Holland, Amsterdam, pp. 341–381.

Beuermann, D., Cristia, J., Cruz-Aguayo, Y., Cueto, S., Malamud, O., 2013. Home Computers and Child Outcomes: Short-Term Impacts from a Randomized Experiment in Peru. NBER Working Paper Series #18818.

Bharadwaj, P., Loken, K., Nielson, C., 2013. Early life health interventions and academic achievement. Am. Econ. Rev. 103 (5), 1862–1891.

Bjorkman, M., Svensson, J., 2009. Power to the people: evidence from a randomized field experiment on community-based monitoring in Uganda. Q. J. Econ. 124 (2), 735–769.

Blimpo, M.P., 2014. Team incentives for education in developing countries: a randomized field experiment in Benin. Am. Econ. J. Appl. Econ. 6 (4), 90–109.

Bloom, N., Van Reenen, J., 2007. Measuring and explaining management practices across firms and countries. Q. J. Econ. 122 (4), 1351–1408.

Bloom, N., Lemos, R., Sadun, R., Van Reenen, J., 2015. Does management matter in schools. Econ. J. 125 (May), 647–674.

Bold, T., Kimenyi, M., Mwabu, G., Ng'ang'a, A., Sandefur, J., 2013. Scaling Up What Works: Experimental Evidence on External Validity in Kenyan Education. Working Paper 321Center for Global Development, Washington, DC.

Borkum, E., 2012. Can eliminating school fees in poor districts boost enrollment? Evidence from South Africa. Econ. Dev. Cult. Chang. 60 (2), 359–398.

Borkum, E., He, F., Linden, L., 2012. School Libraries and Language Skills in Indian Primary Schools: A Randomized Evaluation of the Akshara Library Program. Working Paper, Abdul Latif Jameel Poverty Action Lab, MIT.

Bourdon, J., Frölich, M., Michaelowa, K., 2010. Teacher shortages, teacher contracts and their impact on education in Africa. J. R. Stat. Soc. Ser. A 173, 93–116.

Burde, D., Linden, L.L., 2013. Bringing education to Afghan girls: a randomized controlled trial of village-based schools. Am. Econ. J. Appl. Econ. 5 (3), 27–40.

Carnoy, M., Gove, A., Marshall, J., 2007. Cuba's Academic Advantage: Why Students in Cuba Do Better in School. Stanford University Press, Palo Alto, CA.

Chaudhury, N., Hammer, J., Kremer, M., Muraldhiran, K., Rogers, F.H., 2006. Missing in action: teacher and health worker absence in developing countries. J. Econ. Perspect. 20 (1), 91–116.

Chaudhury, N., Parajuli, D., 2010. Conditional cash transfers and female schooling: the impact of the female school stipend programme on public school enrolments in Punjab, Pakistan. Appl. Econ. 42 (28), 3565–3583.

Chay, K., McEwan, P., Urquiola, M., 2005. The central role of noise in evaluating interventions that use test scores to rank schools. Am. Econ. Rev. 95 (4), 1237–1258.

Chen, Y., Jin, G.Z., 2012. Does health insurance coverage lead to better health and educational outcomes? Evidence from rural China. J. Health Econ. 31 (1), 1–14.

Chetty, R., Friedman, J.N., Hilger, N., Saez, E., Schanzenbach, D.W., Yagan, D., 2011. How does your kindergarten classroom affect your earnings: evidence from Project Star. Q. J. Econ. 126, 1593–1660.

Chin, A., 2005. Can redistributing teachers across schools raise educational attainment: evidence from operation blackboard in India. J. Dev. Econ. 78 (2), 384–405.

Conn, K., 2014. Identifying Effective Education Interventions in Sub-Saharan Africa: A Meta-Analysis of Rigorous Impact Evaluations. Columbia University, New York.

Contreras, D., Rau, T., 2012. Tournament incentives for teachers: evidence from a scaled-up intervention in Chile. Econ. Dev. Cult. Chang. 61 (1), 219–246.

Cristia, J., Czerwonko, A., Garofalo, P., 2014. Does technology in schools affect repetition, dropout and enrollment? Evidence from Peru. J. Appl. Econ. 17, 89–112.

Cullen, J.B., Jacob, B.A., Levitt, S., 2006. The effect of school choice on participants: evidence from randomized lotteries. Econometrica 74, 1191–1230.

Das, J., Dercon, S., Habyarimana, J., Krishnan, P., Muralidharan, K., Sundararaman, V., 2013. School inputs, household substitution, and test scores. Am. Econ. J. Appl. Econ. 5 (2), 29–57.

de Janvry, A., Finan, F., Sadoulet, E., 2012. Local electoral incentives and decentralized program performance. Rev. Econ. Stat. 94 (3), 672–685.

Deaton, A., 2010. Instruments, randomization, and learning about development. J. Econ. Lit. 48 (2), 424–455.

Deaton, A., 2013. The Great Escape: Health, Wealth, and the Origins of Inequality. Princeton University Press, Princeton, NJ.

Duflo, E., 2001. Schooling and labor market consequences of school construction in Indonesia: evidence from an unusual policy experiment. Am. Econ. Rev. 91 (4), 795–813.

Duflo, E., Dupas, P., Kremer, M., 2011. Peer effects, teacher incentives, and the impact of tracking: evidence from a randomized evaluation in Kenya. Am. Econ. Rev. 101, 1739–1774.

Duflo, E., Dupas, P., Kremer, M., 2012a. School governance, teacher incentives, and pupil-teacher ratios: experimental evidence from Kenyan primary schools. No. w17939, National Bureau of Economic Research. (published as Duflo, Dupas and Kremer (2015)).

Duflo, E., Hanna, R., Ryan, S.P., 2012b. Incentives work: getting teachers to come to school. Am. Econ. Rev. 102 (4), 1241–1278.

Duflo, E., Dupas, P., Kremer, M., 2015. School governance, teacher incentives, and pupil-teacher ratios: experimental evidence from Kenyan primary schools. J. Public Econ. 123, 92–110.

Duthilleul, Y., 2005. Lessons Learnt in the Use of 'Contract' Teachers. International Institute for Educational Planning, UNESCO, Paris.

Evans, D., Popova, A., 2015. What Really Works to Improve Learning in Developing Countries: An Analysis of Divergent Findings in Systematic Reviews. Policy Research Working Paper 7203, The World Bank, Washington, DC.

Ferraz, C., Finan, F., Moreira, D.B., 2012. Corrupting learning: evidence from missing federal education funds in Brazil. J. Public Econ. 96 (9-10), 712–726.

Filmer, D., Schady, N., 2014. The medium-term effects of scholarships in a low-income country. J. Hum. Resour. 49 (3), 663–694.

Fiszbein, A., Schady, N., et al., 2009. Conditional Cash Transfers: Reducing Present and Future Poverty. The World Bank, Washington, DC.

Friedman, W., Kremer, M., Miguel, E., Thornton, R., 2011. Education as Liberation?. No. w16939, National Bureau of Economic Research.

Galiani, S., McEwan, P.J., 2013. The heterogeneous impact of conditional cash transfers. J. Public Econ. 103, 85–96.

Gertler, P.J., Patrinos, H.A., Rubio-Codina, M., 2012. Empowering parents to improve education: evidence from rural Mexico. J. Dev. Econ. 99, 68–79.

Gitter, S., Barham, B., 2008. Women and targeted cash transfers in Nicaragua. World Bank Econ. Rev. 22 (2), 271–290.

Glewwe, P., Kassouf, A.L., 2012. The impact of the Bolsa Escola/Familia conditional cash transfer program on enrollment, dropout rates and grade promotion in Brazil. J. Dev. Econ. 97 (2), 505–517.

Glewwe, P., Kremer, M., 2006. Schools, teachers, and education outcomes in developing countries. In: Hanushek, E., Welch, F. (Eds.), Handbook of the Economics of Education. Volume 1, North Holland, Amsterdam.

Glewwe, P., Maïga, E., 2011. The impacts of school management reforms in Madagascar: do the impacts vary by teacher type? J. Dev. Effect. 3 (4), 435–469.

Glewwe, P., Miguel, E., 2008. The impact of child health and nutrition on education in less developed countries. In: Schultz, T.P., Strauss, J. (Eds.), Handbook of Development Economics, Volume 4. Elsevier, Amsterdam.

Glewwe, P., Kremer, M., Moulin, S., Zitzewitz, E., 2004. Retrospective vs. prospective analyses of school inputs: the case of flip charts in Kenya. J. Dev. Econ. 74 (1), 251–268.

Glewwe, P., Kremer, M., Moulin, S., 2009. Many children left behind? Textbooks and test scores in Kenya. Am. Econ. J. Appl. Econ. 1 (1), 112–135.

Glewwe, P., Ilias, N., Kremer, M., 2010. Teacher incentives. Am. Econ. J. Appl. Econ. 2 (3), 205–227.

Glewwe, P., Hanushek, E., Humpage, S., Ravina, R., 2013. School resources and educational outcomes in developing countries. In: Glewwe, P. (Ed.), Education Policy in Developing Countries. University of Chicago Press, Chicago.

Glewwe, P., Park, A., Zhao, M., 2014. A Better Vision for Development: Eyeglasses and Academic Performance in Rural Primary Schools in China. Working Paper, Abdul Lateef Jamil Poverty Action Lab, MIT, Cambridge, MA. Forthcoming, Journal of Development Economics.

Govinda, R., Josephine, Y., 2004. Para-Teachers in India: A Review. National Institute of Educational Planning and Administration, New Delhi.

Goyal, S., Pandey, P., 2009. How Do Government and Private Schools Differ? Findings from Two Large Indian States. World Bank, Washington, D.C.

Handa, S., 2002. Raising primary school enrolment in developing countries: the relative importance of supply and demand. J. Dev. Econ. 69, 103–128.

Hanushek, E.A., Woessmann, L., 2015. The Knowledge Capital of Nations: Education and the Economics of Growth. MIT Press, Cambridge, MA, p. 262.

Hidalgo, D., Onofa, M., Oosterbeek, H., Ponce, J., 2013. Can provision of free school uniforms harm attendance? Evidence from Ecuador. J. Dev. Econ. 103 (2013), 43–51.

Holmstrom, B., Milgrom, P., 1991. Multi-task principal-agent analysis: incentive contracts, asset ownership, and job design. J. Law Econ. Org. 7, 24–52.

Hsieh, C.-T., Urquiola, M., 2006. The effects of generalized school choice on achievement and stratification: evidence from Chile's voucher program. J. Public Econ. 90 (8), 1477–1503.

Huan, W., Chu, J., Loyalka, P., Tao, X., Shi, Y., Qu, Q., Yang, C., Rozelle, S., 2014. Can School Counseling Reduce School Dropout in Developing Countries?. REAP Working Paper #275.

Jackson, C.K., 2012. Single-sex schools, student achievement, and course selection: evidence from rule-based student assignments in Trinidad and Tobago. J. Public Econ. 96 (1–2), 173–187.

Jensen, R., 2010. The (perceived) returns to education and the demand for schooling. Q. J. Econ. 25 (2), 515–548.

Kazianga, H., de Walque, D., Alderman, H., 2012. Educational and child labour impacts of two food-for-education schemes: evidence from a randomized trial in rural Burkina Faso. J. Afr. Econ. 21 (5), 723–760.

Kazianga, H., Levy, D., Linden, L.L., Sloan, M., 2013. The effects of "girl-friendly" schools: evidence from the BRIGHT school construction program in Burkina Faso. Am. Econ. J. Appl. Econ. 5 (3), 41–62.

Kremer, M., 1993. The O-ring theory of economic development. Q. J. Econ. 108, 551–575.

Kremer, M., Muralidharan, K., Chaudhury, N., Rogers, F.H., Hammer, J., 2005. Teacher absence in India: A snapshot. J. Eur. Econ. Assoc. 3, 658–667.

Kremer, M., Miguel, E., Thornton, R., 2009. Incentives to learn. Rev. Econ. Stat. 91 (3), 437–456.

Kremer, M., Brannen, C., Glennerster, R., 2013. The challenge of education and learning in the developing world. Science 340, 297–300.

Krishnaratne, S., White, H., Carpenter, E., 2013. Quality Education for All Children? What Works in Education in Developing Countries. International Initiative for Impact Evaluation (3ie) Working Paper 20, New Delhi.

Kumar, K., Priyam, M., Saxena, S., 2005. The trouble with para-teachers. Frontline 18.

Lai, F., Luo, R., Zhang, L., Huang, X., Rozelle, S., 2011. Does Computer-Assisted Learning Improve Learning Outcomes? Evidence from a Randomized Experiment in Migrant Schools in Beijing. Rural Education Action Program Working Paper 228.

Lai, F., Zhang, L., Qu, Q., Hu, X., Shi, X., Boswell, M., Rozelle, S., 2013. Does Computer-Assisted Learning Improve Learning Outcomes? Evidence from a Randomized Experiment in Public Schools in Rural Minority Areas in Qinghai, China. Rural Education Action Program Working Paper.

Lakshminarayana, R., Eble, A., Bhakta, P., Frost, C., Boone, P., Elbourne, D., Mann, V., 2013. The support to rural India's public education system (STRIPES) trial: a cluster randomised controlled trial of supplementary teaching, learning material and material support. PLoS One. 8 (7), e65775.

LaLonde, R.J., 1986. Evaluating the econometric evaluations of training programs with experimental data. Am. Econ. Rev. 76, 604–620.

Lara, B., Mizala, A., Repetto, A., 2011. The effectiveness of private voucher education: evidence from structural school switches. Educ. Eval. Policy Anal. 33 (2), 119–137.

Lassibille, G., Tan, J.-P., Jesse, C., Nguyen, T., 2010. Managing for results in primary education in Madagascar: evaluating the impact of selected workflow interventions. World Bank Econ. Rev. 24 (2), 303–329.

Lavy, V., 2002. Evaluating the effect of teachers' performance incentives on pupils' achievements. J. Polit. Econ. 110 (6), 1286–1318.

Lavy, V., 2009. Performance pay and teachers' effort, productivity and grading ethics. Am. Econ. Rev., 99 (5), 1979–2011.

Li, T., Han, L., Zhang, L., Rozelle, S., 2014. Encouraging classroom peer interactions: evidence from Chinese migrant schools. J. Public Econ. 111, 29–45.

Linden, L., 2008. Complement or Substitute? The Effect of Technology on Student Achievement in India. J PAL Working Paper.

Loyalka, P., Liu, C., Song, Y., Yi, H., Huang, X., Wei, J., Zhang, L., Shi, Y., Chu, J., Rozelle, S., 2013. Can information and counseling help students from poor rural areas go to high school? Evidence from China. J. Comp. Econ. 41, 1012–1025.

Lucas, A.M., Mbiti, I., 2014. Effects of school quality on student achievement: discontinuity evidence from Kenya. Am. Econ. J. Appl. Econ. 6, 234–263.

Luo, R., Shi, Y., Zhang, L., Liu, C., Rozelle, S., Sharbono, B., Yue, A., Zhao, Q., Martorell, R., 2012. Nutrition and educational performance in rural China's elementary schools: results of a randomized control trial in Shaanxi Province. Econ. Dev. Cult. Chang. 60 (4), 735–772.

Malamud, O., Pop-Eleches, C., 2011. Home computer use and the development of human capital. Q. J. Econ. 126, 987–1027.

McEwan, P., 2013. The impact of Chile's school feeding program on education outcomes. Econ. Educ. Rev. 32, 122–139.

McEwan, P., 2015. Improving learning in primary schools in developing countries: a meta-analysis of randomized experiments. Rev. Educ. Res. 85 (2), 353–394.

Miguel, E., Kremer, M., 2004. Worms: identifying impacts on education and health in the presence of treatment externalities. Econometrica 72 (1), 159–217.

Mo, D., Zhang, L., Yi, H., Luo, R., Rozelle, S., Brinton, C., 2013. School dropouts and conditional cash transfers: evidence from a randomised controlled trial in rural China's junior high schools. J. Dev. Stud. 49 (2), 190–207.

Mo, D., Zhang, L., Wang, J., Huang, W., Shi, Y., Boswell, M., Rozelle, S., 2014. The Persistence of Gains in Learning from Computer Assisted Learning (CAL): Evidence from a Randomized Experiment in Rural Schools in Shaanxi Province in China. REAP Working Paper 268.

Munshi, K., Rosenzweig, M., 2006. Traditional institutions meet the modern world: caste, gender and schooling choice in a globalizing economy. Am. Econ. Rev. 96 (4), 1225–1252.

Muralidharan, K., 2012. Long-Term Effects of Teacher Performance Pay: Experimental Evidence from India. JPAL Working Paper.

Muralidharan, K., 2013. Priorities for primary education policy in India's 12th five-year plan. India Policy Forum 9, 1–46.

Muralidharan, K., 2016a. Field Experiments in Education in Developing Countries. UC San Diego.

Muralidharan, K., 2016b. A New Approach to Public Sector Hiring in India for Improved Service Delivery. UC San Diego.

Muralidharan, K., Kremer, M., 2008. "Public-Private Schools in Rural India". In: Peterson, P., Chakrabarti, R. (Eds.), School Choice International. MIT Press, Cambridge, MA.

Muralidharan, K., Prakash, N., 2013. Cycling to School: Increasing Secondary School Enrollment for Girls in India. NBER Working Paper #19305.

Muralidharan, K., Sundararaman, V., 2010. The impact of diagnostic feedback to teachers on student learning: experimental evidence from India. Econ. J. 120 (546), F187–F203.

Muralidharan, K., Sundararaman, V., 2011. Teacher performance pay: experimental evidence from India. J. Polit. Econ. 119 (1), 39–77.

Muralidharan, K., Sundararaman, V., 2013a. Contract Teachers: Experimental Evidence from India. JPAL Working Paper.

Muralidharan, K., Sundararaman, V., 2013b. The Aggregate Effect of School Choice: Evidence from a Two-Stage Experiment in India. National Bureau of Economic Research Working Paper No. 19441. (published as Muralidharan and Sundararaman (2015)).

Muralidharan, K., Sundararaman, V., 2015. The aggregate effect of school choice: evidence from a two-stage experiment in India. Q. J. Econ. 130 (3), 1011–1066.

Muralidharan, K., Zieleniak, Y., 2014. Chasing the Syllabus: Measuring Learning Trajectories in Developing Countries with Longitudinal Data and Item Response Theory. UC San Diego.

Muralidharan, K., Das, J., Holla, A., Mohpal, A., 2014. The Fiscal Costs of Weak Governance: Evidence from Teacher Absence in India. NBER Working Paper 20299.

Murnane, R., Ganimian, A., 2014. Improving Educational Outcomes in Developing Countries: Lessons from Rigorous Evaluations. NBER Working Paper 20284.

Newman, J., Pradhan, M., Rawlings, L.B., Ridder, G., Coa, R., Evia, J.L., 2002. An impact evaluation of education, health and water supply investments by the Bolivian social investment fund. World Bank Econ. Rev. 16 (2), 241–274.

Olken, B., 2007. Monitoring corruption: evidence from a field experiment in Indonesia. J. Polit. Econ. 115 (2), 200–249.

Olken, B.A., Onishi, J., Wong, S., 2014. Should aid reward performance? Evidence from a field experiment on health and education in Indonesia. Am. Econ. J. Appl. Econ. 6 (4), 1–34.

Orkin, K., 2013. The Effect of Lengthening the School Day on Children's Achievement in Ethiopia. YL-WP119.

Oster, E., Thornton, R., 2011. Menstruation, sanitary products, and school attendance: evidence from a randomized evaluation. Am. Econ. J. Appl. Econ. 3 (1), 91–100.

Ozier, O., 2014. Exploiting Externalities to Estimate the Long-Term Effects of Early Childhood Deworming. World Bank Policy Research Working Paper 7052, World Bank.

Pandey, P., Goyal, S., Sundararaman, V., 2009. Community participation in public schools: impact of information campaigns in three Indian states. Educ. Econ. 17 (3), 355–375.

Pitt, M., Rosenzweig, M., Hassan, M., 2014. Human capital investment and the gender division of labor in a brawn-based economy. Am. Econ. Rev. 102 (7), 3531–3560.

Pop-Eleches, C., Urquiola, M., 2013. Going to a better school: effects of behavioral responses. Am. Econ. Rev. 103 (4), 1289–1324.

Pradhan, M., Suryadarma, D., Beatty, A., Wong, M., Gaduh, A., Alisjahbana, A., Artha, R.P., 2014. Improving educational quality through enhancing community participation: results from a randomized field experiment in Indonesia. Am. Econ. J. Appl. Econ. 6 (2), 105–126.

Pridmore, P., Jere, C., 2011. Disrupting patterns of educational inequality and disadvantage in Malawi. Compare: J. Comp. Intern. Educ. 41 (4), 513–531.

Pritchett, L., Beatty, A., 2012. The Negative Consequences of Over-Ambitious Curricula in Developing Countries. Harvard Kennedy School.

Pritchett, L., Sandefur, J., 2013. Context matters for size: why external validity claims and development practice do not mix. J. Global. Develop. 4 (2), 161–197.

de Ree, J., Muralidharan, K., Pradhan, M., Rogers, H.F., 2015. Double for Nothing: Experimental Evidence on the Impact of an Unconditional Teacher Salary Increase on Student Performance in Indonesia. National Bureau of Economic Research Working Paper 21806.

Reinikka, R., Svensson, J., 2004. Local capture: evidence from a central government transfer program in Uganda. Q. J. Econ. 119 (2), 679–705.

Rodrik, D., 2008. The New Development Economics: We Shall Experiment, But How Shall We Learn?. Working Paper, Kennedy School of Government, Harvard University, Cambridge, MA.

Sabarwal, S., Evans, D.K., Marshak, A., 2014. The Permanent Input Hypothesis: The Case of Textbooks and (No) Student Learning in Sierra Leone. Policy Research Working Paper, No. WPS 7021, World Bank Group, Washington, DC.

Santibanez, L., Abreu-Lastra, R., O'Donoghue, J.L., 2014. School based management effects: resources or governance change? Evidence from Mexico. Econ. Educ. Rev. 39, 97–109.

Schultz, P.T., 2004. School subsidies for the poor: evaluating the Mexican Progresa poverty program. J. Dev. Econ. 74, 199–250.

Sylvia, S., Luo, R., Zhang, L., Shi, Y., Medina, A., Rozelle, S., 2013. Do you get what you pay for with school-based health programs? Evidence from a child nutrition experiment in rural China. Econ. Educ. Rev. 37, 1–12.

Tan, J.-P., Lane, J., Lassibille, G., 1999. Student outcomes in Philippine elementary schools: an evaluation of four experiments. World Bank Econ. Rev. 13 (3), 493–508.

Todd, P., Wolpin, K., 2003. On the specification and estimation of the production function for cognitive achievement. Econ. J. 113 (485), F3–F33.

Todd, P.E., Wolpin, K.I., 2006. Assessing the impact of a school subsidy program in mexico: using a social experiment to validate a dynamic behavioral model of child schooling and fertility. Am. Econ. Rev. 96, 1384–1417.

Tooley, J., 2009. The Beautiful Tree: A Personal Journey into How the World's Poorest People Are Educating Themselves. Penguin, New Delhi.

Tooley, J., Dixon, P., 2007. Private education for low-income families: results from a global reseach project. In: Srivastava, P., Walford, G. (Eds.), Private Schooling in Less Economically Developed Countries: Asian and African Perspectives. Oxford Studies in Comparative Education. Symposium Books. Oxford, UK.

Urquiola, M., 2006. Identifying class size effects in developing countries: evidence from rural Bolivia. Rev. Econ. Stat. 88 (1), 171–177.

Urquiola, M., Verhoogen, E., 2009. Class-size caps, sorting, and the regression discontinuity design. Am. Econ. Rev. 99 (1), 179–215.

Yamauchi, F., 2014. An alternative estimate of school-based management impacts on students' achievements: evidence from the Philippines. Policy Research Working Paper No. WPS 6747; Impact Evaluation Series No. IE 113, World Bank Group, Washington, DC.

Yang, Y., Zhang, L., Zeng, J., Pang, X., Lai, F., Rozelle, S., 2013. Computers and the academic performance of elementary school-aged girls in China's poor communities. Comput. Educ. 60 (2013), 335–346.

Yi, H., Song, Y., Liu, C., Huang, X., Zhang, L., Bai, Y., Ren, B., Shi, Y., Loyalka, P., Chu, J., Rozelle, S., 2014. Giving kids a head start: the impact and mechanisms of early commitment of financial aid on poor students in rural China. J. Dev. Econ. 113, 1–15.

Zhang, H., 2014. The Mirage of Elite Schools: Evidence from Lottery-Based School Admissions in China. Chinese University of Hong Kong, Hong Kong.

INDEX

Note: Page numbers followed by "*f*" indicate figures, "*t*" indicate tables, and "*np*" indicate footnotes.